SOCIAL SECURITY DISABILITY PRACTICE

by Thomas E. Bush

HIGHLIGHTS

Here is your annual update to *Social Security Disability Practice*, the book many Social Security disability practitioners consider the best and most practical work available.

Mr Bush has made substantial changes to these sections:

Chapter 1 Initial Client Contact

Drug Addiction or Alcoholism §176.12
SSA's Appointed Representative Best Practices and Tips §178.8

Chapter 2 Prehearing Procedure

Respiratory Disorders, Listings §233
Neurological Disorders Listings §239
Mental Disorders, Listings §240
Somatic Symptom Disorders §248
Evaluating the Claimant's Statements about Symptoms §257
ODAR'S March 2016 "Best Practices for Claimants' Representatives" §279
Submit Additional Evidence – The Five-Day Rule §285

Chapter 3 The Hearing

Rebuttal Evidence and Argument §359

Chapter 4 Following a Favorable Decision

Points of Comparison and Cessation Month §485
Will SSA Conduct Medical Review During Trial Work Period? §492

Chapter 5 Appeals Council

Reopening by the Appeals Council at the Claimant's Request (HALLEX I-3-9) §531

Appendices

Appendix 10: The Duty to Submit All(?) Evidence

... AND MORE!

We Welcome Your Feedback

Our most useful source of improvements is feedback from our subscribers, so if you have any comments, we would like to hear from you.

Revision Editor
James Publishing, Inc.
3505 Cadillac Ave., Suite P
Costa Mesa, CA 92626

Visit us on the Internet at www.JamesPublishing.com

How To Access Your Digital Forms

Included with your copy of this book is access to all its forms in digital format. So you can easily open and modify the forms, **we have replaced our jamesforms.com website and our old CDs with a convenient ZIP file of Word documents.**

Access is easy.
If you purchased this title on jamespublishing.com, a link to download the ZIP file should have already been delivered to your email inbox. Be sure to add customer-service@jamespublishing.com to your safe sender list so this message doesn't land in a spam folder. You can also access the download link at any time by **logging in at jamespublishing.com and clicking My Account** in the upper right-hand corner.

No account yet? No problem.
If you do not yet have a jamespublishing.com account, or you are having trouble, please contact customer support at **1-866-725-2637** or customer-service@jamespublishing.com. We will get you setup right away.

How to unzip the file:
Once you download the ZIP file, you need to extract the files onto your system. Typically, files are downloaded into your Downloads folder unless another directory was specified. Follow these steps to unzip:

1. **Double-click the ZIP file**. In Windows XP or newer and Mac OS X, you can double-click the ZIP file and it will open in a new window. You can then copy the contents to another folder. OS X will create a new folder next to the ZIP file when you double-click it, but may not open it automatically.

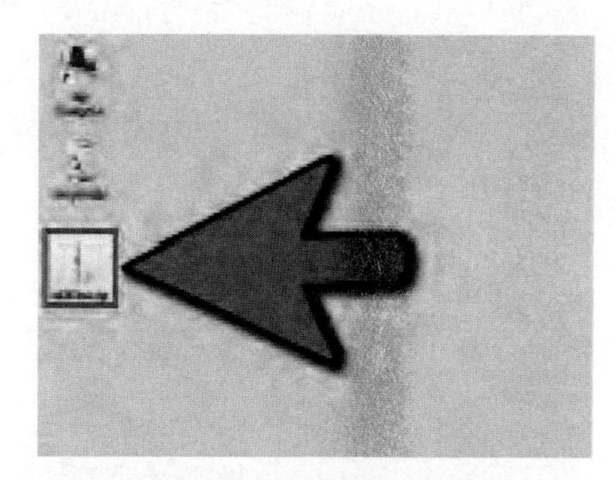

2. **Right-click the ZIP file**. In Windows you can right-click the ZIP file and select *Extract All...* or *Extract Here*. Extract All will allow you to set a path for the extracted folder to go, and Extract Here will decompress the folder and leave it in the same location as the ZIP file.

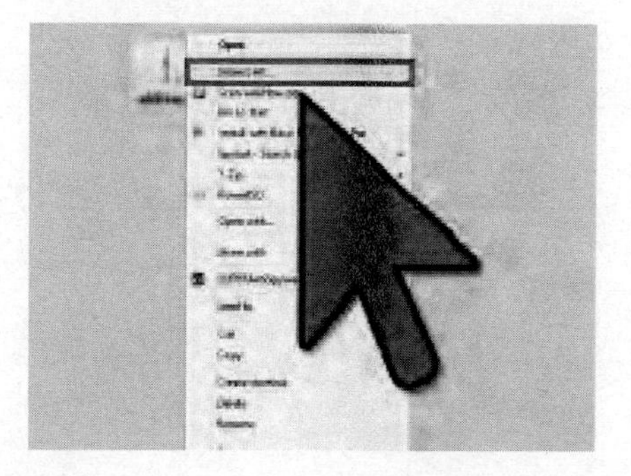

Can I share my digital forms with others?
No. Our forms are copyrighted, and they are licensed to a single individual book purchaser for his or her use only. It is unfair to our book authors if their forms are freely distributed, so please honor their hard work by not sharing their forms. Thank you for understanding.

(This page intentionally left blank.)

Social Security Disability Practice

Volume One

Thomas E. Bush

2nd Edition

Managing Editor: Jim Pawell

Contact us at (866) 72-JAMES or www.jamespublishing.com

Related Texts

Medical Issues in Social Security Disability
Social Security Issues Annotated
Social Security Disability Advocate's Handbook
Social Security Disability Medical Tests

www.JamesPublishing.com or (866) 72-JAMES

ISBN 978-1-945421-40-2

We view the publication of this work as the beginning of a dialogue with our readers. Periodic revisions to it will give us the opportunity to incorporate your suggested changes. Call us at (866) 72-JAMES or send your comments to:

Revision Editor
James Publishing, Inc.
3505 Cadillac Ave., Suite P-101
Costa Mesa, CA 92626

First Edition, 3/85
Revision 1, 3/86
Revision 2, 8/87
Revision 3, 8/88
Revision 4, 6/89
Revision 5, 6/90

Second Edition, 2/92
Revision 1, 4/93
Revision 2, 3/94
Revision 3, 3/95
Revision 4, 2/96
Revision 5, 4/97
Revision 6, 4/98
Revision 7, 7/99
Revision 8, 5/00
Revision 9, 6/01
Revision 10, 5/02
Revision 11, 5/03
Revision 12, 7/04
Revision 13, 10/05
Revision 14, 12/06
Revision 15, 12/07
Revision 16, 12/08
Revision 17, 12/09
Revision 18, 12/10
Revision 19, 12/11
Revision 20, 12/12
Revision 21, 12/13
Revision 22, 12/14
Revision 23, 12/15
Revision 24, 04/17

Summary of Contents

Preface: How to Use This Book and Other Tips for Improving Your Social Security Disability Practice

VOLUME 1

1. Initial Client Contact

2. Prehearing Procedure

VOLUME 2

3. The Hearing

4. Following a Favorable Decision

5. Appeals Council

6. Federal Court Review

7. Attorney's Fees

Detailed Contents

VOLUME 1

Preface: How to Use This Book and Other Tips for Improving Your Social Security Disability Practice

1. Initial Client Contact

2. Prehearing Procedure

VOLUME 2

3. The Hearing

4. Following a Favorable Decision

5. Appeals Council

6. Federal Court Review

7. Attorney's Fees

Appendices

Index

Preface

How to Use This Book and Other Tips for Improving Your Social Security Disability Practice

Learn the Five-Step Sequential Evaluation Process. The five-step Social Security disability sequential evaluation process provides the framework for most arguments to the Social Security Administration about your client's disability. This book is organized around the five-step process. *See* §§110-119 and 20 C.F.R. § 404.1520. Take time to learn how the five steps work. Because the process is *sequential*, if a claimant can be found *not disabled* at any step other than step three, the claimant does not get to proceed to the next step.

Read the First Three Chapters. If you are new to Social Security disability law, sit down and read the first three chapters of this book. This should give you a reasonably good grasp of the unique and often peculiar rules governing this area of practice. You can peruse the other chapters and appendices later, as issues come up.

Use the Forms With Care. This book is absolutely filled with useful forms. The residual functional capacity forms, in particular, are great time savers. You may copy these forms directly out of the book or use Digital Access to adapt them for your word processing program. But beware, forms may need to be modified to address the specific issues in a particular case. A form cannot cover every possible situation. For example, a properly completed interview form will always have comments written in the margins about your client's case.

All of the forms in this book are in use in the author's office, but we are constantly modifying them for individual cases. Sometimes we like a modification so much, we incorporate it into the form. If you make any especially useful modifications, we would appreciate a copy so we can publish improvements.

Check Out the Charts. The charts provide useful summaries of disability concepts. The chart at §121.1 summarizes rules from the Medical Vocational Guidelines. From this chart you can quickly determine what exertional limitations a claimant must have in order to win a disability case. The chart at §135 summarizes differences between the Social Security disability and SSI programs. The chart at §271.1 shows how particular limitations affect ranges of work, and the chart at §349.6 summarizes the different standards for transferability of skills for different ages and exertional levels. The author keeps a copy of this chart in his briefcase for use in questioning vocational experts at hearings.

Do Not Neglect the Appendices. There is a wealth of material in the appendices. The author often begins research on disability issues with Appendix 1, an index to Social Security Rulings. Appendix 8 is an excerpt from the manual given by SSA to medical experts to prepare them to testify. Reading this manual may help prepare you to cross-examine a medical expert. Appendices 4 and 7, excerpts from manuals given by SSA to vocational experts, are required reading when you are preparing to cross-examine a vocational expert (even though they were published by SSA years ago). Appendix 5 is the complete list of unskilled sedentary occupations from the current edition of the *Dictionary of Occupational Titles*. (There are so few of these occupations that vocational experts tend to come up with other jobs which they will testify that they know from "experience" to be unskilled sedentary occupations.) Appendix 9 is a 2007 law review article by Professor Robert E. Rains which tackles the ethical issue that haunts all social security disability practitioners: Must you submit an adverse medical report?

You Will Need Basic Reference Materials. This book provides a place to start. It cannot be used successfully without also reading the regulations and rulings themselves. You can order from the Superintendent of Documents a hard copy of 20 C.F.R. Parts 400-499, which in many circumstances is easier to use than the Internet version. You will also need access to Social Security Rulings and Acquiescence Rulings since 1981, a good medical dictionary and a medical textbook, all of which can be found on the Internet. *See* Appendix 2.

About the Author

Thomas E. Bush has represented Social Security disability claimants since 1977 when he spent a year as a VISTA attorney with the Milwaukee Indian Health Board. At the end of 1977, he opened his own law office. Since then his law practice has concentrated more and more on Social Security disability representation. At present, Bush practices almost exclusively in this area.

Bush received his law degree from the University of Wisconsin where he also did graduate work in Chinese history. He has regularly written and spoken about Social Security disability issues to other lawyers, advocacy groups and the general public. Two brochures he has written, "Social Security Disability and SSI Claims–Your Need for Representation" and "Preparing for Your Social Security Disability or SSI Hearing," are in use all over the country.

A member of the National Organization of Social Security Claimants' Representatives (NOSSCR) since 1980, he served on the Board of Directors from 1988 to 2001. He was the President of NOSSCR for the 1997-98 term.

He may be reached at Thomas E. Bush, S.C., 310 W. Wisconsin Avenue, Suite 930E, Milwaukee, WI 53203, (414) 765-9333.

Chapter 1

Initial Client Contact

§100 "Disabled" — A Term of Art

You cannot always rely on common sense to tell you who is and who is not disabled under Social Security law. Here are some examples:

Example: Lawyer

- He is 35 years old with 10 years of trial experience.
- He is not working, but he is looking for a job.
- He lost his left foot in a car accident a year ago.

Because of stump complications, he is unable to use a prosthetic device to walk one block at a reasonable pace, though he uses it to walk shorter distances, e.g., around an office or around his apartment. When he goes longer distances, he rides a motorized scooter.

He is disabled. *See* C.F.R. Part 404, Subpart P, Appendix 1, § 1.05B.

Example: Bookkeeper

- He has a college education.
- He is a quadriplegic with only limited use of his right hand and arm and no use whatsoever of his legs and left arm.
- He uses an arm brace to write.
- He works a few hours per day as a bookkeeper and earns, after deductions for expenses related to his impairment, about $1,200 per month on average.

Because of his earnings he is not disabled. *See* 20 C.F.R. §§ 404.1520(b) and 404.1574(b)(2).

Example: Construction worker

- He is 48 years old.
- He has done heavy unskilled construction work since age 16.
- He has a fourth grade education and is capable of reading only rudimentary things like inventory lists and simple instructions.
- He has a "low normal" I.Q.
- He is limited to sedentary work because of a heart condition.

He is not disabled unless he has some additional limitations. *See* 20 C.F.R. Part 404, Subpart P, Appendix 2, Rule 201.18.

Example: Machine operator

- He is 38 years old.
- He has done medium exertion level unskilled factory work, operating a machine since he graduated from high school.
- A cardiovascular impairment limits him to sedentary work, and a permanent injury of the right hand limits him to such work not requiring bimanual dexterity.

He is probably disabled. *See* Social Security Rulings 83-10 and 96-9p and the discussion at §126.

Example: Truck driver

- He is 61 years old.
- He worked as a truck driver all his life except that 10 years ago during a downturn in the trucking industry, he worked for 1-1/2 years at a sedentary office job which he got with the help of his brother-in-law.
- He is limited to sedentary work because of a pulmonary impairment.

He is not disabled because he is still capable of doing the office job. *See* 20 C.F.R. §§ 404.1520(f) and 404.1560(b).

Example: Packer

- He is 50 years old.
- He has a high school education.
- He has done unskilled light exertion factory work as a packer for the past 30 years.
- He had a heart attack on January 1 and, after being off work for eight months, he recovered after an angioplasty. His cardiologist gave him a clean bill of health and was ready to send him back to work when he broke his leg in a fall unrelated to his heart condition. In a cast and unable to stand and walk as required by his job, he could not return to work until February. He was off work a total of 13 months.

He is not disabled for the time he was off work. 20 C.F.R. § 404.1522(a) provides that unrelated impairments may not be combined to meet the requirement that a claimant be unable to work for 12 months.

Example: Housewife

- She is 55 years old.
- She has an eleventh grade education.
- She has not worked in the past 15 years. Before that she was a secretary.
- She has a back problem diagnosed as status post laminectomy.
- She is limited to maximum lifting of 50 lbs. with frequent lifting of 25 lbs., is capable of frequent bending, stooping, etc., and has no limitation for standing or walking.

She is disabled for the SSI program as long as she meets the income and asset limitations for that program. *See* 20 C.F.R. Part 404, Subpart P, Appendix 2, Rule 203.10. *See also* 20 C.F.R. § 404.1562(b). (She is not eligible for Social Security disability benefits because she has not worked for so long.)

§101 Regulations and Rulings

These examples are based on the Social Security regulations. A current copy of these regulations is essential to representing disability claimants. Although we will discuss some of the regulations, this book is not a substitute for having your own copy. You can purchase a copy of 20 C.F.R. Parts 400 to 499 from the Government Printing Office, which also puts together an online pdf version that you can download from the Internet for free. For ordering information and where to find the regulations on the Internet, *see* Appendix 2.

This chapter will give you an overview of the regulations that describe how to determine if someone is disabled. (For the Social Security disability program, these appear at 20 C.F.R. §§ 404.1501 to 404.1599, plus two appendices located just after 20 C.F.R. § 404.1599.) It will provide enough information about these disability regulations and some of the nondisability and procedural matters covered in other parts of 20 C.F.R. Parts 400 to 499 for you to be able to conduct a reasonably thorough interview of most claimants. But each claimant's situation is unique. You may run into unusual issues for which it will be necessary to study the regulations themselves or other parts of this book.

Outside of the regulations, the most important body of law for determining disability is found in Social Security Rulings. These are published in the Federal Register by the Social Security Administration and are binding on all components of SSA. 20 C.F.R. § 402.35(b)(1). This book will give you citations to Social Security Rulings that elaborate on the meaning of the regulations. Because there are hundreds of rulings of varying usefulness and because these rulings are poorly indexed, Appendix 1 provides a list of the most important Social Security Rulings pertaining to determining disability. It is essential in representing Social Security disability claimants to have access to the rulings listed in Appendix 1. Rulings are available at SSA's website, www.ssa.gov.

Practice Tip

The Appendix 1 Guide to Important Social Security Rulings and Acquiescence Rulings is on the Internet at http://www.tebush.com/teb/SSRs_files/SSRs.htm with links to individual rulings on SSA's website. The best way to search rulings is to use the search engine at www.google.com and limit your search to rulings on the SSA website. For example, if you want to search for references to widow's benefits, enter your Google search this way: site:www.ssa.gov/OP_Home/rulings widow. Or if you want to include regulations, the statute and everything else on SSA's website except the POMS, enter your Google search this way: site:www.ssa.gov widow. To search the POMS, enter the search this way: site:secure.ssa.gov widow. NOSSCR has set up a page from which you can search SSA documents without entering the site limitation yourself. See http://www.nosscr.org/research-advocates.

The primary purpose of this book is to help you represent your clients in administrative proceedings. We are not going to spend much time talking about the Social Security Act itself because the regulations, along with the Social Security Rulings, constitute the official interpretation of the Act. Nearly everything in the Act appears in the regulations, though there are a few notable exceptions (*e.g.*, attorney fees authorized under the fee agreement process, *see* Chapter 7) where SSA has not yet promulgated regulations.

While you may wish to compare the regulations with the Act in certain unusual circumstances, you will never get a decision in your favor from any level of SSA based on a conflict between the Act and the regulations. If you want to challenge the regulations, you will have to make that challenge in federal court after making your record on the issue when the case is before the agency.

The regulations provide a lot of room to maneuver—a lot of possibilities for winning your client's case at the administrative hearing or maybe even at an earlier stage—so we are going to concentrate on these. But first, let us take a brief look at the definition of "disabled" in the Social Security Act.

§102 Statutory Definition

Congress has defined the term "disability" for both the regular Social Security disability program (which appears in Title II of the Social Security Act) and the SSI disability program (which appears in Title XVI of the Act) as an inability "to engage in any substantial gainful activity by reason of any medically determinable physical or mental impairment which can be expected to result in death or which has lasted or can be expected to last for a continuous period of not less than 12 months." 42 U.S.C. §§ 423(d)(1)(A) and 1382c(a)(3)(A).

> An individual shall be determined to be under a disability only if his physical or mental impairment or impairments are of such severity that he is not only unable to do his previous work but cannot, considering his age, education, and work experience, engage in any other kind of substantial gainful work which exists in the national economy, regardless of whether such work exists in the immediate area in which he lives or whether a specific job vacancy exists for him, or whether he would be hired if he

> applied for work. For purposes of the preceding sentence (with respect to any individual), "work which exists in the national economy" means work which exists in significant numbers either in the region where such individual lives or in several regions of the country.

42 U.S.C. §§ 423(d)(2)(A) and 1382c(a)(3)(B).

The Act defines "physical or mental impairment" as "an impairment that results from anatomical, physiological or psychological abnormalities which are demonstrable by medically acceptable clinical and laboratory diagnostic techniques." 42 U.S.C. §§ 423(d)(3) and 1382c(a)(3)(D). The definition of disability in the Act specifically provides that an individual is not "disabled" if drug addiction or alcoholism would "be a contributing factor material to the Commissioner's determination that the individual is disabled." 42 U.S.C. §§ 423(d)(2)(C) and 1382c(a)(3)(J).

The Act leaves it to the Commissioner of Social Security to prescribe regulations to determine when services performed or earnings demonstrate ability to engage in substantial gainful activity. 42 U.S.C. §§ 423(d)(4) and 1382c(a)(3)(E).

The Act provides somewhat different definitions of disability for those who are blind and, until 1991, for widow(er)s (including surviving divorced spouses), subjects which we will not address in detail in this book. *See* §§142 and 143. The part of the Act dealing with SSI provides a significantly different definition of disability for children requiring "marked and severe functional limitations." 42 U.S.C. § 1382c(a)(3)(C)(i). *See* §145.

For regular Social Security disability and SSI, the Act is much less specific than the regulations and rulings promulgated by the Commissioner. For example, although the Act requires consideration of age, education and work experience, it provides no guidance for weighing these factors to determine capacity for other work.

The Act sets a hypothetical tone for disability determination by excluding consideration of availability of work in the area where the claimant lives, job vacancies and whether the individual claimant would be hired. The Act does not define jobs existing "in significant numbers."

The regulations and rulings provide the official, formal interpretation of the Social Security Act, answering many questions raised by the text of the Act and, as we shall see, leaving many questions unanswered. But this is the stuff of which good lawyering is made.

§103 SSA's Manuals and Other Instructions

The regulations and rulings that interpret the Social Security Act are in turn interpreted by agency manuals, bulletins, emergency messages, and memoranda from various components of SSA. For the first time in 2013, SSA stated that these official but less formal statements of policy are binding on ALJs. SSR 13-2p states: "We require adjudicators at all levels of administrative review to follow agency policy, as set out in the Commissioner's regulations, SSRs, Social Security Acquiescence Rulings (ARs), and other instructions, such as the Program Operations Manual System (POMS), Emergency Messages, and the Hearings, Appeals and Litigation Law manual (HALLEX)."

Although prior to 2013 the POMS was not considered binding on ALJs, it was always the case that a clear statement of SSA policy, even one in the POMS, was likely to be followed at all levels of SSA and any SSA interpretation of the Social Security Act or regulations was likely to be extremely influential in a federal court proceeding. See *Washington State Department of Social and Health Services et al. v. Guardianship Estate of Keffeler et al.*, 537 U.S. 371, 385 (2003), in which the U.S. Supreme Court, citing *Skidmore v. Swift & Co.*, 323 U.S. 134, 139-140 (1944), used the POMS as evidence of the Commissioner's interpretation of the Social Security Act. However, when SSA doesn't follow *procedures* set forth in one of its manuals, courts have not been fast to force SSA to follow the stated procedure. In *Schweiker v. Hansen*, 450 U.S. 785, 789 (1981), the U.S. Supreme Court stated that SSA's former claims manual was "not a regulation. It has no legal force, and it does not bind the SSA." In *Moore v. Apfel*, 216 F.3d 864, 868-69 (9th Cir. 2000), the Ninth Circuit refused to enforce the SSA procedure that requires assignment of a new ALJ after a second court remand.

The largest and most important of SSA's manuals is the Program Operations Manual System (POMS), a huge online handbook for internal use by SSA employees and by the employees of the state agencies who make administrative disability determinations below the hearing level. A section of the POMS deals with determining disability, interpreting the regulations and rulings with which we are concerned in this book. The disability section of the POMS, which contains thousands of pages, is only one part of the POMS. The entire POMS, which deals with every aspect of the many programs operated by SSA, contains tens of thousands of pages. The complete POMS is available online to SSA employees through SSA's intranet, SSA's private computer network.

A public version of the POMS may be accessed from SSA's website, www.socialsecurity.gov, or from SSA's Program Policy Information Site, https://secure.ssa.gov/apps10/. According to SSA, "The public version of POMS is identical to the version used by Social Security employees except that it does not include internal data entry and sensitive content instructions." It is not clear what SSA considers to be "sensitive content instructions." Left out of the public POMS are the glossaries for deciphering SSA computer printouts, which may appear as exhibits in a claimant's hearing exhibit file. For example, the Disability Determination Services Query (DDSQ), which sometimes appears as a hearing exhibit, is explained in a section of the POMS entitled "Parts of a Full Query Response" that appears at SM 06002.200 only in the SSA version of the POMS. This section of the POMS is labeled: "SENSITIVE—NOT TO BE SHARED WITH THE PUBLIC." (Nevertheless, it can be found elsewhere on the Internet. *See* §205.2.)

Another category of documents available only on SSA's intranet are "Q and A's," many of which include detailed discussion of medical impairments. An example of a Q and A about migraine headaches appears at §239.2.1.

At the ALJ hearing level, the manual used by ALJs and their staffs, the HALLEX (Hearings, Appeals and Litigation Law Manual), is much smaller than the POMS. The HALLEX describes hearing office procedures, many of which have due process implications, and it includes discussion of substantive legal issues such as *res judicata* and reopening. Even on procedural matters the HALLEX is sometimes incomplete. Policy changes may be announced by Chief Judge Bulletins, which can be accessed from SSA's Program Policy information website, https://secure.ssa.gov/apps10/. Such formal policy changes are intended to eventually appear in the HALLEX. Sometimes as an administrative expedient intended to expedite cases during a time of backlogs, a stated HALLEX policy may be temporarily suspended by a memorandum from the Chief Administrative Law Judge. Thus, even though such informal policy changes do not happen often, the HALLEX must be used with caution because the stated policy may have been superseded or suspended.

Substantive and procedural issues are also addressed in memoranda from various components of SSA, some of which end up as part of the HALLEX, sometimes starting out as "temporary instructions" in HALLEX Volume I, Division 5, which tend to retain temporary status for years. Current temporary instructions deal with oral bench decisions, HALLEX I-5-1-17; increased dollar cap for fee agreements (beginning in 2009), HALLEX I-5-1-18; instructions for processing appeals involving same-sex marriages, HALLEX I-5-1-19; two temporary instructions regarding video hearings, HALLEX I-5-1-20 and I-5-21; a change that applies only to cases from SSA's Boston region, instructions for eliminating the Decision Review Board and related hearing level processing changes, HALLEX I-5-3-18; instructions for processing cases involving the Benefit Offset National Demonstration (BOND) project, HALLEX I-5-3-20; and instruction dated 2001 for processing a subsequent claim while an earlier claim is pending at the Appeals Council, HALLEX I-5-3-17, a policy that was changed by SSR 11-1p, effective July 28, 2011—the HALLEX section remains applicable to cases in which subsequent applications were filed before the effective date of the change.

A classic example of a substantive legal memorandum is one written in 1993 by Associate Commissioner Daniel L. Skoler, which deals with the Americans with Disabilities Act and the role of employer accommodation in evaluating whether someone is disabled. See §344.1. As a rule, ALJs are not supposed to cite memoranda, even though they are supposed to follow the policies or interpretations of the regulations contained in them. Thus, there exists a hidden but influential body of law interpreting SSA's regulations and rulings.

Many ALJs take the position that although they are bound to follow SSA policy, it is often necessary to determine what SSA policy is, whether exceptions apply, and whether the policy applies to the facts of an individual claimant's case.

The Social Security administrative system is not one built on precedent. Only limited attention is paid to court precedent (see §104), and ALJ decisions have no precedential value at all. Even an Appeals Council decision has no precedential value unless, as occasionally occurs, it is adopted as a Social Security ruling. In this system, one tends to fight the same battles over and over.

ALJs usually know and follow official interpretations such as those stated in the POMS. For this reason, it is usually more important to know how SSA interprets the regulations and rulings than it is to know the position of the federal courts on an issue. Knowing SSA's position gives a fairly reliable basis for predicting how an issue will be decided at the administrative level.

§104 Role of Federal Court Decisions

Most lawyers, when dealing with any new federal legal issue, reflexively look first to the Federal Reporter to see how circuit courts have dealt with the matter. But lawyers and administrative law judges within the Social Security Administration tend to look at circuit court case law last, if at all.

Although there used to be an official short list of circuit court cases, which were decided in SSA's favor, that were sometimes cited by ALJs (and even today a few ALJs have favorite circuit court cases that they cite in decisions), it is the rule within SSA that no significant decision-making weight is accorded a decision of a circuit court of appeals unless that decision has been adopted as an acquiescence ruling. *See* SSR 96-1p. Discussion of a circuit court opinion generally appears in an ALJ decision only in response to a citation by a claimant's attorney. An ALJ will follow circuit court precedent only if it suits the ALJ's purpose in the case.

At the same time, ALJs have been instructed not to cite federal *district* court opinions in their decisions except to distinguish them from the facts of the claimant's case. The decisions of the local United States District Court are thus accorded no precedential value whatsoever by SSA. SSR 96-1p.

When SSA finds a court decision to be an accurate statement of SSA policy, SSA may issue that decision as a Social Security Ruling, which will be identified with the suffix "c." But such rulings are rarely cited by ALJs.

SSA does apply precedential value to decisions of the United States Supreme Court. These also are published as Social Security rulings with the suffix "c." However, whenever a Supreme Court decision is cited, even within SSA, it is invariably cited in the usual manner and not as a Social Security ruling.

For the most part, SSA simply ignores circuit court decisions with which it disagrees, except for those few cases in which SSA issues "acquiescence rulings" by which it agrees to follow that appellate court decision in the circuit where it was decided. *See* §105. In the past, SSA issued "rulings of *nonacquiescence*" concerning such circuit court decisions.

SSA says that it must administer a national program. The agency argues that it cannot apply different rules in every federal district in the country, and, less convincingly, that it cannot apply different rules from circuit to circuit. *See* SSR 96-1p. SSA takes interpretation of the Social Security Act to be its mandate and, essentially, considers federal courts as not sufficiently deferential to agency interpretation.

Needless to say, the low regard with which SSA holds federal court decisions has caused tension between the federal courts and SSA. Federal district judges complain that they decide the same issues over and over. Frustrated by SSA's flagrant practice of ignoring appellate court decisions, a judge once threatened the official in charge of the agency with contempt proceedings "both in her official and individual capacities." *Hillhouse v. Harris,* 715 F.2d 428, 430 (8th Cir. 1983) (McMillan, J., concurring).

If you are new to the practice of representing Social Security disability claimants, you may initially find SSA's treatment of federal court precedent to be bizarre and possibly illegal; but once you get used to it, you will find that it opens myriad possibilities for representing your clients. For one thing, if good, on-point claimant-oriented case law is ignored in the administrative phase of your client's case, you obviously have a great case for federal court review.

It often comes as a revelation to lawyers practicing Social Security disability law that at the administrative level you may treat unfavorable appellate court case law the same way SSA does: ignore it. This is especially true for those cases that are *both* anti-claimant *and* contrary to SSA policy. Although, in court, SSA lawyers often use arguments based on case law contrary to SSA policy, it is unlikely that you will ever see such arguments made in administrative proceedings.

§105 Acquiescence Rulings

In addition to regular Social Security rulings, SSA has developed a species of rulings dealing with federal court decisions—"acquiescence rulings." In the 1980s, SSA was faced with more and more class action lawsuits attempting to enforce appellate court precedent. In response, SSA developed a procedure for issuing "acquiescence rulings" to deal with court of appeals decisions that were contrary to SSA policy but which SSA agreed to follow in the circuit from which the decision was issued. SSA policy on acquiescence rulings, including the circumstances under which SSA will relitigate an issue, appears at 20 C.F.R. § 404.985.

We have included acquiescence rulings pertaining to disability determination in our index of important Social Security rulings, Appendix 1. Acquiescence rulings are published in the Federal Register, as are regular Social Security Rulings; and they appear at SSA's website, www.ssa.gov. Acquiescence rulings are identified AR, are numbered consecutively in the year of issuance, and contain a number in parentheses that indicates the circuit in which the acquiescence ruling is applicable. For example, AR 03-1(7) indicates that this is the first acquiescence ruling issued in 2003 and is applicable in the seventh circuit.

You will find that acquiescence rulings are useful even if they do not apply to your clients' circuits. If an acquiescence ruling addresses an issue present in your client's case in an administrative proceeding, it may provide fodder for an argument to be used later in federal court. Perhaps more important, acquiescence rulings always explain how a court decision differs from SSA policy. Many times, such statements operate to clarify just what SSA policy is.

§106 A Nonadversarial Administrative System

SSA says that it conducts "the administrative review process in an informal, non-adversarial manner." 20 C.F.R. §§ 404.900(b) and 404.1740(a)(2). Thus, you will never deal with an attorney adversary representing

SSA's interest at any level of administrative review. Only if your client loses and you appeal to federal court will a lawyer adversary representing the government become involved.

Hearings are supposed to be conducted in "an informal, non-adversarial manner" by ALJs who are supposed to be neutral fact finders who decide cases by a preponderance of the evidence. The degree to which ALJs in practice have lived up to the neutral fact finder goal has varied over time. In recent years many new ALJs have been recruited who have a worldview that is suspicious of claimants, claimants' doctors, and claimants' representatives.

Nevertheless, as a factfinding system at the ALJ level, the Social Security system is designed to be better at determining who is and is not disabled than any alternative adversarial system. Consider, for example, the adversarial worker's compensation system, which is not known for dispassionate decision-making.

Social Security regulations have a certain logic and symmetry that is supposed to aid accurate decision-making. For example, decision makers are supposed to proceed through the sequential evaluation process, see §§110 - 118, answering the questions presented without regard to whether the end result will be "disabled" or "not disabled." When they don't, when decision makers engage in result-oriented decision making, it is often obvious.

Despite the frustration of claimants by the time delays involved in this system at all levels, properly represented claimants tend to find the ALJ hearing to be non-threatening. They like having the opportunity to tell their stories to a judge. They like not having to deal with a lawyer adversary representing the government.

Attorneys representing claimants could abuse this nonadversarial system, but by and large they do not, though there have been some notable exceptions in recent years. Most attorneys recognize that they have a heightened duty to this system: The attorney must not mislead the ALJ or allow a client to do so on any material fact. See 20 C.F.R. § 404.1740(c)(3). Attorneys have an affirmative duty to "[a]ct with reasonable promptness to help obtain information or evidence that the claimant must submit" under Social Security regulations. 20 C.F.R. § 404.1740(b)(1). Representatives should not "unreasonably delay" the processing of a claim. 20 C.F.R. § 404.1740(c)(4).

Based on § 1129 of the Social Security Act, 42 U.S.C. § 1320a-8, Social Security regulations provide for civil monetary penalties against persons who "[m]ake or cause to be made false statements or representations or omissions or otherwise withhold disclosure of a material fact for use in determining any right to or amount of benefits under title II or benefits or payments under title VIII or title XVI of the Social Security Act." 20 C.F.R. § 498.100(b)(1).

Attorneys schooled in the adversarial system do not like having to submit adverse evidence in their clients' cases. Yet this is required by Social Security regulations, which require the submission of all evidence that "relates to" whether or not a claimant is disabled. 20 C.F.R. § 404.1512(a), 80 Fed Reg 14830 (March 20, 2015).

An article by Professor Robert E. Rains, "The Duty to Submit All(?) Evidence," which was prepared for this book appears at Appendix 10. Professor Rains, an expert on the ethical requirements for attorneys in disability cases whose work was cited by SSA when it published the "all evidence" regulation, concludes:

Although there was a longstanding debate over the duty to submit unfavorable evidence, anecdotal information suggests that most representatives did precisely that. For the relatively few who did not, the rule is now reasonably clear: subject to quite limited exceptions, representatives must submit all evidence in their possession, in its entirety, whether favorable or unfavorable. Representatives who fail to do so risk serious sanctions from SSA.

§107 Informal Procedures

Despite a trend in recent years toward more formality in Social Security disability practice, a trend that is disturbing to many attorneys, the administrative system remains an informal one. Hearings before administrative law judges, held in small conference rooms, are much less formal than court proceedings. Some ALJs wear robes but other judicial trappings such as gavels, bailiffs, and court reporters are absent. The rules of evidence do not apply. Evidence may be submitted even though it would be "inadmissible under rules of evidence applicable to court proceedings." 42 U.S.C. § 405(b)(1). Although witnesses at hearings testify under oath, one can submit an unsworn letter from a doctor as evidence. Medical records are not required to be certified.

There is no special form required for any submission to SSA. Most attorneys use letters for almost everything (briefs, motions, to submit evidence, to make requests, to give notice, etc.). Although not required, most attorneys use the official forms for appeals and to notify SSA of their involvement in a case. While the regulations allow appeal by sending a simple letter, it is best to use the official form. With a letter appeal, one runs the risk that an SSA employee will not recognize it for what it is. *See* the sample Request for Hearing, §178.2.2; and Request for Review of Hearing Decision, §512. The Appointment of Representative form, §178.2.1, is used by most attorneys so that SSA employees will note that there is attorney involvement in the case, despite the fact that the regulations require only that the claimant sign a statement appointing a representative. 20 C.F.R. § 404.1707(a).

§108 SSA: A Bureaucracy

For the most part, attorneys deal with SSA's Office of Disability Adjudication and Review (ODAR), which includes about 150 hearing offices scattered around the country, and the next level of appeal, the Appeals Council, which is located in suburbs of Washington, D.C., and Baltimore. In all, ODAR has approximately 10,000 employees, including about 1,400 administrative law judges and more than 50 administrative appeals judges. Dealing with hearing offices is generally a pleasant experience. Although dealing with the Appeals Council can be frustrating for attorneys, it is nothing compared to dealing with SSA outside of ODAR.

There is a rigidity of rule-following, whether or not application of the rule makes any sense, which characterizes the approach of low-level bureaucrats. This problem exists in all bureaucracies and is present at SSA, for the most part outside of ODAR. It is something that has been known to cause both claimants and lawyers to tear out their hair. To deal with this, you will find that it is best to be firm and persistent but never obnoxious.

A fundamental problem in dealing with SSA outside of ODAR is, of course, the sheer size of the agency, which has approximately 57,000 employees in addition to those employed by ODAR. Also, there are more than 15,000 state agency employees nation-wide involved in making determinations of disability below the ALJ hearing level. It is difficult for a lawyer first to figure out whom to contact about a claimant's particular problem and then to determine how to contact them, whether by phone, fax, mail or, in some limited circumstances, e-mail. Once you figure it out in a particular case, be sure to keep good notes for that particular case; and also start keeping a master list of telephone and fax numbers and addresses for use in future cases. You will discover that there are knowledgeable and helpful people at all levels of SSA. You will do well to cultivate a relationship with them. Treasure their phone numbers.

The problem of SSA's size is compounded by the complexity of its programs, the most complicated of which are the two disability programs, Social Security disability and SSI. When there are program changes, it is a huge task to ensure that everyone within SSA who needs to know gets the information, and often they do not. Sometimes it will be up to you to tell SSA employees about policy changes.

To take just one example of problems created by complexity, consider the Social Security Administration's nationwide toll-free telephone number, 1-800-772-1213 (which SSA likes to write as 1-800-SSA-1213). In theory, the toll-free number is staffed by knowledgeable SSA employees capable of answering a wide variety of questions, including questions about entitlement to disability benefits. However, this is not the reality. One test showed 25 percent wrong answers to questions involving SSI, by far the most complicated of SSA's programs. The toll-free number, if you can get past the busy signals and the recorded messages, is most useful for information about the retirement program, not for questions that a lawyer might have about disability benefit entitlement.

SSA, like all bureaucracies, attempts to routinize complex decisions; however, the more complicated the decision, the less effective this is. It does not work well at all for disability determinations below the administrative law judge hearing level because the medical-vocational issues tend to be complicated and because state agencies are not equipped to assess the actual impact of a medical impairment on a particular claimant, which often involves an evaluation of a claimant's subjective symptoms. *See* SSR 16-3p. State agency disability determinations tend to be inadequate, and many people within SSA remain almost blissfully unaware of state agency decision shortcomings. For example, studies using SSA's own peculiar methodology repeatedly conclude that state agency determinations are correct more than 93% of the time. Such studies are unable to explain why ALJs have always found disabled far more than 7% of the claimants who come before them. These studies have led many state agency employees to believe that ALJs issue mostly wrong decisions, and there is a component within SSA (outside of the Office of Disability Adjudication & Review) that thinks so, too.

It is a mistake to view SSA as being of one mind. For example, there are those within SSA who think that disability determination would be improved by getting rid of lawyers, administrative law judges, due process hearings, and appeals. Thus, there is a component of SSA that is opposed to the very existence of the Office of Disability Adjudication and Review. This tension between different components of SSA tends to produce turf wars and, whenever restructuring of SSA is going on as it has been for the past several years, a search for hidden agendas is made to see if this or that bureaucratic change will ultimately be a benefit or detriment to the future of a particular component of SSA.

§109 Citations

The primary focus of this book is on Social Security disability regulations, with an emphasis on the regulations for determining disability beginning at 20 C.F.R. § 404.1501. For the sake of simplicity, citations to the *identical* disability regulations for the SSI program will not be provided. The SSI regulations for determining disability begin at 20 C.F.R. § 416.901. It is easy to find the parallel SSI regulation. The formula is: 20 C.F.R. § 416.900 plus the last two digits of the Social Security disability regulation. For example, the parallel SSI regulation for the important Social Security disability regulation that describes the sequential evaluation process, 20 C.F.R. § 404.1520, appears at 20 C.F.R. § 416.920. The same sort of conversion works for the regulations dealing with the administrative review process appearing at 20 C.F.R. §§ 404.900 to 404.999 for the Social Security disability program. The parallel SSI regulations, which contain some differences, begin at 20 C.F.R. § 416.1400.

To be technically correct according to the Bluebook system of citation, whenever one cites the Code of Federal Regulations, one is supposed to reference the year of the latest bound volume, e.g., 20 C.F.R. § 404.1520 (2014). If a new regulation was issued after the publication date of the latest bound volume, a Federal Register cite should be provided. We have included some important Federal Register citations; but we have chosen not to state the year of the latest C.F.R. because to do so would require annual changes in virtually every citation in this book and would significantly increase subscriber costs for supplements. When you are writing a federal court brief and you want to use correct citation form, be sure to determine the year of the latest C.F.R. and include this in your citation.

This book will cite the Social Security Act using the U.S. Code system, the system usually used by lawyers. The Social Security Administration, on the other hand, usually cites to a section number of the Social Security Act itself. It is easy to convert to the U. S. Code system references to the Social Security Act for Title II, the title pertaining to the Social Security retirement, survivors and disability programs. Simply add 200. For example, a reference to § 223 of the Social Security Act, the section that contains the definition of disability, is a reference to 42 U.S.C. § 423.

Converting references to Title XVI of the Social Security Act, that part of the Act dealing with SSI, to the U.S. Code System is more complicated. Title XVI appears in the Social Security Act at §§ 1601 through 1635; but these sections are crammed into the U.S. Code system from 42 U.S.C. §§ 1381 through 1383d. You may need to use a conversion table, such as one published by West's Social Security Reporting Service, to find a reference to Title XVI in the U.S. Code system.

§110 Determining Disability Under the Regulations and Rulings

Social Security regulations provide a five-step sequential evaluation process for determining disability. In addition, the claimant's impairment must be expected to result in death or have lasted or be expected to last at least 12 months. This is called the duration requirement. It is a requirement that, although not part of the sequential evaluation process, logically could be inserted into this process following step 2, the severity step. Thus, it is included in the following outline of the disability determination process.

§111 *Diagram: Disability Decision and Sequential Evaluation Process*

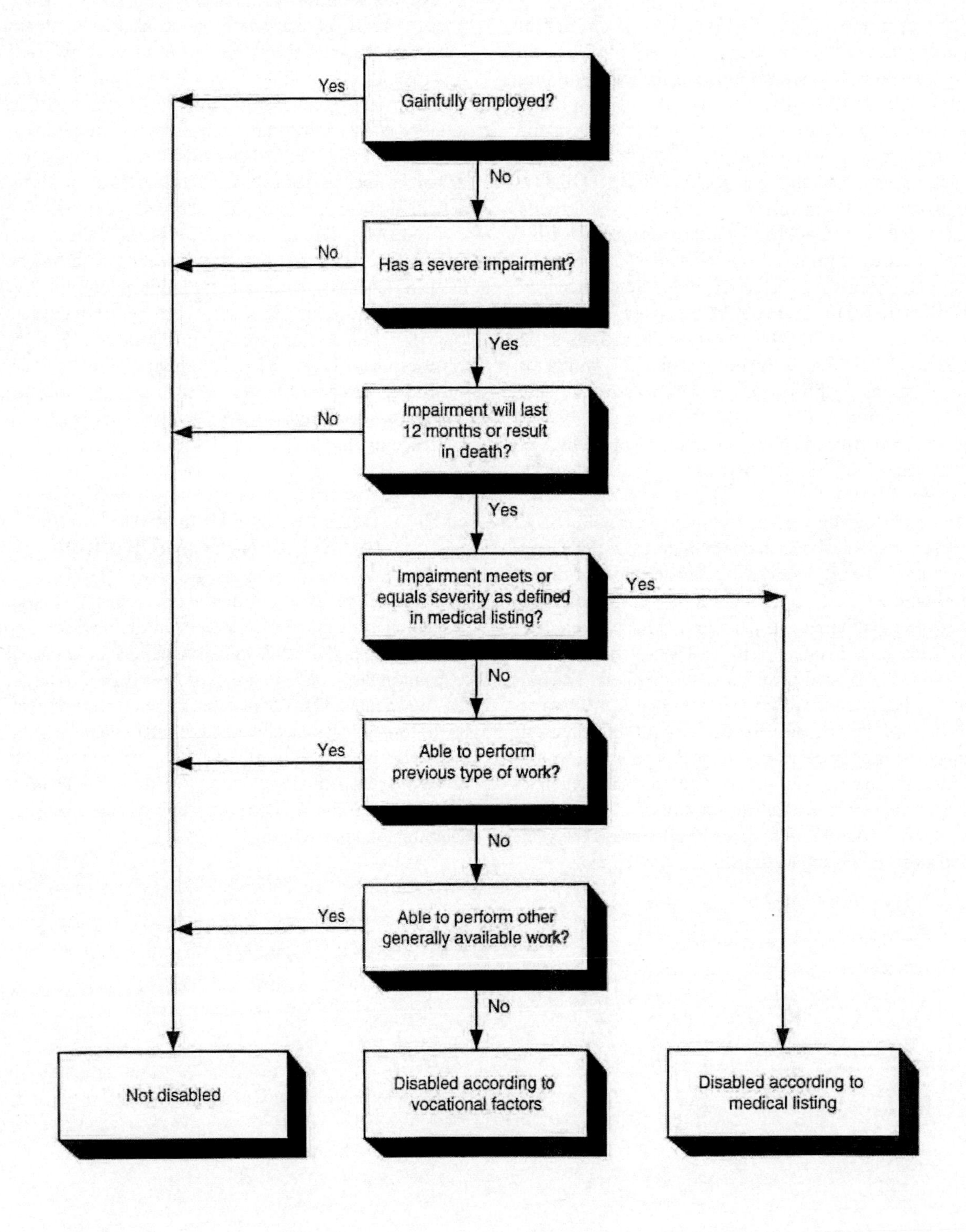

§112 *Sequential Evaluation Process — Overview*

Under the five-step sequential disability evaluation process described in 20 C.F.R. § 404.1520 the following must be proved by a claimant in order to be found disabled:

1. The claimant is not engaging in "substantial gainful activity" (SGA); *and*
2. The claimant has a "severe" impairment; *and*
3. The impairment meets or "equals" one of the impairments described in the Social Security regulations known as the "Listing of Impairments"; *or*
4. Considering the claimant's "residual functional capacity" (RFC), that is, what the claimant can still do even with his or her impairments, the claimant is unable to do "past relevant work" (PRW); *and*
5. Other work within the claimant's RFC, considering age, education and work experience, does not exist in the national economy in significant numbers.

Watch out for the terms identified by quotation marks above and the initials that go with some of them. They have precise meanings in the regulations and rulings that are not necessarily the meanings one would expect. It will be necessary for you to learn these terms if you want to make sense out of Social Security regulations.

§113 *Step 1: Substantial Gainful Activity*

Because it is a sequential process, if the proof fails at any step other than step 3, the process is terminated and the claimant is found not disabled. Thus, if a claimant is working, that is, performing "substantial gainful activity" (SGA), no matter how impaired that claimant is, the claimant cannot be found disabled. This is the reason that our hypothetical bookkeeper in §100 is not disabled.

Work is evaluated "without regard to legality." 20 C.F.R. § 404.1572, 42 U.S.C. §§ 423(d)(4)(B) and 1382c(a)(3)(E). Thus, illegal activity may be substantial gainful activity. *See also* SSR 94-1c, which adopted *Dotson v. Shalala*, 1 F.3d 571 (7th Cir. 1993), as a Social Security ruling.

Work, however, must be both "substantial" and "gainful." "Substantial work activity . . . involves doing significant physical or mental activities." 20 C.F.R. § 404.1572(a). Work may not be substantial when a claimant is unable "to do ordinary or simple tasks satisfactorily without more supervision or assistance than is usually given other people doing similar work" or when a claimant is doing work "that involves minimal duties that make little or no demands" on the claimant and that are of "little or no use" to the employer or to the operation of a self-employed business. 20 C.F.R. § 404.1573(b). But even sheltered work may be substantial. 20 C.F.R. § 404.1573(c).

SSA defines gainful activity broadly: "Work activity is gainful if it is the kind of work usually done for pay or profit, whether or not a profit is realized." 20 C.F.R. § 404.1572(b). Nevertheless, when a claimant is an employee of someone else, whether work is "gainful" is *usually* determined by looking only at the claimant's earnings. But, because SSA does not want to let employed claimants slip past this step if they are in a position to control the timing or amount of their income (*e.g.*, when claimants are working for relatives), SSA will look at factors in addition to the amount of income to make sure such claimants are not cheating. 20 C.F.R. § 404.1574(b)(3)(ii).

This problem is always presented for self-employed claimants, who SSA views very suspiciously. SSA looks carefully at a self-employed person's work activity and its value to the business, even if the person is working at a loss (as so many unimpaired self-employed people do from time to time). *See* 20 C.F.R. § 404.1575(a)(2) and SSR 83-34, which provide evaluation guides for the self-employed. *See also* §176.3 of this book.

Whether the claimant is employed by someone else or is self-employed, to arrive at countable income, SSA allows deduction from earnings for what it calls "impairment-related work expenses," which are usually payments made by the claimant for drugs or medical treatment for the disabling impairment but may also include payments for some transportation costs, vehicle modification, attendant care services, residential modification, *etc.* SSA's impairment-related work expense rules must be reviewed carefully before making a deduction because some expenses you wouldn't expect are included (such as payment for treatment for the disabling impairment that the claimant has to pay whether the claimant works or not) and some expenses that you might expect to qualify are excluded (such as payment for health insurance). *See* 20 C.F.R. § 404.1576, SSR 84-26, and §274 of this book.

In determining if work is substantial gainful activity, SSA averages income according to rules that consider the nature of the work, the period of time worked, and whether the SGA level changed during the time the claimant worked. *See* 20 C.F.R. § 404.1574a and SSR 83-35.

The SGA level, which was $300 per month during all of the 1980s and $500 per month from 1990 until July 1999, when it was raised to $700, is becoming considerably more generous than it used to be because of cost-of-living increases that have been applied beginning with the year 2001. 20 C.F.R. § 404.1574(b)(2)(ii). For example, for the year 2017, average countable earnings of more than $1,170 per month show that work was substantial gainful activity. 20 C.F.R. § 404.1574(b)(2).

You can find the SGA amount for the current year on the Internet at www.ssa.gov/cola/. Because the regulations contain SGA dollar amounts only for years through 2000 (and only a formula for years after that), Appendix 12 of this book provides the SGA amounts (and several other amounts that are based on annual cost-of-living increases) for years beginning with the year 2000. Historical SGA amounts can also be found at POMS DI 10501.015.

§114 Step 2: The Severity Step

At step two of the sequential evaluation process, it is necessary to determine if a claimant's impairments are "severe," a misleading word that encouraged erroneous decisions and spawned much litigation in the past. This step, which incorporates two different concepts, was intended to weed out frivolous cases involving either (1) no medically determinable impairments or (2) *slight* medically determinable impairments that impose only *minor* limitations on ability to work. Virtually any reduction in residual functional capacity (what the claimant can still do even with his or her impairments) satisfies the requirement that there be a severe medically determinable impairment. *See* 20 C.F.R. § 404.1520(c), § 404.1521, SSR 85-28 and SSR 96-3p. As such, medically determinable impairments are divided into two categories: (1) slight impairments that are referred to in SSA's peculiar lingo as "nonsevere" impairments and (2) all other impairments that are, therefore, "severe."

As a practical matter, when you prove a reduction of the claimant's residual functional capacity at step 4, you have effectively proven that the claimant has a severe medically determinable impairment. No separate proof is required to show a significant limitation of ability to do "basic work activities." *See* 20 C.F.R. § 404.1521. SSA is supposed to consider the combined effect of all impairments, including multiple non-severe impairments, in determining if a claimant's overall condition meets the requirement of being "severe." 20 C.F.R. § 404.1523. Note that even subjective symptoms, as long as they arise from a medically determinable impairment, must be considered in assessing whether an impairment, or group of impairments, reduces a claimant's ability to do basic work activity. SSR 96-3p. If an adjudicator is "unable to determine clearly" the effect of an impairment on a claimant's ability to do basic work activities, the adjudicator is directed by SSR 96-3p to proceed with the next steps of the sequential evaluation process. Thus, close cases are to be decided in favor of finding an impairment to be severe.

On the other hand, "[n]o symptom or combination of symptoms can be the basis for a finding of disability, no matter how genuine the individual's complaints may appear to be, unless there are medical signs and laboratory findings demonstrating the existence of a medically determinable physical or mental impairment." SSR 96-4p. When there is no "medically determinable impairment," an individual may be found not disabled at step 2 of the sequential evaluation process. Nevertheless, as a rule, if a doctor has enough information to make a legitimate diagnosis, a claimant has a medically determinable impairment. When there is a controversy over which diagnosis is correct, if medical signs or laboratory findings show any abnormality, the claimant has a medically determinable impairment even if the doctors do not agree on which diagnosis is best.

Step 2 denials are usually hogwash. Do not be intimidated by a step 2 denial if your own eyes tell you that the claimant is significantly impaired and you believe the claimant. Indeed, you should not be intimidated by step 2 denials even after a hearing in a non-frivolous case. Even though the U.S. Supreme Court upheld the facial validity of the step 2 regulation in *Bowen v. Yuckert,* 482 U.S. 137 (1987), federal courts have not treated SSA kindly in step 2 cases. Federal courts usually send step 2 cases back to SSA for completion of the sequential evaluation process. Indeed, after the Supreme Court upheld the facial validity of step 2 in *Bowen v. Yuckert*, it remanded the case to the Ninth Circuit which, in turn, remanded *Yuckert v. Bowen*, 841 F.2d 303 (9th Cir. 1988), refusing to affirm a step 2 denial in that case.

§115 Duration Requirement

Unless an impairment is expected to result in death, it must have lasted or be expected to last for a continuous period of 12 months. 20 C.F.R. § 404.1505(a). *See also* 20 C.F.R. § 404.1522(b).

The regulation implies that the impairment must be continuously "severe." This interpretation is a concern for those impairments that wax and wane or have short periods of remission but have active periods sufficient to preclude engaging in substantial gainful activity on a sustained basis. The regulation, properly interpreted, does not require a denial of disability benefits for failure to meet the duration requirement under such circumstances. *Cf. Moore v. Sullivan,* 895 F.2d 1065, 1069 (5th Cir. 1990).

The regulation specifically prohibits tacking together unrelated severe impairments to meet the duration requirement. 20 C.F.R. § 404.1522(a). This is the reason that our hypothetical packer in §100 is not disabled. This regulation appears to be the unintended consequence of the wording of the definition of disability. 42 U.S.C. § 423(d)(2)(A). It is hard to find a public policy reason for this harsh result.

Denials based on the duration requirement usually occur in those cases where, at the time of the decision, the duration requirement is not met and the impairment is the sort that is likely to improve within 12 months. For those impairments that may or may not improve before the duration requirement is met, sometimes a state agency decision maker will delay a case just to see if the claimant continues to be disabled. Because of the slow progress of the administrative process, the 12 months usually have passed by the time a claimant actually attends a hearing, thus permitting an accurate retrospective evaluation.

Once the twelve-month duration requirement is met, you may ask for a finding of a closed period of disability in the situation where a claimant's condition has improved to the degree that he or she is able to return to work.

§116 Step 3: Listing of Impairments

In order to be found disabled at step 3 of the sequential evaluation process, a claimant's medical signs, findings, and symptoms must meet or "medically equal" one of the set of medical signs, findings and symptoms found in the Listing of Impairments. The Listing of Impairments is a set of medical criteria for disability found at Appendix 1 of the Social Security disability regulations, officially cited as 20 C.F.R. Part 404, Subpart P, Appendix 1.

If a claimant can be found disabled at step 3, there is no inquiry into ability to do past work or other work. This is the reason that our hypothetical lawyer in §100 is disabled despite the fact that he retains the ability to practice law. His impairment meets § 1.05B of the Listings, which deals with amputation of one or both feet.

Although you should look at the issue in every case, you will want to take an especially hard look at the Listings when your client can still perform past relevant work. If your client's impairment meets or equals one of the impairments in the Listings, the ability to perform past work is irrelevant.

It is possible to argue that your client's impairments are medically equivalent to an impairment in the Listing of Impairments. 20 C.F.R. § 404.1526(a). This comes up in four situations: (1) your client does not have one of the essential findings stated in the Listings for your client's particular impairment but your client has other findings; (2) your client has all the essential findings but one or more of the findings is not quite severe enough and your client has other findings; (3) your client's impairment is not described in the Listings but it may be as severe as an analogous impairment that appears in the Listings; or (4) your client has a combination of impairments, none of which meet the Listings but the cumulative total of your client's impairments could still equal the Listings. 20 C.F.R. § 404.1526(b). It is possible to compare medical findings, symptoms and limitations in functioning to see if one claimant, whose impairment does not appear in the Listings, is as disabled as another claimant whose impairment meets a particular Listing. *See* §336. However, before an ALJ or the Appeals Council can find that a claimant's impairment medically equals a Listed Impairment, the decision maker must receive the opinion of a medical expert hired by SSA. *See* SSR 96-6p.

In regular Social Security disability and SSI cases involving adults, if a claimant cannot be found disabled at step 3, the inquiry proceeds to an assessment of residual functional capacity, which, to be technically precise, is determined between steps 3 and 4, 20 C.F.R. § 404.1520(a)(4), and then to step 4. For a discussion of widow(er)'s disability under pre-1991 standards and disabled children's eligibility for SSI, *see* §§142 and 145.

§117 Step 4: Past Relevant Work

In the usual case, attention will focus on steps 4 and 5 of the sequential evaluation process. At step 4 the claimant has the burden of proving that he or she is incapable of doing any "past relevant work." To qualify as past relevant work:

1. The job must have been performed within:
   a. 15 years prior to adjudication; or
   b. if insured status has lapsed, 15 years prior to the date last insured, 20 C.F.R. § 404.1565(a). *See* §131 on insured status.
2. The job must have been "substantial gainful activity," 20 C.F.R. § 404.1565(a). That is,
   a. the job must have involved doing significant physical or mental activities, 20 C.F.R. § 404.1572(a); and
   b. it must have been done at the SGA level. *See* 20 C.F.R. §§ 404.1574-1575.
3. The job must have lasted long enough for the claimant to develop the facility needed for average performance. *See* 20 C.F.R. § 404.1565(a) and SSR 82-62.

Note that a job qualifies as past relevant work even if the job was done only part-time, as long as it was substantial gainful activity. SSR 96-8p, footnote 2. Thus, you have to identify the claimant's easiest full or part time past relevant job and then figure out why the claimant cannot still do it. If the claimant had an easy job in the past 15 years that he or she can still do, the claimant will be found not disabled like our hypothetical truck driver in §100, unless you can put together an argument that the impairments meet or medically equal one of the impairments in the Listing of Impairments.

You must prove that your client cannot do a past relevant job even if that job no longer exists in the economy, an SSA position that was upheld by the U.S. Supreme Court in *Barnhart v. Thomas*, 540 U.S. 20 (2003).

In addition, if a claimant retains the capacity to do a past relevant job as it is ordinarily done, the claimant will be found not disabled even though the claimant's actual past job required greater exertion and the claimant is unable to do that particular job. *See* Social Security Ruling 82-61. The "job as it is ordinarily done" rule will not be applied to a claimant's benefit, however. If a claimant's own past work was easier than the way the job is ordinarily done, even if an employer accommodated the claimant's disability under the Americans with Disabilities Act (*see* §344.1 of this book), SSA will examine the actual job requirements as the claimant performed them in determining whether the claimant can perform past relevant work. *See* SSR 82-62.

Determining whether a claimant can do past relevant work is accomplished by comparing the claimant's current residual functional capacity with the physical and mental demands of past relevant work. 20 C.F.R. § 404.1520(f) and SSR 82-62.

Although criminal activity is considered when determining SGA at step one, SSA will never say that a claimant is not disabled because he or she retains the capacity to return to criminal activity. POMS DI 25005.015 E.

For more about past relevant work, *see* §347.

§118 Step 5: Other Work

Once you have proven that the claimant cannot perform past relevant work, you move on to the most complicated step—determining whether the claimant can make an adjustment to other work that exists in significant numbers in the national economy, considering the claimant's remaining work capacity, age, education and work experience. SSA has provided an important tool for determining whether a claimant is or is not disabled because of medical impairments and vocational factors: the Medical-Vocational Guidelines, discussed in detail beginning at §120. The Medical-Vocational Guidelines, popularly known as the "grids," provide that the older a claimant is, the easier it is to be found disabled. Thus, our hypothetical housewife in §100, is found disabled despite the remaining physical capacity to do most jobs in the economy (sedentary, light and medium work) because of the adversity of age (55), education (less than a high school graduate), and work experience (none in the past 15 years). *See* Rule 203.10 of the Medical-Vocational Guidelines. Indeed, this rule may still be applied if "the work activity performed within this 15-year period does not (on the basis of job content, recency, or duration) enhance present work capability." SSR 82-63.

§119 Summary and Exceptions

As you can see, determining disability involves a multi-step reasoning process. The one-step "he can't work" sort of argument won't get you very far. Common sense can be applied only where there isn't a regulation or Social Security Ruling to the contrary.

Two Main Routes to Disability Finding

The sequential evaluation process provides two main routes for a finding of disability. One route involves a purely medical determination that the claimant's impairment meets or medically equals an impairment described in the Listing of Impairments. The other route to a disability finding involves assessing a combination of medical and vocational factors that culminates at step 5 of the sequential evaluation process and, to one degree or another, uses the Medical-Vocational Guidelines.

Three Special Medical-Vocational Profiles

In addition, there are three other ways to be found disabled without completing the standard five-step sequential evaluation process. If a claimant fits one of three special medical-vocational profiles, the claimant is found disabled without proceeding to step five and without consulting the Medical-Vocational Guidelines. Indeed, for one of the three profiles, it is not even necessary to assess residual functional capacity. A claimant who fits this profile is found disabled by simply showing that he or she has a severe impairment. This profile, which is described at 20 C.F.R. § 404.1562(b), provides that a claimant is disabled who:

- Has a severe, medically determinable impairment;
- Is age 55 or older;
- Has an 11th grade education or less; and
- Has no past relevant work experience.

Another profile, known as the "worn-out worker," describes a claimant who:

- Has no more than a sixth grade education;
- Worked 35 years at arduous unskilled labor; and
- Is unable to do the arduous unskilled labor done in the past.

20 C.F.R. §§ 404.1520(g)(2) and 404.1562(a). *See also* SSR 82-63 and *Walston v. Sullivan*, 956 F.2d 768 (8th Cir. 1992). In effect, the worn-out worker is found disabled at step four with proof that he or she is incapable of performing past relevant work. An article by ALJ Peter J. Lemoine, "The Worn-Out Worker Rule Revisited," 49 West's Social Security Reporting Service 883, presents a well-reasoned analysis that demonstrates that the worn-out worker rule may be more useful than it may appear at first glance.

A claimant may have more formal education than sixth grade and still be considered to have marginal education if he or she functions at the marginal educational level. 20 C.F.R. § 404.1564(b). Even light work "if it demands a great deal of stamina or activity such as repetitive bending and lifting at a very fast pace" (SSR 82-63), may qualify as arduous. The 35 years of qualified work activity need not be continuous and may be interspersed with work activity that does not satisfy the "arduous unskilled labor" requirement. Not all prior work need be unskilled if work at higher skill level is isolated, brief, or remote, or if skills are not transferable. ALJ Lemoine points out that as long as there are 35 years of qualified employment that the claimant can no longer perform, the existence of an unskilled job in the past which the claimant retains the capacity to perform will not make the worn-out worker rule inapplicable.

The third medical-vocational profile, known as the "lifetime commitment" profile, does not appear in 20 C.F.R. § 404.1562. Instead, it appears only in the POMS (along with the other two profiles discussed above), but it is consistent with the principles stated in SSRs 82-63 and 85-15. Like the worn-out worker, this claimant is found disabled at step four with proof of inability to do past relevant work. POMS DI 25010.001B.3 provides:

> A finding of "disabled" will be made for persons who:
>
> • Are not working at SGA level, and
>
> • Have a lifetime commitment (30 years or more) to a field of work that is unskilled, or is skilled or semi-skilled but with no transferable skills, and
>
> • Can no longer perform this past work because of a severe impairment(s), and
>
> • Are closely approaching retirement age (age 60 or older), and
>
> • Have no more than a limited education.
>
> (*See* DI 25001.001 for the definitions of "limited education" and DI 24505.000 for a discussion of severe impairment.)
>
> **NOTE**: To satisfy the requirement for this profile, the 30 years of lifetime commitment work does not have to be at one job or for one employer but rather work in one field of a very similar nature. If the person has a history of working 30 years or more in one field of work, the use of this profile will not be precluded by the fact that the person also has work experience in other fields, so long as that work experience in other fields is not past relevant work which the person is still able to perform.

Six Ways to Be Found Not Disabled

The regulations provide six possibilities for a finding of not disabled. A claimant is not disabled who:

- Is working at the SGA level;
- Has no medically determinable impairment;
- Has an impairment that does not significantly limit the physical or mental ability to do basic work activities;
- Fails to meet the duration requirement;
- Is capable of past relevant work;
- Is capable of other work.

Two Ways to Be Found Disabled But Not Eligible

There are two ways for a claimant to be found *not* disabled *after* the sequential disability evaluation process has been completed and SSA has concluded that the claimant is, in fact, disabled. This can happen when a claimant fails to follow prescribed treatment or when alcoholism or other drug abuse is a contributing factor material to the determination of disability. Although SSA itself never refers to these issues precisely this way, where they apply, you can view these issues as involving additional steps in the sequential evaluation process.

The regulations provide that SSA will not find a claimant disabled if the claimant, without good reason, does not follow prescribed treatment. 20 C.F.R. § 404.1530. Although the regulation doesn't say so, SSR 82-59 makes it clear that a determination finding a claimant not disabled on this basis is made only after SSA finds that the claimant is otherwise disabled. The treatment must be prescribed by the claimant's own physician and, according to SSR 82-59, this treatment must be "clearly expected to restore" the claimant's ability to work. *See* §278 of this book for additional information.

If drug addiction or alcoholism is "a contributing factor material to the determination of disability," a claimant will be found not disabled. 42 U.S.C. §§ 423(d)(2)(C) and 1382c(a)(3)(J). This issue is addressed only after it is determined that the claimant is disabled when considering all impairments, including any impairments involving drug addiction or alcoholism. 20 C.F.R. § 404.1535(a). Then SSA looks at the claimant's impairments again to consider whether the claimant would still be disabled if the claimant stopped using drugs or alcohol. 20 C.F.R. § 404.1535(b)(1) and SSR 13-2p. *See* §249 of this book for additional discussion. (Note that SSA has not amended its regulations after Congress provided that a claimant was not disabled if drug addiction or alcoholism is a contributing factor material to the determination of disability. Thus, regulations that deal with treatment requirements for claimants with drug addiction or alcoholism, 20 C.F.R. §§ 404.1536 to 404.1541, are not applicable.)

Non-Disability Requirements

As we shall see, there are other requirements, which have nothing to do with whether a claimant is disabled—SSA calls these "non-disability requirements"—that may be used by SSA to deny benefits. These issues, "insured status" for Social Security disability claims, and alien status and income/asset limitations for SSI claims, are supposed to be evaluated before SSA looks at medical issues (and they usually are), but sometimes a problem is caught when SSA is getting ready to pay benefits after SSA has already concluded that a claimant meets the disability requirements. *See* §§131, 132, and 136.

§120 Medical-Vocational Guidelines

In determining whether a claimant is capable of performing other work that exists in significant numbers, SSA decision makers are faced with the difficult task of weighing the relative importance of the factors for consideration identified by the Social Security Act: the claimant's remaining work capacity, known as residual functional capacity or RFC; age; education; and work experience, including whether or not the claimant has developed work skills transferable to other work within his or her RFC. Before 1979 SSA relied on vocational expert (VE) testimony to analyze these factors and determine how many jobs existed in the economy for a particular claimant. It was then up to the ALJ to determine whether the number of jobs identified by the vocational expert was "significant." As one might imagine, this procedure yielded disparate results, varying from VE to VE and ALJ to ALJ.

To achieve more consistency in decision-making, SSA promulgated regulations, effective in 1979, known as the Medical-Vocational Guidelines. These appear as Appendix 2 to the Social Security disability regulations cited as 20 C.F.R. Part 404, Subpart P, Appendix 2. The Medical-Vocational Guidelines contain three charts, called grids, which answer the question whether a claimant is or is not disabled for different combinations of maximum physical residual functional capacity, age, education and work experience. If a claimant's profile matches one of the rules in the Medical-Vocational Guidelines, the rules, which are binding on decision-makers, direct the outcome of the case. *See* §121.1 for a chart that shows the maximum residual functional capacity a claimant can have and still be found disabled. You may use this chart to determine to what degree your client must be exertionally limited if he or she is to be found disabled. But do not neglect a careful analysis of age, education and work experience. Your analysis might make a different rule applicable.

If a claimant's profile differs from that described in the grids, the rules do not directly answer the question of whether the claimant is or is not disabled—but they must be used as a "framework" for decision-making. This happens where a claimant's exertional limitations fall between those described by the three grids for sedentary, light and medium work; where a claimant cannot do a full range of sedentary work; and where there are nonexertional limitations such as in cases involving mental, sensory or skin impairments, postural or manipulative limitations or environmental limitations. As a rule, ALJs call vocational experts to testify when the Medical-Vocational Guidelines must be used as a framework.

§121 Maximum Residual Functional Capacity

The following chart is a composite of information from the three grids in the Medical-Vocational Guidelines. The chart focuses on those rules that result in a claimant being found disabled. It shows different combinations of age, education and work experience with the maximum exertional residual functional capacity that a claimant may have and still be found disabled. Thus, the chart shows what you have to prove when, for example, a 55-year-old high school graduate with an unskilled work background comes to your office to discuss a heart impairment: the claimant must have an RFC for light work or less in order to win the case.

§121.1 Chart: Maximum RFC Possible for Disability Finding

Age	Education	Previous work experience	Max. RFC	Rule
60-	6th grade or less	Unskilled	Medium	203.01
	7th to 11th grade	Unskilled	Light	202.01
	11th grade or less	None	Medium	203.02
	11th grade or less	Skilled or semiskilled—skills not transferable	Light	202.02
	High school graduate or more—does not provide for direct entry into skilled work	Unskilled or none	Light	202.04
	High school graduate or more—does not provide for direct entry into skilled work	Skilled or semiskilled—skills not transferable	Light	202.06
55-59	11th grade or less	None	Medium	203.10
	11th grade or less	Unskilled	Light	202.01
	11th grade or less	Skilled or semiskilled—skills not transferable	Light	202.02
	High school graduate or more—does not provide for direct entry into skilled work	Unskilled or none	Light	202.04
	High school graduate or more—does not provide for direct entry into skilled work	Skilled or semiskilled—skills not transferable	Light	202.06
50-54	Illiterate or unable to communicate in English	Unskilled or none	Light	202.09
	11th grade or less—at least literate and able to communicate in English	Unskilled or none	Sedentary	201.09
	High school graduate or more—does not provide for direct entry into skilled work	Unskilled or none	Sedentary	201.12
	High school graduate or more—does not provide for direct entry into skilled work	Skilled or semiskilled—skills not transferable	Sedentary	201.14
45-49	Illiterate or unable to communicate in English	Unskilled or none	Sedentary	201.17
	All educational levels—at least literate and able to communicate in English	Unskilled, none, or skilled or semiskilled—skills not transferable	Sedentary occupational base must be significantly compromised	201.00(h)
18-44	All educational levels including illiterate or unable to communicate in English	Unskilled, none, or skilled or semiskilled—skills not transferable	Sedentary occupational base must be significantly compromised	201.00(h)

§122 Age

Age as a vocational factor is second only to residual functional capacity as a determinant of whether a claimant is found disabled by the Medical-Vocational Guidelines. Age affects whether a claimant can adjust to work other than the claimant's past relevant work. The regulations provide that in determining whether a claimant is disabled, SSA will consider the claimant's chronological age in combination with the claimant's residual functional capacity, education, and work experience. "In determining the extent to which age affects a person's ability to adjust to other work, we consider advancing age to be an increasingly limiting factor in the person's ability to make such an adjustment." But SSA will not consider a claimant's ability to adjust to other work on the basis of the claimant's age alone. 20 C.F.R. § 404.1563(a).

SSA groups claimants into three age categories and two age subcategories. The age categories are "younger individual"—under age 50; "closely approaching advanced age"—age 50–54; and "advanced age"—age 55 or over. The subcategories are "younger individual age 45-49" and "closely approaching retirement age—age 60 or older." POMS DI 25001.001 B.3. Those within each age category or subcategory are treated alike. Thus, a 50-year-old claimant will be treated the same as a 54-year- old claimant.

According to the regulations, age categories will not be applied "mechanically in a borderline situation." 20 C.F.R. § 404.1563(b). The regulation, 20 C.F.R. § 404.1563(b), provides:

> If you are within a few days to a few months of reaching an older age category, and using the older age category would result in a determination or decision that you are disabled, we will consider whether to use the older age category after evaluating the overall impact of all the factors of your case.

At first glance, this looks like a rule that says if a claimant is within a few months of a birthday that puts him or her into a disabled category in the Medical-Vocational Guidelines, the claimant is supposed to get the benefit of the doubt by using the rule for the higher age category. Instead, this rule is interpreted in the stingiest possible way.

The borderline age rule applies only when it makes the difference between winning and losing. It cannot be used merely to give a claimant a few more months of back benefits. Let's take an example. Recall that except for claimants who are illiterate (who may be found disabled at age 45), claimants who have never had a sedentary job and who have no transferable skills to sedentary work are found disabled at age 50 if they are limited to sedentary work. See Medical-Vocational Guidelines Rules 201.09. 201.10, 201.12, and 201.14. If at age 49 years and 10 months, a claimant suffers a back injury that limits him to sedentary work, the borderline age rule can be used to find this claimant disabled only if something, e.g., date last insured, prevents him from being found disabled at age 50. Otherwise, as SSA interprets it, a borderline age situation does not apply. Thus, instead of finding him disabled as of his alleged onset date, SSA will simply find the claimant disabled as of the day before his 50th birthday, applying the SSA rule that says a claimant "attains a particular age on the day before his or her birthday." POMS DI 25015.005 B. *See also* GN 00302.400.

Now let's change the facts a little. Let's say this claimant suffered a back injury on December 20, his insured status expired eleven days later on December 31, and he turned 50 on February 20 of the next year. This clearly is a situation where using the older age category would result in the claimant being found disabled but using the younger age category would result in a denial. Thus, this is a borderline age situation as SSA defines it. But, according to SSA, the analysis is not done. According to 20 C.F.R. § 404.1563(b), SSA "will consider whether to use the older age category after evaluating the overall impact of all the factors of your case."

According to SSA, this language in the regulation means that SSA will "not use the higher age category automatically in a borderline age situation." POMS DI 25015.006E. HALLEX I-2-2-42C instructs ALJs as follows:

> ALJs will consider whether to use the higher age category after evaluating the overall impact of all the factors on the claimant's ability to adjust to doing other work (e.g., residual functional capacity combined with age, education, and work experience as explained in 20 CFR 404.1563, 416.963, and Part 404, Subpart P, Appendix 2). For additional information and examples, see also Program Operations Manual System (POMS) DI 25015.006.

When deciding whether to apply a higher age category in a borderline age situation, the ALJ will:

1. Determine the Time Period Under Review.

> The ALJ will first determine the time period under review. For example, under a particular fact scenario, the time under review may be a "few days to a few months" between the date of adjudication and the date the claimant attains age 55 and would be found disabled under a direct application of the medical-vocational rules. The closer in time the claimant is to the next higher age category, the more disadvantageous the claimant's age.

2. Analyze the Other Factor(s) of the Case.

The ALJ will consider all other factor(s) relevant to the case (e.g., residual functional capacity combined with age, education, and work experience as explained in 20 CFR 404.1563, 416.963, and Part 404, Subpart P, Appendix 2) for each of the medical-vocational rules for chronological age and the higher age category. The ALJ will consider whether an adjudicative factor(s) is relatively more adverse under the criteria of each rule, or whether there is an additional element(s) present that seriously affects a claimant's ability to adjust to other work. Examples of situations where certain factors may impact the case can be found in POMS DI 25015.006E.

ALJs must be careful not to double-weigh a factor if the medical-vocational rule for the higher age category already incorporates the factor. For example, if the applicable medical-vocational rule for the higher age category already considers illiteracy (such as a younger individual age 44 years and 9 months who has a reduced sedentary residual functional capacity, and the adjudicator is considering applying the higher age category (45-49) medical-vocational rule 201.17), then there would need to be factors other than illiteracy to justify application of the higher age category.

3. Determine Whether the Overall Impact of the Factor(s) Justifies Using the Higher Age Category to Find the Claimant "Disabled."

The ALJ will take a "sliding scale" approach when determining which age category to use. To support the use of the higher age category, the claimant must show that the factor(s) have a progressively more adverse impact on his or her ability to adjust to other work as the period between the claimant's actual age and attainment of the next higher age category lengthens.

4. Determine Onset.

If all of the factors support using the higher age category, the ALJ will find the claimant disabled with an established onset date corresponding to the:

- Date of adjudication;
- Date last insured;
- End of disabled widow(er)'s benefit prescribed period;
- End of child disability re-entitlement period; or
- Date of cessation of disability.

If there is no support for the use of the higher age category (e.g., the factors present do not negatively affect or have a more adverse impact on the case), ALJs will use the claimant's chronological age, even when the period under consideration is only a few days.

5. Include in the Decision an Explanation that the Borderline Age Situation Was Considered.

The ALJ will explain in the decision that he or she considered the borderline age situation, state whether he or she applied the higher age category or the chronological age, and note the specific factor(s) he or she considered.

NOTE:

Even when the ALJ is using the higher age category to issue a favorable decision, the ALJ must identify the specific factors that support the use of the higher age category.

If we apply these rules to our hypothetical claimant, note that in order for him to be found disabled as of his date last insured, there must be some vocational adversities to justify use of the higher age rule. It is not enough that there be a borderline age situation. The fact that there are only seven weeks between his date last insured and his 50th birthday is important for applying the "sliding scale" approach. But there must be one or more additional vocational adversities that are not already accounted for in the grid rule you want applied to your client's case in order for the ALJ to justify applying the higher age category. Such additional vocational adversities can come from the claimant's RFC, education or work experience. In most cases, a claimant's representative can usually find some vocational adversity to point to.

The examples given in POMS DI 25001.001B.2 of additional vocational adversities may be useful:

> Consider additional vocational adversities when deciding to use a claimant's chronological age in a borderline age issue. Additional vocational adversities can be in a claimant's residual functional capacity (RFC), education, or work experience. *See* DI

25015.005 for the borderline age issue definition. *See* DI 25015.006 for details on borderline age.

- **RFC:** In borderline age issues, the adjudicator considers if limitations and restrictions in the RFC that affect, but do not substantially erode, a claimant's remaining occupational base are additional vocational adversities. **EXAMPLE:** A claimant aged 49 years and 10 months who cannot do past relevant work (PRW) with a sedentary RFC, 12th grade education, and unskilled work will meet medical-vocational rule 201.12 at attainment of age 50. The claimant has reduced hearing ability. Because this limitation affects, but does not substantially erode, the sedentary occupational base, the adjudicator should consider whether it might be an additional vocational adversity.
- **Education:** When using a medical-vocational rule that expresses education as a continuum, the adjudicator may consider facts falling at the lower end of the continuum to be an additional vocational adversity. **EXAMPLE:** An individual who is 54 years, 9 months of age with a light RFC, unskilled medium work experience and a 5th grade education will meet medical-vocational rule 202.01 at attainment of age 55. The rule requires limited or less education (11th grade or less). The adjudicator should consider whether education may be an additional vocational adversity if the individual has an education at the lower end of the rule continuum.
- **Illiteracy or inability to communicate in English** is defined as the inability to read or write a simple message such as instructions or inventory lists. As such, illiteracy or inability to communicate in English can only be considered to be an additional vocational adversity when using a special medical-vocational profile, or if an individual is a few days to a few months of attaining advanced age, has a medium RFC and no past relevant work, or is a few days to a few months of "closely approaching retirement age," has a medium RFC, cannot do past work, and has unskilled or no work experience (medical-vocational rules 203.10, 203.02, 203.01). In all other instances, illiteracy or inability to communicate in English will already be material to the allowance and cannot be used again as an additional adversity. **EXAMPLE:** A claimant aged 44 years, 10 months with a sedentary RFC, unskilled medium work experience, who is illiterate or unable to communicate in English would meet medical-vocational rule 201.17 at attainment of age 45. Because the claimant must be illiterate or unable to communicate in English to meet this rule, the adjudicator could only consider whether the claimant had additional RFC or work experience-related adversities.
- **Work experience:** Because no past relevant work is more adverse than other work experience categories, the adjudicator considers whether no past relevant work might be an additional vocational adversity except when using a rule that an individual can meet only by having no past relevant work experience. **EXAMPLE:** Medical-vocational rule 203.02 requires no past relevant work, so "no past relevant work" could not be considered an additional adversity when using this rule. Medical-vocational rule 203.01 requires unskilled or no past relevant work experience. No past relevant work could be considered an additional adversity when using this rule because it is a more adverse vocational factor than unskilled past relevant work.
- **Isolated industry:** The adjudicator should consider whether work in an isolated industry might be an additional vocational adversity. **EXAMPLE:** A claimant aged 54 years 11 months with a 10th grade education, a light RFC and past medium skilled work with no transferable skills meets medical-vocational 202.02 at attainment of age 55. If the claimant's past relevant work was as a salmon fisherman, this could be considered a job in an isolated industry. Such work experience could be an additional adversity that could be considered in a borderline age issue.

How age affects a claimant's ability to work is not explained anywhere in the regulations. Instead, it appears in the commentary that was published when the Medical- Vocational Guidelines were first promulgated. "[W] here age is critical to a decision, recognition is taken of increasing physiological deterioration in the senses, joints, eye-hand coordination, reflexes, thinking processes, etc., which diminish a severely impaired person's aptitude for new learning and adaptation to new jobs." 43 Fed. Reg. 55,359 (1978). At another point this commentary refers to age "in terms of how the progressive deteriorative changes which occur as individuals get older affect their vocational capacities to perform jobs." 43 Fed. Reg. 55,353 (1978).

§123 Education

As a rule, SSA uses the highest grade completed in school in evaluating educational level. However, the regulation itself recognizes that a person's actual educational abilities may be higher or lower. SSA will accept evidence that a claimant's actual educational level is lower than the numerical grade completed in school. 20 C.F.R. § 404.1564(b). Achievement testing, such as with the Wide Range Achievement Test (WRAT), may show a low educational level.

§124 Work Experience

SSA classifies work as unskilled, semiskilled and skilled. Unskilled work is work that may be learned in 30 days or less. 20 C.F.R. § 404.1568(a). Everything else is either semiskilled or skilled. For the purposes of the Medical-Vocational Guidelines, semiskilled and skilled work is treated as one category. This treatment has spawned the issue of transferability of work skills. *See* §349 *et seq.*

§125 Full or Wide Range of Work

Under certain circumstances, a claimant can somewhat exceed the maximum residual functional capacity stated in the Medical-Vocational Guidelines (*see* chart at §121.1) and still be found disabled under the rule for the lower RFC. To give an example: a claimant's doctor says the claimant may not lift more than 50 pounds but fails to explain that the claimant may not engage in repetitive lifting of weights of more than about 10 pounds and may not bend or stoop frequently. Based on the 50-pound lifting limitation, SSA may leap to the conclusion that the grid for medium work should be applied and issue a denial decision.

However, to apply a rule from one of the grids in the Medical-Vocational Guidelines to the facts of a particular claimant's case, that claimant must be capable of doing a "full or wide range" of work at the exertional level applicable to that grid. That is, the claimant must be capable of substantially all of the activities at that exertional level. SSRs 83-10 and 83-11.

Medium work requires frequent lifting of 25 pounds and frequent bending or stooping, both of which are beyond the capacity of our hypothetical claimant. Thus, our claimant has the RFC for only slightly more than light work. Therefore, the light grid may be applied, which may require a decision that this claimant is disabled. For more information about how to evaluate an RFC that falls between ranges of work, *see* Social Security Ruling 83-12.

As you can see, understanding the definitions of the exertional levels that appear in 20 C.F.R. § 404.1567 is extremely important to application of the proper grid to your client's case. Social Security Ruling 83-10 provides the most detailed explanation of medium, light and sedentary work. These explanations are set forth below.

§125.1 Definition of Medium Work From SSR 83-10

"The regulations define medium work as lifting no more than 50 pounds at a time with frequent lifting or carrying of objects weighing up to 25 pounds. A full range of medium work requires standing or walking, off and on, for a total of approximately 6 hours in an 8-hour workday in order to meet the requirements of frequent lifting or carrying objects weighing up to 25 pounds. As in light work, sitting may occur intermittently during the remaining time. Use of the arms and hands is necessary to grasp, hold, and turn objects, as opposed to the finer activities in much sedentary work, which require precision use of the fingers as well as use of the hands and arms.

"The considerable lifting required for the full range of medium work usually requires frequent bending-stooping. (Stooping is a type of bending in which a person bends his body downward and forward by bending the spine at the waist.) Flexibility of the knees as well as the torso is important for this activity. (Crouching is bending both the legs and spine in order to bend the body downward and forward.) However, there are relatively few occupations in the national economy which require exertion in terms of weights that must be lifted at times (or involve equivalent exertion in pushing or pulling), but are performed primarily in a sitting position, *e.g.*, taxi driver, bus driver, and tank-truck driver (semiskilled jobs). In most medium jobs, being on one's feet for most of the workday is critical. Being able to do frequent lifting or carrying of objects weighing up to 25 pounds is often more critical than being able to lift up to 50 pounds at a time."

§125.2 Definition of Light Work From SSR 83-10

"The regulations define light work as lifting no more than 20 pounds at a time with frequent lifting or carrying of objects weighing up to 10 pounds. Even though the weight lifted in a particular light job may be very little, a job is in this category when it requires a good deal of walking or standing—the primary difference between sedentary and most light jobs. A job also is in this category when it involves sitting most of the time but with some pushing and pulling of arm-hand or leg-foot controls, which require greater exertion than in sedentary work; *e.g.*, mattress sewing machine operator, motor-grader operator, and road-roller operator (skilled and semiskilled jobs in these particular instances). Relatively few unskilled light jobs are performed in a seated position.

"'Frequent' means occurring from one-third to two-thirds of the time. Since frequent lifting or carrying requires being on one's feet up to two-thirds of a workday, the full range of light work requires standing or walking, off and on, for a total of approximately 6 hours of an 8-hour workday. Sitting may occur intermittently during the remaining time. The lifting requirement for the majority of light jobs can be accomplished with occasional, rather than frequent, stooping. Many unskilled light jobs are performed primarily in one location, with the ability to stand being more critical than the ability to walk. They require use of arms and hands to grasp and to hold and turn objects, and they generally do not require use of the fingers for fine activities to the extent required in much sedentary work."

§125.3 Definition of Sedentary Work From SSR 83-10

"The regulations define sedentary work as involving lifting no more than 10 pounds at a time and occasionally lifting or carrying articles like docket files, ledgers and small tools. Although sitting is involved, a certain amount of walking and standing often is necessary in carrying out job duties. Jobs are sedentary if walking and standing are required occasionally and other sedentary criteria are met. By its very nature, work performed primarily in a seated position entails no significant stooping. Most unskilled sedentary jobs require good use of the hands and fingers for repetitive hand-finger actions.

"'Occasionally' means occurring from very little up to one-third of the time. Since being on one's feet is required 'occasionally' at the sedentary level of exertion, periods of standing or walking should generally total no more than about 2 hours of an 8-hour workday, and sitting should generally total approximately 6 hours of an 8-hour workday. Work processes in specific jobs will dictate how often and how long a person will need to be on his or her feet to obtain or return small articles."

§126 RFC for Less Than Full Range of Sedentary Work

Go back and look at the chart, §121.1, for the age categories under 50. At first glance, proof of disability for almost everyone under age 50 looks like an impossible task. Disability for such individuals requires proof that they can do much less than a full or wide range of sedentary work, described by SSR 83-12 as a "significance compromise" of the sedentary occupational base. This means, according to SSR 96-9p, that jobs for them do not exist in significant numbers. Although this is frequently difficult, it is not impossible.

For example, our hypothetical machine operator in §100 has an RFC for much less than a wide range of sedentary work. He may be found disabled despite his young age and high school education because of a limitation to sedentary work *plus* an impairment that affects bimanual dexterity. This result is based on SSRs 83-10 and 96-9p, which point out that "most sedentary jobs require good use of both hands." However, a note of caution is appropriate here. SSA's position, in effect, is that although a person limited to sedentary work with limited bimanual dexterity will *usually* be found disabled, this conclusion can be rebutted by vocational expert testimony in an individual case.

For most claimants under age 50, as a preliminary matter, it is necessary to show that they can do neither a wide range of sedentary work nor a wide range of light work. It is essential, then, to have a thorough understanding of SSA's definitions of sedentary and light work. *See* §§125.2 and 125.3, from Social Security Ruling 83-10.

In order to prove that the sedentary occupational base is significantly compromised, you will usually look for a combination of exertional and nonexertional impairments. Each additional impairment whittles away the range of sedentary work that a claimant is capable of doing to arrive at the point where jobs do not exist in significant numbers. *See* §§260 *et seq.,* on designing a case for a claimant under age 50. *See* §348.8, on dealing with vocational experts regarding whether significant numbers of jobs exist within the claimant's RFC.

Often, you will find individuals who, for one reason or another, cannot sit for the six hours out of an eight-hour day required to do sedentary work, nor can they stand for six hours out of an eight-hour day required to do light work. A common residual functional capacity describes claimants who must alternate between sitting and standing. Although Social Security Ruling 83-12 analyzes this RFC, this RFC does present several challenges to lawyers representing claimants, a subject dealt with in detail at §§348.4 and 348.9. The SSR 83-12 statement on the subject is reproduced below.

§126.1 Alternate Sitting and Standing From SSRs 83-12 and 96-9p

SSR 83-12 provides:

> In some disability claims, the medical facts lead to an assessment of RFC which is compatible with the performance of either sedentary or light work except that the person must alternate periods of sitting and standing. The individual may be able to sit for a time, but must then get up and stand or walk for a while before returning to sitting. Such an individual is not functionally capable of doing either the prolonged sitting contemplated in the definition of sedentary work (and for the relatively few light jobs which are performed primarily in a seated position) or the prolonged standing or walking contemplated for most light work. (Persons who can adjust sitting

and standing by doing so at breaks, lunch periods, etc., would still be able to perform a defined range of work.)

There are some jobs in the national economy—typically professional and managerial ones—in which a person can sit or stand with a degree of choice. If an individual had such a job and is still capable of performing it, or is capable of transferring work skills to such jobs, he or she would not be found disabled. However, most jobs have ongoing work processes which demand that a worker be in a certain place or posture for at least a certain length of time to accomplish a certain task. Unskilled types of jobs are particularly structured so that a person cannot ordinarily sit or stand at will. In cases of unusual limitation of ability to sit or stand, a V[ocational] S[pecialist] should be consulted to clarify the implications for the occupational base.

SSR 96-9p added the following to the discussion of alternate sitting and standing jobs:

Alternate sitting and standing: An individual may need to alternate the required sitting of sedentary work by standing (and, possibly, walking) periodically. Where this need cannot be accommodated by scheduled breaks and a lunch period, the occupational base for a full range of unskilled sedentary work will be eroded. The extent of the erosion will depend on the facts in the case record, such as the frequency of the need to alternate sitting and standing and the length of time needed to stand. The RFC assessment must be specific as to the frequency of the individual's need to alternate sitting and standing. It may be especially useful in these situations to consult a vocational resource in order to determine whether the individual is able to make an adjustment to other work.

§127 Nonexertional Limitations

Exertional abilities involve sitting, standing, walking, lifting, carrying, pushing and pulling. 20 C.F.R. § 404.1569a. A limitation of any other work-related ability is a nonexertional limitation. A list of categories and examples follows:

Category	Example
Postural:	**Need to alternate sitting and standing; Need to elevate leg; Difficulty turning head; Balance problems; Difficulty bending, stooping or squatting.**
Manipulative:	**Difficulties with reaching, grasping, handling, fingering.**
Environmental:	**Difficulties working around fumes, dust, etc.; Difficulties tolerating noise, heights, humidity or temperature extremes; Inability to be around dangerous machinery.**
Mental:	**Difficulties relating with others; Difficulty understanding, remembering or carrying out simple instructions; Inability to maintain attention or concentration; Poor stress tolerance.**
Sensory:	**Difficulties speaking, hearing, feeling or seeing.**

This list is by no means exhaustive. Note that a nonexertional *impairment* may impose more than one type of nonexertional *limitation*. For example, a skin impairment may impose both environmental and manipulative limitations and may affect work in other ways, also. Some impairments, such as certain gastro-intestinal impairments, impose nonexertional limitations by forcing a worker to be absent from the work area to lie down or go to the restroom, *etc*.

Many impairments have both exertional and nonexertional implications. For example, amputation of an arm will limit the weight a claimant can lift, an exertional impairment, and will limit bimanual dexterity, a nonexertional manipulative impairment.

Nonexertional impairments need to be carefully examined. They are discussed in Social Security Rulings 83-12, 83-14, 85-15, 96-4p, 96-8p and 96-9p. You may need to consult your own vocational expert for help evaluating the impact of such limitations on your client's ability to work.

§128 Transferable Work Skills

You also may need a vocational expert to help you manage the complex problem of transferability of work skills. If you examine the three grids from the Medical-Vocational Guidelines, you will discover that a claimant is never disabled if the claimant has skills transferable to jobs within his or her RFC that exist in significant numbers. On the other hand a finding of no transferable work skills may lead to a finding of disability in certain cases. But note that in only two age categories does the issue of transferability of skills determine the outcome of the case. If a claimant is age 50 or older and is limited to sedentary work, the claimant wins or loses the case based upon whether or not the claimant has skills transferable to sedentary work. If a claimant is age 55 or older, this rule extends to light work—a claimant wins or loses based on whether or not the claimant has skills transferable to a significant range of semiskilled or skilled light work.

Since an unskilled work background produces no transferable skills, the rules about transferability apply only to claimants with histories of semiskilled or skilled work.

The standards for determining transferability differ for age categories beginning with ages 50, 55 and 60, making it easier as a claimant gets older to show that skills are not transferable to a significant range of work within the claimant's RFC. At age 50, garden-variety transferability of skills to sedentary work is all that is required to turn down a case based on the presence of transferable skills. To find that skills of a 55-year-old claimant are transferable to sedentary work, SSA must meet a higher burden. It must show that there is "very little, if any, vocational adjustment required in terms of tools, work settings, or the industry." Rule 201.00(f) of the Medical-Vocational Guidelines. A 55-year-old claimant limited to light work needs only garden-variety transferable work skills in order to be turned down. But at age 60 for claimants limited to light work, SSA must meet a higher burden—the same higher burden that applies to 55-year-olds limited to sedentary work. *See* Rules 202.00(c) and (e) of the Medical-Vocational Guidelines. *See* §349.6 for a chart showing the transferability standards for different ages; *and see* §349 for an extensive discussion of the transferability issue.

In that rare situation where recently completed education provides for direct entry into skilled work, the Guidelines always require a finding of not disabled. *See* Rules 201.05, 201.08, 201.13, 201.16, 202.05, 202.08, 203.09, 203.17 and 203.24.

§129 Medical-Vocational Guidelines as Framework for Decision-Making

The grids govern the outcome of cases where they exactly describe a claimant. But the characteristics of many claimants do not fall squarely within the Guidelines. For example, a claimant's residual functional capacity may fall between ranges of work, a claimant may have only nonexertional impairments, or a claimant may have a combination of exertional and nonexertional impairments. In these cases, the Medical-Vocational Guidelines, by their own terms, are to be used as "an overall structure for evaluation" and a "framework for consideration" of disability. *See* Rules 200.00(d) and (e).

The most important principle of the Medical-Vocational Guidelines may be stated as follows: the more adverse a claimant's vocational factors (age, education and work experience), the more remaining residual functional capacity the claimant may have and still be found disabled. Consider our hypothetical housewife in §100. She is age 55, has a limited education and no relevant work experience. The grids find her disabled despite her residual functional capacity for medium work, a capacity which means that she is physically capable of performing about 2,500 out of the approximately 3,100 unskilled occupations identified in the *Dictionary of Occupational Titles*.

This fundamental principle of the Guidelines is based on the concept of vocational adaptability. Younger, better-educated people with work experience are more adaptable to job changes despite a decline in RFC caused by a medical impairment. Such younger claimants must demonstrate a more restricted RFC in order to be found disabled. Indeed, according to the Medical-Vocational Guidelines, English-speaking claimants with exertional impairments who are under age 50 must have such restricted RFCs that they are limited to much less than a wide range of sedentary work—to the point that jobs do not exist in significant numbers, according to SSR 96-9p. Using the Guidelines as a framework, an English-speaking claimant under age 50 with nonexertional impairments must have a similarly restricted occupational base.

Using the Medical-Vocational Guidelines as a framework for analysis is a slippery concept that is not well understood by claimants' attorneys or even by ALJs. It is the subject of three Social Security Rulings, SSRs 83-12, 83-14 and 85-15. SSR 96-9p, with its emphasis on whether jobs exist in significant numbers, departs somewhat from the earlier rulings. *See* §348, for a detailed discussion.

§130 Social Security Disability and SSI: Nondisability Requirements and Other Differences

§131 Social Security Disability — Worker's Insured Status

The Social Security program for workers functions like an insurance plan. There are requirements that a claimant for disability insurance must have:

- Contributed to the program (paid Social Security taxes) over a sufficiently long period to be "fully insured," and
- Contributed to the program recently enough to have "disability insured status."

In short, a worker must have paid Social Security taxes in order to be "insured," just like paying the premiums for a private insurance policy. After stopping work (and stopping paying Social Security taxes), there will come a time when insured status will lapse, just like with a private insurance policy.

Contributions are counted in "quarters of coverage," abbreviated QC by SSA, with minimum earnings requirements that, since 1978, go up every year. Before 1978 a nonagricultural worker generally could earn only one QC if he or she worked in only one calendar quarter of the year, no matter how great the earnings. (A calendar quarter is one of the following three-month periods: January through March, April through June, July through September, or October through December.) Before 1978 a worker need earn only $50 in wages in a calendar quarter to count as a "quarter of coverage." Thus, to evaluate how many QCs a worker earned prior to 1978, you need to know how much a worker earned and during what months of the year the money was earned. 20 C.F.R. §§ 404.140 through 404.146.

Beginning in 1978, an individual with sufficient earnings in one calendar quarter could earn QCs for the entire year, up to a total of four QCs for a calendar year. Thus, beginning in 1978 you need only consider total annual earnings and compare to the minimum earnings for a quarter of coverage. To take an example, in 2000 minimum earnings for a QC was $780. Therefore, a claimant who earned $3120 or more in wages in 2000 was credited with four QCs, no matter when the money was earned during 2000. 20 C.F.R. §§ 404.143 through 404.146.

Occasionally, you will encounter a case where, in order to meet the insured status rules, a claimant needs those extra quarters of coverage credited during the year he or she stopped working. For example, let's say that a claimant who earned $3120 in 2000 actually stopped working because of disability on March 31, 2000. Because the worker needs all four quarters of coverage in order to meet the insured status rules, the worker does not become insured until October 1, 2000. This is the "date first insured." This worker cannot be found disabled for Social Security disability before this date. Note that a quarter of coverage is acquired on the first day of the quarter in which it is assigned. 20 C.F.R. §§ 404.110(e) and 404.145.

To be *fully insured*, as a rule, a claimant must have one QC for every calendar year after the year in which he or she turned 21, up to the calendar year before becoming disabled, though more than 40 QCs are never required. 20 C.F.R. §§ 404.110 and 404.132.

The rule for *disability insured status* for those over 31 years old is that they must have 20 quarters of coverage out of the 40 calendar quarters before they become disabled. 20 C.F.R. § 404.130. This is referred to as the 20/40 rule. Significant work in five years out of the last 10 years usually satisfies this requirement. For a claimant with a steady work record, insured status will lapse about five years after stopping work. To receive any Social Security disability benefits, such a claimant will have to prove that he or she was disabled before the "date last insured." Our hypothetical housewife described in §100 does not have current insured status because she has not worked for over 15 years. Thus, she is not eligible for Social Security disability benefits even though she is disabled for SSI purposes.

For those who become disabled before age 31 there is a reduced quarter of coverage requirement. Such a younger claimant must have earned QCs in one-half the calendar quarters beginning with the quarter after the quarter in which he or she attained age 21 and ending with the quarter in which he or she became disabled. If the number of elapsing calendar quarters is an odd number, the next lower even number is used. A minimum of 6 QCs is required. If a claimant becomes disabled before age 24, an alternative rule applies. He or she must simply have 6 QCs in the 12-quarter period ending with the quarter in which disability began. Under the alternative rule, there is no requirement that the QCs be earned after attaining age 21. 20 C.F.R. § 404.130(c). *See* section III of SSR 11-2p. *See also* POMS RS 00301.140, which contains a good discussion filled with examples.

As a rule those who have "disability insured status" are also "fully insured." But there are circumstances where this is not so. Evaluating denials based on insured status requires careful reading of the regulations and the claimant's earnings record. *See* 20 C.F.R. §§ 404.101 to 404.146 and §205.4 of this book.

§132 SSI

The Supplemental Security Income (SSI) program is a federal welfare program for the disabled, blind and those over 65. In contrast to Social Security disability, benefits are paid out of general revenues, not out of the Social Security trust fund. Many states supplement the federal SSI benefit. Thus, the SSI benefit amount varies from state to state.

To meet all the requirements to receive SSI a claimant must:

- Be "disabled" using the same definition as is used for the Social Security disability program;
- Meet the income and asset requirements of the SSI program;
- Be a U.S. citizen or fall into the group of limited exceptions to the citizenship rule (*see* §136); and
- File an application

There are both income and asset limitations for eligibility. *See* 20 C.F.R. §§ 416.1100 to 416.1266. The income limit is based upon the SSI benefit amount after several different kinds and amounts of unearned income are "disregarded"; and part of earned income is disregarded under a formula designed to encourage SSI recipients to work. There is also a formula for counting part of the income of parents of minors or spouses who live with the claimant. Application of this formula is called "deeming."

Claimants may receive both Social Security disability and SSI benefits if the Social Security disability benefits are low enough. When both kinds of benefits are received, the recipient's total income from the two programs equals the SSI benefit amount plus $20. However, even where high Social Security disability benefits disqualify a claimant from receiving SSI, he or she still may get SSI during the five-month waiting period when no Social Security disability benefits are paid, assuming assets and any other income are small enough.

The asset limitation beginning in 1989 is $2,000 for an individual and $3,000 for a couple. Several assets are excluded, the most significant of which are the home of any value and one car of any value if it is used for work or to obtain medical care. *See* 20 C.F.R. §§ 416.1210 *et seq.*

§133 Retroactivity of Applications and Waiting Period

During the history of the SSI program, SSI benefits have never been paid for any time before the date of the application; in other words, there is no retroactive effect of an SSI application. Social Security disability, on the other hand, may pay benefits for the 12 months preceding the date of application if all requirements are met. Claimants who are not currently eligible for Social Security disability benefits must be found entitled to at least one month of benefits during this 12-month period in order for a "period of disability" to be established. For example, if a claimant alleges a disability that ended more than about 14 months before the date of application, SSA will not even bother to investigate if the claimant really was disabled during this time because no benefits are payable.

An exception to this rule allows filing up to 36 months after the period of disability ended if a physical or mental condition prevented a claimant from applying. *See* 20 C.F.R. §§ 404.621(d) and 404.320(b)(3). Since it is hard to see how an impairment could be so severe as to prevent application for benefits but not severe enough to make the person unable to work, this exception must be applicable primarily to those whose disabilities begin just before full retirement age, after which there can be no period of disability. They would have until three years after full retirement age to apply under this exception.

There used to be no waiting period for SSI. For applications before August 22, 1996, SSI was paid from the date of application if all requirements were met. For SSI applications filed on or after August 22, 1996, there is an effective waiting period until the first of the next month after all requirements are met. 20 C.F.R. §§ 416.330 and 416.335. For Social Security disability there is a five-month waiting period after the "onset date," the date disability began, during which no Social Security disability benefits are payable. Because only *full* months are counted, the actual waiting period is nearly always more than five months. Only when a person becomes disabled on the first day of the month is the waiting period exactly five months.

§134 Other Differences

A significant procedural difference between the Social Security disability and SSI programs appears in the time limit for requesting reopening of earlier applications based on good cause, such as where there is new evidence or where the earlier decision was wrong on its face. For Social Security disability, that time limit is four years from the date of the notice of the initial determination. 20 C.F.R. § 404.988(b). For SSI, that time limit is two years. 20 C.F.R. § 416.1488(b). *See also* §§370 *et seq.*

Payment processing within the Social Security Administration differs for the two programs, knowledge of which is useful when you are trying to track down and correct a payment delay. SSI payment is processed at the local Social Security office. Social Security disability payment is processed in Baltimore for those under age 55. Payment for those over 55 is processed at regional payment centers. *See also* §§440 *et seq.*

Social Security disability benefits applicable to one month are paid during the next month. For example, a Social Security disability payment for January is paid in February. For SSI, the check received in January is for January.

There also are some differences in the way benefits are paid. These differences are helpful when you're talking to a recipient of disability benefits and trying to figure out whether he or she is receiving Social Security disability or SSI payments, a distinction that many recipients of benefits do not make. SSI benefits arrive in the mail or by direct deposit on the first of the month. An SSI check says SSI on it. A Social Security disability check is very similar to an SSI check but it includes the reference: SOC SEC FOR INS.

In a concurrent claim in which a beneficiary receives both Social Security disability and SSI payments, the Social Security disability portion is paid on the third of the month. If a beneficiary receives only Social Security disability benefits, those benefits are paid on the second, third or fourth Wednesday of the month depending on the beneficiary's birthday. Those born on the 1st through the 10th of the month are paid on the second Wednesday. Those born on the 11th through the 20th are paid on the third Wednesday. The rest are paid on the fourth Wednesday.

§135 Chart: Social Security Disability and SSI Compared

Issue	SS Disability	SSI
Disability standard:	Same for both programs.	
Source of payment:	Social Security trust fund.	General revenue.
Amount of payment:	Based on worker's earnings record.	Federal amount set by Congress plus state supplement, if any, set by state. State supplement amount may vary according to living arrangement.
Payment to children:	Yes, additional payment based on earnings record to children under age 18 or under age 19 and still in high school.	No increased federal payment for child; but some state SSI supplements add money for children. Otherwise, children may receive welfare, which is not counted as income; i.e., welfare does not reduce SSI benefit amount.
Payment to spouse:	Yes, if child in spouse's care is under age 16 or is disabled. There is an income limit for spouse's payment.	No increased federal payment but some state SSI supplements add money for spouse.
Earnings requirement:	Fully insured (1 QC for each year after age 21); and disability insured status (20/40 rule).	None.
Asset limitation:	None.	$2,000 individual; $3,000 couple.
Unearned income limit:	None.	A small amount is disregarded; the rest is deducted from SSI benefit.
Earned income limit:	Same for both programs for claimants; SGA results in step one denial.	After individual is receiving benefits, SSI has more liberal rules designed to encourage work.
Waiting period:	Five full months from date of onset of disability.	For applications on or after August 22, 1996, payment begins with first of month after all requirements are met. For earlier applications, payment begins with date of application if all requirements are met.

Issue	SS Disability	SSI
Retroactivity of application:	12 months if all requirements are met.	No retroactivity.
Time limit for reopening for good cause:	4 years.	2 years.
Payment processing office:	Baltimore or regional payment center.	Local office.
Payment applies to:	Previous month.	Current month.
Payment date:	Varies by birthday except concurrent cases paid on 3rd of month.	1st day of month.
Check says:	SOC SEC FOR INS.	SSI.
Attorney's fees:	Up to 25 percent of past due benefits withheld for direct payment.	Up to 25 percent of back benefits withheld for direct payment.
Medical coverage:	Medicare begins after receipt of 24 months of benefits.	Medicaid coverage in most states begins with entitlement to SSI (sometimes 3 months before).
Eligibility of legal aliens:	Eligible.	Aliens who were lawfully residing in the U.S. on August 22, 1996 are, for the most part, eligible for SSI disability benefits; but those who arrived later are ineligible with limited exceptions.

§136 Eligibility of Aliens

The welfare reform legislation signed into law on August 22, 1996, made legal aliens ineligible for SSI benefits with some limited (and complicated) exceptions. A year later, this law was amended to make most legal aliens who were residing in the United States on August 22, 1996 eligible for SSI disability benefits and to grandfather in those aliens who were eligible to receive benefits on August 22, 1996. Thus, the original law applies only to those aliens who arrive in the United States after August 22, 1996. Public Law 110-328, enacted October 1, 2008, granted a two or three year extension to certain categories of aliens. The result is an odd patchwork that requires careful analysis. A threshold issue is the definition of U.S. "resident" and the acceptable types of evidence for proving status as a U.S. citizen or national. These are provided in 20 C.F.R. §§ 416.1603 and 416.1610.

A good description of which aliens were eligible for SSI appeared in an attachment to a memorandum from the Chief Administrative Law Judge dated August 29, 1997. This is an updated and edited version of that document:

The following is a list of the only categories of people who may be eligible for SSI:

1. Citizens or nationals of the U.S.
2. Aliens who are lawfully admitted for permanent residence under the Immigration and Nationality ACT (INA) and who have worked long enough to have at least a total of 40 qualifying quarters of work. An alien may get the 40 quarters of work himself or herself. Also, work done by a spouse or parent may count toward the 40 quarters of work for getting SSI only. We cannot count any quarter of work acquired after December 31, 1996 if the alien or the worker received certain types of federally funded assistance during that quarter.
3. Certain aliens who are blind or disabled and were lawfully residing in the U.S. on August 22, 1996. Note that this provision creates a new category of claimants who attorneys may be asked to prove disabled: Aliens over age 65. See SSR 99-3p about proving disability for claimants over age 65.
4. Certain aliens who are lawfully residing in the U.S. and who were "receiving" SSI benefits on August 22, 1996. SSA has interpreted this provision to apply to those whose claims were filed before August 22, 1996 and who were eligible to receive benefits for periods prior to August 22, 1996 even if their claims were not finally adjudicated and they were not actually being paid prior to August 22, 1996.
5. American Indians born outside the U.S. who are under section 289 of the INA or who are members of federally recognized Indian tribes under section 4(e) of the Indian Self-Determination and Educational Assistance Act.
6. Aliens admitted as refugees under section 207 of the INA. SSI eligibility is limited to the first 7 years after being admitted as a refugee. The 7-year limit applies even if the alien's status changes to lawfully admitted for permanent residence. Public Law 110-328 granted a two-year extension to most refugees, three years if the refugee has shown good faith in pursuing U.S. citizenship as determined by the Department of Homeland Security. However, the time limit does not apply at all if the alien meets the requirements in category 2, 3, 4, or 11.
7. Aliens granted asylum under section 208 of the INA. SSI eligibility is limited to the first 7 years after asylum is granted. The 7-year limit applies even if the alien's status changes to lawfully admitted for permanent residence. However, this time limit was extended by two or three years by Public Law 110-328, the same as for refugees described in category 6 above. The time limit does not apply at all if the alien meets the requirements in category 2, 3, 4, or 11.
8. Aliens whose deportation has been withheld under section 243(h) of the INA as in effect prior to April 1, 1997, or whose removal has been withheld under section 241(b)(3) of the INA. SSI eligibility is limited to the first 7 years after deportation or removal is withheld. The 7-year limit applies even if the alien's status changes to lawfully admitted for permanent residence. However, no time limit applies if the alien meets the requirements in category 2, 3, 4, or 11. Public Law 110-328 also extended the time limit by two or three years for this category, the same as for those described in categories 6 and 7 above.
9. Aliens who are Cuban or Haitian entrants as defined in section 501(e) of the Refugee Education Assistance Act of 1980. SSI eligibility is limited to the first 7 years after entrant status is granted. The 7-year time limit applies even if the alien's status changes to lawfully admitted for permanent residence. However, the 7-year limit does not apply if the alien meets the requirements in category 2, 3, 4, or 11. Public Law 110-328 also extended

the time limit by two or three years for this category, the same as for those described in categories 6, 7 and 8 above.

10. Aliens who are admitted to the U.S. as Amerasian immigrants under section 584 of the Foreign Operations, Export Financing, and Related Programs Appropriation Act, 1988 (as contained in section 101(e) of Public Law 100-202 and amended by the 9th proviso under "Migration and Refugee Assistance" in title II of the Foreign Operations, Export Financing, and Related programs Appropriations Act, 1989, Public Law 100-461, as amended.) SSI eligibility is limited to the first 7 years after being admitted. The 7-year time limit applies even if the alien's status changes to lawfully admitted for permanent residence. However, the 7-year limit does not apply if the alien meets the requirements in category 2, 3, 4, or 11. Public Law 110-328 also extended the time limit by two or three years for this category, the same as for those described in categories 6, 7, 8 and 9 above.
11. Certain aliens who are:
    - Active duty members of the U.S. Armed Forces (except for training purposes only), or
    - Honorably discharged veterans of the U.S. Armed Forces but not discharged because of alien status, or
    - Spouses, including unremarried widows or widowers, or unmarried dependent children of people in the above two groups.

AND

Under categories 3, 4, 10, and 11, the alien must also be a qualified alien as follows:

- Lawfully admitted for permanent residence under the INA;
- A refugee under section 207 of the INA;
- An asylee under section 208 of the INA;
- A person whose deportation is withheld under section 243(h) of the INA as in effect prior to April 1, 1997, or whose removal has been withheld under section 241(b)(3) of the INA;
- A parolee under section 212(d)(5) of the INA for at least one year;
- A person granted conditional entry under section 203(a)(7) of the INA as in effect prior to April 1, 1980;
- A Cuban or Haitian entrant as defined in section 501(e) of the Refugee Education Assistance Act of 1980; or
- A certain alien, or an alien parent of a child, or an alien child of a parent who has:
    - been battered or subjected to extreme cruelty in the U.S. by a spouse, parent, or certain other family members the alien, parent, and/or child lived with; and
    - been determined to need SSI because of this abuse; and
    - a determination from the Immigration and Natura-lization Service (INS) for a certain change in status.

§140 Special Disability Programs

Special disability programs under both Title II (Social Security disability) and Title XVI (SSI) serve a much smaller group of claimants than the regular Social Security disability and SSI disability claims that are the focus of this book. Nevertheless, for certain claimants these lesser known programs can be a lifeline.

§141 Social Security Disability — Disabled Adult Children

Payment of Social Security benefits to children is well known. When an insured wage earner, that is, someone who has worked and paid enough Social Security taxes to have "insured status" under the Social Security program, receives Social Security disability or retirement benefits, if the wage earner has paid more than a minimum amount of Social Security taxes, SSA will also pay benefits to the wage earner's minor children. In addition, when an insured wage earner dies, a child receives survivor benefits. Whether the parent is retired, disabled or deceased, a minor child, whom SSA calls an auxiliary, receives benefits until age 18 or until age 19 if the child is a full-time elementary or secondary school student.

Less well known is that a disabled *adult* child of a retired, disabled or deceased wage earner may also receive benefits on the account of a parent. For many people, it comes as a complete surprise that it is possible for an adult disabled claimant of *any* age, who has never paid any Social Security taxes at all, to receive disabled adult child benefits on a parent's account beginning when that parent retires, becomes disabled or dies. Knowledge of the rules that allow a disabled adult child to receive benefits on a parent's account is important not only for lawyers who represent claimants in Social Security disability cases, but also for attorneys involved in retirement and estate planning for the parents of disabled children.

Social Security Regulations

Social Security regulations treat disabled adult children as one category of children entitled to benefits on the earnings record of a wage earner parent. Childhood disability benefits, referred to as CDB in SSA's on-line program manual, the POMS, and colloquially at SSA as DAC (pronounced dak) benefits, are a type of auxiliary benefits subject to all the same rules applicable to other auxiliaries. The regulations provide:

> § 404.350 Who is entitled to child's benefits.
> (a) General. You are entitled to child's benefits on the earnings record of an insured person who is entitled to old-age or disability benefits or who has died if—
> (1) You are the insured person's child, based upon a relationship described in §§ 404.355-404.359;
> (2) You are dependent on the insured, as defined in §§ 404.360-404.365;
> (3) You apply;
> (4) You are unmarried; and
> (5) You are under age 18; you are 18 years old or older and have a disability that began before you became 22 years old; or you are 18 years or older and qualify for benefits as a full-time student as described in § 404.367.

20 C.F.R. § 404.350.

Each separate requirement for entitlement to these auxiliary benefits must be met. The insured parent must be entitled to benefits or be dead. The child must be "dependent" but, as we shall see, in most situations proof of dependency does not present a problem because the child is "deemed" to be dependent. There must be an application, but sometimes an application for other benefits may be treated by SSA as an application for childhood disability benefits. A claimant must be unmarried at the time of application. And the claimant's disability must have begun before age 22.

A Public Education Problem

The biggest problem with receipt of childhood disability benefits is that potential claimants do not apply because they do not know the program exists. This is a public education problem for SSA, a problem which lawyers can't significantly alleviate. Indeed, most disabled adult children never need lawyers for their disability cases.

Here's a typical situation. Let's assume, for example, that the disabled child's parents are alive, not disabled and not retired. When the child is under age 18, let's say that because of the parents' income and assets, the child is not eligible for SSI. At age 18, the child applies for SSI because the parents' income and assets are no longer "deemed" to the child. The child is found disabled using the same definition of disability that applies to all the disability programs operated by SSA (except children's SSI). Thus, the child is found entitled to SSI. And the child receives SSI for years. When a parent retires or becomes disabled, SSA advises the child, who now may be middle-aged, to apply for disabled adult child benefits on the parent's account. Because the child was found disabled and has been receiving SSI since before age 22, SSA simply adopts the earlier decision that the child is disabled. In this scenario, receipt of disabled adult child's benefits is virtually automatic.

SSA does a pretty good job of identifying disabled adult children who are eligible to apply for benefits on the accounts of retired or disabled parents. When retirement or disability applications are taken, SSA representatives generally inquire whether there are any disabled adult children who might be eligible on the parent's account. POMS GN 00204.022. They are supposed to do the same after the death of a parent when SSA takes an application for the $255 Lump Sum Death Payment; but local office officials admit that there may be disabled adult children who are not identified in this process, including some who are receiving SSI at the time the parent dies.

When SSA does a redetermination for an SSI recipient, which it does every few years to examine a beneficiary's income, assets, living situation, *etc.*, a claims representative is supposed to inquire about other possible benefits to which the SSI beneficiary may be entitled, including disabled adult child benefits. If a claims representative misses potential eligibility, after it discovers the error, SSA will use the date of the redetermination as a protective filing date for disabled adult child benefits. POMS GN 00204.015.

Representing Disabled Adult Children

Disability cases for disabled adult children that end up with lawyers tend to be those in which SSI applications were never filed or were filed much later than age 22. Sometimes the legal issue is proof of ancient history—that a middle-aged client, who never applied for SSI, has been disabled since before age 22. Or a lawyer could have a 50-year-old client, who began receiving SSI at age 30. In such a case, the lawyer does not usually need to prove more than that the client was disabled from before age 22 until the client was found disabled for SSI. Sometimes there will be periods of what looks like substantial gainful activity that will need to be investigated. Lawyers also have been known to become involved in a disabled adult child case after a beneficiary marries and loses benefits, though, as we shall see, the options for solving this problem are limited.

If you have a client who is between 18 and 22 who has applied for childhood disability benefits, once you've made sure there is no special dependency requirement, proof of the case is the same as in any other adult Social Security disability or SSI case.

After you win a disabled adult child case, you will find that figuring out the first month of entitlement is different from what you may be used to under the regular Social Security disability program. Differences also exist between the programs pertaining to termination of benefits and reentitlement. Otherwise, recipients of childhood disability benefits are treated the same way as those entitled to the regular Social Security disability program; and the same rules that apply for Medicare eligibility also apply to adult Social Security disability cases.

Disability

The definition of disability is the same for childhood disability cases as for any other Social Security disability case (20 C.F.R. § 404.1505(a)) with one additional requirement. In addition to using the five-step sequential evaluation process to prove that the claimant is disabled, you are required to show that a disabled adult child has been continuously disabled since before age 22. 20 C.F.R. § 350(a)(5). Given the odd way SSA treats people as reaching a birthday on the day before, childhood disability claimants must become disabled no later than two days before their actual 22nd birthdays. 20 C.F.R. § 404.102, POMS DI 25501.330.A.4.

Proof of continuous disability since before age 22 presents some problems for claimants who have worked. *Cf.* SSR 68-64c. As a rule, you will need to show that any work:

- was an unsuccessful work attempt (20 C.F.R. § 404.1574(c)),
- was not substantial work activity (20 C.F.R. § 404.1572(a)),
- was not gainful work activity (20 C.F.R. § 404.1572(b)) after deducting impairment-related work expenses (20 C.F.R. § 404.1576) and averaging earnings (20 C.F.R. § 404.1574(a)),
- was done under special conditions (20 C.F.R. § 404.1573(c)), or,
- was subsidized (20 C.F.R. § 404.1574(a)(2)).

Instructions to SSA employees concerning applications advise them to take a disabled adult child's application if there "are lengthy gaps in the claimant's recent work history" or there is "a pattern of low and irregular earnings following a period of substantially higher earnings." POMS GN 00205.035B. Note that if a claimant has "worked only 'off-and-on' or for brief periods of time during the 15-year period," which SSA evaluates for considering whether a claimant can perform past relevant work, SSA generally considers that such work experience does not apply as a vocational factor. 20 C.F.R. § 404.1565(a). Thus, there is a precedent in the regulations for treating sporadic work as no work.

It is SSA policy that claimants for disabled adult child's benefits must show that they have been continuously unable to work since before age 22. It is not sufficient to argue that an impairment, which began before age 22 and became disabling later, qualifies a claimant for childhood disability benefits. *Reyes v. Secretary*, 476 F.2d 910, 914 (D.C. Cir. 1973); *Reading v. Matthews*, 542 F.2d 993, 997 (7th Cir. 1976).

But does it have to be the same disability, that is, the same impairment that disables a claimant all along? Or is it possible to have two different successive impairments that render a claimant continuously unable to work since before age 22? There is no clear statement of SSA policy on this issue; and courts have never been presented with a case in which an ALJ found that a claimant was not entitled to childhood disability benefits because he had two successive disabling impairments—that is, the current disabling impairment did not exist before age 22. Nevertheless, the issue has been addressed by courts in *dicta*. *Reading v. Matthews*, 542 F.2d 993, 997 (7th Cir. 1976), says that the statute "requires that the [current] disability exist as a disability at age 22." *Reyes v. Secretary*, 476 F.2d 910, 914 (D.C. Cir. 1973), required a showing that the current condition was "the same condition that began in 1933 and which at that time and at all times subsequent thereto was equally disabling to such a degree that appellee was prevented from engaging in substantial gainful work." *Reyes* was once issued as Social Security Ruling 74-20c. The SSA summary for the ruling, which was rescinded in 1984, discussed other issues.

The *Reading* and *Reyes* courts came to their conclusions based on statutory construction of the requirement that a disabled adult child be "under a disability (as defined in § 423(d) of this title) which began before he attained the age of 22." 42 U.S.C. § 402(d)(1)(B), emphasis added. Disability is defined as the "inability to engage in any substantial gainful activity by reason of any medically determinable physical or mental impairment which can be expected to result in death or which has lasted or can be expected to last for a continuous period of not less than 12 months." 42 U.S.C. § 423(d). Does "under a disability" refer to one disability that began before age 22, or does it mean simply that a claimant must be disabled since before age 22? What possible public policy could be served by requiring that the continuous disability was always caused by the same impairment?

Relationship	Standard	Dependency Requirement	Citations
Natural child	Could inherit under state inheritance laws	Deemed dependent	20 C.F.R. §§ 404.355(a)(1), 404.361
Natural child	Invalid marriage of parents because of legal impediment	Deemed dependent	20 C.F.R. §§ 404.355(a)(2), 404.361
Natural child	Parents never married. Insured 1) acknowledged paternity in writing; 2) was decreed by court to be parent; or 3) was ordered by court to contribute to support before death of insured	Deemed dependent	20 C.F.R. §§ 404.355(a)(3), 404.361
Natural child	Parents never married but evidence exists other than above that shows insured is parent	Parent was living with child or contributing to support at time child applies for benefits or at time insured died	20 C.F.R. §§ 404.355(a)(4), 404.366(a) and (c)
Natural child	Adopted by someone else during insured's lifetime but after child applies for benefits	Deemed dependent	20 C.F.R. § 404.361(b)(2)(i)
Natural child	Adopted by someone else during insured's lifetime but after beginning of insured's period of disability	Deemed dependent	20 C.F.R. § 404.361(b)(2)(ii)
Natural child	Adopted by someone else at some other time during insured's lifetime	Parent was living with child or contributing to support 1) at time child applies for benefits; 2) at time insured died, or 3) when insured became entitled to retirement benefits or at beginning of insured's period of disability	20 C.F.R. § 404.361(b)(1)
Legally adopted child	Adopted by insured *before* insured became entitled to disability or retirement benefits	Deemed dependent	20 C.F.R. § 404.362(a)
Legally adopted child—adopted *after* insured became entitled to disability or retirement benefits	Child applies for benefits *after* death of insured	Deemed dependent	20 C.F.R. § 404.362(a)

Relationship	Standard	Dependency Requirement	Citations
Legally adopted child—adopted *after* insured became entitled to disability or retirement benefits	Child is natural child or stepchild of insured	Deemed dependent	20 C.F.R. § 404.362(b)(2)
Legally adopted child—adopted *after* insured became entitled to disability or retirement benefits	Child had not attained the age of 18 before adoption proceedings were started *and* adoption was issued by a court in U.S.	Deemed dependent	20 C.F.R. § 404.362(b)(1)(i)
Legally adopted child—adopted *after* insured became entitled to disability or retirement benefits	Child had attained the age of 18 before adoption proceedings were started *and* adoption was issued by a court in U.S.	Child must be living with insured or receiving one-half support from insured for year preceding adoption	20 C.F.R. § 404.362(b)(1)(ii)
Legally adopted child—adopted *after* insured's death by surviving spouse	Insured started adoption before death *or* surviving spouse completed adoption within 2 years of insured's death	Child must be living with insured or receiving one-half support from insured at time of death	20 C.F.R. § 404.362(c)(1)
Legally adopted child—adopted *after* insured's death by surviving spouse	Child is grandchild or step-grandchild of insured *and* adoption took place in U.S. *and* at time of insured's death, the natural, adopting or stepparent was not living in insured's household *and* not making regular contributions toward support	Child must have begun living with insured before age 18 and living with insured in U.S. and receiving one-half of support from insured for the year before insured became entitled to disability or retirement benefits or died; or if the insured had a period of disability before becoming entitled to benefits or died, for the year immediately before the month in which the period of disability began. If the child was born during the one-year period, the child must have lived with the insured and received at least one-half support for substantially all of the period that begins with the date of birth.	20 C.F.R. §§ 404.362(c)(2) and 404.364
Stepchild—insured alive when child applies	Child must have been stepchild for 1 year immediately before applying	Child must be receiving one-half support when child applies or if insured had period of disability that lasted until entitlement to disability or retirement then at the beginning of the period of disability or at the time the insured became entitled to benefits	20 C.F.R. §§ 404.357 and 404.363* and §104 of P.L. 104-121 (Contract with America Advancement Act of 1996)

Relationship	Standard	Dependency Requirement	Citations
Stepchild—insured not alive when child applies	Child must have been stepchild for 9 months before insured died unless death was accidental or occurred in the line of duty while in the U.S. armed services	Child must be receiving one-half support when insured died or if insured had period of disability that lasted until entitlement to disability or retirement, then at the beginning of the period of disability or at the time the insured became entitled to benefits	20 C.F.R. §§ 404.335(a)(2), 404.357 and 404.363* and §104 of P.L. 104-121 (Contract with America Advancement Act of 1996)
Grandchild or step-grandchild	Natural or adoptive parents must have been either deceased or disabled at time grandparent or step grandparent became entitled to retirement or disability benefits or died; or if the grandparent or step grandparent had a period of disability that continued until entitlement to benefits or death, at the time the period of disability began	Child must have begun living with insured before age 18 and living with insured in U.S. and receiving one-half of support from insured for the year before insured became entitled to disability or retirement benefits or died; or if the insured had a period of disability before becoming entitled to benefits or died, for the year immediately before the month in which the period of disability began. If the child was born during the one-year period, the child must have lived with the insured and received at least one-half support for substantially all of the period that begins with the date of birth	20 C.F.R. §§ 404.358 and 404.364
Equitably adopted child—equitable adoption occurred *before* insured's entitlement to benefits	Insured agreed to adopt child but adoption did not occur. Agreement, valid under state law, would allow child to inherit if insured died intestate	Child must be living with insured or receiving contributions for support at time of insured's death or when child applied or if insured had period of disability that lasted until insured became entitled to retirement or disability benefits, then at the beginning of the period of disability or at the time the insured became entitled to benefits	20 C.F.R. §§ 404.359 and 404.365
Equitably adopted child—equitable adoption occurred *after* insured's entitlement to benefits	Insured agreed to adopt child but adoption did not occur. Agreement, valid under state law, would allow child to inherit if insured died intestate	Dependency cannot be established during insured's life. Child must be living with insured or receiving contributions for support at the time of the insured's death	20 C.F.R. §§ 404.359 and 404.365

* 20 C.F.R. § 404.363 is out of date. It was not revised following passage of Section 104 of P.L. 104-121 (Contract with America Advancement Act of 1996), which applies to a stepchild becoming initially entitled in July 1996 or later. This Act removed the opportunity for a stepchild to meet the dependency requirements by living with the stepparent. The regulation still says that the dependency requirement for a stepchild may be met if the child was living with the stepparent at the crucial time. *See* POMS GN 00306.232.

Relationship

A claimant can be a natural child, legally adopted child, stepchild, grandchild, step grandchild, or equitably adopted child of the wage earner. It is necessary to know the precise nature of the relationship in order to figure out if there are any special dependency requirements.

For a natural child, who could inherit from the wage earner under applicable state law, there are no special dependency requirements. 20 C.F.R. § 404.355(a)(1). For a natural child who could not inherit under state law, you'll need to find out if paternity has been adjudicated by a court, whether a court has ordered the parent to contribute to the support of the child, or whether the father has acknowledged in writing that the child is his. 20 C.F.R. § 404.355(a)(3). For all of these situations, there are no special dependency requirements either; but for most other situations involving a natural child, you'll need to look carefully at the circumstances.

For an adopted child you'll need to look at when the child was adopted, how old the child was when adoption proceedings were started, whether the adoption took place in the United States, when the wage earner became entitled to benefits or died, and whether the child was the insured's stepchild before adoption. For a stepchild, determine the date of the wage earner's marriage to the child's parent and the length of marriage before the wage earner became entitled to benefits or died. For a grandchild, examine not only the relationship between the child and grandparent but also whether the parent, that is, the child of the grandparent, was deceased or disabled.

Dependent

For most natural children and legally adopted children, dependency is deemed. That is, you do not need to show that the child was dependent on the wage earner at any time. For a few natural children, some children for whom adoption proceedings were started after they turned age 18 *and* after the wage earner became entitled to disability or retirement benefits, all stepchildren, grandchildren and step grandchildren, proof of the dependency requirement, which was designed to limit eligibility for benefits, may be a challenge. The following chart shows the dependency requirements:

Application

In order to receive disabled adult child's benefits, an application is required. Whenever you are presented with a case in which the application for disabled adult child's benefits is filed long after the parent died or became entitled to disability or retirement benefits, you need to ask your client how it happened that the client didn't apply earlier and what prompted the current application. Explore any earlier contacts with SSA. You may find some transaction with SSA that can be treated as a protective filing or even as an actual application. Or you may find that SSA provided incorrect information to your client, which may allow for a deemed filing date as of the date of the misinformation. 20 C.F.R. § 404.633. *See* §176.5 of this book.

An SSI application is treated as an actual application, not a protective filing, for disabled adult child benefits under Title II of the Social Security Act. POMS SI 00601.035. Unless that Title II "application" is closed out or adjudicated, it is possible that the application will remain open indefinitely. POMS GN 00204.025.

An SSI redetermination, which must be done periodically to make sure an SSI beneficiary is receiving the correct amount of benefits, is treated under SSA policy as a protective filing for all possible benefits under Title II of the Social Security Act, not just Title II benefits on the claimant's own Social Security number. POMS GN 00204.015.

As a rule, a protective filing requires a written statement indicating intent to claim benefits; but SSA is supposed to prepare a statement if a claimant states intent to file an application in a telephone call to SSA. 20 C.F.R. § 404.630(b). After such contact with a claimant, SSA is supposed to send the claimant a notice stating that if the claimant files an actual application within six months of the date of the notice, SSA will use the date of receipt of the claimant's written statement of intent to file or telephone contact as the date of application. 20 C.F.R. § 404.630(c). When SSA fails to send such a notice, filing protection will remain open indefinitely. POMS GN 00204.010A.5.

There may be other kinds of written statements that may constitute protective filings, which apply to disabled adult child benefits. Such protective filings include a statement filed with the Railroad Retirement Board (20 C.F.R. § 404.631) or a statement filed with a hospital (20 C.F.R. § 404.632). *See* POMS GN 00204.010 for an extended discussion of protective filings.

There also may be the possibility of reopening an earlier application that was closed out or adjudicated. *See* §§370-379 of this book.

Retroactivity

If the wage earner is disabled, the application for childhood disability benefits, like all applications for disability benefits, will pay benefits for 12 months before the date of application if all other requirements are met as of that date. 20 C.F.R. § 404.621(a)(1). If the wage earner is deceased or retired, the application will pay benefits only for six months before the date of application if all other requirements are met as of that date. 20 C.F.R. § 404.621(a)(2).

No Waiting Period

Unlike the regular Social Security disability program, there is no five-month waiting period for entitlement to childhood disability benefits. POMS DI 10115.005. But the child cannot become entitled before the parent if the parent is alive or before the month the parent died, if the parent is deceased unless, of course, the parent was receiving disability or retirement benefits before death. 20 C.F.R. § 404.350(a).

Month of Entitlement

If the parent wage earner is deceased, the disabled child's first month of benefits is the month in which all of the requirements for entitlement are met during any part of the month. 20 C.F.R. § 404.352(a)(1). When there is a living wage earner parent, with certain extremely limited exceptions (*see* POMS RS 00203.010), the requirements for entitlement (other than the application requirement) must be met throughout the entire month. 20 C.F.R. § 404.352(a)(2). POMS DI 10115.025. Thus, if a child becomes disabled on the 15th of the month and the wage earner is deceased, the first month of benefits can be the month in which the child became disabled—assuming all other requirements are met. But if the wage earner is alive, the first month of benefits is the next month.

Family Maximum

A retired or disabled wage earner must have paid enough Social Security taxes so that the wage earner's "family maximum" benefit amount, a special calculation done by SSA, exceeds the benefits that the wage earner receives. *See* 20 C.F.R. §§ 404.403 to 404.411. If the family maximum is equal to the wage earner's monthly benefit, there will be no Social Security benefits left to be paid to a disabled adult child.

People with low lifetime earnings tend to have a family maximum benefit amount that is equal to the "primary insurance amount," which is the amount of benefits paid to a disabled person or to someone who retires at full retirement age. Thus, it is possible for a disabled adult child to meet the disability criteria for entitlement and still not receive any benefits while the parent is alive. When the parent dies, though, the disabled adult child would receive benefits on the parent's account (since the parent is no longer using up the family maximum benefit amount).

Benefit Amount

If the wage earner is alive, the disabled adult child is entitled to 50% of the wage earner's primary insurance amount, subject to the family maximum. If the wage earner is deceased, the disabled adult child receives 75% of the wage earner's primary insurance amount, subject to the family maximum. When the family maximum is reached, benefits for auxiliaries are equally divided between them. 20 C.F.R. §§ 404.353(a), 404.304(d), and 404.403.

Marriage

Marriage is a terminating event for disabled adult child's benefits. The only exception is when a disabled adult child marries someone who is also receiving Title II benefits (except child's benefits unless they are childhood disability benefits). *See* 20 C.F.R. § 404.352(b)(4) and 42 U.S.C. § 402(d)(1)(D). Although marriage does not affect benefits for the regular Social Security disability program, marriage terminates benefits for someone who is receiving disabled adult child's benefits; and unless that marriage is voided or annulled, a person cannot become entitled to those benefits again on the same record. A divorce is not sufficient and neither is death of the spouse. *See* 42 U.S.C. § 402(d)(6), 20 C.F.R. § 404.351, Social Security Ruling 84-1 and POMS RS 00203.015.

Although marriage is a *terminating* event for disabled adult child's benefits, for *initial entitlement* the statute requires only that the claimant be unmarried. 42 U.S.C. § 402(d)(1)(B), 20 C.F.R. § 404.350(a)(4). Thus, before applying, a claimant may be married and divorced. It is also possible, where benefits of a disabled adult child are terminated because of marriage and that marriage ends, that the disabled adult child, now unmarried, can apply for benefits on the other parent's account.

In addition, a claimant who is married when the application is filed may be entitled to benefits in the retroactive period before the month of marriage. POMS DI 10115.001.

Termination

Benefits of a disabled adult child will end for all the same reasons an adult beneficiary's benefits end, *e.g.*, end of disability, death. In addition to terminating when a disabled adult child marries, benefits for a disabled adult child end if the insured person's disability or retirement benefits end for a reason other than death. Here's an exception: if the insured lost benefits because drug addiction or alcoholism was found to be material to the insured's disability, as long as the insured remains disabled, the disabled adult child can continue receiving benefits. 20 C.F.R. § 404.352(b)(5).

Reentitlement

If entitlement to childhood disability benefits ends because the child's disability has ceased, a child may be reentitled to benefits on the same earnings record if the child again becomes disabled before 84 months (seven years) after benefits ended. However, in order to encourage work, Congress established an exception: the seven-year time limit was removed for those whose benefits ceased because of performance of substantial gainful activity, effective October 1, 2004. Section 420A of Public Law 108-203, the Social Security Protection Act of 2003.

To be reentitled, a child must not have married unless that marriage is void or was annulled. 20 C.F.R. § 404.351.

A marriage that ends because of divorce or death precludes reentitlement. POMS DI 10115.035. Note that this is different from the requirement for initial entitlement, which requires only that the child not be married when he or she applies.

Reentitlement rules do not apply when the child's benefits end because the parent's disability ended. If the parent becomes entitled to disability benefits again or retires or dies, the initial entitlement provisions apply. POMS DI 10115.035.

Of course, the initial entitlement rules apply if the child applies for benefits on the other parent's account, for example, where a child marries and loses benefits on one parent's account, and, after the marriage ends, applies for benefits on the other parent's account.

An Odd Result

The reentitlement rules highlight an odd result. Let's say there are two equally disabled adult children, each with a deceased parent. The only difference between the two children is that one applies for and receives disabled adult child's benefits. When they both get better and go to work for two years at the substantial gainful activity level, the one who had disabled adult child's benefits, of course, loses the benefits because of work activity. But then let's say they both get worse and are disabled again. The one who received benefits before can apply for reentitlement to disabled adult child's benefits. The other cannot show continuous disability since before age 22 and will never be entitled to disabled adult child's benefits.

Citing the reentitlement provisions, a Pennsylvania district court held in *Axe v. Harris*, 503 F.Supp. 1049, 1051 (ED Pa. 1980), that if a claimant was disabled by an impairment at age 22 and again disabled by the same impairment when he applied for childhood disability benefits, he was entitled to benefits. The court remanded the case for further findings of fact. On remand, SSA found that the claimant was disabled before age 22 and again disabled when he applied, but that he was not disabled from May 1964 until December 1972, a period of 8 and a half years. Given this, SSA found that the claimant was not entitled to benefits. When the case went back to court, without mentioning the reentitlement provisions, the court held that plaintiff Axe was entitled to benefits because the statute did not require that a claimant be continuously disabled. *Axe v. Department of Health and Human Services*, 564 F.Supp. 789 (ED Pa. 1983).

Although the first *Axe* decision is interesting because it mentions the reentitlement provisions, the second decision is virtually useless. It stands as the sole case holding that the statute does not require continuous disability since before age 22. It has never been followed by another district court in a published decision. It was relied on once by the district court in Puerto Rico in an unpublished opinion; but that decision was reversed by the First Circuit Court of Appeals in *Suarez v. Secretary of Health and Human Services*, 755 F.2d 1 (1st Cir. 1985).

Medicare and Medicaid

Medicare works the same for disabled adult children as for recipients of Social Security disability benefits. Both groups have a 24-month waiting period. Both groups are required to pay a Medicare premium to receive Part B, which pays for doctor visits, *etc.*

The Social Security Act also provides for special Medicaid (Title 19) eligibility for some disabled adult children. Recall that, before receiving disabled adult child benefits, a typical beneficiary may receive SSI for many years, including automatic Medicaid eligibility in most states. The amount of disabled adult child benefits is great enough to disqualify many beneficiaries from receiving SSI. Others receive both SSI and disabled adult child benefits for a time and then lose SSI when DAC benefits are increased upon the death of a parent (or sometimes with a cost of living increase). Without a special provision in the Social Security Act, Medicaid benefits would be lost when SSI is lost.

The Social Security Act provides that, when a beneficiary loses SSI because of receipt of childhood disability benefits, for purposes of Medicaid eligibility, the DAC beneficiary is to be treated as if he or she were still receiving SSI benefits and thus eligible for Medicaid "so long as he or she would be eligible for" SSI benefits "in the absence of such child's insurance benefits or such increase." 42 U.S.C. § 1383c(c). Note that to continue Medicaid eligibility: (1) the DAC beneficiary would have to meet the SSI asset limitations, and (2) income from sources other than DAC benefits could not be so great as to disqualify the person for SSI.

§142 Social Security Disability — Widow(er)s and Surviving Divorced Spouses

Disability claims of widow(er)s and surviving divorced spouses require that the deceased spouse be fully insured at the time of death. Only marriage of a required duration confers the right to benefits based on the work history of a spouse: 10 years for a surviving divorced spouse and, with some exceptions, 9 months for a widow(er). Widow(er)s and surviving divorced spouses must be at least 50; and their disabilities must start within seven years of the death of the spouse or within seven years of the time the widow(er) or surviving divorced spouse was last entitled to mother's or father's benefits or to widow(er)'s disability benefits.

The end of the seven years is referred to as the end of the "prescribed period" and functions similar to the way "date last insured" operates in regular Social Security disability cases.

Special rules effective in 1984 allow remarriage in many circumstances without affecting eligibility. *See* 20 C.F.R. §§ 404.335 and 404.336.

Widow(er)s and surviving divorced spouses become entitled to benefits at age 60 without being disabled. Thus, they receive disability benefits only for ages 50-59.

Beginning in 1991, pursuant to an amendment to 42 U.S.C. § 423(d), widow(er)s and surviving divorced spouses are found disabled using the same five-step sequential evaluation process used for the regular Social Security disability program. Entitlement (that is, payment) under this new standard could not begin before January 1991. However, one may use the new standard to find a widow disabled prior to January 1991. Thus, the five-month waiting period requirement may be fulfilled before January 1991; and, even more important for those widows who were unable to work for many years, widows may be found disabled using an onset date occurring many years ago, an onset date that is within the seven-year time limit applicable in such cases.

Sometimes in widow(er)'s cases, SSA evaluates disability as of a "controlling date." The "controlling date" is the latest date by which a widow(er) may become disabled and still be entitled to benefits for the earliest possible month. *See* POMS DI 25501.350. Take the example of a woman who became disabled at age 40 whose husband died when she was 51. Rather than develop 11 years of medical evidence, SSA will look at the controlling date, in this example, five full months before her husband died, to see if she was disabled then. If so, she will be eligible for widow's benefits effective with the month her husband died. *See* §142.1, for a form based on an SSA worksheet for calculating the prescribed period and controlling date.

Proof of disability in widow(er)'s cases for years prior to 1991 remains based on a more stringent statutory definition of disability under which a widow must demonstrate that she is incapable of *any* gainful activity rather than *substantial* gainful activity. Age, education and work experience may not be considered. *Compare* 42 U.S.C. § 423(d)(2)(A) with § 423(d)(2)(B). In the past, SSA took the position that in widow's cases, inquiry under the sequential evaluation process stopped at step 3 with consideration of whether or not the widow's impairment met or equaled the Listings. Because of the litigation spawned by this position that focused on the issue whether SSA must consider residual functional capacity (RFC) in determining if a widow is unable to perform any gainful activity, SSA capitulated and issued Social Security Ruling 91-3p, which describes the process for determining disability in widow(er)s' cases prior to 1991.

SSR 91-3p, in essence, applies the five-step sequential evaluation process and adds a sixth step to determining disability in widow(er)s' cases. If the widow is found disabled at step three, of course, entitlement may be found prior to, as well as after, January 1991. If disability is found at step five, there may be entitlement as of January 1991; but an additional step is required to determine possible entitlement before January 1991. To prove entitlement before January 1991, a widow must show, at step six, that she was incapable of performing a full range of sedentary work.

Practice Tip

Whenever you represent a widow(er), take a careful look at the onset date. If onset of disability can be established five full months before the widow(er)'s spouse died, the five-month waiting period, in effect, is served while the spouse is still alive. Thus, entitlement commences with the month of the spouse's death. Therefore, amend the onset date to five full months before the spouse's death to obtain the most past-due benefits for your client. *See* POMS DI 25501.350A.5.

§142.1 Form: Determining Prescribed Period and Controlling Date for Widow's Claim

PRESCRIBED PERIOD:

Prescribed period ***begins*** with the latest of: (Starting Date) ____________________

a. ______________ Month of wage earner's death

b. ______________ Last month of previous entitlement to Disabled Widow(er)'s Benefits

c. ______________ Last month of entitlement to Mother's benefits

Prescribed period ***ends*** with the earlier of: (Ending Date)

a. ______________ Month before the month widow(er) attains age 60

b. ______________ If filing for Medicare only, the month before the month widow(er) attains age 65

c. ______________ Last day of 84th month following the month the prescribed period began

CONTROLLING DATE:

1. Select the latest of: (Earliest Month of Entitlement)

   a. ___________ 12 months retroactive from filing date

   b. ___________ Wage earner's month of death

   c. ___________ Month widow attains age 50

   d. ___________ Month after last month of entitlement to Mother's or Disabled Widow(er)'s Benefits

2. Indicate 1st day of the 5th month before date of #1 above: ________________________

3. Indicate alleged onset date: ________________________

4. Indicate the later date of #2 and #3 above: ________________________

5. Indicate the date the prescribed period ends: ________________________

6. The earlier of #4 and #5 above is the Controlling Date: ________________________

§143 *Social Security Disability — Blindness*

The Social Security disability program for blind claimants has somewhat different rules from those applied to the regular Social Security disability program. To qualify, a disabled person must meet the strict medical definition of blindness stated in the statute, which requires a central visual acuity of 20/200 or less in the better eye with best corrective lens or a field of vision of 20 degrees or less. There is no opportunity to "equal" this requirement, in contrast to step 3 of the sequential evaluation process applicable to regular Social Security disability claims.

To receive benefits, those who meet this definition must be fully insured; but there is no recent work requirement.

Special rules create much more incentive for a blind person to work than a person receiving regular Social Security disability benefits. The amount of monthly income that constitutes substantial gainful activity is higher for blind people than it is for those eligible for regular disability benefits. Special rules apply for those age 55 and over that allow continuing eligibility during any month with no substantial gainful activity if the claimant is unable to perform work requiring skills or abilities comparable to the work he or she did before reaching age 55 or before becoming blind, whichever occurred later. *See* 20 C.F.R. §§ 404.1581 to 404.1587.

Note, however, that if a person with impaired vision does not meet the peculiar requirements of this program, he or she still may be found disabled for the regular Social Security disability program as a result of vision problems. *See* §232.

§144 *SSI Blind*

If an SSI claimant is blind (under the same medical standards as for the Social Security disability blindness program), he or she does not have to meet the 12-month duration requirement that applies to both regular Social Security disability benefits and regular SSI benefits. Such a claimant also does not have to be unable to do any substantial gainful activity. *See* 20 C.F.R. § 416.983. Note, also, that if a claimant does not meet the test for blindness, impaired vision may still qualify him or her for regular SSI. *See* §232, *infra*.

§145 *SSI Children*

Until 1990 SSA took the position that children's SSI disability cases were to be evaluated the same way that widows' cases used to be evaluated, that is, that the inquiry stopped at step 3 with consideration of whether or not a child's impairments met or equaled the Listings. Limitations in *functioning* were not considered. This led to the anomalous result that a child age 17 who is denied SSI benefits could be awarded benefits as soon as the child turned 18 because at that point SSA continues the sequential evaluation process beyond step 3 and evaluates residual functional capacity.

In *Sullivan v. Zebley,* 493 U.S. 521 (1990), *affirming Zebley v. Bowen,* 855 F.2d 67 (3d Cir. 1988), the United States Supreme Court held in a nationwide class action that SSA must make an individualized functional analysis of child SSI disability claims. The court ordered SSA to find a child disabled if the child's impairment is "of comparable severity" to that which would disable an adult. This ruling was given retroactive effect, requiring SSA to reevaluate denials for SSI children's benefits back to 1980.

In 1996 Congress set a new, stricter standard for SSI children's cases, abandoning the "individualized functional assessment" procedure adopted in the wake of the *Zebley* decision. Under the new standard a child must have a "medically determinable physical or mental impairment which results in marked and severe functional limitations." 42 U.S.C. § 1382c(a)(3)(C)(i). In order for a child to be found disabled, a child's impairment must meet, "medically equal," or "functionally equal" an impairment found in the Listing of Impairments. 20 C.F.R. § 416.924(d).

Proof of children's SSI disability, which is regarded by many lawyers as more difficult than adult cases, is not covered in this book. It is properly the subject of a separate practice manual with forms designed specifically for children's SSI cases. Unfortunately, no such book currently exists. The best resource for SSI children's cases is on the Internet at www.hdadvocates.org/ProgramsChildren/SSI/ssi.htm.

§150 Appeal Process

There are four levels of administrative adjudication of Social Security claims. They are:

(1) The initial determination,
(2) Reconsideration determination,
(3) Hearing before an administrative law judge, and
(4) Review by the Appeals Council.

After this, a case may be filed in federal court.

The time limit for all appeals but one is 60 days from the date of receipt of a decision. Because there is a strong presumption that decisions are received five days from the date on the face of the decision, unless there is evidence to the contrary, the effective time limit is 65 days from the date of the decision.

The only exception to the 65-day effective time limit for appeal applies to appealing an ALJ denial to the Appeals Council *after* there has been a federal court remand. The time limit is 30 days for these appeals. *See* §560.

When the period for requesting the next appellate step ends on a Saturday, Sunday, legal holiday, or any other day of which all or part is a nonworkday for federal employees by statute or Executive Order, the period is extended to include the next full workday. 20 C.F.R. §§ 404.3(b), 416.120(d).

SSA treats an appeal as filed on the day it receives it. However, SSA will use the date a "request or notice is mailed to us by the U.S. mail, if using the date we receive it would result in the loss or lessening of rights. The date shown by a U.S. postmark will be used as the date of mailing. If the postmark is unreadable, or there is no postmark, we will consider other evidence of when you mailed it to us." 20 C.F.R. § 404.614(b)(2).

Take a look at the diagrams in §156, which shows the percentages of claimants approved at various levels of appeal from 2008 to 2012. They show that in recent years approximately one million claimants were found disabled on their initial applications. About 2 million claimants were denied, but fewer than half that number requested reconsideration. Note the low approval percentage on reconsideration (12% to 14%), and that in 2012 52% of hearing decisions were favorable (this is around 350,000 claimants). Note the declining allowance rates at ALJ hearings – dropping from 63% in 2008 to 52% in 2012. Note the declining remand rate at the Appeals Council, which dropped from 22% to 18%, but in absolute numbers the Appeals Council grants relief to about four times the number of claimants granted relief by the federal courts.

§150.1 Disability Service Improvement (DSI)

If you practice in Maine, New Hampshire, Vermont, Massachusetts, Rhode Island, or Connecticut, the administrative appeal process changed on August 1, 2006 under the program named Disability Service Improvement (DSI), which was implemented by regulations in a new part of 20 C.F.R., Part 405. Although the original plan was to gradually extend DSI to the rest of the country, it now appears that only certain aspects of DSI will be made applicable to the rest of the United States through future changes to the regular Social Security disability and SSI regulations found in Parts 404 and 416 of 20 C.F.R.

DSI is designed as an experiment to see if SSA can speed up disability determination at all levels including the initial determination. Based on a predictive model, some cases are automatically referred from the field office to a state agency Quick Disability Determination unit with the goal of making a favorable determination within 20 days. 20 C.F.R. § 405.105. For all initial determinations, not only those referred to the Quick Disability Determination units, SSA will require state agencies to adopt a standard decision-writing format that "will explain in clear and understandable language the specific reasons for and the effect of the initial determination." 20 C.F.R. § 405.115.

DSI initially replaced the reconsideration step with review by a federal reviewing official; but because of budgetary issues and long processing times, sending new cases to federal reviewing officials was suspended in early 2008, reverting to the process that was in effect in these states before DSI.

Some DSI ALJ hearing procedures are more formal with more mandatory time limits than under current practice. *See* §300.1 of this book and 20 C.F.R. §§ 405.301 *ff.*

Under DSI, the Appeals Council was initially replaced by a Decision Review Board, which applied significantly different administrative appeal procedures than the Appeals Council. But the Decision Review Board was abandoned by SSA in 2011 and all pending cases were transferred to the Appeals Council. The Appeals Council applies the same rules to DSI cases that it applies to case from the rest of the country except when a claimant submits new evidence. *See* §524.1.

§151 Initial and Reconsideration Determinations

A Social Security disability claim (but not an SSI disability claim) can be completed on the Internet at https://secure.ssa.gov/iClaim/dib, which is how about half of all claimants file their applications for benefits. Others initiate their claims by telephoning an SSA teleservice center at SSA's toll-free number, 1-800-772-1213. Teleservice center staff will make an appointment for the claimant with an SSA representative from a local office. If a claimant prefers, an appointment can be made to go to a local Social Security office to complete an application in person, though most claimants make a telephone appointment for an SSA claims representative to call the claimant back at an appointed hour. During the appointment, the claimant will be asked basic information, which will be entered into a computer application form that will be printed and, if it is a telephone interview, will be mailed to the claimant for signature, along with other forms to be completed and signed. An application for benefits is one of the few forms in a disability case that may not be signed by a lawyer on behalf of a claimant, unless that lawyer is appointed to do so by a court. *See* 20 C.F.R. §§ 404.612 and 404.613.

The prohibition on a lawyer signing an application for benefits on behalf of a claimant includes a prohibition against a lawyer "electronically signing" an application that is submitted over the Internet, although a lawyer may assist in filing an application. *See* http://www.socialsecurity.gov/representation/. According to SSA's website at http://www.socialsecurity.gov/representation/: "You cannot electronically sign the application on behalf of the applicant. Only the person you are helping can electronically sign his or her Internet Social Security Benefit Application and attest to the accuracy of the information provided."

At the initial and reconsideration levels the Social Security Administration does not make medical determinations of disability. Instead, claims are referred to an agency of the state government that has a contract with SSA for determining disability. At the state agency usually a medical doctor and a layman, called a disability examiner, evaluate the claim, though SSA has been experimenting in pilot projects with having disability examiners make uncomplicated decisions on their own. The Social Security Administration then adopts the determinations at these two levels. *See* 20 C.F.R. §§ 404.900 *et seq*. regarding initial determinations.

If the claimant is dissatisfied with the initial determination, the claimant may appeal. In most states, this appeal is a request for reconsideration. In ten states (Alabama, Alaska, Colorado, Louisiana, Michigan, Missouri, New Hampshire, Pennsylvania, and parts of New York and California), called prototype states, SSA is experimenting with eliminating the reconsideration step. The initial determination will tell a claimant in a prototype state to appeal by requesting a hearing. HALLEX I-2-4-99 contains instructions for processing appeals in those circumstances where a claimant moves into or out of a prototype state while the claim is pending.

If a claimant requests reconsideration, a different team than the one that issued the initial determination will make the reconsideration determination; but the result will probably be the same. Relatively few reconsideration determinations result in a claimant receiving benefits. *See* 20 C.F.R. §§ 404.907 *et seq*. regarding reconsideration. The next step is to request a hearing before an administrative law judge.

There are two ways for a claimant to have, in effect, a reconsideration after a hearing is requested. First, a case may be *informally* remanded to the state agency (or to a special SSA regional screening unit) for "prehearing case review" by a hearing office pursuant to the broad authority granted by 20 C.F.R. § 404.941 if:

> 1) Additional evidence is submitted;
> 2) There is an indication that additional evidence is available,
> 3) There is a change in the law or regulation; or
> 4) There is an error in the file or some other indication that the prior determination may be revised.

20 C.F.R. § 404.941(b).

On informal remand, the state agency (or the special SSA regional screening unit) may issue a fully or partially favorable revised determination. A partially favorable revised determination will notify the claimant that the hearing will be held unless all parties notify SSA that they agree to dismiss the hearing request. If the informal remand does not result in a partially or fully favorable decision, no formal decision will be issued. Thus, no new hearing request will need to be submitted. The case will be returned to the administrative law judge, theoretically without delaying the scheduling of the hearing. HALLEX I-2-5-10.

Second, a case may be *formally* remanded to the state agency to issue a new reconsideration determination where there has been a change in the law, or new evidence has been received that may permit the state agency to issue a fully favorable revised reconsideration determination. 20 C.F.R. § 404.948(c). If the claimant did not request remand, the ALJ must give the claimant notice and the opportunity to object. Any objection must be dealt with in writing. HALLEX I-2-5-12. If after formal remand the new reconsideration determination is unfavorable, a claimant must again request a hearing.

§152 Hearing

After a claimant requests a hearing, but before a hearing is held, an attorney advisor (whose job includes writing decisions for ALJs) may review the file, request additional evidence, conduct an informal prehearing conference (usually a telephone call to the claimant's attorney), and issue a fully favorable decision. The regulation granting decision-signing authority to attorney advisors is one of the few SSA regulations that contains a sunset provision—an expiration date. 20 C.F.R. § 404.942(g). Sometimes it is extended; sometimes not. The current sunset date is August 4, 2017. 80 Fed. Reg. 31990 (2015).

The attorney advisor who looks at your client's case could be in the hearing office where your client's case is assigned, or the attorney advisor could be anywhere in the country. Pursuant to Chief Judge Bulletin, CJB

15-02, SSA assigns attorney advisors from time to time to what it calls a "National Adjudication Team" which looks at electronic-folder cases from all over the country. If you get a telephone call from a senior attorney who says your client's case is being reviewed by the National Adjudication Team, you are being presented with an opportunity. Immediately start building your client's case; order updated medical records and reports and submit them electronically as soon as possible. This new evidence may convince an attorney advisor to issue a favorable decision. Although the authority of attorney advisors to issue favorable decisions has been sharply curtailed by a Chief Judge Bulletin dated November 27, 2013, CJB 07-10 Rev4, there remains the possibility of an attorney advisor favorable decision in your client's case.

Regulations provide that the attorney advisor may issue only a fully favorable decision. 20 C.F.R. § 404.942(a) and (d). If a fully favorable attorney advisor decision is issued, the parties will be allowed 60 days to request that an ALJ reinstate the request for hearing "if they disagree with the decision for any reason." The claimant can then proceed with a hearing. 20 C.F.R. § 404.941(d). On own motion review, the Appeals Council, not an ALJ, has authority to review a fully favorable decision by an attorney advisor. 20 C.F.R. § 404.942(f)(3).

Note that unless a claimant waives a hearing—seldom a good idea—an ALJ has authority to issue only a *fully favorable* decision without holding a hearing. 20 C.F.R. § 404.948. Consider the implications: first, in cases where you think the record supports finding that the claimant became disabled earlier than the claimant originally alleged, you need to send a letter to the hearing office right away asking to amend the "alleged onset date." Otherwise, if your client gets a fully favorable ALJ decision using the onset date originally alleged, getting your client found disabled as of the earlier onset date may be difficult. *Cf.* § 508. Second, in those cases in which a later onset date is justified, amending the alleged onset date may prompt an ALJ to issue a fully favorable decision without a hearing. An unjustified early onset date may be the only thing keeping an ALJ from issuing a fully favorable decision without a hearing. Often in clear cases of disability that allege an onset date that is too early, an attorney advisor or ALJ will telephone the claimant's attorney to inquire whether the claimant's attorney will agree to amend the onset date so that a fully favorable decision can be issued without a hearing. Sometimes a formal prehearing conference will be held concerning this or other issues in the case pursuant to 20 C.F.R. § 404.961.

The claimant may appear in person before the ALJ or by video teleconferencing. If a claimant objects to appearing by video teleconferencing, the ALJ must reschedule the hearing so that the claimant can appear in person. 20 C.F.R. § 404.936(d) and (e). *See* § 304.2 for additional discussion.

At a hearing before an ALJ, evidence may be received even though it would not be admissible in court under the rules of evidence used by the court. 20 C.F.R. § 404.950(c). Vocational or medical experts sometimes testify, appearing in person, by video teleconferencing, or by telephone. 20 C.F.R. § 404.936(c)(2). The hearing is not adversarial in nature. The hearing is recorded and testimony is taken under oath or by affirmation. After the hearing, a written decision is issued by the administrative law judge. *See* Chapter 3 and 20 C.F.R. §§ 404.929 *et seq.* regarding the hearing.

§153 Differences Between State Agency Determinations and Hearing Decisions

There are significant differences between the way disability is evaluated by the state agencies and the way ALJs approach the issue. Although it is the rule at all levels that a disability decision cannot be inconsistent with the medical evidence, the state agency decision-makers, who have only the cold file to review, seldom look beyond medical findings to consider a claimant's actual ability to work. At the state agencies, the Listing of Impairments is used much more often as a basis for a favorable decision. Despite several successful lawsuits challenging this, state agency decision-makers tend to use the Listing of Impairments as the unstated basis for a denial determination, especially for those claimants under age 50.

If a younger claimant's impairment does not meet a Listing, that claimant is unlikely to be found disabled by the state agency. State agency decision makers tend to apply written or unwritten formulas (sometimes found in state agency manuals) to determine residual functional capacity (RFC) for certain medical impairments, thus treating all claimants with similar medical findings the same. Few of the state agency formulas point to a conclusion that a claimant can do less than a wide range of sedentary work.

ALJs, on the other hand, tend to view medical findings as setting the parameters for a range of possible RFCs, some of which may lead to a finding of disabled. They view their role as evaluating the entire case, including the claimant's subjective symptoms, to determine which possible RFC most closely describes the capacity of a particular claimant. ALJs find claimants under age 50 disabled because of inability to perform a wide range of sedentary work much more often than state agency decision makers do.

The charts in §153.1 were created in conjunction with a 2010 Social Security Administration Office of the Inspector General (OIG) study of the differences between state agency decisions and ALJ decisions for impairments most frequently denied by state agencies and subsequently allowed by ALJs. Table 1 shows, for example, that during the period studied, ALJs found claimants with back impairments disabled 70% of the time while the state agency denied 78% of such cases. Look at the entry for claimants under age 50 with back impairments in Table 2. The state agency found them not disabled 94% of the time while ALJs found them disabled 63% of the time. In the same table look at the numbers for diabetes mellitus for claimants under age 50. They were found not disabled by state agencies 95% of the time while ALJs found them disabled 59% of the time. Table 8, which focuses on impairments with 80% or greater hearing level allowance rates, shows that in addition to rare impairments seldom seen and various cancers, claimants with the following impairments were found disabled by ALJs 80% or more of the time: Parkinson's disease, multiple sclerosis, chronic renal failure, and peripheral vascular disease. Note also that the state agency finds disabled the vast majority of claimants with these impairments.

The Social Security Administration has viewed such differences in results and approach to decision-making as a problem. The series of Social Security rulings published in 1996, SSR 96-1p through SSR 96-9p, known as the "process unification rulings," were designed to encourage a unified approach to decision making at all administrative levels. Most observers agree that there were some changes. After promulgation of the process unification rulings, more claimants were found disabled by the state agencies. But as the 2010 OIG study shows, disparities remain. For example, if a claimant is under age 50 and has a back problem that does not meet the Listings, that claimant is likely to be denied by the state agency; but if that claimant is truly unable to work, the claimant may have a pretty good chance of winning before an ALJ.

§153.1 Charts: State Agency and ALJ Disability Decisions Compared

Table 1
Four Impairments Most Frequently Denied by DDSs and Subsequently Allowed at the Hearing Level

Impairment	Number of DDS Denials	DDS Denial Rate	Number of Hearing Level Allowances	Hearing Level Allowance Rate
Disorders of Back	744,602	78%	238,903	70%
Osteoarthrosis and Allied Disorders	204,652	58%	61,118	70%
Diabetes Mellitus	165,411	81%	38,174	67%
Disorders of Muscle, Ligament, and Fascia	138,905	80%	34,693	65%

Table 2
DDS and Hearing Level Allowances by Age of Claimant

Impairment	Age of Claimant	Number of DDS Determinations	Number of DDS Denials (Denial Rate)	Number of Appeals (Appeal Rate)	Number of Hearing Level Allowances (Allowance Rate)
Disorders of Back	Age 50 or Older	433,677	257,574 (59%)	138,617 (54%)	110,311 (80%)
	Under Age 50	516,125	487,028 (94%)	204,253 (42%)	128,592 (63%)
Osteoarthrosis and Allied Disorders	Age 50 or Older	237,566	101,695 (43%)	47,511 (47%)	37,254 (78%)
	Under Age 50	115,371	102,957 (89%)	39,646 (39%)	23,864 (49%)

Table 2 (continued)
DDS and Hearing Level Allowances by Age of Claimant

Impairment	Age of Claimant	Number of DDS Determinations	Number of DDS Denials (Denial Rate)	Number of Appeals (Appeal Rate)	Number of Hearing Level Allowances (Allowance Rate)
Diabetes Mellitus	Age 50 or Older	107,771	74,189 (69%)	29,310 (40%)	22,176 (76%)
	Under Age 50	96,320	91,222 (95%)	27,341 (30%)	15,998 (59%)
Disorders of Muscle, Ligament, and Fascia	Age 50 or Older	75,293	46,488 (62%)	21,941 (44%)	16,708 (76%)
	Under Age 50	97,271	92,417 (95%)	31,405 (34%)	17,985 (57%)

Table 8
Impairments With 80 Percent or Greater Hearing Level Allowance Rates

Impairment	Number of DDS Determinations	DDS Denial Rate	Hearing Level Allowance Rate
Salmonella Bacteremia	13	62%	100%
Pancreatitis	9	89%	100%
Strongyloidiasis	7	29%	100%
Cardiovascular Syphilis	105	50%	94%
Squamous Cell Carcinoma of the Anal Canal or Anal Margin	228	34%	92%
Malignant Neoplasm of Pleura	2,672	3%	91%
Parkinson's Disease	12,359	22%	89%

Table 8 (continued)
Impairments With 80 Percent or Greater Hearing Level Allowance Rates

Impairment	Number of DDS Determinations	DDS Denial Rate	Hearing Level Allowance Rate
Multiple Myeloma	6,530	12%	88%
Malignant Neoplasm of Gallbladder and Extrahepatic Bile Ducts	1,240	3%	88%
Secondary Malignant Neoplasm	1,096	2%	88%
Malignant Neoplasm of Small Intestine	1,896	15%	87%
Liver Transplant	1,440	20%	86%
Malignant Neoplasm of Trachea, Bronchus, or Lung	60,516	3%	85%
Macroglobulinemia or Heavy Chain	156	22%	84%
Multiple Sclerosis	42,614	47%	84%
Neuroblastoma	1,527	10%	83%
Malignant Neoplasm of Colon, Rectum, or Anus	35,825	26%	82%
Malignant Neoplasm of Maxilla, Orbit, or Temporal Fossa	3,649	18%	82%
Kaposi's Sarcoma	142	17%	82%
Leukemia	17,959	13%	82%

Table 8 (continued)
Impairments With 80 Percent or Greater Hearing Level Allowance Rates

Impairment	Number of DDS Determinations	DDS Denial Rate	Hearing Level Allowance Rate
Malignant Neoplasm of Skeletal System	1,502	19%	81%
Malignant Neoplasm of Prostate	10,174	41%	80%
Chronic Renal Failure	69,836	10%	80%
Malignant Neoplasm of Stomach	5,830	9%	80%
Anterior Horn Cell Disease (includ-ing Amyotrophic LateralSclerosis)	4,661	1%	80%
Malignant Neoplasm of Bladder	4,896	25%	80%
Malignant Neoplasm of Bladder Peripheral Vascular (Arterial) Disease	28,325	29%	80%

From Office of the Inspector General, Social Security Administration, DISABILITY IMPAIRMENTS ON CASES MOST FREQUENTLY DENIED BY DISABILITY DETERMINATION SERVICES AND SUBSEQUENTLY ALLOWED BY ADMINISTRATIVE LAW JUDGES, August 2010 A-07-09-19083, Audit Report. Available on the Internet at http://www.ssa.gov/oig/ADOBEPDF/A-07-09-19083.pdf.

§154 Appeals Council Review

If a decision after hearing is unfavorable, the claimant or representative may ask for review of that decision by the Appeals Council, which has its headquarters in Falls Church, Virginia. The Appeals Council may decline to review the decision of the administrative law judge, in which case the decision of the ALJ becomes the final decision of the Commissioner of Social Security on the claim, subject to court review. The Appeals Council may review the decision of the ALJ and affirm it, modify it, reverse it, or remand it for a new hearing.

In some instances, the Appeals Council reviews decisions of administrative law judges, either favorable or unfavorable to the claimant, on its own motion.

New evidence, applicable to the time before the date of the ALJ's decision, may be submitted to the Appeals Council. Review by the Appeals Council is almost always a review of the record. Although there is a provision that allows the claimant or representative to petition to be allowed to appear before the Appeals Council, oral argument is virtually never granted. *See* Chapter 5, and 20 C.F.R. §§ 404.967 *et seq.* regarding Appeals Council review.

§155 Federal Court

If the Appeals Council denies review or makes a decision adverse to the claimant, the claimant may file a civil action in the United States District Court for the district where the claimant resides. The Commissioner of Social Security is named as defendant. *See* Chapter 6. The court has the power to affirm, modify or reverse the decision of the Commissioner, with or without remanding the case for a rehearing. 42 U.S.C. § 405(g).

If the U.S. District Court affirms the decision of SSA and grants judgment to the defendant Commissioner, the claimant may appeal to the United States Court of Appeals for the circuit in which the district court sits. If the Court of Appeals denies the claimant's case, the claimant may file a petition for certiorari with the United States Supreme Court. Recently the Supreme Court has granted certiorari in very few Social Security Act cases.

§156 *Diagrams: The Appeal Process and Outcomes 2008 - 2015*

FISCAL YEAR 2008 WORKLOAD DATA: DISABILITY DECISIONS*

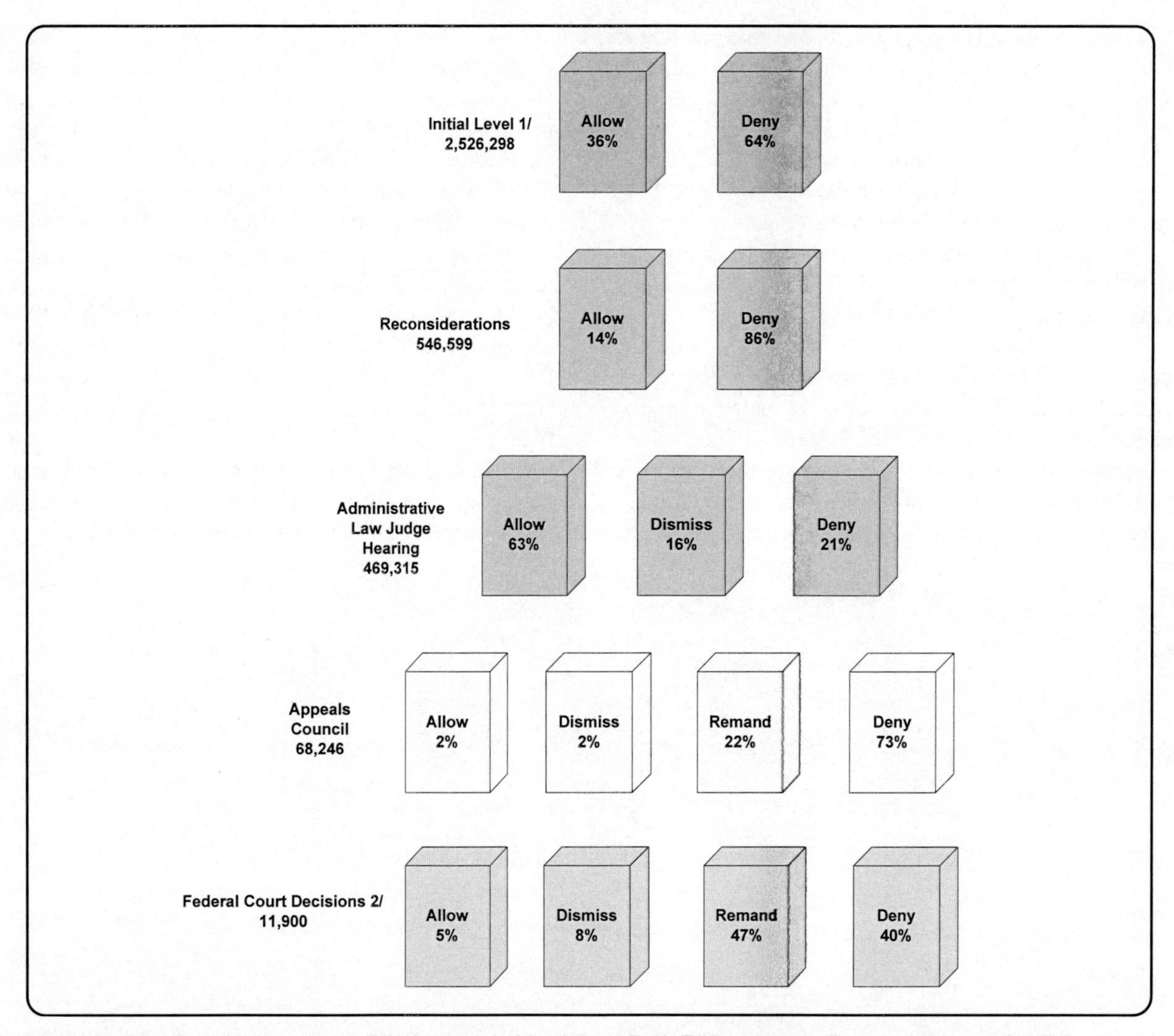

*Data include all disability decisions completed in FY2008 and include claims that were filed in FY08 or prior years. These are decisions on disability eligibility. Other non-disability eligibility factors may affect final eligibility for benefits , i.e., some cases with a favorable disability decision could ultimately be denied for failure to meet other eligibility requirements. Some disability claims not eligible on non-disability grounds will not be referred for a disability decision and are not reflected in the data shown. Decisions include Title II – Social Security Disability Insurance and Title XVI – Supplemental Security Income (SSI) cases. Some claimants may file concurrently for both Title II and Title XVI. Concurrent Title II/XVI cases are counted as one.

1/Approximately 24% of initial level denials are from 10 states using the Prototype process. If appealed, these cases would bypass the reconsideration level and go directly to an Administrative Law Judge hearing.

2/ Data are on applications for persons filing for disability except for Federal Court data which also includes appealed Continuing Disability Review (CDR) decisions.

Prepared by: SSA, ODPMI (Office of Disability Program Management Information)
Date Prepared: October 6, 2009
Data Sources:
1) Initial and Reconsideration Data: SSA State Agency Operations Report
2) Administrative Law Judge and Appeals Council data: SSA Office of Disability Adjudication and Review (ODAR)
3) Federal Court data: SSA Office of General Counsel

FISCAL YEAR 2009 WORKLOAD DATA: DISABILITY DECISIONS*

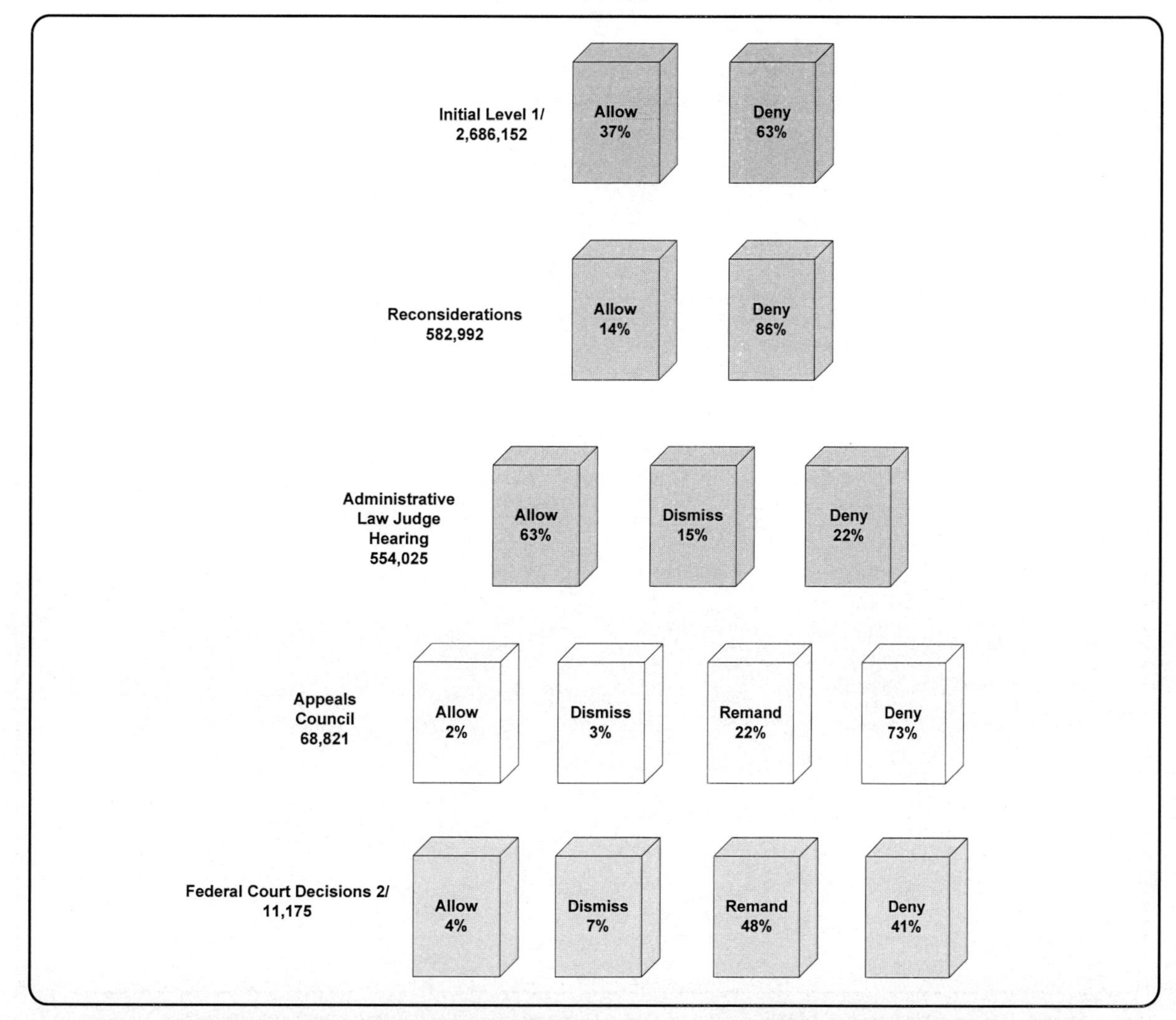

*Data include all disability decisions completed in FY2009 and include claims that were filed in FY09 or prior years. These are decisions on disability eligibility. Other non-disability eligibility factors may affect final eligibility for benefits , i.e., some cases with a favorable disability decision could ultimately be denied for failure to meet other eligibility requirements. Some disability claims not eligible on non-disability grounds will not be referred for a disability decision and are not reflected in the data shown. Decisions include Title II – Social Security Disability Insurance and Title XVI – Supplemental Security Income (SSI) cases. Some claimants may file concurrently for both Title II and Title XVI. Concurrent Title II/XVI cases are counted as one.
1/Approximately 24% of initial level denials are from 10 states using the Prototype process. If appealed, these cases would bypass the reconsideration level and go directly to an Administrative Law Judge hearing.
2/ Data are on applications for persons filing for disability except for Federal Court data which also includes appealed Continuing Disability Review (CDR) decisions.

Prepared by: SSA, ODPMI (Office of Disability Program Management Information)
Date Prepared: November 19, 2009
Data Sources:
1) Initial and Reconsideration Data: SSA State Agency Operations Report
2) Administrative Law Judge and Appeals Council data: SSA Office of Disability Adjudication and Review (ODAR)
3) Federal Court data: SSA Office of General Counsel

FISCAL YEAR 2010 WORKLOAD DATA: DISABILITY DECISIONS*

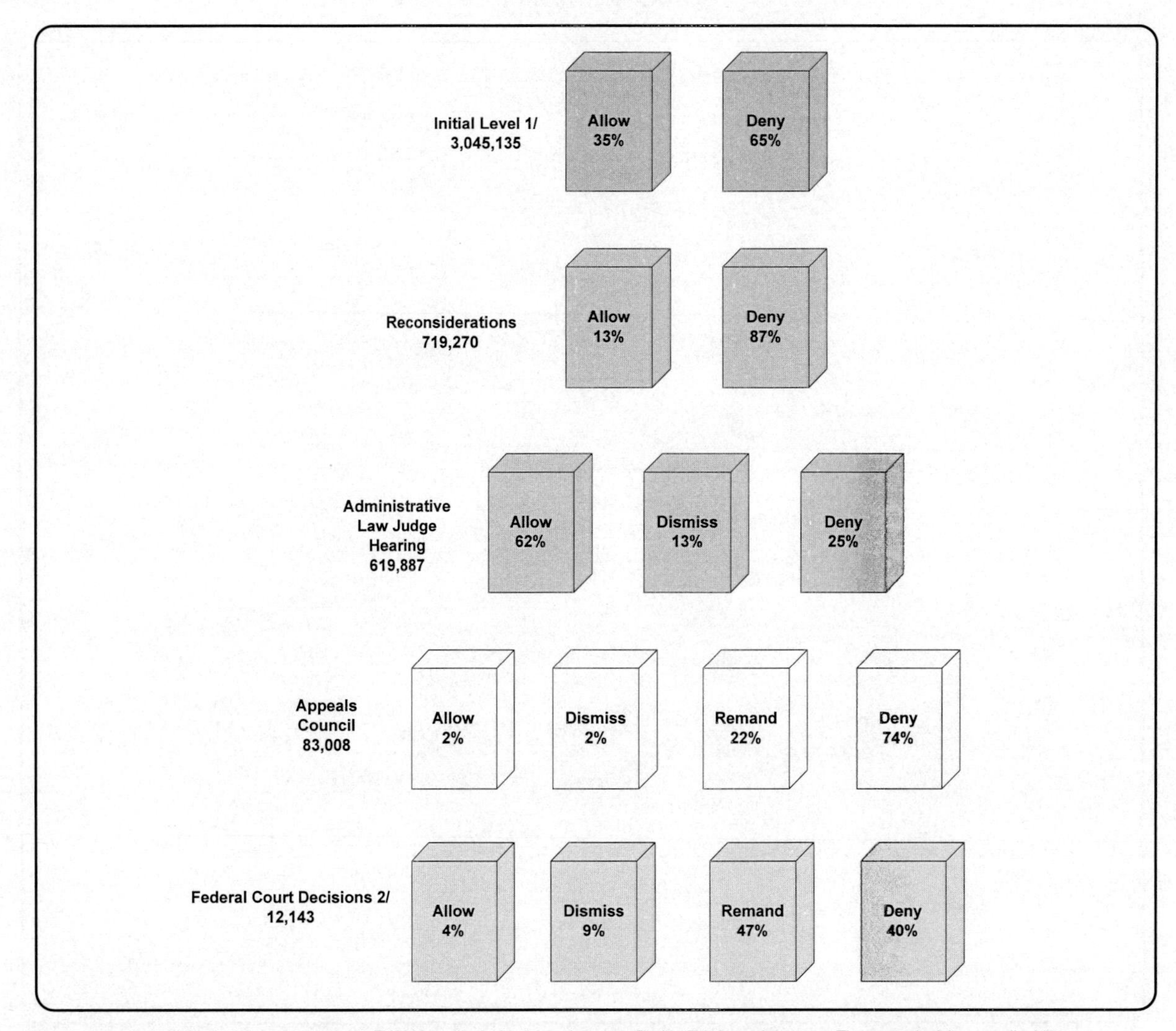

*Data include all disability decisions completed in FY2010 and include claims that were filed in FY10 or prior years. These are decisions on disability eligibility. Other non-disability eligibility factors may affect final eligibility for benefits , i.e., some cases with a favorable disability decision could ultimately be denied for failure to meet other eligibility requirements. Some disability claims not eligible on non-disability grounds will not be referred for a disability decision and are not reflected in the data shown. Decisions include Title II – Social Security Disability Insurance and Title XVI – Supplemental Security Income (SSI) cases. Some claimants may file concurrently for both Title II and Title XVI. Concurrent Title II/XVI cases are counted as one.

1/Approximately 24% of initial level denials are from 10 states using the Prototype process. If appealed, these cases would bypass the reconsideration level and go directly to an Administrative Law Judge hearing.

2/ Data are on applications for persons filing for disability except for Federal Court data which also includes appealed Continuing Disability Review (CDR) decisions.

Prepared by: SSA, ODPMI (Office of Disability Program Management Information)
Date Prepared: November 30, 2010
Data Sources:
1) Initial and Reconsideration Data: SSA State Agency Operations Report
2) Administrative Law Judge and Appeals Council data: SSA Office of Disability Adjudication and Review (ODAR)
3) Federal Court data: SSA Office of General Counsel

FISCAL YEAR 2011 WORKLOAD DATA: DISABILITY DECISIONS*

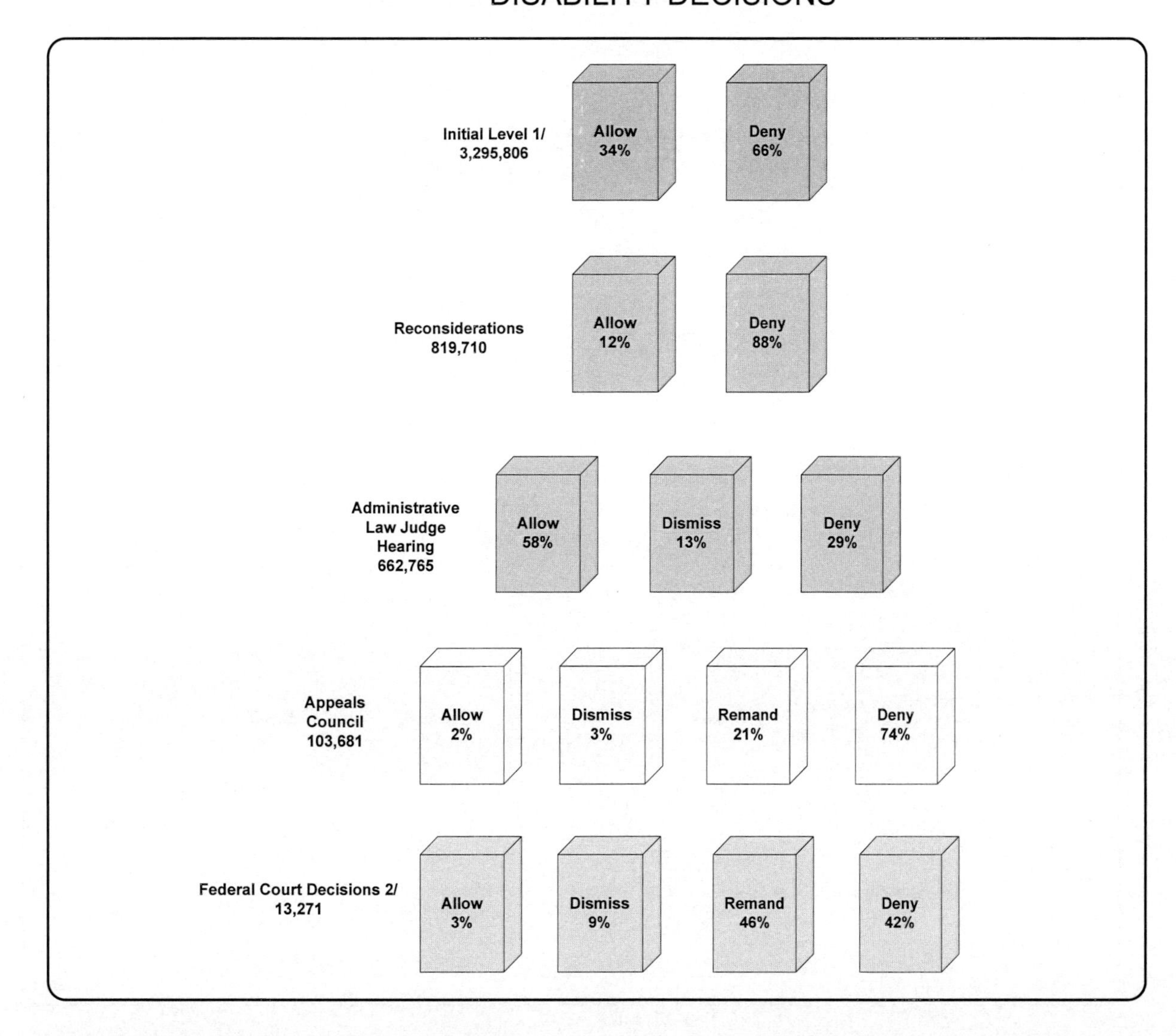

*Includes Title II, Title XVI, and concurrent initial disability determinations and appeals decisions issued in FY 2011, regardless of the year in which the initial claim was filed, and regardless of whether the claimant ever received benefits (in a small number of cases with a favorable disability decision benefits are subsequently denied because the claimant does not meet other eligibility requirements.) Does not include claims where an eligibility determination was reached without a determination of disability. If a determination or appeals decision was made on Title II and Title XVI claims for the same person, the results are treated as one concurrent decision.

1/About 23% of initial level denials are issued in States that use the Disability Prototype process, which eliminates the reconsideration step of the appeals process. The first level of appeal for these cases is a hearing before an Administrative Law Judge.

2/ Federal Court data includes appeals of Continuing Disability Reviews.

Prepared by: SSA, ODPMI (Office of Disability Program Management Information)
Date Prepared: December 20, 2011
Data Sources:
1) Initial and Reconsideration Data: SSA State Agency Operations Report
2) Administrative Law Judge and Appeals Council data: SSA Office of Disability Adjudication and Review (ODAR)
3) Federal Court data: SSA Office of General Counsel

FISCAL YEAR 2012 WORKLOAD DATA: DISABILITY DECISIONS*

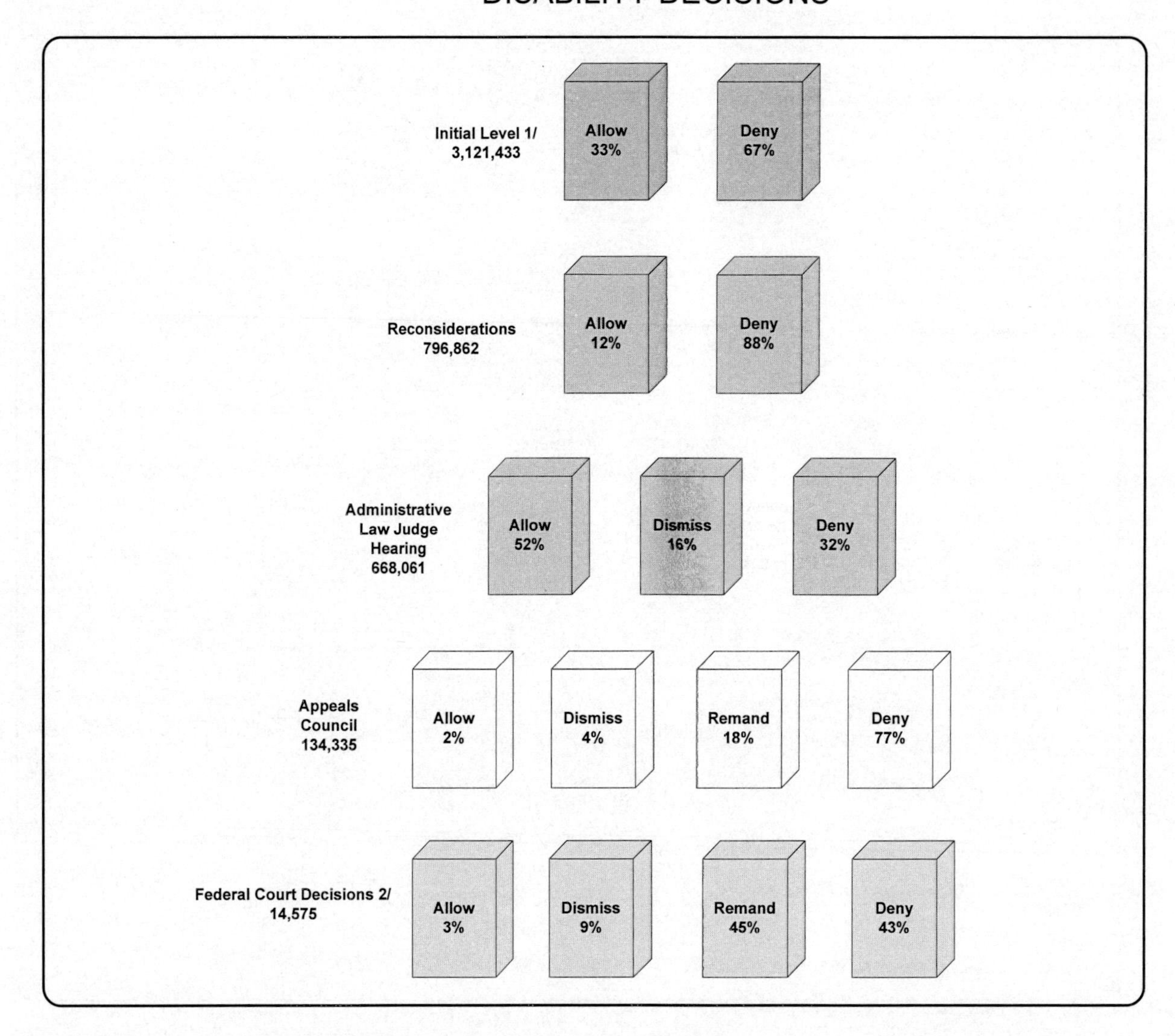

*Includes Title II, Title XVI, and concurrent initial disability determinations and appeals decisions issued in FY 2012, regardless of the year in which the initial claim was filed, and regardless of whether the claimant ever received benefits (in a small number of cases with a favorable disability decision benefits are subsequently denied because the claimant does not meet other eligibility requirements.) Does not include claims where an eligibility determination was reached without a determination of disability. If a determination or appeals decision was made on Title II and Title XVI claims for the same person, the results are treated as one concurrent decision.
1/About 24% of initial level denials are issued in States that use the Disability Prototype process, which eliminates the reconsideration step of the appeals process. The first level of appeal for these cases is a hearing before an Administrative Law Judge.
2/ Federal Court data includes appeals of Continuing Disability Reviews.

Prepared by: SSA, ODPMI (Office of Disability Program Management Information)
Date Prepared: November 26, 2012
Data Sources:
1) Initial and Reconsideration Data: SSA State Agency Operations Report
2) Administrative Law Judge and Appeals Council data: SSA Office of Disability Adjudication and Review (ODAR)
3) Federal Court data: SSA Office of General Counsel

FISCAL YEAR 2013 WORKLOAD DATA: DISABILITY DECISIONS*

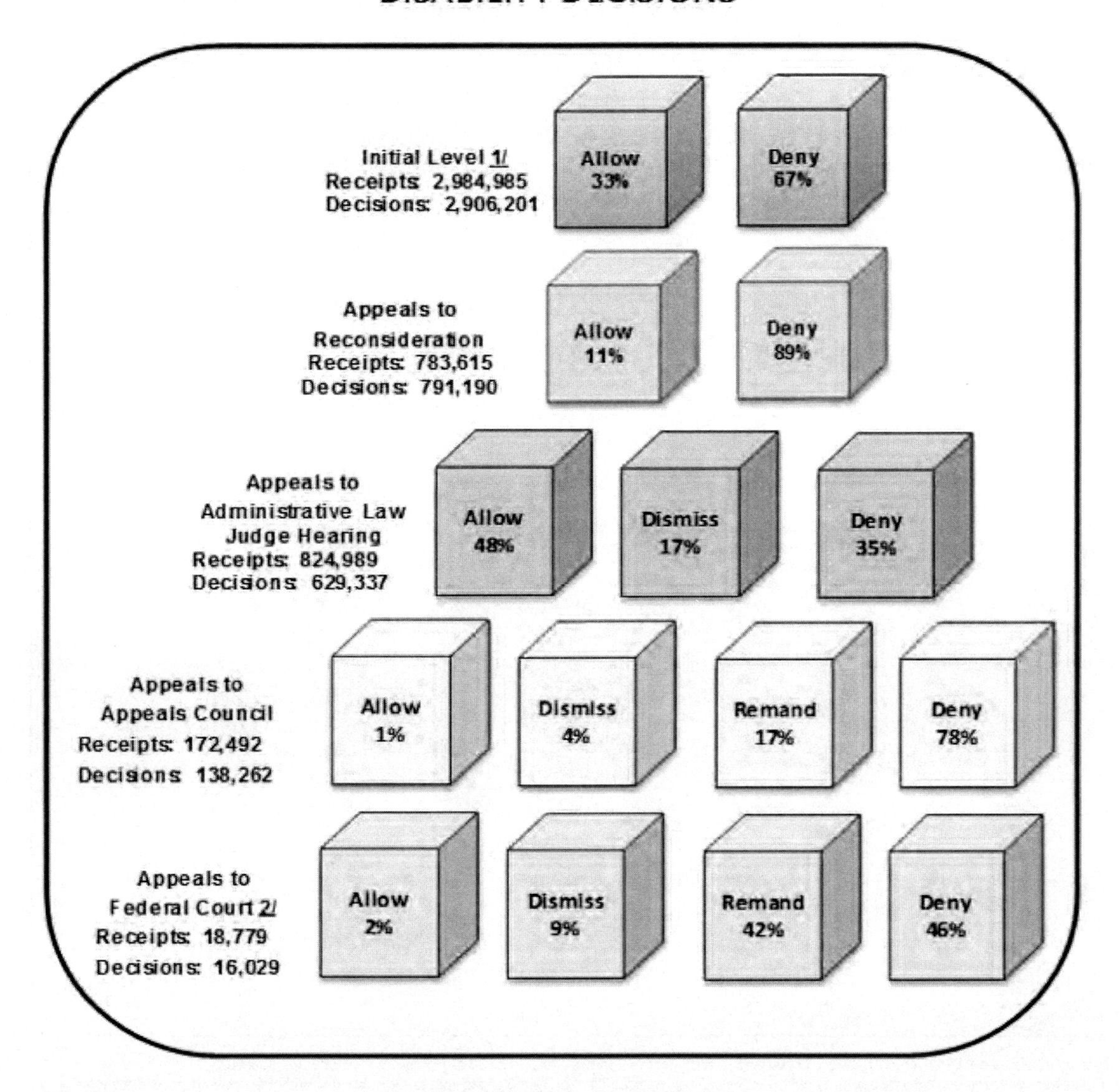

*Includes Title II, Title XVI, and concurrent initial disability determinations and appeals decisions issued in FY 2013, regardless of the year in which the initial claim was filed, and regardless of whether the claimant ever received benefits (in a small number of cases with a favorable disability decision benefits are subsequently denied because the claimant does not meet other eligibility requirements.) Does not include claims where an eligibility determination was reached without a determination of disability. If a determination or appeals decision was made on Title II and Title XVI claims for the same person, the results are treated as one concurrent

1/ About 24% of initial level denials are issued in States that use the Disability Prototype process, which eliminates the reconsideration step of the appeals process. The first level of appeal for these cases is a hearing before an Administrative Law Judge.

2/ Federal Court data includes appeals of Continuing Disability Reviews.

NOTE: Due to rounding, data may not always total 100%.

Prepared by: SSA, Office of Disability Program Management Information, 12/13/13; Office of Budget, 02/06/14
Data Sources: A) Initial and Reconsideration Data: SSA State Agency Operations Report; B) Administrative Law Judge and Appeals Council data: SSA Office of Disability Adjudication and Review (ODAR); C) Federal Court data: SSA Office of General Counsel

FISCAL YEAR 2008 WORKLOAD DATA: DISABILITY DECISIONS*

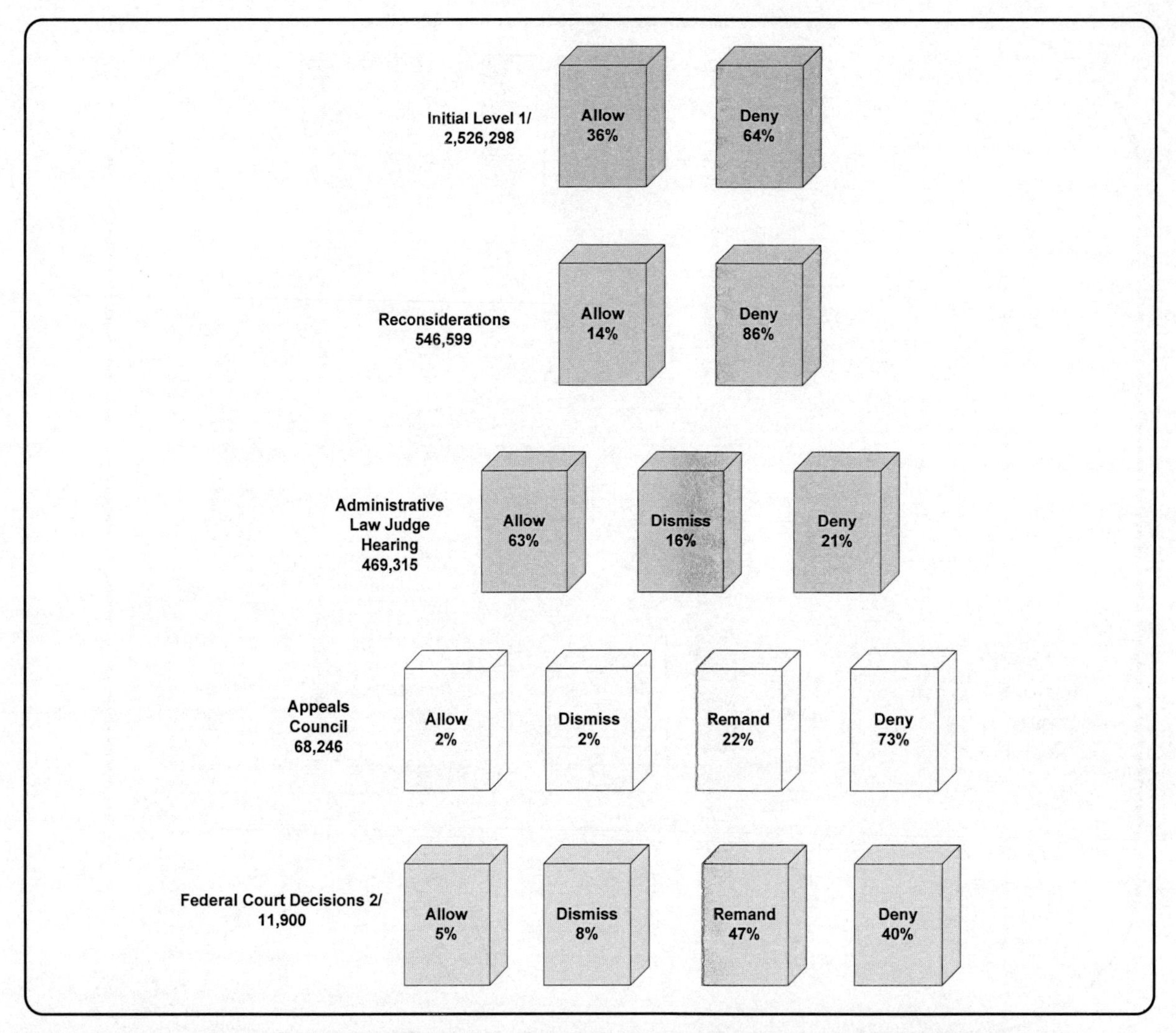

*Data include all disability decisions completed in FY2008 and include claims that were filed in FY08 or prior years. These are decisions on disability eligibility. Other non-disability eligibility factors may affect final eligibility for benefits , i.e., some cases with a favorable disability decision could ultimately be denied for failure to meet other eligibility requirements. Some disability claims not eligible on non-disability grounds will not be referred for a disability decision and are not reflected in the data shown. Decisions include Title II – Social Security Disability Insurance and Title XVI – Supplemental Security Income (SSI) cases. Some claimants may file concurrently for both Title II and Title XVI. Concurrent Title II/XVI cases are counted as one.

1/Approximately 24% of initial level denials are from 10 states using the Prototype process. If appealed, these cases would bypass the reconsideration level and go directly to an Administrative Law Judge hearing.

2/ Data are on applications for persons filing for disability except for Federal Court data which also includes appealed Continuing Disability Review (CDR) decisions.

Prepared by: SSA, ODPMI (Office of Disability Program Management Information)
Date Prepared: October 6, 2009
Data Sources:
1) Initial and Reconsideration Data: SSA State Agency Operations Report
2) Administrative Law Judge and Appeals Council data: SSA Office of Disability Adjudication and Review (ODAR)
3) Federal Court data: SSA Office of General Counsel

FY 2015 DISABILITY WORKLOAD

The following table provides data on the FY 2015 disability claims and appeals workload.

Table 3.34—FY 2015 Workload Data Disability Appeals*

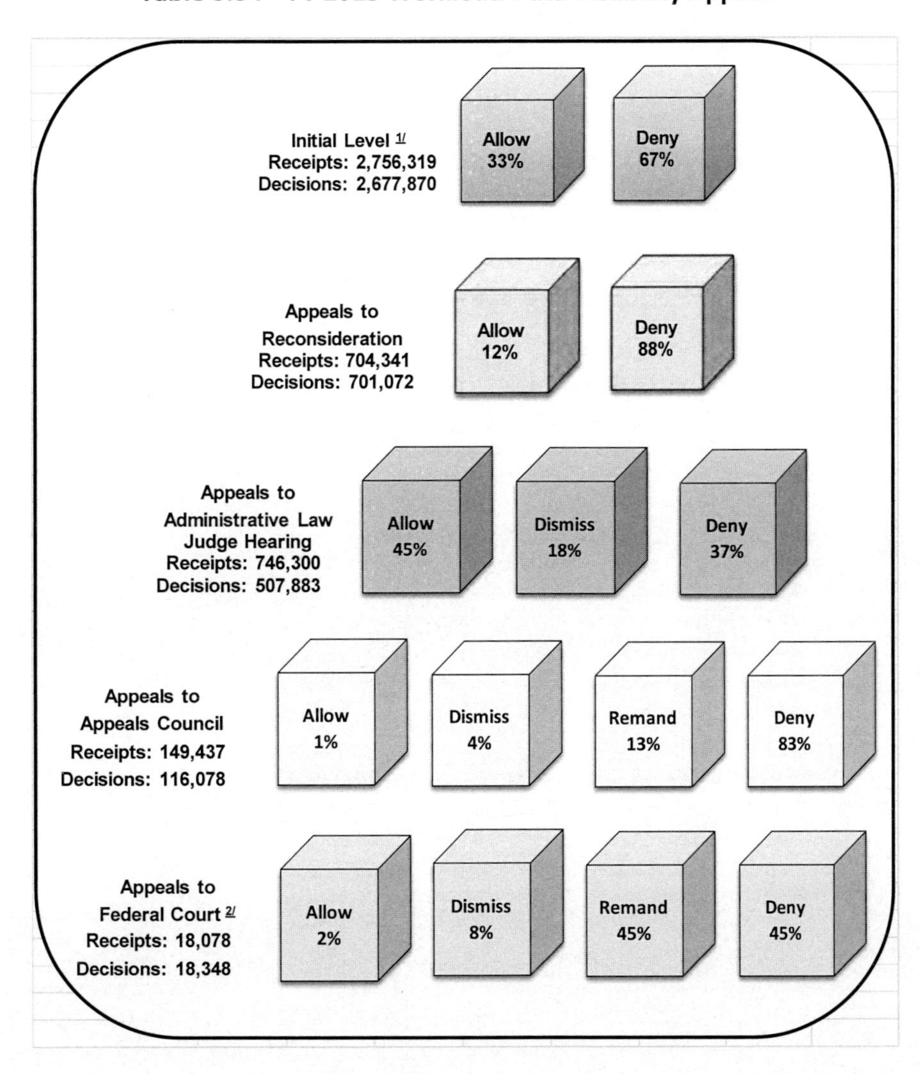

*Includes Title II, Title XVI, and concurrent initial disability determinations and appeals decisions issued in FY 2015, regardless of the year in which the initial claim was filed, and regardless of whether the claimant ever received benefits (in a small number of cases with a favorable disability decision benefits are subsequently denied because the claimant does not meet other eligibility requirements.) Does not include claims where an eligibility determination was reached without a determination of disability. If a determination or appeals decision was made on Title II and Title XVI claims for the same person, the results are treated as one concurrent decision.

1/ About 24% of initial level denials are issued in States that use the Disability Prototype process, which eliminates the reconsideration step of the appeals process. The first level of appeal for these cases is a hearing before an Administrative Law Judge.

2/ Federal Court data includes appeals of Continuing Disability Reviews.

NOTE: Due to rounding, data may not always total 100%.

Prepared by: SSA, ODPMI (Office of Disability Program Management Information) January 14, 2014; Office of Budget, January 29, 2014
Data Sources:
A) Initial and Reconsideration Data: SSA State Agency Operations Report
B) Administrative Law Judge and Appeals Council data: SSA Office of Disability Adjudication and Review (ODAR)
C) Federal Court data: SSA Office of General Counsel

§157 Diagram: How Long Does Appeal Process Take?

Social Security Appeal Process

Initial Determination

114 days

Reconsideration Determination

113 days

Hearing

550 days

Appeals Council

386 days

Approximate national average processing times for 2013-2015. Prepared by the author based on SSA data.

§158 Good Cause for Late Filing

If a claimant does not meet the deadline for appealing, you may ask that SSA extend the deadline by finding that there was good cause for missing the deadline. To do so, send the appeal along with a detailed letter explaining why the request for review of the determination or decision was untimely. Depending on the circumstances, an affidavit from the claimant may be necessary. If SSA finds "good cause" for the delay in appealing, it will extend the time limit. 20 C.F.R. §§ 404.909(b), 404.933(c), and 404.968(b).

POMS GN 03101.020 D provides: "The component with jurisdiction of the appeal request makes the good cause determination." Thus, even if someone at the local office states there is good cause for late filing of a Request for Hearing, an ALJ is not bound by such a determination. The ALJ may decide that good cause does not exist. Pursuant to 20 C.F.R. § 404.968(b), the Appeals Council is given explicit authority to determine good cause if the Request for Review of Hearing Decision is late. See §513. The Appeals Council will determine good cause to extend the deadline to file in federal court pursuant to 20 C.F.R. § 404.982. See 552.

"Good cause" for missing a deadline for requesting review is described in 20 C.F.R. § 404.911. According to that regulation, SSA will consider circumstances preventing a timely appeal, whether any SSA action misled the claimant and whether the claimant failed to understand the requirement of timely appeal. 20 C.F.R. § 404.911(a)(1)-(3). 20 C.F.R. § 404.911(a)(4) provides that SSA will consider:

> Whether you had any physical, mental, educational, or linguistic limitations (including any lack of facility with the English language) which prevented you from filing a timely request or from understanding or knowing about the need to file a timely request for review.

Social Security Ruling 91-5p expands on 20 C.F.R. § 404.911(a)(4). The ruling provides that if a claimant had no one legally responsible for prosecuting the claim, "e.g., a parent of a claimant who is a minor, legal guardian, attorney, or other legal representative," and the claimant shows that mental incapacity prevented the claimant from timely appealing, "regardless of how much time has passed since the prior administrative action, the claimant can establish good cause for extending the deadline to request review of that action." According to the ruling, the evidence must show that the claimant lacked the mental capacity to understand the procedures for requesting review. Reasonable doubt is to be resolved in favor of the claimant.

For those in the Fourth Circuit, AR 90-4(4), which adopted *Culbertson v. Secretary of Health and Human Services*, 859 F.2d 319 (4th Cir. 1988), and *Young v. Bowen*, 858 F.2d 951 (4th Cir. 1988), as an acquiescence ruling, provides essentially the same principal as SSR 91-5p but calls for reopening the earlier decision rather than extending the deadline for appeal.

20 C.F.R. § 404.911(b) provides nine examples of good cause for missing a deadline:

> (b) Examples of circumstances where good cause may exist include, but are not limited to, the following situations:
>
> (1) You were seriously ill and were prevented from contacting us in person, in writing, or through a friend, relative, or other person.
>
> (2) There was a death or serious illness in your immediate family.
>
> (3) Important records were destroyed or damaged by fire or other accidental cause.
>
> (4) You were trying very hard to find necessary information to support your claim but did not find the information within the stated time periods.
>
> (5) You asked us for additional information explaining our action within the time limit, and within 60 days of receiving the explanation you requested reconsideration or a hearing, or within 30 days of receiving the explanation you requested Appeal Council review or filed a civil suit.
>
> (6) We gave you incorrect or incomplete information about when and how to request administrative review or to file a civil suit.
>
> (7) You did not receive notice of the determination or decision.
>
> (8) You sent the request to another Government agency in good faith within the time limit and the request did not reach us until after the time period had expired.
>
> (9) Unusual or unavoidable circumstances exist, including the circumstances described in paragraph (a)(4) of this section, which show that you could not have known of the need to file timely, or which prevented you from filing timely.

Example (7) presents the common situation where a claimant says he or she did not receive the determination or decision. To prevail on this issue, as a rule, you need more than simply the claimant's allegation. 20 C.F.R. § 404.901 provides, "*Date you receive notice* means

5 days after the date on the notice, unless you show us that you did not receive it within the 5-day period." POMS GN 03101.020 C. provides these examples: "e.g., SSA used an incorrect address or the claimant moved." Be sure to ask if the claimant has a theory why the determination or decision was not received.

Another common situation is where a claimant failed to appeal timely because the claimant was confused by information given by SSA. This allegation not only raises the issue of the claimant's mental status but also the quality of the information given by SSA. The POMS makes it clear that information from SSA need not be incorrect or incomplete. If the information was confusing, it could form the basis for an argument that there is good cause for missing the deadline. POMS GN 03101.020 C.

A situation that comes up from time to time is where a claimant thinks that his or her representative filed the appeal. HALLEX I-2-0-60 B., which deals with a late Request for Hearing, includes a this example of good cause: "The claimant relied on a representative to timely file a request, and the representative failed to do so." HALLEX I-2-0-60 B includes this caveat:

> An ALJ must not infer good cause for late filing merely because a claimant has a representative, but must consider a claimant's good cause statement indicating reliance on a representative. If a representative has a pattern of filing untimely appeals, or the claimants of a particular representative develop a pattern of submitting good cause statements for late filing citing reliance on the representative, an ALJ will consider whether circumstances warrant a referral to the Office of the General Counsel (OGC) as a possible violation of our rules. See Hearings, Appeals, and Litigation Law (HALLEX) manual I-1-1-50 for instructions on making referrals to OGC.

A similar HALLEX provision applies to a late Request for Review by the Appeals Council. HALLEX I-3-1-1 E.3.

If SSA refuses to extend the deadline, the late appeal may be treated as a protective filing for a new application. POMS GN 03101.020 D.1.b.2.

§160 Before Initial Interview

Successfully interviewing Social Security disability claimants requires a basic understanding of how SSA determines whether a claimant is or is not disabled and how the administrative appeal system operates. In addition, every lawyer must address basic office policy issues in handling disability cases and interviews.

§161 Office Policy Considerations

Here are some items to think about before setting your office policy:

- Are you going to represent claimants prior to the hearing stage?
- If you are not going to get involved prior to the hearing stage, how are you going to ensure that the claimants will call you back?
- Are you going to represent every claimant who contacts you or are you going to screen cases?
- If you are going to screen cases, are you going to screen out some cases on the telephone?
- Is an attorney or a paralegal going to screen cases?
- If you are going to screen cases, how are you going to do it? Are you going to screen out only the frivolous cases? Or, are you going to select cases using some sort of probability of success or other criteria?
- If a claimant telephones when the 60-day time limit for requesting a hearing has nearly expired, are you going to have the claimant come to your office or are you going to send the claimant directly to the Social Security office?
- Are you going to suggest to all claimants that they file their appeals before they see you or are you going to complete the appeal forms for them when they come in?
- How are you going to handle the problem of expenses of the case? Is your firm going to advance all expenses? What about those long shot cases that can be won only if you get the right medical test results? Who is going to pay for expensive medical testing?
- Are you going to handle cases involving only SSI (where there is no concurrent application for Social Security disability benefits)?
- Are you going to handle continuing disability review (CDR) cases? If so, how will you deal with the problem of attorney's fees?

§162 One Approach to Dealing With Disability Cases

Different lawyers answer the questions in §161 differently. There may be more differences of opinion among lawyers about these issues than there are about how to prove disability. Answers to these questions are subjective and are largely determined by an individual lawyer's style of representation and resources. There may be no "right" answer. Rather than discuss these issues at any length, we're simply going to explain how the author's firm deals with these matters:

- We have experimented with and have had good results with representing claimants at the initial and reconsideration stages. We focus our efforts at these levels on getting a good report from a treating doctor that 1) addresses Listing issues and 2) accurately describes a claimant's residual functional capacity. We ask treating doctors if they are willing to do a consultative examination for the fee provided by SSA, and if so, we ask SSA to use the treating doctor for the consultative examination. *See* 20 C.F.R. § 404.1519h. In addition, because claimants left on their own often do not provide sufficient details, we help our client complete the Function Report and other forms sent to the client by the state agency.
- We do not accept all cases on a contingent fee basis. We decline to represent those relatively few claimants with frivolous cases. There is an additional small group of cases in which we will undertake representation only on a non-contingent fee basis after prepayment of all or part of the fee into our trust account. Rarely does a claimant agree to such a fee arrangement.
- Our paralegals begin screening cases on the telephone using a telephone intake sheet (*see* §165), for taking notes to evaluate the case following the sequential evaluation process. Many callers to our office do not have disability claims or are seeking information about how to file an application. We send literature to such callers.
- While we are alert to earmarks of frivolous cases, it is rare that we can get enough information on the telephone to make this determination. We usually schedule an appointment because, after seeing a claimant and talking with him or her for a while, we may think of ways to win the case that the claimant has not considered.
- We try to schedule appointments no earlier than one week after the date of the telephone call and no later than four weeks after the call. To cut down on the frequency of no shows, we telephone claimants the day before their appointments with us to remind them about their appointments.
- In evaluating a case, we analyze the legal issues, try to estimate the probability of success, expenses involved, attorney time needed, and amount of benefits at stake. We weigh all of these factors. We will take a difficult case on a contingent fee (for example, involving an English-speaking claimant under age 50—overall such cases have odds of about 2 to 1 against the claimant being found disabled) if we have a theory why the claimant is disabled under the law, if the case has average expenses, average attorney time requirements, and average benefits. Where there are significantly lower than average benefits, inordinate attorney time requirements, or potentially high expenses that cannot be borne by the claimant, we may not accept the case with the fee based on our standard two-tiered fee agreement, which appears at §178.3.1.
- We will evaluate the claimant's chances of survival in the real world of work (as opposed to the artificial one concocted by SSA) and if we're convinced the claimant is never going to work again, we will try to figure out a way to represent him or her.
- Anyone who calls us at the eleventh hour about an appeal is sent directly to the Social Security office.
- We normally request that claimants file their appeals before seeing us. Note that this suggestion is in the initial letter to the claimant, §166. However, if a claimant comes in without having first filed an appeal, if we accept the case, we will assist the claimant in filing the appeal. We complete the appeal form online for the claimant. We will also complete online the companion form that goes with the Request for Reconsideration or Request for Hearing, the Disability Report—Appeal (SSA-3441). *See* §178.2.3 for the paper version of this form.
- We usually advance expenses; but it has been our experience that this area of practice has higher expenses as a percentage of attorney's fees than most other areas in which attorneys accept contingent fee cases. If we can anticipate that a case cannot be won without inordinate, and very expensive, medical development, we will explain the problem to the claimant and ask him or her to pay an amount into our trust account to cover such expenses as a condition of representation.
- We accept cases involving SSI where there is no concurrent Social Security disability application; but we do not represent SSI children.
- We will handle continuing disability review (CDR) cases; but we try to make arrangements for the fee, usually a contingent fee of a set amount, to be paid into our trust account before the case is completed. We make a special effort to accommodate former clients.

§163 Telephone Contact

When a claimant telephones with a disability case, the first order of business is to find out how far along the case is and whether there is a problem with the time limit for appeal that needs immediate attention. It is best not to rely on the claimant's description of the administrative process. Instead, ask the claimant to read you portions of the latest denial letter. Reconsideration determinations usually but not always are entitled "Notice of Reconsideration," and usually but not always begin: "Upon receipt of your request for reconsideration . . ." If the denial letter does not start out that way it still could be a reconsideration denial. Ask the claimant to read you what it says about how to appeal. Is the next step to request reconsideration or to request a hearing? Note that the claimant could be involved in a pilot project that skips reconsideration.

Ask the claimant to read you the date on the notice. If the date is more than 65 days ago and the claimant has not yet appealed, find out why no appeal has been made and look for "good cause" for missing the deadline. *See* 20 C.F.R. § 404.911. If no good cause exists for missing the deadline, the claimant will have to start the case over with a new application.

Practice Tip

If the claimant still has time to appeal but is at the 11th hour, advise the claimant to go immediately to the Social Security office. At the local office, all the appeal papers can be completed and the claimant will be given a copy of the appeal form that shows that it was timely filed. A telephone call to the local office will not protect the claimant's rights. SSA requires that the appeal be submitted within 65 days. Although a postmark on the envelope transmitting the appeal showing that it was mailed on the 65th day is acceptable, if that envelope is lost in the mail, it is unlikely that a claimant will be able to prove timeliness to SSA's satisfaction.

Use the Social Security Disability Telephone Intake Form (§165) to gather information from the claimant and to schedule an appointment. This form also may be used as instructions to your secretary to send the claimant a letter confirming the appointment (§166) and to send the claimant a copy of the Client Questionnaire (§167). The questionnaire is a great timesaver for an attorney; but it is long and will take the claimant quite a while to complete. During your telephone call with the claimant, explain about the questionnaire-how long it is and how important it is that you have all this information.

The Claimant Questionnaire asks very few questions about mental impairments. You may ask some claimants with mental impairments to complete an additional questionnaire, the Claimant Psychiatric Questionnaire (§168); but before you give this questionnaire to any claimant, make sure it is appropriate. It is only appropriate for relatively articulate claimants who have insight into their mental problems.

§164 Literature for Prospective Clients

Many people who telephone the office of a Social Security disability attorney are not ready to schedule an appointment. For such people, you need to have some literature, tailored to the practices of your office, available to send them. We send three brochures published by our office, "Social Security Disability and SSI Claims—Your Need for Representation," "Preparing for Your Social Security Disability or SSI Hearing" and "Dealing with the Social Security Administration." In addition, we send the memorandum that is reproduced at §164.1.

§164.1 Memorandum: Common Questions About Applying for Disability Benefits

BUSH LAW OFFICE

REPRESENTING THE DISABLED:
SOCIAL SECURITY DISABILITY
LONG-TERM DISABILITY

SUITE 930E
310 WEST WISCONSIN AVENUE
MILWAUKEE, WISCONSIN 53203

TELEPHONE: (414) 765-9333
FAX: (414) 765-0459

MEMORANDUM No. 1

TO: Social Security Disability/SSI Applicants

FROM: Thomas E. Bush

RE: Common Questions About Applying for Disability Benefits From the Social Security Administration/Appeals/Attorney Representation

This memorandum answers common questions about applying for Supplemetnal Security Income (SSI) or Social Security disability benefits. It should be read along with the two brochures published by this office titled, "Social Security Disability and SSI Claims — Your Need for Representation" and "Preparing for Your Social Security Disability or SSI Hearing."

How can I tell if I am disabled enough to apply for Social Security disability benefits?

Social Security regulations make it easier to be found disabled as you get older. It becomes easier for a few people at age 45 (those unable to read English), for more people at age 50, for most people at age 55, and even more people at age 60. If you're age 55 or over and you cannot do any job you have done in the past 15 years, you should definitely apply. If you're age 50-54 and have a severe impairment that keeps you from doing all but the easiest jobs, you ought to apply.

Even if you're a younger person, you don't have to be bedridden in order to be found disabled. If you're under age 45 or 50 and you cannot do your past jobs and you cannot work full time at any regular job, that ought to be enough.

Nevertheless, being unable to work and being found "disabled" by the Social Security Administration (SSA) are two different things. It is often difficult to convince SSA that someone is "disabled" even when he or she genuinely cannot work. But it is not impossible.

If you really cannot work, apply for disability benefits from SSA. Keep appealing denials at least through the hearing before an administrative law judge.

How do I apply for Social Security or SSI disability benefits?

SSA offers three ways for you to apply for Social Security disability benefits: by telephone, in person at a local Social Security office, or via the Internet. These days, SSA encourages people to use the Internet to apply. If you want to use the Internet to apply for Social Security disability benefits, go to http://www.socialsecurity.gov/disabilityssi/apply.html. If you want to apply for SSA's other disability program—SSI—you cannot complete an SSI application online, but you can complete one of the necessary supporting documents, the Adult Disability and Work History Report, on the Internet.

If you want to complete an application for SSI or Social Security disability by telephone or in person, you must first telephone SSA at 1-800-772-1213. If you choose to go to a Social Security office to complete the application, the person at the 800 number will schedule an appointment for you, give you directions to the Social Security office, and tell you what papers you need to bring along. If you want to apply by phone, you will be given a date and an approximate time to expect a phone call from someone at the Social Security office who will take your application over the phone. The application will then be mailed to you for your signature.

Do you have any advice about applying for disability benefits?

Yes. Give SSA all the information it asks for in a straightforward way. Be truthful. Do not exaggerate or minimize your disability.

When you complete the Adult Disability Report, a form that SSA requests to be completed at the time the application is submitted, be sure to provide a complete list of doctors, clinics and hospitals where you've been treated for your disabling impairments. Also, provide your work history for the past 15 years.

Should I contact a lawyer to help me apply for Social Security Disability or SSI benefits?

As a rule, a person does not need a lawyer's help to file the application. SSA makes this part easy. Many people are found disabled after they file applications on their own. Most people do not hire a lawyer to help with filing the application.

What happens if I am denied benefits and I do not appeal within 60 days?

You'll have to start over with a new application—and it may mean that you'll lose some back benefits. So it's important to appeal all denials within 60 days. It's better if you appeal right away so that you don't forget about the deadline and miss it. The sooner you appeal, the sooner the next decision can be made.

How do I appeal?

Your denial letter will tell you about appealing. The first appeal is called a "reconsideration." You must request reconsideration within 60 days of the date you received the initial denial and then, if reconsideration is denied, you must request a hearing within 60 days of the date you received the reconsideration denial. You are presumed to receive the denial letter within 5 days of the date on the denial letter itself. Thus, you've actually got 65 days from the date on a denial letter to appeal it. But it is best not to wait. Appeal as soon as you get the denial letter.

You can appeal in one of three ways: 1) If possible, SSA prefers that you appeal online at https://secure.ssa.gov/apps6z/iAppeals/ap001.jsp. Be sure to print and retain the receipt for your appeal so that you can prove you appealed on time. 2) Telephone the Social Security Administration and make arrangements for your appeal to be handled by phone and mail. 3) Go to the Social Security office to submit your appeal. If you go to the Social Security office, be sure to take along a copy of your denial letter. Ask the Social Security representative to give you a receipt that will show you appealed on time.

What are the biggest mistakes people make when trying to get disability benefits?

Failing to appeal. More than half of the people whose applications are denied fail to appeal. Many people who are denied on reconsideration fail to request a hearing.

Another mistake, although much less common, is made by people who fail to obtain appropriate medical care. Some people with long-term chronic medical problems feel that they have not been helped much by doctors. Thus, for the most part, they stop going for treatment. This is a mistake for both medical and legal reasons. First, no one needs good medical care more than those with chronic medical problems. Second, medical treatment records provide the most important evidence of disability in a Social Security case.

Since medical evidence is so important, should I have my doctor write a letter to the Social Security Administration and should I gather medical records and send them to SSA?

SSA will gather the medical records, so you don't have to do that. Whether you should ask your doctor to write a letter is a hard question. A few people win their cases by having their doctors write letters. You can try this if you want to. The problem is that the medical-legal issues are so complicated in most disability cases that a doctor may inadvertently give the wrong impression. Thus, obtaining medical reports may be something best left for a lawyer to do.

When is the best time for a lawyer to get involved in my case?

Many people wait until it is time to request a hearing before contacting us to represent them. Although everyone agrees that a lawyer's help is essential at the hearing and the great majority of people who have lawyers win their cases at a hearing, how necessary it is to have the help of a lawyer at the early stages is a subject with arguments on both sides.

More than one-third of those people who apply will be found disabled after filing the initial application without a lawyer's help. About 15% of those who request reconsideration are found disabled at the reconsideration stage, mostly without a lawyer's help. If you are successful in handling the case yourself at the initial or reconsideration steps, you will save having to pay attorney's fees. It is hard to predict which cases may benefit from a lawyer's help early on.

We seldom get involved when someone is just filing an application. SSA makes it difficult for a lawyer to do much at this point. As a rule, we don't get involved in a case until after an initial denial is issued and a legal controversy exists. Every once in awhile a claimant points out an obvious (and quite unusual) legal problem with a case that needs a lawyer's attention early in a claim. We do consider getting involved in such cases before the initial determination is issued.

If a claimant asks us to get involved at the reconsideration stage, we will evaluate the case even though cases are harder to evaluate at this stage than they are at the hearing stage. Sometimes it is even hard to tell if a claimant will be disabled for twelve months, which is required by the Social Security Act. If you want us to consider representing you at the reconsideration stage, we may ask you to do more work gathering records so that we have enough information to evaluate your case.

If you want us to consider becoming involved in your case at the initial or reconsideration steps, please telephone us to discuss your situation. Otherwise, the best time to call us is as soon as you get the reconsideration denial.

How much do you charge?

Almost all of our clients prefer a "contingent fee," a fee paid only if they win. The usual fee is 25% (one-quarter) of back benefits up to a maximum amount set by SSA, which is currently $6,000.00. The fee comes from those benefits that build up by the time you are found disabled and benefits are paid. No fee comes out of current monthly benefits.

Although the usual fee will not normally exceed $6,000.00, if we have to appeal after the first administrative law judge hearing, our contract drops the $6,000.00 limit on fees. Even in this circumstance, though, our fee will not be greater than 25% of back benefits.

Sometimes at the request of a client, we charge a non-contingent hourly or per case fee. There is also the rare case where a contingent 25% fee arrangement is insufficient to allow for an adequate fee. In such a case, we use a different method of calculating the fee.

In addition to the fee, you will be expected to reimburse us for the expense of gathering medical records, obtaining medical opinion letters, etc.

If I have other questions, will you answer them by telephone?

Yes. If this memorandum and the brochures don't answer your questions, please telephone us.

§165 Form: Social Security Disability Telephone Intake

DISABILITY TELEPHONE INTAKE

NAME: ______________________ **Interviewer:** ______________________

ADDRESS: ______________________ **Date:** ______________________

______________________ **Phone:** ______________________

Referred by: ______________________ Name of caller: ______________________

Type of claim: ☐ **SSD** ☐ **SSI** ☐ **SSD/Widow/er** ☐ **Worker's Compensation**

AGE: ______ Education: ____________ Date Last Worked: ____________ Telephoned before: ☐

Prior work experience: ____

Describe impairments/injury: ____

____

____

____

SSA:
- ☐ Initial contact (PF) ______________
- ☐ Initial app ______________
- ☐ Initial denial ______________ Why ______________________
- ☐ Recon not requested
- ☐ Recon requested ______________
- ☐ Recon denial ______________ Why ______________________
- ☐ Hearing not requested
- ☐ Hearing requested ______________
- ☐ Hearing scheduled ______________
- ALJ ______________

AC:
- ☐ Hearing denial ______________ Were you represented ______________
- ALJ ______________ By who ______________
- ☐ Request for review not filed When was your attorney released ________
- ☐ Request for review filed ________ Decision received by ______________

WC:
- Employer ______________ Insurance Carrier ______________
- ☐ Date of injury ______________ Type of Injury ______________
- ☐ No dispute
- ☐ Dispute ____
- ☐ Causation ____
- ☐ IME ______________ DR. ______________________
- ☐ Healing Plateau ______________
- ☐ PPD Conceded ______________
- ☐ Issues ____

____

____

IMPAIRMENTS ____

____

____

____

TREATMENT/DOCTORS ____

____

RESTRICTIONS ____

____

____

____

____

MEDICATIONS ____

____

____

____

ISSUES ____

____

____

____

APPOINTMENT: Day: __________ Date: ____________ Time: __________

Rep: __________ **Scheduler's Initials**: ______ Type of Letter: ____________

Questionnaires: ☐ SSA ☐ WC ☐ TERM ☐ Psych ☐ Supplemental

OTHER: ___________ SEND: ☐ Can't Reach letter ☐ Brochures ☐ Kit

☐ **DECLINE CASE. Reason:** ____

____

§166 Form: Letter to Prospective Client

Client's Name
Address
City, State Zip

Re: Social Security Case

Dear Client's Name:

This letter is to confirm your appointment with me at my office on _________ [*day*], __________ [*date*] at ______ [*time*].

When you come, please bring all of your Social Security papers (especially the denial letters and appeal forms), including any papers related to earlier applications.

Be very careful about appeal deadlines. Please appeal any denial letters as soon as possible. Please submit your appeal before the date of our appointment. You may appeal on the Internet at www.socialsecurity.gov or by going to any Social Security office. Don't forget to bring your copy of the appeal papers to our meeting.

If you have any hospital records or medical reports in your possession, please bring them, too. However, you don't need to go to doctors or hospitals to get medical records if you don't already have them. If you have been involved in any other disability cases (such as short or long term disability, worker's compensation, etc.) please bring papers related to those cases, too. If you received Unemployment Compensation during any time you claim to be disabled, bring papers related to your Unemployment Compensation benefits.

Please complete the enclosed questionnaire before our meeting. This is a long and detailed questionnaire; but all of the information requested on the questionnaire is necessary in order to evaluate your case and effectively represent you.

This questionnaire may take several hours to complete. If you do not have it completed by the time of the appointment, please call and reschedule.

If you need help completing the questionnaire and no one is available to help you, please telephone me so that we can discuss how to deal with this.

Sincerely,

____
(Name of Attorney)

§167 Form: Claimant Questionnaire

QUESTIONNAIRE

NAME:	TELEPHONE:
ADDRESS:	SSN:
	DATE OF BIRTH: AGE:

1. Are you a U.S. Citizen? ☐ Yes ☐ No

2. On what date did you apply for Social Security disability and/or SSI benefits? ____________________

3. In your application for benefits, what date did you state as the date you became unable to work?

____

4.

LIST YOUR HEALTH CONDITIONS	WHEN DID EACH CONDITION *FIRST BOTHER YOU? (APPROXIMATE DATE)*

5. When did you stop working? ______________________________

6. Why did you stop working? ____

____

____

7. Why can't you work now? ____

____

____

8. Please provide your work history for **15 years** before you became unable to work. Approximate dates are acceptable.

Start with your most recent job and then the next most recent job, etc.

DATES WORKED (MONTH & YEAR) FROM:	TO:	NAME ***AND ADDRESS*** OF EMPLOYER	NAME OF JOB & JOB DUTIES	HOURS PER DAY	REASON FOR LEAVING	HOURS PER WEEK	RATE OF PAY
				Sitting: ______ Standing: _____ Walking: _____			
				Sitting: ______ Standing: _____ Walking: _____			
				Sitting: ______ Standing: _____ Walking: _____			
				Sitting: ______ Standing: _____ Walking: _____			
				Sitting: ______ Standing: _____ Walking: _____			
				Sitting: ______ Standing: _____ Walking: _____			
				Sitting: ______ Standing: _____ Walking: _____			

(Use additional sheets of paper, if necessary.)

USUAL WORK:

9. Which work do you consider to be your usual work? ______________________________

MOST RECENT JOB:

10. For your *most recent job* in addition to the information provided on page 2, please answer the following:

a. What was the *greatest* weight you had to lift or carry on this job? ________ pounds

(1) How many times per day would you lift or carry this much? ________ times per day

(2) What object(s) weighed this much? ______________

b. What was the *average* weight you had to lift or carry on this job? ________ pounds

(1) How many times per day would you lift or carry this much? ________ times per day

(2) What object(s) weighed this much? ______________

c. Did you use machines, tools or equipment of any kind? ☐ Yes ☐ No

If yes, describe: ____

____

d. Did you use technical knowledge or skills? ☐ Yes ☐ No

If yes, describe: ____

____

e. Did you do any writing, complete reports, or perform similar duties? ☐ Yes ☐ No

If yes, describe: ____

____

f. Did you have supervisory responsibilities? ☐ Yes ☐ No

If yes, how many people did you supervise? ______________

g. Before you left this job, did your medical problems require you to make any changes in the hours of work, the way you worked, your job duties, absences, etc.? If so, what were these changes?

____

____

____

EASIEST JOB:

11. Which job listed on page two would be the easiest for you to do now, considering your medical problems? (Do not describe any job that lasted less than three months.)

____

For your easiest job, please answer the following:

a. Supervisor's name: ____

b. In an average workday, how many hours were spent: Sitting: ______________
Standing: ______________
Walking: ______________

c. What was the *greatest* weight you had to lift or carry on this job? ______________ pounds

(1) How many times per day would you lift or carry this much? _________ times per day

(2) What object(s) weighed this much? ___________________

d. What was the *average* weight you had to lift or carry on this job? ______________ pounds

(1) How many times per day would you lift or carry this much? _________ times per day

(2) What object(s) weighed this much? ___________________

SEDENTARY/OFFICE WORK:

12. Have you ever had a desk or sit down job? ☐ Yes ☐ No When? _____________________

Where? _____________________

13. Have you ever had an office job? ☐ Yes ☐ No

Office Skills:

☐ Filing ☐ Typing/w.p.m.: _________________
☐ Office Machines ☐ Computers
☐ Dictation ☐ Bookkeeping
☐ Other ____

RECENT WORK:

14. Are you working now? ☐ Yes ☐ No

a. If so, where? ____

b. Earnings per month (gross) $ _________________________

15. Have you worked anywhere since you became disabled? ☐ Yes ☐ No

When? ______________________ What job? ___________________________

Where? ______________________ Why did job end? _____________________

16. Have you applied for unemployment compensation (UC) since the date you became unable to work? ☐ Yes ☐ No

If yes, did you receive UC benefits? ☐ Yes ☐ No

If yes, what dates did you receive UC benefits? _____________________________________

If no, why didn't you receive UC benefits? ____

17. Have you ever lost or quit a job because of your limitations? ☐ Yes ☐ No

    Explain yes answer: ______________________________

18. Have you applied for any jobs since the date you became unable to work? ☐ Yes ☐ No

    If yes, what job(s) did you apply for? ______________________________

19. Are there any of your previous jobs that you think you might be able to do? ☐ Yes ☐ No

    If yes, which one(s)? ______________________________

EDUCATION:

20. What was the highest grade you completed in school? ______________________________

    a. When did you last go to school? ______________________________

    b. Name of last school: ____________________ City & State: ____________________

    c. Did you repeat any grades? ☐ Yes ☐ No If yes, which one(s)? ____________________

    d. Were you in special classes? ☐ Yes ☐ No If yes, describe: ____________________

    e. If you left school before completing high school,

       (1) Did you get a GED? ☐ Yes ☐ No When? ____________________

       (2) What was the reason for leaving school? ______________________________

    f. How well do you read?

       ☐ Above Average ☐ Below Average
       ☐ Average ☐ Illiterate/unable to read English

       If below average or illiterate,

       (1) Are you able to read a menu or list? ☐ Yes ☐ No

       (2) Are you able to read simple instructions? ☐ Yes ☐ No

       (3) Has your reading been tested? If so, where? ______________________________

    g. Are you able to do the following mathematics? (Check all that you can do.)

       ☐ Make Change ☐ Decimals/Fractions
       ☐ Add and Subtract ☐ Higher Mathematics
       ☐ Multiply and Divide

    h. Were you an ☐ A ☐ B ☐ C ☐ D student in high school?

VOCATIONAL TRAINING:

21. For any vocational training you have had in your life, please identify the school, the type of training, dates attended and whether you completed the program: ________________________________
____
____

a. Have you ever been evaluated by the state vocational rehabilitation agency?

☐ Yes ☐ No If no, why not? ____
____

b. If yes, please complete the following:

VOC. REHABILITATION COUNSELOR'S NAME	ADDRESS	DATES

MILITARY:

22. Were you ever in the military? ☐ Yes ☐ No

a. Branch: ________________ When? ________________ Highest Rank: ________________

b. Nature of discharge: ____

c. Describe any special training: ____

VETERANS DISABILITY:

23. Have you ever applied for VA disability? ☐ Yes ☐ No

a. If yes, was it for ☐ service connected or ☐ non-service connected disability?

b. What was the percentage rating? _____ What was the date of the rating? ________________

c. When did benefits begin? ____

d. What were the medical problems that the VA rating was based on? ____________________
____

e. Is your VA disability claim pending now? ☐ Yes ☐ No

If yes, please give us the name and address of your representative (if you have one): __________
____
____

MEDICAL INFORMATION:

24. Current Height: ______________________________ Current Weight: ______________________

    a. How much is your usual weight? ______________________________

    b. When was the last time you weighed this much? ______________________________

25. Do you smoke? ☐ Yes ☐ No If yes, how much? ___________________

26. Have you *ever* been treated by a psychiatrist or psychologist? ☐ Yes ☐ No

    If yes, give details including dates, reasons for treatment, and nature of treatment: _______________

    ____

27. Have you *ever* had any problems with alcohol or drug abuse? ☐ Yes ☐ No

    If so, describe problem: ____

28. Have you *ever* been treated for alcohol or drug abuse? ☐ Yes ☐ No

    a. If yes, when and where? ____

    b. When did you recover from alcohol/drug abuse? ____

CURRENT MEDICAL PROBLEMS

29. Since the date you became disabled, have you been getting better or worse?

    ☐ Better ☐ Worse ☐ Same

30. Will you ever get well enough to work again? ☐ Yes ☐ No If yes, when? _______________

31. Has any doctor told you not to work? ☐ Yes ☐ No If yes, who? __________ When? _______

32. Has any doctor told you to limit your activities? ☐ Yes ☐ No

    a. If yes, please describe the limitations: ____

    ____

    b. Which doctor(s) told you this? ___________________________ When? _____________

33. Do you have a handicapped-parking permit? ☐ Yes ☐ No

    If yes, which doctor signed the papers for it? ____

34. Which doctor knows you best? ____

35. Do you have any *current* problem with any of the following?

Shortness of breath	☐ Yes	☐ No	Alcohol abuse	☐ Yes	☐ No
Coughing up blood	☐ Yes	☐ No	High blood pressure	☐ Yes	☐ No
Hot/cold flashes	☐ Yes	☐ No	Dizziness	☐ Yes	☐ No
Excessive sweating	☐ Yes	☐ No	Swelling of feet/ankles	☐ Yes	☐ No
Heart palpitations	☐ Yes	☐ No	Blackouts	☐ Yes	☐ No
Diarrhea	☐ Yes	☐ No	Fatigue	☐ Yes	☐ No
Controlling your urine	☐ Yes	☐ No	Difficulty sleeping	☐ Yes	☐ No
Vision	☐ Yes	☐ No	Recent weight loss	☐ Yes	☐ No
Drug abuse	☐ Yes	☐ No	Recent weight gain	☐ Yes	☐ No

36. If you answered *Yes* to Drug Abuse in the above question, please explain:

____

____

37. Do you drink any alcohol? ☐ Yes ☐ No

If yes, please answer the following questions:

a. What sort of alcoholic beverage do you usually drink? ______________________

b. How much alcohol do you drink in a typical week? ______________________

c. During the past month, was there any single day in which you had five or more drinks of beer, wine or liquor? ☐ Yes ☐ No

d. During the past six months, have you thought you should cut down on your drinking of alcohol? ☐ Yes ☐ No

e. During the past six months, has anyone complained about your drinking? ☐ Yes ☐ No

f. During the past six months, have you felt guilty or upset about your drinking? ☐ Yes ☐ No

g. As a result of alcohol use, have you ever lost a job? ☐ Yes ☐ No

h. As a result of alcohol use, have you ever lost a friend? ☐ Yes ☐ No

PAIN:

38. If your disability involves physical pain, answer the following: (If physical pain is not your problem, go on to question #39.)

a. Approximate date pain began: ______________________________

b. What event caused the pain (e.g., accident, disease, surgery, unknown)? ______________________________

____

c. What does your pain feel like? ______________________________

____

____

d. What reasons have your doctors given for your pain? ______________________________

____

____

e. Does pain ☐ lessen or ☐ increase when you push on the painful spots?

f. Are any of the following associated with your pain? Check those that apply:

☐ Numbness
☐ Increased sweating
☐ Nausea
☐ Loss of concentration
☐ Tingling (pins and needles)
☐ Muscle spasm
☐ Loss of sleep
☐ Depression
☐ Weakness
☐ Skin discoloration
☐ Crying spells
☐ Agitation

g. Location of pain: Please shade in areas of pain.

BE AS SPECIFIC AS POSSIBLE.

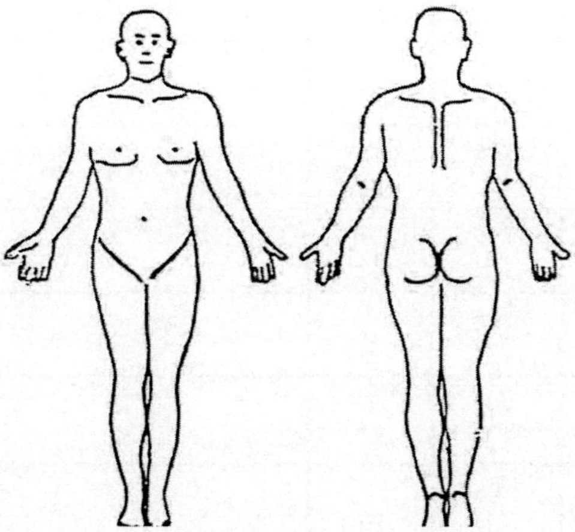

h. Is pain: ☐ Constant? ☐ Often? ☐ Occasional?

i. How many hours per day do you have pain? ____________

j. If you do not have pain every day, estimate how many hours of pain per week, or days per week or month: ___
____

k. Below is a list of activities. For each activity indicate how it affects your pain.

	INCREASES	DECREASES	NO EFFECT
Lying down	☐	☐	☐
Sitting	☐	☐	☐
Rising from sitting	☐	☐	☐
Sitting with legs elevated	☐	☐	☐
Standing	☐	☐	☐
Walking	☐	☐	☐
Bending	☐	☐	☐
Coughing/Sneezing	☐	☐	☐

l. What else increases your pain? ____

____

m. Below is a list of treatments you may have used to relieve pain. For each of these, indicate whether you have tried it and, if you tried it, the degree it helped.

Treatment	Have you tried?		Rate Helpfulness 0 = No Help; 10 = Excellent Relief
Heat	Yes ☐	No ☐	0 1 2 3 4 5 6 7 8 9 10
Massage	Yes ☐	No ☐	0 1 2 3 4 5 6 7 8 9 10
Whirlpool	Yes ☐	No ☐	0 1 2 3 4 5 6 7 8 9 10
Traction	Yes ☐	No ☐	0 1 2 3 4 5 6 7 8 9 10
Prescribed Exercise	Yes ☐	No ☐	0 1 2 3 4 5 6 7 8 9 10
Bed rest	Yes ☐	No ☐	0 1 2 3 4 5 6 7 8 9 10
TENS (electrical stimulation)	Yes ☐	No ☐	0 1 2 3 4 5 6 7 8 9 10
Biofeedback	Yes ☐	No ☐	0 1 2 3 4 5 6 7 8 9 10
Trigger Point Injections	Yes ☐	No ☐	0 1 2 3 4 5 6 7 8 9 10
Nerve Blocks	Yes ☐	No ☐	0 1 2 3 4 5 6 7 8 9 10
Acupuncture	Yes ☐	No ☐	0 1 2 3 4 5 6 7 8 9 10
Chiropractic Treatments	Yes ☐	No ☐	0 1 2 3 4 5 6 7 8 9 10
Cranial Sacral Therapy	Yes ☐	No ☐	0 1 2 3 4 5 6 7 8 9 10

Behavior Modification	Yes ☐	No ☐	0 1 2 3 4 5 6 7 8 9 10
Counseling/ Psychotherapy	Yes ☐	No ☐	0 1 2 3 4 5 6 7 8 9 10
Herbs, Vitamins, Supplements, etc.	Yes ☐	No ☐	0 1 2 3 4 5 6 7 8 9 10
Pain Clinic/Pain Program	Yes ☐	No ☐	0 1 2 3 4 5 6 7 8 9 10

n. What other things relieve your pain? ______________________________

____

____

____

o. Does drinking alcoholic beverages relieve your pain? ☐ Yes ☐ No

p. If you did not have pain, what things would you do that you cannot do now because of the pain?

____

____

____

____

q. **Rating pain**. Circle the ***one*** number that best describes your pain:

I. Pain Severity

A. Rate how severe your pain is **right now, at this moment** when filling out this questionnaire:

0	1	2	3	4	5	6	7	8	9	10
No pain					Most severe pain you can imagine					

B. Rate how severe your pain is **at its worst**:

0	1	2	3	4	5	6	7	8	9	10
No pain					Excruciating					

C. Rate how severe your pain is **on the average**:

0	1	2	3	4	5	6	7	8	9	10
No pain					Excruciating					

D. Rate how much your pain is **aggravated by activity**:

0	1	2	3	4	5	6	7	8	9	10
Activity does not aggravate pain					Excruciating following any activity					

E. Rate how **frequently** you experience pain:

0	1	2	3	4	5	6	7	8	9	10
Rarely										All the time

II. Activity Limitation or Interference

A. How much does your pain interfere with your ability to **walk one block**?

0	1	2	3	4	5	6	7	8	9	10
Does not restrict ability to walk										Pain makes it impossible for me to walk

B. How much does your pain prevent you from **lifting 10 pounds** (a bag of groceries)?

0	1	2	3	4	5	6	7	8	9	10
Does not interfere at all with lifting 10 pounds										Impossible to lift 10 pounds

C. How much does your pain interfere with your ability to **sit for 1/2 hour**?

0	1	2	3	4	5	6	7	8	9	10
Does not restrict ability to sit for 1/2 hour										Impossible to sit for 1/2 hour

D. How much does your pain interfere with your ability to **stand for 1/2 hour**?

0	1	2	3	4	5	6	7	8	9	10
Does not restrict ability to stand for 1/2 hour										Unable to stand at all

E. How much does your pain interfere with your ability to **get enough sleep**?

0	1	2	3	4	5	6	7	8	9	10
Does not prevent me from sleeping										Impossible to sleep

F. How much does your pain interfere with your ability to **participate in social activities**?

0	1	2	3	4	5	6	7	8	9	10
Does not interfere with social activities										Completely interferes with social activities

G. How much does your pain interfere with your ability to **travel up to 1 hour by car**?

0	1	2	3	4	5	6	7	8	9	10
Does not interfere with ability to travel 1 hour by car										Completely unable to travel 1 hour by car

H. In general, how much does your pain interfere with your **daily activities**?

0	1	2	3	4	5	6	7	8	9	10
Does not limit with my daily activities										Completely interferes with my daily activities

I. How much do you **limit your activities to prevent your pain from getting worse**?

0	1	2	3	4	5	6	7	8	9	10
Does not limit activities										Completely limits activities

J. How much does your pain interfere with your **relationship with your family/significant others**?

0	1	2	3	4	5	6	7	8	9	10
Does not interfere with relationships										Completely interferes with relationships

K. In general, how much does your pain interfere with your ability to do **jobs around your home**?

0	1	2	3	4	5	6	7	8	9	10
Does not interfere at all										Completely unable to do any job around home

L. How much does pain interfere with your ability to **bathe without help from someone else**?

0	1	2	3	4	5	6	7	8	9	10
Does not interfere at all										My pain makes it impossible to shower or bathe without help

M. How much does your pain interfere with your ability to **write or type**?

0	1	2	3	4	5	6	7	8	9	10
Does not interfere at all										My pain makes it impossible to write or type

N. How much does your pain interfere with your ability to **dress yourself**?

0	1	2	3	4	5	6	7	8	9	10
Does not interfere at all										My pain makes it impossible to dress myself

O. How much does your pain interfere with your ability to **concentrate**?

0	1	2	3	4	5	6	7	8	9	10
Never										All the time

III. Effect of Pain on Mood

A. Rate your overall mood during the past week.

0	1	2	3	4	5	6	7	8	9	10
Extremely high/good										Extremely low/bad

B. During the past week, how **anxious or worried** have you been because of your pain?

0	1	2	3	4	5	6	7	8	9	10
Not at all anxious/worried										Extremely anxious/worried

C. During the past week, how **depressed** have you been because of your pain?

0	1	2	3	4	5	6	7	8	9	10
Not at all depressed					Extremely depressed					

D. During the past week, how **irritable** have you been because of your pain?

0	1	2	3	4	5	6	7	8	9	10
Not at all irritable					Extremely irritable					

E. In general, how anxious/worried are you about performing activities because they **might make your pain/ symptoms worse**?

0	1	2	3	4	5	6	7	8	9	10
Not at all anxious/worried					Extremely anxious/worried					

MEDICATIONS:

39. For each ***prescription drug*** you are *presently* taking, please complete the following:

NAME OF MEDICATION AND DOSAGE	DAILY AMOUNT TAKEN	FOR WHICH CONDITION	NAME OF PRESCRIBING DOCTOR	APPROX. DATE STARTED	IDENTIFY SIDE EFFECTS YOU ARE HAVING FROM THIS DRUG

40. For each ***non-prescription drug*** you are taking, complete the following:

NAME OF MEDICATION AND DOSAGE	HOW MUCH DO YOU TAKE PER DAY	FOR WHICH CONDITION

41. For each doctor the ***Social Security Administration*** sent you to for examination concerning your disability, please complete the following:

DAILY ACTIVITIES:

NAME AND ADDRESS OF DOCTOR	DOCTOR'S SPECIALTY	APPROX. DATE OF EXAM.	LENGTH OF EXAM (MINUTES)	DESCRIBE THE EXAMINATION AND ANYTHING THE DOCTOR TOLD YOU ABOUT YOUR CONDITION

42. a. What is the amount of your current income? $____________ per month

b. What is the source of your current income? ____________________________

43. a. Where do you currently live?

☐ apartment ☐ duplex ☐ single family home
☐ condominium ☐ trailer ☐ rooming house

b. Do you own or rent? ☐ own ☐ rent

44. a. Please identify all of your children who are now under age 18 or who were under age 18 at the time you became disabled. Please list children even if they do not live with you. For each child who does not live with you, please tell us who the child lives with. Please include each child's date of birth and Social Security Number (SSN).

CHILD'S NAME & SSN	AGE	DATE OF BIRTH	LIVES WITH

45. What are the names of the two people with whom you spend the most time?

a. ____________________________ b. ____________________________

46. At present, how much time do you spend *each day*:

	HOURS PER DAY
Lying down or reclining	
Sitting upright	
Standing/Walking	
TOTAL HOURS PER DAY:	**24**

47. a. How well do you sleep? ☐ good ☐ fair ☐ poor

Explain fair or poor answer: ______________________________

____

b. Do you elevate the head of your bed or sleep on extra pillows? ☐ Yes ☐ No

If yes, how high is the head of the bed elevated or how many pillows do you use?

____

48. a. Indicate if you use any of the following assistive devices:

☐ Regular cane	☐ Special mattress	☐ High toilet seat
☐ Four-footed cane	☐ Hospital bed	☐ Grabber
☐ Walker	☐ Shower bar	☐ Sock tube
☐ Wheelchair	☐ Shower chair	☐ Lift chair

b. Please describe any other assistive devices you use or any home modifications you have done to accommodate your disability:

____

____

49. Please check what you do and how often. If you need help or do a poor job please indicate.
Give examples as appropriate.

	SEVERAL TIMES A DAY	DAILY	WEEKLY	MONTHLY	NEVER	EXAMPLES — NEED HELP, DO A POOR JOB
Drive						
Cook						
Wash Dishes						
Straighten up house						
Dust						
Vacuum						
Mop floor						
Do laundry						
Clean bathroom						
Make bed						
Change bed sheets						
Yard work						
Gardening						
Shovel snow						
Fix things						
Grocery shop						
Pay bills, handle finances						

	SEVERAL TIMES A DAY	DAILY	WEEKLY	MONTHLY	NEVER	EXAMPLES — NEED HELP, DO A POOR JOB
Watch children						
Groom self						
Participate in organizations						
Attend religious services						
Play cards/games						
Attend sports events						
Hobbies (*name*)						
Visit relatives						
Visit friends						
Talk to neighbors						
Go out to eat or to movies						
Use public transportation						
Exercise						
Watch TV or listen to radio	Number of hours per day:					
Read	Number of hours per day:					
Talk on phone	Number of hours per day:					
Sleep/stay in bed	Number of hours per day:					
Sleep/lie on couch	Number of hours per day:					

50. ***ONGOING ASSISTANCE:*** Does anyone have to help you to do things around the house on a regular basis? Who? What do they do?

____

____

____

____

51. ***PHYSICAL LIMITATIONS:***

NOTE: ***If your disability is psychiatric and you have no physical limitations, it is not necessary to complete question 51. Go on to question 52.***

a. ***SITTING:***

What best describes your ability to sit?

☐	I have no problem sitting.
☐	I can sit with some difficulty.
☐	I can sit with great difficulty.
☐	I cannot sit at all.

If you have trouble sitting:

Does it make a difference what kind of chair you sit on?	☐ Yes	☐ No
What kind of chair is best for you?		
Do you elevate your legs while sitting?	☐ Yes	☐ No
Where do you have pain or discomfort when you sit too long?		
What do you do to relieve that pain or discomfort?		

List examples of activities you have trouble performing while sitting:

____

____

(1) What is your best estimate of how long you can sit ***continuously in one stretch*** in a work chair (*not* a recliner) before you must get up and move around or lie down?

Hours/minutes: __________

(2) If you were sitting on and off throughout a workday, how many hours ***total out of an 8-hour workday*** in a regular work setting can you sit?

Hours: __________

b. ***STANDING:***

What best describes your ability to stand?

☐	I have no problem standing.
☐	I can stand with some difficulty.
☐	I can stand with great difficulty.
☐	I cannot stand at all.

If you have trouble standing:

Where do you have pain or discomfort when you sit too long?
What do you do to relieve that pain or discomfort?

List examples of activities you have trouble performing while standing:

____

____

(1) What is your best estimate of how long you can stand ***continuously in one stretch*** without sitting down or walking around?

Hours/minutes: __________

(2) If you were standing on and off throughout a workday, how many hours ***total out of an 8-hour workday*** in a regular work setting can you stand?

Hours: __________

c. ***WALKING:***

What best describes your ability to walk?

☐	I have no problem walking.
☐	I can walk with some difficulty.
☐	I can walk with great difficulty.
☐	I cannot walk at all.

If you have trouble walking:

Do you ever use a cane or other device to help you walk?	☐ Yes	☐ No
Where do you have pain or discomfort when you sit too long?		
What do you do to relieve that pain or discomfort?		

List examples of activities you have trouble performing while walking:

____

____

(1) What is your best estimate of how far you can walk ***continuously in one stretch*** without stopping to rest?

Blocks: __________

(2) How many hours ***total out of an 8-hour workday*** in a regular work setting can you walk?

Hours: __________

d. ***LIFTING AND CARRYING:***

What best describes your ability to lift and carry?

☐	I have no problem lifting and carrying.
☐	I can lift and carry with some difficulty.
☐	I can lift and carry with great difficulty.
☐	I cannot lift and carry at all.

If you have trouble lifting and carrying:

What is the heaviest thing that you encounter in your everyday life, which you can still lift or carry (for example, gallon of milk, six-pack of soda, a bag of groceries, basket of laundry, small children or grandchildren)?	
What happens when you try to lift or carry too much?	

List examples of things you encounter in your daily life that you can no longer lift or carry:

____

____

____

What is your best estimate of the maximum weight you can lift or carry in a regular work situation:

(1) if you had to lift or carry only ***rarely or once in a while***?

__________ pounds

(2) if you had to lift or carry up to ***one-third of the workday***?

__________ pounds

(3) if you had to do it ***from one-third to two-thirds of the workday***?

__________ pounds

e. ***LEGS AND FEET:***

Do you have any trouble using your legs or feet?	☐ Yes	☐ No
Do you have any trouble using your legs and feet to drive a car?	☐ Yes	☐ No

Describe the difficulty.

____

____

f. ***ARMS AND HANDS:***

Are you left or right handed?	☐ Left	☐ Right
Do you have any problems using your hands or arms?	☐ Yes	☐ No
Do the problems occur with repetitive use of your hands or arms?	☐ Yes	☐ No
Can you make a fist with each hand?	☐ Yes	☐ No
Can you touch each finger to the thumb on each hand?	☐ Yes	☐ No
Do your hands shake?	☐ Yes	☐ No
Do you have any trouble with your hands being numb or having pins and needles?	☐ Yes	☐ No
Do you have any trouble with dropping things?	☐ Yes	☐ No
Have you lost strength in your hands or arms?	☐ Yes	☐ No
Can you reach above your head (for example, to put things away in kitchen cupboards)?	☐ Yes	☐ No
Do you have any problems writing a letter?	☐ Yes	☐ No
Do you have any difficulty playing cards?	☐ Yes	☐ No

List examples of activities you have difficulty performing with your hands:

____

____

g. ***OTHER EXERTIONAL LIMITATIONS:***

Do you have trouble doing any of the following things?	☐ Yes	☐ No

*If **yes**, complete the following:*

	CAN'T DO AT ALL	ONCE IS OKAY	A FEW TIMES PER HOUR IS OKAY	REPETITIVELY IS OKAY
Bending:	☐	☐	☐	☐
Twisting:	☐	☐	☐	☐
Squatting:	☐	☐	☐	☐
Climbing stairs:	☐	☐	☐	☐

h. ***ENVIRONMENTAL RESTRICTIONS:*** Are there any restrictions on your activities, or problems which you encounter, having to do with any of the following situations?

Describe the problem:

(1) Unprotected heights: ____

(2) Being around moving machinery: ______________________________________

(3) Exposure to marked changes in temperature or humidity: ________________________

____

(4) Exposure to dust, fumes or gases: ______________________________________

52. Do you have any *current* problem with any of the following?

Depression	☐ Yes	☐ No	Dealing with the public	☐ Yes	☐ No
Anxiety attacks	☐ Yes	☐ No	Relating to other people	☐ Yes	☐ No
Memory	☐ Yes	☐ No	Maintaining attention	☐ Yes	☐ No
Dealing with stress	☐ Yes	☐ No	Loss of concentration	☐ Yes	☐ No

53. ***GOOD DAYS AND BAD DAYS:***

a. Do you have good days and bad days? ☐ Yes ☐ No

b. Approximately how many days per month are good days? __________

Approximately how many days per month are bad days? __________

c. What tends to produce good days? ____

____

____

____

d. What is a good day like? ____

____

____

e. What tends to produce bad days? ____

____

____

f. What is a bad day like? ____

____

____

OTHER:

54. Are the medical providers listed on your denial letters a complete listing of those needed to get a full understanding of your disability? ☐ Yes ☐ No

If no, what other medical providers should be contacted? ________________________________

____

55. What are the name, address and telephone number of someone who doesn't live with you but will always be able to find you?

Name:	
Address:	
Telephone:	
Relationship:	

56. Have you ever been convicted of a felony? ☐ Yes ☐ No

If yes, explain: ______________________________

57. Are you on probation or parole right now? ☐ Yes ☐ No

If yes, please provide the following:

Name of probation/parole officer: ______________________________

Probation/parole officer address: ______________________________

____

Probation/parole officer telephone: ______________________________

58. Please provide the following (if you have them):

a. Your cell phone number: ______________

b. Your fax number: ______________

c. Your email address: ______________

59. Other information you consider important: ______________________________

____

____

____

60. Did you need help to complete this questionnaire? ☐ Yes ☐ No

If yes, who helped you? ______________________________

Name: ________________________ **Date:** ________________________ **THIS IS VERY IMPORTANT**

DOCTORS, ETC.:

1. For each doctor, chiropractor, psychologist, psychological counselor, etc., you have seen, please complete the following chart.

List the doctors you are seeing now first and work your way back to about five years before you became unable to work.

NAME AND ADDRESS OF DOCTOR, ETC.	DATE OF FIRST VISIT (APPROX.)	DATE OF LAST VISIT (APPROX.)	APPROX. HOW MANY VISITS TOTAL?	WHICH CONDITION WAS TREATED	DESCRIBE ANY RESTRICTION OF ACTIVITIES IMPOSED OR WHAT YOU WERE TOLD ABOUT YOUR CONDITION

(CONTINUED ON NEXT PAGE)

DOCTORS, ETC.: — Continued

NAME AND ADDRESS OF DOCTOR, ETC.	DATE OF FIRST VISIT (APPROX.)	DATE OF LAST VISIT (APPROX.)	APPROX. HOW MANY VISITS TOTAL?	WHICH CONDITION WAS TREATED	DESCRIBE ANY RESTRICTION OF ACTIVITIES IMPOSED OR WHAT YOU WERE TOLD ABOUT YOUR CONDITION

(PLEASE USE ADDITIONAL PAPER, IF NECESSARY)

HOSPITALIZATIONS:

2. For each *hospitalization* (where you stayed at least one night), please complete the following chart.

List your most recent hospitalization first and work your way back to about five years before you became unable to work.

NAME AND ADDRESS OF HOSPITAL	APPROX. DATES	WHY WERE YOU HOSPITALIZED	DESCRIBE THE TREATMENT YOU RECEIVED	NAMES OF DOCTORS WHO TREATED YOU

(PLEASE USE ADDITIONAL PAPER, IF NECESSARY)

3. For each *outpatient visit to a hospital, diagnostic center, rehabilitation center or physical therapy clinic* (for example, for emergency room care, physical therapy or other treatment, diagnostic tests, etc.), please complete the following chart:

List your most recent visit first and work your way back to about five years before you became unable to work.

NAME AND ADDRESS OF HOSPITAL, CENTER OR CLINIC	APPROX. DATE	DESCRIBE THE TREATMENT OR DIAGNOSTIC TESTS	NAMES OF DOCTORS OR THERAPISTS

§168 Form: Claimant Psychiatric Questionnaire

Name: ____

1. List names and addresses of ***psychologists*** and ***psychiatrists*** who have evaluated or treated you:

NAME/ADDRESS	DATE OF FIRST VISIT	DATE OF LAST VISIT	NUMBER OF VISITS

2. List names and addresses of psychiatric social workers and counselors who have counseled you:

NAME/ADDRESS	DATE OF FIRST VISIT	DATE OF LAST VISIT	NUMBER OF VISITS

3. List the names and addresses of ***hospitals*** where you have had a psychiatric hospitalization:

HOSPITAL NAME/ADDRESS	APPROX. DATE OF ADMISSION	APPROX. DATE OF DISCHARGE

4. Have you had any of the following tests in the last two years?

5. List all of your psychiatric diagnoses: ______________________________

TEST	YES/ NO	DONE BY WHOM AND WHERE	APPROXIMATE DATE
MMPI (Minnesota Muliphasic Personality Inventory)			
WAIS (Wechsler Adult Intelligence Scale)			
Other psychological tests:			

____

6. When did you ***first*** have someone give you these diagnoses? ______________________________

7. Please place a check mark beside each statement below that describes you.

a._____ I have lost interest in my normal activities
b._____ I feel nervous or anxious a lot
c._____ I sleep fairly well
d._____ I have trouble making my own decisions
e._____ Sometimes I suddenly feel fear or panic
f._____ I like to be with people
g._____ I have trouble understanding directions
h._____ I have considered or attempted suicide
i._____ I lack confidence
j._____ I am sad most of the time
k._____ I am able to pay attention to activities I like
l._____ I have been told in the last two years that I should cut down or stop using alcohol or drugs
m._____ People make me happy
n._____ I make bad decisions in a work setting
o._____ I have trouble remembering recent things
p._____ I sleep too much
q._____ People in the workplace have liked me
r._____ I am intelligent
s._____ I have hope for my future
t._____ I hear voices or see things that other people do not see or hear
u._____ I sometimes use alcohol or street drugs to help myself feel better
v._____ I sometimes overuse my prescriptions to help myself feel better
w._____ I am basically a happy person despite all of my problems
x._____ I can do simple jobs or tasks as long as I do not have to deal with a lot of people
y._____ I depend on others too much
z._____ I feel guilty a lot
aa.____ I have trouble getting along with family, neighbors or others
bb.____ I have trouble with my temper
cc.____ I do not trust people
dd.____ I could do some jobs but people will not hire me
ee.____ Sometimes I lose control over my body parts
ff._____ People are out to get me
gg.____ I have been told that I am in good physical health
hh.____ I think I have a serious undiagnosed illness
ii._____ My appetite or eating has changed
jj._____ I have racing or confusing thoughts
kk.____ I know things will get better
ll._____ I had help filling out this questionnaire

8. If there are any alcohol, drug or abuse of prescription medication issues, please describe:

   Substance(s) used: ______________________________

   How often: ______________________________

   How much: ______________________________

   Describe any treatment for this problem: ______________________________

9. Explain why you could not complete a regular work week without your mental problem(s) interfering:
   ____
   ____
   ____

10. Describe any critical events in your life that contributed to your mental problems (e.g., accidents, victim of crime or abuse, etc.): ______________________________
    ____

11. Please complete the following sentences:

    I have trouble concentrating and paying attention when: ______________________________

    If I had a job, I would need special help from a supervisor to get simple tasks completed because:
    ____

    I could not understand and follow simple instructions on a job because: ______________________________
    ____

    My mental problems would not allow me to work because: ______________________________
    ____

    Examples of how my habits have deteriorated are: ______________________________
    ____

    The biggest difficulty I would have on a job is: ______________________________

    What makes me happiest is: ______________________________

    I am afraid of: ______________________________

    What I like best about myself is: ______________________________

    I get angry with myself when I: ______________________________

    Date completed: ______________

§169 Office Organization

Just as there is wide variation in the way lawyers successfully handle Social Security disability cases, there is variation in the way lawyers set up their offices to organize work, to keep track of cases, to make sure that no deadlines are missed, and to make sure that fees are paid (but not overpaid) by SSA. Most lawyers with more than a few Social Security disability cases use a database to accomplish at least some of these tasks. Many use paralegals for a variety of tasks.

§169.1 Databases

Use of a database is virtually essential to perform some tasks. For example, SSA has a bad habit of sending letters (and sometimes even checks) that fail to mention the name of the client; but such letters always include the Social Security number. Without using a searchable database, it would be necessary to go through your clients' Social Security numbers one by one to discover which client SSA is writing about.

The author uses a custom-built database based on Paradox for Windows that contains all necessary client information, including a picture of the client. Virtually the entire set of attorney forms and letters published in this book can be printed in our office with customized client data automatically inserted. We use Paradox for Windows to generate form letters to medical sources requesting records, letters to doctors requesting reports, letters to our clients, letters to the Social Security office, letters to the ALJ transmitting hearing exhibits, etc. Our letterhead, which is stored in a graphics field, automatically prints on all letters. Many form letters are programmed to provide different information under different circumstances. For example, the "congratulations" letter sent to a client after winning a Title II case (*see* §§403 and 404) automatically includes a paragraph about evaluating appeal if a partially favorable decision is issued.

We print envelopes directly from the database, a great time-saver. With the click of an on-screen button, we also print residual functional capacity (RFC) forms for doctors to complete. All of the RFC forms published in this book can be printed from our database with the client's name, SSN and doctor's name on them.

We manage bank accounts and print checks for client expenses (to pay for medical records, etc.) and for the clients' trust account from the database. When we print a check for a client expense, the program adds an entry for that check to the database from which we generate a bill for expenses to send to the client at the conclusion of the case.

We have a mountain of data stored in the computer. We use this data to track trends in our practice, generating statistics that show the number of open cases at various levels of appeal, the number of intake interviews scheduled, the number of new client cases we open, cases won and lost, cases at the Appeals Council, information about cases in which we are waiting to get paid including the total amount of approved fees outstanding at any time and how long it takes to get paid, to give just a few examples. The computer allows us to carefully track cases in which we are waiting for the check for attorney's fees and follow up sooner rather than later when the check is late (which is essential to keeping a regular cash flow going).

With so much data stored in the computer, it is necessary to worry about disasters. It is essential to have a good backup system. In fact, we use two systems to back up our computers. First, we have a virtually automatic daily digital tape backup. It is necessary only to remember to change the tape every day. Second, we have a fully automatic daily backup system that backs up all important files over the Internet to a computer at the author's home using LogMeIn Backup software. The software includes automatic email notification whether the backup is successful. In addition, our server uses mirrored hard drives, each containing a complete copy of everything stored on the server. This way, if one hard drive crashes, the other is available to run everything.

Every letter or other document we send out is scanned to PDF format. (Most letters are scanned automatically by our database software.) We scan everything we receive. There is a small scanner at almost every work station in our office. One work station is linked to a large scanner that is used for big scanning jobs. Scanned copies of documents are accessible from each work station in our office from a link through the database. Nevertheless, we don't have a "paperless" office because we continue to retain paper files while a case is open, which we regard as essential for backup. At the conclusion of a case, we offer the paper copy of hearing exhibits to our client and shred the rest of the paper file, retaining only the scanned copies of documents as our closed file.

Practice Tips

- The best computerized case management system in the world won't do everything. The human element is extremely important. It is necessary to have a good, well-trained staff that understands the system.
- The system has to be user-friendly. If a system isn't easy to learn and to use, people have a tendency not to use it.
- A system has to be flexible enough to accommodate different work styles. If you are going to buy one of

the commercially available programs, make sure that it will work for every lawyer in the office.

• A good backup system is essential. Using multiple backup systems is a good idea.

• Buy one of the commercially available case management programs rather than trying to build one yourself.

§169.2 Paralegals

In all cases, you need to:

- Screen/schedule clients
- Interview potential clients
- Evaluate potential clients' cases
- Research legal issues
- Gather evidence
- Organize evidence
- Analyze evidence
- Submit evidence

Most offices use paralegals to perform many of these tasks; but different lawyers divide up the work differently.

Many lawyers have found that retired SSA employees are excellent additions to their office staffs. Many former SSA employees, who often retire in their 50s, want to work part-time. They bring an expertise that is invaluable to a law office that handles Social Security disability cases. Our law offices offer one of the few places that former SSA employees can use their specialized knowledge.

§170 Initial Interview

Every Social Security disability case presents a little puzzle to be put together by the claimant's attorney. The pieces of the puzzle include the claimant's age, education, work experience, and current capacity for work. These puzzle pieces need to be put together with the regulations and rulings to make a complete picture showing that the claimant is entitled to Social Security disability benefits. Although not all of the pieces of this puzzle may be available at the initial interview, most are. A thorough interview can usually give you a pretty good idea whether you can win the claimant's case. Sometimes, though, it is necessary to review a claimant's Social Security file first to determine the chances of success.

Even if you're interviewing a claimant to consider involvement in the case at a stage below the hearing level, focus your evaluation on what will be needed to win at a hearing. Then, set about obtaining the necessary evidence to submit to SSA as soon as possible. You may be able to use this evidence to convince a state agency decision-maker, thus making a hearing unnecessary.

§171 Observe the Claimant

When the claimant comes in for the initial interview, take some extra time for observation. Watch the claimant get up from the chair in your waiting room, walk to your office and sit in your office. A few minutes of observation is frequently worth hours of digging through illegible medical records, especially when you realize that claimants' doctors often observe them walking only from a chair to the examining table. By the time you are done with your interview, you may have spent more time with this claimant than his or her doctor has in the past year.

§172 Determine Claim Type and Procedural Issues

The first thing you must determine is what kind of claim(s) you are looking at. From your initial telephone contact, you may have an idea of the medical problem precipitating the claimant's disability claim. It is equally important to check for clues to procedural and other issues that may affect the claim.

Line up all the denial letters in chronological order on your desk. In the past, separate denial letters were issued for Social Security disability and SSI claims, and you will still see cases where virtually identical denial letters are issued in such concurrent claims. Recently, though, SSA has been issuing a single denial letter in concurrent claims that can be identified only by noting that the caption of the letter includes the words "Retirement, Survivors and Disability Insurance" as well as "Supplemental Security Income."

Sometimes when you lay out the denial letters on your desk, it may look at first glance as if SSA sent multiple copies of the same Social Security disability letter to the claimant; but this is unlikely. More likely is that this claimant, in addition to a claim based on his or her own earnings record, has a pending claim based on the Social Security earnings record of someone else, as in a widow(er)'s claim or a surviving divorced spouse's claim (based on the deceased spouse's earnings record), or a disabled adult child's claim (based on a retired, disabled or deceased parent's earnings record). Thus, whenever you see multiple Title II denial letters, compare the Social Security numbers. Since oftentimes claimants do not know what claims they have pending, checking the Social Security numbers may be the only way to figure out that, in addition to a concurrent claim, this claimant has an additional claim pending. SSA employees refer to these as "three-way" cases in which there are pending claims for SSI, regular Social Security disability on the claimant's own account, and disability benefits based on someone else's account.

You will be able to learn from the denial letters whether or not the claimant has a problem with "insured status" in a Social Security disability claim. If there is a problem, the denial letter will state either that the claimant is not insured as of the date disability is alleged, or will identify the "date last insured." The "date last insured" is the date by which this claimant must have been disabled in order for him or her to get any Social Security disability benefits.

When there is a problem with insured status, you'll need to make a note to look at SSA's calculation of the date last insured, something that you will have to do after the initial interview. As a rule, though, SSA does not make many mistakes in calculating date last insured except for when a claimant has had a prior period of disability. So, if date last insured is an issue, be sure to ask the claimant if he or she has ever received Social Security disability benefits before.

Occasionally date last insured is an issue because not all the claimant's earnings show up in SSA's records, something that you'll have to check later to see if there is any way to add quarters of coverage. *See* C.F.R. §§ 404.101 to 404.146. At the initial interview, you can alert the claimant to this problem and ask the claimant to find copies of old tax returns and W-2 forms for your review later. *See* §205.4, on reviewing the claimant's earnings record.

When there is problem with insured status, you also need to consider whether there is a supportable earlier "onset date" for disability, one within the insured period.

§173 Use Denial Letter to Determine Why Claim Was Denied

The next step is to understand why SSA concluded that the claimant was not disabled. Look at the latest denial letter. Try to figure out the step of the sequential evaluation process at which the denial determination was issued. If a denial letter says that the claimant can "engage in normal activities," it is a denial at step 2 based on a non-severe impairment. You should be able to tell by looking at the claimant and talking with him or her for a few minutes whether or not this claimant's case is truly frivolous. As a rule, it will not be. Instead, the finding probably reflects a deficiency in the medical evidence. It will be your job to complete the record.

The denial letter may say that the claimant's impairment is "not severe enough." This may be a step 2 denial or such language may simply indicate that the denial letter was poorly crafted. The denial letter may say that the claimant can still do a former job, often without telling you which job; but you might be able to figure that out by talking with the claimant about his or her easiest job. Or it may concede that the claimant cannot do any former job but can do "lighter work" (which may or may not mean light work as defined by Social Security regulations, it often means medium work) or, in mental impairment cases, that the claimant can do "simple, routine, repetitive, low stress, unskilled work."

Although an ALJ evaluates a disability case *de novo* and all of the elements of proof must be present in order for the claimant to be found disabled, a good place to start your analysis of the case is with the issues raised by a denial determination from the state agency. If you conclude that the denial is wrong, you can figure out what must be proven to win this claimant's case based on the chart at §121.1, or the Medical-Vocational Guidelines. Explain this to the claimant. For example, if disability is denied because the claimant could be found disabled if limited to sedentary work, explain the definition of light work to the claimant and inquire why he or she cannot do it. If the answer is that the claimant cannot be on his or her feet for six hours out of an eight-hour workday, this is your "theory of the case." Set about gathering information to corroborate this.

§174 Analyze Claimant's Answers

There is an art to interviewing a disability claimant. Those lawyers who are most successful at interviewing claimants do whatever is necessary to put the claimant at ease. They frequently start the interview by letting the claimant explain why SSA should have found him or her disabled. Letting the claimant talk while you sit and observe without taking notes allows you to evaluate the claimant, to assess not only the impairments but also the claimant's *perception* of the impairments. It allows you to measure the claimant's understanding of medical problems and the Social Security system.

If you can figure out why SSA denied benefits, you can focus on the crucial issue early in the interview. For example, for literate, English-speaking claimants under age 50, a common issue is the capacity for a wide range of sedentary work. But when you ask a claimant why he or she cannot do a sedentary job, it will probably be necessary to separate the wheat from the chaff of the answer and, in the process, educate the claimant about all those common sense things that SSA or Congress has determined to be irrelevant in a disability case. You are likely to get such answers to the sedentary work question as:

- I'm not qualified for sedentary jobs. (The Medical-Vocational Guidelines make education and work experience irrelevant for literate English-speaking people under age 50.)
- I can't get such a job. (Irrelevant. 20 C.F.R. § 404.1566(c)(1).)
- Employers wouldn't hire me for such a job because of my age, race, sex, etc. (Irrelevant. 20 C.F.R. § 404.1566(c)(3).)
- Even though I could do the job, I would never pass the physical because of all my medical problems. (Irrelevant. 20 C.F.R. § 404.1566(c)(3). But with all those medical problems would the claimant be able to maintain reasonably consistent attendance? Would he or she be able to maintain minimum production standards? These are very relevant.)
- There is no sedentary work around here. (Irrelevant. 20 C.F.R. § 404.1566(c)(2).)
- There aren't any job openings. (Irrelevant. 20 C.F.R. § 404.1566(c)(6).)
- I wouldn't like a job like that. (Irrelevant. *See* 20 C.F.R. § 404.1566(c)(8).)
- The pay is too little. (Irrelevant.)

If these are the only reasons that a literate, English speaking claimant under age 50 cannot do sedentary work, and if the claimant's impairments do not meet or equal a Listed Impairment, the claimant will lose. The claimant will not be found disabled despite the fact that you can be morally certain that because of age, medical problems, poor education, work experience or the availability of sedentary work in your area, the claimant will never get a sedentary job. This is the situation with our hypothetical 48-year-old construction worker in §100.

The key is to direct the claimant's attention to those aspects of his or her situation that are relevant to disability determination. There are lots of valid ways to prove that a claimant cannot do a full range of sedentary work. Claimants, with the help of lawyers who listen carefully to them, come up with new approaches all the time. Your most important function as the claimant's lawyer is to explore the claimant's reasons and circumstances thoroughly, since a claimant's answer often includes valid factors that may result in a disability finding. In many cases you can put together a persuasive argument even for those difficult cases involving claimants under age 50.

Once you have a basic understanding of the claimant's case, it is time to impose more structure on the interview and gather the details necessary to win the case. A sample interview form follows that is designed for use in conjunction with the questionnaire provided in §167.

§174.1 Use Interview and Analysis Forms to Evaluate Claimant's Case

The Interview and Analysis forms, §§175 and 175.1, are designed for use with the Claimant Questionnaire, §167. The purposes of the forms are to: (1) gather a lot of information in manageable form; (2) evaluate and analyze the claimant's case; and (3) outline approaches for winning the case. Also, by asking the claimant questions similar to those an ALJ may ask at a hearing, you will help prepare the claimant to testify.

Question 38, section q. on the Claimant Questionnaire, §167, is based on table 18-4 in Guides to the Evaluation of Permanent Impairment, Fifth Edition, by the American Medical Association, copyright 2001, and is used with permission. If you review your client's answers to these questions, you should develop a sense of your client's situation, especially if you observe your client carefully and use other available information to assess the case. The Guides chapter on pain, which ought to be required reading for Social Security disability lawyers, in fact, provides a numerical scoring system for assessing pain based on a patient's answers to the table 18-4 questions, which some lawyers might find useful.

The Interview form follows the structure of the Questionnaire, covering areas of inquiry in approximately the same order. During the client interview, once you have read through the Claimant Questionnaire from beginning to end, return to the beginning and page through it again as you ask the claimant questions from the Interview form. The two forms are designed to avoid needless repetition; however, some issues need to be approached in more than one way to test the claimant's answers and to make sure you don't miss something really important.

Page 1 of the Analysis form acts as the summary sheet for the claimant's case. It belongs at the top of the papers in the claimant's file. It provides a place for entering the essential facts and conclusions about each element of the proof of disability.

The Analysis form asks you to rank the claimant's medical impairments, that is, the diagnosed medical problems. It also provides a place for you to list the claimant's corresponding symptoms. Having a list of both impairments and symptoms on the summary sheet allows you to tell at a glance exactly what kind of case the claimant has, something which cannot be done in all cases if you listed only impairments or only symptoms.

The most important information you obtain from a claimant is the description of symptoms, not the list of medical impairments. Symptoms are what a claimant knows best. You can usually rely on a claimant's ranking of symptoms, but you cannot always rely on a claimant's ranking of medical impairments. A claimant with multiple medical problems may not be able to identify which medical impairment is causing the most severe symptom, the one primarily responsible for the inability to work. Ranking impairments at the time of the initial interview is tentative. It merely gives you a working hypothesis. Do not hesitate to change the ranking of impairments after you have reviewed the claimant's medical records or spoken with the claimant's doctors.

It is your job to make sure there is a clear link between a medical impairment and the resulting symptom. A symptom unrelated to a diagnosed medical impairment cannot form the basis for a finding of disability. But once this link is established, you can use the symptom in your analysis of the claimant's residual functional capacity (RFC).

Pages 2 and 3 of the Analysis form provide a place to write out a description of the claimant's RFC. Some cases require only a brief description of RFC. Others require a detailed description not only of limitations, but also of the reasons for those limitations. If you write out a description of RFC at the initial interview, your description is likely to be much more accurate and appropriate for the case than if you write it later when composing a letter to the treating doctor requesting an opinion about RFC. In the author's office, the description of RFC is written on the Analysis form at the time of the initial interview. It is then entered into a computerized database and edited as necessary after review of the claimant's medical records or if there are changes in the claimant's condition while the claim is pending. This description is inserted into a letter to a treating doctor (such as the letter at §221.8).

Page 4 of the Analysis form provides a place to list things to do in the claimant's case and to record your first impression of the odds of winning, e.g., 60% chance of winning (which is approximately the chance of winning an average case before an average ALJ). The estimate of the odds of winning is primarily for your own use in refining your interviewing and analysis skills. The author records his impression again after reviewing the file and a third time immediately after the hearing. When a case turns out to be much better (or worse) than one initially thought, it is a useful exercise to go back and look for clues for why your evaluation of the case initially missed the mark.

Although the theory appears on page 1 of the Analysis form, write this last. The theory is one or two sentences that sums up the case and explains why the claimant should be found disabled. Sometimes the theory is as simple as this: "The claimant, whose past work was semi-skilled medium work, is 54 years old and is limited to sedentary work by degenerative disk disease. Because he has no transferable skills, Rule 201.14 of the Medical-Vocational Guidelines requires that he be found disabled." In the author's office, this theory is entered into the computer database and refined as necessary as the case proceeds. Then, in response to a pre-hearing order requesting a statement of the theory of the case, it is put into a letter to the ALJ.

§175 Interview Form

Name: ______________________________ ☐ Mr. ☐ Ms.

Date: ______________________________

Address: ___________________________
____

Time: _______ Rep: _______ Asst. _____

SSN: _____________________

Telephone: ______________________________ DOB: ___________

Message #: ______________________________ Age: ___________

☐ Married ☐ Single ☐ Widowed ☐ Divorced ☐ Separated

Other names used during relevant time period: ________________________________

Total number of children:	Number of children under 18* at any time after onset date:	Number of stepchildren under 18* who reside with claimant:

*or under 19 and still in high school

[Parent's name in child's case]	SSN:* *SSI disabled couple and Widow(er) cases only	Date of Death: [Widow(er)]

Referred By: _________________________________

Type of Claim: ☐ Initial ☐ Term ☐ Other

ALJ: ____

Fee: ☐ Petition ☐ Agreement ☐ Two-Tier ☐ W/holding waived

ALJ Address: ______________________ Stage of Claim: _______________________

Local Office Address:

Awaiting: ___________________________________

Hearing		***Termination Cases***	
Date:	Time:	Date Disability Ceased:	
VE:		Continuing Benefits: ☐ Yes ☐ No	
ME:		Date Last Check:	Amount of Check:

Hearing Preparation Appointment: ***Date:***

Prior Applications: ☐ Yes ☐ No Dates and Results: ____________________________

Identify reopening earlier application as an issue on Analysis form.

Application/Termination	Reconsideration	Hearing Request
Application Date:	Recon. Request Date:	☐ Not Yet Filed
Denial/Term. Date:	Recon. Denial Date:	Date Filed:
Rationale:	Rationale:	Timely: ☐ Yes ☐ No
		Why not?

Identify any problem with timeliness of appeal as issue on Analysis form.

PRESENT SYMPTOMS

	SYMPTOM 1	SYMPTOM 2	SYMPTOM 3	SYMPTOM 4
Location:				
Description: (consider describing occasional radiation of pain as a separate symptom)				
Frequency:				
Duration:				
What starts it?				
What aggravates it?				
Intensity at its worst 1-10:				
Usual Intensity 1-10:				
Intensity at its best 1-10:				
What makes it better?				
Effectiveness of medication:				
Side effects of medication:				

Rank symptoms on Analysis form.

How *often* do you have any of the following?

Nausea:		Crying spells:	
Fainting:		Headaches:	
Dizziness:		Spasms:	
Bladder control problems:		Cramps:	
Seizures:		Diarrhea:	
Dates of most recent seizures:			

At what pharmacies have you purchased seizure medication in the past year?

____

____

____

Can you ask your pharmacist(s) to provide a summary of all seizure medication purchased in the past year?

____

Have you had any of the following tests recently?

TEST	WHERE DONE	APPROX. DATE
Treadmill Stress Test		
Other Heart Tests Identify:		
EMG/Electrodiagnostic Studies		
X-ray/CAT Scan Part of Body:		
MRI Part of Body:		
Myelogram:		
Breathing Tests:		
MMPI		
Other:		

FAMILY, HOUSING AND INCOME:

List all children who were under 18 (or under 19 and still in high school or disabled adult children) at any time after the alleged onset date. Identify custodian.

CHILDREN'S NAMES	RELATIONSHIP	DOB	CUSTODIAN

How many people are in your household? _____________

MONTHLY INCOME	CLAIMANT	SPOUSE
*Emplyment after onset from to		
*Unemployment compensation after onset from to		
Welfare: Type: AFDC GA		
Food Stamps:		
V.A. benefits: Type: Service connected; non-service connected:		
Worker's Compensation after onset from to		
Loans:		
Investments:		
Disability Insurance: (Enter name and address of LTD carrier on Analysis form.)		
Pension Benefits (company):		
SSI (Especially Spouse SSI):		
Social Security Disability/Retirement:		
TOTAL: Family:		

**Identify these as issues on Analysis form.*

Place of birth: ____________________________Resided in state ☐ all life/since ____________________

☐ A U.S. citizen. ☐ Not a U.S. citizen. Resided in U.S. ☐ all life/since: _______________
Immigration Status: ____

DAILY ACTIVITIES:

Do you have a particular chair, couch, etc. that is most comfortable? Describe: ____________________

What floor is bedroom on:		Trouble with stairs?	☐ Yes ☐ No
Which is worse, going up stairs or down?	☐ Up ☐ Down	Rise: a.m.	Retire: p.m.
Do you nap during the day?	☐ Yes ☐ No	Where do you nap?	
How many times?		How long?	
Do you have rest periods during the day?	☐ Yes ☐ No	Where do you rest?	
How many times?	How long?		

____

Summary of typical day: ____
____

____

____

Do you attend religious services? ☐ Yes ☐ No How often? ______________________________

Are you active in any groups, clubs, etc.? ☐ Yes ☐ No Describe:______________________________

Are you involved in any volunteer work? ☐ Yes ☐ No Describe: ______________________________

____

Present hobbies: ____

Former hobbies that you can no longer do: ____

____

PHYSICAL ASSESSMENT:

Rank sitting, standing, walking from easiest to hardest: Easiest: ____________________

Hardest: ____________________

Assuming that everyone, even the most disabled people, can do some sort of work, describe what you think you can do:

____

____

____

If pain is involved, how *often* is your experience of pain severe enough to interfere with attention and concentration?

☐ Never ☐ Seldom ☐ Often ☐ Frequently ☐ Constantly

To what *degree* does it interfere?

☐ Would prevent performance of simplest tasks.

☐ Would only prevent performance of more complicated tasks such as those involved in semi-skilled work.

☐ Would only prevent performance of very complicated tasks such as those involved in skilled work.

ENVIRONMENTAL RESTRICTIONS	**NO RESTRICTION**	**AVOID CONCENTRATED EXPOSURE**	**AVOID EVEN MODERATE EXPOSURE**	**AVOID ALL EXPOSURE**
Extreme cold				
Extreme heat				
Wetness				
High humidity				
Noise				
Chemicals				
Solvents/cleaners				
Soldering fluxes				
Cigarette smoke				
Perfumes				
Fumes, odors, dusts, gases				
List other irritants or allergens:				
Hazards (machinery, heights, etc.)				

Describe how these environmental factors impair activities and identify hazards to be avoided.

____

____

MENTAL RESIDUAL FUNCTIONAL CAPACITY:

I.	MENTAL ABILITIES AND APTITUDES NEEDED TO DO UNSKILLED WORK	Unlimited or Very Good	Limited but satis-factory	**Seriously limited, but not precluded**	**Unable to meet competitive standards**	**No useful ability to function**
A.	Remember work-like procedures					
B.	Understand and remember very short and simple instructions					
C.	Carry out very short and simple instructions					
D.	Maintain attention for two hour segment					
E.	Maintain regular attendance and be punctual within customary, usually strict tolerances					
F.	Sustain an ordinary routine without special supervision					
G.	Work in coordination with or proximity to others without being unduly distracted					
H.	Make simple work-related decisions					
I.	Complete a normal workday and workweek without interruptions from psychologically based symptoms					
J.	Perform at a consistent pace without an unreasonable number and length of rest periods					
K.	Ask simple questions or request assistance					
L.	Accept instructions and respond appropriately to criticism from supervisors					
M.	Get along with coworkers or peers without unduly distracting them or exhibiting behavioral extremes					
N.	Respond appropriately to changes in a routine work setting					
O.	Deal with normal work stress					
P.	Be aware of normal hazards and take appropriate precautions					

II.	MENTAL ABILITIES AND APTITUDES NEEDED TO DO SEMISKILLED AND SKILLED WORK	Unlimited or Very Good	Limited but satis-factory	**Seriously limited, but not precluded**	**Unable to meet competitive standards**	**No useful ability to function**
A.	Understand and remember detailed instructions					
B.	Carry out detailed instructions					
C.	Set realistic goals or make plans independently of others					
D.	Deal with stress of semiskilled and skilled work					

Explain limitations falling in the three most limited categories (identified by **bold type**):

If stress tolerance is an issue, what demands of work do you find stressful?

- ☐ speed
- ☐ precision
- ☐ complexity
- ☐ deadlines
- ☐ working within a schedule
- ☐ making decisions
- ☐ exercising independent judgment
- ☐ completing tasks
- ☐ working with other people
- ☐ dealing with the public (strangers)
- ☐ dealing with supervisors
- ☐ being criticized by supervisors
- ☐ simply knowing that work is supervised
- ☐ getting to work regularly
- ☐ remaining at work for a full day
- ☐ fear of failure at work
- ☐ monotony of routine
- ☐ little latitude for decision-making
- ☐ lack of collaboration on the job
- ☐ no opportunity for learning new things
- ☐ underutilization of skills
- ☐ lack of meaningfulness of work

Meeting The Mental Listing — The B Criteria:

FUNCTIONAL LIMITATION						
A.	Restriction of activities of daily living	None Mild ☐	Moderate ☐	Marked ☐	Extreme ☐
B.	Difficulties in maintaining social functioning	None Mild ☐	Moderate ☐	Marked ☐	Extreme ☐
C.	Deficiencies of concentration, persistence or pace	None Mild ☐	Moderate ☐	Marked ☐	Extreme ☐
D.	Repeated episodes of decompensation within 12 month period, each of at least two weeks duration*	None ☐	One or Two ☐	Three ☐	Four or More ☐

* If within one year client had more than three episodes of decompensation of shorter duration than two weeks or less frequent episodes of decompensation of longer duration than two weeks, state the dates of each episode of decompensation:

____

If at Listing level (2 Marked or 1 Extreme limitation), indicate which Listing is met and describe why you think client meets Listing:

LITIGATION AND OTHER DETAILS (Include Attorney's Name, Address & Telephone)

WORKER'S COMPENSATION: ______________________________

____

INSURANCE AND PENSION: ______________________________

OTHER CLAIMS FOR BENEFITS: ______________________________

POTENTIAL WITNESSES

NAME	TELEPHONE NUMBER	AREA OF TESTIMONY

ATTORNEY'S NOTES

Best indications of inability to work: ______________________________

Potential problems with case* ______________________________

*Summarize issues on Analysis form.

OBSERVATIONS

CHECK ITEM TO INDICATE DIFFICULTY WAS OBSERVED

☐ Reading	☐ Hearing	☐ Using Hands	☐ Walking
☐ Writing	☐ Speaking	☐ Breathing	☐ Sitting
☐ Answering	☐ Understanding	☐ Seeing	☐ Rising

Describe difficulty with checked item(s): ______________________________

Describe posture: ______________________________

Describe unusual appearance, behavior or observed difficulty not noted elsewhere:

____

Assistive devices:

____

GENERAL APPEARANCE

Skin:		Deformities:	
Body build:		Hand calluses:	

§175.1 Form: Analysis

Name: ______________________________ DOB: ______________

Theory: ______________________________

____

Med-Voc Rule: __________ Listings §__________ Alleged Onset: ____________ DLI: __________

Issues: ______________________________

____

____

ATTORNEY'S RANKING OF IMPAIRMENTS	ASSOCIATED SYMPTOMS
1.	1.
2.	2.
3.	3.
4.	4.
5.	5.

Date Last Worked: ___________ Age today: _______ Age at onset: _______

• Past 15 years or 15 years before date last insured, if earlier. * Enter C for customary, E for easiest job.

Dates	Occupation •	Strength Level	Skill Level	DOT No.	C/E*

Unable to do easiest job because: ______________________________

Limited to: ☐ less than sedentary ☐ alt sit/stand ☐ sedentary ☐ light ☐ medium

Mental limitations: ______________________ Work skills: ______________

Highest Grade Completed: ______ Vocational Training: ______________________

☐ Check here if abilities appear less than level of schooling would indicate.

Summary of Physical Residual Functional Capacity

☑ ______________________________ says that s/he can walk about ______ blocks before stopping.
☑ S/he can sit for about ______ minutes at one time and stand for about ______ minutes at one time.
☑ Out of an 8-hour working day, s/he says s/he can sit for a total of _____ hours and stand/walk for a total of ______ hours.
☐ S/he needs to walk around approximately every ______ minutes for about ______ minutes.
☐ S/he needs a job that permits shifting positions at will.

☐ Because of

☐ muscle weakness	☐ pain/paresthesias, numbness	☐ ______________
☐ chronic fatigue	☐ adverse effects of medication	☐ ______________

s/he may need to take unscheduled breaks [" to lie down] during an 8-hour working day. S/he expects this to happen ____________________________; and s/he may need to rest __________ minutes (on average) before returning to work.
☐ If s/he had a sedentary job, because of ____________________________ s/he says s/he would need to elevate his/her legs about ______% of the time during an 8-hour working day. S/he needs to elevate his/her legs about ☐ hip / ☐ heart ______ high.
☐ S/he needs a cane to walk because of

☐ imbalance	☐ pain	☐ weakness	☐ dizziness
☐ insecurity	☐ ______________________________		

☑ S/he can occasionally lift and carry _____ lbs. and frequently lift and carry _____ lbs.
☐ S/he says that because of

☐ pain/paresthesias	☐ motor loss	☐ sensory loss/numbness
☐ muscle weakness	☐ swelling	☐ side effects of medication
☐ limitation of motion	☐ ______________________________	

s/he has significant limitations in reaching, handling, and fingering.

S/he can use her/his **left** hand for
grasping _____% of the time,
fingering _____% of the time,
reaching overhead _____% of the time, and
reaching in front of body _____% of the time.

S/he can use her/his **right** hand for
grasping _____% of the time,
fingering _____% of the time,
reaching overhead _____% of the time, and
reaching in front of body _____% of the time.

☐ S/he says that s/he can

never	rarely	occasionally	frequently	
☐	☐	☐	☐	twist,
☐	☐	☐	☐	stoop (bend),
☐	☐	☐	☐	crouch/squat,
☐	☐	☐	☐	climb ladders, and
☐	☐	☐	☐	climb stairs.

☐ S/he says that s/he can

never	rarely	occasionally	frequently	
☐	☐	☐	☐	look down (sustained flexion of neck),
☐	☐	☐	☐	turn head right or left,
☐	☐	☐	☐	look up, and
☐	☐	☐	☐	hold head in static position.

☐ S/he says that s/he has the following environmental limitations:

____

____

☐ S/he says that her/his symptoms are severe enough to interfere with attention and concentration so that s/he would be "off task" at work ☐ 5% / ☐ 10% / ☐ 15% / ☐ 20% / ☐ 25% or more / of the time.

☐ S/he says that as a result of his/her impairments s/he has a (moderate) (marked) (severe) limitation in dealing with work stress.

☐ Because of bad days, s/he says that if s/he had a full-time job s/he expects that s/he would miss work about/more than _____ times a month.

VISION

☐ S/he says that s/he can

never	rarely	occasionally	frequently	constantly	
☐	☐	☐	☐	☐	utilize near acuity,
☐	☐	☐	☐	☐	utilize far acuity, and
☐	☐	☐	☐	☐	utilize depth perception.

☐ S/he is incapable of avoiding ordinary hazards in the workplace, such as boxes on the floor, doors ajar, approaching people or vehicles.

☐ S/he has difficulty walking up or down stairs because of his/her vision.

☐ S/he says s/he cannot work with small objects such as those involved in doing sedentary work.

☐ S/he can/cannot work with large objects.

☐ Other: ____

____

NOW	DOCTORS TO GET RFC OPINIONS FROM	TYPE OF RFC FORM	OTHER RECORDS THAT SSA MAY NOT HAVE OBTAINED
	1.		1.
	2.		2.
	3.		3.
	4.		4.

LONG TERM DISABILITY CARRIER	OTHER RECORDS NEEDED
Name:	☐ SS file from local office ☐ Work records—employer:________________
Address:	☐ Vocational rehabilitation records ☐ L.T.D. carrier records
	☐ School records ☐ Driving record
	☐ Other:________________________________ ☐ Other:________________________________

☐ Flag to work up for possible on-the-record decision. Impression: ____________________________

☐ Request postponement of hearing scheduled for ________________ with ALJ ___________________

OTHER THINGS TO DO

____

____

____

____

THINGS OUR CLIENT WILL SEND US

____

____

____

§176 Look for Problem Areas and Opportunities

As you are interviewing the claimant, think through the case following the sequential evaluation process, looking for problems and opportunities. Begin with an analysis of issues surrounding the "onset date," the date the claimant became disabled.

§176.1 Onset Date

Ask the claimant how the onset date was selected. Was it the claimant's idea or was it the idea of someone at the Social Security office? Now that you have explained what it means to be disabled, does the claimant have any second thoughts about the onset date? What you want to do, of course, is push the onset date back as far as possible. An onset 18 months before the date of application will pick up 12 full months of retroactive Social Security disability benefits—which are all the months of back benefits available unless you can reopen an earlier application. As a rule, if you can have your client found disabled based on an onset date earlier than 18 months before the date of application, it is beneficial because it usually increases the amount of monthly benefits. Some caution is appropriate, though, because every once in a while you will see a case where an earlier onset date actually decreases the monthly benefit amount. This tends to happen with younger workers whose earnings after the earlier onset date are relatively high compared to their earnings in prior years. *See* 20 C.F.R. §§ 404.211 and 404.212. (To check this, you will need to ask someone at a local Social Security office or use a computer program available from SSA called the PIA Calculator.)

Always consider the possibility that the claimant's last job was not "substantial gainful activity" or was an "unsuccessful work attempt." As a rule, you will need to show that any work after onset of disability:

- was not substantial work activity (20 C.F.R. § 404.1572(a));
- was not gainful work activity (20 C.F.R. § 404.1572(b)) after deducting impairment related work expenses (20 C.F.R. § 404.1576) and averaging earnings (20 C.F.R. § 404.1574a);
- was done under special conditions (20 C.F.R. § 404.1573(c));
- was subsidized (20 C.F.R. § 404.1574 (a)(2)); or
- was an unsuccessful work attempt (20 C.F.R. § 404.1574(c)).

If work was not substantial gainful activity or was an unsuccessful work attempt (*see* §176.2), you may be able to push the onset date back to the time before the claimant did such work.

§176.2 Unsuccessful Work Attempts

Work lasting up to six months, which the claimant had to stop because of an impairment, may qualify as an unsuccessful work attempt. Even a series of unsuccessful work attempts may occur after the onset date. Earnings during unsuccessful work attempts will not be considered in determining whether or not work is substantial gainful activity (SGA). *See* 20 C.F.R. §§ 404.1574(a)(1) and 404.1574(c). *See also* Social Security Ruling 05-02. Where your client's last employment meets this description, the onset date may be moved back to a point before the unsuccessful work effort.

20 C.F.R. § 404.1574(c), which applies to employees, provides specific requirements for a work effort to qualify as an unsuccessful work attempt. 20 C.F.R. § 404.1575(d) provides the requirements for finding that a self-employed claimant's work is an unsuccessful work attempt. The two regulations are similar.

An unsuccessful work attempt must be preceded by a break in the claimant's previous work. 20 C.F.R. §§ 404.1574(c)(2) and 404.1575(d)(2). This requirement may be met if, because of the impairment:

- Claimant is out of work for 30 consecutive days (or perhaps a few days less if the subsequent work attempt is brief "and clearly not successful because of [the] impairment"—SSR 05-02); or
- Claimant was forced to change to another type of work or another employer; or
- Work was reduced so much that it no longer constituted substantial gainful activity (SGA).

SSR 05-02 makes it clear that a claimant does not have to be working before an unsuccessful work attempt in order to qualify. SSR 05-02 provides that an interruption in work activity "could also occur when, before the onset of your impairment, you discontinued (or limited) your work for other reasons, such as retirement, or never engaged in work activity."

Once this threshold requirement is met, the work must end (or be reduced to the non-SGA level) in either of two ways. First, work may end directly because of the impairment. For example, the claimant explains, "Because of my back problem, I just couldn't do the job anymore." Second, work cessation may occur indirectly because of the impairment if there is "removal of special conditions related to the impairment that are essential to the further performance of work."

Special conditions exist, for example, where a claimant receives assistance from other employees in order to do a job. If, for one reason or another, other employees no longer are available to help the claimant do the job, the special conditions related to the impairment (help from other employees) would be removed. Thus, the claimant must quit work. 20 C.F.R. §§ 404.1574(c)(3), 404.1575(d)(3) and 404.1573(c), and SSR 05-02.

According to 20 C.F.R. §§ 404.1574(c)(5), 404.1575(d)(5) and Social Security Ruling 05-02, work that constitutes substantial gainful activity lasting more than six months cannot qualify as an unsuccessful work attempt no matter why it ended. Nevertheless, there can be a string of unsuccessful work attempts spread over a period of time much longer than six months. Whenever a claimant is off work for 30 days, changes to an easier job (either with the same employer or a different employer), or has a period of time where work is at less than SGA level, examine the work efforts after this time to determine if they can be characterized as unsuccessful work attempts.

Note that SSA expects a very precise application of the six-month time limit. Approximation will not do. Although SSR 05-02 was written when different rules applied for unsuccessful work attempts lasting three or six months, the example it provides shows that a six month UWA cannot last longer than from November 5, 2003, through a date no later than May 4, 2004. Thus, you are going to need the exact dates of your client's work attempts. It may be necessary to contact your client's employers for this information, as well as for the reasons any work attempt ended. SSR 05-02 says that SSA does not rely solely on information from the claimant, but instead seeks confirmation from the employer or even from a doctor "or other medical source" who could state "whether, in his or her opinion or according to the records, your work discontinuance or reduction was due to your impairment."

§176.3 *Working Claimants, Closed Period of Disability and Trial-Work Period*

If a claimant is currently working, you need to determine if that work makes it impossible for the claimant to be found disabled. Sometimes this occurs even when that work is not substantial gainful activity (SGA) because, for example, the work may be so inconsistent with a claim for disability benefits that the claimant will likely lose the case. For example, what if a claimant, who must prove inability to do a wide range of sedentary work in order to be found disabled, is working part-time at a heavy job? The issue you face is: How is it that this claimant has the capacity to do a heavy job part-time but cannot do a sedentary job full-time? In SSA terms, the fact that the claimant's "earnings were not substantial will not necessarily show that [the claimant is] not able to do substantial gainful activity." 20 C.F.R. § 404.1574(a)(1).

Working at Less Than SGA Level

Whenever a claimant is working for someone else, that is, the claimant is not self-employed, proof that the work is at less than SGA level is usually a mathematical process. In the past, SSA built into its regulations a gray area of earnings just below the SGA level. When a claimant's earnings fell in the gray area, SSA reserved the right to find that a claimant was, in fact, working at the SGA level even though the claimant's income did not quite meet the SGA guidelines. No more. Now, unless SSA thinks the claimant is actually performing SGA or is in a position to control the timing or amount of earnings (*see* 20 C.F.R. § 404.1574(b)(3)(ii)), SSA simply compares the claimant's earnings from work (after applying appropriate deductions and averaging income) with the SGA earnings guidelines stated in 20 C.F.R. § 404.1574(b)(2).

Because the regulations contain SGA amounts only for years through 2000 (and a formula for years after that—which isn't much practical help), Appendix 12 of this book provides the SGA amounts (and several other amounts that are based on annual cost-of-living increases) for years beginning with the year 2000. The SGA level, which was $500 per month from 1990 until July 1999 when it was raised to $700, is becoming considerably more generous than it used to be because of cost-of-living increases. For the year 2016, SGA has increased to $1,130 per month. SGA for the current year is found on SSA's website at www.ssa.gov/OACT/COLA/SGA.html. Historical and current SGA amounts can also be found at POMS DI 10501.015.

Although gross earnings, not net earnings, are considered, sick pay and vacation pay should be deducted from the claimant's gross earnings. According to POMS DI 10505.010 C:

> When evaluating earnings for substantial gainful activity purposes, consider only earnings derived from actual work activity for the month under consideration. If an individual receives sick or vacation pay for non-work days in a particular month, that pay should not be considered countable income for that month. Rather, the question is what work activity did the individual actually perform in the given month and what earnings did the individual actually receive for that work activity. Only the earnings paid as a result of work activity should be used in determining if the individual has engaged in SGA in a particular month.

However, POMS DI 10505.010 D says that bonuses count when evaluating whether work done was SGA.

Before the hearing, in order to establish exactly how much the claimant is earning, you will need to obtain copies of the claimant's check stubs or ask the claimant's employer for a month-by-month breakdown of the claimant's earnings. *See* §216.2 for a form to send to the employer.

During an initial interview with a claimant, it works best to inquire about hourly wage and number of hours worked per week; then calculate the claimant's earnings yourself. Beware of the mistake that claimants sometimes make when they simply multiply weekly earnings by four to demonstrate that their earnings are less than SGA. There are 4.3 weeks in a month.

Also, for Title II cases, be sure to count income from work when earned, not when paid. POMS DI 10505.005 C.1.d. Sometimes it makes a difference.

If you find an occasional month that exceeds the SGA level, don't worry. Earnings are supposed to be averaged over the time worked unless there is a reason not to average them (such as where work is reduced because of an impairment, or there are distinct periods of work involved, or the SGA level changes). *See* 20 C.F.R. § 404.1574a and SSR 83-35. Since the SGA level has changed annually since 2000, as a rule it is appropriate to average earnings over each calendar year in the current century. The years in the 1990s, before July 1999, however, can be averaged together for a claimant who worked steadily during those years to see if the claimant's earnings exceeded $500 per month, the applicable SGA amount. Note that there is an entire Social Security ruling on the subject of averaging earnings to determine if work is substantial gainful activity, SSR 83-35. The ruling provides more details and existed before the regulation, 20 C.F.R. § 404.1574a, which merely restates the policy found in the ruling. In those rare cases in which a claimant's work is very close to SGA level, it may be necessary to go through both the ruling and the regulation with the claimant during the interview.

Impairment-Related Work Expenses (IRWE)

If a claimant's earnings still appear to be above the SGA level, ask the claimant about out-of-pocket payments for medical expenses to treat the disabling impairment. Such impairment-related work expenses may be deducted from a claimant's monthly earnings when determining if the work constitutes substantial gainful activity. 20 C.F.R. §§ 404.1574(b)(1) and 404.1576. The cost of certain items and services that an impaired person needs in order to work, called impairment-related work expenses (IRWE), may be deducted from earnings when considering if work constitutes substantial gainful activity, even though such items and services are also necessary for normal daily activities. Routine drugs, however, are not deductible unless they are necessary to control the disabling condition so as to enable the individual to work. Deduction may be made only if the cost is actually paid by the individual. Thus, if the cost is paid by insurance, it is not deductible; and neither is the cost of the medical insurance. Insurance co-pays, however, are deductible.

As a rule, IRWEs are deducted in the month the claimant pays the bill, not when they are incurred. But some big ticket items may be spread over many months. There is a lengthy regulation, 20 C.F.R. § 404.1574, and a Social Security Ruling on IRWE, SSR 84-26, which should be studied in these cases. *See also* §274 for more details. A memorandum explaining IRWE, which may be sent to your client as you are gathering information about your client's IRWE, appears at §274.1. A Monthly Income Worksheet appears at §216.3.

Subsidies

Sometimes, even after deducting sick pay, vacation pay and IRWEs and averaging earnings, you will find a claimant who is earning more than the SGA level but the work situation is unusual. Consider whether there is a "marked discrepancy between the amount of pay and the value of the services." SSR 83-33. If so, such work may include a "subsidy." To help SSA employees spot subsidies, POMS DI 10505.010 A.1. provides this list of "circumstances indicating strong possibility of a subsidy":

- The employment is 'sheltered,' as defined in DI 10505.025D.; or
- Childhood disability is involved; or
- Mental impairment is involved; or
- There appears to be a marked discrepancy between the amount of pay and the value of the services; or
- The employer, employee, or other interested party alleges that the employee does not fully earn his or her pay (e.g., the employee receives unusual help from others in doing the work); or
- The nature and severity of the impairment indicates that the employee receives unusual help from others in doing the work; or
- The employee is involved in a government-sponsored job training and employment program (see DI 10505.025B.); or
- The person is in the military service (see DI 10505.023.).

Consider the situation where a claimant is working for a relative. The claimant may be doing very little work but the claimant is being paid more than the claimant's work is actually worth. This is not substantial work. This work involves a subsidy. 20 C.F.R. § 404.1574(a)(2). One way to prove a subsidy is to obtain from the employer an estimate of the true value of the claimant's work. If the true value of the claimant's work is less than the SGA level, the claimant will be found not to be performing gainful activity.

Other situations in which work may not be substantial include work done under special conditions, such as in a sheltered workshop where a claimant might receive special assistance from others; where the claimant is allowed to work irregular hours or take frequent rest breaks; where the claimant is provided special equipment or was assigned work especially suited to the claimant's impairment; where the claimant was able to work because someone helped the claimant prepare for or get to and from work; where the claimant is allowed to work at a lower standard of productivity; or where the claimant was given the opportunity to work because of a family relationship, past association with the employer or the employer's concern with the claimant's welfare. 20 C.F.R. § 404.1573(c).

Although SSA reserves the right to determine that work done under special conditions may actually constitute substantial gainful activity, 20 C.F.R. § 404.1574(a)(3), or "work done under special conditions may show that you have the necessary skills and ability to work at the substantial gainful activity level," 20 C.F.R. § 404.1573(c), usually such insubstantial work is not an impediment to the claimant being found disabled. Whenever you have a client working under special conditions, ask the employer to compare the claimant's work with similar work in the regular work force and to establish the "reasonable worth of the work." 20 C.F.R. § 404.1574(a)(3). SSA does not consider "any income that is not directly related to your productivity. When your earnings exceed the reasonable value of the work you perform, we consider only that part of your pay which you actually earn." 20 C.F.R. § 404.1574(a)(2).

Section 216.1 of this book is a questionnaire that may be sent to an employer to establish that work was done under special conditions. To establish that the worth of the work was below the SGA level, it is best to talk with the employer and obtain a letter from the employer explaining the value of the work to the business. *See* POMS DI 10505.010 A.3.b.

Working at the SGA Level

Sometimes the conclusion is inescapable that a claimant is working at the SGA level even after subsidies, impairment-related work expenses, sick pay and vacation pay are deducted and income is averaged. You cannot argue that the worth of work is less than the SGA level. The claimant's work does not fit the criteria for an unsuccessful work attempt because, by the time of the hearing, it has not stopped (or it has gone on more than six months, too long to fit the unsuccessful work attempt criteria even if it did stop). Should you end the inquiry right there and send the claimant away? No.

The first thing you need to figure out is whether this claimant might be eligible for a "closed period of disability." The crucial question is whether the claimant's impairment meets the 12-month duration requirement. 20 C.F.R. § 404.1509. To meet the duration requirement, the claimant's impairment cannot have improved to the point that the claimant is *capable* of substantial gainful activity, and the claimant cannot have actually returned to substantial gainful activity before 12 months from the date of onset, though it is possible to have an unsuccessful work attempt during the first 12 months.

Take a simple example. Say the claimant is a 52-year-old man with a limited education. His past work was heavy and unskilled. He is now limited to sedentary work because of a back problem. After he was off work for a full year because of his impairment, he took a part-time unskilled sedentary job in which, for the past 8 months, he has earned an amount sufficient to qualify as substantial gainful activity—even after all appropriate deductions are taken. Rule 201.09 of the Medical-Vocational Guidelines requires that he be found disabled with a sedentary RFC. Because he was off work for a full year, he meets the duration requirement. Thus, he is at least eligible for a closed period of disability. But when does the closed period of disability end, and how should the period of time when he was working be treated?

Applicability of Medical Improvement Rules

For the answer to this question, it is SSA's position that we must consult its rules for determining whether a disability continues or ends, the same rules that are applied when someone receiving disability benefits undergoes a "continuing disability review," to see if benefits should be terminated. 20 C.F.R. §§ 404.1594 and 416.994 must be applied to find a closed period of disability. SSR 02-1p, Footnote 2; SSR 02-2p, Footnote 3; POMS DI 28005.001.D.1.b. These rules, which are called the "medical improvement review standard" (MIRS) in the POMS, are usually referred to as the "medical improvement rules" by lawyers. Note that the parts of these rules that actually deal with whether a claimant's disability improved would not cause termination of our hypothetical claimant's benefits because he has not improved. A sedentary RFC requires that he be found disabled, and he is working at the sedentary level.

SSI Medical Improvement Rules

Because there are significant differences between the SSI rules and the Title II rules, SSI and Title II cases need to be evaluated separately. Here is how our hypothetical claimant's case would be evaluated if he applied only for SSI. Congress and SSA have made such a great effort to encourage SSI beneficiaries to work that SSA does "not use substantial gainful activity as a measure for continuing eligibility for SSI benefits." 65 Fed Reg. 82,906 (2000). Note that 20 C.F.R. § 416.994 makes no mention of performance of SGA as a consideration in determining if disability has ended. Compare the evaluation steps for finding medical improvement in the SSI rules, 20 C.F.R. § 416.994(b)(5), with the steps for finding medical improvement in the Title II case, 20 C.F.R. § 404.1594(f). *See also* 42 U.S.C. § 1382h, known as Section 1619 of the Social Security Act.

Thus, there are only two issues to be determined for our hypothetical claimant if he were eligible only for SSI: (1) whether he returned to substantial gainful activity before 12 months from the date of onset of disability, that is, whether he meets the duration requirement; and (2) whether there has been medical improvement. Because our hypothetical claimant meets both requirements, he should be found entitled to continuing benefits. *See* 20 C.F.R. § 416.994. (His monthly SSI benefits, though, will be reduced in accord with the rules for working beneficiaries. *See* 20 C.F.R. §§ 416.261, 416.262, and 416.1111.)

Title II Medical Improvement Rules and Trial Work Period

Let's see what happens if our hypothetical claimant applied for Title II benefits. If a claimant is performing SGA, SSA will find that the claimant's disability has ended at the first step of the sequential evaluation process for medical improvement. 20 C.F.R. § 404.1594(f)(1). However, that first step of the evaluation process applies only if "any applicable trial-work period has been completed." 20 C.F.R. § 404.1594(f)(1). That first step of the medical improvement sequential evaluation process directs one to an "exception" to the medical improvement rules. This exception, which does not appear in the corresponding SSI regulation, applies to beneficiaries who are currently engaging in substantial gainful activity. It states that for such a working individual, "before we determine whether you are no longer disabled because of your work activity, we will consider whether you are entitled to a trial-work period as set out in § 404.1592. We will find that your disability has ended in the month in which you demonstrated your ability to engage in substantial gainful activity (*following completion of a trial-work period, where it applies*)." 20 C.F.R. § 404.1594(d)(5), emphasis added. The question, then, is whether our hypothetical claimant is eligible for a trial-work period, a concept that applies only to Title II cases, not SSI cases. If eligible, a disabled individual is allowed to test his or her ability to return to work for nine months, not necessarily consecutive, during which time full benefits are paid.

It is SSA policy that "a person may be awarded a trial work period as part of the adjudication of an initial application when he or she returns to work more than 12 months from onset." 65 Fed. Reg. 42774 (2000). The 12-month duration requirement must be met. In addition, trial work period rules impose two absolute limitations on eligibility: a trial-work period cannot begin before the five-month waiting period has elapsed, and it cannot begin before the claimant applies for benefits. 20 C.F.R. § 404.1592(d)(2). (Any months of work before the date of application or during the waiting period do not count as part of the trial-work period.) But after the five-month waiting period, any month in which a claimant earns over a certain amount constituting "services" for trial-work period purposes, qualifies as a trial work period month, even if those months of work are also determined to be unsuccessful work attempts, and even if those months of work are performed prior to adjudication.

The "services" amount, $200 during the years 1990 through 2000, was raised to $530 per month beginning in 2001, and indexed annually after that. 20 C.F.R. § 404.1592(b). *See* Appendix 12 for the trial work period services monthly amounts for years after 2001. For 2015, the trial work period services amount is $780 per month. The amount for the current year can be found on SSA's website at www.ssa.gov/OACT/COLA/twp.html. *See also* POMS DI 13010.060A for trial work period services monthly amounts. For Title II purposes, income is considered when earned. For SSI purposes, income is considered when received. *See* POMS DI 10505.005 C.1.d.

Once the claimant works for 9 months in what SSA calls a rolling 60-month period, the trial work period is used up. 20 C.F.R. § 404.1592(e)(2). To determine whether the 9 months of work fall within the 60-month rolling period, take the last month that qualifies as trial work and count backward in time for 60 months. If during that 60-month period there are 9 months of trial work, the trial work period ends. POMS DI 13010.060D.

After the trial work period is over, monthly benefits will end when the claimant performs substantial gainful activity. SSA refers to this as finding that "disability ceased" under 20 C.F.R. § 404.1594(f)(1), step one of the sequential medical improvement review standard. Do not be confused by this. This is not a finding that the claimant no longer has a disabling impairment or that the claimant has medically improved. It is a finding only that the claimant is engaging in SGA after the end of the trial work period. *See* 20 C.F.R. § 404.1594(d)(5).

To determine if the claimant is performing SGA after the trial work period is over, unsuccessful work attempt rules apply, IRWEs, sick pay and vacation pay may be deducted, and income will be averaged to make sure the claimant is performing SGA. 20 C.F.R. § 404.1592a(a)(1). The worksheet at §216.3 may help calculate countable income month-by-month. Once it is determined that the claimant is performing SGA after the trial work period is over, the claimant will be paid for the first month of SGA and the next two months, whether or not the claimant does SGA in those months. 20 C.F.R. §§ 404.401a and 404.1592a(a)(2). Whether the claimant is paid benefits in the months after those three months, though, depends on whether the claimant is actually performing SGA in those months and whether the claimant continues to have a disabling impairment.

Extended Period of Eligibility (EPE)

For 36 months counting from the end of the trial work period, which is called the "re-entitlement period" in the regulations and referred to as the "extended period of eligibility" (EPE) in the POMS, benefits will not be paid for any month in which the claimant is performing substantial gainful activity. Benefits will still be paid for any month in which the claimant is not performing SGA as long as the claimant continues to have a disabling impairment. 20 C.F.R. § 404.1592a(a). Benefits are not averaged for this determination and unsuccessful work attempt rules do not apply, but IRWEs may be deducted. During the re-entitlement period, payment is accomplished without a new application—an excellent arrangement for beneficiaries experiencing starts and stops in their efforts to return to work. 20 C.F.R. § 404.1592a(a)(2)(i).

If a claimant is found to be working at the SGA level at any time during the 36-month re-entitlement period, SSA will find that the claimant's *entitlement* to disability benefits terminates with the very first month of SGA *after* the re-entitlement period. 20 C.F.R. § 404.1592a(a)(3). This is easiest to understand if we assume that a claimant began working and never stopped—that is, the claimant worked in consecutive months at the SGA level throughout the 9-month trial work period, the 36-month re-entitlement period and beyond. If this was the work pattern, actual payment of the claimant's monthly benefits would stop with the 12th month of work (nine months of trial work plus three months after that), which would also happen to be the third month of the re-entitlement period in this example. But *entitlement* to disability benefits does not end for another two and three-quarter years even though the claimant is not getting paid during this time. *See* 20 C.F.R. § 404.325, Example 1 and POMS DI 13010.210. This rather technical "entitlement" that existed during the intervening months is the claimant's right to contact SSA to have benefits paid for any month the claimant's income drops below the SGA level.

If a claimant did not work at the SGA level at all during the 36-month re-entitlement period after the end of the trial work period, that is, benefits were paid during this entire time, SSA:

> will apply all of the relevant provisions of §§ 404.1571-404.1576 including, but not limited to, the provisions for averaging earnings, unsuccessful work attempts, and deducting impairment-related work expenses to determine whether your disability ceased because you performed substantial gainful activity after the re-entitlement period. If we find that your disability ceased because you performed substantial gainful activity in a month after your re-entitlement period ended, you will be paid benefits for the month in which your disability ceased and the two succeeding months. After those three months, your entitlement to a period of disability or to disability benefits terminates (*see* §§ 404.321 and 404.325).

20 C.F.R. § 404.1592a(a)(3). *See also* POMS DI 13010.210.

If the claimant worked enough at the beginning of the 36-month re-entitlement period to have benefits cease because of performance of SGA, and then stops working during the re-entitlement period, the claimant's benefits will resume and continue beyond the 36-month re-entitlement period until the very first month the claimant performs SGA. For this determination, income is not averaged and unsuccessful work attempt rules do not apply, though IRWEs may be deducted and subsidies or special consideration by the employer may be considered. POMS DI 13010.210 D. Benefits will stop with the first month the claimant's earnings, after appropriate deductions, exceed the SGA amount; and they do not resume if, for example, the very next month the claimant stops working again. Entitlement has terminated with that first month of SGA after the end of the 36-month re-entitlement period. 20 C.F.R. § 404.325.

It is worthwhile to pause and reflect on the consequences of using up the trial work period. Note that the 36-month re-entitlement period does not begin until the 9-month trial work period ends. Thus, if a claimant never uses up the trial work period, the 36-month re-entitlement rules never kick in. Note that even if the claimant never works at all during the 36-month extended period of eligibility, and starts working after the 36 months have passed, the claimant's entitlement to disability benefits will end once it is determined that the claimant is performing SGA. At least for this SGA determination, though, all of the rules for evaluating a claimant's work apply including unsuccessful work attempt rules and the rules for averaging earnings.

Expedited Reinstatement (EXR)

If a beneficiary, whose benefits were terminated because of the performance of SGA, stops working after the end of the re-entitlement period, that beneficiary can still request "expedited reinstatement," referred to as EXR in the POMS, for 60 months after entitlement is terminated because the claimant returned to work at the SGA level. To qualify for expedited reinstatement, an individual must:

1. Not be performing SGA in the month he or she applies for EXR;
2. Be unable to work at the SGA level due to his or her medical condition;

3. Have his or her current medical impairment be the same as or related to the original impairment; and
4. Be under a disability based on application of the medical improvement review standards set forth in 20 C.F.R. § 404.1594.

See 20 C.F.R. §§ 404.1592b through 404.1592f.

As you can see, there are significant benefits to our hypothetical claimant being treated in a trial work period while he works part-time at a sedentary job. He will get back pay for all those months he worked. If he stops working or reduces his work income to less than SGA level within 36 months of the end of the trial work period, his benefits will resume. He can request expedited reinstatement within 60 months of when entitlement terminated because he was working at the SGA level. Thus, rather than seeking a closed period that ends when the claimant first went to work, you should ask the ALJ to find this claimant's work to be part of a trial work period and to find that there is no medical improvement. If, after the end of the 9-month trial work period, the claimant has already worked at the SGA level (after considering all deductions from work income—IRWEs, etc., averaging income and applying the rules for unsuccessful work attempts), you need to ask the ALJ to find that the claimant's disability ceased because of performance of SGA within the first month of SGA following the end of the trial work period.

Concurrent Cases

Note that if our hypothetical claimant applied for both Title II and Title XVI benefits and continues working beyond the trial work period, his Title II benefits will end; but his SSI benefits will continue subject to the rules for deducting earned income.

If the Claimant Medically Improves

Let us change the hypothetical situation a little to illustrate the interplay of the trial work period rules and the medical improvement rules. For example, the 52-year-old male hypothetical claimant, with a limited education and a heavy unskilled work background, began a part-time sedentary job when all his doctors agreed he was limited to sedentary work; and he has continued to work at that job. However, after six months of work, his back condition improved to the point that his doctor concluded, based on a functional capacities evaluation, he is capable of light work. Thus, there has been medical improvement to the point that he is no longer disabled under the Medical-Vocational Guidelines. It does not matter that he is in a trial-work period. He is eligible only for a closed period of disability, which ends when he has medically improved. "We may find that your disability has ended at any time during the trial work period if the medical or other evidence shows that you are no longer disabled." 20 C.F.R. § 404.1592(e)(3).

Under Rule 202.10 of the Medical-Vocational Guidelines, his disability ends when he becomes capable of light work; however, the evidence of this improvement must arise from somewhere other than the trial work. There must be "new evidence, other than evidence relating to any work you did during the trial work period, [which] shows that you are not disabled." 20 C.F.R. § 404.1592(e)(3). Note that if the only evidence of the capacity for light work comes from the work he has been doing (*e.g.*, although the job started out as sedentary, the claimant has been doing some light level exertion at work), SSA may not use such evidence, under the theory that to use evidence arising from the trial work itself would discourage attempting to work—and it is SSA policy to encourage trial work.

Return to Work Within 12 Months of Onset

Let us see what happens if we change our hypothetical situation again. For example, all the facts are the same except that our Title II claimant returned to work 11 months after the alleged onset date and there is no medical improvement. In this situation, SSA's position is that the claim must be denied because it does not meet the 12-month duration requirement. *See* 20 C.F.R. § 404.1592(d)(2)(iii) and SSR 82-52. There is no opportunity for a trial work period. In *Barnhart v. Walton*, 535 U.S. 212 (2002), the United States Supreme Court upheld SSA's position on this issue.

But consider this: If SSA had already found this claimant disabled by the time he returned to work, he would be entitled to a trial work period even though he returned to work before 12 months from onset of disability. In this circumstance, the duration requirement would be met at the time of adjudication because SSA would have determined that the impairment was *expected* to last 12 months. *See* 20 C.F.R. § 404.1505(a). SSA's trial work period regulation specifically states that a claimant is not entitled to a trial work period when the claimant returns to work within 12 months of onset "*and before the date of any notice of determination or decision finding*" the claimant disabled. 20 C.F.R. § 404.1592(d)(2)(iii) (emphasis added). *See also* SSR 82-52 and 65 Fed. Reg. 42,774 (2000).

Return to Work During Waiting Period

If a claimant returns to work during the five-month waiting period, the claimant is not entitled to a trial work period, 20 C.F.R. § 404.1592(d)(2)(ii), and, if SSA were to issue a favorable decision before the claimant returned to work during the waiting period, it is SSA's policy that it must reopen the determination finding the claimant disabled and deny the claim. If the work later turns out to be an unsuccessful work attempt, SSA will reopen the claim again and award benefits. SSR 82-52.

Self-Employed Claimants

While determining whether an employee is engaging in substantial gainful activity is largely a mathematical determination, determining whether a self-employed claimant is engaging in SGA is another matter entirely. SSR 83-34 points out:

> In determining whether a self-employed individual is engaging in SGA, consideration must be given to the individual's activities and their value to his or her business. Self-employment income alone is not a reliable factor in determining SGA, since it is influenced not only by the individual's services but also by such things as market conditions, capital investments, the services of other people, and agreements on distribution of profits. An individual's services may help build up capital assets during a period of development when no profits are evident, or they may reduce losses during temporary periods of poor business conditions. On the other hand, a person who is incapable of rendering valuable services may receive a large income solely because of his or her capital investment in the business. Hence, it is necessary to consider the economic value of the individual's services, regardless of whether an immediate income results from such services.

In order to determine if a self-employed person is engaging in SGA, SSA uses three tests:

(1) Significant services and substantial income. The claimant is engaging in SGA if the claimant is providing significant services *and* receiving more than the SGA Earnings Guidelines, the same guidelines used for employees. 20 C.F.R. § 404.1575(a)(1). If the claimant is not receiving substantial income, the claimant can, nevertheless, be found to be engaging in SGA based on tests 2 or 3.

(2) Comparability of work. "The individual's work activity, in terms of all relevant factors such as hours, skills, energy output, efficiency, duties, and responsibilities, is comparable to that of unimpaired individuals in the same community engaged in the same or similar businesses as their means of livelihood." SSR 83-34. 20 C.F.R. § 404.1575(a)(2).

(3) Worth of work. "The individual's work activity, although not comparable to that of unimpaired individuals as indicated above, is, nevertheless, clearly worth more than the amount shown for the particular calendar year in the SGA Earnings Guidelines when considered in terms of its value to the business, or when compared to the salary an owner would pay to an employee for such duties in that business setting." SSR 83-34. 20 C.F.R. § 404.1575(a)(3).

A self-employed person is rendering "significant services" no matter how few hours per month he or she works if the business is a solo operation—a one person business. If more than one person is involved in the business, a self-employed person will be found to be rendering significant services if he contributes more than half the total time required for the management of the business, or he renders "management services for more than 45 hours a month regardless of the total management time required by the business." 20 C.F.R. § 404.1575(b).

Here is the formula from 20 C.F.R. § 404.1575(c) that SSA uses for determining countable income from self employment:

	Gross income
minus	Normal business expenses
equals	Net income
minus	Value of unpaid help at the prevailing wage rate
minus	IRWEs
minus	Business expenses paid by another individual or agency
equals	Actual value of work or countable income

If the countable income exceeds the SGA amount, then, of course, SSA determines that the claimant has received substantial income from the business. However, "even if 'countable income' from the business does not average more than the applicable amount shown in the Guidelines, a self-employed individual will have substantial income from a business if the livelihood which he or she derives from the business is comparable to that which he or she had before becoming disabled, or is comparable to that of unimpaired self-employed individuals in his or her community engaged in the same or similar businesses as their means of livelihood." SSR 83-34. 20 C.F.R. § 404.1575(c)(2).

To establish comparability of work activity under test 2, SSR 83-34 makes it clear that a decision-maker cannot simply describe the claimant's activities and assert that they are comparable to the work of unimpaired persons.

It is necessary to show that the disabled person is performing at a level comparable to that of unimpaired persons considering the following factors: hours, skills, energy output, efficiency, duties and responsibilities. The lack of conclusive evidence as to the comparability of the required factors will result in a finding that work performed is not SGA. SSR 83-34.

This puts the burden on SSA to show comparability. SSR 83-34 also makes clear:

> Each work factor cited above must be described in detail, showing its contribution to the business operation. General descriptions are considered inconclusive evidence for the point-by-point comparison that is required. If only a general description is possible or available, any doubt as to the comparability of the factors should be resolved in favor of the impaired individual.

Even when a self-employed claimant is earning less than the trial work period services month dollar amount in the regulations, if the claimant is working more than 80 hours in a month, the month qualifies as a trial work period services month. The 80 hours per month rule applies since the beginning of 2001. From 1990 through the year 2000, if the self-employed person was working more than 40 hours per month, the month would qualify as a trial work period services month. 20 C.F.R. § 404.1592(b)(2).

Unsuccessful work attempt rules for self-employed claimants are essentially the same as for claimants who are not self-employed. *See* 20 C.F.R. § 404.1575(d).

Somewhat different approaches for evaluating self-employment of farm landlords appear in 20 C.F.R. § 404.1575 and SSR 83-34. If a farm landlord "materially participates in the production or the management of the production of the things raised on the rented farm," the farm landlord will be considered to be rendering "significant services." If the farm landlord was given Social Security earnings credits, the landlord will be considered to be rendering significant services. 20 C.F.R. §§ 404.1575(b)(2) and 404.1082 and SSR 83-34.

There is a higher SGA level for blind claimants and beneficiaries. *See* 20 C.F.R. § 404.1584 and Appendix 12. Self-employed blind beneficiaries do not have to contend with tests 2 and 3. Whether they are working at the SGA level or not is determined solely by comparing their income to the blind SGA amount. SSR 83-34.

§176.4 Prior Applications

Be sure to find out about earlier applications. These might lead you to conclude not to take a case; but often the earlier denial decisions can help you design a winning case, possibly even a winning case that includes past due benefits paid under the first application.

Whenever there is an earlier application, you need to address the issues created by that earlier application. Do not be lulled into inactivity by SSA's general policy, which is to grant a *de novo* hearing on a later application (as long as the last denial decision on the earlier application was not issued *after* the date last insured). Although under SSA's general policy the earlier denial is not considered "evidence" that must be rebutted, most ALJs treat it as a factor for consideration; and ALJs often follow the earlier decision. Thus, *de novo* hearings often yield similar results. Although an ALJ can and sometimes does come to a different conclusion than that arrived at in the earlier denial, even when there is no new evidence, it is your job as the claimant's attorney to answer this usually unstated question: why should the result be any different this time around?

In three circuits, the Fourth, Sixth, and Ninth, acquiescence rulings require an adjudicator in the second claim to treat as evidence the findings (such as a residual functional capacity finding) in the earlier denial decision. *See* ARs 97-4(9), 98-3(6), 98-4(6), and 00-1(4). These acquiescence rulings bring to the forefront the unstated question that lurks in such cases in the other circuits: why should the result be any different this time around? Depending on the facts, a prior finding may make it easier or more difficult for a claimant to be found disabled on a new application. It may be easier, for example, when a prior residual functional capacity (RFC) finding would warrant a conclusion that a claimant is disabled because the claimant moved into a higher age category. It may be more difficult, for example, when the prior RFC finding does not warrant a different result on the new application and there is no new medical evidence demonstrating that the prior RFC finding is wrong. *See* §379, for more information on these acquiescence rulings.

Don't neglect the possibility that an earlier application can be reopened, which will lead to significant additional past-due benefits. You may request reopening of a Social Security disability or SSI case *for any reason* within 12 months of the initial determination. 20 C.F.R. §§ 404.988(a) and 416.1488(a). For *good cause* you may request reopening within four years of an initial denial in a Social Security disability case, 20 C.F.R. § 404.988(b), and within two years in an SSI case, 20 C.F.R. § 416.1488(b). The standards for good cause are the same for both programs. Good cause includes "new and material evidence" and that the "evidence that was considered in making the determination . . . clearly shows on its face that an error was made." 20 C.F.R. §§ 404.989 and 416.1489.

The time limits for reopening run from the date of the initial determination, that is, the initial denial. A claimant's current application, if it contains the same alleged onset date as an earlier application, can be construed as a timely request to reopen the earlier application. *See* HALLEX I-2-9-1.

There are also situations where no time limit applies. 20 C.F.R. § 404.988(c) provides a long list of circumstances where reopening may be had "at any time," the most important of which is 20 C.F.R.

§404.988(c)(8) providing for reopening to correct "an error that appears on the face of the evidence."

No time limit for reopening applies in cases involving claimants who lacked the mental capacity to understand the procedures for appealing an adverse administrative action. SSR 91-5p. This rule applies where there was no one legally responsible for prosecuting the claim such as a parent of a claimant who is a minor, legal guardian, attorney or other representative. Regardless of how much time has passed from the time of the prior administrative action, the case can be reopened if it is established that at the time of the prior administrative action the claimant lacked the mental capacity to understand the procedures for appealing. The adjudicator must consider:

- Inability to read or write
- Lack of facility with the English language
- Limited education
- Any mental or physical condition that limits the claimant's ability to do things for himself or herself

Adjudicators are instructed to "resolve any reasonable doubt in favor of the claimant." SSR 91-5p.

In addition, for those in the Fourth Circuit, SSA must follow an acquiescence ruling as well as SSR 91-5p. *See* AR 90-4(4), pertaining to *Culbertson v. Secretary of Health & Human Services*, 859 F.2d 319 (4th Cir. 1988), and *Young v. Bowen*, 858 F.2d 951 (4th Cir. 1988).

Time limits for reopening, of course, will not apply in cases where class action judgments mandate reopening. The most famous and far reaching such case involves SSI children for decisions made between 1980 and the time of the Supreme Court's decision in *Sullivan v. Zebley*, 493 U.S. 521 (1990), adopted as SSR 91-7c. *See* §145. Since most class actions in the past were brought by agencies funded by the Legal Services Corporation, contact your local legal services agency to find out if other class actions apply to your area.

Neither time limits nor the doctrine of *res judicata* apply to reopening where, after July 1, 1991, the language in an initial or reconsideration denial notice misled a claimant about the consequences of failing to appeal. A denial determination may not be given *res judicata* effect if a claimant demonstrates that he or she failed to appeal "acting in good faith reliance upon incorrect, incomplete, or misleading information, relating to the consequences of reapplying for benefits in lieu of seeking review of an adverse determination. . . ." 42 U.S.C. § 405(b)(3)(A).

This statute has little practical effect because SSA changed the most misleading language in its denial notices prior to July 1, 1991. Before that time denial notices routinely stated: "If you do not request reconsideration of your case within the prescribed time period, you still have the right to file another application at any time." This sentence would be patently false if a claimant's insured status lapsed before the date of the determination, since SSA would apply the doctrine of *res judicata* to a new application to refuse to consider it on the merits in the absence of significant new evidence.

If you find that a denial notice containing such language has been given *res judicata* effect, it is worth challenging the validity of the notice on due process grounds. For those in the Ninth Circuit, SSA has issued an acquiescence ruling, AR 92-7(9), concerning *Gonzalez v. Sullivan*, 914 F.2d 1197 (9th Cir. 1990), stating that time limits for reopening and revising agency determinations do not apply where a denial notice contains the misleading language quoted above. Other decisions finding that this notice language denies due process include *Dealy v. Heckler*, 616 F. Supp. 880 (W.D. Mo. 1984); *Aversa v. Secretary of Health & Human Services*, 672 F. Supp. 775 (D.N.J. 1987); and *Butland v. Bowen*, 673 F. Supp. 638 (D. Mass. 1987). Although SSR 95-1p attempts to limit the impact of *Gonzalez* outside the Ninth Circuit, this ruling should not deter attorneys from challenging due process violations created by defective notices where SSA denies the right to file a new application on *res judicata* grounds. For more on this issue, *see* §378.

For a more detailed analysis of reopening issues, *see* §370 ff. For analysis of *res judicata* from SSA's perspective, *see* two articles written by Administrative Appeals Judge Catherine Ravinski that appear in Volume 1 of *The OHA Law Journal* (November 1990) and in Volume 3, No. 1 of *The OHA Law Journal* (Spring 1992). *See also* HALLEX I-3-3-9, reproduced at §531.

§176.5 Cases Where SSA Misinformation Deters Applying

If the claimant has been disabled for quite some time but never before filed an application for benefits, find out why he or she didn't apply earlier. Inquire whether an SSA employee may have provided misinformation that deterred the claimant from applying for benefits. If you find such a case, you may be able to use the date the misinformation was provided as a "deemed" application date, resulting in months or even years of additional back benefits. The statutory provision authorizing this procedure in Social Security disability cases, 42 U.S.C. § 402(j)(5), applies to misinformation given after December 31, 1982 for benefits payable after December 1982.

In Social Security disability cases, you need look at this issue only when there are more than 17 months between the date of onset and the date of application. If less than that much time has passed, the claimant will receive all benefits due, anyway.

In SSI cases, this rule may have even greater impact because benefits are not paid before the date of the application and because of the quantity of misinformation SSA employees regularly dispense about this complicated welfare program. The SSI provision of the law, 42 U.S.C. § 1383(e)(4), applies to benefits payable for months after December 1989 based on misinformation given on or after December 19, 1989.

According to 20 C.F.R. § 404.633(d), applicable to Social Security disability claims, and 20 C.F.R. § 416.351(d), applicable to SSI claims, preferred evidence that misinformation was provided is "written evidence which relates directly to your inquiry about your eligibility for benefits. . . ." Such written evidence includes a notice or letter from SSA, and SSA telephone or interview records. In the absence of preferred evidence, SSA will consider other evidence, including but not limited to:

- The individual's statements, including information about the date and time of the contact with SSA; how the contact was made; reasons for the contact; who gave the misinformation; questions asked by the individual; facts given and questions asked by the SSA employee and the information the employee gave at the time;
- Statements from others who were present;
- If the individual can identify the employee or the employee recalls the inquiry—
  - Statements from the employee about the contact; and
  - An assessment of the likelihood that the SSA employee gave the misinformation.
- An evaluation of the credibility and validity of the individual's allegation in conjunction with other relevant information; and
- Any other information.

SSA says that it "will not find that we gave you misinformation based solely on your statements." 20 C.F.R. § 404.633(d)(2) and 20 C.F.R. § 416.351(d)(2). SSA explained its policy this way when it published the regulations:

> We will evaluate the individual's allegations and seek corroboration; we will resolve reasonable doubt in the individual's favor if the allegation of misinformation seems credible, is supported by other evidence, and there is no contradictory evidence.

59 Fed. Reg. 44,920 (1994).

If you find a case in which it appears that misinformation from an SSA employee caused a claimant not to apply for benefits, this issue will need to be developed initially at the Social Security office before it is presented to an administrative law judge. Contact the local office and request that it investigate the matter, take an additional application, and rule on the issue.

§176.6 Receipt of Unemployment Compensation Benefits

If the onset date originally alleged is the date the claimant was laid off from work, this may also be the date the claimant started getting unemployment compensation (UC) benefits and telling the UC people he or she was ready, willing and able to work. Because of the apparent conflict between alleging that one is entitled to disability benefits from one program and telling another government program that one can work, it is hard, though not necessarily impossible, to claim benefits from both programs. You may want to discuss with your client whether a later onset date would be appropriate. But before you amend the alleged onset date, be sure you understand the situation surrounding your client's layoff, your client's limitations and the UC system in your state. Ask the claimant how the alleged onset date was determined. Was it the claimant's idea or did an SSA claims representative suggest using the last day of work? Because ALJs have widely divergent views about the receipt of UC benefits during months that a claimant claims to be disabled under the Social Security disability program, it is also useful to try to find out the ALJ's position on this issue.

There are cases where there is no conflict between receipt of unemployment compensation and an application for Social Security disability benefits. For example, a claimant who is available only for light work may legitimately receive unemployment compensation benefits, and if the claimant is age 55 or older, the claimant could be found disabled using rules from the Medical-Vocational Guidelines. *See* Chart: Maximum RFC Permitted for Disability Finding, §121.1. (On the other hand, in many states it may be difficult to claim that there is no conflict even if your 50-year-old client who received UC benefits alleges to SSA that he is limited to sedentary work. In many states a limitation to sedentary work does not qualify a claimant for UC benefits because there is a requirement that the claimant be capable of performing a larger percentage of jobs than the sedentary occupational base contains.)

Even though in most situations there is an apparent inconsistency between receipt of unemployment compensation and a claim for Social Security disability benefits that covers the same period, it is sometimes possible to argue that even though your client would have attempted work during the time he was receiving unemployment compensation benefits (which makes receipt of unemployment compensation benefits legitimate), in retrospect it appears that he would not have been able to sustain work (which provides the basis for the disability claim).

For many judges, the fact that your client was laid off because of lack of work or a plant closing, *etc.* (rather than being terminated because of inability to do the job) is a bigger problem than receipt of unemployment compensation itself. Some ALJs shrug at receipt of unemployment compensation, viewing it from a "person's got to live" perspective. These ALJs do not even ask about receipt of UC benefits at the hearing, though they are likely aware of it because SSA has access to UC payment information, which usually appears in a claimant's hearing exhibit file. Other ALJs will ask you to amend the alleged onset date to the day after your client last received unemployment compensation benefits.

Although there is no statute, regulation or ruling that says your client cannot receive UC and Social Security disability benefits for the same period, some ALJs, who regard receipt of both benefits for the same period as double dipping, simply will not find a claimant disabled during the time a claimant received UC benefits, even if the logic of your argument is that the claimant can receive both benefits, but they will find a claimant disabled the month after UC stops. Other ALJs, who may regard receipt of UC benefits as proof the claimant could work during the time the claimant was receiving UC benefits, expect an amended alleged onset date to be based on medical worsening, not on when UC stopped.

Courts generally view receipt of unemployment compensation as inconsistent with a claim for disability benefits but they do not regard it as conclusive proof that a claimant is not disabled. *See*, for example, *Jernigan v. Sullivan*, 948 F.2d 1070, 1074 (8th Cir. 1991). When an ALJ decision contains legal errors or is not supported by substantial evidence, receipt of unemployment compensation benefits does not alone prevent a court from remanding a case for SSA to address the errors. A U.S. Magistrate Judge addressed the UC issue in *Roberts v. Callahan*, 971 F. Supp. 498, 501-502 (D.N.M. 1997), as follows:

> Receipt of unemployment benefits, however, does not mean that a claimant is able to work. *See, e.g., Alverio v. Chater,* 902 F. Supp. 909, 928 (N.D. Iowa 1995); *Riley v. Heckler*, 585 F. Supp. 278, 285 (S.D. Ohio 1984). A desire to work likewise does not mean that a claimant can actually work. *See, e.g., Talbot v. Heckler*, 814 F.2d 1456, 1461 (10th Cir. Okla. 1987); *Morales v. Bowen*, 664 F. Supp. 75, 79 (S.D.N.Y. 1987); *Rivera v. Schweiker*, 717 F.2d 719, 725 (2d Cir. N.Y. 1983).

In a memorandum dated August 9, 2010, the Chief Administrative Law Judge reminded ALJs that "the receipt of unemployment insurance benefits does not preclude the receipt of Social Security disability benefits. The receipt of unemployment insurance benefits is only one of many factors that must be considered in determining whether the claimant is disabled. 20 C.F.R. §§ 404.1512(b) and 416.912(b)." The Chief ALJ drew an analogy with *Cleveland v. Policy Management Systems Corp.*, 526 U.S. 795 (1999), adopted by SSA as SSR 00-1c, in which the Supreme Court held that receipt of Social Security disability benefits is often consistent with a claim for relief under the Americans with Disabilities Act (ADA). "The Court noted that, under the presumptions embodied in our five-step sequential evaluation process, a person can qualify for Social Security disability benefits even though he or she remains capable of performing some work. Similar logic applies to applications for unemployment insurance benefits." The Chief ALJ continued:

> In addition, it is often uncertain whether we will find a person who applies for unemployment insurance benefits ultimately to be disabled under our rules, and our decision-making process can be quite lengthy. Therefore, it is SSA's position that individuals need not choose between applying for unemployment insurance and Social Security disability benefits.
>
> However, application for unemployment insurance benefits is evidence that the ALJ must consider together with all of the medical and other evidence. Often, the underlying circumstances will be of greater relevance than the mere application for and receipt of the benefits. For instance, the fact that the person has, during his or her alleged period of disability, sought employment at jobs with physical demands in excess of the person's alleged limitations would be a relevant factor that the ALJ should take into account, particularly if the ALJ inquired about an explanation for this apparent inconsistency.

Reprinted at *Social Security Forum*, Vol. 32, No. 8, p. 10, August 2010. *See also* the virtually identical memorandum dated November 15, 2006, which is reprinted at *Social Security Forum*, Vol. 29, No. 11, November 2007, pp. 18-19.

§176.7 Americans With Disabilities Act Claims

If a Social Security disability claimant also filed a claim against a former employer under the Americans with Disabilities Act (ADA), 42 U.S.C. § 12101, do not automatically assume that this means that the claimant is capable of working at a past job. You need to find out the details.

In an ADA claim, an individual must assert that he or she is capable of performing a specific job, with or without accommodation. In a Social Security disability claim, of course, a claimant must prove inability to perform jobs done in the past, as well as inability to perform other work.

SSA's position is it is not relevant to a Social Security disability claim that an individual is capable of returning to a past job as long as certain accommodations are made. *See* §344.1. In fact, the details of the ADA claim may help demonstrate that a claimant needs so much accommodation that jobs for this claimant do not exist in significant numbers. On the other hand, the details of the ADA claim may show that the requested accommodation is so minor or specific to a particular employer, that the claimant is capable of other work.

In *Cleveland v. Policy Management Systems Corp.*, 119 S. Ct. 159 (1999), a case involving an ADA claim in which the plaintiff also filed a Social Security disability application, the Supreme Court held that the ADA and the Social Security Act were often consistent and could comfortably exist side by side. The Court noted that the ADA considered "reasonable accommodation" while the Social Security Act did not. The Supreme Court stated that an ADA plaintiff must explain the apparent contradiction when pursuing claims under both the ADA and the Social Security disability program.

§176.8 Evaluate the Listing of Impairments

Take a look at the appropriate section of the Listing of Impairments during the initial interview. With the claimant's help you may be able to put together an argument that the claimant's impairment meets the Listings.

§176.9 Past Relevant Work

Be sure you understand all the jobs the claimant did for the past 15 years. The dates are important for proof that the job was done more than 15 years ago, or that it wasn't done long enough to learn the job-both of which are reasons to exclude the job from consideration as past relevant work. The amount of earnings is important. If a job was not done at the substantial gainful activity level, it does not count as past relevant work. The exertional and skill levels of the jobs are important both for proof of inability to do the job now and for use of the Medical-Vocational Guidelines. Watch out for transferable skills.

Note that you will need more than 15 years of the claimant's job history in two circumstances. First, if the claimant's insured status has already lapsed, you need to know about the claimant's jobs for 15 years before the date last insured. Second, to evaluate whether the "worn out worker" rule, 20 C.F.R. § 404.1562, applies to claimants with a marginal education, you need 35 years of job history that shows "arduous unskilled work." *See* §119 on the worn out worker and §347 for more about past relevant work.

§176.10 Education

By the time you have completed your interview, especially if you have had the opportunity to review materials written by the claimant, you may have a good idea whether the claimant's highest grade completed in school is commensurate with his or her actual educational abilities. Often you will find significant disparity. There are a few instances, especially for claimants age 60 to 64, where this disparity may affect the result when the Medical-Vocational Guidelines are applied. *See* §121.1. Educational level is a crucial element of the "worn out worker" rule. *See* §119. Also, when cross-examining a vocational expert concerning jobs the claimant is allegedly capable of doing, you can sometimes reduce the number of jobs significantly by pointing out the claimant's actual educational level. Have the claimant's reading and math levels tested using the Wide Range Achievement Test (WRAT) if appropriate for the claimant's case. Attorneys underutilize this very useful approach.

§176.11 SSI Issues: Gifts, In-Kind Support, Loans and Assets

If a claimant is going to have continuing SSI eligibility either because there is only an SSI application or because the claimant's monthly Social Security disability benefit amount will be lower than the SSI benefit rate, take a look at how the claimant is making ends meet while the SSI application is pending:

(1) Is someone simply giving the claimant money to live on with no expectation of ever getting the money back?

(2) Is someone loaning the claimant money? If so, what is the understanding between the parties? Is there a written loan agreement?

(3) Is the claimant living with someone who is subsidizing the claimant by providing food and/or shelter? What is the nature of the arrangement between the parties?

(4) Is someone outside the household where the claimant lives providing what SSA calls "in-kind support" such as free or reduced rent in a house owned by that other person?

(5) Is someone else simply paying the claimant's bills? What sort of arrangement is this? Are these gifts or is there an understanding between the parties that the claimant will pay back the benefactor?

Gifts

There is a big difference between how SSA treats actual money given to a claimant and in-kind support. If someone is simply giving the claimant money to live on, the impact on the claimant's SSI benefits can be devastating. Such cash payments will be deducted from the claimant's potential SSI benefit dollar-for-dollar (except for the first $20, which is disregarded). 20 C.F.R. §§ 416.420 and 416.1124(c)(12). If someone is giving the claimant more than the amount of the federal SSI benefit rate plus any federally administered State SSI supplement plus $20, the claimant will not be eligible for SSI at all because the claimant is receiving too much countable income.

There is a simple solution to the gift problem that results in the claimant not losing more than about one-third of the federal SSI benefit rate. Instead of giving money to the claimant, if the claimant's benefactor directly pays the claimant's bills, SSA treats this as in-kind support. Although claimants probably see little difference between a father giving a claimant $500 to pay rent and the father paying the money directly to the claimant's landlord, the difference in the impact on SSI benefits is dramatic. Under SSA's rules, when someone pays the claimant's bills directly, SSA assumes that the value of such in-kind support is one-third of the federal SSI benefit rate plus $20. 20 C.F.R. § 416.1140. If the money passes through the claimant's hands, it is all treated as income. 20 C.F.R. § 416.1102. The reduction of potential SSI benefits is nearly dollar-for-dollar. Let's see how this works in practice.

Example: The claimant's father is giving the claimant a monthly check for $1,200, which the claimant uses to pay for shelter (rent, utilities, etc.), food, clothing and health insurance. This amount of monthly gift income is sufficient to disqualify the claimant for SSI in all 50 states. But, instead of giving money to the claimant, if the father directly pays the claimant's bills, the reduction in SSI is only one-third the federal benefit rate plus $20. Payment for food and shelter is treated as in-kind support, resulting in the reduction of benefits. Payment for clothing and health insurance doesn't count at all because "[i]ncome is anything you receive in cash or in kind that you can use to meet your needs for food and shelter." 20 C.F.R. § 416.1102.

Loans

There is another possible way to deal with gifts to a claimant which avoids any reduction of SSI at all. If, instead of giving money with no expectation of being paid back, the benefactor loans the claimant money in an arrangement that meets SSA's requirements for a valid loan, there will be no reduction of a claimant's monthly SSI benefit. 20 C.F.R. § 416.1103(f).

Loans do not count as income to a claimant. During the month a claimant receives a loan, SSA does not count it. If the claimant still has money left the next month, that money is counted as part of the claimant's resources, which are limited to $2,000 for an individual or $3,000 for a couple. POMS SI 01120.220C.1.a. Thus, taking out a second mortgage doesn't work if the claimant is going to have thousands of dollars sitting in a bank account. That money in the bank will be treated as a resource, which will disqualify a claimant from receiving SSI benefits. However, this isn't what SSI claimants often do; usually they borrow money monthly to pay bills.

If you discover that an SSI claimant is borrowing money to live on during the time the case is pending, which the claimant plans to repay after winning the case, your job is to make sure the arrangement meets SSA's requirements for a bona fide loan. Although SSA does not require it, it is best to put the loan in writing. A fuzzy understanding of informal loan terms often results in the loan being treated as a gift, even if the loan is ultimately repaid. SSA may quiz both the lender and the borrower about the terms of an oral loan, and if it finds an aspect of the loan that does not meet SSA's stringent loan requirements, it will treat the loan as a gift. The amount of any "gift" will be used to reduce SSI back benefits month-by-month around the time the money was received. *See* 20 C.F.R. § 416.420.

SSA requires that loans, even informal loans among family members, be legally enforceable under state law. If the loan meets all of SSA's requirements, it will not be treated as income and will not reduce the amount of back SSI benefits. *See* POMS SI 01120.220, part of which is reprinted at §426 of this book.

Watch out for this, however: Before you even got involved in the case, SSA may have already made a preemptive strike against money received by the claimant being treated as a loan. Around the time of the SSI application, SSA may have taken a statement from the claimant and from the benefactor that establishes that one or more of the elements of a bona fide loan are missing. *See* POMS SI 01120.220D. Under these circumstances, it is difficult, if not impossible, to argue that a bona fide loan existed from the time money was first received by the claimant from the benefactor. Indeed, in this very situation, SSA has been known to accuse lawyers of coaching a claimant to lie to SSA about the terms of an oral loan. Lawyers who are caught telling claimants to lie to SSA may lose their right to represent claimants before SSA. You need to be very careful. Nevertheless, after receiving legal advice from you, nothing prevents a claimant and benefactor from coming up with a new arrangement that applies from the day the new arrangement is put in writing. If the loan is bona fide, from the date of the new agreement, SSA will have to treat the money received as a loan.

SSA will recognize an informal loan, even an oral loan, if it contains all of the following elements of legal enforceability:

- The loan must be enforceable under state law;
- The agreement must be in effect at the time the money is loaned;
- The agreement must include the borrower's acknowledgment of the obligation to repay;
- The loan cannot be contingent on some event happening in the future such as receipt of SSI benefits;
- There must be a plan for repayment; and
- The repayment plan must be feasible.

See POMS SI 01120.220D reproduced at §426 of this book.

Beware of these problems. If the agreement between the claimant and benefactor is that the claimant will repay the loan *only* if the claimant is found eligible for SSI, SSA will say the loan is not valid because it is contingent. If the loan is impossible to repay even if the claimant gets SSI (because it is for more than the claimant will receive), SSA will say it is not a valid loan. Consider our example of the father who is giving his son $1,200 per month. Unless the claimant is expecting an inheritance or some other future income in addition to SSI, this is too much to be treated as a loan.

If you see to it that the claimant and lender have a bona fide written loan agreement, the loan cannot be treated as a gift by SSA and cannot be used to reduce SSI back benefits. *See* §425 for additional discussion and §176.11.1 for a sample loan agreement.

In-Kind Loans

If, instead of borrowing money, a claimant is supported by someone the claimant intends to repay once the case is won, the same rules apply. *See* §425. The claimant, in essence, is borrowing room and board, something that SSA calls an "in-kind loan." This loan agreement must be enforceable under state law or SSA will treat it as "in-kind income," which triggers reduction of SSI benefits, even where a claimant actually repays the "in-kind loan."

A common in-kind income situation is where a claimant moves in with a relative or friend who provides both room and board during the time the SSI case is pending. SSA calls this "living in another person's household." It requires a reduction of the claimant's SSI benefits of one-third of the federal benefit rate. 20 C.F.R. §§ 416.1131 and 416.1132. But if the claimant has an in-kind loan agreement, there will be no reduction in SSI benefits. *See* §425 and SSR 92-8p. *See* §176.11.2 for a sample loan agreement that will be useful when the claimant is living in another person's household.

When someone outside the claimant's household is paying the claimant's bills or providing a place for the claimant to live for free or at reduced cost, it is also possible to restructure the relationship to turn it into an in-kind loan. Consider our example of a claimant whose father is giving him $1,200 per month which, as we have pointed out, is probably too much to be turned into a loan. As mentioned earlier, if the father directly pays the claimant's bills, the reduction in the claimant's SSI benefits will be limited to one-third of the federal SSI benefit rate plus $20. But it is possible to turn part of this in-kind support into an in-kind loan. In-kind provision of anything other than food and shelter does not count against SSI benefits. 20 C.F.R. §§ 416.1102 and 416.1103(g). Therefore, the claimant could have an in-kind loan agreement with his father for any food and shelter provided by the father. And, consider this, if the father is providing support for the claimant and the claimant's family, SSA will accept a loan agreement for the claimant's *pro rata* share of the cost of food and shelter, which may be a manageable amount for a loan. *Pro rata* share is determined by dividing the value of the food and shelter by the number of people in the claimant's household regardless of age. *Cf.* 20 C.F.R. § 416.1133(b). With such a loan agreement in place, there will be no reduction of the claimant's SSI benefits.

A common situation for SSI claimants is where a claimant is living rent free in a house owned by a relative. SSA will treat this rental arrangement as in-kind income requiring a reduction of SSI benefits amounting to one-third of the federal benefit rate plus $20. 20 C.F.R. §§ 416.1140 and 416.1141. But it is possible to have an in-kind loan agreement so that there is no reduction of the claimant's benefits. This works especially well in the 2nd and 7th Circuits where court-fashioned rules limit the value of such rental agreements to one-third of the federal SSI benefit rate plus $20. *See* §424, 20 C.F.R. § 416.1130(b) and AR 90-2(2). A sample loan agreement appears at §176.11.3.

In other circuits, SSA will insist that there is in-kind income unless the claimant agrees to pay the current market value of the house. However, SSA will accept an agreement to repay the claimant's *pro rata* share of the current market value. Thus, there can be an agreement to repay an in-kind loan of $200 per month for an apartment with a current market value of $600 per month when the apartment is occupied by the claimant, spouse and child. *Cf.* POMS SI 00835.482.

Lawyers outside the 2nd and 7th Circuits have also suggested to claimants that they sign leases with the relative-owners of apartments that they are staying in without paying rent. Those who represent claimants know that it is not uncommon for a non-relative landlord to tell an SSI claimant that the landlord will wait until after the claimant wins the SSI claim to catch up on rent. SSA never challenges these arrangements—it never claims that there is in-kind income in this situation. But it is a different story when the landlord is a relative. The lease with a relative must require rent of at least the claimant's *pro rata* share of the current market value of the property or SSA may argue that there is still in-kind income. POMS SI 00835.380. Claims representatives also have been known to take the position that such a lease is not valid if the relative tells the SSA claims representative that he would never evict the claimant for non-payment of rent.

Assets

If it should come up in your initial interview with an SSI claimant that the claimant has non-exempt assets greater than $2,000 for an individual or $3,000 for a couple, 20 C.F.R. § 416.1205, the claimant will not be eligible for SSI until the claimant's assets get under the asset limit. The best way to reduce assets is for the claimant to buy exempt assets such as a house, household goods and personal effects, a car, a burial plot, *etc. See* 20 C.F.R. § 416.1210. Because there are limits on the value of some exempt assets, be sure to review the regulations before advising your client. It may also be possible, considering the amount at issue, for the claimant simply to spend the money. Be sure to tell the claimant to save receipts so that he or she can show SSA where the excess assets went. Also tell the claimant not to give the money away or transfer assets at less than current market value. This can result in ineligibility for 24 months. 20 C.F.R. § 416.1246.

§176.11.1 Form: Sample SSI Cash Loan Agreement

I, ________________________, agree to pay back ____________________ who has agreed to loan me $____ per month beginning ___________ during the time my SSI application is pending so that I can pay for food and rent. I will repay the loan when I receive payments for back SSI benefits. If I don't receive SSI benefits, I will pay this money back out of other future income.

Date: ________________ ____________________

____

§176.11.2 Form: Sample In-Kind Loan Agreement (Living in the Household of Another)

I, ________________, agree that I will pay back my *pro rata* share of rent, utilities, food and other household expenses to _________________, with whom I live, for each month I receive SSI back benefits beginning with the month of the date of this agreement. I will repay the loan when I receive payments for back SSI benefits. Once I start receiving my monthly SSI checks, I will pay my *pro rata* share of such expenses from that month forward. If I do not receive SSI, I will pay back this loan out of other future income.

My attorney, ___________________, advised me to make this agreement.

Date: ________________ ____________________

____

§176.11.3 Form: Sample In-Kind Loan Agreement With Person Outside the Household (7th and 2nd Circuits Only)

I, ________________, agree that I will pay back "in-kind support" received from ____________, (who is a person that I do not live in the same household with), for each month I receive SSI back benefits beginning with the month of this agreement. The value of the monthly in-kind support, which I will repay, is calculated as follows: one-third of the federal SSI benefit rate plus $20. I will repay the loan when I receive payments for back SSI benefits. If I do not receive SSI, I will pay back this loan out of other future income.

My attorney, ___________________, advised me to make this agreement.

Date: ________________ ____________________

____

§176.12Drug Addiction or Alcoholism

If a claimant's drug addiction or alcoholism is a "contributing factor material to the determination of disability," that claimant will be found ineligible for disability benefits from the Social Security Administration. 42 U.S.C. § 423(d)(2)(C) provides: "An individual shall not be considered to be disabled for purposes of this title if alcoholism or drug addiction would (but for this subparagraph) be a contributing factor material to the Commissioner's determination that the individual is disabled."

SSA applies the drug addiction and alcoholism rules to the sequential evaluation process by going through the sequential evaluation process twice. That is, the five-step sequential evaluation process is applied taking into consideration all of a claimant's limitations, including any that may arise from drug addiction or alcoholism. If the claimant is found not disabled at any point in the five-step process, then, of course, that ends the inquiry. But if the claimant is found disabled under the five-step process when considering all impairments, then the decision maker must apply the sequential evaluation process a second time while considering what limitations would remain if the claimant stopped using drugs or alcohol. This evaluation is described in 20 C.F.R. § 404.1535 as follows:

> (a) *General.* If we find that you are disabled and have medical evidence of your drug addiction or alcoholism, we must determine whether your drug addiction or alcoholism is a contributing factor material to the determination of disability.
>
> (b) *Process we will follow when we have medical evidence of your drug addiction or alcoholism.* (1) The key factor we will examine in determining whether drug addiction or alcoholism is a contributing factor material to the determination of disability is whether we would still find you disabled if you stopped using drugs or alcohol.
>
> (2) In making this determination, we will evaluate which of your current physical and mental limitations, upon which we based our current disability determination, would remain if you stopped using drugs or alcohol and then determine whether any or all of your remaining limitations would be disabling.
>
> (i) If we determine that your remaining limitations would not be disabling, we will find that your drug addiction or alcoholism is a contributing factor material to the determination of disability.
>
> (ii) If we determine that your remaining limitations are disabling, you are disabled independent of your drug addiction or alcoholism and we will find that your drug addiction or alcoholism is not a contributing factor material to the determination of disability.

SSA has set forth the evaluation steps in extensive detail in SSR 13-2p, which it summarized in a chart reproduced at § 176.13. Although the chart is useful for understanding the general principles of the SSA evaluation of drug addiction and alcoholism, when you are working on a case involving these, there is no substitute for reading and rereading SSR 13-2p. Don't rely only on this summary chart. SSR 13-2p contains valuable details that could win your client's case at the hearing. Indeed, SSR 13-2p is so complicated that it is unlikely an ALJ would successfully follow all of its directions, thus opening arguments for appeal.

As a threshold issue, the decision maker must first determine whether drug addiction or alcoholism is involved in the claimant's case. According to SSR 13-2p, there must be medical evidence from an acceptable medical source establishing that the claimant has a Substance Use Disorder as defined in the latest edition of the Diagnostic and Statistical Manual of Mental Disorders. However, the ruling provides that SSA does not include nicotine use disorders (now called Tobacco Use Disorder in DSM-5); and because Substance Use Disorders are diagnosed in part by the presence of maladaptive use of substances, SSA does not include addiction to prescription medications taken as prescribed. A history of binge drinking, or a history of maladaptive use of drugs or alcohol, is not sufficient to establish the diagnosis. Likewise, a history of drug addiction or alcoholism that is not relevant to the period under consideration does not require making a materiality determination.

A Substance Use Disorder, like all impairments, must be established by medical evidence. An individual's own statement that he is a drug addict or alcoholic is not, by itself, sufficient. Neither is an arrest for "driving under the influence" or a third party report. Even a "claimant's occasional maladaptive use" of drugs or alcohol does not establish that the claimant has a medically determinable Substance Use Disorder. Nevertheless, because of the broad nature of the criteria, a Substance Use Disorder is relatively easy for SSA to establish whenever, in DSM-5 terms, a "problematic pattern" of substance use leads to "clinically significant impairment or distress." SSA may order a consultative examination to establish the diagnosis of drug addiction or alcoholism, but SSA will never purchase drug or alcohol testing (because a single test is not sufficient to establish drug addiction or alcoholism as a medically determinable impairment).

The issue of whether drug addiction or alcoholism is material, however, can be considerably more difficult to determine than the diagnosis of a Substance Use Disorder:

Would the claimant be able to work if the claimant stopped using drugs or alcohol? 20 C.F.R. § 404.1535(b)(1). Nevertheless, this determination is easy when drug addiction or alcoholism is the only impairment. It is obviously material. *See* Step 3 on the SSR 13-2p chart in § 249.1.

When the other impairment is disabling by itself and is not medically caused by or affected by drug addiction or alcoholism, the determination that drug addiction or alcoholism is not material is also easy. *See* Step 5 on the SSR 13-2p chart.

When the other impairment is medically caused by or affected by drug addiction or alcoholism, we get to the really difficult determinations that are addressed in some detail by SSR 13-2p. This ruling describes different approaches for when the claimant's other impairment is mental compared to when it is physical.

For example, consider when the other impairment is cirrhosis of the liver medically caused by the claimant's drinking. The relevant inquiry is whether cirrhosis of the liver would continue to be disabling if the claimant stopped drinking now. That is, is it irreversible? To meet the claimant's burden of proving that drug addiction or alcoholism is not material, you may need the claimant's doctor's opinion on this issue. In SSR 13-2p, SSA says that the decision maker "may consider medical opinions from treating or nontreating sources about the likely effects that abstinence from drugs or alcohol would have on the impairment(s)." SSR 13-2p explains in a footnote that while an opinion whether drug addiction or alcoholism is "material" is an issue reserved to the Commissioner under 20 C.F.R. § 404.1527(d), "[i]n cases involving physical impairments, we may ask for medical opinions that project the nature, severity, and functional effects if the claimant were to stop using drugs or alcohol. In cases involving mental impairment(s) we will not ask for projections..."

SSR 13-2p provides: "We do not know of any research data that we can use to predict reliably that any given claimant's co-occurring mental disorder would improve, or the extent to which it would improve, if the claimant were to stop using drugs or alcohol." The ruling notes: "Unlike cases involving physical impairments, we do not permit adjudicators to rely exclusively on medical expertise and the nature of a claimant's mental disorder." Instead, the ruling says that SSA "must have evidence in the case record that establishes that a claimant with a co-occurring mental disorder(s) would not be disabled in the absence of DAA." The ruling says that even a period of abstinence because of hospitalization where the other mental impairment appears to improve is not enough. The other mental disorder "may appear to improve because of the structure and support provided in a highly structured treatment setting." SSR 13-2p says that:

> A single hospitalization or other inpatient intervention is not sufficient to establish that DAA is material when there is evidence that a claimant has a disabling co-occurring mental disorder(s). We need evidence from outside of such highly structured treatment settings demonstrating that the claimant's co-occurring mental disorder(s) has improved, or would improve, with abstinence. In addition, a record of multiple hospitalizations, emergency department visits, or other treatment for the co-occurring mental disorder—with or without treatment for DAA—is an indication that DAA may not be material even if the claimant is discharged in improved condition after each intervention.

The ruling says that SSA "will find that DAA is not material to the determination of disability and allow the claim if the record is fully developed and the evidence does not establish that the claimant's co-occurring mental disorder(s) would improve to the point of nondisability in the absence of DAA." In other words, a preponderance of the evidence other than medical opinions must establish "that a claimant with a co-occurring mental disorder(s) would not be disabled in the absence of DAA." Otherwise the claimant will be found disabled.

One of the biggest problems in representing an alcoholic or drug addict is that ALJs often assume that alcoholics and drug addicts are lying about their limitations from other impairments. Because many ALJs will bend over backwards before they will find an alcoholic or drug addict entitled to disability benefits, their cases present special challenges. SSR 13-2p addresses this issue:

> We do not have special rules for evaluating a claimant's credibility in cases involving DAA. Adjudicators must not presume that all claimants with DAA are inherently less credible than other claimants. We will apply our policy in SSR 96-7p and our regulations as in any other case, considering the facts of each case. In addition, adjudicators must consider a claimant's co-occurring mental disorder(s) when they evaluate the credibility of the claimant's allegations.

SSR 16-3p, which superseded SSR 96-7p, eliminated use of the term "credibility" to clarify that "subjective symptom evaluation is not an examination of an individual's character." Thus, the point made by SSR 13-2p is even stronger. ALJs may not assume that alcoholics and drug addicts are lying about their other impairments.

If drug addiction or alcoholism is found to exist but not to be a contributing factor material to the determination of disability, the claimant will be ordered to have a representative payee if the claimant is also found unable to manage his or her own benefits and referred for treatment. However, under current law there are no sanctions for failure to comply with treatment.

Practice Tip

Tell your client to stop drinking or using drugs. Although your client has probably ignored doctors' advice to stop for years, maybe hearing it from a lawyer will make a difference. After all, the best proof of disability in a case involving drug addiction or alcoholism comes after a claimant has stopped using drugs or alcohol. If, after a significant period of sobriety, a claimant remains incapable of working, the case becomes much easier to prove. Tell your client that lying about stopping will make the case more difficult.

§176.12.1 Chart: Is Drug Addiction or Alcoholism a Contributing Factor Material to the Determination of Disability?

1. Does the claimant have DAA?
   a.) No–No DAA materiality determination necessary.
   b.) Yes–Go to step 2.

2. Is the claimant disabled considering all impairments, including DAA?
   a.) No–Do not determine DAA materiality. (Denial.)
   b.) Yes–Go to step 3.

3. Is DAA the only impairment?
   a.) Yes–DAA material. (Denial.)
   b.) No–Go to step 4.

4. Is the other impairment(s) disabling by itself while the claimant is dependent upon or abusing drugs or alcohol?
   a.) No–DAA material. (Denial.)
   b.) Yes–Go to step 5.

5. Does the DAA cause or affect the claimant's medically determinable impairment(s)?
   a.) No–DAA not material. (Allowance.)
   b.) Yes, but the other impairment(s) is irreversible or could not improve to the point of nondisability–DAA not material. (Allowance.)
   c.) Yes, and DAA could be material–Go to step 6.

6. Would the other impairment(s) improve to the point of nondisability in the absence of DAA?
   a.) Yes–DAA material. (Denial.)
   b.) No–DAA not material (Allowance.)

From SSR 13-2p

§177 Begin Hearing Preparation at Initial Interview

Even if you're getting involved in a case below the hearing level, because most cases will end up going to a hearing, it is a good idea to begin hearing preparation at the initial interview. Explain to the claimant that you will try to win the case without a hearing; but often this is not possible. Anyway, a hearing is nothing to fear.

§177.1 Educate Claimant About Disability Law

At the initial interview, explain the peculiar way SSA looks at disability—the hypothetical approach. The issue is never whether the claimant can get a job. Rather, the issue is whether the claimant is capable of performing a job.

Claimants often think that proof of inability to get a job helps the case. Some uncounseled claimants have even been known to apply for jobs so that they can report to the ALJ: "see, I'm disabled; no one will hire me." In fact, many ALJs view the very fact that a claimant applied for a job as an admission that he or she is capable of doing the job. The ALJ's reasoning is: "why would anyone apply for a job if that person is not capable of doing the job?" Explain the "hireability" versus capability issue to the claimant at the initial interview.

Some claimants have an understandable tendency to exaggerate their impairments. They may have heard that they have to prove that they are "permanently and totally disabled." Explode this myth. Their disability does not have to be "permanent," it only has to last 12 months. And total disability doesn't mean bedridden. Even those who must prove inability to do a full range of sedentary work do not need to be bedridden to be found disabled.

Without confronting the claimant about any exaggerations you may perceive in his or her description of symptoms, work into your conversation the dangers of exaggerating symptoms when describing them to an ALJ—the ALJ simply won't believe it.

Another group of claimants tends to minimize impairments. Careful questioning is necessary to elicit an accurate description of the degree of impairments. If you find areas where a claimant has minimized impairments, point this out to the claimant. Make a note to discuss this problem with other members of the claimant's family.

§177.2 Put Claimant at Ease About Hearing Process

Tell the claimant about the hearing. Stress the informal, non-threatening nature of Social Security hearings, that the ALJ is not an adversary, that rough cross-examination is rare and that no one will try to trick the claimant. Explain that a disability hearing will be nothing like any court hearings the claimant has ever seen and certainly nothing like any television versions of court hearings the claimant may have watched. Do whatever you can to reassure the claimant. Putting the claimant at ease about the hearing is one of your most important jobs.

§177.3 Record Claimant's Strengths and Weaknesses as a Witness

Record your observations of the claimant, how the claimant looks, walks, sits, and how the claimant answers questions. And make a note of any special problems that need to be addressed when you meet the claimant to prepare to testify at the hearing. Such special problems may be identified as issues on the Analysis Form, §175.1.

§177.4 Identify Potential Witnesses

Find out from the claimant who might make a good witness to testify at the hearing. At the least, start the claimant thinking about this issue. Note that the sample letter to the claimant following the initial interview discusses this. *See* §183.

§177.5 Daily Diary

Consider whether or not a daily diary of some sort might be useful. For claimants who have trouble generalizing or providing sufficiently detailed information, the exercise of keeping a daily diary until the time of the hearing is excellent preparation for hearing testimony. You may ask the claimant to keep track of daily symptoms in a notebook.

For episodic impairments, seizures, headaches, or good or bad day issues, a diary helps quantify problems. Sometimes a monthly wall calendar can be used by a claimant to record bad days—days that the claimant would not be going to work if the claimant had a job. When more information is necessary, such as in cases involving seizures or headaches, it works well to provide the claimant with a form to complete. A sample monthly headache diary appears at §177.8.

Whether or not you decide to use the diary as evidence, it will help you and your client clarify issues and prepare for testimony at the hearing.

§177.6 List Things to Do

By the end of your interview, you may have a good idea of some medical or vocational records to order, doctor's reports to request, evaluations to be performed, issues to develop, witnesses to contact, *etc.* It is a good idea to make a list of these things right away. Space has been provided for a brief list on the Analysis Form, §175.1. A more extensive Intake Action Sheet is provided at §177.7. Order records that you are sure SSA has not already obtained. Unless the hearing is already scheduled and coming up soon, hold off ordering other medical records until you have seen SSA's file on your client.

Consider whether you should request a report from the claimant's treating doctor right away. Do not request a report right away if you have any doubts about your understanding of the claimant's impairments or if it will be many months before the duration requirement is met and the claimant's impairment is the kind that might improve. Whenever you learn that the claimant is changing doctors, consider requesting a report right away. If you wait, it is likely that the former doctor will tell you that a report cannot be completed because it has been so many months since the doctor has seen the claimant. If a claimant is planning surgery or some other treatment that might improve his or her condition, requesting a pre-treatment report may give you a snapshot of the claimant's condition at that time, which may form the basis for granting a closed period of disability.

§177.7 Form: Intake Action Sheet

Name: ______________________ Date: _________________

☐ Letter to Local Office:

- ☐ New Application Letter
- ☐ Cover Letter (in a pending case) With:
  - ☐ Request for Reconsideration
  - ☐ Request for Hearing
  - ☐ Disability Report—Appeal
  - ☐ Signed Releases
  - ☐ Appointment of Representative Form
  - ☐ Attorney or Client Fee Agreement
  - ☐ Direct Payment of Authorized Fees Form SSA-1695
  - ☐ cc to Office of Disability Adjudication and Review
  - ☐ cc to Client With Fee Agreement
  - ☐ cc to Disability Determination Bureau With Enclosures
  - ☐ Re-Open Prior Application
  - ☐ Request Local Hearing
  - ☐ Appealing Onset Date Only
  - ☐ Opening Letter to Client
  - ☐ Thank You Letter to Referral Source
  - ☐ Letter to Client With Diary:
    - ☐ Seizure Diary
    - ☐ Headache Diary
    - ☐ MS Diary
    - ☐ Other: ___________________
  - ☐ Letter to Disability Determination Bureau: ☐ Now ☐ Send in 30 Days

☐ Request Medical CE

☐ Request Psych CE

☐ Request State Agency RFCs (both physical and mental)

☐ Request State Agency "Electronic Worksheet" and/or Rationale for Denying Claim

☐ Supply Additional Medical Records

a.

b.

c.

☐ Supply Photos

☐ Other: _______________

☐ Letter to Local Office Requesting eDib File (CD)

☐ Letter to Office of Disability Adjudication and Review

☐ Request DISCO DIB Earnings Record

☐ National Directory New Hire, Wage and Unemployment Report for the Following Years: ______________________

☐ Detailed Earning Report: ___________ to Present

☐ Other: ______________________________

☐ Letter to Former Employer (_______________) Requesting Confirmation of Last Day of Work

☐ Letter to Former Employer Requesting Personnel File (specify portion or specific documents)

☐ Letter to Medical Providers Requesting Records:

a. _______________ covering _______________

b. _______________ covering _______________

c. _______________ covering _______________

d. _______________ covering _______________

☐ Letter to Vocational Rehabilitation Agency Requesting Copy of File

☐ Run Client Through Legal Database

§177.8 Form: Monthly Headache Diary

Month/Year: ______________________

Name: ______________________

Date	1	2	3	4	5	6	7	8	9	10	11	12	13	14	15	16	17	18	19	20	21	22	23	24	25	26	27	28	29	30	31
	Did you have a headache today?																														
Yes																															
No																															
	Intensity of Headache: MILD—able to function; MODERATE—unable to function/bed rest not needed; SEVERE—bed rest req.																														
Mild																															
Moderate																															
Severe																															
	Duration of this headache?																														
Less than 4 Hours																															
4-12 Hours																															
13-24 Hours																															
	Symptoms of this headache. Please mark all that apply.																														
Aura Colors																															
Nausea/Vomiting																															
Light Sensitivity																															
Personality Change																															
Dizziness/Vertigo																															
Numbness/Tingling																															
Motor Impairment																															
Double Vision																															
Other Vision Symptoms																															
Speech Impairment																															
	Medications taken for treatment of this headache. Please also indicate medications taken other than daily medications.																														

§178 Necessary Forms

§178.1 Consent Forms

Have the claimant sign medical consent forms, employment information consent forms and other consent forms as appropriate.

§178.2 SSA Forms

Have the claimant sign an Appointment of Representative form, a sample of which follows at §178.2.1. An individual lawyer is supposed to be named as the representative. SSA will not allow a law firm or other organization to be appointed as the representative (though in recent years SSA has been considering the feasibility of this). If a firm name is entered on the form as the representative, SSA will treat the lawyer who signs accepting the appointment as the appointed representative. POMS GN 03910.040H.3.

Although you're not supposed to name a law firm as the representative, you can name multiple lawyers as representatives if you want (though many lawyers are coming to view this as a bad idea because SSA's rules say that fee petitions must be filed to obtain the fee if an appointed representative leaves the firm). If you appoint multiple lawyers as representatives, you can do so using one form, although SSA suggests using one form for each representative. SSA says that the Appointment of Representative form should indicate which representative is the main representative so that it knows to whom to send copies of notices in the case. SSA policy is to send copies of notices to only one representative. POMS GN 03910.040D.

Although 20 C.F.R. § 404.1707(b) requires only non-attorneys to sign the Appointment of Representative form accepting the appointment, since signing the form is "strongly encouraged" by SSA as a way of indicating that the attorney has the necessary qualifications and will abide by the rules governing attorney fees, most attorneys, in fact, do enter their signatures on the form. SSA accepts rubber stamped signatures. POMS GN 03910.040B.1.

Some law firms appoint only a principal of the firm as the representative even though it is understood from the beginning that an associate will appear at the hearing. Law firms do this in an effort to get the attorney fee check paid in the name of the principal of the firm and to avoid having to file a fee petition if the associate leaves the firm. As a rule, a check for attorney fees will come in the name of the attorney first appointed because when the attorneys are in the same firm, no one at SSA bothers to add a representative in SSA's computer when a different member of the firm shows up at the hearing. The HALLEX provides that if someone else from the firm (other than the attorney named as the representative on the Appointment of Representative form) shows up at the hearing, the ALJ is to treat that person as an additional appointed representative. HALLEX I-1-2-12 C.3.b. However, if SSA does recognize the attorney who showed up at the hearing as an officially appointed representative and SSA applies the rule that says the fee must be divided between appointed representatives, unless the associate attorney files an SSA-1695, *see* §178.4, the associate attorney will not be paid directly by SSA.

Other law firms appoint as representative the associate attorney who will appear at the hearing and also name a principal of the firm as a representative. Firms that do this and firms that appoint only a principal of the firm say either approach is better than appointing only the associate as representative because of potential transition problems if the associate leaves the firm. This practice ensures that someone at the firm is entitled to receive copies of decisions and award letters in the claimant's case, but it does not ensure that the fee will be paid under the fee agreement process.

If an associate who is appointed as one of two or more representatives leaves the firm, the fee is not supposed to be paid under the fee agreement process. Although this does not always happen in practice, the fee agreement is supposed to be disapproved and all appointed representatives are supposed to file fee petitions. This rule illustrates SSA's policy to avoid entanglement in attorney fee disputes between representatives. *See* §709.

The best solution for potential problems with attorney fees when an associate leaves the firm is to deal with them in advance in an employment contract between the firm and the associate. For example, an employment contract could make it clear that all fees received by the associate belong to the firm, could require the associate after leaving the firm to pay to the firm any fees received directly from SSA, could grant the firm authority to sign any checks received from SSA in the associate's name and require the associate to help with submitting a fee petition if one is deemed necessary by SSA.

If clerks, paralegals, associate attorneys, or anyone else from your office (or a copying service hired by your firm) will be involved in obtaining copies of records from SSA, be sure to check the box on the Appointment of Representative form (which we have checked on the sample form at §178.2.1) that allows SSA to release information from the claimant's file to them: "I authorize the Social Security Administration to release information about my pending claim(s) or asserted right(s) to designated associates who perform administrative duties (*e.g.*, clerks), partners and/ or parties under contractual arrangements (*e.g.*, copying services) for or with my representative."

When this box is checked on the Appointment of Representative form, POMS GN 03305.025B applies: "If we receive a notice of appointment (SSA-1696-U4 or equivalent writing) authorizing us to release records to a designated associate, a separate SSA-3288 (or other consent form meeting our requirements) is not required as long as the appointed representative is representing the individual in a matter currently pending with SSA." Because someone at SSA may ask for proof that the person who shows up to copy a file is a "designated associate," it is a good idea for the firm employee to take along a letter signed by the appointed representative that says the employee is a "designated associate."

Although the same procedure should apply if you are using a copying service, see POMS GN 03305.025B, someone at the local office may try to take a more stringent position on copying services based on misinterpreting GN 03305.025A, which provides: "Do not disclose the requested information to a copying service or other company performing administrative services unless that entity is named separately on the consent form." This section of POMS applies if you use a copying service to copy a claimant's file before you have been appointed as the claimant's representative. To avoid arguments, some attorneys make it a practice to obtain a claimant's signature on a Form SSA-3288 when they are using a copying service.

If you want to send an employee or a copying service to copy a claimant's file before you have been appointed as the claimant's representative, you will need to obtain the claimant's signature on a Form SSA-3288. See § 178.2.5 Consent for Release of Information, Form SSA-3288. Although SSA won't allow a law firm to be appointed as a representative, it will release information to a law firm. Thus, a law firm name can be entered on the SSA-3288. See POMS GN 03305.025A and GN 03910.025.2. Note that the instructions for the Form SSA-3288 state that SSA will not honor the form unless all required fields (identified by asterisks) are completed and that SSA "will not honor blanket requests for 'all records' or the 'entire file.'"

The Appointment of Representative form asks you to indicate the nature of your fee arrangement and sign the form a second time. On the sample form in this book, we have checked the box indicating that you will be charging a fee and requesting direct payment, but checking this box is not the only thing you need to do obtain direct payment of your fee. You also need to register (which you generally need to do only once) and you need to submit a form SSA-1695 in every case. *See* §178.4.

If you want direct payment of your entire fee by SSA, do not have a paralegal sign an Appointment of Representative form as a representative in a disability case unless the paralegal has been qualified by SSA as eligible for direct payment of fees. If an attorney and a non-qualified paralegal both submit Appointment of Representative forms, SSA is supposed to send one-half of the approved fee to the attorney and notify the parties that the non-attorney's half of the fee must be collected from the claimant.

SSA will accept a fax or photocopy of the SSA-1696. POMS GN 03910.040B.1.

If an appeal is due, complete a Request for Reconsideration or Request for Hearing along with a Disability Report—Appeal online at SSA's website at https://secure.ssa.gov/apps6z/iAppeals/ap001.jsp. If you want direct payment of your fee, SSA requires you to file appeals and the Disability Report—Appeal online. *See* §178.6. Be sure to print the receipt for the appeal and a copy of the Disability Report—Appeal. It will still be necessary to submit a paper Authorization to Disclose Information to the Social Security Administration (Form SSA-827), §178.2.4, signed by the claimant along with the Appointment of Representative form and contract.

Because you are filing the appeal, your client will not have the option of electronically signing the SSA-827 online. Also note that because you are involved in the case, SSA is unlikely to use the signed authorization to release information to SSA, Form SSA-827. Nevertheless, if you do not provide this signed paper form to SSA, someone from the local office will contact you or your client about submitting a signed authorization and the local office may delay forwarding your client's file to the hearing office until you do so.

You will not be able to appeal online in cases involving disability cessations, partially favorable decisions, date of onset decisions, and non-medical appeals. It will be necessary to submit a paper appeal in such cases. The only other time you need to use a paper Request for Hearing, §178.2.2, or Request for Reconsideration, and paper Disability Report—Appeal, §178.2.3, is when SSA's website or your Internet access is down and your client's time for appeal is running out. Note that SSA will accept faxed appeal requests. POMS GN 03103.010B.5.

The sample letter, which appears at §183, can be used for transmitting documents to the local Social Security office when you request a hearing. If you are requesting reconsideration, use the letter §193.

If a hearing has already been requested, send a completed Appointment of Representative form to the hearing office along with requests that you be notified when the hearing exhibits are numbered, that you be told how you can obtain a copy of your client's hearing exhibit file, and that you be contacted before scheduling the case for hearing so that you can avoid conflicts in your schedule. A sample letter appears at §182. A copy of the Appointment of Representative form and contract with the claimant is also sent to the claimant's Social Security office along with a letter (§184) which encloses an SSA-1695 (§178.4.2), a form required in all cases where you submit an Appointment of Representative form after January 1, 2007, if you want direct payment of your fee. *See* §178.4.

§178.2.1 Form: Appointment of Representative (SSA-1696-U6)

COMPLETING THIS FORM TO APPOINT A REPRESENTATIVE

Choosing to be Represented

You can choose to have a representative help you when you do business with Social Security. We will work with your representative, just as we would with you. It is important that you select a qualified person because, once appointed, your representative may act for you in most Social Security matters. We give more information, and examples of what a representative may do, in the section titled "Information for Claimants."

Privacy Act Statement
Collection and Use of Personal Information

Sections 206(a) and 1631(d) of the Social Security Act, as amended, authorize us to collect this information. We will use the information you provide on this form to verify your appointment of an individual as your representative and his or her acceptance of the appointment. Furnishing us this information is voluntary. However, if you want to use this form to appoint someone to act on your behalf in matters before the Social Security Administration (SSA), then you and that individual must complete the appropriate sections of this form.
We rarely use the information you supply for any purpose other than to verify your appointment of an individual as your representative and his or her acceptance of the appointment. However, we may use the information for the administration of our programs including sharing information:

1. To comply with Federal laws requiring the release of information from our records (e.g., to the Government Accountability Office and Department of Veterans Affairs); and,

2. To facilitate statistical research, audit, or investigative activities necessary to assure the integrity and improvement of our programs (eg., to the Bureau of the Census and to private entities under contract with us).

A complete list of when we may share your information with others, called routine uses, is available in our Privacy Act System of Records Notice entitled, Appointed Representative File, 60-0325. Additional information about this and other system of records notices and our programs are available from our Internet website at www.socialsecurity.gov or at your local Social Security office. We may share the information you provide to other health agencies through computer matching programs. Matching programs compare our records with records kept by other Federal, State, or local government agencies. We use the information from these programs to establish or verify a person's eligibility for federally funded or administered benefit programs and for repayment of incorrect payments or delinquent debts under these programs.

How to Complete this Form

Please print or type your answers on this form. At the top of the form, provide your full name and your Social Security number. If your claim is based on another person's work and earnings, also provide the "wage earner's" name and Social Security number. If you appoint more than one individual as your representative, you may want to complete a form for each of them.

Part I Claimant's Appointment of Representative
Give the name and address of the individual(s) you are appointing. You may appoint an attorney or any other qualified individual to represent you. You also may appoint more than one individual, but please refer to the "Information for Claimants" section "What your Representative(s) May Charge" for more information about payment of fees. You can appoint one or more individuals in a firm, corporation, or other organization as your representative(s), but you may not appoint a law firm, legal aid group, corporation or organization itself.

Check the block(s) showing the program(s) under which you have a claim. You may check more than one block. Check:

- Title II (RSDI), if your claim concerns retirement, survivors, or disability insurance benefits.
- Title XVI (SSI), if your claim concerns Supplemental Security Income.
- Title XVIII (Medicare Coverage), if your claim concerns entitlement to Medicare or enrollment in the Supplementary Medical Insurance (SMI) plan.
- Title VIII (SVB), if your claim concerns entitlement to Special Veterans Benefits.

When you give your permission your representative may designate an associate (e.g. a clerk), or other party or entity (e.g. a copying service) to receive information from your claim file on your representative's behalf for the duration of your claim. If you want to give your representative permission to do that, check the block to authorize this release.

If you will have more than one representative, check the appropriate block and give the name of the individual you want to be your principal representative. SSA will make contacts with, and send notices or requests for development to, only the principal representative. The principal representative will provide copies of notices or requests to other co-representatives.

You must sign and date the form. Print or type your address, area code and telephone number.

If you are appointing a representative to replace a representative that you discharged or who withdrew his or her representation, you must notify us in writing that the prior appointment has ended.

Form **SSA-1696-U4** (07-2014) ef (07-2014)
Use Prior Editions Until Exhausted

Part II Representative's Acceptance of Appointment

Each individual you appoint in Part I should also complete Part II. If the individual is not an attorney, he or she must give his or her name, state that he or she accepts the appointment, and sign the form.

Part III Fee Arrangement

To help in processing benefits and fee payments timely you and your representative should complete this section. Your representative should check a box, sign and date the form. Your representative may choose to receive payment, waive direct payment, or waive payment of the fee altogether. If you and your representative change your arrangement before we decide your claim, you can provide a new or amended form so that we can update our records. If you appoint a second representative or co-counsel who also will not charge a fee, he or she should also complete this part or provide a new form, or if not using the form, give us a separate, written waiver statement. If your representative is not eligible for direct payment, or is an attorney or an eligible non-attorney who waives direct payment, you will be responsible for paying any fee we authorize.

Under certain circumstances, we do not have to authorize the fee. These circumstances include where a Court has awarded a fee based on your representative's actions as a legal guardian or court-appointed representative, or where a business (such as an insurance company), other organization or government agency will pay your representative's fee and you and your beneficiaries have no liability to pay any fees or expenses.

Paperwork Reduction Act Statement - This information collection meets the requirements of 44 U.S.C. § 3507, as amended by Section 2 of the Paperwork Reduction Act of 1995. You do not need to answer these questions unless we display a valid Office of Management and Budget control number. We estimate that it will take about 10 minutes to read the instructions, gather the facts, and answer the questions. **SEND THE COMPLETED FORM TO YOUR LOCAL SOCIAL SECURITY OFFICE. The office is listed under U. S. Government agencies in your telephone directory or you may call Social Security at 1-800-772-1213 (TTY 1-800-325-0778).** *You may send comments on our time estimate above to: SSA, 6401 Security Blvd, Baltimore, MD 21235-6401. Send **only** comments relating to our time estimate to this address, not the completed form.*

References

- 18 U.S.C. §§ 203, 205, and 207; and 42 U.S. C. §§ 406 (a), 1320a-6, and 1383(d)(2)
- 20 CFR §§ 404.1700 et. seq., 408.1101, and 416.1500 et. seq.
- Social Security Rulings 83-27 and 82-39
- 26 U.S.C. §§ 6041 and 6045(f)

Form **SSA-1696-U4** (07-2014) ef (07-2014)

INFORMATION FOR REPRESENTATIVES

Fees for Representation
An attorney or other individual who wants to charge or collect a fee for providing services in connection with a claim before the Social Security Administration (SSA) must generally obtain our prior authorization of the fee for representation. The only exceptions are if:

- certain requirements are met and a third-party entity, such as a business, an insurance carrier, a for profit, or nonprofit organization or a government agency will pay the fee and any expenses from its own funds and the claimant and auxiliary beneficiaries incur no liability, directly or indirectly, for the cost(s); or
- a Federal court awarded a fee based on the representative's activities as the claimant's legal guardian or court-appointed representative;
- a Federal court awarded a fee for representational services provided before the court. In those cases, neither the Federal court nor SSA can authorize a fee for the other.

Obtaining Authorization of a Fee
To charge a fee for services, you must use one of two mutually exclusive fee authorization processes. You must file either a fee petition or a fee agreement with us. In either case, you cannot charge more than the fee amount we authorize.

Fee Petition Process

You may file a fee petition after you complete your services to the claimant. This written request must describe in detail the amount of time you spent on each service provided and the amount of the fee you are requesting. In order to directly pay you under a fee petition, you must either file a fee petition or notify us within 60 days after we decide the claim of your intent to file a fee petition.

You must give the claimant a copy of the fee petition and each attachment. The claimant may disagree with the information shown by contacting a Social Security office within 20 days of receiving his or her copy of the fee petition. We will consider the reasonable value of the services provided, and send you notice of the amount of the fee you can charge.

Fee Agreement Process
If you and the claimant have a written fee agreement, one of you must give it to us before we decide the claim(s). We usually will approve the agreement if:

- you both signed it;
- the fee you agreed on is no more than 25 percent of past-due benefits, or $6,000 (or a higher amount we set and announce in the Federal Register), whichever is less;
- we approve the claim(s); and
- the claim results in past-due benefits.

We will send you a copy of the notice we send the claimant telling him or her the amount of the fee you can charge based on the agreement.

If we do not approve the fee agreement, we will tell you in writing. We also will tell you and the claimant that you must file a fee petition if you wish to charge and collect a fee.

After we tell you the amount of the fee you can charge, you or the claimant may ask us in writing to review the authorized fee. If we approved a fee agreement, the person who decided the claim(s) also may ask us to lower the amount. Someone who did not decide the amount of the fee the first time will review and finally decide the amount of the fee.

Collecting a Fee
You may accept money for your fee in advance, as long as you hold it in a trust or escrow account. The claimant never owes you more than the fee we authorize, except for:

- any fee a Federal court allows for your services before it; and
- out-of-pocket expenses you incur or expect to incur, for example, the cost of getting evidence. Our authorization is not needed for such expenses.

If you are not an attorney and you are ineligible to receive direct payment, you must collect the authorized fee from the claimant. If you are interested in becoming eligible to receive direct payment, you can find more information about this on our "Representing Social Security Claimants" website:
http://www.ssa.gov/representation/.

If you are an attorney or a non-attorney whom SSA has found eligible to receive direct payment and you register with SSA, as described below, we usually withhold 25 percent of any past-due benefits that result from a favorably decided retirement, survivors, disability insurance, or supplemental security income claim. Once we authorize a fee, we pay you all or part of the fee from the funds withheld. We will also charge you the assessment required by section 206(d) and 1631(d)(2)(C) of the Social Security Act. You cannot charge or collect this expense from the claimant. You will need to collect from the claimant:

- **the rest of the fee he or she owes,** if the amount of the authorized fee is more than the amount of money we withheld and paid you for the claimant, plus any amount you held for the claimant in a trust or escrow account.
- **all of the fee he or she owes,** if we did not withhold past-due benefits, (for example, because there are no past-due benefits; you waived direct payment or did not register for direct payment; the claimant discharged you or you withdrew from representing before we issued a favorable decision); or we withheld past-due benefits, but you did not ask us to authorize a fee or tell us that you planned to ask for a fee within 60 days after the date of the notice of award and we released the withheld amount to the claimant.

Registering for Direct Fee Payment

If you are eligible and want to receive direct payment, you must register with us before we effectuate a favorable decision on the claim. To register, you must submit a Form SSA-1699 (Registration of Individuals and Staff for Appointed Representative Services) once and a Form SSA-1695 (Identifying Information for Possible Direct Payment of Authorized Fees) with each appointment. We will use the information you provide on these forms to issue you a Form 1099-MISC if we pay you aggregate fees of $600 or more in a calendar year. The Internal Revenue Code requires that we do this. For information on the registration process, see our "Representing Social Security Claimants" website http://www.ssa.gov/representation/.

Conflict of Interest and Penalties

If you commit improper acts, you can be suspended or disqualified from representing anyone before SSA. You also can face criminal prosecution. Improper acts include:

- If you are or were an officer or employee of the United States, providing services as a representative in certain claims against and other matters affecting the Federal government.
- Knowingly and willingly furnishing false information.
- Charging or collecting an unauthorized fee, or charging or collecting too much for services provided in any claim, including services before a court that made a favorable decision.

References

- 18 U.S.C. §§ 203, 205, and 207; and 42 U.S.C. §§ 406 (a), 1320a-6, and 1383(d)(2)
- 20 CFR §§ 404.1700 et. seq., 408.1101, and 416.1500 et. seq.
- Social Security Rulings 83-27 and 82-39
- 26 U.S.C. §§ 6041 and 6045(f)

Form **SSA-1696-U4** (07-2014) ef (07-2014)

Social Security Administration
Please read the instructions before completing this form.

Form Approved
OMB No. 0960-0527

Name (Claimant) (Print or Type)	Social Security Number
Wage Earner (If Different)	Social Security Number

Part I **CLAIMANT'S APPOINTMENT OF REPRESENTATIVE**

I appoint this individual, ____________________
(Name and Address)

to act as my representative in connection with my claim(s) or asserted right(s) under:

☐ Title II (RSDI) ☐ Title XVI (SSI) ☐ Title XVIII (Medicare) ☐ Title VIII (SVB)

This individual may, entirely in my place, make any request or give any notice; give or draw out evidence or information; get information; and receive any notice in connection with my pending claim(s) or asserted right(s).

☐ I authorize the Social Security Administration to release information about my pending claim(s) or asserted right(s) to designated associates who perform administrative duties (e.g. clerks), partners, and/or parties under contractual arrangements (e.g. copying services) for or with my representative.

☐ I appoint, or I now have, more than one representative. My principal representative is:

____
(Name of Principal Representative)

Signature (Claimant)	Address	
Telephone Number (with Area Code)	Fax Number (with Area Code)	Date

Part II **REPRESENTATIVE'S ACCEPTANCE OF APPOINTMENT**

I, ____________________, hereby accept the above appointment. I certify that I have not been suspended or prohibited from practice before the Social Security Administration; that I am not disqualified from representing the claimant as a current or former officer or employee of the United States; and that I will not charge or collect any fee for the representation, even if a third party will pay the fee, unless it has been approved in accordance with the laws and rules referred to on the reverse side of the representative's copy of this form. If I decide not to charge or collect a fee for the representation, I will notify the Social Security Administration. (Completion of Part III satisfies this requirement.)

Check one: ☐ I am an attorney. ☐ I am a non-attorney eligible for direct payment under SSA law.
☐ I am a non-attorney not eligible for direct payment.

I am now or have previously been disbarred or suspended from a court or bar to which I was previously admitted to practice as an attorney. ☐ YES ☐ NO

I am now or have previously been disqualified from participating in or appearing before a Federal program or agency.
☐ YES ☐ NO

I declare under penalty of perjury that I have examined all the information on this form, and on any accompanying statements or forms, and it is true and correct to the best of my knowledge.

Signature (Representative)	Address	
Telephone Number (with Area Code)	Fax Number (with Area Code)	Date

Part III **FEE ARRANGEMENT**

(Select an option, sign and date this section.)

☐ **I am charging a fee and requesting direct payment** of the fee from withheld past-due benefits. *(SSA must authorize the fee unless a regulatory exception applies.)*

☐ **I am charging a fee but waiving direct payment** of the fee from withheld past-due benefits --I do not qualify for or do not request direct payment. *(SSA must authorize the fee unless a regulatory exception applies.)*

☐ **I am waiving fees and expenses from the claimant and any auxiliary beneficiaries** --By checking this block I certify that my fee will be paid by a third-party entity or government agency, and that the claimant and any auxiliary beneficiaries are free of all liability, directly or indirectly, in whole or in part, to pay any fee or expenses to me or anyone as a result of their claim(s) or asserted right(s). *(SSA does not need to authorize the fee if a third-party entity or a government agency will pay from its funds the fee and any expenses for this appointment. Do not check this block if a third-party individual will pay the fee.)*

☐ **I am waiving fees from any source** --I am waiving my right to charge and collect any fee, under sections 206 and 1631 (d)(2) of the Social Security Act. I release my client and any auxiliary beneficiaries from any obligations, contractual or otherwise, which may be owed to me for services provided in connection with their claim(s) or asserted right(s).

Signature (Representative)	Date

Form SSA-1696-U4 (07-2014) ef (07-2014)
Use Prior Editions Until Exhausted

FILE COPY

Social Security Administration
Please read the instructions before completing this form.

Form Approved
OMB No. 0960-0527

Name (Claimant) (Print or Type)	Social Security Number
Wage Earner (If Different)	Social Security Number

Part I
CLAIMANT'S APPOINTMENT OF REPRESENTATIVE

I appoint this individual, ______________________________
(Name and Address)

to act as my representative in connection with my claim(s) or asserted right(s) under:

☐ Title II(RSDI) ☐ Title XVI (SSI) ☐ Title XVIII (Medicare) ☐ Title VIII (SVB)

This individual may, entirely in my place, make any request or give any notice; give or draw out evidence or information; get information; and receive any notice in connection with my pending claim(s) or asserted right(s).

☐ I authorize the Social Security Administration to release information about my pending claim(s) or asserted right(s) to designated associates who perform administrative duties (e.g. clerks), partners, and/or parties under contractual arrangements (e.g. copying services) for or with my representative.

☐ I appoint, or I now have, more than one representative. My principal representative is:

____
(Name of Principal Representative)

Signature (Claimant)	Address	
Telephone Number (with Area Code)	Fax Number (with Area Code)	Date

Part II
REPRESENTATIVE'S ACCEPTANCE OF APPOINTMENT

I, ______________________________, hereby accept the above appointment. I certify that I have not been suspended or prohibited from practice before the Social Security Administration; that I am not disqualified from representing the claimant as a current or former officer or employee of the United States; and that I will not charge or collect any fee for the representation, even if a third party will pay the fee, unless it has been approved in accordance with the laws and rules referred to on the reverse side of the representative's copy of this form. If I decide not to charge or collect a fee for the representation, I will notify the Social Security Administration. (Completion of Part III satisfies this requirement.)

Check one: ☐ I am an attorney. ☐ I am a non-attorney eligible for direct payment under SSA law.
☐ I am a non-attorney not eligible for direct payment.

I am now or have previously been disbarred or suspended from a court or bar to which I was previously admitted to practice as an attorney. ☐ YES ☐ NO

I am now or have previously been disqualified from participating in or appearing before a Federal program or agency. ☐ YES ☐ NO

I declare under penalty of perjury that I have examined all the information on this form, and on any accompanying statements or forms, and it is true and correct to the best of my knowledge.

Signature (Representative)	Address	
Telephone Number (with Area Code)	Fax Number (with Area Code)	Date

Part III
FEE ARRANGEMENT

(Select an option, sign and date this section.)

☐ **I am charging a fee and requesting direct payment** of the fee from withheld past-due benefits. *(SSA must authorize the fee unless a regulatory exception applies.)*

☐ **I am charging a fee but waiving direct payment** of the fee from withheld past-due benefits —I do not qualify for or do not request direct payment. *(SSA must authorize the fee unless a regulatory exception applies.)*

☐ **I am waiving fees and expenses from the claimant and any auxiliary beneficiaries** —By checking this block I certify that my fee will be paid by a third-party entity or government agency, and that the claimant and any auxiliary beneficiaries are free of all liability, directly or indirectly, in whole or in part, to pay any fee or expenses to me or anyone as a result of their claim(s) or asserted right(s). *(SSA does not need to authorize the fee if a third-party entity or a government agency will pay from its funds the fee and any expenses for this appointment. Do not check this block if a third-party individual will pay the fee.)*

☐ **I am waiving fees from any source** —I am waiving my right to charge and collect any fee, under sections 206 and 1631 (d)(2) of the Social Security Act. I release my client and any auxiliary beneficiaries from any obligations, contractual or otherwise, which may be owed to me for services provided in connection with their claim(s) or asserted right(s).

Signature (Representative)	Date

Form SSA-1696-U4 (07-2014) ef (07-2014)
Use Prior Editions Until Exhausted

CLAIMANT COPY

INFORMATION FOR CLAIMANTS

What Your Representative(s) May Do
We will work directly with your appointed representative unless he or she asks us to work directly with you. Your representative may:

- get information from your claim(s) file;
- with your permission, designate associates who perform administrative duties (e.g. clerks), partners and/or parties under contractual arrangements (e.g., copying services) to receive information from us on his or her behalf (by checking the appropriate block and signing this form, you are providing your permission for your representative to designate such associates, partners, and/or contractual parties);
- give us evidence or information to support your claim;
- come with you, or for you, to any interview, conference, or hearing you have with us;
- request a reconsideration, a hearing, or Appeals Council review; and
- help you and your witnesses prepare for a hearing and question any witnesses.

Also, your representative will receive a copy of the decision(s) we make on your claim(s). We will rely on your representative to tell you about the status of your claim(s), but you still may call or visit us for information.

You and your representative(s) are responsible for giving Social Security accurate information. It is wrong to knowingly and willingly furnish false information. Doing so may result in criminal prosecution.

We usually continue to work with your representative until (1) you notify us in writing that he or she no longer represents you; or (2) your representative tells us that he or she is withdrawing or indicates that his or her services have ended (for example, by filing a fee petition or not pursuing an appeal). We do not continue to work with someone who is suspended or disqualified from representing claimants. We will inform you if we suspend your representative.

What Your Representative(s) May Charge
Each representative you appoint can ask for a fee. To charge you a fee for services, your representative must get our authorization if you or another individual will pay the fee. However, as described in "Completing this form to appoint a representative, Part III Fee Arrangement" section of this form, under certain circumstances, we do not have to authorize the representative's fee. To request a fee, your representative must file a fee agreement or a fee petition. In either case, your representative cannot charge you more than the fee amount we authorize. If he or she does, promptly report this to your Social Security office.

Filing A Fee Petition
Your representative may file a fee petition when his or her work on your claim(s) is complete. This written request describes in detail the amount of time your representative spent on each service he or she provided you. The request also gives the amount of the fee the representative wants to charge for these services. Your representative must give you a copy of the fee petition and each attachment. If you disagree with the information shown in the fee petition, contact your Social Security office. Please do this within 20 days of receiving your copy of the petition.

We will review the petition and consider the reasonable value of the services provided. Then we will tell you in writing the amount of the fee we authorize.

Filing A Fee Agreement
If you and your representative have a written fee agreement, one of you must give it to us before we decide your claim(s). We usually will approve the agreement if:

- you both signed it;
- the fee you agreed on is no more than 25 percent of past-due benefits, or $6,000 (or a higher amount we set and announced in the Federal Register), whichever is less;
- we approve your claim(s); and
- your claim results in past-due benefits.

We will tell you in writing the amount of the fee your representative can charge based on the agreement.

If we do not approve the fee agreement, we will tell you and your representative in writing. If your representative wishes to charge and collect a fee, he or she must file a fee petition.

After we tell you the amount of the fee your representative can charge, you or your representative can ask us to look at it again if either or both of you disagree with the amount. If we approved a fee agreement, the person who decided your claim(s) also may ask us to lower the amount. Someone who did not decide the amount of the fee the first time will review and finally decide the amount of the fee.

How Much You Pay
You never owe more than the fee we authorize, except for:

- any fee a Federal court allows for your representative's services before it; and
- out-of-pocket expenses your representative incurs or expects to incur, for example, the cost of getting your doctor's or hospital's records. Our authorization is not needed for such expenses.

Your representative may accept money in advance as long as he or she holds it in a trust or escrow account. We usually withhold 25 percent of your past-due benefits to pay toward the fee for you if:

- your retirement, survivors, disability insurance, and/or supplemental security income claim(s) results in past-due benefits;
- your representative is an attorney or a non-attorney whom we have determined to be eligible to receive direct payment of fees; and
- your representative registers with us for direct payment before we effectuate a favorable decision on your claim.

You must pay your representative directly:

- **the rest of the fee you owe,** if the amount of the authorized fee is more than the money we withheld and paid to your representative for you plus any amount your representative held for you in a trust or escrow account.
- **all of the fee you owe,** if we did not withhold past-due benefits, (for example, because there are no past-due benefits; your representative waived direct payment, did not register for direct payment, you discharged the representative, or he or she withdrew from representing you, before we issued a favorable decision); or we withheld an amount from your past-due benefits, but your representative did not ask us to authorize a fee or tell us that he or she planned to ask for a fee within 60 days after the date of your notice of award and we released the withheld amount to you.

Form **SSA-1696-U4** (07-2014) ef (07-2014)

Social Security Administration
Please read the instructions before completing this form.

Form Approved
OMB No. 0960-0527

Name (Claimant) (Print or Type)	Social Security Number
Wage Earner (If Different)	Social Security Number

Part I

CLAIMANT'S APPOINTMENT OF REPRESENTATIVE

I appoint this individual, ________________________________
(Name and Address)

to act as my representative in connection with my claim(s) or asserted right(s) under:

☐ Title II (RSDI) ☐ Title XVI (SSI) ☐ Title XVIII (Medicare) ☐ Title VIII (SVB)

This individual may, entirely in my place, make any request or give any notice; give or draw out evidence or information; get information; and receive any notice in connection with my pending claim(s) or asserted right(s).

☐ I authorize the Social Security Administration to release information about my pending claim(s) or asserted right(s) to designated associates who perform administrative duties (e.g. clerks), partners, and/or parties under contractual arrangements (e.g. copying services) for or with my representative.

☐ I appoint, or I now have, more than one representative. My principal representative is:

____
(Name of Principal Representative)

Signature (Claimant)	Address	
Telephone Number (with Area Code)	Fax Number (with Area Code)	Date

Part II

REPRESENTATIVE'S ACCEPTANCE OF APPOINTMENT

I, ________________________________, hereby accept the above appointment. I certify that I have not been suspended or prohibited from practice before the Social Security Administration; that I am not disqualified from representing the claimant as a current or former officer or employee of the United States; and that I will not charge or collect any fee for the representation, even if a third party will pay the fee, unless it has been approved in accordance with the laws and rules referred to on the reverse side of the representative's copy of this form. If I decide not to charge or collect a fee for the representation, I will notify the Social Security Administration. (Completion of Part III satisfies this requirement.)

Check one: ☐ I am an attorney. ☐ I am a non-attorney eligible for direct payment under SSA law.
☐ I am a non-attorney not eligible for direct payment.

I am now or have previously been disbarred or suspended from a court or bar to which I was previously admitted to practice as an attorney. ☐ YES ☐ NO

I am now or have previously been disqualified from participating in or appearing before a Federal program or agency. ☐ YES ☐ NO

I declare under penalty of perjury that I have examined all the information on this form, and on any accompanying statements or forms, and it is true and correct to the best of my knowledge.

Signature (Representative)	Address	
Telephone Number (with Area Code)	Fax Number (with Area Code)	Date

Part III

FEE ARRANGEMENT

(Select an option, sign and date this section.)

☐ **I am charging a fee and requesting direct payment** of the fee from withheld past-due benefits. *(SSA must authorize the fee unless a regulatory exception applies.)*

☐ **I am charging a fee but waiving direct payment** of the fee from withheld past-due benefits —I do not qualify for or do not request direct payment. *(SSA must authorize the fee unless a regulatory exception applies.)*

☐ **I am waiving fees and expenses from the claimant and any auxiliary beneficiaries** —By checking this block I certify that my fee will be paid by a third-party entity or government agency, and that the claimant and any auxiliary beneficiaries are free of all liability, directly or indirectly, in whole or in part, to pay any fee or expenses to me or anyone as a result of their claim(s) or asserted right(s). *(SSA does not need to authorize the fee if a third-party entity or a government agency will pay from its funds the fee and any expenses for this appointment. Do not check this block if a third-party individual will pay the fee.)*

☐ **I am waiving fees from any source** —I am waiving my right to charge and collect any fee, under sections 206 and 1631 (d)(2) of the Social Security Act. I release my client and any auxiliary beneficiaries from any obligations, contractual or otherwise, which may be owed to me for services provided in connection with their claim(s) or asserted right(s).

Signature (Representative)	Date

Form SSA-1696-U4 (07-2014) ef (07-2014)
Use Prior Editions Until Exhausted

REPRESENTATIVE COPY

Social Security Administration
Please read the instructions before completing this form.

Form Approved
OMB No. 0960-0527

Name (Claimant) (Print or Type)	Social Security Number
Wage Earner (If Different)	Social Security Number

Part I **CLAIMANT'S APPOINTMENT OF REPRESENTATIVE**

I appoint this individual, ______________________________
(Name and Address)

to act as my representative in connection with my claim(s) or asserted right(s) under:

☐ Title II (RSDI) ☐ Title XVI (SSI) ☐ Title XVIII (Medicare) ☐ Title VIII (SVB)

This individual may, entirely in my place, make any request or give any notice; give or draw out evidence or information; get information; and receive any notice in connection with my pending claim(s) or asserted right(s).

☐ I authorize the Social Security Administration to release information about my pending claim(s) or asserted right(s) to designated associates who perform administrative duties (e.g. clerks), partners, and/or parties under contractual arrangements (e.g. copying services) for or with my representative.

☐ I appoint, or I now have, more than one representative. My principal representative is:

____
(Name of Principal Representative)

Signature (Claimant)	Address	
Telephone Number (with Area Code)	Fax Number (with Area Code)	Date

Part II **REPRESENTATIVE'S ACCEPTANCE OF APPOINTMENT**

I, ______________________________, hereby accept the above appointment. I certify that I have not been suspended or prohibited from practice before the Social Security Administration; that I am not disqualified from representing the claimant as a current or former officer or employee of the United States; and that I will not charge or collect any fee for the representation, even if a third party will pay the fee, unless it has been approved in accordance with the laws and rules referred to on the reverse side of the representative's copy of this form. If I decide not to charge or collect a fee for the representation, I will notify the Social Security Administration. (Completion of Part III satisfies this requirement.)

Check one: ☐ I am an attorney. ☐ I am a non-attorney eligible for direct payment under SSA law.
☐ I am a non-attorney not eligible for direct payment.

I am now or have previously been disbarred or suspended from a court or bar to which I was previously admitted to practice as an attorney. ☐ YES ☐ NO

I am now or have previously been disqualified from participating in or appearing before a Federal program or agency.
☐ YES ☐ NO

I declare under penalty of perjury that I have examined all the information on this form, and on any accompanying statements or forms, and it is true and correct to the best of my knowledge.

Signature (Representative)	Address	
Telephone Number (with Area Code)	Fax Number (with Area Code)	Date

Part III **FEE ARRANGEMENT**

(Select an option, sign and date this section.)

☐ **I am charging a fee and requesting direct payment** of the fee from withheld past-due benefits. *(SSA must authorize the fee unless a regulatory exception applies.)*

☐ **I am charging a fee but waiving direct payment** of the fee from withheld past-due benefits —I do not qualify for or do not request direct payment. *(SSA must authorize the fee unless a regulatory exception applies.)*

☐ **I am waiving fees and expenses from the claimant and any auxiliary beneficiaries** —By checking this block I certify that my fee will be paid by a third-party entity or government agency, and that the claimant and any auxiliary beneficiaries are free of all liability, directly or indirectly, in whole or in part, to pay any fee or expenses to me or anyone as a result of their claim(s) or asserted right(s). *(SSA does not need to authorize the fee if a third-party entity or a government agency will pay from its funds the fee and any expenses for this appointment. Do not check this block if a third-party individual will pay the fee.)*

☐ **I am waiving fees from any source** —I am waiving my right to charge and collect any fee, under sections 206 and 1631 (d)(2) of the Social Security Act. I release my client and any auxiliary beneficiaries from any obligations, contractual or otherwise, which may be owed to me for services provided in connection with their claim(s) or asserted right(s).

Signature (Representative)	Date

Form SSA-1696-U4 (07-2014) ef (07-2014)
Use Prior Editions Until Exhausted

ODAR COPY

§178.2.2 Form: Request for Hearing (HA-501)

Editor's Note: A paper Request for Hearing should be used only when an appeal cannot be submitted electronically from SSA's website.

SOCIAL SECURITY ADMINISTRATION
OFFICE OF DISABILITY ADJUDICATION AND REVIEW

Form Approved
OMB No. 0960-0269

REQUEST FOR HEARING BY ADMINISTRATIVE LAW JUDGE

(Take or mail the completed original to your local Social Security office, the Veterans Affairs Regional Office in Manila or any U.S. Foreign Service post and keep a copy for your records)

See Privacy Act Notice

1. Claimant Name	2. Claimant SSN	3. Claim Number, if different

4. I REQUEST A HEARING BEFORE AN ADMINISTRATIVE LAW JUDGE. I disagree with the determination because:

An Administrative Law Judge of the Social Security Administration's Office of Disability Adjudication and Review or the Department of Health and Human Services will be appointed to conduct the hearing or other proceedings in your case. You will receive notice of the time and place of a hearing at least 20 days before the date set for a hearing.

5. I have additional evidence to submit. ☐ Yes ☐ No

Name and source of additional evidence, if not included.

Submit your evidence to the hearing office within 10 days. Your servicing Social Security office will provide the hearing office's address. Attach an additional sheet if you need more space.

6. Do not complete if the appeal is a Medicare issue. Otherwise, check one of the blocks

☐ I wish to appear at a hearing.

☐ I do not wish to appear at a hearing and I request that a decision be made based on the evidence in my case. (Complete Waiver Form HA-4608)

Representation: You have a right to be represented at the hearing. If you are not represented, your Social Security office will give you a list of legal referral and service organizations. If you are represented, complete and submit form SSA-1696 (Appointment of Representative) unless you are appealing a Medicare issue.

7. CLAIMANT SIGNATURE (OPTIONAL)		DATE	8. NAME OF REPRESENTATIVE (if any)		DATE
RESIDENCE ADDRESS			ADDRESS		
CITY	STATE	ZIP CODE	CITY	STATE	ZIP CODE
TELEPHONE NUMBER	FAX NUMBER		TELEPHONE NUMBER	FAX NUMBER	

TO BE COMPLETED BY SOCIAL SECURITY ADMINISTRATION- ACKNOWLEDGMENT OF REQUEST FOR HEARING

9. Request received on ________ by: ________________
(Date) (Print Name) (Title)

____
(Address) (Servicing FO Code) (PC Code)

10. Was the request for hearing received within 65 days of the reconsidered determination? ☐ Yes ☐ No
If no, attach claimant's explanation for delay and supporting documents if any.

11. If claimant is not represented, was a list of legal referral service organizations provided? ☐ Yes ☐ No

12. Interpreter needed ☐ Yes ☐ No

Language (including sign language):

13. Check one: ☐ Initial Entitlement Case
☐ Disability Cessation Case or ☐ Other Postentitlement Case

14. HO COPY SENT TO: ________ HO on ________
☐ Claims Folder (CF) Attached: ☐ Title (T) II; ☐ T XVI; ☐ T VIII; ☐ T XVIII; ☐ T II CF held in FO ☐ Electronic Folder
☐ CF requested ☐ T II; ☐ T XVI; ☐ T VIII; ☐ T XVIII
(Copy of email or phone report attached)

16. CF COPY SENT TO: ________ HO on ________
☐ CF Attached: ☐ Title (T) II; ☐ T XVI; ☐ T XVIII
☐ Other Attached:

15. Check all claim types that apply:

☐ Retirement and Survivors Insurance Only	(RSI)
☐ Title II Disability - Worker or child only	(DIWC)
☐ Title II Disability - Widow(er) only	(DIWW)
☐ Title XVI (SSI) Aged only	(SSIA)
☐ Title XVI Blind only	(SSIB)
☐ Title XVI Disability only	(SSID)
☐ Title XVI/Title II Concurrent Aged Claim	(SSAC)
☐ Title XVI/Title II Concurrent Blind	(SSBC)
☐ Title XVI/Title II Concurrent Disability	(SSDC)
☐ Title XVIII Hospital/Supplementary Insurance	(HI/SMI)
☐ Title VIII Only Special Veterans Benefits	(SVB)
☐ Title VIII/Title XVI	(SVB/SSI)
☐ Other - Specify:	

Form HA-501-U5 (01-2015) ef (01-2015)
Use 08-2012 Edition Until Stock is Exhausted

TAKE OR SEND ORIGINAL TO SSA AND RETAIN A COPY FOR YOUR RECORDS

PRIVACY ACT STATEMENT
Request for Hearing by Administrative Law Judge

Sections 205(a) (42 U.S.C. 405 (a)), 702 (42 U.S.C. 902), 1631(e) (1) (A), and; (B) (42 U.S.C. 1383(e) (1) (A) and (B)), 1839(i) (42 U.S.C. 1395r), 1869(b) (1), and (c) (42 U.S.C. 1395ff) of the Social Security Act, as amended, authorize us to collect this information. We will use the information you provide to continue processing your claim.

Providing this information is voluntary. However, failing to provide us with all or part of the requested information may prevent us from making an accurate and timely decision on your claim.

We rarely use the information you supply for any purpose other than for determining problems in Social Security programs. However, we may use it for the administration and integrity of Social Security programs. We may also disclose information to another person or to another agency in accordance with approved routine uses, which include, but are not limited to the following:

1. To enable a third party or an agency to assist Social Security in establishing rights to Social Security benefits and/or coverage;
2. To comply with Federal laws requiring the release of information from Social Security records (e.g., to the Government Accountability Office and the Department of Veterans' Affairs);
3. To make determinations for eligibility in similar health and income maintenance programs at the Federal, State, and local level; and
4. To facilitate statistical research, audit, or investigate activities necessary to assure the integrity of Social Security programs.

We may also use the information you provide in computer matching programs. Matching programs compare our records with records kept by other Federal, State, or local government agencies. Information from these matching programs can be used to establish or verify a person's eligibility for Federally-funded or administered benefit programs and for repayment of payments or delinquent debts under these programs.

A complete list of routine uses for this information is available in System of Records Notices 60-0089, Claims Folder System and 60-0050, Completed Determination-Continuing Disablility Determinations. These notices, additional information regarding this form, and information regarding our programs and systems, are available on-line at www.socialsecurity.gov or any local Social Security office.

Paperwork Reduction Act Statement - This information collection meets the requirements of 44 U.S.C. § 3507, as amended by Section 2 of the Paperwork Reduction Act of 1995. You do not need to answer these questions unless we display a valid Office of Management and Budget control number. We estimate that it will take about 10 minutes to read the instructions, gather the facts, and answer the questions. **SEND OR BRING THE COMPLETED FORM TO YOUR LOCAL SOCIAL SECURITY OFFICE. You can find your local Social Security office through SSA's website at www.socialsecurity.gov. Offices are also listed under U. S. Government agencies in your telephone directory or you may call Social Security at 1-800-772-1213 (TTY 1-800-325-0778).** *You may send comments on our time estimate above to:SSA, 6401 Security Blvd, Baltimore, MD 21235-6401.* ***Send only comments relating to our time estimate to this address, not the completed form.***

Form **HA-501-U5** (01-2015) ef (01-2015)

§178.2.3 Form: Disability Report — Appeal (SSA-3441)

Editor's Note: A paper Disability Report - Appeal should be used only when an appeal cannot be submitted electronically from SSA's website.

DISABILITY REPORT - APPEAL
SSA-3441-BK

PLEASE READ THIS INFORMATION BEFORE COMPLETING THIS REPORT

This report is used to update your information for your disability appeal. Completing this report accurately helps us process your claim. Please complete as much of this report as you can.

IF YOU NEED HELP

Please do **not** ask your health care provider to complete this report. You can get help from other people, such as a friend or family member. If you cannot complete this report, a Social Security representative can assist you. If you make an appointment with us, please complete as much of this report as you can and have it with you for your appointment.

HOW TO COMPLETE THIS REPORT

If you have Internet access, you may be able to complete this report online at www.ssa.gov/disability/appeal

If you complete this report on paper:

- Print or write clearly.
- Include a ZIP or postal code with each address.
- Provide complete phone numbers, including area code. If a phone number is outside the United States, also provide International Direct Dialing (IDD) code and country code.
- If you cannot remember the names and addresses of your health care providers, you may be able to get that information from the telephone book, Internet, medical bills, prescriptions, or prescription medicine containers.
- **ANSWER EVERY QUESTION,** unless this report indicates otherwise. You can write "don't know," or "none," or "does not apply" if you need to.
- If you need more space to answer any question, please use the REMARKS section on the last page, SECTION 10. Include the number of the question you are answering.

YOUR MEDICAL RECORDS

If you have any medical records that you have not given to us, send or bring them to our office with this completed report. Please tell us if you want us to return them to you. If you are having an interview in our office, bring your medical records, your prescription medicine containers (if available), and this completed report with you.

YOU DO NOT NEED TO ASK DOCTORS OR HOSPITALS FOR ANY MEDICAL RECORDS THAT YOU DO NOT ALREADY HAVE. With your permission, we will request your records. The information that you give us on this report tells us where to request your medical and other records.

HOW TO SUBMIT THIS REPORT

Send or bring this completed report to your local Social Security office. If you have Internet access, you can locate your nearest Social Security office by zip code at www.socialsecurity.gov/locator. Our offices are also listed under U.S. Government agencies in your telephone directory or you may call Social Security at 1-800-772-1213 (TTY 1-800-325-0778).

Privacy Act Statement
Disability Report - Appeal
Collection and Use of Personal Information

Sections 205 (42 U.S.C. 405 (a) and (b)), 223 (42 U.S.C. 423 (d)), and 1631 (42 U.S.C. 1383 (e)(1)) of the Social Security Act, as amended, authorize us to collect this information. We will use the information you provide to update your disability report information.

Furnishing us this information is voluntary. However, failing to provide us with all or part of the information may prevent an accurate and timely decision on your appeal for your claim.

We rarely use the information you provide on this form for any purpose other than to update your disability information. However, we may use it for the administration and integrity of Social Security programs. We may also disclose information to another person or to another agency in accordance with approved routine uses, which include but are not limited to the following:

1. To enable a third party or an agency to assist Social Security in establishing rights to Social Security benefits and/or coverage;

2. To comply with Federal laws requiring the release of information from Social Security records (e.g., to the Government Accountability Office and Department of Veterans Affairs);

3. To make determinations for eligibility in similar health and income maintenance programs at the Federal, State, and local level; and

4. To facilitate statistical research, audit, or investigative activities necessary to ensure the integrity of Social Security programs (e.g., to the U.S. Census Bureau and to private entities under contract with us).

A complete list of when we may share your information with others, called routine uses, is available in our Privacy Act Systems of Records Notices entitled, Claims Folder System (60-0089) and Electronic Disability (60-0320). Additional information about these and other system of records notices and our programs are available online at www.socialsecurity.gov or at your local Social Security office.

We may also use the information you provide in computer matching programs. Matching programs compare our records with records kept by other Federal, State, or local government agencies. Information from these matching programs can be used to establish or verify a person's eligibility for Federally funded or administered benefit programs and for repayment of payments or delinquent debts under these programs.

Paperwork Reduction Act

This information collection meets the requirements of 44 U.S.C. § 3507, as amended by Section 2 of the Paperwork Reduction Act of 1995. You do not need to answer these questions unless we display a valid Office of Management and Budget control number. We estimate that it will take about 45 minutes to read the instructions, gather the facts, and answer the questions.

You may send comments on our time estimate above to:
SSA, 6401 Security Boulevard, Baltimore, MD 21235-6401.
Send ONLY comments relating to our time estimate to this address, not the completed form.

AFTER COMPLETING THIS REPORT, REMOVE THIS SHEET AND KEEP IT FOR YOUR RECORDS.

SOCIAL SECURITY ADMINISTRATION

Form Approved
OMB No. 0960-0144

DISABILITY REPORT – APPEAL

For SSA use only. Please do not write in this box.

Related SSN ____________________ Number Holder ____________________

If you are filling out this report for someone else, please provide information about him or her. When a question refers to "you" or "your," it refers to the person who is applying for disability benefits.

SECTION 1 – INFORMATION ABOUT THE DISABLED PERSON

1. A. Name (First, Middle, Last, Suffix)	**1. B.** Social Security Number

1. C. Daytime Phone Number, including area code (include IDD and country codes if outside the U.S. or Canada)

☐ Check this box if you do not have a phone number where we can leave a message.

1. D. Alternate Phone Number – another number where we may reach you, if any

1. E. Email Address (Optional)

SECTION 2 – CONTACTS

Give the name of someone **(other than your doctors)** we can contact who knows about your medical conditions, and can help you with your claim. (e.g., friend or relative)

2. A. Name (First, Middle, Last)	**2. B.** Relationship to Disabled Person

2. C. Mailing Address (Street or PO Box), include apartment number or unit if applicable.

City	State/Province	ZIP/Postal Code	Country (if not U.S.)

2. D. Daytime Phone Number, including area code (include IDD and country codes if outside the U.S. or Canada)

2. E. Can this person speak and understand English?

☐ Yes ☐ No

If no, what language does the contact person prefer? ____________________

2. F. Who is completing this form?

☐ The person who is applying for disability (Go to SECTION 3 - MEDICAL CONDITIONS).
☐ The person listed in 2.A. (Go to SECTION 3 - MEDICAL CONDITIONS).
☐ Someone else (Please complete the information below).

2. G. Name (First, Middle, Last)	**2. H.** Relationship to Disabled Person

2. I. Mailing Address (Street or PO Box) Include apartment number or unit if applicable.

City	State/Province	ZIP/Postal Code	Country (if not U.S.)

2. J. Daytime Phone Number, including area code (include IDD and country codes if outside the U.S. or Canada)

SECTION 3 – MEDICAL CONDITIONS

3. A. **Since you last told us about your medical conditions,** has there been any CHANGE (for better or worse) in your physical or mental conditions?

☐ Yes, approximate date change occurred: ____________________ ☐ No

If yes, please describe in detail: ______________________________

3. B. **Since you last told us about your medical conditions,** do you have any NEW physical or mental conditions?

☐ Yes, approximate date of new conditions: ____________________ ☐ No

If yes, please describe in detail: ______________________________

If you need more space, use SECTION 10 – REMARKS on the last page.

SECTION 4 – MEDICAL TREATMENT

4. A. Have you used any other names on your medical or educational records? Examples are maiden name, other married name, or nickname.

☐ Yes ☐ No

If yes, please list the other names used: ______________________________

4. B. **Since you last told us about your medical treatment**, have you seen a doctor or other health care provider, received treatment at a hospital or clinic, or **do you have a future appointment scheduled?**

☐ Yes ☐ No (Go to SECTION 6 – MEDICINES)

4. C. What type(s) of condition(s) were you treated for, or will you be seen for?

☐ Physical ☐ Mental (including emotional or learning problems)

If you answered "Yes" to 4.B., please tell us who may have NEW medical records about any of your **physical or mental** conditions (including emotional or learning problems).

Use the following pages to provide information for up to three (3) providers. **Complete one page for each provider.** If you have more than three providers, list them in SECTION 10 - REMARKS on the last page.

Please include:

- doctors' offices
- hospitals (including emergency room visits)
- clinics
- mental health center
- other health care facilities.

Only list the providers you have seen since you last told us about your medical treatment.

SECTION 4 – MEDICAL TREATMENT (continued)

Provider 1

4. D. Name of facility or office	Name of health care provider who treated you

ALL OF THE QUESTIONS ON THIS PAGE REFER TO THE HEALTH CARE PROVIDER ABOVE.

Phone Number	Patient ID# (if known)

Address

City	State/Province	ZIP/Postal Code	Country (if not U.S.)

Dates of Treatment (approximate date, if exact date is unknown)

Office, Clinic or Outpatient visits at this facility	Emergency Room visits at this facility	Overnight hospital stays at this facility
First Visit ________	Date ________	Date in _____ Date out _____
Last Visit ________	Date ________	Date in _____ Date out _____
Next scheduled appointment	Date ________	Date in _____ Date out _____
(if any) ________	☐ None	☐ None

What medical conditions were treated or evaluated?

What treatment did you receive for the above conditions? (Do not list medicines or tests in this box.)

Has this provider performed or sent you to any tests? Please include tests you are scheduled to have in the future. ☐ Yes (Please complete the information below.) ☐ No (Go to the next page.)

KIND OF TEST	DATES OF TESTS	KIND OF TEST	DATES OF TESTS
☐ Biopsy (list body part) ________		☐ MRI/CT Scan (list body part) ________	
☐ Blood Test (not HIV)		☐ Speech/Language Test	
☐ Breathing Test		☐ Treadmill (exercise test)	
☐ Cardiac Catheterization		☐ Vision Test	
☐ EEG (brain wave test)		☐ X-ray (list body part)	
☐ EKG (heart test)		________	
☐ Hearing Test		☐ Other (please describe)	
☐ HIV Test		________	
☐ IQ Testing			

If you need to list more tests, use SECTION 10 - REMARKS on the last page.

If you do not have any more providers to describe,

go to SECTION 5 – OTHER MEDICAL INFORMATION on page 6.

SECTION 4 – MEDICAL TREATMENT (continued)
Provider 2

4. D. Name of facility or office	Name of health care provider who treated you

ALL OF THE QUESTIONS ON THIS PAGE REFER TO THE HEALTH CARE PROVIDER ABOVE.

Phone Number	Patient ID# (if known)

Address

City	State/Province	ZIP/Postal Code	Country (if not U.S.)

Dates of Treatment (approximate date, if exact date is unknown)

Office, Clinic or Outpatient visits at this facility	Emergency Room visits at this facility	Overnight hospital stays at this facility
First Visit ____________	Date ____________	Date in _____ Date out _____
Last Visit ____________	Date ____________	Date in _____ Date out _____
Next scheduled appointment	Date ____________	Date in _____ Date out _____
(if any) ____________	☐ None	☐ None

What medical conditions were treated or evaluated?

What treatment did you receive for the above conditions? (Do not list medicines or tests in this box.)

Has this provider performed or sent you to any tests? Please include tests you are scheduled to have in the future. ☐ Yes (Please complete the information below.) ☐ No (Go to the next page.)

KIND OF TEST	DATES OF TESTS	KIND OF TEST	DATES OF TESTS
☐ Biopsy (list body part) ____________		☐ MRI/CT Scan (list body part) ____________	
☐ Blood Test (not HIV)		☐ Speech/Language Test	
☐ Breathing Test		☐ Treadmill (exercise test)	
☐ Cardiac Catheterization		☐ Vision Test	
☐ EEG (brain wave test)		☐ X-ray (list body part)	
☐ EKG (heart test)		____________	
☐ Hearing Test		☐ Other (please describe)	
☐ HIV Test		____________	
☐ IQ Testing			

If you need to list more tests, use SECTION 10 - REMARKS on the last page.

If you do not have any more providers to describe,

go to SECTION 5 – OTHER MEDICAL INFORMATION on page 6.

SECTION 4 – MEDICAL TREATMENT (continued)
Provider 3

4. D. Name of facility or office	Name of health care provider who treated you

ALL OF THE QUESTIONS ON THIS PAGE REFER TO THE HEALTH CARE PROVIDER ABOVE.

Phone Number	Patient ID# (if known)

Address

City	State/Province	ZIP/Postal Code	Country (if not U.S.)

Dates of Treatment (approximate date, if exact date is unknown)

Office, Clinic or Outpatient visits at this facility	Emergency Room visits at this facility	Overnight hospital stays at this facility
First Visit ________	Date ________	Date in _____ Date out _____
Last Visit ________	Date ________	Date in _____ Date out _____
Next scheduled appointment (if any) ________	Date ________	Date in _____ Date out _____
	☐ None	☐ None

What medical conditions were treated or evaluated?

What treatment did you receive for the above conditions? (Do not list medicines or tests in this box.)

Has this provider performed or sent you to any tests? Please include tests you are scheduled to have in the future. ☐ Yes (Please complete the information below.) ☐ No (Go to the next page.)

KIND OF TEST	DATES OF TESTS	KIND OF TEST	DATES OF TESTS
☐ Biopsy (list body part) ________		☐ MRI/CT Scan (list body part) ________	
☐ Blood Test (not HIV)		☐ Speech/Language Test	
☐ Breathing Test		☐ Treadmill (exercise test)	
☐ Cardiac Catheterization		☐ Vision Test	
☐ EEG (brain wave test)		☐ X-ray (list body part) ________	
☐ EKG (heart test)			
☐ Hearing Test		☐ Other (please describe) ________	
☐ HIV Test			
☐ IQ Testing			

If you need to list more tests, use SECTION 10 - REMARKS on the last page.

If you have been treated by more providers, use section 10 - REMARKS on the last page.

Form **SSA-3441-BK** (03-2015) ef (03-2015) Page 5

SECTION 5 – OTHER MEDICAL INFORMATION

5. **Since you last told us about your other medical information**, does anyone else have **medical information** about any of your **physical or mental** conditions (including emotional and learning problems) or are you scheduled to see anyone else?

This may include:

- workers' compensation
- vocational rehabilitation services
- insurance companies who have paid you disability benefits
- prisons and correctional facilities
- attorneys
- social service agencies
- welfare agencies
- school/education records

☐ Yes (Please complete the information below.)
☐ No (Go to SECTION 6 – MEDICINES)

Name of Organization			Claim or ID Number (if any)
Address			
City	State/Province	ZIP/Postal Code	Country (if not U.S.)
Name of Contact Person			Phone Number
Date of First Contact	Date of Last Contact	Date of Next Contact (if any)	
Reasons for Contacts			

If you need to list more people or organizations, use SECTION 10 – REMARKS on the last page.

SECTION 6 – MEDICINES

6. Are you currently taking any medicines (prescription or non-prescription)?

☐ Yes (Please complete the information below. You may need to look at your medicine containers.)
☐ No (Go to SECTION 7 – ACTIVITIES)

NAME OF MEDICINE	IF PRESCRIBED, NAME OF DOCTOR	REASON FOR MEDICINE	SIDE EFFECTS YOU HAVE

If you need to list more medicines, use SECTION 10 – REMARKS on the last page.

SECTION 7 - ACTIVITIES

7. **Since you last told us about your activities,** has there been any **change** (for better or worse) in your daily activities due to your **physical** or **mental** conditions? (Examples of daily activities are household tasks, personal care, getting around, hobbies and interests, social activities, etc.)

☐ Yes ☐ No

If yes, please describe in detail: ____________________

____

____

____

If you need more space, use SECTION 10 – REMARKS on the last page.

SECTION 8 – WORK AND EDUCATION

8. A. **Since you last told us about your work,** have you worked or has your work changed?

☐ Yes ☐ No

If yes, you will be asked to provide additional information.

8. B. **Since you last told us about your education,** have you completed or are you enrolled in any type of specialized job training, trade school, or vocational school?

☐ Yes ☐ No

If yes, what type? ____________________

Date(s) attended: ____________________

If you need more space, use SECTION 10 – REMARKS on the last page.

SECTION 9 – VOCATIONAL REHABILITATION, EMPLOYMENT, OR OTHER SUPPORT SERVICES

9. Since you last told us about your vocational rehabilitation, have you participated, or are you participating in:

- an individual work plan with an employment network under the Ticket to Work Program?
- an individualized plan for employment with a vocational rehabilitation agency or any other organization?
- a Plan to Achieve Self-Support (PASS)?
- an individualized education program (IEP) through an educational institution (if a student age 18-21)?
- any program providing vocational rehabilitation, employment services, or other support services to help you go to work?

☐ Yes (Please complete the information below.)
☐ No (Go to SECTION 10 – REMARKS)

Name of Organization or School			
Name of Counselor, Instructor, or Job Coach			Phone Number
Address			
City	State/Province	ZIP/Postal Code	Country (if not U.S.)

Date when you started participating in the plan or program:

If you need more space, use SECTION 10 – REMARKS on the last page.

SECTION 10 – REMARKS

Use this space to provide any information you could not show in earlier sections of this form or any additional information you feel we should know about. Please be sure to include the number of the question you are answering (For example, 3A, 4D, etc.).

Date Report Completed MM/DD/YYYY:

§178.2.4 Form: Authorization to Disclose Information to the Social Security Administration (SSA-827)

Form Approved
OMB No. 0960-0623

WHOSE ***Records to be Disclosed***

NAME *(First, Middle, Last, Suffix)*	
SSN - -	Birthday *(mm/dd/yy)*

AUTHORIZATION TO DISCLOSE INFORMATION TO THE SOCIAL SECURITY ADMINISTRATION (SSA)

**** PLEASE READ THE ENTIRE FORM, BOTH PAGES, BEFORE SIGNING BELOW ****

I voluntarily authorize and request disclosure (including paper, oral, and electronic interchange):
OF WHAT ***All my medical records;*** **also education records and other information related to my ability to perform tasks. This includes specific permission to release:**

1. **All records and other information regarding my treatment, hospitalization, and outpatient care for my impairment(s)** ***including*****, and not limited to :**
   - Psychological, psychiatric or other mental impairment(s) (excludes "psychotherapy notes" as defined in 45 CFR 164.501)
   - Drug abuse, alcoholism, or other substance abuse
   - Sickle cell anemia
   - Records which may indicate the presence of a communicable or noncommunicable disease; and tests for or records of HIV/AIDS
   - Gene-related impairments (including genetic test results)
2. **Information about how my impairment(s) affects my ability to complete tasks and activities of daily living, and affects my ability to work.**
3. **Copies of educational tests or evaluations, including Individualized Educational Programs, triennial assessments, psychological and speech evaluations, and any other records that can help evaluate function; also teachers' observations and evaluations.**
4. **Information created within 12 months after the date this authorization is signed, as well as past information.**

FROM WHOM

- **All medical sources** (hospitals, clinics, labs, physicians, psychologists, etc.) including mental health, correctional, addiction treatment, and VA health care facilities
- All educational sources (schools, teachers, records administrators, counselors, etc.)
- Social workers/rehabilitation counselors
- Consulting examiners used by SSA
- Employers, insurance companies, workers' compensation programs
- Others who may know about my condition (family, neighbors, friends, public officials)

THIS BOX TO BE COMPLETED BY SSA/DDS (as needed) Additional information to identify the subject (e.g., other names used), the specific source, or the material to be disclosed:

TO WHOM **The Social Security Administration and to the State agency authorized to process my case** (usually called "disability determination services"), **including contract copy services, and doctors or other professionals consulted during the process.** [Also, for international claims, to the U.S. Department of State Foreign Service Post.]

PURPOSE Determining my **eligibility for benefits**, including looking at the combined effect of any impairments that by themselves would not meet SSA's definition of disability; and whether I can manage such benefits.

☐ Determining whether I am **capable of managing benefits ONLY** (check only if this applies)

EXPIRES WHEN This authorization is good for 12 months from the date signed (below my signature).

- I authorize the use of a copy (including electronic copy) of this form for the disclosure of the information described above.
- I understand that there are some circumstances in which this information may be redisclosed to other parties (see page 2 for details).
- I may write to SSA and my sources to revoke this authorization at any time (see page 2 for details).
- SSA will give me a copy of this form if I ask; I may ask the source to allow me to inspect or get a copy of material to be disclosed.
- **I have read both pages of this form and agree to the disclosures above from the types of sources listed.**

PLEASE SIGN USING BLUE OR BLACK INK ONLY		**IF not signed by subject of disclosure, specify basis for authority to sign**		
INDIVIDUAL authorizing disclosure **SIGN ▶**		☐ **Parent of minor** ☐ **Guardian** ☐ **Other personal representative (explain)** (Parent/guardian/personal representative sign here if two signatures required by State law) ▶		
Date Signed	Street Address			
Phone Number (with area code)	City		State	ZIP

WITNESS *I know the person signing this form or am satisfied of this person's identity:*

SIGN ▶	IF needed, second witness sign here (e.g., if signed with "X" above) **SIGN ▶**
Phone Number (or Address)	Phone Number (or Address)

This general and special authorization to disclose was developed to comply with the provisions regarding disclosure of medical, educational, and other information under P.L. 104-191 ("HIPAA"); 45 CFR parts 160 and 164; 42 U.S. Code section 290dd-2; 42 CFR part 2; 38 U.S. Code section 7332; 38 CFR 1.475; 20 U.S. Code section 1232g ("FERPA"); 34 CFR parts 99 and 300; and State law.

Form **SSA-827** (11-2012) ef (11-2012) Use 4-2009 and Later Editions Until Supply is Exhausted Page1 of 2

Explanation of Form SSA-827,
"Authorization to Disclose Information to the Social Security Administration (SSA)"

We need your written authorization to help get the information required to process your claim, and to determine your capability of managing benefits. Laws and regulations require that sources of personal information have a signed authorization before releasing it to us. Also, laws require specific authorization for the release of information about certain conditions and from educational sources.

You can provide this authorization by signing a form SSA-827. Federal law permits sources with information about you to release that information if you sign a single authorization to release all your information from all your possible sources. We will make copies of it for each source. A covered entity (that is, a source of medical information about you) may not condition treatment, payment, enrollment, or eligibility for benefits on whether you sign this authorization form. A few States, and some individual sources of information, require that the authorization specifically name the source that you authorize to release personal information. In those cases, we may ask you to sign one authorization for each source and we may contact you again if we need you to sign more authorizations.

You have the right to revoke this authorization at any time, except to the extent a source of information has already relied on it to take an action. To revoke, send a written statement to any Social Security Office. If you do, also send a copy directly to any of your sources that you no longer wish to disclose information about you; SSA can tell you if we identified any sources you didn't tell us about. SSA may use information disclosed prior to revocation to decide your claim.

It is SSA's policy to provide service to people with limited English proficiency in their native language or preferred mode of communication consistent with Executive Order 13166 (August 11, 2000) and the Individuals with Disabilities Education Act. SSA makes every reasonable effort to ensure that the information in the SSA-827 is provided to you in your native or preferred language.

Privacy Act Statement
Collection and Use of Personal Information

Sections 205(a), 233(d)(5)(A), 1614(a)(3)(H)(i), 1631(d)(l) and 1631(e)(l)(A) of the Social Security Act as amended, [42 U.S.C. 405(a), 433(d)(5)(A), 1382c(a)(3)(H)(i), 1383(d)(l) and 1383(e)(l)(A)] authorize us to collect this information. We will use the information you provide to help us determine your eligibility, or continuing eligibility for benefits, and your ability to manage any benefits received. The information you provide is voluntary. However, failure to provide the requested information may prevent us from making an accurate and timely decision on your claim, and could result in denial or loss of benefits.

We rarely use the information you provide on this form for any purpose other than for the reasons explained above. However, we may use it for the administration and integrity of Social Security programs. We may also disclose information to another person or to another agency in accordance with approved routine uses, including but not limited to the following:

1. To enable a third party or an agency to assist us in establishing rights to Social Security benefits and/or coverage;
2. To comply with Federal laws requiring the release of information from our records (e.g., to the Government Accountability Office, General Services Administration, National Archives Records Administration, and the Department of Veterans Affairs);
3. To make determinations for eligibility in similar health and income maintenance programs at the Federal, State, and local level; and
4. To facilitate statistical research, audit, or investigative activities necessary to assure the integrity and improvement of our programs (e.g., to the U.S. Census Bureau and to private entities under contract with us).

We may also use the information you provide in computer matching programs. Matching programs compare our records with records kept by other Federal, State, or local government agencies. We use the information from these programs to establish or verify a person's eligibility for Federally funded or administered benefit programs and for repayment of incorrect payments or delinquent debts under these programs.

A complete list of routine uses of the information you gave us is available in our Privacy Act Systems of Records Notices entitled, Claims Folder System, 60-0089; Master Beneficiary Record, 60-0090; Supplemental Security Income record and Special Veterans benefits, 60-0103; and Electronic Disability (eDIB) Claims File, 60-0340. The notices, additional information regarding this form, and information regarding our systems and programs, are available on-line at www.socialsecurity.gov or at any Social Security office.

Paperwork Reduction Act Statement - This information collection meets the requirements of 44 U.S.C. § 3507, as amended by section 2 of the Paperwork Reduction Act of 1995. You do not need to answer these questions unless we display a valid Office of Management and Budget control number. We estimate that it will take about 10 minutes to read the instructions, gather the facts, and answer the questions. **SEND OR BRING THE COMPLETED FORM TO YOUR LOCAL SOCIAL SECURITY OFFICE.** You can find your local Social Security office through SSA's website at www.socialsecurity.gov. Offices are also listed under U.S. Government agencies in your telephone directory **or you may call Social Security at 1-800-772-1213 (TTY 1-800-325-0778).** *You may send comments on our time estimate above to: SSA, 6401 Security Blvd, Baltimore, MD 21235-6401.* ***Send only comments relating to our time estimate to this address, not the completed form.***

§178.2.5 Form: Consent for Release of Information (SSA-3288)

Social Security Administration
Consent for Release of Information

Form Approved
OMB No. 0960-0566

Instructions for Using this Form

Complete this form only if you want us to give information or records about you, a minor, or a legally incompetent adult, to an individual or group (for example, a doctor or an insurance company). If you are the natural or adoptive parent or legal guardian, acting on behalf of a minor child, you may complete this form to release only the minor's non-medical records. We may charge a fee for providing information unrelated to the administration of a program under the Social Security Act.

NOTE: Do not use this form to:

- Request the release of medical records on behalf of a minor child. Instead, visit your local Social Security office or call our toll-free number, 1-800-772-1213 (TTY-1-800-325-0778), or
- Request detailed information about your earnings or employment history. Instead, complete and mail form SSA-7050-F4. You can obtain form SSA-7050-F4 from your local Social Security office or online at www.ssa.gov/online/ssa-7050.pdf.

How to Complete this Form

We will not honor this form unless all required fields are completed. An asterisk (*) indicates a required field. Also, we will not honor blanket requests for "any and all records" or the "entire file." You must specify the information you are requesting and you must sign and date this form. We may charge a fee to release information for non-program purposes.

- Fill in your name, date of birth, and social security number or the name, date of birth, and social security number of the person to whom the requested information pertains.
- Fill in the name and address of the person or organization where you want us to send the requested information.
- Specify the reason you want us to release the information.
- Check the box next to the type(s) of information you want us to release including the date ranges, where applicable.
- You, the parent or the legal guardian acting on behalf of a minor child or legally incompetent adult, must sign and date this form and provide a daytime phone number.
- If you are not the individual to whom the requested information pertains, state your relationship to that person. We may require proof of relationship.

PRIVACY ACT STATEMENT

Section 205(a) of the Social Security Act, as amended, authorizes us to collect the information requested on this form. We will use the information you provide to respond to your request for access to the records we maintain about you or to process your request to release your records to a third party. You do not have to provide the requested information. Your response is voluntary; however, we cannot honor your request to release information or records about you to another person or organization without your consent. We rarely use the information provided on this form for any purpose other than to respond to requests for SSA records information. However, the Privacy Act (5 U.S.C. § 552a(b)) permits us to disclose the information you provide on this form in accordance with approved routine uses, which include but are not limited to the following:

1. To enable an agency or third party to assist Social Security in establishing rights to Social Security benefits and or coverage;
2. To make determinations for eligibility in similar health and income maintenance programs at the Federal, State, and local level;
3. To comply with Federal laws requiring the disclosure of the information from our records; and,
4. To facilitate statistical research, audit, or investigative activities necessary to assure the integrity of SSA programs.

We may also use the information you provide when we match records by computer. Computer matching programs compare our records with those of other Federal, State, or local government agencies. We use information from these matching programs to establish or verify a person's eligibility for Federally-funded or administered benefit programs and for repayment of incorrect payments or overpayments under these programs. Additional information regarding this form, routine uses of information, and other Social Security programs is available on our Internet website, www.socialsecurity.gov, or at your local Social Security office.

PAPERWORK REDUCTION ACT STATEMENT

This information collection meets the requirements of 44 U.S.C. § 3507, as amended by section 2 of the Paperwork Reduction Act of 1995. You do not need to answer these questions unless we display a valid Office of Management and Budget control number. We estimate that it will take about 3 minutes to read the instructions, gather the facts, and answer the questions. **SEND OR BRING THE COMPLETED FORM TO YOUR LOCAL SOCIAL SECURITY OFFICE. You can find your local Social Security office through SSA's website at www.socialsecurity.gov. Offices are also listed under U.S. Government agencies in your telephone directory or you may call 1-800-772-1213 (TYY 1-800-325-0778).** You may send comments on our time estimate above to: SSA, 6401 Security Blvd., Baltimore, MD 21235-6401. ***Send only comments relating to our time estimate to this address, not the completed form.***

Form SSA-3288 (07-2013) EF (07-2013) Destroy Prior Editions

Social Security Administration

Consent for Release of Information

Form Approved
OMB No. 0960-0566

Instructions for Using this Form

Complete this form only if you want us to give information or records about you, a minor, or a legally incompetent adult, to an individual or group (for example, a doctor or an insurance company). If you are the natural or adoptive parent or legal guardian, acting on behalf of a minor child, you may complete this form to release only the minor's non-medical records. We may charge a fee for providing information unrelated to the administration of a program under the Social Security Act.

NOTE: Do not use this form to:

- Request the release of medical records on behalf of a minor child. Instead, visit your local Social Security office or call our toll-free number, 1-800-772-1213 (TTY-1-800-325-0778), or
- Request detailed information about your earnings or employment history. Instead, complete and mail form SSA-7050-F4. You can obtain form SSA-7050-F4 from your local Social Security office or online at www.ssa.gov/online/ssa-7050.pdf.

How to Complete this Form

We will not honor this form unless all required fields are completed. An asterisk (*) indicates a required field. Also, we will not honor blanket requests for "any and all records" or the "entire file." You must specify the information you are requesting and you must sign and date this form. We may charge a fee to release information for non-program purposes.

- Fill in your name, date of birth, and social security number or the name, date of birth, and social security number of the person to whom the requested information pertains.
- Fill in the name and address of the person or organization where you want us to send the requested information.
- Specify the reason you want us to release the information.
- Check the box next to the type(s) of information you want us to release including the date ranges, where applicable.
- You, the parent or the legal guardian acting on behalf of a minor child or legally incompetent adult, must sign and date this form and provide a daytime phone number.
- If you are not the individual to whom the requested information pertains, state your relationship to that person. We may require proof of relationship.

PRIVACY ACT STATEMENT

Section 205(a) of the Social Security Act, as amended, authorizes us to collect the information requested on this form. We will use the information you provide to respond to your request for access to the records we maintain about you or to process your request to release your records to a third party. You do not have to provide the requested information. Your response is voluntary; however, we cannot honor your request to release information or records about you to another person or organization without your consent. We rarely use the information provided on this form for any purpose other than to respond to requests for SSA records information. However, the Privacy Act (5 U.S.C. § 552a(b)) permits us to disclose the information you provide on this form in accordance with approved routine uses, which include but are not limited to the following:

1. To enable an agency or third party to assist Social Security in establishing rights to Social Security benefits and or coverage;
2. To make determinations for eligibility in similar health and income maintenance programs at the Federal, State, and local level;
3. To comply with Federal laws requiring the disclosure of the information from our records; and,
4. To facilitate statistical research, audit, or investigative activities necessary to assure the integrity of SSA programs.

We may also use the information you provide when we match records by computer. Computer matching programs compare our records with those of other Federal, State, or local government agencies. We use information from these matching programs to establish or verify a person's eligibility for Federally-funded or administered benefit programs and for repayment of incorrect payments or overpayments under these programs. Additional information regarding this form, routine uses of information, and other Social Security programs is available on our Internet website, www.socialsecurity.gov, or at your local Social Security office.

PAPERWORK REDUCTION ACT STATEMENT

This information collection meets the requirements of 44 U.S.C. § 3507, as amended by section 2 of the Paperwork Reduction Act of 1995. You do not need to answer these questions unless we display a valid Office of Management and Budget control number. We estimate that it will take about 3 minutes to read the instructions, gather the facts, and answer the questions. **SEND OR BRING THE COMPLETED FORM TO YOUR LOCAL SOCIAL SECURITY OFFICE. You can find your local Social Security office through SSA's website at www.socialsecurity.gov. Offices are also listed under U.S. Government agencies in your telephone directory or you may call 1-800-772-1213 (TYY 1-800-325-0778).** You may send comments on our time estimate above to: SSA, 6401 Security Blvd., Baltimore, MD 21235-6401. ***Send only comments relating to our time estimate to this address, not the completed form.***

Form SSA-3288 (07-2013) EF (07-2013) Destroy Prior Editions

§178.3 Attorney Fees Contract

Have your client sign a contract for attorney representation. We recommend using the two-tiered fee agreement at §178.3.1. Below is a brief explanation of the two-tiered fee agreement and SSA's Byzantine attorney fee rules so that you can fulfill your duty of explaining the contract and SSA's rules to your client. An entire chapter of this book, Chapter 7, deals with the subject of attorney fees in more detail.

SSA Fee Approval Required

SSA must approve attorney fees. There are criminal penalties applicable if you accept a fee that has not been approved by SSA. Approval is simple if, in a typical case where back benefits accumulate, you agree to limit your fee to 25 percent of past-due benefits or $6,000, whichever is less. With this limitation in your agreement, the fee agreement can be approved under the "fee agreement process," *see* §§700-719, which was created to provide for expedited approval and payment of attorney fees and is used by most attorneys these days. You will not have to use the fee petition process, *see* §§720-739, which is stingy, cumbersome and slow.

If the fee agreement is signed by the representative and claimant, the fee agreement is submitted to SSA before the date of the favorable decision, and no "exceptions" apply, the fee agreement will be approved by SSA. If the case is decided by an ALJ or the Appeals Council, along with the favorable decision, the decision maker will issue an order approving the fee agreement. If the case is decided at the initial or reconsideration levels, approval of your fee agreement will appear in the award notice. Once your fee agreement is approved under the fee agreement process, SSA will pay your fee directly to you using an automated procedure that pays you around the time the notice of award is issued. If you have any other fee arrangement with your client, it will be necessary for you to submit a fee petition to SSA, wait for its approval, and then wait for your fee to be paid by SSA.

25% of Past-Due Benefits

When a favorable decision is issued by SSA at any level of administrative review, the benchmark for computing back benefits subject to attorney fees is not the date your client was found disabled. Instead, the benchmark is the date SSA does payment calculations, which is called effectuation. When calculating attorney fees, Social Security disability back benefits are computed up to the month before the month of effectuation. SSI back benefits include the month of effectuation. *See* §741. Social Security disability back benefits subject to attorney fees include benefits paid to auxiliaries unless, for some reason, an auxiliary is separately represented. POMS GN 03920.035B.

Direct Payment of the Fee

For cases where you began representation after December 31, 2006, whether your fee is approved under the fee agreement process or it is approved after filing a fee petition, in order to receive direct payment, you must have registered with SSA by completing a Form SSA-1699 (§178.4.1), and you must submit a Form SSA-1695 (§178.4.2) in every case. *See* §178.4.

For cases in which you submitted an Appointment of Representative Form SSA-1696 to SSA before January 1, 2007, SSA will send your fee to you out of your client's back benefits (unless you waive direct payment of the fee in an individual case) without you having ever filed an SSA-1699 or filing an SSA-1695 in the individual case. The only exception is for cases in which a federal court awards a fee after December 31, 2006. For such cases you must file an SSA-1695 in the individual case and you must have signed up for direct payment by submitting an SSA-1699.

Waiver of Direct Payment

If you want to waive direct payment of the fee, this may be accomplished by checking a box and signing Part III of the Appointment of Representative Form, §178.2.1, indicating that you are "charging a fee but waiving direct payment," or by sending a letter to SSA. Waiving direct payment of the fee is usually not a good idea. Before August 31, 2004, in order to avoid the 6.3% deduction from the fee for direct payment, a number of attorneys experimented with waiving direct payment of the fee in selected cases, and collected fees directly from their clients. After August 31, 2004, when the 6.3% "user fee" was capped at $75 (plus an annual COLA adjustment), few attorneys waived direct payment figuring that paying a capped user fee is worth avoiding the risk of non-payment of the fee. *See* §748 for additional information about the user fee.

Two-Tiered Fee Agreement

The fee agreement process works well for the typical case in which a favorable decision is issued by SSA at or below the ALJ hearing level. In protracted cases, cases with perhaps more than one ALJ denial decision and multiple appeals, which can take years to resolve, a $6,000 fee, when you finally get it, is probably inadequate. In such cases, you may find yourself wishing you had used the fee petition process. For this reason we recommend using a two-tiered fee agreement that combines use of the two fee approval systems into one contract. With this fee agreement, most cases will be processed under the fee agreement process. But in a protracted case, you can request a full 25% fee by filing a fee petition.

A sample two-tiered fee agreement follows at §178.3.1. This fee agreement meets the requirements of the "fee agreement process" (because it calls for a fee of 25 percent of past-due benefits or $6,000, whichever is less) if the favorable decision is issued at any level of administrative review through the first ALJ decision after the date of the contract—the first tier. If the first tier is applicable, the decision maker must approve the fee agreement. If the second tier is applicable, that is, if a favorable decision is issued later, the fee is 25% of past-due benefits. When the second tier applies, because the fee agreement process is no longer available, a decision maker must disapprove the fee agreement. A fee petition must be submitted to obtain approval of a fee. *See* §§700, 703 and 727.

First ALJ Decision After the Date of the Agreement

Although SSA has never required specific language in a fee agreement, it has provided some samples, including sample language for a two-tiered fee agreement. *See* HALLEX I-1-2-15. Our contract, §178.3.1, is more versatile than the sample provided in the HALLEX, which establishes the first tier as any SSA decision in the case through the first ALJ hearing decision and the second tier as the decisions after that. Thus, if you first get involved in a case at the Appeals Council level or after remand by the Appeals Council, use of SSA's sample agreement would require you to file a fee petition no matter at what level the favorable decision is issued.

Our two-tiered contract, which makes the fee agreement process tier apply to a decision at any administrative level through the first ALJ decision *after the date of the agreement*, may be used when you first become involved in a case after an ALJ decision has already been issued. The first tier applies until the next ALJ decision is issued.

It has another advantage, too. You can submit a contract with the same language again that is signed after the date of the ALJ decision and effectively return to the fee agreement process tier through the next ALJ decision. In practice, because of a low benefit rate, eligibility only for a closed period or a relatively fast remand by the Appeals Council, it happens frequently that the fee would not be more than $6,000 even after the second ALJ decision. Under these circumstances, why stick with a contract that requires you to file a fee petition? Your client will be happy that you are once more limiting your fee to $6,000.

Escalator Clause

So that you won't have to renegotiate all your existing contracts if in the future the Commissioner exercises the statutorily granted discretion to increase the $6,000 cap, the contract provides for this possibility using language that has been approved by SSA. See POMS GN 03940.003 A.3. Note 3. The cap was last raised with an effective date of June 22, 2009.

Claimant and Representative Must Sign the Fee Agreement

The claimant and representative must sign the fee agreement. Although it is acceptable to SSA for the fee agreement to be between the client and the firm, the appointed representative must sign the agreement. If more than one attorney from the firm is appointed as a representative, all must sign a single fee agreement. HALLEX I-1-2-12. Because SSA treats extra signers on the fee agreement as irrelevant, many law firms have every potential representative sign the fee agreement. HALLEX I-1-2-12 A.2. Since SSA will treat someone from the firm who shows up at the hearing as an appointed co-representative even if he or she did not sign the Appointment of Representative form, if that person signed the fee agreement, the agreement will be approved under the fee agreement process. HALLEX I-1-2-12 C.3.b. If the person who appears at the hearing did not sign the fee agreement, the fee agreement in the file is not supposed to be approved. However, a superseding fee agreement with all the appropriate signatures may be submitted before the date of the favorable decision and approved by the ALJ. In the days of paper files, it was known to happen that right at the hearing an ALJ would let the co-representative sign the fee agreement in the file.

Submit Fee Agreement Before Favorable Decision Is Issued

For the "fee agreement process" to apply, the fee agreement must be received by SSA at least a day before the favorable decision is issued. It is good practice to have a way of proving when SSA got your fee agreement.

Exceptions to the Fee Agreement Process—Multiple Representatives

If the fee agreement is signed by the representative and claimant and submitted to SSA before the date of the favorable decision and no exceptions apply, the fee agreement will be approved by SSA. The most common exceptions involve multiple representatives in three circumstances: 1) where the claimant had a prior representative; 2) where the claimant appoints multiple representatives from the same firm and all do not sign a common fee agreement; and 3) where the claimant appoints multiple representatives and all are not members of a single firm. SSA says that these exceptions themselves will not apply if the problem-representative waives his or her fee. But this works only in a situation involving successive representatives. If your client had a representative before you, make a note to contact the prior representative to ask him or her to sign a waiver of the fee.

In the other situations, those involving co-representatives, although a fee waiver will allow the fee to be paid under the fee agreement process, it will also reduce the total fee by the amount of the proportionate share of the waiving co-representative. Thus, it is a bad idea for anyone other than a former representative to waive a fee in a Social Security case. *See* §709. Therefore, be careful who is appointed as representative. Make sure no one from outside the firm is appointed and make sure all appointed representatives sign a common fee agreement.

See §705 for other exceptions that seldom arise in practice.

Attorney Appeals for Fee Greater Than $6,000

The sample contract refers to the possibility that the attorney may seek administrative review of a maximum fee set under the fee agreement process cap (currently $6,000) to request a fee of 25% of past-due benefits. You need to consider the implications of this clause to determine if it is appropriate for your practice. Lawyers generally want to appeal a fee determined under the fee agreement process in only two situations: First, to obtain a fee greater than $6,000; and second, to obtain a minimum fee, that is, either a specific minimum (*e.g.*, $2,500) or a specific rate per hour (*e.g.*, $150). With this clause in your contract, you'll be able to appeal to request a fee greater than $6,000 (up to 25% of past-due benefits), but you won't be able to appeal to request a minimum fee.

Note also that you won't be able to request a fee greater than 25% of back benefits. Thus, this clause limits what you can ask for on administrative review. This clause is much easier to explain to a claimant than if the contract included a provision that raised the possibility that you might even ask for more than 25% of back benefits as your fee.

Having a clause in your fee agreement that tells your client what to expect if you appeal is advantageous when you request administrative review of the amount of your fee. You can point out this clause to the decision maker. One of the things that a decision maker must consider when reviewing a fee appeal is the "expectation of the parties when they entered into the fee agreement, as expressed in the written agreement filed with SSA." HALLEX I-1-2-47 A.4. You can tell your client when you negotiate the contract that the fee may be the full 25% of past-due benefits, even if this amount exceeds $6,000.

Appeals to Obtain a Minimum Fee

Appeals to obtain a minimum fee are usually more trouble than they are worth. Indeed, most minimum fee situations can be anticipated. You can negotiate a contract with your client initially, or possibly even later in the case, *see* §708, that uses the fee petition process to obtain your fee. On the other hand, if you want to use a minimum fee appeal clause under the fee agreement process, *see* §703, for language that has been approved by SSA.

Fee Appeals Are Rare

Although the sample fee agreement contains the clause pertaining to administrative review of the amount of the fee determined under the fee agreement process, lawyers rarely invoke it. Most lawyers will appeal only under truly unusual circumstances. Such appeals are not regarded with favor by most ALJs. Caution on fee appeals is also advised because if you appeal, SSA may reduce your fee below the amount approved under the fee agreement process. *See* §715.

Expenses

Be sure to explain that expense reimbursement is not part of the fee and that SSA will not pay expenses directly to the attorney. The client must pay these expenses directly to you whether the case is won or lost.

Administrative Representation Only

Note that this contract applies only to representation before the Social Security Administration, which is governed by 42 U.S.C. § 406(a). If your client loses before SSA and you decide to take the case to federal court, a new contract governed by 42 U.S.C. § 406(b), which includes language for how to treat attorney fees awarded under the Equal Access to Justice Act, will have to be negotiated. Using two contracts, one for representation before SSA and one for federal court representation, has the advantage of allowing use of a much simpler contract for the usual case that will never go to federal court rather than trying to incorporate all features into one contract. A two-contract approach avoids the implication that you will certainly take the case to federal court if your client loses; and it gives you the opportunity to have your client come to your office at the time the case is taken to federal court to negotiate payment of expenses, or even negotiate a new contract for administrative representation that will be applicable if the federal court remands the case. *See* §758, for a sample federal court contract.

Scope of Representation Clause

Some disability claimants more or less assume that because you have agreed to represent them in their Social Security disability or SSI claims, you will be representing them in all cases having to do with their disabilities, *e.g.*, Medicaid appeals, long-term disability claims, mortgage or auto disability insurance claims, COBRA issues, worker's compensation claims, *etc.* The contract includes a scope of representation clause designed to avoid such misunderstanding.

§178.3.1 Form: Two-Tiered Fee Agreement

TWO-TIERED FEE AGREEMENT — SOCIAL SECURITY DISABILITY/SSI

ATTORNEY FEES: I employ [*name of firm*] to represent me before the Social Security Administration (SSA) in my disability case. If I win at any administrative level through the first administrative law judge (ALJ) decision after the date of this agreement, I agree that the attorney fee will be the lesser of twenty-five percent (25%) of all past-due benefits awarded **to my family** and me, or the dollar amount established pursuant to 42 U.S.C. § 406(a)(2)(A), which is currently $6,000, but may be increased from time to time by the Commissioner of Social Security. I understand that my attorney has the right to seek administrative review to increase the amount of the fee set under the preceding sentence of this agreement; but if that happens, my attorney will not ask for a fee of more than 25% of total back benefits awarded in my case. If the first ALJ decision after the date of this agreement is a denial and my attorney agrees to appeal and I win my case later, my attorney will ask SSA to approve a fee no greater than twenty-five percent (25%) of all back benefits awarded in my case. If I receive both Social Security disability and SSI benefits, I understand that my total fee will not be more than 25% of all past-due benefits, or no more than the limit set by 42 U.S.C. § 406(a)(2)(A), if the limit applies. I understand that if I do not win benefits, then the attorneys get no fee.

SCOPE OF REPRESENTATION: I have employed my attorneys to represent me in my Social Security disability and/or SSI claim. I understand that my attorneys do not represent me in any other public or private claim related to my disability, or with any other government agency or any insurance company unless separate arrangements, including a separate contract, have been made for representation on any other claim.

PAYMENT OF ATTORNEY FEES: I understand that SSA will hold out money from my past-due benefits and pay my attorneys for their work on my case unless my attorneys waive withholding and direct payment. If SSA does not withhold and pay all approved attorney fees, I will pay them promptly.

I WILL PAY EXPENSES: In addition to fees, I agree to pay my attorneys for reasonable expenses that they pay in my case. These may include medical records and reports, photocopying, travel expenses, transcript preparation, and the like. I will get a bill for expenses that shows how and when my attorneys spent the money. In a case in which I get benefits, I agree to pay my attorneys back for these expenses as soon as I get a check for back benefits. I agree to pay expenses whether we win or lose.

COMPLIANCE WITH SOCIAL SECURITY REGULATIONS: I understand that Social Security regulations require me and my representative to submit to SSA no later than 5 days before the hearing all evidence related to my disability even if unfavorable. I will inform my representative about all evidence related to my disability.

I HAVE NOT BEEN PROMISED THAT I WILL WIN: My attorneys promised that they will do their best to help me. They did not promise me that I will win.

I accept and approve this agreement:

	____________________ Date
____________________ Attorney Signature	____________________ Signature
____________________ Attorney Signature	____________________ Name (*printed or typed*)
	____________________ Social Security Number

§178.4 Direct Payment of Attorney Fees

In order to comply with an IRS mandate that SSA provide Form 1099s to representatives for fees paid by SSA, SSA requires representatives to register and to submit a special form in every case in which you began representing a claimant after December 31, 2006 and for cases in which a federal court approves a fee out of a claimant's back benefits after December 31, 2006. In order to receive direct payment of the fee, you must do two things. First, you must register. That is, you must complete and submit to SSA a Form SSA-1699 Registration for Appointed Representative Services and Direct Payment (§178.4.1). (For direct payment, this form needs to be submitted only once unless information on the form changes.) Second, you must submit to the claimant's local office Form SSA-1695 Identifying Information for Possible Direct Payment of Authorized Fees (§178.4.2) in every case.

If you are employed by a law firm, so that SSA can send your firm a Form 1099 showing total fees received by all firm employees, your firm should submit to SSA a Form SSA-1694 Request for Business Entity Taxpayer Information (§178.4.3). Like the SSA-1699, this form needs to be completed only once unless information provided on the form changes. The SSA-1694 can be completed online by first registering as a "Business Services Online" user at www.socialsecurity.gov/bso/. Or the form may be printed from SSA's website, completed on paper and submitted to any local Social Security office.

SSA-1699

The SSA-1699 can be completed online by starting at www.ssa.gov/employer/representatives/af1699WelcomePage.htm. Once the form is completed, you must print it out and fax it to SSA's Office of Central Operations at 1-877-268-3827. Do not fax more than one Form SSA-1699 at a time. Note that the form asks for four addresses: your home mailing address, which is used to verify your identity; an "Address for Receipt of Notices," which is where you want SSA to send letters, decisions, etc., and the check for attorney fees in your clients cases (unless you choose direct deposit); a "Tax Address," which is the address to which you want the IRS Form 1099 sent; and a firm or organization address.

Although most lawyers choose to receive attorney fee checks by mail rather than direct deposit, the proportion of those choosing direct deposit is growing. The SSA-1699 itself appears to limit direct deposit to the owner or co-owner of the bank account into which you want the direct deposits made; however, SSA says it will treat as a co-owner anyone who has signature authority on a firm bank account. Thus, unless they have signature authority, associates in a firm cannot request direct deposit into a firm bank account. Some lawyers who have tried direct deposit of fees complain that their bank statements do not provide sufficient information to distinguish deposits of fees from different clients. SSA says that many banks apparently do not pass on all the information provided by SSA. When it makes a direct deposit, SSA provides the bank with the first four letters of the claimant's first name, the first 13 letters of the claimant's last name and the claimant's SSN. SSA says that lawyers need to consult with their banks about obtaining all the information provided by SSA.

Some attorneys have arranged to get an e-mail from their bank whenever a direct deposit is made in a Social Security case. The e-mail contains the information provided to the bank by SSA, including the claimant's SSN. These attorneys say this option works well; their only complaint, however, is that their banks charge them extra for the e-mail notification service. Before you sign up for direct deposit with SSA, be sure you have thoroughly discussed all the issues and the charges with your bank.

SSA-1695

The SSA-1695 must be sent to the claimant's local office for any case begun after December 31, 2006. A transmittal letter is provided at §184. The form, which must include your SSN and your firm's Employer Identification Number (EIN), must be submitted prior to effectuation of a favorable decision. If more than one attorney is listed on the Appointment of Representative Form SSA-1696, an SSA-1695 must be submitted for each appointed representative.

When the local office receives the form, it is supposed to enter information from the form into SSA's database, mask your SSN, scan the form, destroy the original, place the scanned SSA-1695 in your client's electronic file, and send you an acknowledgement notice that it was received. A sample acknowledgement notice appears at POMS GN 03910.090, Exhibit 9. POMS GN 03910.042 A.2, Note says, "This notice must be sent." You need to make sure your office develops a system for confirming that the acknowledgement notice is received in every case in which you submit an SSA-1695.

Save the acknowledgement notice. You may need it if SSA refuses to pay you because it says you did not timely submit an SSA-1695. If an SSA-1695 is not submitted to SSA before effectuation, SSA policy is not to pay the attorney directly. POMS GN 03920.017 C.3. provides:

> If the claimant signs the Appointment of Representative after December 31, 2006, and the attorney or the non-attorney, is not registered for direct payment when the favorable decision is

effectuated, SSA is not responsible for paying the fee directly to the representative. In these cases:

- There is no provision for establishing good cause for late registration.
- SSA will not withhold past-due benefits to permit a representative to register after we effectuate a favorable decision.
- After SSA effectuates the favorable decision, the agency will not subsequently establish an overpayment for the claimant in order to pay the fee to the representative who registered after the date we effectuated the favorable decision.
- SSA will advise the representative that he/she must look to the claimant for payment of the fee.

Nevertheless, if you are able to prove that the SSA-1695 was timely submitted, SSA says it will follow the procedures set forth in POMS GN 03920.055 for seeing to it that you are paid your fee. *See* POMS GN 03910.042B.5.

Auxiliaries

The SSA-1695 provides a place to list the names and SSNs of "other claimants you are representing in connection with this claim," i.e., auxiliaries—the claimant's spouse and children. Most attorneys find this part of the SSA-1695 puzzling since they do not usually separately represent auxiliaries. POMS GN 03910.042 A.2, Step 5, states that providing these auxiliary SSNs is "optional." SSA has informally told representatives that it will not refuse to pay attorney fees from auxiliary benefits simply because the names and SSNs of the auxiliary beneficiaries were not listed on this form. Indeed, it is SSA policy that attorney fees are withheld and paid from auxiliary past due benefits unless for some reason the auxiliary was separately represented by some other representative. POMS GN 03920.035 B.

§178.4.1 Form: Registration for Appointed Representative Services and Direct Payment (SSA-1699)

Social Security Administration

Form Approved
OMB No. 0960-0732

REGISTRATION FOR APPOINTED REPRESENTATIVE SERVICES AND DIRECT PAYMENT

Complete all sections that apply to you. We will return incomplete or inaccurate forms.

Section I: Your Personal Identification and Home Contact Information

- All fields in this section are required unless indicated as optional. For your protection, we collect your home contact information to check against our records.
- If you need to update information you provided on or after 10/31/09, include your name, Rep ID, and all information that has changed. You must attest, sign, and date the updated form.
- Enter your name in the boxes below exactly as it appears on your Social Security card. If you want to use a different name, contact your local Social Security office to change the name currently in our records. You must either receive a new card or receive confirmation that we processed your name change prior to completing this form.

If you registered as an Appointed Representative on or after 10/31/09 and need to update your information, enter your Rep ID below:

Your First Name | **Your Middle Name**

Your Last Name | **Your Suffix** (if any)

Your Date of Birth (MM/DD/YYYY) | **Your Social Security Number**

Your Home Mailing Address

Street Line 1

Line 2

City | **State**

ZIP/Postal Code

Country (if outside the U.S.)

Your Daytime Telephone Number

Country/Area Code | Phone Number | Extension

Your Home Fax Number (Optional)

Country/Area Code | Fax Number

Your Email Address (Optional - Used for registration purposes and Social Security online service messages.)

Section II: Your Representational Standing

Check one of the boxes below.

Are you currently in good standing and admitted to practice law before the U.S. Supreme Court; a U.S. Federal, state, territorial, insular possession, or District of Columbia court; or a member of a state bar if that membership carries with it the authority to practice law in that state?

☐ Yes **(Go to Section III)** ☐ No **(Go to Section IV)**

NOTE: If you are not in the business of providing services to Social Security claimants and beneficiaries, but will be appointed as a representative for a relative, friend, or other acquaintance, **YOU DO NOT NEED TO COMPLETE THIS FORM.**

Section III: Your Bar and Court Information

Provide information for one state, U.S. territory, or U.S. Federal Court in which you **currently** are in good standing and have the right to practice law.

Court or Bar	Year Admitted (YYYY)	Court or Bar License Number (If one issued)

Section IV: Your Information as a Representative

All representatives must complete this section.

1. **Your Address for Receipt of Notices** ☐ Same as Home Address in Section I

Street Line 1

Line 2

City **State**

ZIP/Postal Code

Country(if outside the U.S.)

2. **Business Telephone Number** (if different from that provided in Section I.)

Country/Area Code Phone Number Extension

Business Fax Number (Optional)

Country/Area Code Fax Number

3. **Business Email Address** (Optional)

4. **Did you check "Yes" in Section II OR have you been notified by us that you are eligible for direct payment of your fees?**

☐ Yes

☐ No **(Go to Section VI)**

5. **What is your preferred payment method?**

☐ **Direct Deposit** to U.S. Bank – I am the owner or co-owner of this account. (You must be the owner or co-owner)

Type of Financial Account: ☐ Checking ☐ Savings

Routing Number **Account Number**

OR

☐ **Check –** Will be mailed to the **Notice Address**

6. **Your Tax Address** (This is the address where we will send your FORM 1099-MISC)

☐ Same as Home Address

☐ Same as Notice Address in 1 in this section

Street Line 1

Line 2

City **State**

ZIP/Postal Code

Country(if outside the U.S.)

SECTION V: Your Information When You Are Working for a Firm or Organization

Complete this section if your work as a representative will be affiliated with a firm or organization. If you work for more than one firm or organization complete and attach as many copies of this section as needed. You will need an EIN in order to complete this section.

Complete 1 through 5 below.

1. **Employer Identification Number (EIN)** ☐☐ ☐☐☐☐☐☐☐
   (See your W-2 or contact the firm or organization to get this number.)

   Name of Firm or Organization ____________________

2. **Your Address for Receipt of Notices** ☐ Same as home address in Section I
   ☐ Same as notice address in Section IV

   Street Line 1 ☐☐☐☐☐☐☐☐☐☐☐☐☐☐☐☐☐☐☐☐☐☐

   Line 2 ☐☐☐☐☐☐☐☐☐☐☐☐☐☐☐☐☐☐☐☐☐☐

   City ☐☐☐☐☐☐☐☐☐☐☐☐☐☐☐☐☐☐☐☐☐☐ **State** ☐☐

   ZIP/Postal Code ☐☐☐☐☐☐☐☐☐☐☐☐☐☐☐

Country (if outside the U.S.) ☐☐☐☐☐☐☐☐☐☐☐☐☐☐☐☐☐☐☐☐☐☐

3. **Business Telephone Number**

   ☐ Same as home number in Section I

   ☐ Same as business number in Section IV

   ____________ ____________ ____________
   Country/Area Code Phone Number Extension

   Business Fax Number (Optional)

   ____________ ____________
   Country/Area Code Fax Number

4. **Business Email Address** (Optional)

5. **What is your preferred payment method?**

   ☐ **Direct Deposit** to U.S. Bank

   ☐ Same bank information as provided in Section IV

   OR

   ☐ Direct deposit to the account shown below. I am the owner or co-owner of this account. (You must be the owner or co-owner of the account)

   Type of Financial Account: ☐ Checking ☐ Savings

   Routing Number ☐☐☐☐☐☐☐☐☐ **Account Number** ☐☐☐☐☐☐☐☐☐☐☐☐☐☐☐☐☐

   OR

   ☐ **Check** – Will be mailed to the **Notice Address**

Section VI: Attestations and Questions for Representation

You **MUST ATTEST** to these statements and complete the following questions.

1. **I understand and will comply with** SSA laws and rules relating to the representation of parties, including the Rules of Conduct and Standards of Responsibility for Representatives.

   I will not charge, collect, or retain a fee for representational services that SSA has not approved or that is more than SSA approved, unless a regulatory exclusion applies.

   I will not threaten, coerce, intimidate, deceive, or knowingly mislead a claimant or prospective claimant, or beneficiary, regarding benefits or other rights under the Social Security Act.

   I will not knowingly make or present, or participate in making or presenting, false or misleading oral or written statements, assertions, or representations about a material fact or law concerning a matter within SSA's jurisdiction.

   I am aware that if I fail to comply with any SSA laws and rules relating to representation, I may be suspended or disqualified from practicing as a representative before SSA.

   ☐ **I attest to all of the above.**

2. **Have you ever been:**

a.	**Suspended or prohibited** from practice before SSA or any other Federal program or agency?	☐ Yes (Explain below.) ☐ No
b.	**Disbarred or suspended** from a court or bar to which you were previously admitted to practice as an attorney?	☐ Yes (Explain below.) ☐ No
c.	**Convicted of a violation** under Section 206 or 1631(d) of the Social Security Act?	☐ Yes (Explain below.) ☐ No
d.	**Disqualified** from representing a claimant as a current or former officer or employee of the United States?	☐ Yes (Explain below.) ☐ No

3. **For each Yes answer in 2, provide the information below regarding that event** (Attach copies of this page if you need more space.)

Federal Program or Agency; or Court or Bar Name:

Bar Number (provide the Bar Number if you have one AND you answered "Yes" to 2b):

Year Admitted (provide the year if you answered "Yes" to 2b):

Beginning Date of:	**Ending Date:** (if ended)

Brief Description of Circumstances:

Section VII: General Attestations

You **MUST ATTEST** to these statements.

I will not divulge any information that SSA has furnished or disclosed about a claim or prospective claim, unless I have the claimant's consent or there is a Federal law or regulation authorizing me to divulge this information.

I have in place reasonable administrative, technical, and physical security safeguards to protect the confidentiality of all personal information I receive from SSA, to avoid its loss, theft, or inadvertent disclosure.

I will not omit or otherwise withhold disclosure of information to SSA that is material to the benefit entitlement or eligibility of claimants or beneficiaries, nor will I cause someone else to do so, if I know or should know, that this would be false or misleading.

I will not use Social Security program words, letters, symbols, branding, or emblems in my advertising or other communications, in a way that conveys the false impression that SSA has approved, endorsed, or authorized me, my communications, or my organization, or that I have some connection with or authorization from SSA.

I will update this registration if my personal, professional or business affiliation information changes, including information related to disbarments, suspensions or sanctions.

I am aware that if I fail to comply with SSA laws and rules, I could be criminally punished by a fine or imprisonment or both, and I could be subject to civil monetary penalties.

I understand that SSA will validate the information I provide.

☐ **I attest to all of the above.**

Perjury Statement

I agree that a copy of this signed Form SSA-1699 will have the same force and effect as the original.

I declare under penalty of perjury that I have examined all of the information on this application and it is true and correct to the best of my knowledge.

Signature of Person Identified in Section I (You must sign your OWN name.)	Date
▶	

§178.4.2 Form: Identifying Information for Possible Direct Payment of Authorized Fees (SSA-1695)

Social Security Administration

Form Approved
OMB No. 0960-0730

Identifying Information For Possible Direct Payment of Authorized Fees

Information About the Claimant

First Name

Middle Name

Last Name

Suffix

Social Security Number

Wage Earner's Name (if different than above)

Wage Earner's Social Security Number (if different)

Type of Benefits ☐ Title II (RSDI) ☐ Title XVI (SSI)

Information about You, the Representative

Name

Social Security Number

P.O. Box, Street, Apt.,or Suite No.

City

State

ZIP Code or Postal Zone

Country

Phone Number (including area code)

Fax Number (optional)

Employer Identification Number (EIN), if applicable. If you are representing the claimant(s) as a partner or an employee of a firm or other business entity, you may provide the EIN of the firm or business. See instructions on Page 2 for more information.

Information about Other Claimants You are Representing in Connection with this Claim

List below the Social Security Numbers and names of all other claimants not mentioned above. If all claimants will not fit on this form, list on a separate form or blank paper.

Claimant's Social Security Number	Claimant's Name
- -	
- -	
- -	
- -	
- -	

Form **SSA-1695-F3** (07-2013) Page 1
Destroy Prior Editions

IMPORTANT INFORMATION

Purpose of Form

An attorney or other person who wishes to charge or collect a fee for providing services in connection with a claim before the Social Security Administration (SSA) must first obtain approval from SSA. The request for appointment is generally made using the SSA-1696-U4, Appointment of Representative, or equivalent written statement. An attorney or other person who wishes to receive direct payment of authorized fees from SSA must have completed an SSA-1699, Request for Appointed Representative's Direct Payment Information, in order to provide the identifying information that will be used to process these direct payments, including the possible use of direct deposit to a financial institution, and to meet any requirements for issuance of a Form 1099-MISC. It is important to complete a new SSA-1699 whenever there are changes to identifying information. In addition, an attorney or other person must complete this SSA-1695, Identifying Information for Possible Direct Payment of Authorized Fees, for each claim in which a request is being made to receive direct payment of authorized fees.

Instructions for Completing the Form

Claimant Information - Please provide the Social Security Number (SSN) and name of the claimant that you will represent before SSA.

Wage Earner Information - If the claim is being filed on the Social Security record of someone other than the claimant, please provide the SSN and name of that wage earner.

Type of Benefits Information - Please specify the type of benefits for which you are representing the claimant(s). **Representative Information -** Please enter your SSN and name as shown on your Social Security card and your mailing address. If you have changed your last name (e.g., due to marriage), please contact your local SSA office to make this change to your Social Security record. In addition, if you are representing the claimant(s) as a partner or employee of a firm or other business entity, you may provide the EIN of that entity. This will allow SSA to issue a Form 1099-MISC to that entity to reflect that the direct payment of authorized fees you receive is actually income to that entity for tax purposes.

Information About Other Claimants - If you are representing other claimants in this claim that are not mentioned above, please provide their SSNs and names. If there are more than five individuals, please provide this information on a separate attachment to this form.

Privacy Act Statement

Collection and Use of Personal Information

Sections 206(a) and 1631(d) of the Social Security Act, as amended, authorize us to collect the information on this form. We will use the information you provide to facilitate direct payment of authorized fees and to meet the reporting requirements of the law.

Your response is voluntary. However, failing to provide us with all or part of the information could result in nonpayment for your service.

We rarely use the information you provide for any purpose other than for determining continuing eligibility. In accordance with 5 U.S.C. § 552a(b) of the Privacy Act, however, we may disclose the information provided on this form in accordance with approved routine uses, which include but are not limited to the following:

1. To enable a third party or an agency to assist Social Security in establishing rights to Social Security benefits and/or coverage;

2. To comply with Federal laws requiring the release of information from Social Security records (e.g., to the Government Accountability Office and Department of Veterans' Affairs);

3. To make determinations for eligibility in similar health and income maintenance programs at the Federal, State, and local level; and,

4. To facilitate statistical research, audit, or investigative activities necessary to assure the integrity and improvement of Social Security programs.

We may also use the information you provide in computer matching programs. Computer matching programs compare our records with those of other Federal, State, or local government agencies. We can use information from these matching programs to establish or verify a person's eligibility for federally-funded or administered benefit programs and for repayment of payments or delinquent debts under these programs.

A complete list of routine uses for this information is available in our System of Records Notices entitled, Attorney Fee File, 60-0003 and Master Representative Payee File, 60-0222. These notices, additional information regarding this form, and information regarding our programs and systems, are available on-line at http://www.socialsecurity.gov or at your local Social Security office.

Paperwork Reduction Act Statement - This information collection meets the requirements of 44 U.S.C. § 3507, as amended by section 2 of the Paperwork Reduction Act of 1995. You do not need to answer these questions unless we display a valid Office of Management and Budget control number. We estimate that it will take about 10 minutes to read the instructions, gather the facts, and answer the questions. **SEND OR BRING THE COMPLETED FORM TO YOUR LOCAL SOCIAL SECURITY OFFICE.** You can find your local Social Security office through SSA's website at www.socialsecurity.gov. Offices are also listed under U.S. Government agencies in your telephone directory or you may call Social Security at 1-800-772-1213 (TTY 1-800-325-0778). You may send comments on our time estimate above to: SSA, 6401 Security Blvd, Baltimore, MD 21235-6401. ***Send only comments relating to our time estimate to this address, not the completed form.***

§178.4.3 Form: Request for Business Entity Taxpayer Information (SSA-1694)

Social Security Administration

Form Approved
OMB No. 0960-0731

Request for Business Entity Taxpayer Information

BUSINESS INFORMATION

Employer Identification Number (EIN)

Name of the Business Entity

Tax Mailing Address
P.O. Box, Street, Apt., or Suite No.

City

State

ZIP Code or Postal Zone

Country

PERJURY STATEMENT

I declare under penalty of perjury that I have examined all of the information on this request and it is true to the best of my knowledge. I am aware that if I knowingly and willingly make any false representation about any material fact provided herein or knowingly and willingly make any false representation to obtain information from Social Security records, and/or attempt to deceive the Social Security Administration as to my true identity, I could be criminally punished by a fine or imprisonment or both.

Printed Name

Signature

Date / /

Contact Name

Phone Number (including area code)

FOR AGENCY USE ONLY:

IMPORTANT INFORMATION

Purpose of Form

The Social Security Administration (SSA) is required to file an information return (i.e., Form 1099-MISC) with the Internal Revenue Service (IRS) when payments of $600 or more have been made to appointed representatives associated with a business entity as employees or partners. In order to meet this requirement, SSA must obtain the name, employer identification number (EIN), and address of the business entity.

Instructions for Completing the Form

Employer Identification Number

Please enter your EIN. If you do not have an EIN, please apply for one immediately by filing an SS-4, Application for Employer Identification Number, with the IRS. You can apply for an EIN online by accessing the IRS website at www.irs.gov.

Name of Business Entity

Enter your business name as shown on required Federal tax documents. Normally, this will match the name used when you filed a Form SS-4 to apply for an EIN.

Tax Mailing Address

Please enter your tax mailing address. SSA will mail Form 1099-MISC to you at this address if payments of $600 or more are made to appointed representatives associated with your business entity during a tax year.

Privacy Act Notice

Request for Business Entity Taxpayer Information
Sections 206(a) and 1631(d) of the Social Security Act, as amended, authorize us to collect this information. We will use the information you provide to identify appointed representatives associated with a business entity as employees or partners and to facilitate issuance of appropriate return information for reporting purposes.

Furnishing us this information is voluntary. However, failing to provide us with all or part of the information could prevent us from sending you Form 1099-MISC.

We rarely use the information you supply for any purpose other than to identify appointed representatives associated with a business entity as employees or partners and to facilitate issuance of appropriate return information for reporting purposes. We may also disclose information to another person or to another agency in accordance with approved routine uses, which include but are not limited to the following:
1. To enable a third party or an agency to assist Social Security in establishing rights to Social Security benefits and/or coverage;
2. To comply with Federal laws requiring the release of information from Social Security records (e.g., to the Government Accountability Office and Department of Veterans' Affairs);
3. To make determinations for eligibility in similar health and income maintenance programs at the Federal, State, and local level; and,
4. To facilitate statistical research, audit, or investigative activities necessary to assure the integrity and improvement of Social Security programs (e.g., to the Bureau of the Census and private concerns under contract to Social Security).

We may also use the information you provide in computer matching programs. Matching programs compare our records with records kept by other Federal, State, or local government agencies. Information from these matching programs can be used to establish or verify a person's eligibility for federally-funded or administered benefit programs and for repayment of payments or delinquent debts under these programs.

A complete list of routine uses for this information is available in the Systems of Records Notice entitled, Master Representative Payee File, 60-0222. The notice, additional information regarding this form, and information regarding our programs and systems, are available on-line at www.socialsecurity.gov or at your local Social Security office.

Paperwork Reduction Act Statement

This information collection meets the requirements of 44 U.S.C. 3507, as amended by section 2 of the Paperwork Reduction Act of 1995. You do not need to answer these questions unless we display a valid Office of Management and Budget control number. We estimate that it will take 20 minutes to read the instructions, gather the facts, and answer the questions. **SEND THE COMPLETED FORM TO YOUR LOCAL SOCIAL SECURITY OFFICE. The office is listed under U.S. Government agencies in your telephone directory or you may call Social Security at 1-800-772-1213.** You may send comments on our time estimate above to SSA, 6401 Security Boulevard, Baltimore, MD, 21235-6401. **Send only comments relating to our time estimate to this address, not the completed form.**

§178.5 Appointed Representative Services — Online Access to Clients' Electronic Files

"Appointed Representative Services," which you may sign up for by completing a form SSA-1699 (§178.4.1) after being invited to do so by SSA, is SSA's way of referring to granting a representative online access to his or her clients' electronic files. When you are cleared for online access, you will be able to look at your client's file on SSA's server using your Internet connection by entering at http://www.ssa.gov/ar/. When you enter your user ID and a password, you will instantly receive a 10-digit number by text message on your cell phone. Once you enter that number and your client's Social Security number, you will be able to view your client's file in two versions. If exhibits have been numbered you will be able to view your client's hearing exhibit file starting from a list of exhibits; and you will also be able to look at the "Case Documents" version, which, before exhibits are numbered, looks like a raw file. After exhibits are numbered, by looking at the Case Documents version, you will be able to see all the exhibits, including exhibit numbers, plus you will be able to see everything that was left out of the exhibit file (which is usually junk but every once in a while someone makes a mistake).

You will be able to download a PDF version of the file or download the hearing exhibit file in its tiff format so that you end up with a file on your computer that looks similar to an SSA hearing exhibit file on CD-ROM, complete with a list of exhibits that is opened with an Internet browser. After you submit an exhibit electronically to SSA, you will be able to check to see that it is included in the file, whether it has been numbered and, if so, what exhibit number it was given. Following a hearing, you can check the online file to see if a decision has been issued and download a copy of the decision before you receive the paper copy in the mail. You can also download a copy of the recording of the hearing shortly after the hearing is held. (To listen to the recording you will need to download and install on your computer the FTR player from www.fortherecord.com.)

You can also obtain lists of all your cases at the hearing or Appeals Council levels that show the status of each case.

To sign up for online access, contact a hearing office and ask to be placed on the list of representatives who would like to receive an invitation to enroll. To sign up you must be an attorney or a non-attorney representative who has been qualified to receive direct payment of attorney fees. You must have at least one case pending at a hearing office where you are the primary appointed representative or pending at the Appeals Council. You must also have a cell phone that can receive text messages. If SSA invites you to sign up, it will ask you to complete a form SSA-1699, Registration for Appointed Representative Services and Direct Payment, and fax it to SSA prior to meeting in person with an SSA employee at a hearing office. *See* §178.4.1. Although most representatives completed this form (or an earlier version) when they signed up for direct payment of attorney fees, it will be necessary to complete the form again when instructed by SSA. The form now does double duty. Any qualified representative can complete and submit form SSA-1699 to sign up for direct payment of fees or to update a form SSA-1699 previously submitted to SSA. But to use form SSA-1699 to sign up for online access to your client's file—the "appointed representative services"—you must have an invitation. For additional information, *see* POMS GN 03913.000 – GN 03913.025.

As part of the sign-up process, you will be given a representative ID, a user ID and you will be asked to select a password, which you will have to change every 90 days.

Many lawyers want their paralegals and secretaries also to have online access to a firm's Social Security clients' electronic files. Although SSA has no problem giving firm employees a user ID and password so that they can *submit* electronic documents to a claimant's file, at this time SSA refuses to allow anyone other than the primary appointed representative to *view* a claimant's file online. If your firm appoints more than one lawyer as representatives for a claimant, only the primary representative will have online access to that particular claimant's file, even if the other appointed representatives have also signed up for online access. When someone who is not the primary representative tries to access a claimant's electronic file, the website generates an error message.

In the future SSA plans to extend online access to other qualified firm members. Online access currently applies only to cases pending at a hearing office (and for three months after the ALJ decision is issued) and, if review is requested, at the Appeals Council. Online access is not available for cases at the initial and reconsideration stages, though SSA plans to extend online access to those stages in the future.

§178.6 Requirement That Appeals Be Filed Online

20 C.F.R. § 404.1713 provides that a "representative must conduct business with us electronically at the times and in the manner we prescribe on matters for which the representative requests direct fee payment." This regulation cross references 20 C.F.R. § 404.1740(b)(4), which is part of the "rules of conduct and standards of responsibility for representatives." That subsection

provides that it is an affirmative duty for a representative to "[c]onduct business with us electronically at the times and in the manner we prescribe on matters for which the representative requests direct fee payment." Effective March 16, 2012, pursuant to these regulations SSA requires that the Request for Reconsideration and Request for Hearing along with the Disability Report—Appeal be filed online. 77 Fed. Reg. 4653 (Jan. 31, 2012) and 77 Fed. Reg. 13968 (Mar. 8, 2012).

A 2015 upgrade to the iAppeals system allows an Appointment of Representative form and medical evidence to be submitted electronically at the time the appeal is filed. However, the appeal is not considered filed until the Disability Report is completed along with the Request for Reconsideration or Request for Hearing. POMS GN 03101.125.

Note that because this requirement to submit appeals electronically is included in SSA's rules of conduct, in addition to refusing to pay the representative directly, SSA may invoke sanctions against a representative who fails to conduct business with it electronically. *See* 76 Fed. Reg. 56108 (Sept. 12, 2011). Thus, whenever it is necessary to file a paper appeal, be sure to document your file well enough that you will be able to explain later why an Internet appeal was not used.

§178.7 Changing Your Address With SSA

When you change your address or change your firm affiliation, you must complete a new SSA-1699 with the new information. The SSA-1699 can be completed online from a link at http://www.socialsecurity.gov/ar/, printed and faxed to SSA. According to POMS GN 03913.015C.1, if you registered with SSA for appointed representative services and direct payment of fees after October 30, 2009, you need to put on the SSA-1699 only your name, Rep ID, and the information that has changed. You must also complete the attestation sections and sign the form.

If you registered for appointed representative services and direct payment of fees before October 31, 2009 (which means you do not have a Rep ID), you must complete the entire SSA-1699.

Fax the completed and signed form to 1-570-270-7307 or 1-570-831-1312. SSA-1699s must be faxed to one of these dedicated fax numbers one form at a time.

According to POMS GN 03913.015A, submitting a new SSA-1699 will change your address for all future cases. For all pending cases, it will be necessary to submit a new SSA-1695 for each case.

§ 178.8 SSA's Appointed Representative Best Practices and Tips

From: https:// www.ssa.gov

We value our relationship with the appointed representative community and provide the following recommended best practices for use when conducting business with the agency.

Online Services

- Become familiar with our website at www.socialsecurity.gov/representation and sign up for email updates to stay informed of developments that affect representatives.
- Use Electronic Records Express (ERE) at www.ssa.gov/ere to expedite the disability decision process. Ask the Disability Determination Services (DDS) or Office of Disability Adjudication and Review (ODAR) handling your client's claim to give you the barcode required for submitting records online.
- Request access to your client's electronic folder for cases pending at the hearings level and above by visiting: www.socialsecurity.gov/representation.

Initial Claims

- File the initial disability claim online. Expedite processing of the claim by having as much disability-related and medical information available and complete the SSA-3368 (Medical Disability Report) at the same time of the filing.
- Provide the SSA-820 (Work Activity Report – Self-Employed Person) or SSA-821(Work Activity Report – Employee) for all work done after the alleged onset date, as appropriate. Find helpful information for filing complete online applications at Apply Online for Disability Benefits.
- Ensure your client has attested or has personally signed the application.
- Submit Worker's Compensation information as soon as possible to expedite case and fee payment.
- Mail or fax your notice of appointment (i.e., SSA-1696 (Appointment of Representative) or writing) and the SSA-1695 (Identifying Information for Possible Direct Payment of

Authorized Fees) to the servicing field office, as determined by the claimant's zip code at www.socialsecurity.gov/agency/contact/. File these documents with the claim or after the claim is filed, never before.

Reconsideration and Hearing Requests

- File your appeal online on our Disability Appeal portal at https://secure.ssa.gov/iApplsRe/start and be ready to complete the SSA-3441 (Disability Report – Appeal) with the request. (If you are eligible for and seek direct fee payment, you are required to do so.)
- Submit medical documentation, appointment forms and other documents electronically with the appeal request online.
- Include a statement with the reason why the appeal was not filed timely, if you or your client files the appeal after the 60-day appeal period. If we cannot establish "good cause for late filing," we cannot process the appeal. If we establish "good cause" submit a new notice of appointment if you want to represent or continue representing a client on the appeal.

Submitting Documents

- Prevent delays by avoiding duplicate submissions. Use one channel only (online, mail, or fax), when submitting appointment-related forms or other evidentiary documents to prevent delays.
- Include or resubmit a notice of appointment or fee payment forms (e.g., SSA-1695) only if you want to give us new or updated information. We will notify you when we process the documents.
- Fax your non-electronic submissions of 30 pages or less, to the servicing field office.
- Mail your non-electronic submissions over 30 pages, to the servicing field office.

Status Inquiries and Field Office Contacts

- Be prepared to answer personally identifiable questions when you call our field offices, so that we can confirm your identity and protect the claimant's privacy. Visit our Public Program Operations Manual Section GN 03360.005 at https://secure.ssa.gov/apps10/poms.nsf/partlist for additional information on disclosure.
- Know that for privacy and security reasons we are unable to respond to email inquiries.

Representative Issues

- We only recognize individual representatives, not entities.
- We only accept appointment and fee documents such as withdrawals and fee petitions relating to an appointed representative submitted by the appointed representative.
- Be aware that the fee payment process becomes "manual" and may require additional time when multiple representatives are involved in a case.
- Secure a new notice of appointment from the claimant, with a new date and signature and submit it to us, when substituting representatives during the administrative review process.
- Submit a new 1695 for each of your pending cases, when any of your personal or banking information or employer affiliations change.
- Always keep your information, including your address(es) and telephone number(s) updated using form SSA-1699.

Updated 3/31/2016

§179 Begin Keeping Time Records

If you use a "two-tier" attorney fee agreement, in most cases, filing a fee petition with SSA will be unnecessary, but be prepared for those few cases that you lose at the ALJ hearing but win later. It will be necessary to submit a fee petition. Begin keeping time records at the conclusion of the initial interview. Good time records are essential for completion of a fee petition. You also may have to file a fee petition in the unlikely event that the ALJ or claimant objects to your fee under the fee agreement process.

In addition, time records will help you assess the profitability of Social Security disability representation. Time records also ought to be used by an attorney when, at the conclusion of the case, the attorney evaluates the value of representation so that the attorney may avoid accepting excessive fees from disability claimants, something which would violate the Rules of Professional Conduct even if neither the claimant nor the ALJ objected to the fee. *See* Chapter 7 for more information about attorney's fees.

§180 After Initial Interview — Hearing Stage

After the interview, send your client a letter that explains hearing procedure, etc. *See* §181.

If the Request for Hearing has already been filed, prepare a letter notifying the hearing office that you will be representing the claimant and transmitting an Appointment of Representative form SSA-1696. *See* sample letter §182. Note that even if the claimant's case uses an electronic folder at SSA, initial documents must be submitted on paper. (In response to receipt of your letter, the hearing office will provide you with a bar code and instructions how to file subsequent documents, including medical records, electronically.) If you are planning on using the "fee agreement process" for obtaining your fee, send your fee agreement with the initial letter to the hearing office. If you intend to use the fee petition process for obtaining your fee, delete the second paragraph in the sample letter, §182, since it is not necessary to send your contract to SSA. If you want direct payment of your fee, send a form SSA-1695 to the local office. *See* sample letter §184.

If the Request for Hearing was not filed by the claimant before your interview, unless you file the Request for Hearing and Disability Report—Appeal online, send a completed Request for Hearing and Disability Report—Appeal along with an Appointment of Representative form, and a signed Authorization to Disclose Information to the Social Security Administration (Form SSA-827) to the claimant's social security office. *See* sample letter §183. If you want to use the "fee agreement process" to obtain your fee, enclose your signed fee agreement. If you are not going to use the fee agreement process to obtain your fee, delete the second paragraph in the sample letter, §183. If you want direct payment of your fee, send the sample letter §184 to the local office with its enclosures. You can send letters §183 and §184 in the same envelope as long as you staple to letter §184 a form SSA-1695, another copy of the contract and another copy of the Appointment of Representative form.

§181 Form: Letter to Claimant Following Initial Interview — Hearing Stage

Client's Name
Street Address
City, State Zip

Re: Disability Case

Dear ***Client's Name:***

Enclosed with this letter please find the following:

- A copy of my letter notifying the Social Security Administration that I will be representing you at your hearing

- Your copy of the Appointment of Representative form

- A copy of our contract

Please review the contract again. If you have any questions about any of the contract's provisions, please telephone my office and ask to speak with me personally.

This letter attempts to answer some questions people often have when they are going to have a disability hearing. Please read the letter now and keep it as a reference.

How long will it take for a hearing to be held, a decision to be issued and for benefits to be paid?
It varies a lot. Lately, our hearing office has been averaging about [*enter your local number*] months from the date a person requests a hearing until a decision is issued; but this is an average. Some hearings don't take that long and some take longer. After the hearing, unless we are lucky enough to get a bench decision at the hearing, it often takes two or three months for a decision to be issued. After that, if we win, it takes a month or two for current benefits to start being paid. From the date of the decision, it can take from one to five or six months for all back benefits to be paid, sometimes longer when there is SSI involved. Thus, all this takes a long time, much longer than it should. I've discovered that there are few opportunities for a representative to speed things up. About all I can do is try not to slow things down. I'll try to do my best.

How will I be notified of when my hearing is?
You should hear from me first. Hearing office staff will telephone me before scheduling your hearing to make sure I don't have any conflicts on my calendar. As soon as I hear from the hearing scheduler, I'll send you a letter. After you get the letter from me, you'll get a Notice of Hearing from the hearing office.

What happens if I get a Notice of Hearing before I get a letter from my representative telling me about the date?
It may be that someone failed to call me about your hearing. So, if you get a Notice of Hearing before you get a letter from me telling you the date of your hearing, ***call me immediately.***

Is there anything that I should not do, anything that might harm my case?
Although judges and hearing office staff are not supposed to search the Internet for information about claimants, it is a good idea to avoid putting any personal information on the Internet where everyone, including someone from the Social Security Administration, could see it. Do not discuss your disability case online. It is possible that something you say online could create the wrong impression.

Is there anything I can do during the time I'm waiting for a hearing that would help my case?
Here's some important things you can do:

1. Continue with regular medical treatment. ***Be a model patient.*** Do everything your doctor asks you to do.

2. ***Be sure your doctor understands your symptoms and limitations***, including any that arise from side effects of medication. Be sure your doctor understands the impact of your symptoms on your daily activities.

At the same time, though, remember that anything you say to your doctor might show up in your medical records, which will be read by the judge. So, it is best not to talk with your doctor about what your representative has told you about your disability case. Also, don't talk with your doctor about how frustrated you are with the Social Security Administration or how slow the process is. When such things appear in medical records, they can give the wrong impression.

3. ***Keep track of your medical appointments.*** We'll ask you for a list from time to time.

4. Be sure to provide us with complete names and addresses of all treating sources (including clinic names). Gather ***business cards*** for all doctors, therapists, etc., and send them to us when we ask for a medical care update.

5. If you have ***disability forms*** or work release forms in your possession that your doctor completed describing your work limitations, which you have not already given us, please send me copies right away. Such forms are often not included in the records we get from your doctor (despite the fact that we always ask for them). Such forms sometimes win cases.

Do I need to get medical records or reports for my representative?
No. You don't have to get any medical records or reports yourself. In fact, it's better if you do not even try to get such things unless I ask you to.

But what if my doctor gives me a report?
If you happen to get something such as a disability form completed by your doctor for an insurance company, etc., be sure to send me a copy.

What if the hearing office sends me a form to be completed by my doctor?
Sometimes a claimant may be sent a form to be completed by a doctor concerning how much work the claimant can do. If the hearing office sends you a form to be completed by your doctor, telephone me so that we can discuss how to deal with this. I may want you to send the form to me; but call me first so we can discuss it.

Should I send anything to the hearing office?
No. As a rule, do not send anything of any substance to the Social Security Administration without your representative seeing it first.

Should I send my representative the "acknowledgment" that comes with the Notice of Hearing?
No. There will be a paper sent to you with your Notice of Hearing that you must mark to indicate that you'll be coming to the hearing. This paper is called an Acknowledgment of Notice of Hearing. You may send the "acknowledgment" directly back to the hearing office. I don't have to see it. But don't send anything else to the Social Security Administration without me seeing it first.

Will I have to fill out any forms before my hearing?
Yes. Usually the hearing office will send you some forms to complete about recent medical treatment, what medications you're taking, etc. Complete these forms as soon as possible after you get them and send them to me. I'll forward them to the hearing office.

What will my representative do to prepare for the hearing?
I will review your Social Security file. I will figure out what we need to prove to win your case and how to prove it. I will get the necessary medical records and other records. I will obtain reports from your doctors, if necessary. And I will meet with you a day or so before your hearing to get you prepared to testify. I will also talk with any witnesses from whom we may want to present testimony at your hearing.

What can I do to help get ready for my hearing?
Think about who might be a good witness—someone who knows you well, who knows all the problems you've been having lately and who can describe them for the judge. Most people use as witnesses their spouse, other family member or a close friend because usually they are the ones who know them the best and there really isn't anyone else. Such witnesses are fine. I think they are truthful, good witnesses; but sometimes a judge will think that close friends or family members bend over backwards to help a claimant. Therefore, often the very best witnesses are people who are not as close and who might be considered more objective. In the past my clients have suggested as witnesses former supervisors, coworkers, social workers, vocational rehabilitation counselors, ministers, landlords, neighbors, etc. If you have an idea for having someone like this to be a witness, call me about it when you receive the letter from me notifying you of your hearing date.

Should I try to get letters from friends and relatives about my disability?
Letters from friends, relatives and other people can be very useful in a disability case. As a rule, the more such letters we have, the better. If you want, I can provide you with a memo to distribute to friends and relatives that explains how to prepare such a letter.

Should I telephone my representative whenever I see a doctor?
No. It is not necessary to telephone me to tell me about routine medical care. But keep track of the dates of all medical treatment between now and the time we go to your hearing. When I send you the letter about your hearing date, I'll probably send you a form to complete to tell me about all of the medical care you've received since I first saw you.

Under what circumstances should I telephone my representative?
There probably will be little need for you to telephone me to discuss your case prior to the time I notify you of when your hearing will be held. However, if one of the following things happens, please telephone me:

- There is a dramatic change in your condition—for the worse or the better.
- Your doctor gives you a ***new*** diagnosis of your medical condition.
- You are hospitalized.
- You go back to work.
- You are thinking about going to work full-time or part-time. (We have a memo about working part-time. Please call us if you want a copy.)
- You change your address and/or telephone.
- Someone from SSA contacts you.
- You get a letter from SSA that you don't understand.
- You get a Notice of Hearing without first getting a letter from me telling you the date of your hearing.
- You get a form from the hearing office to be completed by your doctor.

But if at any time you have a question about your case, please telephone me.

Sincerely,

Attorney
Enclosures

§182 Form: Initial Letter to Hearing Office (When Request for Hearing Has Already Been Filed)

Office of Disability Adjudication and Review, SSA

Address

Re: ***Client's Name***

SSN:

Dear Office of Disability Adjudication and Review:

I have been retained to represent ___________________ [***Client's Name***] in an appeal presently pending in your office.

Enclosed is a signed Appointment of Representative form. Also enclosed is a contract signed by our client so that the fee agreement process will apply to the fee in this case. Please note that our client has been provided with a copy of this contract.

Please let me know when the hearing exhibits are numbered and how we may obtain a copy of the exhibit file. Also, so that I can avoid conflicts on my calendar, please have the scheduler contact me when the case is ready to be scheduled.

Sincerely,

____

Attorney

Enclosures

cc: Client's Name

Social Security Office

§183 Form: Initial Letter to Social Security Office (With Alternative Language — Enclosing Request for Hearing or Request for Hearing Filed Via Internet)

Social Security Office

Address

Re: ***Claimant's Name***

SSN:

Dear Social Security Office:

I have been retained to represent ______________________ [***Client's Name***] in an appeal for disability benefits from the Social Security Administration. Please note that a Request for Hearing and Disability Report—Appeal were completed online on [***date***]. I enclose the following signed forms:

- Appointment of Representative
- Authorization to Disclose Information to the Social Security Administration (Form SSA-827)

Because I would like to use the "fee agreement process" for obtaining approval of my fee in this case, I enclose the original contract signed by my client and me. Please note that my client has been provided with a copy of this contract.

If you need any other forms signed by my client, you may send them directly to my client.

Please send this letter along with my client's file to the hearing office.

Note to Hearing Office:

1. Please let me know when the hearing exhibits are numbered and how we may obtain a copy of the exhibit file.

2. Please have the scheduler contact me before setting a hearing date so that I may avoid conflicts in my schedule.

Sincerely,

____
Attorney

cc: Client's Name

§184 Form: Letter to Social Security Office Transmitting Form SSA-1695

Social Security Office

Address

Re: ***Claimant's Name***

SSN:

Dear Social Security Office:

Enclosed is Form SSA-1695 in the case of ______________ [***Client's Name***]. Once you have entered the appropriate data into SSA's computer system, please send us a letter acknowledging receipt of the SSA-1695 in accordance with the requirements of POMS GN 03910.042A.2.

Please note that we have stapled to the SSA-1695 a copy of the Appointment of Representative Form SSA-1696 and a copy of the contract with our client.

Sincerely,

____

Attorney

Enclosures

§190 After Initial Interview — Below Hearing Stage

Some lawyers never get involved in a case below the hearing stage. A few are so heavily involved from the beginning that they help the claimant submit the Social Security disability application and Disability Report online and before the state agency acts on the claimant's case, they submit all medical records and reports from the claimant's doctors.

Many lawyers who get involved below the hearing stage take a middle position. They let the state agency gather medical records; and they try to focus their attention on what the state agency does poorly: 1) obtain opinions about capacity for working from treating doctors; 2) obtain medical and other records that the state agency rarely gets such as relevant medical records more than a year old (*see* 20 C.F.R. § 404.1512(d)), long term disability insurance carrier records, employment records, school records, and sometimes vocational rehabilitation records; and 3) monitor the state agency's use of consultative examinations and insist, as appropriate, that the claimant's doctor perform the consultative exam. *See* 20 C.F.R. § 404.1519h. In addition, many lawyers find it useful to talk with the disability examiner at the state agency.

Being involved at this stage allows you to monitor how SSA forms are completed by your client and assist if necessary. When the state agency asks your client to complete a Function Report—Adult (*see* sample at § 206.8), if you or a member of your staff does not assist with completion of the form, send your client the memorandum at § 195, which will answer questions claimants often have about completing this form.

One of the great advantages of lawyer involvement below the hearing stage, even in those cases that must ultimately go to a hearing, is that it gives you the opportunity to influence the choice of consultative examiners. SSA's regulations state that the treating doctor, if that doctor is "qualified, equipped and willing" to accept the fee paid for such exams, is the "preferred" consultative examiner. 20 C.F.R. § 404.1519h. To accomplish this, though, you must move quickly. Generally, you will find out that someone at the state agency feels a consultative examination is necessary only when your client receives a notice saying that an exam is scheduled with someone other than the claimant's doctor. As soon as you find out that an exam is scheduled, you need to contact the claimant's doctor to find out if the doctor is "qualified, equipped and willing" to accept the fee for such exams. If so, you need to contact the disability examiner and insist, pursuant to 20 C.F.R. § 404.1519h, that the claimant's doctor perform the consultative examination. The claimant's doctor brings greater knowledge of the claimant to such an examination. As a rule, the claimant's doctor will provide a more thorough examination report than the typical consultative examiner.

When the claimant's doctor is not available to perform the consultative examination, you need to monitor the consultative examination process. You need to learn about consultative examiners in your area so that you know who to object to. Consider going along with your clients to some consultative examinations. Set up files for individual consultative examiners. Include copies of consultative examination reports and notes gathered from your clients, who are excellent sources of information about consultative examiners. A form is provided at §194, that you may send to your client before the client is to attend a consultative examination. Use the data you collect to determine which consultative examiners to object to. Note that SSA's regulations state that if there is a good reason for an objection to a consultative examiner, it will schedule the examination with another physician or psychologist.

The rules, for the most part, contemplate situations where the claimant has had experience with the particular consultative examiner, such as where the examiner performed an adverse medical exam for an insurance carrier. However, the rules also contemplate objections based on lack of objectivity in general. If this objection is raised, to "avoid a delay in processing" the claim, the consultative examiner will be changed while a review is conducted. "However, if we had previously conducted such a review and found that the reports of the consultative physician or psychologist in question conformed to our guidelines, we will not change [the] examination." 20 C.F.R. § 404.1519j.

Perhaps the biggest problem with being involved at this stage is that SSA has a bad habit of failing to send copies of initial and reconsideration determination letters to the claimant's attorney. This is a potentially serious problem that you need to alert the claimant to at the initial interview and remind the claimant about in the initial letter. Claimants tend to assume that the lawyer will take care of the appeal—something that is impossible if the lawyer doesn't know that a denial has been issued. SSA will likely find good cause for missing the deadline for appeal in cases where the lawyer was not sent a copy of the denial letter and the claimant assumed that the lawyer was taking care of the appeal. *Cf.* HALLEX I-2-0-60 B. But this is still a hassle.

Ask your client to telephone you whenever the client receives a determination from SSA and remind your client about this at every available opportunity. Also, set up a system in your office for regularly checking the status of cases below the hearing stage by contacting your client, the state agency or the local office.

Some lawyers do nothing more than submit an Appointment of Representative form and a contract to SSA in cases below the hearing stage. They figure that the case will be denied at that level anyway and that whatever they do is a waste of time. This is a mistake for several reasons. First, even if you are unable to convince the state agency that your client is disabled, there are things that you can do when the case is at the state agency that may make a difference in the outcome of the hearing, *e.g.,* obtaining a report from the treating doctor or insisting that the treating doctor conduct the consultative examination.

Second, if you do nothing and you win below the hearing stage, SSA's rules (POMS GN 03960.010 B.2) provide that a fee under the fee agreement process may be protested (even though this doesn't happen often in practice); and if you take a $6,000 fee for nothing more than interviewing the claimant, you may be in violation of your state bar's rules on excessive fees.

Third, if you lose below the hearing level, appeal and win at the hearing, you run the risk that an ALJ will object to your inactivity below the hearing stage, arguing that if you had done your job, the case might not have needed to go to the hearing level. Some ALJs have challenged fees on this basis.

§191 Form: Letter to Claimant Following Initial Interview — Below Hearing Stage

Client Name
Street Address
City, State Zip

Re: Disability Case

Dear ***Client's Name:***

Enclosed is a copy of my letter notifying the Social Security Administration (SSA) that I will be representing you [and a copy of your Request for Reconsideration]. Also enclosed for your records are a copy of our contract and your copy of the Appointment of Representative form.

Please review the contract again. If you have any questions about any of the contract's provisions, please telephone my office and ask to speak with me personally.

This letter attempts to answer some questions people often have about their disability cases. Please read the letter now and keep it as a reference.

How long will it take for a determination to be issued?
It varies a lot. It usually takes only a few months for a denial to be issued. Sometimes it takes less than one month. It often takes longer for a decision to be issued finding you disabled.

Do you think we have a chance of winning?
I am always hopeful. However, less than 40 percent of people who apply are found disabled at the initial or reconsideration stages. Although this does not mean that I will not try to win your case at this level, do not be discouraged if we receive a denial notice. I agreed to represent you because I thought you had a good case. It may be necessary to go to a hearing to win your case.

What happens when I get a denial notice?
The first thing you need to do is make sure that I received a copy. It is necessary for you to do this because the Social Security Administration frequently fails to send me a copy of the determination. If I do not get a copy of the notice from Social Security, I won't know that a decision has been made on your case unless you tell me. Therefore, please telephone me when you get the notice of determination in your case. I will then send you the necessary forms to sign for appealing.

Is there anything that I should not do, anything that might harm my case?
Avoid putting any personal information on the Internet where everyone, including someone from the Social Security Administration, could see it. Do not discuss your disability case online. It is possible that something you say online could create the wrong impression.

Is there anything I can do during the time I'm waiting for a hearing that would help my case?
Here's some important things you can do:

1. Continue with regular medical treatment. ***Be a model patient.*** Do everything your doctor asks you to do.

2. ***Be sure your doctor understands your symptoms and limitations***, including any that arise from side effects of medication. Be sure your doctor understands the impact of your symptoms on your daily activities.

At the same time, though, remember that anything you say to your doctor might show up in your medical records, which will be read by the judge. So, it is best not to talk with your doctor about what your representative has told you about your disability case. Also, don't talk with your doctor about how frustrated you are with the Social Security Administration or how slow the process is. When such things appear in medical records, they can give the wrong impression.

3. ***Keep track of your medical appointments.*** We'll ask you for a list from time to time.

4. Be sure to provide us with complete names and addresses of all treating sources. Gather ***business cards*** for all doctors, therapists, etc., and send them to us when we ask for a medical care update.

5. If you have ***disability forms*** or work release forms in your possession that your doctor completed describing your work limitations, which you have not already given us, please send me copies right away. Such forms are often not included in the records we get from your doctor (despite the fact that we always ask for them). Such forms sometimes win cases.

Do I need to get medical records or reports for my representative?
No. You don't have to get any medical records or reports yourself. In fact, it's better if you do not even try to get such things unless I ask you to.

But what if my doctor gives me a report?
If you happen to get something such as a disability form completed by your doctor for an insurance company, etc., be sure to send me a copy.

Should I send anything to the Social Security Administration?
No. As a rule, do not send anything of any substance to the Social Security Administration without your representative seeing it first. The only exception to this rule is if SSA asks you to sign medical consent forms, you may sign them and send them directly back to SSA. I don't need to see those.

Will I have to fill out any additional forms?
Sometimes SSA will send you a form to complete about your daily activities, etc. Sometimes SSA asks you to complete other forms that ask about your symptoms. If you want to discuss a form with me before completing it, please call me; but here's the advice I always give: Be truthful. Don't exaggerate; but don't minimize your problems either. Include plenty of details and examples that show your limitations; but don't go on and on. Complete any form as soon as possible after you get it and send it to me. I'll review it and forward it to SSA.

Will SSA ask me to see one of their doctors?
Sometimes SSA will ask you to see a private doctor who is paid by SSA for what they call a "consultative examination." However, the quality of such examinations varies widely. SSA's rules state that your own doctor can perform such an examination if your doctor is able to do it and agrees to accept the payment offered by SSA. If SSA wants to send you for a consultative examination, we may ask that your own doctor do this exam. If you get a notice to go to a consultative examination, please telephone us to make sure we received a copy of the notice.

What will my representative do to represent me at this stage?
I will review your case. I will figure out what we need to prove to win your case and figure out how to prove it. I will make sure that the Social Security Administration gets the necessary medical records and other records. I will obtain reports from your doctors, if necessary.

Should I telephone my representative whenever I see a doctor?
No. It is not necessary to telephone me to tell me about *routine* medical care. But keep track of the dates of all medical treatment from now on. I will gather this information from you when we request your hearing; and I may periodically request updated medical information from you.

Under what circumstances should I telephone my representative?
If one of the following things happens, please telephone me:

- There is a dramatic change in your condition—for the worse or the better.
- Your doctor gives you a new diagnosis of your medical condition.
- You start seeing a new doctor.
- You are hospitalized.

- You go back to work.
- You change your address and/or telephone.
- Someone from SSA contacts you.
- You get a notice asking you to attend a consultative examination.
- You get a letter from SSA that you don't understand.
- You get a notice from SSA telling you that you are or are not disabled.

But if at any time you have a question about your case, please telephone me.

Sincerely,

____
Attorney

§192 Form: Initial Letter to SSA — No Appeal Due, Case Below Hearing Stage

Social Security Office

Street Address
City, State Zip

Re: ***Client's Name***

SSN:

Dear Social Security Office:

I represent ___________________________ [***Client's Name***] in a disability claim that is pending with the Social Security Administration. Please see that I get a copy of all future notices and determinations regarding my client. I enclose the original Appointment of Representative form.

In addition, I enclose an original contract signed by our client so that the fee agreement process will apply to the fee in this case. Please note that our client has been provided with a copy of this contract.

Please provide me with a CD-ROM containing my client's electronic file. I make this request pursuant to provisions of the Privacy Act, 5 U.S.C. § 552a.

If you need any information from me, please do not hesitate to contact me.

It is my understanding from discussing this case with my client that no appeal is currently due; however, if this is not correct, please treat this letter as a request to appeal this case to the next level of administrative review.

Sincerely,

____
Attorney

§193 Form: Initial Letter to SSA — Request for Reconsideration Filed Via Internet)

Social Security Office

Street Address
City, State Zip

Re: ***Client's Name***

SSN:

Dear Social Security Office:

I have been retained to represent ______________________ [***Client's Name***] in an appeal for disability benefits from the Social Security Administration. Please note that a Request for Reconsideration and Disability Report—Appeal were completed online on [***date***]. I enclose the following signed forms:

- Appointment of Representative
- Authorization to Disclose Information to the Social Security Administration (Form SSA-827)

Because I would like to use the fee agreement process for obtaining approval of my fee in this case, I enclose the original contract signed by my client and me. Please note that my client has been provided with a copy of this contract.

If you need any other forms signed by my client, you may send them directly to my client.

Please provide me with a CD-ROM containing my client's electronic file. I make this request pursuant to provisions of the Privacy Act, 5 U.S.C. § 552a.

If you need any information from me, please do not hesitate to contact me.

Sincerely,

____
Attorney

§194 Form: Claimant's Consultative Examination Questionnaire

To: ___________________________ [Client's Name]

CONSULTATIVE EXAMINATION QUESTIONNAIRE

Appointment scheduled with ____________________ [Doctor], on __________, _____ [Date], at [Time].

1) Did you actually see the doctor named above? ___ Yes ___ No
If no, please state the name of the doctor you saw:

2) What is the doctor's specialty? (Orthopedic, cardiac, etc.) ______________________________

3) Was this the first time you have ever seen this doctor? ___ Yes ___ No

4) Did the doctor examine you in an office or in an examining room? ______________________

5) Was anyone else present during the exam? (Nurse or assistant) ______________________

6) What did the doctor do? ____

7) Did the doctor draw blood or take x-rays? If x-rays, what part of the body? ______________
____

8) Did the doctor have you do any test with a machine? ___ Yes ___ No
Explain: ____

9) Were you asked to fill out any forms or questionnaires related to your disability?
___ Yes ___ No Explain: ______________________________________

10) Did you feel the doctor gave you a thorough exam? ___ Yes ___ No
Explain: ____

11) How much time did the doctor spend with you? ______________________________

12) Did the doctor have any of your medical records from your treating physicians?
___ Yes ___ No Explain: ______________________________________

13) Was the doctor _____ rude or _____ nice? Explain: ______________________

14) Did you ask Social Security to send a copy of the exam to your doctor? ___ Yes ___ No
Which doctor? ____

15) Are there any comments that you would like to make about this exam? ___ Yes ___ No
Explain: ____
____
____

Please complete this form after your exam and return it to us as soon as possible.
A self-addressed stamped envelope is enclosed for your use.

§195 Form: Memorandum to Claimant Re: Completing Function Report

When claims are at the initial or reconsideration steps of the disability appeal process, the Social Security Administration (SSA) usually asks claimants to complete a Function Report—Adult. This questionnaire asks how your medical condition limits your ability to work; it asks what you do during a typical day; it asks about specific daily activities; and it asks about your ability to perform activities such as sitting, standing, walking, lifting, etc. This memorandum is designed to answer questions claimants often have about completing the Function Report—Adult, form SSA-3373-BK dated January 2013. (If you have an earlier or later version of the Function Rcport, this memorandum may not be fully applicable.)

Will this memorandum give me some stock paragraphs to insert into the Function Report so that I can be sure to win my case?
Absolutely not. The surest way to lose a case is for you to use stock paragraphs written by someone else. The best way to win a case is to write the absolute truth about your life, written in your own words.

I am not a very good writer. I can't even spell many words correctly. Shouldn't I get some help?
If you're capable of writing a letter that a family member can understand, you don't need help completing the questionnaire. If your answers on the Function Report are honest and genuine, that's more important than any misspellings or grammatical errors. A Function Report obviously written by a claimant is often more powerful and convincing than a questionnaire completed by, for example, a claimant's lawyer.

But my handwriting is illegible. Should I have someone with better handwriting write down what I say?
Yes. If your handwriting is truly illegible, ask a friend with better handwriting to help you. It is important for your case that SSA decision makers are able to read what you write.

Do you have any general advice for completing this questionnaire?
Tell the truth. Be sure the questionnaire describes not only your daily activities but also your limitations. Describe both without exaggerating and without minimizing. Details help someone who reads the questionnaire understand what your life is like. When you're done, ask a friend or relative to read the questionnaire and answer this question: Have I given an accurate description of my limitations and my daily life?

Do you have any advice for answering this question on page 1: "How do your illnesses, injuries, or conditions limit your ability to work?"
The biggest mistake made by claimants in answering this question is failing to provide enough details about their limitations. The more specific details about how your medical condition limits your ability to work, the better.
Another mistake sometimes made by claimants when answering this question is that they explain only why they cannot do their former work. To win a disability case, you usually need to prove much more than inability to do your prior job. Many claimants, including almost everyone under age 50, must prove they cannot do a full-time easy job.

Because it gives so little space at the top of page 2, question 6 makes it look like SSA wants me to describe in a few sentences what I do from the time I wake up until going to bed. Should I write only a few sentences?
No. You need to write as much as is necessary so that the reader will understand what your life is like. You can use the page 8 "Remarks" section to provide additional information, but even that isn't very large. You may have to add a page. It is important to take as much space as needed to give a good description of your daily activities; but at the same time, do not go on and on. Some people have been known to write a "book." While such "books" can provide valuable information, there is such a thing as overkill. And such "books" sometimes make SSA decision makers wonder how it is that someone who can write so much can be unable to work.

The mistake made by most people, though, is writing too little.

The best approach is to answer question 6 after you've answered all the other questions on the Function Report—Adult. The questionnaire asks a lot of specific questions. If you describe something in answer to a specific question, you don't need to repeat it when answering question 6. You can use question 6 to give an overview of what your life is like. But it might be a good idea to conclude your answer to question 6 with this: "See my answers to other questions."

But I don't really do anything during a typical day. I heat up food and wash a few dishes daily. I do a little cleaning once in a while. I do laundry and grocery shopping once a week. Is this what I should describe?
Yes, but cooking, cleaning, laundry and shopping will be addressed in answers to specific questions on pages 3 and 4. In answering question 6, it is important for you to describe "not really doing anything." That is, what are you doing in between such activities? How are you spending the majority of your time? Are you watching television? Are you reading? Are you looking out the window? It is also important to fully explain all of your "down time"—the time you spend in bed, the recliner, on the sofa, in the bathroom, or taking daytime naps.

As for laundry, cleaning, etc., it is important to describe anything you do differently now. If you do things for only a few minutes at a time and then rest, be sure to explain that either in answer to question 6 or question 14.b. Note that question 14.b. asks how much time house work takes you. Some disabled people have been known to honestly answer question 14.b. saying that housework takes them "all day." This is true because they do it only for a few minutes at a time and then rest and keep going back to it all day. It takes all day to get a little housework done. But SSA will likely conclude from such answers that these claimants spend the entire day doing housework without a break—they could work as house cleaners. Thus, a complete description of how housework gets done is important to keep SSA from getting the wrong impression.

What do daily activities have to do with being disabled?
Although there are some disabled people whose daily activities at home are completely normal (for example, those with certain mental impairments), most claimants have organized their home life to accommodate their disabilities. A description of how you organize your life around your disability can win your case.
For example, sometimes people with back impairments have to spend time lying down or sitting in a recliner. Some people get relief lying on the floor. Some people use a heating pad or ice. Some people do daily back exercises. This is important information. If people with such impairments leave out a description of how they try to get relief from pain during the day, if they describe only the few activities they actually do (laundry, cleaning, shopping, etc.), they are missing an opportunity to provide information that might convince SSA decision makers that they cannot work a regular job.

How much detail should I provide on page 6 in the "Information About Abilities" section of the Disability Report—Adult?
As much as possible. Use the Remarks section at the end of the questionnaire to provide details and, if necessary, add another page. Thoughtful, honest, realistic descriptions of how your medical condition affects your "abilities" can help win your case. Describe how long you can do various activities. Beware of underestimating or overestimating your capacity.

Although SSA does not say so, the relevant issue is this: What is your capacity for doing these activities in a normal work situation. For example, let's say you can walk one mile if you really push yourself but then you'd have to go home and lie down. Do you have the capacity to walk one mile in a normal work situation? No, you don't. Walking one mile is over-doing it. Walking this far exceeds your normal work limitations. You need to keep this in mind when you estimate how far you can walk.

Estimates of sitting and standing should also be based on a normal work situation. Sitting tolerances should be estimated for sitting in a work chair, not a recliner. A better way to ask about sitting is: How long can you sit in a work chair in a normal work situation before you need to get up? Does standing and stretching for a minute or two take care of the problem? If so, describe what you need to do when you get up. Or do you need to walk around? If so, describe it. How long do you need to walk around? If you add together all your sitting time, what is the grand total number of hours out of an 8-hour working day that you can sit?

Standing tolerance should be estimated based on standing in a slow moving line or the way a worker moves around a little when standing at a machine in a factory. A worker doesn't stand at attention like a soldier. Estimate standing at one time and also estimate the grand total number of hours out of an 8-hour working day that you can stand.

Should I give the lowest possible estimates for my capacity for sitting, standing and walking?
No. You should give the most accurate and honest estimates possible. If your tolerance for these activities varies from day to day, state a range of minutes you can do an activity and estimate how often the shorter time applies and how often the longer time applies.
My problem comes and goes. Some days I can do most normal daily activities but other days I can hardly do anything.
Many claimants are disabled by such episodic impairments. It is important that you explain what happens on bad days and how often you have problems. Think back over the last month or the last year. Count how many bad days you have had. Estimate how many days per month are bad days—so bad you would not be going to work (or would have to leave work early) even if you had a really easy job.

It is important to give SSA a balanced picture of your life. If you describe only the bad days, it is likely SSA won't believe you. If you describe only the good days, you'll lose your case because SSA will conclude that you function normally.

I am disabled because of mental illness. Should I skip all the questions about physical limitations and doing things at home?
No. Answer these questions honestly. If you have no limitation in a particular area, say so. Check only the boxes in the "Information About Abilities" section on page 6 having to do with your limitations. This section offers several choices that may or may not apply to your situation: memory, completing tasks, concentration, understanding, following instructions, getting along with others. Sometimes it helps to discuss your limitations with a spouse or friend. When you describe your limitations, provide details and examples. Details and examples win cases.

Why does SSA want to know about side effects of medications (page 8)?
Sometimes side effects of medications impose significant work restrictions. Thus, it is important to describe these side effects. Sometimes when you are taking many medications, you and your doctor don't know exactly which medication is causing the side effect or if it is a combination of medications that causes the side effect. It would be wise to explain this on the Function Report—Adult.

Note that SSA needs to know only about the side effects you are actually having from medications, not the possible ones listed by the drug manufacturers.

It is important that you have discussed any side effects with your doctor. Many people assume that they have to put up with the side effects in order to get the therapeutic benefit of the drugs. And they don't describe side effects in any detail when their doctor asks. Unless your side effects are described in your medical records, SSA may not accept that you actually suffer the side effects even if they are listed by the drug manufacturer.

Important: Before you send your completed Function Report—Adult to SSA, make a copy for yourself.

(This page intentionally left blank.)

Chapter 2

Prehearing Procedure

§200 Hearing Preparation — Theory of the Case

Even in those cases where you get involved long before the hearing stage, approach the case as if you were preparing it for presentation at a hearing. Think about the theory of the case that you developed at the initial interview with your new client. *See* §174.1. What evidence needs to be gathered to prove this theory of the case? Virtually anything that you can think of that helps show your client is disabled is encompassed by the Social Security Administration's broad definition of evidence: "Evidence is anything you or anyone else submits to us or that we obtain that relates to your claim." 20 C.F.R. § 404.1512(b). *See also* 20 C.F.R. § 404.702: "*Evidence* means any record, document, or signed statement that helps to show whether you are eligible for benefits or whether you are still entitled to benefits."

To prove the typical case, you need to do the things that are the subject of this chapter: review the Social Security file (§§201-208), analyze the legal and medical issues (§§230-268), gather records (§§210-219), obtain opinion evidence about your client's capacity for working (§§220-221), and prepare witnesses, including your client, to testify (§§290-297). As you do these things, keep focused on the theory of the case. Doing so will keep you from wasting your time and your client's money gathering unnecessary medical records, and it will direct your energy to where it matters most in winning your client's case.

Be prepared to refine the theory of why your client is disabled. That is, seek evidence that supports the theory of the case, but when things turn up that don't quite fit, don't try to make the facts fit the theory. Don't say, "Here is the conclusion on which I will base the facts." Instead, when the facts don't fit, rethink the theory.

You will find that revising the theory is essential in a number of your cases. For example, some cases that start out looking as if they involve only physical impairments, turn out in the end to be mental impairment cases—either because they involve somatic symptom disorders, that is, mental impairments that manifest themselves with physical symptoms, or because the real reason your client cannot work is, say, depression associated with a physical impairment that your client's doctor says ought not to be disabling.

The theory of the case does not have to be complicated. In fact, it is better if it can be described in a few sentences. But it must answer the central question in the case—why is your client disabled? In simple cases, the theory may address only residual functional capacity and issues presented by step five of the sequential evaluation process, the step that asks whether the claimant is capable of performing other work in the economy. Here is a simple example: *The claimant, who is age 52 and has an unskilled medium work background, is limited to sedentary work by spinal stenosis. Thus, Rule 201.12 of the Medical-Vocational Guidelines requires that he be found disabled.* In actual practice, you would probably include references to the evidence that show that the claimant is limited to sedentary work; but beyond this, nothing more is needed.

In more difficult cases, such as those involving literate claimants under age 50, the theory, in essence, is an explanation why your client cannot do a broad range of sedentary work. *See* §§260-268. And if there is alcoholism or other drug abuse (AODA) involved, since Congress has seen fit to include as part of the definition of disability the requirement that AODA not "be a contributing factor material to the Commissioner's determination," 42 U.S.C. § 423(d)(2)(C), include in the theory of the case the explanation why this is not "material." *See* §176.12.

Whenever the facts of your client's case contain an impediment to reaching a conclusion that he or she is disabled, it helps to explain the way around the problem as part of the theory of the case. For example, if the claimant is working at what appears at first glance to be the substantial gainful activity level, include a reference to deducting impairment-related work expenses as part of the theory. If the state agency found that the claimant could return to past relevant work, include as part of the theory an explanation why the claimant cannot do the past job.

The theory of the case gives focus to development of the evidence and to hearing testimony. It is the engine that runs the case. As such, write out a tentative theory when you first interview a claimant. It can be entered on the Analysis Form in this book (*see* §175.1). Update it as you go along so that everyone in your office who works on the case has access to the latest version of the theory. The final version of the theory may be sent to the judge (or to the state agency if you become involved in the case below the hearing level).

In addition to a brief theory statement, it is also useful to maintain a current detailed description of your client's residual functional capacity. The Analysis Form, §175.1, also provides a place to record your initial impression. If you make significant changes to the theory, update the detailed description of your client's residual functional capacity, too. You'll need this detailed description to send to your client's doctor when you request an opinion from the doctor about what your client can still do despite your client's impairments. *See* §§221-221.9.

§201 Obtaining a Copy of the File and Submitting Evidence

§201.1 Obtaining a Copy of the File — Cases Below the Hearing Stage

All new claims use the electronic disability folder. There are no paper files for new claims. When your client's case is at any level of review below the hearing stage, it's easy to obtain a copy of the file by requesting a CD-ROM containing it from the local office that has jurisdiction of your client's case. Your client has a right to get a copy of his or her Social Security file under provisions of the Privacy Act. 5 U.S.C. § 552a. You exercise this right on behalf of your client. *See generally* 20 C.F.R. §§ 401.35-401.55 and 404.1710.

The local office has instructions to provide one CD-ROM copy of your client's file for free if the request for the copy is for "program purposes," such as in connection with a claim for benefits. If you make multiple requests for copies of the file, e.g., once when the case is at the initial stage and again when the case is at the reconsideration stage, POMS instructions provide that the local office may charge $10 for each CD-ROM prepared after the first one if the total cost to the agency is over $25. If the cost to the agency is less than $25, then the CD-ROM is free. POMS DI 81001.035E. The POMS does not explain how to calculate the cost to the agency.

§201.2 Submitting Evidence — Cases Below Hearing Stage

Shortly after you have submitted your Appointment of Representative form SSA-1696 to the local Social Security office that has jurisdiction of your client's case, you should receive instructions from the state agency describing how to submit records electronically. If you do not receive these instructions, ask for them. SSA has designed two methods for electronic submission of records—by fax to a special fax number or by submission of scanned documents to SSA's Electronic Records Express (ERE). But state agencies request only submission by fax. You fax records to the state agency using as the cover sheet the claim-specific bar code provided by the state agency.
documents);

- The ALJ or senior attorney decision in the pending case; and
- Representative fee authorization(s).

§201.3 Obtaining a Copy of the File — Cases at the Hearing Stage

For cases at the hearing level in which you want to be paid directly by SSA, if your client's case uses an electronic folder, you are required to download your copy of the hearing exhibit file from the ERE. The hearing office will not provide you with a CD-ROM. *See* 81 Fed. Reg. 22697 (2016) and HALLEX I-5-1-22. Therefore, if you have not already done so, you must sign up for access to your clients' electronic folders on SSA's Electronic Records Express (ERE). *See* § 178.5.

If the case uses an electronic folder, the hearing office will send you a bar code and instructions for adding exhibits to the file. When an electronic hearing exhibit file is set up, the hearing office will notify you that it is ready for you to download. Note that the initial letter to the hearing office, § 182, asks that you be notified how to obtain a copy as soon as the hearing exhibits are numbered. If you want a copy of the file earlier (for example, if you want to review the file to see if the case is appropriate for requesting an on-the-record decision), you can download the raw file from the Case Documents section of the ERE. A raw electronic file, like a raw paper file, will be organized into five sections (see § 202) but it will have no exhibit numbers.

The hearing office will not provide a copy of a client's file on CD-ROM to any lawyer who wants to be paid with only very limited exceptions. An exception applies where although a claim is electronic, representatives have no ERE access to it. For example, where a claimant has two claims pending, which is something that can happen with SSA permission, ERE access to either claim is precluded because of "systems limitations." SSA also says that an exception applies when "technology limitations do not permit a representative to register for ARS (e.g., no cell phone coverage)." HALLEX I-5-1-22 III.

When there are multiple appointed representatives from the same firm, only the principal representative is given ERE access. Other representatives who use the same EIN as the principal representative are expected to obtain their copies of the file from the principal representative. When there are extenuating circumstances that prevent the secondary representative from getting a copy of the file from the principal representative, the hearing office is supposed to provide a copy after determining the legitimacy of the extenuating circumstances. *See* HALLEX 1-5-1-22 IV.B & C.

When there are two representatives from different firms, the hearing office will provide a CD-ROM to the secondary representative. HALLEX I-5-1-22.

If you want to look at a claimant's file before you sign the claimant up as a client, the hearing office will provide you with a copy of the file on CD-ROM if you submit a consent form, see § 178.2.5, signed by the claimant. Any CD-ROM you receive from SSA is supposed to be encrypted. See § 201.6 for decrypting instructions.

When you show up for a hearing in a case using an electronic file, the hearing office will not provide you with a CD-ROM containing the latest edition of the hearing exhibit file. The hearing office will not provide you with access to the ERE through SSA's computer system and it will not provide you with Wi-Fi Internet access so that you can log on to the ERE from the hearing room.

Before you go to the hearing office you will have to download the latest hearing exhibit file yourself. If you put it on a CD-ROM, you will be able to use a computer in the hearing room to view the CD-ROM. Many lawyers download the latest copy of the hearing exhibit file to a laptop, which they use during the hearing.

If your client's file is a paper file, which are still seen in very old disability claims, in some continuing disability review cases and sometimes in cases involving post-entitlement issues such as overpayments, you will have to make arrangements for copying the hearing exhibit file. As a rule, it is best to wait until the exhibits are numbered before copying the file. Otherwise, after the exhibits have been numbered it is necessary either to number your copy by going through the file page by page or to copy the file again—both time consuming processes. Without exhibit numbers, communication about the contents of the exhibit file with the administrative law judge (ALJ) or the Appeals Council is cumbersome.

In practice, hearing offices are generally accommodating in providing the claimant's paper file for review and copying, though sometimes the file with numbered exhibits is not available until around the time someone calls you from the hearing office to schedule the hearing. If you are located near the hearing office, you may arrange for access to the file at that office. If the hearing office is too distant, you can arrange to review the file by asking that it be sent to a Social Security office closer to you and made available for examination and copying during office hours. If it cannot be arranged to review and copy the file at either the hearing office or a local office, according to HALLEX I-2-1-35 B.2, "H[earing] O[ffice] staff must send photocopies of the file and proposed exhibits . . . ."

The claimant's right of access to the file, which you exercise on the claimant's behalf, includes the right to obtain copies. See the Privacy Act, 5 U.S.C. § 552a(d). It is essential that you obtain a copy of the entire hearing exhibit file in virtually every case. Often, because of the nature of the medical issues involved, you will find that you need details from records that at first may not seem significant—things you may miss when you take notes. Such details assume greater importance after medical research and discussing a claimant's case with doctors. Or you may need to provide copies of records to medical consultants of your own, a need that may not be immediately apparent. Therefore, the best practice is to obtain a copy of all hearing exhibits as soon as possible.

Each administrative law judge and hearing office works a little differently from the others, as they are allowed considerable discretion. Most hearing offices provide copy machines that may be used by attorneys and claimants for copying files. HALLEX I-2-1-35 C states, "Per provisions in the Privacy Act, the H[earing] O[ffice] will provide one free copy of a file to the claimant when access is for program purposes (i.e., for the purpose of obtaining a Social Security benefit). A representative is also entitled to a free copy of the claim(s) file, unless the claim(s) file is electronic and the representative is subject to the instructions in HALLEX I-5-1-22." Nevertheless, because of budgetary constraints, some hearing offices ask that attorneys provide copy paper and some restrict use of the copy machine. With broad use of electronic files at hearing offices, demand for use of the copy machine is reduced, thus making it more readily available for copying the few paper files.

§201.4 Submitting Evidence — Cases at the Hearing Stage

If your client's file is a paper file, you will not be allowed to submit records electronically directly into your client's electronic disability folder. Instead, you will need to submit paper records to the hearing office by mail or hand delivery. You can also fax records to the hearing office's regular fax number, not the special fax number that is used only for electronic records submission. Whichever way you submit records, develop a system for making sure that you get an acknowledgement that the records were received, such as a fax confirmation, certified mail receipt or a hearing office "received" stamp on a copy of your transmittal letter.

If the case file is electronic, you are required to submit exhibits electronically. You can submit electronically by fax or by using the Electronic Records Express. The hearing office will send you a special fax number and one or more sheets of paper with bar codes for your client's case that must be placed as the first page of any evidence you send to SSA via fax. Take a close look at the sheets of paper with bar codes: one sheet may be specifically for submitting medical evidence, another for non-medical evidence, and another for a request for an on-the-record decision. When you fax evidence to SSA by using the special fax number and the bar code, the evidence is automatically placed in your client's electronic file, though the quality of the images is degraded slightly. Someone at the hearing office must identify the records and add an exhibit number.

If you use the Electronic Records Express (ERE) to submit records online, there is no quality degradation of the images. You are also able to identify the records yourself right in your client's electronic folder, though someone at the hearing office still needs to number the exhibits. When an appointed representative submits records on the ERE, as long as you have been given access by SSA to your client's electronic folder, you won't need information from the bar code to file documents, though anyone else in your office who is signed up to submit documents on the ERE will need such information to successfully file documents on the ERE.

Practice Tip

Sign up your office staff so that they can submit exhibits on the Electronic Records Express at http://eme.ssa.gov. Although your office staff will not be given direct access to your client's electronic folder, that is, they will not be able to look at your client's electronic folder or download anything from it, they will be able to submit documents directly into your client's electronic folder. Everyone who submits records to a claimant's file must have his or her own user ID and password.

In order to file records at the hearing level, your office staff will need a bar code sheet from the hearing office. Located beneath the bar code are letters and numbers that must be entered on the website in order to file documents. Although most lawyers scan and save documents in PDF format, the website allows you to file documents in any of the following formats: .wpd, .doc, .docx, .jpg, .bmp, .mdi, .txt, .rtf, .xls, .xlsx, .pdf, .tiff, .tif. This means that in addition to PDF documents, you can submit word processing documents created in Word Perfect, Microsoft Word (2007 and earlier versions), and other word processing programs (if they use .txt or .rtf formats). You can submit documents created with Microsoft Office Document Imaging (.mdi). You can submit Excel spreadsheets (2007 and earlier versions) and pictures of documents or actual pictures in four different formats—.jpg, .bmp, .tiff and .tif. Color pictures, though, are displayed in black and white by SSA's system.

Although the website asks you to select a category for each document filed, the website does not provide sufficient categories for the kinds of things lawyers often file such as letters from friends and family, a letter from an employer, a vocational expert opinion or earnings information. It does not even provide the choice of medical source statement. It will be necessary to choose the closest category and provide further identification of the evidence in the notes field.

You will be able to print a confirmation that the documents were filed. Someone at the hearing office will add a hearing exhibit number to the records you filed, but unless someone at the hearing office changes it, your description of a particular document will appear in the electronic file.

SSA recommends that you submit a transmittal letter that shows all the records you are submitting. See § 279. Such a letter helps hearing office staff better identify records and it gives you a list of what you submitted. Such a letter is filed as a separate document.

§201.5 Working With an Electronic Disability File

Once the hearing exhibits are numbered, you will receive a letter telling you that hearing exhibits are ready to be downloaded. An electronic hearing exhibit file contains the same records that appear in a paper hearing exhibit file and is organized the same way. Electronic hearing exhibits are in .tiff format, which are recognized and can be opened by any computer.

Although you can successfully continue to use paper files in your office while SSA uses an electronic disability folder, many lawyers have taken the opportunity to convert to using electronic files in PDF format rather than .tiff, which is used by SSA, because PDF offers much more functionality. The .tiff files you get from SSA can be converted to PDF using the Create PDF feature available in Adobe Acrobat Professional DC.

Many lawyers use one of two programs purchased on the Internet from Atlasware, www.atlasware.com/, or from Nooksoft at www.nooksoft.net/, which makes conversion of the file to PDF even easier. The programs automatically convert all the files in a downloaded zip file or on an SSA CD-ROM to one huge PDF file complete with bookmarks identifying each individual exhibit with page and exhibit numbers on each page. Then, using Adobe Acrobat, you can add post-it notes to individual exhibits, you can underline things or you can add additional bookmarks, making the electronic file easier to navigate than a paper file. You can also run OCR Text Recognition on the PDF file to make it searchable.

§201.6 Decrypting a CD-ROM Containing an Electronic Disability File

The following is based on an article originally written by Attorney Peter H. D. McKee, which was published in the NOSSCR Social Security Forum, Vol. 33, No. 1, January 2011, p. 1. It is used with the permission of NOSSCR and the author. The article has been updated because in 2016 SSA switched to using McAfee CD encryption/decryption software.

A. Overview

ODAR E-file CDs are encrypted (or password-locked) by SSA. Without knowing how to "decrypt" them, the disks are useless. Many practitioners use a third-party software—Atlasware —to convert the E-file to a more useable PDF format. Whether you use this software or not, you still need to "decrypt" the CD.

The files on the disk have to be decrypted and then sent as a group to a folder on your computer. Once this is done, Atlasware can be used to convert the collection of TIFF files into the more useable PDF file the software creates. Once these decrypted files are in the folder on your computer, you may treat that folder as if it were an unencrypted E-file CD. It is that folder (rather than the CD) that Atlasware will convert from the massive set of TIFF files into the familiar bookmarked PDF file that we end up with when converting the E-file CD.

If you do use Atlasware, there is one more thing to remember. Once you have "decrypted" the files and then converted those files using Atlasware into a new, saved PDF file, you still have the unconverted files of the decrypted CD on your hard drive which were created when you went through the decryption process. If you use Atlasware, you do not need to keep these decrypted files, so you should delete them.

B. How to Decrypt a CD

Put the encrypted EDIB disk in the DVD drive of your computer. (If you use Atlasware, decrypt the disk on a computer on which Atlasware is installed.) The CD will run, and either a menu will pop up and you will choose "Open folder to view files" or the files on the CD will just show up.

Double click the MfeEERM.exe file. You will get a McAfee dialog box that asks for a password. The password for each client's encrypted CD is: the first four letters of the client's first name, followed by the # (number sign) followed by the last four numbers of the client's Social Security Number (SSN). No punctuation or spaces. It should look like this: edwa#3568. It is not case sensitive. If the client's first name is not 4 letters long, enter as many letters as is in the name and then add the symbol # to make 4 entries for this part of the password (before the mandatory # which separates the name and the numbers). So for Tom Smith, the password would be "tom##7483" (assuming Tom's last four digits of his SS number is 7483).

If you mess up and fail to complete this authentication screen properly, the dialog box goes away. You'll need to start over.

Click the OK button. A larger McAfee Removable Media Protection screen will pop up. From this screen, you may simply select the files, copy the files and paste them into a folder.

You can make a new folder or reuse a previous folder from which you have deleted the contents.

Name the folder what you want. (I decided to name my folder "Decrypted E-File.") It will always stay there on your computer and you can use it over and over, if you clean it out at the end of this process. If you want, you can make a new folder every time with the client's name. However, this will clutter your computer up with too many folders with TIFF files.

If you do not use Atlasware, just open the folder on your computer where you extracted the contents of the CD-ROM and double click the file named "index." This will open the Disability Case Document Index from which you can open individual exhibits.

C. Converting the Decrypted File with Atlasware

Go to your desktop and double click on the Atlasware icon. Select the source folder that you have established into which the decrypted contents of the CD were sent as the source from which Atlasware will get the data to convert. Select the whole folder, not a particular file in that folder. Then pick the location on your computer to which you want Atlasware to send the converted PDF file. Convert it to PDF and save it. Now you are done with the Atlasware conversion. All you now have to do is delete the decrypted but unconverted files still on your computer.

D. Conclusion

Decrypting a CD is a bit of a hassle, but once you have done it a few times, it is manageable. Once it is decrypted, conversion to PDF format using Atlasware works fine.

§202 Contents of the Disability File

For years SSA used a modular color-coded paper file folder called a five-part folder, which was organized to hold six groups of documents. When a hearing exhibit list was prepared, any documents found in the third group, the C section called "Current Development/ Temporary," were purged or moved to other sections. The other groups were lettered A, B, D, E and F and individual items within each group were identified with a letter and number, e.g., 1A, 2A, etc. The file folder itself contained instructions for filing and examples of the kinds of documents filed in each section.

The subdivisions of the file were the following:

A — Payment Documents/Decisions
B — Jurisdictional Documents/Notices
D — Non-Disability Development
E — Disability Related Development
F — Medical Records

Paper files will continue to exist at hearing offices for a number of years for older files, such as cases that have been appealed and remanded for a new hearing, but new claims are all paperless.

The electronic file displays exhibits in a way that mimics paper files. These exhibits are pulled by hearing office staff out of another part of the electronic file called "Case Documents" and placed into the A, B, D, E, or F subdivisions of the electronic file and numbered in the same way paper files are numbered. Thus, the discussion of the contents of the various sections of the file is identical for paper and electronic files. Although there are some variations from hearing office to hearing office and sometimes from ALJ to ALJ in the way hearing exhibit files are set up, for the most part these variations are minor.

§203 Section A: Payment Documents/ Decisions

HALLEX I-2-1-15 B.1. provides the following example of what goes into the A section of a file:

Part A—Payment Documents/Decisions

HO staff will generally exhibit:

- SSA-831 (Disability Determination and Transmittal);
- Disability Determination Explanation (DDE);
- SSA-832 and SSA-833 (title II and XVI Cease/ Continue Disability Determination and Transmittal);
- Previous decisions, dismissals, and revised determinations (including Appeals Council action documents);
- The ALJ or senior attorney decision in the pending case; and
- Representative fee authorization(s).

§203.1 Disability Determination and Transmittal

After the disability determination is made, it is recorded on Form SSA-831, Disability Determination and Transmittal. (*See* sample following this section at §203.2.) Separate forms are used for the initial and reconsideration determinations, and for each type of claim. The form states that the claimant is disabled and gives the date that disability began (block #15), or it states that through the date of the determination (or other pertinent date, such as expiration of insured status), the claimant is not disabled (block #19).

You'll find the citation to the sequential evaluation regulation under which a claim is denied in block 22 labeled REG-BASIS CODE. Sometimes, such as when your client receives a poorly written denial letter, this block is the only source for determining that the state agency found that the claimant's impairment was not severe or that the claimant was or was not capable of performing past relevant work. You may find, for example, the code H1. This is a denial at step four of the sequential evaluation process—the claimant is capable of performing past relevant work. In an SSI case, a denial based on capacity for past relevant appears as N31. *See* §203.3, for POMS DI 26510.045, which provides instructions for completing item 22 and shows all of the regulation basis codes.

Another useful code found on the Disability Determination and Transmittal is the specialty code for the doctor who signed the form. *See* item 32B. A chart based on POMS DI 26510.090, which translates these codes, appears at §203.4. If you make a regular practice of figuring out the state agency doctor's specialty, you may be astounded to discover, for example, that a gynecologist wrote your client's RFC assessment based on an orthopedic impairment. SSR 96-6p states that the "adjudicator must also consider all other factors that could have a bearing on the weight to which an opinion is entitled, including any specialization of the State agency medical or psychological consultant." *See also* 20 C.F.R. § 404.1527(e)(2)(ii).

You won't find any reference on the Disability Determination and Transmittal form to consideration of whether your client's impairment might equal an impairment found in the Listing of Impairments. And in most cases you won't find any mention of this issue elsewhere in the record. Instead, according to SSR 96-6p, "The signature of a State agency medical or psychological consultant on an SSA-831-U5 (Disability Determination and Transmittal Form) . . . ensures that consideration by a physician (or psychologist) designated by the Commissioner has been given to the question of medical equivalence at the initial and reconsideration levels of administrative review."

§203.2 Form: Disability Determination and Transmittal (SSA-831)

DEPARTMENT OF HEALTH AND HUMAN SERVICES
SOCIAL SECURITY ADMINISTRATION

DISABILITY DETERMINATION AND TRANSMITTAL

1. DESTINATION: DDS ☐ ODO ☐ DRS ☐ DQB ☐ INTPSC ☐
2. DDS CODE
3. FILING DATE
4. SSN
BIC (if CDB or DWB CLAIM)
5. NAME AND ADDRESS OF CLAIMANT (include ZIP Code)
6. WE'S NAME (if CDB or DWB CLAIM)
7. TYPE CLAIM (Title II): DIB ☐ FZ ☐ DWB ☐ CDB-R ☐ CDB-D ☐ RD-R ☐ RD-D ☐ RD ☐ P-R ☐ P-D ☐ MQFE ☐
8. TYPE CLAIM (Title XVI): DI ☐ DS ☐ DC ☐ BI ☐ BS ☐ BC ☐
9. DATE OF BIRTH
10. PRIOR ACTION: PD ☐ PT ☐
11. REMARKS
12. DISTRICT-BRANCH OFFICE ADDRESS (include ZIP Code)
DO-BO CODE
13. DO-BO REPRESENTATIVE
14. DATE
11A. ☐ Presumptive Disability ______
11B. ☐ Impairment ______

DETERMINATION PURSUANT TO THE SOCIAL SECURITY ACT, AS AMENDED

15. CLAIMANT DISABLED
A. ☐ Disability Began
B. ☐ Disability Ceased
16A. PRIMARY DIAGNOSIS
BODY SYS.
CODE NO.
16B. SECONDARY DIAGNOSIS
CODE NO.
17. DIARY TYPE | MO./YR. | REASON
18. CASE OF BLINDNESS AS DEFINED IN SEC. 1614(a)(2)/(216)(i)
A. ☐ Not Disab. for Cash Bene. Purp.
B. ☐ Disab. for Cash Benefit Purp. Beg.
19. CLAIMANT NOT DISABLED
A. ☐ Through Date of Current Determination
B. ☐ Through ______
C. ☐ Before Age 22 (CDB only)
20. VOCATIONAL BACKGROUND
OCC YRS.
ED YRS.
21. VR ACTION: SC IN A. ☐ SC OUT B. ☐ Prev Ref C. ☐
22. REG-BASIS CODE
23. MED LIST NO.
24. MOB CODE
25. REVISED DET ☐
25A. Initial A. ☐ Recon B. ☐ Recon DHU C. ☐ ALJ Hearing D. ☐ Appeals Council E. ☐ U.S. District Court F. ☐
26. LIST NO. ▶ A. B. C. D. E. F.
27. RATIONALE: ☐ See Attached SSA-4268-U4/C4 ☐ Check if Vocational Rule Met. Cite Rule ▶
28. A. ☐ Period of Disability B. ☐ Disability Period C. ☐ Estab Beg. ______ AND D. ☐ Continues E. ☐ Term. ______
29. LTR/PAR NO.
30. DISABILITY EXAMINER–DDS
31. DATE
32. PHYSICIAN OR MEDICAL SPEC. SIGNATURE
33. DATE
32A. PHYSICIAN OR MEDICAL SPEC. NAME (*Stamp, Print or Type*)
32B. SPEC. CODE
34. REMARKS
MULTIPLE IMPAIRMENTS CONSIDERED
34A COMBINED MULTIPLE NONSEVERE-SEVERE
34B COMBINED MULTIPLE NONSEVERE-NONSEVERE
35. BASIS CODE
36. REV.DET. CODES
37. SSA REPRESENTATIVE
SSA CODE
38. DATE

§203.3 Form: DI 26510.045 Completing Item 22 (Regulation Basis Code) on theSSA-831

A. Title II

Enter the appropriate "Regulation-Basis" code under which the claimant is allowed or denied.

NOTE: The Reg-Basis Code should reflect the nature of the allowance or denial at the time of adjudication. However, in denials, when a technical requirement is no longer met, the Reg-Basis Code should reflect the nature of the denial at the time the technical requirement was last met.

Select the appropriate code from the reference charts in DI 26510.045C, in this section.

- In closed period cases, enter the appropriate Reg-Basis Code applicable to that portion of the determination which reflects that the claimant was found to be disabled. Whenever the Central Office or Disability Quality Branch returns a determination for further consideration, enter the Regulation-Basis Code that is applicable to any new determination that is prepared. For a description of the various bases for determination refer to DI 26510.045C in this section.
- When the regulation basis code of the original determination is unavailable, enter "CE" in Item 22. See "Collateral Estoppel – New Regulation Basis Codes" in DI 27515.060. See "Collateral Estoppel – New Regulation Basis Codes" in DI 27515.060. However, if known, the original regulation basis code should be entered here.
- A claim denied on the basis of res judicata requires the entry "S1" in Item 22. (See DDS Action on Subsequent Title II Claim -- Claimant Previously Denied Through Date Last Insured/Prescribed Period/Age 22, DI 27516.005B.3.)

NOTE: It is no longer necessary to code a regulation number along with the Regulation Basis code because the National Disability Determination Services System only captures the Regulation Basis code for management information purposes.

NOTE: When adjudicating CDB re-entitlement claims, refer to notes in Childhood Disability Beneficiary (CDB) Re-entitlement, DI 23505.010A and Requirements for Re-entitlement, DI 10115.035A for a change in the re-entitlement period.

[1] ER (earnings requirement); PP (prescribed period).

DIB/DWB Claim—Denial		
Basis for Decision	**Enter in Item 22 Reg-Basis Code**	
	ER[1] or PP[1] Last met on or after date of current decision	**ER[1] or PP[1] last met prior to date of current decision**
Impairment Not Severe—Medical Consideration Alone	F1[2]	F2
Capacity for SGA—Any Relevant Past Work	H1	H2
Capacity for SGA—Other Than Relevant Past Work	J1	J2
Engaging in SGA—(DIB claims only)	N1[3]	N2[3]
Impairment Prevented SGA for a Period of Less Than 12 Months	E1	E2

DIB/DWB Claim—Denial (continued)		
Basis for Decision	**Enter in Item 22 Reg-Basis Code**	
	ER[1] or PP[1] Last met on or after date of current decision	**ER[1] or PP[1] last met prior to date of current decision**
Impairment Prevents SGA at Time of Adjudication but is not Expected to Prevent SGA for a Period of 12 Months	E3	E4
Insufficient Evidence Furnished	M5[4]	M6[5]
DAA Is Material to the Determination of Disability	Z1	Z2
Failure or Refusal to Submit to Consultative Examination and Insufficient Evidence	L1	L2
NH Does Not Want to Continue Development of Claim—Wants Decision Made on Evidence in File	M3	M4
NH Does Not Want to Continue Development of Claim—Does Not Indicate Decision to be Made on Evidence in File	M7	M8
NH Willfully Fails to Follow Prescribed Treatment	K1	K2
DWB Medicare Only Case—EOD at or after Age 62 Years and 7 Months—No Prior Disability Benefit Entitlement or Not Disabled, Whereabouts Unknown	X3	X3

[2] Also use this Reg-Basis Code in situations where the claimant only meets the fully insured requirement at AOD or later, has alleged a visual impairment, and the claimant does not meet the definition of statutory blindness.

[3] Use this code if the FO has determined that the claimant is engaging in SGA, the claimant alleges a visual impairment and the DDS determines that the claimant is not statutorily blind.(See Item 22 (Regulation Basis Code – Procedure – Title II – DIB-SGA Alleged, DI 26010.040C.)

[4] Do not use M5 when the claimant cooperated but there is insufficient evidence of disability. In these situations, use F1..

[5] Do not use M6 when the claimant cooperated but there is insufficient evidence of disability relating to the period before the insured status requirement was last met. In these situations, use F2.

DIB/DWB Claim—Allowance	
Basis for Decision	**Enter in Item 22 Reg-Basis Code**
Impairment Meets Level of Severity of Listings	A1[1]
Impairment Equals Level of Severity of Listings	B1
Medical and Vocational Considerations	C1
Medical and Vocational Considerations (35-40 Years of Arduous Unskilled Work, Marginal Education, and Significant Impairment)	D1

[1] When the date of onset (in item 15A) is based on statutory blindness, but the claimant is found not disabled for cash benefit purposes (item 18A), enter Regulation-Basis code "A1."

CDB Claim—Denial		
Basis for Decision	**Enter in Item 22 Reg-Basis Code**	
	CDB Claim, or reentitlement CDB claim and RP last met on or after date of current decision	**Reentitlement CDB claim and RP last met prior to date of current decision**
Impairment Not Severe—Medical Consideration Alone or Condition Disabling but did not Exist Before Age 22	F1	F2
Capacity for SGA—Vocational Considerations	G1	G2
Impairment Prevented SGA for a Period of Less Than 12 Months	E1	E2
Impairment Prevents SGA at Time of Adjudication but is Not Expected to Prevent SGA for a Period of 12 Months	E3	E4
Insufficient Evidence Provided	M5[1]	M6[2]
Failure or Refusal to Submit to Consultative Examination and Insufficient Evidence	L1	L2
Claimant Does not Want to Continue Development of Claim	M3	M4
Claimant Willfully Fails to Follow Prescribed Treatment	K1	K2
Drug Addiction and/or Alcoholism Is Material to the Determination of Disability	Z1	Z2

[1] M5 is not used when the claimant has cooperated but there is insufficient evidence before age 22 to establish disability - use F1 instead.

[2] M6 is not used when the claimant has cooperated but there is insufficient evidence before the end of the reentitlement period to establish disability - use F2 instead.

CDB Claim—Allowance	
Basis for Decision	**Enter in Item 22 Reg-Basis Code**
Impairment Meets Level of Severity of Listings	A1
Impairment Equals Level of Severity of Listings	B1
Medical and Vocational Considerations	C1

Parent Determination—Denial	
Basis for Decision	**Enter in Item 22 Reg-Basis Code**
Impairment Not Severe—Medical Considerations Alone	F1
Capacity for SGA—Any Relevant Past Work	H1
Capacity for SGA—Other Than Relevant Past Work	J1
Impairment Prevented SGA for a Period of Less Than 12 Months	E1
Impairment Prevents SGA at Time of Adjudication But Is Not Expected to Prevent SGA for a Period of 12 Months	E3
Insufficient Evidence Furnished	M5
Failure or Refusal to Submit to Consultative Examination and Insufficient Evidence	L1
NH Does Not Want to Continue Development of Claim	M3
NH Willfully Fails to Follow Prescribed Treatment	K1

Parent Determination—Allowance	
Basis for Decision	**Enter in Item 22 Reg-Basis Code**
Impairment Meets Level of Severity of Listings	A1
Impairment Equals Level of Severity of Listings	B1
Medical and Vocational Considerations	C1
Medical and Vocational Considerations (35-40 Years of Arduous Unskilled Work, Marginal Education, and Significant Impairment)	D1

B. Title XVI

- Enter the appropriate Regulation-Basis Code. The code should reflect the nature of the allowance or denial **at the time of adjudication**.
- Use a regulation basis code that **reflects disability rather than blindness** if the claimant was disabled in the month of filing and became statutorily blind in a later month.
- In **closed period cases**, enter the appropriate regulation basis code applicable to the portion of the determination that reflects that the claimant was found to be disabled.

DI, or DS, AI, AS Claim—Denial DC Claim and Claimant Age 18-21—Denial		
Basis for Decision is	**Enter in Item 22 Reg-Basis Code**	
	No Visual Impairment[1]	**Visual Impairment**[2]
Impairment Not Severe—Medical Consideration Alone	N30	N41[4]
Capacity for SGA—Any Relevant Past Work	N31	N42
Capacity for SGA—Other Than Relevant Past Work	N32[3]	N43[3]
Engaging in SGA	N33	N33[5]
Impairment Prevented SGA for a Period of Less Than 12 Months	N34	N45
Impairment Prevented SGA at Time of Adjudication But Is *Not* Expected to Prevent SGA for a Period of 12 Months	N35	N46
Insufficient Evidence Furnished	N36	N36
Failure or Refusal to Submit to Consultative Examination and Insufficient Evidence	N37	N37
Applicant Does Not Want to Continue Development of Claim	N38	N38
Applicant Willfully Fails to Follow Prescribed Treatment	N39[6]	N39[6]

- When the regulation basis code of the original determination is unavailable, enter "ACE" in Item 22. See "Collateral Estoppel – New Regulation Basis Codes" in DI 27515.060". However, if known, the original regulation basis code should be entered here
- Enter the regulation basis code that is applicable to any new determination prepared whenever a determination is **returned by CO or DQB** for further consideration.

NOTE: It is no longer necessary to code a regulation number along with the Regulation Basis code because the National Disability Determination Services System only captures the Regulation Basis code for management information purposes.

[1] Enter the applicable Reg-Basis Code from this column when the applicant does not allege a visual impairment.

[2] Enter the applicable Reg-Basis Code from this column when the applicant alleges a visual impairment.

[3] Also use this code when the applicant has the capacity for SGA but does not have a work history.

[4] Also use this code in a multi-category case when a disability recipient is determined not to be statutorily blind.

[5] Use this code if the FO has determined that the claimant is engaging in SGA, the claimant alleges a visual impairment and the DDS determines that the claimant is not statutorily blind. Use code N33 for both Engaging in SGA Without or With a Visual Impairment denials. Complicated systems changes prevent a new Regulation Basis Code from being created at this time. Code N44, formerly used in Engaging in SGA with a Visual Impairment denials, was redefined for use in DC Under Age 18 Impairment Not Severe denials.

[6] Also use this code along with the appropriate DAA indicator code, when DAA is material to the determination of disability.

DI, or DS, AI, AS Claim—Allowance DC Claims and Claimant Age 18-21—Allowance	
Basis for Decision	**Enter in Item 22 Reg-Basis Code**
Impairment Meets Level of Severity of Listings	A61
Impairment Equals Level of Severity of Listings	A62
Medical and Vocational Considerations	A63
Medical and Vocational Considerations (35-40 Years of Arduous Unskilled Work, Marginal Education, and Significant Impairment)	A64

BI or BS Claim—Allowance	
Basis for Decision	**Enter in Item 22 Reg-Basis Code**
Statutory Blindness	A61

DC Claim and Claimant Under Age 18-21—Denial		
Basis for Decision	**Enter in Item 22 Reg-Basis Code**	
	No Visual Impairment[1]	**Visual Impairment**[2]
Engaging in SGA	N33	N33
Impairment(s) Disabling for a Period of Less Than 12 Months	N34	N45
Impairment(s) Disabling at Time of Adjudication But Is Not Expected to Be Disabling for a Period of 12 Months	N35	N46
Insufficient Evidence Furnished	N36	N36
Failure or Refusal to Submit to Consultative Examination and Insufficient Evidence	N37	N37
Applicant Does Not Want to Continue Development of Claim	N38	N38
Applicant Willfully Fails to Follow Prescribed Treatment	N39[3]	N39[3]
Impairment(s) Severe But Does Not Cause Marked and Severe Functional limitations; i.e., does not meet or medically or functionally equal the severity of a listing	N43	N43
Impairment Not Severe	N44	N44

[1] Enter the applicable Reg-Basis Code from this column when the applicant does not allege a visual impairment.

[2] Enter the applicable Reg-Basis Code from this column when the applicant alleges a visual impairment.

[3] Also, use this code along with the appropriate DAA indicator, when DAA is material to the determination of disability.

DC Claim and Claimant under Age 18—Allowance	
Basis for Decision	**Enter in Item 22 Reg-Basis Code**
Impairment Meets Level of Severity of Listings	A61
Impairment(s) Medically Equals Level of Severity of Listings	A65
Impairment(s) Functionally Equals Levels of Severity of Listings	A66

BC Claim—Allowance	
Basis for Decision	**Enter in Item 22 Reg-Basis Code**
Statutory Blindness	A61

C. Description of Basis for Decision

1. Allowance

a. Impairment meets listings

Description of Basis for Decision	Type of Claim	Reg. Basis Code[1]
The individual is disabled on medical considerations alone because the disability is caused by an impairment specifically listed in the "Listing of Impairments" and the medical evidence contains the specific findings listed for the impairment. This entry will also include cases of "statutory blindness. No allowance should be coded as meeting the listings unless the specific medical criteria of one or more of the listed impairments are met, as shown by the medical evidence in file.	DIB, DWB, CDB Parent Determination DI, DS, AI, AS DC age 18-21 DC Under 18 BI/BS/BC	A1 A61 A61 A61

b

Description of Basis for Decision	Type of Claim	Reg. Basis Code[1]
The individual is disabled on medical considerations alone (or for DCs under 18, functional considerations as well) because of an impairment or a combination of impairments of severity equal to the level of severity contemplated in the "Listing of Impairments," but where all the specific requirements of the Listing are not met on the basis of the medical evidence in file. No allowance should be coded as equaling the listings on the basis of medical evidence which is inadequate to describe impairment severity; the medical evidence should be adequate albeit somewhat different from the specific listing requirements.	DIB, DWB, CDB Parent Determination DI/DS, AI, AS DC Age 18-21 DC under 18 Medically Equals DC Under 18 functionally equals	B1 A62 A65 A66

c. Severe impairment(s) short of the Listings plus adverse vocational factors

Description of Basis for Decision	Type of Claim	Reg. Basis Code[1]
The individual is disabled as defined in Regulation 404.1520(f) or 416.920(f) on the basis of a severe impairment(s) short of the severity in the "Listing of Impairments," together with adverse vocational factors.	DIB, DWB, CDB Parent Determination DI/DS, AI, AS DC Age 18-21	CI A63

d. 35-40 years of arduous unskilled work

Description of Basis for Decision	Type of Claim	Reg. Basis Code[1]
The individual with 35-40 years of arduous unskilled work and a marginal education who cannot work at the customary level of physical exertion because of a significant impairment(s) is disabled.	DIB, DWB Parent Determination DI/DS, AI, AS	D1 A64

2. Denial

a. Impairment prevents(ed) SGA (GA) for a period of less than 12 months

Description of Basis for Decision	Type of Claim	Reg. Basis Code[1]
The impairment is (or was) severe enough to prevent SGA (GA) at or after AOD but is not expected to (or did not) prevent SGA (GA) for a period of 12 months and is not expected to result in death.	DIB, CDB, DWB Parent Determination DI/DS, AI, AS DC Age 18-21	E1, E2, E3 or E4[2,4] E1 or E3[2,4] N34 or N45 N35 or N464

b. Impairment(s) causes (or caused) marked and severe functional limitations for a period of less than 12 months

Description of Basis for Decision	Type of Claim	Reg. Basis Code[1]
The impairment(s) did (or does) cause marked and severe functional limitations at or after AOD but is not expected to (or did not) cause marked and severe functional limitations for a period of 12 months and is not expected to result in death.	DC Under 18	N34, N35[5] N45 or N46[4]

c. Impairment not severe

Description of Basis for Decision	Type of Claim	Reg. Basis Code[1]
The individual is found not disabled on medical considerations alone because the impairment is not severe. The criteria of a non-severe impairment are met when the impairment(s) does not significantly limit the individual's physical or mental capacity to perform basic work-related functions. For DCs under age 18, the criteria of a nonsevere impairment are met when the impairment(s) does not cause more than a minimal limitation in the individual's ability to function in an age -appropriate manner.	DIB, DWB, CDB Parent Determination DI/DS, AI, AS DC Age 18-21 DC Under 18	F1 or F2 F1 N30 or N41 N44

d. Child's impairment(s) is not severe before age 22 or the end of the CDB re-entitlement period

Description of Basis for Decision	Type of Claim	Reg. Basis Code[1]
The individual is found to have a disabling impairment, but the condition was not disabling before age 22.	CDB	F1 or F2

e. Impairment(s) severe but does not cause marked and severe functional limitations; i.e., does not meet or medically or functionally equal the severity of a listing

Description of Basis for Decision	Type of Claim	Reg. Basis Code[1]
The impairment is severe but not disabling because it does not cause marked and severe functional limitations (i.e. it does not meet or medically or functionally equal the severity of a listing).	DC Under 18	N43

f. Capacity for SGA (CDB case)

Description of Basis for Decision	Type of Claim	Reg. Basis Code[1]
The child has a severe impairment(s) but is found not disabled because he or she has a functional and vocational capacity to engage in substantial gainful activity.	CDB	G1 or G2

g. Capacity for SGA—relevant past work

Description of Basis for Decision	Type of Claim	Reg. Basis Code[1]
The individual has a severe impairment(s) but is found not disabled because he or she has the functional and vocational capacity to engage in substantial gainful activity in relevant past work.	DIB, DWB Parent Determination DI/DS, AI, AS and DC Age 18-21	H1 or H2 H1 N31 or 42

h. Capacity for SGA—other than relevant past work

Description of Basis for Decision	Type of Claim	Reg. Basis Code[1]
The individual has a severe impairment(s) but is found not disabled because he or she has the functional and vocational capacity to engage in substantial gainful activity in other than relevant past work for which he or she is capable by past education, training or work experience.	DIB, DWB Parent Determination DI/DS, AI, AS and DC Age 18-21 DC Under 18	J1 or J2 J1 N32 or N43

i. Failure to follow prescribed treatment

Description of Basis for Decision	Type of Claim	Reg. Basis Code[1]
The individual willfully, without justifiable cause, fails to follow therapy prescribed by the treatment source for a disabling impairment which is amenable to treatment that could be expected to restore ability to work, or, if a DC under 18, to function in an age-appropriate manner.	DIB, CDB, DWB Parent Determination DI/DS, AI, AS and DC Age 18-21 DC Under 18	K1 or K2 K1 N39[6]

j. Refusal or failure to appear for a consultative examination

Description of Basis for Decision	Type of Claim	Reg. Basis Code[1]
The individual refuses or fails to present him or herself for a consultative examination which is considered essential to a proper determination and there is insufficient evidence in file to make a determination..	DIB, CDB, DWB Parent Determination DI/DS, AI, AS and DC Age 18-21 DC Under 18	L1 or L2 L1 N37

k. Failure to cooperate in submitting evidence of disability

Description of Basis for Decision	Type of Claim	Reg. Basis Code[1]
The individual is found not disabled because of failure to cooperate in submitting medical, functional, or vocational evidence necessary for a determination.	DIB, CDB, DWB Parent Determination DI/DS, AI, AS and DC Age 18-21 DC Under 18	M5 or M6[3] M5 N36

l. Does not wish to continue development of claim

Description of Basis for Decision	Type of Claim	Reg. Basis Code[1]
1) Wants Decision Made on Evidence in File—The individual does not wish to continue development of the claim, wants a decision made on the evidence in file and the evidence does not establish that the individual is disabled.	DIB, CDB, DWB Parent Determination DI/DS, AI, AS and DC Age 18-21 DC Under 18	M3 or M4 M3 N38
2) Does Not Indicate Decision to Be Made on Evidence in File—The individual does not wish to continue development of the claim, does not indicate that he/she wants a decision to be made on the evidence in file and the evidence does not establish that the individual is disabled.	DIB, DWB CDB Parent Determination DI/DS, AI, AS and DC Age 18-21 DC Under 18	M7 or M8 M3 or M4 M3 N38

m. SGA

Description of Basis for Decision	Type of Claim	Reg. Basis Code[1]
Engaging in SGA—The individual is found not disabled because he/she is engaging in substantial gainful activity.	DIB, DWB DI/DS, AI, AS and DC Age 18-21	N1 or N2 N33

n. DAA

Description of Basis for Decision	Type of Claim	Reg. Basis Code[1]
Drug addiction and/or alcoholism is material to the determination of disability.	DIB, DWB, CDB	Z1 or Z2

[1] The numerical codes "1," "3," "5" and "7" (e.g., "A1" or "E3") signify that the earnings requirement (in DIB cases) or the prescribed period requirement (in DWB and CDB re-entitlement cases) is not at issue. The numerical codes "2," "4," "6" and "8" indicate that in addition to the basis for the disability determination, the earnings requirement, prescribed period requirement, or re-entitlement period requirement expired before the date of the current decision; e.g., claimant is not disabled through the date the earnings requirement was last met.

[2] These codes are used to differentiate between an impairment that prevents SGA at time of adjudication but is not expected to prevent SGA for 12 months as opposed to an impairment that no longer prevented SGA at time of adjudication and did not prevent SGA for 12 months.

[3] Do not use M6 when the claimant cooperated but there is insufficient evidence of a disability relating to the period before the insured status or prescribed period requirement was last met. In these situations, use F2.

[4] These codes are used to differentiate between an impairment that results in marked and severe functional limitations at time of adjudication but is not expected to do so for 12 months (N35, N46), as opposed to an impairment that no longer causes marked and severe functional limitations at time of adjudication and did not do so for 12 months (N34, N45).

[5] Also use this code along with the appropriate DAA indicator when DAA is material to the determination of disability.

§203.4 Chart: DDS Medical Specialty Codes

Code	Specialty	Code	Specialty
01	Anesthesiology	25	Obstetrics
02	Ambulatory Medicine	26	Occupational Medicine
03	Audiology	27	Oncology
04	Cardiology	28	Ophthalmology
05	Cardiopulmonary	29	Orthopedics
06	Dermatology	30	Osteopathy
07	E.E.N.T.	31	Pathology
08	E.N.T.	32	Pediatrics
09	E.T.	33	Physiatry
10	Emergency Room Medicine	34	Physical Medicine
11	Endocrinology	35	Plastic Surgery
12	Family or General Practice	36	Preventative Medicine
13	Gastroenterology	37	Psychiatry
14	Geriatrics	38	Psychology
15	Gynecology	39	Public Health
16	Hematology	40	Pulmonary
17	Industrial Medicine	41	Radiology
18	Infectious Diseases	42	Rehabilitative Medicine
19	Internal Medicine	43	Rheumatology
20	Neurology	44	Special Senses
21	Neuro-Ophthalmology	45	Surgery
22	Neuro-Psychiatry	46	Urology
23	Neonatology	47	Other
24	Nephrology	48	Speech—Language Pathology
		49	Child and Adolescent Psychiatry

From POMS DI 24501.004B.

§203.5 eCAT: Disability Determination Explanation

State agencies use a web-based automated Electronic Claims Analysis Tool (eCAT), to document the analysis made by disability adjudicators and ensure that all relevant agency policies are considered during the adjudication process. eCAT produces a Disability Determination Explanation, consisting of many pages, that documents the analysis and rationale for finding a claimant disabled or denying a claim. The Disability Determination Explanation replaces the state agency worksheets, the Psychiatric Review Technique form (PRTF) (§241.1), the Mental Residual Functional Capacity Assessment (§245.4), and the physical Residual Functional Capacity Assessment (§207.2). The Disability Determination Explanation summarizes the medical evidence and addresses every issue in the 5-step sequential evaluation of disability.

The Disability Determination Explanation is filed in the A section of the electronic hearing exhibit file. The PRTF, RFC assessments, etc., no longer appear in the F section.

Do not treat the Disability Determination Explanation as a procedural document that can be safely ignored. Study this document. It can show you where the holes are in your client's case and it may also show you where the state agency went wrong in its analysis.

§204 Section B: Jurisdictional Documents and Notices

HALLEX I-2-1-15 B.2 provides the following example of what goes into the B section of a file:

Part B—Jurisdictional Documents/Notices

HO staff will generally exhibit:

- Initial determination form and notice;
- Request for reconsideration and notice;
- Request for hearing;
- A cessation notice of planned action;
- An initial notice of overpayment;
- Representative appointment and fee agreement;
- Notice of withdrawal of representative (submitted prior to finalized exhibit list);
- Waiver of right to appear;
- Substitute party form; and
- Withdrawal of a request for hearing.

If received, the HO will also add the following documents to the B section but will generally not exhibit the documents:

- Representative fee petition request;
- Notice of withdrawal of representative received after ALJ issues decision;
- Acknowledgement of request for hearing and any attachments;
- Continuance of hearing;
- Notice of hearing;
- Professional Qualification Statements sent with notice of hearing; and
- Request for Appeals Council review.

§204.1 Denial Letters

Some state agencies do a good job of explaining the reasons for denial. Others do not. If your state agency does a good job, you may find that the denial letter contains the most succinct explanation of why the claim was denied available anywhere in the record. Although a denial letter may be a few pages long, it is only the paragraph that explains the reasons for denial that is worth reading. The list of evidence considered tends to be unreliable. The rest is boiler plate—stock paragraphs that appear in all denial letters.

§204.2 Request for Reconsideration and Hearing

The appeal forms appear as hearing exhibits mostly for jurisdictional reasons. They require little more than a glance at the reasons stated for disagreement with the prior denial determination to make sure that the claimant did not write something stupid that may need to be explained at the hearing.

Make sure that the Request for Hearing was timely filed. If the Request for Hearing was not timely filed, look for documents that explain the late filing and whether local office personnel recommend finding good cause for late filing. Note, though, ALJs consider the decision on whether to find good cause for late filing of a Request for Hearing to be within their jurisdiction. Thus, even though local office personnel may have written a document that looks like a finding of good cause for late filing, ALJs do not feel bound to accept the conclusion of local office personnel on this score. Instead, an ALJ may decide this issue using the guidelines set forth at 20 C.F.R. § 404.911. Whenever there is an untimely Request for Hearing that is not adequately explained in the file, ask your client about the reasons. Because ALJs have been known to dismiss cases involving late Requests for Hearing without ever scheduling a hearing, it is good practice to send the ALJ an affidavit from your client explaining the late filing when this may be an issue in your client's case.

§205 Section D: Non-Disability Development

HALLEX I-2-1-15 B.4 provides the following example of what goes into the D section of a file:

Part D—Non-Disability Development

HO staff will generally exhibit:

- The application;
- A written statement or record of oral inquiry indicating an intent to claim benefits (for protective filing purposes);
- Birth certificate or other proof of age;
- Earnings records and proof of any non-posted wages or self-employment income;
- Workers' Compensation, Department of Veterans Affairs, or other relevant federal agency award information (with any medical records from these sources filed in Part F).
- Evidence of death and relationship in auxiliary and survivor cases (for purposes of non-disability development);
- Verification of any work activity engaged in by the claimant after the alleged onset date;
- Pertinent statements or reports of contact (not disability related); and
- Congressional inquiries and responses

§205.1 Application for Benefits

Most applications are computer-generated, based on answers given by the claimant to an SSA employee either in person or by telephone or based on an Internet application submitted by the claimant. The computer-generated Social Security disability (Title II) application prints only information applicable to your client, so it is usually much shorter than the older Form SSA-16. It takes just a minute to read. Make a practice of doing so, looking for errors that need to be corrected.

The most important item on a Title II application is the alleged "onset date," the date the claimant says he or she became disabled. In many cases this crucial date may be wrong as a result of being chosen by an SSA representative based upon a claimant's incomplete description of problems, or by a claimant with inadequate information about what it means to be disabled. Such incorrect onset dates need to be amended, which may be accomplished simply by writing a letter to the ALJ. Sometimes the alleged onset date that appears in the application is a date chosen by a claims representative for a legal reason—*res judicata*. *See* §§370-379.

SSI (Title XVI) applications, which primarily concern financial eligibility for this federal welfare program, for many years did not contain an alleged onset date. Since SSI benefits never were paid before the date of application, the onset date does not have the same impact on payment of SSI back benefits as it has had in Social Security disability cases.

Both the Title II and Title XVI applications may contain an important date in the upper right hand corner of the first page, the filing date of the application. This may be a "protective filing" date, that is, the effective filing date, usually the date the claimant first contacted SSA about submitting the application. Sometimes, though, you will find in the hearing exhibits a record of a claimant's contact with SSA without any reference to the protective filing date on the application itself. In these situations, a protective filing date may be established by asking the ALJ to make reference to the date of contact as the protective filing date in the final paragraph of the ALJ decision, known as the "decisional paragraph."

For a protective filing date to be established, the application must be filed within a certain time limit calculated from the date SSA, in response to contact by the claimant, sends notice of the need to file an application. The time limit is 60 days for SSI and 6 months for Social Security disability claims. *See* 20 C.F.R. §§ 404.630(c), 416.340(c) and 416.345. *See also* 20 C.F.R. § 416.350, which treats filing a Title II application as an inquiry about SSI. Note that if SSA fails to send the required notice, which it often does, arguably there is no time limit for using the date of contact as a protective filing date. This is especially useful in Title II claims in which, for one reason or another, it is determined later that there is an advantage to having an SSI application filed, too. If the requirements of 20 C.F.R. § 416.350 are met, an SSI application may be filed even after a favorable Title II decision is received. The Title II application date is used as the SSI protective filing date. *See* §410.

The protective filing date is important in an SSI case because benefits may be paid to otherwise qualified claimants from the protective filing date for claims filed before August 22, 1996, or the first of the month after the protective filing date for more recent applications. In a Social Security disability case, the protective filing date is important only where it has been more than 17 months between the onset date and the date on the Title II application. (All potential back benefits will be paid anyway for applications filed within 17 months of onset of disability.)

Other things to look for on an application include:

1. Reference to prior applications.
2. Reference to claims filed under other programs such as black lung, worker's compensation, and government pension, which may affect the amount of benefits.
3. Reference to children who may be eligible for benefits if the claim is successful. (If a child is omitted, this omission needs to be corrected as soon as possible by bringing it to SSA's attention in writing.)

§205.2 Full DIB Review Sheet (DIBWIZ)

The Full DIB Review Sheet and its shorter version, the Partial DIB Review Sheet—either of which may appear on an exhibit list as "DIBWIZ"—contain a summary of procedural aspects of the claimant's case created from queries of multiple SSA databases. A sample appears at §205.3.

Although the DIBWIZ is hard to read because of abbreviations, acronyms and various codes, it is worthwhile to spend some time trying to understand the information it contains about your client's claims. Just paying attention to which database or query the information comes from gives you a head start and a basis for educated guesses about the meaning of various things that appear on the DIBWIZ. These database queries, which are identified by acronyms on the DIBWIZ, include the following:

- Numident (NUMI), the master file based on SSN, contains all names used by the number holder, mother and father's names, date of birth, etc.;
- Master Beneficiary Record (MBR), SSA's major administrative database for Title II records, which contains information about claimants and beneficiaries including payment history and is used for the calculation of benefits; queries of this database are identified as MBR or FACT;
- Modernized Claims System (MCS) will show information about Title II applications;
- Supplemental Security Income Display (SSID), a query showing SSI information from the database known as the Supplemental Security Record (SSR);
- Modernized Supplemental Security Income Claims System (MSSICS) shows information about SSI applications similar to the MCS for Title II claims;
- Summary Earnings Query (SEQY) shows annual income reported to SSA;
- Detailed Earnings Query (DEQY) shows annual income by employer;
- Disability Determination Service Query (DDSQ) shows when the state agency acted on a claim and the basis of its action;
- OHAQ shows the status of a case at the hearing office;
- Prisoner Update Processing System (PUPS) provides prisoner information.

Note that the DIBWIZ begins on page 1 with demographic information from the Numident database. The DIBWIZ calculates when a claimant reaches certain "critical ages": 18, 22, 31, 50, 55, 60, 62 and full retirement age (FRA). Age 22 is important for disabled adult child cases (*see* §141); age 31 is where the 20/40 rule for disability insured status first applies (*see* §205.4); ages 50, 55 and 60 are important for application of rules from the Medical-Vocational Guidelines; ages 62 and full retirement age are important for retirement claims. Note that for SSA purposes, a person reaches a particular age on the day before the person's birthday (*see* §122). The claimant in the sample DIBWIZ was born on 12/26; she reaches all the critical ages on 12/25.

Appearing immediately after the "critical ages" is data from the Modernized Claims System (MCS) showing the alleged onset date, date last worked, date first insured, date last insured and some information about representation. (The sample provides outdated information showing that this claimant is represented by a non-attorney. This shows that representation information in the MCS can be wrong. Later in this DIBWIZ sample, you will see the author's name and address as this claimant's representative, which appears as part of the SSI Display.)

The "Recent Work" section provides annual earnings for the claimant for the past 5 years. Sometimes the DIBWIZ includes some recent quarterly wage information in this section. ALJs sometimes use this section of the DIBWIZ as a basis for questioning the claimant about work after the alleged onset date.

One of the most useful sections of the DIBWIZ titled "Prior Disability Claim Denials" gathers information about previous and current Title II and SSI claims. This information is valuable sometimes for understanding the procedural status of the current claim. It is most important for identifying prior applications that possibly could be reopened. Note that information about Title II denials is not as complete as SSI but it does show Title II date of filing, alleged onset date, level of denial and basis of denial for all claims, including the current one. For the latest denial on the current claim, it provides the month and year for the date adjudicated and gives the "Basis of Denial" in cryptic English, as well as a denial code. We give the key for these codes in §203.3 of this book.

SSI information about prior applications is better because whenever a new SSI claim is filed, a new SSR record is created and numbered sequentially. This appears as "Record Number" in a subsection of the DIBWIZ labeled "SSID Data (Title XVI)." When there are multiple claims, the presence of these record numbers makes it easier to keep track of which claim you're looking at. The highest record number will be the latest (probably current) application. In this part of the DIBWIZ you can find not only the dates of application for each SSI claim but also the "Basis for Denial," which is provided in cryptic English as well as a denial code. This section of the DIBWIZ shows the level of appeal, date of appeal and date of decision for the current application and prior applications.

In the "DDSQ and OHAQ Data" section of the DIBWIZ you can find more details about the current claim and prior claims when they were at the state agency level for the initial and reconsideration determinations. This section does not show the official date of a determination. Instead, it shows the "Date Claim Cleared DDS," which is not usually very useful information for a lawyer. The OHAQ subsection shows the date of the request for hearing, when the claim arrived at the hearing office, when the case was assigned to an ALJ, the ALJ's name and code number, and the disposition date.

The section titled "Current or Prior Disability Entitlement" is blank on our sample (because this claimant was never before entitled to disability benefits). When there was prior entitlement, information about it from the MBR in a Title II case or from the SSI Display (SSID) appears in this area. This section will show date of onset on the prior claim, date of entitlement, date the claim was adjudicated, disability cessation date and date benefits ceased. If applicable, it will show the date an Extended Period of Eligibility (EPE) began. This section will also show the primary and secondary diagnoses and the reason for disability cessation, e.g., medical.

The "Folder Locations" section of the DIBWIZ will show which local Social Security office took the request for hearing and therefore will be responsible for paying SSI if the claim is successful. Local offices are shown by codes, which like so many other items that appear on the DIBWIZ, are not accessible in the public POMS or on SSA's website. However, at the Centers for Disease Control website, there is an SSA codebook that contains this information and translates many other SSA codes —http://www.cdc.gov/nchs/data/datalinkage/nchs_ssa_data_codebook_2009.pdf. If you are puzzling over an entry on the DIBWIZ and cannot find it by searching the POMS, look in this codebook.

Beginning on page 4 of the sample DIBWIZ is even more cryptic computer generated information than appears on the first three pages. These pages provide additional details. So that you can tell what kind of data you're looking at, it helps to pay attention to the name of the query from which the information is drawn. For example, the demographic information at the top of page 4 is from the Numident (NUMI); the next section provides state agency information from the DDSQ, followed by a FACT query from the MBR at the top of page 5. An SSI Display (SSID) starts at the bottom of page 5. SEQY data showing annual earnings appears in the lower third of page 6. The DEQY, which provides annual income by employer, begins at the bottom of page 6 and concludes on page 9. At the bottom of page 9 is OHAQ data.

The very last line on page 9 identifies that the next set of data is from MCS, the Title II Modernized Claims System, which continues on page 10. Note that some information about representation and attorney fees appears here. For example, this section shows that the author's SSA-1695 was received by the local office on November 28, 2008. There is a notation about the fee agreement: "25%/5300." You cannot tell from looking at this, though, whether the SSA-1695 and contract were sent to SSA by the author or by the previous non-attorney representative.

Additional SSI information from the Modernized SSI Claims System (MSSICS) begins at the bottom of page 10. There is a note on page 11 that says this claimant has two children in the household, one is a minor, and the claimant is working part time and gets W2, which is the Wisconsin version of Temporary Assistance to Needy Families (TANF).

§205.3 *Sample: Full DIB Review Sheet (DIBWIZ)*

Refer to: [redacted] **SSN:** [redacted]

Full DIB Review Sheet Page 1 Query

Date: 5/22/2009

SSN: [redacted] Unit: EZTOOL

Name: [redacted]

Other Last Names (from NUMI):

Date of Birth (from NUMI): 12/26/1964 **Date of Death (from NUMI):**

Attainment of Critical Ages (GN 00302.400A for attainment; RS 00615.003A for Full Retirement Age

Age 18: 12/25/1982	Age 31: 12/25/1995	Age 55: 12/25/2019	Age 62: 12/25/2026
Age 22: 12/25/1986	Age 50: 12/25/2014	Age 60: 12/25/2024	FRA: 12/25/2031

MCS displays an "alleged" onset date 9/12/2006 and date last worked of Work not ended.
MCS also displays a date first insured 07/01 and date last insured (DLI) 12/12
MCS also displays a title II issue of 1696 and a title II remark of NON-AT - MELISA GONZALEZ
Please verify an SSA-1696 form is in file, and if so, follow the procedures found in POMS GN 03910.000.
MCS also displays a title II issue of 1696 and a title II remark of
Please verify an SSA-1696 form is in file, and if so, follow the procedures found in POMS GN 03910.000.

RECENT WORK

SEQY and DEQY Data

Year:	2004	Covered Earnings:	$21,420.00	MQGE Earnings:	$0.00	Non-Covered Earnings:	$0.00
Year:	2005	Covered Earnings:	$5,355.00	MQGE Earnings:	$0.00	Non-Covered Earnings:	$0.00
Year:	2006	Covered Earnings:	$5,315.52	MQGE Earnings:	$0.00	Non-Covered Earnings:	$0.00
Year:	2007	Covered Earnings:	$8,772.16	MQGE Earnings:	$0.00	Non-Covered Earnings:	$0.00
Year:	2008	Covered Earnings:	$0.00	MQGE Earnings:	$0.00	Non-Covered Earnings:	$0.00

Note - to view the complete SEQY and last 15 years of the DEQY, please go to the Queries Menu and select query 'G. SEQY

PRIOR DISABILITY CLAIM DENIALS

MBR Data (Title II)

SSN: [redacted] **BIC:** A **Date of Birth:** 12/26/64 **Debit Run Date (DRD):** 2/9/2007 **X-REF AN:**

MBR DIB Line(s) Data

Date of Onset (DDO): 09/12/06 **Date Adjudicated(DSD):** 05/2007
Level of Denial (LOD): 2 Reconsideration
Basis of Denial (BDC): J1 [DIB] Capacity for SGA - other work (Earnings req. last met on or after date of current decision)

MBR BEN DENY Data

Date of Filing: 09/12/06 **DIB Onset:** 09/12/2006 **Level of Denial:** RECON **Disalow/Den RSN:** 0J1
Date of Filing: 09/12/06 **DIB Onset:** 09/12/2006 **Level of Denial:** INITIAL **Disalow/Den RSN:** 0J1

SSID Data (Title XVI)

Record Number: 1 **Application Date:** 9/12/2006 **Date of Onset:** 9/12/2006
Date of Denial: 02/07/07 **Basis for Denial:** N32 Capacity for SGA-other work, no visual impairment
Appeal Type: I *Initial Claims* **Appeal Level:** H *Hearing*
Appeal Reason: DI *Initial Disability* **Date Appeal Filed:** 7/4/2007
Appeal Decision: **Date of Decision:**

Record Number: 1 **Application Date:** 9/12/2006 **Date of Onset:** 9/12/2006
Date of Denial: 02/07/07 **Basis for Denial:** N32 Capacity for SGA-other work, no visual impairment
Appeal Type: I *Initial Claims* **Appeal Level:** R *Reconsideration*
Appeal Reason: DI *Initial Disability* **Date Appeal Filed:** 3/23/2007
Appeal Decision: UF *Unfavorable* **Date of Decision:** 5/10/2007

DDSQ and OHAQ DATA

DDSQ Data

Claim Level/Type: RC-DIB reconsideration-disability insurance benefits **Program:** 02 **STATUS:** CLOSED
Application 9/12/2006 **Recon Date:** 3/23/2007
Basis Code for J1 [DIB] Capacity for SGA - other work (Earnings req. last met on or after date of current decision)
Decision Code: DE denial
Date Claim Cleared DDS: 5/10/2007 **State:** WI **X-Ref:**

Refer to: [redacted] **SSN:** [redacted]

Full DIB Review Sheet

Page 2 Query

Date: 5/22/2009

SSN: [redacted]

Unit: EZTOOL

Claim Level/Type: RC-DI reconsideration-disabled individual **Program:** 16 **STATUS:** CLOSED
Application 9/12/2006 **Recon Date:** 3/23/2007
Basis Code for N32 Capacity for SGA-other work, no visual impairment
Decision Code: DE denial
Date Claim Cleared DDS: 5/10/2007 **State:** WI **X-Ref:**

DDSQ Development History Data

Claim Level: IN *initial claim* **Title:** 02
Basis Code for Decision: J1 *[DIB] Capacity for SGA - other work (Earnings req. last met on or after date of current decision)*
Decision Code: DE *denial*
Date Claim Cleared DDS: 2/7/2007 **State:** WI **X-Ref:**

Claim Level: IN *initial claim* **Title:** 16
Basis Code for Decision: N32 *Capacity for SGA-other work, no visual impairment*
Decision Code: DE *denial*
Date Claim Cleared DDS: 2/7/2007 **State:** WI **X-Ref:**

OHAQ Data **(For additional Hearing and Appeals information, use the CPMS or ARPS websites)**
Claim Type: SSDC Supplemental Security Income Disabled Claimant Concurrent with **Issue:**
Last Action Taken: 310 Case Assigned to ALJ **Date Action Taken:** 02/02/09
Hearing Section:
Hearing Type: NRH-REG 10 New request for hearing - Regular
Hearing Request Date: 07/04/07 **Disposition Date (DID):** **ALJ:** 1143 AHLGREN S J
ALJ Disposition Title II:
ALJ Disposition Title XVI:
Appeals Council (AC) Section:
AC Request Date: **AC Disposition Date (ADD):** **AAJ:**
AC Disposition Title II:
AC Disposition Title XVI:
(AC Review information updated after 03/03/08 will no longer be on the OHAQ; use the ARPS website to view this
Court Section:
Advised of Suit Date: **Court Disposition Date (CDD):** **District Court Code:**
Attorney ServedDate:
Court Disposition Title II:
Court Disposition Title XVI:

Remember-- If the ALJ dismissed a request for hearing, treat any new application as if no hearing request was ever filed. If the AC (without issuing decision) denies or dismisses a request for review of the ALJ's decision, the period adjudicated reverts to the ALJ decision (DID). (Refer to POMS DI 27510.001B, Exhibit 2)

When a prior claim is at the ALJ level and a new claim (initial or CDR) under the same title is filed, the new claim should generally be routed to the ALJ (via the FO). If the prior claim is at the AC level and a new claim under the same or different title is filed, the subsequent claim will be processed as a new initial claim. However, if the AC remands the prior claim back to the ALJ, the DDS should stop development and forward the subsequent claim to the appropriate HO for association. (Refer to POMS DI 20101.025)

CURRENT OR PRIOR DISABILITY ENTITLEMENT

FOLDER LOCATIONS

MCS WMS Query - Claim Status/Movement

MCS indicates a HEARING claim was TRANSFERRED from office 535 on 9/4/2007 to office X10.

SSID Data (Title XVI)

RN: 01X01 **Current Folder Location:** X10
Receipt Date: 09/01/07-C **Prior Folder Location:** 535

DDSQ Data

Claim Level/Type: RC-DIB **Program:** 02 **SLC Code:**
LTJ Code: EDC (EDC indicates an EDCS claim) **LTG Code:**
Date Received in DDS 3/28/2007 **Date Case Cleared** 5/10/2007 **Destination of Case at Closure:** 535

Refer to: [redacted] **SSN:** [redacted]

Full DIB Review Sheet

Page 3 Query

Date: 5/22/2009

SSN: [redacted]

Unit: EZTOOL

Claim Level/Type: RC-DI **Program:** 16 **SLC Code:**
LTJ Code: EDC (EDC indicates an EDCS claim) **LTG Code:**
Date Received in DDS 3/28/2007 **Date Case Cleared** 5/10/2007 **Destination of Case at Closure:** 535

OHAQ Hearings and Appeals Data
Last Action Taken: 310 Case Assigned to ALJ **Date Action Taken:** 02/02/09
Hearings Office Where Last Action Taken: 5059 MILWAUKEE WI (Office Code: X10)
Social Security Office: 535
Title II Claims File Transferred to: **Title XVI Claims File Transferred to:**

eFolder Information

SSN: [redacted] **Name:** [redacted]

A check in the EDCS Claim box indicates an eView folder exists. To determine if a paper folder also exists, go to eView by Only the most recent MCS/MSSICS DWO1 data is displayed. If the individual filed only a DWB or CDB claim, MCS data will not be selecting the "Open eView, DISCO or CPMS with SSNs" button from the DIBwiz Menu. displayed in the MCS DWO1 section because DIBwiz only works with BOANs. However, if the claim is on EDCS, it will appear in

MCS DW01: Yes **T2Attest:** Yes **MCS message:**
MSSICS DW01: Yes **T16Attest:** Yes **MSSICS message:**
DDSQ indicates: **EDCS Claim:** **Claim Type:** RC-DIB

DDSQ indicates: **EDCS Claim:** **Claim Type:** RC-DI

PCACS indicates Record is being controlled by the PSC paperless No
OHAQ indicates CPMS Interface: Yes

PRISONER STATUS - Refer to POMS DI 10105.100-.105, 11010.285-.305 or 23501ff for the documentation
needed when prisoner data exists.

No PUPS record exists.

Refer to: **SSN:**

Full DIB Review Sheet

Page 4 Query

Date: 5/22/2009

SSN:

Unit: EZTOOL

```
NUMI      DTE:05/22/09     SSN:                 XC:B   UNIT:EZTOOL    PG:001+
 ACCOUNT    SSN:              ETC:0 RFN:30249006812 DOC:535 IDN:P
 NAME       NAA:
 BIRTH      DOB:12/26/1964 PLB: MILWAUKEE , WI SEX:F ETB:2 CSP:A
 PARENT     MNA:
            FNA:
 INTERNAL   FMC:1 CYD:02/02/1983
 ACCOUNT    SSN:              ETC:2 RFN:06289027473 DOC:535 IDN:D
 NAME       NAA:
 BIRTH      DOB:12/26/1964 PLB: MILWAUKEE , WI SEX:F ETB:2 CSP:A
 PARENT     MNA:
            FNA:
 INTERNAL   CYD:10/16/2006
            NO CORRESPONDENCE RECORDS FOUND
 XR SSNS    NO MULTIPLE SSNS LOCATED
MSG-0416891    DTE:05/22/09    TIME:180248                          PG:001+
DDSQ     SSN:              BIC:      ST: WI SA: X10 UNIT: EZTOOL
AN:           BIC:HA   DB:12/26/1964  RI:NKL STATE:WI  SA:S56  STATUS:CLOSED
AH:                                MCS REF: 02004     MDT: 032607    PGM:02
AD:                          MILWAUKEE          WI
APD: 09/12/06      TYP: RC-DIB        DO: 535       ZIP: 53218      SCI:  CCI:Y
RCD: 03/23/07      DEC: DE BAS: J1    LUN: A1       TEL:            NP:    QA:N
SRD: 03/28/07      OND:               LEX: MJH      SLC:            VOC:N  FS:N
PSD:               ABO:               LMC:          CDF:            RLB:  EOR:N
MDF1:              DSI: 0-2780-0      DST: 535      SCF:            APL:C CER:N
                   DIA:               FMD:                          SC1:  SC4:
ESD: 05/10/07      CSD:               RTN:      CDT:       RTG:     SC2:  SC5:
MSD: 05/10/07      SCD: 05/10/07       SO: N    BOD: 09             SC3:  SBI:
LTI:      LTJ:EDC  REM:
OCC:      SDI: 2960      SPC: 30              J1:   /        RFC:        LB:
EDU: 12   MOB:           ESC:                J1B:   /        DAA:        LD:
                    * * DEVELOPMENT HISTORY * *
    S E C                * * ST-WI * *
    L O E
LEV C R R DEC  OND      CSD  BAS  DSI    LEX  LIT  DST   SCD      XAN     BOD
IN   7 Y N DE                J1  024800 KKS        535 020707             20
AN:           BIC:HA   DB:12/26/1964  RI:NKL STATE:WI  SA:S56  STATUS:CLOSED
AH:                                MCS REF:           MDT: 032307    PGM:16
AD:                          MILWAUKEE          WI
APD: 09/12/06      TYP: RC-DI         DO: 535       ZIP: 53218      SCI:  CCI:Y
RCD: 03/23/07      DEC: DE BAS: N32   LUN: A1       TEL:            NP:    QA:N
SRD: 03/28/07      OND:               LEX: MJH      SLC:            VOC:N  FS:N
PSD:               ABO:               LMC:          CDF:            RLB:  EOR:N
MDF1:              DSI: 0-2780-0      DST: 535      SCF:            APL:C CER:N
                   DIA:               FMD:                          SC1:  SC4:
ESD: 05/10/07      CSD:               RTN:      CDT:       RTG:     SC2:  SC5:
MSD: 05/10/07      SCD: 05/10/07       SO: N    BOD: 09             SC3:  SBI:
LTI:      LTJ:EDC  REM:N VILLARREAL 414-463-7146 EXT 1276
OCC:      SDI: 2960      SPC: 30              J1:   /        RFC:        LB:
EDU: 12   MOB:           ESC:                J1B:   /        DAA:        LD:
                    * * DEVELOPMENT HISTORY * *
    S E C                * * ST-WI * *
    L O E
LEV C R R DEC  OND      CSD  BAS  DSI    LEX  LIT  DST   SCD      XAN     BOD
IN   7 Y N DE                N32 024800 KKS        535 020707             20
```

Refer to: [redacted] **SSN:** [redacted]

Full DIB Review Sheet

Date: 5/22/2009 Page 5 Query

SSN: [redacted] Unit: EZTOOL

```
FACT     DTE:05/22/09  SSN:[redacted]  BIC:    DOC:X10 UNIT:EZTOOL  PG: 001+
STATUS   MBR YES LOU-05/22 DATA FILES YES LOU-05/21 SSACCS NO  LOU-05/21
         CPS NO
ACCOUNT    PCOC-7 NOP-01 SP-F TAC-D LUM-05 LMM-05/09 FLI-M  SEC-D CDY-0
           SSI INVOLVED  DRAMS READ  INACTIVE ACCT
PRIMARY    [redacted] DOB-12/26/1964 LSPA-$0.00
INSURED    CLAIM TYPE-DISABILITY DATE OF FILING-09/12/2006
           FIRST MET-07/2001  LAST MET-09/2011  WAIT PER START-10/2006
           NONX NO GMS USED-10/2001  EXC NO GMS USED-07/2001
           20/40 EXCLUSION-TEST MET  20/40 NON EXCL-TEST MET
           DIB QC REQUIRE-20  DIB QC EARNED-40  FULL INS EXCL-TEST MET
           FULL INS NONEXCL-TEST MET  FULL QC REQUIRE-20  FULL QC EARNED-40
           CURR QC EARNED-00  HLTHBEN QC EARN-00
PMT CYC    CYI-4 PCEFD-02/09/2007 PCCOM-02/07 PCCR-I
PAYMENT    PIC-A  MPA-$0.00 DOC-535 SCC-52390  RD-04/28/09 LAP-U F/LLOA-2/3
           EDA-02/09/07 EDL-02/09/07
TELE NO    BTN-[redacted] BTC1-O CPND-05/07
PAYEE      [redacted]
ADDRESS    [redacted]   MILWAUKEE WI 53218-####
ZIP FLAG   ZF-1 ZFDT-02/07
BENEFIT    BIC-A [redacted] SB-F DOB-12/26/1964 B  ABN-DXEP
           LAF-ND MBP-$0.00 DRD-02/09/07 LANG-E TOC-5
BEN DENY   DATE OF FILING-09/12/2006 APP RECEIPT-11/06/2006 ID CODE-A
           CUR ENT CODE-DISABLED  DIB ONSET-09/12/2006  DISALOW/DEN RSN-0J1
           LEVEL OF DENIAL-INITIAL
           DATE OF FILING-09/12/2006 APP RECEIPT-03/23/2007 ID CODE-A
           CUR ENT CODE-DISABLED  DIB ONSET-09/12/2006  DISALOW/DEN RSN-0J1
           LEVEL OF DENIAL-RECON
DIB        DDO-09/12/06 LOD-2 BDC-J1 DSD-05/07
CITIZEN    START-12/26/1964 COUNTRY-UNITED STATES PROVEN
ST EXCH    SEWC-520 SECAC-K SEAD-03/09 SEAC-X SEWN-7502648771Y1
SID        SIFT-D SIED-02/07 SISC-D XIXEC-I SCCR-52390 RZIP-53218 SIAD-12/04
+++ TRANS UPDATED THRU 05/21 +++
TRANS    RD-5/28/08 LAP-U   ST EXCHG ANNOT PIC-A
         RD-7/01/08 LAP-U   ST EXCHG ANNOT PIC-A
         RD-7/29/08 LAP-U   ST EXCHG ANNOT PIC-A
         RD-8/26/08 LAP-U   ST EXCHG ANNOT PIC-A
         RD-9/30/08 LAP-U   ST EXCHG ANNOT PIC-A
         RD-10/28/08 LAP-U   ST EXCHG ANNOT PIC-A
         RD-12/02/08 LAP-U   ST EXCHG ANNOT PIC-A
         RD-12/30/08 LAP-U   ST EXCHG ANNOT PIC-A
         RD-1/27/09 LAP-U   ST EXCHG ANNOT PIC-A
         RD-3/03/09 LAP-U   ST EXCHG ANNOT PIC-A
         RD-3/31/09 LAP-U   ST EXCHG ANNOT PIC-A
         RD-4/28/09 LAP-U   ST EXCHG ANNOT PIC-A
---------------------------------------------------------------------------
MSG:          DTE:05/22/09 SSID   QN:[redacted] RN:01X01 UN:EZTOOL PG: 001+
 CCTL FUN:[redacted] CFL:X10  MV:09/01/07-C PFL:535
    [redacted] PSY:N32 DS:N32-02/07/07 TMR:DI ID:DI
         TDA:03/31/09 SEQ:1
 CMSC HUN:[redacted] RIC:G VER:3 CPD:11/28/08-G MSI:3-1-11/06/06
 PRSN AP:09/12/06 DF:11/06/06 DB:12/26/1964-B SX:F AR:A-      -  -
         LPS:ENGLISH LPW:ENGLISH DOE:09/06 MEF:09/12/2006 MCI:N
 AUTH T:A NME:THOMAS EDMOND BUSH ADR:161 W WISCONSIN AVE, SUITE 5185
         CTY:MILWAUKEE STN:WI 53203-#### TEL:414-765-9333 MAR:N
         DP:D FST:U
```

Refer to: **SSN:**

Full DIB Review Sheet

Page 6 Query

Date: 5/22/2009

SSN:

Unit: EZTOOL

```
RCRD EST:11/06/06 XDO:535 IDD:02/07/07 SNV:3 CNV:5 LAF:ND QCR:20 QCE:40
       QCI:Y PCO:7 ECI:LA FS1:Y FS2:N
ADDR                CTY:MILWAUKEE STN:WI 53218-#### TL:
       DIS:535 ST:52390A ACD:03/23/07
RADR                CTY:MILWAUKEE STN:WI 53218-0000
     DIAR:JR DATE:03/29/09-1
DISB DPC:R SAC:S56 DSA:11/06/06 DDO:09/12/06
NOTC  02/07/07 -1131 0000
APPE ASI C T L RSN   FIL       DSN          OFC   EFT        SBC BEG   END
     01    I R DI    03/23/07 UF-05/10/07 S56
     02    I H DI    07/04/07              X10
TRAN UN:W85
TRAN DY-03/31/09,
TRAN OL-11/28/08-535,
TRAN MB-09/26/07,
TRAN MB-09/06/07,
TRAN OL-09/04/07-535,
TRAN OL-09/04/07-535,
TRAN OL-05/10/07-L24,
TRAN MB-03/27/07,
TRAN OL-03/23/07-535,
TRAN OL-03/23/07-535
ENIH
ENIH  T ENP  ENS   ENA      F V
ENIH  W 0906 0000  550.00 C 1
UMIH
UMIH  T  UMP  UMS  UMA     F UMI         PV
UMIH  A  0906 0906     .00 R             71
UMIH  F  0906 0000  336.50 C              0
CMPH+      FAM     SAM     SUP    UMC     ENC     PCI      PS  BELGPF FO
CMPH  1006     .00     .00 52390     .00     .00     .00 N32         *Z 3NN R 4
SEQY  DTE:05/22/09    AN:             DOC:X10    UNIT:EZTOOL        PG: 001
 MEF: QN:            NA:             DB: 12/1964 SX: F AK:
 SUMMARY FICA EARNINGS FOR YEARS REQUESTED
```

YEAR	EARNINGS	YEAR	EARNINGS	YEAR	EARNINGS	YEAR
1983	414.10	1990	.00	1996	7324.76	2002
1984	5053.17	1991	.00	1997	10378.80	2003
1985	5233.25	1992	2140.02	1998	11532.51	2004
1986	267.75	1993	6806.80	1999	9287.38	2005
1987	.00	1994	10020.14	2000	19120.00	2006
1988	484.73	1995	6911.69	2001	21813.25	2007
1989	.00					

```
 SUMMARY MQGE EARNINGS FOR YEARS REQUESTED
 NO MQGE EARNINGS FOR YEARS REQUESTED
 REMARKS
 CLAIMS ACTIVITY -- SEE MBR
 CLAIMS ACTIVITY -- SEE SSR
---------------------------------------------------------------------------

QRY  DATE: 05/22/09  AN:             DOC: X10 UNIT: EZTOOL  PG: 001+ DEQR
 INPUT: YRS REQ: 1994-1998; COVERED DETAILS; NON-COVERED DETAILS; PENSION;
   SPECIAL WAGE PAYMENT; EMPLOYER ADDRESS
 MEF: NA:            DB: 12/1964 SX: F AK:
 DETAIL COVERED FICA EARNINGS AND EMPLOYER NAME AND ADDRESS FOR YEARS
 REQUESTED
```

Refer to: [redacted] **SSN:** [redacted]

Full DIB Review Sheet

Date: 5/22/2009 Page 7 Query

SSN: [redacted] Unit: EZTOOL

```
EIN: [redacted]              J C PENNY CORP INC
                             % TAX DEPT
                             6501 LEGACY DR
                             PLANO                  TX  75024-3612
RPYR  REO LOAC  NAME         EARNINGS       TOTAL COMP  CONTROL NUMBER  PR
0094  AA  1394  [redacted]       10020.14       10020.14 4136-86-30203
                WAGE TOTAL       10020.14
       OASDI EMPLOYER TOTAL      10020.14
      94 OASDI YEARLY TOTAL      10020.14
EIN: [redacted]  J C PENNY CORP INC
RPYR  REO LOAC  NAME         EARNINGS       TOTAL COMP  CONTROL NUMBER  PR
0095  AA  1394  [redacted]        6911.69        6911.69 5192-85-46119
                WAGE TOTAL        6911.69
       OASDI EMPLOYER TOTAL       6911.69
      95 OASDI YEARLY TOTAL       6911.69
EIN: [redacted]  J C PENNY CORP INC
RPYR  REO LOAC  NAME         EARNINGS       TOTAL COMP  CONTROL NUMBER  PR
0096  AA  1394  [redacted]        7324.76        7324.76 6274-85-39882
                WAGE TOTAL        7324.76
       OASDI EMPLOYER TOTAL       7324.76
      96 OASDI YEARLY TOTAL       7324.76
EIN: [redacted]  J C PENNY CORP INC
RPYR  REO LOAC  NAME         EARNINGS       TOTAL COMP  CONTROL NUMBER  PR
0097  IA  1394  [redacted]       10378.80       10378.80 8141-85-61179
                WAGE TOTAL       10378.80
       OASDI EMPLOYER TOTAL      10378.80
      97 OASDI YEARLY TOTAL      10378.80
EIN: [redacted]  J C PENNY CORP INC
RPYR  REO LOAC  NAME         EARNINGS       TOTAL COMP  CONTROL NUMBER  PR
0098  AA        [redacted]       11532.51       11532.51 8123-86-65013
                WAGE TOTAL       11532.51
       OASDI EMPLOYER TOTAL      11532.51
      98 OASDI YEARLY TOTAL      11532.51
DETAIL NON-COVERED EARNINGS AND W-2 PENSION DATA AND EMPLOYER NAME AND
 ADDRESS  FOR YEARS REQUESTED
 NO NON-COVERED EARNINGS AND W-2 PENSION DATA POSTED FOR YEARS REQUESTED
REMARKS
 CLAIMS ACTIVITY--SEE MBR
 CLAIMS ACTIVITY--SEE SSR
QRY  DATE: 05/22/09  AN: [redacted]  DOC: X10 UNIT: EZTOOL  PG: 001+ DEQR
 INPUT: YRS REQ: 1999-2003; COVERED DETAILS; NON-COVERED DETAILS; PENSION;
   SPECIAL WAGE PAYMENT; EMPLOYER ADDRESS
MEF: NA: [redacted] DB: 12/1964 SX: F AK:
DETAIL COVERED FICA EARNINGS AND EMPLOYER NAME AND ADDRESS FOR YEARS
REQUESTED
EIN: [redacted]              J C PENNY CORP INC
                             % TAX DEPT
                             6501 LEGACY DR
                             PLANO                  TX  75024-3612
RPYR  REO LOAC  NAME         EARNINGS       TOTAL COMP  CONTROL NUMBER  PR
0099  AA        [redacted]        2486.88        2486.88 9154-85-24267
                WAGE TOTAL        2486.88
       OASDI EMPLOYER TOTAL       2486.88
EIN: [redacted]              DAUGHTERS OF LUKE LIMITED-D O L L
                             % ROEPSCH LAW OFFICES
                             1545 N 7TH STREET
```

Refer to: [redacted] **SSN:** [redacted]

Date:

Full DIB Review Sheet

5/22/2009

SSN: [redacted]

Page 8 Query

Unit: EZTOOL

```
                    MILWAUKEE             WI  53205-2347
0099  AA   [redacted]         6800.50       6800.50 9068-69-31171
              WAGE TOTAL        6800.50
     OASDI EMPLOYER TOTAL       6800.50
    99 OASDI YEARLY TOTAL       9287.38
EIN: [redacted]  DAUGHTERS OF LUKE LIMITED-D O L L
RPYR  REO LOAC  NAME          EARNINGS      TOTAL COMP  CONTROL NUMBER  PR
0000  AA   [redacted]        19120.00      19120.00 0092-67-13104
              WAGE TOTAL       19120.00
     OASDI EMPLOYER TOTAL      19120.00
    00 OASDI YEARLY TOTAL      19120.00
EIN: [redacted]  DAUGHTERS OF LUKE LIMITED-D O L L
RPYR  REO LOAC  NAME          EARNINGS      TOTAL COMP  CONTROL NUMBER  PR
0001  AA   [redacted]        21813.25      21813.25 1071-65-62525
              WAGE TOTAL       21813.25
     OASDI EMPLOYER TOTAL      21813.25
    01 OASDI YEARLY TOTAL      21813.25
EIN: [redacted]  DAUGHTERS OF LUKE LIMITED-D O L L
RPYR  REO LOAC  NAME          EARNINGS      TOTAL COMP  CONTROL NUMBER  PR
0002  AA   [redacted]        21367.50      21367.50 2061-67-65622
              WAGE TOTAL       21367.50
     OASDI EMPLOYER TOTAL      21367.50
    02 OASDI YEARLY TOTAL      21367.50
EIN: [redacted]  DAUGHTERS OF LUKE LIMITED-D O L L
RPYR  REO LOAC  NAME          EARNINGS      TOTAL COMP  CONTROL NUMBER  PR
0003  AA   [redacted]        21792.75      21792.75 3177-69-55579
              WAGE TOTAL       21792.75
     OASDI EMPLOYER TOTAL      21792.75
    03 OASDI YEARLY TOTAL      21792.75
DETAIL NON-COVERED EARNINGS AND W-2 PENSION DATA AND EMPLOYER NAME AND
 ADDRESS  FOR YEARS REQUESTED
 NO NON-COVERED EARNINGS AND W-2 PENSION DATA POSTED FOR YEARS REQUESTED
REMARKS
 CLAIMS ACTIVITY--SEE MBR
 CLAIMS ACTIVITY--SEE SSR
QRY  DATE: 05/22/09  AN: [redacted]  DOC: X10 UNIT: EZTOOL  PG: 001+ DEQR
 INPUT: YRS REQ: 2004-2008; COVERED DETAILS; NON-COVERED DETAILS; PENSION;
   SPECIAL WAGE PAYMENT; EMPLOYER ADDRESS
 MEF: NA: [redacted]  DB: 12/1964 SX: F AK:
DETAIL COVERED FICA EARNINGS AND EMPLOYER NAME AND ADDRESS FOR YEARS
REQUESTED
EIN: [redacted]         DAUGHTERS OF LUKE LIMITED-D O L L
                        % ROEPSCH LAW OFFICES
                        1545 N 7TH STREET
                        MILWAUKEE             WI  53205-2347
RPYR  REO LOAC  NAME          EARNINGS      TOTAL COMP  CONTROL NUMBER  PR
0004  AA   [redacted]        21420.00      21420.00 4209-65-16550
              WAGE TOTAL       21420.00
     OASDI EMPLOYER TOTAL      21420.00
    04 OASDI YEARLY TOTAL      21420.00
EIN: [redacted]         BURLINGTON COAT FACTORY WAREHOUSE
                         CORPORATION
                        1830 ROUTE 130 N
                        BURLINGTON            NJ  08016-3017
RPYR  REO LOAC  NAME          EARNINGS      TOTAL COMP  CONTROL NUMBER  PR
0005  AA   [redacted]         4095.00        4095.00 5116-85-87821
```

Refer to: [redacted] **SSN:** [redacted]

Full DIB Review Sheet Page 9 Query

Date: 5/22/2009

SSN: [redacted] Unit: EZTOOL

```
                WAGE TOTAL          4095.00
      OASDI EMPLOYER TOTAL          4095.00
EIN: [redacted]  DAUGHTERS OF LUKE LIMITED-D O L L
0005  AA   [redacted]               1260.00        1260.00 5142-75-09183
      AA1  [redacted]               1260.00        1260.00 5142-75-09207
      1A1  [redacted]              -1260.00       -1260.00 5142-75-09207
                WAGE TOTAL          1260.00
      OASDI EMPLOYER TOTAL          1260.00
     05 OASDI YEARLY TOTAL          5355.00
EIN: [redacted]            TJX COMPANIES INC
                           770 COCHITUATE RD
                           FRAMINGHAM          MA  01701-4666
RPYR  REO LOAC  NAME          EARNINGS      TOTAL COMP  CONTROL NUMBER  PR
0006  AA   [redacted]               3495.52        3495.52 6087-90-28362
                WAGE TOTAL          3495.52
      OASDI EMPLOYER TOTAL          3495.52
EIN: [redacted]  BURLINGTON COAT FACTORY WAREHOUSE
0006  AA   [redacted]               1820.00        1820.00 6262-85-03562
                WAGE TOTAL          1820.00
      OASDI EMPLOYER TOTAL          1820.00
     06 OASDI YEARLY TOTAL          5315.52
EIN: [redacted]  TJX COMPANIES INC
RPYR  REO LOAC  NAME          EARNINGS      TOTAL COMP  CONTROL NUMBER  PR
0007  AA   [redacted]               8772.16        8772.16 8091-BP-69960
                WAGE TOTAL          8772.16
      OASDI EMPLOYER TOTAL          8772.16
     07 OASDI YEARLY TOTAL          8772.16
  08 NONE
DETAIL NON-COVERED EARNINGS AND W-2 PENSION DATA AND EMPLOYER NAME AND
 ADDRESS  FOR YEARS REQUESTED
 NO NON-COVERED EARNINGS AND W-2 PENSION DATA POSTED FOR YEARS REQUESTED
REMARKS
 CLAIMS ACTIVITY--SEE MBR
 CLAIMS ACTIVITY--SEE SSR
-----------------------------------------------------------------------------
[redacted] - PCACS - SSN NOT FOUND
-----------------------------------------------------------------------------
DATE: 05/22/09  SUMM  UN: EZTOOL  AN: [redacted]     PG:   1
 SUMMARY              REC:   1 ACD: 02/02/09 LOU: 02/02/09            PHT:
 AH : [redacted]               CLT: SSDC HGT: NRH-REG 10   BIC:       SSO:
 OFC: 5059 MILWAUKEE WI        ACC: CASE ASSIGNED/REASSIGNED      310
 XAH:                          XAN:              XBI: A      SPC:     HRD:
 HSD:                          HHD:              CST: WI     ISI:     CIF:
 CFL: 5059 MILWAUKEE WI        FLD: 09/04/07     FOC: X10
 ALJ: 1143 AHLGREN S J         RIN:              HO1: 5059
 AAJ:                          RRD:              OAO:
 ASD:                          AVD:              HRM:        CRT:
 DID:                          ADD:                          CDD:
                         TITLE 2/MEDICARE/BLACK LUNG/MISC
  HEARING           APPEAL           COURT
 DSP:              DSP:             DSP:                     CTT:
                                    TITLE 16
 2SP:              2SP:             2SP:                     2TT:
-----------------------------------------------------------------------------

 MCS                            DEVELOPMENT WORKSHEET
```

§205.4 Earnings Record and Insured Status

The Earnings Comp Determination form (*see* sample in §205.5), one of several similar earnings record reports that can be generated by SSA, contains a record of the claimant's reported earnings from wages and self-employment since the inception of the program. It displays the computation of the claimant's PIA (Primary Insurance Amount), which is the amount of monthly benefits payable to a disabled beneficiary. It is a computer-generated document that combines into one record all earnings and quarters of coverage information from all Social Security numbers assigned to the claimant. Because this document contains a wealth of information, if you can decipher the abbreviations and winnow the useful entries from the items of value only to SSA actuaries, §205.5 presents an annotated copy of an Earnings Comp Determination.

Quarters of Coverage

The QC column on the Earnings Comp Determination form shows whether the claimant earned a quarter of coverage for each calendar quarter of the year. These symbols may appear in this column:

N — no quarter of coverage;

C — a quarter of coverage based on wages;

L — for "lag" quarters, which means that earnings have not yet been entered into the computer system for that year but earnings information has been provided to SSA showing a quarter of coverage;

F — Medicare earnings only.

The following apply to years before 1978:

S — a quarter of coverage based on self-employment;

A — a quarter of coverage based on agricultural labor;

M — military wages prior to 1957 credited as a QC;

D — deemed QC based on military service;

R — railroad QC;

J — QC based on deemed wages for interned Americans of Japanese ancestry;

* — a "frozen" quarter, considered a valid QC;

$ — a valid QC;

— appears for earnings 1955-77; earnings posted for that quarter may have been less than $50, which was the amount required for a quarter of coverage during those years;

G — stands for a "gift" or "gratuitous" quarter of coverage, in instances when the claimant did not earn a quarter of coverage for that quarter but the claimant's earnings for the year were over the maximum for which Social Security tax was withheld.

Analysis. If there is a problem with insured status, the claimant's attorney must learn everything possible from the Earnings Record. *See* §131 of this book and review 20 C.F.R. §§ 404.101-404.146 on insured status. Seek help, if necessary, from a knowledgeable hearing office employee or claims representative. Then compare the earnings record information with the claimant's records and recollection. *See* 20 C.F.R. §§ 404.820-404.823 on correcting an earnings record.

In the usual case where there is no problem with insured status, the following entries on the Earnings Comp Determination deserve attention:

Date Last Insured. The date last insured is the date by which a claimant must be found disabled in order to receive any disability benefits. This date is so important that, when you see it on a printout in the hearing exhibit file, an SSA employee may have already highlighted or circled it. If this is a date in the future, you may rest easy. If it is a date in the past, all evidence including testimony in the case must relate to this date or earlier.

Date of Onset. Make sure that SSA entered the correct date. If it's wrong, it may affect SSA's calculations. If you amend the alleged onset date, the new date may affect insured status or the amount of benefits.

Date of Entitlement. The date of entitlement will let you know how far back benefits will be paid based on the current application and alleged onset date.

Primary Insurance Amount (PIA). This amount represents the monthly disability benefit before the "dollar down adjustment" is made. 20 C.F.R. §§ 404.317 and 404.304(f). That is, if the PIA is $1,460.90, the monthly benefit is $1,460. The PIA also represents the amount of benefits for a retiree at regular retirement age. 20 C.F.R. § 404.312.

Family Maximum (Fam Max). This amount is the maximum amount payable on the claimant's account to all family members including the claimant. The PIA or family maximum will let you know how much is at stake in the claimant's case, something in which both claimants and their attorneys are always interested. Since the early 1980s the family maximum has been limited to 150 percent of the PIA in a disability case, but it may be less in cases of claimants with a limited earnings history. *See* 20 C.F.R. § 404.403(d-1).

Regular Earnings. Glance down the regular earnings column that shows the claimant's annual earnings during the claimant's lifetime. If there are big gaps or widely fluctuating income, ask the claimant about any substantial periods of unemployment. ALJs have been known to check this column when evaluating a claimant's work history.

Average Current Earnings (ACEH)/Derived 80% ACE. Although the ACEH does not appear on the sample in §205.5, it often appears on similar printouts as ACEH or as "Derived 80% ACE" in the Alert and Informational sections. This represents 80% of average current earnings, a number that is important in Social Security disability cases where there is also a worker's compensation claim or public disability offset. 80% of average current earnings is the maximum amount a claimant may receive per month from both Social Security disability, worker's compensation, and public disability benefit. In most states SSA reduces Social Security disability benefits so that worker's compensation benefits plus public disability benefits, if any, plus Social Security disability benefits equals 80% of the average current earnings. In a few states, called "reverse offset states," the worker's compensation insurance carrier reduces its payment so that the total payment from both programs equals 80% of the average current earnings. *See* §438 of this book and 20 C.F.R. § 404.408.

Practice Tip—Calculating Date Last Insured

If an earnings record appears in your client's file that does not include date last insured, you can calculate it easily from the information provided. First, determine your client's age at the alleged onset date. If your client was younger than age 31, special rules apply. *See* below. Otherwise, if your client was age 31 or older at the alleged onset date, the 20/40 rule applies. Here's how to figure out if your client meets this rule: Find the QC column. From the most recent entry, count backward in time 20 QCs, which are usually identified with a C. Then, beginning with the 20th QC you counted, calling it number 1, count forward in time 40 calendar quarters. The end of the 40th calendar quarter is the date last insured.

Flexible QCs. If it makes a difference to the calculation, QCs can be moved within a year. *See* POMS RS 00301.230 and 20 C.F.R. § 404.143(b). (After 1977 earnings are reported annually, not quarterly. There is no way for SSA to know in which calendar quarter a claimant had earnings, so the claimant is given the benefit of the doubt.) When you count back 20 QCs in the sample Earnings Comp Determination in §205.5, the 20th QC appears in the first quarter of 1994. The other three quarters in 1994 are each designated N, indicating that no QC was earned. If you count the 20th QC as if it really were in the first quarter of 1994, this claimant's date last insured would be December 31, 2003. But by moving this QC to the last quarter of 1994, this claimant's date last insured becomes September 30, 2004, the date calculated by SSA.

Shortcut. From the most recent entry, count backward in time 20 QCs. Then, go back one more calendar quarter. Determine the date that quarter ends. From that date, add ten years. In the sample at §205.5, when you count back to the 20th QC, it appears in the first quarter of 1994. Since there is only one QC for 1994, move the 20th QC to the fourth quarter of 1994. Then count back one more quarter to the third quarter of 1994, which ends on September 30, 1994. Adding ten years yields a date last insured of September 30, 2004.

Beware. If the date last insured you arrive at does not include all 20 QCs that you counted, the claimant is not insured.

Younger Than Age 31. If your client was not yet age 31 at the alleged onset date, different rules apply. A younger claimant must have QCs equal to one-half the calendar quarters in the period beginning with the quarter after the quarter the claimant became age 21 and ending when the claimant became disabled, with a minimum of 6 QCs. If there are an odd number of quarters between age 21 and becoming disabled, you get to round down when calculating one-half the quarters. *See* 20 C.F.R. § 404.130(c) and SSR 11-2p.

Fully Insured. Every once in a while you will run across a case in which a claimant meets the 20/40 disability insured status rule but does not meet the fully insured status rule. To be fully insured a claimant must have one QC for each calendar year after the claimant turns 21. This is a separate requirement. For example, a claimant is 51 when he becomes disabled. He can meet the 20/40 rule by working for the 5 years before he becomes disabled, accumulating 20 QCs. But he needs 30 QCs to be fully insured: age 51 minus age 21 equals 30. To be fully insured, one is never required to have more than 40 QCs. *See* 20 C.F.R. §§ 404.110 and 404.132.

Date First Insured. Another problem that can affect those with spotty work records is the date first insured. 20 C.F.R. § 404.321 provides: "Your period of disability begins on the day your disability begins if you are insured for disability on that day. If you are not insured for disability on that day, your period of disability will begin on the first day of the first calendar quarter after your disability began in which you become insured for disability." This is easiest to illustrate with the following example: Your 40-year-old client becomes disabled and stops working on July 31, 2006. At that point, he has 19 QCs, all earned within the last 5 years. He returns to work part-time in the first quarter of 2007 (at less than SGA level), earning one more QC. Thus, he becomes insured with the first quarter of 2007, but his period of disability cannot begin on July 31, 2006. Instead, it begins on January 1, 2007, which is the first day of the first calendar quarter after his disability began in which he became insured for disability. January 1, 2007 is his date first insured. Because the waiting period cannot begin before the date first insured, his first month of benefits is five months later—June 2007.

Practice Tip—Prior Period of Disability

When a claimant has had a prior period of disability, SSA's calculation of date last insured is frequently wrong. SSA is supposed to exclude the prior period of disability from the date last insured calculation, but often fails to do so. You may have to do this calculation yourself by following SSA's rules. When calculating date last insured, 20 C.F.R. § 404.130(f) provides that SSA does "not count any quarter all or part of which is in a prior period of disability. . . ." According to 20 C.F.R. § 404.321, a period of disability begins with the onset date and ends the month "immediately preceding your termination month." Termination month is defined in 20 C.F.R. § 404.325 as the third month following the month in which an impairment ends. The month immediately preceding the "termination month" is, in fact, the last month for which the claimant was paid on the prior period of disability. (Since Social Security disability benefits are received in the month after the month to which they apply, the termination month is the month the last check was received.) To do this calculation yourself, first, figure out the actual dates of the prior period of disability. Next, count the calendar quarters all *or part of which* are included between these dates. This is the number of excluded quarters. Then, using the claimant's earnings record, count back 20 quarters of coverage as described above, and count forward 40 calendar quarters plus the number of excluded quarters. The end of the last quarter is the date last insured.

Practice Tip—Missing PIA

If the PIA is missing from the earnings record, it's much easier to request the PIA from the local office than to use the computer program that you can obtain from SSA (called the PIA Calculator) to calculate the PIA yourself. Ask for an "Earnings Comp Determination" or an "Informational Earnings Record Estimate." (An Earnings Comp Determination appears in §205.5.) Send along a copy of your Appointment of Representative form just in case your name has not yet been entered into SSA's computer system as the claimant's representative.

§205.5 Sample: Earnings Comp Determination

```
*** REC 2001138   150739  HB0C0EE0  ARWF    CIPCMA4    PCA4    (F-ARW)  ***

MCS                     EARNINGS COMP DETERMINATION                 MCR1

NH SSN:                 NH NAME: JOHN                          [1] 05/18/01
                                                               COM: 05/01

CASE DISPLAY      1. ALL            4. CIVIL SERVICE       7. APPROVE
                  2. REMARKS        5. PIA CALCS           8. PRINT
                  3. EARNGS, I/S    6. WC/PDB
--------------------------------------------------------------------------
[2] PIA: 1460.90   [3] FAMILY MAX: 2191.40   COMPUTATION TYPE: NS 78 DIS EX
PIA REDUCED FOR AGE:                         LOW TWO YEARS: 1960  16579.95 IND
[4] DATE LAST INSURED: 09/04                                1962   9359.50 IND
--------------------------------------------------------------------------
CLAIM [5]                [6] CLAIM  [7] ENTITLED    [8] NEXT PAYMENT [9] ONGOING
DISPLAY  BIC CL  NAME        TYPE       DATE   LAF      AMT—DATE          PAYMENT
         HA      JOHN        DIB     Y  11/99   C    19207.50 05/01      1460.00
--------------------------------------------------------------------------
CLAIM DISPLAY       1. ALL          3. ENTITLEMENT/ELIGIBILITY
OPTIONS             2. REMARKS      4. PAYMENT CALCULATIONS MORE (Y/N): N
ALERT CASE—SEE REMARKS

MCS          TRANSFER TO:            REMARKS                        DRMK
NH SSN:        NH NAME: JOHN
```

---

1. Date the Earnings Comp Determination was printed. Some of the information on the form applies only to this date.
2. PIA—Primary Insurance Amount. Amount of disability benefits at the time the report was printed.
3. Family Max—Family Maximum. This is the total amount payable to claimant and family.
4. Date Last Insured. A disability claimant must prove that he or she was disabled on or before this date.
5. BIC—Benefit identification. HA indicates that this is a claim for a disabled individual. W is used in a disabled widow's claim. HC indicates that this is a claim for a disabled adult child.
6. Claim Type. DIB indicates that this is a disability insurance benefits claim. SURSPO is used in a widow's disability claim.
7. Entitled Date. Date of entitlement. This is the first month for which benefits are payable based on the alleged onset date and application date.
8. Next Payment Amt—Date. This is the amount of back benefits payable if they are paid in the month indicated.
9. Ongoing Payment. This is the claimant's monthly benefit applicable at the time the Earnings Comp Determination was printed.

10 ALERT

POSSIBLE DUPLICATES PRIOR TO 1978

POSSIBLE DUPLICATES 1996 1998

POSSIBLE INCOMPLETES PRIOR TO 1978

POSSIBLE INCOMPLETES 1994 1997

EARNINGS AFTER ONSET—CHECK DATE OF ONSET OR DEVELOP SGA OR UWA

NH HAS 30 YOC'S FOR NONCOVERED PENSION PIA

MORE (Y/N): Y

ALERT CASE—SEE REMARKS

MCS TRANSFER TO: REMARKS DRMK
NH SSN: NH NAME: JOHN

NH HAS 30 DIS EX YOC'S FOR NONCOVERED PENSION PIA

11 BIC A ATTORNEY INV-DIARY

INFORMATIONAL

12 DISABILITY NON-EXCLUSION 20/40 INSURED TEST MET

DISABILITY EXCLUSION FULLY INSURED STATUS MET

DISABLED NH IS FULLY INSURED RIB

13 DISABILITY NON-EXCLUSION FULLY INSURED STATUS MET

MORE (Y/N): Y

ALERT CASE—SEE REMARKS

MCS TRANSFER TO: REMARKS DRMK
NH SSN: NH NAME: JOHN

PRIOR CLAIM STATUS—A

14 PAYMENT CYCLE 4

NO RECOMPUTATION INCREASE JAN 2000

NO RECOMPUTATION INCREASE JAN 2001

DISABILITY EXCLUSION 20/40 INSURED TEST MET

MORE (Y/N): N

---

10. Alert. This can show many different things. This record shows possible duplicate postings of earnings, gaps in earnings, earnings after alleged onset date. Such alerts are often wrong as is this one: "NH has 30 YOC's for noncovered pension PIA." This translates as "Number holder has 30 years of coverage for noncovered pension PIA," i.e., the claimant worked for 30 years outside the system covered by FICA taxes, e.g., city, county or federal government.
11. BIC A Attorney Inv-Diary. This means that someone has made the appropriate entry into SSA's computer system of your involvement in the case.
12. Disability Non-Exclusion Insured Status Met. The claimant has QCs for at least 20 quarters out of the 40 calendar quarters before becoming disabled. "Disability Exclusion" pertains to those with prior periods of disability that are excluded.
13. Disability Non-Exclusion Fully Insured Status Met. Claimant is "fully insured." *See* §131.
14. Payment Cycle 4. Based on the claimant's date of birth, the claimant will receive checks on the 4th Wednesday of the month.

ALERT CASE—SEE REMARKS

MCS TRANSFER TO: INSURED STATUS DEI1
NH SSN: NH NAME: JOHN

NHID: BIRTHDATE: 07/22/1940 B SEX: M [15] FILE: 05/25/00 MOE:
DEATH: [16] ALG ONSET 06/01/99 ADJ BLIND ONSET:

---

[17] DATE FIRST INSURED: 01/95 TOTAL QUARTERS OF COVERAGE:
MAXIMUM QC'S: SIMPLIFIED QC'S:
WAGE AFTER 194G: 150 WAGE AFTER 1950: 150
SELF EMPLOYED: 000 AGRICULTURAL: 000

		REQ	HAS		REQ	HAS
[18] DIB FULLY INSURED	EXCLUDED	37	40	NON-EXCLUDED	37	40
CURRENTLY INSURED	EXCLUDED			NON-EXCLUDED		
[19] DIB SPECIAL INSURED						
20/40	EXCLUDED	20	36	NON-EXCLUDED	20	36
	EXCLUDED			NON-EXCLUDED		
	EXCLUDED			NON-EXCLUDED		
HIB INSURED						

ALERT CASE—SEE REMARKS
MCS TRANSFER TO: ADDITIONAL EARNINGS DATA DE12
NH SSN: NH NAME: JOHN

SELECTED LAG EARNINGS	**LAG YEAR EARNINGS CONSIDERED**
YEAR TYPE AMOUNT PRF CONS	
	[20] **MILITARY SERVICE** FROM TO PRF CONS
EARNINGS CORRECTIONS PERIOD TYPE AMOUNT + / - CONS	
	JAPANESE INTERNMENT FROM TO HOURLY WAGE PRF CONS
	MORE (Y/N): N

---

15. File. Date of filing of application.
16. Alg Onset. Alleged onset date.
17. Date First Insured. Date first insured is a problem only for claimants with spotty work records who do not meet the insured status rules until this date. They cannot be found disabled before this date.
18. DIB Fully Insured. This shows that the claimant requires 37 QCs to be fully insured. (One QC for every year after age 21.) The claimant in the example was 58 as of the alleged onset date. 58 minus 21 = 37. This shows that the claimant "Has" 40 QCs. In fact, this claimant has a lot more than 40 QCs. 40 QCs is the maximum that could be required. Excluded and Non-Excluded are the same because this claimant had no prior period of disability.
19. DIB Special insured 20/40. This shows that the claimant requires 20 QCs, the same number that everyone who is over age 31 requires. This claimant has 36 QCs.
20. Military Service. Dates of military service will show up here.

ALERT CASE—SEE REMARKS
MCS TRANSFER TO: EARNINGS DATA DEIE
NH SSN: NH NAME: JOHN

TOTAL EARNINGS: AFTER 1936: 742467.66 AFTER 1950: 742467.66

COMPUTATIONAL YEARLY EARNINGS

[21] MAX	[22] QC AMT	YR	[23] QC PATN	[24] REGULAR EARNINGS	U 1	U 2	U 3	INDEXED EARNINGS	EARNINGS U	DMW	SE	AG
4800		59	NCNN	670.52				4769.36		0000	0	0
4800		60	NCCC	2422.44	L			16579.95		0000	0	0
4800		61	CCCN	1034.73				6944.01		0000	0	0
4800		62	CCCC	1464.50	L			9359.50		0000	0	0
4800		63	CCCC	3595.67	H			22429.59		0000	0	0
4800		64	CCCC	3983.56	H			23873.57		0000	0	0
4800		65	CCCC	4692.31	H			27623.75		0000	0	0
6600		66	CCCC	6513.33	H			36172.86		0000	0	0
6600		67	CCCC	7814.12	H			34720.18		0000	0	0
7800		68	CCCC	7529.02	H			37060.27		0000	0	0
7800		69	CCCC	8314.14	H			36296.49		0000	0	0
7800		70	CCCC	11052.02	H			34580.42		0000	0	0
7800		71	CCCG	7800.00	H			32925.99		0000	0	0

MORE (Y/N): Y

ALERT CASE—SEE REMARKS

MCS TRANSFER TO: EARNINGS DATA DEIE
NH SSN: NH NAME: JOHN

TOTAL EARNINGS: AFTER 1936: 742467.66 AFTER 1950: 742467.66

COMPUTATIONAL YEARLY EARNINGS (CONTINUED)

MAX	QC ANT	YR	QC PATN	REGULAR EARNINGS	U 1	U 2	U 3	[25] INDEXED EARNINGS	EARNINGS U	[26] DMW	[27] SE	[28] AG
9000	72		CCGG	9000.00	H			34600.63		0000	0	0
10800	73		CCCC	12276.19	H			39075.80		0000	0	0
13200	74		CCCG	13200.00	H			45079.57		0000	0	0
14100	75		CCCC	14100.00	H			44804.79		0000	0	0
15300	76		CCCC	15300.00	H			45479.73		0000	0	0
16500	77		CCCG	16500.00	H			46273.51		0000	0	0
17700	250	78	CCCC	17700.00	H			45987.00		0000	N	N
22900	260	79	CCCC	22900.00	H			54711.23		0000	N	N
25900	290	80	CCCC	25900.00	H			56765.55		0000	N	N
29700	310	81	CCCC	29700.00	H			59140.80		0000	N	N
32400	340	82	CCCC	32400.00	H			61150.75		0000	N	N
35700	370	83	CCCC	35700.00	H			64249.15		0000	N	N
37800	390	84	CCCC	50507.15	H			64251.52		0000	N	N

MORE (Y/N):

---

21. Max. This is the maximum amount of earnings on which a person pays FICA taxes during the applicable year.
22. QC Amt. This is the amount of earnings necessary to earn one QC. Before 1978 this amount was $50. The column is blank until the 1978 entry.
23. QC. This shows whether there are QCs for each of the four calendar quarters for the year. An N indicates no QC.
24. Regular Earnings. The claimant's earnings are usually shown only up to the amount of the maximum on which FICA taxes are payable.
25. Indexed Earnings. SSA indexes earnings for inflation for their calculation purposes.
26. DMW. Deemed military wages.
27. SE. Self-employment earnings.
28. AG. Agricultural wages.

ALERT CASE—SEE REMARKS
MCS TRANSFER TO: EARNINGS DATA DEIE
NH SSN: NH NAME: JOHN

TOTAL EARNINGS: AFTER 1936: 742467.66 AFTER 1950: 742467.66

COMPUTATIONAL YEARLY EARNINGS (CONTINUED)

MAX	QC ANT	YR	QC PATN	REGULAR EARNINGS	U 1	U 2	U 3	INDEXED EARNINGS	EARNINGS U	DMW	SE	AG
39600	410	85	CCCC	39600.00	H			64560.50		0000	N	N
42000	440	86	CCCC	42000.00	H			66499.48		0000	N	N
43800	460	87	CCCC	43800.00	H			65191.88		0000	N	N
45000	470	88	CCCC	59285.20	H			63834.05		0000	N	N
48000	500	89	CCCC	48000.00	H			65496.39		0000	N	N
51300	520	90	CCCC	51300.00	H			66908.65		0000	N	N
53400	540	91	CCCC	53400.00	H			67145.39		0000	N	N
55500	570	92	CCCC	18546.69	H			22177.99		0000	N	N
57600	590	93	CCCC	4948.00				5866.33		0000	N	N
60600	620	94	CNNN	800.00				923.69		0000	N	N
61200	630	95	CCCC	2887.80				3205.78		0000	N	N
62700	640	96	CCCC	4800.00				5080.08		0000	N	N
65400	670	97	CCCN	2490.00				2490.00		0000	N	N

MORE (Y/N): Y

ALERT CASE SEE REMARKS
MCS TRANSFER TO: EARNINGS DATA DEIE
NH SSN: NH NAME: JOHN
TOTAL EARNINGS: AFTER 1936: 742467.66 AFTER 1950: 742467.66

COMPUTATIONAL YEARLY EARNINGS (CONTINUED)

MAX	QC AMT	YR	QC PATN	REGULAR EARNINGS	U 1	U 2	U 3	INDEXED EARNINGS	EARNINGS U	DMW	SE	AG
68400	700	98	CCCC	5261.07				5261.07		0000	N	N
72600	740	99	CCNN	1600.00				1600.00		0000	N	N
76200	780	00	CCNN	1679.20				1679.20		0000	N	N

MORE (Y/N): N

ALERT CASE—SEE REMARKS
MCS TRANSFER TO: PRIMARY INSURANCE AMOUNT (PIA) CALCULATIONS DPIA

NH SSN: NH NAME: JOHN

CLAIM TYPE: DISABILITY PAYMENT PIA COMPUTATION
[29] COMPUTATION TYPE: NS 78 DIS EX ELG: 1999 YEARS OF COVERAGE:
BASE YEARS: 1951-1998 DIVIDEND: 1455006.93 DROPOUT YEARS:
5
FACTOR CODE: L DIVISOR MONTHS: 384 CHILD-CARE DROPOUT YEARS:
TYPE OF MAX: D AIME: 3789 INCREMENT YEARS:

29. These lines show information about the type of computation used to derive the PIA. *See* 20 C.F.R. §404.204 and following. In this case the computation is based on the average indexed monthly earnings (AIME). *See* 20 C.F.R. §404.210.

	EFFECTIVE DATE:	PIA	FAMILY MAX:	EFFECTIVE DATE:	PIA	FAMILY MAX:
30	11/99	1378.50	2067.70	12/99	1411.50	2117.30
	12/00	1460.90	2191.40			

MORE (Y/N): N

ALERT CASE—SEE REMARKS

MCS TRANSFER TO: TRIAL PIA COMPUTATIONS DTPC

NH SSN: NH NAME: JOHN

12/00	1460.90	NS	78	600.90	SP	MIN	
	1460.90	NS	78R	1460.90	NS	78R	DIS EX
	1460.90	NS	78R	1460.90	NS	78R	DIS EX

MORE (Y/N): N

ALERT CASE—SEE REMARKS

MCS TRANSFER TO: ELIGIBILITY DATA DEE1

NH JOHN CL JOHN

BIC: HA
DATE OF FILING: 05/25/00
DATE OF BIRTH: 07/22/1940
AGE ATTAINMENT DATE:
FULL RETIREMENT AGE: YEARS MONTHS
FULL RETIREMENT DATE:
LAST MONTHLY EARNINGS TEST YEAR:

ELIGIBILITY FACTORS

FACTOR	APPLICABLE	MET	MET	DATE
AGE PROOF	Y	Y		
AGE	N			
MOEL	N			
ONSET	Y	Y		11/99

DISALLOWANCE

CODE REASON

HI/SMI ELIGIBILITY FACTORS

FACTOR	APPLICABLE	MET	MET	DATE
SMI ENROLLMENT				
NON-CRIMINAL				

ALERT CASE—SEE REMARKS

MCS TRANSFER TO: ENTITLEMENT DATA DEE2

NH JOHN CL JOHN

BIC: HA
CLAIM TYPE: DIB
DATE OF FILING: 05/25/00
ENTITLED: Y
DATE OF ENTITLEMENT: 11/99

ALG ONSET 06/01/99
ADJ BLIND ONSET:
31 WAITING PERIOD START DATE: 06/99
END DATE: 10/99
32 PRESCRIBED PERIOD START DATE:
END DATE:

30. This group of dates and numbers shows the PIA and Family Maximum as of the date of entitlement and as of the effective date of each annual COLA increase.

31. Waiting Period Start and End Dates. This shows the beginning and end of the five-month waiting period.

32. Prescribed Period Start and End Dates. In a widow's case the start date is the month of death of the wage earner or the last month of entitlement to mother's benefits, whichever is later. The end date is 84 months after the start date or the month before the month the widow turns 60, whichever is earlier.

HOSPITAL INSURANCE, SUPPLEMENTARY MEDICAL INSURANCE

ENTITLEMENT DATES	ENROLLMENTPERIODS
HOSPITAL INSURANCE:	INITIAL START DATE:
SUPP MEDICAL INSURANCE:	END DATE:
THIRD PARTY START:	GENERAL START DATE:
THIRD PARTY STOP:	END DATE:
PREMIUM PENALTY PERCENTAGE	SPECIAL START DATE:
HOSPITAL INSURANCE:	END DATE:
SUPP MEDICAL INSURANCE:	

ALERT CASE—SEE REMARKS

MCS TRANSFER TO: PAYMENT CALCULATIONS DPC1
NH JOHN CL JOHN

PIC: HA NUMBER OF BENEFICIARIES: 01
MONTHLY PAYMENT AMT: 1460.00
ACCRUAL DATE: 05/01
PRIOR MONTH ACCRUAL AMT: 19207.50
CURRENT AMT: 1460.00

DEFERRED PAYMENT DATE:
SPECIAL PAYMENT AMT:
SPECIAL PAYMENT CODE:
LUMP SUM PAYMENT DATE:
LUMP SUM AMOUNT PAID:

BIC: HA LAF: C
MONTHLY BENEFIT PAYABLE: 1460.00
ACCRUAL DATE: 05/01
PRIOR AMT: 19207.50
CURRENT AMT: 1460.00
LEGAL PAYMENT DED. AMT: 6402.50
CRITICAL PAYMENT AMT:

DEFERRED PAYMENT DATE:
SPECIAL PAYMENT AMT:
SPECIAL PAYMENT CODE:
UNPD. MARITIME TAX AMT:
WINDFALL TOTAL AMT:
ADJUSTED TREASURY AMT:
PREMIUM DEDUCTED/REFUNDED:

DELAYED RETIREMENT CREDITS

RETIREMENT CURRENT:
RET 1ST PRIOR: RET 2ND PRIOR:
RET 3RD PRIOR:

WORK CESSATION DIARY DATE:
WORK RESUMPTION DATE 1:
WORK RESUMPTION DATE 2:

ALERT CASE—SEE REMARKS

MCS TRANSFER TO: HISTORY DBPH
NH JOHN CL JOHN

DATE	PIA	FMAX	AB	OB	MBA	RFD	WIC	HSA	DDA	AMWA	MBC
11/99	1378.50	2067.70	1378.50	1378.50	1378.50		0	0.00	.50	.00	1378.00
12/99	1411.50	2117.30	1411.50	1411.50	1411.50		0	0.00	.50	.00	1411.00
12/00	1460.90	2191.40	1460.90	1460.90	1460.90		0	0.00	.90	.00	1460.00

MORE (Y/N): N

ALERT CASE—SEE REMARKS

MCS TRANSFER TO: XREF ADJUSTED HISTORY DAPH

NH SSN: NH NAME:

EC HAS ADJUSTED THE PAYMENTS AND HISTORY ON THE EXISTING MBR

SCH PAY -- PMA: THRU:
CMA: FOR:
SPC PAY -- SPA: DPD:
BENEFIT -- MBP:
HISTORY --DATE MBA HSA DDA1 DDA2 RFD WIC MBC

MORE (Y/N): N

ALERT CASE—SEE REMARKS

§205.6 Correcting an Earnings Record

If all of the claimant's earnings do not appear on the claimant's earnings record (E/R), it is possible for the claimant to ask SSA to make corrections especially if the wrong year is within the same time limit that the IRS uses for amending a tax return—three years, three months and 15 days from the end of the tax year. 20 C.F.R. §§ 404.802 and 404.821. If the claimant files an application for disability benefits, which has not been finally adjudicated, the time limit is tolled. 20 C.F.R. § 404.822(c)(2).

Even after the time limit runs, a claimant may request that SSA correct its records so that SSA's records correspond with the claimant's tax returns. 20 C.F.R. § 404.822(b). Errors that appear on the face of the record or entries posted for the wrong person or the wrong period may also be corrected by SSA at any time. *See* 20 C.F.R. §§ 404.822(e)(2) and (e)(4).

Note that the claimant must sign the request for correction of the earnings record; it cannot be signed by the representative. 20 C.F.R. § 404.820(b)(2).

When you have a case in which the earnings record needs to be corrected, review 20 C.F.R. §§ 404.820 to 404.823. A valuable POMS section, which summarizes the rules and provides POMS cross-references, is reproduced at §205.7. A sample Form SSA-7008, Request for Correction of Earnings Record, appears at §205.8.

§205.7 POMS RS 02201.008 — Exceptions to the Statute of Limitations

Citations:

Social Security Act Section 205(c)(5).

A. POLICY

After the expiration of the time limitation, the E/R may be revised only for one of the following reasons:

1. Application for Benefit

An application for monthly benefits (including DIB), HIB, LSDP, or SSI is filed before the expiration of the time limitation and a final decision on the application has not been made (see RS 02201.010); or

2. Written Request for Revision

The individual or his/her survivor files a written request for revision of the E/R before the end of the time limitation and a final decision on the request has not been made (see RS 02201.010); or

3. Apparent Error

There is an error apparent on the face of the record (see RS 02201.012); or

4. RRB Interchange

To transfer items to or from RRB records when the items were reported to the wrong agency (see RS 02201.014); or

5. Fraud

To reduce or delete any entry in SSA records established through fraud (see RS 02201.015); or

6. Conforming to Tax Returns

To conform SSA records to tax returns of wages, to wage reports and contributions returns filed by a State (see RS 02201.017) and to SE tax returns filed with IRS (see RS 02201.018); or

7. Errors in Allocation

To correct errors made in allocation of earnings entered in SSA records to individuals or periods (see RS 02201.022); or

8. No Entry or Incomplete Entry of Wages

To credit wages paid to an SSA record when no entry of the wages exists (see RS 02201.016) or where the employer reported less than the correct amount of wages (see RS 02201.013); or

9. Compensation Certified by RRB

To enter on the E/R RRB certified compensation (see RS 02201.014); or

10. SEI Included in Place of Wrongly Reported Wages

To enter SEI in place of erroneously reported wages (see RS02201.026); or

11. SE Returns Filed No SEI on E/R

To enter SEI when SE tax returns were filed, but no SEI is entered on the E/R (see RS 02201.018, RS 02201.019).

B. PROCEDURE

More than one exception may apply to a case. It is only necessary to establish that an exception applies in order to revise the E/R.

§205.8 Form: Request for Correction of Earnings Record (SSA-7008)

SOCIAL SECURITY ADMINISTRATION

Form Approved
OMB No. 0960-0029

REQUEST FOR CORRECTION OF EARNINGS RECORD

I have examined your statement (or record) of my Social Security earnings and it is not correct. I am providing the following information and accompanying evidence so that you can correct my record.

1. Print your name (First Name, Middle Initial, Last Name)

2. Enter your date of birth (Month, Day, Year)

3. Print your name as shown on your Social Security number card

4. Print any other name used in your work. (If you have used no other name enter "None.")

5. (a) Enter your Social Security number

5. (b) Enter any other Social Security number(s) used by you or your employer to report your wages or self-employment. If none, check "None." ☐ None
(1)
(2)
(3)

6. IF NECESSARY, SSA MAY DISCLOSE MY NAME TO MY EMPLOYERS: ☐ YES ☐ NO
(Without permission to use your name, SSA cannot make a thorough investigation.)

- If you disagree with wages reported to your earnings record, complete Item 7.
- If you disagree with self-employment income recorded on your earnings record, go to Item 8.

7. **Print** below in date order your employment **only** for year(s) (or months) you believe our records are not correct. If you need more space, attach a separate sheet. Please make only one entry per calendar **period** employed. Show quarterly wage periods and amounts for years prior to 1978; annual amounts, 1978 on.

1 - Year(s) (or months) of employment 2 - Type of employment (e.g., agricultural)	Employer's business name, address, and phone number *(include number, city, state, and ZIP code)*	My correct Social Security (FICA) wages were:	My evidence of my correct earnings (enclosed)
(a) 1. 2.		$	☐W2 or W-2C ☐Other (specify)
(b) 1. 2.		$	☐W2 or W-2C ☐Other (specify)
(c) 1. 2.		$	☐W2 or W-2C ☐Other (specify)

- If you do not have evidence of these earnings, you must explain why you are unable to submit such evidence in the remarks section of Item 10.
- If you do not have self-employment income that is incorrect go on to item 10 for any remarks, and then complete Item 11.

8. Print below in date order your self-employment earnings **only** for years you believe our records are not correct. Please make only one entry per year.

	Trade or business name and business address	Year(s) of self-employment	My correct self-employment earnings were:
(a)			$
(b)			$

Form **SSA-7008** (03-2015) ef (03-2015) Page 1
Destroy Prior Editions

9. Regarding your earnings from self-employment: a. Did you file an income tax return reporting your self-employment income?	☐ YES (If "YES," go on to Item 9b.)	☐ NO (If "NO," explain why in Item 10).
b. Do you have a copy of your income tax return and evidence of filing such as a canceled check?	☐ YES (If "YES," please enclose copies.)	☐ NO (If "NO," go on to Item 9c.)
c. Have you asked the Internal Revenue Service to furnish you copies from their records?	☐ YES (But none available)	☐ NO (If "NO," please do so if your return was filed less than 6 years ago.)

d. If you are unable to submit a copy of your self-employment tax return, please explain in the remarks section (Item 10).

10. Remarks - You may use this space for any explanations. (If you need more space, please attach a separate sheet).

11. I declare under penalty of perjury that I have examined all the information on this form, and on any accompanying statements or forms, and it is true and correct to the best of my knowledge. I understand that anyone who knowingly gives a false statement about a material fact in this information, or causes someone else to do so, commits a crime and may be subject to a fine or imprisonment.

Signature of person making statement *(First Name, Middle Initial, Last Name)*

Mailing Address *(Number & Street, Apt. No., P.O. Box, Rural Route)*

City	State	ZIP Code

Date	Telephone Number (Include Area Code): 1. Work 2. Home

When you have filled out this form, mail it in an envelope addressed to:

Social Security Administration
6100 Wabash Ave.
Baltimore, Maryland 21215

Form **SSA-7008** (03-2015) ef (03-2015) Page 2

Privacy Act Statement
Collection and Use of Personal Information

Sections 205(c)(4) and (5) of the Social Security Act, as amended, allow us to collect this information. We will use the information you provide to correct your earnings record where any discrepancy exists. Furnishing us this information is voluntary. However, failing to provide us with all or part of the information could affect your future eligibility for benefits and the amounts of benefits to which you may become entitled.

We rarely use the information you supply for any purpose other than to correct your earnings record where any discrepancy exists. However, we may use the information for the administration of our programs including sharing information:

1. To comply with Federal laws requiring the release of information from our records (e.g., to the Government Accountability Office and Department of Veterans Affairs); and,
2. To facilitate statistical research, audit, or investigative activities necessary to assure the integrity and improvement of our programs (e.g., to the Bureau of the Census and to private entities under contract with us).

A complete list of when we may share your information with others, called routine uses, is available in our Privacy Act System of Records Notice entitled, Earnings Recording and Self-Employment Income System, 60-0059. Additional information about this and other system of records notices and our programs are available from our Internet website at www.socialsecurity.gov or at your local Social Security office.

We may share the information you provide to other health agencies through computer matching programs. Matching programs compare our records with records kept by other Federal, State, or local government agencies. We use the information from these programs to establish or verify a person's eligibility for federally funded or administered benefit programs and for repayment of incorrect payments or delinquent debts under these programs.

Paperwork Reduction Act Statement - This information collection meets the requirements of 44 U.S.C. § 3507, as amended by section 2 of the Paperwork Reduction Act of 1995. You do not need to answer these questions unless we display a valid Office of Management and Budget control number. We estimate that it will take about 10 minutes to read the instructions, gather the facts, and answer the questions. **SEND OR BRING THE COMPLETED FORM TO YOUR LOCAL SOCIAL SECURITY OFFICE. You can find your local Social Security office through SSA's website at www.socialsecurity.gov. Offices are also listed under U. S. Government agencies in your telephone directory or you may call Social Security at 1-800-772-1213 (TTY 1-800-325-0778).** *You may send comments on our time estimate above to: SSA, 6401 Security Blvd, Baltimore, MD 21235-6401.* ***Send only comments relating to our time estimate to this address, not the completed form.***

§206 Section E: Disability Related Development

HALLEX I-2-1-15 B.5. provides the following example of what goes into the E section of a file:

Part E — Disability Related Development and Documentation

HO staff will generally exhibit:

- SSA-3368 (Disability Report - Adult);
- SSA-3369 (Work History Report);
- SSA-3441 (Disability Report-Appeal);
- SSA-3820 (Disability Report-Child);
- SSA-454 (Report of Continuing Disability);
- SSA-455 (Disability Update Report);
- SSA-821 (Work Activity Report- Employee);
- SSA-820 (Work Activity Report-Self Employed);
- School records (including teacher evaluations);
- Supplemental requests for more information about activities of daily living, pain, seizures, medication, recent medical treatment, or work history;
- Letters from employers, family members, or other individuals describing the claimant's impairments and limitations;
- Vocational expert interrogatories and the received response;
- A written summary of the case, or written statements about the facts and law material to the case, sub-mitted by the claimant or the claimant's representative;
- Pertinent reports of contact related to disability development;
- Unsuccessful attempts to obtain necessary disability documentation;
- Any other documentation relating to development of disability;
- State vocational reports;
- Disability Determination Services worksheet(s); and
- Electronic Disability Collect System (EDCS) routing form.

The claimant completes a number of items in a hearing exhibit file, most of which appear in the E section. Many attorneys give these documents short shrift. Don't make this mistake. It may come back to haunt you if, for example, the claimant appears to say one thing on an SSA form and another in testimony at the hearing. Read everything written by your client. Flag anything that appears inconsistent or wrong and ask your client for an explanation.

§206.1 Disability Report

The Disability Report, Form SSA-3368, is filled out at the time the claim is filed. It calls for information about the claimant's impairments, treatment sources, medical tests, medications, vocational rehabilitation, work information and educational background.

The Disability Report asks, "When did your illnesses, injuries or conditions **first bother you**?" and "When did you become **unable to work** because of your illnesses, injuries, or conditions?" Pay attention to the claimant's answers to these questions. These answers may help explain a puzzling alleged onset date on the application.

Part II of the Disability Report covers the claimant's medical records, medical tests and medications. Always look here for medical providers that the claimant may have failed to tell you about and from whom SSA may have failed to obtain records.

The full Disability Report, Form SSA-3368-F6, is reproduced at §206.5. It, and many other forms, may be found on the Internet at www.ssa.gov/ online/ forms.html. SSA personnel complete another form, Disability Report—Field Office, Form SSA-3367-F4. It is reproduced at §206.6. This form provides a place for SSA personnel to record observations of a claimant. SSR 16-3p provides, "We will consider any statements in the record noted by agency personnel who previously interviewed the individual, whether in person or by telephone."

§206.2 Work History Report

SSR 82-62 states: "The claimant is the primary source for vocational documentation, and statements by the claimant regarding past work are generally sufficient for determining skill level, exertional demands and nonexertional demands of such work." Form SSA-3369, the Work History Report, is the form used by SSA to gather information about past relevant work. It asks the claimant to describe all jobs he or she has had in the past 15 years. Make sure that the claimant gave complete and correct information on this form. For example, make sure the claimant did not underestimate the duties and exertional and nonexertional requirements of past jobs.

In the usual case it is the claimant's burden at step four of the sequential evaluation process to prove that he or she is incapable of performing each job the claimant has had in the past fifteen years if the job in question lasted long enough for the claimant to learn to do it and was performed at the substantial gainful activity level. *See* §§117 and 347. A relatively brief easy job can present a serious problem for the claimant's case if it appears to be within the claimant's current residual functional capacity. *See* the example in §100 of the truck driver who had a brief office job. Even though he was unable to work as a truck driver, he was found not disabled because he retained the capacity to perform the office job that he performed for a short period during a downturn in the trucking industry. This is exactly the sort of job that, because of its brevity, a claimant might neglect to tell you about. Be sure to look for such jobs on this form.

Carrying the claimant's burden at step four of the sequential evaluation process also can be a problem if the claimant gave one description of a past job on the Work History Report and then describes the job as more difficult at the hearing. If the claimant does not have a satisfactory explanation for the error, you may need to develop evidence from coworkers or supervisors concerning the requirements of past work. Form SSA-3369-BK is reproduced at §206.7.

§206.3 Disability Report—Appeal

A Disability Report—Appeal, Form SSA-3441-BK, is completed at the time the Request for Reconsideration is filed and another one is completed at the time the Request for Hearing is filed to update the information in SSA's file. A copy of this form appears at §178.2.3.

§206.4 Daily Activities Questionnaire

Sometimes you will find a form completed by the claimant, or by someone who knows the claimant well, describing the claimant's daily activities. Some state agencies use a Daily Activities Questionnaire reproduced at the state agency. Others use the Function Report—Adult (SSA-3373). *See* sample at §206.8. Make a note of good and bad examples given on such questionnaires. The good examples make great hearing testimony. At the hearing, ask for more details about the good examples. Bad examples may require explanation from your client. Inarticulate clients who have trouble explaining their daily activities may be sent the Activities Questionnaire from this book, §291, to help prepare them to testify.

§206.5 Form: Disability Report (SSA-3368)

DISABILITY REPORT - ADULT
SSA-3368-BK

PLEASE READ THIS INFORMATION BEFORE COMPLETING THIS REPORT

The information you give us on this report will be used by the office that makes the disability decision on your disability claim. Completing this report accurately and completely will help us expedite your claim. Please complete as much of the report as you can.

IF YOU NEED HELP

You can get help from other people, such as a friend or family member. Please do **not** ask your health care provider to complete this report. If you cannot complete the report, a Social Security Representative will assist you. If you have an appointment, please have the completed report ready when we contact you. If we ask you to do so, please mail the completed report to us ahead of time.

Note: If you are assisting someone else with this report, please answer the questions as if that person were completing the report.

HOW TO COMPLETE THIS REPORT

- Print or write clearly.
- Include a ZIP or postal code with each address.
- Provide complete phone numbers including area code. If a phone number is outside the United States, also provide International Direct Dialing (IDD) code and country code.
- If you cannot remember the names and addresses of your health care providers, you may be able to get that information from the telephone book, Internet, medical bills, prescriptions, or prescription medicine containers.
- **ANSWER EVERY QUESTION,** unless the report indicates otherwise. If you do not know an answer, or the answer is "none" or "does not apply," please write: "don't know," or "none," or "does not apply."
- Be sure to explain an answer if the question asks for an explanation, or if you want to give additional information.
- If you need more space to answer any question, please use Section 11 - Remarks on the last page to finish your answer. Write the number of the question you are answering.

YOUR MEDICAL RECORDS

If you have any of your medical records, send or bring them to our office with this completed report. Please tell us if you want to keep your records so we can return them to you. If you are having an interview in our office, bring your medical records, your prescription medicine containers (if available), and the completed report with you.

YOU DO NOT NEED TO ASK DOCTORS OR HOSPITALS FOR ANY MEDICAL RECORDS THAT YOU DO NOT ALREADY HAVE. With your permission, we will request your records. The information that you give us on this report tells us where to request your medical and other records.

WHAT WE MEAN BY "DISABILITY"

"Disability" under Social Security is based on your inability to work. For purposes of this claim, we want you to understand that "disability" means you are unable to work as defined by the Social Security Act. You will be considered disabled if you are unable to do any kind of work for which you are suited and if your disability is expected to last (or has lasted) for at least a year or is expected to result in death. So when we ask "when did you become unable to work," we are asking when you became disabled as defined by the Social Security Act.

Privacy Act Statement
Collection and Use of Personal Information

Section 205(a), 223(d), and 1631(e)(1) of the Social Security Act, as amended, authorize us to collect this information. We will use the information you provide to make a decision on the named claimant's claim.

Furnishing us this information is voluntary. However, failing to provide us with all or part of the information could prevent us from making an accurate and timely decision on the named claimant's claim.

We rarely use the information you supply for any purpose other than to make decisions regarding claims. We may also disclose information to another person or to another agency in accordance with approved routine uses, which include but are not limited to the following:

1. To enable a third party or an agency to assist Social Security in establishing rights to Social Security benefits and/or coverage;

2. To comply with Federal laws requiring the release of information from Social Security records (e.g., to the Government Accountability Office and Department of Veterans' Affairs);

3. To make determinations for eligibility in similar health and income maintenance programs at the Federal State, and local level; and,

4. To facilitate statistical research, audit, or investigative activities necessary to assure the integrity and improvement of Social Security programs (e.g., to the Bureau of the Census and private concerns under contract to Social Security).

We may also use the information you provide in computer matching programs. Matching programs compare our records with records kept by other Federal, State, or local government agencies. Information from these matching programs can be used to establish or verify a person's eligibility for federally-funded or administered benefit programs and for repayment of payments or delinquent debts under these programs.

A complete list of routine uses for this information is available in Systems of Records Notice entitled, Claims Folders Systems, 60-0089. This notice, additional information regarding this form, and information regarding our programs and systems, are available on-line at www.socialsecurity.gov or at your local Social Security office.

Paperwork Reduction Act Statement - This information collection meets the requirements of 44 U.S.C. § 3507, as amended by section 2 of the Paperwork Reduction Act of 1995. You do not need to answer these questions unless we display a valid Office of Management and Budget control number. We estimate that it will take about 90 minutes to read the instructions, gather the facts, and answer the questions. **SEND OR BRING THE COMPLETED FORM TO THE OFFICE THAT REQUESTED IT. You can find your local Social Security office through SSA's website at www.socialsecurity.gov. Offices are also listed under U. S. Government agencies in your telephone directory or you may call Social Security at 1-800-772-1213 (TTY 1-800-325-0778).** *You may send comments on our time estimate above to: SSA, 6401 Security Blvd, Baltimore, MD 21235-6401.* ***Send only comments relating to our time estimate to this address, not the completed form.***

AFTER COMPLETING THIS REPORT, REMOVE THIS SHEET AND KEEP IT FOR YOUR RECORDS

Form **SSA-3368-BK** (10-2015) UF (10-2015)

SOCIAL SECURITY ADMINISTRATION

Form Approved
OMB No. 0960-0579

DISABILITY REPORT ADULT

For SSA Use Only- Do not write in this box.
Related SSN ____________
Number Holder ____________

Anyone who makes or causes to be made a false statement or representation of material fact for use in determining a payment under the Social Security Act, or knowingly conceals or fails to disclose an event with an intent to affect an initial or continued right to payment, commits a crime punishable under Federal law by fine, imprisonment, or both, and may be subject to administrative sanctions.

If you are filling out this report for someone else, please provide information about him or her. When a question refers to "you" or "your," it refers to the person who is applying for disability benefits.

SECTION 1 - INFORMATION ABOUT THE DISABLED PERSON

1.A. Name (First, Middle Initial, Last)	**1.B.** Social Security Number

1.C. Mailing Address (Street or PO Box) Include apartment number or unit if applicable.

City	State/Province	ZIP/Postal Code	Country (If not USA)

1.D. Email Address

1.E. Daytime Phone Number, including area code, and the IDD and country codes if you live outside the USA or Canada. Phone number ____________

☐ Check this box if you do not have a phone or a number where we can leave a message .

1.F. Alternate Phone Number - another number where we may reach you, if any.

Alternate phone number ____________

1.G. Can you speak and understand English? ☐ Yes ☐ No

If no, what language do you prefer? ____________

If you cannot speak and understand English, we will provide an interpreter, free of charge.

1.H. Can you read and understand English? ☐ Yes ☐ No

1.I. Can you write more than your name in English? ☐ Yes ☐ No

1.J. Have you used any other names on your medical or educational records? Examples are maiden name, other married name, or nickname. ☐ Yes ☐ No

If yes, please list them here: ____________

SECTION 2 - CONTACTS

Give the name of someone **(other than your doctors)** we can contact who knows about your medical conditions, and can help you with your claim.

2.A. Name (First, Middle Initial, Last)	**2.B.** Relationship to you

2.C. Daytime Phone Number (as described in 1.E. above)

____

2.D. Mailing Address (Street or PO Box) Include apartment number or unit if applicable.

City	State/Province	ZIP/Postal Code	Country (If not USA)

2.E. Can this person speak and understand English? ☐ Yes ☐ No

If no, what language is preferred? ____________

SECTION 2 - CONTACTS (continued)

2.F. Who is completing this report?

- ☐ The person who is applying for disability. (Go to Section 3 - Medical Conditions)
- ☐ The person listed in 2.A. (Go to Section 3 - Medical Conditions)
- ☐ Someone else (Complete the rest of Section 2 below)

2.G. Name (First, Middle Initial, Last)	**2.H.** Relationship to Person Applying

2.I. Daytime Phone Number ______________________

2.J. Mailing Address (Street or PO Box) Include apartment number or unit if applicable.

City	**State/Province**	**ZIP/Postal Code**	**Country (If not USA)**

SECTION 3 - MEDICAL CONDITIONS

3.A. List all of the physical or mental conditions (including emotional or learning problems) that limit your ability to work. If you have cancer, please include the stage and type. List each condition separately.

1.
2.
3.
4.
5.

If you need more space, go to Section 11-Remarks on the last page

3.B. What is your height without shoes? ____ feet ____ inches OR ____________ centimeters (if outside USA)

3.C. What is your weight without shoes? ____________ pounds OR ____________ kilograms (if outside USA)

3.D. Do your conditions cause you pain or other symptoms? ☐ Yes ☐ No

SECTION 4 - WORK ACTIVITY

4.A. Are you currently working?

- ☐ No, I have never worked (Go to question **4.B.** below)
- ☐ No, I have stopped working (Go to question **4.C.** below)
- ☐ Yes, I am currently working (Go to question **4.F.** on page 3)

IF YOU HAVE NEVER WORKED:

4.B. When do you believe your condition(s) became severe enough to keep you from working (even though you have never worked)? (month/day/year) ____________ (Go to Section 5 on page 3)

IF YOU HAVE STOPPED WORKING:

4.C. When did you stop working? (month/day/year) ____________

Why did you stop working?

- ☐ Because of my condition(s).
- ☐ Because of other reasons. Please explain why you stopped working (for example: laid off, early retirement, seasonal work ended, business closed)

____

Even though you stopped working for other reasons, when do you believe your condition(s) became severe enough to keep you from working? (month/day/year) ____________

4.D. Did your condition(s) cause you to make changes in your work activity? (for example: job duties, hours, or rate of pay)

- ☐ No (Go to Section 5 - Education and Training on page 3)
- ☐ Yes When did you make changes? (month/day/year) ____________

SECTION 4 - WORK ACTIVITY (continued)

4.E. Since the date in 4.D. above, have you had gross earnings greater than $1,090 in any month? Do not count sick leave, vacation, or disability pay. (We may contact you for more information.)

☐ No (Go to Section 5) ☐ Yes (Go to Section 5)

IF YOU ARE CURRENTLY WORKING:

4.F. Has your condition(s) caused you to make changes in your work activity? (for example: job duties or hours)

☐ No When did your condition(s) first start bothering you? (month/day/year) ______________

☐ Yes When did you make changes? (month/day/year) ______________

4.G. Since your condition(s) first bothered you, have you had gross earnings greater than $1,090 in any month? Do not count sick leave, vacation, or disability pay. (We may contact you for more information.)

☐ No ☐ Yes

SECTION 5 - EDUCATION AND TRAINING

5.A. Check the highest grade of school completed.

0	1	2	3	4	5	6	7	8	9	10	11	12	GED	College: 1	2	3	4 or more
☐	☐	☐	☐	☐	☐	☐	☐	☐	☐	☐	☐	☐	☐	☐	☐	☐	☐

Date completed: ______________________

5.B. Did you attend special education classes? ☐ Yes ☐ No (Go to 5.C.)

Name of School ______________________________

City ______________ State/Province ______ Country (If not USA) ______________

Dates attended special education classes: from ______________ to ______________

5.C. Have you completed any type of specialized job training, trade, or vocational school?

☐ Yes ☐ No

If "Yes," what type? ______________________ Date completed: ______________

If you need to list other education or training use Section 11 - Remarks on the last page.

SECTION 6 - JOB HISTORY

6.A. List the jobs (up to 5) that you have had in the 15 years before you became unable to work because of your physical or mental conditions. List your most recent job first.

☐ Check here and go to Section 7 on page 5 if you did not work at all in the 15 years before you became unable to work.

	Job Title	Type of Business	Dates Worked		Hours Per Day	Days Per Week	Rate of Pay	
			From MM/YY	To MM/YY			Amount	Frequency
1.								
2.								
3.								
4.								
5.								

SECTION 6 - JOB HISTORY (continued)

Check the box below that applies to you.

☐ I had **only one job** in the last 15 years before I became unable to work. Answer the questions below.

☐ I had **more than one job** in the last 15 years before I became unable to work. Do **not** answer the questions on this page; go to Section 7 on page 5. (We may contact you for more information.)

Do not complete this page if you had **more than one job** in the last 15 years before you became unable to work.

6.B. Describe this job. What did you do all day?

(If you need more space, use Section 11 - Remarks on the last page.)

6.C. In this job, did you:

Use machines, tools or equipment? ☐ Yes ☐ No

Use technical knowledge or skills? ☐ Yes ☐ No

Do any writing, complete reports, or perform any duties like this? ☐ Yes ☐ No

6.D. In this job, how many total hours each day did you do each of the tasks listed:

Task	Hours	Task	Hours	Task	Hours
Walk		Stoop *(Bend down & forward at waist.)*		Handle large objects	
Stand		Kneel *(Bend legs to rest on knees.)*		Write, type, or handle small objects	
Sit		Crouch *(Bend legs & back down & forward.)*		Reach	
Climb		Crawl *(Move on hands & knees.)*			

6.E. Lifting and carrying *(Explain in the box below, what you lifted, how far you carried it, and how often you did this in your job.)*

6.F. Check **heaviest** weight lifted:

☐ Less than 10 lbs. ☐ 10 lbs. ☐ 20 lbs. ☐ 50 lbs. ☐ 100 lbs. or more ☐ Other ____________

6.G. Check weight **frequently** lifted: *(by frequently, we mean from 1/3 to 2/3 of the workday.)*

☐ Less than 10 lbs. ☐ 10 lbs. ☐ 25 lbs. ☐ 50 lbs. or more ☐ Other ____________

6.H. Did you supervise other people in this job? ☐ Yes (Complete items below.) ☐ No (if No, go to **6.I.**)

How many people did you supervise? ____________

What part of your time did you spend supervising people? ____________

Did you hire and fire employees? ☐ Yes ☐ No

6.I. Were you a lead worker? ☐ Yes ☐ No

SECTION 7 - MEDICINES

7. Are you taking any medicines (prescription or non-prescription)?

☐ Yes (Give the information requested below. You may need to look at your medicine containers.)

☐ No (Go to Section 8-Medical Treatment.)

Name of Medicine	If prescribed, give name of doctor	Reason for medicine

If you need to list other medicines, go to Section 11 - Remarks on the last page.

SECTION 8 - MEDICAL TREATMENT

Have you seen a doctor or other health care professional or received treatment at a hospital or clinic, or **do you have a future appointment scheduled**?

8.A. For any **physical** condition(s)?

☐ Yes ☐ No

8.B. For any **mental** condition(s) **(including emotional or learning problems)**?

☐ Yes ☐ No

If you answered "No" to both 8.A. and 8.B., go to Section 9 - Other Medical Information on page 11.

SECTION 8 - MEDICAL TREATMENT (continued)

Tell us who may have medical records about any of your **physical and/or mental** condition(s) (including emotional or learning problems). This includes doctors' offices, hospitals **(including emergency room visits)**, clinics, and other health care facilities. Tell us about your next appointment, if you have one scheduled.

8.C. Name of Facility or Office	Name of health care professional who treated you

ALL OF THE QUESTIONS ON THIS PAGE REFER TO THE HEALTH CARE PROVIDER ABOVE.

Phone Number	Patient ID# (if known)

Mailing Address

City	State/Province	ZIP/Postal Code	Country (If not USA)

Dates of Treatment

1. Office, Clinic or Outpatient visits	**2. Emergency Room visits** List the most recent date first	**3. Overnight hospital stays** List the most recent date first	
First Visit	A.	A. Date in	Date out
Last Visit	B.	B. Date in	Date out
Next scheduled appointment (if any)	C.	C. Date in	Date out

What medical conditions were treated or evaluated?

What treatment did you receive for the above conditions? (Do not describe medicines or tests in this box.)

Check the boxes below for any tests this provider performed or sent you to, or has scheduled you to take. Please give the dates for past and future tests. If you need to list more tests, use Section 11-Remarks on the last page.

☐ **Check this box if no tests by this provider or at this facility.**

Kind of Test	Dates of Tests	Kind of Test	Dates of Tests
☐ EKG (heart test)		☐ EEG (brain wave test)	
☐ Treadmill (exercise test)		☐ HIV Test	
☐ Cardiac Catheterization		☐ Blood Test (not HIV)	
☐ Biopsy (list body part)		☐ X-Ray (list body part)	
☐ Hearing Test		☐ MRI/CT Scan (list body part)	
☐ Speech/Language Test			
☐ Vision Test		☐ Other (please describe)	
☐ Breathing Test			

If you do not have any more doctors or hospitals to describe, go to Section 9 on page 11.

SECTION 8 - MEDICAL TREATMENT (continued)

Tell us who may have medical records about any of your **physical and/or mental** condition(s) (including emotional or learning problems). This includes doctors' offices, hospitals **(including emergency room visits)**, clinics, and other health care facilities. Tell us about your next appointment, if you have one scheduled.

8.D. Name of Facility or Office	Name of health care professional who treated you

ALL OF THE QUESTIONS ON THIS PAGE REFER TO THE HEALTH CARE PROVIDER ABOVE.

Phone Number	Patient ID# (if known)

Mailing Address

City	State/Province	ZIP/Postal Code	Country (If not USA)

Dates of Treatment

1. Office, Clinic or Outpatient visits	**2. Emergency Room visits** List the most recent date first	**3. Overnight hospital stays** List the most recent date first	
First Visit	A.	A. Date in	Date out
Last Visit	B.	B. Date in	Date out
Next scheduled appointment (if any)	C.	C. Date in	Date out

What medical conditions were treated or evaluated?

What treatment did you receive for the above conditions? (Do not describe medicines or tests in this box.)

Tell us about any tests this provider performed or sent you to, or has scheduled you to take. Please give the dates for past and future tests. If you need to list more tests, use Section 11 - Remarks on the last page.

☐ **Check this box if no tests by this provider or at this facility.**

Kind of Test	Dates of Tests	Kind of Test	Dates of Tests
☐ EKG (heart test)		☐ EEG (brain wave test)	
☐ Treadmill (exercise test)		☐ HIV Test	
☐ Cardiac Catheterization		☐ Blood Test (not HIV)	
☐ Biopsy (list body part)		☐ X-Ray (list body part)	
☐ Hearing Test		☐ MRI/CT Scan (list body part)	
☐ Speech/Language Test			
☐ Vision Test		☐ Other (please describe)	
☐ Breathing Test			

If you do not have any more doctors or hospitals to describe, go to Section 9 on page 11.

SECTION 8 - MEDICAL TREATMENT (continued)

Tell us who may have medical records about any of your **physical and/or mental** condition(s) (including emotional or learning problems). This includes doctors' offices, hospitals **(including emergency room visits)**, clinics, and other health care facilities. Tell us about your next appointment, if you have one scheduled.

8.E. Name of Facility or Office	Name of health care professional who treated you

ALL OF THE QUESTIONS ON THIS PAGE REFER TO THE HEALTH CARE PROVIDER ABOVE.

Phone Number	Patient ID# (if known)

Mailing Address

City	State/Province	ZIP/Postal Code	Country (If not USA)

Dates of Treatment

1. Office, Clinic or Outpatient visits	**2. Emergency Room visits** List the most recent date first	**3. Overnight hospital stays** List the most recent date first	
First Visit	A.	A. Date in	Date out
Last Visit	B.	B. Date in	Date out
Next scheduled appointment (if any)	C.	C. Date in	Date out

What medical conditions were treated or evaluated?

What treatment did you receive for the above conditions? (Do not describe medicines or tests in this box.)

Tell us about any tests this provider performed or sent you to, or has scheduled you to take. Please give the dates for past and future tests. If you need to list more tests, use Section 11 - Remarks on the last page.

☐ **Check this box if no tests by this provider or at this facility.**

Kind of Test	**Dates of Tests**	**Kind of Test**	**Dates of Tests**
☐ EKG (heart test)		☐ EEG (brain wave test)	
☐ Treadmill (exercise test)		☐ HIV Test	
☐ Cardiac Catheterization		☐ Blood Test (not HIV)	
☐ Biopsy (list body part)		☐ X-Ray (list body part)	
☐ Hearing Test		☐ MRI/CT Scan (list body part)	
☐ Speech/Language Test			
☐ Vision Test		☐ Other (please describe)	
☐ Breathing Test			

If you do not have any more doctors or hospitals to describe, go to Section 9 on page 11.

SECTION 8 - MEDICAL TREATMENT (continued)

Tell us who may have medical records about any of your **physical and/or mental** condition(s) (including emotional or learning problems). This includes doctors' offices, hospitals **(including emergency room visits)**, clinics, and other health care facilities. Tell us about your next appointment, if you have one scheduled.

8.F. Name of Facility or Office	Name of health care professional who treated you

ALL OF THE QUESTIONS ON THIS PAGE REFER TO THE HEALTH CARE PROVIDER ABOVE.

Phone Number	Patient ID# (if known)

Mailing Address

City	State/Province	ZIP/Postal Code	Country (If not USA)

Dates of Treatment

1. Office, Clinic or Outpatient visits	**2. Emergency Room visits** List the most recent date first	**3. Overnight hospital stays** List the most recent date first	
First Visit	A.	A. Date in	Date out
Last Visit	B.	B. Date in	Date out
Next scheduled appointment (if any)	C.	C. Date in	Date out

What medical conditions were treated or evaluated?

What treatment did you receive for the above conditions? (Do not describe medicines or tests in this box.)

Tell us about any tests this provider performed or sent you to, or has scheduled you to take. Please give the dates for past and future tests. If you need to list more tests, use Section 11 - Remarks on the last page.

☐ **Check this box if no tests by this provider or at this facility.**

Kind of Test	Dates of Tests	Kind of Test	Dates of Tests
☐ EKG (heart test)		☐ EEG (brain wave test)	
☐ Treadmill (exercise test)		☐ HIV Test	
☐ Cardiac Catheterization		☐ Blood Test (not HIV)	
☐ Biopsy (list body part)		☐ X-Ray (list body part)	
☐ Hearing Test		☐ MRI/CT Scan (list body part)	
☐ Speech/Language Test			
☐ Vision Test		☐ Other (please describe)	
☐ Breathing Test			

If you do not have any more doctors or hospitals to describe, go to Section 9 on page 11.

SECTION 8 - MEDICAL TREATMENT (continued)

Tell us who may have medical records about any of your **physical and/or mental** condition(s) (including emotional or learning problems). This includes doctors' offices, hospitals **(including emergency room visits)**, clinics, and other health care facilities. Tell us about your next appointment, if you have one scheduled.

8.G. Name of Facility or Office	Name of health care professional who treated you

ALL OF THE QUESTIONS ON THIS PAGE REFER TO THE HEALTH CARE PROVIDER ABOVE.

Phone Number	Patient ID# (if known)

Mailing Address

City	State/Province	ZIP/Postal Code	Country (If not USA)

Dates of Treatment

1. Office, Clinic or Outpatient visits	**2. Emergency Room visits** List the most recent date first	**3. Overnight hospital stays** List the most recent date first	
First Visit	A.	A. Date in	Date out
Last Visit	B.	B. Date in	Date out
Next scheduled appointment (if any)	C.	C. Date in	Date out

What medical conditions were treated or evaluated?

What treatment did you receive for the above conditions? (Do not describe medicines or tests in this box.)

Tell us about any tests this provider performed or sent you to, or has scheduled you to take. Please give the dates for past and future tests. If you need to list more tests, use Section 11 - Remarks on the last page.

☐ **Check this box if no tests by this provider or at this facility.**

Kind of Test	Dates of Tests	Kind of Test	Dates of Tests
☐ EKG (heart test)		☐ EEG (brain wave test)	
☐ Treadmill (exercise test)		☐ HIV Test	
☐ Cardiac Catheterization		☐ Blood Test (not HIV)	
☐ Biopsy (list body part)		☐ X-Ray (list body part)	
☐ Hearing Test		☐ MRI/CT Scan (list body part)	
☐ Speech/Language Test			
☐ Vision Test		☐ Other (please describe)	
☐ Breathing Test			

If you have been treated by more than five doctors or hospitals, use Section 11 - Remarks on the last page and give the same detailed information as above for each healthcare provider.

SECTION 9 - OTHER MEDICAL INFORMATION

9. Does **anyone else** have medical information about your physical and/or mental condition(s) (including emotional and learning problems), or are you scheduled to see anyone else? (This may include places such as workers' compensation, vocational rehabilitation, insurance companies who have paid you disability benefits, prisons, attorneys, social service agencies and welfare.)

☐ Yes (Please complete the information below.)

☐ No (If you are receiving Supplemental Security Income (SSI) and have been asked to complete this report, go to Section 10 - Vocational Rehabilitation; if not, go to Section 11 on the last page.)

Name of Organization			Phone Number
Mailing Address			
City	State/Province	ZIP/Postal Code	Country (If not USA)
Name of Contact Person			Claim or ID number (if any)
Date of First Contact	Date of Last Contact		Date of Next Contact (if any)
Reasons for Contacts			

If you need to list other people or organizations use Section 11 - Remarks on the last page and give the same detailed information as above for each one you list.

COMPLETE THIS SECTION ONLY IF YOU ARE ALREADY RECEIVING SSI.

SECTION 10 - VOCATIONAL REHABILITATION, EMPLOYMENT, OR OTHER SUPPORT SERVICES

10.A. Have you participated, or are you participating in:

- An individual work plan with an employment network under the Ticket to Work Program;
- An individualized plan for employment with a vocational rehabilitation agency or any other organization;
- A Plan to Achieve Self-Support (PASS);
- An Individualized Education Program (IEP) through a school (if a student age 18-21); or
- Any program providing vocational rehabilitation, employment services, or other support services to help you go to work?

☐ Yes (Complete the following information) ☐ No (Go to Section 11)

10.B. Name of Organization or School			
Name of Counselor, Instructor, or Job Coach			Phone Number
Mailing Address			
City	State/Province	ZIP/Postal Code	Country (If not USA)

10.C. When did you start participating in the plan or program?

SECTION 10 - VOCATIONAL REHABILITATION, EMPLOYMENT, OR OTHER SUPPORT SERVICES (continued)

10.D. Are you still participating in the plan or program?

- ☐ Yes, I am scheduled to complete the plan or program on: ____________________
- ☐ **No.** I completed the plan or program on: ____________________
- ☐ **No.** I stopped participating in the plan or program before completing it because:

10.E. List the types of services, tests, or evaluations that you received (for example: intelligence or psychological testing, vision or hearing test, physical exam, work evaluations, or classes).

If you need to list another plan or program use Section 11 - Remarks and give the same detailed information as above.

SECTION 11 - REMARKS

Please write any additional information you did not give in earlier parts of this report. If you did not have enough space in the sections of this report to write the requested information, please use this space to tell us the additional information requested in those sections. Be sure to show the section to which you are referring.

Date Report Completed ____________________

month, day, year

§206.6 Form: Disability Report — Field Office (SSA-3367)

Social Security Administration

DISABILITY REPORT - FIELD OFFICE

IDENTIFYING INFORMATION

1. Name of person on whose Social Security Record this claim is being filed | His or Her Social Security Number

Name of Claimant (*if different from above*) | SSN (*if different from above*)

☐ Male ☐ Female DOB

2. Claimant's Alleged Onset Date (AOD)

3. Potential Onset Date (*see DI 25501.220 Potential Onset Date (POD)*) (*check type of claim(s) and enter potential onset date*) ☐ SSI

☐ DIB/Freeze ☐ DWB ☐ CDB ☐ OTHER

4. Reason for Potential Onset Date

☐ SSI Application Date ☐ Controlling Date ☐ Other (explain in item 5)

☐ SSI Alien ☐ Statutorily Blind

☐ Date Last Insured ☐ Work Before/After AOD

☐ Date First Insured ☐ UWA ☐ SGA ☐ Not SGA ☐ 823 In File

5. Explanation for Potential Onset Date, when applicable:

☐ 820/821 Pending Date Requested

MISCELLANEOUS INFORMATION

6. Protective filing date Non-blind date last insured (DIB/Freeze case)

Beginning of Prescribed Period (DWB) End of Prescribed Period

Controlling date Blind date last insured (if applicable)

Closed period case ☐ Yes ☐ No

PRIOR FILING INFORMATION - Use Remarks, if additional space is needed

7. Prior filing(s) ☐ Yes ☐ No

If yes, and you are not sending the prior folder(s) to the DDS, enter the following;

Type of prior claim(s)

SSN(s) of prior claim(s)

Date of last decision Level of last decision ☐ Allowance ☐ Denial

Location of prior folder

Prior folder requested ☐ Yes (date requested) ☐ No

Form SSA-3367 (09-2014) ef (09-2014) Page 1
Destroy Prior Editions

Disability Report - Field Office Form SSA-3367

Social Security Administration

DISABILITY REPORT - FIELD OFFICE

IDENTIFYING INFORMATION

1. Name of person on whose Social Security Record this claim is being filed | His or Her Social Security Number

Name of Claimant (*if different from above*) | SSN (*if different from above*)

☐ Male ☐ Female DOB

2. Claimant's Alleged Onset Date (AOD)

3. Potential Onset Date (*see DI 25501.220 Potential Onset Date (POD)*) (*check type of claim(s) and enter potential onset date*) ☐ SSI

☐ DIB/Freeze ☐ DWB ☐ CDB ☐ OTHER

4. Reason for Potential Onset Date

☐ SSI Application Date ☐ Controlling Date ☐ Other (explain in item 5)

☐ SSI Alien ☐ Statutorily Blind

☐ Date Last Insured ☐ Work Before/After AOD

☐ Date First Insured ☐ UWA ☐ SGA ☐ Not SGA ☐ 823 In File

5. Explanation for Potential Onset Date, when applicable:

☐ 820/821 Pending Date Requested

MISCELLANEOUS INFORMATION

6. Protective filing date Non-blind date last insured (DIB/Freeze case)

Beginning of Prescribed Period (DWB) End of Prescribed Period

Controlling date Blind date last insured (if applicable)

Closed period case ☐ Yes ☐ No

PRIOR FILING INFORMATION - Use Remarks, if additional space is needed

7. Prior filing(s) ☐ Yes ☐ No

If yes, and you are not sending the prior folder(s) to the DDS, enter the following;

Type of prior claim(s)

SSN(s) of prior claim(s)

Date of last decision Level of last decision ☐ Allowance ☐ Denial

Location of prior folder

Prior folder requested ☐ Yes (date requested) ☐ No

Form SSA-3367 (09-2014) ef (09-2014) Page 1
Destroy Prior Editions

Disability Report - Field Office Form SSA-3367

Social Security Administration

DISABILITY REPORT - FIELD OFFICE

IDENTIFYING INFORMATION

1. Name of person on whose Social Security Record this claim is being filed | His or Her Social Security Number

Name of Claimant (*if different from above*) | SSN (*if different from above*)

☐ Male ☐ Female DOB ________

2. Claimant's Alleged Onset Date (AOD)

3. Potential Onset Date (*see DI 25501.220 Potential Onset Date (POD)*) (*check type of claim(s) and enter potential onset date*) ☐ SSI ________

☐ DIB/Freeze ________ ☐ DWB ________ ☐ CDB ________ ☐ OTHER ________

4. Reason for Potential Onset Date

☐ SSI Application Date ☐ Controlling Date ☐ Other (explain in item 5)

☐ SSI Alien ☐ Statutorily Blind

☐ Date Last Insured ☐ Work Before/After AOD

☐ Date First Insured ☐ UWA ☐ SGA ☐ Not SGA ☐ 823 In File

5. Explanation for Potential Onset Date, when applicable:

☐ 820/821 Pending Date Requested

MISCELLANEOUS INFORMATION

6. Protective filing date ________ Non-blind date last insured (DIB/Freeze case) ________

Beginning of Prescribed Period (DWB) ________ End of Prescribed Period ________

Controlling date ________ Blind date last insured (if applicable) ________

Closed period case ☐ Yes ☐ No

PRIOR FILING INFORMATION - Use Remarks, if additional space is needed

7. Prior filing(s) ☐ Yes ☐ No

If yes, and you are not sending the prior folder(s) to the DDS, enter the following;

Type of prior claim(s) ________

SSN(s) of prior claim(s) ________

Date of last decision ________ Level of last decision ________ ☐ Allowance ☐ Denial

Location of prior folder ________

Prior folder requested ☐ Yes ________ (date requested) ☐ No

Form SSA-3367 (09-2014) ef (09-2014) Page 1

Destroy Prior Editions

Disability Report - Field Office Form SSA-3367

Social Security Administration

DISABILITY REPORT - FIELD OFFICE

IDENTIFYING INFORMATION

1. Name of person on whose Social Security Record this claim is being filed | His or Her Social Security Number

Name of Claimant (*if different from above*) | SSN (*if different from above*)

☐ Male ☐ Female DOB

2. Claimant's Alleged Onset Date (AOD)

3. Potential Onset Date (*see DI 25501.220 Potential Onset Date (POD)*) (*check type of claim(s) and enter potential onset date*) ☐ SSI

☐ DIB/Freeze ☐ DWB ☐ CDB ☐ OTHER

4. Reason for Potential Onset Date

☐ SSI Application Date ☐ Controlling Date ☐ Other (explain in item 5)

☐ SSI Alien ☐ Statutorily Blind

☐ Date Last Insured ☐ Work Before/After AOD

☐ Date First Insured ☐ UWA ☐ SGA ☐ Not SGA ☐ 823 in File

5. Explanation for Potential Onset Date, when applicable:

☐ 820/821 Pending Date Requested

MISCELLANEOUS INFORMATION

6. Protective filing date Non-blind date last insured (DIB/Freeze case)

Beginning of Prescribed Period (DWB) End of Prescribed Period

Controlling date Blind date last insured (if applicable)

Closed period case ☐ Yes ☐ No

PRIOR FILING INFORMATION - Use Remarks, if additional space is needed

7. Prior filing(s) ☐ Yes ☐ No

If yes, and you are not sending the prior folder(s) to the DDS, enter the following;

Type of prior claim(s)

SSN(s) of prior claim(s)

Date of last decision Level of last decision ☐ Allowance ☐ Denial

Location of prior folder

Prior folder requested ☐ Yes (date requested) ☐ No

Form SSA-3367 (09-2014) ef (09-2014) Page 1
Destroy Prior Editions

Disability Report - Field Office Form SSA-3367

Social Security Administration

DISABILITY REPORT - FIELD OFFICE

IDENTIFYING INFORMATION

1. Name of person on whose Social Security Record this claim is being filed | His or Her Social Security Number

Name of Claimant (*if different from above*) | SSN (*if different from above*)

☐ Male ☐ Female DOB

2. Claimant's Alleged Onset Date (AOD)

3. Potential Onset Date (*see DI 25501.220 Potential Onset Date (POD)*) (*check type of claim(s) and enter potential onset date*) ☐ SSI

☐ DIB/Freeze ☐ DWB ☐ CDB ☐ OTHER

4. Reason for Potential Onset Date

☐ SSI Application Date ☐ Controlling Date ☐ Other (explain in item 5)

☐ SSI Alien ☐ Statutorily Blind

☐ Date Last Insured ☐ Work Before/After AOD

☐ Date First Insured ☐ UWA ☐ SGA ☐ Not SGA ☐ 823 in File

5. Explanation for Potential Onset Date, when applicable:

☐ 820/821 Pending Date Requested

MISCELLANEOUS INFORMATION

6. Protective filing date Non-blind date last insured (DIB/Freeze case)

Beginning of Prescribed Period (DWB) End of Prescribed Period

Controlling date Blind date last insured (if applicable)

Closed period case ☐ Yes ☐ No

PRIOR FILING INFORMATION - Use Remarks, if additional space is needed

7. Prior filing(s) ☐ Yes ☐ No

If yes, and you are not sending the prior folder(s) to the DDS, enter the following;

Type of prior claim(s)

SSN(s) of prior claim(s)

Date of last decision Level of last decision ☐ Allowance ☐ Denial

Location of prior folder

Prior folder requested ☐ Yes (date requested) ☐ No

Disability Report - Field Office Form SSA-3367

Form SSA-3367 (09-2014) ef (09-2014) Page 1
Destroy Prior Editions

§206.7 Form: Work History Report (SSA-3369-BK)

WORK HISTORY REPORT- Form SSA-3369-BK

READ ALL OF THIS INFORMATION BEFORE YOU BEGIN COMPLETING THIS FORM

IF YOU NEED HELP

If you need help with this form, complete as much of it as you can. Then call the phone number provided on the letter sent with the form or the phone number of the person who asked you to complete the form for help to finish it.

HOW TO COMPLETE THIS FORM

The information that you give us on this form will be used by the office that makes the disability decision on your disability claim. You can help them by completing as much of the form as you can.

- Print or type.
- A reference to "you," "your," or "the Disabled Person," or "claimant" means the person who is applying for disability benefits. If you are filling out the form for someone else, provide information about him or her.
- **ANSWER ALL OF THE QUESTIONS FOR EACH JOB YOU DESCRIBE.** If you do not know the answer or the answer is "none" or "does not apply," please write "don't know" or "none" or "does not apply."
- Be sure to explain an answer if the question asks for an explanation, or if you think you need to explain an answer.
- If more space is needed to answer any questions, use the "REMARKS" section on Page 8, and show the number of the question being answered.

WHY THIS INFORMATION IS IMPORTANT

The information we ask for on this form will help us understand how your illnesses, injuries, or conditions might affect your ability to do work for which you are qualified. The information tells us about the kinds of work you did, including the types of skills you needed and the physical and mental requirements of each job. In Section 2, be sure to give us all of the different jobs you did in the 15 years before you became unable to work because of your illnesses, injuries, or conditions. There is a separate page to describe each different job.

REMEMBER TO GIVE US THE NAME AND ADDRESS OF THE PERSON COMPLETING THIS FORM ON PAGE 8

Privacy Act Statement
Collection and Use of Personal Information

Sections 205(a), 223(d), and 1631(e)(1) of the Social Security Act, as amended, authorize us to collect this information. We will use the information you provide to make a determination of eligibility for Social Security benefits.

Furnishing us this information is voluntary. However, failing to provide us with all or part of the information may prevent an accurate and timely decision on any claim filed.

We rarely use the information you supply us for any purpose other than to make a determination regarding benefits eligibility. However, we may use the information for the administration of our programs including sharing information:

1. To comply with Federal laws requiring the release of information from our records (e.g., to the Government Accountability Office and Department of Veterans Affairs); and,

2. To facilitate statistical research, audit, or investigative activities necessary to ensure the integrity and improvement of our programs (e.g., to the Bureau of the Census and to private entities under contract with us).

A complete list of when we may share your information with others, called routine uses, is available in our Privacy Act System of Records Notices 60-0089, entitled, Claims Folders Systems; and, 60-0090, entitled, Master Beneficiary Record. Additional information about these and other system of records notices and our programs are available online at www.socialsecurity.gov or at your local Social Security office.

We may share the information you provide to other health agencies through computer matching programs. Matching programs compare our records with records kept by other Federal, State or local government agencies. We use the information from these programs to establish or verify a person's eligibility for federally funded or administered benefit programs and for repayment of incorrect payments or delinquent debts under these programs.

Paperwork Reduction Act Statement - This information collection meets the requirements of 44 U.S.C.§ 3507, as amended by Section 2 of the Paperwork Reduction Act of 1995. You do not need to answer these questions unless we display a valid Office of Management and Budget control number. We estimate that it will take about 1 hour to read the instructions, gather the facts, and answer the questions. **SEND OR BRING THE COMPLETED FORM TO THE STATE AGENCY THAT REQUESTED IT. If you have questions about how to complete the form, contact the State Agency that requested it. If you need the address or phone number for your State Agency, you can get it by calling Social Security at 1-800-772-1213 (TTY 1-800-325-0778).** *You may send comments on our time estimate above to: SSA, 6401 Security Blvd., Baltimore, MD 21235-6401.* ***Send only comments relating to our time estimate to this address, not the completed form.***

PLEASE REMOVE THIS SHEET BEFORE RETURNING THE COMPLETED FORM.

SOCIAL SECURITY ADMINISTRATION

Form Approved
OMB No. 0960-0578

WORK HISTORY REPORT

For SSA Use Only
Do not write in this box.

SECTION 1 - INFORMATION ABOUT THE DISABLED PERSON

A. NAME (First, Middle Initial, Last)

B. SOCIAL SECURITY NUMBER

C. **DAYTIME TELEPHONE NUMBER** *(If you have no number where you can be reached, give us a daytime number where we can leave a message for you.)*

( ) -
Area Code Phone Number

☐ Your Number ☐ Message Number ☐ None

SECTION 2 - INFORMATION ABOUT YOUR WORK

List all the jobs that you have had in the 15 years before you became unable to work because of your illnesses, injuries, or conditions.

Job Title	Type of Business	Dates Worked	
		From	To
1.			
2.			
3.			
4.			
5.			
6.			
7.			
8.			
9.			
10.			

Work History Report - Form SSA-3369-BK

Give us more information about Job No. 1 listed on Page 1. Estimate hours and pay, if you need to.

JOB TITLE NO. 1

Rate of Pay	Per *(Check One)*	Hours per day	Days Per Week
$	☐ Hour ☐ Day ☐ Week ☐ Month ☐ Year		

Describe this job. What did you do all day? *(If you need more space, write in the"Remarks" section.)*

In this job, did you:

Use machines, tools, or equipment?	☐ YES	☐ NO
Use technical knowledge or skills?	☐ YES	☐ NO
Do any writing, complete reports, or perform duties like this?	☐ YES	☐ NO

In **this job**, how many total hours each day did you:

Walk? ____
Stand? ____
Sit? ____
Climb? ____
Stoop? *(Bend down and forward at waist)* ____
Kneel? *(Bend legs to rest on knees)* ____
Crouch? *(Bend legs & back down & forward)* ____
Crawl? *(Move on hands & knees)* ____
Handle, grab, or grasp big objects? ____
Reach? ____
Write, type, or handle small objects? ____

Lifting and Carrying *(Explain what you lifted, how far you carried it, and how often you did this.)*

Check the **heaviest** weight lifted:

☐ Less than 10 lbs ☐ 10 lbs ☐ 20 lbs ☐ 50 lbs ☐ 100 lbs. or more ☐ Other ____

Check weight you **frequently** lifted: *(By frequently, we mean from 1/3 to 2/3 of the workday.)*

☐ Less than 10 lbs ☐ 10 lbs ☐ 25 lbs ☐ 50 lbs or more ☐ Other ____

Did you supervise other people in this job? ☐ YES (Complete the next 3 items.) ☐ NO (Skip to the last question on this page.)

How many people did you supervise? ____

What part of your time was spent supervising people? ____

Did you hire and fire employees? ☐ YES ☐ NO

Were you a lead worker? ☐ YES ☐ NO

Give us more information about Job No. 2 listed on Page 1. Estimate hours and pay, if you need to.

JOB TITLE NO. 2

Rate of Pay	Per *(Check One)*	Hours per day	Days per week
$	☐ Hour ☐ Day ☐ Week ☐ Month ☐ Year		

Describe this job. What did you do all day? *(If you need more space, write in the"Remarks" section.)*

In this job, did you:

Use machines, tools, or equipment?	☐ YES	☐ NO
Use technical knowledge or skills?	☐ YES	☐ NO
Do any writing, complete reports, or perform duties like this?	☐ YES	☐ NO

In **this job**, how many total hours each day did you:

Walk? ______
Stand? ______
Sit? ______
Climb? ______
Stoop? *(Bend down and forward at waist)* ______
Kneel? *(Bend legs to rest on knees)* ______
Crouch? *(Bend legs & back down & forward)* ______
Crawl? *(Move on hands & knees)* ______
Handle, grab, or grasp big objects? ______
Reach? ______
Write, type, or handle small objects? ______

Lifting and Carrying *(Explain what you lifted, how far you carried it, and how often you did this.)*

Check the **heaviest** weight lifted:

☐ Less than 10 lbs ☐ 10 lbs ☐ 20 lbs ☐ 50 lbs ☐ 100 lbs. or more ☐ Other ______

Check weight you **frequently** lifted: *(By frequently, we mean from 1/3 to 2/3 of the workday.)*

☐ Less than 10 lbs ☐ 10 lbs ☐ 25 lbs ☐ 50 lbs or more ☐ Other ______

Did you supervise other people in this job? ☐ YES (Complete the next 3 items.) ☐ NO (Skip to the last question on this page.)

How many people did you supervise? ______

What part of your time was spent supervising people? ______

Did you hire and fire employees? ☐ YES ☐ NO

Were you a lead worker? ☐ YES ☐ NO

Give us more information about Job No. 3 listed on Page 1. Estimate hours and pay, if you need to.

JOB TITLE NO. 3

Rate of Pay	Per *(Check One)*	Hours per day	Days per week
$ ______	☐ Hour ☐ Day ☐ Week ☐ Month ☐ Year		

Describe this job. What did you do all day? *(If you need more space, write in the"Remarks" section.)*

In this job, did you:

Use machines, tools, or equipment? ☐ YES ☐ NO

Use technical knowledge or skills? ☐ YES ☐ NO

Do any writing, complete reports, or perform duties like this? ☐ YES ☐ NO

In **this job**, how many total hours each day did you:

Walk? ______
Stand? ______
Sit? ______
Climb? ______
Stoop? *(Bend down and forward at waist)* ______

Kneel? *(Bend legs to rest on knees)* ______
Crouch? *(Bend legs & back down & forward)* ______
Crawl? *(Move on hands & knees)* ______
Handle, grab, or grasp big objects? ______
Reach? ______
Write, type, or handle small objects? ______

Lifting and Carrying *(Explain what you lifted, how far you carried it, and how often you did this.)*

Check the **heaviest** weight lifted:

☐ Less than 10 lbs ☐ 10 lbs ☐ 20 lbs ☐ 50 lbs ☐ 100 lbs. or more ☐ Other ______

Check weight you **frequently** lifted: *(By frequently, we mean from 1/3 to 2/3 of the workday.)*

☐ Less than 10 lbs ☐ 10 lbs ☐ 25 lbs ☐ 50 lbs or more ☐ Other ______

Did you supervise other people in this job? ☐ YES (Complete the next 3 items.) ☐ NO (Skip to the last question on this page.)

How many people did you supervise? ______

What part of your time was spent supervising people? ______

Did you hire and fire employees? ☐ YES ☐ NO

Were you a lead worker? ☐ YES ☐ NO

Give us more information about Job No. 4 listed on Page 1. Estimate hours and pay, if you need to.

JOB TITLE NO. 4

Rate of Pay	Per *(Check One)*	Hours per day	Days per week
$	☐ Hour ☐ Day ☐ Week ☐ Month ☐ Year		

Describe this job. What did you do all day? *(If you need more space, write in the"Remarks" section.)*

In this job, did you:

Use machines, tools, or equipment? ☐ YES ☐ NO
Use technical knowledge or skills? ☐ YES ☐ NO
Do any writing, complete reports, or perform duties like this? ☐ YES ☐ NO

In **this job**, how many total hours each day did you:

Walk? ____
Stand? ____
Sit? ____
Climb? ____
Stoop? *(Bend down and forward at waist)* ____
Kneel? *(Bend legs to rest on knees)* ____
Crouch? *(Bend legs & back down & forward)* ____
Crawl? *(Move on hands & knees)* ____
Handle, grab, or grasp big objects? ____
Reach? ____
Write, type, or handle small objects? ____

Lifting and Carrying *(Explain what you lifted, how far you carried it, and how often you did this.)*

Check the **heaviest** weight lifted:

☐ Less than 10 lbs ☐ 10 lbs ☐ 20 lbs ☐ 50 lbs ☐ 100 lbs. or more ☐ Other ____

Check weight you **frequently** lifted: *(By frequently, we mean from 1/3 to 2/3 of the workday.)*

☐ Less than 10 lbs ☐ 10 lbs ☐ 25 lbs ☐ 50 lbs or more ☐ Other ____

Did you supervise other people in this job? ☐ YES (Complete the next 3 items.) ☐ NO (Skip to the last question on this page.)

How many people did you supervise? ____

What part of your time was spent supervising people? ____

Did you hire and fire employees? ☐ YES ☐ NO

Were you a lead worker? ☐ YES ☐ NO

Form **SSA-3369-BK** (04-2014) ef (04-2014) PAGE 5

Give us more information about Job No. 5 listed on Page 1. Estimate hours and pay, if you need to.

JOB TITLE NO. 5

Rate of Pay	Per *(Check One)*	Hours per day	Days per week
$ ______	☐ Hour ☐ Day ☐ Week ☐ Month ☐ Year		

Describe this job. What did you do all day? *(If you need more space, write in the"Remarks" section.)*

In this job, did you:

Use machines, tools, or equipment? ☐ YES ☐ NO

Use technical knowledge or skills? ☐ YES ☐ NO

Do any writing, complete reports, or perform duties like this? ☐ YES ☐ NO

In **this job**, how many total hours each day did you:

Walk? ______

Stand? ______

Sit? ______

Climb? ______

Stoop? *(Bend down and forward at waist)* ______

Kneel? *(Bend legs to rest on knees)* ______

Crouch? *(Bend legs & back down & forward)* ______

Crawl? *(Move on hands & knees)* ______

Handle, grab, or grasp big objects? ______

Reach? ______

Write, type, or handle small objects? ______

Lifting and Carrying *(Explain what you lifted, how far you carried it, and how often you did this.)*

Check the **heaviest** weight lifted:

☐ Less than 10 lbs ☐ 10 lbs ☐ 20 lbs ☐ 50 lbs ☐ 100 lbs. or more ☐ Other ______

Check weight you **frequently** lifted: *(By frequently, we mean from 1/3 to 2/3 of the workday.)*

☐ Less than 10 lbs ☐ 10 lbs ☐ 25 lbs ☐ 50 lbs or more ☐ Other ______

Did you supervise other people in this job? ☐ YES (Complete the next 3 items.) ☐ NO (Skip to the last question on this page.)

How many people did you supervise? ______

What part of your time was spent supervising people? ______

Did you hire and fire employees? ☐ YES ☐ NO

Were you a lead worker? ☐ YES ☐ NO

Give us more information about Job No. 6 listed on Page 1. Estimate hours and pay, if you need to.

JOB TITLE NO. 6

Rate of Pay	Per *(Check One)*	Hours per day	Days per week
$	☐ Hour ☐ Day ☐ Week ☐ Month ☐ Year		

Describe this job. What did you do all day? *(If you need more space, write in the"Remarks" section.)*

In this job, did you:

Use machines, tools, or equipment? ☐ YES ☐ NO
Use technical knowledge or skills? ☐ YES ☐ NO
Do any writing, complete reports, or perform duties like this? ☐ YES ☐ NO

In **this job**, how many total hours each day did you:

Walk? ____
Stand? ____
Sit? ____
Climb? ____
Stoop? *(Bend down and forward at waist)* ____
Kneel? *(Bend legs to rest on knees)* ____
Crouch? *(Bend legs & back down & forward)* ____
Crawl? *(Move on hands & knees)* ____
Handle, grab, or grasp big objects? ____
Reach? ____
Write, type, or handle small objects? ____

Lifting and Carrying *(Explain what you lifted, how far you carried it, and how often you did this.)*

Check the **heaviest** weight lifted:

☐ Less than 10 lbs ☐ 10 lbs ☐ 20 lbs ☐ 50 lbs ☐ 100 lbs. or more ☐ Other ____

Check weight you **frequently** lifted: *(By frequently, we mean from 1/3 to 2/3 of the workday.)*

☐ Less than 10 lbs ☐ 10 lbs ☐ 25 lbs ☐ 50 lbs or more ☐ Other ____

Did you supervise other people in this job? ☐ YES (Complete the next 3 items.) ☐ NO (Skip to the last question on this page.)

How many people did you supervise? ____

What part of your time was spent supervising people? ____

Did you hire and fire employees? ☐ YES ☐ NO

Were you a lead worker? ☐ YES ☐ NO

SECTION 3 - REMARKS

Use this section to add any information you did not have space for in other parts of the form. Show the page number of the part you are continuing.

BE SURE TO COMPLETE THE BOTTOM OF THIS PAGE.

Name of person completing this form if other than the disabled *person (Please print)*	Date *(Month, day, year)*	
Address *(Number and Street)*	Email address *(optional)*	
City	State	ZIP Code

§206.8 Form: Function Report — Adult (SSA-3373)

FUNCTION REPORT - ADULT - Form SSA-3373-BK

READ ALL OF THIS INFORMATION BEFORE YOU BEGIN COMPLETING THIS FORM

IF YOU NEED HELP

If you need help with this form, complete as much of it as you can and call the phone number provided on the letter sent with the form, or contact the person who asked you to complete the form. If you need the address or phone number for the office that provided the form, you can get it by calling Social Security at 1-800-772-1213.

HOW TO COMPLETE THIS FORM

The information that you give us on this form will be used by the office that makes the disability decision on your disability claim. You can help them by completing as much of the form as you can.

It is important that you tell us about your activities and abilities.

- Print or type.
- **DO NOT LEAVE ANSWERS BLANK.** If you do not know the answer or the answer is "none" or "does not apply," please write "don't know" or "none" or "does not apply."
- Do not ask a doctor or hospital to complete this form.
- Be sure to explain an answer if the question asks for an explanation, or if you think you need to explain an answer.
- If more space is needed to answer any questions, use the "REMARKS" section on Page 8, and show the number of the question being answered.

REMEMBER TO GIVE US THE NAME AND ADDRESS OF THE PERSON COMPLETING THIS FORM ON PAGE 8

Privacy Act Statements
Collection and Use of Personal Information

Sections 205(a), 223(d)(5)(A), 1631(d)(1), and 1631(e)(1) of the Social Security Act, as amended, authorize us to collect this information. We will use the information you provide to assist us in making a decision on your claim.

Furnishing us this information is voluntary. However, failing to provide us with all or part of the information could prevent us from making a decision on your claim.

We rarely use the information you supply for any purpose other than the reason stated above. However, we may use it for the administration and integrity of Social Security programs. We may also disclose information to another person or to another agency in accordance with approved routine uses, which include but are not limited to:

1. To comply with Federal laws requiring the release of information from our records (e.g., to the Government Accountability Office and Department of Veterans Affairs); and,

2. To facilitate statistical research, audit, or investigative activities necessary to ensure the integrity and improvement of our programs (e.g., to the Bureau of the Census and private entities under contract with us).

A list of when we may share your information with others, called routine uses, is available in our System of Records Notices entitled, Master Files of Social Security Number (SSN) Holders and SSN Applications System, 60-0058; Claims Folders System, 60-0089; and Master Beneficiary Record, 60-0090. Additional information about these and other system of records notices and our programs are available online at www.socialsecurity.gov or at your local Social Security office.

We may also share the information you provide to other agencies through computer matching programs. Matching programs compare our records with records kept by other Federal, State, or local government agencies. We use the information from these programs to establish or verify a person's eligibility for federally funded or administered benefit programs and for repayment of incorrect payments or delinquent debts under these programs.

Paperwork Reduction Act Statement - This information collection meets the requirements of 44 U.S.C. § 3507, as amended by section 2 of the Paperwork Reduction Act of 1995. You do not need to answer these questions unless we display a valid Office of Management and Budget control number. We estimate that it will take about 61 minutes to read the instructions, gather the facts, and answer the questions. **SEND OR BRING THE COMPLETED FORM TO THE OFFICE THAT REQUESTED IT. If you do not have that address, you may call Social Security at 1-800-772-1213 (TTY 1-800-325-0778).** *You may send comments on our time estimate above to:* SSA, 6401 Security Blvd., Baltimore, MD 21235-6401. ***Send only comments relating to our time estimate to this address, not the completed form.***

PLEASE REMOVE THIS SHEET BEFORE RETURNING THE COMPLETED FORM.

SOCIAL SECURITY ADMINISTRATION

Form Approved
OMB No. 0960-0681

FUNCTION REPORT - ADULT

How your illnesses, injuries, or conditions limit your activities

For SSA Use Only
Do not write in this box.

Anyone who makes or causes to be made a false statement or representation of material fact for use in determining a payment under the Social Security Act, or knowingly conceals or fails to disclose an event with an intent to affect an initial or continued right to payment, commits a crime punishable under Federal law by fine, imprisonment, or both, and may be subject to administrative sanctions.

SECTION A - GENERAL INFORMATION

1. **NAME OF DISABLED PERSON** *(First, Middle Initial, Last)*	2. **SOCIAL SECURITY NUMBER**

3. **YOUR DAYTIME TELEPHONE NUMBER** *(If there is no telephone number where you can be reached, please give us a daytime number where we can leave a message for you.)*

______ __________ ☐ Your Number ☐ Message Number ☐ None
Area Code *Phone Number*

4. a. Where do you live? *(Check one.)*

☐ House ☐ Apartment ☐ Boarding House ☐ Nursing Home
☐ Shelter ☐ Group Home ☐ Other *(What?)* ______________

b. With whom do you live? *(Check one.)*

☐ Alone ☐ With Family ☐ With Friends
☐ Other *(Describe relationship.)* ______________

SECTION B - INFORMATION ABOUT YOUR ILLNESSES, INJURIES, OR CONDITIONS

5. How do your illnesses, injuries, or conditions limit your ability to work?

SECTION C - INFORMATION ABOUT DAILY ACTIVITIES

6. Describe what you do from the time you wake up until going to bed.

7. Do you take care of anyone else such as a wife/husband, children, grandchildren, parents, friend, other? ☐ Yes ☐ No

   If "YES," for whom do you care, and what do you do for them?

8. Do you take care of pets or other animals? ☐ Yes ☐ No

   If "YES," what do you do for them?

9. Does anyone help you care for other people or animals? ☐ Yes ☐ No

   If "YES," who helps, and what do they do to help?

10. What were you able to do before your illnesses, injuries, or conditions that you can't do now?

11. Do the illnesses, injuries, or conditions affect your sleep? ☐ Yes ☐ No

    If "YES," how?

12. **PERSONAL CARE** (Check here ☐ if **NO PROBLEM** with personal care.)

    a. Explain how your illnesses, injuries, or conditions affect your ability to:

    Dress

    Bathe

    Care for hair

    Shave

    Feed self

    Use the toilet

    Other

b. Do you need any special reminders to take care of personal needs and grooming? ☐ Yes ☐ No

If "YES," what type of help or reminders are needed?

c. Do you need help or reminders taking medicine? ☐ Yes ☐ No

If "YES," what kind of help do you need?

13. **MEALS**

a. Do you prepare your own meals? ☐ Yes ☐ No

If "Yes," what kind of food do you prepare? (For example, sandwiches, frozen dinners, or complete meals with several courses.)

How often do you prepare food or meals? (For example, daily, weekly, monthly.)

How long does it take you?

Any changes in cooking habits since the illness, injuries, or conditions began?

b. If "No," explain why you cannot or do not prepare meals.

14. **HOUSE AND YARD WORK**

a. List household chores, both indoors and outdoors, that you are able to do. (For example, cleaning, laundry, household repairs, ironing, mowing, etc.)

b. How much time does it take you, and how often do you do each of these things?

c. Do you need help or encouragement doing these things? ☐ Yes ☐ No

If "YES," what help is needed?

d. If you don't do house or yard work, explain why not.

15. **GETTING AROUND**

a. How often do you go outside?

If you don't go out at all, explain why not.

b. When going out, how do you travel? *(Check all that apply.)*

☐ Walk ☐ Drive a car ☐ Ride in a car ☐ Ride a bicycle

☐ Use public transportation ☐ Other *(Explain)*

c. When going out, can you go out alone? ☐ Yes ☐ No

If "NO," explain why you can't go out alone.

d. Do you drive? ☐ Yes ☐ No

If you don't drive, explain why not.

16. **SHOPPING**

a. If you do any shopping, do you shop: *(Check all that apply.)*

☐ In stores ☐ By phone ☐ By mail ☐ By computer

b. Describe what you shop for.

c. How often do you shop and how long does it take?

17. **MONEY**

a. Are you able to:

Pay bills ☐ Yes ☐ No Handle a savings account ☐ Yes ☐ No

Count change ☐ Yes ☐ No Use a checkbook/money orders ☐ Yes ☐ No

Explain all "NO" answers.

b. Has your ability to handle money changed since the illnesses, injuries, or conditions began? ☐ Yes ☐ No

If "YES," explain how the ability to handle money has changed.

18. **HOBBIES AND INTERESTS**

a. What are your hobbies and interests? (For example, reading, watching TV, sewing, playing sports, etc.)

b. How often and how well do you do these things?

c. Describe any changes in these activities since the illnesses, injuries, or conditions began.

19. **SOCIAL ACTIVITIES**

a. Do you spend time with others? *(In person, on the phone, on the computer, etc.)* ☐ Yes ☐ No

If "YES," describe the kinds of things you do with others.

How often do you do these things?

b. List the places you go on a regular basis. (For example, church, community center, sports events, social groups, etc.)

Do you need to be reminded to go places? ☐ Yes ☐ No

How often do you go and how much do you take part?

Do you need someone to accompany you? ☐ Yes ☐ No

c. Do you have any problems getting along with family, friends, neighbors, or others? ☐ Yes ☐ No

If "YES," explain.

d. Describe any changes in social activities since the illnesses, injuries, or conditions began.

SECTION D - INFORMATION ABOUT ABILITIES

20. a. Check any of the following items that your illnesses, injuries, or conditions affect:

☐ Lifting	☐ Walking	☐ Stair Climbing	☐ Understanding
☐ Squatting	☐ Sitting	☐ Seeing	☐ Following Instructions
☐ Bending	☐ Kneeling	☐ Memory	☐ Using Hands
☐ Standing	☐ Talking	☐ Completing Tasks	☐ Getting Along With Others
☐ Reaching	☐ Hearing	☐ Concentration	

Please explain how your illnesses, injuries, or conditions affect each of the items you checked. (For example, you can only lift [how many pounds], or you can only walk [how far])

b. Are you: ☐ Right Handed? ☐ Left Handed?

c. How far can you walk before needing to stop and rest?

If you have to rest, how long before you can resume walking?

d. For how long can you pay attention?

e. Do you finish what you start? *(For example, a conversation, chores, reading, watching a movie.)* ☐ Yes ☐ No

f. How well do you follow written instructions? (For example, a recipe.)

g. How well do you follow spoken instructions?

h. How well do you get along with authority figures? (For example, police, bosses, landlords or teachers.)

i. Have you ever been fired or laid off from a job because of problems getting along with other people? ☐ Yes ☐ No

If "YES," please explain.

If "YES," please give name of employer.

j. How well do you handle stress?

k. How well do you handle changes in routine?

l. Have you noticed any unusual behavior or fears? ☐ Yes ☐ No

If "YES," please explain.

21. Do you use any of the following? *(Check all that apply.)*

☐ Crutches ☐ Cane ☐ Hearing Aid
☐ Walker ☐ Brace/Splint ☐ Glasses/Contact Lenses
☐ Wheelchair ☐ Artificial Limb ☐ Artificial Voice Box
☐ Other (Explain)

Which of these were prescribed by a doctor?

When was it prescribed?

When do you need to use these aids?

22. Do you currently take any medicines for your illnesses, injuries, or conditions? ☐ Yes ☐ No

If "YES, "do any of your medicines cause side effects? ☐ Yes ☐ No

If "YES," please explain. (Do not list all of the medicines that you take. List only the medicines that cause side effects.)

NAME OF MEDICINE	SIDE EFFECTS YOU HAVE

SECTION E - REMARKS

Use this section for any added information you did not show in earlier parts of this form. When you are done with this section (or if you didn't have anything to add), be sure to complete the fields at the bottom of this page.

Name of person completing this form (Please print)	Date *(month, day, year)*	
Address (Number and Street)	Email address (optional)	
City	State	ZIP Code

§207 Section F: Medical Records

HALLEX I-2-1-15 B.6. provides the following example of what goes into the F section of a file:

Part F—Medical Records

HOs will generally exhibit:

- A Cooperative Disability Investigations Unit Report of Investigation (filed on top in a paper claim(s) file);
- Treatment records (with cover letter if not otherwise identified);
- Hospital records;
- Laboratory/imaging reports and findings;
- Outpatient notes;
- Consultative examination reports;
- Medical opinions, analyses, and residual functional capacity assessments;
- School records of multi-discipline evaluations and/or psychologist evaluations.
- Letters of unsuccessful attempts to obtain medical evidence;
- SSA-4734 (Residual Functional Capacity Assessment);
- SSA-2506 (Psychiatric Review Technique - PRT Form);
- Death certificate (for the purposes of assessing disability);
- Medical expert interrogatories and received responses; and
- Professional Qualification Statements attached to medical evidence, SSA-831 or SSA-833.

§207.1 Residual Physical Functional Capacity Assessment

If exertional impairments are involved, the file will contain an appraisal of the claimant's physical residual functional capacity (RFC), unless it is found that the claimant is actually engaged in substantial gainful activity, or that the claimant's impairments are not severe. The Residual Physical Functional Capacity Assessment, Form SSA-4734, (*see* the following sample, §207.2), appears as a medical exhibit. For mental RFC assessments, *see* sample form SSA-4734-F4-SUP at §245.4.

At the hearing level, the RFC assessment is to be made by the administrative law judge. ALJs are required to treat state agency doctor RFC determinations as opinion evidence, 20 C.F.R. § 404.1512(b)(6), SSR 96-6p, and will evaluate such opinions taking into account contrary opinions from treating and examining doctors, which may be entitled to more weight. 20 C.F.R. § 404.1527(c). "[B]ecause nonexamining sources have no examining or treating relationship with [the claimant], the weight [SSA] will give their opinions will depend on the degree to which they provide supporting explanations for their opinions." 20 C.F.R. § 404.1527(c)(3). When you review an RFC form completed by a state agency doctor, look at the explanations provided for the conclusions, which are usually written in state agency worksheets. More than likely you will find the explanations to be inadequate.

According to HALLEX I-2-1-15 B.5, state agency worksheets are to be filed in the E section of the disability file. However, many hearing offices put them in the F section, recognizing that they contain medical opinion evidence.

If the file does not contain RFC assessment forms, it is likely that the RFC assessment is included in the Disability Determination Explanation, which appears in the A section.

§207.2 Form: Residual Functional Capacity Assessment (SSA-4734)

FORM APPROVED
OMB NO. 0960-0431

PHYSICAL RESIDUAL FUNCTIONAL CAPACITY ASSESSMENT

CLAIMANT:	SOCIAL SECURITY NUMBER:
NUMBERHOLDER (IF CDB OR DWB CLAIM):	_ _

PRIMARY DIAGNOSIS:	RFC ASSESSMENT IS FOR:
SECONDARY DIAGNOSIS:	☐ Current Evaluation ☐ Date 12 Months After Onset: ______ (Date)
OTHER ALLEGED IMPAIRMENTS:	☐ Date Last Insured: ______ (Date) ☐ Other (Specify): ______

PRIVACY ACT NOTICE: The information requested on this form is authorized by Section 223 and Section 1633 of the Social Security Act. The information provided will be used in making a decision on this claim. Failure to complete this form may result in a delay in processing the claim. Information furnished on this form may be disclosed by the Social Security Administration to another person or governmental agency only with respect to Social Security programs and to comply with Federal laws requiring the exchange of information between Social Security and other agencies.

PAPERWORK REDUCTION ACT: This information collection meets the requirements of 44 U.S.C. § 3507, as amended by Section 2 of the Paperwork Reduction Act of 1995. You do not need to answer these questions unless we display a valid Office of Management and Budget control number. We estimate that it will take about 20 minutes to read the instructions, gather the facts, and answer the questions. *You may send comments on our time estimate above to: SSA, 6401 Security Blvd., Baltimore, MD 21235-6401.* ***Send only comments relating to our time estimate to this address, not the completed form.***

I. LIMITATIONS:

For Each Section A - F

Base your conclusions on **all evidence** in file (clinical and laboratory findings; symptoms; observations, lay evidence; reports of daily activities; etc.).

Check the blocks which reflect your **reasoned judgment**.

Describe how the **evidence substantiates your conclusions** (Cite specific clinical and laboratory findings, observations, lay evidence, etc.).

Ensure that you have:

- Requested appropriate medical source statements regarding the individual's capacities (DI 22505.000ff. and DI 22510.000ff.) and that you have given appropriate **weight to treating source conclusions** (See Section III.).
- Considered and responded to **any alleged limitations imposed by symptoms** (pain, fatigue, etc.) attributable, in your judgment, to a medically determinable impairment. Discuss your assessment of symptom-related limitations in the explanation for your conclusions in A - F below (See also Section II.).
- Responded to all allegations of physical limitations or factors which can cause physical limitations.

Frequently means occurring one-third to two-thirds of an 8-hour workday (cumulative, not continuous). **Occasionally** means occurring from very little up to one-third of an 8-hour workday (cumulative, not continuous).

Continued on Page 2

A. EXERTIONAL LIMITATIONS

☐ None established. (Proceed to section B.)

1. **Occasionally** lift and/or carry (including upward pulling)
(maximum) - when less than one-third of the time or less than 10 pounds, explain the amount (time/pounds) in item 6.

☐ less than 10 pounds

☐ 10 pounds

☐ 20 pounds

☐ 50 pounds

☐ 100 pounds or more

2. **Frequently** lift and/or carry (including upward pulling)
(maximum) - when less than two-thirds of the time or less than 10 pounds, explain the amount (time/pounds) in item 6.

☐ less than 10 pounds

☐ 10 pounds

☐ 25 pounds

☐ 50 pounds or more

3. Stand and/or walk (with normal breaks) for a total of -

☐ less than 2 hours in an 8-hour workday

☐ at least 2 hours in an 8-hour workday

☐ about 6 hours in an 8-hour workday

☐ medically required hand-held assistive device is necessary for ambulation

4. Sit (with normal breaks) for a total of -

☐ less than about 6 hours in an 8-hour workday

☐ about 6 hours in an 8-hour workday

☐ must periodically alternate sitting and standing to relieve pain or discomfort. (If checked, explain in 6.)

5. Push and/or pull (including operation of hand and/or foot controls) -

☐ unlimited, other than as shown for lift and/or carry

☐ limited in upper extremities (describe nature and degree)

☐ limited in lower extremities (describe nature and degree)

6. Explain how and why the evidence supports your conclusions in item 1 through 5.
Cite the specific facts upon which your conclusions are based.

Continued on Page 3

6. Continue (NOTE: MAKE ADDITIONAL COMMENTS IN SECTION IV)

B. POSTURAL LIMITATIONS

☐ None established. (Proceed to section C.)

	Frequently	Occasionally	Never
1. Climbing - ramp/stairs	☐	☐	☐
- ladder/rope/scaffolds	☐	☐	☐
2. Balancing	☐	☐	☐
3. Stooping	☐	☐	☐
4. Kneeling	☐	☐	☐
5. Crouching	☐	☐	☐
6. Crawling	☐	☐	☐

7. When less than two-thirds of the time for frequently or less than one-third for occasionally, fully describe and explain. Also explain how and why the evidence supports your conclusions in items 1 through 6. Cite the specific facts upon which your conclusions are based.

Continued on Page 4

C. MANIPULATIVE LIMITATIONS

☐ None established. (Proceed to section D.)

	LIMITED	UNLIMITED
1. Reaching all directions (including overhead)	☐	☐
2. Handling (gross manipulation)	☐	☐
3. Fingering (fine manipulation)	☐	☐
4. Feeling (skin receptors)	☐	☐

5. Describe how the activities checked "limited" are impaired. Also, explain how and why the evidence supports your conclusions in item 1 through 4. Cite the specific facts upon which your conclusions are based.

D. VISUAL LIMITATIONS

☐ None established. (Proceed to section E.)

	LIMITED	UNLIMITED
1. Near acuity	☐	☐
2. Far acuity	☐	☐
3. Depth perception	☐	☐
4. Accommodation	☐	☐
5. Color vision	☐	☐
6. Field of vision	☐	☐

7. Describe how the faculties checked "limited" are impaired. Also explain how and why the evidence supports your conclusions in items 1 through 6. Cite the specific facts upon which your conclusions are based.

Continued on Page 5

E. COMMUNICATIVE LIMITATIONS

☐ None established. (Proceed to section F.)

	LIMITED	UNLIMITED
1. Hearing	☐	☐
2. Speaking	☐	☐

3. Describe how the faculties checked "limited" are impaired. Also, explain how and why the evidence supports your conclusions in items 1 and 2. Cite the specific facts upon which your conclusions are based.

F. ENVIRONMENTAL LIMITATIONS

☐ None established. (Proceed to section II.)

	UNLIMITED	AVOID CONCENTRATED EXPOSURE	AVOID EVEN MODERATE EXPOSURE	AVOID ALL EXPOSURE
1. Extreme cold	☐	☐	☐	☐
2. Extreme heat	☐	☐	☐	☐
3. Wetness	☐	☐	☐	☐
4. Humidity	☐	☐	☐	☐
5. Noise	☐	☐	☐	☐
6. Vibration	☐	☐	☐	☐
7. Fumes, odors, dusts, gases, poor ventilation, etc.	☐	☐	☐	☐
8. Hazards (machinery, heights, etc.)	☐	☐	☐	☐

9. Describe how these environmental factors impair activities and identify hazards to be avoided. Also, explain how and why the evidence supports your conclusions in items 1through 8. Cite the specific facts upon which your conclusions are based.

Continued on Page 6

9. Continue (NOTE: MAKE ADDITIONAL COMMENTS IN SECTION IV)

II. SYMPTOMS

For symptoms alleged by the claimant to produce physical limitations, and for which the following have not previously been addressed in section I, discuss whether:

A. The symptom(s) is attributable, in your judgment, to a medically determinable impairment.

B. The severity or duration of the symptom(s), in your judgment, is disproportionate to the expected severity or expected duration on the basis of the claimant's medically determinable impairment(s).

C. The severity of the symptom(s) and its alleged effect on function is consistent, in your judgment, with the total medical and nonmedical evidence, including statements by the claimant and others, observations regarding activities of daily living, and alterations of usual behavior or habits.

Continued on Page 7

III. MEDICAL SOURCE STATEMENT(S)

A. Is a medical source statement(s) regarding the claimant's physical capacities in file?

☐ Yes

☐ No (Includes situations in which there was no source or when the source(s) did not provide a statement regarding the claimant's physical capacities.)

B. If yes, are there medical source conclusions about the claimant's limitations or restrictions which are significantly different from your findings?

☐ Yes

☐ No

C. If yes, explain why those conclusions are not supported by the evidence in file. Cite the source's name and the statement date.

Continued on Page 8

IV. ADDITIONAL COMMENTS:

V. SIGNATURE

A. Signatory's Role

☐ Medical Consultant **(MC)**

OR

☐ Single Decisionmaker **(SDM)**

B. MC's Statement

The MC does **not** check this block when the MC's assessment is preliminary, advisory or partial.

☐ THESE FINDINGS COMPLETE THE MEDICAL PORTION OF THE DISABILITY DETERMINATION.

SIGNATURE:	MEDICAL CONSULTANT'S CODE:	DATE:

§208 Analysis of Hearing Exhibit File

As you are going through the Social Security file, watch for references to the existence of other medical evidence that your client may not have told you about.

When a medical summary refers to relevant treatment, positive test results, etc., make sure these records appear in the file. If they do not, make a note to obtain them. Make sure records have been obtained from all relevant treating sources. Compare the list of treating sources provided by your client to SSA to what your client told you. Your client may have forgotten to tell you about a treating source.

As you are reviewing the Social Security file, try to determine as precisely as possible 1) why the claim was denied, and 2) what additional facts or opinions are necessary to change that denial into an allowance of benefits. Pay special attention to the state agency worksheets and the Disability Determination Explantions, which include notes written about your client's case by disability examiners and state agency doctors. These notes often include questions written by a disability examiner and answers written by the state agency doctor. You may want to ask the claimant's doctor any good questions that you find in the notes. Often you'll get a different answer or, at least, an explanation that leads to a different result from that reached by the state agency.

If you think your client's impairment meets the criteria set forth for one of the impairments found in the Listing of Impairments, be sure to look at the state agency worksheets to see how this issue was addressed by the disability examiner and state agency physician. Sometimes you will find that the state agency doctor missed the issue or made an error in interpreting medical records. More often, however, except for those Listings that incorporate subjective determinations (such as the mental Listings), you'll either end up agreeing that your client's impairment does not meet the Listings (state agency physicians, in fact, make relatively few errors on this score) or you will learn exactly what evidence is missing to prove that your client's impairment really does meet a Listing.

Perhaps the most common single reason for an erroneous denial is that the state agency overestimated the claimant's residual functional capacity. For example, the state agency may have determined that the claimant is capable of medium work, but the claimant is actually limited to light work, an RFC that may, if the claimant is old enough, lead to a finding of disabled under the Medical-Vocational Guidelines. If this is an issue in the case, concentrate on obtaining medical opinion evidence and other evidence that demonstrates your client's correct RFC.

Other common examples of erroneous reasons for denial are:

- an impairment was determined to be "not severe";
- the claimant's mental impairment was determined not to meet the Listings;
- additional impairments were not considered;
- the claimant's allegations of pain were not properly evaluated;
- the state agency did not gather evidence showing that the claimant's impairment meets the Listings;
- the claimant was determined to be capable of past work but the state agency underestimated the exertional level of the past work both as the claimant actually performed it and as the occupation is usually performed; and
- the state agency used the claimant's years of formal schooling for establishing educational level but testing shows the claimant's educational level is considerably lower.

Other possibilities are virtually limitless.

By understanding how the state agency came to its conclusion that your client was not disabled, you may find discrete issues in the case on which to focus in developing proof that your client is disabled. Sometimes the state agency's error is so obvious that you may want to point it out to the ALJ well in advance of the hearing in conjunction with a request for an on-the-record favorable decision. *See* §282.

At the same time, it is important not to neglect the rest of the proof that your client is disabled. The ALJ does not always have to accept conclusions arrived at by the state agency that are favorable to your client. *See* §289.

§209 Form: Initial File Review Action Sheet

Client: ____________________ Date: ________________

I. Treatment Records

1. Treatment Source:
   a. Medical Conditions:
   b. Records Since: _____________ (Date)
      ☐ Get updated records now
      ☐ Get updated records later

2. Treatment Source:
   a. Medical Conditions:
   b. Records Since: _____________ (Date)
      ☐ Get updated records now
      ☐ Get updated records later

3. Treatment Source:
   a. Medical Conditions:
   b. Records Since: _____________ (Date)
      ☐ Get updated records now
      ☐ Get updated records later

4. Treatment Source:
   a. Medical Conditions:
   b. Records Since: _____________ (Date)
      ☐ Get updated records now
      ☐ Get updated records later

5. Treatment Source:
   a. Medical Conditions:
   b. Records Since: _____________ (Date)
      ☐ Get updated records now
      ☐ Get updated records later

6. Treatment Source:
   a. Medical Conditions:
   b. Records Since: _____________ (Date)
      ☐ Get updated records now
      ☐ Get updated records later

II. Missing or Incomplete Medical Records:

1.

2.

3.

4.

III. Vocational Issues:

☐ Have client complete "Work History Report"
☐ Request Earnings Comp Determination
☐ Request Detailed Earnings Report
☐ Request letter from employer confirming last day worked
☐ Request letter from employer explaining compensation paid after last day of work
☐ Obtain personnel files for years ________

IV. Additional Information From Client:

☐ Current medications
☐ Doctors since ______________
☐ Hospitalizations since ______________
☐ Copies of diaries previously sent to client
☐ Work History Report
☐ Recent work activity since ____________
☐ Pharmacy printout for last _____ years
☐ Have client supply W2 for tax years ________
☐ Have client supply most recent paycheck stub showing year-to-date wages
☐ ______________________________
☐ ______________________________

V. Areas of Concern:

____
____
____

VI. Plan:

☐ Pursue "on the record"
☐ Obtain medical source statement/RFC Form ☐ Now ☐ Later

1.

2.

3.

4.

☐ Expect that case will go to hearing

§210 Obtaining Medical and Other Documentation

Regulations effective April 20, 2015 require a claimant to inform SSA about or submit all known evidence that "relates to" whether or not a claimant is disabled. 20 C.F.R. § 404.1512(a). A representative must help obtain the evidence that a claimant must submit, 20 C.F.R. § 404.1740(b)(1), or possibly face sanctions. 20 C.F.R. § 404.1745(b).

While there are exceptions to the "all evidence" regulation under the attorney-client privilege and attorney work product doctrines, these exceptions do not allow withholding factual information, medical source opinions or medical evidence that relates to whether or not a claimant is disabled. See 20 C.F.R. § 404.1512(b)(2).

Making sure that the hearing exhibit file contains all the evidence that relates to whether or not a claimant is disabled requires careful cross-checking. Many claimants, especially those with complicated medical histories, fail to provide a complete list of medical providers. To develop a complete list, you need to compare what the claimant told you with what the claimant told SSA and crosscheck with medical histories that appear in the medical records themselves. Although claimants make frequent errors on dates of treatment, it is rare that a claimant will claim to have been treated by a medical provider that he or she never saw. Whenever a medical source tells you (or the state agency) that the claimant was never seen, don't assume that the medical source is correct. Double-check with your client and double-check with the medical source. Common explanations are that the claimant used a different name, the medical provider's records contain a wrong name or date of birth, the claimant was treated by the medical source at a different address, or the wrong medical care provider was contacted at the address given by the claimant. (E.g., when a claimant is seen by a private doctor for outpatient treatment at a hospital, does the hospital or the doctor have the medical records? What if the doctor is an employee of a medical school?)

Most attorneys pay for copies of a client's medical records and are reimbursed by the client at the conclusion of the case. Although charges for such records can be significant, many states have laws limiting the cost of such records in disability cases. If your state has such a law, be sure to invoke it when ordering records. For a list of state laws that limit medical records charges, see the Social Security Forum, which publishes an annually updated list. In many instances records are copied and sent to you by nation-wide medical record copy services that have employees stationed at local hospitals and clinics. Some of these medical record copy services offer delivery of medical records over the Internet.

Be sure your office has an efficient system for tracking payments you have made for medical records. In the author's office, it is common to get requests for double payment for the same medical records, especially from the nationwide medical record copy services.

SSA has always required a lot of medical documentation. Conclusions are not enough, especially if the issue is whether your client's impairment meets a Listing. SSA wants to see the medical test results themselves. See 20 C.F.R. §§ 404.1508, 404.1512(b)(1)(i), 404.1513, 404.1527(c)(3), 404.1528. It is good practice to make sure the file contains the actual test results for all significant positive tests. Note that the introductory sections to the Listing of Impairments contain specific requirements for particular kinds of medical evidence. For example, in cardiac cases SSA requires copies of the electrocardiogram tracings as well as the cardiologist's interpretation of them. Listing § 4.00C.2. In pulmonary impairment cases SSA requires copies of the spirometric tracings. Listing § 3.00E.

Gather medical evidence that is related to your client's disabling impairments and does not duplicate what is already in the hearing exhibit file. As a rule, it is not necessary to request records concerning routine medical care for matters having nothing do to with your client's disability such as gynecological records (although a gynecologist's observations about the claimant's disabling impairments is "related to" the claimant's disability). Because gynecological records seldom provide relevant evidence -- even if they might sometimes provide evidence that "relates to" a claimant's disability -- many attorneys do not request them. They take the position that they have fulfilled their responsibilities under the all evidence rule by providing to SSA the name and address of the gynecologist so that SSA can obtain the records if it wants them.

You do not need to request all records pertaining to the disabling impairments. For example, nurse's notes, doctors' orders and other miscellaneous records from a hospitalization seldom add anything to a case. SSA says that it did not intend "to impose a duty on claimants or their representatives to request and submit all evidence (medical and non-medical) from all sources . . . . For example, if claimants or their representatives request only the discharge summary from a hospital chart, we require them to submit only what they receive in response to that request in its entirety. We would not require them to request and pay for all of the other records from that hospitalization." 80 Fed. Reg. 14834 (March 20, 2015). If, as sometimes happens, you are sent more records than you requested, you are supposed to submit them.

As a rule, records from more than a year before the alleged onset date are not very helpful in proving that your client has been disabled since the onset date (though this is a rule with exceptions for slowly progressing impairments and worsening episodic impairments when you want to provide a longitudinal view of increasing disability resulting from these impairments).

Sometimes, though, there are cases where you want to obtain absolutely every scrap of medical evidence that exists. For example, consider a case involving chronic fatigue or fibromyalgia with a date last insured of five years ago. In such a case you must prove that your client was disabled by an impairment with few objective signs five years ago or your client will lose. Because medical records sometimes provide more than just medical evidence, such as statements from the claimant about activities of daily living, work activity, and work capacity, it is useful to obtain all treatment records, even those involving gynecological examinations, etc.

Unless records are not "related to" a claimant's disability, Social Security regulations provide no basis for not submitting any records you obtain, especially records that detract from your theory of the case. Obtaining such adverse evidence, after all, was SSA's goal in promulgating the all evidence regulations. Submit adverse records and deal with them in your argument. You may refine the theory of why your client is disabled to account for the existence of such records, or explain that a preponderance of the evidence supports a finding that the claimant is disabled despite the existence of some adverse evidence, or you may be able to deal with them in other ways.

§211 Hospital Records

SSA imposes no requirement that hospital records be certified. Thus, attorneys usually do not request certified hospital records for submission to SSA.

Sometimes, in unusual cases such as those where you want to see every shred of medical evidence, it is most efficient for the attorney to go through medical records at the hospital and request copies of selected pages. This procedure may be faster, more thorough, and much less expensive than requesting a copy of *all* records by mail.

If you're new at reviewing hospital records, it is a useful exercise to review records at the hospital a few times so that you can see the sorts of things that routinely are not included in response to a medical records request. For example, you may discover that the most complete history and physical examination report in a hospital record is a handwritten one by a resident or medical student that may not routinely be included in copies prepared by the hospital. If you go through the hospital record yourself, you can be sure that no significant information is missed and you can also sift out irrelevant laboratory test results, and other unnecessary items.

At a minimum, gather the emergency room records, admission histories and physicals, all reports by medical consultants, physical therapy evaluations and reports, surgical/operative reports, pathologist's reports, discharge summaries and test results pertaining to the claimant's impairment, such as laboratory reports, radiologist reports, nerve condition/EMG reports, nuclear medicine reports, etc.

What you order from the hospital, of course, depends on your theory of the case. In many cases, hospital records concerning an acute illness are less important than the records generated by the claimant's doctor or therapist after the claimant has stabilized. After all, there is no controversy over whether the claimant can work when hospitalized with an acute illness. Everyone agrees that the claimant cannot work then. The issue in most cases is whether the claimant can work after recovering from the acute phase.

On the other hand, there are cases where the claimant is hospitalized so often that the frequency of hospitalization is part of your theory of the case. At a minimum, you need to obtain copies of all the discharge summaries. In such cases you can also obtain a copy of a list of all admissions that is maintained by most hospitals and available only by special request. Such a summary sheet makes a dramatic exhibit and saves you the trouble of compiling a list of your own.

§211.1 Veterans Administration Hospital

It is important to tell a VA hospital that you are representing the veteran in a Social Security disability claim when you are requesting medical records. If you do, ordinarily you will be provided records free of charge. And if you do not, there may be a delay while the VA hospital scrutinizes your request for medical records to see if VA might have a subrogated claim for medical expense reimbursement in a personal injury case.

Veterans Administration hospital records usually do not contain VA rating exam reports and VA disability ratings. You may need to request these from the appropriate Veterans Administration Regional Office, the addresses of which can be found using the Facilities Locator on the Internet at www.va.gov. Although VA disability determinations are not binding on SSA (20 C.F.R. § 404.1504), they are considered to be "evidence" pursuant to 20 C.F.R. § 404.1512(b)(5), and according to SSR 06-3p, a decision by another governmental agency "cannot be ignored and must be considered." SSR 06-3p states that a decision maker "should explain the consideration given to these decisions in the notice of decision." *See also Morrison v. Apfel*, 146 F.3d 625, 628 (8th Cir. 1998); *Baca v. Department of Health & Human Servs.*, 5 F.3d 476, 480 (10th Cir. 1993); *Davel v. Sullivan*, 902 F.2d 559, 560 n.1 (7th Cir. 1990); and *Hankerson v. Harris*, 636 F.2d 893, 897 (2d Cir. 1980).

Because of the similarity between a VA finding of unemployability and what it means to be disabled under the Social Security disability program, it is the rule in four circuits that such VA disability ratings are entitled to "great weight." *See McCartey v. Massanari*, 298 F.3d 1072 (9th Cir. 2002); *Chambliss v. Massanari*, 269 F.3d 520, 522 (5th Cir. 2001); *Brady v. Heckler*, 724 F.2d 914, 921 (11th Cir. 1984); and *De Loatche v. Heckler*, 715 F.2d 148, 150 n.1 (4th Cir. 1983). One circuit court has said that VA disability ratings were entitled to "substantial weight." *See Kane v. Heckler*, 776 F.2d 1130, 1135 (3d Cir. 1985). SSR 06-3p says that the decision and the evidence used to make the decision "may provide insight into the individual's mental and physical impairment(s) and show the degree of disability determined by these agencies based on their rules. We will evaluate the opinion evidence from medical sources, as well as 'non-medical sources' who have had contact with the individual in their professional capacity, used by other agencies, that are in our case record, in accordance with 20 C.F.R. 404.1527, 416.927, Social Security Rulings 96-2p and 96-5p and the applicable factors" for weighing opinion evidence identified in SSR 06-3p (which is essentially the same factors that are set forth in 20 C.F.R. § 404.1527(c)).

§212 Doctors' Records

§212.1 Physicians, Osteopaths, Podiatrists, Optometrists

Physicians, osteopaths, podiatrists and optometrists are recognized as acceptable medical sources by 20 C.F.R. § 404.1513(a). Where examination or treatment by such health care providers is pertinent, always obtain a copy of the doctors' notes. A skeptical ALJ may insist that you submit the notes so the ALJ can make sure the notes support the doctor's conclusions contained in a medical report. If they are difficult to read or contain special shorthand notations, sometimes, if you ask, a doctor's office will transcribe the notes or explain the notation system in a letter to you. Since not all doctor's offices give you reports when you just request "records," always ask for a copy of all reports the doctor has written concerning your client.

§212.2 Psychologists

Psychologists are also acceptable medical sources according to 20 C.F.R. § 404.1513(a). When you obtain office records from a psychologist, be sure to request copies of all test results. These are required by the mental Listings. *See* Listing § 12.00D.

The Minnesota Multiphasic Personality Inventory (MMPI), an objective personality test, can be a valuable test in a disability case. Although results are sometimes referred to in reports with a series of numbers, always ask for a copy of the MMPI profile sheet or "graph." The graph will show how much your client's personality traits deviate from the mean score of 50, which is the middle black line on the profile sheet.

Sometimes the validity scales of the MMPI raise questions about a claimant's tendency to exaggerate or minimize impairments, something that an ALJ may point to as a sign of a lack of credibility. When the MMPI raises such questions, be sure to go back to the psychologist to inquire about the significance of the validity scales. As a rule, psychologists offer a more sophisticated evaluation of the MMPI validity scales than simply concluding that the claimant is not credible.

§212.3 Chiropractors

Chiropractors do not appear on SSA's list of "acceptable medical sources." Instead, they appear on the list of "other" medical sources that may "show the severity of your impairment(s) and how it affects your ability to work." 20 C.F.R. § 404.1513(a) and (d). Although a few district courts have held that a treating chiropractor's opinion is entitled to the same weight as a treating physician's opinion, the circuit courts of appeals have followed SSA's regulation. *See*, for example, *Walters v. Commissioner of Social Security*, 127 F.3d 525 (6th Cir. 1997), and *Diaz v. Shalala*, 59 F.3d 307 (2d Cir. 1995).

In practice, the weight given to a chiropractor's records and opinion by an ALJ may be less than that given to other professionals listed along with chiropractors as "other medical sources," such as nurse-practitioners, physicians' assistants, audiologists and therapists. 20 C.F.R. § 404.1513(d). Most ALJs give little weight to a chiropractor's explanation that your client's problem is due to spinal misalignment. You will need an opinion concerning your client's back problem from an "acceptable" medical source. Nevertheless, do not neglect a chiropractor's records. If nothing else, they may demonstrate that your client was in enough pain to seek frequent chiropractic manipulation.

§213 Physical and Occupational Therapists

Physical and occupational therapists' summaries, evaluations, and notes of treatment, if properly interpreted, may be invaluable even though they appear on SSA's list of "other medical sources" rather than the list of "acceptable medical sources." 20 C.F.R. § 404.1513(d). These records may provide the best description of your client's symptoms and the best source of information about your client's range of motion for particular joints. Sometimes occupational therapists' records contain a detailed evaluation of your client's former job and explain why your client is not now capable of performing that job. SSA has recognized that "depending on the particular facts in a case, and after applying the factors for weighing opinion evidence, an opinion from a medical source who is not an 'acceptable medical source' may outweigh the opinion of an 'acceptable medical source,' including the medical opinion of a treating source. For example, it may be appropriate to give more weight to the opinion of a medical source who is not an 'acceptable medical source' if he or she has seen the individual more often than the treating source and has provided better supporting evidence and a better explanation for his or her opinion. Giving more weight to the opinion from a medical source who is not an 'acceptable medical source' than to the opinion from a treating source does not conflict with the treating source rules in 20 CFR 404.1527(c)(2)." SSR 06-3p.

But beware that physical therapists are under pressure from insurance carriers, especially HMOs, to demonstrate continued improvement as a result of therapy; and often their records indicate improvement where, in fact, it is minimal or non-existent. And many times where there is improvement during a physical therapy program, a claimant is unable to retain the gains made once the program has ended.

Also, see the discussion of functional capacity evaluations at §231.

§214 Pharmacies

In a case where your client's compliance with prescribed medical treatment is at issue, as it often is in seizure cases, one source of evidence is your client's pharmacy records. These may show that your client has purchased the appropriate amount of medication to be taken as prescribed. Sometimes a pharmacy's list of pain medication refills can underscore your client's testimony about the frequency of taking pain pills. Pharmacy records are also useful for crosschecking your client's list of treating sources.

Rather than requesting pharmacy records by mail, it works best to have your client obtain these records directly from the pharmacist. Pharmacies are used to preparing such printouts for their customers. When an attorney makes a request to a pharmacy, the request may be routed through the home office, thus delaying response.

§215 Insurance Carriers

If your client has been privately insured, a long-term disability carrier may well have an extensive collection of medical records that it may make available to you. It may also have had your client evaluated by a physician whose report could be useful. SSR 06-3p states that a disability decision of a nongovernmental agency "cannot be ignored and must be considered." *See* 20 C.F.R. § 404.1504. The evidence used by a long-term disability carrier to find your client disabled "may provide insight into the individual's mental and physical impairment(s) and show the degree of disability determined" by the LTD carrier. SSR 06-3p.

If your client was denied long term disability benefits by an insurance carrier, it is necessary to obtain the LTD carrier's records to avoid any claim that you're violating the "all evidence" rule found in 20 C.F.R. § 404.1512(a). Sometimes an LTD denial can be explained by the different standards of disability used by the LTD carrier. Other times you will have to explain why the LTD carrier's conclusion is wrong.

§216 Former and Current Employers

You may be able to obtain from former employers copies of the following:

1. Attendance records;
2. Performance evaluations;
3. Statements of medical limitations; and
4. Records explaining reasons for your client's termination/medical leave.

When an issue in your client's case is whether your client's brief work qualifies as an unsuccessful work attempt, especially if the work lasted more than three months but less than six months (*see* §176.2), it may be useful to send the former employer a questionnaire to complete. A sample Employment Questionnaire appears at §216.1.

When you have a working client whose earnings are close to the substantial gainful activity level (*see* 20 C.F.R. § 404.1574), documentation from the employer may be essential to show that your client is not actually performing substantial gainful activity. Your client's W-2 form may work fine for last year, especially if there is no question concerning the dates your client worked. If there is a question about the dates worked last year, you may need information from the employer. If your client is working in the current year and a recent paystub does not show all necessary information, you may need earnings information from the employer. A Monthly Wage Information form appears at §216.2. Note that the form asks about vacation and sick pay. According to POMS DI 10505.010 C, only earnings paid as a result of actual work activity count. Thus, sick pay and vacation pay do not count, although according to POMS DI 10505.010 D, bonuses do count.

Once you obtain monthly earnings information, you'll need to apply SSA's rules to figure out if your client is en-gaging in SGA after deducting impairment related work expenses (IRWE) and averaging earnings, as appropriate. See §§176.3 and 274. A worksheet that can be submitted as an exhibit is provided at §216.3.

§216.1 Form: Employment Questionnaire

To: ____________________
Re: ____________________
SSN: ____________________

Please answer the following questions.

Did you grant any of the following special considerations to allow this employee to work? (Check all that apply.)

Fewer or easier duties	____	Frequent absences	____
Special supervision	____	Extra help from co-workers	____
Lower quality	____	More rest periods	____
Lower production	____	Special equipment	____
Fewer hours	____	Lower efficiency	____
Irregular hours	____	Special transportation	____

Please explain any items checked above and describe any other special considerations granted:

____
____

Was the employee hired because of family relationship, past association with the employer or other altruistic reason?
Yes ____ No ____
Explain Yes answer:

____
____

Did the employee have trouble relating to co-workers? Yes ____ No ____
Explain Yes answer:

____
____

Did the employee have trouble relating to the public? Yes ____ No ____
Explain Yes answer:

____
____

Did the employee have trouble dealing with normal work stress? Yes ____ No ____
Explain Yes answer:

____
____

Did the employee have trouble following directions? Yes ____ No ____
Explain Yes answer:

____
____

Did the employee have trouble maintaining attention and concentration? Yes ____ No ____ Explain Yes answer:

____
____

Was the employee frequently absent from work? Yes ____ No ____

Was the employee's work satisfactory? Yes ____ No ____

If the employee no longer works for you, when did his/her employment end and why?

____

____

____

____

Space for any additional remarks you may wish to provide:

____

____

____

____

Signature: ____________________
Title: ____________________
Date: ____________________
Telephone Number: ____________

§216.2 Form: Monthly Wage Information

To: ______________________________

Re: ______________________________

SSN: ______________________________

Please show monthly gross income & income from vacation/ sick pay for the months and years indicated:

Date work began:______________ Date work ended: ____________

	Year ______		**Year ______**	
Month	**Gross Income**	**Vacation/ sick pay**	**Gross Income**	**Vacation/ sick pay**
January				
February				
March				
April				
May				
June				
July				
August				
September				
October				
November				
December				

Date ______________________ Signature ______________________

Title ______________________ Print Name: ______________________

Telephone: ________________

§216.3 Form: Monthly Income Worksheet

2008: SGA = $940 TWP = $670

2008	Gross Wages	TWP?	IRWE	Net Wages	Avg Wage	SGA?
January						
February						
March						
April						
May						
June						
July						
August						
September						
October						
November						
December						

2009: SGA = $980 TWP = $700

2009	Gross Wages	TWP?	IRWE	Net Wages	Avg Wage	SGA?
January						No
February						No
March						No
April						No
May						No
June						No
July						No
August						No
September						No
October						No
November						No
December						No

2010: SGA = $1,000 TWP = $720

2010	Gross Wages	TWP?	IRWE	Net Wages	Avg Wage	SGA?
January						No
February						No
March						No
April						No
May						No
June						No
July						No
August						No
September						No
October						No
November						No
December						No

2011: SGA = $1,000 TWP = $720

2011	Gross Wages	TWP?	IRWE	Net Wages	Avg Wage	SGA?
January						No
February						No
March						No
April						No
May						No
June						No
July						No
August						No
September						No
October						No
November						No
December						No

2012: SGA = $1,010 TWP = $720

2012	Gross Wages	TWP?	IRWE	Net Wages	Avg Wage	SGA?
January						
February						
March						
April						
May						
June						
July						
August						
September						
October						
November						
December						

2013: SGA = $1,040 TWP = $750

2013	Gross Wages	TWP?	IRWE	Net Wages	Avg Wage	SGA?
January						
February						
March						
April						
May						
June						
July						
August						
September						
October						
November						
December						

2014: SGA = $1,070 TWP = $770

2014	Gross Wages	TWP?	IRWE	Net Wages	Avg Wage	SGA?
January						
February						
March						
April						
May						
June						
July						
August						
September						
October						
November						
December						

§217 Vocational Rehabilitation Agencies

Request copies of the following from vocational rehabilitation agencies:

- Results of all medical and psychological evaluations done at the request of the agency;
- All vocational evaluation reports;
- Results of reading, math and other aptitude tests; and
- Vocational rehabilitation plan or determination of ineligibility for services.

§218 Law Enforcement Agencies

In some mental impairment cases, arrest and conviction records are useful. Police reports may contain good narrative descriptions of the claimant's irrational conduct. Contact your local police department to find out how best to obtain these.

If your client has had a period of incarceration, obtain jail or prison records. They may show important evidence of impairments even if the medical care provided is less than optimal.

§219 Other Sources

§219.1 Social Welfare Agencies

Sometimes social welfare agencies have information that can be used in a Social Security disability case. Such information may include forms for medical exemption from welfare work programs, assessments by disabled housing programs and homemaker programs, and observations of your client in social worker notes.

§219.2 Other Attorneys

If another attorney represented your client in a worker's compensation or personal injury case, the attorney's records may be useful.

§219.3 Schools

There are two circumstances where obtaining your client's school records can be invaluable: where you need to prove that your client is illiterate (SSA decision makers don't necessarily accept the testimony of the claimant and the claimant's friends and family on this score, except when it doesn't matter to the outcome of the case) and where you need to show that your client has a mild intellectual disability, which requires proof of onset before age 22. *See* §244.

School records may be helpful in other circumstances as well. In cases involving long-term psychological problems, there may be helpful special education records, school psychologist and other records. The older your client is the less likely that helpful school records will have been retained. But it never hurts to ask; and sometimes you will be surprised at the useful information that you find.

§220 Obtaining and Dealing With Opinion Evidence

The records you obtain are important for preparing your client's case for hearing. Indeed, some cases are won just because an attorney tracked down all of a client's records. But in most cases it is even more important for you to present medical opinion evidence.

Beware, though, if you obtain a medical opinion, under the all evidence rule you are required to submit it. 20 C.F.R. § 404.1512(b)(2)(iv). Thus, caution is appropriate. Do not request medical opinions willy-nilly. Read the doctor's records first. Talk with your client about whether the client thinks the doctor will support the case. If your client is unsure, ask your client to discuss the issues with the doctor at an upcoming appointment and report back to you before you request a report.

Note that if your client tells you something the doctor said that is potentially harmful to the case, your conversation with your client is protected by the attorney-client privilege. You do not have to report to SSA what your client told you the doctor said. 20 C.F.R. § 404.1512(b)(2)(i). Often, though, when the subject is disability, claimants and doctors fail to fully communicate. For example, doctors have been known to respond to a question about disability by saying: "I think you can do some sort of work." Whether the doctor's opinion supports the case depends on what the doctor means by "some sort of work." A limitation to part time work, after all, wins a case unless a claimant's past relevant work includes part time work. Likewise, a limitation to full time sedentary work for a claimant over age 50, will win the case if the claimant has no past relevant sedentary work and has no transferable skills to sedentary work. There are many other possibilities where a doctor thinks a claimant can "do something," but SSA will find the claimant disabled. Thus, you need to try to talk with the doctor on the telephone. Such conversations are protected from disclosure by the work product doctrine. *See* 20 C.F.R. § 404.1512(b)(2).

If you get an ambiguous or a negative opinion from a doctor who you later convince to change the opinion, under the all evidence rule, you must submit both reports. If a doctor sends you a *draft* of a report, e.g., an unsigned letter, an unsigned medical source statement, or an opinion that is otherwise not "completed," the draft is protected by the work product doctrine. You do not have to submit the draft. *See* 20 C.F.R. § 404.1512(b)(2)(iv).

In addition to obtaining opinions from treating doctors, sometimes it is necessary to hire your own medical or vocational consultant. *See* §§224 and 225. You also have to be prepared to deal with the opinions expressed by state agency physicians and consultative examiners and prepare yourself for cross-examining any medical or vocational experts called by the ALJ. *See* §§222, 223, 226 and 227.

§221 The Claimant's Doctor

The most important thing you do in a case may be getting an opinion from a treating doctor about the nature and severity of your client's impairments—symptoms, diagnosis, prognosis and what your client can still do despite these impairments and any physical or mental restrictions. *See* 20 C.F.R. §§ 404.1513(b) and (c) and 404.1527(a)(2). Such an opinion is called a "medical source statement." "Medical source statements are medical opinions submitted by acceptable medical sources, including treating sources and consultative examiners, about what an individual can still do despite a severe impairment(s), in particular about an individual's physical or mental abilities to perform work-related activities on a sustained basis." SSR 96-5p. Indeed, under Social Security regulations, the claimant's doctor provides the most important medical opinion evidence in the case. A medical opinion from a treating doctor about the nature and severity of your client's impairment is entitled to deference and may be entitled to "controlling weight." *See* 20 C.F.R. § 404.1527(c)(2) and SSR 96-2p. If an opinion is entitled to controlling weight, SSA must adopt the doctor's opinion as its own.

But even if SSA does not give the doctor's opinion controlling weight, SSA must weigh the opinion using rules that recognize the special status of treating doctors and accord their opinions greater weight—even when they are unsupported or contradicted—than such opinions would be entitled to if they came from a doctor who never treated the claimant. Whenever SSA does not find a treating doctor's opinion to be controlling, the decision maker must provide good reasons for the weight given to the doctor's opinion. *See* 20 C.F.R. §404.1527(c)(2).

Acceptable Medical Sources

Not all doctors qualify to give an opinion deserving of controlling weight. The doctor must be an "acceptable medical source." Acceptable medical sources are: a physician (a medical or osteopathic doctor), psychologist (including a school psychologist), podiatrist, optometrist, and qualified speech-language pathologist. 20 C.F.R. § 404.1513(a). Other medical professionals fall into the category of "other sources," whose opinions do not carry the same weight as those professionals deemed "acceptable" by SSA. These include chiropractors (*see* §212.3), nurse practitioners, audiologists, therapists, etc. 20 C.F.R. § 404.1513(d). According to SSR 06-3p, opinions from other sources are evaluated using the same factors used in weighing the opinion of an acceptable medical source described in 20 C.F.R. § 404.1527(c); and although it is possible, depending on the facts of the case, for an opinion from an "other source" to be given the greatest weight of any opinion in the case, even greater weight than that of a treating source, such an opinion can never be given "controlling weight," which is a term of art in the regulations that applies only to opinions from acceptable medical sources.

Medically Determinable Impairment

An opinion on diagnosis can come only from an "acceptable medical source." That is, only an "acceptable medical source" can provide an opinion that establishes whether your client has a "medically determinable impairment." 20 C.F.R. § 404.1513(a). Thus, because a chiropractor is not an acceptable medical source, if your client's chiropractor gives an opinion that your client's disabling impairment is "vertebral subluxation," without confirmation from an acceptable medical source, SSA may conclude that your client does not have a medically determinable impairment and deny the case at step 2 of the sequential evaluation process. Such denials are rare, though, because most claimants for disability benefits, even those who are not treated by acceptable medical sources, usually have some signs or laboratory findings (*cf.* 20 C.F.R. § 404.1508) from which an acceptable medical source employed by SSA (a state agency doctor or consultative examiner) can conclude that the claimant has a medically determinable impairment.

Likewise, the opinion from an acceptable medical source may be necessary to show that your client's symptoms (such as pain) arise from a medically determinable impairment that could reasonably be expected to cause the symptoms. Without evidence of some sort showing that the symptoms arise from a medically determinable impairment, the symptoms and the limitations that flow from them may not be accepted by SSA. 20 C.F.R. § 404.1529(b). This is usually not a problem, though. *See* §253 of this book.

Controlling Weight

In order for a medical opinion to be given controlling weight, the doctor giving the opinion must not only be an acceptable medical source, the doctor must be a "treating source." Second, the doctor's opinion must be a "medical opinion." Third, the medical opinion must be well-supported and, fourth, not inconsistent with other substantial evidence. When these criteria are met, the doctor's opinion "must be given controlling weight, *i.e.*, it must be adopted." SSR 96-2p. "[W]hen all of the factors [for controlling weight] are satisfied, the adjudicator must adopt a treating source's medical opinion irrespective of any finding he or she would have made in the absence of the medical opinion." SSR 96-2p. Alternatively, when these criteria are not met, the opinion will not be entitled to controlling weight, which is not to say that it must be rejected. Instead, it must be weighed using criteria set forth in 20 C.F.R. § 404.1527(c) that give deference to the opinion of a treating doctor.

Controlling Weight: Treating Source

A doctor qualifies as a "treating source" only if the patient's purpose for seeing the doctor is to receive treatment. Thus, you cannot send a claimant to be evaluated by a doctor for the claimant's disability claim and expect that the doctor's opinion will be given controlling weight. "[We] will not consider an acceptable medical source to be your treating source if your relationship with the source is not based on your medical need for treatment or evaluation, but solely on your need to obtain a report in support of your claim for disability." 20 C.F.R. § 404.1502. Such a doctor, just like the consultative physician who examines the claimant for SSA, is referred to in SSA's lexicon as a "nontreating source." (In disability cases there are also doctors who neither treat nor examine a claimant, such as a state agency doctor, referred to as a "nonexamining source." *See* §222. Sometimes lawyers hire a "nonexamining source" doctor to review the claimant's file and prepare an opinion.)

Controlling Weight: Medical Opinion

In addition to being an acceptable medical source and treating source, the doctor's opinion must be a "medical opinion"—an opinion about the nature and severity of a claimant's impairments, including symptoms, diagnosis and prognosis, what the claimant can still do despite the impairments, and the claimant's physical or mental restrictions. 20 C.F.R. § 404.1527(a)(2). Opinions on other subjects, such as whether a claimant is "disabled," are not considered to be medical opinions. *See* 20 C.F.R. § 404.1527(d).

Controlling Weight: Well-Supported

To be given controlling weight, the treating doctor's opinion must also be well-supported by medically acceptable clinical and laboratory diagnostic techniques. 20 C.F.R. § 404.1527(c)(2). "Medically acceptable" means that "the clinical and laboratory diagnostic techniques that the medical source uses are in accordance with the medical standards that are generally accepted within the medical community as the appropriate techniques to establish the existence and severity of an impairment." SSR 96-2p.

According to SSR 96-2p, to be "well-supported" by medically acceptable clinical and diagnostic techniques, it is not necessary that it be "fully supported." Thus, informed judgment must be exercised to determine the extent to which the opinion is supported. SSR 96-2p states that "in cases at the administrative law judge (ALJ) or Appeals Council (AC) level, the ALJ or the AC may need to consult a medical expert to gain more insight into what the clinical signs and laboratory findings signify in order to decide whether a medical opinion is well-supported . . . "

To be well-supported, a doctor's opinion should be supported by the doctor's own records. That is, do the doctor's records support the degree of limitation described by the doctor? Are the medications prescribed and treatment provided consistent with the opinion? Are the daily activities reported by the claimant to the doctor consistent with the doctor's opinion? If you can answer these questions affirmatively, you have a strong argument that the doctor's opinion is well-supported.

Controlling Weight: Not Inconsistent With Other Substantial Evidence

Finally, to be accorded controlling weight, a treating doctor's opinion must be "not inconsistent with other substantial evidence" in the case record. 20 C.F.R. § 404.1527(c)(2). SSA chose the words "not inconsistent" with other substantial evidence to indicate that the medical opinion need not be consistent with all other evidence as long as no other substantial evidence contradicts or conflicts with the opinion. SSR 96-2p. The definition of substantial evidence is from *Richardson v. Perales*, 402 U.S. 389, 401 (1971): "more than a mere scintilla. It means such relevant evidence as a reasonable mind might accept as adequate to support a conclusion." SSR 96-2p. An ALJ or the Appeals Council may need to consult a medical expert to decide whether a medical opinion "is not inconsistent with other substantial evidence in the case record." SSR 96-2p.

Frequently you will see cases at the hearing level in which the *only* evidence that is inconsistent with the treating doctor's opinion are the opinions of state agency doctors. At the initial and reconsideration levels of review, the state agency doctors make administrative findings of fact in a case—RFC assessments; but, once the case arrives at the ALJ level, those administrative findings of fact are to be treated as expert medical opinions from nonexamining sources that cannot be ignored by ALJs. SSR 96-6p. With state agency doctor opinions in the file, can you make the argument that the treating doctor's opinion should be given controlling weight? That is, can you say that the treating doctor's opinion is not inconsistent with other substantial evidence in the case record despite a contrary state agency doctor's opinion? The answer must be yes.

The Sixth Circuit Court of Appeals addressed this issue in *Gayheart v. Commissioner of Social Security*, 710 F.3d 365, 377 (6th Cir. 2013) as follows:

> Surely the conflicting substantial evidence must consist of more than the medical opinions of the [state agency] nontreating and nonexamining doctors. Otherwise the treating-physician rule would have no practical force because the treating source's opinion would have controlling weight only when the other sources agreed with that opinion. Such a rule would turn on its head the regulation's presumption of giving greater weight to treating sources because the weight of such sources would hinge on their consistency with nontreating, nonexamining sources.

Also consider what would have happened if the treating doctor's opinion, which is otherwise entitled to controlling weight, had been submitted to the state agency. SSR 96-2p says, in effect, that even though the state agency doctor would have come to a different conclusion, the state agency doctor would have had to adopt the treating source's opinion. Thus, it would make no sense for the ALJ to conclude that the state agency doctor's opinion is substantial evidence that contradicts the treating doctor's opinion. The same argument could be made if the state agency doctor had the treating source's opinion but improperly evaluated it.

Further, although an ALJ must consider state agency doctor opinions, 20 C.F.R. § 404.1527(e)(2)(ii) explicitly provides for this exception: a decision maker must provide an explanation in the decision for the weight given to a state agency doctor's opinion "[u]nless a treating source's opinion is given controlling weight." Thus, when controlling weight is given to a treating doctor's opinion, the regulations implicitly acknowledge that a state agency doctor's opinion must not constitute substantial evidence. SSR 96-6p, which requires decisions made by ALJs to address the weight given to state agency doctor opinions, is not to the contrary because it does not say anything about what happens when a treating doctor's opinion is given controlling weight. SSR 96-6p does not mention the exception stated in 20 C.F.R. § 404.1527(e)(2)(ii).

If you make the above argument to SSA or to a federal court, if possible, couple it with an additional argument that says this: Even if a state agency doctor RFC opinion can constitute substantial evidence that is inconsistent with the treating doctor's opinion, in your client's particular case, the state agency doctor's opinion is not substantial evidence because of the poor quality of the explanation for the RFC opinion, failure to consider subjective symptoms, failure to consider a combination of impairments, new evidence, etc. Most state agency doctor opinions, when carefully examined, do not meet the *Richardson v. Perales* definition of substantial evidence.

Treating Doctor's Opinion Entitled to Deference

If a treating doctor's opinion is not given controlling weight because it is not well-supported by medically acceptable clinical and laboratory diagnostic techniques or it is inconsistent with other substantial evidence in the case record, it doesn't mean that the opinion must be rejected. SSR 96-2p says, "a finding that a treating source medical opinion is not well-supported by medically acceptable clinical and laboratory diagnostic techniques or is inconsistent with the other substantial evidence in the case record means only that the opinion is not entitled to 'controlling weight,' not that the opinion should be rejected." Instead, an opinion that is not entitled to controlling weight is still entitled to deference and must be weighed by evaluating factors set forth in the regulations. 20 C.F.R. § 404.1527(c)(2). In many cases, a treating doctor's medical opinion will be entitled to the greatest weight and should be adopted by SSA even if it does not meet the test for "controlling weight." SSR 96-2p. SSA evaluates the weight to be given a treating source's opinion by considering:

- Length of the Treating Relationship and the Frequency of Examination. Generally, the longer a treating source has treated a claimant and the more times the claimant has been seen, the more weight SSA will give to that source's medical opinion. If the treating source has obtained a longitudinal picture of the claimant's impairment, the treating source's opinion is entitled to more weight than the opinion of a nontreating source. 20 C.F.R. § 404.1527(c)(2)(i).
- Nature and Extent of the Treatment Relationship. Generally, the more knowledge a treating source has

about the claimant's impairment, the more weight SSA will give that source's medical opinion. 20 C.F.R. § 404.1527(c)(2)(ii).

- Supportability. The more a medical source presents relevant evidence to support an opinion, particularly medical signs and laboratory findings, the more weight SSA will give that opinion. The better an explanation a medical source provides for an opinion, the more weight SSA will give it. 20 C.F.R. § 404.1527(c)(3).
- Consistency. Generally, the more consistent an opinion is with the record as a whole, the more weight SSA will give to that opinion. 20 C.F.R. § 404.1527(c)(4).
- Specialization. SSA generally gives more weight to the opinion of a specialist about medical issues related to the area of the specialty than to the opinion of a source that is not a specialist. 20 C.F.R. § 404.1527(c)(5).
- Other Factors. SSA considers other factors that tend to support or contradict a medical opinion. For example, SSA says it will consider the medical source's amount of understanding of the disability program and evidentiary requirements and whether the medical source is familiar with "other information," that is, non-medical information, in a claimant's case record. 20 C.F.R. § 404.1527(c)(6).

Issues Reserved to the Commissioner

20 C.F.R. § 404.1527(d) says that certain opinions from doctors are not "medical opinions," within the meaning of 20 C.F.R. § 404.1527(a)(2), but rather are "opinions on issues reserved to the Commissioner because they are administrative findings that are dispositive of a case; *i.e.*, that would direct the determination or decision of disability." "A medical source opinion that an individual is 'disabled' or 'unable to work,' has an impairment(s) that meets or equals the requirements of a listing, has a particular residual functional capacity (RFC), that concerns whether an individual's RFC prevents him or her from doing past relevant work, or that concerns the application of vocational factors, is an opinion on an issue reserved to the Commissioner." SSR 03-2p, note 3. See also SSR 14-1p. Such opinions, of course, cannot be given controlling weight; moreover, SSA does not give any special significance to fact that the opinion came from a treating doctor. 20 C.F.R. § 404.1527(d)(3). Nevertheless, 20 C.F.R. § 404.1527(d) itself requires that the decision maker consider such opinions, and SSR 96-5p requires that the decision explain the consideration given to such opinions.

As we explain below, this regulation has only minimal impact on how we prepare a case for hearing. But because SSA decision makers make so many mistakes when rejecting medical opinions as "reserved to the Commissioner," it is important to have a thorough understanding. Thus, we provide an extensive discussion.

Issue Reserved: Claimant is Disabled

Although 20 C.F.R. § 404.1527(d)(1), which says that an opinion from a doctor that says a claimant is disabled is an opinion on an issue reserved to the Commissioner, may affect how you make arguments to the ALJ, the Appeal Council and federal court, it should have little or no impact on how you prepare a case for hearing. There are many reasons (other than it's an issue reserved to the Commissioner) why we do not ask a doctor whether a claimant is "disabled." A statement from a treating doctor saying a patient is disabled, without explanation, is not worth much. There are many reasons that a claimant can be "disabled." Without some explanation, there is usually no way to follow the doctor's reasoning.

By not asking a doctor whether a claimant is disabled, you may avoid two real problems. First, when a doctor thinks your client is disabled, you will avoid giving the impression that your primary concern is the bottom-line conclusion about disability, which could cause the treating doctor to ignore your other questions and respond with a useless one-line letter saying your client is disabled. Second, when a doctor thinks your client is not disabled, not raising the disabled issue could potentially keep the treating doctor from ignoring your other questions and sending you a useless (and wrong) opinion that your client is not disabled. After all, not many doctors think that a 55-year-old man is disabled who, although incapable of his past work, is nevertheless capable of a full range of light work. But such a person, if he doesn't have any transferable skills, is disabled according to the Medical-Vocational Guidelines. See Rules 202.01, 202.02, 202.04 and 202.06.

Although it is good practice never to ask a doctor to state that a claimant is disabled, if you happen to get such a statement, your decision whether or not to submit it depends on the facts of your client's case. That SSA considers the statement an issue "reserved to the Commissioner" should play little or no role in your decision. Does the statement add anything to your client's case? For example, let's say your client's doctor wrote a note saying your client was disabled dated around the time of your client's alleged onset date, which is a couple of years before the date of a full medical source statement you obtained from the doctor recently. Doesn't the existence of this statement help establish onset date?

Do not fail to submit such a statement merely because you think the ALJ will not consider it. Statements on issues reserved to the Commissioner are required to be considered by the decision maker. SSR 96-5p provides that "opinions from any medical source about issues reserved to the Commissioner must never be ignored, and that the notice of the determination or decision must explain the consideration given to the treating source's opinion(s)." When an ALJ decision says only that an opinion will not be considered because it is an issue reserved to the Commissioner, the ALJ has committed error. The ALJ has not considered the opinion.

Issue Reserved: Application of Vocational Factors

The application of vocational factors, another issue reserved to the Commissioner, is also a subject not to address with doctors. Whether a claimant can do past relevant work and how a claimant's age, education and work experience affect the claimant's ability to perform jobs existing in significant numbers are questions outside the expertise of doctors. These issues would be outside doctors' expertise even if they were not reserved to the Commissioner. Never ask a doctor about vocational factors.

Issue Reserved: Claimant Meets Listings

Seeking an opinion about whether a claimant's impairment meets the Listings, however, is another story entirely. Such opinions can be valuable, pointing the way to a decision finding that, in fact, your client's impairment meets the Listings. The regulation says SSA will consider opinions from medical sources on the issue of meeting the Listings. 20 C.F.R. § 404.1527(d)(2). SSR 96-5p says that "[w]hen a treating source provides medical evidence that demonstrates that an individual has an impairment that meets a listing, and the treating source offers an opinion that is consistent with this evidence, the adjudicator's administrative finding about whether the individual's impairment(s) meets the requirements of a listing will generally agree with the treating source's opinion."

What to ask a doctor about meeting the Listings depends on the case, but do not ask a question that will yield only a conclusory opinion that a claimant meets a particular Listing. An opinion which is simply a conclusion saying, without explanation, that a claimant meets a particular section of the Listings is the sort of reserved-to-the-Commissioner opinion to which 20 C.F.R. § 404.1527(d)(2) applies. Such an opinion is not much more valuable than an opinion that a claimant is "disabled." But when the doctor describes *elements* of a specific Listing that your client meets, the doctor is likely giving a medical opinion about the nature and severity of your client's impairment.

When the record demonstrates that all of the elements of a particular Listing are met, you don't need to ask a doctor. Simply point out the elements to the ALJ. Many Listings, though, include elements that do not commonly appear in medical records, at least not in the same language used by the Listings. For example, Listing 1.04A: Is there "evidence of nerve root compression characterized by neuro-anatomic distribution of pain"? *See* §231.1 of this book. The answer to this question is an opinion about the nature and severity of the claimant's impairment. Thus, it does not come within the purview of the reserved-to-the-Commissioner rule.

Many Listings contain elements for which treating doctor opinions may be helpful. For example, several musculoskeletal Listings (1.02A, 1.03, 1.04C, 1.05B, 1.05C, 1.06B) require that a claimant be unable to ambulate effectively, a subject that can be addressed by a treating doctor. See questionnaires pertaining to Listings 1.02A, 1.03 and 1.04C at §§231.1.1, 231.1.3 and 231.1.5 of this book. This is an opinion about what the claimant can still do despite the impairment and thus qualifies as a "medical opinion," not an opinion on an issue reserved to the Commissioner.

Meeting the "B criteria" of the mental Listings is a classic example of where opinions could be crucial. For example, is the claimant's restriction of activities of daily living moderate, marked or extreme? Are the claimant's difficulties maintaining social functioning moderate, marked or extreme? Etc. *See* §§240 – 248.1 of this book. Are opinions on these issues about the nature and severity of the claimant's impairment? Or are they opinions about whether a claimant meets a particular Listing, which pulls them within the purview of the reserved-to-the-Commissioner rule? The answers to these questions are not clear.

Issue Reserved: Claimant Equals Listings

Seeking an opinion about whether a claimant's impairment equals the Listings can also be valuable, though such an opinion clearly addresses a subject reserved to the Commissioner. Although 20 C.F.R. § 404.1527(d)(2) says SSA will consider opinions from medical sources on the issue of equaling the Listings, SSR 96-5p states: "A finding of equivalence involves more than findings about the nature and severity of medical impairments. It also requires a judgment that the medical findings equal a level of severity set forth in 20 CFR 404.1525(a) and 416.925(a); i.e., that the impairment(s) is '. . . severe enough to prevent a person from doing any gainful activity.' This finding requires familiarity with the regulations and the legal standard of severity set forth in 20 CFR 404.1525(a), 404.1526, 416.925(a), and 416.926."

Nevertheless, a treating doctor's opinion can be valuable if you obtain answers to specific questions that ask about issues which SSA itself says show that a Listing is equaled. SSA has a number of rulings and memoranda that explain how particular impairments may equal the Listings. An SSA Q & A says migraine headaches may equal epilepsy Listing 11.03 appears at §239.2.1; SSR 02-1p says that obesity may equal a musculoskeletal listing if the claimant is unable to ambulate effectively; SSR 12-2p says fibromyalgia may equal inflammatory arthritis Listing 14.09D; SSR 14-11 says chronic fatigue syndrome may equal mixed connective tissue disease Listing 14.06B.

Note, though, that an ALJ can find that a claimant's impairment equals a Listing only after seeking an opinion from a medical expert. SSR 96-6p. A treating doctor's opinion that a Listing is equaled alone cannot be the basis of an ALJ finding of equivalence. Note that SSR 96-5p requires the ALJ to resolve the issue. "If the case record contains an opinion from a medical source on an issue reserved to the Commissioner, the adjudicator must evaluate all the evidence in the case record to determine the extent to which the opinion is supported by the record."

Issue Reserved: RFC

An opinion from a medical source on a claimant's "residual functional capacity" is listed in 20 C.F.R. § 404.1527(d)(2) as an issue reserved to the Commissioner. This means that if the claimant's doctor says the claimant has a particular residual functional capacity (sedentary, light, medium, etc.), although SSA will consider the doctor's opinion, such an opinion is not accorded the deference SSA gives to opinions from treating doctors and it is not eligible to be given controlling weight. SSR 96-5p. The same is true if a doctor's opinion is that the claimant's RFC prevents him or her from doing past relevant work. SSR 03-2p, note 3.

But if the claimant's doctor describes "what [the claimant] can still do despite impairment(s), and [the claimant's] physical or mental restrictions," 20 C.F.R. § 404.1527(a)(2), which includes a description of the claimant's ability "to do work-related activities such as sitting, standing, walking, lifting, carrying, handling objects, hearing, speaking, and traveling," 20 C.F.R. § 404.1513(c)(1), and the claimant's "ability to understand, to carry out and remember instructions, and to respond appropriately to supervision, coworkers, and work pressures in a work setting," 20 C.F.R. § 404.1513(c)(2), the opinion is entitled to the deference given treating doctors' opinions and may be entitled to controlling weight. That is, if the requirements for controlling weight are met, the decision maker must adopt the doctor's opinion as SSA's RFC assessment. SSRs 96-5p and 06-1p.

According to SSA, the words "residual functional capacity" apply only to the residual functional capacity assessment, the administrative finding of what a claimant can still do despite the claimant's limitations. SSR 96-5p and 20 C.F.R. § 404.1545. SSA takes the position that a medical source statement (which describes what a claimant can still do) and a residual functional capacity assessment (which makes a finding about what a claimant can still do) are two different things. SSR 96-5p.

Although these two different things look to us lawyers like they both describe RFC (one is an administrative finding of RFC, and the other is an opinion about what the RFC finding ought to be), reserving the RFC finding to the Commissioner is SSA's way of underscoring that its job is to make findings concerning whether a claimant is disabled. Although the treating doctor's opinion may be adopted as the RFC finding, the doctor's job is to provide the raw material for such a finding, not conclusions about the finding.

If the doctor calls the opinion about what a claimant can still do an "RFC opinion," does that make it an opinion on an issue reserved to the Commissioner? No. SSA has said, "We did not intend to suggest a policy that would permit adjudicators to ignore or reject any opinion evidence on the grounds that the opinions used the wrong terminology." 56 Fed. Reg. 36951 (1991).

SSR 96-5p summarizes this issue as follows:

> Even though the adjudicator's RFC assessment may adopt the opinions in a medical source statement, they are not the same thing: A medical source statement is evidence that is submitted to SSA by an individual's medical source reflecting the source's opinion based on his or her own knowledge, while an RFC assessment is the adjudicator's ultimate finding based on a consideration of this opinion and all the other evidence in the case record about what an individual can do despite his or her impairment(s).

In SSR 96-5p, SSA also points out that a medical source statement "may provide an incomplete picture of the individual's abilities." A claimant's doctor may not know about all medical evidence; and a claimant's doctor may not know about "other evidence" in a case. On the other hand, an RFC assessment is supposed to be based on "all relevant evidence in the case record, including medical evidence and relevant nonmedical evidence, such as observations of lay witnesses of an individual's apparent symptomatology, an individual's own statement of what he or she is able or unable to do, and many other factors that could help the adjudicator determine the most reasonable findings in light of all the evidence." SSR 96-5p.

Issue Reserved: Drug Addiction and Alcoholism (DAA) Materiality

According to SSR 13-2p, the issue whether drug addiction or alcoholism is a contributing factor material to the determination of disability is an issue reserved to the Commissioner; however the ruling itself explains what to ask the treating doctor in a case involving a physical impairment. SSR 13-2p, fn 19 provides:

> The finding about materiality is an opinion on an issue reserved to the Commissioner . . .. Therefore, we will not ask a treating source, a CE provider, a medical expert, or any other source for an opinion about whether DAA is material. We will instead ask for medical opinions about the nature, severity, and functional effects of a claimant's impairment(s). In cases involving physical impairments, we may ask for medical opinions that project the nature, severity, and functional effects if the claimant were to stop using drugs or alcohol. In cases involving mental impairment(s) we will not ask for projections, as we explain in Question 7.

Decision Requirements

When rejecting a treating doctor's opinion on an issue reserved to the Commissioner, it is not enough for an SSA decision maker to reject it solely on the grounds that "this is an issue reserved to the Commissioner." Instead, the opinion must be carefully considered and weighed. "If the case record contains an opinion from a medical source on an issue reserved to the Commissioner, the adjudicator must evaluate all the evidence in the case record to determine the extent to which the opinion is supported by the record." SSR 96-5p. The "decision must explain the consideration given to the treating source's opinion(s)." SSR 96-5p.

Opinions from Other Health Care Providers

Nurse Practitioners

When your client is treated only by a nurse practitioner, SSA says that an opinion from the nurse practitioner is not entitled to the special weight that could be accorded if the opinion were from a physician because a nurse practitioner is not an "acceptable medical source." 20 C.F.R. § 404.1513(a). Nevertheless, SSA says the same factors that are used in evaluating treating physician opinions found in 20 C.F.R. § 404.1527(c) are used to evaluate the opinion of an "other source." And under the right facts, an opinion from an "other source" may be accorded more weight than that of a treating physician. SSR 06-3p. After all, the nurse practitioner probably has seen the claimant more and knows more about the claimant's condition than anyone else. Thus, it is important to obtain the opinion of a nurse practitioner.

SSR 06-3p says:

> With the growth of managed health care in recent years and the emphasis on containing medical costs, medical sources who are not "acceptable medical sources," such as nurse practitioners, physician assistants, and licensed clinical social workers, have increasingly assumed a greater percentage of the treatment and evaluation functions previously handled primarily by physicians and psychologists. Opinions from these medical sources, who are not technically deemed "acceptable medical sources" under our rules, are important and should be evaluated on key issues such as impairment severity and functional effects, along with the other relevant evidence in the file.

When your client is treated by both a physician and a nurse practitioner, be sure to get a separate opinion from the physician or, if that's not possible, have the opinion from the nurse practitioner counter-signed by the physician. Even if the physician saw the claimant only once but supervised additional treatment by the nurse practitioner, the physician's opinion ought to be treated as from a "treating source." *See Benton ex rel. Benton v. Barnhart*, 331 F.3d 1030, 1035-1039 (9th Cir. 2003).

But what happens when the nurse practitioner is supervised by a physician who has never actually seen the claimant? Such a supervising physician, in fact, is involved in treatment of the claimant as part of a treatment team. Does getting the opinion from the nurse practitioner counter-signed by the supervising physician make it an opinion from an acceptable medical source? Since the nurse practitioner is an agent of the physician, is the nurse practitioner's opinion, when counter-signed by the supervising physician, the same as an opinion from a treating physician? *Cf. Gomez v. Chater*, 74 F.3d 967, 971 (9th Cir. 1996). There are no clear answers to these questions; they are not addressed by SSR 06-3p. It is probably best to always ask that the opinion of a nurse practitioner be counter-signed by the supervising physician, whether the supervising physician has seen the claimant or not.

Licensed Clinical Social Workers

The same principles apply to the opinions of licensed clinical social workers, also mentioned in SSR 06-3p, who provide psychotherapy and often know more about a claimant's mental issues than the treating psychiatrist. Indeed, in the commentary to the new mental impairment

Listings that took effect on January 17, 2017, 81 Fed. Reg. 66142 (2016), SSA stated:

> We believe that these other medical professionals—because they typically see patients regularly— are important sources of the evidence we need to assess the severity of a person's mental disorder and the resulting limitations in the person's functioning.

See also section 12.00C.2 of the Mental Listings.

Practice Tips

VA Doctors

When your client's treating source is a doctor employed by the Veterans Administration, do not let anyone tell you that VA doctors are prohibited from completing reports for use in Social Security disability cases. Although the VA had such a policy at one time, it is current VA policy that VA doctors are expected to complete such reports at the request of a claimant. *See* VHA Directive 2008-071, which is available on the Internet at http://www1.va.gov/VHAPUBLICATIONS/ViewPublication.asp?pub_ID=1790. Although VHA Directive 2008-071 is beyond its expiration date (October 31, 2013) and a later VHA Directive 2013-002 does not mention completing forms for use in Social Security disability cases, VA policy appears to be that VA doctors are expected to assist. Completion of non-VA disability forms by VA treating physicians is part of the veteran's medical benefits package. *See* 38 C.F.R. § 17.38(a)(1)(xiv). *See also* VHA Handbook 1605.1, Section 34f(3), available at http://www1.va.gov/vhapublications/ViewPublication.asp?pub_ID=1423.

However, in a stunning example of non-cooperation between government agencies, VA doctors may not complete reports at the request of the Social Security Administration. *See* 38 C.F.R. § 17.38(a)(1)(xiv), which provides for completion of forms including "non-VA disability program forms," *i.e.*, forms for use in Social Security disability cases, "but not including the completion of forms for examinations if a third party customarily will pay health care practitioners for the examination but will not pay VA." (SSA's rules allow it to pay private doctors but do not allow it to pay government doctors. 20 C.F.R. § 404.1514.)

Even though there is no prohibition against VA doctors completing disability forms, it is the consensus among lawyers that getting a VA doctor to actually complete a form for use in a Social Security disability case is often more difficult than getting forms completed by other doctors. It usually works best to send your client any form that you want completed by a VA doctor so that your client can ask the doctor to complete the form.

Some lawyers have reported success sending to VA doctors the Disability Benefits Questionnaires used by the VA itself. The VA's specific impairment questionnaires are found on the Internet at http://benefits.va.gov/COMPENSATION/dbq_ListByDBQFormName.asp. These questionnaires usually include a question asking the doctor to describe the impact of the impairment on the veteran's ability to work.

Reports of Contact

SSA gathers medical information from treating sources in a variety of ways. Sometimes it merely requests copies of office notes and test results. Sometimes it sends detailed questions in interrogatory form. Sometimes a state agency physician telephones the treating doctor and writes down what is said in a "report of contact."

Beware of these "reports of contact." They may contain implicit or explicit conclusions not intended by the treating doctor, despite the fact that the "report of contact" may have been sent to the doctor for signature and it may have been signed and returned to the state agency. Needless to say, the existence of an inaccurate "report of contact" presents a very delicate problem to be dealt with by the attorney when requesting a report from the treating doctor, but deal with it you must. If you ignore the "report of contact" you're likely to get a decision from the ALJ questioning the credibility of a doctor who tells the state agency one thing and the claimant's attorney another. Explaining a misleading "report of contact" is one issue that must be addressed by the treating doctor in a report obtained for submission as a hearing exhibit.

§221.1 Hearing Testimony by the Treating Doctor

Presenting live testimony of the treating doctor at a hearing may be the most effective way to get the treating doctor to address all the issues and win your client's case. Unfortunately, most doctors have difficulty fitting an appearance at a hearing into their busy schedules. And the relatively small amount of back benefits in a disability case may not justify the expense to your client. Thus, in the usual case, it is necessary to seek a more economical way of obtaining the doctor's opinion. Indeed, in fiscal year 2000, treating doctors testified in only 1.5 percent of disability cases, according to SSA statistics.

There probably is no single best way to obtain the opinion of a treating source. The following sections describe some options.

§221.2 Taking the Doctor's "Deposition"

In complicated cases, where you want to be sure that the doctor answers numerous questions, you can take the doctor's deposition and submit the transcript as a hearing exhibit. If you want to avoid the expense of paying a court reporter, you may simply record a conversation with the doctor, in person or by telephone, and have the recording transcribed by your secretary. Then have the doctor sign the transcript and submit the transcript as a hearing exhibit.

Attorneys who have video cameras and playback equipment sometimes record an interview of the physician and play the video for the ALJ at the hearing. Preparing a written transcript is optional in this circumstance, since the hearing is recorded. The hearing recording will include the doctor's previously recorded testimony.

§221.3 Specific Questions

Another approach is to develop specific medical questions based on the issues in your client's case. These questions may be sent to the treating doctor in a letter or they may be developed into interrogatories or forms for the doctor to complete. Keep in mind that medical issues may be complex and attorneys often have difficulty framing medical questions. For these reasons, as well as for the good lawyering rule—"Never ask a question to which you do not know the answer"—it is often best to telephone the doctor to discuss the issues before writing the questions for your chosen method of obtaining this information, whether deposition, forms, letter or interrogatories.

§221.4 General Medical Report

Some attorneys use a form letter request for a medical report that asks the doctor to address all the elements identified in SSA's regulations on the content of medical reports, 20 C.F.R. § 404.1513(b) and (c):

> (b) *Medical reports.* Medical reports should include—
>
> (1) Medical history;
>
> (2) Clinical findings (such as the results of physical or mental status examinations);
>
> (3) Laboratory findings (such as blood pressure, x-rays);
>
> (4) Diagnosis (statement of disease or injury based on its signs and symptoms);
>
> (5) Treatment prescribed with response, and prognosis; and
>
> (6) A statement about what you can still do despite your impairment(s) based on the acceptable medical source's findings on the factors under paragraphs (b)(1) through (b)(5) of this section (except in statutory blindness claims) . . . .
>
> (c) *Statements about what you can still do. . . .* Statements about what you can still do (based on the acceptable medical source's findings on the factors under paragraphs (b)(1) through (b)(5) of this section) should describe, but are not limited to, the kinds of physical and mental capabilities listed as follows ....
>
> (1) The acceptable medical source's opinion about your ability, despite your impairment(s), to do work-related activities such as sitting, standing, walking, lifting, carrying, handling objects, hearing, speaking, and traveling; and
>
> (2) In cases of mental impairment(s), the acceptable medical source's opinion about your ability to understand, to carry out and remember instructions, and to respond appropriately to supervision, coworkers, and work pressures in a work setting.

Such a report, if well done, can be invaluable to your client's case. Often, however, most of the reports of this sort will repeat uncontroverted facts already of record in your client's case rather than focusing on the contested issues. The best reports of this genre are also time-consuming for the doctor to prepare, thus adding additional expense to your client's case. When you ask a doctor to prepare an extensive report, you run the risk that your request will be put aside to be done later when the doctor has more time, which may mean there will be a delay in getting the report.

§221.5 Medical Opinion Forms

We give medical opinion forms mixed reviews. They can be great time savers for both the attorney and the doctor, but they must be used with care. Forms may not be appropriate at all in complex cases; and they need to be supplemented in many cases so that all issues are addressed. The best forms are clear and complete but not too long.

This book contains a set of medical source statement forms, some for specific impairments, that, in the author's experience, usually work better than any alternative. Nevertheless, when using one of these forms, make sure it is appropriate for your client's case; and make sure that there are no additional issues that must be addressed. For example, onset date is a common additional issue that is not addressed in most of the specific impairment forms. Indeed, onset date is not an issue in perhaps a majority of cases. If you ask an onset date question in each case, you may inadvertently create an onset date issue based, for example, on a doctor's answer that merely states the first date the doctor saw your client. Therefore, when you need a doctor's opinion about onset date, it is best to add a question. In the author's office, many of the medical source statement forms exist in two versions—one with and one without an onset date question. Both versions are included on Digital Access; the onset version is identified by the word "Onset" following the form number (*e.g.*, §231.2 Onset).

As we explained in §221, according to SSA, the words residual functional capacity (RFC), which is "the most [a claimant] can still do despite [the claimant's] limitations," 20 C.F.R. § 404.1545(a), apply only to the RFC assessment. Thus, SSA never asks a doctor for an opinion about RFC. Instead, SSA asks that medical reports include, among other things, "[a] statement about what [the claimant] can still do despite [the claimant's] impairment(s)." 20 C.F.R. § 404.1513(b)(6). See also 20 C.F.R. § 404.1527(a)(2). SSA calls a doctor's opinion about residual functional capacity a "medical source statement." According to SSA, a medical source statement is not to be confused with an "RFC assessment," which is "an adjudicator's finding about the ability of an individual to perform work-related activities." SSR 96-5p. SSA reserves to itself the job of making an RFC assessment. 20 C.F.R. § 404.1546.

A treating doctor's opinion must be considered by SSA and, under appropriate circumstances, given controlling weight. 20 C.F.R. § 404.1527(c)(2), SSRs 96-5p and 96-2p. It doesn't matter whether the doctor's opinion is called a medical source statement, an RFC opinion, or a medical assessment, a term formerly used by SSA but now disfavored. When SSA first promulgated the regulation that now appears as 20 C.F.R. § 404.1527(d), it stated in the Federal Register in response to a comment, "We did not mean to require medical sources to use proper terminology, as some commenters inferred. However, we did mean to reserve the ultimate determination of disability" to the Commissioner. 56 Fed. Reg. 36937 (1991).

Anyone who tells you that SSA may disregard a treating doctor's opinion on a form with "residual functional capacity" or anything else in its title has misinterpreted the regulations and SSR 96-5p. Indeed, even if a doctor's opinion is considered to be an opinion about RFC (*e.g.*, the doctor says that a claimant is limited to light work), such an opinion still cannot be disregarded. 20 C.F.R. § 404.1527(d)(2) and SSR 96-5p say that SSA will consider such opinions.

This book contains the following medical opinion forms dealing with physical impairments:

- §221.7 Medical Opinion Re: Ability to Do Work-Related Activities (Physical)
- §221.9 Medical Opinion Regarding Physical Capacity for Work
- §221.11 Physical Medical Source Statement
- §221.12 Follow-up Medical Source Statement
- §230.1 Bladder Problem Medical Source Statement
- §230.1.1 Interstitial Cystitis Medical Source Statement
- §230.2 Lupus (SLE) Medical Source Statement
- §230.3 Chronic Fatigue Syndrome Medical Source Statement
- §230.4 Dizziness Medical Source Statement
- §230.5 Post Cancer Treatment Medical Source Statement
- §231.1 Listing § 1.04A—Spinal Nerve Root Compression
- §231.1.1 Listing § 1.02A — Major Dysfunction of a Weight-Bearing Joint
- §231.1.2 Listing § 1.02B — Major Dysfunction of a Major Peripheral Joint
- §231.1.3 Listing § 1.03 — Reconstructive Surgery or Surgical Arthrodesis of a Major Weight-Bearing Joint
- §231.1.4 Listing § 1.04B — Spinal Arachnoiditis
- §231.1.5 Listing § 1.04C — Lumbar Spinal Stenosis
- §231.2 Lumbar Spine Medical Source Statement
- §231.3 Fibromyalgia Medical Source Statement
- §231.4 Arthritis Medical Source Statement
- §231.5 Cervical Spine Medical Source Statement
- §232.1 Meniere's Disease Medical Source Statement
- §232.3 Vision Medical Source Statement
- §232.4 Vision Impairment Medical Source Statement
- §233.1 Pulmonary Medical Source Statement
- §233.2 Sleep Disorders Medical Source Statement
- §234.3 Cardiac Medical Source Statement
- §234.4 Cardiac Arrhythmia Medical Source Statement
- §235.1 Crohn's and Colitis Medical Source Statement
- §235.2 Hepatitis C Medical Source Statement
- §237.1 Skin Disorders Medical Source Statement
- §238.1 Diabetes Mellitus Medical Source Statement
- §238.2 Obesity Medical Source Statement
- §239.1 Seizures Medical Source Statement
- §239.2 Headaches Medical Source Statement
- §239.3 Stroke Medical Source Statement
- §239.4 Multiple Sclerosis Medical Source Statement
- §239.5 Myasthenia Gravis Medical Source Statement
- §239.6 Parkinsonian Syndrome Medical Source Statement
- §239.7 Peripheral Neuropathy Medical Source Statement
- §239.8 Postpolio Syndrome Medical Source Statement
- §239.9 Reflex Sympathetic Dystrophy (RSD)/Complex Regional Pain Syndrome, Type 1 Medical Source Statement
- §239.10 Muscular Dystrophy Medical Source Statement
- § 239.11 Neurological Listings Medical Source Statement
- § 239.12 Seizures Listings Medical Source Statement
- §263.1.1 Manipulative Limitations Medical Source Statement
- §265.1 Environmental Limitations Medical Source Statement

The Physical Medical Source Statement, §221.11, is a more general form for use where there are multiple physical impairments. The Manipulative Limitations Medical Source Statement, §263.1.1, is used where you need only an opinion about manipulative limitations.

Additional forms are included on Digital Access. One is 235A Irritable Bowel Syndrome Medical Source Statement, which is a lightly edited version of the Crohn's and Colitis form, §235.1, that appears in this book. In addition, Digital Access includes sample RFC forms prepared by other lawyers.

A cover letter for sending a specific impairment form appears at §221.8. It is usually a good idea to describe to the doctor what your client has told you about his or her limitations so that the doctor has the patient's description handy when completing the form. Accordingly, the cover letter in §221.8 has a place to insert it. It is good practice to write out this description when you first interview a claimant and update it as you refine your theory of the case. The Analysis Form, §175.1, provides a useful format.

Educating the claimant's doctor about the treating doctor's role in a disability case is an important function of the claimant's attorney. To assist you with this task, we have prepared a memorandum that you can send along with a request to complete a medical source statement in a physical case. The memorandum appears at §221.10.

Forms also may be useful to demonstrate that the medical signs and findings are consistent with your client's symptoms. (A sample form appears at §255.1.) This conclusion is implicit in most medical reports. It usually does not occur to doctors to make it explicit. The form at §255.1 is particularly useful for gathering medical support for limitations arising from impairments such as diabetes that tend to produce multiple complaints (such as fatigue, malaise, blurred vision, dizziness, *etc.*), the cumulative impact of which can have a devastating effect on a claimant's ability to work. You can tailor this form precisely to your client's symptoms. Note that this form asks simply whether the symptom or limitation is consistent with the impairment, an approach that some doctors prefer to a request to describe a claimant's RFC.

Some ALJs want a doctor to explain all the factors considered when completing a medical source statement. It often works best to send a follow-up letter to a doctor after receiving a completed medical source statement from the doctor. Ask for completion of an additional one-page medical source statement – Follow-up Medical Source Statement, §221.12.

ALJs sometimes use Form HA-1151, Medical Source Statement of Ability to Do Work-Related Activities (Physical), a copy of which is reproduced at §221.6. The mental impairment version, Form HA-1152, Medical Source Statement of Ability To Do Work-Related Activities (Mental), appears at §245.3. These are an improvement over older check-off forms, which have been criticized by courts as having inherent interpretation problems. *See O'Leary v. Schweiker,* 710 F.2d 1334, 1341 (8th Cir. 1983). They are also an improvement over the medical assessment forms used by SSA for several years; however, these medical source statement forms are not useful in many cases because they do not ask enough questions that focus on real world limitations from an impairment. They do not ask about the need for breaks, missing work, or interference with attention and concentration. They force a choice between "never" being able to do an activity and "occasionally" being able to do it, that is, being able to do the activity up to one-third of the workday. If a patient can do something, say, 5 percent of the workday, the doctor will choose occasionally because the patient's capacity falls into the occasional range. But this will be interpreted by most ALJs as a doctor's opinion that the patient can do the activity up to one-third of the workday.

Also, some doctors, especially in physical impairment cases, interpret SSA's reference to findings on the physical medical source statement form as a request to state the limitations that an "average man" would have if he had the claimant's findings. If you are going to use SSA's forms, you must explain the correct standard to such doctors. The standard is that there must be a link between the findings and the claimant's limitations, but it is okay to allow for differing individual tolerances for pain and other symptoms. *See* 20 C.F.R. § 404.1545(e).

A revised version of SSA's outdated medical assessment form appears at §221.7. The revision sought to address the criticisms of SSA's form and focus on some common limitations, especially those involving back impairments that require alternating positions. In the author's office, this was at one time the most often used form. Now the four-page Physical Medical Source Statement, §221.11, is used most frequently. The form at §221.7 is currently sent only to doctors who balk at completing a four-page form but will agree to complete a shorter one.

In cases involving older claimants, where all you need to win the case is a treating doctor's opinion on which to base an argument that the claimant is limited to sedentary or light (or, in rare cases, medium) work, a simple form is provided in §221.9. This form addresses only lifting and standing/walking limitations.

Forms also may be developed for obtaining a doctor's opinion whether a particular impairment meets or equals the Listings. Sample forms based on meeting §§ 1.02 through 1.04C of the Listings appear at §§231.1 to 231.1.5. The Sleep Disorders Medical Source Statement, §233.2, seeks the treating doctor's opinion on whether the claimant's sleep disorder is equal in severity to the impairment of a person whose minor motor seizures meet § 11.03 of the Listings. Although opinions on Listings issues may never be given controlling weight, they still must be considered, and the decision "must explain the consideration given to the treating source's opinion(s)." SSR 96-5p. *See also* 20 C.F.R. § 404.1527(d)(2).

This book contains the following mental impairment questionnaires:

- §243.2 Mental Impairment Questionnaire (Listings)
- §245.7 Medical Opinion Re: Ability to Do Work-Related Activities (Mental)
- §245.8 Mental Impairment Questionnaire (RFC and Listings)
- §245.9 Mental Medical Source Statement
- §248.1 Somatic Symptom and Related Disorders Impairment Questionnaire (RFC & Listings)

See §245 for discussion of the mental medical source statement form used by ALJs, which appears at §245.3. The Medical Opinion form that appears at §245.7 is a revised version of the ALJs' mental medical source statement form. In the author's office, the mental questionnaire most commonly used is the one at §245.9, Mental Medical Source Statement, which addresses only mental residual functional capacity. The Mental Impairment Questionnaire at §245.8, which deals with both mental residual functional capacity and Listings issues is also used frequently. The Listings-only form, §243.1, is used only in unusual circumstances.

Before you submit any completed form to the ALJ, make sure it is reasonable in light of the objective findings, internally consistent, and consistent with other evaluations by the same author. If it appears inconsistent, ask the doctor for clarification.

Practice Tip

When is the best time to request an opinion from a doctor? Many attorneys wait until they have reviewed the file and the hearing is scheduled before requesting an opinion from the treating doctor. This has two advantages. First, by waiting until you have fully reviewed the file, you will be able to refine the theory of why your client cannot work and will be better able to seek support for this theory from the treating doctor. Second, the report will be fresh at the time of the hearing.

But this approach also has some disadvantages. When there is a long time between the time you first see your client and the time of the hearing, a lot of things can happen. Your client can improve and go back to work. Although you can seek evidence supporting a finding that your client was disabled for a certain length of time, this puts you in the position of asking the doctor to give a description of your client's ability to work at some time in the past, something that not all doctors are good at. Your client can change doctors, or worse yet, stop seeing doctors altogether because your client's medical insurance has run out. When you write to a doctor who has not seen your client recently, you run the risk that the doctor will be reluctant to complete the form. Doctors seem much more willing to provide opinions about current patients than about patients whom they have not seen for a long time.

Here is an alternative. Consider requesting completion of a medical source statement by the treating doctor on the day your client retains you. This will provide a snapshot description of your client's capacity for working early in the case. If your client improves and returns to work, the description of your client's capacity for working provides a basis for showing that your client was disabled during a closed period of disability. If your client changes doctors, you can get an opinion from the new doctor, too. If your client stops seeing doctors, at least you have one treating doctor opinion and you can present your client's testimony at the hearing to establish that your client has not improved. If your client continues seeing the doctor and it has been a long time since the doctor's opinion was obtained, just before the hearing send the doctor a copy of the form completed earlier, along with a blank form and a cover letter asking for completion of a new form if there are significant changes in the patient's condition. If none, ask the doctor to send you a one-line letter that says there have been no significant changes since the date the earlier form was completed.

There are times, though, that you need to consider *not* requesting a report early in the case. First, depending on the impairment, if your client has not been disabled for twelve months, it is usually better to wait until the twelve-month duration requirement is met. Second, if your client just began seeing a new doctor, it is usually best to wait until the doctor is more familiar with the patient before requesting an opinion. Third, if there are competing diagnoses or other diagnostic uncertainties, it is usually best to wait until the medical issues are resolved before requesting an opinion. Fourth, a really difficult judgment is involved for a client whose medical history has many ups and downs, e.g., several acute phases, perhaps including hospitalizations, followed by significant improvement. You need to request an opinion at a time when the treating doctor will have the best longitudinal perspective on your client's impairment.

§221.6 Form: Medical Source Statement of Ability to Do Work-Related Activities (Physical) (HA-1151)

Editor's Note: This form is provided to show what SSA uses. It is not recommended for use by claimants' representatives. See §221.5

SOCIAL SECURITY ADMINISTRATION
OFFICE OF DISABILITY ADJUDICATION AND REVIEW

Form Approved
OMB No.0960-0662

MEDICAL SOURCE STATEMENT OF ABILITY TO DO WORK-RELATED ACTIVITIES (PHYSICAL)

NAME OF INDIVIDUAL **SOCIAL SECURITY NUMBER**

\- -

To determine this individual's ability to do **work-related activities on a regular and continuous basis**, please give us your opinions for each activity shown below:

The following terms are defined as:

- **REGULAR AND CONTINUOUS BASIS** means 8 hours a day, for 5 days a week, or an equivalent work schedule.
- **OCCASIONALLY** means very little to one-third of the time.
- **FREQUENTLY** means from one-third to two-thirds of the time.
- **CONTINUOUSLY** means more than two-thirds of the time.

Age and body habitus of the individual should not be considered in the assessment of limitations. It is important that you relate particular medical or clinical findings to any assessed limitations in capacity: The usefulness of your assessment depends on the extent to which you do this.

I. LIFTING/CARRYING

Check the boxes representing the amount the individual can lift and how often it can be lifted.

Lift	Never	Occasionally (up to 1/3)	Frequently (1/3 to 2/3)	Continuously (over 2/3)
A. Up to 10 lbs:				
B. 11 to 20 lbs:				
C. 21 to 50 lbs:				
D. 51 to 100 lbs:				

Check the boxes representing the amount the individual can carry and how often it can be carried.

Carry	Never	Occasionally (up to 1/3)	Frequently (1/3 to 2/3)	Continuously (over 2/3)
A. Up to 10 lbs:				
B. 11 to 20 lbs:				
C. 21 to 50 lbs:				
D. 51 to 100 lbs:				

Identify the particular medical or clinical findings (i.e., physical exam findings, x-ray findings, laboratory test results, history, and symptoms including pain, etc.) which support your assessment or any limitations and why the findings support the assessment.

II. SITTING/STANDING/WALKING

Please check how many hours the individual can (if less than one hour, how many minutes):

At One Time without Interruption

	Minutes	Hours							
A. Sit	________	☐ 1	☐ 2	☐ 3	☐ 4	☐ 5	☐ 6	☐ 7	☐ 8
B. Stand	________	☐ 1	☐ 2	☐ 3	☐ 4	☐ 5	☐ 6	☐ 7	☐ 8
C. Walk	________	☐ 1	☐ 2	☐ 3	☐ 4	☐ 5	☐ 6	☐ 7	☐ 8

Total in an 8 hour work day

	Minutes	Hours							
A. Sit	________	☐ 1	☐ 2	☐ 3	☐ 4	☐ 5	☐ 6	☐ 7	☐ 8
B. Stand	________	☐ 1	☐ 2	☐ 3	☐ 4	☐ 5	☐ 6	☐ 7	☐ 8
C. Walk	________	☐ 1	☐ 2	☐ 3	☐ 4	☐ 5	☐ 6	☐ 7	☐ 8

If the total time for sitting, standing and walking does not equal or exceed 8 hours, what activity is the individual performing for the rest of the 8 hours?

Does the individual require the use of a cane to ambulate? ☐ **Yes** ☐ **No**

If the answer is "yes" please answer the following:

- How far can the individual ambulate without the use of a cane?
- Is the use of a cane medically necessary? ☐ **Yes** ☐ **No**
- With a cane, can the individual use his/her free hand to carry small objects? ☐ **Yes** ☐ **No**

Identify the particular medical or clinical findings (i.e., physical exam findings, x-ray findings, laboratory test results, history, and symptoms including pain etc.) which support your assessment or any limitations and why the findings support the assessment.

III. USE OF HANDS

Indicate how often the individual can perform the following activites:

ACTIVITY	Right Hand				Left Hand			
	Never	Occasionally (up to 1/3)	Frequently (1/3 to 2/3)	Continuously (over 2/3)	Never	Occasionally (up to 1/3)	Frequently (1/3 to 2/3)	Continuously (over 2/3)
REACHING (Overhead)								
REACHING (All Other)								
HANDLING								
FINGERING								
FEELING								
PUSH/PULL								

Which is the individual's dominant hand? ☐ Right Hand ☐ Left Hand

Identify the particular medical or clinical findings (i.e., physical exam findings, x-ray findings, laboratory test results, history, and symptoms including pain, etc.) which support your assessment or any limitations and why the findings support this assessment.

IV. USE OF FEET

Indicate how often the individual can perform the following activities:

ACTIVITY	Right Foot				Left Foot			
	Never	Occasionally (up to 1/3)	Frequently (1/3 to 2/3)	Continuously (over 2/3)	Never	Occasionally (up to 1/3)	Frequently (1/3 to 2/3)	Continuously (over 2/3)
Operation of Foot Controls								

Identify the particular medical or clinical findings (i.e., physical exam findings, x-ray findings, laboratory test results, history, and symptoms including pain, etc.) which support your assessment or any limitations and why the findings support the assessment.

V. POSTURAL ACTIVITIES

How often can the individual perform the following activities:

ACTIVITY	Never	Occasionally (up to 1/3)	Frequently (1/3 to 2/3)	Continuously (over 2/3)
Climb stairs and ramps				
Climb ladders or scaffolds				
Balance				
Stoop				
Kneel				
Crouch				
Crawl				

Identify the particular medical or clinical findings (i.e., physical exam findings, x-ray findings, laboratory test results, history, and symptoms including pain etc.) which support your assessment or any limitations and why the findings support the assessment.

VI. DO ANY OF THE IMPAIRMENTS AFFECT THE CLAIMANT'S HEARING OR VISION?

☐ **No** ☐ **Yes** ☐ **Not Evaluated**

If "yes" please complete the following questions (where appropriate)

1. If a **hearing impairment** is present,

   a. Does the individual retain the ability to hear and understand simple oral instructions and to communicate simple information? ☐ Yes ☐ No

   b. Can the individual use a telephone to communicate? ☐ Yes ☐ No

2. If a **visual impairment** is present,

   a. Is the individual able to avoid ordinary hazards in the workplace, such as boxes on the floor, doors ajar, or approaching people or vehicles? ☐ Yes ☐ No

   b. Is the individual able to read very small print? ☐ Yes ☐ No

   c. Is the individual able to read ordinary newspaper or book print? ☐ Yes ☐ No

   d. Is the individual able to view a computer screen? ☐ Yes ☐ No

   e. Is the individual able to determine differences in shape and color of small objects such as screws, nuts or bolts? ☐ Yes ☐ No

   Identify the particular medical or clinical findings (i.e., physical exam findings, x-ray findings, laboratory test results, history, and symptoms including pain etc.) which support your assessment or any limitations and why the findings support the assessment.

VII. ENVIRONMENTAL LIMITATIONS

How often can the individual tolerate exposure to the following conditions:

Condition	Never	Occasionally (up to 1/3)	Frequently (1/3 to 2/3)	Continuously (over 2/3)
Unprotected Heights				
Moving Mechanical Parts				
Operating a motor vehicle				
Humidity and wetness				
Dust, odors, fumes and pulmonary irritants				
Extreme cold				
Extreme heat				
Vibrations				
Other: (Identify)				

Condition	Quiet (Library)	Moderate (Office)	Loud (Heavy Traffic)	Very Loud (Jackhammer)
Noise				

Identify the particular medical or clinical findings (i.e., physical exam findings, x-ray findings, laboratory test results, history, and symptoms including pain, etc.) which support your assessment or any limitations and why the findings support the assessment.

VIII. PLEASE PLACE A CHECK IN APPROPRIATE BOXES BASED SOLELY ON THE CLAIMANT'S PHYSICAL IMPAIRMENTS

ACTIVITY	YES	NO
Can the individual perform activities like shopping?		
Can the individual travel without a companion for assistance?		
Can the individual ambulate without using a wheelchair, walker, or 2 canes or 2 crutches?		
Can the individual walk a block at a reasonable pace on rough or uneven surfaces?		
Can the individual use standard public transportation?		
Can the individual climb a few steps at a reasonable pace with the use of a single hand rail?		
Can the individual prepare a simple meal & feed himself/herself?		
Can the individual care for their personal hygiene?		
Can the individual sort, handle, or use paper/files?		

Please identify the medical findings that support this assessment and why the findings support the assessment (unless a narrative report is attached).

IX. STATE ANY OTHER WORK-RELATED ACTIVITIES, WHICH ARE AFFECTED BY ANY IMPAIRMENTS, AND INDICATE HOW THE ACTIVITIES ARE AFFECTED. WHAT ARE THE MEDICAL FINDINGS THAT SUPPORT THIS ASSESSMENT?

X. THE LIMITATIONS ABOVE ARE ASSUMED TO BE YOUR OPINION REGARDING CURRENT LIMITATIONS ONLY.

HOWEVER, IF YOU HAVE SUFFICIENT INFORMATION TO FORM AN OPINION WITHIN A REASONABLE DEGREE OF MEDICAL PROBABILITY AS TO PAST LIMITATIONS, ON WHAT DATE WERE THE LIMITATIONS YOU FOUND ABOVE FIRST PRESENT? ____________

XI. HAVE THE LIMITATIONS YOU FOUND ABOVE LASTED OR WILL THEY LAST FOR 12 CONSECUTIVE MONTHS? ☐ Yes ☐ No

XII. DID YOU EXAMINE THE CLAIMANT? ☐ Yes ☐ No

I DECLARE UNDER PENALTY OF PERJURY THAT I HAVE EXAMINED ALL THE INFORMATION ON THIS FORM, AND ON ANY ACCOMPANYING STATEMENTS OR FORMS, AND IT IS TRUE AND CORRECT TO THE BEST OF MY KNOWLEDGE.

____________________ ____________

SIGNATURE DATE

____

Print Name, Title and Medical Specialty (Legibly Please)

Privacy Act Statement

Medical Source Statement of Ability to do Work-Related Activities (Physical)

Sections 205(a), 223(d), 1614(a)(3)(H)(I) and 1631(d)(1) of the Social Security Act, as amended, authorize us to collect this information. We will use the information you provide to determine the individual's ability to perform (mental) work-related activities on a sustained basis.

The information you furnish on this form is voluntary. However, failure to provide the requested information may affect our ability to make an accurate assessment of the individual's mental ability to perform a work related activity.

We rarely use the information you supply for any purpose other than for the reasons explained above. However, we may use it for the administration and integrity of Social Security programs. We may also disclose information to another person or to another agency in accordance with approved routine uses, which include, but are not limited to the following:

1. To enable a third party or an agency to assist Social Security in establishing rights to Social Security benefits and/or coverage;

2. To comply with Federal laws requiring the release of information from Social Security records (e.g., to the Government Accountability Office and Department of Veterans' Affairs);

3. To make determinations for eligibility in similar health and income maintenance programs at the Federal, state and local level; and

4. To facilitate statistical research, audit or investigative activities necessary to assure the integrity of Social Security programs.

We may also use the information you provide in computer matching programs. Matching programs compare our records with records kept by other Federal, State, or local government agencies. Information from these matching programs can be used to establish or verify a person's eligibility for Federally-funded or administered benefit programs and for repayment of payments of delinquent debts under these programs.

A complete list of routine uses for this information is available in our System of Records Notice entitled, Completed Determination Record - Continuing Disability Determinations, 60-0050. This notice, additional information regarding this form, and information regarding our programs and systems, is available on-line at http://www.socialsecurity.gov or at your local Social Security office.

Paperwork Reduction Act Statement - This information collection meets the requirements of 44 U.S.C. § 3507, as amended by section 2 of the Paperwork Reduction Act of 1995. You do not need to answer these questions unless we display a valid Office of Management and Budget control number. We estimate that it w ill take about 15 minutes to read the instructions, gather the facts, and answer the questions. SEND OR BRING THE COMPLETED FORM TO YOUR LOCAL SOCIAL SECURITY OFFICE. The office is listed underU. S. Government agencies in your telephone directory or you may call Social Security at 1-800-772-1213 (TTY 1-800-325-0778). You may send comments on our time estimate above to: SSA, 6401 Security Blvd, Baltimore,MD 21235-6401. Send only comments relating to our time estimate to this address, not the completed form.

§221.7 Form: Medical Opinion Re: Ability to Do Work-Related Activities (Physical)

MEDICAL OPINION RE: ABILITY TO DO WORK-RELATED ACTIVITIES (PHYSICAL)

NAME:______________________________ DOB: ______________________________

To determine your patient's ability to do *work-related activities on a day-to-day basis in a regular work setting*, please give us your opinion -- **based on your examination** -- of how your patient's physical capabilities are affected *by the impairment(s)*. Do not consider your patient's age, sex or work experience. Consider the medical history, the chronicity of findings (or lack thereof), symptoms *(including differing individual tolerances for pain, etc.)*, and the expected duration of any work-related limitations.

For each activity shown below:

(1) Indicate your patient's ability to perform the activity; and

(2) Identify the particular medical findings (e.g., physical examination findings, x-ray findings, laboratory test results, history, symptoms (including pain), etc.) that support your opinion regarding any limitations.

IT IS IMPORTANT THAT YOU RELATE PARTICULAR MEDICAL FINDINGS TO ANY REDUCTION IN CAPACITY; THE USEFULNESS OF YOUR OPINION DEPENDS ON THE EXTENT TO WHICH YOU DO THIS.

==

1. Maximum ability to lift and carry on an *occasional* basis (no more than 1/3 of an 8-hour day).

   No limitation 100# 50# 20# 10# less than 10#

2. Maximum ability to lift and carry on a *frequent* basis (1/3 to 2/3 of an 8-hour day).

   No limitation 50# 25# 10# less than 10#

3. Maximum ability to stand and walk (with normal breaks) during an 8-hour day.

   No limit about 6 hrs. about 4 hrs. about 3 hrs. about 2 hrs. less than 2 hrs.

4. Maximum ability to sit (with normal breaks) during an 8-hour day.

   No limit about 6 hrs. about 4 hrs. about 3 hrs. about 2 hrs. less than 2 hrs.

5. If your patient must periodically alternate sitting, standing or walking to relieve discomfort:

   How long can your patient ***sit*** before changing position? 0 5 10 15 20 30 45 60 90 Minutes

   How long can your patient ***stand*** before changing position? 0 5 10 15 20 30 45 60 90 Minutes

   How ***often*** must your patient ***walk around***? Frequency: 0 5 10 15 20 30 45 60 90 Minutes

   How ***long*** must your patient ***walk each time***? Duration: 0 5 10 15 20 30 45 60 90 Minutes

Does your patient need the opportunity to shift ***at will*** from sitting or standing/walking? ☐ Yes ☐ No

6. Will your patient sometimes need to lie down at unpredictable intervals during an 8 hour working shift? ☐ Yes ☐ No

   If yes, how often do you think this will happen? ____________________

7. What medical findings support the limitations described above? ____________________

8. How often can your patient perform the following **POSTURAL ACTIVITIES?**

	Rarely	**Occasionally**	**Frequently**	**Constantly**
Twist	☐	☐	☐	☐
Stoop (Bend)	☐	☐	☐	☐
Crouch	☐	☐	☐	☐
Climb stairs	☐	☐	☐	☐
Climb ladders	☐	☐	☐	☐

Rarely: from 1% to 5% of an 8-hour day
Occasionally: from 6% to 33% of an 8-hour day
Frequently: from 34% to 66% of an 8-hour day
Constantly: more than 66% of an 8-hour workday

What medical findings support this? ____________________

9. Are the following **PHYSICAL FUNCTIONS** affected by the impairment?

Reaching overhead	☐ **Yes** ☐ **No**	Handling (gross manipulation)	☐ **Yes** ☐ **No**
Reaching forward or to side	☐ **Yes** ☐ **No**	Feeling	☐ **Yes** ☐ **No**
Fingering (fine manipulation)	☐ **Yes** ☐ **No**	Pushing/pulling	☐ **Yes** ☐ **No**

A. How are these physical functions affected? ____________________

B. What medical findings support this? ____________________

10. Please assess **ENVIRONMENTAL RESTRICTIONS**:

	NO RESTRICTION	**AVOID CONCENTRATED EXPOSURE**	**AVOID EVEN MODERATE EXPOSURE**	**AVOID ALL EXPOSURE**
Extreme cold	☐	☐	☐	☐
Extreme heat	☐	☐	☐	☐
High humidity	☐	☐	☐	☐
Fumes, odors, dusts, gases	☐	☐	☐	☐
Perfumes	☐	☐	☐	☐
Soldering fluxes	☐	☐	☐	☐
Solvents/cleaners	☐	☐	☐	☐
Chemicals	☐	☐	☐	☐
List other irritants or allergens: ____________	☐	☐	☐	☐

§221.8 Form: Letter to Treating Source Transmitting Medical Source Statement

Date

Doctor
Address
City, State Zip

Re: **Client**
DOB:**Date of Birth**

Dear **Doctor**:

I represent **Client** on a claim for disability benefits from the Social Security Administration; and I need your help.

Please complete the enclosed form titled **[Title of Form]**. This form need not be typewritten; but I'd appreciate it if you'd answer all questions. This form asks about ability to do activities in a competitive work situation which means: What are your patient's limitations if the patient were required to perform activities 40 hours per week, 50 weeks a year?

You patient has told me about the following limitations:

[Insert claimant's description of limitations from Analysis Form, §175.1.]

I enclose a signed medical release for your records. Please bill me for your time in responding to this letter.

Please note that I need to submit this form to the Social Security judge by **[Insert Date]**. I will need the completed form by that date.

Please note that the Social Security Administration (SSA) views the opinion of a treating doctor as extremely valuable in a disability claim. It does not expect you to order a functional capacity evaluation. Instead, SSA expects that you will provide an opinion based on your understanding of your patient's symptoms and knowledge of your patient's impairments. Estimates are acceptable.

Sincerely,

Attorney
Enclosure

§221.9 *Form: Medical Opinion Regarding Physical Capacity for Work*

From: ______________________ (Physician)

Re: ______________________ (Patient)

DURING AN 8-HOUR WORKDAY, on a REGULAR AND CONTINUING BASIS, that is, 8 hours per day, 5 days per week, or an equivalent work schedule, can your patient:

1. **Lift and Carry** 25 pounds for up to 2/3 of an 8-hour workday and 50 pounds for up to 1/3 of an 8-hour workday throughout an eight-hour workday? ☐ Yes ☐ No

   If not, how much would you estimate that your patient can lift?

   ___ pounds 2/3 of the day

   ___ pounds 1/3 of the day

   What is the reason for any limitation on lifting?

2. **Stand or Walk** 6 hours out of an 8-hour workday (with breaks)? ☐ Yes ☐ No

   If not, how many minutes or hours could your patient stand or walk at one time without a break? _____ minutes or _____hours

   If not, how many hours total could your patient stand or walk (with breaks) in an 8-hour workday? ______ hours

   What is the reason for any limitation on standing or walking?

Regarding Qualifications as Examining and Treating Physician:

Have you examined the patient often enough to obtain a view over time of the patient's medical conditions, abilities, and limitations, to a reasonable degree of medical certainty? ☐ Yes ☐ No

Is your knowledge of the nature and severity of the patient's conditions and limitations based on your examinations, patient's response to treatment, and results of examinations or testing you have ordered? ☐ Yes ☐ No

Date First Examined: ________________________ Date Last Examined: _________________

Physician Signature: ________________________ Date of this Statement: _________________

Board Certification: ____

§221.10 Memorandum: The Role of the Treating Doctor in Social Security Disability Determinations

The Social Security Administration (SSA) and attorneys for claimants routinely ask treating doctors to provide information and opinions about their patients' impairments. This memorandum answers questions doctors have about responding to such requests.

Why does a patient need the opinion of a treating doctor in making a Social Security disability claim?

According to SSA, the treating doctor is the medical professional most able to provide a detailed, longitudinal picture of a claimant's medical impairments. The treating doctor may bring a unique perspective to the medical evidence that cannot be obtained from the objective medical findings alone or from reports of individual examinations, such as consultative examinations arranged by SSA or brief hospitalizations. 20 C.F.R. § 404.1527(c)(2). SSA gives the opinion of the treating doctor special consideration. 20 C.F.R. § 404.1527, SSR 96-2p.

What information does SSA need from the treating doctor?

According to SSA, a treating doctor may be asked about the nature, severity, extent and duration of a patient's impairments, including observations and opinions about how well the patient is able to function, the effects of any treatment, including side effects, and how long the impairments are expected to limit the patient's ability to function. A treating doctor may be asked about the effects of impairments on the patient's ability to function in a sustained manner when performing work activities and when performing activities of daily living. Such opinions help SSA adjudicators draw accurate conclusions about the severity of the impairments and the patient's remaining capacity for work. 20 C.F.R. §§ 404.1513 and 404.1527, SSRs 96-2p, 96-5p, *cf.* 99-2p.

Isn't an opinion about a patient's capacity to do sustained work activities very subjective?

Yes. SSA recognizes that claimants are limited by symptoms and that symptoms are subjective and difficult to quantify. 20 C.F.R. § 404.1529(c)(3). Symptoms cannot always be measured objectively through clinical or laboratory diagnostic techniques. SSR 16-3p. According to SSA, a doctor may be asked for an opinion about the nature and severity of a patient's symptoms, what the patient can still do despite his or her impairments, and the patient's physical or mental restrictions. Determining what a patient can still do requires the exercise of professional judgment first, to figure out whether the patient's symptoms can be reasonably attributed to a medical diagnosis, and second, if a patient's claimed symptom-related limitations are reasonably consistent with the medical signs and findings. 42 U.S.C. § 423(d)(5)(a), 20 C.F.R. § 404.1527 and SSR 96-8p.

To decide if claimed limitations are reasonable for a particular patient, should I consider whether the average person with the same impairment would be so impaired?

No. SSA's rules recognize that an "average man" test is not appropriate. SSA acknowledges that symptoms limit some people more than they do others. SSA offers the example of someone with a low back disorder who may be fully capable of sustained medium work activity, but another person with the same disorder, because of pain, may not be capable of more than light work activity on a sustained basis. 20 C.F.R. § 404.1545(e). Some people have less tolerance for pain. Some people's ability to cope with an impairment is less than others. Individual differences need to be considered.

Should I refer the patient for a functional capacity evaluation?

Probably not. SSA itself never asks a claimant to undergo a functional capacity evaluation. As a rule, functional capacity evaluations, which last at most only a few hours, do not reliably answer the essential question: What is your patient's capacity to *sustain* work activities 8 hours per day, 5 days per week, 50 weeks per year? In many cases, especially for those under age 50, the crucial issue is a claimant's capacity to perform an easy job such as full time sedentary work, which requires the capacity to sit for 6 hours out of an 8-hour working day, stand or walk intermittently for 2 hours per day, occasionally lift about 10 pounds and frequently lift lighter objects. Many functional capacity evaluations assign the capacity to do sedentary work by default. That is, they assume a sedentary capacity when work at higher levels of exertion is ruled out. To truly test a patient's capacity to sustain sedentary work, the patient would need to be observed in work simulation for several weeks—something which would be very expensive.

Doesn't a doctor need special expertise to estimate a patient's capacity for performing work-related activities?

No. While SSA considers a doctor's expertise when weighing the doctor's opinion, SSA does not require a treating doctor to have special expertise or training to provide a relevant opinion about a patient's ability to work. SSA says that a treating doctor who has developed a longitudinal perspective on a patient's problems is in a position to make a valuable contribution to determining whether a patient is or is not disabled. It depends on the case, of course, but usually a treating doctor who has treated a patient for a long time can provide a more valuable opinion than a specialist who sees the patient only once. This is particularly true if the specialist sees the patient only for a disability evaluation rather than treatment. 20 C.F.R. § 404.1527.

How important are objective medical findings?

Objective medical findings are very important. Such findings, in effect, determine the range of possibilities. But, as a rule, one cannot determine a claimant's capacity for working by looking only at the medical findings for a claimant whose impairment does not meet the Listing of Impairments, SSA's special set of medical findings discussed below. For example, SSA itself acknowledged that there is a lack of correlation between x-ray findings and function of a joint. 66 Fed. Reg. 58,017 (2001). Researchers have concluded that there is no correlation between lumbar range of motion and disability. *See* Parks, *et al.*, "A Comparison of Lumbar Range of Motion and Functional Ability Scores in Patients with Low Back Pain," *Spine*, Vol 28, No. 4, pp. 380-384, 2003.

What is the best way to approach preparing an opinion about a patient's capacity to do work-related activities?

Talk with your patient. Obtain your patient's own opinion about his or her ability to do work-related activities. Exercise professional judgment to determine whether your patient's stated limitations are reasonably consistent with what you know about your patient's medical impairments and what you know about your patient.

Should I simply endorse whatever the patient says about his or her limitations?

No. Then there would be no exercise of professional judgment. And let's face it, sometimes patients describe symptoms that cannot be reasonably attributed to a medical diagnosis or side effects of medication. Such symptoms should not be considered. And sometimes patients claim limitations so severe that they are outside the realm of possibility created by the patient's impairments, medical findings, history and personality.

Functional capacity forms these days seem to ask for an inordinate number of details about a patient's capacity for working. Is all this necessary?

The short answer is yes. SSA requires a lot of detailed information about a claimant's capacity for performing work-related activities. This is especially necessary for those cases in which hearings are held before administrative law judges where vocational experts may testify about whether jobs exist in significant numbers for claimants with certain limitations. Although we realize that not all questions on a form may relate to a particular claimant's case, relevant details often make the difference between winning and losing a case.

Sometimes an answer to a question on a form is "it depends." How can I convey this?

Explain it in the margins. The more information SSA has, the better. The author of many such forms has commented that no form is ever complete without things written in the margins. But be sure to provide enough information so that the reader knows exactly what you mean. SSA says that the better the explanation a doctor provides, the more weight SSA will give that opinion. 20 C.F.R. § 404.1527(c)(3).

My personal opinion is that virtually everyone, unless bedridden, ought to be able to do some sort of work, whether it be part-time work or work with accommodation such as using a wheelchair, etc. Is this a bias that I need to consider when I answer questions about my patient?

This opinion is shared by many claimants' lawyers and judges who work in the Social Security disability area. It isn't a bias. In fact, it provides a useful perspective that may produce the very sort of information SSA is looking for. If you think a claimant is limited to part time work, say so. If you think in order to work full time a claimant needs special accommodations, describe the necessary accommodations—*e.g.*, a flexible work schedule, special allowance for missing work, extra work breaks to rest, the opportunity to lie down on a work break, work at home, *etc.*

In close cases I worry that I'll inadvertently say the wrong thing or that I will harm my patient's case if I describe my patient as capable of doing any work-related activities at all. Should I be concerned about this?

Probably not. The source of this worry oftentimes is the misperception that a patient needs to be virtually bedridden to be found disabled by SSA. Although this is not the case, sometimes the best thing a doctor can do is telephone the claimant's attorney to discuss the issues.

What is the worst thing a doctor can do when completing a disability form describing a patient's capacity for work?

Describing a patient as more disabled than he or she actually is. It is worse than erring in the other direction because it tends to make the doctor's opinion useless for determining whether the patient meets the requirements of the Social Security Act to be found disabled.

If I really think my patient can sustain work at a regular full-time job, should I fill out the form anyway? (I'd hate to have my patient charged for my work on this form if it will be essentially useless for the claim.)

It depends on the age of the claimant and the claimant's attorney's theory of the case. Because of age, especially if over age 50 or 55, some claimants can actually be capable of performing a surprising number of jobs and still be found disabled. It is also possible the claimant's attorney is looking to document the impact of a few physical limitations to be used in combination with a mental impairment to establish eligibility. The claimant's attorney will appreciate a telephone call from you before you fill out the form.

What is the definition of disability for the Social Security disability program?

Here are the elements of the definition of disability found in the Social Security Act. To be found disabled a claimant must have:

- a medically determinable impairment, that is, a physical or mental impairment that results from anatomical, physiological or psychological abnormalities which are demonstrable by medically acceptable clinical and laboratory diagnostic techniques; and
- which meets the duration requirement, that is, the impairment can be expected to result in death or it must have already lasted or can be expected to last for a continuous period of not less than 12 months; and
- which prevents the performance of past relevant work; and
- which prevents the performance of any other substantial gainful work that exists in the economy in significant numbers,
- considering the claimant's age, education and work experience.

42 U.S.C. § 423(d).

The definition of disability in the Act specifically provides that an individual is not disabled if drug addiction or alcoholism would "be a contributing factor material to the . . . determination that the individual is disabled." 42 U.S.C. § 423(d)(2)(C).

Is the definition of disability the same for the SSI program?

Yes, it is. The same definition of disability is used for SSI, the Supplemental Security Income program—a welfare program operated by SSA. This program provides a minimum income level to disabled people who have not worked enough to be entitled to higher Social Security disability benefits—though SSI benefits are still well below the federal poverty threshold. 42 U.S.C. § 1382c.

Is there anything I should know about the term "medically determinable impairment"?

SSA has taken a common sense approach: If a doctor can make a legitimate diagnosis based on anything more than a patient's description of symptoms, SSA almost always will find that the patient has a medically determinable impairment.

In some circumstances, SSA says that a patient's description of symptoms may constitute findings. For example, SSA agrees that migraine headaches are medically determinable based on the peculiar group of symptoms described by the patient when the physician rules out other causes for the symptoms. A similar approach is taken for the diagnosis of fibromyalgia when there are an insufficient number of tender points. SSR 12-2p.

Does SSA expect treating doctors to know the precise legal definition of disability?

No. In fact, SSA assumes that treating doctors know nothing about determining whether someone is disabled. SSA says that figuring out whether a claimant is disabled or not is its job—this is a legal determination. So if a treating doctor offers the opinion that a patient is disabled, even if the opinion is dressed up with all the statutory jargon, SSA barely considers the opinion. These are issues reserved to SSA. 20 C.F.R. § 404.1527(d) and SSR 96-5p. SSA is most interested in the doctor's opinion about what a patient can do.

How does the Social Security Administration find someone disabled?

SSA has two sets of regulations that are very important in determining disability. One set, called the Listing of Impairments, consists of medical findings, which, if present, require that a claimant be found disabled even without looking at whether a claimant can do his or her past relevant work. The other set of regulations, called the Medical-Vocational Guidelines, are used only when a claimant cannot be found disabled using the Listing of Impairments and only after a claimant shows that he or she cannot do any past relevant work. The Medical-Vocational Guidelines directly apply only to physical impairments that cause exertional limitations, but they are to be used as a framework for decision making in other cases, as well. These rules state whether a claimant is or is not disabled when a claimant has certain combinations of age, education, work experience and residual functional capacity.

What is the Listing of Impairments?

It is a set of medical findings for many common physical and mental impairments (and some that are not so common). The Listings are available on the Internet at http://www.socialsecurity.gov/disability/professionals/bluebook/index.htm. When a claimant's impairment meets the criteria set forth in the Listing of Impairments, the claimant is said to "meet the Listings" and is found disabled. It is also possible for a claimant to be found disabled because his or her impairment is as severe as a particular impairment in the Listing of Impairments. The claimant is then said to "equal the Listings."

Does the treating doctor's opinion play any role in deciding whether a claimant's impairment meets or equals the Listings?

Although SSA says that it will not ignore any opinion from a treating doctor, SSA describes the issue of meeting the Listings as one more of medical fact than medical opinion. When dealing with the Listings, SSA regards the treating doctor mostly as a source of medical evidence. Although SSA will consider an opinion from a treating doctor that a claimant meets the Listings and agree with it if the claimant's findings coincide with those in the Listings, SSA is quick to point out that whether or not a claimant meets the Listings is an issue reserved to SSA. SSA says that an opinion that a claimant's impairment equals the Listings requires special expertise not possessed by treating doctors. SSR 96-5p. In actual practice, though, SSA's administrative law judges will carefully consider any well-supported opinion that a claimant's impairment meets or equals the Listings.

How does SSA find someone disabled using medical-vocational rules?

SSA first determines what work-related activities a claimant can still do despite his or her impairments, which SSA calls a residual functional capacity (RFC) assessment. SSA then uses the RFC assessment to decide if the claimant can do any significant job the claimant has done in the past 15 years. If not, SSA translates the RFC into a work level defined in the Dictionary of Occupational Titles—*e.g.,* sedentary, light or medium work. Then a decision maker literally looks up the claimant's combination of RFC, age, education and work experience on a table, which tells whether a claimant with that combination of factors is or is not disabled.

How does SSA determine whether drug addiction or alcoholism is "material"?

The test is this: If hypothetically the claimant were to stop abusing drugs or alcohol, would the claimant's ability to work be restored? Let's illustrate this with an example. Let's say that alcohol caused a claimant's disabling liver disease. If stopping drinking will restore the claimant's ability to work, SSA will find that alcoholism is material and therefore this claimant will be ineligible for benefits. But if stopping drinking would *not* restore the claimant's ability to work, SSA will find that alcoholism is *not* material, even though it was alcoholism that caused the damage in the first place and even though this claimant is still drinking. This claimant will be eligible for benefits.

§221.11 Form: Physical Medical Source Statement

PHYSICAL MEDICAL SOURCE STATEMENT

From: ______________________________

Re: ______________________________(Name of Patient)

______________________________(Date of Birth)

Please answer the following questions concerning your patient's impairments:

1. Frequency and length of contact: ______________________________

2. Diagnoses: ______________________________

3. Prognosis: ______________________________

4. List your patient's ***symptoms***, including pain, dizziness, fatigue, etc:

____

____

5. If your patient has pain, characterize the nature, location, frequency, precipitating factors, and severity of your patient's pain:

____

____

6. Identify the clinical findings and objective signs:

____

____

7. Describe the treatment and response including any side effects of medication that may have implications for working, *e.g.*, drowsiness, dizziness, nausea, etc.:

____

____

8. Have your patient's impairments lasted or can they be expected to last at least twelve months? □ Yes □ No

9. Do emotional factors contribute to the severity of your patient's symptoms and functional limitations? ☐ Yes ☐ No

10. Identify any psychological conditions affecting your patient's physical condition:

☐ Depression	☐ Anxiety
☐ Somatic symptom disorder	☐ Personality disorder
☐ Psychological factors affecting physical condition	☐ Other: ________________

11. As a result of your patient's impairments, estimate your patient's functional limitations if your patient were placed in a ***competitive work situation***.

a. How many city blocks can your patient walk without rest or severe pain? __________

b. Please circle the hours and/or minutes that your patient can sit ***at one time***, *e.g.*, before needing to get up, *etc.*

Sit: 5 10 15 20 30 45 (Minutes) 1 2 More than 2 (Hours)

c. Please circle the hours and/or minutes that your patient can stand ***at one time***, *e.g.*, before needing to sit down, walk around, *etc.*

Stand: 5 10 15 20 30 45 (Minutes) 1 2 More than 2 (Hours)

d. Please indicate how long your patient can sit and stand/walk ***total in an 8-hour working day*** (with normal breaks):

Sit	**Stand/walk**	
☐	☐	less than 2 hours
☐	☐	about 2 hours
☐	☐	about 4 hours
☐	☐	at least 6 hours

e. Does your patient need a job that permits shifting positions at will from sitting, standing or walking? ☐ Yes ☐ No

f. Does your patient need to include periods of walking around during an 8-hour working day? ☐ Yes ☐ No

If yes, how ***often*** must your patient walk? 1 5 10 15 20 30 45 60 90 (Minutes)

How ***long*** must your patient walk each time? 1 2 3 4 5 6 7 8 9 10 11 12 13 14 15 (Minutes)

g. In addition to normal breaks every two hours, will your patient sometimes need to take *unscheduled* breaks during a working day? □ Yes □ No

If yes, 1) approx. how ***often*** do you think this will happen? ________________

2) approx. how ***long*** (on average) will each break last?________________

3) what symptoms cause a need for breaks?

□ Muscle weakness □ Pain/ paresthesias, numbness
□ Chronic fatigue □ Adverse effects of medication
□ Other: ____

h. With prolonged sitting, should your patient's leg(s) be elevated? □ Yes □ No

If yes, 1) how ***high*** should the leg(s) be elevated? ________________

2) if your patient had a sedentary job***, what percentage of time*** during an 8-hour working day should the leg(s) be elevated? ______________%

3) what symptoms cause a need to elevate leg(s)? _____________

i. While engaging in occasional standing/walking, must your patient use a cane or other hand-held assistive device? Yes No

If yes, what symptoms cause the need for a cane?

□ Imbalance □ Pain □ Weakness
□ Insecurity □ Dizziness
□ Other: ____

For this and other questions on this form, "rarely" means 1% to 5% of an 8-hour working day; "occasionally" means 6% to 33% of an 8-hour working day; "frequently" means 34% to 66% of an 8-hour working day.

j. How many pounds can your patient lift and carry in a competitive work situation?

	Never	**Rarely**	**Occasionally**	**Frequently**
Less than 10 lbs.	□	□	□	□
10 lbs.	□	□	□	□
20 lbs.	□	□	□	□
50 lbs.	□	□	□	□

k. How often can your patient perform the following activities?

	Never	Rarely	Occasionally	Frequently
Twist	□	□	□	□
Stoop (bend)	□	□	□	□
Crouch/ squat	□	□	□	□
Climb stairs	□	□	□	□
Climb ladders	□	□	□	□

l. Does your patient have significant limitations with reaching, handling or fingering?
□ Yes □ No

If yes, please indicate the percentage of time during an 8-hour working day that your patient can use hands/fingers/arms for the following activities:

	HANDS: Grasp, Turn Twist Objects	**FINGERS: Fine Manipulations**	**ARMS: Reaching In Front of Body**	**ARMS: Reaching Overhead**
Right:	**%**	**%**	**%**	**%**
Left:	**%**	**%**	**%**	**%**

m. How much is your patient likely to be ***"off task"***? That is, what percentage of a typical workday would your patient's symptoms likely be severe enough to interfere with ***attention and concentration*** needed to perform even simple work tasks?

□ 0% □ 5% □ 10% □ 15% □ 20% □ 25% or more

n. To what degree can your patient tolerate work stress?

□ Incapable of even "low stress" work □ Capable of low stress work
□ Capable of moderate stress - normal work □ Capable of high stress work

Please explain the reasons for your conclusion: ______________________________

o. Are your patient's impairments likely to produce "good days" and "bad days"?
□ Yes □ No

If yes, assuming your patient was trying to work full time, please estimate, on the average, how many days per month your patient is likely to be absent from work as a result of the impairments:

☐ Never	☐ About three days per month
☐ About one day per month	☐ About four days per month
☐ About two days per month	☐ More than four days per month

12. Are your patient's impairments (physical impairments plus any emotional impairments) as demonstrated by signs, clinical findings and laboratory or test results ***reasonably consistent*** with the symptoms and functional limitations described above in this evaluation?

☐ Yes ☐ No

If no, please explain: ______________________________

13. Please describe any other limitations (such as psychological limitations, limited vision, difficulty hearing, need to avoid temperature extremes, wetness, humidity, noise, dust, fumes, gases or hazards, etc.) that would affect your patient's ability to work at a regular job on a sustained basis:

____

____

____

______________________ ______________________

Date *Signature*

Printed/Typed Name: ______________________

Address: ______________________

____

____

7-28

7/16
§221.11

§221.12 Form: Follow-up Medical Source Statement

FOLLOW-UP MEDICAL SOURCE STATEMENT

From: ______________________________

Re: ______________________________(Name of Patient)

______________________________(Date of Birth)

You completed a medical source statement dated ________________, a copy of which is attached. Please identify all factors you considered in coming to your conclusions about your patient's capacity – what your patient can still do despite his/her impairments:

☐ Longitudinal perspective, i.e., experience with patient over time treating patient
☐ Patient's complaints
☐ Consistency of patient's complaints over time
☐ Patient's response to treatment
☐ Reports from other medical care providers; identify providers:

____

☐ Consistency of patient's complaints with clinical and laboratory findings; identify findings:

____

____

____

____

____

☐ Other factors; identify:

____

____

____

____

______________________________ ______________________________

Date *Signature*

Printed/Typed Name: ______________________________

Address: ______________________________

____

§222 State Agency Doctors

According to SSR 96-6p and 20 C.F.R. § 404.1527(e), an ALJ may not ignore the opinions of state agency doctors and other program physicians and psychologists, who are referred to in SSA's lexicon as "non-examining sources." Their opinions may appear in the Disability Determination Explanation, on state agency RFC forms or along with disability examiner notes in a typewritten document known as the "electronic worksheet" (EWS). You may need to pay attention to the individual's initials to figure out which are the notes of the doctor and which are the notes of the non-physician disability examiner, whose opinion carries no weight. Sometimes the state agency doctor's opinion appears in barely legible handwritten notes near the EWS in the exhibit file. These often cryptic notes by state agency doctors are supposed to be treated as expert opinions by the ALJ; and the decision must explain the weight given to these opinions unless the treating doctor's opinion is given controlling weight. The regulations below set forth rules for weighing the opinions of non-examining sources:

- The weight given to the opinions of nonexamining sources "will depend on the degree to which they provide supporting explanations for their opinions." 20 C.F.R. § 404.1527(c)(3).
- SSA considers the degree to which nonexamining sources' opinions "consider all of the pertinent evidence in [the] claim, including opinions of treating and other examining sources." 20 C.F.R. § 404.1527(c)(3).
- "Generally, the more consistent an opinion is with the record as a whole, the more weight [SSA] will give to that opinion." 20 C.F.R. § 404.1527(c)(4).
- SSA considers the doctor's medical specialty. 20 C.F.R. § 404.1527(c)(5) and (e)(2)(ii). *See* §§203.1 and 203.4 of this book for how to determine the state agency doctor's medical specialty.
- SSA considers the medical source's "amount of understanding of [SSA's] disability programs and their evidentiary requirements." 20 C.F.R. § 404.1527(c)(6) and (e)(2)(ii). "State agency medical or psychological consultants or other program physicians and psychologists are highly qualified physicians and psychologists who are also experts in Social Security disability evaluation." 20 C.F.R. § 404.1527(e)(2)(i).
- Generally SSA gives more weight to the opinion of a doctor who has examined the claimant than to the opinion of a doctor who has not. 20 C.F.R. § 404.1527(c)(1).
- Generally SSA gives more weight to a treating doctor's opinion. 20 C.F.R. § 404.1527(c)(2).

Most attorneys, at one time or another, have the impulse to ask an ALJ to subpoena state agency physicians whose unrealistic RFC evaluations appear in a client's hearing exhibit file. This impulse is understandable given that the rule in most circuits, at least in some circumstances, allows such opinions to constitute "substantial evidence." If your impression of case law is driving your desire to subpoena state agency doctors, review your circuit's cases carefully, since a close look at the case law may allay your fears. For example, it is difficult to find a case that uses a state agency doctor's opinion as substantial evidence supporting a denial decision when that opinion contradicts all other evidence on the record.

Requesting a subpoena of a state agency physician usually accomplishes little more than alienating the ALJ. Only in the most extreme and unusual circumstances will the ALJ consider calling a state agency physician to testify, and even then the ALJ must obtain special approval from the Social Security Administration. You will be expected to demonstrate the need to cross-examine a state agency physician at your client's hearing, state what you hope to establish through such testimony, and explain why interrogatories will not suffice.

In the usual case, by the time of the hearing both you and the ALJ know the answers to most questions concerning the state agency physician evaluation. For example, there is no controversy over whether the state agency physician has ever seen your client. State agency doctors are "nonexamining sources." 20 C.F.R. § 404.1527(e).

Although SSR 96-6p refers to state agency doctors as "highly qualified physicians and psychologists who are experts in the evaluation of the medical issues in disability claims," a state agency doctor probably had no special expertise prior to employment by the state agency, something you may discover from the American Medical Directory used in hearing offices. Whatever special expertise a state agency doctor has, it was gained on the job. The non-physician disability examiner, in fact, may have completed the RFC form signed by the state agency physician, which is allowed by SSA's rules. *See* POMS DI 24510.066A.

State agency physicians rely often exclusively on objective evidence in arriving at their conclusions about RFC. Indeed, despite Social Security regulations and rulings that require subjective complaints to be considered, an Iowa class action demonstrated that state agency physicians "place an undue emphasis on objective evidence at the expense of subjective complaints." *Laird v. Stilwill*, 969 F. Supp. 1167, 1185 (N.D. Iowa 1997). This class action revealed that three state agency physicians spent an average of less than 20 minutes reviewing each claim file. Disability examiners had highlighted the objective evidence with paper clips before giving the files to the doctors. The court concluded, "a twenty-minute review of a Social Security file cannot provide the scrutiny that most claimants' cases deserve." *Laird v. Stilwill*, 969 F. Supp. 1167, 1185 (N.D. Iowa 1997).

Regulations concerning the weight of medical evidence state that although the ALJ is not bound by the findings of state agency doctors, the ALJ is to consider them and weigh them against other medical opinions in the record, using rules that generally accord more weight to a treating source's opinion. 20 C.F.R. § 404.1527. One of the rules states that "because nonexamining sources have no examining or treating relationship with [the claimant], the weight [SSA] will give their opinions will depend on the degree to which they provide supporting explanations for their opinions." 20 C.F.R. § 404.1527(c)(3). State agency physicians are notorious for providing conclusory RFC opinions. By subpoenaing a state agency physician you may give the doctor the opportunity to provide a supporting explanation for the opinion.

The regulations also provide that the ALJ must consider the degree to which the opinion considered all of the pertinent evidence in the claim. 20 C.F.R. § 404.1527(c)(3). In most cases, some new evidence is submitted at the ALJ level, evidence that was not considered by the state agency physician. If the state agency physician is subpoenaed, the doctor will, of course, have the opportunity to review this new evidence, testify that it has been considered, and opine that it does not change the state agency doctor's conclusion about your client's RFC.

However, there is one fact that, if you could demonstrate it through cross-examination, could be worth the effort of trying to get the ALJ to subpoena a state agency physician: The state agency physician's opinion may, in fact, be based on little more than informal medical guidelines. These guidelines are similar to a Social Security Ruling that was withdrawn when it became the focus of litigation, SSR 82-51: "Guidelines for Residual Functional Capacity Assessment in Musculoskeletal and Cardiovascular Impairments." But be forewarned: Although the use of such guidelines probably denies claimants their right to individualized RFC assessments under the Social Security Act, the complexity of this issue and the difficulty of establishing it through cross-examination of only one or two state agency physicians, suggests that this issue is better left to a class action directed against state agencies.

If your client's case is appealed to federal court (depending on which circuit's case law applies and the facts that form the basis for your argument that cross-examination is essential), denial of your request to subpoena a state agency physician may be sufficient to prevent the state agency physician's RFC evaluation from being considered substantial evidence in support of an ALJ denial decision. Denial of this request denies your client's right to cross-examine an adverse witness. *See Richardson v. Perales,* 402 U.S. 389, 402 (1971). That is why many attorneys advise requesting a subpoena of the state agency physician. The ALJ will probably think that the *only* reason you requested a subpoena of a state agency physician is to permit you to argue later that the claimant was denied the right to cross examine an adverse witness. ALJs tend to view this strategy as legal shenanigans, especially, they say, since most ALJs don't put much stock in state agency physician RFC evaluations anyway.

Although many ALJs say that state agency physician RFC evaluations are close to useless in determining residual functional capacity, SSR 96-6p provides that ALJs "may not ignore these opinions and must explain the weight given to the opinions in their decisions." Nevertheless, SSR 96-6p notes that the:

> regulations provide progressively more rigorous tests for weighing opinions as the ties between the source of the opinion and the individual become weaker. For example, the opinions of physicians or psychologists who do not have a treatment relationship with the individual are weighed by stricter standards, based on a greater degree of medical evidence, qualifications, and explanations for the opinions, than are required of treating sources.

Some ALJs, if they pay attention to the state agency RFC evaluations at all, use the rule of thumb that state agency physicians usually overestimate RFC by approximately one exertional level. This assumption is rarely stated, however, and cannot be counted upon.

Requesting subpoenas of state agency physicians should be reserved for unusual situations. If you have such a situation, learn as much as possible about how your state agency operates. Do so by obtaining a copy of the state agency manuals. It is more useful to review the unofficial manuals, rather than the official SSA manual, POMS, because the unofficial ones will provide fodder for genuine cross-examination. Follow the procedures for requesting subpoenas described in §284. Note that you will need to explain why a subpoena is necessary, what the testimony of the witness is expected to prove and why this cannot be proved without issuing a subpoena, that is, why interrogatories are not a satisfactory alternative. For an example of a case in which a court upheld SSA's refusal to issue a subpoena for state agency doctors, *see Butera v. Apfel*, 173 F.3d 1049, 1058-1059 (7th Cir. 1999). *But see Calvin v. Chater*, 73 F.3d 87, 92 (6th Cir. 1996), which upheld an ALJ's refusal to subpoena an SSA consultative doctor; *Flatford v. Chater*, 93 F.3d 1296, 1307 (6th Cir. 1996), which upheld an ALJ's refusal to subpoena a medical expert who submitted answers to interrogatories from the ALJ; and *Yancey v. Apfel*, 145 F.3d 106, 113-114 (2d Cir. 1998), which upheld an ALJ's refusal to subpoena a treating doctor who gave an adverse opinion.

A memorandum from the Chief Administrative Law Judge dated January 28, 1997 reiterated SSA's policy on issuance of subpoenas to state agency doctors. It stated that claimants' representatives were requesting subpoenas to refute state agency doctor opinions following the publication of SSRs 96-5p and 96-6p. The memorandum, which was written long before SSA imposed the requirement that subpoenas be requested no later than10 business days before the date of the hearing, states:

> By virtue of the regulations at 20 C.F.R. 404.950(d) and 416.1450(d), the Commissioner has delegated to ALJs qualified discretionary authority to issue subpoenas in those situations "[w]hen it is reasonably necessary for the full presentation of a case." The regulations also provide that parties to a hearing may request a subpoena to compel testimony or documents, providing they file a written request with an ALJ at least five days before the hearing date. The request must include a justification for the need for a subpoena by stating the "important facts" that the witness or document is expected to prove, and explaining why such facts cannot be proven without issuing a subpoena.
>
> HALLEX section I-2-5-78 implements the qualified discretionary subpoena authority noted above. Section I-2-578B provides that an ALJ must issue a subpoena if the claimant shows that the evidence cannot be obtained without a subpoena and that it is reasonably necessary to the full presentation of the case. To make this determination, the full documentary evidence in the file must be reviewed. Only when the file does not contain the information sought, after development is completed (and all means of obtaining the information has been exhausted) should the ALJ determine whether the information is reasonably necessary for the full presentation of the case. HALLEX Section I-2-5-78C.
>
> An opportunity to confront and cross-examine adverse witnesses and present rebuttal evidence and to have a full and fair hearing before an impartial decision maker are longstanding requisites of procedural due process. Subpoena power is a tool to ensure adjudicative administrative procedural due process. *Goldberg v. Kelly,* 397 U.S. 254 (1970); *Richardson v. Perales,* 402 U.S. 389 (1971).
>
> Whenever the ALJ must discuss the non-treating source opinion evidence provided by the State Agency medical and psychological consultants at the initial or reconsideration level, the ALJ must first review the documentary evidence in the file. Only if the nontreating source opinion is critical to the decision making process, should the ALJ consider obtaining testimony from the State Agency consultant for purposes of cross-examination. If the opinion evidence can be discounted because it conflicts with the preponderance of the other evidence in the record (or if it simply adds to the body of other documentary evidence) which, standing alone, would be sufficient to support a decision, there would be no purpose served in obtaining the testimony of the State Agency consultant. Further, if there is little or no rationale describing how the consultant weighed the evidence and made the determination at the earlier level of adjudication, the probative value of the opinion is extremely limited and may not, therefore, require the opportunity to rebut the opinion.
>
> It should be noted that Acquiescence Ruling 91-1(5), acquiescing in the decision in *Lidy v. Sullivan,* 911 F.2d 1075 (5th Cir. 1990), requires the ALJ, in states in the Fifth Circuit, to issue a subpoena to consultants who have examined the claimant. The ruling is silent with regard to nonexamining medical or psychological consultants.
>
> We consider the subpoena a "last resort" measure. In the rare circumstance where the ALJ finds that the requirements for compelling the appearance of a State Agency consultant are met, Social Security Administration instructions in POMS DI 29501.030B provide that the ALJ will first send a memorandum to the State Agency through the Assistant Regional Commissioner (ARC), Programs, with a copy to the OHA Regional Office, requesting the appearance of the individual. The ALJ allows 15 days for clearance and response through the ARC, Programs, to the State Agency. POMS cautions the State Agency to respond promptly to the ALJ, as the ALJ has the authority to issue a subpoena to State Agency consultant or employees.

Some attorneys have achieved good results by sending thorough interrogatories to the ALJ for submission to the state agency physician. Others have obtained productivity records and copies of the medical consultant's contracts from their state agencies that show how little time state agency doctors spend on each case. (State agency doctors are proud of this!) Such records may be submitted to the ALJ with a request to weigh the doctor's opinion accordingly.

§223 Consultative Doctors — Hired by SSA

SSA's guidelines for health professionals preparing consultative examination reports appears on the Internet in something SSA calls the Green Book. See http://www.ssa.gov/disability/professionals/greenbook/ce-adult.htm. This document details the requirements of the examination and report both generally and for specific impairments. Sometimes the Green Book provides fodder for arguing that a particular CE report is insufficient under SSA's rules.

When you find that an SSA consultative doctor disagrees with your client's treating doctor, ask the treating doctor to address the medical issues raised by the consultant. If the treating physician can provide a plausible explanation for the differing conclusion, the treating doctor's opinion ought to be accepted. *See* 20 C.F.R. § 404.1527(c). The last thing you want to do is to bring in the consultative physician for cross-examination. Doing so risks providing the consultative physician the opportunity to convince the ALJ that the treating doctor is wrong.

But what do you do when the record contains a biased, potentially devastating consultative physician's report? Where circumstances present no choice but to request that the ALJ subpoena the consultative physician for cross-examination, you must follow the rules for requesting subpoenas (20 C.F.R. § 404.950(d); *see* §284), and fully explain why interrogatories are not an adequate substitute for the live testimony of the doctor. In *Solis v. Schweiker,* 719 F.2d 301, 302 (9th Cir. 1983), the Ninth Circuit Court of Appeals held that "[a]lthough interrogatories can adequately replace in-court testimony where factual questions such as foundation or expertise are at issue, we agree with appellant that bias is better elicited through rigorous in-court scrutiny." If your request is denied, HALLEX I-2-5-78 D requires that the ALJ give you written notification and that your request and the notification denying the request be made a hearing exhibit. Consider whether you need to submit a written objection to the ALJ. At the least, plan on making your record at the hearing, including a request that the consultative physician's report be stricken because the claimant has been denied the right to cross-examine an adverse witness.

An agonizing dilemma is presented by the ambiguous consultative doctor's report. For example, a report filled with the words "mild," "minimal," or "moderate" that does not specifically delineate limitations may come from a doctor whose fully explained view of a "mild limitation" may, in fact, help your case. A mild limitation in the ability to stand may mean to some doctors that the claimant can stand, but not for more than a half hour at one time. This limitation, of course, is sufficient to support an RFC for sedentary work. Then again, it could be the consultative doctor's opinion that this mild limitation limits the claimant to standing for no more than two hours at one time nor for more than six hours out of an eight hour working day, a position that moves the claimant's RFC into the light range and beyond.

Before you ask the ALJ to obtain a clarification of the consultative doctor's opinion, try to obtain a preview. The doctor may be willing to talk to you by telephone. Be sure to send a medical consent form in advance of your call.

While some consultative doctors are happy to clarify ambiguities in their reports, many state agencies have told such doctors not to talk to attorneys for claimants. Indeed, the state agency may even have led the doctor to believe that it is illegal to talk to you. This, of course, is not a correct interpretation of any law or regulation.

When SSA published regulations on consultative examinations on August 1, 1991, SSA stated in the preamble when discussing comments to proposed regulations:

> One commenter stated that this section should include provisions that the claimant or his representative may submit questions to the consultative examiner. . . . We have no objection to the claimant or his or her representative submitting questions to a consultative examiner. We believe, however, that this does not have to be included in the regulations.

56 Fed. Reg. 36,946 (1991). In addition, a letter dated April 10, 1997 from the Director, Division of Medical and Vocational Policy of the Office of Disability to Attorney Daniel Schorsch, available from NOSSCR, says:

> There has been no change in our policy that it neither requires nor prohibits consultative examination (CE) physicians from discussing the examination results with the claimant or the claimant's representative. There has also been no change in our policy that the CE physician may conduct additional tests requested by the claimant or the claimant's representative at their expense.

Once you have satisfied yourself that the consultative doctor's opinion will help your client's case, draft interrogatories for the doctor to complete. Send the interrogatories to the ALJ with a request that the ALJ review them and forward them to the doctor.

If you cannot get the consultative doctor to talk with you, you may be able to find another doctor, perhaps the treating physician, to help you clarify the ambiguities in the consultative doctor's report. It's also possible another lawyer may have some experience interpreting this particular doctor's reports.

If you can get no advance reading on the consultative doctor's opinion, your client's case may be better if you do not ask for clarification of ambiguities, since, in the end, the doctor really has very little information about your client.

§224 Consultative Doctors — Hired by You

Before you hire a physician to evaluate your client, make sure it's necessary to do so. If you are seeking information or an opinion that can be obtained from the treating doctor, it is better to get it from that source whose opinion is entitled to more weight. Even when it is necessary to hire a consultant, send the treating physician a copy and try to get the treating doctor's imprimatur on the consultant's report.

Generally, the only times you will be hiring specialists is when you need them to corroborate and supplement the treating doctor's conclusions. For example, when the treating physician is a psychiatrist and your client has never had a full battery of the more objective tests that psychologists administer, it may be beneficial to refer your client for a thorough psychological evaluation.

Psychological evaluations may be the type most frequently requested by attorneys. They are useful in many kinds of cases, not just those cases involving mental illness. For example, a psychological evaluation that includes an MMPI can assist with the evaluation of pain in cases involving physical impairments alone, physical impairments with an "emotional overlay" and cases involving somatic symptom disorders, those psychological disorders that have pain as their primary symptom. *See* §§250-259, regarding proof of pain and §248, on somatic symptom disorders.

Always hire reputable, well-respected specialists. A medical school is a good source of consultants. Doctors who provide reliable evaluations for SSA may also perform evaluations for you. The judges will probably know from experience and reputation which doctors' opinions are not to be trusted. Stay away from them.

Some ALJs distrust the opinions of any doctor hired by the claimant's attorney, no matter how reputable. Although the regulations provide that more weight will be accorded to the opinion of a treating doctor, the opinion of an examining doctor is accorded more weight than is the opinion of a doctor who never examined the claimant. 20 C.F.R. § 404.1527(c). Nothing in the regulations or rulings states that the value of a doctor's opinion is less because the claimant's attorney hired the doctor. The opinion of such a doctor should be weighed in the same way the opinion of any examining source is weighed. If the opinion is from a specialist who considered all the pertinent evidence, is consistent with the record as a whole and is supported by medical signs and findings, the opinion is entitled to substantial weight.

When an ALJ depreciates the value of a doctor's report because the claimant's attorney hired the doctor, the ALJ must go outside the record for support for the conclusion that the doctor's report is entitled to less weight. The Eleventh Circuit Court of Appeals remanded a case solely because an ALJ noted that a certain doctor "consistently finds disability in cases of clients represented by [the plaintiff's] attorney." The court found that such a conclusion compromised the disability determination process and remanded the case for "an unbiased reconsideration of [plaintiff's] application for benefits before a different ALJ." *Miles v. Chater,* 84 F.3d 1397, 1400-1401 (11th Cir. 1996). *But cf. Miller v. Commissioner of Social Security,* 172 F.3d 303, 305 (3d Cir. 1999).

According to *Van Nguyen v. Chater,* 100 F.3d 1462, 1464 (9th Cir. 1996), "the fact that the examination was conducted at the request of an attorney is relevant where the opinion itself provides grounds for suspicion as to its legitimacy." Where there are no such grounds, the court noted, it doesn't mean that the opinion must prevail, "but it does mean that [the doctor's] credibility is not subject to attack on the basis of the source of his patient's referral." *Nguyen* at 1465. "[I]n the absence of other evidence to undermine the credibility of a medical report, the purpose for which the report was obtained does not provide a legitimate basis for rejecting it." *Reddick v. Chater*, 157 F.3d 715, 726 (9th Cir. 1998). "There is nothing fundamentally wrong with a lawyer sending a client to a doctor, especially when the capacity of that client to care for himself is questionable." *Blankenship v. Bowen*, 874 F.2d 1116, 1122 n. 8 (6th Cir. 1989).

§225 Vocational Experts — Hired by You

Occasionally it will be necessary for you to hire a vocational expert to evaluate your client's case. Try to find one who is on SSA's panel, who has a thorough understanding of Social Security regulations and rulings, and whose opinion is respected by the ALJs.

Some attorneys hire vocational experts to review exhibit files and render opinions in virtually all of their cases. Although good results may be obtained by such a practice, it is very expensive and, in fact, very few cases *require* vocational expert evaluation.

Consider hiring a vocational expert only to address those two issues on which the claimant has the burden of proof: with the claimant's RFC, is the claimant capable of returning to past relevant work 1) as the claimant actually performed it and 2) as that work is *generally* performed in the economy?

But let us pause for a moment to consider whether it is necessary to hire a vocational expert to address even these limited issues. If the claimant is a good witness and is capable of offering a convincing explanation why past relevant work as he or she actually did it cannot be performed now, why hire a vocational expert? If the ALJ is not calling a vocational expert to testify, the only way the second issue can come up is if the ALJ finds, in the DICTIONARY OF OCCUPATIONAL TITLES (DOT), easier demands for one of the claimant's past jobs than the claimant describes. You may be able to save the expense of hiring a vocational expert by consulting the DOT yourself.

At the fifth step of the sequential evaluation process, the step where SSA has the burden of proof, vocational issues are frequently presented. Vocational experts may be necessary to address the following:

1) Proving that a literate claimant under age 50 is not capable of performing jobs that exist in significant numbers in the economy;
2) Using the Medical-Vocational Guidelines as a "framework" in evaluating cases where the claimant's RFC does not exactly fit the categories established by the grids; and
3) Dealing with the knotty issue of transferability of skills.

Unless you have an exceptionally strong opinion from a claimant's doctor that explains why your client is unable to do any sort of work, a vocational expert's help in a case involving a literate claimant under age 50 or an illiterate claimant under age 45 can be valuable. *See* §§260-268.

Upon close analysis, it is a rare claimant whose RFC exactly matches the RFC necessary for a full range of sedentary, light or medium work; but by reviewing Social Security Rulings 83-12 and 83-14, the rulings that deal with using the grids as a framework in cases involving exertional impairments and cases involving combinations of exertional and nonexertional limitations, you may have a pretty good idea of "framework analysis" without having the assistance of a vocational expert. Those Social Security Rulings will help you determine whether you really need to hire a vocational expert.

When you are dealing with solely nonexertional impairments, addressed in SSR 85-15, you may have more difficulty using the grids as a framework without having the help of a vocational expert, especially if your client retains the capacity for unskilled work. The issue in such cases is whether your client will be able to adapt to unskilled work, considering your client's age, education and work experience. When your client is more restricted than this, a treating doctor or a medical consultant hired by you may be able to describe your client's mental residual functional capacity in such a way as to lead readily to the conclusion that your client is disabled, especially if you get the doctor to assess your client's abilities using SSA's list of critical requirements for unskilled work. *See* §§245 and 246. If not, you may need a vocational expert's help.

The problematic issue of transferability of work skills, discussed in SSR 82-41, in several regulations and in the introductory texts to the grids (*see* §349), may present issues with which a vocational expert can help. In close cases, particularly those that may involve differing degrees of transferability because of the claimant's age, it may be extremely useful to hire a vocational expert to assist you, though advanced practitioners tend to rely on written resources alone to plan cross examination of the vocational expert called by the ALJ. Advanced practitioners use the DOT and SELECTED CHARACTERISTICS OF OCCUPATIONS DEFINED IN THE REVISED DICTIONARY OF OCCUPATIONAL TITLES (SCO), the same publications relied upon by SSA to determine the requirements of work in the national economy. SSR 00-4p. Advanced practitioners use these publications to try to identify similar jobs with easier demands to which a claimant might transfer skills.

There are some shortcuts that you can use to determine if transferability of skills is going to be a problem in your client's case. First, always ask your client if there are any jobs within his or her current capacity for work where work skills could be used. Second, note that the DOT groups jobs by industry. When you find your client's job, look around in the DOT on the pages near that job to familiarize yourself with the constellation of jobs in that industry. Also identify the GOE code found in the definition trailer of the DOT job description. This will lead you to a group of similar jobs in SCO. Examine similar jobs to see if you can identify reasons, based on your client's RFC and the requirements of those jobs, that your client is not capable of doing those jobs. If you find some jobs in which it appears possible your client's skills could be utilized, it is time to seek vocational expert assistance. Because this area is so complicated, a good vocational expert can usually come up with reasons why your client's skills cannot be transferred to jobs that may at first glance appear to be problematic.

The vocational expert you hire may testify at the hearing, prepare a report, or simply assist you in preparing to cross-examine a vocational expert called by the ALJ. When you are dealing with transferable skills, though, unless your client's transferable skills are obvious or the state agency has raised the issue, it is best to hold any vocational expert report for rebuttal. If you submit a vocational expert's report arguing that there are no transferable skills, you may prompt the vocational expert called by the ALJ to take a contrary position. If you do not raise the issue, it may not come up.

Practice Tip

Whenever you receive a report on an issue addressed by a vocational expert in a particular case, consider whether you can have the vocational expert also write a more generic version that you can use in many cases. A vocational expert may effectively address a few issues that come up often in disability cases. The expert can prepare a report that may be submitted over and over in different clients' cases. A sample report dealing with one-arm work from Dr. Brent C. Evans follows. A sample report dealing with alternate sitting and standing jobs appears at §348.4.

December 1, 1995

VOC-EVAL
ASSOCIATES, INC.

Mr. Thomas E. Bush
Attorney at Law
161 West Wisconsin Avenue
Milwaukee, WI 53203

Re: One-Arm Jobs

Dear Mr. Bush:

You have asked me to state my opinion concerning the existence of unskilled (SVP1 or 2) occupations in the economy which can be performed by a person with one arm.

I have approached this problem in several different ways using the Dictionary of Occupational Titles, a computerized data base, and my years of experience as a vocational expert. I have also examined the position of the Social Security Administration on this issue which appears in Social Security Ruling 83-12 and in POMS DI 25020.005.

I note that it is SSA's position that loss of use of an upper extremity "would reduce the total number of unskilled occupations within the person's RFC to a little more than the number represented by the full range of sedentary work." POMS DI 25020.005A.5.b. My research does not support this conclusion.

If we limit our inquiry to "occupations" which appear in the DOT and require that every function of each "occupation" be capable of performance at competitive speed by an individual with average manual dexterity of the remaining arm, it is my professional opinion that such occupations are relatively rare. There are nowhere near as many DOT occupations which can be performed by a person with one arm as there are sedentary unskilled occupations.

I would like to see the Social Security Administration's official list of one-arm occupations; but I understand that SSA has no such list. You once provided me with what you termed to be an "unofficial" list of 18 one-arm occupations which you obtained from the Wisconsin State Agency.

Let me take a few examples from this list to illustrate my conclusion. The list includes the job of "ticketer (any industry) 652.685-098." According to the DOT, such a ticketer

10708 W. Janesville Rd.
Suite 104
Hales Corners, WI 53130
(414) 529-2211
Fax (414) 529-9731

2949 N. Mayfair Rd.
Suite 105
Wauwatosa, WI 53222
(414) 476-2277
Fax (414) 476-3781

333 Buchner Place
Wing C
La Crosse, WI 54603
(608) 784-2299
Fax (608) 784-2421

306 S. Barstow St.
Suite 212
Eau Claire, WI 54701
(715) 832-5032
Fax (715) 832-4832

tends the machine that prints information, such as price, size, etc., on ID tags. This job includes the following which could not be done by a one-arm person at competitive speed: "mounts roll of tags or labeling material on machine brackets and threads end of roll through feeding device." When there is defective printing this individual "turns knobs or repositions printing plate, using hand tools, to adjust machine." This job also, by the way, in the 1991 revision of the DOT is a semiskilled job (SVP3).

The State Agency's list includes "nailing machine operator, automatic (any industry) 669.685-066." Depending on the make of the machine a one-arm person may not be able to perform at competitive speed because the job includes the following: "positions reel of nail wire on spindle of machine and pulls wire through rollers into driving mechanism." The DOT also notes: "depresses pedal or button to drive nails into stock." Sometimes the stock parts to be nailed together have to be held in position by hand. Obviously, under such circumstances a one-arm person would be able to operate only the machine equipped with the foot pedal.

A "clinching-machine operator (elec. equip.) 616.685-014" may use pliers to strip rubber insulation off wire cord. This cannot be done by a one-arm person without some arrangement for positioning the wire while pliers are held in hand.

It is necessary to examine each function of a DOT occupation in order to determine whether or not a one-arm person can do each and every operation at competitive speed. The fact that the "unofficial" list of such jobs fails this test supports my position that there are relatively few occupations in which each of the functions described in the DOT can be performed by a one-arm person.

This conclusion, however, doesn't fully answer the question of how many "jobs" exist which can be performed by a person with one arm. The Social Security Administration pointed out in Social Security Ruling 83-12 that "individuals with this impairment have been known to perform selected occupations [i.e., jobs] at nearly all exertional levels..." It is true, especially for those individuals with above average strength and above average remaining manual dexterity, that many one-arm individuals work. In fact, some people are capable of performing quite remarkable dexterous activities with one arm, as a result of years of experience and practice. One cannot assume that their performance can be matched by the average person on an entry level job. In fact, one can assume exactly the opposite.

There are some individual jobs which exist in the economy which can be performed by a one-arm person because a particular machine or the work process of a particular employer accommodates one-arm operation. I know that there are such individual jobs. However, I know of no studies which total their numbers.

You want to know if the total number of all unskilled one-arm jobs in the economy is greater than, less than, or equal to the total number of unskilled sedentary jobs in the economy. Here, we are dealing with the total number of positions, not occupational titles. As such, my conclusion cannot be based solely on the Dictionary of Occupational Titles. I must rely on training, experience and personal observation. One of the things that I have learned from experience placing individuals and discussing this issue with other vocational counselors is that it is hard to place a person in unskilled sedentary work; but it is even harder to place a one-arm person in a suitable unskilled job. The accepted fact that unskilled work primarily involves working with things, objects which must be manipulated, rather than data or people, corroborates this experience.

In conclusion, it is my opinion that there are many fewer one-arm unskilled jobs existing in the economy than there are unskilled sedentary jobs.

I am attaching to this letter a copy of my resume, a copy of the portion of Social Security Ruling 83-12 dealing with one-arm jobs, the Wisconsin State Agency's list of one-arm jobs and the section from POMS DI 25020.005A.5 dealing with this issue.

Please feel free to contact me if you have any questions regarding this matter.

Respectfully,

Dr. Brent C. Evans

Dr. Brent C. Evans, CVE, CWA
Diplomate, ABVE
President, VOC-EVAL Associates, Inc.

BCE/krn

§226 Vocational Experts Called by the ALJ

Vocational experts testify in more than half of all Social Security disability cases nationwide. Because there is some additional preparation that must be done when a vocational expert is called to testify at your client's hearing, don't forget to ask whether the ALJ is calling any experts when a hearing office staff member telephones you to schedule the hearing. Otherwise, you won't find out whether an expert will testify until you receive the notice of hearing, which, unless there is a clerical error, should include a copy of any notice to the vocational expert called by the ALJ.

Try to predict what issues the vocational expert will be asked to address. Anticipate, if you can, the ALJ's questions and the vocational expert's answers. Be sure that the claimant's doctor has given a clear description of the claimant's residual functional capacity. Work out one or more hypothetical questions for the vocational expert to answer based on the claimant's doctor's description of the claimant's residual functional capacity. And figure out why the vocational expert's answer ought to be that the claimant is incapable of performing jobs in significant numbers in the economy. Work out a plan for cross-examination if the vocational expert's answer goes awry.

To prepare, *see* §§340-349 regarding cross-examination of vocational experts. In addition, pay special attention to anything that explains SSA's viewpoint on vocational issues and vocational expert testimony. Familiarize yourself with all the Social Security rulings pertaining to vocational issues. *See* the list of rulings at §271. Read the Vocational Expert Self-Study Guide excerpted in Appendix 4, Phrasing Hypothetical Questions to Vocational Experts Training Guide in Appendix 6, and the Vocational Expert Handbook reproduced in Appendix 8.

Make every effort to have the record closed on the day of the hearing because, if you submit significant evidence after the hearing, the ALJ will most likely send the new evidence to the vocational expert with an interrogatory rather than schedule a supplemental hearing. Although HALLEX I-2-5-58 gives you the right to call for a supplemental hearing when you do not like the vocational expert's answer to the interrogatory, the very act of having the vocational expert write answers to an interrogatory solidifies the vocational expert's answers and makes later cross examination quite difficult.

§227 Medical Expert

Attached to your client's notice of hearing may be a notice indicating that a medical expert will be testifying at your client's hearing. Medical experts testify at about 20 percent of disability hearings. When a medical expert is scheduled to appear at a hearing, you must be prepared. First, make sure the exhibit file is complete, preferably well in advance of the hearing date, so that the hearing is not delayed while the medical expert is reading all the records you brought in on the day of the hearing.

Second, try to anticipate the questions the ALJ will ask the medical expert. These questions could revolve around the issue of whether or not your client's impairments meet the Listings. If so, try to submit as hearing exhibits sufficient documentation and perhaps the treating physician's analysis of the appropriate Listings.

Try to resolve as many medical issues as possible before the hearing by asking the treating physician to prepare a thorough report. If the issues are of the sort over which there is medical disagreement, review medical texts and journal articles and consult with your own expert in preparation to cross-examine the medical expert. Obtain copies of medical text pages or journal articles for submission as hearing exhibits if the medical expert takes a position contrary to your position.

The attorney in a Social Security case has no formal way of getting an advance reading on a medical expert's opinion. You cannot subpoena the expert for a deposition, for example. Although there is no written SSA prohibition against talking with a medical expert before a hearing, which may tempt you to take advantage of an opportunity to approach the medical expert informally, many ALJs may take offense at such efforts.

See §§330-337 regarding cross-examination of a medical expert at a hearing.

§230 Analysis of Medical Impairments

In this book, the discussion of medical impairments follows the organization of the Listing of Impairments, with the exception of impairments seldom seen in a Social Security disability hearing, discussed below, and obesity, which no longer appears in the Listings but appears in this book along with discussion of the endocrine system Listing, §238. The Listings themselves are intended to be only one small aspect of our discussion, because in the usual case you will focus on step 5 of the sequential evaluation process to show that your client is incapable of performing jobs existing in significant numbers, not the Listing step, step 3. The more medical knowledge you have about these impairments, the better you will be able to understand medical reports, identify medical issues, and discuss medical matters with doctors.

SSA likes to pretend that disability analysis is predominantly a medical determination. While it is true that it is a medical determination to find that a claimant's impairment meets a Listing, it is usually a hoax when SSA uses "medical signs and findings" to deny a claimant's case. Medical signs and findings are an essential element of a claimant's case; but they only set the parameters. Within limits dictated by the medical impairment, RFC determinations are matters subject to proof at a hearing at which the claimant's testimony and lay witness evidence are considered. *Cf.* SSRs 96-2p and 96-7p and 20 C.F.R. § 404.1527(c) on credibility and weighing medical opinions. To recognize when SSA is overreaching in characterizing its determinations as based on "medical signs and findings," or, on the other hand, to know when a treating physician is "leaning over backwards" [*cf. Stephens v. Heckler*, 766 F.2d 284, 289 (7th Cir. 1985)] to conclude that a claimant has an extremely restricted RFC, you must be familiar with the medical limits.

The same medical issues surface again and again in Social Security disability cases. You will inevitably collect medical articles, charts, your own notes, and other materials pertinent to particular conditions that you will use over and over. Set up a filing system for such things following the organization of the Listing Impairments.

We provide the most extensive discussion on the four most common causes of disability—low back pain, heart conditions, neurological impairments and mental impairments—the longest of which is that for mental impairments, §§240-249. Not only are there many mental impairment cases that reach hearing level, but also perhaps a majority of physical impairment cases include hidden psychological issues. Chronic physical problems take their psychological toll.

For several reasons, including their relative rarity at hearings, we have omitted a full discussion of the following impairments:

- **Genito-Urinary System, Listings §§ 6.00-6.09**

Although rarely seen at hearings, kidney problems that do not meet the Listings can, nevertheless, be disabling. Bladder problems that do not appear in the Listings are frequently brought up at hearings, either alone or in combination with other impairments.

Interstitial cystitis (IC), a chronic bladder condition with symptoms of urinary frequency (the need to urinate frequently), urinary urgency (an urgent need to urinate), and pelvic pain, which afflicts women 10 times more often than men, can limit a person's ability to work in a variety of ways: It can cause a person to need to urinate as often as every 10 to 15 minutes, requiring a nearby restroom, taking a worker away from the work station and disrupting work tasks. Associated pain, if severe, can interfere with attention and concentration needed to perform even simple tasks. Urinary frequency at night, called nocturia, can disrupt sleep, cause daytime drowsiness and impair concentration. Depression and anxiety, which often accompany this impairment, can limit social functioning and affect ability to complete tasks in a timely manner. Interstitial cystitis can affect a person's ability to perform exertional activities. It also may affect ability to do postural functions, such as climbing, balancing, stooping, and crouching. Many people with interstitial cystitis are essentially housebound.

SSR 15-1p, focuses on establishing whether a claimant's diagnosed interstitial cystitis meets SSA's criteria for a medically determinable impairment (MDI). SSR 15-1p notes:

> IC constitutes an MDI when producing appropriate symptoms and medical signs or laboratory findings, and may result in a disabling impairment. There are some signs and findings that could indicate IC, but there are no specific signs or findings that are universally accepted. However, for our program purposes, we are choosing to rely upon certain signs and findings to establish the existence of an MDI of IC.

While an earlier ruling, SSR 02-2p, noted that IC was a diagnosis of exclusion, SSR 15-1p states that SSA "cannot rely on the physician's diagnosis alone to establish an MDI of IC," observing that the "physician may make a diagnosis of IC based only on the person's reported symptoms, after examining the person and ruling out other diseases that could cause the symptoms." SSR 15-1p demands that there be medical signs or laboratory findings supporting the diagnosis, but lists the clinical finding, "suprapubic tenderness on physical examination," with "other symptoms." Here is the crucial part of SSR 15-1p that sets forth the medical signs or findings that SSA will accept:

> C. Medical signs. Medical signs can support a diagnosis of IC and help establish the MDI. These signs include the following, which can be detected during a medical procedure that stretches the bladder with fluid (cystoscopy under anesthesia with bladder distention):
>
> 1. Fibrosis (bladder-wall stiffening);
> 2. Diffuse glomerulations (pinpoint bleeding caused by recurrent irritation) on the bladder wall; and
> 3. Hunner's ulcers (patches of broken skin) on the bladder wall.
>
> D. Laboratory findings. Laboratory test findings can also support a diagnosis of IC. We will make every reasonable effort to obtain the results of appropriate laboratory testing. However, we will not purchase complex, costly, or invasive tests. Some laboratory tests and findings are more widely used and accepted than others. The following laboratory findings can help establish an

MDI of IC:

1. Repeated sterile urine cultures while IC symptoms continue;
2. Positive potassium sensitivity test (Parson's test); and
3. Antiproliferative factor (APF) accumulation in the urine.

E. Other signs and findings. Because of the ongoing research into the etiology and manifestations of IC, the medical criteria discussed above are only examples of signs and laboratory findings that help establish an MDI of IC; they are not all-inclusive. As medical research advances regarding IC, we may rely on other signs and laboratory findings to help establish an MDI of IC. For example, gene studies are exploring whether there are various subtypes of IC. Thus, we may document the existence of IC as an MDI with medical signs and laboratory findings other than those listed above, provided such evidence is consistent with medically accepted clinical practice and the other evidence in the case record.

Note that all of the medical signs listed in SSR 15-1p are discovered during cystoscopy under anesthesia with bladder distention. Yet, there may be many cases, perhaps a majority of cases, in which this procedure is not done. The American Urological Association says that "[c]ystoscopy and/or urodynamics should be considered as an aid to diagnosis only for complex presentations; these tests are not necessary for making the diagnosis in uncomplicated presentations." http://www.auanet.org/common/pdf/education/clinical-guidance/IC-Bladder-Pain-Syndrome-Revised.pdf. Thus, there will be many cases where the only clinical finding on physical examination is suprapubic tenderness and the only laboratory finding is repeated sterile urine cultures while symptoms of IC continue. Although such findings, along with a patient's history and description of symptoms, are enough to satisfy the American Urological Association and the National Institute of Digestive and Kidney Diseases at the National Institutes of Health (http://kidney.niddk.nih.gov/KUDiseases/pubs/interstitialcystitis/index.aspx), in cases with these findings, you may find yourself arguing with the ALJ over whether your client's diagnosed interstitial cystitis is a medically determinable impairment.

Don't forget that when dealing with other impairments tenderness on palpation is a finding. Thus, there is no basis for treating suprapubic tenderness on physical examination as a symptom. In addition, sometimes patients' descriptions of symptom complexes, when interpreted by physicians, can be a considered signs. See SSR 96-4p, footnote 2, and the Daniels memorandum, Appendix 13.

A general Bladder Problem Medical Source Statement, which includes limitations as a result of incontinence, appears at §230.1. A specific Interstitial Cystitis Medical Source Statement that includes the requirements of SSR 15-1p appears at §230.1.1, except that we show suprapubic tenderness on examination as a clinical finding. See also §268.

- Cancer (Malignant **Neoplastic Diseases), Listings §§ 13.00-13.29**

Cancer is usually found to be disabling based on medical signs and findings by the state agency. When the cancer is in remission, fatigue may remain as a residual symptom of the disease, resulting from treatment or psychological factors. *See* the discussion of fatigue at §239, accompanying our discussion of multiple sclerosis (M.S.). A Post Cancer Treatment Medical Source Statement appears at §230.5. A Leukemia Medical Assessment form is included on Digital Access as 230C.

- **Immune System Disorders, Listings §§ 14.00-14.10**

Impairments involving the immune system—including systemic lupus erythematosus, systemic vasculitis, systemic sclerosis (scleroderma), polymyositis or dermatomyositis, undifferentiated and mixed connective tissue disease, immune deficiency disorders, HIV infection, inflammatory arthritis, and Sjögren's syndrome—appear in section 14 of the Listings. Each of the immune system disorders provides alternate criteria for meeting the Listings that includes at least two of the constitutional symptoms (severe fatigue, fever, malaise, or involuntary weight loss) and "marked" functional limitations in either activities of daily living, maintaining social functioning or completing tasks in a timely manner due to deficiencies in concentration, persistence, or pace.

An Auto Immune Disorder Medical Assessment form is included as 230A on Digital Access. A questionnaire for Connective Tissue Disorder, an immune system disorder, Listing 14.06, is included on Digital Access as 230D.

- **Systemic Lupus Erythematosus (SLE)**

Systemic lupus erythematosus (SLE), which appears in § 14.02 of the Listings, is a chronic inflammatory disease that can affect virtually any organ or body system. Claimants usually complain about fatigue, fever, or malaise. Musculoskeletal complaints are common. Sometimes claimants with SLE complain about what SSA calls "fluctuating cognition ('lupus fog')," which SSA accepts as a sign of mental involvement. *See* § 14.00D.1.a. A rheumatologist usually is in charge of treatment of the disease, but other doctors may be involved in treating lupus flares that affect other organs or body systems. To meet § 14.02A of the Listings, a claimant must have involvement of two or more organs or body systems with one of them involved to at least a moderate level of severity. In addition, at least two of what SSA calls the "constitutional symptoms or signs" must be present—severe fatigue, fever, malaise, or involuntary weight loss. *See* § 14.00C.2.

To meet Listing § 14.02B, a claimant must have *repeated* manifestations of SLE, at least two of the constitutional symptoms (severe fatigue, fever, malaise, or involuntary weight loss) and "marked" functional limitations in either activities of daily living, maintaining social functioning, or completing tasks in a timely manner due to deficiencies in concentration, persistence, or pace. "Repeated" is defined in § 14.00I.3 of the Listings as follows:

> 3. As used in these listings, "repeated" means that the manifestations occur on an average of three times a year, or once every 4 months, each lasting 2 weeks or more; or the manifestations do not last for 2 weeks but occur substantially more frequently than three times in a year or once every 4 months; or they occur less frequently than an average of three times a year or once every 4 months but last substantially longer than 2 weeks. Your impairment will satisfy this criterion regardless of whether you have the same kind of manifestation repeatedly, all different manifestations, or any other combination of manifestations; for example, two of the same kind of manifestation and a different one. You must have the required number of manifestations with the frequency and duration required in this section. Also, the manifestations must occur within the period covered by your claim.

A Lupus (SLE) Medical Source Statement designed to also address some Listings issues appears at §230.2. Lupus in its manifestation at less than Listing level often involves fatigue as a primary symptom. In this way Lupus is like chronic fatigue syndrome, an impairment that does not appear in the Listings. Both impairments must be evaluated based on the totality of the evidence.

- **HIV Infection**

Fatigue also can be an issue in evaluating the severity of HIV infection in the sort of HIV case one is most likely to see at a hearing. Listing §14.08K provides for a finding of disability where there are repeated manifestations of HIV infection that do not meet the other very specific HIV Listings (§14.08A-J) resulting in "significant documented symptoms or signs (for example, severe fatigue, fever, malaise, involuntary weight loss, pain, night sweats, nausea, vomiting, headaches, or insomnia)" and one of the following at the "marked" level:

> 1. Limitation of activities of daily living; or
> 2. Limitations in maintaining social functioning; or
> 3. Limitation in completing tasks in a timely manner due to deficiencies in concentration, persistence, or pace.

Social Security Ruling 93-2p provides that one who has documentation of HIV infection as described in former Listing §14.00D3, now §14.00F1, (which appears to be broad enough to include any legitimate diagnosis of HIV infection, even where definitive laboratory evidence is unavailable) has an impairment that is considered permanent or is expected to result in death. Thus, no separate finding concerning the duration of the impairment is required. An HIV Medical Assessment form is included as 230B on Digital Access.

- **Chronic Fatigue Syndrome**

SSR 14-1p, a ruling addressing the requirements for proving disability based on chronic fatigue syndrome, is primarily concerned with the requirement stated in the Social Security Act and regulations that a " physical or men-tal impairment must be established by medical evidence consisting of signs, symptoms, and laboratory findings, not only by your statement of symptoms." 20 C.F.R. § 404.1508. The ruling provides a long list of possible objective findings, any one of which will demonstrate the existence of a medically determinable impairment. As a rule, in any genuine chronic fatigue syndrome case, you will discover the necessary objective findings in the medical records. For example, many people with chronic fatigue syndrome may have "tender point" findings similar to those in fi-bromyalgia cases. SSR 14-1p, note 21, states that while fibromyalgia has a requirement of a minimum number of tender points to establish the diagnosis, SSA "may still find that a person with CFS has [a medically determinable impairment] if he or she does not have the specified number of tender points to establish" fibromyalgia.

The Chronic Fatigue Syndrome Medical Source Statement, §230.3, includes questions to demonstrate that the medically determinable impairment requirement of SSR 14-1p is met.

- **Dizziness**

Sometimes you'll see a claim where the primary disabling impairment is dizziness but there are diagnostic uncertainties about the source of the dizziness. Dizziness can be related to many different impairments—labyrinthine-vestibular dysfunction (such as Meniere's disease, see §232), cardiac, neurological disorders, a tumor, metabolic disorders, side-effects of medication or even psychiatric disorders. When you don't know what specific medical source statement to send to a doctor, use the Dizziness Medical Source Statement form at §230.4.

§230.1 Form: Bladder Problem Medical Source Statement

BLADDER PROBLEM MEDICAL SOURCE STATEMENT

From: ______________________________

Re: ______________________________ (Name of Patient)

______________________________ (Date of Birth)

Please answer the following questions concerning your patient's impairments:

1. Frequency and length of contact: ______________________________
2. Diagnoses: ______________________________
3. Prognosis: ______________________________
4. List your patient's symptoms, including urinary frequency, urinary incontinence, etc.:

   ____

   ____

5. Identify the clinical findings and objective signs:

   ____

   ____

6. Describe the treatment and response including any side effects of medication that may have implications for working, e.g., drowsiness, dizziness, nausea, etc.:

   ____

   ____

7. Have your patient's impairments lasted or can they be expected to last at least twelve months? ☐ Yes ☐ No

8. Do emotional factors contribute to the severity of your patient's symptoms and functional limitations? ☐ Yes ☐ No

9. Identify any psychological conditions affecting your patient's physical condition:

□ Depression □ Anxiety
□ Psychological factors affecting physical condition □ Personality disorder
□ Other: ____________________

10. Does your patient have urinary frequency? □ Yes □ No

If yes, please estimate approximately how often your patient must urinate. __________

11. Does your patient have urinary incontinence? □ Yes □ No

If yes, a) please estimate approximately how often your your patient is incontinent: __________

b) please estimate the volume of urine involved: __________

12. What makes your patient's urinary frequency/ incontinence better?

____

13. What makes your patient's urinary frequency/ incontinence worse?

____

14. To what degree can your patient tolerate work stress?

□ Incapable of even "low stress" work □ Capable of low stress work
□ Capable of moderate stress - normal work □ Capable of high stress work

Please explain the reasons for your conclusion: ____________________

15. As a result of your patient's impairments, estimate your patient's functional limitations if your patient were placed in a ***competitive work situation.***

a. How many city blocks can your patient walk without stopping? ______

b. Please circle the hours and/or minutes that your patient can sit ***at one time,*** e.g., before needing to get up, etc.

Sit: 0 5 10 15 20 30 45 (Minutes) 1 2 More than 2 (Hours)

c. Please circle the hours and/or minutes that your patient can stand ***at one time***, e.g., before needing to sit down, walk around, etc.

Stand: 0 5 10 15 20 30 45 (Minutes) 1 2 More than 2 (Hours)

d. Please indicate how long your patient can sit and stand/ walk ***total in an 8 hour working day*** (with normal breaks):

Sit	Stand/walk	
□	□	less than 2 hours
□	□	about 2 hours
□	□	about 4 hours
□	□	at least 6 hours

e. Does your patient need a job that permits shifting positions ***at will*** from sitting, standing or walking? □ Yes □ No

f. Does your patient need a job that permits ready access to a restroom?
□ Yes □ No

g. Will your patient sometimes need to take *unscheduled* restroom breaks during a working day? □ Yes □ No

If yes, 1) how ***often*** do you think this will happen? ____________________

2) how ***long*** will your patient be away from the work station for an average unscheduled restroom break? ____________________

3) how much advance notice does your patient have of the need for a restroom break? ____________________

h. Will your patient sometimes need to clean up and change clothes following urinary incontinence during an 8-hour working day? □ Yes □ No

If yes, how ***often*** do you think this will happen? ____________________

For this and other questions on this form, "rarely" means 1% to 5% of an 8-hour working day; "occasionally" means 6% to 33% of an 8-hour working day; "frequently" means 34% to 66% of an 8-hour working day.

i. How many pounds can your patient lift and carry in a competitive work situation?

	Never	**Rarely**	**Occasionally**	**Frequently**
Less than 10 lbs.	□	□	□	□
10 lbs.	□	□	□	□
20 lbs.	□	□	□	□
50 lbs.	□	□	□	□

j. How often can your patient perform the following activities?

	Never	**Rarely**	**Occasionally**	**Frequently**
Twist	□	□	□	□
Stoop (bend)	□	□	□	□
Crouch/ squat	□	□	□	□
Climb ladders	□	□	□	□
Climb stairs	□	□	□	□

k. How much is your patient likely to be ***"off task"***? That is, what percentage of a typical workday would your patient's symptoms likely be severe enough to interfere with ***attention and concentration*** needed to perform even simple work tasks?

□ 0% □ 5% □ 10% □ 15% □ 20% □ 25% or more

l. Are your patient's impairments likely to produce "good days" and "bad days"?

□ Yes □ No

If yes, assuming your patient was trying to work full time, please estimate, on the average, how many days per month your patient is likely to be absent from work as a result of the impairments:

□ Never □ About three days per month
□ About one day per month □ About four days per month
□ About two days per month □ More than four days per month

16. Are your patient's impairment's (physical impairments plus any emotional impairments) as demonstrated by signs, clinical findings and laboratory or test results ***reasonably consistent*** with the symptoms and functional limitations described in this evaluation?

☐ Yes ☐ No

If no, please explain: ______________________________

17. Please describe any other limitations (such as limitations using hands, arms, fingers, psychological limitations, limited vision, difficulty hearing, need to avoid temperature extremes, wetness, humidity, noise, dust, fumes, gases or hazards, etc.) that would affect your patient's ability to work at a regular job on a sustained basis:

____

____

____

______________________ ______________________
Date *Signature*

Printed/Typed Name: ______________________

Address: ______________________

____

____

§230.1.1 Form: Interstitial Cystitis Medical Source Statement

INTERSTITIAL CYSTITIS MEDICAL SOURCE STATEMENT

From: ______________________________

Re: ______________________________ (Name of Patient)

______________________________ (Date of Birth)

Please answer the following questions concerning your patient's impairments:

1. Frequency and length of contact: ____

2. Does your patient have Interstitial Cystitis? □ Yes □ No

3. Identify your patient's ***symptoms***:

□ Urinary frequency
□ Urinary urgency
□ Anxiety
□ Depression
□ Sexual dysfunction
□ Bladder/ pelvic pain
□ Low back pain
□ Thigh pain
□ Vaginal pain
□ Chronic fatigue or tiredness
□ Nocturia with disrupted sleep
□ Daytime drowsiness & lack of mental clarity

Other symptoms: ____

4. Identify the clinical findings and objective signs:

□ Suprapubic tenderness on physical examination
□ Fibrosis (bladder wall stiffening) detected during hydrodistention
□ Hunner's ulcers on the bladder wall detected during hydrodistention
□ Diffuse glomerulations (pinpoint bleeding caused by recurrent irritation on the bladder wall) detected during hydrodistention
□ Absence of infection or other disorders that could cause the symptoms

Other findings: ____

5. Identify any associated disorders:

□ Inflammatory bowel disease
□ Chronic fatigue syndrome
□ Systemic lupus erythematosus
□ Chronic headaches
□ Allergies
□ Irritable bowel syndrome
□ Vulvodynia
□ Sjögren's syndrome
□ Fibromyalgia
□ Endometriosis

6. Other diagnoses: ____

7. Prognosis:____

8. Describe the treatment and response including any side effects of medication that may have implications for working, e.g., drowsiness, dizziness, nausea, etc.:

____

____

9. Have your patient's impairments lasted or can they be expected to last at least twelve months? □ Yes □ No

10. Do emotional factors contribute to the severity of your patient's symptoms and functional limitations? □ Yes □ No

11. Identify any psychological conditions affecting your patient's physical condition:

□ Depression
□ Somatoform disorder
□ Psychological factors affecting physical condition
□ Anxiety
□ Personality disorder
□ Other: ____________________

12. If your patient has urinary frequency, please estimate approximately how often your patient must urinate. __________

13. As a result of your patient's impairments, estimate your patient's functional limitations if your patient were placed in a ***competitive work situation***.

a. How many city blocks can your patient walk without stopping? ________________

b. Please circle the hours and/or minutes that your patient can sit ***at one time,*** e.g., before needing to get up, etc.

Sit: 0 5 10 15 20 30 45 (Minutes) 1 2 More than 2 (Hours)

c. Please circle the hours and/or minutes that your patient can stand ***at one time***, e.g., before needing to sit down, walk around, etc.

Stand: 0 5 10 15 20 30 45 (Minutes) 1 2 More than 2 (Hours)

d. Please indicate how long your patient can sit and stand/walk ***total in an 8 hour working day*** (with normal breaks):

Sit	Stand/walk	
☐	☐	less than 2 hours
☐	☐	about 2 hours
☐	☐	about 4 hours
☐	☐	at least 6 hours

e. Does your patient need a job that permits shifting positions ***at will*** from sitting, standing or walking? ☐ Yes ☐ No

f. Does your patient need a job that permits ready access to a restroom?
☐ Yes ☐ No

g. Will your patient sometimes need to take *unscheduled* restroom breaks during a working day? ☐ Yes ☐ No

If yes, 1) how ***often*** do you think this will happen? ______________________

2) how ***long*** will your patient be away from the work station for an average unscheduled restroom break? ______________________

3) how much advance notice does your patient have of the need for a restroom break? ______________________

For this and other questions on this form, "rarely" means 1% to 5% of an 8-hour working day; "occasionally" means 6% to 33% of an 8-hour working day; "frequently" means 34% to 66% of an 8-hour working day.

h. How many pounds can your patient lift and carry in a competitive work situation?

	Never	Rarely	Occasionally	Frequently
Less than 10 lbs.	☐	☐	☐	☐
10 lbs.	☐	☐	☐	☐
20 lbs.	☐	☐	☐	☐
50 lbs.	☐	☐	☐	☐

i. How often can your patient perform the following activities?

	Never	Rarely	Occasionally	Frequently
Twist	□	□	□	□
Stoop (bend)	□	□	□	□
Crouch/ squat	□	□	□	□
Climb ladders	□	□	□	□
Climb stairs	□	□	□	□

j. How much is your patient likely to be ***"off task"***? That is, what percentage of a typical workday would your patient's symptoms likely be severe enough to interfere with ***attention and concentration*** needed to perform even simple work tasks?

□ 0% □ 5% □ 10% □ 15% □ 20% □ 25% or more

Please explain the reasons for your conclusion: ______________________________

____

k. To what degree can your patient tolerate work stress?

□ Incapable of even "low stress" jobs □ Capable of low stress jobs
□ Moderate stress is okay □ Capable of high stress work

Please explain the reasons for your conclusion: ______________________________

____

l. Are your patient's impairments likely to produce "good days" and "bad days"?
□ Yes □ No

If yes, assuming your patient is trying to work full time, please estimate, on the average, how many days per month your patient is likely to be absent from work as a result of the impairments:

□ Never □ About three days per month
□ About one day per month □ About four days per month
□ About two days per month □ More than four days per month

16. Are your patient's impairment's (physical impairments plus any emotional impairments) as demonstrated by signs, clinical findings and laboratory or test results ***reasonably consistent*** with the symptoms and functional limitations described in this evaluation?

If no, please explain:____

17. Please describe any other limitations (such as limitations involving urinary incontinence, limitations using hands, arms, fingers, psychological limitations, limited vision, difficulty hearing, need to avoid temperature extremes, wetness, humidity, noise, dust, fumes, gases or hazards, etc.) that would affect your patient's ability to work at a regular job on a sustained basis:

____

____

____

____

______________________ ______________________

Date *Signature*

Printed/Typed Name: ______________________

Address: ______________________

____

____

7-51IC
7/16
§230.1.1

§230.2 Form: Lupus (SLE) Medical Source Statement

LUPUS (SLE) MEDICAL SOURCE STATEMENT

From: ______________________________

Re: ______________________________(Name of Patient)

______________________________(Date of Birth)

Please answer the following questions concerning your patient's impairments:

1. Frequency and length of contact: ______________________________

2. Does your patient fulfill the diagnostic criteria for systemic lupus erythematosus (SLE) identified by the American College of Rheumatology?

   □ Yes □ No

3. Other diagnoses: ______________________________

   ____

4. Identify clinical findings, laboratory and test results that show the severity of your patient's impairment:

   ____

   ____

   ____

5. Identify any constitutional symptoms:

□	Severe fatigue	□	Fever
□	Involuntary weight loss	□	Malaise[1]

6. List your patient's other symptoms:

   ____

   ____

   ____

7. Do emotional factors contribute to the severity of your patient's symptoms and functional limitations? □ Yes □ No

____

1 Malaise is defined as frequent feelings of illness, bodily discomfort, or lack of well-being that result in significantly reduced physical activity or mental function.

8. Identify prescribed medications and side effects that may affect working, *e.g.*, sedation, drowsiness, fatigue, lethargy, malaise, irritability, nausea, dizziness, *etc.*

____

____

9. Identify Major Organ or Body System Involvement ***at least to a moderate degree:***

☐		**Respiratory**	☐		**Renal** - Glomerulonephritis
	☐	Pleuritis	☐		**Neurologic** - Seizures
	☐	Pneumonitis	☐		**Mental**
☐		**Cardiovascular**		☐	Anxiety
	☐	Endocarditis		☐	Fluctuating cognition – lupus fog
	☐	Myocarditis		☐	Mood disorders
	☐	Pericarditis		☐	Organic brain syndrome
	☐	Vasculitis		☐	Psychosis
☐		**Hematologic**	☐		**Other immune system disorder**
	☐	Anemia		☐	Inflammatory arthritis
	☐	Leukopenia		☐	Sjögren's syndrome
	☐	Thrombocytopenia	☐		**Skin**

10. Have your patient's impairments lasted or can they be expected to last at least 12 months?
☐ Yes ☐ No

11. Prognosis: ____

12. As a result of your patient's impairments, estimate your patient's functional limitations if your patient were placed in a ***competitive work situation***:

a. Does your patient have the stamina and endurance to work an easy job 8 hours per day 5 days per week (with normal breaks every two hours)?
☐ Yes ☐ No

If no, please explain the reasons for your conclusion: ______________________

b. Does your patient need a job that permits shifting positions ***at will*** from sitting, standing or walking? ☐ Yes ☐ No

c. Does your patient need to include periods of walking around during an 8-hour working day? ☐ Yes ☐ No

1) If yes, approximately how ***often*** must your patient walk?

1 5 10 15 20 30 45 60 90
Minutes

2) How ***long*** must your patient walk each time?

1 2 3 4 5 6 7 8 9 10 11 12 13 14 15
Minutes

d. In addition to normal breaks every two hours, will your patient sometimes need to take *unscheduled* breaks during a working day? □ Yes □ No

If yes, 1) approx. how ***often*** do you think this will happen? ________________

2) approx. how ***long*** (on average) will each break last? ________________

3) what symptoms cause a need for breaks?

□ Muscle weakness □ Pain/ paresthesias, numbness
□ Chronic fatigue □ Adverse effects of medication
□ Other: ______________________________________

e. While engaging in occasional standing/walking, must your patient use a cane or other assistive device? Yes No

If yes, what symptoms cause the need for a cane?

□ Imbalance □ Pain □ Weakness
□ Insecurity □ Dizziness
□ Other: ______________________________________

f. With prolonged sitting, should your patient's leg(s) be elevated? □ Yes □ No

If yes, 1) how ***high*** should the leg(s) be elevated? ________________

2) if your patient had a sedentary job, ***what percentage of time*** during an 8-hour working day should the leg(s) be elevated? ________________%

3) what symptoms cause a need to elevate leg(s)? ________________

g. If your patient has significant limitations with reaching, handling or fingering, please indicate the percentage of time during an 8-hour working day that your patient can use hands/fingers/arms for the following activities

	HANDS: Grasp, Turn Twist Objects	**FINGERS: Fine Manipulations**	**ARMS: Reaching In Front of Body**	**ARMS: Reaching Overhead**
Right:	%	%	%	%
Left:	%	%	%	%

h. State the degree to which your patient should avoid the following:

ENVIRONMENTAL RESTRICTIONS	**NO RESTRICTIONS**	**AVOID CONCENTRATED EXPOSURE**	**AVOID EVEN MODERATE EXPOSURE**	**AVOID ALL EXPOSURE**
Extreme cold	☐	☐	☐	☐
Extreme heat	☐	☐	☐	☐
High humidity	☐	☐	☐	☐
Wetness	☐	☐	☐	☐
Cigarette smoke	☐	☐	☐	☐
Perfumes	☐	☐	☐	☐
Soldering fluxes	☐	☐	☐	☐
Solvents/cleaners	☐	☐	☐	☐
Fumes, odors, gases	☐	☐	☐	☐
Dust	☐	☐	☐	☐
Chemicals	☐	☐	☐	☐
List other irritants:	☐	☐	☐	☐

i. How much is your patient likely to be ***"off task"***? That is, what percentage of a typical workday would your patient's symptoms likely be severe enough to interfere with ***attention and concentration*** needed to perform even simple work tasks?

☐ 0% ☐ 5% ☐ 10% ☐ 15% ☐ 20% ☐ 25% or more

j. To what degree can your patient tolerate work stress?

☐ Incapable of even "low stress" work ☐ Capable of low stress work
☐ Capable of moderate stress - normal work ☐ Capable of high stress work

Please explain the reasons for your conclusion: ____________________________

k. Are your patient's impairments likely to produce "good days" and "bad days"?

□ Yes □ No

If yes, assuming your patient was trying to work full time, please estimate, on the average, how many days per month your patient is likely to be absent from work as a result of the impairments:

□ Never	□ About three days per month
□ About one day per month	□About four days per month
□ About two days per month	□More than four days per month

l. Indicate to what degree the following functional limitations exist as a result of your patient's impairments. *Note*: **Marked** means more than moderate but less than extreme. A marked limitation my arise when several activities or functions are impaired or even when only one is impaired, so long as the degree of limitation is such as to seriously interfere with the ability to function independently, appropriately, effectively, and on a sustained basis.

	FUNCTIONAL LIMITATION				
A.	Limitation of activities of daily living	None or Mild	Moderate	Marked	Extreme
B.	Limitation in maintaining social functioning	None or Mild	Moderate	Marked	Extreme
C.	Limitation in completing tasks in a timely manner due to deficiencies in concentration, persistence or pace	None or Mild	Moderate	Marked	Extreme

13. Are your patient's impairments (physical impairments plus any emotional impairments) as demonstrated by signs, clinical findings and laboratory or test results ***reasonably consistent*** with the symptoms and functional limitations described above in this evaluation?

□ Yes □ No

If no, please explain: ____

14. Please describe any other limitations (such as psychological limitations, limited vision, difficulty hearing, etc.) that would affect your patient's ability to work at a regular job on a sustained basis:

____

____

____

______________________ ______________________

Date *Signature*

7-48
§230.2
2/17

Printed/Typed Name: ______________________

Address: ______________________

____

____

§230.3 Form: Chronic Fatigue Syndrome Medical Source Statement

CHRONIC FATIGUE SYNDROME MEDICAL SOURCE STATEMENT

From: ______________________________

Re: ______________________________(Name of Patient)

______________________________(Date of Birth)

Please answer the following questions concerning your patient's impairments:

1. Frequency and length of contact:______________________________

2. Does your patient have Chronic Fatigue Syndrome? □ Yes □ No

3. Other diagnoses:______________________________

4. Prognosis:______________________________

5. Have your patient's impairments lasted or can they be expected to last at least twelve months? □ Yes □No

6. Does your patient have unexplained persistent or relapsing chronic fatigue that is of new or definite onset (has not been lifelong), is not the result of ongoing exertion, and results in substantial reduction in previous levels of occupational, educational, social, or personal activities? □ Yes □ No

   If yes, please describe your patient's history of fatigue.

   ____

   ____

   ____

7. Have you been able to exclude any other impairments as a cause for your patient's fatigue such as HIV-AIDS, malignancy, parasitic disease (Lyme Disease), psychiatric disease, rheumatoid arthritis, drug or alcohol addiction or abuse, side effects of medications, etc.? □ Yes □ No

If yes, identify which impairments you have excluded and on what basis.

____

____

____

8. Does your patient have ***concurrent occurrence of four or more*** of the following symptoms that persisted or recurred during six or more consecutive months of illness and did not predate the fatigue? Yes No

If yes, identify the ***symptoms***:

- ☐ Post-exertional malaise lasting more than 24 hours;
- ☐ Self-reported impairment in short-term memory or concentration severe enough to cause substantial reduction in previous levels of occupational, educational, social or personal activities:
- ☐ Sore throat;
- ☐ Tender cervical or axillary lymph nodes;
- ☐ Muscle pain;
- ☐ Multiple joint pain without joint swelling or redness;
- ☐ Headaches of a new type, pattern or severity;
- ☐ Unrefreshing sleep.

9. Indicate which, if any, of the following additional symptoms are present:

☐ Muscle weakness;

☐ Disturbed sleep patterns (for example, insomnia, prolonged sleeping, frequent awakenings, or vivid dreams or nightmares);

☐ Visual difficulties (for example, trouble focusing, impaired depth perception, severe photosensitivity, or eye pain);

☐ Orthostatic intolerance (for example, lightheadedness, fainting, dizziness, or increased fatigue with prolonged standing);

☐ Respiratory difficulties (for example, labored breathing or sudden breathlessness);

☐ Cardiovascular abnormalities (for example, palpitations with or without cardiac arrhythmias);

☐ Gastrointestinal discomfort (for example, nausea, bloating, or abdominal pain); and

☐ Urinary or bladder problems (for example, urinary frequency, nocturia, dysuria, or pain in the bladder region).

10. Indicate which, if any, of the following are present:

☐ Fever; ☐ Involuntary weight loss; ☐ Malaise (defined as frequent
☐ feelings of illness, bodily discomfort, or lack of well-being that result in significantly reduced physical activity or mental function).

11. Indicate which, if any, of the following ***medical signs*** have been clinically documented over a period of at least six consecutive months:

☐ Palpably swollen or tender lymph nodes on physical examination;

☐ Nonexudative pharyngitis;

☐ Persistent reproducible muscle tenderness on repeated examinations, including the presence of positive tender points.

List any other ***medical signs*** that are consistent with medically acceptable clinical practice and are consistent with other evidence in the case record including frequent viral infections with prolonged recovery; sinusitis; ataxia; extreme pallor; and pronounced weight change:

____

____

12. Indicate which, if any, of the following ***laboratory findings*** are present:

    □ An elevated antibody titer to Epstein-Barr virus (EBV) capsid antigen equal to or greater than 1:5120, or early antigen equal to or greater than 1:640;

    □ An abnormal magnetic resonance imaging (MRI) brain scan;

    □ Neurally mediated hypotension as shown by tilt table testing or another clinically accepted form of testing.

    List any other ***laboratory findings*** that are consistent with medically accepted clinical practice and are consistent with other evidence in the case record; for example, an abnormal exercise stress test or abnormal sleep studies, appropriately evaluated and consistent with the other evidence in the case record:

    ____

13. Indicate which, if any, of the following ***mental findings*** have been documented by mental status examination or psychological testing:

    □ Short term memory deficit □ Information processing limitations

    □ Visual-spatial difficulties □ Comprehension problems

    □ Concentration limitations □ Anxiety

    □ Depression

    Identify any ***other mental findings*** suggesting persisting neurocognitive impairment:

    ____

14. Do emotional factors contribute to the severity of your patient's symptoms and functional limitations? □ Yes □ No

15. Treatment and response, including list of prescribed medications and their ***side effects***:

____

16. As a result of your patient's impairments, estimate your patient's functional limitations if your patient were placed in a ***competitive work situation***:

a. Does your patient have the stamina and endurance to work an easy job 8 hours per day 5 days per week (with normal breaks every two hours)?

☐ Yes ☐ No

If no, please explain the reasons for your conclusion: ______________________________

____

b. Does your patient need a job that permits shifting positions ***at will*** from sitting, standing or walking? ☐ Yes ☐ No

c. Does your patient need to include periods of walking around during an 8-hour working day? ☐ Yes ☐ No

1) If yes, approximately how ***often*** must your patient walk?

1 5 10 15 20 30 45 60 90
Minutes

2) How ***long*** must your patient walk each time?

1 2 3 4 5 6 7 8 9 10 11 12 13 14 15
Minutes

d. In addition to normal breaks every two hours, will your patient sometimes need to take *unscheduled* breaks during a working day? ☐ Yes ☐ No

If yes, 1) approx. how ***often*** do you think this will happen? ________________

2) approx. how ***long*** (on average) will each break last?________________

3) what symptoms cause a need for breaks?

☐ Muscle weakness ☐ Pain/ paresthesias, numbness
☐ Chronic fatigue ☐ Adverse effects of medication
☐ Other: ______________________________

e. With prolonged sitting, should your patient's leg(s) be elevated? □ Yes □ No

If yes, 1) how ***high*** should the leg(s) be elevated? ________________

2) if your patient had a sedentary job, ***what percentage of time*** during an 8-hour working day should the leg(s) be elevated? ________________%

f. Does your patient have significant limitations with reaching, handling or fingering?
□ Yes □ No

If yes, please indicate the percentage of time during an 8-hour working day that your patient can use hands/fingers/arms for the following activities:

	HANDS: Grasp, Turn Twist Objects	**FINGERS: Fine Manipulations**	**ARMS: Reaching In Front of Body**	**ARMS: Reaching Overhead**
Right:	%	%	%	%
Left:	%	%	%	%

g. How much is your patient likely to be ***"off task"***? That is, what percentage of a typical workday would your patient's symptoms likely be severe enough to interfere with ***attention and concentration*** needed to perform even simple work tasks?

□ 0% □ 5% □ 10% □ 15% □ 20% □ 25% or more

h. To what degree can your patient tolerate work stress?

□ Incapable of even "low stress" jobs □ Capable of low stress jobs
□ Moderate stress is okay □ Capable of high stress work

Please explain the reasons for your conclusion:________________________________

i. Are your patient's impairments likely to produce "good days" and "bad days"?
□ Yes □ No

If yes, assuming your patient was trying to work full time, please estimate, on the average, how many days per month your patient is likely to be absent from work as a result of the impairments:

□ Never
□ About one day per month
□ About two days per month
□ About three days per month
□ About four days per month
□ More than four days per month

j. Indicate to what degree the following functional limitations exist as a result of your patient's impairments. *Note*: **Marked** means more than moderate but less than extreme. A marked limitation my arise when several activities or functions are impaired or even when only one is impaired, so long as the degree of limitation is such as to seriously interfere with the ability to function independently, appropriately, effectively, and on a sustained basis.

FUNCTIONAL LIMITATION					
A.	Limitation of activities of daily living	None or Mild □	Moderate □	Marked □	Extreme □
B.	Limitation in maintaining social functioning	None or Mild □	Moderate □	Marked □	Extreme □
C.	Limitation in completing tasks in a timely manner due to deficiencies in concentration, persistence or pace	None or Mild □	Moderate □	Marked □	Extreme □

17. Are your patient's impairments (physical impairments plus any emotional impairments) as demonstrated by signs, clinical findings and laboratory or test results ***reasonably consistent*** with the symptoms and functional limitations described in this evaluation?

□ Yes □ No

If no, please explain:______________________________________

18. Please describe any other limitations (such as limited vision, difficulty hearing, need to avoid temperature extremes, wetness, humidity, noise, dust, fumes, gases or hazards, etc.) that would affect your patient's ability to work at a regular job on a sustained basis:

____

____

____

§230.4 Form: Dizziness Medical Source Statement

DIZZINESS MEDICAL SOURCE STATEMENT

From: ______________________________

Re: ______________________________ (Name of Patient)

______________________________ (Date of Birth)

Please answer the following questions concerning your patient's dizziness:

1. Frequency and length of contact:____

2. Diagnoses:____

____

____

____

____

____

3. Does your patient have dizziness? Yes No

4. If yes, what diagnosis is this dizziness related to? ________________________

____

____

5. What is the average frequency of your patient's dizziness episodes?

________ per week ________ per month

6. How long does a typical episode last? ______________________________

7. Does your patient always have a warning of impending dizziness? Yes No

If yes, how long is it between the warning and the onset of the dizziness?
________minutes

Can your patient always take safety precautions when he/she feels an episode coming on?
Yes No

8. Does dizziness occur at a particular time of the day? Yes No

   If yes, explain when dizziness occurs:______________________________

   ____

9. Are there precipitating factors such as stress, exertion? Yes No

   If yes, explain:______________________________________

10. Identify symptoms associated with your patient's dizziness episodes?

    Nausea/vomiting
    Malaise
    Photosensitivity
    Sensitivity to noise
    Hot flashes
    Visual disturbances
    Mood changes
    Mental confusion/inability to concentrate
    Fatigue/exhaustion
    Falling
    Other: ____

    ____

11. After the episode ends, are there any after effects?

    Check those that apply:

    Confusion
    Exhaustion
    Irritability
    Severe headache
    Muscle strain
    Paranoia
    Other: ______________________________

12. How long after an episode do these after effects last?____________________

13. Describe the degree to which dizziness episodes interfere with your patient's daily activities:

    ____

    ____

14. Does your patient have a history of injury during an episode? Yes No

15. Type of medication and response:________________________________

    ____

16. Will your patient need more supervision at work than an unimpaired worker?
Yes No

17. Can your patient work at heights? Yes No

18. Can your patient work with power machines that require an alert operator?
Yes No

19. Can your patient operate a motor vehicle? Yes No

20. Can your patient take a bus alone? Yes No

21. If your patient has any associated mental problems, please check those that apply:

Depression	Short attention span
Irritability	Memory problems
Social isolation	Behavior extremes
Poor self-esteem	Other: ________________

22. To what degree can your patient tolerate work stress?

Incapable of even "low stress" work	Capable of low stress work
Capable of moderate stress - normal work	Capable of high stress work

Please explain the reasons for your conclusion:________________

23. Will your patient sometimes need to take unscheduled breaks during an 8-hour working day?
Yes No

If yes, 1) how ***often*** do you think this will happen? ________________

2) how ***long*** (on average) will your patient have to rest before returning to work? ________________

24. How much is your patient likely to be ***"off task" while working***? That is, what percentage of a typical workday would your patient's symptoms likely be severe enough to interfere with ***attention and concentration*** needed to perform even simple work tasks?

0% 5% 10% 15% 20 % 25% or more

25. Are your patient's impairments likely to produce "good days" and "bad days"?
Yes No

If yes, assuming your patient was attempting to work full time, please estimate, on the average, how many days per month your patient is likely to be absent from work as a result of the impairments:

Never About three days per month
About one day per month About four days per month
About two days per month More than four days per month

26. Are your patient's impairments (physical impairments plus any emotional impairments) as demonstrated by signs, clinical findings and laboratory or test results ***reasonably consistent*** with the symptoms and functional limitations described above in this evaluation?

Yes No

If no, please explain: ____________________

27. Please describe any other limitations (such as limitations in the ability to sit, stand, walk, lift, bend, stoop, limitations in using arms, hands, fingers, limited vision, difficulty hearing, need to avoid temperature extremes, wetness, humidity, noise, dust, fumes, gases or hazards, etc.) that would affect your patient's ability to work at a regular job on a sustained basis.

____

____

28. Please describe any additional testing that would help clarify the severity of your patient's impairments and limitations.

____

____

____________________ ____________________
Date *Signature*

Printed/Typed Name: ____________________

Address: ____________________

____

____

7/16
230.4
7-58

§230.5 Form: Post Cancer Treatment Medical Source Statement

POST CANCER TREATMENT MEDICAL SOURCE STATEMENT

From: ______________________________

Re: ______________________________(Name of Patient)

______________________________(Date of Birth)

Please answer the following questions concerning your patient's impairments:

1. Frequency and length of contact:____

2. If your patient has been diagnosed with and treated for cancer,

   a. Please identify the type of cancer: ______ ________________________

b. Cancer status: □ Remission □ Other: ____________________________

c. Does your patient have ***chronic fatigue*** as a result of cancer or treatment (including radiation and/or chemotherapy)? □ Yes □ No

   d. Please identify your patient's other impairments that could cause or exacerbate your patient's chronic fatigue:

   □ HIV-AIDS □ Rheumatoid arthritis □ Depression
   □ Fibromyalgia □ Lyme disease □ Side effects of medications
   □ Chronic fatigue syndrome (CFS)
   □ Other ____

3. Other Diagnoses:____

4. Prognosis: ____

5. Please list ***signs and symptoms*** (other than fatigue) your patient has as a result of cancer or treatment?

   □ Muscle pain □ Chronic headaches □ Disturbed sleep
   □ Depression □ Anxiety □ Impaired memory
   □ Muscle weakness □ Impaired attention/concentration
   □ Lower extremity edema
   □ Other: ____

6. Identify any side effects of current medication that may have implications for working:___

____

7. Have your patient's impairments lasted or can they be expected to last at least twelve months? ☐ Yes ☐ No

8. Do emotional factors contribute to the severity of your patient's symptoms and functional limitations? ☐ Yes ☐ No

9. Identify any psychological conditions affecting your patient's physical condition:

☐ Depression	☐ Anxiety
☐ Somatic symptom disorder	☐ Personality disorder
☐ Psychological factors affecting physical condition	☐ Other: ____________________

10. As a result of your patient's impairments, estimate your patient's functional limitations if your patient were placed in a ***competitive work situation***.

a. How many city blocks can your patient walk ***at one time*** before stopping? ________

b. Please circle the hours and/or minutes that your patient can sit ***at one time,*** e.g., before needing to get up, etc.

Sit: 0 5 10 15 20 30 45 (Minutes) 1 2 More than 2 (Hours)

c. Please circle the hours and/or minutes that your patient can stand ***at one time***, e.g., before needing to sit down, walk around, etc.

Stand: 0 5 10 15 20 30 45 (Minutes) 1 2 More than 2 (Hours)

d. Please indicate how long your patient can sit and stand/walk ***total in an 8-hour working day*** (with normal breaks):

Sit	**Stand/walk**	
☐	☐	less than 2 hours
☐	☐	about 2 hours
☐	☐	about 4 hours
☐	☐	at least 6 hours

e. Is your patient capable of working an 8-hour working day, 40 hours per week?

□ Yes □ No

If no, approximately ***how many hours per week*** can your patient work?

10 15 20 25 30
Hours

f. Does your patient need a job that permits shifting positions at will from sitting, standing or walking? □ Yes □ No

g. If your patient's symptoms would likely cause the need to take ***unscheduled breaks*** to rest during a workday,

1) ***How many times*** during an average workday do you expect this to happen?

0 1 2 3 4 5 6 7 8 9 10, More than 10

2) ***How long*** (on average) will your patient have to rest before returning to work?

2 3 5 10 20 30 45 — Minutes
1 2 More than 2 — Hours

3) What symptoms cause a need for breaks?

□ Pain/arthralgia □ Fatigue □ Nausea
□ Medication side effects □ Other:______________________

h. With prolonged sitting, should your patient's leg(s) be elevated? □ Yes □ No

If yes, 1) how *high* should the leg(s) be elevated? _______________

2) if your patient had a sedentary job, *what percentage of time* during an 8 hour working day should the leg(s) be elevated? _______________%

For this and other questions on this form, "rarely" means 1% to 5% of an 8-hour working day; "occasionally" means 6% to 33% of an 8-hour working day; "frequently" means 34% to 66% of an 8-hour working day.

i. How many pounds can your patient lift and carry in a competitive work situation?

	Never	**Rarely**	**Occasionally**	**Frequently**
Less than 10 lbs.	□	□	□	□
10 lbs.	□	□	□	□
20 lbs.	□	□	□	□
50 lbs.	□	□	□	□

j. How often can your patient perform the following activities?

	Never	Rarely	Occasionally	Frequently
Twist	□	□	□	□
Stoop (bend)	□	□	□	□
Crouch/ squat	□	□	□	□
Climb ladders	□	□	□	□
Climb stairs	□	□	□	□

k. If your patient has significant limitations with reaching, handling or fingering, please indicate the percentage of time during an 8-hour working day that your patient can use hands/fingers/arms for the following activities:

	HANDS: **Grasp, Turn** **Twist Objects**	**FINGERS:** **Fine** **Manipulations**	**ARMS:** **Reaching** **In Front of Body**	**ARMS:** **Reaching** **Overhead**
Right:	%	%	%	%
Left:	%	%	%	%

l. How much is your patient likely to be ***"off task"***? That is, what percentage of a typical workday would your patient's symptoms likely be severe enough to interfere with ***attention and concentration*** needed to perform even simple work tasks?

□ 0% □ 5% □ 10% □ 15% □ 20% □ 25% or more

m. To what degree can your patient tolerate work stress?

□ Incapable of even "low stress" work □ Capable of low stress work
□ Capable of moderate stress - normal work □ Capable of high stress work

Please explain the reasons for your conclusion: ______________________________

n. Are your patient's impairments likely to produce "good days" and "bad days"?

□ Yes □ No

If yes, assuming your patient was trying to work full time, please estimate, on the average, how many days per month your patient is likely to be absent from work as a result of the impairments:

□ Never	□ About three days per month
□ About one day per month	□ About four days per month
□ About two days per month	□ More than four days per month

11. Are your patient's impairments (physical impairments plus any emotional impairments) as demonstrated by signs, clinical findings and laboratory or test results ***reasonably consistent*** with the symptoms and functional limitations described above in this evaluation?

□ Yes □ No

If no, please explain: ____

12. Please describe any other limitations (such as psychological limitations, limited vision, difficulty hearing, need to avoid temperature extremes, wetness, humidity, noise, dust, fumes, gases or hazards, etc.) that would affect your patient's ability to work at a regular job on a sustained basis:

____

____

____

______________________________ ______________________________

Date *Signature*

Printed/Typed Name: ______________________________

Address: ______________________________

____

____

7-49-1
1/17
§230.5

§231 Musculoskeletal System, Listings §§ 1.00-1.08

Listings

Note that when symptoms such as pain appear as an element in the musculoskeletal Listings, any pain will do. It is not necessary to quantify it, or to evaluate its intensity or functionally limiting effects to determine if the Listing is met unless the Listing itself states otherwise. *See* 20 C.F.R. § 404.1529(d)(2). None of the musculoskeletal Listings require anything more than the presence of pain, though § 1.04A (spinal nerve root compression) requires "neuro-anatomic distribution of pain"; § 1.04B (arachnoiditis) requires "severe burning or painful dysesthesia"; and § 1.04C (spinal stenosis) requires "chronic nonradicular pain."

Six of the thirteen musculoskeletal Listings focus on inability to ambulate effectively on a sustained basis. This is described in the introductory section of the musculoskeletal Listing, § 1.00B2b, as follows:

> b. *What We Mean by Inability to Ambulate Effectively*
>
> (1) *Definition.* Inability to ambulate effectively means an extreme limitation of the ability to walk; *i.e.*, an impairment(s) that interferes very seriously with the individual's ability to independently initiate, sustain, or complete activities. Ineffective ambulation is defined generally as having insufficient lower extremity functioning (see 1.00J) to permit independent ambulation without the use of a hand-held assistive device(s) that limits the functioning of both upper extremities. (Listing 1.05C is an exception to this general definition because the individual has the use of only one upper extremity due to amputation of a hand.)
>
> (2) *To ambulate effectively.* Individuals must be capable of sustaining a reasonable walking pace over a sufficient distance to be able to carry out activities of daily living. They must have the ability to travel without companion assistance to and from a place of employment or school. Therefore, examples of ineffective ambulation include, but are not limited to, the inability to walk without the use of a walker, two crutches or two canes, the inability to walk a block at a reasonable pace on rough or uneven surfaces, the inability to use standard public transportation, the inability to carry out routine ambulatory activities, such as shopping and banking, and the inability to climb a few steps at a reasonable pace with the use of a single hand rail. The ability to walk independently about one's home without the use of assistive devices does not, in and of itself, constitute effective ambulation.

Despite the language in § 1.00B2b(1) that appears at first glance to require a walker or two canes to meet the criteria, when these musculoskeletal Listings were published in the Federal Register, SSA said that the "criteria do not require an individual to use an assistive device on any kind. The first sentence of final § 1.00B2b stresses that '[i]nability to ambulate effectively means an extreme limitation of the ability to walk.' The ensuing explanation and examples should make it clear that this applies to anyone who cannot walk adequately. The explanation is intended to mean that individuals who can only walk with the aid of hand-held assistive devices requiring the use of both upper extremities would meet the definition of inability to ambulate effectively. In addition, anyone with an ineffective gait who cannot use assistive devices would also meet the definition of inability to ambulate effectively .... Thus, we recognize that individuals with extreme inability to ambulate do not necessarily use assistive devices. Furthermore, we recognize that an individual who uses a cane may be disabled." 66 Fed. Reg. 58026-58027 (2001).

SSA's Office of Disability issued a series of Q & A's as part of a training program on the musculoskeletal Listings. One question was: "Can there be situations where there is ineffective ambulation that meets Listing § 1.02A when only one extremity is involved and only one cane or crutch is used?" Answer: "The use of a cane(s) or crutch(es) is not a requirement to meet this listing .... It is important to remember that it is the medical inability to ambulate effectively, not the use of an assistive device(s), that establishes listing level severity. Therefore, when the listing criteria are met, a claimant's impairment can meet § 1.02A even if he or she is not using any assistive device."

Another question: "Since the new listings require the use of two canes, how do we evaluate a person who uses only one cane?" Answer: "The use of two canes was given as an example. The key to the new listings is the inability to ambulate effectively. An individual can meet the listings by virtue of being unable to ambulate effectively even if [he or she] use[s] no assistive device."

Thus, always ask your client if he or she can walk a block at a reasonable pace on rough or uneven surfaces.

With the exception of lumbar spinal stenosis resulting in pseudoclaudication, § 1.04C, disorders of the spine do not require proof of inability to ambulate effectively to meet the Listings. To meet the criteria of § 1.04A, quoted at §231.1, which deals with spinal nerve root compression, SSA says that all of the elements of the Listing must be simultaneously present on examination and this level of severity must have continued or be expected to continue for 12 months. In *Radford v. Colvin,* 734 F.3d 288 (4th Cir. 2013), the Fourth Circuit held that 1.04A did not require that all of the clinical signs or symptoms be documented as present simultaneously. In AR 15-1(4), applicable to cases in the Fourth Circuit, SSA agreed to apply the holding of *Radford* in other cases. When there are significant objective findings concerning your client's back, don't overlook the possibility that your client's impairment may meet the Listings. Often this can best be established using a questionnaire that incorporates the elements of the Listing at issue. A sample questionnaire based on § 1.04A of the Listings appears at §231.1. Other sample questionnaires for meeting sections of the musculoskeletal Listings are also provided:

- §231.1.1 Form: Listing §1.02A—Major Dysfunction of a Weight-Bearing Joint
- §231.1.2 Form: Listing §1.02B—Major Dysfunction of a Major Peripheral Joint
- §231.1.3 Form: Listing §1.03 — Reconstructive Surgery or Surgical Arthrodesis of a Major Weight-Bearing Joint
- §231.1.4 Form: Listing §1.04B — Spinal Arachnoiditis
- §231.1.5 Form: Listing §1.04C — Lumbar Spinal Stenosis

RFC Evaluation

SSA is in the dark ages in its approach to evaluating disability from low back pain. Part of the problem lies in SSA's approach to the evaluation of pain, to which we devote a separate discussion. *See* §§250-259. The way SSA deals with osteoarthritis and degenerative joint disease also contributes. SSA does not treat these impairments as disabling, at least in the early stages when claimants may be suffering pain, muscle spasms and some limitation of motion but may not have significant neurological findings.

Doctors will tell you that x-ray findings for osteoarthritis and degenerative joint disease do not correlate well with symptoms. Some people with x-ray evidence of severe osteoarthritis or degenerative joint disease may have no symptoms whatsoever. Others, who have x-ray findings characterized as mild, suffer excruciating pain. For those people who are symptomatic, x-ray findings often seem to lag far behind symptoms. SSA acknowledged that "there is a relative lack of correlation between findings on imaging and function of the joint" in the introductory comments to the musculoskeletal Listings that took effect on February 19, 2002. 66 Fed. Reg. 58,017 (2001).

Indeed, there is little or no correlation between lumbar range of motion and residual functional capacity. Studies have found a large variation in lumbar range of motion of those who have no back impairment whatsoever. Age, gender and time of day of testing also influence lumbar range of motion. Spinal stability has been found to be more important for the performance of everyday activities than is the ability to touch one's toes. One study concluded that lumbar flexion was not reduced in patients with chronic low back pain. Another study found no correlation between lumbar range of motion and functional ability. *See* Parks, *et al.*, "A Comparison of Lumbar Range of Motion and Functional Ability Scores in Patients with Low Back Pain," *Spine*, Vol 28, No. 4, pp. 380-384, 2003.

ALJs frequently explain denial decisions in low back pain cases on the grounds that the "mild" x-ray findings or lack of significant limitation of lumbar range of motion do not support the claimant's allegation of pain and reduced residual functional capacity. This is despite the fact that the record contains a report from the treating physician reciting findings and describing a significantly limited RFC. In order to avoid this problem, it is necessary to have the treating physician provide maximum detail and explanation. You must ask the treating physician to explain *why* the findings support the diagnosis, and *why* the medical signs and findings caused the physician to conclude the claimant's RFC was so limited.

There may be additional factors that help to explain the claimant's symptoms. For example, if the treating physician concludes that the claimant does have a back problem but that the claimant's symptoms are out of proportion to the findings and that an "emotional" or "psychogenic" overlay accounts for the claimant's increased symptoms, develop evidence concerning this "overlay." Have the treating physician explain what this means. An emotional overlay is defined as "the emotionally determined increment to an existing organic symptom or disability." DORLAND'S ILLUSTRATED MEDICAL DICTIONARY, 29th ed., p. 1295.

When the treating physician suggests that your client has an emotional overlay, corroboration may be obtained through a psychological evaluation. Be sure the psychologist administers an MMPI, attaches a copy of the MMPI graph to the report, and explains its significance. Ask the psychologist to address the issue of possible malingering. Most often the combination of the underlying back problem and the emotional overlay will explain your client's symptoms. *See also* the discussion of medical issues and pain, §254.

In those rare cases where there are no objective findings whatsoever supporting your client's back complaints, have a psychologist evaluate the possibility that your client has a somatic symptom disorder. *See* §248.

This book contains eight medical source statement forms that may be used in cases involving musculoskeletal impairments. For simple cases involving older claimants where you need to establish little more than that the claimant is limited to a full range of sedentary, light (or in rare cases medium) work, use the ALJ's medical assessment form, §221.6, or the form that appears at §221.9. In more difficult cases involving younger claimants who must alternate sitting, standing and walking, use the medical opinion form that appears at §221.7, or the more detailed form at §231.2, if the claimant's impairment primarily involves the lumbar spine. If the case involves the cervical spine, use the Cervical Spine Medical Source Statement that appears at §231.5. If other joints are involved, use the Arthritis Medical Source Statement at §231.4, or the Physical Medical Source Statement, a questionnaire that is also useful in chronic pain cases, which appears at §221.11.

If fibromyalgia, also known as fibrositis and fibromyositis, is the diagnosis, use the questionnaire from §231.3 (which is based on diagnostic criteria set forth in SSR 12-2p). Fibromyalgia, an impairment characterized by a lack of objective findings other than eighteen specific tender points, can have a devastating impact on a claimant's ability to work. A study published in the Journal of Rheumatology compared the quality of life of patients with fibromyalgia to other patients with rheumatoid arthritis, osteoarthritis, permanent ostomies, chronic obstructive pulmonary disease, insulin dependent diabetes and healthy controls. The patients with fibromyalgia consistently scored among the poorest quality of life. *See,* Burckhardt, Clark and Bennett, "Fibromyalgia and Quality of Life: A Comparative Analysis," *The Journal of Rheumatology,* 1993; 20:475-479. *See also, Cline v. Sullivan*, 939 F.2d 560 (8th Cir. 1991), *Lisa v. Secretary of HHS*, 940 F.2d 40 (2d Cir. 1991), and *Sarchet v. Chater,* 78 F.3d 305 (7th Cir. 1996).

File Review—Low Back Cases

In any back case, objective evidence is extremely important. But let us not make the same mistake that SSA so often makes: SSA elevates the importance of objective evidence so much that it often fails to consider the subjective things, the history, the consistency of the complaints, and the credibility of the claimant. It is possible for there to be very little objective evidence of a back impairment, yet a claimant may be disabled. For example, chronic back strain where there is no evidence of any x-ray changes still can be disabling. (One would expect a history of back spasm, however. Back spasm is an objective finding.)

When reviewing a record, look at the overall consistency of the claimant's subjective complaints. Are the complaints consistent over time? Or does the claimant appear to tell one doctor one thing and another doctor another thing? Can such differences be explained by changes in symptoms over time?

Are the claimant's complaints consistent with your theory of why this claimant is disabled? That is, does the claimant appear to be telling you one thing and the doctors another? Although this may be a problem of physician perception or physician note taking, you need to look at this carefully and ask your client about it.

If the claimant is obese, don't forget that the Listings instruct decision makers that the "combined effects of obesity with musculoskeletal impairments can be greater than the effects of each of the impairments considered separately." Listing § 1.00Q. The Listings state that when assessing RFC, "adjudicators must consider any additional and cumulative effects of obesity." Listing § 1.00Q. *See also* Fanuele, et al., "Association Between Obesity and Functional Status in Patients with Spine Disease," *Spine*, volume 27, No. 3, pp. 306-312 (2002), which concluded that for spine patients, the heavier they are, the more disabled they are.

Every back case needs to be evaluated using sections 1.04A, B and C of the Listing of Impairments. Even though few cases at the hearing level actually meet this Listing, if any of the elements set forth in this Listing are present in you client's case, it is important to make note of them. Section 1.04 requires "neuro-anatomic distribution of pain." Generalized pain complaints are usually found in so many places in a client's record that it is not fruitful to make a list of all of them; but anything that shows a "neuro-anatomic distribution of pain" needs to be noted. It is also important to make a notation if there is a complete absence of your client's pain complaints in the medical records.

The § 1.04A issues you should note are the following: neuro-anatomic distribution of pain, limitation of motion of the spine (note that the limitation of motion does not have to be "significant" to meet this Listing), motor loss shown by atrophy with muscle weakness or muscle weakness alone, positive straight-leg raising test both sitting and supine, sensory loss or reflex changes. (The Listing itself refers to reflex "loss" but doctors generally find any reflex *change* to be significant. Reflex changes are usually illustrated by different findings for each leg.)

Muscle spasm is a significant finding. *See* § 1.00E1 of the Listings and the pain regulation, 20 C.F.R. § 404.1529(c)(2). However, muscle spasm was not made part of § 1.04A because, according to SSA, it "usually reflects an acute condition that will not persist for a year. Moreover, because spasm is often an intermittent finding, it may not be present on a given examination even though an individual might otherwise be significantly limited." 66 Fed. Reg. 58,018 (2001).

According to section 1.00E1 of the Listings:

> Inability to walk on the heels or toes, to squat, or to arise from a squatting position, when appropriate, may be considered evidence of significant motor loss. However, a report of atrophy is not acceptable as evidence of significant motor loss without circumferential measurements of both thighs and lower legs, or both upper or lower arms, as appropriate, at a stated point above and below the knee or elbow given in inches or centimeters. Additionally, a report of atrophy should be accompanied by measurement of the strength of the muscle(s) in question generally based on a grading system of 0 to 5, with 0 being complete loss of strength and 5 being maximum strength.

The pain regulation, 20 C.F.R. § 404.1529(c)(3), contains a list of factors that SSA will consider when evaluating pain:

> (i) Your daily activities;
> (ii) The location, duration, frequency, and intensity of your pain or other symptoms;
> (iii) Precipitating and aggravating factors;
> (iv) The type, dosage, effectiveness and side effects of any medication you take or have taken to alleviate your pain or other symptoms;
> (v) Treatment, other than medication, you receive or have received for relief of your pain or other symptoms;
> (vi) Any measures you use or have used to relieve your pain or other symptoms (e.g., lying flat on your back, standing for 15 to 20 minutes every hour, sleeping on a board, etc.); and
> (vii) Other factors concerning your functional limitations and restrictions due to pain or other symptoms.

Although a decision maker must consider all evidence in assessing residual functional capacity, SSR 96-8p provides a list of factors to consider:

1) Medical history;
2) Medical signs and laboratory findings;
3) The effects of treatment, including limitations or restrictions imposed by the mechanics of treatment (e.g., frequency of treatment, duration, disruption to routine, side effects of medication);
4) Reports of daily activities;
5) Lay evidence;
6) Recorded observations;
7) Medical source statements;
8) Effects of symptoms, including pain, that are reasonably attributed to a medically determinable impairment;
9) Evidence from attempts to work;
10) Need for structured living environment; and
11) Work evaluations, if available.

Functional Capacity Evaluations

Although functional capacity evaluations done by physical therapists can identify some people who are so disabled that they are incapable of performing sedentary work, such evaluations are generally not sufficient to determine whether most claimants can sustain the performance of a wide range of sedentary work. A conclusion based on a functional capacity evaluation that your client can perform sedentary work is not reliable. There is no good way to test tolerance for sedentary activity other than a full work simulation—eight hours per day over a period of weeks. And this is seldom done. You may find that a conclusion by a physical therapist that a patient is capable of sedentary work is based on nothing more than testing that shows the patient is incapable of light and medium work—without the patient's capacity for sedentary work ever being tested. Thus, the patient is found able to do sedentary work simply by default.

Don't necessarily accept therapists' conclusions that your client did not give full effort or failed to cooperate with a test. Assessment of cooperation and sincerity of effort during functional capacity evaluations has never been validated. *See* Lechner, Roth and Straaton, "Functional Capacity Evaluation in Work Disability," 1 *Work* 37 (Spring 1991); Lechner, Bradbury and Bradley, "Detecting Sincerity of Effort: A Summary of Methods and Approaches," 78 *Physical Therapy* 867 (August 1998); and King, Tuckwell and Barrett, "A Critical Review of Functional Capacity Evaluations," 78 *Physical Therapy* 852 (August 1998). In fact, you may discover that your client really did not give full effort. You may find that your client was too afraid of additional injury to give full effort during a functional capacity evaluation. Your client's position is not necessarily unreasonable. *See* chapter 14 of NOSSCR's Social Security Practice Guide.

Deconditioning

In some back cases (and in some cardiac cases as well), you may find that a doctor attributes some or all of your client's apparent limitations to "deconditioning." Deconditioning, of course, is not a medically determinable impairment. If the reason your client cannot do, say, heavy work is that your client has had a sedentary lifestyle for the past 20 years, (even if your client, like the hypothetical housewife in §100, is one of the few people who win a disability case with a medium RFC), your client will be denied at step 2 of the sequential evaluation process. Deconditioning in this circumstance is an attribute of body habitus, which, according to SSR 96-8p, is not to be considered when evaluating RFC.

It is rare, though, to see a disability case in which the only thing that accounts for the claimant's reduced RFC is deconditioning. More often, the claimant will have a significant impairment that may account for the deconditioning. Consider this. Suppose a claimant with a back impairment had a spinal fusion followed by an extended period of convalescence that continued through the tenth month of disability. This was followed by three months of work hardening physical therapy, after which the claimant returned to work. In all, the claimant had been off work for thirteen months. It is unlikely that SSA would deny this claim based on failure to meet the duration requirement of twelve months of disability by claiming that after ten months the claimant's limitations were attributable to deconditioning. Indeed, if it is appropriate at all to refer to deconditioning as preventing work after ten months, that deconditioning was a direct result of the claimant's spinal impairment. Thus, the time when the claimant was regaining strength to work should be considered part of the disability associated with the spinal fusion.

Let's look at a claimant with similar facts but consider what happens if work hardening fails. Here too, whatever role deconditioning plays in the claimant's RFC, it arises directly from the claimant's back impairment. As long as the failure of work hardening does not constitute a failure to follow prescribed treatment within the meaning of 20 C.F.R. § 404.1530 and SSR 82-59, any limitations that may be attributed to deconditioning ought to be considered as part of the claimant's RFC.

In most cases, you will also find certain vagueness about the role played by deconditioning. In *Bladow v. Apfel*, 205 F.3d 356, 361 (8th Cir. 2000), the Eighth Circuit Court of Appeals remanded the case with directions to the ALJ to "seek to focus the blurry connection between Bladow's general deconditioning and his work limitations."

Symptom Magnification — Waddell Signs

Watch out for Waddell signs, also called non-organic signs, behavioral signs, inappropriate signs and medically incongruent signs. Representatives have been known to erroneously cite Waddell signs as positive findings showing a severe back problem. In fact, there is a whole group of tests used by doctors to discover if a patient, rather than having a straightforward physical problem, may need psychological evaluation. The Waddell signs include superficial tenderness, non-anatomic tenderness, axial loading, simulated rotation, distraction straight leg raising, regional weakness, regional sensory change and overreaction to examination. If three or more of these signs are positive, doctors regard it as clinically significant. Usually these signs represent patient responses to examination affected by fear of injury, poor coping, unusual beliefs about pain or psychological distress. Nevertheless, these behavioral signs do not contradict organic findings. Instead, they help a doctor assess how best to treat a patient. The signs have been misinterpreted and misused by many people, including some ALJs, as signs of malingering, lack of credibility or veracity, or as a substitute for psychological assessment. None of these things are true according to an author of the article that originally proposed using these behavioral signs, Dr. Waddell himself. *See* Main and Waddell, *"Behavioral Responses to Examination: A Reappraisal of the Interpretation of 'Nonorganic Signs."'* *Spine,* Vol. 23, No. 21, pp. 2367-2371, 1998. *See also* Lechner, Bradbury and Bradley, "Detecting Sincerity of Effort: A Summary of Methods and Approaches," 78 *Physical Therapy* 867 (August 1998). A good description of Waddell signs with illustrative pictures is available on the Internet at http://nursing.bellarmine.edu/pt/orthospecialtests/text/waddell. Questions for cross-examination appear on the Internet in an article, "The Use of 'Waddell' in Workers' Compensation Claims," by Attorney Jon L. Gelman and Myron E. Brazin, M.D., at http://www.gelmans.com/Articles/Waddell97.

§231.1 Form: Listing § 1.04A — Spinal Nerve Root Compression

Listing §1.04A – Spinal Nerve Root Compression

From: ______________________________

Re: ______________________________(Name of Patient)

______________________________(Date of Birth)

Please comment on whether your patient has the following impairment:

> Disorders of the spine (e.g., herniated nucleus pulposus, spinal arachnoiditis, spinal stenosis, osteoarthritis, degenerative disc disease, facet arthritis, vertebral fracture), resulting in compromise of a nerve root (including the caudal equina) or the spinal cord. With:
>
> A. Evidence of nerve root compression characterized by neuro-anatomic distribution of pain, limitation of motion of the spine, motor loss (atrophy with associated muscle weakness or muscle weakness) accompanied by sensory or reflex loss and, if there is involvement of the lower back, positive straight-leg raising test (sitting and supine).

1. Does your patient have a disorder of the spine? ☐ Yes ☐ No

   If yes, please identify the disorder: ______________________________

2. Does your patient have evidence of nerve root compression? ☐ Yes ☐ No

3. Does your patient have neuro-anatomic distribution of pain? ☐ Yes ☐ No

   If yes, please describe: ______________________________

   ____

4. Does your patient have any limitation of motion of the spine? ☐ Yes ☐ No

   If yes, indicate range of motion with the following movements:

   Flexion ____°   Lateral bending - right ____°
   Extension ____°   Lateral bending - left ____°

   Other: ______________________________

5. Does your patient have any muscle weakness? ☐ Yes ☐ No

   If yes, please identify the affected muscles and describe using the grading system 0 to 5:

   ____

   Identify any positive signs of motor loss:

   ☐ Inability towalk on heels   ☐ Inability to squat
   ☐ Inability to walk on toes   ☐ Inability to arise from squatting position
   ☐ Atrophy: Indicate circumferential measurements of both thighs and lower legs or upper and lower arms as appropriate:

   ____

6. Does your patient have sensory *or* reflex loss? ☐ Yes ☐ No

   If yes, please describe: ______________________________

   ____

7. Is there involvement of the lower back? ☐ Yes ☐ No

   If yes, does your patient have a positive straight-leg raising test *both* sitting and supine? ☐ Yes ☐ No

   Please describe: ______________________________

   ____

8. If the clinical findings do not match ***all*** of the findings required above, are your patient's combined impairments medically ***equivalent*** to the severity of conditions in the above listed impairment? ☐ Yes ☐ No

   If yes, please explain in detail how your patient's impairments are equivalent to the impairment listed above, with reference to ***specific supporting clinical findings.***

   ____

   ____

   ____

   ____

   ____

   ____

   ____

   ____

   ____

______________________________ ______________________________
Date *Signature*

Printed/Typed Name: ______________________________

Address: ______________________________

____

7-32

12/13
§231.1

§231.1.1 Form: Listing § 1.02A — Major Dysfunction of a Weight-Bearing Joint

LISTING §1.02A – MAJOR DYSFUNCTION OF A WEIGHT BEARING JOINT

From: ______________________________

Re: ______________________________

DOB: ______________________________

Please comment on whether your patient has the following impairment:

> 1.02 Major dysfunction of a joint(s) (due to any cause): Characterized by gross anatomical deformity (e.g., subluxation, contracture, bony or fibrous ankylosis, instability) and chronic joint pain and stiffness with signs of limitation of motion or other abnormal motion of the affected joint(s), and findings on appropriate medically acceptable imaging of joint space narrowing, bony destruction, or ankylosis of the affected joint(s). With:
> A. Involvement of one major peripheral weight-bearing joint (i.e., hip, knee or ankle), resulting in inability to ambulate effectively, as defined in 1.00B2b;

1. Does your patient have major dysfunction of a weight bearing joint characterized by gross anatomical deformity (e.g., subluxation, contracture, bony or fibrous ankylosis, instability)? ☐ Yes ☐ No

   If yes, please identity affected joint(s): ______________________________

   and please identify the dysfunction: ______________________________

2. Is dysfunction confirmed by findings or appropriate medically acceptable imaging? ☐ Yes ☐ No

   If yes, please attach findings or describe type of imaging and date performed:

   ____

3. Does your patient have evidence of chronic joint pain and stiffness in the affected joint(s)? ☐ Yes ☐ No

4. Does your patient have any limitation of motion of the affected joint(s)? ☐ Yes ☐ No

   If yes, indicate ranges of motion that are limited: ______________________________

   ____

5. Concerning your patient's ability to "ambulate effectively," is your patient able to do the following on a *sustained* basis *without companion assistance*?

   A. walk a block at a reasonable pace on rough or uneven surfaces?
   ☐ Yes ☐ No

   B. use standard public transportation including climbing into/out of a bus and tolerate the typical jostling on a bus? ☐ Yes ☐ No

   C. carry out routine ambulatory activities including grocery and clothes shopping and banking? ☐ Yes ☐ No

   D. climb several stairs at a reasonable pace with use of only a single hand rail?
   ☐ Yes ☐ No

6. Does your patient need an assistive device to ambulate? ☐ Yes ☐ No

   If yes, what type of assistive device:______________________________

7. If the clinical findings do not match ***all*** of the findings required above, are your patient's combines impairments medically ***equivalent*** to the severity of conditions in the above listed impairment? ☐ Yes ☐ No

   If yes, please explain in detail how your patient's impairments are equivalent to the impairment listed above, with reference to ***specific supporting clinical findings***.

   ____
   ____
   ____
   ____
   ____
   ____

Date: ____________________ Signed: ____________________

Print Name: ____________________

Address: ____________________

____

7-32-1

8/14

§231.1.1

§231.1.2 Form: Listing § 1.02B — Major Dysfunction of a Major Peripheral Joint

LISTING §1.02B – MAJOR DYSFUNCTION OF A MAJOR PERIPHERAL JOINT

From: ______________________________

Re: ______________________________

DOB: ______________________________

Please comment on whether your patient has the following impairment:

> 1.02 Major dysfunction of a joint(s) (due to any cause): Characterized by gross anatomical deformity (e.g., subluxation, contracture, bony or fibrous ankylosis, instability) and chronic joint pain and stiffness with signs of limitations of motion or other abnormal motion of the affected joint(s), and findings on appropriate medically acceptable imagining of joint space narrowing, bony destruction, or ankylosis of the affected joint(s). With:
> B. Involvement of one major peripheral joint in each upper extremity (i.e., shoulder, elbow, or wrist-hand), resulting in inability to perform fine and gross movements effectively, as defined in 1.00B2c.

1. Does your patient have major dysfunction of a major peripheral joint in each upper extremity (e.g., shoulder, elbow, or wrist-hand)? ☐ Yes ☐ No

   If yes, please identity affected joints: ______________________________
   and please identify the dysfunction: ______________________________

2. Is dysfunction confirmed by findings or appropriate medically acceptable imaging? ☐ Yes ☐ No

   If yes, please attach findings or describe type of imaging and date performed:

   ____

3. Does your patient have evidence of chronic joint pain and stiffness in the affected joints? ☐ Yes ☐ No

4. Does your patient have any limitations of motion or other abnormal motion of the affected joints? ☐ Yes ☐ No

   If yes, indicate ranges of motion that are limited: ______________________________

   ____

5. If your patient's unable to perform fine and gross movements effectively[1]?
☐ Yes ☐ No

A. *If yes*, please explain: ____________________

____

6. If the clinical findings do not match ***all*** of the findings required above, are your patient's combines impairments medically ***equivalent*** to the severity of conditions in the above listed impairment? ☐ Yes ☐ No

If yes, please explain in detail how your patient's impairments are equivalent to the impairment listed above, with reference to ***specific supporting clinical findings***.

____

____

____

____

____

____

Date: ____________________ Signed: ____________________

Print Name: ____________________

Address: ____________________

____

7-32-2
12/13
§231.1.2

[1] Ability to perform fine and gross movements effectively means ability to sustain such functions as reaching, pushing, pulling, grasping, and fingering to carry out activities of daily living. Examples of inability include, but are not limited to inability to sort and handle papers or files, to place files in a file cabinet at or above waist level, inability to effectively and independently take care of personal hygiene or prepare a simple meal and feed oneself.

§231.1.3 *Form: Listing § 1.03 — Reconstructive Surgery or Surgical Arthrodesis of a Major Weight-Bearing Joint*

LISTING §1.03 – RECONSTRUCTIVE SURGERY OR SURGICAL ARTHRODESIS OF A MAJOR WEIGHT-BEARING JOINT

From: ______________________________

Re: ______________________________

DOB: ______________________________

Please comment on whether your patient has the following impairment:

> 1.03 Reconstructive surgery or surgical arthrodesis of a major weight-bearing joint, with inability to ambulate effectively, as defined in 1.00B2b, and return to effective ambulation did not occur, or is not expected to occur, within 12 months of onset.

1. Has your patient had reconstructive surgery of a major weight bearing joint(s)?
☐ Yes ☐ No

If yes, please identity the affected joint(s): ______________________________

Please state the date(s) of reconstructive surgery: ______________________________

2. Does your patient have surgical arthrodesis of a major weight-bearing joint?
☐ Yes ☐ No

If yes, please identify the affected joint(s): ______________________________

Please explain the basis for your opinion: ______________________________

____

3. Concerning your patient's ability to "ambulate effectively," is your patient able to do the following on a *sustained* basis *without companion assistance*?

A. walk a block at a reasonable pace on rough or uneven surfaces?
☐ Yes ☐ No

B. use standard public transportation including climbing into/out of a bus and tolerate the typical jostling on a bus? ☐ Yes ☐ No

C. carry out routine ambulatory activities including grocery and clothes shopping and banking? ☐ Yes ☐ No

D. climb several stairs at a reasonable pace with use of only a single hand rail?
☐ Yes ☐ No

4. Does your patient need an assistive device to ambulate? ☐ Yes ☐ No

   If yes, identify the type of assistive device needed: ____________________

5. If the clinical findings do not match ***all*** of the findings required above, are your patient's combines impairments medically ***equivalent*** to the severity of conditions in the above listed impairment? ☐ Yes ☐ No

   If yes, please explain in detail how your patient's impairments are equivalent to the impairment listed above, with reference to ***specific supporting clinical findings***.

   ____
   ____
   ____
   ____
   ____
   ____

Date: ____________________ Signed: ____________________

Print Name: ____________________

Address: ____________________

____

7-32-3
7/14
§231.1.3

§231.1.4 Form: Listing § 1.04B — Spinal Arachnoiditis

LISTING §1.04B – SPINAL ARACHNOIDITIS

From: ____________________________________

Re: ____________________________________

DOB: ____________________________________

Please comment on whether your patient has the following impairment:

> Disorder of the spine (e.g., herniated nucleus pulposus, spinal arachnoiditis, spinal stenosis, osteoarthritis, degenerative disc disease, facet arthritis, vertebral fracture) resulting in compromise of a nerve root (including the caudal equina) or the spinal cord. With:
>
> B. Spinal arachnoiditis, confirmed by an operative note or pathology report of tissue biopsy, or by appropriate medically acceptable imaging, manifested by severe burning or painful dysesthesia, resulting in the need for changes in position or posture more than once ever two hours;

1. Does your patient have spinal arachnoiditis? ☐ Yes ☐ No

2. If yes, how has this disorder been confirmed (e.g., operative note, pathology report of tissue biopsy, or imaging)? ____________________________________

   ____________________________________ (if available please attach).

3. If yes, does your patient have compromise of a nerve root or the spinal cord? ☐ Yes ☐ No

4. Does your patient have severe burning or painful dysesthesia? ☐ Yes ☐ No

   If yes, please indicate location of these symptoms: ____________________________________

   ____

5. If yes, do these symptoms result in the need for changes in position or posture more than once every two hours? ☐ Yes ☐ No

6. If the clinical findings do not match ***all*** of the findings required above, are your patient's combines impairments medically ***equivalent*** to the severity of conditions in the above listed impairment? ☐ Yes ☐ No

If yes, please explain in detail how your patient's impairments are equivalent to the impairment listed above, with reference to ***specific supporting clinical findings***.

____

____

____

____

____

____

Date: ____________________ Signed: ____________________

Print Name: ____________________

Address: ____________________

____

§231.1.5 Form: Listing § 1.04C — Lumbar Spinal Stenosis

LISTING §1.04C – LUMBAR SPINAL STENOSIS

From: ______________________________

Re: ______________________________

DOB: ______________________________

Please comment on whether your patient has the following impairment:

> Disorder of the spine (e.g., herniated nucleus pulposus, spinal arachnoiditis, spinal stenosis, osteoarthritis, degenerative disc disease, facet arthritis, vertebral fracture) resulting in compromise of a nerve root (including the caudal equina) or the spinal cord. With:
>
> C. Lumbar spinal stenosis resulting in pseudoclaudication, established by findings on appropriate medically acceptable imaging, manifested by chronic nonradicular pain and weakness, and resulting in inability to ambulate effectively, as defined in 1.00B2b.

1. Does your patient have lumbar spinal stenosis? ☐ Yes ☐ No

   If yes, has this disorder been confirmed by an appropriate imaging? ☐ Yes ☐ No

   Please attach or identify the date and type of such imaging: ______________________

2. If yes, does this disorder result in pseudoclaudication? ☐ Yes ☐ No

3. Does your patient have chronic nonradicular pain? ☐ Yes ☐ No

   If yes, please describe the location of pain: ______________________________

   ____

4. Does your patient have any muscle weakness? ☐ Yes ☐ No

   If yes, please identify the affected muscles and describe using the grading system 0 to 5:

   ____

5. Concerning your patient's ability to "ambulate effectively", is your patient able to do the following on a *sustained* basis *without companion assistance*?

A. walk a block at a reasonable pace on rough or uneven surfaces?
☐ Yes ☐ No

B. use standard public transportation including climbing into/out of a bus and tolerate the typical jostling on a bus? ☐ Yes ☐ No

C. carry out routine ambulatory activities including grocery and clothes shopping and banking? ☐ Yes ☐ No

D. climb several stairs at a reasonable pace with use of only a single hand rail?
☐ Yes ☐ No

6. Does your patient need an assistive device to ambulate? ☐ Yes ☐ No

If yes, what type of assistive device:______________________________

7. If the clinical findings do not match ***all*** of the findings required above, are your patient's combines impairments medically ***equivalent*** to the severity of conditions in the above listed impairment? ☐ Yes ☐ No

If yes, please explain in detail how your patient's impairments are equivalent to the impairment listed above, with reference to ***specific supporting clinical findings***.

____

____

____

____

____

____

Date: ______________________ Signed: ______________________________

Print Name: ______________________________

Address: ______________________________

____

§231.2 Form: Lumbar Spine Medical Source Statement

LUMBAR SPINE MEDICAL SOURCE STATEMENT

From: ______________________________

Re: ______________________________(Name of Patient)

______________________________(Date of Birth)

Please answer the following questions concerning your patient's impairments:

1. Frequency and length of contact:______________________________

2. Diagnoses:______________________________

____

3. Prognosis: ______________________________

4. Identify the ***clinical findings***, laboratory and test results that show your patient's medical impairments:

____

____

____

5. Have your patient's impairments lasted or can they be expected to last at least twelve months? □ Yes □ No

6. Identify all of your patient's ***symptoms***, including pain, insomnia, fatigue, etc.:

____

____

7. If your patient has pain:

a. Characterize the nature, location, radiation, frequency, precipitating factors, and severity of your patient's pain:

____

____

b. Does your patient have neuro-anatomic distribution of pain?

□ Yes □ No

c. Identify any positive objective signs:

Reduced range of motion: Description ______________________________

□	Positive supine straight leg raising test:	□	Swelling
□	Left at_____° Right at______°	□	Muscle spasm
□	Positive seated straight leg raising test	□	Motor loss
□	Abnormal gait	□	Muscle atrophy
□	Sensory loss	□	Muscle weakness
□	Reflex loss	□	Impaired appetite
□	Tenderness	□	Weight change
□	Crepitus	□	Impaired sleep

Other signs: ____

8. Do emotional factors contribute to the severity of your patient's symptoms and functional limitations? □ Yes □ No

9. Identify the side effects of any medication that may have implications for working, e.g., dizziness, drowsiness, stomach upset, etc.:

____

____

10. As a result of your patient's impairments, estimate your patient's functional limitations if your patient were placed in a ***competitive work situation***:

a. How many city blocks can your patient walk without rest or severe pain? __________

b. Please circle the hours and/or minutes that your patient can sit ***at one time,*** e.g., before needing to get up, etc.

Sit:	0 5 10 15 20 30 45	1 2 More than 2
	Minutes	Hours

c. Please circle the hours and/or minutes that your patient can stand ***at one time***, e.g., before needing to sit down, walk around, etc.

Stand:	0 5 10 15 20 30 45	1 2 More than 2
	Minutes	Hours

d. Please indicate how long your patient can sit and stand/walk ***total in an 8- hour working day*** (with normal breaks):

Sit	**Stand/walk**	
□	□	less than 2 hours
□	□	about 2 hours
□	□	about 4 hours
□	□	at least 6 hours

e. Does your patient need a job that permits shifting positions ***at will*** from sitting, standing or walking? □ Yes □ No

f. Does your patient need to include periods of walking around during an 8-hour working day? □ Yes □ No

If yes, how ***often*** must your patient walk?
1 5 10 15 20 30 45 60 90
Minutes

How ***long*** must your patient walk each time?
1 2 3 4 5 6 7 8 9 10 11 12 13 14 15
Minutes

g. In addition to normal breaks every two hours, will your patient sometimes need to take *unscheduled* breaks during a working day? □ Yes □ No

If yes, 1) approx. how ***often*** do you think this will happen? _______________

2) approx. how ***long*** (on average) will each break last?_______________

h. With prolonged sitting, should your patient's leg(s) be elevated? □ Yes □ No

If yes, 1) how ***high*** should the leg(s) be elevated? ___________

2) if your patient had a sedentary job, ***what percentage of time*** during an 8-hour working day should the leg(s) be elevated? ___________%

i. While engaging in occasional standing/walking, must your patient use a cane or other assistive device? □ Yes □ No

For this and other questions on this form, "rarely" means 1% to 5% of an 8-hour working day; "occasionally" means 6% to 33% of an 8-hour working day; "frequently" means 34% to 66% of an 8-hour working day.

j. How many pounds can your patient lift and carry in a competitive work situation?

	Never	**Rarely**	**Occasionally**	**Frequently**
Less than 10 lbs.	☐	☐	☐	☐
10 lbs.	☐	☐	☐	☐
20 lbs.	☐	☐	☐	☐
50 lbs.	☐	☐	☐	☐

k. How often can your patient perform the following activities?

	Never	**Rarely**	**Occasionally**	**Frequently**
Twist	☐	☐	☐	☐
Stoop (bend)	☐	☐	☐	☐
Crouch/ squat	☐	☐	☐	☐
Climb ladders	☐	☐	☐	☐
Climb stairs	☐	☐	☐	☐

l. If your patient has significant limitations with reaching, handling or fingering, please indicate the percentage of time during an 8-hour working day that your patient can use hands/fingers/arms for the following activities:

	HANDS: Grasp, Turn Twist Objects	**FINGERS:** Fine Manipulations	**ARMS:** Reaching In Front of Body	**ARMS:** Reaching Overhead
Right:	%	%	%	%
Left:	%	%	%	%

m. How much is your patient likely to be **"*off task*"**? That is, what percentage of a typical workday would your patient's symptoms likely be severe enough to interfere with ***attention and concentration*** needed to perform even simple work tasks?

☐ 0% ☐ 5% ☐ 10% ☐ 15% ☐ 20% ☐ 25% or more

n. To what degree can your patient tolerate work stress?

☐ Incapable of even "low stress" work ☐ Capable of low stress work
☐ Capable of moderate stress - normal work ☐ Capable of high stress work

Please explain the reasons for your conclusion: ______________________________

o. Are your patient's impairments likely to produce "good days" and "bad days"?
□ Yes □ No

If yes, assuming you patient was trying to work full time, please estimate, on the average, how many days per month your patient is likely to be absent from work as a result of the impairments:

□	Never	□	About three days per month
□	About one day per month	□	About four days per month
□	About two days per month	□	More than four days per month

11. Are your patient's impairments (physical impairments plus any emotional impairments) as demonstrated by signs, clinical findings and laboratory or test results ***reasonably consistent*** with the symptoms and functional limitations described above in this evaluation? □ Yes □ No

If no, please explain: ____________________

12. Please add an additional page to describe any other limitations (such as psychological limitations, limited vision, difficulty hearing, need to avoid temperature extremes, wetness, humidity, noise, dust, fumes, gases or hazards, etc.) that would affect your patient's ability to work at a regular job on a sustained basis.

____________ ____________________
Date *Signature*

Printed/Typed Name: ____________________

Address: ____________________

____

7-35
7/16
§231.2

§231.3 Form: Fibromyalgia Medical Source Statement

FIBROMYALGIA MEDICAL SOURCE STATEMENT

From: ______________________________

Re: ______________________________(Name of Patient)

______________________________(Date of Birth)

Please answer the following questions concerning your patient's impairments:

1. Frequency and length of contact: ____

2. a. Does your patient meet the 1990 American College of Rheumatology Criteria for the Classification of Fibromyalgia (which includes tender point criteria)?

   ☐ Yes ☐ No

   b. If no, does your patient meet the 2010 American College of Rheumatology Preliminary Diagnostic Criteria for Fibromyalgia (which does not include tender point criteria)?

   ☐ Yes ☐ No

3. Identify your patient's symptoms, signs and associated conditions:

☐ History of widespread pain > 3 months	☐ Severe fatigue
☐ 11 of 18 specific tender points – see page 3	☐ Depression
☐ Cognitive dysfunction ("fibro fog")	☐ Anxiety disorder
☐ Irritable Bowel Syndrome	☐ Waking unrefreshed
☐ Muscle pain	☐ Numbness or tingling
☐ Muscle weakness	☐ Abdominal pain/ cramps
☐ Frequent severe headaches	☐ Constipation
☐ Dizziness	☐ Nausea
☐ Palpitations	☐ Nervousness
☐ Shortness of breath	☐ Chest pain
☐ Frequent urination	☐ Blurred vision
☐ Insomnia	☐ Fever
☐ Pain in upper abdomen	☐ Diarrhea
☐ Raynaud's Phenomenon	☐ Dry mouth
☐ Hives or welts	☐ Itching
☐ Ringing in the ears	☐ Wheezing
☐ Oral ulcers	☐ Vomiting
☐ Change in taste	☐ Heartburn
☐ Dry eyes	☐ Loss of taste
☐ Shortness of breath	☐ Seizures
☐ Loss of appetite	☐ Sun sensitivity
☐ Hearing difficulties	☐ Easy bruising
☐ Frequent urination	☐ Hair loss

Symptoms, signs and associated conditions (continued):

- ☐ Bladder spasms
- ☐ Irritable bladder syndrome
- ☐ Gastroesophageal reflux disorder (GERD)
- ☐ Chronic Fatigue Syndrome
- ☐ Restless leg syndrome
- ☐ Temporomandibular Joint Disorder (TMJ)
- ☐ Involuntary weight loss
- ☐ Interstitial cystitis
- ☐ Migraines
- ☐ Dysmenorrhea
- ☐ Multiple Chemical Sensitivity
- ☐ Carpal Tunnel Syndrome
- ☐ Panic attacks
- ☐ Malaise[1]
- ☐ Other:____

____

4. Other diagnosed impairments: ______________________________

____

5. Were other disorders that could cause repeated manifestations of symptoms, signs or co-occurring conditions *excluded*? (Such disorders include rheumatologic disorders, myofascial pain syndrome, polymyalgia rheumatica, chronic Lyme disease, and cervical hyperextension-associated or hyperflexion-associated disorders.)

☐Yes ☐No

6. a. Identify the location of pain including, where appropriate, an indication of right or left side or bilateral areas affected:

	RIGHT	LEFT	BILATERAL
☐ Lumbosacral spine			
☐ Cervical spine			
☐ Thoracic spine			
☐ Chest			
☐ Shoulders	☐	☐	☐
☐ Arms	☐	☐	☐
☐ Hands/fingers	☐	☐	☐
☐ Hips	☐	☐	☐
☐ Legs	☐	☐	☐
☐ Knees/ankles/feet	☐	☐	☐

b. Describe the nature, frequency, and severity of your patient's pain:

____

c. Identify any factors that precipitate pain:

☐ Changing weather ☐ Fatigue ☐ Movement/Overuse ☐ Cold
☐ Hormonal Changes ☐ Stress ☐ Sleep problems ☐ Static Position

1 Malaise is defined as frequent feelings of illness, bodily discomfort, or lack of well-being that result in significantly reduced physical activity or mental function.

7. Do emotional factors contribute to the severity of your patient's symptoms and functional limitations? ☐ Yes ☐No

8. Circle your patient's tender points:

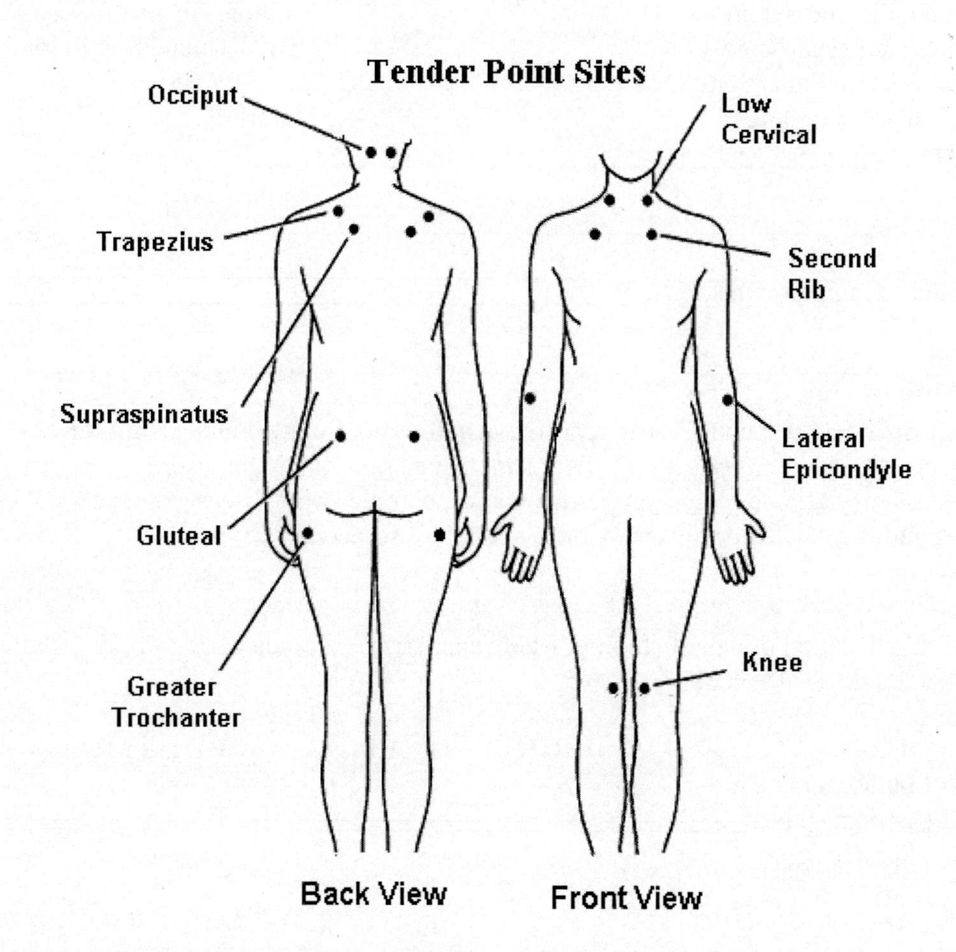

9. Describe the treatment and response including any side effects of medication that may have implications for working, *e.g.*, drowsiness, dizziness, nausea, etc.:

____

____

10. Prognosis: ____

11. Has your patient's fibromyalgia lasted or can it be expected to last at least twelve months? ☐ Yes ☐No

12. As a result of your patient's impairments, estimate your patient's functional limitations if your patient were placed in a ***competitive work situation***.

a. Does your patient have the stamina and endurance to work an easy job 8 hours per day 5 days per week (with normal breaks every two hours)?

☐ Yes ☐ No

If no, please explain the reasons for your conclusion: ______________________________

____

b. Does your patient need a job that permits shifting positions ***at will*** from sitting, standing or walking? ☐ Yes ☐ No

c. Does your patient need to include periods of walking around during an 8-hour working day? ☐ Yes ☐ No

1) If yes, approximately how ***often*** must your patient walk?

1 5 10 15 20 30 45 60 90
Minutes

2) How ***long*** must your patient walk each time?

1 2 3 4 5 6 7 8 9 10 11 12 13 14 15
Minutes

d. In addition to normal breaks every two hours, will your patient sometimes need to take *unscheduled* breaks during a working day? ☐Yes ☐No

If yes, 1) approx. how ***often*** do you think this will happen? ________________

2) approx. how ***long*** (on average) will each break last?________________

3) what symptoms cause a need for breaks?

☐ Muscle weakness ☐ Pain/ paresthesias, numbness
☐ Chronic fatigue ☐ Adverse effects of medication
☐ Other: ____

e. With prolonged sitting, should your patient's leg(s) be elevated? ☐Yes ☐No

If yes, 1) how ***high*** should the leg(s) be elevated? ________________

2) if your patient had a sedentary job, ***what percentage of time*** during an 8-hour working day should the leg(s) be elevated? ________________%

3) what symptoms cause a need to elevate leg(s)? ______________

f. Does your patient have significant limitations with reaching, handling or fingering?
☐Yes ☐No

If yes, please indicate the percentage of time during an 8-hour working day that your patient can use hands/fingers/arms for the following activities:

	HANDS: Grasp, Turn Twist Objects	**FINGERS: Fine Manipulations**	**ARMS: Reaching In Front of Body**	**ARMS: Reaching Overhead**
Right:	%	%	%	%
Left:	%	%	%	%

g. How much is your patient likely to be ***"off task"***? That is, what percentage of a typical workday would your patient's symptoms likely be severe enough to interfere with ***attention and concentration*** needed to perform even simple work tasks?

☐ 0% ☐ 5% ☐ 10% ☐ 15% ☐ 20.00 % ☐ 25% or more

h. To what degree can your patient tolerate work stress?

☐ Incapable of even "low stress" work ☐ Capable of low stress work
☐ Capable of moderate stress - normal work ☐ Capable of high stress work

i. Are your patient's impairments likely to produce "good days" and "bad days"?
☐ Yes ☐No

If yes, assuming your patient was trying to work full time please estimate, on the average, how many days per month your patient is likely to be absent from work as a result of the impairments:

☐Never ☐About three days per month
☐About one day per month ☐About four days per month
☐About two days per month ☐More than four days per month

j. Indicate to what degree the following functional limitations exist as a result of your patient's impairments. *Note*: **Marked** means more than moderate but less than extreme. A marked limitation may arise when several activities or functions are impaired or even when only one is impaired, so long as the degree of limitation is such as to seriously interfere with the ability to function independently, appropriately, effectively, and on a sustained basis.

	FUNCTIONAL LIMITATION				
A.	Limitation of activities of daily living	None or Mild ☐	Moderate ☐	Marked ☐	Extreme ☐
B.	Limitation in maintaining social functioning	None or Mild ☐	Moderate ☐	Marked ☐	Extreme ☐
C.	Limitation in completing tasks in a timely manner due to deficiencies in concentration, persistence or pace	None or Mild ☐	Moderate ☐	Marked ☐	Extreme ☐

13. Are your patient's impairments (physical impairments plus any emotional impairments) as demonstrated by signs, clinical findings and laboratory or test results ***reasonably consistent*** with the symptoms and functional limitations described above in this evaluation? ☐ Yes ☐No

    If no, please explain: ______________________________

14. Please describe any other limitations (such as psychological limitations, limited vision, difficulty hearing, need to avoid temperature extremes, wetness, humidity, noise, dust, fumes, gases or hazards, etc.) that would affect your patient's ability to work at a regular job on a sustained basis:

____

____

____

______________________ ______________________

Date *Signature*

Print/Type Name: ______________________

Address: ______________________

____

____

§231.4 *Form: Arthritis Medical Source Statement*

ARTHRITIS MEDICAL SOURCE STATEMENT

From: ________________________________

Re: ________________________________(Name of Patient)

________________________________(Date of Birth)

Please answer the following questions concerning your patient's impairments:

1. Frequency and length of contact:________________________________

2. Diagnoses:________________________________

3. Prognosis:________________________________

4. Identify all of your patient's ***symptoms***, including pain, dizziness, fatigue, etc.:

   ____

5. If your patient has pain, characterize the nature, location, frequency, precipitating factors, and severity of your patient's pain:

   ____

   ____

6. Identify any positive objective signs:

☐ Reduced range of motion:	☐ Sensory changes	☐ Reduced grip strength
Joints affected:	☐ Reflex changes	☐ Redness
____________________	☐ Impaired sleep	☐ Swelling
____________________	☐ Weight change	☐ Muscle spasm
☐ Joint warmth	☐ Impaired appetite	☐ Muscle weakness
☐ Joint deformity	☐ Abnormal posture	☐ Muscle atrophy
☐ Joint instability	☐ Tenderness	☐ Abnormal gait
☐ Myofascial trigger points	☐ Crepitus	☐ Positive straight leg raising test
☐ Fibromyalgia tender points		

   Other clinical findings: ________________________________

7. Do emotional factors contribute to the severity of your patient's symptoms and functional limitations? ☐ Yes ☐ No

8. Identify any psychological conditions affecting your patient's physical condition:

☐ Depression ☐ Anxiety
☐ Somatoform disorder ☐ Personality disorder
☐ Psychological factors affecting physical condition
☐Other: ________________________________

9. Identify the side effects of any medication that may have implications for working, e.g., dizziness, drowsiness, stomach upset, etc.:

____

____

10. Have your patient's impairments lasted or can they be expected to last at least twelve months? ☐ Yes ☐ No

11. As a result of your patient's impairments, estimate your patient's functional limitations if your patient were placed in a ***competitive work situation:***

a. How many city blocks can your patient walk without rest or severe pain? ________

b. Please circle the hours and/or minutes that your patient can sit ***at one time,*** e.g., before needing to get up, etc.

Sit: 0 5 10 15 20 30 45 (Minutes) 1 2 More than 2 (Hours)

c. Please circle the hours and/or minutes that your patient can stand ***at one time***, e.g., before needing to sit down, walk around, etc.

Stand: 0 5 10 15 20 30 45 (Minutes) 1 2 More than 2 (Hours)

d. Please indicate how long your patient can sit and stand/walk ***total in an 8-hour working day*** (with normal breaks):

Sit	Stand/walk
☐	☐ less than 2 hours
☐	☐ about 2 hours
☐	☐ about 4 hours
☐	☐ at least 6 hours

e. Does your patient need a job that permits shifting positions ***at will*** from sitting, standing or walking? ☐ Yes ☐ No

f. Does your patient need to include periods of walking around during an 8-hour working day? ☐ Yes ☐ No

If yes, how ***often*** must your patient walk? 1 5 10 15 20 30 45 60 90 Minutes

How ***long*** must your patient walk each time? 1 2 3 4 5 6 7 8 9 10 11 12 13 14 15 Minutes

g. In addition to normal breaks every two hours, will your patient sometimes need to take *unscheduled* breaks during a working day? ☐ Yes ☐ No

If yes, 1) approx. how ***often*** do you think this will happen? ________________

2) approx. how ***long*** (on average) will each break last?________________

3) on such a break, will your patient need to ☐lie down or ☐sit quietly?

h. With prolonged sitting, should your patient's leg(s) be elevated? ☐ Yes ☐ No

If yes, 1) how ***high*** should the leg(s) be elevated? ________________

2) if your patient had a sedentary job, ***what percentage of time*** during an 8-hour working day should the leg(s) be elevated? ________________%

i. While engaging in occasional standing/walking, must your patient use a cane or other assistive device? ☐ Yes ☐ No

For this and other questions on this form, "rarely" means 1% to 5% of an 8-hour working day; "occasionally" means 6% to 33% of an 8-hour working day; "frequently" means 34% to 66% of an 8-hour working day.

j. How many pounds can your patient lift and carry in a competitive work situation?

	Never	**Rarely**	**Occasionally**	**Frequently**
Less than 10 lbs.	☐	☐	☐	☐
10 lbs.	☐	☐	☐	☐
20 lbs.	☐	☐	☐	☐
50 lbs.	☐	☐	☐	☐

k. How often can your patient perform the following activities?

	Never	**Rarely**	**Occasionally**	**Frequently**
Twist	☐	☐	☐	☐
Stoop (bend)	☐	☐	☐	☐
Crouch/ squat	☐	☐	☐	☐
Climb ladders	☐	☐	☐	☐
Climb stairs	☐	☐	☐	☐

l. Does your patient have significant limitations with reaching, handling or fingering?
☐ Yes ☐ No

If yes, please indicate the percentage of time during an 8-hour working day that your patient can use hands/fingers/arms for the following activities:

	HANDS: Grasp, Turn Twist Objects	**FINGERS: Fine Manipulations**	**ARMS: Reaching In Front of Body**	**ARMS: Reaching Overhead**
Right:	%	%	%	%
Left:	%	%	%	%

m. How much is your patient likely to be ***"off task"***? That is, what percentage of a typical workday would your patient's symptoms likely be severe enough to interfere with ***attention and concentration*** needed to perform even simple work tasks?

☐ 0% ☐ 5% ☐ 10% ☐ 15% ☐ 20% ☐ 25% or more

n. To what degree can your patient tolerate work stress?

☐ Incapable of even "low stress" work
☐ Capable of low stress work
☐ Capable of moderate stress - normal work
☐ Capable of high stress work

o. Are your patient's impairments likely to produce "good days" and "bad days"?
☐ Yes ☐ No

If yes, assuming your patient was trying to work full time, please estimate, on the average, how many days per month your patient is likely to be absent from work as a result of the impairments:

☐Never About three days per month
☐About one day per month
☐About two days per month
☐About four days per month
☐More than four days per month

12. Are your patient's impairments (physical impairments plus any emotional impairments)) as demonstrated by signs, clinical findings and laboratory or test results ***reasonably consistent*** with the symptoms and functional limitations described in this evaluation?
☐Yes ☐No

If no, please explain: ____________________

13. Please describe any other limitations (such as psychological limitations, limited vision, difficulty hearing, need to avoid temperature extremes, wetness, humidity, noise, dust, fumes, gases or hazards, etc.) that would affect your patient's ability to work at a regular job on a sustained basis:

____

____

____

____________________ ____________________

Date *Signature*

Printed/Typed Name: ____________________

Address: ____________________

____

____

§231.5 Form: Cervical Spine Medical Source Statement

CERVICAL SPINE MEDICAL SOURCE STATEMENT

From: ______________________________

Re: ______________________________ (Name of Patient)

______________________________ (Date of Birth)

Please answer the following questions concerning your patient's impairments:

1. Frequency and length of contact: ______________________________

2. Diagnoses: ______________________________

3. Prognosis: ______________________________

4. Does your patient have chronic pain/paresthesia? Yes No

   a. If yes, describe the nature, location, frequency, precipitating factors, and severity of your patient's pain/paresthesia:

   ____

   ____

   b. Does your patient have neuro-anatomic distribution of pain?

   □ Yes □No

   c. Identify signs, findings, and associated symptoms of your patient's impairments:

□ Tenderness	□ Weight change	□ Reflex loss
□ Crepitus	□ Sensory loss	□ Swelling
□ Muscle spasm	□ Impaired sleep	□ Atrophy
□ Muscle weakness	□ Impaired appetite	□ Motor loss
□ Chronic fatigue	□ Lack of coordination	□ Drops things
□ Spastic gait	□ Abnormal posture	□ Reduced grip strength

   □other: ______________________________

   d. Does your patient have limitation of motion?

   □ Yes □No

   If yes, please indicate cervical range of motion (ROM):

Extension	______%	Flexion	______%
Left rotation	______%	Right rotation	______%
Left lateral bending	______%	Right lateral bending	______%

5. Does your patient have severe headache pain associated with impairment of the cervical spine? ☐ Yes ☐No

If yes:

a. Please characterize the nature, location and intensity/severity (mild to severe) of your patient's headaches:

____

____

____

b. Identify any other symptoms associated with your patient's headaches:

☐ Vertigo	☐ Weight change	☐ Visual disturbances
☐ Nausea/vomiting	☐ Inability to concentrate	☐ Mood changes
☐ Malaise	☐ Impaired sleep	☐ Mental confusion
☐ Photosensitivity	☐ Exhaustion	☐ Impaired appetite

☐ Other:____

____

c. What is the approximate frequency of headaches? _______per week/ ____ per month

d. What is the approximate duration of a typical headache? minutes/ ____ hours

e.. What makes your patient's headaches better?

☐ Lie down	☐ Quiet place	☐ Hot pack
☐ Take medication	☐ Dark room	☐ Cold pack

Other____

6. Identify any other clinical findings and objective signs not mentioned above:

____

____

7. Describe the treatment and response including any side effects of medication that may have implications for working, e.g., drowsiness, dizziness, nausea, etc:

____

____

8. Have your patient's impairments lasted or can they be expected to last at least twelve months? □ Yes □ No

9. Do emotional factors contribute to the severity of your patient's symptoms and functional limitations? □ Yes □ No

10. Identify any psychological conditions affecting your patient's physical condition:

□ Depression	□ Anxiety
□ Somatoform disorder	□ Personality disorder
□ Psychological factors affecting physical condition	□ Other: ____________

11. As a result of your patient's impairments, estimate your patient's functional limitations if your patient were placed in a ***competitive work situation***.

a. How many city blocks can your patient walk without rest or severe pain? ________

b. Please circle the hours and/or minutes that your patient can sit ***at one time,*** e.g., before needing to get up, etc.

Sit: 0 5 10 15 20 30 45 Minutes | 1 2 More than 2 Hours

c. Please circle the hours and/or minutes that your patient can stand ***at one time***, e.g., before needing to sit down, walk around, etc.

Stand: 0 5 10 15 20 30 45 Minutes | 1 2 More than 2 Hours

d. Please indicate how long your patient can sit and stand/walk ***total in an 8-hour working day*** (with normal breaks):

Sit	**Stand/walk**	
		less than 2 hours
		about 2 hours
		about 4 hours
		at least 6 hours

e. Does your patient need a job that permits shifting positions ***at will*** from sitting, standing or walking? □ Yes □ No

f. Does your patient need to include periods of walking around during an 8-hour working day? □ Yes □ No

If yes, how ***often*** must your patient walk?
1 5 10 15 20 30 45 60 90
Minutes

How ***long*** must your patient walk each time?
1 2 3 4 5 6 7 8 9 10 11 12 13 14 15
Minutes

g. In addition to normal breaks every two hours, will your patient sometimes need to take *unscheduled* breaks during a working day? ☐ Yes ☐ No

If yes, 1) approx. how ***often*** do you think this will happen? ________________

2) approx. how ***long*** (on average) will each break last? ________________

3) what symptoms cause a need for breaks?

☐ Muscle weakness ☐ Pain/ paresthesias, numbness
☐ Chronic fatigue ☐ Adverse effects of medication
☐ Other: ________________________________

h. While engaging in occasional standing/walking, must your patient use a cane or other assistive device? ☐ Yes ☐ No

For this and other questions on this form, "rarely" means 1% to 5% of an 8-hour working day; "occasionally" means 6% to 33% of an 8-hour working day; "frequently" means 34% to 66% of an 8-hour working day.

i. How many pounds can your patient lift and carry in a competitive work situation?

	Never	**Rarely**	**Occasionally**	**Frequently**
Less than 10 lbs.	☐	☐	☐	☐
10 lbs.	☐	☐	☐	☐
20 lbs.	☐	☐	☐	☐
50 lbs.	☐	☐	☐	☐

j. How often can your patient perform the following activities?

	Never	**Rarely**	**Occasionally**	**Frequently**
Look down (sustained flexion of neck)	☐	☐	☐	☐
Turn head right or left	☐	☐	☐	☐
Look up	☐	☐	☐	☐
Hold head in static position	☐	☐	☐	☐

k. How often can your patient perform the following activities?

	Never	**Rarely**	**Occasionally**	**Frequently**
Twist	☐	☐	☐	☐
Stoop (bend)	☐	☐	☐	☐
Crouch/ squat	☐	☐	☐	☐
Climb ladders	☐	☐	☐	☐
Climb stairs	☐	☐	☐	☐

l. If your patient has significant limitations with reaching, handling or fingering:

What symptoms cause limitations of use of the upper extremities?

☐ Pain/ paresthesias ☐ Incoordination ☐ Sensory loss/ numbness
☐ Muscle weakness ☐ Spasticity ☐ Fatigue
☐ Tremor ☐ Other: ____________________

Please indicate the percentage of time during an 8-hour working day that your patient can use hands/fingers/arms for the following activities:

	HANDS: Grasp, Turn Twist Objects	**FINGERS: Fine Manipulations**	**ARMS: Reaching In Front of Body**	**ARMS: Reaching Overhead**
Right:	%	%	%	%
Left:	%	%	%	%

m. How much is your patient likely to be ***"off task"***? That is, what percentage of a typical workday would your patient's symptoms likely be severe enough to interfere with ***attention and concentration*** needed to perform even simple work tasks?

☐ 0% ☐ 5% ☐ 10% ☐ 15% ☐ 20% ☐ 25% or more

n. To what degree can your patient tolerate work stress?

☐ Incapable of even "low stress" work ☐ Capable of low stress work
☐ Capable of moderate stress - normal work ☐ Capable of high stress work

Please explain the reasons for your conclusion: ____________________

o. Are your patient's impairments likely to produce "good days" and "bad days"?
☐ Yes ☐ No

If yes, assuming your patient was trying to work full time, please estimate, on the average, how many days per month your patient is likely to be absent from work as a result of the impairments:

☐ Never ☐ About three days per month
☐ About one day per month ☐ About four days per month
☐ About two days per month ☐ More than four days per month

12. Are your patient's impairments (physical impairments plus any emotional impairments) as demonstrated by signs, clinical findings and laboratory or test results ***reasonably consistent*** with the symptoms and functional limitations described above in this evaluation? Yes ☐ No ☐

If no, please explain: ____________________

13. Please describe any other limitations (such as psychological limitations, limited vision, difficulty hearing, need to avoid temperature extremes, wetness, humidity, noise, dust, fumes, gases or hazards, etc.) that would affect your patient's ability to work at a regular job on a sustained basis:

____

____

________________________ ________________________

Date *Signature*

Printed/Typed Name: ________________________

Address: ________________________

____

____

7-31
7/16
§231.5

§232 *Special Senses and Speech, Listings §§2.00-2.11*

Vision

To meet the requirements for "statutory blindness" and to be eligible for the special benefits available to blind beneficiaries under both Title II and Title XVI of the Act (*see* §§ 143 and 144), a claimant's impairment must strictly meet §§2.02 or 2.03A of the Listings. *See* Listing §2.00A.2. Equaling §§2.02 or 2.03A is not good enough to meet the requirements for statutory blindness. Visual impairments that *equal* §§2.02 or 2.03A or are decided under other vision Listings will qualify a claimant for regular Social Security disability or SSI benefits.

The Listings point out that there are different requirements for proof of statutory blindness under Title II and Title XVI of the Act. For the Social Security disability program, it is necessary to have proof of the cause of the loss of vision. Listing §2.00A.4. For SSI, there is no requirement to prove the cause of loss of vision. All that is necessary is evidence showing that visual acuity or loss of visual field in the better eye meets the statutory requirement. Listing §2.00A.3.

Claimants whose visual impairments fall just short of meeting the Listings usually find it difficult to be found disabled based upon limited RFC caused by the visual limitations alone. It is SSA's policy, as stated in SSR 85-15, that as "a general rule, even if a person's visual impairment(s) were to eliminate all jobs that involve very good vision (such as working with small objects or reading small print), as long as he or she retains sufficient visual acuity to be able to handle and work with rather large objects (and has the visual fields to avoid ordinary hazards in the workplace), there would be a substantial number of jobs remaining across all exertional levels." SSR 83-14 notes that where a claimant,

> has a visual impairment which is not of Listing severity but causes the person to be a hazard to self and others—usually a constriction of visual fields rather than a loss of visual acuity—the manifestations of tripping over boxes while walking, inability to detect approaching persons or objects, difficulty in walking up and down stairs, etc., will indicate to the decisionmaker that the remaining occupational base is significantly diminished for light work (and medium work as well).

See also POMS DI 25020.005A.10 at §272.

Limitations of near visual acuity in combination with other limitations, especially a limitation to sedentary work which usually involves working with smaller objects, may cause a claimant to be found disabled. SSR 96-9p states that if "a visual limitation prevents an individual from seeing the small objects involved in most sedentary unskilled work, or if an individual is not able to avoid ordinary hazards in the workplace, such as boxes on the floor, doors ajar, or approaching people or vehicles, there will be significant erosion of the sedentary occupational base." Nevertheless, demonstrating the vocational implications of limited vision is challenging for the claimant's representative.

Visual acuity is tested under ideal circumstances with ideal contrast—sharp black letters on a bright white background. Acuity testing does *not* measure the smallest type one would be *comfortable* reading in a work situation. Instead, it measures the smallest type one is *capable* of pulling into focus without a time limit. Like any other test of maximum capacity, significant adjustment of the results is necessary to reflect a claimant's ability in a work situation.

Near visual acuity is often described by doctors in terms of the smallest point type a claimant is capable of reading, something with which most lawyers are familiar because of resizable fonts used by computer word processing programs. For example, near visual acuity may be described for a particular claimant as "10 point." This means that the smallest type this claimant can read is 10 point, that which is used in this sentence. (This means, of course, that this claimant is *not capable* of performing a job involving a good deal of reading or working with comparably small objects. To be capable of spending much of the working day reading 10-point type, one must have considerably better visual acuity.)

The other system in use by physicians is the Jaeger's test type, usually abbreviated in doctors' notes as "J." Because some translation is required to interpret Jaeger numbers, we provide this chart:

Point	Jaeger	Distance Equivalent
26	16	20/200
14	10	20/100
10	7	20/70
8	5	20/50
6	3	20/40
5	2	20/30
4	1	20/25
3	1+	20/20

A major problem in assessing the vocational impact of visual limitations is that visual acuity testing may not address the real problem. For example, a claimant with diabetic retinopathy may have one or more blind spots near the center of vision. Testing the visual acuity of vision outside the blind spots does not necessarily tell much about a claimant's ability to read or do other work requiring good near acuity. Many claimants with diabetic retinopathy say that looking through their eyes is as if one were looking through a paint splattered window screen. When reading, as the eyes follow a sentence, words seem to disappear as they go behind the paint splatters. Such claimants also complain about difficulty going from the end of one line on the right side of the page to the beginning of the next line on the left side of the page. They may also have poor contrast sensitivity. That is, they can see the black letters on the white background of the eye chart very well, but they may have great difficulty distinguishing objects of different colors when the contrast is not as great as that between black and white. These problems make work requiring good near visual acuity very difficult despite the fact that such claimants' tested visual acuity may be very good.

Some cases involving blurred vision present an even greater challenge for the claimant's representative. Often a claimant with certain kinds of blurred vision can get the blurring to clear enough to do well on visual acuity testing even though the blurred vision may be bad enough and frequent enough to prevent any work requiring good near visual acuity. Objective testing of visual acuity is largely irrelevant in this circumstance. In such cases you need the claimant's eye doctor to explain why the claimant's eye condition could reasonably be expected to produce blurred vision, the cause of the blurred vision, the fact that there is no test for blurred vision, that the complaints of blurred vision are consistent with objective evidence concerning the claimant's eyes, etc. Blurred vision is the sort of symptom that may suggest "greater severity of impairment than can be shown by objective evidence alone." 20 C.F.R. § 404.1529(c)(3). In short, blurred vision, like pain, is a symptom subject to the same sort of proof as any other subjective symptom. The same rules apply. *Cf.* SSRs 96-7p and 96-8p.

If your client is limited to sedentary work, a letter, such as the one at §232.2, to the treating ophthalmologist or optometrist may elicit the necessary information to win your client's case. Or you may send your client's eye doctor a copy of the shorter Vision Medical Source Statement at §232.3. Because some eye problems limit a claimant's exertional capacity as well as vision, and because in some cases the shorter questionnaire is insufficient to obtain information about all of your client's limitations from an eye problem, a longer Vision Impairment Medical Source Statement is provided at §232.4.

Note that the two vision questionnaires, §§232.3 and 232.4, ask whether a claimant can use near acuity, far acuity, depth perception, accommodation, color vision and field of vision constantly, frequently, or occasionally. These categories appear in Selected Characteristics of Occupations Defined in the Revised Dictionary of Occupational Titles, a companion volume to the Dictionary of Occupational Titles. They may be used to assess whether your client's vision limitations preclude performance of certain jobs. You may find that although your client's vision limitations alone do not prevent your client from performing all work, the vision limitations in combination with other limitations reduce your client's occupational base to the point that a vocational expert will agree that jobs do not exist in significant numbers within your client's residual functional capacity.

Meniere's Disease

Meniere's disease is characterized by recurrent attacks of disabling vertigo, tinnitus and fluctuating but progressive hearing loss over time, usually in only one ear. The Listings incorporate these characteristics of Meniere's disease plus one other. In its relentless search for objective support for diagnoses, SSA also requires "[d]isturbed function of vestibular labyrinth demonstrated by caloric or other vestibular tests." Listing §2.07A. Meniere's disease cases seen at the hearing level tend to be those where no vestibular testing was done or the result of such testing is negative. Many doctors say that a negative vestibular test does not disprove a diagnosis of Meniere's disease. A Meniere's Disease Medical Source Statement, which addresses both Listings and RFC issues, appears at §232.1. A Vestibular Disorder Medical Assessment Form is included as 232A on Digital Access.

§232.1 Form: Meniere's Disease Medical Source Statement

MENIERE'S DISEASE MEDICAL SOURCE STATEMENT

From: ______________________________

Re: ______________________________(Name of Patient)

______________________________(Date of Birth)

Please answer the following questions concerning your patient's impairments:

1. Nature, frequency and length of contact:______________________________

____

2. Diagnoses:____

____

____

3. Does your patient have Meniere's Disease? ☐ Yes ☐No

4. Does your patient have:

   a. History of frequent attacks of balance disturbance? ☐Yes ☐No

   b. Tinnitus? ☐Yes ☐No

   c. Progressive hearing loss? ☐Yes ☐No

   If yes, is the hearing loss established by audiometry? ☐Yes ☐No

   If no, explain how the hearing loss was established:______________________

   ____

   ____

   d. Disturbed function of vestibular labyrinth demonstrated by caloric or other vestibular tests? ☐ Yes ☐No

If no, explain how the absence of vestibular tests or a negative vestibular test affects the diagnosis and assessment of severity of the impairment:

____

____

____

5. Identify symptoms associated with your patient's Meniere's attacks:

- ☐ Vertigo
- ☐ Nausea/vomiting
- ☐ Malaise
- ☐ Photosensitivity
- ☐ Sensitivity to noise
- ☐ Visual disturbances
- ☐ Mood changes
- ☐ Mental confusion/inability to concentrate
- ☐ Fatigue/exhaustion

☐ Other:____

____

____

6. What is the average frequency of your patient's Meniere's attacks?

_____ per week _____ per month

7. How long does a typical attack last? _____________

8. Does your patient always have a warning of an impending attack? ☐Yes ☐ No

If yes, how long is it between the warning and the onset of the attack? ______ minutes

Can your patient always take safety precautions when he/she feels an attack coming on? ☐Yes ☐ No

9. Do attacks occur at a particular time of the day? ☐Yes ☐ No

If yes, explain when attacks occur:____

10. Are there precipitating factors such as stress, exertion, sudden movement, certain kinds of light, computer monitors, etc.? ☐Yes ☐ No

If yes, explain:____

11. What makes your patient's attack worse?

☐ Bright lights ☐ Moving around
☐ Noise ☐ Other:______________________

12. What makes your patient's attack better?

☐ Lying in a dimly lit room ☐ Cold/hot packs
☐ Other:____

____

13. What are the post-attack manifestations? *Check those that apply:*

☐Confusion ☐Severe headache
☐Exhaustion ☐Paranoia
☐Irritability ☐Other:___________________________

14. How long after an attack do these manifestations last? ___________________________

15. Describe the degree to which having an attack interferes with your patient's daily activities following an attack:____

____

16. To what degree do emotional factors contribute to the severity of your patient's attacks?

☐ Not at all ☐ Somewhat ☐ Very much

17. To what degree can your patient tolerate work stress?

☐ Incapable of even "low stress" work ☐ Capable of low stress work
☐ Capable of moderate stress - normal work ☐ Capable of high stress work

Please explain the reasons for your conclusion:_____ ___________________________

____ ___________________________

18. Describe the treatment and response:____

____ ___________________________

19. List your patient's current medications used for control/treatment of Meniere's disease:

____ ___________________________

____ ___________________________

20. Identify any side effects of these medications experienced by your patient:

____

____

21. Prognosis:____

____

22. Have your patient's impairments lasted or can they be expected to last at least twelve months? ☐ Yes ☐ No

23. During times your patient has an attack, would your patient generally be precluded from performing even basic work activities and need a break from the workplace?
☐ Yes ☐ No
If no, please explain:__________________________________

____

24. In addition to normal breaks every two hours, will your patient sometimes need to take *unscheduled* breaks during a working day? ☐ Yes ☐ No

If yes, 1) approx. how ***often*** do you think this will happen? ____________

2) approx. how ***long*** (on average) will each break last?____________

25. Other than unscheduled breaks, how much is your patient likely to be ***"off task" while working***? That is, what percentage of a typical workday would your patient's symptoms likely be severe enough to interfere with ***attention and concentration*** needed to perform even simple work tasks?

☐ 0% ☐ 5% ☐ 10% ☐ 15% ☐ 20 % ☐ 25% or more

26. Are your patient's impairments likely to produce "good days" and "bad days"?
☐ Yes ☐ No

If yes, assuming your patient was trying to work full time, please estimate, on the average, how many days per month your patient is likely to be absent from work as a result of the impairments:

☐ Never	☐ About three days per month
☐ About one day per month	☐ About four days per month
☐ About two days per month	☐ More than four days per month

27. Are your patient's impairments (physical impairments plus any emotional impairments) as demonstrated by signs, clinical findings and laboratory or test results ***reasonably consistent*** with the symptoms and functional limitations described in this evaluation?

☐ Yes ☐ No

If no, please explain:____

28. Please describe any other limitations (such as limitations in the ability to sit, stand, walk, lift, bend, stoop, crouch, limited vision, difficulty hearing, need to avoid temperature extremes, wetness, humidity, noise, dust, fumes, gases or hazards, etc.) that would affect your patient's ability to work at a regular job on a sustained basis:

____

____

____

____________________ ____________________________

Date *Signature*

Printed/Typed Name: ____________________________

7-52

Address: ____________________________

7/16
§232.1

____

____

§232.2 Form: Letter to Doctor re: Vision When Claimant Limited to Sedentary Work

Date

Doctor's Name
Doctor's Address

Re: **Client's Name**
DOB:**Client's DOB**

Dear Dr. **Name**:

I represent **Client's Name** in a Social Security disability claim in which my client's vision is an issue. Because I have great difficulty figuring out the vocational implications of vision testing, I need your help. When I review a vision case, I always have difficulty figuring out how to translate ophthalmology notes into work limitations. I hope you will be able to explain my client's limitations in layman's terms.

At issue in this case is my client's ability to do sedentary work. SSA's rules say that most sedentary jobs require working with small objects. From the information you have, would it be possible for you to describe my client's capacity for working at a sedentary job? For example, would s/he be able to do a job that required reading regular size print? Could s/he fill out reports such as those filled out by a security guard, checking IDs, reading time clocks, etc.? What about working as a cashier which requires making change, filling out and reading charge slips, reading price tags, etc.? What about her capacity to do, say, bench assembly with relatively small parts, small screws, follow diagrams, solder wires, etc.? How about working as an inspector examining small parts for defects?

Is my client able to avoid ordinary hazards in the workplace, such as boxes on the floor, doors ajar, approaching people or vehicles?

I enclose a signed medical consent form for your records. Please bill me for your time in responding to this letter.

Please note that I need to send your response to the Social Security judge by **Date**.

Sincerely,

Attorney
Enclosure

§232.3 Form: Vision Medical Source Statement

VISION MEDICAL SOURCE STATEMENT

From: ______________________________

Re: ______________________________(Name of Patient)

______________________________(Date of Birth)

Please answer the following questions concerning your patient's impairments.

1. Frequency and length of contact: ______________________________

2. Diagnoses: ______________________________

3. Prognosis: ______________________________

4. After best correction visual acuity right eye: __________

5. After best correction visual acuity left eye: __________

6. Describe contraction of peripheral visual fields in the better eye:

____

____

7. Describe your patient's vision ***symptoms***:

____

____

"Rarely" means 1% to 5% of an 8-hour working day; "occasionally" means 6% to 33% of an 8-hour working day; "frequently" means 34% to 66% of an 8-hour working day.

8. As a result of your patient's impairments, estimate your patient's functional limitations if your patient were placed in a ***competitive work situation***.

   a. How often can your patient perform work activities involving the following?

	Never	**Rarely**	**Occasionally**	**Frequently**	**Constantly**
Near Acuity	☐	☐	☐	☐	☐
Far Acuity	☐	☐	☐	☐	☐
Depth Perception	☐	☐	☐	☐	☐
Accommodation	☐	☐	☐	☐	☐
Color Vision	☐	☐	☐	☐	☐
Field of Vision	☐	☐	☐	☐	☐

b. Does your patient have exertional or postural limitations related to vision problems?
☐ Yes ☐ No

If yes, how many pounds can your patient lift and carry?

	Never	**Rarely**	**Occasionally**	**Frequently**
Less than 10 lbs.	☐	☐	☐	☐
10 lbs.	☐	☐	☐	☐
20 lbs.	☐	☐	☐	☐
50 lbs.	☐	☐	☐	☐

c. How often can your patient perform the following activities?

	Never	**Rarely**	**Occasionally**	**Frequently**
Stoop (bend)	☐	☐	☐	☐
Crouch/ squat	☐	☐	☐	☐
Climb ladders	☐	☐	☐	☐

9. Please describe any other limitations that would affect your patient's ability to work at a regular job on a sustained basis:

____

____

____

______________________ ______________________

Date *Signature*

*Printed/Typed Name:*______________________

*Address:*______________________

232-3
7/16
7-50s

____

____

§232.4 Form: Vision Impairment Medical Source Statement

VISION IMPAIRMENT MEDICAL SOURCE STATEMENT

From: ______________________________

Re: ______________________________(Name of Patient)

______________________________(Date of Birth)

Please answer the following questions concerning your patient's impairments. *Attach relevant treatment notes, laboratory and test results as appropriate.*

Please answer the following questions concerning your patient's impairments.

1. Frequency and length of contact:______________________________

2. Diagnoses:______________________________

3. Prognosis:______________________________

4. Visual acuity after best correction right eye:________

5. Visual acuity after best correction left eye: ________

6. Describe any contraction of peripheral visual fields:

____

____

____

7. Describe your patient's vision ***symptoms***:

____

____

"Rarely" means 1% to 5% of an 8-hour working day; "occasionally" means 6% to 33% of an 8-hour working day; "frequently" means 34% to 66% of an 8-hour working day.

8. As a result of your patient's impairments, estimate your patient's vision limitations if your patient were placed in a ***competitive work situation***.

   a. How often can your patient perform work activities involving the following?

	Never	**Rarely**	**Occasionally**	**Frequently**	**Constantly**
Near Acuity	☐	☐	☐	☐	☐
Far Acuity	☐	☐	☐	☐	☐
Depth Perception	☐	☐	☐	☐	☐
Accommodation	☐	☐	☐	☐	☐
Color Vision	☐	☐	☐	☐	☐
Field of Vision	☐	☐	☐	☐	☐

b. Is your patient capable of avoiding ordinary hazards in the workplace, such as boxes on the floor, doors ajar, approaching people or vehicles? ☐ Yes ☐ No

c.. Does your patient have any difficulty walking up or down stairs? ☐ Yes ☐ No

d. Can your patient work with small objects such as those involved in doing sedentary work? ☐ Yes ☐ No

e. Can your patient work with large objects? ☐ Yes ☐ No

9. Please identify any exertional limitations; and please explain the relationship of these limitations to your patient's vision:

a. How many pounds can your patient ***lift and carry*** in a competitive work situation?

	Never	**Rarely**	**Occasionally**	**Frequently**
Less than 10 lbs.	☐	☐	☐	☐
10 lbs.	☐	☐	☐	☐
20 lbs.	☐	☐	☐	☐
50 lbs.	☐	☐	☐	☐

b. How often can your patient perform the following activities?

	Never	**Rarely**	**Occasionally**	**Frequently**
Stoop (bend)	☐	☐	☐	☐
Crouch/ squat	☐	☐	☐	☐

c. Please explain the medical basis for the above limitations and whether they are related to your patient's eye problem:

____

____

____

____

10. In addition to normal breaks every two hours, will your patient sometimes need to take *unscheduled* breaks during a working day? ☐ Yes ☐ No

If yes, 1) approx. how ***often*** do you think this will happen? ____________

2) approx. how ***long*** (on average) will each break last?________________

3) please explain why such breaks are necessary:

____

____

11. How much is your patient likely to be "***off task***"? That is, what percentage of a typical workday would your patient's symptoms likely be severe enough to interfere with ***attention and concentration*** needed to perform even simple work tasks?

☐ 0% ☐ 5% ☐ 10% ☐ 15% ☐ 20% ☐ 25% or more

12. Please describe any other limitations that would affect your patient's ability to work at a regular job on a sustained basis:

____

____

____

____

______________________________ ______________________________

Date *Signature*

Printed/Typed Name ______________________________

Address: ______________________________

____

7/16

7-501 ______________________________

232-4

§233 Respiratory Disorders, Listings §§ 3.00-3.11

Listings

A claimant with the most common respiratory impairment, asthma, will meet § 3.03B of the Listings if attacks requiring hospitalization meet the following requirements:

> Exacerbations or complications requiring three hospitalizations within a 12-month period and at least 30 days apart (the 12-month period must occur within the period we are considering in connection with your application or continuing disability review). Each hospitalization must last at least 48 hours, including hours in a hospital emergency department immediately before the hospitalization. Consider under a disability for 1 year from the discharge date of the last hospitalization; after that, evaluate the residual impairment(s) under 3.03 or another appropriate listing.

In a case involving a respiratory impairment, send a copy of the appropriate section of the Listings to your client's pulmonary specialist. Ask the doctor to look at three Listings issues: 1) Do the claimant's medical records contain evidence that the claimant meets any of the medical criteria for this particular impairment? 2) Is it probable that additional testing would show that the claimant meets one of the medical criteria (and would the doctor be willing to order the necessary testing)? 3) If the claimant's impairment does not meet the Listings, does the doctor think that the claimant is as impaired as one who does meet the Listings?

RFC Evaluation

Ask the treating physician for a more detailed description of RFC than that which is usually given in response to forms, such as the one used by ALJs (*see* §221.6). Respiratory impairments cause limitations that are exertional, environmental and sometimes mental. A Pulmonary Medical Source Statement appears at §233.1. Supplement this questionnaire where appropriate.

Environmental Limitations

See SSRs 83-14 and 85-15 for a limited discussion of the impact of environmental limitations.

Sleep Disorders

Sleep-related breathing disorders are mentioned in the introductory part of the Respiratory Disorders Listings at § 3.00P as follows:

P. What are sleep-related breathing disorders and how do we evaluate them?

1. Sleep-related breathing disorders (for example, sleep apnea) are characterized by transient episodes of interrupted breathing during sleep, which disrupt normal sleep patterns. Prolonged episodes can result in disorders such as hypoxemia (low blood oxygen) and pulmonary vasoconstriction (restricted blood flow in pulmonary blood vessels). Over time, these disorders may lead to chronic pulmonary hypertension or other complications.
2. We evaluate the complications of sleep-related breathing disorders under the listings in the affected body system(s). For example, we evaluate chronic pulmonary hypertension due to any cause under 3.09; chronic heart failure under 4.02; and disturbances in mood, cognition, and behavior under 12.02 or another appropriate mental disorders listing. We will not purchase polysomnography (sleep study).

Narcolepsy, an impairment that does not appear in the Listings, is discussed in POMS DI 24580.005. This POMS section says that narcolepsy is a chronic neurological disorder.

A Sleep Disorders Medical Source Statement appears at §233.2.

§233.1 Form: Pulmonary Medical Source Statement

PULMONARY MEDICAL SOURCE STATEMENT

From: ______________________________

Re: ______________________________(Name of Patient)

______________________________(Date of Birth)

Please answer the following questions concerning your patient's impairments. *Attach relevant treatment notes, radiologist reports, laboratory and test results as appropriate.*

1. Frequency and length of contact: ______________________________

2. Diagnoses: ______________________________

____

3. Identify the clinical findings, laboratory and pulmonary function test results that show your patient's medical impairments: ______________________________

____

4. Identify all of your patient's ***symptoms***:

☐Shortness of breath ☐Rhonchi ☐Episodic pneumonia
☐Orthopnea ☐Edema ☐Fatigue
☐Chest tightness ☐Episodic acute asthma ☐Palpitations
☐Wheezing ☐Episodic acute bronchitis ☐Coughing
Other symptoms: ______________________________

____

5. If your patient has acute asthma attacks,

a. Identify the precipitating factors:

☐Upper respiratory infection ☐Emotional upset/stress
☐Allergens ☐Irritants
☐Exercise ☐Cold air/change in weather
☐Aspirin ☐Foods
☐Tartrazine

b. Characterize the nature and severity of your patient's attacks: ________________

____

c. How often does your patient have asthma attacks? ____________________

d. How long is your patient incapacitated during an average attack? ____________

6. Do emotional factors contribute to the severity of your patient's symptoms and functional limitations? ☐ Yes ☐ No

If no, please explain: ____

7. a. List of prescribed medications:

b. Describe any side effects of your patient's medications (particularly of steroids, if applicable) that may have implications for working, e.g., dizziness, fatigue, drowsiness, stomach upset, etc.:

8. Prognosis: ____

9. Have your patient's impairments lasted or can they be expected to last at least twelve months? ☐ Yes ☐ No

10. As a result of your patient's impairments, estimate your patient's functional limitations if your patient were placed in a ***competitive work situation:***

a. How many city blocks can your patient walk without rest or severe pain? _______

b. Please circle the hours and/or minutes that your patient can sit ***at one time,*** e.g., before needing to get up, etc.

Sit: 0 5 10 15 20 30 45 (Minutes) 1 2 More than 2 (Hours)

c. Please circle the hours and/or minutes that your patient can stand ***at one time***, e.g., before needing to sit down, walk around, etc.

Stand: 0 5 10 15 20 30 45 Minutes | 1 2 More than 2 Hours

d. How long can your patient sit and stand/walk ***total in an 8-hour working day*** (with normal breaks)?

Sit	Stand/walk	
☐	☐	less than 2 hours
☐	☐	about 2 hours
☐	☐	about 4 hours
☐	☐	at least 6 hours

e. In addition to normal breaks every two hours, will your patient sometimes need to take *unscheduled* breaks during a working day? Yes No

If yes, 1) approx. how ***often*** do you think this will happen? ________________

2) approx. how ***long*** (on average) will each break last?________________

3) on such a break, will your patient need to ☐ lie down / ☐ sit quietly?

For this and other questions on this form, "rarely" means 1% to 5% of an 8-hour working day; "occasionally" means 6% to 33% of an 8-hour working day; "frequently" means 34% to 66% of an 8-hour working day.

f. How many pounds can your patient lift and carry in a competitive work situation?

	Never	**Rarely**	**Occasionally**	**Frequently**
Less than 10 lbs.	☐	☐	☐	☐
10 lbs.	☐	☐	☐	☐
20 lbs.	☐	☐	☐	☐
50 lbs.	☐	☐	☐	☐

g. How often can your patient perform the following activities?

	Never	**Rarely**	**Occasionally**	**Frequently**
Twist	☐	☐	☐	☐
Stoop (bend)	☐	☐	☐	☐
Crouch/ squat	☐	☐	☐	☐
Climb ladders	☐	☐	☐	☐
Climb stairs	☐	☐	☐	☐

h. State the degree to which your patient should avoid the following:

ENVIRONMENTAL RESTRICTIONS	NO RESTRICTIONS	AVOID CONCENTRATED EXPOSURE	AVOID EVEN MODERATE EXPOSURE	AVOID ALL EXPOSURE
Extreme cold	☐	☐	☐	☐
Extreme heat	☐	☐	☐	☐
High humidity	☐	☐	☐	☐
Wetness	☐	☐	☐	☐
Cigarette smoke	☐	☐	☐	☐
Perfumes	☐	☐	☐	☐
Soldering fluxes	☐	☐	☐	☐
Solvents/cleaners	☐	☐	☐	☐
Fumes, odors, gases	☐	☐	☐	☐
Dust	☐	☐	☐	☐
Chemicals	☐	☐	☐	☐
List other irritants:				
________________	☐	☐	☐	☐

i. How much is your patient likely to be ***"off task"***? That is, what percentage of a typical workday would your patient's symptoms likely be severe enough to interfere with ***attention and concentration*** needed to perform even simple work tasks?

☐ 0% ☐ 5% ☐ 10% ☐ 15% ☐ 20% ☐ 25% or more

j. To what degree can your patient tolerate work stress?

☐ Incapable of even "low stress" jobs ☐ Capable of low stress jobs
☐ Moderate stress is okay ☐ Capable of high stress work

Please explain the reasons for your conclusion: ______________________________

k. Are your patient's impairments likely to produce "good days" and "bad days"?
☐ Yes ☐ No

If yes, assuming your patient was trying to work full time, please estimate, on the average, how many days per month your patient is likely to be absent from work as a result of the impairments:

☐Never ☐About three days per month
☐About one day per month ☐About four days per month
☐About two days per month ☐More than four days per month

11. Are your patient's impairments (physical impairments plus any emotional impairments) as demonstrated by signs, clinical findings and laboratory or test results ***reasonably consistent*** with the symptoms and functional limitations described in this evaluation?
□ Yes □No

If no, please explain: ______________________________

12. Please describe any other limitations (such as psychological limitations, limited vision, difficulty hearing, etc.) that would affect your patient's ability to work at a regular job on a sustained basis:

____

____

______________________________ ______________________________
Date *Signature*

Printed/Typed Name: ______________________________

Address: ______________________________

____

§233.2 *Form: Sleep Disorders Medical Source Statement*

SLEEP DISORDERS MEDICAL SOURCE STATEMENT

From: ______________________________

Re: ______________________________(Name of Patient)

______________________________(Date of Birth)

Please answer all the following questions concerning your patient's sleep disorders and other health problems. *Attach relevant treatment notes, laboratory and test results as appropriate.*

1. Frequency and length of contact: ______________________________

2. Diagnoses:______________________________

3. Prognosis:______________________________

4. Identify your patient's ***symptoms and signs***:

□ Cataplexy	□Sinus arrhythmia	□Hypnogogic phenomenon
□ Insomnia	□Extreme bradycardia	□Ventricular tachycardia
□ Atrial flutter	□Sleep paralysis	□Excessive daytime sleepiness
□ Cognitive problems	□Automatic behavior	□Hypercapnia
□ Hypoxia	□Pulmonary insufficiency	□Obesity

□ Sleep apnea:	a. □ Obstructive	b. □ Centralc.	c. □ Mixed

□ Other: ______________________________

5. Does your patient have ***recurrent daytime sleep attacks***? □ Yes □ No

If yes,

a. Can these attacks occur suddenly and in hazardous conditions (e.g., driving, while exposed to heights or moving machinery)? □ Yes □ No

b ***How often*** do these attacks typically occur: _______ per day or _______ per week or ______ per month?

c. ***How long*** does your patient typically sleep with each attack? ______________

d. Identify situations that can precipitate attacks:

□ Quiet
□ Emotion
□ Sleep disturbance
□ Laughter
□ Exertion
□ Side effects of medications
□ Repetitive activity

□ Other ______________________

e. If your patient was working at the time of a sleep attack, would the attack likely disrupt the work of coworkers or supervisors in your patient's vicinity?

□ Yes □ No

6. Identify positive clinical findings and test results (e.g., multiple sleep latency test, MSLT, MWT, REM testing, EEG, polysomnographic studies, etc.):

____

____

7. Identify any ***side effects*** of medications that may have implications for working:
□ Drowsiness/sedation □ Other: _________________________________

8. Have your patient's impairments lasted or can they be expected to last at least twelve months?

□ Yes □ No

9. As a result of your patient's impairments, estimate your patient's functional limitations assuming your patient was placed in a ***competitive work situation*** on an ongoing basis:

a. In addition to normal breaks every two hours, will your patient sometimes need to take *unscheduled* breaks during a working day? □ Yes No

If yes, 1) approx. how ***often*** do you think this will happen? ________________

2) approx. how ***long*** (on average) will each break last?________________

3) what symptoms cause a need for breaks?

□ Daytime sleep attacks □ Adverse effects of medication
□ Chronic fatigue
□ Other: ____________________________________

b. State the degree to which your patient should avoid the following:

ENVIRONMENTAL RESTRICTIONS	NO RESTRICTIONS	AVOID CONCENTRATED EXPOSURE	AVOID EVEN MODERATE EXPOSURE	AVOID ALL EXPOSURE
Driving	□	□	□	□
Heights	□	□	□	□
Moving machinery	□	□	□	□
Working alone without supervision	□	□	□	□
Power tools	□	□	□	□
Routine, repetitive tasks	□	□	□	□

c. How much is your patient likely to be ***"off task"***? That is, what percentage of a typical workday would your patient's symptoms likely be severe enough to interfere with ***attention and concentration*** needed to perform even simple work tasks?

□ 0% □ 5% □ 10% □ 15% □ 20% □ 25% or more

d. To what degree can your patient tolerate work stress?

□ Incapable of even "low stress" work □ Capable of low stress work
□ Capable of moderate stress - normal work □ Capable of high stress work

Please explain the reasons for your conclusion: ______________________

e. Are your patient's impairments likely to produce "good days" and "bad days"?
□ Yes □ No

If yes, assuming your patient was trying to work full time, please estimate, on the average, how many days per month your patient is likely to be absent from work as a result of the impairments:

□ Never □ About three days per month
□ About one day per month □ About four days per month
□ About two days per month More than four days per month

10. Are your patient's impairments (physical impairments plus any emotional impairments) as demonstrated by signs, clinical findings and laboratory or test results ***reasonably consistent*** with the symptoms and functional limitations described above in this evaluation? □ Yes □ No

If no, please explain: ____

11. We understand your patient has a sleep disorder, not a seizure disorder. However, Social Security describes a seizure disorder that it considers disabling as follows:

> 11.02B Epilepsy—Dyscognitive seizures (formerly complex partial seizures), occurring at least once a week for at least 3 consecutive months despite adherence to prescribed treatment

In your opinion, is your patient's sleep disorder in combination with any other impairments ***at least as medically severe*** as the condition described above? □ Yes □ No

If yes, please explain: ____

____

12. Please describe any other limitations that would affect your patient's ability to work at a regular job on a sustained basis or any testing that would help to clarify the severity of your patient's impairment(s) or limitations:

____

____

____

Date: ____________________ *Signed:* ______________________________

Print Name: ______________________________

Address ______________________________

____

____

§233.2

7-59

1/17

§234 Cardiovascular System, Listings §§ 4.00-4.12

Listings

The cardiac Listings, effective April 13, 2006, continue the pivotal role of exercise testing in evaluating ischemic heart disease and, to a somewhat lesser degree of importance, in evaluating chronic heart failure, the two cardiac impairments seen most often at hearings. Although some substantive changes were made to the Listings, these Listings are recognizable to anyone who worked with the earlier version. Changes mostly involve updating for new test procedures.

SSA removed what it calls reference Listings, which merely referred to other sections of the Listings. When the reference Listings were removed, SSA did not renumber the remaining Listings. Thus, for example, the Listing dealing with ischemic heart disease remains § 4.04, despite the fact that there is now no § 4.03 of the Listings.

The introductory section of the cardiac Listings has been completely rewritten, making it much more useful in understanding your client's impairment and in understanding SSA's approach to evaluating that impairment. It is required reading for claimants' advocates.

SSA changed a Listing dealing with chronic heart failure, which previously required "an inability to carry on any physical activity." SSA noted that this "implied that the individual must be bedridden. Our program experience shows that this listing was set at too high a level of severity and was little used." Instead, SSA noted that the final criteria for the revised § 4.02B1 describes an "extreme" limitation, "that is, an impairment that very seriously limits your ability to independently initiate, sustain, or complete activities of daily living. This is modeled after our other rules that define listing-level severity in terms of an 'extreme' limitation; for example, the definition of 'inability to ambulate effectively' in the musculoskeletal listings, section 1.00B2b(1)." 71 Fed. Reg. 2318 (2006). This formulation also appears in § 4.04C2 dealing with ischemic heart disease. To meet the chronic heart failure Listing § 4.02B1, or the ischemic heart disease Listing § 4.04C2, a state agency doctor must first determine that exercise testing would present a significant risk to the individual.

A new section of the ischemic heart disease Listing provides that three "ischemic episodes" in one year, each requiring revascularization, defined as an angioplasty or bypass surgery (*see* § 4.00E9f), will meet § 4.04B.

The introductory section of the cardiac Listings discusses lymphedema but states that lymphedema does not meet § 4.11 "although it may medically equal the severity of that listing." Listing § 4.00G4(a). This section also states that lymphedema may equal §§ 1.02A or 1.03 of the musculo-skeletal Listing. A Lymphedema Medical Assessment form appears as 234A on Digital Access.

§234.1 Dealing With Exercise Tolerance Test Results

An exercise tolerance test is positive if one group of configurations, identified in § 4.04A of the Listings, is noted on the electrocardiogram at 5 METs or less. One MET is that amount of energy expended by an individual sitting quietly. This amount varies from individual to individual because of physical conditioning, weight or underlying pathology. Because it is not practical to measure the oxygen uptake of everyone who takes an exercise tolerance test, averages are used. These averages may differ significantly from your client's actual MET measurement. In addition, cardiologists disagree about these average values.

Whenever you have a client with ischemic heart disease, whose impairment has been deemed by state agency doctors not to meet the Listings, you are likely to find a negative exercise tolerance test in the records gathered by SSA that, at first glance, appears inconsistent with your client's claim. Indeed, it might be inconsistent with a finding that your client is disabled. But many times such exercise tests can be properly placed in context and are not inconsistent with your client being found disabled.

Such exercise tolerance tests, abbreviated ETT in the introductory section of the Listings, have limitations that were acknowledged by SSA in § 4.00C4 as follows:

> 4. *Do ETTs have limitations?* An ETT provides an estimate of aerobic capacity for walking on a grade, bicycling, or moving one's arms in an environmentally controlled setting. Therefore, ETT results do not correlate with the ability to perform other types of exertional activities, such as lifting and carrying heavy loads, and do not provide an estimate of the ability to perform activities required for work in all possible work environments or throughout a workday. Also, certain medications (such as beta blockers) and conduction disorders (such as left or right bundle branch blocks) can cause false-negative or false-positive results. Therefore, we must consider the results of an ETT together with all the other relevant evidence in your case record.

SSA also acknowledged that a negative test is not necessarily dispositive. Section 4.00C11 provides:

> 11. *How do we evaluate ETT results?* We evaluate ETT results on the basis of the work level at which the test becomes abnormal, as documented by onset of signs or symptoms and any ECG or imaging

abnormalities. The absence of an ischemic response on an ETT alone does not exclude the diagnosis of ischemic heart disease. We must consider the results of an ETT in the context of all of the other evidence in your case record.

SSA states that if a claimant's impairment does not meet or equal an impairment found in the Listings, the claimant "may or may not have the residual functional capacity to engage in substantial gainful activity." § 4.00I3b. Thus, your client could be disabled despite a negative exercise tolerance test.

Also note that SSA states that the results of an exercise test are "timely" only for 12 months after the date performed "provided there has been no change in your clinical status that may alter the severity of your cardiovascular impairment." § 4.00C9a. When SSA evaluates a test that is more than 12 months old, it "must consider the results in the context of all the relevant evidence, including why the test was performed and whether there has been an intervening event or improvement or worsening of your impairment." § 4.00C9c. Do not ignore the possibility that your client's condition worsened after the date of a negative exercise tolerance test.

Also do not ignore the possibility that there is a psychological component to the claimant's cardiac disability. If there is evidence supporting this, consider whether the claimant's cardiologist can address the claimant's psychological limitations or whether you need to refer the claimant for a psychological evaluation.

In most cases that reach the hearing level, it will be necessary to obtain a detailed description of the claimant's RFC from the treating cardiologist. It generally works best to send the treating cardiologist a medical source statement form, such as the one at §234.3. If the cardiologist describes an RFC that appears inconsistent with the results of an exercise tolerance test, send a follow-up letter inquiring about this. Supplement with the following questions to the treating cardiologist, as appropriate:

- Is the claimant so afraid of having another heart attack that this fear, in itself, will interfere with the ability to work?
- What implications for the claimant's ability to work are demonstrated by the claimant's dramatic rise in blood pressure during the exercise tolerance test?
- Do the exercise tolerance test results give an accurate picture of this claimant's ability to work on a sustained basis, day in and day out?
- Are there other cardiac test results that give a more accurate picture of the claimant's limitations than the exercise tolerance test?
- What is the role played by the claimant's obesity on the claimant's ability to perform activities day in and day out?
- Is the combined effect of the claimant's cardiovascular impairment and obesity greater than the effects of each impairment considered separately? (*Cf.* § 4.00I1 of the Listings and SSR 02-1p.)

At the ALJ level there has always been more room for argument, more opportunities for a treating cardiologist to explain why in the claimant's case an exercise tolerance test is not dispositive. But understanding how the decisions are made at the initial and reconsideration stages is useful in developing your argument to the ALJ. Consider this: SSA has never recognized a limitation to sedentary work because of ischemic heart disease. One would assume that SSA chose 5 METs to be the cutoff point for meeting the Listings because it determined that an individual, whose exercise tolerance test was positive at that level, was incapable of performing all work, including sedentary work. Thus, it would be logical to assume that someone whose test was positive at somewhat more than 5 METs would be limited to sedentary work, and so on. This argument does work with ALJs when you are trying to prove a limitation to sedentary work; but SSA uses the following informal rule of thumb that skips over a limitation to sedentary work altogether:

— Ability to complete 9 or more METs (Stage III of the Bruce protocol), without the occurrence of any of the findings in § 4.04A or a precipitous fall in blood pressure, would be consistent with ability to work at heavy exertional levels.

— Ability to complete 7 METs of exercise, without the occurrence of any of the findings in § 4.04A, but with the occurrence of one or more of these findings or precipitous fall in blood pressure at a higher level of exercise (9 or 10 METs), would be consistent with ability to perform at medium exertional levels.

— Ability to complete 5 METs of exercise, without the occurrence of the findings in § 4.04A, but with the occurrence of one or more of these changes at exercise between 5 and 7 METs, would be consistent with ability to perform at light exertional levels.

§234.2 *New York Heart Association Standards*

Sometimes doctors assess functional classification according to the following standards set by the New York Heart Association:

THE FUNCTIONAL AND THERAPEUTIC CLASSIFICATIONS
OF PATIENTS WITH DISEASES OF THE HEART

Functional Classification

Note: The classification of patients according to their cardiac functional capacity gives only a part of the information needed to plan the management of the patient's activities. A recommendation or prescription regarding physical activity should be based on information derived from many sources. The functional classification is an estimate of what the patient's heart will allow him to do and should not be influenced by the character of the structural lesions nor by an opinion as to treatment or prognosis.

Class I — Patients with cardiac disease but without resulting limitations of physical activity. Ordinary physical activity does not cause undue fatigue, palpitation, dyspnea, or anginal pain.

Class II — Patients with cardiac disease resulting in slight limitation of physical activity. They are comfortable at rest. Ordinary physical activity results in fatigue, palpitation, dyspnea, or anginal pain.

Class III — Patients with cardiac disease resulting in marked limitation of physical activity. They are comfortable at rest. Less than ordinary physical activity causes fatigue, palpitation, dyspnea, or anginal pain.

Class IV — Patients with cardiac disease resulting in inability to carry on any physical activity without discomfort. Symptoms of cardiac insufficiency or of the anginal syndrome may be present even at rest. If any physical activity is undertaken, discomfort is increased.

Therapeutic Classification

Note: The therapeutic classification is intended as a guide to the management of the activities of cardiac patients. It gives a prescription for the amount of physical activity which is advised for those in each functional class. From a practical point of view, it should be translated into terms of daily physical activity, such as walking a certain number of yards, climbing a specified number of stairs, lifting a certain number of pounds, and standing for an unlimited or limited part of the working day. For children it is necessary to individualize with permissible play programs, specifying the type and duration of outdoor and indoor activity which may be performed.

Class A — Patients with cardiac disease whose physical activity need not be restricted in any way.

Class B — Patients with cardiac disease whose ordinary physical activity need not be restricted, but who should be advised against severe or competitive efforts.

Class C — Patients with cardiac disease whose ordinary physical activity should be moderately restricted, and whose more strenuous efforts should be discontinued.

Class D — Patients with cardiac disease whose ordinary physical activity should be markedly restricted.

Class E — Patients with cardiac disease who should be at complete rest, confined to bed or chair.

Note: The functional capacity of the patient does not always determine the amount of physical activity that should be permitted. For example, although a child at the onset of active rheumatic carditis may not experience discomfort on playing baseball, rest in bed is imperative. Such a patient would be designated as Class I (Functional), E (Therapeutic). There is frequently a difference between the amount of activity which a patient can undertake in terms of his functional capacity and that which he should attempt in order to prevent aggravation of his disease. The recommendation of physical activity is based not only upon the amount of effort possible without discomfort but also upon the nature and severity of the cardiac disease.

(Excerpted from DISEASES OF THE HEART AND BLOOD VESSELS—NOMENCLATURE AND CRITERIA FOR DIAGNOSIS, 6th ed., Boston: Little, Brown and Company, copyright 1964 by the New York Heart Association, Inc.)

When these classifications are translated to MET levels we get a better understanding of both of the classifications and the MET levels. Class I patients are capable of 7 METs and more. Class II patients are capable of 5 to 6 METS. Class III patients are capable of 2 to 4 METs; and Class IV less than 2 METs. *See* the AMA GUIDES TO THE EVALUATION OF PERMANENT IMPAIRMENT, 5th ed., p. 27.

§234.3 Form: Cardiac Medical Source Statement

CARDIAC MEDICAL SOURCE STATEMENT

From: ______________________________

Re: ______________________________(Name of Patient)

______________________________(Date of Birth)

Please answer the following questions concerning your patient's impairments. *Attach relevant treatment notes, radiologist reports, laboratory and test results as appropriate.*

1. Frequency and length of contact: ______________________________

2. Diagnosis (with New York Heart Association functional classification):

____

3. Prognosis:____

4. Identify clinical findings, laboratory and test results that show your patient's impairments:

____

____

5. Identify your patient's signs and symptoms:

- □ Chest pain
- □ Weakness
- □ Arrhythmia
- □ Exertional dyspnea
- □ Loss of appetite
- □ Syncope
- □ Hepatomegaly
- □ Paroxysmal nocturnal dyspnea
- □ Anginal equivalent pain
- □ Exercise intolerance
- □ Orthopnea
- □ Rest dyspnea
- □ Peripheral edema
- □ Near syncope
- □ Prinzmetal's angina
- □ Chronic fatigue
- □ Nausea
- □ Dizziness
- □ Nocturia
- □ Pulmonary edema
- □ Chronic cough
- □ Palpitations

Other: ____

6. If your patient has angina:

a. Describe nature, location and radiation of symptoms: ____________________

____

b. How often do angina episodes typically occur? ________________________

c. If your patient must typically rest after an episode of angina, how long will your patient typically rest? ____________________________

7. Describe the treatment and response including any side effects of medication that may have implications for working, *e.g.*, drowsiness, dizziness, nausea, etc.:

____

____

8. a. What is the role of stress in bringing on your patient's symptoms?

____

b. To what degree can your patient tolerate work stress?

□ Incapable of even "low stress" work
□ Capable of low stress work
□ Capable of moderate stress - normal work
□ Capable of high stress work

Please explain the reasons for your conclusion: ____________________

9. Do your patient's physical symptoms and limitations cause emotional difficulties such as depression or chronic anxiety? □ Yes □ No

Please explain: ______________________________________

10. Do emotional factors ***contribute*** to the severity of your patient's subjective symptoms and functional limitations? □ Yes □ No

11. Have your patient's impairments lasted or can they be expected to last at least twelve months? □ Yes □ No

12. As a result of your patient's impairments, estimate your patient's functional limitations if your patient were placed in a ***competitive work situation.***

a. How many city blocks can your patient walk without rest or severe pain? _____

b. Please indicate how long your patient can sit and stand/walk ***total in an 8-hour working day*** (with normal breaks):

Sit	**Stand/walk**	
□	□	less than 2 hours
□	□	about 2 hours
□	□	about 4 hours
□	□	at least 6 hours

c. Does your patient need a job that permits shifting positions at will from sitting, standing or walking? □ Yes □ No

d. In addition to normal breaks every two hours, will your patient sometimes need to take *unscheduled* breaks during a working day? □ Yes □ No

If yes, 1) approx. how ***often*** do you think this will happen? ___________

2) approx. how ***long*** (on average) will each break last?__________

3) on such a break, will your patient need to lie down or sit quietly?

e. With prolonged sitting, should your patient's leg(s) be elevated? □ Yes □ No

If yes, 1) how ***high*** should the leg(s) be elevated? _________________

2) if your patient had a sedentary job***, what percentage of time*** during an 8-hour working day should the leg(s) be elevated? ______________________%

3) what symptoms cause a need to elevate the leg(s)? ___________

For this and other questions on this form, "rarely" means 1% to 5% of an 8-hour working day; "occasionally" means 6% to 33% of an 8-hour working day; "frequently" means 34% to 66% of an 8-hour working day.

f. How many pounds can your patient lift and carry in a competitive work situation?

	Never	**Rarely**	**Occasionally**	**Frequently**
Less than 10 lbs.	□	□	□	□
10 lbs.	□	□	□	□
20 lbs.	□	□	□	□
50 lbs.	□	□	□	□

g. How often can your patient perform the following activities?

	Never	**Rarely**	**Occasionally**	**Frequently**
Twist	□	□	□	□
Stoop (bend)	□	□	□	□
Crouch/ squat	□	□	□	□
Climb stairs	□	□	□	□
Climb ladders	□	□	□	□

h. State the degree to which your patient should avoid the following:

ENVIRONMENTAL RESTRICTIONS	**NO RESTRICTIONS**	**AVOID CONCENTRATED EXPOSURE**	**AVOID EVEN MODERATE EXPOSURE**	**AVOID ALL EXPOSURE**
Extreme cold	□	□	□	□
Extreme heat	□	□	□	□
High humidity	□	□	□	□
Wetness	□	□	□	□
Cigarette smoke	□	□	□	□
Perfumes	□	□	□	□
Soldering fluxes	□	□	□	□
Solvents/cleaners	□	□	□	□
Fumes, odors, gases	□	□	□	□
Dust	□	□	□	□
Chemicals	□	□	□	□
List other irritants:				
________________	□	□	□	□
________________	□	□	□	□

i. How much is your patient likely to be **"*off task*"**? That is, what percentage of a typical workday would your patient's symptoms likely be severe enough to interfere with ***attention and concentration*** needed to perform even simple work tasks?

□ 0% □ 5% □ 10% □ 15% □ 20 % □ 25% or more

j. Are your patient's impairments likely to produce "good days" and "bad days"?

□ Yes □ No

If yes, assuming your patient was trying to work full time, please estimate, on the average, how many days per month your patient is likely to be absent from work as a result of the impairments:

□ Never
□ About one day per month
□ About two days per month
□ About three days per month
□ About four days per month
□ More than four days per month

13. Are your patient's impairments (physical impairments plus any emotional impairments) as demonstrated by signs, clinical findings and laboratory or test results ***reasonably consistent*** with the symptoms and functional limitations described above in this evaluation? □ Yes □ No

If no, please explain: ____

14. Please describe any other limitations (such as psychological limitations, limited vision,

difficulty hearing, etc.) that would affect your patient's ability to work at a regular job on a sustained basis:

____

____

____

________________ ______________________

Date *Signature*

Printed/Typed Name: ______________________

Address: ______________________

7-45 ______________________

 ____

§234.4 Cardiac Arrhythmia Medical Source Statement

CARDIAC ARRHYTHMIA MEDICAL SOURCE STATEMENT

From: ______________________________

Re: ______________________________(Name of Patient)

______________________________(Date of Birth)

Please answer the following questions concerning your patient's impairments. *Attach relevant treatment notes, radiologist reports, laboratory and test results as appropriate.*

1. Frequency and length of contact: ______________________________

2. Does your patient have arrhythmias? □ Yes □ No

   If yes, are they atrial/ supraventricular arrhythmias or ventricular arrhythmias?

3. Other cardiac diagnoses (with New York Heart Association functional classification):

   ____

4. Prognosis: ______________________________

5. If your patient has episodes of arrhythmia,

   a. Identify your patient's symptoms:

   □ Chest pain □ Syncope □ Chronic fatigue
   □ Weakness □ Palpitations □ Nausea
   □ Shortness of breath □ Edema □ Dizziness
   □ Near syncope □ Light headedness

   b. How often do episodes typically occur?

   □ Seldom or never □ Daily
   □ Several times a week but less often than daily □ Several times a day

   c. How long do episodes typically last? ______________________________

   d. If your patient must typically rest after an episode, how long will your patient typically rest?

   ____

6. Identify clinical findings, laboratory and test results that show your patient's impairments:

____

____

7. If your patient has an implanted defibrillator and experiences frequent shocks,

   a. What is the frequency of shocks? ______________________

   b. What are the reasons for frequent shocks? ______________________

8. Describe the treatment and response including any side effects of medication that may have implications for working, *e.g.*, drowsiness, dizziness, nausea, etc:

____

____

9. a. What is the role of stress in bringing on your patient's symptoms?

____

   b. To what degree can your patient tolerate work stress?

   □ Incapable of even "low stress" work □ Capable of low stress work
   □ Capable of moderate stress - normal work □ Capable of high stress work

   Please explain the reasons for your conclusion: ______________________

10. Do your patient's physical symptoms and limitations cause emotional difficulties such as depression or chronic anxiety? □ Yes □ No

    Please explain: ______________________________

11. Do emotional factors *contribute* to the severity of your patient's subjective symptoms and functional limitations? □ Yes □ No

12. Have your patient's impairments lasted or can they be expected to last at least twelve months? Yes No

13. As a result of your patient's impairments, estimate your patient's functional limitations if your patient were placed in a ***competitive work situation***.

    a. How many city blocks can your patient walk ***at one time*** before stopping? ____

b. Please circle the hours and/or minutes that your patient can sit ***at one time***, *e.g.*, before needing to get up, *etc.*

Sit: 0 5 10 15 20 30 45 Minutes — 1 2 More than 2 Hours

c. Please circle the hours and/or minutes that your patient can stand ***at one time***, *e.g.*, before needing to sit down, walk around, *etc.*

Stand: 0 5 10 15 20 30 45 Minutes — 1 2 More than 2 Hours

d. Please indicate how long your patient can sit and stand/walk ***total in an 8-hour working day*** (with normal breaks):

Sit	Stand/walk	
□	□	less than 2 hours
□	□	about 2 hours
□	□	about 4 hours
□	□	at least 6 hours

e. Does your patient need a job that permits shifting positions at will from sitting, standing or walking? □ Yes □ No

f. Will your patient sometimes need to take unscheduled breaks during a working day? □ Yes □ No

If yes, 1) how ***often*** do you think this will happen? ________________
2) how ***long*** (on average) will your patient have to rest before returning to work? ________________

g. With prolonged sitting, should your patient's leg(s) be elevated? □ Yes □ No

If yes, 1) how ***high*** should the leg(s) be elevated? ________________
2) if your patient had a sedentary job***, what percentage of time*** during an 8-hour working day should the leg(s) be elevated? ________________%

For this and other questions on this form, "rarely" means 1% to 5% of an 8-hour working day; "occasionally" means 6% to 33% of an 8-hour working day; "frequently" means 34% to 66% of an 8-hour working day.

h. How many pounds can your patient lift and carry in a competitive work situation?

	Never	**Rarely**	**Occasionally**	**Frequently**
Less than 10 lbs.	□	□	□	□
10 lbs.	□	□	□	□
20 lbs.	□	□	□	□
50 lbs.	□	□	□	□

i. State the degree to which your patient should avoid the following:

ENVIRONMENTAL RESTRICTIONS	**NO RESTRICTIONS**	**AVOID CONCENTRATED EXPOSURE**	**AVOID EVEN MODERATE EXPOSURE**	**AVOID ALL EXPOSURE**
Extreme cold	□	□	□	□
Extreme heat	□	□	□	□
High humidity	□	□	□	□
Wetness	□	□	□	□
Cigarette smoke	□	□	□	□
Perfumes	□	□	□	□
Soldering fluxes	□	□	□	□
Solvents/cleaners	□	□	□	□
Fumes, odors, gases	□	□	□	□
Dust	□	□	□	□
Chemicals	□	□	□	□
List other irritants:				
____________________	□	□	□	□

j. How much is your patient likely to be ***"off task"***? That is, what percentage of a typical workday would your patient's symptoms likely be severe enough to interfere with ***attention and concentration*** needed to perform even simple work tasks?

□ 0% □ 5% □ 10% □ 15% □ 20% □ 25% or more

k. Are your patient's impairments likely to produce "good days" and "bad days"?

□ Yes □ No

If yes, assuming your patient was trying to work full time, please estimate, on the average, how many days per month your patient is likely to be absent from work as a result of the impairments:

□ Never
□ About one day per month
□ About two days per month
□ About three days per month
□ About four days per month
□ More than four days per month

14. Are your patient's impairments (physical impairments plus any emotional impairments) as demonstrated by signs, clinical findings and laboratory or test results ***reasonably consistent*** with the symptoms and functional limitations described above in this evaluation? □ Yes □ No

If no, please explain: ____________________

15. Please describe any other limitations (such as psychological limitations, limited vision, difficulty hearing, need to avoid temperature extremes, wetness, humidity, noise, dust, fumes, gases or hazards, etc.) that would affect your patient's ability to work at a regular job on a sustained basis:

____

____

____

____________________ ____________________

Date *Signature*

Printed/Typed Name: ____________________

Address: ____________________

____

____

§235 Digestive System, Listings §§ 5.00-5.09

Inflammatory Bowel Disease: Crohn's Disease and Ulcerative Colitis

The most common digestive system problems seen in ALJ hearings are those in which the primary symptoms are abdominal pain and diarrhea, sometimes with fecal incontinence. The most serious of these impairments are the ones that fall into the category of inflammatory bowel disease, usually Crohn's disease or ulcerative colitis. Irritable bowel syndrome, which has some similar symptoms but no findings of inflammatory bowel disease, is discussed separately below.

Work limitations of claimants with inflammatory bowel disease of the sort seen at ALJ hearings often result from missing work and while at work having to spend so much time, unpredictably, in the lavatory and away from the workstation. Symptoms and signs include "diarrhea, fecal incontinence, rectal bleeding, abdominal pain, fatigue, fever, nausea, vomiting, arthralgia, abdominal tenderness, palpable abdominal mass (usually inflamed loops of bowel) and perineal disease." § 5.00E2. There may be findings indicating malnutrition in severe cases. § 5.00E2. Because an inflammatory process is involved, other body systems may be affected in a variety of ways but SSA notes that the extraintestinal manifestations "may not correlate with the severity of your" inflammatory bowel disease. *See* § 5.00E3.

To meet § 5.06A of the Listing of Impairments two hospitalizations for bowel obstruction are required. The two hospitalizations must be at least 60 days apart within a 6-month period. To meet § 5.06B:

> B. Two of the following despite continuing treatment as prescribed and occurring within the same consecutive 6-month period:
>
> 1. Anemia with hemoglobin of less than 10.0 g/dL, present on at least two evaluations at least 60 days apart; or
> 2. Serum albumin of 3.0 g/dL or less, present on at least two evaluations at least 60 days apart; or
> 3. Clinically documented tender abdominal mass palpable on physical examination with abdominal pain or cramping that is not completely controlled by prescribed narcotic medication, present on at least two evaluations at least 60 days apart; or
> 4. Perineal disease with a draining abscess or fistula, with pain that is not completely controlled by prescribed narcotic medication, present on at least two evaluations at least 60 days apart; or
> 5. Involuntary weight loss of at least 10 percent from baseline, as computed in pounds, kilograms, or BMI, present on at least two evaluations at least 60 days apart; or
> 6. Need for supplemental daily enteral nutrition via a gastrostomy or daily parenteral nutrition via a central venous catheter.

The lives of claimants with inflammatory bowel disease at less than Listing level are often completely disrupted by their impairments. Their symptoms often make it difficult for them to cope with life, let alone working. Even claimants whose impairments are viewed by SSA (with its emphasis on objective findings) as relatively mild are often unable to sustain full-time work in a regular work setting.

There may be associated psychological problems that can be corroborated by a psychological evaluation. Or the claimant may simply exhibit poor coping with the impairment that may not rise to the level of a diagnosable psychological impairment but is nevertheless part of the picture that needs to be displayed for the ALJ. These cases often need to be developed primarily with lay evidence concerning attempts to work, and frequency and intensity of symptoms. Have the claimant keep a diary for a month or so before the hearing describing and keeping track of the frequency of diarrhea and other symptoms. Sometimes a vocational expert may be retained to give an opinion on the claimant's ability to work.

When you find someone whose impairment worsens while waiting for a hearing to the point that the inflammatory bowel disease now meets the Listings, it is a challenge to develop the claim in such a way that the claimant will be found disabled from the originally alleged onset date. It is difficult to obtain medical opinions about how severe the impairment was before it got worse since doctors tend to focus on treating immediate problems. For this reason, if you are involved in an inflammatory bowel disease case early on, don't wait until the hearing has been scheduled to obtain an opinion from the claimant's doctor.

Sometimes for certain claimants a colostomy or ileostomy disrupts the daily routine enough to interfere with work, which in combination with other limitations may contribute to a finding that the claimant is disabled. Sometimes a claimant has a difficult time coping with an ileostomy or colostomy as well as other stressors, which makes the claimant's case one more about the claimant's ability to cope with stressors than simply dealing with an ileostomy or colostomy. SSA's position, which may be true as far as it goes, is that an ileostomy or colostomy "does not preclude any gainful activity if [the claimant is] able to maintain adequate nutrition and function of the stoma." § 5.00E4. Meeting Listing level for weight loss, which is how SSA evaluates "adequate nutrition," requires a BMI of 17.5 or less calculated on two occasions at least 60 days apart during a 6-month period. § 5.08. A BMI of 17.5 is extremely skinny. A BMI of less than 18.5 is considered underweight; normal weight is BMI of 18.5 to 24.9. The formula for calculating BMI appears in §238 in the discussion of obesity. A National Institutes of Health BMI calculator is on the Internet at http://www.nhlbisupport.com/bmi/.

A Crohn's & Colitis Medical Source Statement appears at §235.1.

Irritable Bowel Syndrome

Irritable bowel syndrome is considered to be a functional bowel disorder with few objective findings on laboratory tests, x-rays, and biopsies. Emotional factors, stress, diet, drugs, or hormones may aggravate symptoms. There may be associated anxiety disorders, depression, or sometimes a somatization disorder. Frequently there are sleep disturbances. Doctors have come to view IBS as not purely psychosomatic. The gastrointestinal symptoms such as diarrhea provide objective evidence that something physical is going on.

Like cases involving inflammatory bowel disease, when developing a case for a hearing, the emphasis should be on disruption of work routine and missing work. Psychological impairments may need to be investigated.

An Irritable Bowel Syndrome Medical Source Statement, which is identical to the Crohn's and Colitis form in §235.1 except for the title, appears as 235A on Digital Access.

Hepatitis C

Even though it infects less that 2% of the total United States population, hepatitis C, an inflammation of the liver due to the hepatitis C virus (HCV), is a diagnosis that appears relatively frequently among disability claimants, either as the primary impairment or as a secondary diagnosis. The hepatitis C virus is generally contracted through direct contact with infected blood. For example, IV drug users sharing needles with an infected person can contract it. Thus, although some people contracted it when they had blood transfusions before 1992, the year that blood banks began effectively screening for hepatitis C, there is often a stigma associated with the diagnosis.

Many people who have been infected by the hepatitis C virus for years have no symptoms whatsoever. Thus, when you see hepatitis C as a secondary diagnosis in your client's medical records, chances are that your client may have no symptoms attributable to hepatitis C. Some people never develop symptoms. With others, hepatitis C may be quietly damaging their livers and symptoms may emerge in later years in conjunction with serious liver damage, which is addressed by § 5.05 of the Listings. As a rule, cases involving serious liver damage do not end up at the hearing level. Such claimants are found disabled by the state agency.

There is a group of people who do not have serious liver damage but are symptomatic. These are the problematic hepatitis C cases that are being seen more and more at disability hearings. Doctors speculate that symptoms may occur as part of the immune system's response to the virus. This would explain why laboratory studies do not show that the livers of these symptomatic people are worse than the livers of those with hepatitis C who are not symptomatic. For the group of people whose hepatitis C is symptomatic, fatigue, sometimes disabling fatigue, may be the primary symptom. Another common symptom is musculoskeletal pain. Not everyone in the symptomatic group progresses to cirrhosis and end stage liver disease. And, although hepatitis C is recognized by doctors as being capable of causing disabling fatigue, there is no correlation between the degree of fatigue and the degree of abnormality of liver function studies. *See* Barkhuizen, et al., "Musculoskeletal Pain and Fatigue Are Associated With Chronic Hepatitis C," 94 *American Journal of Gastroenterology* 1355 (1999); Foster, et al., "Chronic Hepatitis C Virus Infection Causes a Significant Reduction in Quality of Life in the Absence of Cirrhosis," 27 *Hepatology* 209 (1998); Goh, et al., "Fatigue Does Not Correlate With the Degree of Hepatitis or the Presence of Autoimmune Disorders in Chronic Hepatitis C Infection," 11 *European Journal of Gastroenterology and Hepatology* 833 (1999).

SSA recognizes that "[s]ymptoms of chronic liver disease may have a poor correlation with the severity of liver disease and functional ability." § 5.00D3a. It recognizes that "abnormal lab tests, such as liver enzymes, serum total bilirubin, or ammonia levels, may have a poor correlation with the severity of liver disease and functional ability." § 5.00D3c.

Combined interferon and ribavirin treatment for hepatitis C, which can last nearly a year, itself often produces disabling side effects. Claimants have been known to say that the cure is worse than the disease. The side effects are acknowledged by SSA at Listing § 5.00D4c(ii).

Because fatigue can play such a prominent role, proving disability from hepatitis C is often similar to proving disability for a claimant with chronic fatigue syndrome, *see* §230, or multiple sclerosis, *see* §239. Obtain reports from the claimant's doctors that address the critical issues. *See* §235.2 for a Hepatitis C Medical Source Statement. Be sure the record contains a full longitudinal medical history, and obtain statements from the claimant's family and friends that describe the claimant's ability to function. A paper by Attorney Ann W. Cook, "Tired and True Measures in Hepatitis C Claims," presented at a seminar in October 2000 still provides good advice even though the digestive system Listings were revised in 2007. Attorney Cook's paper is available from NOSSCR. *See also* the American Liver Foundation website at www.liverfoundation.org; Centers for Disease Control, www.cdc.gov/ncidod/diseases/hepatitis; and the Hepatitis C Foundation, www.hepcfoundation.org.

Other Digestive System Impairments

Medical Assessment forms for Cirrhosis, Gastritis, and Pancreatitis appear as 235B, 235C, and 235D on Digital Access

.§235.1 *Form: Crohn's & Colitis Medical Source Statement*

CROHN'S & COLITIS MEDICAL SOURCE STATEMENT

From: ______________________________

Re: ______________________________(Name of Patient)

______________________________(Date of Birth)

Please answer the following questions concerning your patient's impairments:

1. Frequency and length of contact:______________________________

2. Diagnoses: ______________________________

3. Prognosis: ______________________________

4. Identify your patient's symptoms:

□ Chronic diarrhea	□ Anal fissures
□ Bloody diarrhea	□ Nausea
□ Abdominal pain and cramping	□ Peripheral arthritis
□ Fever	□ Kidney problems
□ Weight loss	□ Malaise
□ Loss of appetite	□ Fatigue
□ Bowel obstruction	□ Mucus in stool
□ Vomiting	□ Ineffective straining at stool
□ Abdominal distention	□ (rectal tenesmus)
□ Fistulas	□ Sweatiness

Other: ______________________________

5. If your patient has pain, characterize the nature, location, frequency, precipitating factors, and severity of your patient's pain:

____

____

6. If aspects of your patient's impairment are episodic, describe the nature, precipitating factors, severity, frequency and duration of the episodic aspects:

____

____

7. Identify the clinical findings and objective signs:

____

____

8. Describe the treatment and response including any side effects of medication that may have implications for working, e.g., drowsiness, dizziness, nausea, etc.:

____

____

____

9. Have your patient's impairments lasted or can they be expected to last at least twelve months? □ Yes □ No

10. Do emotional factors contribute to the severity of your patient's symptoms and functional limitations? □ Yes □ No

11. Identify any psychological conditions affecting your patient's physical condition:

□ Depression
□ Somatoform disorder
□ Psychological factors affecting physical condition
□ Anxiety
□ Personality disorder
□ Other ____________

12. As a result of your patient's impairments, estimate your patient's functional limitations if your patient were placed in a ***competitive work situation:***

a. How many city blocks can your patient walk? ________

b. Please circle the hours and/or minutes that your patient can sit ***at one time,*** e.g., before needing to get up, etc.

Sit: 0 5 10 15 20 30 45 Minutes   1 2 More than 2 Hours

c. Please circle the hours and/or minutes that your patient can stand ***at one time***, e.g., before needing to sit down, walk around, etc.

Stand: 0 5 10 15 20 30 45 Minutes   1 2 More than 2 Hours

d. Please indicate how long your patient can sit and stand/walk ***total in an 8-hour working day*** (with normal breaks):

Sit	Stand/walk	
□	□	less than 2 hours
□	□	about 2 hours
□	□	about 4 hours
□	□	at least 6 hours

e. Does your patient need a job that permits shifting positions ***at will*** from sitting, standing or walking? □ Yes □ No

f. Does your patient need a job that permits ready access to a restroom? □ Yes □ No

g. In addition to normal breaks every two hours, will your patient need to take *unscheduled restroom* breaks during a working day? □ Yes □ No

If yes, 1) approx. how ***often*** do you think this will happen? ________________

2) approx. how ***long*** (on average) will each break last?________________

3) how much advance notice does your patient have of the need for a restroom break? ________________

h. Will your patient also sometimes need to lie down or rest at unpredictable intervals during a working day? □ Yes □ No

If yes, 1) how ***often*** do you think this will happen? ____________________

2) how ***long*** (on average) will your patient have to rest before returning to work? ____________________

3) what symptoms cause a need for such breaks? ____________________

____

For this and other questions on this form, "rarely" means 1% to 5% of an 8-hour working day; "occasionally" means 6% to 33% of an 8-hour working day; "frequently" means 34% to 66% of an 8-hour working day.

i. How many pounds can your patient lift and carry in a competitive work situation?

	Never	**Rarely**	**Occasionally**	**Frequently**
Less than 10 lbs.	□	□	□	□
10 lbs.	□	□	□	□
20 lbs.	□	□	□	□
50 lbs.	□	□	□	□

j. How often can your patient perform the following activities?

	Never	**Rarely**	**Occasionally**	**Frequently**
Twist	□	□	□	□
Stoop (bend)	□	□	□	□
Crouch/ squat	□	□	□	□
Climb ladders	□	□	□	□
Climb stairs	□	□	□	□

k. Does your patient have significant limitations with reaching, handling or fingering?
□Yes □No

If yes, please indicate the percentage of time during an 8-hour working day that your patient can use hands/fingers/arms for the following activities:

	HANDS: **Grasp, Turn** **Twist Objects**	**FINGERS:** **Fine** **Manipulations**	**ARMS:** **Reaching** **In Front of Body**	**ARMS:** **Reaching** **Overhead**
Right:	%	%	%	%
Left:	%	%	%	%

l. How much is your patient likely to be ***"off task"***? That is, what percentage of a typical workday would your patient's symptoms likely be severe enough to interfere with ***attention and concentration*** needed to perform even simple work tasks?

□ 0% □ 5% □ 10% □ 15% □ 20% □ 25% or more

m. To what degree can your patient tolerate work stress?

□ Incapable of even "low stress" work
□ Capable of low stress work
□ Capable of moderate stress - normal work
□ Capable of high stress work

Please explain the reasons for your conclusion: ____________________

n. Are your patient's impairments likely to produce "good days" and "bad days"?
□ Yes □ No

If yes, assuming your patient was trying to work full time, please estimate, on the average, how many days per month your patient is likely to be absent from work as a result of the impairments:

□ Never
□ About one day per month
□ About two days per month
□ About three days per month
□ About four days per month
□ More than four days per month

13. Are your patient's impairments (physical impairments plus any emotional impairments) as demonstrated by signs, clinical findings and laboratory or test results ***reasonably consistent*** with the symptoms and functional limitations described above in this evaluation?
□ Yes □ No

If no, please explain: ____

14. Please describe any other limitations (such as psychological limitations, limited vision, difficulty hearing, need to avoid temperature extremes, wetness, humidity, noise, dust, fumes, gases or hazards, etc.) that would affect your patient's ability to work at a regular job on a sustained basis:

____

____

____

________________________ ________________________

Date *Signature*

Printed/Typed Name: ________________________

Address: ________________________

____

____

7-43
7/16
§235.1

§235.2 Form: Hepatitis C Medical Source Statement

HEPATITIS C MEDICAL SOURCE STATEMENT

From: ______________________________

Re: ______________________________(Name of Patient)

______________________________(Date of Birth)

Please answer the following questions concerning your patient's impairments:

1. Frequency and length of contact:______________________________

2. Does your patient have hepatitis C? □ Yes □ No

   If yes, is your patient's hepatitis C symptomatic? □ Yes □ No

3. Other Diagnoses:______________________________

4. Prognosis: ______________________________

5. Identify your patient's symptoms and signs:

□ Chronic fatigue
□ Right upper quadrant pain
□ Recurrent fevers
□ Enlarged liver
□ Cholangitis
□ Skin rashes
□ Dizzy spells
□ Nausea/vomiting
□ Muscle & joint aches
□ Abdominal pain
□ Difficulty concentrating
□ Weakness
□ Neuropathy
□ Hot/cold spells
□ Tremor
□ Enlarged spleen
□ Jaundice
□ Esophageal varices
□ Ascites
□ Loss of appetite
□ Urinary frequency
□ Confusion
□ Sleep disturbance
□ Recurrent/persistent diarrhea
□ Bowel incontinence
□ Muscle wasting
□ Anemia
□ Spider nevi
□ Hematemesis
□ Peripheral edema
□ Weight loss
□ Urinary incontinence
□ Blackouts

□ other: ______________________________

6. If your patient has fatigue, please state whether it is true that as a rule the degree of fatigue does not correlate with the severity of hepatitis C or with the degree of elevation of laboratory tests. □ Yes □ No

   If no, please explain what studies correlate with fatigue:

   ____

7. Describe the treatment and response including any side effects of medication (e.g., interferon/ ribavirin) that may have implications for working:

____

8. Have your patient's impairments lasted or can they be expected to last at least twelve months? □ Yes □ No

9. Do emotional factors contribute to the severity of your patient's symptoms and functional limitations? □ Yes □ No

10. Identify any psychological conditions affecting your patient's physical condition:

□ Depression	□ Anxiety
□ Somatoform disorder	□ Personality disorder
□ Psychological factors affecting physical condition	□ Other: ______________________

11. As a result of your patient's impairments, estimate your patient's functional limitations if your patient were placed in a ***competitive work situation***.

a. How many city blocks can your patient walk without rest? ________

b. Please circle the hours and/or minutes that your patient can sit ***at one time***, e.g., before needing to get up, etc.

Sit: 0 5 10 15 20 30 45 (Minutes) 1 2 More than 2 (Hours)

c. Please circle the hours and/or minutes that your patient can stand ***at one time***, e.g., before needing to sit down, walk around, etc.

Stand: 0 5 10 15 20 30 45 (Minutes) 1 2 More than 2 (Hours)

d. Please indicate how long your patient can sit and stand/walk ***total in an 8-hour working day*** (with normal breaks):

Sit	**Stand/walk**	
□	□	less than 2 hours
□	□	about 2 hours
□	□	about 4 hours
□	□	at least 6 hours

e. Is your patient capable of working an 8-hour working day, 40 hours per week? □ Yes □ No

If no, approximately ***how many hours per week*** can your patient work?
10 15 20 25 30
Hours

f. Does your patient need a job that permits shifting positions at will from sitting, standing or walking? □ Yes □ No

g. In addition to normal breaks every two hours, will your patient sometimes need to take *unscheduled* breaks during a working day? □ Yes □ No

If yes, 1) approx. how ***often*** do you think this will happen? ________________

2) approx. how ***long*** (on average) will each break last?________________

3) what symptom(s) cause a need for breaks?

□ Pain/arthralgia □ Fatigue □ Nausea
□ Medication side effects □ Other:________________________

h. With prolonged sitting, should your patient's leg(s) be elevated? □ Yes □ No

If yes, 1) how ***high*** should the leg(s) be elevated? ________________

2) if your patient had a sedentary job, ***what percentage of time*** during an 8 hour working day should the leg(s) be elevated? ________________%

For this and other questions on this form, "rarely" means 1% to 5% of an 8-hour working day; "occasionally" means 6% to 33% of an 8-hour working day; "frequently" means 34% to 66% of an 8-hour working day.

i. How many pounds can your patient lift and carry in a competitive work situation?

	Never	**Rarely**	**Occasionally**	**Frequently**
Less than 10 lbs.	□	□	□	□
10 lbs.	□	□	□	□
20 lbs.	□	□	□	□
50 lbs.	□	□	□	□

j. How often can your patient perform the following activities?

	Never	**Rarely**	**Occasionally**	**Frequently**
Twist	□	□	□	□
Stoop (bend)	□	□	□	□
Crouch/ squat	□	□	□	□
Climb ladders	□	□	□	□
Climb stairs	□	□	□	□

k. If your patient has significant limitations with reaching, handling or fingering, please indicate the percentage of time during an 8-hour working day that your patient can use hands/fingers/arms for the following activities:

	HANDS: Grasp, Turn <u>Twist Objects</u>	**FINGERS: Fine <u>Manipulations</u>**	**ARMS: Reaching <u>In Front of Body</u>**	**ARMS: Reaching <u>Overhead</u>**
Right:	%	%	%	%
Left:	%	%	%	%

l. How much is your patient likely to be "***off task***"? That is, what percentage of a typical workday would your patient's symptoms likely be severe enough to interfere with ***attention and concentration*** needed to perform even simple work tasks?

□ 0% □ 5% □ 10% □ 15% □ 20% □ 25% or more

m. To what degree can your patient tolerate work stress?

□ Incapable of even "low stress" work □ Capable of low stress work
□ Capable of moderate stress - normal work □ Capable of high stress work

Please explain the reasons for your conclusion: ____________________

n. Are your patient's impairments likely to produce "good days" and "bad days"?
□ Yes □ No

If yes, assuming your patient was trying to work full time, please estimate, on the average, how many days per month your patient is likely to be absent from work as a result of the impairments:

□ Never □ About three days per month
□ About one day per month □ About four days per month
□ About two days per month □ More than four days per month

12. Are your patient's impairments (physical impairments plus any emotional impairments) as demonstrated by signs, clinical findings and laboratory or test results ***reasonably consistent*** with the symptoms and functional limitations described above in this evaluation? □ Yes □ No

If no, please explain: ____________________

13. Please describe any other limitations (such as psychological limitations, limited vision, difficulty hearing, need to avoid temperature extremes, wetness, humidity, noise, dust, fumes, gases or hazards, etc.) that would affect your patient's ability to work at a regular job on a sustained basis:

____

______________________ ______________________________

Date *Signature*

Printed/Typed Name: ______________________________

Address: ______________________________

____

____

7-37
7/16

235.2

§236 Hematological Disorders, Listings §§ 7.00-7.18

Hematolgical Disorders Listings, effective May 18, 2015, include § 7.18 titled "Repeated complications of hematological disorders," which provides functional criteria to indicate Listing-level severity. Here is section 7.18 in its entirety:

> 7.18 Repeated complications of hematological disorders (see 7.00G2), including those complications listed in 7.05, 7.08, and 7.10 but without the requisite findings for those listings, or other complications (for example, anemia, osteonecrosis, retinopathy, skin ulcers, silent central nervous system infarction, cognitive or other mental limitation, or limitation of joint movement), resulting in significant, documented symptoms or signs (for example, pain, severe fatigue, malaise, fever, night sweats, headaches, joint or muscle swelling, or shortness of breath), and one of the following at the marked level (see 7.00G4):
>
> A. Limitation of activities of daily living (see 7.00G5).
>
> B. Limitation in maintaining social functioning (see 7.00G6).
>
> C. Limitation in completing tasks in a timely manner due to deficiencies in concentration, persistence, or pace (see 7.00G7).

Hematological disorders not of Listing level usually involve fatigue as the primary limiting symptom. These include anemia, sickle cell disease, thrombocytopenia, hemophilia, and polycythemia vera. Even when these impairments do not meet Listing § 7.18, you can provide proof of fatigue by lay evidence and corroboration from the treating physician that someone with the claimant's findings can indeed have fatigue that prevents full time work. See the discussion of fatigue at §239, in conjunction with the discussion of M.S.

§237 Skin Disorders, Listings §§ 8.00-8.08

Whenever you are presented with a case involving skin disease, review the Listings carefully and, if possible, go over them with the claimant's treating dermatologist. Note that most of the skin Listings, which were revised effective July 9, 2004, require proof of extensive lesions (*see* § 8.00 C.1.) that persist despite continuing prescribed treatment after three months. *See* §§ 8.02-8.06. The Listings for genetic photosensitivity disorders, which are almost never seen at hearings, and burns, which are sometimes seen, require proof that extensive skin lesions will last for 12 months. *See* §§ 8.07-8.08. The Listing for genetic photosensitivity disorders may also be met by proof of inability to function outside of a highly protective environment for at least 12 months. § 8.07 B.2.

A Skin Disorders Medical Source Statement, which addresses Listing as well as residual functional capacity issues, appears at §237.1. In a skin case that goes to a hearing, the claimant can usually give a convincing demonstration of limitations. Document the file with photographs.

§237.1 Form: Skin Disorders Medical Source Statement

SKIN DISORDERS MEDICAL SOURCE STATEMENT

From: ______________________________

Re: ______________________________ (Name of Patient)

______________________________ (Date of Birth)

Please answer the following questions concerning your patient's impairments:

1. Frequency and length of contact:______________________________

2. Diagnoses:______________________________

3. Prognosis:______________________________

4. Identify symptoms your patient has had in the past two years:

□ Skin lesions on multiple body sites	□ Pain
□ Skin lesions that interfere with motion of	□ Skin lesions that interfere with use of
□ one joint □ two or more joints	□ one extremity □ two extremities
□ Skin lesions on the palm(s) of	□ Skin lesions affecting
□ one hand □ two hands	□ one □ both axillae
□ Skin lesions on the sole(s) of	□ Skin lesions affecting
□ one foot □ two feet	□ one □ both inguinal areas
□ Skin lesions affecting the perineum	□ Difficulty walking
□ Loss of manual dexterity	□ Difficulty sitting
□ Chronic skin infections	□ Easily irritated skin
□ Skin fissures	□ Skin blisters
□ Skin ulcers	□ Skin scaling
□ Skin inflammation	□ Skin redness
□ Swelling	□ Skin crusting
□ Skin weeping	□ Skin cracking
□ Skin bleeding	□ Hives
□ Thick leathery skin	□ Pruritus

Other symptoms:______________________________

5. Approximate frequency and duration of flare-ups:______________________________

____

6. Describe skin lesions:____

____

7. Describe the treatment and response including any side effects of medication that may have implications for working, *e.g.*, drowsiness, dizziness, nausea, etc.:

____

____

8. Does your patient have extensive skin lesions that persist for at least 3 months despite continuing treatment as prescribed? □ Yes □ No

9. Do emotional factors contribute to the severity of your patient's symptoms and functional limitations? □ Yes □ No

10. Identify any psychological conditions affecting your patient's physical condition:

□ Depression	□ Anxiety
□ Somatic symptom disorder	□ Personality disorder
□ Psychological factors affecting physical condition	□ Other: ________________

11. As a result of your patient's impairments, estimate your patient's functional limitations if your patient were placed in a ***competitive work situation:***

a. How many city blocks can your patient walk without rest or severe pain? ________

b. Please circle the hours and/or minutes that your patient can sit ***at one time,*** e.g., before needing to get up, etc.

	Minutes	Hours
Sit:	0 5 10 15 20 30 45	1 2 More than 2

c. Please circle the hours and/or minutes that your patient can stand ***at one time***, e.g., before needing to sit down, walk around, etc.

	Minutes	Hours
Stand:	0 5 10 15 20 30 45	1 2 More than 2

d. Please indicate how long your patient can sit and stand/walk ***total in an 8- hour working day*** (with normal breaks):

Sit	Stand/walk	
□	□	less than 2 hours
□	□	about 2 hours
□	□	about 4 hours
□	□	at least 6 hours

e. In addition to normal breaks every two hours, will your patient sometimes need to take *unscheduled* breaks during a working day? □ Yes □ No

If yes, 1) approx. how ***often*** do you think this will happen? ________________

2) approx. how ***long*** (on average) will each break last? ________________

3) on such a break, will your patient need to □lie down or □sit quietly?

For this and other questions on this form, "rarely" means 1% to 5% of an 8-hour working day; "occasionally" means 6% to 33% of an 8-hour working day; "frequently" means 34% to 66% of an 8-hour working day.

f. How often can your patient perform the following activities?

	Never	Rarely	Occasionally	Frequently
Twist	□	□	□	□
Stoop (bend)	□	□	□	□
Crouch/ squat	□	□	□	□

g. If your patient has significant limitations with reaching, handling or fingering, please indicate the percentage of time during an 8-hour working day that your patient can use hands/fingers/arms for the following activities:

	HANDS: Grasp, Turn Twist Objects	**FINGERS: Fine Manipulations**	**ARMS: Reaching In Front of Body**	**ARMS: Reaching Overhead**
Right:	**%**	**%**	**%**	**%**
Left:	**%**	**%**	**%**	**%**

h. State the degree to which your patient should avoid the following:

ENVIRONMENTAL RESTRICTIONS	NO RESTRICTIONS	AVOID CONCENTRATED EXPOSURE	AVOID EVEN MODERATE EXPOSURE	AVOID ALL EXPOSURE
Extreme cold	□	□	□	□
Extreme heat	□	□	□	□
High humidity	□	□	□	□
Wetness	□	□	□	□
Dryness	□	□	□	□
Cigarette smoke	□	□	□	□
Perfumes	□	□	□	□
Cosmetics	□	□	□	□
Soldering fluxes	□	□	□	□
Solvents/cleaners	□	□	□	□
Fumes, odors, gases	□	□	□	□
Dust	□	□	□	□
Sand	□	□	□	□
Metals	□	□	□	□
Chemicals	□	□	□	□
Glues	□	□	□	□
Wool	□	□	□	□
Rubber products	□	□	□	□
Synthetic fibers	□	□	□	□
Working around food	□	□	□	□
Public contact	□	□	□	□
Co-worker contact	□	□	□	□
List other irritants:				
____________________	□	□	□	□

i. How much is your patient likely to be ***"off task"***? That is, what percentage of a typical workday would your patient's symptoms likely be severe enough to interfere with ***attention and concentration*** needed to perform even simple work tasks?

□ 0% □ 5% □ 10% □ 15% □ 20% □ 25% or more

j. To what degree can your patient tolerate work stress?

□ Incapable of even "low stress" work □ Capable of low stress work
□ Capable of moderate stress - normal work □ Capable of high stress work

Please explain the reasons for your conclusion: ______________________________

k. Are your patient's impairments likely to produce "good days" and "bad days"?
□ Yes □ No

If yes, assuming your patient was trying to work full time, please estimate, on the average, how many days per month your patient is likely to be absent from work as a result of the impairments:

□ Never	□ About three days per month
□ About one day per month	□ About four days per month
□ About two days per month	□ More than four days per month

12. Are your patient's impairments (physical impairments plus any emotional impairments) as demonstrated by signs, clinical findings and laboratory or test results ***reasonably consistent*** with the symptoms and functional limitations described above in this evaluation? □ Yes □ No

    If no, please explain: ____

13. Please describe any other limitations (such as psychological limitations, limited vision, difficulty hearing, etc.) that would affect your patient's ability to work at a regular job on a sustained basis:

____

____

____

____________________ ____

Date *Signature*

Printed/Typed Name: ____

Address: ____

____

____

§238 Endocrine Disorders, Listing § 9.00 and Obesity

Endocrine disorders were removed from the Listing of Impairments effective June 7, 2011. 76 Fed. Reg. 19,696 (2011). The endocrine disorders Listings were replaced by Listing 9.00, which is a reference Listing. That is, it directs that endocrine disorders must be evaluated under the Listing for the body system affected by the endocrine disorder and identifies the other Listings that could be involved. In addition, SSA has promulgated two rulings:

- SSR 14-2p Evaluating Diabetes Mellitus
- SSR 14-3p Evaluating Endocrine Disorders Other Than Diabetes Mellitus

Diseases of the endocrine system involve overproduction or underproduction of hormones that control bodily functions. These cause various complications in the body. The endocrine disorder most commonly seen in disability cases is diabetes mellitus (DM). Other such diseases include thyroid and adrenal disorders. A Medical Assessment form for Thyroid Disorder is included as 238A on Digital Access. A form for use with Graves Disease is included on Digital Access as 238B.

Diabetes Mellitus

Diabetes mellitus, which does not meet one of the Listings for an affected body system, presents a variety of symptoms that are frequently diffuse in nature. It is very important to get a complete description of symptoms including a description of precipitating factors, location, frequency and duration. Send this list of symptoms to the treating physician along with an inquiry whether or not the claimant's diabetes mellitus could be reasonably expected to cause these symptoms. Have the claimant testify in detail about symptoms at the hearing.

The following is an outline for your inquiry:

- **Head**
  - headaches
  - dizziness/loss of balance/falls
- **Vision**
  - retinopathy: spots
  - episodic blurriness
- **Extremities**
  - neuropathy: burning pain, numbness, clumsiness, dropping things, difficulty walking
  - vascular disease: leg cramping with walking
- **Internal**
  - thirst
  - cardiac involvement: chest pain
  - abdominal pain
  - diarrhea
  - frequency of urination
  - bed wetting
  - infections/fevers
  - kidney problems
- **General**
  - chronic skin infections
  - history of vascular disease
  - excessive eating with weight loss
  - obesity
  - sensitivity to light, heat, cold
  - muscle weakness
  - fatigue
  - general malaise
  - associated psychological problems
- **Hypo/hyperglycemic attacks**
  - hot flashes
  - difficulty thinking concentrating
  - loss of manual dexterity
  - sweating
  - fast heart rate
  - nausea/vomiting
  - dizziness
  - blurred vision
  - convulsions
  - insulin shock/coma
  - post-attack fatigue

For those with poorly controlled diabetes, find out why your client has had such difficulty with control. Listing § 9.00 B.5 states: "While both type 1 and type 2 DM are usually controlled, some persons do not achieve good control for a variety of reasons including, but not limited to, hypoglycemia unawareness, other disorders that can affect blood glucose levels, inability to manage DM due to a mental disorder, or inadequate treatment." Be sure to inquire whether you client is aware when blood sugar drops. Listing § 9.00 B.5.b provides: "Persons with DM may experience episodes of hypoglycemia, which is an abnormally low level of blood glucose. Most adults recognize the symptoms of hypoglycemia and reverse them by consuming substances containing glucose; however, some do not take this step because of hypoglycemia unawareness." A Diabetes Mellitus Medical Source Statement appears at §238.1.

Obesity

The Social Security Administration removed obesity from the Listing of Impairments effective October 25, 1999. 64 Fed. Reg. 46,122 (1999). A ruling, SSR 02-1p, outlines SSA's approach to evaluating disability based on obesity.

Although SSR 02-1p acknowledges that obesity could play a role in *equaling* a Listing, and the ruling gave one example in which obesity could play a role in *meeting* a Listing, it is unlikely that many hearing decisions will be issued in which obesity plays a role at step 3. Thus, removal of the obesity Listing changes the focus of proving disability for obese claimants from step 3 to step 5.

That is, in most cases it will be necessary to show that the claimant's limited residual functional capacity prevents the claimant from performing jobs existing in significant numbers considering age, education and work experience. An Obesity Medical Source Statement is provided at §238.2, to assist you in gathering information about RFC from the claimant's doctor.

SSA says that obesity is a medically determinable impairment and, if it imposes more than minimal functional limitations, it is a "severe" impairment at step 2 of the sequential evaluation process. SSA added paragraphs to the introductory sections of the Listings pertaining to musculoskeletal, respiratory and cardiovascular impairments to remind adjudicators that the combined effect of obesity with one of the other impairments can be greater than the effects of each of the impairments considered separately. SSA instructed adjudicators to consider the cumulative effects not only when considering whether a claimant's impairments meet or medically equal the Listings but also when assessing residual functional capacity. *See* sections 1.00Q, 3.00F, and 4.00F of the Listing of Impairments.

Obesity is evaluated using body mass index (BMI). A 1999 report by the National Heart, Lung and Blood Institute of the National Institutes of Health, *Clinical Guidelines on the Identification, Evaluation, and Treatment of Overweight and Obesity in Adults,* available on the Internet at www.nhlbi.nih.gov/guidelines/obesity/ob_home.htm, recommended use of BMI for evaluation of obesity. The report also noted that waist circumference demonstrating excess fat in the abdomen was an independent predictor of risk factors and morbidity for those with BMIs less than 35 kg/m^2. No reference to waist circumference appears in the Obesity Medical Source Statement at §238.2; but there may be a few cases where you will want to ask a claimant's doctor whether the claimant's disproportionately large waist size demonstrates a greater impact from obesity than is shown by BMI alone.

BMI is weight in kilograms divided by height in meters squared. The formula for BMI using pounds and inches is: [weight (pounds)/ height (inches)^2] x 704.5. That is, calculate weight in pounds divided by height in inches squared and multiply the result by 704.5. According to the National Institutes of Health, a person with a BMI of 25 to 29.9 kg/m^2 is considered overweight but not obese unless that person has a waist size of greater than 40 inches in men and greater than 35 inches in women. A BMI of 30 kg/m^2 or greater is considered obese. The study divided obesity into three classes: level I, BMIs of 30.0 to 34.9 kg/m^2; level II, BMIs of 35 to 39.9 kg/m^2; and level III, extreme obesity, a BMI of 40.0 kg/m^2 or greater. As an example of how to use these different levels of obesity, note that the study recommends that weight loss surgery is considered an option only for those at level III (BMI of 40 kg/m^2 or more) and for those at level II (BMI of 35 to 39.9 kg/m^2) with comorbid conditions.

SSA's former obesity Listing, converted to BMI, ranges from 43.7 for tall women to 48.0 for short men.

Obesity at any level, because it is a medically determinable impairment, must be considered in assessing RFC. Do not be misled by the statement in SSR 96-8p that "body habitus" is not a factor to be considered in assessing RFC. Body habitus is not a medically determinable impairment. *See* SSR 02-1p. If a claimant is limited in any way by the medically determinable impairment obesity, then those limitations must be considered in assessing RFC. Indeed, not that it will get you very far in most cases, but if the claimant has another "severe" impairment or if the claimant's combination of impairments is "severe" any limitation arising from obesity must be considered, even if the limitation from obesity, by itself, would not be considered severe. 20 C.F.R. § 404.1523.

Obesity can affect residual functional capacity in many ways. Obesity may limit the seven physical demands of work: sitting, standing, walking, lifting, carrying, pushing, and pulling. It may affect manipulative and postural functions of work: reaching, handling, stooping and crouching. It may affect climbing. There may be environmental limitations such as the need to avoid extreme heat or humidity. There may be associated depression. Fatigue may be a factor. Many obese claimants have sleep apnea, which can lead to drowsiness and lack of mental acuity during the day, affecting a claimant's cognitive abilities. *See* SSR 02-1p.

Some obese people may require special chairs or workstations in order to work. If such accommodation is necessary for an obese claimant to work, then arguably because SSA does not consider the possibility of such accommodation, the need for accommodation proves that the claimant is disabled. *See* §§344 and 344.1.

Continuing Disability Reviews

Removal of the obesity Listing should have no impact on continuing disability reviews. In most cases, SSA must show that a beneficiary's condition has improved medically and that the medical improvement is related to the ability to work. In determining whether any medical improvement is related to the ability to work, SSA uses "the same listing section used to make our most recent favorable decision." 20 C.F.R. § 404.1594(c)(3)(i). *See also* SSR 02-1p.

Failure to Follow Prescribed Treatment

Although SSR 00-3p states, "We will rarely use 'failure to follow prescribed treatment' for obesity to deny or cease benefits," be prepared to have the claimant testify at the hearing about efforts to lose weight. You may want to have the claimant's physician comment on the claimant's difficulty losing weight; but note that a simple statement that a person should lose weight probably does not qualify as "prescribed treatment." SSR 02-1p states, "A treating source's statement that an individual 'should' lose weight or has 'been advised' to get more exercise is not prescribed treatment."

A physician must prescribe treatment and that treatment must be expected to restore the claimant's ability to work. SSR 82-59.

§238.1 Form: Diabetes Mellitus Medical Source Statement

DIABETES MELLITUS MEDICAL SOURCE STATEMENT

From: ______________________________

Re: ______________________________(Name of Patient)

______________________________(Date of Birth)

Please answer the following questions concerning your patient's impairments:

1. Frequency and length of contact:____

2. Diagnoses: Type 1 Diabetes Mellitus; Type 2 DM; Other:____________________

3. Prognosis:____

4. Identify your patient's ***symptoms***:

□ Fatigue	□ General malaise	□ Extremity pain and numbness
□ Difficulty walking	□ Muscle weakness	□ Loss of manual dexterity
□ Episodic vision blurriness	□ Retinopathy	□ Diarrhea
□ Bladder infections	□ Kidney problems	□ Frequency of urination
□ Bed wetting	□ Hot flashes	□ Sweating
□ Infections/fevers	□ Psychological problem	□ Difficulty concentrating
□ Excessive thirst	□ Abdominal pain	□ Headaches
□ Rapid heartbeat/chest pain	□ Vascular disease/ leg cramping	□ Dizziness/loss of balance
□ Swelling		□ Hypoglycemia
□ Chronic skin infections	□ Insulin shock/coma	□ Hypoglycemia unawareness
□ Sensitivity to light, heat or cold	□ Nausea/vomiting	□ Other: _______________ _______________

5. Clinical findings: ____

6. Describe the treatment and response including any side effects of medication that may have implications for working, *e.g.*, drowsiness, dizziness, nausea, etc.:

____

7. Have your patient's impairments lasted or can they be expected to last at least twelve months? □ Yes □ No

8. Do emotional factors contribute to the severity of your patient's symptoms and functional limitations? □ Yes □ No

9. Identify any psychological conditions affecting your patient's physical condition:

☐Depression ☐Somatic symptom disorder
☐Anxiety ☐Personality disorder ☐Other: ________________

10. As a result of your patient's impairments, estimate your patient's functional limitations if your patient were placed in a ***competitive work situation:***

a. How many city blocks can your patient walk without rest or severe pain?______

b. Please circle the hours and/or minutes that your patient can sit ***at one time,*** e.g., before needing to get up, etc.

Sit: 0 5 10 15 20 30 45 (Minutes) 1 2 More than 2 (Hours)

c. Please circle the hours and/or minutes that your patient can stand ***at one time***, e.g., before needing to sit down, walk around, etc.

Stand: 0 5 10 15 20 30 45 (Minutes) 1 2 More than 2 (Hours)

d. Please indicate how long your patient can sit and stand/walk ***total in an 8- hour working day*** (with normal breaks):

Sit	Stand/walk	
☐	☐	less than 2 hours
☐	☐	about 2 hours
☐	☐	about 4 hours
☐	☐	at least 6 hours

e. Does your patient need a job that permits shifting positions ***at will*** from sitting, standing or walking? ☐ Yes ☐No

f. Does your patient need to include periods of walking around during an 8-hour working day? ☐ Yes ☐ No

If yes, how ***often*** must your patient walk? How ***long*** must your patient walk each time?

1 5 10 15 20 30 45 60 90 (Minutes) 1 2 3 4 5 6 7 8 9 10 11 12 13 14 15 (Minutes)

g. In addition to normal breaks every two hours, will your patient sometimes need to take *unscheduled* breaks during a working day? ☐ Yes ☐ No

If yes, 1) approx. how ***often*** do you think this will happen? ________________

2) approx. how ***long*** (on average) will each break last?________________

3) what symptoms cause a need for breaks?

☐ Muscle weakness ☐ Pain/ paresthesias, numbness
☐ Chronic fatigue ☐ Adverse effects of medication
☐ Other: ____

h. With prolonged sitting, should your patient's leg(s) be elevated? ☐Yes ☐ No

If yes, 1) how ***high*** should the leg(s) be elevated? _________________

2) if your patient had a sedentary job, ***what percentage of time*** during an 8-hour working day should the leg(s) be elevated? _______________%

3) what symptoms cause a need to elevate leg(s)? ______________

i. While engaging in occasional standing/walking, must your patient use a cane or other assistive device? Yes No

For this and other questions on this form, "rarely" means 1% to 5% of an 8-hour working day; "occasionally" means 6% to 33% of an 8-hour working day; "frequently" means 34% to 66% of an 8-hour working day.

j. How many pounds can your patient lift and carry in a competitive work situation?

	Never	**Rarely**	**Occasionally**	**Frequently**
Less than 10 lbs.	☐	☐	☐	☐
10 lbs.	☐	☐	☐	☐
20 lbs.	☐	☐	☐	☐
50 lbs.	☐	☐	☐	☐

k. How often can your patient perform the following activities?

	Never	**Rarely**	**Occasionally**	**Frequently**
Twist	☐	☐	☐	☐
Stoop (bend)	☐	☐	☐	☐
Crouch/ squat	☐	☐	☐	☐
Climb ladders	☐	☐	☐	☐
Climb stairs	☐	☐	☐	☐

l. If your patient has significant limitations with reaching, handling or fingering, please indicate the percentage of time during an 8-hour working day that your patient can use hands/fingers/arms for the following activities:

	HANDS: Grasp, Turn Twist Objects	**FINGERS: Fine Manipulations**	**ARMS: Reaching In Front of Body**	**ARMS: Reaching Overhead**
Right:	%	%	%	%
Left:	%	%	%	%

m. State the degree to which your patient should avoid the following:

ENVIRONMENTAL RESTRICTIONS	**NO RESTRICTIONS**	**AVOID CONCENTRATED EXPOSURE**	**AVOID EVEN MODERATE EXPOSURE**	**AVOID ALL EXPOSURE**
Extreme cold	□	□	□	□
Extreme heat	□	□	□	□
High humidity	□	□	□	□
Wetness	□	□	□	□
Cigarette smoke	□	□	□	□
Perfumes	□	□	□	□
Soldering fluxes	□	□	□	□
Solvents/cleaners	□	□	□	□
Fumes, odors, gases	□	□	□	□
Dust	□	□	□	□
Chemicals	□	□	□	□
List other irritants:				
____________________	□	□	□	□

n. How much is your patient likely to be ***"off task"***? That is, what percentage of a typical workday would your patient's symptoms likely be severe enough to interfere with ***attention and concentration*** needed to perform even simple work tasks?

□ 0% □ 5% □ 10% □ 15% □ 20% □ 25% or more

o. To what degree can your patient tolerate work stress?

□ Incapable of even "low stress" work □ Capable of low stress work
□ Capable of moderate stress - normal work □ Capable of high stress work

Please explain the reasons for your conclusion: ____________________________

p. Are your patient's impairments likely to produce "good days" and "bad days"?
□ Yes □ No

If yes, assuming your patient was trying to work full time, please estimate, on the average, how many days per month your patient is likely to be absent from work as a result of the impairments:

☐ Never	☐ About three days per month
☐ About one day per month	☐ About four days per month
☐ About two days per month	☐ More than four days per month

11. Are your patient's impairment's (physical impairments plus any emotional impairments) as demonstrated by signs, clinical findings and laboratory or test results ***reasonably consistent*** with the symptoms and functional limitations described in this evaluation?

☐ Yes ☐ No

If no, please explain: ______________________________

12. Please describe any other limitations (such as psychological limitations, limited vision, difficulty hearing, etc.) that would affect your patient's ability to work at a regular job on a sustained basis:

____

____

____

______________ ______________________________
Date *Signature*

Printed/Typed Name: ______________________________

Address: ______________________________

____

§238.2 Form: Obesity Medical Source Statement

OBESITY MEDICAL SOURCE STATEMENT

From: ______________________________

Re: ______________________________(Name of Patient)

______________________________(Date of Birth)

Please answer the following questions concerning your patient's impairments.

1. Frequency and length of contact:____

2. Does your patient meet the criteria for the diagnosis of obesity as defined by the National Institutes of Health (a Body Mass Index* of 30.0 kg/m^2)? ☐ Yes ☐ No
   *BMI is the ratio of patient weight in kilograms to the square of the patient's height in meters.

3. a. What is your patient's current weight? ________ b. Current height? _____________

4. Other Diagnoses: ____

5. Prognosis: ____

6. List your patient's ***symptoms***, including pain, shortness of breath, fatigue, etc:

   ____

7. If your patient has pain, shortness of breath, fatigue, etc., characterize the nature, location, frequency, precipitating factors, and severity of your patient's symptoms:

   ____

   ____

8. Identify the clinical findings and objective signs:

   ____

   ____

9. Describe the treatment and response including any side effects of medication that may have implications for working, e.g., drowsiness, dizziness, nausea, etc:

   ____

   ____

10. Have your patient's impairments lasted or can they be expected to last at least twelve months? ☐ Yes ☐ No

11. Do emotional factors contribute to the severity of your patient's symptoms and functional limitations? ☐ Yes ☐ No

12. Identify any psychological conditions affecting your patient's physical condition:

- ☐ Depression
- ☐ Anxiety
- ☐ Somatic Symptom disorder
- ☐ Personality disorder
- ☐ Psychological factors affecting physical condition
- ☐ Other: ____________________

13. As a result of your patient's impairments, estimate your patient's functional limitations if your patient were placed in a ***competitive work situation***.

a. How many city blocks can your patient walk without rest or severe pain? ___________

b. Please circle the hours and/or minutes that your patient can sit ***at one time,*** e.g., before needing to get up, etc.

Sit: 0 5 10 15 20 30 45 (Minutes) 1 2 More than 2 (Hours)

c. Please circle the hours and/or minutes that your patient can stand ***at one time***, e.g., before needing to sit down, walk around, etc.

Stand: 0 5 10 15 20 30 45 (Minutes) 1 2 More than 2 (Hours)

d. Please indicate how long your patient can sit and stand/walk ***total in an 8-hour working day*** (with normal breaks):

Sit	Stand/walk	
☐	☐	less than 2 hours
☐	☐	about 2 hours
☐	☐	about 4 hours
☐	☐	at least 6 hours

e. Does your patient need a job that permits shifting positions ***at will*** from sitting, standing or walking? ☐ Yes ☐ No

f. Does your patient need to include periods of walking around during an 8-hour working day? ☐ Yes ☐ No

If yes, how ***often*** must your patient walk?
1 5 10 15 20 30 45 60 90 (Minutes)

How ***long*** must your patient walk each time?
1 2 3 4 5 6 7 8 9 10 11 12 13 14 15 (Minutes)

g. In addition to normal breaks every two hours, will your patient sometimes need to take *unscheduled* breaks during a working day? ☐ Yes☐ No

If yes, 1) approx. how ***often*** do you think this will happen? ______________

2) approx. how ***long*** (on average) will each break last?______________

3) what symptoms cause a need for breaks? ____________________

h. With prolonged sitting, should your patient's leg(s) be elevated? ☐ Yes ☐ No

If yes, 1) how ***high*** should the leg(s) be elevated? ______________

2) if your patient had a sedentary job, ***what percentage of time*** during an 8-hour working day should the leg(s) be elevated? ________%

3) what symptoms cause a need to elevate leg(s)? ______________

i. While engaging in occasional standing/walking, must your patient use a cane or other assistive device? ☐ Yes ☐ No

If yes, what symptoms cause a need for an assistive device? ______________

For this and other questions on this form, "rarely" means 1% to 5% of an 8-hour working day; "occasionally" means 6% to 33% of an 8-hour working day; "frequently" means 34% to 66% of an 8-hour working day.

j. How many pounds can your patient lift and carry in a competitive work situation?

	Never	**Rarely**	**Occasionally**	**Frequently**
Less than 10 lbs.		☐	☐	☐
10 lbs.	☐	☐	☐	☐
20 lbs.	☐	☐	☐	☐
50 lbs.	☐	☐	☐	☐

k. How often can your patient perform the following activities?

	Never	**Rarely**	**Occasionally**	**Frequently**
Twist	☐	☐	☐	☐
Stoop (bend)	☐	☐	☐	☐
Crouch/ squat	☐	☐	☐	☐
Climb ladders	☐	☐	☐	☐
Climb stairs	☐	☐	☐	☐

l. Does your patient have significant limitations with reaching, handling or fingering? ☐ Yes ☐ No

If yes, what symptoms cause these limitations?

____

____

If yes, please indicate the percentage of time during an 8-hour working day that your patient can use hands/fingers/arms for the following activities:

	HANDS: Grasp, Turn Twist Objects	**FINGERS: Fine Manipulations**	**ARMS: Reaching In Front of Body**	**ARMS: Reaching Overhead**
Right:	%	%	%	%
Left:	%	%	%	%

m. How much is your patient likely to be ***"off task"***? That is, what percentage of a typical workday would your patient's symptoms likely be severe enough to interfere with ***attention and concentration*** needed to perform even simple work tasks?

☐ 0% ☐ 5% ☐ 10% ☐ 15% ☐ 20% ☐ 25% or more

n. To what degree can your patient tolerate work stress?

☐ Incapable of even "low stress" work ☐ Capable of low stress work
☐ Capable of moderate stress - normal work ☐ Capable of high stress work

Please explain the reasons for your conclusion: ______________________________

o. Are your patient's impairments likely to produce "good days" and "bad days"?
☐ Yes ☐ No

If yes, assuming your patient was trying to work full time, please estimate, on the average, how many days per month your patient is likely to be absent from work as a result of the impairments:

☐ Never ☐ About three days per month
☐ About one day per month ☐ About four days per month
☐ About two days per month ☐ More than four days per month

14. Are your patient's impairments (physical impairments plus any emotional impairments) ***reasonably consistent*** with the symptoms and functional limitations described in this evaluation? ☐ Yes ☐ No

15. Please describe any other limitations (such as psychological limitations, limited vision, difficulty hearing, need to avoid temperature extremes, wetness, humidity, noise, dust, fumes, gases or hazards, etc.) that would affect your patient's ability to work at a regular job on a sustained basis:

____

____

____

______________________ ______________________________
Date *Signature*

Printed/Typed Name: ______________________________

Address: ______________________________

____

____

7-39
1/17
§238.2

§239 Neurological Disorders, Listings § § 11.00-11.22

With only the exceptions of § 11.02 epilepsy, § 11.10 ALS, and § 11.20 coma, all of the neurological disorders Listings effective September 29, 2016 can be met by showing that the claimant has a combination of physical and mental limitations consisting of marked limitation in physical functioning and a *marked* limitation in one of the following: understanding, remembering or applying information; interacting with others; concentrating, persisting, or maintaining pace; or adapting or managing oneself. *See* § 11.00G. These are the same mental functions used in evaluating the B criteria of the mental Listings effective January 17, 2017. *See* §242. (The epilepsy Listing includes an alternative route to meeting the Listings with a reduced seizure frequency *plus* marked physical or one of the B criteria mental limitations at the marked level. See Epilepsy discussion below.)

With the same exceptions, all the other neurological disorders Listings can also be met by showing that the claimant has disorganization of motor functioning in two extremities resulting in an extreme limitation in the ability to stand up from a seated position, balance while standing or walking, or use the upper extremities. *See* § 11.00D.

For Listings involving § 11.05 benign brain tumors, § 11.06 Parkinsonian syndrome, § 11.09 multiple sclerosis, § 11.13 muscular dystrophy, § 11.14 peripheral neuropathy, § 11.17 neurodegenerative disorders of the central nervous system, § 11.18 traumatic brain injury, the two ways for meeting the Listings described above are the only ways to meet those Listings. Other Listings offer other possibilities.

Duration Requirement

All disability cases, of course, require the claimant to meet the 12-month duration requirement – the claimant's impairment either must have already lasted 12 months or be expected to last 12 months. Some Listings accept that proof of meeting the Listings for a shorter period of time satisfies the duration requirement. In effect, where the Listings provide a shorter length of time, SSA has determined that the claimant is not going to improve. For example, Listing § 11.10 ALS is met when the diagnosis requirements of the Listings are established by clinical and laboratory findings. The Listing for ALS includes no functional requirements. Listing § 11.20 is met when a claimant is in a coma or persistent vegetative state for one month.

Listing § 11.04 "vascular insult to the brain," usually called stroke or CVA, may be met if Listing-level limitations persist for at least three consecutive months after the stroke. Likewise, Listing § 11.08 spinal cord disorders may be met if Listing-level limitations persist for three consecutive months as does Listing § 11.18 traumatic brain injury.

Requirement to Follow Prescribed Treatment

Three of the neurological Listings may be met if Listing-level limitations persist for at least three months despite adherence to prescribed treatment – § 11.02 epilepsy, § 11.06 Parkinsonian syndrome, and § 11.12 myasthenia gravis. *See* 11.00C.

Medical Source Statements

The medical source statements for neurological disorders in this book focus on residual functional capacity. If it appears that a neurological Listing other than epilepsy is met in one of the ways described above, to obtain a treating doctor's opinion about Listings issues, use the Neurological Listings Medical Source Statement at §239.11. For epilepsy, use the Seizures Listings Medical Source Statement at §239.12. Most cases, though, especially those at hearing level, don't involve meeting the Listings. Instead you will need to establish your client's residual functional capacity.

This book includes the following medical source statement for neurological disorders:

- §239.1 Seizures (Epilepsy)
- §239.2 Headaches
- §239.3 Stroke (Vascular insult to the brain)
- §239.4 Multiple Sclerosis
- §239.5 Myasthenia Gravis
- §239.6 Parkinsonian Syndrome
- §239.7 Peripheral Neuropathy
- §239.8 Post-polio Syndrome
- §239.9 Reflex Sympathetic Dystrophy (RSD)/ Complex Regional Pain Syndrome, Type 1 (CRPS)
- §239.10 Muscular Dystrophy

Listings — Epilepsy

Cases involving epilepsy or seizures typically present the issue of whether the claimant is following prescribed treatment, a requirement that appears in the Listings itself. Thus, it is necessary to resolve the issue of noncompliance in any seizure case. Obtain the opinion of the treating physician on this issue. Sometimes it is necessary for the attorney to assist the treating physician in figuring out whether the claimant is, in fact, taking medication as prescribed. A good source of such information is the claimant's pharmacist who will be able to provide information whether the claimant is purchasing the necessary amount of anticonvulsant medication.

Another issue frequently lurking in a case involving seizures is alcohol and drug abuse. Use of alcohol is sometimes the reason for a claimant's failure to properly follow prescribed treatment." If alcohol abuse is found to be a problem, it should be evaluated also. *See* SSR 13-2p.

In a seizure case, the issue of failure to follow prescribed treatment may come up twice as a decision maker proceeds through the sequential evaluation process, once at step 3 and once again at step 5. At step 3 a decision maker deals with this issue for purposes of determining whether or not the claimant's impairment meets the Listings. If the claimant's impairment does not meet the Listings because the claimant is not following prescribed treatment, decision makers are required to complete the sequential evaluation process by assessing RFC, determining whether the claimant is capable of past relevant work and determining whether other work exists in the economy in significant numbers. Then, after the claimant is found disabled, the decision maker must turn again to the issue of failure to follow prescribed treatment.

A denial after step 5 of the sequential evaluation process based on failure to follow prescribed treatment requires specific findings that are set forth in SSR 82-59 as follows:

> 1. The evidence establishes that the individual's impairment precludes engaging in any substantial gainful activity (SGA),... and
>
> 2. The impairment has lasted or is expected to last for 12 continuous months from onset of disability or is expected to result in death; and
>
> 3. Treatment which is clearly expected to restore capacity to engage in any SGA...has been prescribed by a treating source; and
>
> 4. The evidence of record discloses that there has been refusal to follow prescribed treatment.

Where SSA makes a determination of "failure," a determination must also be made as to whether or not failure to follow prescribed treatment is justifiable.

Examples of acceptable reasons for failure to follow prescribed treatment appear at 20 C.F.R. § 404.1530(c) and are expanded upon in SSR 82-59, but none of the examples are particularly relevant to seizure cases.

The explanation most often given by claimants is that they cannot tolerate the side effects, usually extreme drowsiness, of the medication given to control the seizures. They have, in effect, chosen to have occasional seizures rather than constant drowsiness. Cases for such claimants should have a dual focus: whether this is an acceptable reason to refuse to take medication, and also whether the claimant would be able to work if the claimant were taking the prescribed seizure medication and suffering extreme side effects. In other words, address not only the "refusal" issue but also address the SSR 82-59 issue of whether this treatment "is clearly expected to restore capacity to engage in" substantial gainful activity.

For generalized tonic-clonic seizures, Listing § 11.02A requires a frequency of more than one seizure per month for at least three consecutive months despite adherence to prescribed treatment. Listing § 11.02C may be met if generalized tonic-clonic seizures occur *at least once every two months for at least four consecutive months* despite adherence to prescribed treatment if the claimant *also* has a marked limitation in physical functioning or a marked limitation in one of the four areas of mental functioning that appear in the B criteria of the mental Listings. *See* above.

For dyscognitive seizures (formerly called complex partial seizures) to meet Listing § 11.02B such seizures must occur at least once a week for at least three consecutive months despite adherence to prescribed treatment. To meet § 11.02D such seizures must occur *at least once every two weeks* for at least three consecutive months despite adherence to prescribed treatment and the claimant has a marked limitation in physical functioning or a marked limitation in one of the four areas of mental functioning that appear in the B criteria of the mental Listings. *See* above.

Pay attention to SSA's rules for counting seizures. § 11.02H4 provides:

> 4. Counting seizures. The period specified in 11.02A, B, or C cannot begin earlier than one month after you began prescribed treatment. The required number of seizures must occur within the period we are considering in connection with your application or continuing disability review. When we evaluate the frequency of your seizures, we also consider your adherence to prescribed treatment (see 11.00C). When we determine the number of seizures you have had in the specified period, we will:
>
> a. Count multiple seizures occurring in a 24-hour period as one seizure.

b. Count status epilepticus (a continuous series of seizures without return to consciousness between seizures) as one seizure.

c. Count a dyscognitive seizure that progresses into a generalized tonic-clonic seizure as one generalized tonic-clonic seizure.

d. We do not count seizures that occur during a period when you are not adhering to prescribed treatment without good reason. When we determine that you had good reason for not adhering to prescribed treatment, we will consider your physical, mental, educational, and communicative limitations (including any language barriers). We will consider you to have good reason for not following prescribed treatment if, for example, the treatment is very risky for you due to its consequences or unusual nature, or if you are unable to afford prescribed treatment that you are willing to accept, but for which no free community resources are available. We will follow guidelines found in our policy, such as § § 404.1530(c) and 416.930(c) of this chapter, when we determine whether you have a good reason for not adhering to prescribed treatment.

e. We do not count psychogenic nonepileptic seizures or pseudoseizures under 11.02. We evaluate these seizures under the mental disorders body system, 12.00.

RFC Evaluation — Seizures

For those individuals whose impairments would meet the Listings except for the fact that the frequency of their seizures is somewhat less than that required, it is necessary to assess the vocational impact of the seizures. One of the more ridiculous positions taken by SSA is that all individuals with seizures have the capacity to do all jobs that do not involve workplace hazards such as heights, dangerous machinery, etc. This position may be true only in cases involving infrequent seizures having very little vocational impact. You'll probably need the help of a vocational expert to assess the full extent of the vocational impact of most seizure disorders.

A Seizures Medical Source Statement, which covers most vocational issues raised by seizures, appears at §239.1.

File Review — Seizures

In any seizure case, the most important thing is documentation of the seizures themselves. When you review a file involving seizures, make a list of every reference to each individual seizure. Include date, time, observers, description and where the reference to this seizure is found in the hearing exhibits/medical records. But be sure that you don't limit yourself to medical records. Include any seizures described in SSA forms, letters, etc., completed by the claimant, the claimant's family or friends. When you are finished you should end up with a chronological list of all seizures that are in any way referred to in the records.

Watch out for references to alcohol abuse. Alcohol abuse can cause seizures. A claimant whose seizures are caused by alcohol abuse will be denied disability benefits unless it can be shown that even if the claimant stopped drinking, the claimant would still have disabling seizures.

Following prescribed treatment is very important in a seizure case. Make a note of all references in the file indicating that the claimant is not following prescribed treatment or not taking seizure medications as prescribed. Watch for lab test results that show blood levels of seizure medications at less than therapeutic levels and include them in your summary. If blood levels of seizure medications are often at less than therapeutic levels, scour the records to find out if a doctor has explained this on any basis other than failure to follow prescribed treatment.

Strokes

The residuals of central nervous system vascular accidents, usually referred to as strokes, present difficult problems for representation because the effects of strokes can be varied and subtle. Every case is different. It is often necessary for additional testing to be done concerning the claimant's mental and physical capacity. There may be a fatigue factor that must be proven with lay evidence or, in some circumstances, a workshop evaluation. A psychologist who does neuropsychological testing may be able to provide useful test results and evaluation.

A Stroke Medical Source Statement appears at §239.3.

Multiple Sclerosis

Multiple sclerosis (MS) cases, especially those involving the common relapsing-remitting MS, often involve exacerbations followed by periods of improvement called remissions. SSA refers to this type of MS as "milder" than the steadily progressive form of MS. *See* 11.09N1. With relapsing remitting MS, remissions vary in duration and the extent of improvement. Some people improve so much that they are capable of working during remissions. Others do not. In cases of claimants who are capable of working during remissions, one must look carefully at the frequency, duration, nature, and severity of the exacerbations.

Many people with relapsing-remitting MS describe a sort of stair step progression to their impairment. Every exacerbation leaves them worse. Some people, half or more by some estimates, who start out with relapsing-remitting MS develop what is called secondary progressive MS in which the patient's condition worsens without exacerbations. Primary progressive MS, which affects about 10 percent of those diagnosed with the disease, involves gradual worsening over time. Least common is progressive relapsing MS, which affects 5 percent of those diagnosed with MS

According to SSA, because of weakness, spasticity, incoordination, imbalance, tremor, or a combination of these, people with MS most often become disabled as a result of impaired gait. POMS DI 24580.015A. To meet § 11.09A of the Listings, a claimant must have disorganization of motor functioning in two extremities resulting in an *extreme* limitation in the ability to stand up from a seated position, balance while standing or walking, or use the upper extremities. Often you will find claimants with MS who have difficulty walking, perhaps because of a problem with one leg, but who don't meet § 11.09A of the Listings. Such claimants are limited to sedentary work; and because MS strikes at an age less than 50, in order to win their cases, they must prove that they are not capable of performing a wide range of sedentary work.

Problems with vision (blindness in one eye and double vision, in particular), which is not mentioned in the MS Listing, and mental limitations, which are addressed in Listing 11.09B, are common. When claimants have visual limitations be sure to consider whether your client meets § §2.02, 2.03 or 2.04 of the Listings dealing with impairment of central visual acuity, contraction of peripheral visual fields in the better eye, and loss of visual efficiency.

By its nature, MS can impair different parts of the body or brain and affect functioning in myriad ways. It is necessary to carefully go through your client's explanation why full-time sedentary work would not be possible. Keep an open mind about symptoms and limitations arising from MS. Only the more common symptoms are listed in the Multiple Sclerosis Medical Source Statement at §239.4. Sometimes it is necessary to ask the claimant's neurologist whether a particular symptom is related to MS

Many times you will find that the claimant's explanation of why he or she cannot do full time sedentary work involves fatigue. Be sure to ask enough questions about what the claimant means by fatigue. As a rule, MS claimants describe something other than muscle fatigue. Although many MS claimants may have fatigue of motor function, MS claimants most often complain about a sort of total physical and mental fatigue better referred to as lassitude.

The neurological disorders Listings address fatigue at 11.00T as follows:

> *How do we consider symptoms of fatigue in these listings?* Fatigue is one of the most common and limiting symptoms of some neurological disorders, such as multiple sclerosis, post-polio syndrome, and myasthenia gravis. These disorders may result in physical fatigue (lack of muscle strength) or mental fatigue (decreased awareness or attention). When we evaluate your fatigue, we will consider the intensity, persistence, and effects of fatigue on your functioning. This may include information such as the clinical and laboratory data and other objective evidence concerning your neurological deficit, a description of fatigue considered characteristic of your disorder, and information about your functioning. We consider the effects of physical fatigue on your ability to stand up, balance, walk, or perform fine and gross motor movements using the criteria described in 11.00D. We consider the effects of physical and mental fatigue when we evaluate your physical and mental functioning described in 11.00G.

It has become well accepted among neurologists who deal with MS patients that MS itself accounts for fatigue with or without significant on-going neurological deficits. Therefore, the diagnosis of MS, which is usually documented by findings of white matter on brain or spinal MRIs usually along with a classic history of exacerbations, provides the necessary findings to show "the existence of a medical impairment[s]... which could reasonably be expected to produce the...symptoms alleged." 20 C.F.R. § 404.1529(b).

The treating neurologist may be able to state only that there is no medical reason to doubt the claimant's description of fatigue because fatigue is such a common symptom of MS. Such an opinion should be enough to help the claimant's case.

A useful medical journal article by L. Krupp, et al., "Fatigue in Multiple Sclerosis," 45 *Archives of Neurology* 435 (April 1988), notes that fatigue is a common and frequently disabling symptom in MS. The authors conclude that there is no direct relationship between fatigue severity and neurologic disability. Thus, "fatigue is a distinct symptom complex whose disabling effect on patients cannot be predicted from their underlying neurologic deficits." Severity of fatigue also did not correlate well with depression. 45 *Archives of Neurology* 435, 437 (April 1988). Thus, determining whether or not a claimant with MS is disabled, depends on proper assessment of the claimant's symptoms under SSR 16-3p. Because there is little or no correlation of fatigue severity with medical signs and findings, a denial based on objective evidence makes no sense.

Headaches

A neurological impairment that does not appear in the Listings is headaches. Headaches, particularly migraine headaches, can be vocationally devastating. Don't let anyone tell you that headaches are not a medically determinable impairment observable by "medically acceptable clinical diagnostic techniques." A headache is one of those symptoms that can be considered a sign when reported to a physician in a clinical setting. A thorough discussion, including criteria for a medically determinable impairment and when migraine headaches may be considered equal to dyscognitive seizures in section 11.02B of the Listings, appears in the SSA Q&A 09-036, which is reprinted at §239.2.1. *See also* SSR 96-4p, footnote 2. A Headaches Medical Source Statement appears at §239.2.

Post-polio Syndrome

Many people who had polio when they were young develop related problems later in life—post-polio syndrome (also known as the late effects of poliomyelitis), early advanced degenerative arthritis, sleep disorders, respiratory insufficiency, and a variety of mental disorders—that SSA refers to as "postpolio sequelae" in SSR 03-1p and as post-polio syndrome in § 11.11 of the Listings. According to SSA, "'postpolio sequelae' includes the documented residuals of acute infection as well as all other documented clinical conditions that have an etiological link to either the acute infection or to its residual deficits." SSA says that "postpolio syndrome is characterized by a further weakening of muscles that were previously affected by the polio infection. The signs and symptoms include fatigue, slowly progressive muscle weakness, and, at times, muscular atrophy." Joint pain and skeletal deformities, such as scoliosis, are common.

SSR 03-1p provides:

> Once postpolio sequelae has been documented as a medically determinable impairment, the impact of any of the symptoms of postpolio sequelae, including fatigue, weakness, pain, intolerance to cold, etc., must be considered both in determining the severity of the impairment and in assessing the individual's RFC. The adjudicator must make a comprehensive assessment of the cumulative and interactive effects of all of the individual's impairments and related symptoms, including the effects of postpolio sequelae.

A Post-polio Syndrome Medical Source Statement is provided at §239.8.

Reflex Sympathetic Dystrophy

Reflex sympathetic dystrophy (RSD), also known as complex regional pain syndrome, type 1 (CRPS), is an impairment involving complaints of severe, disabling pain, usually in one extremity following a relatively minor trauma. The pain complaints, which have been known to spread to other extremities, are invariably assessed to be out of proportion to the trauma – an assessment that is usually problematic in Social Security disability cases except that with RSD/CRPS, it is a typical feature of the syndrome. Signs and findings are often transient, present at one evaluation but not present at another. Because dysfunction of the sympathetic nervous system is thought to be the cause, the most significant findings include evidence of abnormal sympathetic stimulation, which may produce changes in blood vessels, skin, musculature and bone. *See* Social Security Ruling 03-2p, which focuses on proof that RSD/CRPS is a medically determinable impairment. Questions about medical findings to show a medically determinable impairment set forth in SSR 03-2p have been incorporated into the Reflex Sympathetic Dystrophy (RSD)/Complex Regional Pain Syndrome, Type 1 Medical Source Statement, which appears at §239.9.

§239.1 Form: Seizures Medical Source Statement

SEIZURES MEDICAL SOURCE STATEMENT

From: ________________________________

Re: ________________________________(Name of Patient)

________________________________(Date of Birth)

Please answer the following questions concerning your patient's seizures:

1. Frequency and length of contact:____
____
____
____

2. Does your patient have seizures? ☐ Yes ☐ No

Other diagnoses:____
____
____
____
____

3. If your patient has seizures:

A. What type of seizures does your patient have?

☐ Generalized tonic-clonic seizures
☐ Dyscognitive seizures (formerly complex partial seizures)
☐ Pseudoseizures
☐ Psychogenic nonepileptic seizures
☐ Other - identify: ____

B. Is there loss of consciousness during seizure? ☐ Yes ☐ No

If no, is there alternation of awareness during seizure? ☐ Yes ☐ No

C. Does your patient always have a warning of an impending seizure? ☐ Yes ☐ No

If yes, how long is it between the warning and onset of the seizure? ______minutes

Can your patient always take safety precautions when a seizure is coming on?
☐ Yes ☐ No

D. What is the average frequency of seizures? _____ per week _____ per month

E. Do seizures occur at a particular time of the day? ☐ Yes ☐ No

If yes, explain when seizures occur:____

F. Please provide a detailed description of a typical seizure: __________________

____

____

____

G. Identify ***symptoms or signs*** associated with your patient's seizure disorder:

☐ Presence of aura ☐ Tongue bites or other injures
☐ Loss of sphincter control ☐ Loss of bladder control
☐ Other: _______________________________

H. Identify postictal phenomena:

☐ Confusion ☐ Muscle strain ☐ Exhaustion
☐ Paranoia ☐ Irritability ☐ Difficulties communicating
☐ Severe headaches ☐ Other: ______________________________________

How long after a seizure do these postictal phenomena last? ________________

I. Does your patient typically need to rest after a seizure? ☐ Yes ☐ No

If yes, for approximately how long:__________________

J. Describe the degree to which having a seizure interferes with your patient's daily activities following a seizure:

____

____

____

K. What sort of action must others take during and immediately after your patient's seizure?

☐ Put something soft under the head ☐ Remove glasses
☐ Clear the area of hard or sharp objects ☐ Loosen tight clothing
☐ After seizure, turn patient on side to allow saliva to drain from mouth
☐ Other: ____

4. Identify positive test results (e.g., EEG): ______________________________

5. Can stress precipitate your patient's seizures? ☐ Yes ☐ No

   If yes, to what degree can your patient tolerate work stress?

   ☐ Incapable of even "low stress" work
   ☐ Capable of low stress work
   ☐ Capable of moderate stress - normal work
   ☐ Capable of high stress work

6. Can exertion precipitate your patient's seizures? ☐ Yes ☐ No

   If yes, if your patient was placed in a competitive job,

   A. Please indicate how long your patient can sit and stand/walk ***total in an 8-hour working day*** (with normal breaks):

Sit	Stand/walk	
☐	☐	less than 2 hours
☐	☐	about 2 hours
☐	☐	about 4 hours
☐	☐	at least 6 hours

For this question "rarely" means 1% to 5% of an 8-hour working day; "occasionally" means 6% to 33% of an 8-hour working day; "frequently" means 34% to 66% of an 8-hour working day.

   B. How many pounds can your patient lift and carry in a competitive work situation?

	Never	Rarely	Occasionally	Frequently
Less than 10 lbs.	☐	☐	☐	☐
10 lbs.	☐	☐	☐	☐
20 lbs.	☐	☐	☐	☐
50 lbs.	☐	☐	☐	☐

7. Type of medication and response: ______________________________

   ____

8. Is your patient compliant with taking medication? ☐ Yes ☐ No

9. Please identify any side effects of seizure medication:

   ☐ Dizziness
   ☐ Double vision
   ☐ Eye focusing problems
   ☐ Coordination disturbance
   ☐ Lethargy
   ☐ Lack of alertness
   ☐ Other: ______________________________

10. If your patient's blood levels of anticonvulsant medication have recently been at less than therapeutic levels, please explain why there has been difficulty controlling blood levels.

____

____

____

11. Does your patient currently abuse alcohol or street drugs? ☐ Yes ☐ No

    A. If no, to the best of your knowledge, when was the last time your patient abused alcohol or street drugs? ☐ Never ☐ ____________________

    B. If yes, if you were to assume your patient was able to maintain complete sobriety, would your patient continue to exhibit the symptoms and limitation described in this questionnaire? ☐ Yes ☐ No

    Please explain: ____

12. Does your patient have any associated mental problems? ☐ Yes ☐ No

    If yes, please check those that apply:

    ☐ Depression ☐ Short attention span
    ☐ Irritability ☐ Memory problems
    ☐ Social isolation ☐ Behavior extremes
    ☐ Poor self-esteem ☐ Other: ______________________________

13. In addition to time away from work for seizures and postictal phenomena, will your patient otherwise need to take ***unscheduled breaks*** during an 8-hour working day? ☐ Yes ☐ No

    If yes, 1) approx. how ***often*** do you think this will happen? ______________________

    2) approx. how ***long*** (on average) will each break last? ____________________

    3) what are the reasons for such breaks? ______________________________

14. Are your patient's impairments likely to produce "good days" and "bad days"? ☐ Yes ☐ No

If yes, assuming your patient was attempting to work full time, please estimate, on the average, how many days per month your patient is likely to be absent from work as a result of the impairments:

☐ Never	☐ About three days per month
☐ About one day per month	☐ About four days per month
☐ About two days per month	☐ More than four days per month

15. Please describe any other limitations (such as limitations in the ability to bend, stoop, limitations in using arms, hands, fingers, limited vision, difficulty hearing, need to avoid temperature extremes, wetness, humidity, noise, dust, fumes, gases or hazards, etc.) that would affect your patient's ability to work at a regular job on a sustained basis:

____

____

____

____________________ ______________________________

Date *Signature*

Printed/Typed Name: ______________________________

Address: ______________________________

____

____

§239.2 Form: Headaches Medical Source Statement

HEADACHES MEDICAL SOURCE STATEMENT

From: ______________________________

Re: ______________________________(Name of Patient)

______________________________(Date of Birth)

Please answer the following questions concerning your patient's headaches.

1. Frequency and length of contact:______________________________

2. Diagnoses:______________________________

____

3. Does your patient have headaches? Yes ☐ No ☐

   a. If yes, what ***type*** of headache does your patient have?

   ☐ Migraine ☐ Vascular tension ☐ Cluster ☐ Post concussion syndrome

   ☐ Other: ______________________________

   b. Please describe the ***intensity*** your patient's headaches:

   ☐ Mild ☐ Moderate -- inhibits but does not wholly prevent usual activity

   ☐ Severe – prevents all activity

4. Identify any other signs and symptoms associated with your patient's headaches:

   ☐ Nausea
   ☐ Vomiting
   ☐ Phonophobia
   ☐ Photophobia
   ☐ Throbbing pain
   ☐ Alteration of awareness
   ☐ Mental confusion
   ☐ Inability to concentrate
   ☐ Mood changes
   ☐ Exhaustion
   ☐ Malaise
   ☐ Vertigo
   ☐ Numbness
   ☐ Visual disturbances
   ☐ Impaired sleep
   ☐ Impaired appetite
   ☐ Weight change
   ☐ Pain worse with activity
   ☐ Causes avoidance of activity

   ☐ Other: ______________________________

   ____

5. If there are premonitory symptoms or aura, please describe:

____

____

6. What is the approximate ***frequency*** of headaches? _______ per week/ _______ per month

7. What is the approximate ***duration*** of a typical headache? ____ minutes/ _____ hours

8. Identify any impairments that could reasonably be expected to explain your patient's headaches:

- ☐ Anxiety/tension
- ☐ Cerebral hypoxia
- ☐ Cervical disc disease
- ☐ History of head injury
- ☐ Hypertension
- ☐ Intracranial infection or tumor
- ☐ Primary migraines
- ☐ Seizure disorder
- ☐ Sinusitus
- ☐ Substance abuse

☐ Other ____

____

9. What triggers your patient's headaches?

- ☐ Alcohol
- ☐ Bright lights
- ☐ Hunger
- ☐ Food - identify:

____

____

____

- ☐ Lack of sleep
- ☐ Menstruation
- ☐ Noise
- ☐ Stress
- ☐ Strong odors
- ☐ Vigorous exercise
- ☐ Weather changes

☐ Other: ____

____

10. What makes your patient's headaches worse?

- ☐ Bright lights
- ☐ Coughing, straining/bowel movement
- ☐ Moving around
- ☐ Noise

☐ Other ____

____

11. What makes your patient's headaches better?

- ☐ Lie down
- ☐ Take medication
- ☐ Quiet place
- ☐ Dark room
- ☐ Hot pack
- ☐ Cold pack

☐ Other ____

____

12. To what degree do emotional factors contribute to the severity of your patient's headaches?

☐ Not at all ☐ Somewhat ☐ Very much

Please explain: ____

13. To what degree can your patient tolerate work stress?

☐ Incapable of even "low stress" work ☐ Capable of low stress work
☐ Capable of moderate stress - normal work ☐ Capable of high stress work

Please explain the reasons for your conclusion: ____________________

____

14. Describe the treatment and response: ____________________

____

____

____

____

15. Identify side effects of medications experienced by your patient:

☐ Sedation ☐ Confusion ☐ Inattention

Other: ____________________

____

16. Prognosis: ____________________

17. Have your patient's impairments lasted or can they be expected to last at least twelve months? Yes ☐ No ☐

18. Do your patient's headaches cause significant interference with activity during the day? Yes ☐ No ☐

19. During the time your patient has a headache:

a. Is there alteration of awareness? Yes ☐ No ☐

b. Would your patient generally be precluded from performing even basic work activities and need a break from the workplace? Yes ☐ No ☐

If no, please explain: ____________________

20. If your patient will sometimes need to take unscheduled breaks during a working day:

a. how ***often*** do you think this will happen? ____________________

b. how ***long*** (on average) will your patient have to rest before returning to work? ____________________

c. on such a break, will your patient need to ☐ lie down or ☐ sit quietly?

21. Not counting breaks, how much is your patient likely to be ***"off task" while at work***? That is, what percentage of a typical workday would your patient's symptoms likely be severe enough to interfere with ***attention and concentration*** needed to perform even simple work tasks?

☐ 0% ☐ 5% ☐ 10% ☐ 15% ☐ 20% ☐ 25% or more

22. Are your patient's impairments likely to produce "good days" and "bad days"?
Yes ☐ No ☐

If yes, assuming your patient was trying to work full time, please estimate, on the average, how many days per month your patient is likely to be absent from work as a result of the impairments:

☐ Never
☐ About one day per month
☐ About two days per month
☐ About three days per month
☐ About four days per month
☐ More than four days per month

23. Please describe any other limitations (such as limitations in the ability to sit, stand, walk, lift, bend, stoop, crouch, limitations in using arms, hands, fingers, limited vision, difficulty hearing, need to avoid temperature extremes, wetness, humidity, noise, dust, fumes, gases or hazards, etc.) that would affect your patient's ability to work at a regular job on a sustained basis:

____
____
____
____
____

________________ ______________________________
Date *Signature*

Printed/Typed Name: ______________________________

Address: ______________________________
____

§239.2.1 Q & A 09-036 Evaluation of Migraine Headaches

Q&A - 09-036

National

Question & Answer

Tracking number: 09-036
This revises Q&A 09-028

Only active Q&As may be used as guidance in the adjudication of a current claim.

Brief Question: **Please provide guidance regarding the evaluation of migraine headaches.**

Detailed Question:

The regulations state that we cannot establish a disabling condition based on symptoms alone. According to the medical literature, there are no laboratory findings or clinical signs to substantiate the presence of migraine headaches in most cases. The diagnosis of migraine headache is usually established through patients' reported symptoms (pain, photophobia, nausea). Previous guidance from the Office of Disability from the early 1990's stated that, although migraine headaches that are disabling for 12 continuous months in spite of treatment are extremely rare, there are some cases that do not respond to treatment. The guidance said to consider whether the impairment medically equals listing 11.03 based on "altered awareness."

Our questions are:

> What criteria should we use to determine that migraine headaches are a medically determinable impairment (MDI)? Is a diagnosis from an acceptable medical source sufficient, even if it is based only on a claimant's reported symptoms? If not, what evidence establishes the MDI?
> If we use listing 11.03 to evaluate migraine headaches, should we use POMS DI 24580.001/Social Security Ruling (SSR) 87-06 to evaluate migraine headaches? If so, what constitutes appropriate treatment and an ongoing treatment relationship?
> The POMS/SSR also say that we need a description of a seizure from professional observation or a third party. Does this guidance apply to migraine headaches?

The POMS/SSR also say that we need a record of anticonvulsant blood levels in every case before we can allow it unless there is convincing evidence that subtherapeutic drug levels are due to abnormal absorption or metabolism and the prescribed drug dosage is adequate. Is there an analogous medically acceptable way to determine if an individual is taking headache medications appropriately? If not, how should we assess compliance with treatment?
What is "altered awareness" and how is it measured?

Answer:
Because of significant changes in the diagnosis and treatment of migraine headaches since we provided guidance in memorandums from the early 1990's, we are rescinding that guidance and temporarily replacing it with the guidance in this Q & A while we prepare proposed updates to the neurological listings. However, as we explain below, there is little change in the guidance we originally provided.

Under our general policy, you cannot establish the existence of any MDI based solely on a diagnosis in the evidence or on a claimant's reported symptoms. There must be clinical signs or laboratory findings to support the finding.
A diagnosis of migraine headaches requires a detailed description from a physician of a typical headache event (intense headache with more than moderate pain and with associated migraine characteristics and phenomena) that includes a description of all associated phenomena; for example, premonitory symptoms, aura, duration, intensity, accompanying symptoms, and effects of treatment. The diagnosis should be made only after the claimant's history and neurological and any other appropriate examinations rule out other possible disorders that could be causing the symptoms. There are other clinically accepted indicators of the diagnosis, including:

Headache event that lasts from 4 to 72 hours if untreated or unsuccessfully treated.
Two of the following: Unilateral, pulsating (throbbing) quality; moderate (inhibits but does not wholly prevent usual activity) or severe (prevents all activity) pain intensity, worsened by routine physical activity (or

causing avoidance of activity).
At least one of the following during the headache: Nausea, vomiting, photophobia, or phonophobia.

Once other possible causes have been ruled out and a pattern has been established, we consider the foregoing findings reported by a physician to be "signs" that establish the existence of migraine headaches as an MDI. This is consistent with the way we establish the existence of some mental disorders and other physical disorders that are characterized by complaints reported by acceptable medical sources based on their examinations.

As in our earlier guidance regarding migraine headaches, we continue to recognize that migraine headaches will rarely prevent a person from working for a continuous 12 months but that there are exceptions. Likewise, listing 11.03 (Epilepsy - nonconvulsive epilepsy) is still the most analogous listing for considering medical equivalence. However, the guidance in POMS DI 24580.001/ SSR 87-06 is specific to epilepsy and not applicable to the evaluation of migraine headaches. We do not consider treatment non-compliance or therapeutic levels of medication in the blood because, unlike treatment for epilepsy, which seeks to maintain a steady level of medication in the blood, there is no such standard of care in the treatment of migraine headaches. Also, therapeutic blood levels for migraine medication have not been established. Nor do we require a professional observation or third-party description of a migraine headache event, although such observations are helpful. We require a professional observation or third-party description of a seizure partly because the person having the seizure is unaware of it and cannot describe how s/he looks during a seizure. This is not the case for migraine headaches.
It may be helpful to review the essential components of listing 11.03 as they may be related to migraine headaches:

"Documented by detailed description of a typical" headache event pattern
"Including all associated phenomena"; for example, premonitory symptoms, aura, duration, intensity, accompanying symptoms, treatment.
"Occurring more frequently than once weekly." Count characteristic headache events.

Q&A - 09-036

"In spite of at least 3 months of prescribed treatment." Inapplicable, as we explain above.

"With alteration of awareness." This means a condition of being inattentive, or not cognizant of one's surroundings and external phenomena as well as one's personal state. Many psychotropic and neuroleptic medications used for treating migraines can produce sedation, confusion, or inattention. However, it is not necessary for a person with migraine headaches to have alteration of awareness as long as s/he has an effect (e.g., one or more of the problems described in the next bullet) that significantly interferes with activity during the day.

"Significant interference with activity during the day." Same meaning as in listing 11.03. May be the result, e.g., of a need for a darkened, quiet room, lying down without moving, or a sleep disturbance that impacts on daytime activities.

Did this document help answer your question?

Category: **Medical Policy**
Subcategory:**Neurological**
Purpose: **Policy Clarification**
Answered by: **ODP** Posted: **Tue 12/15/2009**
Responsible CO Component: **ODP**
Reference:
Link to reference:

Link to this section:
http://policynet.ba.ssa.gov/pnqa.nsf/links/09-036This%20revises%20Q&A%2009-028

---

§239.3 Form: Stroke Medical Source Statement

STROKE MEDICAL SOURCE STATEMENT

From: ______________________________

Re: ______________________________(Name of Patient)

______________________________(Date of Birth)

Please answer the following questions concerning your patient's impairments:

1. Frequency and length of contact:____

2. Did your patient have a stroke/ CVA? ☐ Yes ☐ No

   If yes, type of stroke:____

3. Other diagnoses:____

4. Identify your patient's symptoms and signs:

☐ Balance problems	☐ Vertigo/dizziness
☐ Poor coordination	☐ Headaches
☐ Loss of manual dexterity	☐ Difficulty remembering
☐ Weakness	☐ Confusion
☐ Slight paralysis	☐ Depression
☐ Unstable walking	☐ Emotional lability
☐ Falling spells	☐ Personality change
☐ Numbness or tingling	☐ Difficulty solving problems
☐ Other sensory disturbance	☐ Problems with judgment
☐ Pain	☐ Double or blurred vision
☐ Fatigue	☐ Partial or complete blindness
☐ Bladder problems	☐ Shaking tremor
☐ Nausea	☐ Speech/communication difficulties

5. Other symptoms and clinical findings:_________________________________

6. Treatment and response:____

7. Prognosis:____

8. Do emotional factors contribute to the severity of your patient's symptoms and functional limitations? ☐ Yes ☐ No

9. Have your patient's impairments lasted or can they be expected to last at least twelve months? ☐ Yes ☐ No

10. As a result of your patient's impairments, estimate your patient's functional limitations if your patient were placed in a ***competitive work situation***:

   a. How many city blocks can your patient walk without rest? ________________

   b. Please circle the hours and/or minutes that your patient can sit ***at one time,*** e.g., before needing to get up, etc.

   Sit: 0 5 10 15 20 30 45 (Minutes) 1 2 More than 2 (Hours)

   c. Please circle the hours and/or minutes that your patient can stand ***at one time***, e.g., before needing to sit down, walk around, etc.

   Stand: 0 5 10 15 20 30 45 (Minutes) 1 2 More than 2 (Hours)

   d. Please indicate how long your patient can sit and stand/walk ***total in an 8-hour working day*** (with normal breaks):

Sit	Stand/walk	
☐	☐	less than 2 hours
☐	☐	about 2 hours
☐	☐	about 4 hours
☐	☐	at least 6 hours

   e. Does your patient need a job that permits shifting positions at will from sitting, standing or walking? ☐ Yes ☐ No

   f. In addition to normal breaks every two hours, will your patient sometimes need to take *unscheduled* breaks during a working day? ☐ Yes ☐ No

   If yes, 1) approx. how ***often*** do you think this will happen? ____________

   2) approx. how ***long*** (on average) will each break last?________________

   3) on such a break, will your patient need to lie down or sit quietly?

   g. With prolonged sitting, should your patient's leg(s) be elevated? ☐ Yes ☐ No

   If yes, 1) how ***high*** should the leg(s) be elevated? ________________

   2) if your patient had a sedentary job, ***what percentage of time*** during an 8 hour working day should the leg(s) be elevated? ________________%

h. While engaging in occasional standing/walking, must your patient use a cane or other assistive device? ☐ Yes ☐ No

For this and other questions on this form, "rarely" means 1% to 5% of an 8-hour working day; "occasionally" means 6% to 33% of an 8-hour working day; "frequently" means 34% to 66% of an 8-hour working day.

i. How many pounds can your patient lift and carry in a competitive work situation?

	Never	**Rarely**	**Occasionally**	**Frequently**
Less than 10 lbs.	☐	☐	☐	☐
10 lbs.	☐	☐	☐	☐
20 lbs.	☐	☐	☐	☐
50 lbs.	☐	☐	☐	☐

j. How often can your patient perform the following activities?

	Never	**Rarely**	**Occasionally**	**Frequently**
Twist	☐	☐	☐	☐
Stoop (bend)	☐	☐	☐	☐
Crouch/ squat	☐	☐	☐	☐
Climb ladders	☐	☐	☐	☐
Climb stairs	☐	☐	☐	☐

k. Does your patient have significant limitations with reaching, handling or fingering?
Yes No

If yes, please indicate the percentage of time during an 8-hour working day that your patient can use hands/fingers/arms for the following activities:

	HANDS: Grasp, Turn Twist Objects	**FINGERS: Fine Manipulations**	**ARMS: Reaching In Front of Body**	**ARMS: Reaching Overhead**
Right:	%	%	%	%
Left:	%	%	%	%

l. State the degree to which your patient should avoid the following:

ENVIRONMENTAL RESTRICTIONS:	NO RESTRICTIONS	AVOID CONCENTRATED EXPOSURE	AVOID EVEN MODERATE EXPOSURE	AVOID ALL EXPOSURE
Extreme cold	☐	☐	☐	☐
Extreme heat	☐	☐	☐	☐
High humidity	☐	☐	☐	☐
Wetness	☐	☐	☐	☐
Fumes, odors, gases	☐	☐	☐	☐
Soldering fluxes	☐	☐	☐	☐
Dust	☐	☐	☐	☐
Hazards (heights, etc.)	☐	☐	☐	☐

m. To what degree can your patient tolerate work stress?

☐ Incapable of even "low stress" work
☐ Capable of low stress work
☐ Capable of moderate stress - normal work
☐ Capable of high stress work

Please explain the reasons for your conclusion: ______________________

____

n. How much is your patient likely to be ***"off task"***? That is, what percentage of a typical workday would your patient's symptoms likely be severe enough to interfere with ***attention and concentration*** needed to perform even simple work tasks?

☐ 0% ☐ 5% ☐ 10% ☐ 15% ☐ 20% ☐ 25% or more

o. Are your patient's impairments likely to produce "good days" and "bad days"?

☐ Yes ☐ No

If yes, assuming your patient was trying to work, please estimate, on the average, how many days per month your patient is likely to be absent from work as a result of the impairments:

☐ Never
☐ About one day per month
☐ About two days per month
☐ About three days per month
☐ About four days per month
☐ More than four days per month

11. Are your patient's impairments (physical impairments plus any emotional impairments) as demonstrated by signs, clinical findings and laboratory or test results ***reasonably consistent*** with the symptoms and functional limitations described in this evaluation?

☐ Yes ☐ No

If no, please explain:____

12. Please describe any other limitations (such as psychological limitations, limited vision, difficulty hearing, etc.) that would affect your patient's ability to work at a regular job on a sustained basis:

____

____

______________________________ ______________________________

Date *Signature*

*Printed/Typed Name:*______________________________

Address: ______________________________

____

____

§239.4 Form: Multiple Sclerosis Medical Source Statement

MULTIPLE SCLEROSIS MEDICAL SOURCE STATEMENT

From: ______________________________

Re: ______________________________ (Name of Patient)

______________________________ (Date of Birth)

Please answer the following questions concerning your patient's impairments:

1. Frequency and length of contact: ______________________________

2. Does your patient have multiple sclerosis? Yes No

   If yes, how was this diagnosis made? ______________________________
   —

3. Identify your patient's ***symptoms and signs***:

☐ Flaccidity	☐ Trouble sleeping	☐ Loss of manual dexterity
☐ Spasticity	☐ Mental fatigue	☐ Muscle atrophy
☐ Spasms	☐ Impaired attention	☐ Bladder problems
☐ Incoordination	☐ Impaired concentration	☐ Bowel problems
☐ Imbalance	☐ Impaired memory	☐ Speech difficulties
☐ Tremor	☐ Impaired judgment	☐ Nystagmus
☐ Physical fatigue	☐ Mood swings	☐ Visual loss
☐ Muscle weakness	☐ Depression	☐ Double vision
☐ Dizziness	☐ Emotional lability	☐ Pain in one eye
☐ Tingling	☐ Personality change	☐ Dimness of vision
☐ Numbness	☐ Confusion	☐ Partial blindness
☐ Pain	☐ Sensitivity to heat	☐ Other vision disturbance
☐ Increased deep reflexes	☐ Unstable walking	☐ Difficulty solving problems

   Other symptoms, signs and clinical findings: ______________________________

   ____

4. Have your patient's impairments lasted or can they be expected to last at least twelve months? ☐ Yes ☐ No

5. Treatment and response:

____

____

____

____

6. Prognosis: ____

7. As a result of your patient's impairments, estimate your patient's functional limitations if your patient were placed in a ***competitive work situation:***

   a. How many city blocks can your patient walk without rest or severe pain? ______

   b. Please circle the hours and/or minutes that your patient can sit ***at one time,*** *e.g.*, before needing to get up, *etc.*

      Sit: 0 5 10 15 20 30 45 Minutes 1 2 More than 2 Hours

   c. Please circle the hours and/or minutes that your patient can stand ***at one time***, *e.g.*, before needing to sit down, walk around, *etc.*

      Stand: 0 5 10 15 20 30 45 Minutes 1 2 More than 2 Hours

   d. Please indicate how long your patient can sit and stand/walk ***total in an 8-hour working day*** (with normal breaks):

Sit	Stand/walk	
☐	☐	less than 2 hours
☐	☐	about 2 hours
☐	☐	about 4 hours
☐	☐	at least 6 hours

   e. Does your patient need a job that permits shifting positions ***at will*** from sitting, standing or walking? ☐ Yes ☐ No

   f. In addition to normal breaks every two hours, will your patient sometimes need to take *unscheduled* breaks during a working day? ☐ Yes ☐ No

If yes, 1) approx. how ***often*** do you think this will happen? ________________

2) approx. how ***long*** (on average) will each break last?________________

3) what symptoms cause a need for breaks?

☐ Muscle weakness ☐ Pain/ paresthesias, numbness
☐ Chronic fatigue ☐ Adverse effects of medication
☐ Other:____

g. While engaging in occasional standing/walking, must your patient use a cane or other assistive device? ☐ Yes ☐ No

If yes, what symptoms cause a need to use a cane?

☐ Muscle weakness ☐ Spasticity ☐ Chronic fatigue
☐ Incoordination ☐ Imbalance ☐ List others in margin

For this and other questions on this form, "rarely" means 1% to 5% of an 8-hour working day; "occasionally" means 6% to 33% of an 8-hour working day; "frequently" means 34% to 66% of an 8-hour working day.

h. How many pounds can your patient lift and carry in a competitive work situation?

	Never	**Rarely**	**Occasionally**	**Frequently**
Less than 10 lbs.	☐	☐	☐	☐
10 lbs.	☐	☐	☐	☐
20 lbs.	☐	☐	☐	☐
50 lbs.	☐	☐	☐	☐

i. How often can your patient perform the following activities?

	Never	**Rarely**	**Occasionally**	**Frequently**
Twist	☐	☐	☐	☐
Stoop (bend)	☐	☐	☐	☐
Crouch/ squat	☐	☐	☐	☐

j. If your patient has significant limitations with reaching, handling or fingering:

What symptoms cause limitations of use of the upper extremities?

☐ Pain/ paresthesias ☐ Incoordination ☐ Sensory loss/ numbness
☐ Muscle weakness ☐ Spasticity ☐ Fatigue
☐ Tremor ☐ Other: ________________________________

Please indicate the percentage of time during an 8-hour working day that your patient can use hands/fingers/arms for the following activities:

	HANDS: Grasp, Turn Twist Objects	**FINGERS: Fine Manipulations**	**ARMS: Reaching In Front of Body**	**ARMS: Reaching Overhead**
Right:	%	%	%	%
Left:	%	%	%	%

k. How much is your patient likely to be ***"off task"***? That is, what percentage of a typical workday would your patient's symptoms likely be severe enough to interfere with ***attention and concentration*** needed to perform even simple work tasks?

☐ 0% ☐ 5% ☐ 10% ☐ 15% ☐ 20% ☐ 25% or more

l. Do emotional factors contribute to the severity of your patient's symptoms and functional limitations? Yes No

m. To what degree can your patient tolerate work stress?

☐ Incapable of even "low stress" work ☐ Capable of low stress work
☐ Capable of moderate stress - normal work ☐ Capable of high stress work

Please explain the reasons for your conclusion: ____________________________

n. Are your patient's impairments likely to produce "good days" and "bad days"?
☐ Yes ☐ No

If yes, assuming your patient was trying to work full time, please estimate, on the average, how many days per month your patient is likely to be absent from work as a result of the impairments:

☐ Never ☐ About three days per month
☐ About one day per month ☐ About four days per month
☐ About two days per month ☐ More than four days per month

8. Are your patient's impairments (physical impairments plus any emotional impairments) as demonstrated by signs, clinical findings and laboratory or test results ***reasonably consistent*** with the symptoms and functional limitations described above in this evaluation? ☐ Yes ☐ No

If no, please explain: ______________________________

9. Please describe any other limitations (such as psychological limitations, limited vision, difficulty hearing, difficulty speaking, need to avoid temperature extremes, wetness, humidity, noises, dust, fumes, gases or hazards, etc.) that would affect your patient's ability to work at a regular job on a sustained basis.

____

____

____

____

10. What is the earliest date that the description of ***symptoms and limitations*** in this questionnaire applies? ____________________

____________________ ______________________________

Date *Signature*

Printed/Typed Name: ______________________________

Address: ______________________________

____

____

§239.5 *Form: Myasthenia Gravis Medical Source Statement*

MYASTHENIA GRAVIS MEDICAL SOURCE STATEMENT

From: ______________________________

Re: ______________________________(Name of Patient)

______________________________(Date of Birth)

Please answer the following questions concerning your patient's impairments:

1. Frequency and length of contact:____

2. Does your patient have myasthenia gravis? ☐ Yes ☐ No

   If yes, how was this diagnosis made?______________________________________

3. Prognosis:____

4. Identify your patient's ***symptoms and signs***:

   ☐ Fatigability of muscles after exercise
   ☐ Limb weakness
   ☐ General fatigue
   ☐ Double vision
   ☐ Drooping upper eyelid
   ☐ Difficulty speaking
   ☐ Alteration in voice
   ☐ Other:____
   ☐ Difficulty swallowing
   ☐ Difficulty breathing
   ☐ Diarrhea
   ☐ Stomach cramping
   ☐ Facial muscle weakness
   ☐ Nasal regurgitation of food
   ☐ Choking

5. Do your patient's symptoms and signs fluctuate in intensity over the course of hours to days? ☐ Yes ☐ No

   Is it common for symptoms and signs to fluctuate in patients with myasthenia gravis?
   ☐ Yes ☐ No

6. Does your patient have significant difficulty with speaking, swallowing or breathing ***while on prescribed therapy***? ☐ Yes ☐ No

   If yes, please describe the degree of difficulty: ____________________________

   ____

7. Does your patient have significant motor weakness of muscles of extremities on repetitive activity against resistance ***while on prescribed therapy***?
   ☐ Yes No

If yes, describe the repetitive activity and the severity of the resulting muscle weakness:

____

____

8. Do emotional factors contribute to the severity of your patient's symptoms and functional limitations? ☐ Yes ☐ No

9. Has your patient taken medications or followed other prescribed treatment for at least three consecutive months? ☐ Yes ☐ No

10. Have your patient's impairments lasted or can they be expected to last at least twelve months? ☐ Yes ☐ No

11. As a result of your patient's impairments, estimate your patient's functional limitations if your patient were placed in a ***competitive work situation***:

 a. How many city blocks can your patient walk without rest? ________________

 b. Please circle the hours and/or minutes that your patient can sit ***at one time,*** e.g., before needing to get up, etc.

 Sit: 0 5 10 15 20 30 45 (Minutes) 1 2 More than 2 (Hours)

 c. Please circle the hours and/or minutes that your patient can stand ***at one time***, e.g., before needing to sit down, walk around, etc.

 Stand: 0 5 10 15 20 30 45 (Minutes) 1 2 More than 2 (Hours)

 d. Please indicate how long your patient can sit and stand/walk ***total in an 8-hour working day*** (with normal breaks):

Sit	**Stand/walk**	
☐	☐	less than 2 hours
☐	☐	about 2 hours
☐	☐	about 4 hours
☐	☐	at least 6 hours

 e. Does your patient need a job that permits shifting positions at will from sitting, standing or walking? ☐` Yes ☐ No

 f. In addition to normal breaks every two hours, will your patient sometimes need to take *unscheduled* breaks during a working day? ☐ Yes ☐ No

If yes, 1) approx. how ***often*** do you think this will happen? ________________

2) approx. how ***long*** (on average) will each break last?________________

3) what symptoms cause a need for breaks?

☐ Muscle weakness ☐ Pain/ paresthesias, numbness
☐ Chronic fatigue ☐ Adverse effects of medication
☐ Other: ________________________________

g. With prolonged sitting, should your patient's leg(s) be elevated? ☐ Yes ☐ No

If yes, 1) how ***high*** should the leg(s) be elevated? ________________

2) if your patient had a sedentary job, ***what percentage of time*** during an 8-hour working day should the leg(s) be elevated?________________%

h. While engaging in occasional standing/walking, must your patient use a cane or other assistive device? ☐ Yes ☐ No

For this and other questions on this form, "rarely" means 1% to 5% of an 8-hour working day; "occasionally" means 6% to 33% of an 8-hour working day; "frequently" means 34% to 66% of an 8-hour working day.

i. How many pounds can your patient lift and carry in a competitive work situation?

	Never	**Rarely**	**Occasionally**	**Frequently**
Less than 10 lbs.	☐	☐	☐	☐
10 lbs.	☐	☐	☐	☐
20 lbs.	☐	☐	☐	☐
50 lbs.	☐	☐	☐	☐

j. How often can your patient perform the following activities?

	Never	**Rarely**	**Occasionally**	**Frequently**
Twist	☐	☐	☐	☐
Stoop (bend)	☐	☐	☐	☐
Crouch/ squat	☐	☐	☐	☐
Climb ladders	☐	☐	☐	☐
Climb stairs	☐	☐	☐	☐

k. Does your patient have significant limitations with reaching, handling or fingering?
☐ Yes ☐ No

If yes, please indicate the percentage of time during an 8-hour working day that your patient can use hands/fingers/arms for the following activities:

	HANDS: Grasp, Turn Twist Objects	**FINGERS: Fine Manipulations**	**ARMS: Reaching In Front of Body**	**ARMS: Reaching Overhead**
Right:	%	%	%	%
Left:	%	%	%	%

l. State the degree to which your patient should avoid the following:

ENVIRONMENTAL RESTRICTIONS:	**NO RESTRICTIONS**	**AVOID CONCENTRATED EXPOSURE**	**AVOID EVEN MODERATE EXPOSURE**	**AVOID ALL EXPOSURE**
Extreme cold	☐	☐	☐	☐
Extreme heat	☐	☐	☐	☐
High humidity	☐	☐	☐	☐
Wetness	☐	☐	☐	☐
Fumes, odors, gases	☐	☐	☐	☐
Soldering fluxes	☐	☐	☐	☐
Dust	☐	☐	☐	☐
Hazards (heights, etc.)	☐	☐	☐	☐

m. How much is your patient likely to be ***"off task"***? That is, what percentage of a typical workday would your patient's symptoms likely be severe enough to interfere with ***attention and concentration*** needed to perform even simple work tasks?

☐ 0% ☐ 5% ☐ 10% ☐ 15% ☐ 20% ☐ 25% or more

n. To what degree can your patient tolerate work stress?

☐ Incapable of even "low stress" work ☐ Capable of low stress work
☐ Capable of moderate stress - normal work ☐ Capable of high stress work

Please explain the reasons for your conclusion:________________________

____

o. Are your patient's impairments likely to produce "good days" and "bad days"?
☐ Yes ☐ No

If yes, assuming your patient was trying to work full time, please estimate, on the average, how many days per month your patient is likely to be absent from work as a result of the impairments:

☐ Never
☐ About one day per month
☐ About two days per month
☐ About three days per month
☐ About four days per month
☐ More than four days per month

12. Are your patient's impairments (physical impairments plus any emotional impairments) as demonstrated by signs, clinical findings and laboratory or test results ***reasonably consistent*** with the symptoms and functional limitations described in this evaluation?
☐ Yes ☐ No

If no, please explain:____

13. Please describe any other limitations (such as psychological limitations, limited vision, difficulty hearing, etc.) that would affect your patient's ability to work at a regular job on a sustained basis:

____

____

14. What is the earliest date that the description of ***symptoms and limitation*** in this questionnaire applies? ______________

______________________ ______________________
Date *Signature*

*Printed/Typed Name:*______________________

Address: ______________________

____

____

§239.6 Form: Parkinsonian Syndrome Medical Source Statement

PARKINSONIAN SYNDROME MEDICAL SOURCE STATEMENT

From: ______________________________

Re: ______________________________(Name of Patient)

______________________________(Date of Birth)

Please answer the following questions concerning your patient's impairments:

1. Frequency and length of contact: ______________________________

2. Does your patient suffer from Parkinsonian Syndrome? ☐ Yes ☐ No

3. List any other diagnosed impairments: ______________________________

4. Identify your patient's symptoms and signs:

   ☐ Tremors
   ☐ Rigidity
   ☐ Bradykinesia – slow movement
   ☐ Impaired gait
   ☐ Signs of autonomic nervous dysfunction
   ☐ Soft/ poorly modulated voice
   ☐ Impaired control of distal musculature
   ☐ Muscular aches
   ☐ Tremors enhanced by stress/ fatigue
   ☐ Hypokinesia – decreased movement
   ☐ Falls
   ☐ Postural instability
   ☐ Impaired ability to rise from seated
   ☐ Difficulty to start walking
   ☐ Chronic fatigue
   ☐ Saliva drooling
   ☐ Impaired ability to perform rapid successive movements

   Other symptoms, signs and clinical findings: ______________________________

   ____

5. Please describe treatment and response: ______________________________

   ____

6. Prognosis: ______________________________

7. Has your patient taken medications or followed other prescribed treatment for at least three consecutive months? ☐ Yes ☐ No

8. Have your patient's impairments lasted or can they be expected to last at least twelve months? ☐ Yes ☐ No

9. Identify any associated psychological problems/ limitations:

☐ Cognitive limitations	☐ Personality change
☐ Impaired attention and concentration	☐ Depression
☐ Impaired short term memory	☐ Social withdrawal
☐ Reduced ability to attend to tasks	☐ Anxiety
☐ Reduced ability to persist in tasks	☐ List others in margin:

10. Identify ***side effects*** of any medications that may have implications for working:

☐ Drowsiness/ sedation ☐ Other: ______________________________

11. As a result of your patient's impairments, estimate your patient's functional limitations if your patient were placed in a ***competitive work situation***.

a. How many city blocks can your patient walk without rest or severe pain? ______

b. Please circle the hours and/or minutes that your patient can sit ***at one time,*** *e.g.*, before needing to get up, *etc.*

Sit:	0 5 10 15 20 30 45 Minutes	1 2 More than 2 Hours

c. Please circle the hours and/or minutes that your patient can stand ***at one time***, *e.g.*, before needing to sit down, walk around, *etc.*

Stand:	0 5 10 15 20 30 45 Minutes	1 2 More than 2 Hours

d. Please indicate how long your patient can sit and stand/walk ***total in an 8-hour working day*** (with normal breaks):

Sit	Stand/walk	
☐	☐	less than 2 hours
☐	☐	about 2 hours
☐	☐	about 4 hours
☐	☐	at least 6 hours

e. Does your patient need a job that permits shifting positions at will from sitting, standing or walking? ☐ Yes ☐ No

f. Does your patient need to include periods of walking around during an 8-hour working day? ☐ Yes ☐ No

If yes, how ***often*** must your patient walk?
1 5 10 15 20 30 45 60 90
Minutes

How ***long*** must your patient walk each time?
1 2 3 4 5 6 7 8 9 10 11 12 13 14 15
Minutes

g. In addition to normal breaks every two hours, will your patient sometimes need to take *unscheduled* breaks during a working day? ☐ Yes ☐ No

If yes, 1) approx. how ***often*** do you think this will happen? ________________

2) approx. how ***long*** (on average) will each break last?________________

3) what symptoms cause a need for breaks?

☐ Muscular aches ☐ Tremor enhanced by stress
☐ Chronic fatigue ☐ Adverse effects of medication
☐ Other: ____

h. With prolonged sitting, should your patient's leg(s) be elevated? ☐ Yes ☐ No

If yes, 1) how ***high*** should the leg(s) be elevated? __________________

2) if your patient had a sedentary job, ***what percentage of time*** during an 8 hour working day should the leg(s) be elevated? ________________%

3) what symptoms cause a need to elevate leg(s)? __________

i. While engaging in occasional standing/walking, must your patient use a cane or other assistive device? ☐ Yes ☐ No

For this and other questions on this form, "rarely" means 1% to 5% of an 8-hour working day; "occasionally" means 6% to 33% of an 8-hour working day; "frequently" means 34% to 66% of an 8-hour working day.

j. How many pounds can your patient lift and carry in a competitive work situation?

	Never	**Rarely**	**Occasionally**	**Frequently**
Less than 10 lbs.	☐	☐	☐	☐
10 lbs.	☐	☐	☐	☐
20 lbs.	☐	☐	☐	☐
50 lbs.	☐	☐	☐	☐

k. How often can your patient perform the following activities?

	Never	Rarely	Occasionally	Frequently
Twist	☐	☐	☐	☐
Stoop (bend)	☐	☐	☐	☐
Crouch/ squat	☐	☐	☐	☐

l. If your patient has significant limitations with reaching, handling or fingering:

Please indicate the percentage of time during an 8-hour working day that your patient can use hands/fingers/arms for the following activities:

	HANDS: Grasp, Turn Twist Objects	**FINGERS: Fine Manipulations**	**ARMS: Reaching In Front of Body**	**ARMS: Reaching Overhead**
Right:	**%**	**%**	**%**	**%**
Left:	**%**	**%**	**%**	**%**

What symptoms cause limitations of use of the upper extremities?

☐ Tremor
☐ Fatigue
☐ Muscular aches
☐ Rigidity
☐ Bradykinesia
☐ Other: ____________________
☐ Impaired muscle control
☐ Side effects of medication

m. How much is your patient likely to be ***"off task"***? That is, what percentage of a typical workday would your patient's symptoms likely be severe enough to interfere with ***attention and concentration*** needed to perform even simple work tasks?

☐ 0% ☐ 5% ☐ 10% ☐ 15% ☐ 20% ☐ 25% or more

n. To what degree can your patient tolerate work stress?

☐ Incapable of even "low stress" jobs
☐ Moderate stress is okay
☐ Capable of low stress jobs
☐ Capable of high stress work

Please explain the reasons for your conclusion: ____________________

o. Are your patient's impairments likely to produce "good days" and "bad days"?
☐ Yes ☐ No

If yes, assuming you patient was trying to work full time, please estimate, on the average, how many days per month your patient is likely to be absent from work as a result of the impairments:

☐ Never	☐ About three days per month
☐ About one day per month	☐ About four days per month
☐ About two days per month	☐ More than four days per month

12. Are your patient's impairments (physical impairments plus any emotional impairments) as demonstrated by signs, clinical findings and laboratory or test results ***reasonably consistent*** with the symptoms and functional limitations described above in this evaluation? ☐ Yes ☐ No

    If no, please explain: ______________________________

13. Please attach another page to describe any other limitations (such as limited vision, difficulty hearing, difficulty speaking, need to avoid temperature extremes, wetness, humidity, noise, dust, fumes, gases or hazards, etc.) that would affect your patient's ability to work at a regular job on a sustained basis.

______________________ ______________________________

Date *Signature*

Printed/Typed Name: ______________________________

Address: ______________________________

____

____

§239.7 Form: Peripheral Neuropathy Medical Source Statement

PERIPHERAL NEUROPATHY MEDICAL SOURCE STATEMENT

From: ______________________________

Re: ______________________________(Name of Patient)

______________________________(Date of Birth)

Please answer the following questions concerning your patient's impairments.

1. Frequency and length of contact: ______________________________

2. Does your patient have peripheral neuropathy? ☐ Yes ☐ No

3. List any other diagnosed impairments: ______________________________

   ____

4. Prognosis: ______________________________

5. Identify your patient's symptoms and signs:

   ☐ Pain
   ☐ Weakness
   ☐ Paresthesias
   ☐ Sensory loss
   ☐ Abnormal gait
   ☐ Decreased deep tendon reflexes
   ☐ Deficiencies in joint proprioception
   ☐ Chronic fatigue
   ☐ Urinary incontinence
   ☐ Fecal incontinence
   ☐ Diarrhea
   ☐ Cramping, burning calves & feet
   ☐ Postural hypotension
   ☐ Muscle atrophy

   Other symptoms, signs and clinical findings: ______________________________

   ____

   ____

6. If your patient has pain/ paresthesias, characterize the severity of the pain/ paresthesias:

   ☐ Mild ☐ Moderate ☐ Severe

   Describe the location and frequency of your patient's pain/ paresthesias:

   ____

7. Have your patient's impairments lasted or can they be expected to last at least twelve months? ☐ Yes ☐ No

8. Identify any associated psychological problems/ limitations:

☐ Cognitive limitations
☐ Impaired attention and concentration
☐ Impaired short term memory
☐ Reduced ability to attend to tasks
☐ Reduced ability to persist in tasks
☐ Personality change
☐ Depression
☐ Social withdrawal
☐ Anxiety
☐ List others in margin:

9. Identify **side effects** of any medications that may have implications for working:

☐ Drowsiness/ sedation ☐ Other: ______________________________

10. As a result of your patient's impairments, estimate your patient's functional limitations if your patient were placed in a ***competitive work situation***.

a. How many city blocks can your patient walk without rest or severe pain? ___________

b. Please circle the hours and/or minutes that your patient can sit ***at one time***, *e.g.*, before needing to get up, *etc*.

Sit: 0 5 10 15 20 30 45 Minutes 1 2 More than 2 Hours

c. Please circle the hours and/or minutes that your patient can stand ***at one time***, *e.g.*, before needing to sit down, walk around, *etc*.

Stand: 0 5 10 15 20 30 45 Minutes 1 2 More than 2 Hours

d. Please indicate how long your patient can sit and stand/walk ***total in an 8-hour working day*** (with normal breaks):

Sit	Stand/walk	
☐	☐	less than 2 hours
☐	☐	about 2 hours
☐	☐	about 4 hours
☐	☐	at least 6 hours

e. Does your patient need a job that permits shifting positions at will from sitting, standing or walking? ☐ Yes ☐ No

f. Does your patient need to include periods of walking around during an 8-hour working day? ☐ Yes ☐ No

If yes, how *often* must your patient walk? How *long* must your patient walk each time?

1 5 10 15 20 30 45 60 90 Minutes

1 2 3 4 5 6 7 8 9 10 11 12 13 14 15 Minutes

g. In addition to normal breaks every two hours, will your patient sometimes need to take *unscheduled* breaks during a working day? ☐ Yes ☐ No

If yes, 1) approx. how ***often*** do you think this will happen? ________________

2) approx. how ***long*** (on average) will each break last?________________

3) what symptoms cause a need for breaks?

☐ Muscle weakness ☐ Pain/ paresthesias, numbness
☐ Chronic fatigue ☐ Adverse effects of medication
☐ Other: ______________________________

h. With prolonged sitting, should your patient's leg(s) be elevated? ☐ Yes ☐ No

If yes, 1) how ***high*** should the leg(s) be elevated? ______________
2) if your patient had a sedentary job, ***what percentage of time*** during an 8-hour working day should the leg(s) be elevated? ______________

3) what symptoms cause a need to elevate the leg(s)? ______________

i. While engaging in occasional standing/walking, must your patient use a cane or other hand-held assistive device? ☐ Yes ☐ No

For this and other questions on this form, "rarely" means 1% to 5% of an 8-hour working day; "occasionally" means 6% to 33% of an 8-hour working day; "frequently" means 34% to 66% of an 8-hour working day.

j. How many pounds can your patient lift and carry in a competitive work situation?

	Never	**Rarely**	**Occasionally**	**Frequently**
Less than 10 lbs.		☐	☐	☐
10 lbs.	☐	☐	☐	☐
20 lbs.	☐	☐	☐	☐
50 lbs.	☐	☐	☐	☐

k. How often can your patient perform the following activities?

	Never	**Rarely**	**Occasionally**	**Frequently**
Twist	☐	☐	☐	☐
Stoop (bend)	☐	☐	☐	☐
Crouch/ squat	☐	☐	☐	☐

l. Does your patient have significant limitations with reaching, handling or fingering?
☐ Yes ☐ No

If yes, what symptoms cause limitations of use of the upper extremities?

☐ Pain/ paresthesias ☐ Motor loss ☐ Sensory loss/ numbness
☐ Muscle weakness ☐ Swelling ☐ Side effects of medication
☐ Limitation of motion ☐ Other: ______________________________

Please indicate the percentage of time during an 8-hour working day that your patient can use hands/fingers/arms for the following activities:

	HANDS: Grasp, Turn Twist Objects	**FINGERS:** Fine Manipulations	**ARMS:** Reaching In Front of Body	**ARMS:** Reaching Overhead
Right:	%	%	%	%
Left:	%	%	%	%

m. How much is your patient likely to be ***"off task"***? That is, what percentage of a typical workday would your patient's symptoms likely be severe enough to interfere with ***attention and concentration*** needed to perform even simple work tasks?

☐ 0% ☐ 5% ☐ 10% ☐ 15% ☐ 20% ☐ 25% or more

n. To what degree can your patient tolerate work stress?

☐ Incapable of even "low stress" work ☐ Capable of low stress work
☐ Capable of moderate stress - normal work ☐ Capable of high stress work

Please explain the reasons for your conclusion: ______________________________

o. Are your patient's impairments likely to produce "good days" and "bad days"?
☐ Yes ☐ No

If yes, assuming your patient was trying to work full time, please estimate, on the average, how many days per month your patient is likely to be absent from work as a result of the impairments:

☐ Never ☐ About three days per month
☐ About one day per month ☐ About four days per month
☐ About two days per month ☐ More than four days per month

11. Are your patient's impairments (physical impairments plus any emotional impairments) as demonstrated by signs, clinical findings and laboratory or test results ***reasonably consistent*** with the symptoms and functional limitations described above in this evaluation?
☐ Yes ☐ No

If no, please explain: ____

12. Please describe any other limitations (such as limited vision, difficulty hearing, need to avoid temperature extremes, wetness, humidity, noise, dust, fumes, gases or hazards, *etc.*) that would affect your patient's ability to work at a regular job on a sustained basis:

____

____

____

____

______________________________ ______________________________
Date *Signature*

Printed/Typed Name: ______________________________

Address: ______________________________

____

____

7-36
1/17
§239.7

§239.8 *Form: Postpolio Syndrome Medical Source Statement*

POST-POLIO SYNDROME MEDICAL SOURCE STATEMENT

From: ______________________________

Re: ______________________________(Name of Patient)

______________________________(Date of Birth)

Please answer the following questions concerning your patient's impairments:

1. Frequency and length of contact: ______________________________

2. Does your patient suffer from post-polio syndrome? ☐ Yes ☐ No

   If yes, identify impairments associated with the residuals of polio:

   ☐ Early advanced degenerative arthritis related to long-standing postural imbalance
   ☐ Respiratory insufficiency linked to weakening of respiratory musculature
   ☐ Sleep disorders related to respiratory insufficiency
   ☐ Mental disorder related to any of the above

3. List any other diagnosed impairments: ______________________________

   ____

4. Prognosis: ______________________________

5. Identify your patient's symptoms and signs:

   ☐ Slowly progressive weakness of muscles previously affected by polio
   ☐ Muscle atrophy
   ☐ Reduced peripheral reflexes
   ☐ Muscle pain
   ☐ Joint pain
   ☐ Abnormal gait
   ☐ Abnormal posture
   ☐ Fatigue
   ☐ Scoliosis
   ☐ Musculoskeletal deformity
   ☐ Intolerance to cold
   ☐ Speech difficulty
   ☐ Shortness of breath
   ☐ Sleep apnea
   ☐ Excessive daytime drowsiness
   ☐ Cognitive changes
   ☐ Behavioral changes
   ☐ Abnormal pulmonary function study
   ☐ Abnormal polysomnography
   ☐ Abnormal imaging study
   ☐ Positive EMG

   Other symptoms, signs and clinical findings: ______________________________

   ____

6. Have your patient's impairments lasted or can they be expected to last at least twelve months? ☐ Yes ☐ No

7. Identify any associated psychological problems/ limitations:

☐ Cognitive limitations	☐ Personality change
☐ Impaired attention and concentration	☐ Depression
☐ Impaired short term memory	☐ Social withdrawal
☐ Reduced ability to attend to tasks	☐ Anxiety
☐ Reduced ability to persist in tasks	☐ List others in margin:

8. Identify **side effects** of any medications that may have implications for working:

☐ Drowsiness/ sedation ☐ Other: ______________________________

9. As a result of your patient's impairments, estimate your patient's functional limitations if your patient were placed in a ***competitive work situation***.

a. How many city blocks can your patient walk without rest or severe pain? __________

b. Please circle the hours and/or minutes that your patient can sit ***at one time***, *e.g.*, before needing to get up, *etc*.

Sit: 0 5 10 15 20 30 45 (Minutes) 1 2 More than 2 (Hours)

c. Please circle the hours and/or minutes that your patient can stand ***at one time***, *e.g.*, before needing to sit down, walk around, *etc*.

Stand: 0 5 10 15 20 30 45 (Minutes) 1 2 More than 2 (Hours)

d. Please indicate how long your patient can sit and stand/walk ***total in an 8-hour working day*** (with normal breaks):

Sit	**Stand/walk**	
☐	☐	less than 2 hours
☐	☐	about 2 hours
☐	☐	about 4 hours
☐	☐	at least 6 hours

e. Does your patient need a job that permits shifting positions ***at will*** from sitting, standing or walking? ☐ Yes ☐ No

f. Does your patient need to include periods of walking around during an 8-hour working day? ☐ Yes ☐ No

If yes, how ***often*** must your patient walk? 1 5 10 15 20 30 45 60 90 Minutes

How ***long*** must your patient walk each time? 1 2 3 4 5 6 7 8 9 10 11 12 13 14 15 Minutes

g. In addition to normal breaks every two hours, will your patient sometimes need to take *unscheduled* breaks during a working day? ☐ Yes ☐ No

If yes, 1) approx. how ***often*** do you think this will happen? ________________

2) approx. how ***long*** (on average) will each break last?________________

3) what symptoms cause a need for breaks?

☐ muscle weakness ☐ pain/ paresthesias, numbness
☐ chronic fatigue ☐ adverse effects of medication
☐ other: ______________________________

h. With prolonged sitting, should your patient's leg(s) be elevated? ☐ Yes ☐ No

If yes, 1) how ***high*** should the leg(s) be elevated? ________________

2) if your patient had a sedentary job, ***what percentage of time*** during an 8-hour working day should the leg(s) be elevated? ______________%

3) what symptoms cause a need to elevate leg(s)? ______________

i. While engaging in occasional standing/walking, must your patient use a cane or other assistive device? ☐ Yes ☐ No

For this and other questions on this form, "rarely" means 1% to 5% of an 8-hour working day; "occasionally" means 6% to 33% of an 8-hour working day; "frequently" means 34% to 66% of an 8-hour working day.

j. How many pounds can your patient lift and carry in a competitive work situation?

	Never	**Rarely**	**Occasionally**	**Frequently**
Less than 10 lbs.	☐	☐	☐	☐
10 lbs.	☐	☐	☐	☐
20 lbs.	☐	☐	☐	☐
50 lbs.	☐	☐	☐	☐

k. How often can your patient perform the following activities?

	Never	**Rarely**	**Occasionally**	**Frequently**
Twist	☐	☐	☐	☐
Stoop (bend)	☐	☐	☐	☐
Crouch/ squat	☐	☐	☐	☐

l. Does your patient have significant limitations with reaching, handling or fingering?
☐ Yes ☐ No

If yes, what symptoms cause limitations of use of the upper extremities?

☐ Pain/ paresthesias ☐ Motor loss ☐ Sensory loss/ numbness
☐ Muscle weakness ☐ Swelling ☐ Side effects of medication
☐ Limitation of motion ☐ Other: ____________________

Please indicate the percentage of time during an 8-hour working day that your patient can use hands/fingers/arms for the following activities:

	HANDS: Grasp, Turn <u>Twist Objects</u>	**FINGERS:** Fine <u>Manipulations</u>	**ARMS:** Reaching <u>In Front of Body</u>	**ARMS:** Reaching <u>Overhead</u>
Right:	%	%	%	%
Left:	%	%	%	%

m. How much is your patient likely to be ***"off task"***? That is, what percentage of a typical workday would your patient's symptoms likely be severe enough to interfere with ***attention and concentration*** needed to perform even simple work tasks?

☐ 0% ☐ 5% ☐ 10% ☐ 15% ☐ 20% ☐ 25% or more

n. To what degree can your patient tolerate work stress?

☐ Incapable of even "low stress" jobs ☐ Capable of low stress jobs
☐ Moderate stress is okay ☐ Capable of high stress work

Please explain the reasons for your conclusion: ____________________

o. Are your patient's impairments likely to produce "good days" and "bad days"?
☐ Yes ☐ No

If yes, assuming your patient was trying to work full time, please estimate, on the average, how many days per month your patient is likely to be absent from work as a result of the impairments:

☐ Never	☐ About three days per month
☐ About one day per month	☐ About four days per month
☐ About two days per month	☐ More than four days per month

10. Are your patient's impairments (physical impairments plus any emotional impairments) as demonstrated by signs, clinical findings and laboratory or test results ***reasonably consistent*** with the symptoms and functional limitations described in this evaluation?
☐ Yes ☐ No

If no, please explain: ______________________________

11. Please describe any other limitations (such as limited vision, difficulty hearing, need to avoid temperature extremes, wetness, humidity, noise, dust, fumes, gases or hazards, etc.) that would affect your patient's ability to work at a regular job on a sustained basis:

____

____

12. What is the earliest date that the description of ***symptoms and limitation*** in this questionnaire applies? ______________________________

______________________________ ______________________________
Date *Signature*

Printed/Typed Name: ______________________________

Address: ______________________________

____

____

§239.8

1/17

7-44

§239.9 Form: Reflex Sympathetic Dystrophy (RSD)/Complex Regional Pain Syndrome (CRPS), Type 1 Medical Source Statement

REFLEX SYMPATHETIC DYSTROPHY (RSD)/ COMPLEX REGIONAL PAIN SYNDROME, TYPE 1 (CRPS) MEDICAL SOURCE STATEMENT

From: ______________________________

Re: ______________________________ (Name of Patient)

______________________________ (Date of Birth)

Please answer the following questions concerning your patient's impairments.

1. Frequency and length of contact: ______________________________

2. Does your patient suffer from RSD/ CRPS? ☐ Yes ☐ No

   If yes, does your patient have persistent complaints of pain that are typically out of proportion to the severity of any documented precipitant? ☐ Yes ☐No

   If yes, please identify which of the following clinically documented signs in the affected region have been present ***at any time*** following the documented precipitant:

   ☐ Swelling
   ☐ Decreased or increased sweating
   ☐ Osteoporosis
   ☐ Abnormal hair or nail growth – too slow or too fast
   ☐ Changes in skin color or texture
   ☐ Skin temperature changes
   ☐ Abnormal pilomotor erection (gooseflesh)
   ☐ Involuntary movements of the affected region

3. List any other diagnosed impairments: ______________________________

4. Prognosis: ______________________________

5. Have your patient's impairments lasted or can they be expected to last at least twelve months? ☐ Yes ☐ No

6. Identify your patient's symptoms and signs:

   ☐ Burning, aching or searing pain initially localized to the site of injury
   ☐ Increased sensitivity to touch
   ☐ Joint stiffness
   ☐ Restricted mobility
   ☐ Muscle spasm
   ☐ Impaired appetite
   ☐ Pain complaints that spread to involve other extremities
   ☐ Abnormal sensations of heat or cold
   ☐ Muscle pain
   ☐ Muscle atrophy
   ☐ Impaired sleep
   ☐ Chronic fatigue

   Other symptoms, signs and clinical findings: ______________________________

   ____

7. Identify any associated psychological problems/ limitations:

☐ Cognitive limitations	☐ Personality change
☐ Impaired attention and concentration	☐ Depression
☐ Impaired short term memory	☐ Social withdrawal
☐ Reduced ability to attend to tasks	☐ Anxiety
☐ Reduced ability to persist in tasks	☐ List others in margin:

8. Identify ***side effects*** of any medications that may have implications for working:

☐ Drowsiness/ sedation ☐ Other: ______________________________

9. As a result of your patient's impairments, estimate your patient's functional limitations if your patient were placed in a ***competitive work situation***.

a. How many city blocks can your patient walk without rest or severe pain? __________

b. Please circle the hours and/or minutes that your patient can sit ***at one time,*** e.g., before needing to get up, *etc*.

Sit: 0 5 10 15 20 30 45 Minutes 1 2 More than 2 Hours

c. Please circle the hours and/or minutes that your patient can stand ***at one time***, e.g., before needing to sit down, walk around, *etc*.

Stand: 0 5 10 15 20 30 45 Minutes 1 2 More than 2 Hours

d. Please indicate how long your patient can sit and stand/walk ***total in an 8-hour working day*** (with normal breaks):

Sit	Stand/walk	
☐	☐	less than 2 hours
☐	☐	about 2 hours
☐	☐	about 4 hours
☐	☐	at least 6 hours

e. Does your patient need a job that permits shifting positions at will from sitting, standing or walking? ☐ Yes ☐ No

f. Does your patient need to include periods of walking around during an 8-hour working day? ☐ Yes ☐ No

If yes, how ***often*** must your patient walk? 1 5 10 15 20 30 45 60 90 Minutes

How ***long*** must your patient walk each time? 1 2 3 4 5 6 7 8 9 10 11 12 13 14 15 Minutes

g. In addition to normal breaks every two hours, will your patient sometimes need to take *unscheduled* breaks during a working day? ☐ Yes ☐ No

If yes, 1) approx. how ***often*** do you think this will happen? __________

2) approx. how ***long*** (on average) will each break last? __________

3) what symptoms cause a need for breaks?

☐ Muscle weakness ☐ Pain/ paresthesias, numbness
☐ Chronic fatigue ☐ Adverse effects of medication
☐ Other: ______________________________

h. With prolonged sitting, should your patient's leg(s) be elevated? ☐ Yes ☐ No

If yes, 1) how ***high*** should the leg(s) be elevated? ______________

2) if your patient had a sedentary job, ***what percentage of time*** during an 8-hour working day should the leg(s) be elevated? ______________

3) what symptoms cause a need to elevate the leg(s)? ______________

i. While engaging in occasional standing/walking, must your patient use a cane or other hand-held assistive device? ☐ Yes ☐ No

For this and other questions on this form, "rarely" means 1% to 5% of an 8-hour working day; "occasionally" means 6% to 33% of an 8-hour working day; "frequently" means 34% to 66% of an 8-hour working day.

j How many pounds can your patient lift and carry in a competitive work situation?

	Never	**Rarely**	**Occasionally**	**Frequently**
Less than 10 lbs.		☐	☐	☐
10 lbs.	☐	☐	☐	☐
20 lbs.	☐	☐	☐	☐
50 lbs.	☐	☐	☐	☐

k. How often can your patient perform the following activities?

	Never	**Rarely**	**Occasionally**	**Frequently**
Twist	☐	☐	☐	☐
Stoop (bend)	☐	☐	☐	☐
Crouch/ squat	☐	☐	☐	☐

l. If your patient has significant limitations with reaching, handling or fingering:

What symptoms cause limitations of use of the upper extremities?

☐ Pain/ paresthesias ☐ Motor loss ☐ Sensory loss/ numbness
☐ Muscle weakness ☐ Swelling ☐ Side effects of medication
☐ Limitation of motion ☐ Other: ______________________

Please indicate the percentage of time during an 8-hour working day that your patient can use hands/fingers/arms for the following activities:

	HANDS: Grasp, Turn Twist Objects	**FINGERS: Fine Manipulations**	**ARMS: Reaching In Front of Body**	**ARMS: Reaching Overhead**
Right:	%	%	%	%
Left:	%	%	%	%

m. How much is your patient likely to be ***"off task"***? That is, what percentage of a typical workday would your patient's symptoms likely be severe enough to interfere with ***attention and concentration*** needed to perform even simple work tasks?

☐ 0% ☐ 5% ☐ 10% ☐ 15% ☐ 20% ☐ 25% or more

n. To what degree can your patient tolerate work stress?

☐ Incapable of even "low stress" work ☐ Capable of low stress work
☐ Capable of moderate stress - normal work ☐ Capable of high stress work

o. Are your patient's impairments likely to produce "good days" and "bad days"?
☐ Yes ☐ No

If yes, assuming your patient was trying to work full time, please estimate, on the average, how many days per month your patient is likely to be absent from work as a result of the impairments:

☐ Never ☐ About three days per month
☐ About one day per month ☐ About four days per month
☐ About two days per month ☐ More than four days per month

10. Are your patient's impairments (physical impairments plus any emotional impairments) as demonstrated by signs, clinical findings and laboratory or test results ***reasonably consistent*** with the symptoms and functional limitations described above in this evaluation?
☐ Yes ☐ No

If no, please explain: ______________________________

11. Please describe any other limitations (such as limited vision, difficulty hearing, need to avoid temperature extremes, wetness, humidity, noise, dust, fumes, gases or hazards, etc.) that would affect your patient's ability to work at a regular job on a sustained basis:

____
____
____
____

______________________ ______________________
Date *Signature*

Printed/Typed Name: ______________________

Address: ______________________
____
____

7-34
7/16

§239.9

§239.10 Form: Muscular Dystrophy Medical Source Statement

MUSCULAR DYSTROPHY MEDICAL SOURCE STATEMENT

From: ______________________________

Re: ______________________________ (Name of Patient)

______________________________ (Date of Birth)

Please answer the following questions concerning your patient's impairments:

1. Frequency and length of contact: ____

2. Does your patient have muscular dystrophy? ☐ Yes ☐ No

   If yes, what type of muscular dystrophy? ______________________________

   How was this diagnosis made? ______________________________

3. Identify your patient's ***symptoms and signs***:

☐ Generalized weakness	☐ Delayed muscle relaxation	☐ Gastrointestinal problems
☐ Muscle wasting	☐ Unstable walking	☐ Vision disturbance
☐ Exercise intolerance	☐ Joint stiffness	☐ Heart involvement
☐ Paralysis	☐ Joint looseness	☐ Respiration difficulty
☐ Balance problems	☐ Muscle fatigue of limb	☐ Swallowing difficulty
☐ Tremor	☐ Cerebellar ataxia	☐ Depression
☐ Increased deep reflexes	☐ Loss of manual dexterity	☐ Learning disability
☐ Chronic fatigue	☐ Scoliosis	☐ Problems with judgment
☐ Paresthesias	☐ Numbness	☐ Emotional lability
☐ Poor coordination	☐ Pain	☐ Confusion
☐ Muscle spasticity	☐ Speech difficulty	☐ Difficulty remembering
☐ Sensitivity to heat	☐ Difficulty solving problems	

   Other symptoms, signs and clinical findings: ______________________________

   ____

4. Have your patient's impairments lasted or can they be expected to last at least twelve months? ☐ Yes ☐ No

5. Treatment and response:

____

____

____

____

6. Prognosis: ____

7. Do emotional factors contribute to the severity of your patient's symptoms and functional limitations? ☐ Yes ☐ No

8. Identify any psychological conditions affecting your patient's physical condition:

☐ Depression	☐ Anxiety
☐ Somatic symptom disorder	☐ Personality disorder
☐ Psychological factors affecting physical condition	☐ Other:________________________

9. As a result of your patient's impairments, estimate your patient's functional limitations if your patient were placed in a ***competitive work situation:***

   a. How many city blocks can your patient walk without rest or severe pain? _____

   b. Please circle the hours and/or minutes that your patient can sit ***at one time,*** *e.g.*, before needing to get up, *etc.*

	Minutes	Hours
Sit:	0 5 10 15 20 30 45	1 2 More than 2

   c. Please circle the hours and/or minutes that your patient can stand ***at one time***, *e.g.*, before needing to sit down, walk around, *etc.*

	Minutes	Hours
Stand:	0 5 10 15 20 30 45	1 2 More than 2

   d. Please indicate how long your patient can sit and stand/walk ***total in an 8-hour working day*** (with normal breaks):

Sit	**Stand/walk**	
☐	☐	less than 2 hours
☐	☐	about 2 hours
☐	☐	about 4 hours
☐	☐	at least 6 hours

e. Does your patient need a job that permits shifting positions ***at will*** from sitting, standing or walking? ☐ Yes ☐ No

f. In addition to normal breaks every two hours, will your patient sometimes need to take *unscheduled* breaks during a working day? ☐ Yes ☐ No

If yes, 1) approx. how ***often*** do you think this will happen? ________________

2) approx. how ***long*** (on average) will each break last? ________________

3) what symptoms cause a need for breaks?

☐ Muscle weakness ☐ Pain/ paresthesias, numbness
☐ Chronic fatigue ☐ Adverse effects of medication
☐ Other: ____

g. With prolonged sitting, should your patient's leg(s) be elevated? ☐ Yes ☐ No

If yes, 1) how ***high*** should the leg(s) be elevated? ________________

2) if your patient had a sedentary job, ***what percentage of time*** during an 8 hour working day should the leg(s) be elevated? ________________%

3) what symptoms cause a need to elevate the leg(s)? _______

h. While engaging in occasional standing/walking, must your patient use a cane or other assistive device? Yes No

If yes, what symptoms cause a need to use a cane?

☐ Muscle weakness ☐ Spasticity ☐ Chronic fatigue
☐ Incoordination ☐ Imbalance ☐ List others in margin

For this and other questions on this form, "rarely" means 1% to 5% of an 8-hour working day; "occasionally" means 6% to 33% of an 8-hour working day; "frequently" means 34% to 66% of an 8-hour working day.

i. How many pounds can your patient lift and carry in a competitive work situation?

	Never	**Rarely**	**Occasionally**	**Frequently**
Less than 10 lbs.	☐	☐	☐	☐
10 lbs.	☐	☐	☐	☐
20 lbs.	☐	☐	☐	☐
50 lbs.	☐	☐	☐	☐

j. How often can your patient perform the following activities?

	Never	Rarely	Occasionally	Frequently
Twist	☐	☐	☐	☐
Stoop (bend)	☐	☐	☐	☐
Crouch/ squat	☐	☐	☐	☐

k. If your patient has significant limitations with reaching, handling or fingering:

What symptoms cause limitations of use of the upper extremities?

☐ Pain/ paresthesias ☐ Incoordination ☐ Sensory loss/ numbness
☐ Muscle weakness ☐ Spasticity ☐ Fatigue
☐ Tremor ☐ Other: ____________________

Please indicate the percentage of time during an 8-hour working day that your patient can use hands/fingers/arms for the following activities:

	HANDS: Grasp, Turn <u>Twist Objects</u>	**FINGERS: Fine <u>Manipulations</u>**	**ARMS: Reaching <u>In Front of Body</u>**	**ARMS: Reaching <u>Overhead</u>**
Right:	%	%	%	%
Left:	%	%	%	%

l. How much is your patient likely to be "***off task***"? That is, what percentage of a typical workday would your patient's symptoms likely be severe enough to interfere with ***attention and concentration*** needed to perform even simple work tasks?

☐ 0% ☐ 5% ☐ 10% ☐ 15% ☐ 20% ☐ 25% or more

m. To what degree can your patient tolerate work stress?

☐ Incapable of even "low stress" work ☐ Capable of low stress work
☐ Capable of moderate stress - normal work ☐ Capable of high stress work

Please explain the reasons for your conclusion: ____________________

n. Are your patient's impairments likely to produce "good days" and "bad days"?
☐ Yes ☐ No

If yes, assuming your patient was trying to work full time, please estimate, on the average, how many days per month your patient is likely to be absent from work as a result of the impairments:

☐ Never
☐ About one day per month
☐ About two days per month
☐ About three days per month
☐ About four days per month
☐ More than four days per month

10. Are your patient's impairments (physical impairments plus any emotional impairments) as demonstrated by signs, clinical findings and laboratory or test results ***reasonably consistent*** with the symptoms and functional limitations described above in this evaluation? ☐ Yes ☐ No

If no, please explain: ______________________________

11. Please describe any other limitations (such as psychological limitations, limited vision, difficulty hearing, difficulty speaking, need to avoid temperature extremes, wetness, humidity, noises, dust, fumes, gases or hazards, etc.) that would affect your patient's ability to work at a regular job on a sustained basis.

____

____

______________________________ ______________________________
Date *Signature*

Printed/Typed Name: ______________________________

Address: ______________________________

____

____

§239.11 Form: Neurological Listings Medical Source Statement

NEUROLOGICAL LISTINGS MEDICAL SOURCE STATEMENT

From: ______________________________

Re: ______________________________ (Name of Patient)

______________________________ (Date of Birth)

Please answer the following questions concerning your patient's impairments.

1. Frequency and length of contact: ______________________________

2. Identify your patient's neurological impairments:

☐ Traumatic brain injury	☐ Benign brain tumor	☐ Parkinsonian syndrome
☐ Cerebral palsy	☐ Spinal cord disorder	☐ Multiple sclerosis
☐ Post-polio syndrome	☐ Myasthenia gravis	☐ Muscular dystrophy
☐ Vascular insult to the brain	☐ Motor neuron disorder other than ALS	☐ Neurodegenerative disease of the central nervous system
☐ Peripheral neuropathy		

3. Other impairments: ______________________________

4. Identify your patient's **symptoms and signs**:

☐ Flaccidity	☐ Trouble sleeping	☐ Loss of manual dexterity
☐ Spasticity	☐ Mental fatigue	☐ Muscle atrophy
☐ Spasms	☐ Impaired attention	☐ Bladder problems
☐ Incoordination	☐ Impaired concentration	☐ Bowel problems
☐ Imbalance	☐ Impaired memory	☐ Sensitivity to heat
☐ Tremor	☐ Impaired judgment	☐ Nystagmus
☐ Physical fatigue	☐ Depression	☐ Visual loss
☐ Muscle weakness	☐ Anxiety	☐ Double vision
☐ Dizziness	☐ Emotional lability	☐ Pain in one eye
☐ Tingling	☐ Personality change	☐ Dimness of vision
☐ Numbness	☐ Confusion	☐ Partial blindness
☐ Pain	☐ Dementia	☐ Other vision disturbance
☐ Increased deep reflexes	☐ Unstable walking	☐ Difficulty solving problems
☐ Nausea	☐ Balance problems	☐ Speech difficulties
☐ Headaches	☐ Falling spells	☐ Ineffective communication
☐ Poor proprioception	☐ Abnormal stereognosis	☐ Bulbar dysfunction
☐ Chorea	☐ Athetosis	☐

Other symptoms, signs and clinical findings: ______________________________

5. Treatment and response:

____

____

6. Prognosis:____

7. Have your patient's impairments lasted or can they be expected to last at least twelve months? Yes No

8. Rate the degree to which your patient is physically limited.

☐ None ☐ Mild ☐ Moderate ☐ Marked ☐ Extreme

Note: A **marked** limitation means that, due to the signs and symptoms of your patient's neurological disorder, your patient is seriously limited in the ability to independently initiate, sustain, and complete work-related physical activities. Your patient may have a marked limitation in physical functioning when the neurological disease process causes persistent *or* intermittent symptoms that affect your patient's abilities to independently initiate, sustain, and complete work-related activities, such as standing, balancing, walking, using both upper extremities for fine and gross movements, or results in limitations in using one upper and one lower extremity. The persistent and intermittent symptoms must result in a serious limitation in your patient's ability to do a task or activity on a sustained basis. "Marked" is not defined by a specific number of different physical activities or tasks that demonstrate your patient's ability, but by the overall effects of neurological symptoms on your patient's ability to perform such physical activities on a consistent and sustained basis. Your patient need not be totally precluded from performing an activity to have a marked limitation, as long as the degree of limitation seriously limits your patient's ability to independently initiate, sustain, and complete work-related physical activities.

9. Does your patient have disorganization of motor function in two extremities resulting in an **extreme** limitation in the ability to stand up from a seated position? That is, once seated is your patient unable to stand and maintain an upright position without the assistance of another person or the use of an assistive device, such as a walker, two crutches, or two canes? ☐ Yes ☐ No

10. Does your patient have disorganization of motor function in two extremities resulting in an **extreme** limitation in balance while standing or walking? That is, is your patient unable to maintain an upright position while standing or walking without the assistance of another person or an assistive device, such as a walker, two crutches, or two canes? ☐ Yes ☐ No

11. Does your patient have disorganization of motor function in two extremities resulting in an **extreme** limitation in the ability to use the upper extremities? That is, does your patient have a loss of function of both upper extremities (including fingers, wrists, hands, arms, and shoulders) that very seriously limits your patient's ability to independently initiate, sustain, and complete work-related activities involving fine and gross motor movements? (Inability to perform fine and gross motor movements could include not being able to pinch, manipulate, and use fingers; or not being able to use hands, arms, and shoulders to perform gross motor movements, such as handling, gripping, grasping, holding, turning, and reaching; or not being able to engage in exertional movements such a lifting, carrying, pushing, and pulling.) ☐ Yes ☐ No

12. Rate your patient's mental limitations as a result of the neurological impairment using the following scale:

Moderate means the ability to function independently, appropriately, effectively, and on a sustained basis is **fair**;
Marked means the ability to function independently, appropriately, effectively, and on a sustained basis is **seriously limited**;
Extreme means **not able** to function independently, appropriately, effectively, and on a sustained basis, but it does not mean a total loss of ability to function.

RATE THE DEGREE OF LIMITATION IN THE FOLLOWING AREAS:					
A.1.	Understanding information:	None-Mild	Moderate	Marked	Extreme
A.2.	Remembering information	None-Mild	Moderate	Marked	Extreme
A.3.	Applying information	None-Mild	Moderate	Marked	Extreme
B.	Interacting with others:	None Mild	Moderate	Marked	Extreme
C.1.	Concentrating	None Mild	Moderate	Marked	Extreme
C.2.	Persisting	None Mild	Moderate	Marked	Extreme
C.3	Maintaining pace	None Mild	Moderate	Marked	Extreme
D.1.	Adapting in the workplace	None Mild	Moderate	Marked	Extreme
D.2.	Managing oneself in the workplace	None Mild	Moderate	Marked	Extreme

13. What is the earliest date that the description of **limitations** in this questionnaire applies?

____

____________________ ______________________________

Date *Signature*

Printed/Typed Name: ______________________________

Address: ______________________________

____

____

7-30
1/17
§239.11

§239.12 Form: Seizures Listings Medical Source Statement

SEIZURES LISTINGS MEDICAL SOURCE STATEMENT

From: ______________________________

Re: ______________________________(Name of Patient)

______________________________(Date of Birth)

Please answer the following questions concerning your patient's seizures:

1. Frequency and length of contact:______________________________
____
____
____

2. Does your patient have seizures? ☐ Yes ☐ No

3. If your patient has seizures:

A. What type of seizures does your patient have?

☐ Generalized tonic-clonic seizures
☐ Dyscognitive seizures (formerly complex partial seizures)
☐ Pseudoseizures
☐ Psychogenic nonepileptic seizures
☐ Other - identify: ______________________________

B. What is the average frequency of seizures? _____ per week _____ per month

4. Does your patient follow prescribed treatment? ☐ Yes ☐ No

5. Please describe a typical seizure:

____
____
____
____
____
____
____

6. Rate the degree to which your patient's **physical functioning** is limited.

☐ None ☐ Mild ☐ Moderate ☐ Marked ☐ Extreme

Note: A **marked** limitation means that, due to the signs and symptoms of your patient's seizure disorder, your patient is seriously limited in the ability to independently initiate, sustain, and complete work-related physical activities. Your patient may have a marked limitation in physical functioning when the neurological disease process causes persistent *or* intermittent symptoms that affect your patient's abilities to independently initiate, sustain, and complete work-related activities, such as standing, balancing, walking, using both upper extremities for fine and gross movements, or results in limitations in using one upper and one lower extremity. The persistent and intermittent symptoms must result in a serious limitation in your patient's ability to do a task or activity on a sustained basis. "Marked" is not defined by a specific number of different physical activities or tasks that demonstrate your patient's ability, but by the overall effects of neurological symptoms on your patient's ability to perform such physical activities on a consistent and sustained basis. Your patient need not be totally precluded from performing an activity to have a marked limitation, as long as the degree of limitation seriously limits your patient's ability to independently initiate, sustain, and complete work-related physical activities.

7. On the next page, rate your patient's **mental limitations** in a work setting as a result of the seizure disorder using the following scale:

> **Moderate** means the ability to function independently, appropriately, effectively, and on a sustained basis is **fair**;
> **Marked** means the ability to function independently, appropriately, effectively, and on a sustained basis is **seriously limited**;
> **Extreme** means **not able** to function independently, appropriately, effectively, and on a sustained basis, but it does not mean a total loss of ability to function.

RATE THE DEGREE OF LIMITATION IN THE FOLLOWING AREAS:					
A.1.	Understanding information:	None-Mild	Moderate	Marked	Extreme
A.2.	Remembering information	None-Mild	Moderate	Marked	Extreme
A.3.	Applying information	None-Mild	Moderate	Marked	Extreme
B.	Interacting with others:	None Mild	Moderate	Marked	Extreme
C.1.	Concentrating	None Mild	Moderate	Marked	Extreme
C.2.	Persisting	None Mild	Moderate	Marked	Extreme
C.3	Maintaining pace	None Mild	Moderate	Marked	Extreme
D.1.	Adapting in the workplace	None Mild	Moderate	Marked	Extreme
D.2.	Managing oneself in the workplace	None Mild	Moderate	Marked	Extreme

_______________________ _______________________

Date *Signature*

Printed/Typed Name: _______________________

Address: _______________________

____

§240 Mental Impairments, Listings § § 12.00-12.15

Because a somewhat different procedure is followed to evaluate mental impairments, and because mental impairment issues are so frequently seen in Social Security disability cases, we provide an expanded discussion.

In the Social Security Disability Benefits Reform Act of 1984, P.L. 98-460, Congress mandated that mental impairment criteria in the Listing of Impairments be revised to permit realistic evaluation of a claimant's ability to engage in a competitive work environment. The revised mental criteria, which were published in 1985, were based on the Diagnostic and Statistical Manual of Mental Disorders, Third Edition, by the American Psychiatric Association, known as DSM-III. 50 Fed. Reg. 35038 (1985). With minor changes, the Listing criteria for determining if a claimant had a particular mental impairment were based on the 1985 rules until January 17, 2017, the effective date of a sweeping revision of the mental Listings based on DSM-5 (which was published by the American Psychiatric Association in 2013). 81 Fed. Reg. 66138 (2016)

There are eleven Listings of mental impairments:

12.02 Neurocognitive Disorders
12.03 Schizophrenia Spectrum and Other Psychotic Disorders
12.04 Depressive, Bipolar and Related Disorders
12.05 Intellectual Disorder
12.06 Anxiety and Obsessive-Compulsive Disorders
12.07 Somatic Symptom and Related Disorders
12.08 Personality and Impulse-Control Disorders
12.10 Autistic Spectrum Disorder
12.11 Neurodevelopmental Disorders
12.13 Eating Disorders
12.15 Trauma- and Stressor-Related Disorders

Each Listing, except § 12.05 (intellectual disorder), consists of the A criteria—a set of medical criteria (based on DSM-5) used to determine if a claimant has a particular mental impairment, and the B criteria—a set of work-related functional limitations that are rated on a scale. In Listings § § 12.02, 12.03, 12.04, 12.06 and 12.15, there are additional functional criteria—the C criteria, assessed when the B criteria are not satisfied. To meet one of the Listings except § 12.05, a claimant must meet the A and B criteria or the A and C criteria.

To meet the requirements of § 12.05, intellectual disorder, one must meet the requirements of either paragraph A or B from that Listing, which apply only to intellectual disorder. Each paragraph of § 12.05 requires significantly subaverage intellectual functioning, significant deficits in adaptive functioning, and evidence consistent with a conclusion that the intellectual disorder began before age 22. *See* §244.

Although Substance-Related and Addictive Disorders are mental impairments included in DSM-5, because such disorders cannot form the basis for a finding of disability, they are not included in the Listing of Impairments. For discussion of alcoholism and drug abuse, *see* § 176.12.

§241 Procedure for Evaluation of Mental Impairments

The first requirement for evaluation of mental impairments is to determine that the claimant, in fact, has a medically determinable mental impairment. This is done by deciding whether certain medical findings are present using the A criteria, or, in the case of § 12.05, whether certain medical findings are present using the A or B paragraphs. Once this hurdle is crossed, one may move on to an evaluation of whether or not the mental impairment is "severe," step 2 of the sequential evaluation process. *See* § 114.

For physical impairments, the Listings are used only in adjudicating step 3 of the sequential evaluation process, that is, determining whether a claimant's impairment meets or equals a Listed impairment. For mental impairments, the Listings criteria are also used determine whether the impairment is severe. This is determined under the mental Listings by evaluating not only the medical evidence pertaining to that impairment, but also by evaluating the degree of functional limitations caused by the impairment, addressed in most Listings in the B criteria.

Functional limitations as set forth in the B criteria are evaluated in four areas by rating a claimant's ability to:

1. Understand, remember or apply information;
2. Interact with others;
3. Concentrate, persist, or maintain pace;
4. Adapt or manage oneself.

The regulation requires application of a specific scale to functional limitations in these areas. The scale is "none," "mild," "moderate," "marked," and "extreme." The regulation states:

> If we rate the degree of your limitation as "none" or "mild," we will generally conclude that your impairment(s) is not severe, unless the evidence otherwise indicates that there is more than a minimal limitation in your ability to do basic work activities (*see* § 404.1521).

20 C.F.R. § 404.1520a(d)(1).

The regulation states that the last point on the scale, i.e., "extreme," "represents a degree of limitation that is incompatible with the ability to do any gainful activity." 20 C.F.R. § 404.1520a(c)(4). Thus, a rating at the "extreme" level of only one of the B criteria calls for a finding that the claimant's impairment meets the Listing. The Listings otherwise may be met if two of the B criteria are at the "marked" level. The following chart, to which we have added columns, is based on SSA's Psychiatric Review Technique Form:

FUNCTIONAL LIMITATION		Column 1		Column 2	Column 3	Column 4
1.	Understand, remember or apply information	None	Mild	Moderate	Marked	Extreme
2.	Interact with others	None	Mild	Moderate	Marked	Extreme
3.	Concentrate, persist, or maintain pace	None	Mild	Moderate	Marked	Extreme
4.	Adapt or manage oneself	None	Mild	Moderate	Marked	Extreme

The degree of limitation shown in Column 1 is considered "generally...not severe, unless the evidence otherwise indicates that there is more than a minimal limitation in your ability to do basic work activities." 20 C.F.R. § 404.1520a(d)(1). The degree of limitation shown in Column 2 indicates a severe impairment, but one that does not meet or equal a Listed impairment. The degree of limitation shown in Column 3 is of Listing-level severity. The Listings are met or equaled when two of the four B criteria are at this level. The Listings also may be met or equaled when only one of the B criteria is at the level of severity shown by Column 4.

Note that each of the B criteria except "interact with others," contains more than one part. Listing 12.00F3f says that for these paragraphs "the greatest degree of limitation of any part of the area of mental functioning directs the rating of limitation to that whole area of mental functioning." In other words, if a claimant has only mild limitations in understanding and remembering information but marked limitation in applying information, the limitation for this part of the B criteria must be ranked as marked. But the Listings say, "Marked limitation in more than one part of the same paragraph B area of mental functioning does not satisfy the requirement to have marked limitation in two paragraph B areas of mental functioning." 12.00F3f(iii).

If the B Criteria are not met, one moves on to evaluate the C Criteria when the claimant's impairment involves one of five Listings: § § 12.02, 12.03, 12.04, 12.06, or 12.15. The C Criteria for all five Listings are identical. In the C criteria SSA recognizes that "mental health interventions may control the more obvious symptoms and signs" of a mental disorder so that the B criteria would not be met. The C Criteria provides an alternative. It requires a medically documented two-year history of the existence of a chronic mental impairment plus two other requirements: C1 requires that the claimant relies "on an ongoing basis, upon medical treatment, mental health therapy, psychosocial support(s), or a highly structured setting(s) to diminish the signs and symptoms" of the mental impairment. This requires medical treatment "with a frequency consistent with accepted medical practice" for the particular impairment. 12.00G2b. C2 is met when the evidence shows that despite diminished symptoms and signs, the claimant has achieved only "marginal adjustment," which means that the claimant has minimal capacity to adapt to changes in his or her environment or "to demands that are not already part of" the claimant's daily life. *See* §243, for more about the C Criteria.

According to § 12.00J2, "If you have a severe medically determinable impairment(s) that does not meet a listing, we will determine whether your impairment(s) medically equals a listing." Presumably, equivalence may be found when a claimant's impairment meets the B or C criteria, even when the A criteria are not met. *See* 20 C.F.R. § § 404.1520a(d)(2) and 404.1526.

Limitations falling in Column 2 require a residual functional capacity (RFC) assessment. 20 C.F.R. § 404.1520a(d)(3). Section 12.00J3 of the Listings provides:

> If your impairment(s) does not meet or medically equal a listing, we will assess your residual functional capacity for engaging in substantial gainful activity (*see* § § 404.1545 and 416.945 of this chapter). When we assess your residual functional capacity, we consider all of your impairment-related mental and physical limitations.

Determining RFC requires a more detailed assessment than that required when considering the B and C Criteria:

> The psychiatric review technique described in 20 CFR 404.1520a and 416.920a and summarized on the Psychiatric Review Technique

Form (PRTF) requires adjudicators to assess an individual's limitations and restrictions from a mental impairment(s) in categories identified in the "paragraph B" and "paragraph C" criteria of the adult mental disorders listings. The adjudicator must remember that the limitations identified in the "paragraph B" and "paragraph C" criteria are not an RFC assessment but are used to rate the severity of mental impairment(s) at steps 2 and 3 of the sequential evaluation process. The mental RFC assessment used at steps 4 and 5 of the sequential evaluation process requires a more detailed assessment by itemizing various functions contained in the broad categories found in paragraphs B and C of the adult mental disorders listings in 12.00 of the Listing of Impairments, and summarized on the PRTF.

SSR 96-8p.

Regulations specify that the adjudicative process must be documented on "a standard document" at the initial and reconsideration levels. This document is known as the Psychiatric Review Technique Form or PRTF, which in recent years it has been incorporated into the electronic eCAT: Disability Determination Explanation. *See* §203.5. A copy of the PRTF appears in the next section.

At the initial and reconsideration levels, the "standard document" must be completed and signed by SSA's "medical or psychological consultant," usually a state agency doctor, unless a disability hearing officer makes the reconsideration determination. 20 C.F.R. § 404.1520a(e)(1) – (e)(3). At the ALJ and Appeals Council levels, completion of the "standard document" is optional but the written decision must incorporate "pertinent findings and conclusions" from the technique mandated by 20 C.F.R. § 404.1520a for the evaluation of mental impairments. 20 C.F.R. § 404.1520a(e)(4).

§241.1 Form: Psychiatric Review Technique (SSA-2506-BK)

Form **SSA-2506-BK** (01-2017) UF
Discontinue Prior Editions
Social Security Administration

PSYCHIATRIC REVIEW TECHNIQUE

Name	SSN
NH (If different from above)	SSN

I. MEDICAL SUMMARY

A. Assessment is from: ______________________ **to** ______________________

B. Medical Disposition(s):

1. ☐ No Medically Determinable Impairment
2. ☐ Impairment(s) Not Severe
3. ☐ Impairment(s) Severe But Not Expected to Last 12 Months
4. ☐ Meets Listing ____________ ____________ ____________ (Cite Listing)
5. ☐ Equals Listing ____________ ____________ ____________ (Cite Listing)
6. ☐ RFC Assessment Necessary
7. ☐ Coexisting Nonmental Impairment(s) that Requires Referral to Another Medical Specialty
8. ☐ Insufficient Evidence

C. Category(ies) Upon Which the Medical Disposition is Based:

1. ☐ 12.02 Neurocognitive disorders
2. ☐ 12.03 Schizophrenia spectrum and other psychotic disorders
3. ☐ 12.04 Depressive, bipolar and related disorders
4. ☐ 12.05 Intellectual disorder
5. ☐ 12.06 Anxiety and obsessive-compulsive disorders
6. ☐ 12.07 Somatic symptom and related disorders
7. ☐ 12.08 Personality and impulse-control disorders
8. ☐ 12.10 Autism spectrum disorder
9. ☐ 12.11 Neurodevelopmental disorders
10. ☐ 12.13 Eating disorders
11. ☐ 12.15 Trauma- and stressor-related disorders

☐ **These findings complete the medical portion of the disability determination.**

MC/PC's Signature	Date
MC/PC's Printed Name	Code

II. DOCUMENTATION OF FACTORS THAT EVIDENCE THE DISORDER

A. 12.02 Neurocognitive Disorders

☐ Medical documentation of a significant cognitive decline from a prior level of functioning in one or more of the cognitive areas:

1. ☐ Complex attention
2. ☐ Executive function
3. ☐ Learning and memory
4. ☐ Language
5. ☐ Perceptual-motor
6. ☐ Social cognition

☐ A medically determinable impairment is present that does not precisely satisfy the criteria above.

Disorder ____________________________________

Pertinent symptoms, signs, and laboratory findings that substantiate the presence of this impairment:

☐ Insufficient evidence to substantiate the presence of the disorder (explain in Part IV, Consultant's Notes).

B. 12.03 Schizophrenia Spectrum and Other Psychotic Disorders

☐ Medical documentation of one or more of the following:

1. ☐ Delusions or hallucinations
2. ☐ Disorganized thinking (speech)
3. ☐ Grossly disorganized behavior or catatonia

☐ A medically determinable impairment is present that does not precisely satisfy the criteria above.

Disorder ______________________________

Pertinent symptoms, signs, and laboratory findings that substantiate the presence of this impairment:

☐ Insufficient evidence to substantiate the presence of the disorder (explain in Part IV, Consultant's Notes).

C. 12.04 Depressive, Bipolar and Related Disorders

☐ Medical documentation of the requirements of paragraph 1 or 2:

1. ☐ Depressive disorder, characterized by <u>five</u> or more of the following:

   a. ☐ Depressed mood

   b. ☐ Diminished interest in almost all activities

   c. ☐ Appetite disturbance with change in weight

   d. ☐ Sleep disturbance

   e. ☐ Observable psychomotor agitation or retardation

   f. ☐ Decreased energy

   g. ☐ Feelings of guilt or worthlessness

   h. ☐ Difficulty concentrating or thinking

   i. ☐ Thoughts of death or suicide

2. ☐ Bipolar disorder, characterized by <u>three</u> or more of the following:

   a. ☐ Pressured speech

   b. ☐ Flight of ideas

   c. ☐ Inflated self-esteem

   d. ☐ Decreased need for sleep

   e. ☐ Distractibility

   f. ☐ Involvement in activities that have a high probability of painful consequences that are not recognized

   g. ☐ Increase in goal-directed activity or psychomotor agitation

☐ A medically determinable impairment is present that does not precisely satisfy the criteria above.

Disorder ______________________________

Pertinent symptoms, signs, and laboratory findings that substantiate the presence of this impairment (explain in Part IV, Consultant's Notes, if necessary):

☐ Insufficient evidence to substantiate the presence of the disorder (explain in Part IV, Consultant's Notes).

D. 12.05 Intellectual Disorder

☐ Satisfied by A or B:

☐ A. Satisfied by 1, 2, and 3:

1. ☐ Significantly subaverage general intellectual functioning evident in a cognitive inability to function at a level required to participate in standardized testing of intellectual functioning

2. ☐ Significant deficits in adaptive functioning currently manifested by dependence upon others for personal needs (for example, toileting, eating, dressing, or bathing)

3. ☐ The evidence about current intellectual and adaptive functioning and about the history of the disorder demonstrates or supports the conclusion that the disorder began prior to attainment of age 22

OR

☐ B. Satisfied by 1, 2, and 3:

1. ☐ Significantly subaverage general intellectual functioning evidenced by: (a) A full scale (or comparable) IQ score of 70 or below on an individually administered standardized test of general intelligence; or (b) a full scale (or comparable) IQ score of 71-75 accompanied by a verbal or performance IQ score (or comparable part score) of 70 or below on an individually administered standardized test of general intelligence

2. ☐ Significant deficits in adaptive functioning currently manifested by extreme limitation of one, or marked limitation of two, of the areas of mental functioning

3. ☐ The evidence about current intellectual and adaptive functioning and about the history of the disorder demonstrates or supports the conclusion that the disorder began prior to attainment of age 22

☐ A medically determinable impairment is present that does not precisely satisfy the criteria above.

Disorder ______________________________

Pertinent symptoms, signs, and laboratory findings that substantiate the presence of this impairment:

☐ Insufficient evidence to substantiate the presence of the disorder (explain in Part IV, Consultant's Notes).

E. 12.06 Anxiety and Obsessive-Compulsive Disorders

☐ Medical documentation of the requirements of paragraph 1, 2, or 3:

1. ☐ Anxiety disorder, characterized by three or more of the following:
   - a. ☐ Restlessness
   - b. ☐ Easily fatigued
   - c. ☐ Difficulty concentrating
   - d. ☐ Irritability
   - e. ☐ Muscle tension
   - f. ☐ Sleep disturbance
2. ☐ Panic disorder or agoraphobia, characterized by one or both:
   - a. ☐ Panic attacks followed by a persistent concern or worry about additional panic attacks or their consequences
   - b. ☐ Disproportionate fear or anxiety about at least two different situations (for example, using public transportation, being in a crowd, being in a line, being outside of one's home, being in open spaces)
3. ☐ Obsessive-compulsive disorder, characterized by one or both:
   - a. ☐ Involuntary, time-consuming preoccupation with intrusive, unwanted thoughts
   - b. ☐ Repetitive behaviors aimed at reducing anxiety

☐ A medically determinable impairment is present that does not precisely satisfy the criteria above.

Disorder ______________________________

Pertinent symptoms, signs, and laboratory findings that substantiate the presence of this impairment:

☐ Insufficient evidence to substantiate the presence of the disorder (explain in Part IV, Consultant's Notes).

F. 12.07 Somatic Symptom and Related Disorders

☐ Medical documentation of <u>one</u> or more of the following:

1. ☐ Symptoms of altered voluntary motor or sensory function that are not better explained by another medical or mental disorder

2. ☐ One or more somatic symptoms that are distressing, with excessive thoughts, feelings, or behaviors related to the symptoms

3. ☐ Preoccupation with having or acquiring a serious illness without significant symptoms present

☐ A medically determinable impairment is present that does not precisely satisfy the criteria above.

Disorder ______________________________

Pertinent symptoms, signs, and laboratory findings that substantiate the presence of this impairment:

☐ Insufficient evidence to substantiate the presence of the disorder (explain in Part IV, Consultant's Notes).

G. 12.08 Personality and Impulse-Control Disorders

☐ Medical documentation of a pervasive pattern of <u>one</u> or more of the following:

1. ☐ Distrust and suspiciousness of others
2. ☐ Detachment from social relationships
3. ☐ Disregard for and violation of the rights of others
4. ☐ Instability of interpersonal relationships
5. ☐ Excessive emotionality and attention seeking
6. ☐ Feelings of inadequacy
7. ☐ Excessive need to be taken care of
8. ☐ Preoccupation with perfectionism and orderliness
9. ☐ Recurrent, impulsive, aggressive behavioral outbursts

☐ A medically determinable impairment is present that does not precisely satisfy the criteria above.

Disorder ______________________________

Pertinent symptoms, signs, and laboratory findings that substantiate the presence of this impairment:

☐ Insufficient evidence to substantiate the presence of the disorder (explain in Part IV, Consultant's Notes).

H. 12.10 Autism Spectrum Disorder

☐ Medical documentation of both of the following:

1. ☐ Qualitative deficits in verbal communication, nonverbal communication, and social interaction
2. ☐ Significantly restricted, repetitive patterns of behavior, interests, or activities

☐ A medically determinable impairment is present that does not precisely satisfy the criteria above.

Disorder ______________________________

Pertinent symptoms, signs, and laboratory findings that substantiate the presence of this impairment:

☐ Insufficient evidence to substantiate the presence of the disorder (explain in Part IV, Consultant's Notes).

I. 12.11 Neurodevelopmental Disorders

☐ Medical documentation of the requirements of paragraph 1, 2, or 3:

1. ☐ One or both of the following:

   a. ☐ Frequent distractibility, difficulty sustaining attention, and difficulty organizing tasks

   b. ☐ Hyperactive and impulsive behavior (for example, difficulty remaining seated, talking excessively, difficulty waiting, appearing restless, or behaving as if being "driving by a motor")

2. ☐ Significant difficulties learning and using academic skills

3. ☐ Recurrent motor movement or vocalization

☐ A medically determinable impairment is present that does not precisely satisfy the criteria above.

Disorder ______________________________

Pertinent symptoms, signs, and laboratory findings that substantiate the presence of this impairment:

☐ Insufficient evidence to substantiate the presence of the disorder (explain in Part IV, Consultant's Notes).

J. 12.13 Eating Disorders

☐ Medical documentation of a persistent alteration in eating or eating-related behavior that results in a change in consumption or absorption of food and that significantly impairs physical or psychological health

☐ A medically determinable impairment is present that does not precisely satisfy the criteria above.

Disorder ______________________________

Pertinent symptoms, signs, and laboratory findings that substantiate the presence of this impairment:

☐ Insufficient evidence to substantiate the presence of the disorder (explain in Part IV, Consultant's Notes).

K. 12.15 Trauma- and Stressor-Related Disorders

☐ Medical documentation of all of the following:

1. ☐ Exposure to actual or threatened death, serious injury, or violence
2. ☐ Subsequent involuntary re-experiencing of the traumatic event (for example, intrusive memories, dreams, or flashbacks)
3. ☐ Avoidance of external reminders of the event
4. ☐ Disturbance in mood and behavior
5. ☐ Increases in arousal and reactivity (for example, exaggerated startle response, sleep disturbance)

☐ A medically determinable impairment is present that does not precisely satisfy the criteria above.

Disorder ______________________________

Pertinent symptoms, signs, and laboratory findings that substantiate the presence of this impairment:

☐ Insufficient evidence to substantiate the presence of the disorder (explain in Part IV, Consultant's Notes).

III. RATING OF FUNCTIONAL LIMITATIONS

A. "B Criteria" of the Listings

Indicate to what degree the following areas of mental functioning (which are found in paragraph B of listings 12.02, 12.03, 12.04, 12.06, 12.07, 12.08, 12.10, 12.11, 12.13, or 12.15 and paragraph B2 of 12.05) are limited as a result of the individual's mental disorder(s).

Specify the listing(s) (i.e., 12.02, 12.03, 12.04, 12.05, 12.06, 12.07, 12.08, 12.10, 12.11, 12.13, or 12.15) under which the items below are being rated ______________________________

AREAS OF MENTAL FUNCTIONING	DEGREE OF LIMITATION					
	None	Mild	Moderate	Marked*	Extreme*	Insufficient Evidence
1. Understand, remember, or apply information	☐	☐	☐	☐	☐	☐
2. Interact with others	☐	☐	☐	☐	☐	☐
3. Concentrate, persist, or maintain pace	☐	☐	☐	☐	☐	☐
4. Adapt or manage oneself	☐	☐	☐	☐	☐	☐

*Two marked limitations satisfy, or one extreme limitation satisfies, the paragraph B criteria.

Form **SSA-2506-BK** (01-2017) UF Page 14 of 15

B. "C Criteria" of the Listings

1. Complete this section if applicable, for 12.02, 12.03, 12.04, 12.06, or 12.15.

☐ Medically documented history of the existence of the disorder over a period of at least 2 years, and there is evidence of both:

1. ☐ Medical treatment, mental health therapy, psychosocial support(s), or highly structured setting(s) that is ongoing and that diminishes symptoms and signs of the mental disorder

2. ☐ Marginal adjustment, that is, minimal capacity to adapt to changes in the environment or to demands that are not already part of daily life

☐ Evidence does not establish the presence of the "C Criteria"

☐ Insufficient evidence to establish the presence of the "C Criteria" (explain in Part IV, Consultant's Notes).

IV. CONSULTANT'S NOTES

§242 Mental Impairment "B Criteria" Outline

The five-point rating scale for the B criteria is defined in § 12.00F2 as follows:

> 2. The five-point rating scale. We evaluate the effects of your mental disorder on each of the four areas of mental functioning based on a five-point rating scale consisting of none, mild, moderate, marked, and extreme limitation. To satisfy the paragraph B criteria, your mental disorder must result in extreme limitation of one, or marked limitation of two, paragraph B areas of mental functioning. Under these listings, the five rating points are defined as follows:
>
> a. *No limitation (or none)*. You are able to function in this area independently, appropriately, effectively, and on a sustained basis.
>
> b. *Mild limitation.* Your functioning in this area independently, appropriately, effectively, and on a sustained basis is slightly limited.
>
> c. *Moderate limitation.* Your functioning in this area independently, appropriately, effectively, and on a sustained basis is fair.
>
> d. *Marked limitation.* Your functioning in this area independently, appropriately, effectively, and on a sustained basis is seriously limited.
>
> e. *Extreme limitation.* You are not able to function in this area independently, appropriately, effectively, and on a sustained basis.

Note that under these standards, which focus on functioning "independently, appropriately, effectively, and on a sustained basis," someone who is unable to regularly sustain a 40-hour work week has at least a marked limitation. Section 12.00F4a provides that SSA "will consider whether you can use the area of mental functioning on a regular and continuing basis (8 hours a day, 5 days a week, or an equivalent work schedule)."

The four B criteria are described in sections 12.00E1 through E4. Examples are given to illustrate the nature of each area of mental functioning, but SSA notes that it does not require documentation of all of the examples. The next four sections of this book are drawn from 12.00E1 through E4 with bullets added to each example.

§242.1 Understand, Remember or Apply Information

1. *Understand, remember, or apply information (paragraph B1)*. This area of mental functioning refers to the abilities to learn, recall, and use information to perform work activities. Examples include:

- Understanding and learning terms, instructions, procedures;
- following one- or two-step oral instructions to carry out a task;
- describing work activity to someone else;
- asking and answering questions and providing explanations;
- recognizing a mistake and correcting it;
- identifying and solving problems;
- sequencing multi-step activities; and
- using reason and judgment to make work-related decisions.

§242.2 Interact with Others

2. *Interact with others (paragraph B2)*. This area of mental functioning refers to the abilities to relate to and work with supervisors, co-workers, and the public. Examples include:

- cooperating with others;
- asking for help when needed;
- handling conflicts with others;
- stating own point of view;
- initiating or sustaining conversation;
- understanding and responding to social cues (physical, verbal, emotional);
- responding to requests, suggestions, criticism, correction, and challenges; and
- keeping social interactions free of excessive irritability, sensitivity, argumentativeness, or suspiciousness.

§242.3 Concentrate, Persist or Maintain Pace

3. *Concentrate, persist, or maintain pace (paragraph B3)*. This area of mental functioning refers to the abilities to focus attention on work activities and stay on task at a sustained rate. Examples include:

- Initiating and performing a task that you understand and know how to do;
- working at an appropriate and consistent pace;
- completing tasks in a timely manner;
- ignoring or avoiding distractions while working;

- changing activities or work settings without being disruptive;
- working close to or with others without interrupting or distracting them;
- sustaining an ordinary routine and regular attendance at work; and
- working a full day without needing more than the allotted number or length of rest periods during the day.

§242.4 Adapt or Manage Oneself

4. *Adapt or manage oneself (paragraph B4).* This area of mental functioning refers to the abilities to regulate emotions, control behavior, and maintain well-being in a work setting. Examples include:

- Responding to demands;
- adapting to changes;
- managing your psychologically based symptoms;
- distinguishing between acceptable and unacceptable work performance;
- setting realistic goals;
- making plans for yourself independently of others;
- maintaining personal hygiene and attire appropriate to a work setting; and
- being aware of normal hazards and taking appropriate precautions.

§243 Meeting the Mental Listings

Since the mental Listings contain more subjective evaluation than any other Listing, never overlook the possibility that your client's impairment may meet one of the mental Listings.

Although the Listings define a "marked" limitation as "functioning in this area independently, appropriately, effectively, and on a sustained basis is seriously limited," it is often a judgment call whether a claimant's ability to understand, remember or apply information, to interact with others, to concentrate, persist or maintain pace, or adapt or manage oneself is moderately or markedly limited. Whether individual elements of the B criteria are moderately or markedly limited are opinions on the "nature and severity" of the claimant's impairments. *See* 20 C.F.R. § 404.1527(a)(2) and compare § 404.1527(d)(2). When there is any chance of meeting the mental Listings, ask for an opinion on these issues from the treating psychiatrist or psychologist, but don't ask the treating doctor to complete a PRTF. SSA has been known to take the position that because completing a PRTF requires expertise and understanding of special terms, a PRTF completed by a treating doctor may be entitled to little weight. Instead, send the treating doctor one of the forms from this book, either the Mental Impairment Questionnaire (Listings), §243.1, or the Mental Impairment Questionnaire (RFC & Listings), §245.8. We have endeavored to explain the terms on the form itself.

Note also that the forms in this book ask about each element of the B criteria separately because a conclusion that one *element* of a B criteria is at the "marked" level, establishes that one of the four B criteria is at the marked level. Thus, a claimant who is markedly limited in the ability to persist, satisfies the B3 criteria even if the claimant's ability to concentrate or maintain pace is only moderately limited. But recall that if more than one of an individual B criterion is at the marked level, for example, if your client's limitations in the ability to concentrate and maintain pace are both at the marked level, your client still needs another one of the B criteria to be at the marked level to meet the Listings.

Although the forms in this book were designed for sending to doctors, the best sources of information and opinions about the B criteria, might not be the claimant's doctor. Psychiatrists who manage a claimant's psychotropic medications, these days, often don't spend enough time with a patient to know how the patient will respond in a work situation. When the psychiatrist works with a counselor who sees the patient frequently and knows the patient well, it may be that the counselor is in a better position to give an opinion about the B criteria. SSA acknowledges that opinions from such sources "are important and should be evaluated on key issues such as impairment severity and functional effects." SSR 06-3p. *See also* 12.00C2. Indeed, SSR 06-3p states that "it may be appropriate to give more weight to the opinion of a medical source who is not an 'acceptable medical source' if he or she has seen the individual more often than the treating source and has provided better supporting evidence and a better explanation for his or her opinion." Nevertheless, because SSA's rules accord more weight to the opinions of treating doctors, *see* §221, whenever possible, see if it can be worked out that the psychiatrist and counselor work together on the opinion or that the psychiatrist counter-signs the opinion from the counselor.

Since the B criteria focuses on work activity, another good source, when available, is evidence from school, vocational training, work and work-related programs, which is acknowledged as a source of evidence in § 12.00C4. Also, don't ignore the claimant's family, friends, and neighbors, who are acknowledged as a source of evidence in § 12.00C3. Sometimes they can provide information and observations that win cases.

Often the claimant himself or herself may be able to provide useful information; but sometimes in mental impairment cases, claimants have so little insight into their limitations that one must be prepared for widely diverging views between the claimant and those who know the claimant well. This problem in itself can turn out to be a major issue in a mental impairment case. Sometimes denial decisions in such cases are based on little more than uncritical acceptance of a claimant's grandiose statements about the ability to understand, remember or apply information, etc. It is important to look beyond what the claimant says about level of functioning in these areas.

§243.1 C Criteria

Don't neglect the C criteria. As a rule, the C criteria must be assessed when a claimant appears to function too well to meet the B criteria. This level of functioning may be a result of the claimant's medical treatment, psychosocial support and highly structured living environment, which SSA acknowledges as part of the C criteria itself. *See* C1. Here are the C criteria:

> C. Your mental disorder in this listing category is "serious and persistent;" that is, you have a medically documented history of the existence of the disorder over a period of at least 2 years, and there is evidence of both:
>
> 1. Medical treatment, mental health therapy, psychosocial support(s), or a highly structured setting(s) that is ongoing and that diminishes the symptoms and signs of your mental disorder (see 12.00G2b); and
> 2. Marginal adjustment, that is, you have minimal capacity to adapt to changes in your environment or to demands that are not already part of your daily life (*see* 12.00G2c).

Even more than the B Criteria, deciding whether a claimant's impairment meets the C Criteria, especially C2, may depend on expert opinion, particularly from the claimant's treating doctors. Marginal adjustment and "minimal capacity to adapt," are not the sorts of things that can be established by one mental status examination.

§243.2 Form: Mental Impairment Questionnaire (Listings)

MENTAL IMPAIRMENT QUESTIONNAIRE
(LISTINGS)

From: ______________________ Re: ______________________

DOB: ______________________

Please answer the following questions concerning your patient's impairments.

1. Frequency and length of contact: ______________________

____

2. DSM-5 Mental Disorders/Principal Diagnoses: Other Conditions / Focus of Clinical Attention:

______________________ ______________________

______________________ ______________________

______________________ ______________________

3. Treatment and response: ______________________

____

____

4. a. List prescribed medications:

b. Identify your patient's side effects of medications that may affect working, *e.g.*, sedation, drowsiness, fatigue, lethargy, malaise, irritability, nausea, dizziness, *etc.*

5. List the *clinical findings* including those from mental status examination that demonstrate the severity of your patient's mental impairment and symptoms:

____

____

____

6. Prognosis: ______________________

7. Identify your patient's signs and symptoms:

	Significant cognitive decline from a prior level of functioning in *one* or more of the cognitive areas: Complex attention; Executive function; Learning and memory; Language; Perceptual-motor; or Social cognition.		Hyperactive and impulsive behavior (e.g., difficulty remaining seated, talking excessively, difficulty waiting, appearing restless, or behaving as if being "driven by a motor")
	Delusions or hallucinations		Irritability
	Qualitative deficits in verbal communication, nonverbal communication, and social interaction		Preoccupation with having or acquiring a serious illness without significant symptoms present
	Increase in goal-directed activity or psychomotor agitation		Disregard for and violation of the rights of others
	Depressed mood		Detachment from social relationships
	Diminished interest in almost all activities		Distrust and suspiciousness of others
	Restlessness t		Instability of interpersonal relationships
	Sleep disturbance		Pressured speech
	Observable psychomotor agitation or retardation		Preoccupation with perfectionism and orderliness
	Decreased energy		Easily fatigued
	Feelings of guilt or worthlessness		Muscle tension
	Difficulty concentrating or thinking		Disorganized thinking (speech)
	Thoughts of death or suicide		Recurrent motor movement or vocalization
	Excessive emotionality and attention seeking		Repetitive behaviors aimed at reducing anxiety
	Flight of ideas		Inflated self-esteem
	Decreased need for sleep		Distractibility
	Involvement in activities that have a high probability of painful consequences that are not recognized		One or more somatic symptoms that are distressing, with excessive thoughts, feelings, or behaviors related to the symptoms
	Grossly disorganized behavior or catatonia		Appetite disturbance with change in weigh
	Panic attacks followed by a persistent concern or worry about additional panic attacks or their consequences		Symptoms of altered voluntary motor or sensory function that are not better explained by another medical or mental disorder
	Disproportionate fear or anxiety about at least two different situations (for example, using public transportation, being in a crowd, being in a line, being outside of your home, being in open spaces)		Persistent alteration in eating or eating-related behavior that results in a change in consumption or absorption of food and that significantly impairs physical or psychological health s
	Recurrent, impulsive, aggressive behavioral outbursts		Significantly restricted, repetitive patterns of behavior, interests, or activities
	Frequent distractibility, difficulty sustaining attention, and difficulty organizing tasks		Significant difficulties learning and using academic skills
	Involuntary, time-consuming preoccupation with intrusive, unwanted thought		
	Medical documentation of *all* of the following: 1. Exposure to actual or threatened death, serious injury, or violence; 2. Subsequent involuntary re-experiencing of the traumatic event (for example, intrusive memories, dreams, or flashbacks); 3. Avoidance of external reminders of the event; 4. Disturbance in mood and behavior; and 5. Increases in arousal and reactivity (for example, exaggerated startle response, sleep disturbance).		

8. Is your patient's intellectual functioning limited?

Yes No

If yes, please explain:

9. Rate the degree of your patient's expected limitations in a work setting using the following scale:

Moderate means the ability to function independently, appropriately, effectively, and on a sustained basis is **fair;**
Marked means the ability to function independently, appropriately, effectively, and on a sustained basis is **seriously limited;**
Extreme means **not able** to function independently, appropriately, effectively, and on a sustained basis, but it does not mean a total loss of ability to function.

RATE THE DEGREE OF LIMITATION IN THE FOLLOWING AREAS:					
A.1.	Understanding information:	None-Mild	Moderate	Marked	Extreme
A.2.	Remembering information	None-Mild	Moderate	Marked	Extreme
A.3.	Applying information	None-Mild	Moderate	Marked	Extreme
B.	Interacting with others:	None Mild	Moderate	Marked	Extreme
C.1.	Concentrating	None Mild	Moderate	Marked	Extreme
C.2.	Persisting	None Mild	Moderate	Marked	Extreme
C.3	Maintaining pace	None Mild	Moderate	Marked	Extreme
D.1.	Adapting in the workplace	None Mild	Moderate	Marked	Extreme
D.2.	Managing oneself in the workplace	None Mild	Moderate	Marked	Extreme

10. If your patient has a neurocognitive disorder; schizophrenia or other psychotic disorder; depressive, bipolar or related disorder; anxiety or obsessive compulsive disorder; or trauma or stress-related disorder, please indicate if any of the following apply to your patient:

A. ☐ Your patient's chronic mental disorder is "serious and persistent;" that is, your patient has a medically documented history of the existence of the disorder over a period of at least 2 years.

B. ☐ Your patient relies on ongoing medical treatment, mental health therapy, psychosocial support, or a highly-structured setting to diminish the symptoms and signs of his or her mental disorder.

C. ☐ Despite your patient's diminished symptoms and signs, your patient has only marginal adjustment, that is, your patient has minimal capacity to adapt to changes in his or her environment or to demands that are not already part of daily life.

11. Assuming your patient was trying to work full time, on the average, how often do you anticipate that your patient's impairments would cause your patient to be absent from work?

Never	About two days per month	About four days per month
About one day per month	About three days per month	More than four days per month

12. Has your patient's impairment lasted or can it be expected to last at least twelve months?
Yes No

13. Please describe any additional reasons not covered above why your patient would have difficulty working at a regular job on a sustained basis.

14. Can your patient manage benefits in his or her own best interest? Yes No

____________________ ______________________________
Date Signature

Printed/Typed Name: ____________________

Address: ____________________

____

243.2
7.64 1/17

§244 Intellectual Disorder

To meet section 12.05, a claimant must meet either paragraph A or paragraph B. Paragraph A provides:

> A. Satisfied by 1, 2, and 3 (*see* 12.00H):
>
> 1. Significantly subaverage general intellectual functioning evident in your cognitive inability to function at a level required to participate in standardized testing of intellectual functioning; and
>
> 2. Significant deficits in adaptive functioning currently manifested by your dependence upon others for personal needs (for example, toileting, eating, dressing, or bathing); and
>
> 3. The evidence about your current intellectual and adaptive functioning and about the history of your disorder demonstrates or supports the conclusion that the disorder began prior to your attainment of age 22.

The claimant described in 12.05A, who is dependent on others for personal needs and whose cognitive ability is so low that he or she is incapable of taking a standardized test to assess intellectual functioning, is profoundly disabled. Most claimants this disabled are found eligible for benefits at the initial level. Because you're unlikely to see many such cases at the hearing level, we are going to focus on 12.05B.

You may see claimants in your practice who meet paragraph B of section 12.05, which provides:

> B. Satisfied by 1, 2, and 3 (*see* 12.00H):
>
> 1. Significantly subaverage general intellectual functioning evidenced by a or b:
>
> a. A full scale (or comparable) IQ score of 70 or below on an individually administered standardized test of general intelligence; or
>
> b. A full scale (or comparable) IQ score of 71-75 accompanied by a verbal or performance IQ score (or comparable part score) of 70 or below on an individually administered standardized test of general intelligence; and
>
> 2. Significant deficits in adaptive functioning currently manifested by extreme limitation of one, or marked limitation of two, of the following areas of mental functioning:
>
> a. Understand, remember, or apply information (*see* 12.00E1); or
>
> b. Interact with others (*see* 12.00E2); or
>
> c. Concentrate, persist, or maintain pace (*see* 12.00E3); or
>
> d. Adapt or manage oneself (*see* 12.00E4); and
>
> 3. The evidence about your current intellectual and adaptive functioning and about the history of your disorder demonstrates or supports the conclusion that the disorder began prior to your attainment of age 22.

§244.1 Significantly Subaverage General Intellectual Functioning -- IQ Requirements

Section 12.05B provides IQ requirements for meeting the Listing, which focuses on full scale IQ. If the full scale IQ is 70 or below, the IQ requirements are met. *See* section 12.05B1a. But 12.05B1b provides another way to meet the IQ requirements. If the full scale IQ score is 71 to 75 and there is a verbal or performance IQ score of 70 or below, the claimant meets the IQ requirements of section 12.05B1b.

Although the Listings in effect before January 17, 2017 also had (somewhat different) IQ requirements, IQ test results were often rejected. They were found invalid or found to not reflect a claimant's actual level of functioning by state agency doctors, consultative examiners, medical experts or sometimes by ALJs acting alone. Such determinations tended to be conclusory. The determinations appeared to be based on little more than a desire to find that a claimant does not meet the Listings.

In the new mental Listings SSA agreed that adjudicators do not have the expertise to draw such conclusions about IQ scores but retained a significant amount of discretion for SSA medical and psychological experts. *See* 81 Fed. Reg. 66148 (2016). Section 12.00H2d addresses the responsibility for conclusions based on testing:

> d. *Responsibility for conclusions based on testing.* We generally presume that your obtained IQ score(s) is an accurate reflection of your general intellectual functioning, unless evidence in the record suggests otherwise. Examples of this evidence include: a statement from the test administrator indicating that your

obtained score is not an accurate reflection of your general intellectual functioning, prior or internally inconsistent IQ scores, or information about your daily functioning. Only qualified specialists, Federal and State agency medical and psychological consultants, and other contracted medical and psychological experts may conclude that your obtained IQ score(s) is not an accurate reflection of your general intellectual functioning. This conclusion must be well supported by appropriate clinical and laboratory diagnostic techniques and must be based on relevant evidence in the case record, such as:

(i) The data obtained in testing;

(ii) Your developmental history, including when your signs and symptoms began;

(iii) Information about how you function on a daily basis in a variety of settings; and

(iv) Clinical observations made during the testing period, such as your ability to sustain attention, concentration, and effort; to relate appropriately to the examiner; and to perform tasks independently without prompts or reminders.

Because only "qualified specialists" may conclude that a claimant's IQ score is not an accurate reflection of the claimant's general intellectual functioning, an ALJ, acting alone, cannot make such a finding. Note that the conclusion about the IQ score "must be well supported by appropriate clinical and laboratory diagnostic techniques and must be based on relevant evidence in the case record."

§244.2 Deficits in Adaptive Functioning

Note that section 12.05B2, in fact, incorporates all the elements of the "B criteria" used in evaluating the other Listings, though SSA never refers to it this way (probably because of fear of confusion). SSA always refers to the two parts of this section—12.05A and 12.05B—as "paragraphs."

If the claimant has a work record, in the past state agency doctors often referred to the mere fact of a work record as proof of a lack of deficits in adaptive functioning without any inquiry into the nature of the work. The new mental Listings calls for them to do better. Section 12.00H3e provides:

e. *How we consider work activity.* The fact that you have engaged in work activity, or that you work intermittently or steadily in a job commensurate with your abilities, will not always mean that you do not have deficits in adaptive functioning as required by 12.05B2. When you have engaged in work activity, we need complete information about the work, and about your functioning in the work activity and work setting, before we reach any conclusions about your adaptive functioning. We will consider all factors involved in your work history before concluding whether your impairment satisfies the criteria for intellectual disorder under 12.05B. We will consider your prior and current work history, if any, and various other factors influencing how you function. For example, we consider whether the work was in a supported setting, whether you required more supervision than other employees, how your job duties compared to others in the same job, how much time it took you to learn the job duties, and the reason the work ended, if applicable.

§244.3 Onset Before Age 22

Both paragraphs of § 12.05 require that the evidence "supports the conclusion that the disorder began prior to [the claimant's] attainment of age 22." Thus, although evidence, e.g., IQ test results, from before age 22 is probably dispositive (and you should always try to obtain it if it is available), such evidence is not required to meet § 12.05.

Establishing onset before age 22 is discussed in Listings section 12.00H4 as follows:

4. *Establishing that the disorder began before age 22.* We require evidence that demonstrates or supports (is consistent with) the conclusion that your mental disorder began prior to age 22. We do not require evidence that your impairment met all of the requirements of 12.05A or 12.05B prior to age 22. Also, we do not require you to have met our statutory definition of disability prior to age 22. When we do not have evidence that was recorded before you attained age 22, we need evidence about your current intellectual and adaptive functioning and the history of your disorder that supports the conclusion that the disorder began before you attained age 22. Examples of

evidence that can demonstrate or support this conclusion include:

a. Tests of intelligence or adaptive functioning;

b. School records indicating a history of special education services based on your intellectual functioning;

c. An Individualized Education Program (IEP), including your transition plan;

d. Reports of your academic performance and functioning at school;

e. Medical treatment records;

f. Interviews or reports from employers;

g. Statements from a supervisor in a group home or a sheltered workshop; and

h. Statements from people who have known you and can tell us about your functioning in the past and currently.

For claimants somewhat older than age 22, SSA seldom gathers any information about adaptive functioning before age 22. Instead, state agencies tend to gather evidence for the twelve months prior to the date of application as required by 20 C.F.R. § 404.1512(d) but ignoring the provision of that regulation that says "unless there is reason to believe that development of an earlier period is necessary." The real problem here is that you don't know what evidence you're going to find until you look.

Practice Tip

In a case where meeting § 12.05 of the Listings is an issue, get the claimant's school records and present other evidence showing deficits in adaptive functioning before age 22. Also obtain information about the claimant's work history that shows difficulties or accommodation on the job as a result of intellectual disorder. Assess the degree to which the claimant has needed extra supervision, guidance and assistance.

§244.4 Borderline Intellectual Functioning

SSA has said in the past that "[b]orderline intellectual functioning is a medically determinable impairment. Although it will not meet a listing and may not be disabling as a single impairment, it may be disabling in combination with other mental or physical impairments." *See* AM-14056. This is likely to remain SSA's position despite the fact that borderline intellectual functioning, which in the past has been defined by an IQ in the 71 to 85 range, is not a DSM-5 diagnosis. Borderline intellectual functioning appears in DSM-5 only in chapters at the back of the book that include codes used by the World Health Organization's *International Classification of Diseases* (ICD), which recognizes the diagnosis of borderline intellectual functioning.

DSM-5, in fact, takes a different approach to diagnosis of Intellectual Disability (Intellectual Developmental Disorder) than SSA's Listing 12.05 "intellectual disorder." DSM-5 does not use IQ scores for the diagnosis or for severity levels. The DSM-5 diagnosis of Intellectual Disability (Intellectual Developmental Disorder) provides for severity levels ranging from mild to profound. DSM-5, p. 33, states that "[t]he various levels of severity are defined on the basis of adaptive functioning, and not IQ scores, because it is adaptive functioning that determines the level of supports required. Moreover, IQ scores are less valid in the lower end of the IQ range." Thus, those individuals whose IQs fall within the borderline intellectual functioning range who do not meet the IQ requirements of section 12.05 of the Listings but who have low levels of adaptive functioning are included in the DSM-5 Intellectual Disability (Intellectual Developmental Disorder) diagnosis.

If someone with an IQ in the borderline range, 71-85, has low level of adaptive functioning, that person has a significant non-exertional impairment that limits his or her ability to work. Thus, this is a severe impairment. *See*, for example, *Lucy v. Chater*, 113 F.3d 905, 908 (8th Cir. 1997) and *Hunt v. Massanari*, 250 F.3d 622 (8th Cir. 2001). Some people who function at this level have difficulty adapting to a new job or adapting to routine changes in a regular work setting. Some may have difficulty learning all but the simplest jobs. Some with borderline IQs may need more supervision than those with higher IQs. Some may perform slowly and may find it impossible to meet production standards on most jobs. Some people functioning at this level, on the other hand, may have no greater limitations than that they are limited to performing "routine, repetitive work." *See Howard v. Massanari*, 255 F.3d 577, 583 (8th Cir. 2001).

The limitations imposed by borderline intellectual functioning vary from individual to individual. Often you will find that, not only does borderline intellectual functioning limit a claimant's ability to work, but also it limits the claimant's ability to cope with having another physical or mental impairment, thus compounding the claimant's disability.

Where claimants have a significant work history, it may be necessary to contact former employers for assessment of the claimant's job functioning. You need to explain why the claimant used to be able to work but cannot work now. You may discover that the claimant had serious difficulty working in the past. If you do not present evidence of difficulty functioning on prior jobs or some other explanation (e.g., the claimant actually functioned well on prior jobs but is now unable to cope with additional impairments), it is likely the ALJ will assume that the claimant has little or no current limitation from borderline intelligence because, after all, borderline intelligence is a lifelong condition.

In the past, an example in the Medical-Vocational Guidelines found disabled an illiterate 41-year old claimant with an IQ of 78 who was limited to sedentary work. This example was one of two examples withdrawn in 2001 because said SSA, "the examples have led to overly broad generalizations." 66 Fed. Reg. 45,166 (2001). Thus, SSA emphasized that individualized determinations of claimants' residual functional capacities are necessary.

§245 Assessing Mental Residual Functional Capacity

Even if a claimant's mental impairment does not meet the Listings, the claimant's mental residual functional capacity may, nevertheless, be so constricted that the claimant must be found disabled at step five of the sequential evaluation process. Also, note that because of adversities in age, education and work experience, a mentally impaired claimant may be found disabled even when limited to the large job base of unskilled jobs at all levels of exertion. For example, a claimant age 55 or older with a limited education and no relevant work experience generally would be found disabled if the claimant has a severe mental impairment. Likewise, a claimant age 60 or older with a limited education and an unskilled work background may be found disabled despite the capacity for a wide range of unskilled work as long as the claimant is incapable of performing past relevant work because of a severe mental impairment. *See* SSR 85-15.

As a rule, lawyers and SSA use forms to gather information concerning a claimant's mental RFC. State agency doctors assess mental RFC on form SSA-4734-F4-SUP, reproduced at §245.4 for informational purposes. Note that the official POMS instructions for completing this form, which are included at §245.5, recognizing the limitations of the check-off format, state that the check-off section of the form, section I, is merely a worksheet and "does not constitute the RFC assessment." The residual functional capacity assessment is actually the narrative that appears in section III. This form, SSA-4734-F4-SUP, is not useful in your practice for gathering opinions from doctors. Do not send it to the claimant's doctors for completion.

Sometimes ALJs ask for the completion of a flawed form known as Medical Source Statement of Ability to Do Work-Related Activities (Mental), Form HA-1152, reproduced at §245.3 for informational purposes. Avoid using this form if you can. It does not provide enough choices on the continuum between disabled and not disabled. There is no choice between "ability . . . not precluded" and "no useful ability to function."

We have prepared a revised version of the medical assessment form used by ALJs titled Medical Opinion Re: Ability to Do Work-Related Activities (Mental), which appears at §245.7. This form incorporates elements of the form used by state agencies and is organized following POMS DI 25020.010, reprinted at §245.6, that explains the effect of mental limitations on ranges of work. The core of this mental RFC form is also included in two other forms in this book—Mental Medical Source Statement, §245.9, and Mental Impairment Questionnaire (RFC & Listings), §245.8. Note that the list of mental abilities deemed "critical" by SSA for performing unskilled work, POMS DI 25020.010.B.3, appears on these forms as "mental abilities and aptitudes needed to do unskilled work." *Also see* §246. If a claimant is unable to meet competitive standards on any one of these mental abilities and aptitudes, as a rule, a vocational expert will agree that the claimant is incapable of working at a regular job. You may be able to get a vocational expert to agree that if a claimant's abilities are "seriously limited, but not precluded" in all or most of these areas, the claimant is likewise incapable of working a regular job because of substantial loss of ability to perform in so many areas.

Practice Tip — Percentile Ranking

Whenever any mental aptitude testing is done, ask that the results be translated into percentile ranking. Percentile ranking of certain job aptitudes has been done by the Department of Labor and is available in computer programs and companion volumes to the DOT. For example, from the chart in §346.6, prepared from a computer program, we learn that there are *no* sedentary unskilled jobs for a person with a General Learning Ability in the lowest 10% of the population (corresponding to an IQ of 81 or less); there are only five unskilled sedentary occupations suitable for one whose verbal ability is in the lowest 10%; there are only two unskilled sedentary occupations for one whose form perception is in the lowest 10%; and there are only 12 unskilled sedentary occupations available to one whose spatial perception is in the lowest 10% of the population. Indeed, if you search a DOT program such as OccuBrowse, you will learn that there are no jobs at any exertional level for a person whose General Learning Ability is in the lowest 10% of the population.

Percentile ranking information is useful in cross-examining vocational experts and in demonstrating a conflict between the vocational expert's answer and the DICTIONARY OF OCCUPATIONAL TITLES under SSR 00-4p. It is no substitute for obtaining a complete description of your client's mental residual functional capacity.

Practice Tip — Global Assessment of Functioning (GAF)

Although the multiaxial evaluation system of DSM-IV was abandoned by DSM-5, it is still used by some psychiatrists and psychologists and it appears in older medical records. When reviewing medical reports by psychiatrists and psychologists, watch for the doctors' "global assessment of functioning," which is stated on "Axis V" of the multiaxial evaluation system of DSM-IV, the key to which is provided at §245.2. This is a measure of severity of the impairment that is supposed to assess psychological, social and occupational functioning. By paying attention to the doctor's conclusions on Axis V, you will gather clues to how the doctor views the claimant's functional abilities and limitations.

Even though the official SSA position on Axis V, that the GAF "does not have a direct correlation to the severity requirements in [SSA's] mental disorders listings," SSA 65 Fed. Reg. 50,764-50,765 (2000), is probably unassailable, SSA considers a GAF rating to be opinion evidence. Most ALJs pay close attention to GAF scores. You need to do so also.

SSA's most thorough explanation of how GAF should be used in disability adjudication appears in an administrative message dated July 22, 2013 titled "Global Assessment of Functioning (GAF) Evidence in Disability Adjudication," which we reproduce at §245.1. Although this document has a "retention date" that makes it obsolete in early 2014, it is nevertheless likely to remain valuable for understanding the uses and limitations of GAF scores.

While a very low GAF score does not necessarily prove your client cannot work, a high GAF score does not necessarily prove your client can work. It is often necessary to ask the doctor about the meaning of GAF scores. You may discover that GAF scores from one doctor are most useful for tracking your client's ups and downs over a period of time. The doctor may give your client a relatively high GAF score once your client is stabilized on medication and is coping relatively well with daily life even though the doctor may think your client could not withstand the stress of regular work. In other words, when considering GAF scores for patients who are not actually working, many doctors do not include possible occupational functioning in the GAF assessment.

§245.1 AM-13066: Global Assessment of Functioning (GAF) Evidence in Disability Adjudication

Instruction

Identification Number	**AM-13066-REV**	**Effective Date: 10/14/2014**
Intended Audience:	All RCs/ARCs/ADs/FOs/TSCs/PSCs/OCO/OCO-CSTs/ODAR/DDSs/OMVE/OQP/CO	
Originating Office:	ORDP ODP	
Title:	**Global Assessment of Functioning (GAF) Evidence in Disability Adjudication**	
Type:	AM - Admin Messages	
Program:	**Disability**	
Link To Reference:	See **References** at the end of this AM.	

Retention Date: April 14, 2015

REVISION: We revised this AM to include guidance for considering any instrument that allows for estimation of the Global Assessment of Functioning (GAF) ratings.

A. Purpose

This AM provides guidance to all State and Federal adjudicators (including administrative law judges) on how to consider Global Assessment of Functioning (GAF) ratings, and instruments that allow for estimated GAF ratings (for example, the Daily Living Activities Functional Assessment (DLA-20)), when assessing disability claims involving mental disorders. We consider a GAF rating as opinion evidence. As with other opinion evidence, the extent to which an adjudicator can rely on the GAF rating as a measure of impairment severity and mental functioning depends on whether the GAF rating is consistent with other evidence, how familiar the rater is with the claimant, and the rater's expertise.

B. Background

The Diagnostic and Statistical Manual of Mental Disorders (DSM), published periodically by the American Psychiatric Association (APA), provides the common language and standard criteria for classification of mental disorders. The DSM, Fourth Edition, Text Revision (DSM-IV-TR) provided a multi-axial assessment of mental disorders:
Axis I – clinical disorders
Axis II – personality disorders and mental retardation
Axis III – general medical conditions
Axis IV – psychosocial and environmental problems
Axis V – GAF

NOTE: The APA published a fifth edition (DSM-5) on June 1, 2013, that does not include GAF rating for assessment of mental disorders. However, we continue to receive and consider GAF in medical evidence.

C. What is the GAF?

The GAF is a rating reporting the clinician's, or case manager's, judgment of a person's ability to function in daily life. It reflects the clinician's subjective judgment about the person's symptom severity and psychological, social, and occupational functioning. The rating does not reflect impairment in function caused by physical or environmental limitations.

Each 10-point range within the GAF has two components:

1. Symptom severity, and
2. Functioning.

If a person's symptom severity and level of functioning differ, the GAF rating reflects the lower rating. In other words, a person with a number of psychological symptoms and very few functional limitations would get a GAF rating consistent with his or her reported psychological symptoms.

D. Problems with using the GAF to evaluate disability

The problem with using the GAF to evaluate disability is that there is no way to standardize measurement and evaluation.

Some clinicians give inflated or unrealistically low GAF ratings because the GAF rating instructions in the DSM-IV-TR are unclear. In general, inter-rater reliability ratings are low in the clinical setting because there is great variability of training and experience levels amongst clinicians. These rating problems, alone or in combination, can lead to improper assessment of impairment severity.

1. GAF ratings are not standardized

GAF ratings lack standardization, meaning adjudicators cannot draw reliable inferences from differences in GAF ratings assigned by different clinicians or from a single GAF rating. A GAF rating compares the patient with the distinctive population of patients the clinician has known. This limits direct comparability of GAF ratings assigned by different evaluators or even by the same evaluator at substantially different points in time.

Although the GAF rating is numerical, the actual number assigned can be misleading because the score does not quantify differences in function between people. For example, a GAF score of 75 does not mean a person is functioning 10 units better than a person with a score of 65, nor does a GAF of 40 indicate a person is functioning half as well as a person with a score of 80.

2. GAF ratings are not designed to predict outcome

Clinicians use the GAF to help plan and measure the impact of treatment. It is of limited value for assessing prognosis or treatment outcome and other measures are better indicators of outcome.

3. GAF ratings need supporting detail

The GAF scale anchors are very general and there can be a significant variation in how clinicians rate a GAF. For example, if a claimant has a GAF of 20, it could mean that he or she is not maintaining minimal personal hygiene (a clinical observation), or that the claimant has some potential to hurt himself or others (a clinical judgment). Evaluators rarely note whether the score reflects function, symptoms, or both.

E. Weighing GAF ratings as opinion evidence

For purposes of the Social Security disability programs, when it comes from an acceptable medical source, a GAF rating is a medical opinion as defined in 20 CFR §§ 404.1527(a)(2) and 416.927(a)(2). An adjudicator considers a GAF score with all of the relevant evidence in the case file and weighs a GAF rating as required by 20 CFR §§ 404.1527(c), 416.927(c), and SSR 06-03p, while keeping the following in mind:

GAF ratings are opinion evidence and need supporting evidence to give them weight. By itself, the GAF rating cannot be used to "raise" or "lower" someone's level of function. A GAF rating is only a snapshot opinion about the level of functioning. It is one opinion that we consider with all the evidence about a person's functioning. Unless the clinician clearly explains the reasons behind his or her GAF rating, and the period to which the rating applies, it does not provide a reliable longitudinal picture of the claimant's mental functioning for a disability analysis.

Unless the GAF rating is well supported and consistent with other evidence in the file, it is entitled to little weight under our rules. A GAF rating is usually an estimate of the best level of functioning over the last week or so, or over the entirety of the past year. It rarely overrides a more specific longitudinal picture. Because of its drawbacks, you should not rely on GAF evidence as the primary support for findings of impairment severity or of mental limitations.

A GAF score is never dispositive of impairment severity. **DO NOT:**

1. Rely solely upon a GAF rating to support a disability determination or decision.
   When case evidence includes a GAF rating from a treating source, adjudicators must consider the GAF rating and the treating source's support for assigning that specific rating, along with all of the relevant evidence in the case file, and provide good reasons in the personalized disability explanation or decision notice why you assigned it the weight you assigned. In cases where there are multiple GAF ratings from a provider, the articulation requirement can be addressed through a "representative" GAF rating if the GAF scores are similar or, when the GAF ratings are significantly divergent, by addressing whether the range of GAF ratings is supported by the evidence of record.
2. Equate any particular GAF rating with a listing-level limitation.
   You cannot use a GAF rating to determine whether a claimant's impairment meets the diagnostic criteria of mental retardation in listing 12.05, because the rating lacks specificity, may not reflect a claimant's functioning over time, and is not a standardized measure of anything, including intelligence and adaptive behavior.
3. Equate a particular GAF rating with a particular mental residual functional capacity assessment.
   The GAF does not measure the ability to meet the mental demands of unskilled work. There have been no published studies of how, or if, GAF ratings relate to meeting the demands of unskilled work. Additionally, there is no correlation between GAF ratings and the B criteria in the mental disorders listings.

Questions

Direct all program-related and technical questions to your RO support staff or PSC OA staff. RO support staff or PSC OA staff may refer questions or problems to their Central Office contacts.

References:

20 CFR 404.1502 General definitions and terms for subpart P
20 CFR 416.902 General definitions and terms for subpart I
20 CFR 404.1520a Evaluation of mental impairments
20 CFR 416. 920a Evaluation of mental impairments
20 CFR 404.1527 Evaluating opinion evidence
20 CFR 416.927 Evaluating opinion evidence
SSR 96-2p Titles II and XVI: Giving controlling Weight to Treating Source Medical Opinions

SSR 06-03p Titles II and XVI: Considering Opinions and Other Evidence from Sources Who Are Not "Acceptable Medical Sources" in Disability Claims; Considering Decisions on Disability by Other Governmental and Nongovernmental Agencies
DI 22505.001 Medical Evidence of Record (MER) Policies
DI 22505.003 Medical and Other Evidence of an Individual's Impairment(s)
DI 22505.007 Developing Initial Evidence from Medical Sources
DI 24510.065 Section III of SSA-4734-F4-SUP Functional Capacity Assessment
DI 24515.002 Evaluating Opinion Evidence - Basic Policy
DI 24515.003 Weighing Medical Opinions from Treating Sources and Other Medical Sources
DI 24515.004 Giving Controlling Weight to Treating Source Medical Opinions (SSR 96-2p)
DI 24515.005 Evaluating Noncontrolling Treating Source Medical Opinions
DI 24515.006 Evaluating Nontreating Source Medical Opinions
DI 24515.008 Titles II and XVI: Considering Opinions and Other Evidence from Sources Who Are Not "Acceptable Medical Sources" in Disability Claims; Considering Decisions on Disability by Other Governmental and Nongovernmental Agencies (SSR 06-03p)
DI 26530.015 Personalized Disability Explanation in Initial Closed Period, Unfavorable Onset Date, and DWB Allowances Where the Month Of Entitlement is Restricted to January 1991 Under P.L. 101-508
DI 26530.020 Personalized Disability Explanation in Initial Denials
DI 33015.020 Writing the Disability Hearing Officer's (DHO's) Decision
HALLEX 1-2-5-1 Evidence - General
HALLEX 1-2-5-14 Obtaining Medical Evidence from a Treating Source or Other Medical Source
Acta Psychiatr Scand. 2007 Apr; 115(4):326-30. Are GAF scores reliable in routine clinical use? Vatnaland T, Vatnaland J, Friis S, Opjordsmoen S.
Psychiatr Serv. 2002 Jun 53(6) 730-7. Global Assessment of Functioning Ratings and the Allocation and Outcomes of Mental Health Services. Moos RH, Nichol AC, Moos BS.
Journal of Evaluation in Clinical Practice Volume 18, Issue 2, pages 502â€"507, April 2012 Reliability and validity of the Global Assessment of Functioning Scale in clinical outpatients with depressive disorders, Esther M. V. Grootenboer MD, Erik J. Giltay MD PhD, Rosalind van der Lem MD, Tineke van Veen MD PhD, Nic J. A. van der Wee MD PhD, Frans G. Zitman MD PhD.
Ann Gen Psychiatry. 2010 May 7;9:20. doi: 10.1186/1744-859X-9-20. Global Assessment of Functioning (GAF): properties and frontier of current knowledge. Aas IH.
Journal of Mental Health Counseling, Jul 1, 2002. Does the Global Assessment of Functioning assess functioning? (Research), Plake, Edmund V.
The Diagnostic and Statistical Manual of Mental Disorders, Fourth Edition, Text Revision (DSM-IV-TR), American Psychiatric Association (2000).

§245.2 Chart: DSM-IV Axis V

Global Assessment of Functioning (GAF) Scale

Consider psychological, social, and occupational functioning on a hypothetical continuum of mental health–illness. Do not include impairment in functioning due to physical (or environmental) limitations.

Code (**Note:** Use intermediate codes when appropriate, e.g., 45, 68, 72.)

100–91 **Superior functioning in a wide range of activities, life's problems never seem to get out of hand, is sought out by others because of his or her many positive qualities. No symptoms.**

90–81 **Absent or minimal symptoms** (e.g., mild anxiety before an exam), **good functioning in all areas, interested and involved in a wide range of activities, socially effective, generally satisfied with life, no more than everyday problems or concerns** (e.g., an occasional argument with family members).

80–71 **If symptoms are present, they are transient and expectable reactions to psychosocial stressors** (e.g., difficulty concentrating after family argument); **no more than slight impairment in social, occupational, or school functioning** (e.g., temporarily falling behind in schoolwork).

70–61 **Some mild symptoms** (e.g., depressed mood and mild insomnia) **OR some difficulty in social, occupational, or school functioning** (e.g., occasional truancy, or theft within the household), **but generally functioning pretty well, has some meaningful interpersonal relationships.**

60–51 **Moderate symptoms** (e.g., flat affect and circumstantial speech, occasional panic attacks) **OR moderate difficulty in social, occupational, or school functioning** (e.g., few friends, conflicts with peers or co-workers).

50–41 **Serious symptoms** (e.g., suicidal ideation, severe obsessional rituals, frequent shoplifting) **OR any serious impairment in social, occupational, or school functioning** (e.g., no friends, unable to keep a job).

40–31 **Some impairment in reality testing or communication** (e.g., speech is at times illogical, obscure, or irrelevant) **OR major impairment in several areas, such as work or school, family relations, judgment, thinking, or mood** (e.g., depressed man avoids friends, neglects family, and is unable to work; child frequently beats up younger children, is defiant at home, and is failing at school).

30–21 **Behavior is considerably influenced by delusions or hallucinations OR serious impairment in communication or judgment** (e.g., sometimes incoherent, acts grossly inappropriately, suicidal preoccupation) **OR inability to function in almost all areas** (e.g., stays in bed all day; no job, home, or friends).

20–11 **Some danger of hurting self or others** (e.g., suicide attempts without clear expectation of death; frequently violent; manic excitement) **OR occasionally fails to maintain minimal personal hygiene** (e.g., smears feces) **OR gross impairment in communication** (e.g., largely incoherent or mute).

10–1 **Persistent danger of severely hurting self or others** (e.g., recurrent violence) **OR persistent inability to maintain minimal personal hygiene OR serious suicidal act with clear expectation of death.**

0 Inadequate information.

§245.3 Form: Medical Source Statement of Ability to Do Work-Related Activities (Mental) (HA-1152)
Editor's Note: This form is provided to show what SSA uses. It is not recommended for use by claimants' representatives. See 245.

SOCIAL SECURITY ADMINISTRATION
OFFICE OF DISABILITY ADJUDICATION AND REVIEW

Form Approved
OMB No. 0960-0662

MEDICAL SOURCE STATEMENT OF ABILITY TO DO WORK-RELATED ACTIVITIES (MENTAL)

NAME OF INDIVIDUAL	SOCIAL SECURITY NUMBER

INSTRUCTIONS:

Please assist us in determining this individual's ability to do work-related activities on a sustained basis. "Sustained basis" means the ability to perform work-related activities eight hours a day for five days a week, or an equivalent work schedule. (SSR 96-8p). Please give us your professional opinion of what the individual can still do despite his/her impairment(s). The opinion should be based on your findings with respect to medical history, clinical and laboratory findings, diagnosis, prescribed treatment and response, and prognosis.

For each activity shown below, respond to the questions about the individual's ability to perform the activity. When doing so, use the following definitions for the rating terms:

- None - Absent or minimal limitations. If limitations are present they are transient and/or expected reactions to psychological stresses.
- Mild - There is a slight limitation in this area, but the individual can generally function well.
- Moderate - There is more than a slight limitation in this area but the individual is still able to function satisfactorily.
- Marked - There is serious limitation in this area. There is a substantial loss in the ability to effectively function.
- Extreme - There is major limitation in this area. There is no useful ability to function in this area.

IT IS VERY IMPORTANT TO DESCRIBE THE FACTORS THAT SUPPORT YOUR ASSESSMENT. WE ARE REQUIRED TO CONSIDER THE EXTENT TO WHICH YOUR ASSESSMENT IS SUPPORTED.

(1) Is ability to understand, remember, and carry out instructions affected by the impairment? If "no," go to question #2. If "yes," please check the appropriate block to describe the individual's restriction for the following work-related mental activities. ☐ No ☐ Yes

	None	Mild	Moderate	Marked	Extreme
Understand and remember simple instructions.	☐	☐	☐	☐	☐
Carry out simple instructions.	☐	☐	☐	☐	☐
The ability to make judgments on simple work-related decisions.	☐	☐	☐	☐	☐
Understand and remember complex instructions.	☐	☐	☐	☐	☐
Carry out complex instructions.	☐	☐	☐	☐	☐
The ability to make judgments on complex work-related decisions.	☐	☐	☐	☐	☐

Identify the factors (e.g., the particular medical signs, laboratory findings, or other factors described above) that support your assessment.

(2) Is ability to interact appropriately with supervisors, co-workers, and and the public, as well as respond to changes in a routine work setting, affected by the impairment? If "no," go to question #3. If "yes," please check the appropriate block to describe the individual's restriction for the following work-related mental activities. ☐ No ☐ Yes

	None	Mild	Moderate	Marked	Extreme
Interact appropriately with the public.	☐	☐	☐	☐	☐
Interact appropriately with supervisor(s).	☐	☐	☐	☐	☐
Interact appropriately with co-workers.	☐	☐	☐	☐	☐
Respond appropriately to usual work situations and to changes in a routine work setting.	☐	☐	☐	☐	☐

Identify the factors (e.g., the particular medical signs, laboratory findings, or other factors described above) that support your assessment.

(3) Are any other capabilities affected by the impairment? ☐ No ☐ Yes
If "yes," please identify the capability and describe how it is affected.

Identify the factors (e.g., the particular medical signs, laboratory findings, or other factors described above) that support your assessment.

(4) The limitations above are assumed to be your opinion regarding current limitations only.

However, if you have sufficient information to form an opinion within a reasonable degree of medical or psychological probability as to past limitations, on what date were the limitations you found above first present? ____________

(5) If the claimant's impairment(s) include alcohol and/or substance abuse, do these impairments contribute to any of the claimant's limitations as set forth above? If so, please identify and explain what changes you would make to your answers if the claimant was totally abstinent from alcohol and/or substance use/abuse.

(6) Can the individual manage benefits in his/her own best interest? ☐ No ☐ Yes

Signature Date

Print Name, Title, and Medical Specialty (Legibly Please)

PRIVACY ACT STATEMENT

Collection and Use of Personal Information

Sections 205(a), 223(d), 1614(a)(3)(H)(I) and 1631(d)(1) of the Social Security Act, as amended, authorize us to collect this information. The information you provide will be used to complete processing of the named patient's claim. The information you furnish on this form is voluntary. However, failure to provide the requested information may prevent an accurate or timely decision on the named patient's claim.

We rarely use the information you supply for any purpose other than for determining eligibility for benefits. However, we may use it for the administration and integrity of Social Security programs. We may also disclose information to another person or to another agency in accordance with approved routine uses, which include but are not limited to the following:

1. To enable a third party or an agency to assist Social Security in establishing rights to Social Security benefits and/or coverage;
2. To comply with Federal laws requiring the release of information from Social Security records (e.g., to the Government Accountability Office and Department of Veterans' Affairs);
3. To make determinations for eligibility in similar health and income maintenance programs at the Federal, state and local level; and
4. To facilitate statistical research, audit or investigative activities necessary to assure the integrity of Social Security programs.

We may also use the information you provide in computer matching programs. Matching programs compare our records with records kept by other Federal, state or local government agencies. Information from these matching programs can be used to establish or verify a person's eligibility for Federally funded or administered benefit programs and for repayment of payments or delinquent debts under these programs.

Additional information regarding this form, routine uses of information, and our programs and systems, is available on-line at www.ssa.gov or at your local Social Security office.

PAPERWORK REDUCTION ACT STATEMENT - This information collection meets the requirements of 44 U.S.C. § 3507, as amended by section 2 of the Paperwork Reduction Act of 1995. You do not need to answer these questions unless we display a valid Office of Management and Budget control number. We estimate that it will take about 15 minutes to read the instructions, gather the facts, and answer the questions. **SEND OR BRING THE COMPLETED FORM TO YOUR LOCAL SOCIAL SECURITY OFFICE. The office is listed under U.S. Government agencies in your telephone directory or you may call Social Security at 1-800-772-1213 (TTY 1-800-325-0778).** *You may send comments on our time estimate above to: SSA, 6401 Security Blvd, Baltimore, MD 21235-6401.* ***Send only comments relating to our time estimate to this address, not the completed form.***

§245.4 Form: Mental Residual Functional Capacity Assessment (SSA-4734-F4-Sup)

FORM APPROVED
OMB No. 0960-0431

MENTAL RESIDUAL FUNCTIONAL CAPACITY ASSESSMENT

NAME	SOCIAL SECURITY NUMBER
	– –

CATEGORIES *(From 1C of the PRTF)*

ASSESSMENT IS FOR:
☐ Current Evaluation ☐ 12 Months After Onset: ________ *(Date)*
☐ Date Last Insured: ________ *(Date)*
☐ Other: ________ *(Date)* to ________ *(Date)*

I. SUMMARY CONCLUSIONS

This section is for recording summary conclusions derived from the evidence in file. Each mental activity is to be evaluated within the context of the individual's capacity to sustain that activity over a normal workday and workweek, on an ongoing basis. Detailed explanation of the degree of limitation for each category (A through D), as well as any other assessment information you deem appropriate, is to be recorded in Section III (Functional Capacity Assessment).

If rating category 5 is checked for any of the following items, you MUST specify in Section II the evidence that is needed to make the assessment. If you conclude that the record is so inadequately documented that no accurate functional capacity assessment can be made, indicate in Section II what development is necessary, but DO NOT COMPLETE SECTION III.

	Not Significantly Limited	Moderately Limited	Markedly Limited	No Evidence of Limitation in this Category	Not Ratable on Available Evidence
A. UNDERSTANDING AND MEMORY					
1. The ability to remember locations and work-like procedures.	1. ☐	2. ☐	3. ☐	4. ☐	5. ☐
2. The ability to understand and remember very short and simple instructions.	1. ☐	2. ☐	3. ☐	4. ☐	5. ☐
3. The ability to understand and remember detailed instructions.	1. ☐	2. ☐	3. ☐	4. ☐	5. ☐
B. SUSTAINED COCENTRATION AND PERSISTENCE					
4. The ability to carry out very short and simple instructions.	1. ☐	2. ☐	3. ☐	4. ☐	5. ☐
5. The ability to carry out detailed instructtions.	1. ☐	2. ☐	3. ☐	4. ☐	5. ☐
6. The ability to maintain attention and concentration for extended periods.	1. ☐	2. ☐	3. ☐	4. ☐	5. ☐
7. The ability to perform activities within a schedule, maintain regular attendance, and be punctual within customary tolerances.	1. ☐	2. ☐	3. ☐	4. ☐	5. ☐
8. The ability to sustain an ordinary routine without special supervision.	1. ☐	2. ☐	3. ☐	4. ☐	5. ☐
9. The ability to work in coordination with or proximity to others without being distracted by them.	1. ☐	2. ☐	3. ☐	4. ☐	5. ☐
10. The ability to make simple work-related decisions.	1. ☐	2. ☐	3. ☐	4. ☐	5. ☐

	Not Significantly Limited	Moderately Limited	Markedly Limited	No Evidence of Limitation in this Category	Not Ratable on Available Evidence
Continued - **SUSTAINED CONCENTRATION AND PERSISTENCE**					
11. The ability to complete a normal workday and workweek without interruptions from psychologically based symptoms and to perform at a consistent pace without an unreasonable number and length of rest periods.	1. ☐	2. ☐	3. ☐	4. ☐	5. ☐
C. SOCIAL INTERACTION					
12. The ability to interact appropriately with the general public.	1. ☐	2. ☐	3. ☐	4. ☐	5. ☐
13. The ability to ask simple questions or request assistance.	1. ☐	2. ☐	3. ☐	4. ☐	5. ☐
14. The ability to accept instructions and respond appropriately to criticism from supervisors.	1. ☐	2. ☐	3. ☐	4. ☐	5. ☐
15. The ability to get along with coworkers or peers without distracting them or exhibiting behavioral extremes.	1. ☐	2. ☐	3. ☐	4. ☐	5. ☐
16. The ability to maintain socially appropriate behavior and to adhere to basic 17. standards of neatness and cleanliness.	1. ☐	2. ☐	3. ☐	4. ☐	5. ☐
D. ADAPTATION					
17. The ability to respond appropriately to changes in the work setting.	1. ☐	2. ☐	3. ☐	4. ☐	5. ☐
18. The ability to be aware of normal hazards and take appropriate precautions.	1. ☐	2. ☐	3. ☐	4. ☐	5. ☐
19. The ability to travel in unfamiliar places or use public transportation.	1. ☐	2. ☐	3. ☐	4. ☐	5. ☐
20. The ability to set realistic goals or make plans independently of others.	1. ☐	2. ☐	3. ☐	4. ☐	5. ☐

II. REMARKS: If you checked box 5 for any of the preceding items or if any other documentation deficiencies were identified, you MUST specify what additional documentation is needed. Cite the item number(s), as well as any other specific deficiency, and indicate the development to be undertaken.

Continued on Page 3

☐ Continued on Page 4

III. FUNCTIONAL CAPACITY ASSESSMENT

Record the elaborations on the preceding capacities in this section. Complete this section ONLY after the SUMMARY CONCLUSIONS section has been completed. Explain your summary conclusions in narrative form. Include any information which clarifies limitation or function. Be especially careful to explain conclusions that differ from those of treating medical sources or from the individual's allegations.

Continued on Page 4

☐ THESE FINDINGS COMPLETE THE MEDICAL PORTION OF THE DISABILITY DETERMINATION.

MEDICAL CONSULTANT'S SIGNATURE	DATE:

Continuation Sheet Indicate section(s) being continued.

Privacy Act Notice: The information requested on this form is authorized by Section 223 and Section 1633 of the Social Security Act. The information provided will be used in making a decision on this claim. Failure to complete this form may result in a delay in processing the claim. Information furnished on this form may be disclosed by the Social Security Administration to another person or governmental agency only with respect to Social Security programs and to comply with federal laws requiring the exchange of information between Social Security and other agencies.

Paperwork Reduction Act: This information collection meets the requirements of 44 U.S.C. § 3507, as amended by Section 2 of the Paperwork Reduction Act of 1995. You do not need to answer these questions unless we display a valid Office of Management and Budget control number. We estimate that it will take about 20 minutes to read the instructions, gather the facts, and answer the questions. *You may send comments on our time estimate above to: SSA, 6401 Security Blvd , Baltimore, MD 21235-640 / . Send only comments relating to our time estimate to this address, not the completed form.*

§245.5 Form: POMS DI 24510.060 — DI 24510.065 Mental RFC Assessment

MENTAL RFC Social Security Act—Section 1613(a)(3);

Citation Regulations—20 CFR 404.1520a/416.920a; 404.1545/416.945; Appendix 1, Section 12.00A.

DI 24510.060 Mental Residual Functional Capacity Assessment

A. Operating Policy

1. SPECIAL FORM
Because of the complexity of mental disorder evaluation, **a special Form** SSA-4734-F4-SUP is to be used to document the mental residual functional capacity (RFC) decision, i.e., what an individual can do despite his / her impairment.

2. MEDICAL CONSULTANT COMPLETION

a. **Unfavorable and Partially Favorable Decisions**
In decisions that are not fully favorable, only a psychiatrist or psychologist is to perform the analysis and decide the mental functional capacity.

b. **Fully Favorable Decisions**
In fully favorable determinations, the medical consultant (MC) who completes the mental RFC assessment, to the extent possible, should be a psychiatrist or psychologist.

c. **When Physical Impairment Involved**
Refer the claim to a physician of the appropriate medical specialty after all mental RFC considerations have been accomplished.

B. Description of Form SSA-4734-F4-SUP

Form SSA-4734-F4-SUP is divided into four sections:

- Heading,
- Section I, Summary Conclusions,
- Section II, Remarks,
- Section III, Functional Capacity Assessment and MC signature.

1. HEADING
The **Heading** provides space to record claimant and claim identification data.

2. SECTION I
Section I—Summary Conclusions is designed to record the MC's analysis of the evidence and his/her conclusions about:

- the presence and degree of specific functional limitations, and
- the adequacy of documentation.

a. **Section I is merely a worksheet** to aid in deciding the presence and degree of functional limitations and the adequacy of documentation and does not constitute the RFC assessment.

b. **Twenty mental function items** are grouped under **four main categories:**

- Understanding and Memory,
- Sustained Concentration and Persistence,
- Social Interaction, and
- Adaptation

c. **To the right of each of the items** is a series of **decision checkblocks** under the headings:

- Not Significantly Limited
- Moderately Limited
- Markedly Limited
- No Evidence of Limitation in This Category, and
- Not Ratable on Available Evidence

3. SECTION II

Section II—Remarks, provides for discussion of evidence needed to rate particular items in section I.

4. SECTION III

a. **Section III—Functional Capacity Assessment**, is for recording the mental RFC determination. It is in this section that the **actual mental RFC assessment is recorded**, explaining the conclusions indicated in section I, in terms of the extent to which these mental capacities or functions could or could not be performed in work settings.
b. The **discussion** of all mental capacities and limitations in this section **must be in narrative format.** The MC must also include any other information that he/she believes is necessary to present a complete picture of mental RFC.
c. The **Narrative must not** present estimates of capacities for mental functions that **could not be rated** because of insufficient evidence. Such would represent speculation.
d. The completed SSA-4734-F4-SUP must be signed by the MC who conducted the analysis and prepared the mental RFC assessment.

[DDS POMs]

DI 24510.061 Summary Conclusions and Narrative Statement of Mental RFC

A. Introduction

To assure a comprehensive assessment of mental RFC, the SSA-4734-F4-SUP requires the MC **first** to record preliminary conclusions about the effect of the impairment(s) on **each** of **four** general areas of mental function (described in B.1-4 below), **then** to prepare a narrative statement of mental RFC.

B. Operating Policy

The MC is to **analyze each** of the **mental activities** within the following four general mental functional areas and to indicate on the SSA-4734-F4-SUP:

- **Whether** the **evidence** is **sufficient** to permit assessment or, if not, the evidence needed.
- The **extent** to which the individual **can** still **perform** and **sustain** specific mental activities and mental functions.

1. UNDERSTANDING AND MEMORY

a. **Understanding and memory** can be evaluated through evidence from the mental status examination(s) or from elements of standardized psychological tests (such as IQ tests) that assess the ability to understand and remember, as well as evidence available
from other medical and nonmedical sources, e.g., reports of prior work attempts or work evaluations.

b. The ability to understand and remember may be at least partially assessed through answers to some of the following questions:

- Is the individual able to complete forms, respond to two or three-step instructions for filling out applications, or follow instructions given by someone?
- Did the individual have difficulty in the process of filing for disability, going for examinations, or remembering appointments?
- Is there any **history of work or school failures** due to inability to remember and understand?
- Was the individual involved in **special education** or **training programs?** (These might indicate some impairment of the ability to understand and remember.)
- Is there any evidence that the claimant **requires supervision** or **assistance** to perform activities of daily living because of problems with understanding or remembering?
- Did the individual **come to appointments without supervision**, finding his/her own way without unusual supervision?

2. SUSTAINED CONCENTRATION AND PERSISTENCE

a. The individual's ability to sustain ongoing mental performance for a full workday is essential. **These may be evaluated through:**

- Medical history and reports, and
- Reports of performance at past work, recent work attempts, recreational or volunteer activities, or vocational evaluations.

b. **Limitations** in these areas may be **demonstrated** in typically **less demanding settings**, such as sheltered work, vocational training, or school (i.e., in any situation demanding performance of tasks requiring concentration or task persistence).

c. **Use care in inferring** an individual's **ability to sustain** the mental demands of work in a competitive setting from his/her performance in a less demanding setting, such as sheltered work.

NOTE: Discussion with the disability examiner of the performance required in competitive work environments may clarify this distinction.

3. SOCIAL INTERACTION

The items in this subsection deal with socially acceptable behavior and the individual's capacity to relate to others in a work setting. To assess these factors, important considerations are:

- Historical information about interpersonal interactions with others, particularly in an employment or work-like setting.
- Indications, on mental status examinations or psychological testing, of withdrawal, bizarre or unusual behavior, emotional liability, paranoid ideas, or faulty insight and judgment.
- Observed behavior, in terms of how the individual relates to various interviewers or behaves when exposed to a stressful circumstance or situation.

4. ADAPTATION

Adaptive functions reflect the individual's ability to integrate other areas of functioning.

a. **The items in this section pertain to the individual's ability** to:

- plan,
- respond to changes,
- deal appropriately with mental demands (stress),
- avoid hazards and maintain safe behavior,
- follow rules,
- adhere to schedules and to time constraints, and
- travel.

b. **The area of mental demands of work** ("stress") is difficult to assess. Some mentally impaired individuals may be unusually sensitive to changes in their environment and may become anxious, depressed, confused, or even psychotic when confronted with seemingly slight mental demands.

"Stress" is a highly individualized phenomenon and **can only be assessed** with regard to **each individual's experiences** and **limitations.** Even work activities usually considered to entail low stress may produce adverse responses in some individuals.

c. **Data in the medical file may demonstrate sensitivity to change** , e.g., resistance to try a new activity, treatment or medication, or exacerbation of symptoms when a therapist leaves, changes schedule, or goes on vacation.

d. **Most health care settings have rules**, schedules, and hazards. **Limitations** in conforming to acceptable behavior may sometimes emerge in the reports from hospital, or clinics.

[DDS POMS]

DI 24510.062 Completion of Heading of SSA-4734-F4-SUP

A. Operating Policy
The heading must be completed.

B. Operating Procedure

- Obtain this information from the PRTF and the claim folder.
- Insert the individual's name, Social Security Number, categories from section IC of the Psychiatric Review Technique Form (PRTF), and the appropriate period for which the assessment is being made.

[Last Change: 01/01]

DI 24510.063 Completion of Section I of SSA-4734-F4-SUP

A. Operating Policy

For each of the items under the four headings, A through D, **one** of the five boxes to the right of each item **must** be checked.

B. Operating Procedure

Complete Section I by checking the appropriate boxes.

1. CHECK BOX 1
"Not Significantly Limited," when the effects of the mental disorder **do not prevent** the individual from consistently and usefully performing the activity.

2. CHECK BOX 2
"Moderately Limited," when the evidence supports the conclusion that the individual's **capacity to perform** the activity is **impaired**.
NOTE: The **degree and extent** of the capacity or **limitation** must be described in narrative format in Section III.

3. CHECK BOX 3
"Markedly Limited," when the evidence supports the conclusion that the individual cannot usefully perform or sustain the activity.

4. CHECK BOX 4
When there is **no allegation of limitation** of this activity, or the **medical evidence does not indicate limitations** in a particular area and no limitation would be expected, based on the nature of the illness and the rater's clinical experience.

5. CHECK BOX 5
When there is **insufficient evidence** and either a problem in this aspect of work function has been alleged, the evidence suggests a problem, or the MC's clinical judgment suggests the likelihood of a problem.
NOTE: Absence of a rating (i.e., checking blocks 1, 2, or 3) for one or more items in a subsection in section I **does not automatically preclude** a narrative RFC statement for that subsection. **Other items** in the subsection **may be ratable** and may indicate such a level of functional loss that the disability examiner can conclude that the individual's capacity for work is severely compromised, in spite of the absence of a rating for other items.

Discussion with the disability examiner will resolve whether additional information about a subsection is necessary for a useful assessment of mental RFC.
[DDS POMS]

DI 24510.064 Completion of Section II of SSA-4734-F4-SUP—Remarks

A. Introduction

This section is for the identification of any **deficiencies** of evidence, the **type of evidence** needed, and any recommendations of the **source(s)** from which the evidence is to be obtained.

B. Operating Procedure

1. BOX 5 IS CHECKED
a. **When box 5 is checked** for several items within a subsection, **consider** the **possibility** that the **record is inadequate** to permit an RFC statement for that subsection.
b. **When this is the case, do not write a functional assessment** for that subsection in section III. Instead, **write a rationale in section II** , explaining why the narrative assessment is missing for that subsection.

2. ADDITIONAL MEDICAL DEVELOPMENT
a. **Current evidence is insufficient.**
When the evidence in file is insufficient to permit the MC to make assessments of critical mental functional capacities, the MC will **record the medical development to be undertaken** in section II of the SSA-4734-F4-SUP.
NOTE: In addition to permitting new judgments on items that were not initially ratable, the **new evidence may cause the MC to reconsider judgments on other items.**

b. **Additional evidence Obtained.**

- When **additional medical evidence is obtained**, a **new** SSA-4734-F4-SUP **must be prepared** to replace the preliminary SSA-4734-F4-SUP.
- **The new, signed SSA-4734-F4-SUP** is to be **filed on the left** side of the folder.
- **Clearly mark** the preliminary SSA-4734-F4-SUP "PRELIMINARY ONLY" on the first page, then **file** on the **right** side of the folder.
- **Do not file** preliminary SSA-4734-F4-SUP's on the **left** side of the folder.

[DDS POMs]

DI 24510.065 Section III of SSA-4734-F4-SUP - Functional Capacity Assessment

A. Introduction
Section III is for recording the formal narrative mental RFC assessment and **provides** for the MC to prepare a **narrative statement** for **each** of the subsections (A through D) in section I.

B. Operating Procedure
In preparing the formal narrative statement, the MC is to address each of the four mental categories (Understanding and Memory, Concentration and Persistence, Social Interaction, and Adaptation) by:

- Identifying each mental category in turn; and
- Providing a narrative discussion of the individual's capacities and limitations.

1. Writing the Narrative Statement

a. **Identify** the subsection (e.g., Understanding and Memory), then **discuss** the **functions** that the individual has demonstrated that he/she **can do,** as well as any **limitations** of those functions.
   - o **Describe,** in detail, the mental capacities, limitations, and any other information that is important in the comprehensive expression of mental RFC.
   - o **Indicate** the extent to which the individual could be **expected to perform and sustain** the activity.
   - o **Include** any additional information or consideration that is necessary to give a **clear description** of the individual's mental functional capacity.

   Examples:

   - o The claimant can understand, remember, and carry out a two-step command involving simple instructions.
   - o The claimant can understand complex instructions but can only recall at a span of two-step commands. The claimant, therefore, would be limited to this span.
   - o The claimant can understand and remember a four-step command, but the disruption of executive functions is such that he can carry out only a single step before confusing the order.

b. **Record conclusions of functional capacity** provided by examining physicians that are **appropriate** and **consistent** with the documented medical and nonmedical evidence, along with the supporting findings. **Confine** discussion to the **effects** of the impairment(s) on function.

c. **Include no severity ratings** or **nonspecific** qualifying **terms** (e.g., moderate, moderately severe) to describe limitations. Such terms do not describe function and do not usefully convey the extent of capacity limitation.

d. Offer no opinion as to whether the individual is **disabled** or whether the individual **can** or might perform or **qualify** for **levels** of work (e.g., unskilled) or **specific jobs**
(e.g., truck driver).

2. Signature and Date

a. **After completing** the narrative statement in section III, sign and date the SSA-4734-F4-SUP in the spaces provided.

b. The MC's name is to be typed or stamped below the signature.

§245.6 Form: POMS DI 25020.010 — Mental Limitations

DI 25020.010 Mental Limitations

A. POLICY

1. Nonexertional vs. Exertional

Mental limitations are generally considered to be nonexertional, but depression and conversion disorders may also limit exertion.

2. Medical Listing Not Met or Equaled

a. It cannot be assumed that a failure to meet or equal one of the medical listings for mental impairments equates with the capacity to do at least unskilled work.

b. If a medical listing is not met or equaled, the process must continue to consider whether the individual can meet the mental demands of PRW and, if not, whether he/she has the ability to adjust to other work considering his /her remaining mental and other functional capacities and vocational factors.

3. Mental Demands or Unskilled Work

a. The **basic mental demands of** competitive, remunerative, **unskilled work** include the abilities (on a sustained basis) to:

- understand, carry out, and remember simple instructions;
- make judgments that are commensurate with the functions of unskilled work, i.e., simple work-related decisions.
- respond appropriately to supervision, coworkers and work situations; and
- deal with changes in a routine worksetting.

b. A **substantial loss of ability to meet** any of the **basic mental demands** listed in DI 25020.010A.3.a.:

- severely limits the potential occupational base and thus,
- would justify a finding of inability to perform other work even for persons with favorable age, education and work experience.

NOTE: "Substantial loss" cannot be precisely defined. It does not necessarily relate to any particular adjective, number, or percentage. In practical terms, an individual has a substantial loss of ability to perform a basic mental activity when he/she cannot perform the particular activity in regular, competitive employment but, at best, could do so only in a sheltered work setting where special considerations and attention are provided. This requires professional judgment, on the basis of the evidence in file in each case. The impairment in a claim of this type may meet or equal the listed medical criteria. Therefore, before making a determination that includes vocational evaluation, the adjudicator should discuss the case with a psychiatrist or psychologist to learn whether a significant part of the evidence had been previously overlooked or underrated.

c. A person who can meet all of the mental demands listed in DI 25020.010A.3.a. and has only a mental limitation(s) will almost always be capable of adjusting to other work since his/her potential occupational base would be the unskilled jobs at all exertional levels.

EXCEPTION: In a few **rare** instances where a person's vocational profile is **extremely** adverse (e.g., closely approaching retirement age, limited education or less, and essentially a lifetime commitment to a field of **unskilled** work that is now precluded by a mental impairment), a finding of "disabled" may be appropriate. (This would be adjudicated under the Lifetime Commitments Special Medical-Vocational Profile. *See* DI 25010.001B.3.).

B. PROCEDURE

1. Introduction

In DI 25020.010B.2. through DI 25020.010B.5. it shows how the specific abilities listed in section I ("Summary Conclusions") on the mental RFC assessment form (SSA-4734-F4-SUP) relate to:

- the basic mental demands of work listed in DI 25020.010A.3.a. and
- the ability to perform work at various exertional levels and for specific jobs.

NOTE: The purpose of section I ("Summary Conclusion") on the SSA-4734-F-SUP is chiefly to have a worksheet to ensure that the psychiatrist or psychologist has considered each of these pertinent mental activities and the claimant's or beneficiary's degree of limitation for sustaining these activities over a normal workday and workweek on an ongoing, appropriate, and independent basis. **It is the narrative** written by the psychiatrist or psychologist **in section III** ("Functional Capacity Assessment") of form SSA-4734-F4-Sup **that adjudicators are to use as the assessment of RFC**. Adjudicators must take the RFC assessment **in section III** and decide what significance the elements discussed in this RFC assessment have in terms of the person's ability to meet the mental demands of past work or other work. This must be done carefully using the adjudicator's informed professional judgment.

2. Mental Abilities Needed For Any Job

a. Understanding, carrying out, and remembering simple instructions

- The ability to remember locations and worklike procedures.
- The ability to understand and remember very short and simple instructions.
- The ability to carry out very short and simple instructions.
- The ability to maintain concentration and attention for extended periods (the approximately 2-hour segments between arrival and first break, lunch, second break, and departure).
- The ability to perform activities within a schedule, maintain regular attendance, and be punctual within customary tolerances.
- The ability to sustain an ordinary routine without special supervision.
- The ability to work in coordination with or proximity to others without being (unduly) distracted by them.
- The ability to complete a normal workday and workweek without interruptions from psychologically based symptoms and to perform at a consistent pace without an unreasonable number and length of rest periods.

b. Use of judgment

- The ability to make simple work-related decisions.
- The ability to be aware of normal hazards and take appropriate precautions.

c. Responding appropriately to supervision, coworkers, and usual work situations

- The ability to ask simple questions or request assistance.
- The ability to accept instructions and respond appropriately to criticism from supervisors.
- The ability to get along with coworkers or peers without (unduly) distracting them or exhibiting behavioral extremes.

d. Dealing with changes in a routine worksetting—the ability to respond appropriately to changes in (a routine) work setting.

3. Mental Abilities Critical For Performing Unskilled Work

The claimant/beneficiary must show the ability to:

a. remember work-like procedures (locations are not critical).
b. understand and remember very short and simple instructions.
c. carry out very short and simple instructions.
d. maintain attention for extended periods of 2-hour segments (concentration is not critical).
e. maintain regular attendance and be punctual within customary tolerances. (These tolerances are usually strict.) Maintaining a schedule is not critical.
f. sustain an ordinary routine without special supervision.
g. work in coordination with or proximity to others without being (unduly) distracted by them.
h. make simple work-related decisions.
i. complete a normal workday and workweek without interruptions from psychologically based symptoms and perform at a consistent pace without an unreasonable number and length of rest periods. (These requirements are usually strict.)
j. ask simple questions or request assistance.
k. accept instructions and respond appropriately to criticism from supervisors.
l. get along with coworkers or peers without (unduly) distracting them or exhibiting behavioral extremes.
m. respond appropriately to changes in a (routine) work setting.
n. be aware of normal hazards and take appropriate precautions.

4. Mental Abilities Needed To Do Semiskilled and Skilled Work

a. The basic abilities listed in DI 25020.010B.2. (i.e., the "abilities needed to perform any job") are necessary.
b. Often, there is an **increasing requirement for understanding** and **memory** and for **concentration** and **persistence**, e.g.: the ability to:

- understand and remember detailed instructions,
- carry out detailed instructions, and
- set realistic goals or make plans independently of others.

c. Other special abilities may be needed depending upon the type of work and specific functions it involves.

5. Degrees of Mental Limitations vs. Specific Jobs

Different jobs require different degrees of mental ability.

EXAMPLE 1: Most competitive jobs require the **ability to meet basic standards of neatness and cleanliness**. However, the standards that must be met vary greatly depending upon whether the job(s) being considered involve dealing with the public; or working in a factory, a coal mine, a stock yard, etc.

EXAMPLE 2: Most competitive jobs require the ability to travel to and from work and thus, would be precluded by **extreme agoraphobia** in which the person is incapable of leaving his/her home. However, a mild case of agoraphobia may not preclude the ability to travel to and from work or preclude work performed in the same (and thus, familiar) setting each day.

[DDS POMS]

§245.7 *Form: Medical Opinion Re: Ability to Do Work-Related Activities (Mental)*

MEDICAL OPINON RE: ABILITY TO DO WORK-RELATED ACTIVITIES (MENTAL)

To: ______________________ Re: ______________________

DOB: ______________________

To determine your patient's ability to do *work-related activities on a day-to-day basis in a regular work setting,* please give us your opinion **based on your examination** of how your patient's mental/emotional capabilities are affected by the impairment(s). Consider the medical history, the chronicity of findings (or lack thereof), and the expected duration of any work-related limitations, but not your patient's age, sex or work experience.

- *Limited but satisfactory* means your patient has noticeable difficulty (e.g., distracted from job activity) no more than 10 percent of the workday or work week.
- *Seriously limited* means your patient has noticeable difficulty (e.g., distracted from job activity) from 11 to 15 percent of the workday or work week.
- *Unable to meet competitive standards* means your patient has noticeable difficulty (e.g., distracted from job activity) from 16 to 25 percent of the workday or work week.
- *No useful ability to function*, an extreme limitation, means your patient cannot perform this activity on a regular, reliable and sustained schedule in a regular work setting.

I.	MENTAL ABILITIES AND APTITUDES NEEDED TO DO UNSKILLED WORK	Unlimited or Very Good	Limited but satisfactory	**Seriously limited**	**Unable to meet competitiv e standards**	**No useful ability to function**
A.	Remember work-like procedures					
B.	Understand and remember very short and simple instructions					
C.	Carry out very short and simple instructions					
D.	Maintain attention for two hour segment					
E.	Maintain regular attendance and be punctual within customary, usually strict tolerances					
F.	Sustain an ordinary routine without special supervision					
G.	Work in coordination with or proximity to others without being unduly distracted					
H.	Make simple work-related decisions					
I.	Complete a normal workday and workweek without interruptions from psychologically based symptoms					
J.	Perform at a consistent pace without an unreasonable number and length of rest periods					
K.	Ask simple questions or request assistance					
L.	Accept instructions and respond appropriately to criticism from supervisors					
M.	Get along with co-workers or peers without unduly distracting them or exhibiting behavioral extremes					
N.	Respond appropriately to changes in a routine work setting					
O.	Deal with normal work stress					
P.	Be aware of normal hazards and take appropriate precautions					

Q. Explain limitations falling in the three most limited categories (identified by **bold type)** and include the medical/clinical findings that support this assessment:

II.	MENTAL ABILITIES AND APTITUDES NEEDED TO DO SEMISKILLED AND SKILLED WORK	Unlimited or Very Good	Limited but satisfactory	**Seriously limited**	**Unable to meet competitive standards**	**No useful ability to function**
A.	Understand and remember detailed instructions					
B.	Carry out detailed instructions					
C.	Set realistic goals or make plans independently of others					
D.	Deal with stress of semiskilled and skilled work					

E.Explain limitations falling in the three most limited categories (identified by **bold type**) and include the medical/clinical findings that support this assessment:

III.	MENTAL ABILITIES AND APTITUDE NEEDED TO DO PARTICULAR TYPES OF JOBS	Unlimited or Very Good	Limited but satisfactory	**Seriously limited**	**Unable to meet competitive standards**	**No useful ability to function**
A.	Interact appropriately with the general public					
B.	Maintain socially appropriate behavior					
C.	Adhere to basic standards of neatness and cleanliness					
D.	Travel in unfamiliar place					
E.	Use public transportation					

F. Explain limitations falling in the three most limited categories (identified by **bold type**) and include the medical/clinical findings that support this assessment:

IV. Please describe any additional reasons not covered above why your patient would have difficulty working at a regular job on a sustained basis.

V. If your patient was trying to work, on the average, how often do you anticipate that your patient's impairments would cause your patient to be absent from work?

☐ Never ☐About two days per month ☐About four days per month
☐About one day per month ☐About three days per month ☐More than four days per month

VI. Can your patient manage benefits in his or her own best interest? Yes No

_______________________ _______________________________________

Date Signature

7-67 245.7
2/17

§245.8 Form: Mental Impairment Questionnaire (RFC & Listings)

MENTAL IMPAIRMENT QUESTIONNAIRE
(RFC & LISTINGS)

From: ______________________ Re: ______________________

DOB: ______________________

Please answer the following questions concerning your patient's impairments:

1. Frequency and length of contact: ______________________

____

2. DSM-5 Mental Disorders/Principal Diagnoses: Other Conditions / Focus of Clinical Attention:

______________________ ______________________

______________________ ______________________

______________________ ______________________

3. Treatment and response: ______________________

____

____

4. a. List prescribed medications:

   b. Identify your patient's side effects of medications that may affect working, *e.g.*, sedation, drowsiness, fatigue, lethargy, malaise, irritability, nausea, dizziness, *etc.*

5. List the *clinical findings* including those from mental status examination that demonstrate the severity of your patient's mental impairment and symptoms:

____

____

____

6. Prognosis: ______________________

7. Identify your patient's signs and symptoms:

	Significant cognitive decline from a prior level of functioning in *one* or more of the cognitive areas: Complex attention; Executive function; Learning and memory; Language; Perceptual-motor; or Social cognition.		Hyperactive and impulsive behavior (e.g., difficulty remaining seated, talking excessively, difficulty waiting, appearing restless, or behaving as if being "driven by a motor")
	Delusions or hallucinations		Irritability
	Qualitative deficits in verbal communication, nonverbal communication, and social interaction		Preoccupation with having or acquiring a serious illness without significant symptoms present
	Increase in goal-directed activity or psychomotor agitation		Disregard for and violation of the rights of others
	Depressed mood		Detachment from social relationships
	Diminished interest in almost all activities		Distrust and suspiciousness of others
	Restlessness t		Instability of interpersonal relationships
	Sleep disturbance		Pressured speech
	Observable psychomotor agitation or retardation		Preoccupation with perfectionism and orderliness
	Decreased energy		Easily fatigued
	Feelings of guilt or worthlessness		Muscle tension
	Difficulty concentrating or thinking		Disorganized thinking (speech)
	Thoughts of death or suicide		Recurrent motor movement or vocalization
	Excessive emotionality and attention seeking		Repetitive behaviors aimed at reducing anxiety
	Flight of ideas		Inflated self-esteem
	Decreased need for sleep		Distractibility
	Involvement in activities that have a high probability of painful consequences that are not recognized		One or more somatic symptoms that are distressing, with excessive thoughts, feelings, or behaviors related to the symptoms
	Grossly disorganized behavior or catatonia		Appetite disturbance with change in weigh
	Panic attacks followed by a persistent concern or worry about additional panic attacks or their consequences		Symptoms of altered voluntary motor or sensory function that are not better explained by another medical or mental disorder
	Disproportionate fear or anxiety about at least two different situations (for example, using public transportation, being in a crowd, being in a line, being outside of your home, being in open spaces)		Persistent alteration in eating or eating-related behavior that results in a change in consumption or absorption of food and that significantly impairs physical or psychological health s
	Recurrent, impulsive, aggressive behavioral outbursts		Significantly restricted, repetitive patterns of behavior, interests, or activities
	Frequent distractibility, difficulty sustaining attention, and difficulty organizing tasks		Significant difficulties learning and using academic skills
	Involuntary, time-consuming preoccupation with intrusive, unwanted thought		
	Medical documentation of *all* of the following: 1. Exposure to actual or threatened death, serious injury, or violence; 2. Subsequent involuntary re-experiencing of the traumatic event (for example, intrusive memories, dreams, or flashbacks); 3. Avoidance of external reminders of the event; 4. Disturbance in mood and behavior; and 5. Increases in arousal and reactivity (for example, exaggerated startle response, sleep disturbance).		

8. To determine your patient's ability to do **work-related activities on a day-to-day basis in a regular work setting,** please give us your opinion **based on your examination** of how your patient's mental/emotional capabilities are affected by the impairment(s). Consider the medical history, the chronicity of findings (or lack thereof), and the expected duration of any work-related limitations, but not your patient's age, sex or work experience.

- **Limited but satisfactory** means your patient has noticeable difficulty (e.g., distracted from job activity) no more than 10 percent of the workday or work week.
- **Seriously limited** means your patient has noticeable difficulty (e.g., distracted from job activity) from 11 to 15 percent of the workday or work week.
- **Unable to meet competitive standards** means your patient has noticeable difficulty (e.g., distracted from job activity) from 16 to 25 percent of the workday or work week.
- **No useful ability to function**, an extreme limitation, means your patient cannot perform this activity on a regular, reliable and sustained schedule in a regular work setting.

I.	MENTAL ABILITIES AND APTITUDES NEEDED TO DO UNSKILLED WORK	Unlimited or Very Good	Limited but satisfactory	**Seriously limited**	**Unable to meet competitive standards**	**No useful ability to function**
A.	Remember work-like procedures					
B.	Understand and remember very short and simple instructions					
C.	Carry out very short and simple instructions					
D.	Maintain attention for two-hour segment					
E.	Maintain regular attendance and be punctual within customary, usually strict tolerances					
F.	Sustain an ordinary routine without special supervision					
G.	Work in coordination with or proximity to others without being unduly distracted					
H.	Make simple work-related decisions					
I.	Complete a normal workday and workweek without interruptions from psychologically based symptoms					
J.	Perform at a consistent pace without an unreasonable number and length of rest periods					
K.	Ask simple questions or request assistance					
L.	Accept instructions and respond appropriately to criticism from supervisors					
M.	Get along with co-workers or peers without unduly distracting them or exhibiting behavioral extremes					
N.	Respond appropriately to changes in a routine work setting					
O.	Deal with normal work stress					
P.	Be aware of normal hazards and take appropriate precautions					

Q Explain limitations falling in the three most limited categories (identified by **bold type)** and include the medical/clinical findings that support this assessment:

II.	MENTAL ABILITIES AND APTITUDES NEEDED TO DO SEMISKILLED AND SKILLED WORK	Unlimited or Very Good	Limited but satisfactory	**Seriously limited**	**Unable to meet competitive standards**	**No useful ability to function**
A.	Understand and remember detailed instructions					
B.	Carry out detailed instructions					
C.	Set realistic goals or make plans independently of others					
D.	Deal with stress of semiskilled and skilled work					

E.Explain limitations falling in the three most limited categories (identified by **bold type)** and include the medical/clinical findings that support this assessment:

III.	MENTAL ABILITIES AND APTITUDE NEEDED TO DO PARTICULAR TYPES OF JOBS	Unlimited or Very Good	Limited but satisfactory	**Seriously limited**	**Unable to meet competitive standards**	**No useful ability to function**
A.	Interact appropriately with the general public					
B.	Maintain socially appropriate behavior					
C.	Adhere to basic standards of neatness and cleanliness					
D.	Travel in unfamiliar place					
E.	Use public transportation					

F Explain limitations falling in the three most limited categories (identified by **bold type)** and include the medical/clinical findings that support this assessment:

9. Is your patient's intellectual functioning limited?

☐Yes ☐No

If yes, please explain:

10. Does the psychiatric condition exacerbate your patient's experience of pain or any other physical symptom? ☐Yes ☐No

If yes, please explain:

11. Rate the degree of your patient's expected limitations in a work setting using the following scale:

- **Moderate** means the ability to function independently, appropriately, effectively, and on a sustained basis is **fair;**
- **Marked** means the ability to function independently, appropriately, effectively, and on a sustained basis is **seriously limited;**
- **Extreme** means **not able** to function independently, appropriately, effectively, and on a sustained basis, but it does not mean a total loss of ability to function.

RATE THE DEGREE OF LIMITATION IN THE FOLLOWING AREAS:					
A.1.	Understanding information:	None-Mild	Moderate	Marked	Extreme
A.2.	Remembering information	None-Mild	Moderate	Marked	Extreme
A.3.	Applying information	None-Mild	Moderate	Marked	Extreme
B.	Interacting with others:	None Mild	Moderate	Marked	Extreme
C.1.	Concentrating	None Mild	Moderate	Marked	Extreme
C.2.	Persisting	None Mild	Moderate	Marked	Extreme
C.3	Maintaining pace	None Mild	Moderate	Marked	Extreme
D.1.	Adapting in the workplace	None Mild	Moderate	Marked	Extreme
D.2.	Managing oneself in the workplace	None Mild	Moderate	Marked	Extreme

12. If your patient has a neurocognitive disorder; schizophrenia or other psychotic disorder; depressive, bipolar or related disorder; anxiety or obsessive compulsive disorder; or trauma or stress-related disorder, please indicate if any of the following apply to your patient:

A. ☐ Your patient's chronic mental disorder is "serious and persistent;" that is, your patient has a medically documented history of the existence of the disorder over a period of at least 2 years.

B. ☐ Your patient relies on ongoing medical treatment, mental health therapy, psychosocial support, or a highly-structured setting to diminish the symptoms and signs of his or her mental disorder.

C. ☐ Despite your patient's diminished symptoms and signs, your patient has only marginal adjustment, that is, your patient has minimal capacity to adapt to changes in his or her environment or to demands that are not already part of daily life.

13. Assuming your patient was trying to work full time, on the average, how often do you anticipate that your patient's impairments would cause your patient to be absent from work?

☐ Never	☐About two days per month	☐About four days per month
☐About one day per month	☐About three days per month	☐More than four days per month

14. Has your patient's impairment lasted or can it be expected to last at least twelve months?
☐Yes ☐ No

15. Are your patient's impairments (as demonstrated by signs, clinical findings or test results) reasonably consistent with the symptoms and functional limitations described in this evaluation?
☐Yes ☐ No

If no, please explain:

16. Please describe any additional reasons not covered above why your patient would have difficulty working at a regular job on a sustained basis.

17. Can your patient manage benefits in his or her own best interest? ☐Yes ☐No

____________________ ______________________________

Date Signature

Printed/Typed Name: ______________________________

1/17 Address: ______________________________

____

§245.9 Form: Mental Medical Source Statement

MENTAL MEDICAL SOURCE STATEMENT

From: ______________________________ Re: ______________________________

DOB: ______________________________

Please answer the following questions concerning your patient's impairments:

1. Frequency and length of contact: ______________________________

____

2. DSM-5 Mental Disorders/Principal Diagnoses: ______________________________

____

____

Other Conditions / Focus of Clinical Attention: ______________________________

____

____

3. Treatment and response: ______________________________

____

____

4. a. List of prescribed medications:

   b. Identify your patient's side effects of medications that may affect working, *e.g.*, sedation, drowsiness, fatigue, lethargy, malaise, irritability, nausea, dizziness, *etc*.

5. List the *clinical findings* including those from mental status examination that demonstrate the severity of your patient's mental impairment and symptoms:

____

____

____

6. Prognosis: ______________________________

7. Identify your patient's signs and symptoms:

	Significant cognitive decline from a prior level of functioning in *one* or more of the cognitive areas: Complex attention; Executive function; Learning and memory; Language; Perceptual-motor; or Social cognition.		Hyperactive and impulsive behavior (e.g., difficulty remaining seated, talking excessively, difficulty waiting, appearing restless, or behaving as if being "driven by a motor")
	Delusions or hallucinations		Irritability
	Qualitative deficits in verbal communication, nonverbal communication, and social interaction		Preoccupation with having or acquiring a serious illness without significant symptoms present
	Increase in goal-directed activity or psychomotor agitation		Disregard for and violation of the rights of others
	Depressed mood		Detachment from social relationships
	Diminished interest in almost all activities		Distrust and suspiciousness of others
	Restlessness t		Instability of interpersonal relationships
	Sleep disturbance		Pressured speech
	Observable psychomotor agitation or retardation		Preoccupation with perfectionism and orderliness
	Decreased energy		Easily fatigued
	Feelings of guilt or worthlessness		Muscle tension
	Difficulty concentrating or thinking		Disorganized thinking (speech)
	Thoughts of death or suicide		Recurrent motor movement or vocalization
	Excessive emotionality and attention seeking		Repetitive behaviors aimed at reducing anxiety
	Flight of ideas		Inflated self-esteem
	Decreased need for sleep		Distractibility
	Involvement in activities that have a high probability of painful consequences that are not recognized		One or more somatic symptoms that are distressing, with excessive thoughts, feelings, or behaviors related to the symptoms
	Grossly disorganized behavior or catatonia		Appetite disturbance with change in weigh
	Panic attacks followed by a persistent concern or worry about additional panic attacks or their consequences		Symptoms of altered voluntary motor or sensory function that are not better explained by another medical or mental disorder
	Disproportionate fear or anxiety about at least two different situations (for example, using public transportation, being in a crowd, being in a line, being outside of your home, being in open spaces)		Persistent alteration in eating or eating-related behavior that results in a change in consumption or absorption of food and that significantly impairs physical or psychological health s
	Recurrent, impulsive, aggressive behavioral outbursts		Significantly restricted, repetitive patterns of behavior, interests, or activities
	Frequent distractibility, difficulty sustaining attention, and difficulty organizing tasks		Significant difficulties learning and using academic skills
	Involuntary, time-consuming preoccupation with intrusive, unwanted thought		
	Medical documentation of *all* of the following: 1. Exposure to actual or threatened death, serious injury, or violence; 2. Subsequent involuntary re-experiencing of the traumatic event (for example, intrusive memories, dreams, or flashbacks); 3. Avoidance of external reminders of the event; 4. Disturbance in mood and behavior; and 5. Increases in arousal and reactivity (for example, exaggerated startle response, sleep disturbance).		

8. To determine your patient's ability to do **work-related activities on a day-to-day basis in a regular work setting,** please give us your opinion **based on your examination** of how your patient's mental/emotional capabilities are affected by the impairment(s). Consider the medical history, the chronicity of findings (or lack thereof), and the expected duration of any work-related limitations, but not your patient's age, sex or work experience.

- **Limited but satisfactory** means your patient has noticeable difficulty (e.g., distracted from job activity) no more than 10 percent of the workday or work week.
- **Seriously limited** means your patient has noticeable difficulty (e.g., distracted from job activity) from 11 to 15 percent of the workday or work week.
- **Unable to meet competitive standards** means your patient has noticeable difficulty (e.g., distracted from job activity) from 16 to 25 percent of the workday or work week.
- **No useful ability to function**, an extreme limitation, means your patient cannot perform this activity on a regular, reliable and sustained schedule in a regular work setting.

	I.	MENTAL ABILITIES AND APTITUDES NEEDED TO DO UNSKILLED WORK	Unlimited or Very Good	Limited but satisfactory	**Seriously limited**	**Unable to meet competitiv e standards**	**No useful ability to function**
A.		Remember work-like procedures					
B.		Understand and remember very short and simple instructions					
C.		Carry out very short and simple instructions					
D.		Maintain attention for two-hour segment					
E.		Maintain regular attendance and be punctual within customary, usually strict tolerances					
F.		Sustain an ordinary routine without special supervision					
G.		Work in coordination with or proximity to others without being unduly distracted					
H.		Make simple work-related decisions					
		Complete a normal workday and workweek without interruptions from psychologically based symptoms					
		Perform at a consistent pace without an unreasonable number and length of rest periods					
K.		Ask simple questions or request assistance					
L.		Accept instructions and respond appropriately to criticism from supervisors					
M.		Get along with co-workers or peers without unduly distracting them or exhibiting behavioral extremes					
N.		Respond appropriately to changes in a routine work setting					
O.		Deal with normal work stress					
P.		Be aware of normal hazards and take appropriate precautions					

Q Explain limitations falling in the three most limited categories (identified by **bold type)** and include the medical/clinical findings that support this assessment:

	II.	MENTAL ABILITIES AND APTITUDES NEEDED TO DO SEMISKILLED AND SKILLED WORK	Unlimited or Very Good	Limited but satisfactory	**Seriously limited**	**Unable to meet competitive standards**	**No useful ability to function**
A.		Understand and remember detailed instructions					
B.		Carry out detailed instructions					
C.		Set realistic goals or make plans independently of others					
D.		Deal with stress of semiskilled and skilled work					

E. Explain limitations falling in the three most limited categories (identified by **bold type)** and include the medical/clinical findings that support this assessment:

	III.	MENTAL ABILITIES AND APTITUDE NEEDED TO DO PARTICULAR TYPES OF JOBS	Unlimited or Very Good	Limited but satisfactory	**Seriously limited**	**Unable to meet competitive standards**	**No useful ability to function**
A.		Interact appropriately with the general public					
B.		Maintain socially appropriate behavior					
C.		Adhere to basic standards of neatness and cleanliness					
D.		Travel in unfamiliar place					
E.		Use public transportation					

F. Explain limitations falling in the three most limited categories (identified by **bold type)** and include the medical/clinical findings that support this assessment:

9. Is your patient's intellectual functioning limited?

☐Yes ☐No

If yes, please explain:

10. Does the psychiatric condition exacerbate your patient's experience of pain or any other physical symptom? ☐Yes ☐No

If yes, please explain:

11. If stress tolerance is an issue, what demands of work does this patient find stressful?

☐ speed	☐ being criticized by supervisors
☐ precision	☐ simply knowing that work is supervised
☐ complexity	☐ getting to work regularly
☐ deadlines	☐ remaining at work for a full day
☐ working within a schedule	☐ fear of failure at work
☐ making decisions	☐ monotony of routine
☐ exercising independent judgment	☐ little latitude for decision-making
☐ completing tasks	☐ lack of collaboration on the job
☐ working with other people	☐ no opportunity for learning new things
☐ dealing with the public (strangers)	☐ underutilization of skills
☐ dealing with supervisors	☐ lack of meaningfulness of work

12. Assuming your patient was trying to work full time, on the average, how often do you anticipate that your patient's impairments would cause your patient to be absent from work?

☐ Never	☐About two days per month	☐About four days per month
☐About one day per month	☐About three days per month	☐More than four days per month

13. Has your patient's impairment lasted or can it be expected to last at least twelve months? ☐Yes ☐No

14. Are your patient's impairments (as demonstrated by signs, clinical findings or test results) reasonably consistent with the symptoms and functional limitations described in this evaluation? ☐Yes ☐No

If no, please explain:

15. Please describe any additional reasons not covered above why your patient would have difficulty working at a regular job on a sustained basis.

§246 *Evaluating Ability to Work Based on Mental RFC*

Once you have gathered opinions on your client's mental residual functional capacity, try to go as far as you can in determining the implications before hiring a vocational expert (VE). You may discover that you do not need to hire a VE; and if you find that you must hire a VE, you will have already refined the issues.

Social Security Ruling 85-15 discusses using the Medical-Vocational Guidelines as a framework for evaluating solely nonexertional impairments:

> Where a person's only impairment is mental, is not of listing severity, but does prevent the person from meeting the mental demands of past relevant work and prevents the transferability of acquired work skills, the final consideration is whether the person can be expected to perform unskilled work. The basic mental demands of competitive, remunerative, unskilled work include the abilities (on a sustained basis) to understand, carry out, and remember simple instructions; to respond appropriately to supervision, coworkers, and usual work situations; and to deal with changes in a routine work setting. *A substantial loss of ability to meet any of these basic work-related activities would severely limit the potential occupational base. This, in turn, would justify a finding of disability because even favorable age, education, or work experience will not offset such a severely limited occupational base.*

(Emphasis added.)

An expanded list of mental abilities critical for performing unskilled work appears in POMS DI 25020.010B3 included at §245.6. This POMS section is SSA's clearest and best description of the essential mental requirements that one must possess in order to be capable of unskilled work.

In conjunction with the POMS instructions for completing the official mental RFC form (which appear in §245.5), the POMS section at §245.6 provides an explanation of the concepts that appear on the mental REC form used by state agency doctors, form SSA-4734-F4-SUP, §245.4.

The state agency mental RFC form contains every item from the list of mental abilities critical for performing unskilled work in POMS DI 25020.010B3, plus six others that are numbered on the form 3, 5, 12, 16, 19 and 20. Nos. 3, 5, 12 and 20 deal generally with mental demands of semiskilled and skilled work. These are:

> 3. The ability to understand and remember detailed instructions.
>
> 5. The ability to carry out detailed instructions.
>
> 12. The ability to interact appropriately with the general public.
>
> 20. The ability to set realistic goals or make plans independently of others.

A substantial loss of any of these mental abilities will *not* prove an inability to do unskilled work, although it might prove inability to return to former semi-skilled or skilled work.

The remaining two mental abilities on form SSA-4734-F4-SUP, which do not appear on the POMS list of critical mental abilities, are nos. 16 and 19:

> 16. The ability to maintain socially appropriate behavior and to adhere to basic standards of neatness and cleanliness.
>
> 19. The ability to travel in unfamiliar places or use public transportation.

Nevertheless, according to POMS DI 25020.010B5, most competitive jobs require both of these abilities.

Substantial loss of ability to perform any one of the critical mental abilities identified on SSA-4734-F4-SUP as nos. 1, 2, 4, 6, 7, 8, 9, 10, 11, 13, 14, 15, 17, or 18 requires a finding that the claimant is disabled. The critical aspects of these 14 mental abilities and aptitudes for unskilled work are described in POMS DI 25020.010B3 as follows:

The claimant/beneficiary must show the ability to:

> a. remember work-like procedures (locations are not critical).
>
> b. understand and remember very short and simple instructions.
>
> c. carry out very short and simple instructions.
>
> d. maintain attention for extended periods of 2-hour segments (concentration is not critical).
>
> e. maintain regular attendance and be punctual within customary tolerances. (These tolerances are usually strict.) Maintaining a schedule is not critical.
>
> f. sustain an ordinary routine without special supervision.
>
> g. work in coordination with or proximity to others without being (unduly) distracted by them.
>
> h. make simple work-related decisions.
>
> i. complete a normal workday and workweek without interruptions from psychologically based symptoms and perform at a consistent pace without an unreasonable number and length of rest periods. (These requirements are usually strict).
>
> j. ask simple questions or request assistance.
>
> k. accept instructions and respond appropriately to criticism from supervisors.

l. get along with coworkers or peers without (unduly) distracting them or exhibiting behavioral extremes.

m. respond appropriately to changes in a (routine) work setting.

n. be aware of normal hazards and take appropriate precautions.

According to POMS DI 25020.010A3, *see* §245.6, when there is a substantial loss of ability to meet any of the basic mental demands of unskilled work, as outlined in POMS DI 25020.010A3 and elaborated upon in the above list of critical abilities, the claimant may be found disabled.

The form *Medical Opinion Re: Ability to do Work-Related Activities (Mental)*, §245.7, incorporates significant elements from POMS DI 25020.010B3 with a modified rating system that allows more shades of gray than the rating system found in the mental medical source statement form used by ALJs, §245.3. The revised form adds only two questions, both of which concern the ability to deal with stress, always a significant issue in a mental impairment case. *See* §247. The Mental Impairment Questionnaire (RFC & Listings), §245.8, and the Mental Medical Source Statement, §245.9, incorporate this approach, but the Mental Medical Source Statement goes a step further by asking about specific things that the patient finds stressful.

Whenever a claimant has the capacity to do basic work-related activities, the grids are used as a framework to determine if the claimant is or is not still capable of performing jobs existing in significant numbers in the economy. This is usually no easy task, and SSR 85-15 is not much help because the examples given are at both ends of the spectrum—clearly disabled or clearly not disabled. The cases in the middle are difficult.

It is for these cases in the middle that you may need the assistance of a vocational expert to deal with the particular facts of your client's case. Make sure that the vocational expert understands how to use the grids as a framework: that is, age, education and work experience must be factored into the analysis by drawing analogies from the Medical-Vocational Guidelines. For example, consider the situation of a 50-year-old, poorly educated man with an unskilled work background who has only a mental impairment. If, because of his impairment, he is determined in the opinion of a vocational expert to be capable of performing only 200 occupations that appear in the DOT, the size of his occupational base is reduced to approximately the same size as the occupational base for sedentary work. Rule 201.00(a) of the Medical-Vocational Guidelines. Thus, when the decision-maker considers his age, education and work experience by using the "framework" of the Medical-Vocational Guidelines, he ought to be found disabled using Rule 201.09 of the Medical-Vocational Guidelines as the "framework" rule. This sort of case presents a serious challenge for the claimant's attorney, first in establishing the size of the claimant's occupational base and second in getting an SSA decision maker to use Rule 201.09 as a framework to find the claimant disabled rather than using the framework of Rule 204.00 of the Medical-Vocational Guidelines to find the claimant not disabled.

§247 Stress and Mental Impairments

A common issue in mental impairment cases is the role of poor stress tolerance. When determining RFC for mental impairments, the state agency frequently and ALJs occasionally may conclude that a claimant who alleges poor stress tolerance is capable of generic low stress work, usually referred to as "routine, repetitive, low stress work." Sometimes you'll see this conclusion scrawled on a mental RFC form by a state agency physician as simply: RRLSW.

Certainly some mentally impaired people may be able to deal with so-called routine, repetitive, low stress work. Others, perhaps the majority, find such work quite stressful. *See* HEALTHY WORK by Robert Karasek and Tores Theorell published by Basic Books, Inc., which contends that such work is stressful for most people.

An ALJ must specifically describe the nature of that which the claimant finds stressful, circumstances that trigger a stress response, the stress response itself and how it affects the individual's ability to work. SSR 85-15 provides:

> *Stress and Mental Illness*—Since mental illness is defined and characterized by maladaptive behavior, it is not unusual that the mentally impaired have difficulty accommodating to the demands of work and work-like settings. Determining whether these individuals will be able to adapt to the demands or "stress" of the workplace is often extremely difficult. This section is not intended to set out any presumptive limitations for disorders, but to emphasize the importance of thoroughness in evaluation on an individualized basis.
>
> Individuals with mental disorders often adopt a highly restricted and/or inflexible lifestyle within which they appear to function well. Good mental health services and care may enable chronic patients to function adequately in the community by lowering psychological pressure, by medication, and by support from services such as outpatient facilities, day-care programs, social work programs and similar assistance.
>
> The reaction to the demands of work (stress) is highly individualized, and mental illness is characterized by adverse responses to seemingly trivial circumstances. The mentally impaired may

cease to function effectively when facing such demands as getting to work regularly, having their performance supervised, and remaining in the workplace for a full day. A person may become panicked and develop palpitations, shortness of breath, or feel faint while riding in an elevator; another may experience terror and begin to hallucinate when approached by a stranger asking a question. Thus, the mentally impaired may have difficulty meeting the requirements of even so-called "low stress" jobs.

Because response to the demands of work is highly individualized, the skill level of a position is not necessarily related to the difficulty an individual will have in meeting the demands of the job. A claimant's condition may make performance of an unskilled job as difficult as an objectively more demanding job. For example, a busboy need only clear dishes from tables. But an individual with a severe mental disorder may find unmanageable the demands of making sure that he removes all the dishes, does not drop them, and gets the table cleared promptly for the waiter or waitress. Similarly, an individual who cannot tolerate being supervised may not be able to work even in the absence of close supervision; the *knowledge* that one's work is being judged and evaluated, even when the supervision is remote or indirect, can be intolerable for some mentally impaired persons. Any impairment-related limitations created by an individual's response to demands of work, however, must be reflected in the RFC assessment.

For a good case on the subject of stress tolerance, *see Lancellotta v. Secretary of Health & Human Services*, 806 F.2d 284 (1st Cir. 1986). For a list of demands of work that some people find stressful, *see* §316.2. Note that the Mental Medical Source Statement, §245.9, includes a list of potentially stressful activities for the psychiatrist or psychologist to choose when completing the form.

§248 Somatic Symptom Disorders

Somatic symptom disorders, mental disorders with physical symptoms such as pain, present special problems. The method SSA commonly uses to evaluate somatoform disorders, a mental status examination, is completely irrelevant. Orientation, memory, affect, etc., all may be totally normal despite the presence of a disabling Somatic symptom disorder. If a medically determinable impairment can be established that is reasonably expected to produce pain, it doesn't matter if the impairment is a physical impairment or a mental impairment. Either kind of impairment can produce exertional or nonexertional limitations. It is the nature of the limitations that determines how the Medical-Vocational Guidelines are used. *See* SSRs 96-4p and 96-8p. Thus, Somatic symptom disorders must be evaluated by determining a physical RFC. *See* SSR 85-15 and *cf.* POMS DI 25020.010A.1 at §245.6. A Somatic symptom impairment questionnaire appears at §248.1.

§248.1 Form: SOMATIC SYMPTOM AND RELATED DISORDERS IMPAIRMENT QUESTIONNAIRE (RFC & LISTINGS)

SOMATIC SYMPTOM AND RELATED DISORDERS IMPAIRMENT QUESTIONNAIRE (RFC & LISTINGS)

From: ______________________________

Re: ____ (Name of Patient)

____ (Date of Birth)

Please answer the following questions concerning your patient's impairments:

1. Frequency and length of contact: ____

2. DSM-5 Mental Disorders/Principal Diagnoses: Other Conditions / Focus of Clinical Attention:

___________________________________ ___________________________________

___________________________________ ___________________________________

___________________________________ ___________________________________

3. **If your patient has a Somatic Symptom and Related Disorders diagnosis**, identify the signs and symptoms:

	History of pain; identify sites		Menstrual irregularities
	Site:		History of sexual difficulties
	Site:		Urinary complaints
	Site:		History of neurologic symptoms or conversion:
	Site:		Site:
	Site:		Site:
	Site:		Site:
	Gastrointestinal:		Gait or arm problems
	Loss of appetite		Sleep disturbances
	Nausea, vomiting		Associated depression
	Bloating, gas		Associated anxiety
	Abdominal pain		Preoccupation with own health condition(s)
	Other (specify)		Vision, speech or hearing disturbance
	Chronic fatigue		Disturbance in movement, control or sensation
	Weakness		Preoccupation or belief there is a serious illness
	Heartbeat irregularities (racing, pounding)		Other symptoms: *(specify)*

a. Does your patient have symptoms of altered voluntary motor or sensory function that are not better explained by another medical or mental disorder?

□ Yes □ No

b. Does your patient have one or more somatic symptoms that are distressing, with excessive thoughts, feelings, or behaviors related to the symptoms?

□ Yes □ No

c. Does your patient have preoccupation with having or acquiring a serious illness without significant symptoms present?

□ Yes □ No

4. Describe the *clinical findings* (onset, duration and results of mental status exam) that demonstrate the severity of your patient's mental impairment and symptoms:

5. Treatment and response:

6. a. List prescribed medications:

b. Identify your patient's side effects of medications that may affect working, *e.g.*, sedation, drowsiness, fatigue, lethargy, malaise, irritability, nausea, dizziness, *etc.*

7. Prognosis: ____

8. Has your patient's impairment lasted or can it be expected to last at least twelve months?

□ Yes □ No

9. Does the psychiatric condition exacerbate your patient's experience of pain or any other physical symptom? □ Yes □ No

If yes, please explain:

10. Is your patient's intellectual functioning limited?

□ Yes □ No

If yes, please explain:

11. If your patient was trying to work full time, please estimate, on the average, how many days per month your patient is likely to be absent from work as a result of the impairments:

□ Never
□ About one day per month
□ About two days per month
□ About three days per month
□ About four days per month
□ More than four days per month

12. To determine your patient's ability to do **work-related activities on a day-to-day basis in a regular work setting**, please give us your opinion **based on your examination** of how your patient's mental/emotional capabilities are affected by the impairment(s). Consider the medical history, the chronicity of findings (or lack thereof), and the expected duration of any work-related limitations, but not your patient's age, sex or work experience.

- **Limited but satisfactory** means your patient has noticeable difficulty (e.g., distracted from job activity) no more than 10 percent of the workday or work week.
- **Seriously limited** means your patient has noticeable difficulty (e.g., distracted from job activity) from 11 to 15 percent of the workday or work week.
- **Unable to meet competitive standards** means your patient has noticeable difficulty (e.g., distracted from job activity) from 16 to 25 percent of the workday or work week.
- **No useful ability to function**, an extreme limitation, means your patient cannot perform this activity on a regular, reliable and sustained schedule in a regular work setting.

I.	MENTAL ABILITIES AND APTITUDES NEEDED TO DO UNSKILLED WORK	Unlimited or Very Good	Limited but satisfactory	**Seriously limited**	**Unable to meet competitiv e standards**	**No useful ability to function**
A.	Remember work-like procedures					
B.	Understand and remember very short and simple instructions					
C.	Carry out very short and simple instructions					
D.	Maintain attention for two-hour segment					
E.	Maintain regular attendance and be punctual within customary, usually strict tolerances					
F.	Sustain an ordinary routine without special supervision					
G.	Work in coordination with or proximity to others without being unduly distracted					
H.	Make simple work-related decisions					
I.	Complete a normal workday and workweek without interruptions from psychologically based symptoms					
J.	Perform at a consistent pace without an unreasonable number and length of rest periods					
K.	Ask simple questions or request assistance					
L.	Accept instructions and respond appropriately to criticism from supervisors					
M.	Get along with co-workers or peers without unduly distracting them or exhibiting behavioral extremes					
N.	Respond appropriately to changes in a routine work setting					
O.	Deal with normal work stress					
P.	Be aware of normal hazards and take appropriate precautions					

(Q) Explain limitations falling in the three most limited categories (identified by **bold type)** and include the medical/clinical findings that support this assessment:

II.	MENTAL ABILITIES AND APTITUDES NEEDED TO DO SEMISKILLED AND SKILLED WORK	Unlimited or Very Good	Limited but satisfactory	**Seriously limited**	**Unable to meet competitive standards**	**No useful ability to function**
A.	Understand and remember detailed instructions					
B.	Carry out detailed instructions					
C.	Set realistic goals or make plans independently of others					
D.	Deal with stress of semiskilled and skilled work					

(E) Explain limitations falling in the three most limited categories (identified by **bold type)** and include the medical/clinical findings that support this assessment:

III.	MENTAL ABILITIES AND APTITUDE NEEDED TO DO PARTICULAR TYPES OF JOBS	Unlimited or Very Good	Limited but satisfactory	**Seriously limited**	**Unable to meet competitive standards**	**No useful ability to function**
A.	Interact appropriately with the general public					
B.	Maintain socially appropriate behavior					
C.	Adhere to basic standards of neatness and cleanliness					
D.	Travel in unfamiliar place					
E.	Use public transportation					

(F) Explain limitations falling in the three most limited categories (identified by **bold type)** and include the medical/clinical findings that support this assessment:

13. Rate the degree of your patient's expected limitations in a work setting using the following scale:

- **Moderate** means the ability to function independently, appropriately, effectively, and on a sustained basis is **fair**;
- **Marked** means the ability to function independently, appropriately, effectively, and on a sustained basis is **seriously limited**;
- **Extreme** means **not able** to function independently, appropriately, effectively, and on a sustained basis, but it does not mean a total loss of ability to function.

RATE THE DEGREE OF LIMITATION IN THE FOLLOWING AREAS:					
A.1.	Understanding information:	None-Mild	Moderate	Marked	Extreme
A.2.	Remembering information	None-Mild	Moderate	Marked	Extreme
A.3.	Applying information	None-Mild	Moderate	Marked	Extreme
B.	Interacting with others:	None Mild	Moderate	Marked	Extreme
C.1.	Concentrating	None Mild	Moderate	Marked	Extreme
C.2.	Persisting	None Mild	Moderate	Marked	Extreme
C.3	Maintaining pace	None Mild	Moderate	Marked	Extreme
D.1.	Adapting in the workplace	None Mild	Moderate	Marked	Extreme
D.2.	Managing oneself in the workplace	None Mild	Moderate	Marked	Extreme

14. If your patient has a neurocognitive disorder; schizophrenia or other psychotic disorder; depressive, bipolar or related disorder; anxiety or obsessive compulsive disorder; or trauma or stress-related disorder, please indicate if any of the following apply to your patient:

1. □ Your patient's chronic mental disorder is "serious and persistent;" that is, your patient has a medically documented history of the existence of the disorder over a period of at least 2 years.

2. □ Your patient relies on ongoing medical treatment, mental health therapy, psychosocial support, or a highly-structured setting to diminish the symptoms and signs of his or her mental disorder.

3. □ Despite your patient's diminished symptoms and signs, your patient has only marginal adjustment, that is, your patient has minimal capacity to adapt to changes in his or her environment or to demands that are not already part of daily life.

15. Please describe your patient's ability to perform the following activities at a regular job on a sustained (8 hours per day, 5 days a week) basis:

a. Maximum ability to lift and carry on an **occasional** basis (no more than 1/3 of an 8-hour day).

☐ No limitation ☐100# ☐50# ☐20# ☐10# ☐less than 10#

b. Maximum ability to lift and carry on a **frequent** basis (1/3 to 2/3 of an 8-hour day).

☐ No limitation ☐50# ☐25# ☐10# ☐less than 10#

c. Maximum ability to stand and walk (with normal breaks) during an 8-hour day.

☐ No limitation ☐ about 6 hours ☐ about 4 hours ☐ about 3 hours ☐about 2 hours ☐ less than 2 hours

d. Maximum ability to sit (with normal breaks) during an 8-hour day.

☐ No limitation ☐ about 6 hours ☐ about 4 hours ☐ about 3 hours ☐ about 2 hours ☐ less than 2 hours

16. Must your patient periodically alternate sitting, standing, or walking to relieve discomfort?
☐ Yes ☐ No

If yes, please answer the following:

a) How long can your patient **sit** before changing position? 0 5 10 15 20 30 45 60 90 Minutes

b) How long can your patient **stand** before changing position? 0 5 10 15 20 30 45 60 90 Minutes

c) How often must your patient **walk around**? Frequency: 0 5 10 15 20 30 45 60 90 Minutes

d) How long must your patient **walk each time**? Duration: 0 5 10 15 20 30 45 60 90 Minutes

e) Does your patient need the opportunity to shift **at will** from sitting or standing/walking?
☐ Yes ☐ No

17. Will your patient sometimes need to lie down at unpredictable intervals during a work shift?
☐ Yes ☐ No

If yes, please answer the following:

a) How often do you think this will happen? ____________

b) How long will your patient need to be away from the work station each time? ____________

18. Please describe any other limitations (such as limitations in doing repetitive reaching, handling or fingering, difficulty hearing, need to avoid temperature extremes, wetness, humidity, noise, dust, fumes, gases or hazards, etc.) that would affect your patient's ability to work at a regular job on a sustained basis.

19. Can your patient manage benefits in his or her own best interest? □ Yes □ No

____________________ ________________________
Date *Signature*

Printed/Typed Name: ________________________

Address: ________________________

____

____

248-1
1/17
7-77

§250 Pain and Other Symptoms and Their Impact on Residual Functional Capacity

For claimants whose impairments do not meet or equal an impairment found in SSA's Listing of Impairments, disability cases are about *symptoms*. Symptoms—pain, fatigue, dizziness, nervousness, shortness of breath, etc.—keep claimants from doing past relevant work and other work. It is symptoms that make claimants disabled.

Many SSA decision makers, on the other hand, may tell you that *all* disability cases, not only those where claimants' impairments meet or equal the Listings, are really about objective medical evidence. They say that objective medical evidence is the most important category of evidence. Objective medical evidence is what they look to first to figure out if a claimant is disabled. Many SSA decision makers decide cases as if objective medical evidence were required to show the *degree* of symptoms alleged by a claimant or that a claimant could be denied solely because objective evidence does not substantiate the claimant's statements about symptoms. Indeed, as we shall see, many SSA decision makers give objective medical an importance in their decisions beyond that which is required by the Social Security Act and regulations.

The Social Security Act and regulations require only that objective medical evidence show that the claimant has a medically determinable impairment, which *could cause* the sort of symptom alleged by the claimant. Although SSA regulations require that a claimant's limitations be *consistent with* objective medical evidence, they also require consistency with all other evidence in the record. Thus, the importance of objective medical evidence is not elevated above the importance of other evidence in the record. And a requirement that limitations be *consistent with* objective evidence is vastly different from requiring objective evidence to support the *degree* of impairment. The regulations require that a claimant's statements about symptoms not be rejected solely because objective evidence does not substantiate them.

SSA's symptom regulation is summarized in 20 C.F.R. § 404.1529(a) as follows:

> (a) *General.* In determining whether you are disabled, we consider all your symptoms, including pain, and the extent to which your symptoms can reasonably be accepted as consistent with the objective medical evidence and other evidence. By objective medical evidence, we mean medical signs and laboratory findings as defined in § 404.1528 (b) and (c). By other evidence, we mean the kinds of evidence described in §§ 404.1512(b)(2) through (8) and 404.1513(b)(1), (4), and (5), and (d). These include statements or reports from you, your treating or nontreating source, and others about your medical history, diagnosis, prescribed treatment, daily activities, efforts to work, and any other evidence showing how your impairment(s) and any related symptoms affect your ability to work. We will consider all of your statements about your symptoms, such as pain, and any description you, your treating source or nontreating source, or other persons may provide about how the symptoms affect your activities of daily living and your ability to work. However, statements about your pain or other symptoms will not alone establish that you are disabled; there must be medical signs and laboratory findings which show that you have a medical impairment(s) which could reasonably be expected to produce the pain or other symptoms alleged and which, when considered with all of the other evidence (including statements about the intensity and persistence of your pain or other symptoms which may reasonably be accepted as consistent with the medical signs and laboratory findings), would lead to a conclusion that you are disabled. In evaluating the intensity and persistence of your symptoms, including pain, we will consider all of the available evidence, including your medical history, the medical signs and laboratory findings and statements about how your symptoms affect you. (Section 404.1527 explains how we consider opinions of your treating source and other medical opinions on the existence and severity of your symptoms, such as pain.) We will then determine the extent to which your alleged functional limitations and restrictions due to pain or other symptoms can reasonably be accepted as consistent with the medical signs and laboratory findings and other evidence to decide how your symptoms affect your ability to work.

This regulation provides a two-step test for evaluating any symptom. At the first step, there must be objective evidence of some sort showing the claimant has a "medically determinable impairment" that could cause the symptom. To satisfy this first step, if the claimant alleges pain, there must be a medically determinable impairment that could cause some pain, any pain. This first-step finding does not address the "intensity, persistence, or functionally limiting effects" of the symptom. 20 C.F.R. § 404.1529(b). That comes later.

At the first step, a mere allegation of pain or other symptoms is insufficient. The claimant must have a medically determinable impairment "which could reasonably be expected to produce the pain or other symptoms alleged." 20 C.F.R. § 404.1529(b). This threshold requirement, which we will discuss in more detail in §253, is the only point where objective medical evidence is absolutely required.

At the second step, the determination as to the intensity, persistence and functionally limiting effects of pain or other symptoms is made. For this, the decision maker must evaluate the evidence in the record *as a whole*. 20 C.F.R. § 404.1529(c). At the second step objective evidence of the *degree* of symptoms is not required. All the evidence must be evaluated, including the objective medical evidence. So while objective medical evidence does not drop out of consideration for the second step, a claimant's allegations about symptoms may not be discredited *solely* because they are not substantiated by objective evidence. Nevertheless, allegations about symptoms need not be accepted to the extent they are inconsistent with the available evidence, including objective evidence of the underlying impairment.

The difference between the first step and the second step is the difference between "could cause" the alleged symptom (step 1) and "does cause" the alleged symptom (step 2).

Once you have shown that the claimant does have the alleged symptom, your job is not finished. Proving that someone has symptoms, of course, is not an end in itself. Because symptoms reduce a claimant's capacity for work, any discussion of symptoms must therefore include a discussion of symptoms' effect on residual functional capacity (RFC). *See* §258. And any discussion of RFC must include weighing medical opinions (*see* §256) and evaluating a claimant's symptoms. *See* §257.

Before we look at these issues, we will look at the role of pain in SSA's five-step sequential evaluation process for evaluating disability at step 2—the severity step—and step 3—whether a claimant's impairments meet or equal an impairment in SSA's Listing of Impairments.

§251 Symptoms and the Severity Step

The severity step of the sequential evaluation process (*see* 20 C.F.R. § 404.1520(c) and §114 of this book), which existed before the symptom regulation, initially required that the claimant have a medically determinable impairment that imposed more than minor limitations on the ability to work. The symptom regulation added the additional requirement that the medically determinable impairment could cause the claimant's symptoms, which is discussed in detail at §253.

The symptom regulation also addressed the issue of how the adjudicator evaluates symptoms when trying to figure out if an impairment is severe. That is, when determining whether an impairment significantly limits a claimant's physical or mental ability to do basic work activities, does the adjudicator consider the symptoms? Or is step 2 purely an objective evaluation?

At the severity step of the sequential evaluation process, subjective symptoms must be considered in determining whether an otherwise medically determinable impairment significantly limits a claimant's physical or mental ability to do basic work activities. 20 C.F.R. § 404.1529(d)(1). SSR 96-3p provides: "If the adjudicator finds that such symptoms cause a limitation or restriction having more than a minimal effect on an individual's ability to do basic work activities, the adjudicator must find that the impairment(s) is severe and proceed to the next step in the process even if the objective medical evidence would not in itself establish that the impairment(s) is severe."

Close cases are resolved in a claimant's favor. SSR 96-3p says that "if, after completing development and considering all of the evidence, the adjudicator is unable to determine clearly the effect of an impairment(s) on the individual's ability to do basic work activities, the adjudicator must continue to follow the sequential evaluation process until a determination or decision about disability can be reached."

§252 Symptoms and the Listing of Impairments

When pain is required to meet the Listings, any pain will do. If any symptom is a criterion for meeting a Listing, all that is required is that the symptom be present. "It is not necessary, unless the listing specifically states otherwise, to provide information about the intensity, persistence, or limiting effects of the symptom as long as all other findings required by the specific listing are present." 20 C.F.R. § 404.1529(d)(2).

The regulation also states that a claimant cannot use intense pain as a substitute for "a missing or deficient sign or laboratory finding to raise the severity of" the claimant's impairments to equal one of the impairments found in the Listing of Impairments. 20 C.F.R. § 404.1529(d)(3).

§253 A Medically Determinable Impairment that Could Cause the Claimant's Symptoms

To be found disabled, the Social Security Act requires a claimant to be "under a disability." 42 U.S.C. § 423(a)(l). That term is defined in § 423(d)(l)(A) as "inability to engage in any substantial gainful activity by reason of any medically determinable physical or mental impairment" of required duration. 42 U.S.C. § 423(d)(3) requires that a physical or mental impairment be "an impairment that results from anatomical, physiological or psychological abnormalities which are demonstrable by medically acceptable clinical and laboratory diagnostic techniques."

The Social Security Act also provides at 42 U.S.C. § 423(d)(5)(A):

> An individual's statement as to pain or other symptoms shall not alone be conclusive evidence of disability as defined in this section; there must be medical signs and findings, established by medically acceptable clinical or laboratory diagnostic techniques, which show the existence of a medical impairment that results from anatomical, physiological, or psychological abnormalities which could reasonably be expected to produce the pain or other symptoms alleged and which, when considered with all evidence required to be furnished under this paragraph (including statements of the individual or his physician as to the intensity and persistence of such pain or other symptoms which may reasonably be accepted as consistent with the medical signs and findings), would lead to a conclusion that the individual is under a disability. Objective medical evidence of pain or other symptoms established by medically acceptable clinical or laboratory techniques (for example, deteriorating nerve or muscle tissue) must be considered in reaching a conclusion as to whether the individual is under a disability.

20 C.F.R. § 404.1529(b) includes the requirement from the Social Security Act:

> (b) *Need for medically determinable impairment that could reasonably be expected to produce your symptoms, such as pain.* Your symptoms, such as pain, fatigue, shortness of breath, weakness, or nervousness, will not be found to affect your ability to do basic work activities unless medical signs or laboratory findings show that a medically determinable impairment(s) is present. Medical signs and laboratory findings, established by medically acceptable clinical or laboratory diagnostic techniques, must show the existence of a medical impairment(s) which results from anatomical, physiological, or psychological abnormalities and which could reasonably be expected to produce the pain or other symptoms alleged. In cases decided by a State agency (except in disability hearings under §§ 404.914 through 404.918 of this part and in fully favorable determinations made by State agency disability examiners alone under § 404.1615(c)(3) of this part), a State agency medical or psychological consultant or other medical or psychological consultant designated by the Commissioner, directly participates in determining whether your medically determinable impairment(s) could reasonably be expected to produce your alleged symptoms. In the disability hearing process, a medical or psychological consultant may provide an advisory assessment to assist a disability hearing officer in determining whether your impairment(s) could reasonably be expected to produce your alleged symptoms. At the administrative law judge hearing or Appeals Council level of the administrative review process, the adjudicator(s) may ask for and consider the opinion of a medical or psychological expert concerning whether your impairment(s) could reasonably be expected to produce your alleged symptoms. The finding that your impairment(s) could reasonably be expected to produce your pain or other symptoms does not involve a determination as to the intensity, persistence, or functionally limiting effects of your symptoms. We will develop evidence regarding the possibility of a medically determinable mental impairment when we have information to suggest that such an impairment exists, and you allege pain or other symptoms but the medical signs and laboratory findings do not substantiate any physical impairment(s) capable of producing the pain or other symptoms.

It is useful in our analysis to take a look at the definitions of symptoms and signs, which appear in 20 C.F.R. § 404.1528 as follows:

> (a) *Symptoms* are your own description of your physical or mental impairment. Your statements alone are not enough to establish that there is a physical or mental impairment.
>
> (b) *Signs* are anatomical, physiological, or psychological abnormalities which can be observed, apart from your statements (symptoms). Signs must be shown by medically acceptable clinical diagnostic techniques. Psychiatric signs are medically demonstrable phenomena that indicate specific psychological abnormalities, e.g., abnormalities of behavior, mood, thought, memory, orientation, development, or perception. They must also be shown by observable facts that can be medically described and evaluated.

SSR 96-4p states that "under no circumstances may the existence of an impairment be established on the basis of symptoms alone. Thus, regardless of how many symptoms an individual alleges, or how genuine the individual's complaints may appear to be, the existence of a medically determinable physical or mental impairment cannot be established in the absence of objective medical abnormalities; i.e., medical signs and laboratory findings."

Nevertheless, there are situations where it is difficult to tell if something is a symptom or a sign. A doctor's observation of psychiatric symptoms, including the patient's own description of symptoms, may be signs of psychiatric illness. *See* 20 C.F.R. § 404.1528(b).

Sometimes doctors regard a description of a group of physical symptoms to constitute signs of an impairment. SSA's rules allow for this. SSR 96-4p provides in footnote 2: "20 CFR 404.1528, 404.1529, 416.928, and 416.929 provide that symptoms, such as pain, fatigue, shortness of breath, weakness or nervousness, are an individual's own perception or description of the impact of his or her physical or mental impairment(s). . . . However, when any of these manifestations is an anatomical, physiological, or psychological abnormality that can be shown by medically acceptable clinical diagnostic techniques, it represents a medical 'sign' rather than a 'symptom.'"

When an ALJ questioned whether fibromyalgia and chronic fatigue syndrome were medically determinable impairments, SSA's response, in part, relied on SSR 96-4p, footnote 2:

> Your argument based on the Rulings seems to misinterpret the explanation in Footnote 2 to SSR 96-4p, which explains our longstanding policy, consistent with 20 CFR §§ 404.1528(b) and 416.928(b), that some symptoms, when appropriately reported by a physician or psychologist in a clinical setting, can also be considered "signs" because sometimes these observations constitute "medically acceptable clinical diagnostic techniques." This is true for mental impairments in general and for such widely accepted and recognizable disorders as migraine headaches.

See the Daniels memorandum reprinted in Appendix 13 of this book. *Also see* SSR 12-2p, titled Evaluation of Fibromyalgia, which uses the same approach noting in footnote 9 that some "somatic symptoms" were considered to be "signs" under 20 C.F.R. § 404.1528(b).

SSA tends to follow generally accepted medical practice when it decides whether certain impairments are medically determinable. This is what the Daniels memorandum does with fibromyalgia:

> Fibromyalgia is a disorder defined by the American College of Rheumatology (ACR) and we recognize it as medically determinable if there are signs that are clinically established by the medical record. The signs are primarily the tender points. The ACR defines the disorder in patients as "widespread pain in all four quadrants of the body for a minimum duration of 3 months and at least 11 of the 18 specified tender points which cluster around the neck and shoulder, chest, hip, knee, and elbow regions." Other typical symptoms, some of which can be signs if they have been clinically documented over time, are irritable bowel syndrome, chronic headaches, temporomandibular joint dysfunction, sleep disorder, severe fatigue, and cognitive dysfunction.

In SSR 12-2p, SSA adopted an alternative diagnostic criteria for fibromyalgia published in 2010 by the American College of Rheumatology that is not based on tender points. The alternative criteria is based on co-occurring conditions and symptoms, some of which SSA considers to be signs.

In a series of Social Security rulings addressing impairments that have few objective findings, SSA sets forth its criteria for deciding whether an impairment is medically determinable:

- SSR 02-2p Evaluation of Interstitial Cystitis
- SSR 03-1p Development and Evaluation of Disability Claims Involving Postpolio Sequelae
- SSR 03-2p Evaluating Cases Involving Reflex Sympathetic Dystrophy Syndrome/Complex Regional Pain Syndrome
- SSR 06-1p Evaluating Cases Involving Tremolite Asbestos-Related Impairments
- SSR 12-2p Evaluation of Fibromyalgia
- SSR 14-1p Evaluating Cases Involving Chronic Fatigue Syndrome (CFS)

Sometimes you will see a case in which medical signs or laboratory findings show abnormalities but doctors cannot agree on a specific diagnosis. The Daniels memorandum, Appendix 13, makes the important point that a specific diagnosis is unnecessary:

> Establishing the existence of a medically determinable impairment does not necessarily require that the claimant or the medical evidence establish a specific diagnosis. This is especially true when the medical community has not reached agreement on a single set of diagnostic criteria. All the Act and regulations require is that some physical or mental impairment be established through medically acceptable clinical and laboratory diagnostic techniques. In some cases, the record may not establish the diagnosis, but there will be medical signs established by medically acceptable clinical techniques that show that there is an impairment, and that there is a relationship between the findings and the symptoms alleged; i.e., that the

existence of a medically determinable impairment that could reasonably be expected to produce the symptoms has been established.

Remember, the determination at this point in the analysis is whether the medically determinable impairment could cause *any* pain, not whether it could cause pain in the degree alleged. In other words, once adjudicators determine that an impairment could "produce some pain, they must consider all of the evidence relevant to the individual's allegations of pain, even if the alleged pain is more severe or persistent than would be expected." *See* 56 Fed. Reg. 57932 (1991), which explained the symptom regulation when it was promulgated in 1991. The finding that the claimant's medically determinable impairment "could reasonably be expected to produce your pain or other symptoms does not involve a determination as to the intensity, persistence, or functionally limiting effects of your symptoms." 20 C.F.R. § 404.1529(b). That determination comes later in the analysis when *everything* is considered. See below.

§254 Evaluating the Intensity and Persistence of Symptoms — The Role of Objective Evidence and Other Evidence

20 C.F.R. § 404.1529(c)(1) provides:

(c) *Evaluating the intensity and persistence of your symptoms, such as pain, and determining the extent to which your symptoms limit your capacity for work*—(1) *General.* When the medical signs or laboratory findings show that you have a medically determinable impairment(s) that could reasonably be expected to produce your symptoms, such as pain, we must then evaluate the intensity and persistence of your symptoms so that we can determine how your symptoms limit your capacity for work. In evaluating the intensity and persistence of your symptoms, we consider all of the available evidence, including your history, the signs and laboratory findings, and statements from you, your treating or nontreating source, or other persons about how your symptoms affect you. We also consider the medical opinions of your treating source and other medical opinions as explained in § 404.1527. Paragraphs (c)(2) through (c)(4) of this section explain further how we evaluate the intensity and persistence of your symptoms and how we determine the extent to which your symptoms limit your capacity for work, when the medical signs or laboratory findings show that you have a medically determinable impairment(s) that could reasonably be expected to produce your symptoms, such as pain.

At the time the symptom regulation was promulgated, SSA stated: "We do not require objective medical evidence to establish a direct cause and effect relationship between the individual's medically determinable impairment and the intensity, persistence, or functional effects of his or her symptoms, nor do we disregard the individual's allegations about his or her symptoms simply because the allegations are not fully corroborated by objective medical evidence." 56 Fed. Reg. 57932 (1991). "We recognize that individuals with the same impairment may experience different levels of pain." 56 Fed. Reg. 57933 (1991).

Objective Evidence
20 C.F.R. § 404.1529(c)(2) provides:

Consideration of objective medical evidence. Objective medical evidence is evidence obtained from the application of medically acceptable clinical and laboratory diagnostic techniques, such as evidence of reduced joint motion, muscle spasm, sensory deficit or motor disruption. Objective medical evidence of this type is a useful indicator to assist us in making reasonable conclusions about the intensity and persistence of your symptoms and the effect those symptoms, such as pain, may have on your ability to work. We must always attempt to obtain objective medical evidence and, when it is obtained, we will consider it in reaching a conclusion as to whether you are disabled. However, we will not reject your statements about the intensity and persistence of your pain or other symptoms or about the effect your symptoms have on your ability to work solely because the available objective medical evidence does not substantiate your statements.

At the time the symptom regulation was promulgated, SSA stated, "we agree that not all painful conditions will produce muscle spasm, reduced joint motion, or sensory and motor disruption. We also agree that objective medical evidence from which we can draw reasonable conclusions about the intensity, persistence, or functional effects of alleged symptoms may not be available in all cases." 56 Fed. Reg. 57934 (1991).

Objective medical evidence alone does not direct a conclusion about the intensity of symptoms unless it is in the claimant's favor. SSR 16-3p provides: "We will not evaluate an individual's symptoms based solely on objective medical evidence unless that objective medical evidence supports a finding that the individual is disabled."

Practice Tip

When you are analyzing a case, be sure to pay attention to the clinical findings that SSA says show that a claimant is in pain—reduced joint motion, muscle spasm, sensory or motor disruption. 20 C.F.R. § 404.1529(c)(2). These findings can form the basis of an argument that a favorable decision should be issued based solely on the objective evidence.

Other Evidence
20 C.F.R. § 404.1529(c)(3) provides:

> *Consideration of other evidence.* Since symptoms sometimes suggest a greater severity of impairment than can be shown by objective medical evidence alone, we will carefully consider any other information you may submit about your symptoms. The information that you, your treating or nontreating source, or other persons provide about your pain or other symptoms (e.g., what may precipitate or aggravate your symptoms, what medications, treatments or other methods you use to alleviate them, and how the symptoms may affect your pattern of daily living) is also an important indicator of the intensity and persistence of your symptoms. Because symptoms, such as pain, are subjective and difficult to quantify, any symptom-related functional limitations and restrictions which you, your treating or nontreating source, or other persons report, which can reasonably be accepted as consistent with the objective medical evidence and other evidence, will be taken into account as explained in paragraph (c)(4) of this section in reaching a conclusion as to whether you are disabled. We will consider all of the evidence presented, including information about your prior work record, your statements about your symptoms, evidence submitted by your treating or nontreating source, and observations by our employees and other persons. Section 404.1527 explains in detail how we consider and weigh treating source and other medical opinions about the nature and severity of your impairment(s) and any related symptoms, such as pain. Factors relevant to your symptoms, such as pain, which we will consider include:
>
> (i) Your daily activities;
>
> (ii) The location, duration, frequency, and intensity of your pain or other symptoms;
>
> (iii) Precipitating and aggravating factors;
>
> (iv) The type, dosage, effectiveness, and side effects of any medication you take or have taken to alleviate your pain or other symptoms;
>
> (v) Treatment, other than medication, you receive or have received for relief of your pain or other symptoms;
>
> (vi) Any measures you use or have used to relieve your pain or other symptoms (e.g., lying flat on your back, standing for 15 to 20 minutes every hour, sleeping on a board, etc.); and
>
> (vii) Other factors concerning your functional limitations and restrictions due to pain or other symptoms.

Some judges erroneously approach evaluating disability as if it primarily involved evaluating objective evidence—signs and laboratory findings that are described in 20 C.F.R. § 404.1528(b) and (c). While it is true that a decision maker must evaluate the extent to which a claimant's "symptoms can reasonably be accepted as consistent with the objective medical evidence," the regulation adds this important phrase "and other evidence." 20 C.F.R. § 404.1529(a). The regulation specifically refers to regulations that describe "other evidence" including 20 C.F.R. §§ 404.1512(b)(2) through (6). It is useful to take a look at 20 C.F.R. § 404.1512(b):

> (b) *What we mean by "evidence."* Evidence is anything you or anyone else submits to us or that we obtain that relates to your claim. This includes, but is not limited to:
>
> (1) Objective medical evidence, that is, medical signs and laboratory findings as defined in § 404.1528 (b) and (c);
>
> (2) Other evidence from medical sources, such as medical history, opinions, and statements about treatment you have received;
>
> (3) Statements you or others make about your impairment(s), your restrictions, your daily activities, your efforts to work, or any other relevant statements you make to medical sources during the course of examination or treatment, or to us

during interviews, on applications, in letters, and in testimony in our administrative proceedings;

(4) Information from other sources, as described in § 404.1513(d);

(5) Decisions by any governmental or nongovernmental agency about whether you are disabled or blind; [and]

. . .

(8) At the administrative law judge and Appeals Council levels, findings, other than the ultimate determination about whether you are disabled, made by State agency medical or psychological consultants and other program physicians or psychologists, or other medical specialists, and opinions expressed by medical experts or psychological experts that we consult based on their review of the evidence in your case record. *See* §§ 404.1527(e)(2)-(3).

The symptom regulation at 20 C.F.R. § 404.1529(a) also refers to § 404.1513(b)(1), (4), and (5), and (d), which provide:

(b) *Medical reports.* Medical reports should include—

(1) Medical history;

. . .

(4) Diagnosis (statement of disease or injury based on its signs and symptoms);

(5) Treatment prescribed with response, and prognosis; and

. . .

(d) *Other sources.* In addition to evidence from the acceptable medical sources listed in paragraph (a) of this section, we may also use evidence from other sources to show the severity of your impairment(s) and how it affects your ability to work. Other sources include, but are not limited to—

(1) Medical sources not listed in paragraph (a) of this section (for example, nurse-practitioners, physicians' assistants, naturopaths, chiropractors, audiologists, and therapists);

(2) Educational personnel (for example, school teachers, counselors, early intervention team members, developmental center workers, and daycare center workers);

(3) Public and private social welfare agency personnel; and

(4) Other non-medical sources (for example, spouses, parents and other caregivers, siblings, other relatives, friends, neighbors, and clergy).

In short, the "other evidence" in the symptom regulation that must be considered is *everything* other than objective evidence. Not only must this other evidence be considered, but the decision maker must evaluate the degree to which the claimant's symptoms are consistent with this other evidence.

The regulation sets up "other evidence" as equal to the objective evidence. Nothing in the regulations or rulings says that one is more important than the other. "Your symptoms, including pain, will be determined to diminish your capacity for basic work activities to the extent that your alleged functional limitations and restrictions due to symptoms, such as pain, can reasonably be accepted as consistent with the objective medical evidence *and other evidence*." 20 C.F.R. § 404.1529(c)(4), emphasis added.

§255 Issue: Is the Impairment Reasonably Consistent With the Objective Evidence?

The regulations state: "Because symptoms, such as pain, are subjective and difficult to quantify, any symptom-related functional limitations and restrictions which you, your treating or nontreating source, or other persons report, which can reasonably be accepted *as consistent with the objective medical evidence and other evidence*, will be taken into account...in reaching a conclusion as to whether you are disabled." 20 C.F.R. § 404.1529(c)(3), emphasis added. "Your symptoms, including pain, will be determined to diminish your capacity for basic work activities to the extent that your alleged functional limitations and restrictions due to symptoms, such as pain, *can reasonably be accepted as consistent with the objective medical evidence and other evidence*." 20 C.F.R. § 404.1529(c)(4), emphasis added.

Considering the wide variation in symptoms from similar impairments, it ought not to present an insurmountable obstacle in the usual case to demonstrate reasonable consistency between the objective evidence and the alleged symptoms. Most claimants present symptoms which are, in fact, reasonably consistent with the objective medical evidence. The claimants whose symptoms are not reasonably consistent with the objective medical evidence either 1) have an undiagnosed additional physical impairment, 2) need to have more medical tests exploring a diagnosed impairment, or 3) have an undiagnosed mental impairment that accounts for the alleged symptom. The only other possibility is that the claimant is malingering.

In the usual case it is the ALJ's job to weigh the medical opinions on the consistency of symptoms with the objective evidence; and it is, of course, the ALJ's job to examine the consistency of the alleged symptoms with other evidence in the record. But often the record contains no medical opinion whatsoever on whether or not the alleged symptoms are reasonably consistent with the objective medical evidence. Although some ALJs may take upon themselves the task of assessing the degree to which symptoms are reasonably consistent with the objective evidence, this evaluation often requires a medical opinion. (The occasional case is so obvious that no medical opinion is necessary.) It is up to you as the claimant's attorney to be sure the record contains such opinion evidence in support of your client's claim. For this reason, all of the medical source statement forms in this book ask if symptoms and limitations described by the doctor are reasonably consistent with the claimant's impairments.

Where there is a void on this issue, a simple form such as the one at §255.1 may suffice. (This form also may be sent to doctors who resist describing a patient's capacity for performing work-related activities, saying such opinions are outside their area of expertise. For example, consider a claimant who says she is limited to standing and walking no more than two hours out of eight. Some doctors may say they do not know how many hours per day this patient can stand and walk but they are willing to say that the patient's allegation is reasonably consistent with the objective evidence.)

Where there is already a medical opinion in the record that raises a question about the degree to which a claimant's symptoms are consistent with the objective evidence, it may be necessary for the treating doctor to address this issue in more detail.

Questions for the treating doctor include:

- What factors indicate that the claimant's symptoms are reasonably consistent with the objective evidence?
- Has the objective evidence been correctly analyzed by SSA's doctor?
- Why does the treating doctor *not* conclude that the claimant is malingering?
- Has the treating doctor seen patients with similar objective findings who describe similar symptoms?
- What is the range of symptoms which could be described as reasonably consistent with the objective evidence in this case?
- Are there additional indicia of reliability (other than the objective medical evidence) that lend credence to the claimant's description of symptoms?
- Are there personality factors that help explain any possible discrepancy between symptoms and objective evidence?
- Is there a "functional overlay"?
- Is there depression, anxiety or any other mental impairment that may enhance the claimant's symptoms?
- If the claimant's symptoms really are inconsistent with the objective medical evidence, is there the possibility of a somatoform disorder?

§255.1 Form: Doctor's Opinion Re: Consistency of Symptoms and Limitations

From: ______________________

Re: ______________________ (Name of patient)

______________________ (Date of Birth)

In medical reports previously prepared by you or other physicians which are on file with the Social Security Administration, the following findings and diagnoses were made:

Recognizing that an impairment may affect individuals differently, please state whether your patient's symptoms and limitations are *reasonably consistent* with the medical signs and findings.

The patient reports the following symptoms and limitations:

Are these symptoms and limitations *reasonably consistent* with the medical signs and findings?

1. ____ Yes ___ No

2. ____ Yes ___ No

3. ____ Yes ___ No

4. ____ Yes ___ No

5. ____ Yes ___ No

____
Date

____
Signature

Printed/Typed Name: ______________________

Address: ______________________

____

____

§256 Evaluation of Medical Opinions

As explained in §253, only when the medical signs and laboratory findings show that the claimant has a medically determinable impairment that could reasonably be expected to produce the type of symptoms alleged, such as pain, does SSA evaluate the intensity and persistence of the symptoms and how they limit the capacity for work. In evaluating the intensity and persistence of symptoms, SSA must consider all available evidence. This includes the claimant's medical history, the medical signs and laboratory findings, and statements from the claimant, treating or examining physicians or psychologists, or other persons about how the symptoms affect the claimant. SSA also must consider medical opinions of the treating doctors and other medical opinions as explained in 20 C.F.R. § 404.1527. The question is, how much do the claimant's symptoms reduce the claimant's ability to work? Evidence evaluating the intensity and persistence of symptoms is necessary in determining a claimant's residual functional capacity (RFC). SSA will look first to the claimant's treating doctor (whom SSA calls a "treating source") for an opinion. SSA has recognized that such opinions have a special intrinsic value by virtue of the treating source's relationship with the claimant.

SSA's regulation on weighing medical opinions, 20 C.F.R. § 404.1527, recognizes that because opinions always have a subjective component, the effects of medical conditions on individuals vary so widely, and no two cases are ever exactly alike, it is not possible to create rules that prescribe the weight to be given to each piece of evidence that SSA considers in every case. This regulation also recognizes that the weighing of any evidence, including opinions, is a process of comparing the intrinsic value, persuasiveness, and internal consistency of each piece of evidence and then evaluating all of the evidence together to determine which findings of fact are best supported by all of the evidence.

The key factors in weighing medical opinions found in 20 C.F.R. § 404.1527 are the following:

- Regardless of its source, SSA will evaluate every medical opinion it receives.
- Generally, SSA gives **more weight to the opinion of a source who has examined the claimant** than to the opinion of a source who has not examined the claimant. SSR 96-6p notes that the "regulations provide progressively more rigorous tests for weighing opinions as the ties between the source of the opinion and the individual become weaker."
- Generally, SSA gives **more weight to opinions from treating sources** (as defined in 20 C.F.R. § 404.1502) because these sources are likely to be the medical professionals most able to provide a detailed, longitudinal picture of the claimant's medical impairments and may bring a unique perspective to the medical evidence that cannot be obtained from the objective medical findings alone or from reports of individual examinations.
- If a treating source's opinion on the issues of the nature and severity of the claimant's impairments is well-supported by the medically acceptable clinical and laboratory diagnostic techniques and is not inconsistent with the other substantial evidence in the case record, SSA will give it **controlling weight**. 20 C.F.R. § 404.1527(c)(2). This means it is dispositive on the issues of the nature and severity of the impairments. SSA has devoted the entire Social Security Rulings 96-2p to the issue of giving controlling weight to treating source medical opinions in order, it says, to emphasize the following:

1. A case cannot be decided in reliance on a medical opinion without some reasonable support for the opinion.
2. Controlling weight may be given only in appropriate circumstances to medical opinions, i.e., opinions on the issue of the nature and severity of an individual's impairment, from treating sources.
3. Controlling weight may not be given to a treating source's medical opinion unless the opinion is well-supported by medically acceptable clinical and laboratory diagnostic techniques.
4. Even if a treating source's medical opinion is well-supported, controlling weight may not be given to the opinion unless it also is "not inconsistent" with the other substantial evidence in the case record. 20 C.F.R. § 404.1527(c)(2) and SSR 96-2p.
5. The judgment whether a treating source's medical opinion is well-supported and not inconsistent with the other substantial evidence in the case record requires an understanding of the clinical signs and laboratory findings and what they signify. SSR 96-2p.
6. If a treating source's medical opinion is well-supported and not inconsistent with the other substantial evidence in the case record, it *must* be given controlling weight; i.e., it must be adopted. 20 C.F.R. § 404.1527(c)(2) and SSR 96-2p.
7. A finding that a treating source's medical opinion is not entitled to controlling weight does not mean that the opinion is rejected. It may still be entitled to deference and be adopted by the adjudicator.

- SSA is supposed to give **good reasons in the decision for the weight it gives the treating sources opinion**. 20 C.F.R. § 404.1527(c)(2).
- When SSA does not give a treating physician's opinion on the nature and severity of the impairments

controlling weight, it applies the factors listed below in **determining the weight** to give the opinion:

1. **Length of the Treating Relationship and the Frequency of Examination.** Generally, the longer a treating source has treated a claimant and the more times he or she has been seen, the more weight SSA will give to that source's medical opinion. 20 C.F.R. § 404.1527(c)(2)(i).
2. **Nature and Extent of the Treatment Relationship.** Generally, the more knowledge a treating source has about the claimant's impairment, the more weight SSA will give that source's medical opinion. 20 C.F.R. § 404.1527(c)(2)(ii).
3. **Supportability.** The more a medical source presents relevant evidence to support an opinion, particularly medical signs and laboratory findings, the more weight SSA will give that opinion. 20 C.F.R. § 404.1527(c)(3).
4. **Consistency.** Generally, the more consistent an opinion is with the record as a whole, the more weight SSA will give to that opinion. 20 C.F.R. § 404.1527(c)(4).
5. **Specialization.** SSA generally gives more weight to the opinion of a specialist about medical issues related to the area of the specialty than to the opinion of a source that is not a specialist. 20 C.F.R. § 404.1527(c)(5).
6. **Other Factors.** SSA considers other factors that tend to support or contradict a medical opinion. For example, this is meant to cover the situation where a physician or psychologist has been submitting identical medical reports for different individuals. This would clearly affect the weight SSA would give to any opinions expressed in those reports. 20 C.F.R. § 404.1527(c)(6).

- **Opinions that the Claimant is Disabled.** SSA says that it is responsible for making the decision about whether the claimant meets the statutory definition of disability. To do so it looks at all of the evidence that supports a medical source's statement as to disability. A statement that the claimant is disabled or is unable to work does not mean that SSA will determine that the claimant is disabled. 20 C.F.R. § 404.1527(d)(1).
- **Opinions on Certain Issues Reserved to the Commissioner.** Although SSA considers opinions from treating and examining sources on issues such as whether the impairment meets or equals the requirements of any impairment in the Listing of Impairments, residual functional capacity (e.g., a statement that the claimant is limited to light work), or the application of vocational factors, the final responsibility for deciding these issues is reserved to the Commissioner. SSA will not give any special significance to the source of the opinions on these issues. *See* 20 C.F.R. § 404.1527(d)(2) and SSR 96-5p.
- SSA considers all **evidence from nonexamining physicians and psychologists** (including medical experts) to be opinion evidence. It will evaluate every medical opinion it receives. 20 C.F.R. § 404.1527(e). SSA uses the same rules set forth in 20 C.F.R. § 404.1527(a) through (d) to evaluate these opinions.
- At the ALJ level, the ALJ is required to specifically **explain the weight accorded to a state agency medical consultant's opinion** if the ALJ determines that the opinion of a treating source is not to be given controlling weight. The opinions of state agency physicians are treated the same as opinions of other nonexamining physicians and psychologists and are evaluated using the same factors. 20 C.F.R. § 404.1527(e)(2).

As you can see from the above outline which is drawn from the regulations and SSR 96-2p, it will not be easy for an ALJ to reject an opinion of a treating doctor that is consistent with the claimant's allegations and consistent with other evidence in the record. Consistency and credibility are key issues in any disability case involving pain.

§257 Evaluating the Claimant's Symptoms

20 C.F.R. § 404.1529(c)(4) provides:

> How we determine the extent to which symptoms, such as pain, affect your capacity to perform basic work activities. In determining the extent to which your symptoms, such as pain, affect your capacity to perform basic work activities, we consider all of the available evidence described in paragraphs (c)(1) through (c)(3) of this section. We will consider your statements about the intensity, persistence, and limiting effects of your symptoms, and we will evaluate your statements in relation to the objective medical evidence and other evidence, in reaching a conclusion as to whether you are disabled. We will consider whether there are any inconsistencies in the evidence and the extent to which there are any conflicts between your statements and the rest of the evidence, including your history, the signs and laboratory findings, and statements by your medical sources or other persons about how your symptoms affect you. Your symptoms, including pain, will be determined to diminish your capacity for basic work activities to the extent that your alleged functional

> limitations and restrictions due to symptoms, such as pain, can reasonably be accepted as consistent with the objective medical evidence and other evidence.

Evaluation of a claimant's symptoms must be based on all the evidence including objective medical evidence and all other evidence. In the past pursuant to a now superseded ruling, SSA said that this evaluation involved making a credibility finding about the claimant's statements concerning symptoms even though the word "credibility" does not appear in the regulations or the Social Security Act. With the publication of SSR 16-3p, SSA abandoned use of the term "credibility" in what it calls its "sub-regulatory policy." SSA noted that the word "credibility" had been misinterpreted as requiring an examination of a claimant's character.

Once it is established that there is an underlying medically determinable impairment that could produce the claimant's symptoms, SSA will evaluate the intensity and persistence of those symptoms to determine the extent to which the symptoms limit an individual's ability to perform work-related activities." SSR 16-3p clarifies how SSA considers the following:

- The intensity, persistence, and functionally limiting effects of symptoms,
- Objective medical evidence when evaluating symptoms,
- Other evidence when evaluating symptoms,
- The factors set forth in 20 CFR 404.1529(c)(3) and 416.929(c)(3), [which is daily activities, etc., see § 254 above],
- The extent to which an individual's symptoms affect his or her ability to perform work-related activities or function independently, appropriately, and effectively in an age-appropriate manner for a child with a title XVI disability claim, and
- Adjudication standards for evaluating symptoms in the sequential evaluation process.

SSR 16-3p directs adjudicators to conduct a careful examination of the consistency of the claimant's statements, both internally and with other evidence in the case record. SSR 16-3p provides:

> We will consider statements an individual made to us at each prior step of the administrative review process, as well as statements the individual made in any subsequent or prior disability claims under titles II and XVI. If an individual's various statements about the intensity, persistence, and limiting effects of symptoms are consistent with one another and consistent with the objective medical evidence and other evidence in the record, we will determine that an individual's symptoms are more likely to reduce his or her capacities for work-related activities or reduce the abilities to function independently, appropriately, and effectively in an age-appropriate manner. However, inconsistencies in an individual's statements made at varying times does not necessarily mean they are inaccurate. Symptoms may vary in their intensity, persistence, and functional effects, or may worsen or improve with time. This may explain why an individual's statements vary when describing the intensity, persistence, or functional effects of symptoms.

Careful attention must be paid to the longitudinal medical record. SSA says that it "will consider an individual's attempts to seek medical treatment for symptoms and to follow treatment once it is prescribed when evaluating whether symptom intensity and persistence affect the ability to perform work-related activities...Persistent attempts to obtain relief of symptoms, such as increasing dosages and changing medications, trying a variety of treatments, referrals to specialists, or changing treatment sources may be an indication that an individual's symptoms are a source of distress and may show that they are intense and persistent." SSR 16-3p.

SSR 16-3p states:

> In contrast, if the frequency or extent of the treatment sought by an individual is not comparable with the degree of the individual's subjective complaints, or if the individual fails to follow prescribed treatment that might improve symptoms, we may find the alleged intensity and persistence of an individual's symptoms are inconsistent with the overall evidence of record. We will not find an individual's symptoms inconsistent with the evidence in the record on this basis without considering possible reasons he or she may not comply with treatment or seek treatment consistent with the degree of his or her complaints. We may need to contact the individual regarding the lack of treatment or, at an administrative proceeding, ask why he or she has not complied with or sought treatment in a manner consistent with his or her complaints.

SSR 16-3p also provides examples to illustrate possible reasons a claimant may not have pursued frequent treatment. A claimant may have structured daily activities to minimize symptoms. Symptoms may have plateaued. Side effects of medication may be less tolerable than the symptoms themselves. A claimant may not be able to afford treatment and may not have access to free or low cost medical treatment. A claimant's doctor may have said there was no further effective treatment. A claimant's religious beliefs may interfere with treatment. A claimant may not understand the need for consistent treatment. A claimant with a mental impairment "may not be aware that he or she has a disorder that requires treatment."

At the hearing, the best ALJs will ask the claimant about apparent inconsistencies in the record. When the judge does not ask about these things, it is up to you to give the claimant the opportunity to explain. Potential inconsistencies include such things as:

- Vacations or travel;
- Daily activities that are so poorly explained on the Function Report that they sound normal;
- Caring for others at home (for example, children, a disabled spouse, elderly parents);
- Overuse of prescribed drugs;
- Use of street drugs;
- Lack of treatment;
- Receipt of unemployment compensation benefits;
- Job searches;
- Attempts to work;
- How past jobs ended; and
- Hobbies (for example, hunting, motorcycle riding, golf).

SSR 16-3p states: "The determination or decision must contain specific reasons for the weight given to the individual's symptoms, be consistent with and supported by the evidence, and be clearly articulated so the individual and any subsequent reviewer can assess how the adjudicator evaluated the individual's symptoms."

§258 Impact of Symptoms on RFC

20 C.F.R. § 404.1529(c)(4), the same paragraph that explains evaluation of a claimant's symptoms, also explains how SSA determines a claimant's residual functional capacity. Basing the evaluation on the entire record, a claimant's "symptoms, including pain, will be determined to diminish [the claimant's] capacity for basic work activities to the extent that [the claimant's] alleged functional limitations and restrictions due to symptoms, such as pain, *can reasonably be accepted as consistent with the objective medical evidence and other evidence*." (Emphasis added.)Evaluating a claimant's symptoms and determining a claimant's residual functional capacity are based on the same principles.

20 C.F.R. § 404.1545, which deals with determining RFC, was amended at the same time the pain regulation was promulgated. 20 C.F.R. § 404.1545(e) provides:

> Pain or other symptoms may cause a limitation of function beyond that which can be determined on the basis of the anatomical, physiological, or psychological abnormalities considered alone; e.g., someone with a low back disorder may be fully capable of the physical demands consistent with those of sustained medium work activity, but another person with the same disorder, because of pain, may not be capable of more than the physical demands consistent with those of light work activity on a sustained basis.

This regulation should not be interpreted as limiting the choices of RFC for a back disorder to light or medium work. This is merely an example showing that two claimants with similar back disorders can have different RFCs.

Social Security Ruling 96-8p provides a detailed discussion of determining residual functional capacity. SSR 96-8p provides:

> The RFC assessment must be based on *all* of the relevant evidence in the case record, such as:
>
> - Medical history,
> - Medical signs and laboratory findings,
> - The effects of treatment, including limitations or restrictions imposed by the mechanics of treatment (e.g., frequency of treatment, duration, disruption to routine, side effects of medication),
> - Reports of daily activities,
> - Lay evidence,
> - Recorded observations,
> - Medical source statements,
> - Effects of symptoms, including pain, that are reasonably attributed to a medically determinable impairment,
> - Evidence from attempts to work,
> - Need for a structured living environment, and
> - Work evaluations, if available.

SSR 96-8p also sets forth narrative discussion requirements for the RFC assessment:

> The RFC assessment must include a narrative discussion describing how the evidence supports each conclusion, citing specific medical facts (e.g., laboratory findings) and nonmedical evidence (e.g., daily activities, observations). In assessing RFC, the adjudicator must discuss the individual's ability to perform sustained work activities in an ordinary work setting on a regular and continuing basis (i.e., 8 hours a day, for 5 days a week, or an equivalent work schedule), and describe the maximum amount of

each work-related activity the individual can perform based on the evidence available in the case record. The adjudicator must also explain how any material inconsistencies or ambiguities in the evidence in the case record were considered and resolved.

Symptoms. In all cases in which symptoms, such as pain, are alleged, the RFC assessment must:

- Contain a thorough discussion and analysis of the objective medical and other evidence, including the individual's complaints of pain and other symptoms and the adjudicator's personal observations, if appropriate;
- Include a resolution of any inconsistencies in the evidence as a whole; and
- Set forth a logical explanation of the effects of the symptoms, including pain, on the individual's ability to work.

The RFC assessment must include a discussion of why reported symptom-related functional limitations and restrictions can or cannot reasonably be accepted as consistent with the medical and other evidence. In instances in which the adjudicator has observed the individual, he or she is not free to accept or reject that individual's complaints *solely* on the basis of such personal observations.

Medical opinions. The RFC assessment must always consider and address medical source opinions. If the RFC assessment conflicts with an opinion from a medical source, the adjudicator must explain why the opinion was not adopted.

Medical opinions from treating sources about the nature and severity of an individual's impairment(s) are entitled to special significance and may be entitled to controlling weight. If a treating source's medical opinion on an issue of the nature and severity of an individual's impairment(s) is well-supported by medically acceptable clinical and laboratory diagnostic techniques and is not inconsistent with the other substantial evidence in the case record, the adjudicator must give it controlling weight. (*See* SSR 96-2p, "Titles II and XVI: Giving Controlling Weight to Treating Source Medical Opinions," and SSR 96-5p, "Titles II and XVI: Medical Source Opinions on Issues Reserved to the Commissioner."

§259 Summary: Proof of Pain or Other Symptoms

The two steps for proof of pain or other symptoms can be divided into sub-steps:

1) The claimant has
   a) a medically determinable impairment
   b) that can cause the type of alleged symptom, such as pain; and
2) the claimant's symptoms
   a) are reasonably consistent with the objective evidence and
   b) reasonably consistent with other evidence in the record, and are therefore credible, and
   c) limit the claimant's RFC to the degree alleged.

The first step presents primarily medical issues on which there must be medical evidence in the record. Although these issues have a tendency to take care of themselves by the time a lawyer gets involved in a case, some cases will need your attention.

The second step presents medical opinion issues on which you need to seek medical source statements from the claimant's doctors concerning the claimant's limitations and matters subject to proof by testimony of the claimant and lay witnesses at the hearing. Objective medical evidence is not dispositive unless it is in the claimant's favor. The regulations and rulings require the fact finder to look beyond the objective evidence and consider everything in the case. *See* §§315 to 319 of this book for questions to ask the claimant about symptoms and limitations. *See* §§294 to 297 on letters from lay observers and §§320 to 328 on lay witness testimony. Note that in a case where pain is the primary limiting factor, at the hearing all testimony, in essence, is testimony about pain. The same principle applies to any other symptom.

§260 Proving a Case for a Claimant Under Age 50

A claimant who is less than 50 years old has a difficult case. Although, according to SSR 96-9p, "a finding of 'disabled' usually applies when the full range of sedentary work is significantly eroded," inability to perform substantially all sedentary occupations may not be good enough in all cases. SSR 96-9p notes:

> When there is a reduction in an individual's exertional or nonexertional capacity so that he or she is unable to perform substantially all of the occupations administratively noticed in Table No. 1 [the sedentary grid], the individual will be unable to perform the full range of sedentary work: the occupational base will be 'eroded' by the additional limitations or restrictions. However, the mere inability to perform substantially all sedentary unskilled occupations does not equate with a finding of disability. There may be a number of occupations from the approximately 200 occupations administratively noticed, and jobs that exist in significant numbers, that an individual may still be able to perform even with a sedentary occupational base that has been eroded.

Rule 201.00(h)(3) of the Medical-Vocational Guidelines provides:

> Whether an individual will be able to make an adjustment to other work requires an adjudicative assessment of factors such as the type and extent of the individual's limitations or restrictions and the extent of the erosion of the occupational base. It requires an individualized determination that considers the impact of the limitations or restrictions on the number of sedentary, unskilled occupations or the total number of jobs to which the individual may be able to adjust, considering his or her age, education and work experience, including any transferable skills or education providing for direct entry into skilled work.

SSR 96-9p provides:

> The impact of an RFC for less than a full range of sedentary work is especially critical for individuals who have not yet attained age 50. Since age, education, and work experience are not usually significant factors in limiting the ability of individuals under age 50 to make an adjustment to other work, the conclusion whether such individuals who are limited to less than the full range of sedentary work are disabled will depend primarily on the nature and extent of their functional limitations or restrictions.

Thus, it is the nature and extent of the functional limitations, that is, the claimant's RFC, that are critical in determining whether significant numbers of jobs exist that a claimant under age 50 can do. According to SSA, this must be addressed by vocational expert testimony in most cases when there is significant erosion of the sedentary occupational base. It is SSA's position that all of the examples of limitations that *usually* result in a finding of disabled for someone under age 50, except for those that appear in the Medical-Vocational Guidelines themselves, in effect, may be rebutted by vocational expert opinion in an individual case. It is your job as the claimant's attorney to see that the usual rule rather than the exception applies in your client's case. *See* §§340-349 for dealing with vocational expert testimony.

It is important to identify which limitations recognized by SSA will erode the sedentary occupational base so much as to *usually* require a finding that a claimant is disabled. Here is a list of avenues to explore.

§261 Illiteracy

As of age 45, Rule 201.17 of the Medical-Vocational Guidelines requires a finding of disabled for a claimant who is incapable of performing past relevant work (or has no past relevant work), is limited to sedentary work, has no transferable work skills, and is unable to read or write in English. *See* Medical-Vocational Guidelines Rule 201.00(h)(1). Rule 201.17 is not subject to rebuttal by vocational expert testimony; but sometimes an ALJ who thinks that such a claimant can do a sedentary job will refuse to find that the claimant is, in fact, illiterate. If you're dealing with an ALJ who holds such views, you will need to provide an extra measure of proof that your client is unable to read or write English.

At younger ages, a limitation to sedentary work plus illiteracy is insufficient for a finding of disability. Some additional limitation is required. Medical-Vocational Guidelines, Rule 201.00(i).

§262 Inability to Communicate in English

Similarly, a claimant who is limited to sedentary work and is unable to communicate in English may be found disabled if he or she is age 45 or older. Rule 201.17. *See also* Rule 201.00(h)(1). If the claimant is younger than 45, some additional limitation is required in order to be found disabled.

When an individual under age 45 is *both* illiterate *and* unable to communicate in English, what rule applies? SSA takes the position that when it created the Medical-Vocational Guidelines, it assumed that someone who was unable to communicate in English was also illiterate and that Rule 201.23 of the Medical-Vocational Guidelines requires a finding of "not disabled" for those under age 45. But doesn't someone who is *both* illiterate *and* unable to communicate in English have more adverse vocational factors than an individual who is only illiterate? The Fifth Circuit in *Martinez v. Heckler*, 735 F.2d 795 (5th Cir. 1984), decided that vocational expert testimony was necessary, that the Medical-Vocational Guidelines could not be used to deny benefits to an individual who was both illiterate and unable to communicate in English. This decision has been adopted as an acquiescence ruling, AR 86-3(5), applicable only in the Fifth Circuit.

§263 Postural and Manipulative Limitations

§263.1 Manipulative Limitations

SSR 96-9p notes that most unskilled sedentary jobs require "good use of both hands and the fingers; i.e., bilateral manual dexterity. Fine movements of small objects require use of the fingers; e.g., to pick or pinch. Most unskilled sedentary jobs require good use of the hands and fingers for repetitive hand-finger actions."

SSR 96-9p states that "[a]ny significant manipulative limitation of an individual's ability to handle and work with small objects with both hands will result in a significant erosion of the unskilled sedentary occupational base." But SSR 96-9p also notes that "[w]hen the limitation is less significant, especially if the limitation is in the non-dominant hand, it may be useful to consult a vocational expert."

An expanded explanation of manipulative limitations appears in SSR 85-15:

> Reaching, handling, fingering, and feeling require progressively finer usage of the upper extremities to perform work-related activities. Reaching (extending the hands and arms in any direction) and handling (seizing, holding, grasping, turning or otherwise working primarily with the whole hand or hands) are activities required in almost all jobs. Significant limitations of reaching or handling, therefore, may eliminate a large number of occupations a person could otherwise do. Varying degrees of limitations would have different effects, and the assistance of a V[ocational] S[pecialist] may be needed to determine the effects of the limitations. "Fingering" involves picking, pinching, or otherwise working primarily with the fingers. It is needed to perform most unskilled sedentary jobs and to perform certain skilled and semiskilled jobs at all levels of exertion. As a general rule, limitations of fine manual dexterity have greater adjudicative significance—in terms of relative numbers of jobs in which the function is required—as the person's exertional RFC decreases. Thus, loss of fine manual dexterity narrows the sedentary and light ranges of work much more than it does the medium, heavy, and very heavy ranges of work. The varying degrees of loss which can occur may require a decision-maker to have the assistance of a V[ocational] S[pecialist]. However, a V[ocational] S[pecialist] would not ordinarily be required where a person has a loss of ability to feel the size, shape, temperature, or texture of an object by the fingertips, since this is a function required in very few jobs.

See also 20 C.F.R. § 404.1567(b) and SSR 83-14.

SSR 83-12 provides that individuals who have lost the use of an upper extremity "would generally not be expected to perform sedentary work . . ."

SSR 87-11c, which adopted as a Social Security Ruling *Odle v. Secretary of Health & Human Services*, 788 F.2d 1158 (6th Cir. 1985), states SSA's position that loss of use of an arm or hand is not disabling *per se*. Nevertheless, it is SSA's position that loss of use of an upper extremity would reduce the total number of unskilled occupations within the claimant's RFC to a little more than the number represented by the full range of sedentary work. *See* POMS DI 25020.005A5 at §272. What this means is that if the sedentary grid directs a finding of disabled for an individual with the same age, education and work experience as the one-armed claimant, that claimant also ought to be found disabled using the Medical-Vocational Guidelines as a framework. (In fact, a limitation to one arm work probably reduces a claimant's job base to the equivalent of less than a full range of sedentary work. *See* the analysis by Dr. Brent Evans at §225.)

Several of the Medical Source Statement forms in this book include questions on manipulative limitations, which ask the doctor to estimate the percentage of time during an 8-hour working day that the claimant can use hands for grasping, fingers for fine manipulation and arms for reaching. This corresponds with "handling," "fingering," and "reaching," the required frequency of which is indicated for DOT occupations in Selected Characteristics of Occupations Defined in the Revised Dictionary of Occupational Titles, as well as in DOT computer programs. Use these resources to determine if your client can perform certain jobs with the manipulative limitations established by the treating doctor. Note the significant degree to which manipulative limitations reduce the sedentary occupational base, *see* §346.6, and the light occupational base, *see* §348.1.1.

Because one sometimes needs to send a form to a hand specialist that asks *only* about manipulative limitations, a Manipulative Limitations Medical Source Statement is provided at §263.1.1.

§263.1.1 Form: Manipulative Limitations Medical Source Statement

MANIPULATIVE LIMITATIONS MEDICAL SOURCE STATEMENT

From: ______________________________

Re: ______________________________ (Name of Patient)

______________________________ (Date of Birth)

1. Identify any signs or symptoms your patient exhibits that affect shoulders, elbows, wrists, hands or fingers:

☐ tenderness	☐ paresthesia	☐ joint warmth
☐ pain	☐ soft tissue swelling	☐ joint deformity
☐ muscle spasm	☐ muscle weakness	☐ reduced grip strength
☐ redness	☐ limitation of motion	☐ muscle atrophy

☐ other:____

2. If your patient has pain/paresthesia, please characterize the nature of the

pain/paresthesia:____

____

3. Please identify the location and frequency of pain/paresthesia by shading the relevant areas and labeling as constant (C), frequent (F), or intermittent (I):

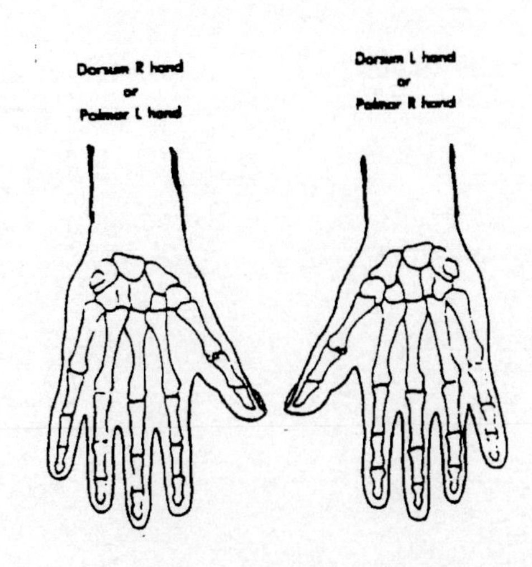

4. Please state any weight lifting limitations:

   Left arm: ________ Right arm: ________ Both: ________

5. Please indicate the percentage of total time during an 8-hour working day that your patient can use hands/fingers/arms for the following activities:

	HANDS: Grasp, Turn Twist Objects	**FINGERS: Fine Manipulations**	**ARMS: Reaching In Front of Body**	**ARMS: Reaching Overhead**
Right:	___%	___%	___%	___%
Left:	___%	___%	___%	___%

6. Please indicate the number of minutes your patient can use hands and fingers continuously in one stretch before needing a rest break; and indicate how long the rest break would have to be before resuming another period of continuous use:

	Use Hand Continuously	**Length of Rest**	**Use Fingers Continuously**	**Length of Rest**
Right:	____**Minutes**	____**Minutes**	___**Minutes**	___**Minutes**
Left:	____**Minutes**	____**Minutes**	___**Minutes**	___**Minutes**

7. Are your patient's impairments as demonstrated by signs, clinical findings and laboratory or test results ***reasonably consistent*** with the symptoms and functional limitations described above in this evaluation?

   ☐ Yes ☐ No

   If no, please explain: ____

________________________ ________________________________
Date *Signature*

Printed/Typed Name: ________________________________

Address: ________________________________

____

____

7-29
12/13
§ 263.1.1

§263.2 Postural Limitations

Sitting Limitations

In order to do a full range of sedentary work, one must have the capacity for prolonged sitting. *See* SSR 83-12. According to SSR 83-10, "sitting should generally total approximately six hours of an eight-hour workday." SSR 83-12 discusses an RFC that is compatible with either sedentary or light work except that the person must alternate sitting and standing. It notes, "most jobs have ongoing work processes which demand that a worker be in a certain place or posture for at least a certain length of time to accomplish a certain task. Unskilled types of jobs are particularly structured so that a person cannot ordinarily sit or stand at will."

SSR 96-9p says this about the need to alternate sitting and standing:

> An individual may need to alternate the required sitting of sedentary work by standing (and, possibly, walking) periodically. Where this need cannot be accommodated by scheduled breaks and a lunch period, the occupational base for a full range of unskilled sedentary work will be eroded. The extent of the erosion will depend on the facts in the case record, such as the frequency of the need to alternate sitting and standing and the length of time needed to stand. The RFC assessment must be specific as to the frequency of the individual's need to alternate sitting and standing. It may be especially useful in these situations to consult a vocational resource in order to determine whether the individual is able to make an adjustment to other work.

As a rule, whenever the need to alternate sitting and standing is presented in a case, the ALJ will call a vocational expert to testify. If an ALJ does not rely on vocational expert testimony but concludes nevertheless that a claimant who must alternate sitting and standing is not disabled, as a rule, the Appeals Council or the federal court will remand the case. *See Wilson v. Heckler,* 743 F.2d 218 (4th Cir. 1984); *Wages v. Secretary of Health & Human Services,* 755 F.2d 495 (6th Cir. 1985); *Howse v. Heckler,* 782 F.2d 626 (6th Cir. 1986); *Cantrell v. Secretary of Health & Human Services,* 867 F.2d 1137 (8th Cir. 1989); *Hammock v. Bowen,* 867 F.2d 1209 (9th Cir. 1989); *Peterson v. Chater,* 96 F.3d 1015 (7th Cir. 1996); *Shultz v. Bowen,* 662 F. Supp. 1074 (E.D. Pa. 1986); *Cummings v. Bowen,* 677 F. Supp. 975 (N.D. Ill. 1988); *Jennings v. Bowen,* 703 F. Supp. 833 (D. Ariz. 1988); and *Nguyen v. Chater*, 172 F.3d 31, 36 (1st Cir. 1999).

In a case where a claimant's lawyer tried to argue that SSR 83-12 conflicted with the vocational expert's opinion that stated a number of jobs that could be done while alternating sitting and standing, the Seventh Circuit Court of Appeals said that SSR 83-12's "description of what the case is 'ordinarily' does not refute, by itself, the opinion of an expert in response to a specific question." *Powers v. Apfel*, 207 F.3d 431, 436 (7th Cir. 2000). Thus, in order to win the case, vigorous cross examination of the vocational expert is essential. For examples of questions to ask a vocational expert on this issue, *see* §348.9. *See also* the evaluation of this issue by vocational expert Dr. Brent Evans at §348.4, which remains a good analysis even though it was written before SSR 96-9p was issued.

Standing and Walking Limitations

Because one is expected to be capable of being on one's feet, standing and walking, intermittently for a total of about two hours out of an eight hour workday, SSR 83-10, any significant reduction of standing and walking capacity below this limited amount will reduce the sedentary occupational base. *See, e.g., Johnson v. Bowen*, 687 F. Supp. 1284, 1301 (W.D. Wis. 1988). SSR 96-9p says that the occupational base of one who can stand and walk for only a few minutes out of the workday would be significantly eroded. For those who can stand and walk more than a few minutes out of the workday, it is appropriate to consult a vocational resource to determine if standing and walking limitations preclude an adjustment to sedentary work.

Use of Cane

Because sedentary work requires one to be able to obtain and return objects, being on one's feet, standing and walking, for approximately two hours out of an eight hour working day, SSR 83-10, it follows that use of a cane would limit capacity for a full range of sedentary work because one sometimes needs two free hands to carry some objects encountered on sedentary jobs. *See Walker v. Bowen,* 826 F.2d 996, 1003 (11th Cir. 1987). SSR 96-9p says that if a cane, which it calls a "medically required hand-held assistive device" is needed only for prolonged ambulation, walking on uneven terrain or slopes, the sedentary occupational base will not be significantly eroded; and if the need for a cane arises because of an impairment that affects only one lower extremity, one "may still have the ability to make an adjustment to sedentary work that exists in significant numbers. On the other hand, the occupational base for an individual who must use such a device for balance because of significant involvement of both lower extremities (e.g., because of a neurological impairment) may be significantly eroded." Note that if there is "significant involvement of both lower extremities" because of a neurological impairment as required by SSR 96-9p to significantly erode the sedentary occupational base, the impairment probably meets or equals § 11.04B of the Listing of Impairments. *See also* § 1.00B.2.b.(2) of the Listings.

The need to use a cane would preclude work at higher exertional levels than sedentary work.

Need to Walk Around

If a claimant needs to periodically walk around (as many with back problems do), it is likely that this is a disabling limitation, depending on the frequency and duration of the need to walk around, because this takes a claimant away from the work station. *Cf.* SSRs 83-12 and 96-9p and *see also* §348.4.

Need to Elevate Leg

A limitation caused by the need to elevate one or both legs when sitting is not discussed in Social Security regulations or rulings but, depending on how high the leg needs to be elevated and for how long during a working day, such a requirement may significantly limit the full range of sedentary work. *See, e.g., Mazzella v. Secretary of United States Dep't of Health & Human Services,* 588 F. Supp. 603 (S.D.N.Y. 1984); *Brown v. Bowen,* 710 F. Supp. 1303 (W.D. Wash. 1989); *Stewart v. Sullivan*, 881 F.2d 740 (9th Cir. 1989); *Dean v. Sullivan*, 735 F.Supp. 401 (M.D. Fla. 1990); *Smalls v. Shalala,* 996 F.2d 413 (1993); and *Laird v. Stilwill*, 969 F. Supp. 1167, 1177 (N.D. Iowa 1997). Note, though, that if a vocational expert testifies that a claimant can still do a number of jobs even while elevating a leg, a court is unlikely to disturb an ALJ's finding that the claimant is capable of performing jobs existing in significant numbers. *See Shramek v. Apfel*, 226 F.3d 809, 815 (7th Cir. 2000).

Inability to Stoop

SSR 83-14 defines stooping as bending "the body downward and forward by bending the spine at the waist." *See also* SSRs 83-10 and 85-15. SSR 96-9p notes that a "complete inability to stoop would significantly erode the unskilled sedentary occupational base and a finding that the individual is disabled would usually apply." But since most unskilled sedentary jobs require only occasional stooping, a reduction to occasional stooping would only minimally erode the sedentary occupational base.

Despite the helpful language in SSR 96-9p that a finding of disabled would usually apply when a claimant is totally unable to stoop, one court has specifically rejected the argument that an inability to stoop automatically results in a finding of disabled for a younger claimant who was restricted to unskilled sedentary work. *See Lauer v. Apfel*, 169 F.3d 489 (7th Cir. 1999).

Need to Lie Down During the Day

Obviously a need to lie down during the day will be accommodated in few unskilled sedentary jobs.

§264 Visual Impairment

According to SSR 96-9p:

> Most sedentary unskilled occupations require working with small objects. If a visual limitation prevents an individual from seeing the small objects involved in most sedentary unskilled work, or if an individual is not able to avoid ordinary hazards in the workplace, such as boxes on the floor, doors ajar, or approaching people or vehicles, there will be a significant erosion of the sedentary occupational base. These cases may require the use of vocational resources.

See also Gordon v. Schweiker, 725 F.2d 231, 236-7 (4th Cir. 1984), SSRs 85-15 and 83-14 and *see* §232. Use the letter to the treating ophthalmologist at §232.2, the short Vision Medical Source Statement at §232.3, or the longer Vision Impairment Medical Source Statement at §232.4 to gather information about your client's limitations resulting from reduced vision.

§265 Environmental Restrictions

Certain types of environmental restrictions, if extreme, may significantly limit the ability to do a full range of sedentary work. SSR 96-9p states:

> In general, few occupations in the unskilled sedentary occupational base require work in environments with extreme cold, extreme heat, wetness, humidity, vibration, or unusual hazards. The "hazards" defined in the [Selected Characteristics of Occupations Defined in the Revised Dictionary of Occupational Titles] are considered unusual in unskilled sedentary work. They include: moving mechanical parts of equipment, tools, or machinery; electrical shock; working in high, exposed places; exposure to radiation; working with explosives; and exposure to toxic, caustic chemicals. Even a need to avoid all exposure to these conditions would not, by itself, result in a significant erosion of the occupational base.
>
> Since all work environments entail some level of noise, restrictions on the ability to work in a noisy workplace must be evaluated on an individual basis. The unskilled sedentary occupational base may or

> may not be significantly eroded depending on the facts in the case record. In such cases, it may be especially useful to consult a vocational resource.
>
> Restrictions to avoid exposure to odors or dust must also be evaluated on an individual basis. The RFC assessment must specify which environments are restricted and state the extent of the restriction; e.g., whether only excessive or even small amounts of dust must be avoided.

In *Warmoth v. Bowen,* 798 F.2d 1109, 1112 (7th Cir. 1986), which involved a limitation to sedentary work without exposure to "respiratory irritants," the Seventh Circuit Court of Appeals concluded:

> Approximately 85 percent of the 200 unskilled sedentary occupations that exist throughout the national economy are in the machine trades and bench work categories. 20 C.F.R. Part 404, Subpart P, Appendix 2, § 201.00(a) (1985). But the Secretary's regulations do not further contain such relevant evidence or other material to support the finding that Warmoth can still perform a significant number of these jobs. The Fifth Circuit, on the other hand, observed that "[m]achine trades and bench work by their nature often involve exposure to dust, fumes and other suspended particulates irritating or intolerable to persons afflicted with respiratory ailments." *Thomas v. Schweiker*, 666 F.2d 999, 1005 n.8 (5th Cir. 1982) *(per curiam).* Similarly, it is hard to conceive of many unskilled, sedentary jobs that are performed in surroundings free of cigarette smoke, perfume and other like irritants which Warmoth cannot tolerate.

See also SSRs 83-14 and 85-15.

Some of the medical source statement forms in this book ask about environmental limitations, e.g., §233.1 Pulmonary Medical Source Statement and §234.3 Cardiac Medical Source Statement. Sometimes when you're dealing with a case involving chemical intolerance or environmental allergies, it is necessary to have a form that focuses on environmental limitations. For this reason, we provide an Environmental Limitations Medical Source Statement at §265.1.

§265.1 Form: Environmental Limitations Medical Source Statement

ENVIRONMENTAL LIMITATIONS MEDICAL SOURCE STATEMENT

From: ______________________________

Re: ______________________________(Name of Patient)

______________________________(Date of Birth)

Please answer the following questions concerning your patient's impairments. *Attach relevant treatment notes, laboratory and test results as appropriate.*

1. Frequency and length of contact: ______________________________

2. Diagnoses: ______________________________

____

____

3. List your patient's ***symptoms***, including fatigue, shortness of breath, dizziness, pain, etc:

____

____

____

4. Identify the clinical findings, laboratory and test results that show your patient's medical impairments:

____

____

____

5. Describe the treatment and response including any side effects of medication that may have implications for working, *e.g.*, drowsiness, dizziness, nausea, etc:

____

____

____

6. Have your patient's impairments lasted or can they be expected to last at least twelve months? ☐ Yes ☐ No

7. Is your patient a malingerer? ☐ Yes ☐ No

8. Do emotional factors contribute to the severity of your patient's symptoms and functional limitations? ☐ Yes ☐ No

If yes, please explain: ______________________________

____

9. State the degree to which your patient should avoid the following:

ENVIRONMENTAL RESTRICTIONS	NO RESTRICTIONS	AVOID CONCENTRATED EXPOSURE	AVOID EVEN MODERATE EXPOSURE	AVOID ALL EXPOSURE
Extreme cold	☐	☐	☐	☐
Extreme heat	☐	☐	☐	☐
High humidity	☐	☐	☐	☐
Wetness	☐	☐	☐	☐
Cigarette smoke	☐	☐	☐	☐
Perfumes	☐	☐	☐	☐
Soldering fluxes	☐	☐	☐	☐
Solvents/cleaners	☐	☐	☐	☐
Fumes, odors, gases	☐	☐	☐	☐
Dust	☐	☐	☐	☐
Chemicals	☐	☐	☐	☐
List other irritants:				
______________		☐	☐	☐
______________		☐	☐	☐
______________		☐	☐	☐
______________		☐	☐	☐

10. How much is your patient likely to be ***"off task"***? That is, what percentage of a typical workday would your patient's symptoms likely be severe enough to interfere with ***attention and concentration*** needed to perform even simple work tasks?

☐ 0% ☐ 5% ☐ 10% ☐ 15% ☐ 20% ☐ 25% or more

11. To what degree can your patient tolerate work stress?

☐ Incapable of even "low stress" work ☐ Capable of low stress work
☐ Capable of moderate stress - normal work ☐ Capable of high stress work

Please explain the reasons for your conclusion: ______________________________

12. Are your patient's impairments likely to produce "good days" and "bad days"?
☐ Yes ☐ No

If yes, assuming your patient was trying to work full time, please estimate, on the average, how many days per month your patient is likely to be absent from work as a result of the impairments or treatment:

☐ Never
☐ About one day per month
☐ About two days per month
☐ About three days per month
☐ About four days per month
☐ More than four days per month

13. Are your patient's impairments (physical impairments plus any emotional impairments) as demonstrated by signs, clinical findings and laboratory or test results ***reasonably consistent*** with the functional limitations described in this evaluation?
☐ Yes ☐ No

If no, please explain: ______________________________

14. Please describe any other limitations (such as exertional limitations, psychological limitations, limited vision, difficulty hearing, etc.) that would affect your patient's ability to work at a regular job on a sustained basis:

____

____

____

____

______________ ______________________________
Date *Signature*

Printed/Typed Name: ______________________________

Address: ______________________________

____

7-74
11/13
265.1

§266 Mental Impairments

SSR 96-9p provides:

> A substantial loss of ability to meet any one of several basic work-related activities on a sustained basis (i.e., 8 hours a day, 5 days a week, or an equivalent work schedule), will substantially erode the unskilled sedentary occupational base and would justify a finding of disability. These mental activities are generally required by competitive, remunerative, unskilled work:
>
> - Understanding, remembering, and carrying out simple instructions.
> - Making judgments that are commensurate with the functions of unskilled work—e.g., simple work-related decisions.
> - Responding appropriately to supervision, co-workers and usual work situations.
> - Dealing with changes in a routine work setting.
>
> A less than substantial loss of ability to perform any of the above basic work activities may or may not significantly erode the unskilled sedentary occupational base. The individual's remaining capacities must be assessed and a judgment made as to their effects on the unskilled occupational base considering the other vocational factors of age, education, and work experience. When an individual has been found to have a limited ability in one or more of these basic work activities, it may be useful to consult a vocational resource.

See also SSRs 85-16, 85-15 and 83-14 for the limited help that they give. *See* the discussion at §246. On the issue of stress tolerance, *see* §247.

§267 Part-Time and Sporadic Work

Social Security Ruling 96-8p states, "Ordinarily, RFC is an assessment of an individual's ability to do sustained work-related physical and mental activities in a work setting on a regular and continuing basis. A 'regular and continuing basis' means 8 hours a day, for 5 days a week, or an equivalent work schedule." *See also* SSR 96-9p, which notes, for example, a substantial loss of ability to do any one of several basic mental work-related activities "on a sustained basis (i.e., 8 hours a day, 5 days a week, or an equivalent work schedule), will substantially erode the unskilled sedentary occupational base and would justify a finding of disability."

The requirement that work be full-time is consistent with court decisions. Some courts have said that a "physical limitation which prevents a claimant from working a full workday, minus a reasonable time for lunch and breaks, constitutes a disability within the meaning of the Act." *Johnson* v. *Harris,* 612 F.2d 993, 998 (5th Cir. 1980). The capacity to perform work only sporadically because of exacerbations of a medical condition, with or without requiring hospitalization, may also significantly compromise the range of work at all exertional levels. *See Totten v. Califano,* 624 F.2d 10, 12 (4th Cir. 1980).

In evaluating the ability to sustain work, POMS DI 24510.005C.2.b. instructs decision makers to "[c]onsider an **8-hour workday** and a 5 day work week (with normal breaks, e.g., lunch, morning and afternoon breaks)." (Emphasis in original.) *See also* POMS DI 24510.061B.2., reprinted at §245.5, which notes that an "individual's ability to sustain ongoing mental performance for a full workday is essential."

Although there are a number of court cases affirming findings of non-disability at step five based on an ability to do part-time work, those cases are inconsistent with SSR 96-8p. Therefore, those cases should not be followed. While part-time work may establish non-disability at step one and, in some situations, at step four, SSA does not consider the ability to do part-time work as relevant to a finding of non-disability at step five.

§268 Some Additional Possibilities

The Effects of Treatment

Social Security Ruling 96-8p recognizes that the effects of treatment must be considered in making an RFC assessment, "including limitations or restrictions imposed by the mechanics of treatment (e.g., frequency of treatment, duration, disruption to routine, side effects of medication)." It is possible that treatment could be too disruptive to allow sustained work.

Side Effects of Medication

For the proposition that drowsiness as a side effect of medication diminishes the number of sedentary jobs a claimant would be able to perform, *see Shultz v. Bowen,* 662 F. Supp. 1074, 1078 (E.D. Pa. 1986).

Varney v. Secretary of HHS, 846 F.2d 581, 585 (9th Cir. 1988) held:

> Like pain, the side effects of medications can have a significant impact on an individual's ability to work and should figure in the disability determination process. *Cf. Howard v. Heckler,* 782 F.2d 1484, 1488 (9th Cir. 1986). Also like pain, side effects can be a "highly idiosyncratic phenomenon" and a claimant's testimony as to their limiting effects should not be trivialized. *Cf. Id.*

In the case quoted above, which is usually referred to as *Varney I*, the claimant petitioned for rehearing asking that, instead of remanding the case for further proceedings before SSA, the court instead remand the case for payment of benefits. This was granted in *Varney II*. In a footnote, the court noted that the findings on side effects were not necessary for proper disposition of the case since benefits were being awarded. *Varney v. Secretary of Health & Human Services*, 859 F.2d 1396, 1400 n.3 (9th Cir. 1988).

Dizziness

Dizziness may limit the capacity for a full range of sedentary work. *See Bellamy v. Secretary of Health & Human Services*, 755 F.2d 1380, 1383 (9th Cir. 1985). A Dizziness Medical Source Statement appears at §230.4.

Bladder Problems

In *Cruz v. Bowen*, 643 F. Supp. 1088, 1092 (D. Mass. 1986) an ALJ found that the claimant had the RFC to perform "sedentary work which would not preclude him from voiding as necessary." The court concluded that substantial evidence did not indicate that the claimant could perform a full range of sedentary work if he had to void about every hour. *Cruz* was remanded for vocational expert testimony as was *Gonzalez v. Sullivan*, 914 F.2d 1197, 1202 (9th Cir. 1990), on a similar limitation to sedentary work plus a bladder problem.

See also Quijano v. Secretary of HHS, 791 F. Supp. 39, 41 (D.P.R. 1992) *and Mac v. Sullivan*, 811 F. Supp. 194, 199 (E.D. Pa. 1993). A Bladder Problem Medical Source Statement appears at §230.1. An Interstitial Cystitis Medical Source Statement appears at §230.1.1.

Diarrhea

For a case in which Crohn's disease with periodic flare-ups involving diarrhea and abdominal pain was found by a court to be disabling, *see Dix v. Sullivan,* 900 F.2d 135, 138 (8th Cir. 1990). *See also Bulpett v. Heckler*, 617 F. Supp. 850, 857 (D. Mass. 1985) *and Rambo v. Heckler*, 728 F.2d 1583, 1584 (11th Cir. 1984). Fecal incontinence, which was brushed aside by an ALJ, was found to warrant a remand in *Crowley v. Apfel*, 197 F.3d 194, 199 (5th Cir. 1999).

A Crohn's and Colitis Medical Source Statement appears at §235.1. An Irritable Bowel Syndrome Medical Source Statement appears as 235A on Digital Access.

Need to Maintain a Colostomy or Ileostomy

See Mackinaw v. Bowen, 866 F.2d 1023, 1024 (8th Cir. 1989), in which the court remanded the case for vocational expert testimony where the claimant had been denied disability benefits based on a capacity for sedentary work despite frequent need to maintain an ileostomy bag.

Skin Impairment

Skin impairments may prevent a claimant from doing a full range of sedentary work. *See Channel v. Heckler*, 747 F.2d 577, 582 (10th Cir. 1984). A Skin Disorders Medical Source Statement appears at §237.1.

Headaches

In *Johnson v. Secretary of Health & Human Services*, 872 F.2d 810, 814 (8th Cir. 1989), the ALJ found Johnson capable of unskilled sedentary work and denied benefits. The Eight Circuit of Appeals found the evidence concerning Johnson's disabling headaches to be so compelling that it ordered judgment entered for Johnson. A Headaches Medical Source Statement appears at §239.2.

The Nonexertional Aspects of Pain

Pain affects a claimant's exertional capacity for work. But, in a variety of ways, pain has an impact on a claimant's ability to do a wide range of work at any exertional level. For example, it may affect a claimant's ability to do repetitive activities. It may limit the number of consecutive hours he or she can work. It may affect the ability to concentrate or pay attention, causing the claimant to be "off task" at work. It may have an impact on mood, making someone irritable and difficult to get along with.

Seizures

See §239.

Inability to Hold Head in Flexed Forward Position

Some people with cervical spine impairments find it impossible to look down at a desk for long while sitting. Since this is the usual work position for sedentary work, you ought to be able to get a vocational expert to agree that someone with this limitation cannot perform most sedentary jobs. Claimants who have this problem go to extraordinary lengths to avoid situations where they must hold their heads in a flexed forward position. Be sure to take testimony about this at the hearing. Also be sure to ask the claimant's doctor about it. Note that the Cervical Spine Medical Source Statement in §231.5 and the Physical Medical Source Statement at §221.11 include a question that addresses this issue.

§269 Limitations that Do Not Significantly Erode the Occupational Base for Work

The following list is from ALJ training materials. For our purposes, it is a useful to have a list of limitations that you probably should not spend much time developing.

The following limitations do not significantly erode the occupational bases for work at all exertional levels:

- "[L]imitations on the ability to crawl" (SSR 85-15)
- Limitations on the ability to kneel (SSR 85-15)
- A restriction "only from being on unprotected elevations and near dangerous moving machinery" (SSR 85-15)
- Inability "to feel the size, shape[,] temperature, or texture of an object by the fingertips" (SSR 85-15)
- A need "to avoid excessive amounts of noise, dust, etc." (SSR 85-15)

The following limitations do not significantly erode the occupational base for sedentary work:

- A restriction against "frequent contact with petroleum based solvents" (SSR 83-12)
- A restriction against "exposure to ragweed pollen" (SSR 83-14)
- A restriction against crouching (SSR 83-14, SSR 96-9p)
- A restriction to no more than occasional stooping (SSR 85-15, 96-9p)
- "[A]n ability to lift or carry slightly less than 10 pounds, with no other limitations or restrictions in the abil-ity to perform the requirements of sedentary work" (SSR 96-9p)
- "Limitations or restrictions on the ability to push or pull" (SSR 96-9p)
- An ability to "stand and walk for a total of slightly less than 2 hours per 8-hour workday," where this is the only limitation (SSR 96-9p)
- A need to alternate sitting and standing (or walking) that can "be accommodated by scheduled breaks and a lunch period" (SSR 96-9p)
- Where "a medically required hand-held assistive device is needed only for prolonged ambulation, walking on uneven terrain, or ascending or descending slopes" (SSR 96-9p)
- Limitations on "climbing ladders, ropes, or scaffolds" (SSR 96-9p)
- "The ability to hear and understand simple oral instructions or to communicate simple information" (SSR 96-9p)
- "[A] need to avoid all exposure" to hazards such as "moving mechanical parts of equipment, tools, or ma-chinery; electrical shock; working in high, exposed places; exposure to radiation; working with explosives; and ex-posure to toxic, caustic chemicals" (SSR 96-9p)

The following limitations do not significantly erode the occupational base for light work:

- A restriction against crouching (SSR 83-14)
- A restriction to no more than occasional stooping (SSR 83-14, 85-15)
- An "inability to ascend or descend scaffolding, poles, and ropes" (SSR 83-14)
- An "inability to crawl on hands and knees" (SSR 83-14)
- A "need to avoid exposure to feathers" (SSR 83-14)

The following limitations do not significantly erode the occupational base for medium work:

- A limitation on "the ability to ascend or descend ladders and scaffolding" (SSR 83-14)
- "The need to avoid environments which contain objects or substances commonly known not to exist in most workplaces" (SSR 83-14)

§270 Preparation Tips

§271 Learn SSA's Approach to Vocational Issues

SSA's approach to vocational issues is set forth in the Medical-Vocational Guidelines, especially the introductory sections to the grids, in 20 C.F.R. §§ 404.1560 through 404.1569a, and in several Social Security Rulings:

SSR 82-40 The Vocational Relevance of Past Work Performed in a Foreign Country

SSR 82-41 Work Skills and Their Transferability as Intended by the Expanded Vocational Factors Regulations Effective February 26, 1979

SSR 82-6 1 Past Relevant Work—The Particular Job or the Occupation as Generally Performed

SSR 82-62 Disability Claimant's Capacity to Do Past Relevant Work, In General

SSR 82-63 Medical-Vocational Profiles Showing an Inability to Make an Adjustment to Other Work

SSR 83-5a Medical-Vocational Guidelines—Conclusiveness of Rules

SSR 83-10 Determining the Capability to Do Other Work—The Medical-Vocational Rules of Appendix 2

SSR 83-11 Capability to Do Other Work—The Exertionally Based Medical Rules Met

SSR 83-12 Capability to Do Other Work—The Medical-Vocational Rules as a Framework for Evaluating Exertional Limitations within a Range of Work or Falling Between Ranges of Work

SSR 83-14 Capability to Do Other Work—The Medical-Vocational Rules as a Framework for Evaluating A Combination of Exertional and Nonexertional Impairments

SSR 85-15 Capability to Do Other Work—The Medical Vocational Rules as a Framework for Evaluating Solely Nonexertional Impairments

SSR 86-8 The Sequential Evaluation Process

SSR 96-8p Assessing Residual Functional Capacity in Initial Claims

SSR 96-9p Determining Capacity to Do Other Work—Implications of a Residual Functional Capacity for Less Than a Full Range of Sedentary Work

SSR 00-4p Use of Vocational Expert and Vocational Specialist Evidence, and Other Reliable Occupational Information in Disability Decisions

SSR 03-3p Evaluation of Disability and Blindness in Initial Claims for Individuals Age 65 or Older

SSR 11-2p Documenting and Evaluating Disability in Young Adults

When preparing your client's case for a hearing, review the appropriate regulations and rulings. Also, it may be beneficial to review §§340-349 concerning vocational expert testimony and the OHA Training Series Manual titled "Vocational Experts—Testifying at Disability Hearings: A Self Study Guide" published in 1984, a portion of which is reprinted in Appendix 4; Phrasing Hypothetical Questions to Vocational Experts Training Guide, Appendix 6; and the Vocational Expert Handbook which is reprinted in Appendix 8.

A good summary of issues discussed in SSRs 83-12, 83-14, and 85-15 appears in a section of the POMS titled "Functional Limitations and Their Effects on Ranges of Work" DI 25020.001-DI 25020.015. This portion of the POMS pertaining to mental limitations appears in this book at §245.6. The rest of this useful item is reproduced at §272. A chart summarizing the effects of physical limitations on ranges of work appears at §271.1.

§271.1 Chart: Physical Limitations and Their Effects on Ranges of Work

<table>
<tr><th></th><th colspan="4">RANGES OF PHYSICAL EXERTION</th><th>CITATIONS</th></tr>
<tr><th></th><th>Heavy</th><th>Medium</th><th>Light</th><th>Sedentary</th><th></th></tr>
<tr><td>Lifting
Carrying</td><td>100 lbs. max.
50 lbs. freq.</td><td>50 lbs. max.
25 lbs. freq.</td><td>20 lbs. max.
10 lbs. freq.</td><td>10 lbs. max. An inability to lift or carry more than 1 or 2 lbs. would erode the sedentary occupational base significantly.</td><td>20 C.F.R. § 404.1567, SSR 96-9p</td></tr>
<tr><td>Standing
Walking</td><td>6 hours/day</td><td>6 hours/day</td><td>6 hours/day</td><td>2 hours/day. A limitation to standing and walking for a total of only a few minutes during the workday would erode the sedentary occupational base significantly.</td><td>SSRs 83-10, 96-9p</td></tr>
<tr><td>Pushing
Pulling</td><td></td><td></td><td>Arm and/or leg controls</td><td>Inability to push/pull will generally have little effect.</td><td>SSR 96-9p</td></tr>
<tr><td>Sitting/
Need to alternate sitting and standing</td><td></td><td></td><td></td><td>6 hours/day. The need to alternately sit and stand erodes the sedentary occupational base but the extent of erosion will depend on the facts such as the frequency of the need to alternate sitting and standing and the length of time needed to stand.</td><td>SSRs 83-10, 83-12, 83-14, 96-9p</td></tr>
<tr><td>Stooping
Crouching</td><td colspan="2">Ability to frequently stoop and crouch is required for most heavy and- medium work.</td><td colspan="2">Crouching is not required for most sedentary and light jobs. Only occasional stooping is required for light and sedentary work.
A complete inability to stoop would significantly erode the unskilled sedentary occupational base and a finding that the individual is disabled would usually apply.</td><td>SSRs 83-10, 83-14, 85-15, 96-9p, POMS DI 25020.005A.9</td></tr>
<tr><td>Climbing
Balancing
Kneeling
Crawling</td><td colspan="3">Relatively few jobs require climbing ladders. Limitations of ability to balance on a slippery or moving surface, crawl, or kneel would be of little significance in the broad world of work.</td><td>Would not usually erode the occupational base for a full range of sedentary work because these activities are not usually required in sedentary work. However, if balancing is limited even when walking on level terrain, there may be significant erosion.</td><td>SSRs 83-14, 85-15, 96-9p, POMS DI 25020.005A.1, POMS DI 25020.005A.4</td></tr>
<tr><td>Fine manual dexterity</td><td colspan="2">Significant loss of fine manual dexterity does not usually impact heavy and medium work except for certain skilled and semi-skilled jobs.</td><td colspan="2">Loss of fine manual dexterity narrows light and sedentary work more than it does heavy and medium work. Loss of bimanual dexterity significantly compromises sedentary occupational base.</td><td>SSRs 83-10, 83-12, 83-14, 85-15, 96-9p, POMS DI 25020.005A.2.c</td></tr>
<tr><td>Reaching
Handling</td><td colspan="4">Reaching and handling are activities required in almost all jobs. Significant limitations of reaching and handling may eliminate a large number of occupations.</td><td>SSRs 85-15, 96-9p POMS DI 25020.005A.8</td></tr>
</table>

<table>
<tr><td>Feeling</td><td colspan="2">The ability to feel the size, shape, temperature or texture of an object by the fingertips is a function required in very few jobs.</td><td>SSRs 85-15, 96-9p, POMS DI 25020.005A.2.b</td></tr>
<tr><td>Loss of use of arm</td><td colspan="2">Greatly impinges on unskilled sedentary work and generally reduces occupational base similar to the number represented by a full range of sedentary work.</td><td>SSR 83-12, POMS DI 25020.005A.5</td></tr>
<tr><td>Visual</td><td>Little impact if there is sufficient visual acuity to handle large objects and visual fields necessary to avoid hazards in the work place.</td><td>If a visual limitation prevents an individual from seeing the small objects involved in most sedentary work or if an individual is not able to avoid hazards in the workplace, there will be a significant erosion of the sedentary occupational base.</td><td>SSRs 83-14, 85-15, 96-9p, POMS DI 25020.005A.10</td></tr>
<tr><td>Commun-icative</td><td colspan="2">Basic communication is all that is needed to do unskilled work. The ability to hear and understand simple oral instructions or to communicate simple information is sufficient. However, hearing impairments do not necessarily prevent communication and differences in types of work may be compatible with various degrees of hearing loss. Impact on occupational base may need to be individually assessed.</td><td>SSR 85-15, 96-9p, POMS DI 25020.005A.3</td></tr>
<tr><td>Environ-mental</td><td colspan="2">Where a person has a medical restriction to avoid excessive amounts of noise, dust, etc., the impact on the broad world of work would be minimal because most job environments do not involve great noise, amounts of dust, etc. Where an individual can tolerate very little noise, dust, etc., the impact on the ability to work would be considerable because very few job environments are entirely free of irritants, pollutants, and other potentially damaging conditions. Where the environmental restriction falls between very little and excessive, resolution of the issue will generally require consultation of occupational reference materials or the services of a vocational expert.</td><td>SSRs 83-14, 85-15, 96-9p, POMS DI 25020.015</td></tr>
<tr><td>Use of cane</td><td>Use of cane precludes the ability to perform most unskilled jobs above the sedentary level.</td><td>The sedentary occupational base for one who must use a cane for balance because of significant involvement of both lower extremities may be significantly eroded. One who needs to use a cane because of an impairment that affects only one leg may still have the ability to make an adjustment to sedentary work that exists in significant numbers.</td><td>20 C.F.R. § 404.1567(a), SSRs 83-10, 96-9p</td></tr>
</table>

§272 Form: POMS DI 25020.005 and DI 25020.015 — Functional Limitations and Their Effects on Ranges of Work — Physical and Environment Limitations

DI 25020.005 Physical Limitations

A. POLICY

1. Climbing and Balancing

a. As a general rule, a small degree of limitation (e.g., the person retains the capacity to ascend and descend ramps and stairs but cannot maintain balance on a ladder) would not significantly impact on any range(s) of work.

b. Can be critical in certain specific types of occupations, e.g., occupations that require climbing ladders, ropes, poles, etc.

2. Fingering and Feeling

a. Fingering is needed to perform most unskilled sedentary jobs and to perform certain skilled and semiskilled jobs at all levels of exertion.

b. The mere ability to feel the size, shape, temperature or texture of an object by the fingertips, is a function required in very few jobs.

c. A loss of fine manual dexterity narrows the sedentary and light ranges of work more than it does the medium, heavy and very heavy ranges of work.

3. Hearing

a. The inability to hear, because it vitally affects communication, may (depending upon the extent of hearing loss) significantly impinge on all range(s) of work.

b. There are many possible medical variables of hearing loss and thus, the exact type and degree of loss must be considered.

c. The overall impact of a hearing loss (or a degree of hearing loss) also depends upon the type of occupations being considered.

EXAMPLE: Certain degrees of hearing loss may preclude the performance of some occupations that require good hearing (e.g., bus driver) without precluding the performance of other occupations (e.g., printing press operator).

4. Kneeling and Crawling

a. Are relatively rare activities even in arduous work.

b. Limitations in kneeling and crawling, in themselves, would have very little impact on the sedentary, light and medium occupational bases.

c. A limitation(s) may affect the ability to perform certain specific occupations, e.g., a carpet layer.

5. Loss of Use of an Upper Extremity

a. Greatly impinges on the unskilled sedentary occupational base since such jobs usually require good use of the hands.

b. Would reduce the total number of unskilled occupations within the person's RFC to a little more than the number represented by the full range of sedentary work.

c. **Amputation above the elbow** may reduce the effectiveness in use of the other hand due to the loss of bimanual manipulation and difficulty or inability to handle bulky objects.

d. **Amputation below the elbow** or partial loss of use of the extremity requires consideration of:
   - the condition of the remaining stump;
   - the person's ability to use a prosthesis; and
   - the person's remaining ability for fine and gross manipulation.

6. Medically-Necessary Hand-Held Assistive Device

See DI 25015.020B.6. [SSR 96-9p.]

7. Need to Alternately Sit and Stand

See DI 25015.020B.6. [SSR 96-9p.]

8. Reaching and Handling

a. Are activities required in almost all jobs.

b. Significant limitations may eliminate large numbers of occupations a person could otherwise perform.

c. Depending upon the degree of limitation—may significantly impinge on any range of work.

9. Stooping and Crouching

a. Some stooping is required to do almost any kind of work.

b. Only **occasional** stooping and no crouching are required to perform most sedentary and light occupations. (*See* DI 25001.001 for definition of "occasionally.")

c. The ability to **frequently** stoop and crouch is required to perform most medium, heavy and very heavy occupations because of the lifting requirements involved. (*See* DI 25001.001 for definition of "frequently.")

d. No crouching is required to perform most sedentary or light work.

10. Visual

a. Given only a visual impairment, a substantial occupational base will usually be found for a person who:
   - retains sufficient visual acuity to handle and work with rather large objects; and
   - has the visual fields necessary to avoid ordinary hazards in the workplace.

b. Even if the criteria in "a." above are met, however, a finding of disabled could be appropriate in a few rare instances in which the claimant's profile is extremely adverse, e.g.:
   - closely approaching retirement age;
   - limited or less education;
   - no transferable skills; and
   - essentially a lifetime commitment to a field of work in which good vision is essential.

   (This would be adjudicated under the Lifetime Commitments Special Medical-Vocational Profile. *See* DI 25010.001B.3.)

B. PROCEDURES

When appropriate, consult a Vocational Specialist to determine the effects of a particular limitation on the range(s) of work or particular occupation(s) being considered.

C. REFERENCES

- Residual Functional Capacity (RFC), DI 24510.000.
- Terms Used in Medical-Vocational Evaluation, DI25001.001.
- Determining Capacity to Do Other Work—Implications of a Residual Functional Capacity for Less Than a Full Range of Sedentary Work (SSR 96-9p), DI 25015.020.

[Last Change: 9/14/12]

DI 25020.015 Environmental Limitations

A. INTRODUCTION

A person may have the physical and mental capacity to perform the functions of certain jobs, but to do so may aggravate his/her impairment(s) or subject the individual or others to the risk of bodily injury due to the environment in which the job is performed. Thus, the effects of any environmental limitation(s) on performing a job and/or a range(s) of work, must also be carefully considered.

See DI 25001.001 for definition of environmental limitation.

B EXAMPLES OF ENVIRONMENTAL LIMITATIONS

Need to avoid being near dangerous moving machinery.

Need to avoid certain chemicals such as petroleum derivatives.

Need to avoid excessive dust or noise.

Need to avoid extreme heat or cold.

C. POLICY

An environmental limitation ordinarily would not significantly affect the range of work existing in the national economy for individuals with the physical capacity for heavy or very heavy work.

A **need to avoid only excessive amounts** of environmental pollutants that exist to some degree in most work places (e.g., dust, noise, etc.) does not significantly impact on any range(s) of work.

An inability to tolerate very little dust, noise, etc., significantly impinges on all ranges of work since very few job environments are entirely free of irritants, pollutants and other potentially damaging conditions.

[Last Change: 9/14/12]

§273 Memorandum to Claimant Re: Working While Your Disability Claim Is Pending

This memorandum is designed to answer questions asked by claimants for Social Security disability or SSI benefits who are considering working part-time during the long wait for their hearings.

Will working part-time make my claim more difficult?

It depends on the facts of your case. As a rule, working a part-time job does not make a case more difficult, but it does once in a while. Sometimes working actually helps a case. Most often, working a part-time job is a neutral factor, neither helping nor harming a case. Occasionally, a judge will draw the wrong conclusions from a claimant's work effort; but this possibility ought not be a reason not to work.

If you earn too much money working at a part-time job, it can cause you to lose your case or limit your back benefits. So, if you are going to work, you need to carefully watch how much you earn. See the discussion below.

If you work, the judge will look closely at your ability to perform work activities. If the job you do part-time is inconsistent with what you have to prove in order to win your disability case, your case will be more difficult—maybe impossible if the part-time job is really inconsistent. For example, if you are under age 50, to win your case you probably must prove that you cannot do any kind of easy job on a full-time basis. So if you are doing a very hard job part-time, the judge will wonder how it is you can do a hard job part-time but you cannot do an easy job full-time. To avoid this problem, be sure to discuss with your lawyer the part-time job you are thinking of doing to make sure the job is not inconsistent with your disability claim.

Usually, though, claimants for disability benefits who work part-time do not work at jobs that are inconsistent with their claims for disability. Working part-time at a job that is totally consistent with your disability claim may actually help your case by illustrating what you are capable of doing and showing your work limitations.

How much can I earn per month?

If you ask employees of the Social Security Administration (SSA) this question, they are likely to tell you to keep your income below what is called the "substantial gainful activity" amount, which for 2015 is $1090 per month. The substantial gainful activity amount is an absolute cut-off point. For example, if you were earning more than the substantial gainful activity amount when you applied for benefits, even $1 more, SSA would deny your claim without even looking at how disabled you are. If you start earning more than the substantial gainful activity amount after you've been off work for less than 12 months, your claim can also be denied outright. After you've been off work for at least 12 months, if you start earning more than the substantial gainful activity amount and you keep earning that much, eventually this will cause your Social Security disability benefits to stop no matter how disabled you are. SSI, however, works differently.

If you are going to work, it is best to keep your income far below the substantial gainful activity amount. The closer your income is to the substantial gainful activity amount, the more likely that problems will arise in your case. In fact, because there are advantages to keeping your income below what SSA calls the "trial work period services" amount, which in 2015 is $780 per month, then we recommend you do just that if your claim is for Social Security disability benefits.

If your claim is for SSI, the trial work period rules do not apply. But because it helps to keep your income well below the "substantial gainful activity" amount while your case is pending, it wouldn't be a bad idea to use the same rule of thumb. Those with SSI claims, however, do not have to compulsively watch every penny when they get close to the trial work period services monthly amount.

What are the advantages to keeping income below the "trial work period services" amount?

The trial work period rules, which were designed for people already receiving benefits, allow a person to earn any amount per month for nine months and still receive their monthly disability benefits. These rules allow you to test your ability to return to full-time work without having your monthly disability benefits stop. For example, if after you've already been found disabled, you use your trial work months by working full-time for eight months and decide you don't want to continue working, there is no harm done to your on-going disability benefits. You'll keep your benefits as long as you don't medically improve.

But it is possible to use up your trial work period months even before SSA has found you disabled. If your income exceeds the trial work period services monthly amount (which is $780 in 2015—it goes up a little every year) for nine months at any time since five full months after you became disabled, even if those nine months are not consecutive, you will have used up your trial work period. Once you use up your nine-month trial work period, it is gone.

If you have already used up your nine-month trial work period by working part-time, you may be surprised when SSA stops your benefits abruptly. For example, if your trial work period has already been used up and then you go to work full-time for eight months, your benefits will be stopped after only three months of work. You'll probably be able to get your benefits back if you stop working within three years of the time when you used up your nine-month trial work period; but then if you work again at the substantial gainful activity level more than three years after you used up your trial-work period, SSA will stop your benefits following the first month of work. If you're unable to continue working at that point more than three years after the end of the trial work period, you'll have more difficulty getting your benefits reinstated.

In short, it is best not to use up your trial work period until you are ready. Because the trial work period can be valuable, we recommend that you do not waste it on part-time work. To keep from wasting the trial work period, you need to keep your monthly income below the trial work period services amount.

When I am trying to keep my income below the trial work period services monthly amount, is it gross income or take-home pay that counts?

Gross income. The trial work period services monthly income rules are very strict. There are no deductions that can be taken against your gross income to reduce it below the trial work period services monthly amount. Because income is not averaged, if you are paid weekly or bi-weekly, you may have some months where you earn more than other months since some months have more paydays.

If I need more income than the trial work period rules allow, what are the rules for working at less than the "substantial gainful activity" level?

Gross income counts but income is averaged. Theoretically, you get to subtract sick pay, vacation pay, and what SSA calls "impairment-related work expenses," which, as a rule, is the amount of out-of-pocket payments you make in order to treat your disabling impairment, but there may be some other work expenses that can be deducted, too. You'll need to consult with your attorney about these deductions because many things you might think are deductible, like health insurance, are not deductible. These deductions can be used to reduce your income below the substantial gainful activity level. However, if you rely on such deductions to keep your income below the substantial gainful activity amount, you're really living dangerously. It is better just to use the substantial gainful activity amount as your guideline and make sure your average monthly earnings do not exceed this amount.

Is it possible to work part-time at my own business?

It is possible but we don't recommend it. SSA's rules allow it to find that a person who is working part-time in his or her own business and actually losing money is engaging in substantial gainful activity. A claim can be denied on this basis alone. Also, even if you are not making much money (or even losing money) but you are working more than 80 hours per month, SSA will find that you are performing trial work period services. Thus, you will be using up your trial work period without making any significant money.

Although trying to start your own business after you have already been found disabled may be a different story, it is not a good idea before you have been found disabled. Telephone your lawyer before you get very far into starting your own business while your disability case is pending.

Does working part-time change how we handle the hearing?

We will take testimony about your work. You will probably be asked to explain it in detail. We also need to provide income records in your possession such as W-2 forms or check stubs. Be sure to save these documents and provide them to your attorney when we are gathering evidence to prepare for your hearing. If these do not provide sufficient information, we may need to request a month-by-month income summary from your employer.

§274 Impairment-Related Work Expenses

Impairment-related work expenses may be deducted from a claimant's earnings in determining if the work constitutes substantial gainful activity. 20 C.F.R. § 404.1574(b)(1). The cost of certain items and services that an impaired person needs in order to work, called impairment related work expenses (IRWE), may be deducted from earnings when considering if work constitutes substantial gainful activity, even though such items and services are also necessary for normal daily activities. 20 C.F.R. § 404.1576(a). But the item or service must be directly related to the disabling impairment.

The costs of routine drugs and medical services are not deductible unless the drugs or services are necessary to control the disabling conditions so as to enable the individual to work. 20 C.F.R. § 404.1576(c)(5). Expenses that are not directly related to the impairments cannot be deducted as IRWE. Thus, the cost of routine annual medical examinations is not deductible. 20 C.F.R. § 404.1576(c)(5)(iii).

It is possible to have the expense of residential modification treated as an IRWE if the claimant works at home, though it may not be treated as an IRWE if the claimant is self-employed and deducts the cost from taxes as a work expense. If the claimant works outside the home, the cost of a wheelchair ramp would qualify because it helps the claimant get to work. 20 C.F.R. § 404.1576(c)(4)(ii). The cost of such large-ticket items can be spread over 12 months or over the period of time that the claimant actually makes payments. 20 C.F.R. § 404.1576(e). Sometimes a portion of payments made in anticipation of work can be deducted if the payment was made within 11 months of starting work. 20 C.F.R. § 404.1576(e)(4).

Attendant care services can also qualify as an IRWE if assistance is needed getting ready for work or getting to and from work or if assistance is needed while at work. 20 C.F.R. § 404.1576(c)(1). But special rules apply if the attendant is a relative. Payment to a relative may be deducted as an IRWE "only if such person, in order to perform the services, suffers an economic loss by terminating his or her employment or by reducing the number of hours he or she worked." 20 C.F.R. § 404.1576(c)(1)(iii)(A).

Deduction may be made only if the cost is actually paid by the individual. Thus, if the cost is paid by insurance, it is not deductible. 20 C.F.R. § 404.1576(b)(3). Payment must be made in the month a claimant is working. 20 C.F.R. § 404.1576(b)(4). Payment must be made in money; payment in kind is not acceptable. 20 C.F.R. § 404.1576(b)(5).

Many claimants struggle to work solely to earn enough money to pay health insurance premiums. They say that they could not control their disabling impairments without medical insurance and that the cost of treatment of their disabling impairments if paid directly would be greater than the cost of the medical insurance. Thus, they argue, the cost of medical insurance ought to be deductible. They are surprised to learn that SSA's position is to the contrary. POMS DI 10520.001A. SSA says the cost of insurance may not be deducted as an IRWE because the cost of medical insurance is not directly related to treatment for the disabling impairment since medical insurance also pays for routine medical care and care unrelated to the disabling impairment. This is a policy that SSA ought to rethink.

There is a lengthy Social Security ruling on IRWE, SSR 84-26, which should be reviewed in these cases along with the extensive explanation provided in the regulations, 20 C.F.R. § 404.1576. *See also* POMS DI 10520.010.

A worksheet for calculating countable income after deducting IRWE is provided at §216.3.

Practice Tip

When IRWE are an issue in your client's case, send your client a copy of the memorandum at §274.1 and ask your client to gather relevant documentation. Then you will need to go through your client's expenses with your client to make a decision whether each item provided by your client may be deducted as an IRWE.

§274.1 Memorandum Re: Impairment-Related Work Expenses (IRWE)

What are IRWE?

Impairment-related work expenses (IRWE) are the cost of *certain* items that you need in order to work, which the Social Security Administration (SSA) deducts from your gross earnings.

How does IRWE help you?

SSA deducts the cost of certain impairment-related items and services that you need to work from your gross earnings when, for purposes of the Social Security disability program, SSA decides if your "countable earnings" demonstrate performance of substantial gainful activity (SGA). It does not matter if you also use these items and services for non-work activities.

SSA also excludes IRWE from your earned income when SSA figures your SSI monthly payment amount. If you are initially filing for SSI disability payments, IRWE may be used to reduce income in order to meet the SSI federal income test.

When will SSA deduct Your IRWE?

SSA deducts IRWE in determining substantial gainful activity for purposes of the Social Security disability program when:

1. The item or service enables you to work;
2. You need the item or service because of your disabling impairment;
3. You paid the cost and are not reimbursed by another source (*e.g.*, Medicare, Medicaid, private insurance);
4. The cost is "reasonable"—that is, it represents the standard charge for the item or service in your community; and
5. You paid the expense in a month in which you were working, except that the cost of durable goods purchased during the eleven months before you started working may be spread over some months of work activity using an SSA formula. Also SSA's rules allow an IRWE deduction for an expense paid in the month after you stopped working to be applied during your last month of work.

For the SSI program, SSA deducts IRWE when SSA figures SSI payment amounts when requirements 1 through 4 above are met, and

- You paid the expense in a month in which you received earned income or performed work while you used the impairment-related item or service.

EXAMPLES OF EXPENSES LIKELY AND NOT LIKELY TO BE DEDUCTIBLE	
DEDUCTIBLE	**NOT DEDUCTIBLE**
1. Attendant Care Services • Performed in the work setting. • Performed to help you prepare for work, the trip to and from work and immediately after work (*e.g.*, bathing, dressing, cooking, and eating). • Services performed by your family member for a cash fee where your family member suffers an economic loss by reducing or ending work in order to help you, (*e.g.*, your spouse reduces work hours to help you get ready for work). • Services are deductible even though they *incidentally* also benefit your family (*e.g.*, meals shared by you and your family).	**1. Attendant Care Services** • Performed on non-workdays or helping you with shopping or general homemaking (*e.g.*, cleaning, laundry). • Performed for someone else in your family (*e.g.*, babysitting). • Services performed by your family member for a cash fee where your family member suffers no economic loss, (*e.g.*, your non-working spouse provides service). • Services performed by your family member for payment "in-kind" (*e.g.*, room and board) regardless if the family member suffers economic loss.
2. Transportation Costs • The cost of structural or operational modifications to your vehicle, which you need in order to travel to work, even if you also use the vehicle for non-work purposes. • The cost of driver assistance or taxicabs where unimpaired individuals in the community do not generally require such special transportation. • Mileage expenses at a rate determined by SSA for an approved vehicle and limited to travel to and from employment.	**2. Transportation Costs** • All transportation costs if your impairment does not prevent driving an unmodified vehicle. • The cost of the vehicle itself whether modified or not, even if you have special transportation needs. • The cost of modification to your vehicle not directly related to your impairment or critical to your operation of the vehicle (*e.g.*, paint or decor preferences). • Your travel expenses related to obtaining medical items or services. • Cost of maintenance and repair of vehicles used for transportation to and from work, since these costs are included in the mileage rates.
3. Work-Related Equipment and Assistants • One-handed typewriters, typing aide (*e.g.*, page-turning devices), measuring instruments, reading aids for visual impairments, electronic visual aids, Braille devices, telecommunications devices for hearing impairments and special work tools.	**3. Work-Related Equipment and Assistants** • If you are self-employed, equipment previously deducted as a business expense. • Reader services if you are visually impaired; interpreter services if you are hearing impaired; expenses for a job coach.
4. Prosthesis • Artificial hip, artificial replacement of an arm, leg, or other parts of the body.	**4. Prosthesis** • Any prosthetic device that is primarily for cosmetic purposes.

DEDUCTIBLE	NOT DEDUCTIBLE
5. Residential Modifications **If you are employed outside of home:** • Modifications to the exterior of your house that permit access to the street or to transportation (*e.g.*, exterior ramps, railings, and pathways). **If you are self-employed at home:** • Modifications made inside your home in order to create a workspace to accommodate your impairment (*e.g.*, enlarge doorway into an office or workroom, the modification of office space to accommodate your problems in dexterity).	**5. Residential Modifications** **If you are employed outside of home:** • Modifications to your house to help you in your home (*e.g.*, enlarge interior doorframes, lower kitchen appliances and bathroom facilities, interior railings, stairway chair lift). **If you are self-employed at home:** • Any modification expenses you previously deducted as a business expense in determining substantial gainful activity.
6. Routine Drugs and Routine Medical Services • Regularly prescribed medical treatment or therapy that is necessary to control your disabling condition (even if control is not achieved), such as anti-convulsant drugs or blood level monitoring; radiation treatment or chemotherapy; corrective surgery for spinal disorders; anti-depressant medication, *etc*. Your physician's fee relating to these services is deductible.	**6. Routine Drugs and Routine Medical Services** • Drugs and/or medical services used for your minor physical or mental problems (*e.g.*, routine physical examinations, allergy treatment, dental examinations, and optician services).
7. Diagnostic Procedures • Any procedure related to the control, treatment, or evaluation of your disabling condition (*e.g.*, brain scans, and electroencephalograms).	**7. Diagnostic Procedures** • Procedures not related to your disabling condition (*e.g.*, allergy testing if allergy is not your disabling impairment).
8. Non-Medical Appliance and Devices • In unusual circumstances, when devices or appliances are essential for the control of your disabling condition either at home or at work (*e.g.*, an electric air cleaner if you have severe respiratory disease), and this need is verified by a physician.	**8. Non-Medical Appliances and Devices** • Devices you use at home or at the office, which are not ordinarily used for medical purposes (*e.g.*, portable room heaters, air conditioners, dehumidifiers, and humidifiers) and for which your doctor has not verified a medical work-related need.
9. Other Items and Services • Expendable medical supplies (*e.g.*, incontinence pads, elastic stockings, and catheters). • The cost of a guide dog including food, licenses, and veterinary services.	**9. Other Items and Services** • An exercise bicycle or other device you use for physical fitness unless verified as necessary by your physician. • Health insurance premiums.
Because it is necessary to go through IRWE with your attorney, gather the necessary documentation to show the amounts paid, what for, and when the payments were made.	

§275 Obtain Information From Your Client

After the judge's assistant telephones you to schedule your client's hearing, notify your client right away. Because a few months may have passed since you first met with your client and reviewed your client's medical history, it will be necessary to obtain information about your client's recent medical treatment. A form for gathering information about recent medical treatment appears at §277. A letter to your client is provided at §276. In addition to notifying your client about the hearing date, it reminds him not to send medical records or reports to SSA without you first seeing them.

§276 Form: Letter to Client re: Hearing Date

Date

Client
Address
City, State Zip

Re: Date of Social Security Hearing

Dear Client:

YOUR SOCIAL SECURITY HEARING IS SCHEDULED FOR ____________________ AT _____. If you cannot come to the hearing, let me know **today.** I will try to set a new date and time for the hearing.

I will do the work needed to make your case ready for the hearing. I will review your Social Security file and get the medical records we need, including reports we need from your doctors.

I need to meet with you to get you ready to testify at your hearing. Please meet me at my office on____________________ at _____. Write this date and time on your calendar and call my office today to let us know that you will be here.

> **You can help prepare for your hearing.** It is very important that you have at least one friend or relative at the hearing who knows you well -- this person will be a witness. I want to ask this person about what you do every day, and the problems caused by your condition. This person should be someone who knows you well. Your witness can be your spouse, other family member, or a close friend. If you want to talk about who should be your witness, please call me.
>
> **I need recent information about your medical treatment.** Please fill out the enclosed form about your doctor and hospital visits since __________. ***Return this form to me TODAY in the enclosed envelope.***
>
> **Mail to the judge the "Acknowledgment of Notice of Hearing" form that comes with the official Notice of Hearing.** An "Acknowledgment of Notice of Hearing" form comes with the Notice of Hearing. I do not have to see it. This is the only thing that you should ever send to the Social Security Administration without letting me see it first.
>
> **All evidence must be submitted at least five days before the hearing.** SSA requires that we submit everything related to your disability even if it is something that says you're not disabled. We will be submitting medical records and reports that we know about, but if there is any medical evidence that you have not told us about, please tell us about it now. If you think of any evidence other than medical evidence that you believe we should submit, please tell us about that too.
>
> **You may have to fill out forms before the hearing.** The judge may also send you forms to fill out before the hearing. These forms ask about your recent medical treatment, your medications, and recent work history. Fill out these forms as soon as you get them, and **send them to me**. I will send them to the judge for you.

There are some things that you **should not** do to get ready for your hearing.

> **Do not get medical records for me unless I ask you to**. I will get the records we need. If both of us ask for the same records, we may pay twice for records, or get records that we cannot use.
>
> **Do not send medical reports to Social Security.** If your doctor gives you a report, send me a copy. If the Social Security judge sends you a form for your doctor to fill out, call me so that we can discuss how to handle this.

Please call me if you have any questions.

Sincerely,

[attorney]

Enclosures

§277 Form: Recent Medical Treatment and Examination

Name: ___________________________________

Tell us about all your medical treatment and examinations after ____________________.

TREATMENT AND EXAMINATION BY DOCTORS, PSYCHOLOGISTS, COUNSELORS, CHIROPRACTORS, PHYSICAL THERAPISTS, ETC.

DOCTOR, ETC. NAME & ADDRESS:	WHICH CONDITION WAS TREATED?	APPROXIMATE DATE:

What have these people told you about your condition? ______________________________

____

____

____

____

INPATIENT AND OUTPATIENT HOSPITAL TREATMENT AND EXAMINATION

NAME AND ADDRESS OF HOSPITAL:	WHY DID YOU GO TO THE HOSPITAL? DESCRIBE THE TREATMENT OR TEST:	APPROXIMATE DATE:

PLEASE RETURN THIS TODAY TO YOUR ATTORNEY

§278 *Imperfect Medical Compliance and Failure to Follow Prescribed Treatment*

Medical Compliance

When you review your client's medical records, if you discover that a treating doctor has indicated your client has had a significant problem with "compliance" with doctor's orders, this may be an issue that needs to be addressed at the hearing. Find out as much as you can about the reasons for the claimant's problems following doctor's orders. Sometimes you will discover that the problem perceived by the doctor is little more than the difference between the doctor's expectation of perfection and the real world in which the claimant tries to do everything the doctor says, but for one reason or another cannot. Compliance, after all, exists on a continuum running from perfection to true refusal to follow prescribed treatment.

Many times, doctors' prescriptions include not only medications and other therapy but also lifestyle changes in diet and exercise or smoking cessation, none of which are easy to accomplish. A patient's success often depends on the patient's intelligence, sophistication, and understanding of medical issues. If the claimant was a C or D student in school, it is unrealistic to expect the claimant to get an A at following a medical regimen.

Unsupervised exercise and even supervised physical therapy sometimes makes the most diligent patients hurt more before they see long-term improvement. Most people, even relatively sophisticated ones, need a lot of encouragement to consistently follow an exercise regimen. This is, after all, one reason rich people hire workout trainers. The poor have no such opportunity.

Poor compliance may be little more than poor understanding or mere remissness. Fatalism, a claimant's bleak outlook on life and feeling that he will never get better no matter what he does, may reduce motivation for treatment. Undiagnosed clinical depression could be at the heart of the matter. Poverty is often a factor that makes it difficult to do everything the doctor says. Many times, you will discover, your client is doing the best he can under the circumstances.

Sometimes it will be necessary to ask the doctor to explain why the doctor thinks the patient is doing a poor job of complying with medical directions. If the issue of medical compliance is raised repeatedly in the medical records, you may need to address it in testimony at the hearing. Often the claimant can offer an explanation that satisfies the administrative law judge.

Rarely are decisions issued that find the claimant failed to follow prescribed treatment within the meaning of 20 C.F.R. § 404.1530 and that the claimant is therefore not disabled. However, poor compliance with medical instructions does crop up in credibility determinations in denial decisions, which conclude, in effect, that the claimant must not be as disabled as the claimant claims to be, otherwise he would do a better job of following prescribed treatment. SSR 96-7p addresses the issue as follows:

> On the other hand, the individual's statements may be less credible if the level or frequency of treatment is inconsistent with the level of complaints, or if the medical reports or records show that the individual is not following the treatment as prescribed and there are no good reasons for this failure. However, the adjudicator must not draw any inferences about an individual's symptoms and their functional effects from a failure to seek or pursue regular medical treatment without first considering any explanations that the individual may provide, or other information in the case record, that may explain infrequent or irregular medical visits or failure to seek medical treatment. The adjudicator may need to recontact the individual or question the individual at the administrative proceeding in order to determine whether there are good reasons the individual does not seek medical treatment or does not pursue treatment in a consistent manner. The explanations provided by the individual may provide insight into the individual's credibility. For example:
>
> - The individual's daily activities may be structured so as to minimize symptoms to a tolerable level or eliminate them entirely, avoiding physical or mental stressors that would exacerbate the symptoms. The individual may be living with the symptoms, seeing a medical source only as needed for periodic evaluation and renewal of medications.
> - The individual's symptoms may not be severe enough to prompt the individual to seek ongoing medical attention or may be relieved with over-the-counter medications.
> - The individual may not take prescription medication because the side effects are less tolerable than the symptoms.
> - The individual may be unable to afford treatment and may not have access to free or low-cost medical services.
> - The individual may have been advised by a medical source that there is no further effective treatment that can be prescribed and undertaken that would benefit the individual.
> - Medical treatment may be contrary to the teaching and tenets of the individual's religion.

Although courts tend to defer to an ALJ's credibility finding, some courts have found adverse credibility determinations based on failure to follow prescribed treatment to be wrong. Here are some examples:

Nguyen v. Chater, 100 F.3d 1462, 1465 (9th Cir. 1996), stated:

> it is common knowledge that depression is one of the most underreported illnesses in the country because those afflicted often do not recognize that their condition reflects a potentially serious mental illness. *See*, e.g., Warren E. Leavy, Hidden Depression, Chi. Trib., Feb. 1, 1996 at 7 (noting that nearly 17 million adult Americans suffer from depression in a given year and that two-thirds of them do not get treatment). Thus, the fact that claimant may be one of millions of people who did not seek treatment for a mental disorder until late in the day is not a substantial basis on which to conclude that Dr. Brown's assessment of claimant's condition is inaccurate. As the Sixth Circuit has noted in finding invalid an ALJ's reasons for rejecting claimant's assertions about his depression, "[a]ppellant may have failed to seek psychiatric treatment for his mental condition, but it is a questionable practice to chastise one with a mental impairment for the exercise of poor judgment in seeking rehabilitation." *Blankenship v. Bowen*, 874 F.2d 1116, 1124 (6th Cir.1989).

In *Shramek v. Apfel*, 226 F.3d 809, 813 (7th Cir. 2000), the court rejected an ALJ's credibility finding based on failure to stop smoking:

> We note that even if medical evidence had established a link between smoking and her symptoms, it is extremely tenuous to infer from the failure to give up smoking that the claimant is incredible when she testifies that the condition is serious or painful. Given the addictive nature of smoking, the failure to quit is as likely attributable to factors unrelated to the effect of smoking on a person's health. One does not need to look far to see persons with emphysema or lung cancer—directly caused by smoking—who continue to smoke, not because they do not suffer gravely from the disease, but because other factors such as the addictive nature of the product impacts their ability to stop. This is an unreliable basis on which to rest a credibility determination.

In *Orn v. Astrue*, 495 F.3d 625, 638 (9th Cir. 2007), the Ninth Circuit stated:

> Our case law is clear that if a claimant complains about disabling pain but fails to seek treatment, or fails to follow prescribed treatment, for the pain, an ALJ may use such failure as a basis for finding the complaint unjustified or exaggerated. *See*, e.g., *Fair*, 885 F.2d at 603. In the case of a complaint of pain, such failure may be probative of credibility, because a person's normal reaction is to seek relief from pain, and because modern medicine is often successful in providing some relief. But in the case of impairments where the stimulus to seek relief is less pronounced, and where medical treatment is very unlikely to be successful, the approach to credibility makes little sense. This second case is probably best exemplified by a claimant whose obesity adversely affects his or her health and activities. *See* S.S.R. 02-1p at 9 (defining "prescribed treatment" narrowly and stating that failure to follow treatment for obesity will "rarely" affect disability determinations). Thus, the failure to follow treatment for obesity tells us little or nothing about a claimant's credibility. In the case before us, there is no reason to conclude from Orn's failure to adhere to an 1800 calorie-per-day diet that he is not telling the truth about his medical problems that are exacerbated by his obesity.

Although it is possible to find some court cases requiring the ALJ to make the same findings for an adverse credibility determination as are required for a determination that a claimant is not disabled because of failure to follow prescribed treatment within the meaning of 20 C.F.R. § 404.1520 and SSR 82-59, discussed below, SSA intended to allow ALJs to conclude simply from a claimant's poor compliance with medical treatment that the claimant's impairment must not be as bad as alleged. A challenge for representing claimants is that it is sometimes true that poor compliance may be a sign that the problems are not as bad as alleged. But this conclusion is one that should be arrived at only after all the others are ruled out, which, in effect, is what SSR 96-7p requires.

Failure to Follow Prescribed Treatment

In order to deny a case based on failure to follow prescribed treatment under 20 C.F.R. § 404.1530, an ALJ must follow the rules of SSR 82-59. The ruling requires that the issue of failure to follow prescribed treatment be addressed only after the claimant is found disabled using the five-step sequential evaluation process and only after SSA has found that the impairment has lasted or is expected to last 12 months. Treatment, which must be prescribed by a treating source, must be "clearly expected to restore" the claimant's capacity to work. There must be "refusal to follow prescribed treatment."

Finally, there must be a determination whether or not failure to follow prescribed treatment was justifiable.

Prescribed by a Treating Doctor

Treatment must be prescribed by a treating source, usually the claimant's doctor. When a claimant does not have a treating doctor but is treated, for example, at an emergency room, SSA says that it is the emergency room doctor who is the treating source whose prescribed treatment must be followed. SSR 82-59 reminds the reader that state agency physicians and consultative examiners are not treating sources. If they should indicate that a specific treatment would restore the claimant's capacity to work, their opinions do not count in an initial disability determination.

Treatment Must Be Prescribed

The treating doctor must prescribe a course of treatment. When a doctor gives a patient treatment options and the patient chooses one rather than another, the treatment that the patient did not choose was not prescribed. SSR 02-1p, the ruling on obesity, stated that treatment must be prescribed, "not simply recommended. A treating source's statement that an individual 'should' lose weight or has 'been advised' to get more exercise is not prescribed treatment." Thus, a mere recommendation to lose weight is not prescribed treatment, though a specific diet could be prescribed, or taking diet medication could be prescribed.

A recommendation for surgery can be prescribed treatment. But when one of the claimant's doctors recommends surgery and another recommends against it, "failure to follow the recommended treatment was justifiable. (Where an individual chooses to follow treatment recommended by one treating source, to the exclusion of alternate treatment recommended by one or more other treating sources, the issue of 'failure' does not arise.)" SSR 82-59.

Clearly Expected to Restore Ability to Work

It is required that prescribed treatment be *clearly* expected to restore the claimant's ability to work. Although SSA says the finding whether following prescribed treatment can be clearly expected to restore the claimant's ability to work will be made by SSA, SSA will consider the opinion of the claimant's doctor on this issue. SSR 82-59.

Whether following prescribed treatment would be clearly expected to restore the claimant's ability to work requires a medical opinion from someone—a state agency doctor or a medical expert. Where no opinion on the subject appears in the record, can an ALJ make such a determination without the assistance of a medical expert? It would seem not. Note that the issue is not merely whether the claimant might improve if the claimant followed a particular treatment. The issue is whether the treatment clearly would restore the claimant's ability to work.

Refusal to Follow Prescribed Treatment

SSR 82-59 uses the word "refusal" to follow prescribed treatment more than once. Thus, it is clear that the sort of failure to follow prescribed treatment SSA has in mind is a willful one. Simply doing a poor job of following treatment, which may be the source of most physician complaints of poor compliance, does not qualify as a willful refusal to follow the treatment.

Consider Claimant's Limitations

Before a claimant can be denied benefits because of failure to follow a prescribed course of treatment, an inquiry must be conducted into the circumstances surrounding the failure. The regulation states that SSA will "consider your physical, mental, educational, and linguistic limitations (including any lack of facility with the English language) when determining if you have an acceptable reason for failure to follow prescribed treatment." 20 C.F.R. § 404.1530(c). SSR 82-59 states that claimants "should be asked to describe whether they understand the nature of the treatment and the probable course of the medical condition (prognosis) with and without the treatment prescribed. The individuals should be encouraged to express in their own words why the recommended treatment has not been followed."

Good Cause Not to Follow Prescribed Treatment

The regulation, 20 C.F.R. § 404.1530(c), provides the following examples of good reasons not to follow prescribed treatment:

(1) The specific medical treatment is contrary to the established teaching and tenets of your religion.

(2) The prescribed treatment would be cataract surgery for one eye, when there is an impairment of the other eye resulting in a severe loss of vision and is not subject to improvement through treatment.

(3) Surgery was previously performed with unsuccessful results and the same surgery is again being recommended for the same impairment.

(4) The treatment because of its magnitude (e.g. open heart surgery), unusual nature (e.g., organ transplant), or other reason is very risky for you; or

(5) The treatment involves amputation of an extremity, or a major part of an extremity.

Three additional examples of "justifiable cause" for failure to follow prescribed treatment are stated in SSR 82-59. HALLEX II-5-3-1 contains this note: "The terms 'justifiable cause' as used in SSR 82-59 and 'good reason' as used in 20 CFR 404.1530(b) and 416.930(b) should be considered synonymous." The numbers are those that appear in SSR 82-59:

> 3. In an unusual case, a claimant's or beneficiary's fear of surgery may be so intense and unrelenting that it is, in effect, a contraindication to surgery. *If a treating source who had advised surgery later decides that the individual's fear is so great that the individual is not a satisfactory candidate for surgery, there is no issue of "failure."*
>
> Where fear of surgery is suggested to be extreme, but the treating source has limited contact with the person and is unable to indicate the significance of the fear, an independent examination by a psychiatrist may be warranted as a means of resolving whether the fear contraindicates surgery.
>
> Attendant to allegations of fear, it is not uncommon to see surgery refused on the grounds that the absolute success of such treatment has not been "guaranteed." No physician can guarantee the results of a major surgical procedure since any surgery generally entails some degree of risk. An individual may also attempt to justify refusal of surgery on the grounds of alleged personal or third-party knowledge of persons who did not improve, or perhaps worsened, following surgery similar to that recommended to the individual by a treating physician. However, such reason(s) for nonacceptance of surgical treatment will not, in and of itself, negate a finding of "failure."
>
> 4. *The individual is unable to afford prescribed treatment which he or she is willing to accept, but for which free community resources are unavailable.* Although a free or subsidized source of treatment is often available, the claim may be allowed where such treatment is not reasonably available in the local community. All possible resources (e.g., clinics, charitable and public assistance agencies, etc.), must be explored. Contacts with such resources and the claimant's financial circumstances must be documented. Where treatment is not available, the case will be referred to VR.
>
> 5. *Any duly licensed treating medical source who has treated the claimant or beneficiary advises against the treatment prescribed for the currently disabling condition.* Thus, if a person has two treating sources who take opposing views regarding treatment, one recommending and one advising against the same treatment, failure to follow the recommended treatment was justifiable. (Where an individual chooses to follow treatment recommended by one treating source, to the exclusion of alternative treatment recommended by one or more other treating sources, the issue of "failure" does not arise.)

Opportunity to Follow the Prescribed Treatment

SSR 82-59 provides that before a determination is made that the claimant has failed to follow prescribed treatment, the individual "will be informed of this fact and of its effect on eligibility for benefits. The individual will be afforded an opportunity to undergo the prescribed treatment . . . ."

Duration Requirement Met

Where the failure to follow prescribed treatment does not arise until after the 12-month duration requirement is met, SSR 82-59 says that the claimant is to be found entitled to a closed period of disability. Disability ends when there is refusal to follow prescribed treatment. The ruling suggests that where the duration requirement is met, it is permissible for an ALJ or the Appeals Council to issue a favorable decision and refer the claim for a continuing disability review to develop the issue of failure to follow prescribed treatment.

Seizure Cases

In the usual case it is rare that a decision is issued that finds a claimant not disabled on the grounds of failure to follow prescribed treatment. However, this does regularly occur in seizure cases. Social Security Ruling 87-6 makes failure to follow prescribed treatment a central issue in every seizure case. *See* §239 of this book.

Obesity

SSR 02-1p provides:

> 10. How Do We Evaluate Failure To Follow Prescribed Treatment in Obesity Cases?
>
> Before failure to follow prescribed treatment for obesity can become an issue in a case, we must first find that the individual is disabled because of obesity or a combination of obesity and another impairment(s). Our regulations at 20 CFR 404.1530 and 416.930 provide that, in order to get benefits, an individual must follow treatment prescribed by his or her physician if the treatment can restore the ability to work, unless the individual has an acceptable reason for failing to follow the prescribed treatment. We will rarely use "failure to follow prescribed treatment" for obesity to deny or cease benefits.
>
> SSR 82-59, "Titles II and XVI: Failure To Follow Prescribed Treatment," explains that we will find

failure to follow prescribed treatment only when all of the following conditions exist:

- The individual has an impairment(s) that meets the definition of disability, including the duration requirement, and
- A treating source has prescribed treatment that is clearly expected to restore the ability to engage in substantial gainful activity, and
- The evidence shows that the individual has failed to follow prescribed treatment without a good reason.

If an individual who is disabled because of obesity (alone or in combination with another impairment(s)) does not have a treating source who has prescribed treatment for the obesity, there is no issue of failure to follow prescribed treatment.

The treatment must be prescribed by a treating source, as defined in our regulations at 20 CFR 404.1502 and 416.902, not simply recommended. A treating source's statement that an individual "should" lose weight or has "been advised" to get more exercise is not prescribed treatment.

When a treating source has prescribed treatment for obesity, the treatment must clearly be expected to improve the impairment to the extent that the person will not be disabled. As noted in question 13, the goals of treatment for obesity are generally modest, and treatment is often ineffective. Therefore, we will not find failure to follow prescribed treatment unless there is clear evidence that treatment would be successful. The obesity must be expected to improve to the point at which the individual would not meet our definition of disability, considering not only the obesity, but any other impairment(s).

Finally, even if we find that a treating source has prescribed treatment for obesity, that the treatment is clearly expected to restore the ability to engage in SGA, and that the individual is not following the prescribed treatment, we must still consider whether the individual has a good reason for doing so. In making this finding, we will follow the guidance in our regulations and SSR 82-59, which provide that acceptable justifications for failing to follow prescribed treatment include, but are not limited to, the following:

- The specific medical treatment is contrary to the teaching and tenets of the individual's religion.
- The individual is unable to afford prescribed treatment that he or she is willing to accept, but for which free community resources are unavailable.
- The treatment carries a high degree of risk because of the enormity or unusual nature of the procedure.

In this regard, most health insurance plans and Medicare do not defray the expense of treatment for obesity. Thus, an individual who might benefit from behavioral or drug therapy might not be able to afford it. Also, because not enough is known about the long-term effects of medications used to treat obesity, some people may be reluctant to use them due to the potential risk.

Because of the risks and potential side effects of surgery for obesity, we will not find that an individual has failed to follow prescribed treatment for obesity when the prescribed treatment is surgery.

Smoking

Also, lung impairment cases may be denied on the grounds that the claimant failed to follow prescribed treatment to cease smoking.

In *Rousey v. Heckler* 771 F.2d 1065, 1069 (7th Cir. 1985), the Seventh Circuit addressed smoking:

> Essential to a denial of benefits pursuant to Section 404.1530 is a finding that if the claimant followed her prescribed treatment she could return to work. No such finding was made in this case. Indeed, the evidence in the record is to the contrary. . . . The Secretary argues that we can affirm the ALJ nonetheless because "[t]he adverse effect of smoking on chronic obstructive pulmonary disease is well documented." Appellee's br. at 14. But this argument ignores the reality of the Secretary's role in making disability determinations. These decisions must be based on testimony and medical evidence in the record or on the regulations. The ALJ cannot make his own independent medical determinations about the claimant. *Freeman v. Schweiker*, 681 F.2d 727, 731 (11th Cir.1982). It was therefore improper for the ALJ to make his own determination regarding the prognosis of recovery should Mrs. Rousey stop smoking, when the record was devoid of any evidence that she could return to work if she quit smoking.

Mental Impairments

HALLEX II-5-3-1, which is an "Appeals Council Interpretation" effective May 20, 1982, provides:

> Social Security Administration Regulations at 20 CFR 404.1530 and 416.930 and Social Security Ruling 82-59 provide that a claimant will be found not disabled if he fails, without good reason, to follow prescribed treatment which can restore the

ability to work. While these sources give examples of good reasons for not following prescribed treatment, none of the examples mentions or addresses psychiatric causes. However, neither the regulations nor the ruling specifically gives an all-inclusive list of good reasons. Moreover, SSR 82-59 states that a full evaluation must be made in each case to determine whether the individual's reason(s) for failure to follow prescribed treatment is justifiable. The ruling also provides that if the issue of "failure" arises at the hearing or Appeals Council levels, and such issue has not been fully developed through testimony and/or evidence submitted, a favorable decision will be issued provided 12 months have expired since onset. The case will then be referred for development of failure to follow prescribed treatment.

The existence of a psychiatric impairment may provide good reason for a claimant's failure to follow prescribed treatment. An example of such would be a paranoid schizophrenic with a highly organized delusional system which leads him to believe that people are attempting to poison him, and that medication prescribed by a physician is part of the poisoning 'plot.'

If a claimant has a psychiatric impairment and his refusal to follow prescribed treatment is based on that impairment or that impairment and a combination of other impairments, the Appeals Council may find that such impairment is a good reason for not following prescribed treatment.

The principle stated by the Appeals Council is broader than the example in the Appeals Council Interpretation. A more common situation is simply where someone with a mental impairment does not believe he has a mental impairment. Or he understands he has a mental impairment but his insight is so limited that he does not realize the necessity for regularly taking medication.

In practice, it is rare to see a denial decision based on someone with a mental impairment refusing to follow prescribed treatment.

§279 ODAR's March 2016 Best Practices For Claimants' Representatives

ODAR's March 2016 Best Practices For Claimants' Representatives

Introduction

We are pleased to provide the revised *Best Practices for Claimants' Representatives*. It is our hope that all claimants' representatives will use these best practices as an aid when advocating and appearing before the Office of Disability Adjudication and Review (ODAR).

ODAR is one of the largest administrative adjudicatory systems in the world. The claimants who appear before us may feel overwhelmed by the legal and administrative requirements associated with pursuing a Social Security claim. Therefore, it is important for those most closely associated with this effort to work together in a collegial and professional manner to make this process as efficient as possible. With those goals in mind, we share these best practices so that we can successfully fulfill our joint mission to provide the best possible service to the public.

Debra Bice
Chief Administrative Law Judge
Social Security Administration
Office of Disability Adjudication and Review

Patricia A. Jonas
Executive Director
Social Security Administration
Office of Disability Adjudication and Review

March 2016

1.01 Be familiar with and follow the rules of conduct and standards of responsibility for representatives.

All claimant representatives should be familiar with, and follow, the rules set forth at 20 CFR 404.1740 and 416.1540. These rules identify both the affirmative duties of a representative and the prohibited actions. *See also* Hearings, Appeals, and Litigation Law Manual (HALLEX) I-1-1-40.

1.02 Obtain as much information as possible from our website, http://www.ssa.gov/appeals/index.html

This practice is a general rule for all dealings with SSA. At the hearing level, the majority of claimants are represented, and we encourage our employees to cooperate as much as possible with requests for information or assistance from representatives. Every personal request for information from hearing office personnel, however, diverts the employee from performing responsibilities relating to other hearing requests. The time saved when representatives obtain information from the website can mean thousands of saved hours that can be devoted to processing other claims. Additional information is available on SSA's website for representatives.

1.03 Timely and properly submit all necessary forms.

This practice should include forms SSA-1696 (Appointment of Representative) and SSA-827 (Authorization to Disclose Information to the Social Security Administration), as well as any fee agreement. If applicable, obtain and submit withdrawals and waivers from prior representatives to avoid possible delay in payment. Moreover, representatives must submit a form SSA-1695 (Identifying Information for Possible Direct Payment of Authorized Fees) to the SSA field office, not the hearing office, even if the case is pending at the hearing level.

1.04 Establish and maintain a good working relationship with hearing office staff and management.

Participate in periodic group meetings with the Hearing Office Chief Administrative Law Judge and Hearing Office Director in the offices in which you practice. Open dialogue allows both representatives and hearing offices to exchange suggestions as to how to improve service in the local area.

1.05 Timely notify the hearing office of any change of address or phone number for either yourself or the claimant.

This ensures that claimants and representatives receive timely notifications and limits the potential for a non-appearance at a scheduled hearing.

1.06 When withdrawing representation, provide sufficient written notice to the claimant as well as to the hearing office.

If you decide to withdraw as representative, please notify the hearing office and claimant as far in advance of the hearing date as possible. Use HALLEX I-2-4-25 C.1.c. and D.1., as well as section I-1-1-30, as a guide.

1.07 Ensure a fee agreement or a fee petition is consistent with Social Security law and policy.

Using the language contained in the sample fee agreement on our website reduces the chance of a fee agreement being disapproved by an administrative law judge (ALJ) for failing to meet the statutory requirements.

See Social Security Act §§206(a) and (b), 1631(d)(2); 20 CFR 404.1700 *et seq.* and 416.1500 *et seq.*; and HALLEX I-1-2.

1.08 If the claimant decides to withdraw his or her Request for Hearing, provide timely and sufficient written notice of the withdrawal request to the hearing office.

Notifying the hearing office in a timely fashion, and preferably as far in advance of the hearing date as possible, may allow the hearing slot to be given to another claimant.

Prior to an Administrative Law Judge Hearing

Under 20 CFR 404.935 and 416.1435, claimants have a duty to submit additional evidence or a summary of the evidence with a Request for Hearing or within 10 days after filing the request, if possible. Under 20 CFR 405.331, claimants in Region 1 (Maine, New Hampshire, Vermont, Massachusetts, Connecticut and Rhode Island) must submit any written evidence no later than five business days before the date of the scheduled hearing. Therefore, we encourage all representatives to review the file and submit evidence as early in the hearing process as possible. Do not wait until the case is scheduled to submit evidence.

Submitting Evidence

2.01 Take advantage of your ability to access a claimant's electronic folder.

Appointed representatives who have registered for the Appointed Representative Services and who request eFolder access can view and download documents in Sections A, B, D, E, and F of the Case Documents and Exhibit List tabs of their clients' Certified Electronic Folders. Representatives can also download any digital hearing recordings in the electronic folder to their personal computers. Please remember that you must be the primary representative of record in order to access the electronic file.

2.02 Do not submit duplicative or illegible evidence.

Agency regulations require claimants and representatives to submit all evidence that relates to the claimant's disability claim received from any source in its entirety, unless the same evidence was previously submitted to the Agency. *See* 20 CFR 404.1512(c) and 416.912(c).

These regulations also require the claimant's representative to help the claimant obtain the information or evidence that we require the claimant to submit under our regulations. Submitting duplicative or illegible evidence significantly delays preparation of cases for hearing. Hearing office staff often spend several hours on any given case sorting out duplicate evidence. The sooner a case is prepared and exhibited, the sooner the hearing office can schedule the case. If a document is not readable because it is illegible or a poor copy, provide a typed and legible version or a clearer copy, when possible.

2.03 Submit or inform us about all known evidence relating to whether the claimant is disabled.

A claimant and representative must inform us about or submit all known evidence that relates to whether the claimant is disabled, subject to two narrow exceptions for privileged communications. These exceptions are oral and written communications protected by the attorney client privilege, and information subject to the attorney work-product doctrine. Failure to comply with the Rules of Conduct may lead to sanctions against a representative.

A representative may ask the hearing office for assistance in obtaining existing medical evidence from a medical source after he or she has made a good faith effort to obtain that evidence, or when the representative is unable to obtain the evidence for reasons beyond his or her control. *See* HALLEX I-2-5-14. These requests for assistance should be submitted no later than 30 days before the hearing, to allow time for the hearing office to request and receive the evidence in time for the hearing. Failure to do so could result in case processing delays.

2.04 Submit evidence as far in advance of the hearing as possible, using Electronic Records Express (ERE).

Representatives should provide sufficient time for hearing office staff to associate the evidence with the file. Please submit evidence via the ERE more than 15 working days before the hearing, as this practice allows hearing office personnel to exhibit the evidence and ensures that the claimant's copy of the file includes a copy of all the evidence that has been received. It also gives the ALJ time to review all the evidence, and helps to ensure that all relevant evidence is timely provided to experts scheduled to appear at hearing. As noted above, in Region 1, evidence must be submitted no later than five days before the hearing.

2.05 Do not submit voluminous records as one document.

Up to 200 pages at one time can be faxed into the electronic folder using the fax number and bar code supplied with the Acknowledgment of Hearing notice. However, we recommend smaller submissions when possible. Instead of submitting new evidence into the record as one large exhibit, divide the evidence into separate exhibits containing the records from a single medical source, preferably less than 30 pages, for ease of processing and identification. This practice assists hearing office staff in reviewing the evidence for duplicates and exhibiting the records.

2.06 Before submitting evidence, check to ensure the evidence submitted belongs to the claimant.

This simple precaution significantly reduces the time hearing offices spend contacting representatives and re-associating evidence with the appropriate file.

2.07 When faxing evidence from different sources into the electronic folder, separate sources by placing a bar code as the first document for each source and submit in chronological order.

Submitting evidence separately by source is the most effective way to assist the hearing office in completing a timely and accurate review of the record, and allows the hearing office to associate new evidence with any previous medical or opinion evidence from the same source and helps the hearing office to review the claimant's case faster. Organizing records by date of medical service, oldest to newest, likewise assists the hearing office in quickly and accurately reviewing the claimant's course of treatment with a particular source. This practice also assists hearing office staff with reviewing the evidence for duplicates and in exhibiting the records.

Ensure that the barcode is the first item faxed in order to ensure proper identification of all records. If you do not have a barcode for a particular case, please ask the hearing office to provide you with one. Bar codes may be photocopied and used more than once, but only for the same claimant.

2.08 Submit a cover letter with the evidence identifying what is being submitted and the date of the evidence.

Submitting evidence with a cover letter and the dates of the evidence will assist hearing office staff in identifying duplicates and in exhibiting the records. Clearly label newly submitted evidence with the source's name, the dates covered, and number of pages. For example: Attachment A – records from Mercy General Hospital, Topeka, KS, for the period 1/2012 through 6/2013, 16 pages; Attachment B – records from treating physician John Smith, M.D., Topeka, KS, for the period 12/2011 through 1/2013, 5 pages.

2.09 Do not submit medical evidence with non-medical evidence documents such as appointment of representative forms or fee agreements.

Because these documents are included in different sections of the folder, it requires more time to separate documents if they are submitted together.

Pre-hearing Brief

2.10 Address employment (substantial gainful activity, unsuccessful work attempts, sheltered work environments, etc.) and earnings issues in a pre-hearing brief or at the hearing.

Be sure to distinguish long-term disability, vacation, or bonus pay, which may appear as earnings after alleged onset.

2.11 Address worker's compensation issues in a pre-hearing brief or at the hearing.

If there has been a settlement, provide appropriate proof.

2.12 Submit concise pre-hearing briefs whenever possible.

This practice assists an ALJ in preparing for the hearing and focusing on the issues or arguments you wish to raise.

Submitting On-The-Record (OTR) Requests

2.13 Clearly label an OTR request "OTR Request," and submit as early as possible (but only when a request is appropriate).

OTR requests are not appropriate in every case, and you should only request an OTR when the evidence in the record unequivocally supports a favorable outcome.

2.14 Identify evidence that supports the OTR.

OTR requests should include a concise summary at the beginning of the brief outlining the argument, followed by a more detailed explanation specifically directing the reviewer's attention to evidence supporting a favorable decision.

2.15 Make sure the evidence supports the alleged onset date.

Onset issues are one of the most frequent reasons an OTR request cannot be granted.

2.16 When contacted, work with attorney advisors to expedite decisions.

Attorney advisors review and screen cases for an OTR, and some senior attorney advisors have the authority to issue a fully favorable OTR decision when it is warranted. If you are contacted by an attorney advisor regarding substantial gainful activity or onset issues in a particular case, discuss the matter with the attorney advisor to see if the issue can be resolved without a hearing.

2.17 Submit updated evidence with an OTR request.

With updated evidence, an ALJ may issue a fully favorable decision without a hearing in a case, which saves time and resources for both the claimant and the hearing office.

Submitting Dire Need and Terminal Illness requests, or information regarding incarcerated individuals

2.18 Notify the hearing office when the claimant has a terminal condition, or is homeless or in dire need. Include appropriate documentation supporting these allegations.

If the allegation is supported, notifying a hearing office of these circumstances can expedite the processing of a case. You must provide sufficient documentation to support the request. The criteria for critical case processing are located in HALLEX I-2-1-40.

2.19 If the claimant is incarcerated, know our procedures and keep the hearing office informed.

It is very important that the hearing office be apprised of the status of an incarcerated claimant and the anticipated duration of the incarceration.

Scheduling, logistical and other issues arise when a claimant is incarcerated. These may include the manner of appearance available at the correctional facility, and issues with scheduling a consultative examination, among others. As stated in HALLEX I-2-3-10 A, a claimant's confinement in a prison or other institution may require an ALJ to schedule the hearing at the place of confinement, by video teleconferencing (VTC), or by telephone when neither an in-person nor VTC hearing is possible.

Scheduling Hearings

2.20 Provide scheduling availability

Hearings require the participation of numerous individuals. These include the ALJ, the claimant, the hearing reporter, the expert witnesses, and possibly a claimant representative, other witnesses, or an interpreter. As requested by the hearing office or National Hearing Center, please provide your scheduling availability to ease the scheduling process for all involved.

2.21 Do not request postponements unless essential.

Be flexible when providing dates and times for hearings, and timely request postponements in writing whenever possible. When you have already agreed to the time of a scheduled hearing, avoid requesting a postponement for a conflict that arises later.

2.22 Consider appearing at the hearing by VTC.

We encourage you to appear at hearings by video teleconferencing (VTC). When a hearing is held by VTC, the claimant may appear at a field office, hearing office, or his or her representative's office if the representative has signed up for the

Representative Video Project (RVP). RVP allows a claimant and his or her representative to appear at the hearing from the representative's office using the representative's video equipment that has been certified by SSA's Office of Systems. More information on RVP can be obtained at www.ssa.gov/appeals/odar_pubs/70-070.pdf. In addition, please see the pamphlet "Why You Should Have Your Hearing by Video Teleconference," available at http://www.ssa.gov/appeals/odar_pubs/70-067.pdf, which discusses the advantages of having a hearing by video.

2.23 When representing a child, have an adult available to care for the child during the entirety of the hearing.

A child claimant may not be able, or required, to remain present in the hearing room for the entire hearing. An adult must be present to care for the child outside of the hearing room. SSA staff will not provide care for the child.

2.24 Notify the hearing office in advance if any special accommodations or assistance is needed.

The agency will provide an interpreter free of charge, when requested, if a claimant has difficulty understanding or communicating in English. However, interpreters for some languages are more difficult to obtain. Please ensure that the request is submitted as far in advance as possible. Additionally, under Section 504 of the Rehabilitation Act, other accommodations may be possible to ensure that claimants are able to fully participate in the hearing. Make such requests as far in advance of the hearing as possible. For more information, see HALLEX I-2-0-8.

After an Administrative Law Judge Hearing

3.1 Submit post-hearing evidence as soon as possible, and include a written brief identifying how the evidence supports a favorable decision.

This practice will assist the ALJ in reviewing the records and appropriately focus attention on the information supporting your arguments, resulting in the issuance of a timely decision. If you are unable to submit evidence within the time period allotted by the ALJ, timely advise the hearing office of the circumstances, including whether you are requesting additional time, or if you need our assistance in obtaining the evidence (see information in 2.03).

3.2 Submit fee petitions within 60 days of a decision or as soon as possible after your services have been terminated or withdrawn.

Submitting fee documents within this period will have a significant impact on the time a representative waits for payment. This practice reduces the number of follow-ups necessary to determine if a fee petition will be submitted, allowing the ALJ to act on the fee authorization at an earlier date. It reduces the likelihood that funds withheld for direct payment will be released to the claimant, and reduces the wait time if administrative review of an authorized fee is requested.

Actions Before the Appeals Council

Requests for Review

4.1 Requests for review must be in writing.

We make available Form HA-520, Request for Review of Hearing Decision/Order, for this purpose, but a written request in any form is acceptable.

4.2 A request for review cannot be submitted via the Internet.

This Appointed Representative Guide to Requesting Appeals Council Review chart describes the three best methods to submit a request for review.

Using any other method, including submission by Electronic Records Express or by fax with a barcode can cause significant delays in processing because Appeals Council (AC) staff does not receive an alert that a request was filed.

4.3 Candor and truthfulness is necessary in any submission to the AC, including the request for review.

Please note that submissions to the AC, including the request for review, additional arguments, and any additional evidence, are governed by 18 USC §§ 1001 and 1621. These statutes, as well as our regulations, require representatives to be forthright in their dealings with us and prohibit a representative from knowingly making false or misleading oral or written statements, assertions, or representations to us about a material fact or law (20 CFR 404.1740 and 416.1540).

Requesting Critical/Terminal Illness (TERI) Case Status

4.4 If a claimant's case is critical, let us know when you file the request for review.

If you believe a claimant's case qualifies for expedited processing under our critical case procedures in Hearings, Appeals, and Litigation Law (HALLEX) manual I-3-1-5, clearly state this in the request for review. Point to or provide evidence to support your request. You can follow up on the request by calling the Congressional and Public Affairs Branch (CPAB) at 1-877-670-2722.

4.5 If you later learn that a claimant's situation is critical, contact us immediately.

If you believe a claimant's medical condition or financial situation becomes critical after you file the request for review, fax a brief statement and supporting documents to CPAB staff at (703) 605-8021. You can also contact the CPAB staff by phone at 1-877-670-2722. A specialist on the CPAB staff will evaluate the claimant's situation under HALLEX I-3-1-5 and take appropriate action.

Procedural Requests

4.6 If you are requesting a copy of the record, submit a clear request.

If you wish to receive a copy of exhibits or the hearing recording in a case, please clearly state this request **at the beginning** of your correspondence to facilitate support staff screening and action on your request. Our letter responding to your request will grant you a 25-day extension of time and will include two AC level barcodes that you can use to submit additional evidence or arguments.

4.7 Be specific in requesting an extension of time.

Requests for an extension of time should explain how much additional time you need and why the AC should grant the request. For second requests, or requests for more than 40 days, the AC will consider the particular set of circumstances in each case. The AC does not grant extensions automatically and will grant additional time only if there are extenuating circumstances present in the case. If the AC grants an extension of time, we will provide you with barcodes to submit additional evidence or arguments.

4.8 If you want barcodes, request an extension of time.

Since the AC only sends barcodes when specifically asked, the best way to ensure that you get AC level barcodes is to request an extension of time when you submit the request for review.

Representative Access to Electronic Folders

4.9 Take advantage of your ability to access a claimant's electronic folder.

Appointed representatives who have registered with the Social Security Administration (SSA) for the Appointed Representative Services and who request eFolder access are able to view and download documents in Sections A, B, D, E, and F of the Case Documents and Exhibit List tabs of their clients' certified electronic folders. As long as the case is pending before the AC, representatives can also download any digital hearing recordings in the electronic folder to their personal computers.

4.10 Make the AC aware of any changes in representation.

If a claimant has appointed more than one representative, only the main representative (as indicated on the Form SSA-1696 with the most recent date) will have access to the electronic folder. If a claimant's main representative changes, it is very important that you notify the AC right away so we can update our records.

4.11 Other issues to note about access to the electronic folder:

- If our records indicate that you have access to the electronic folder, we will not send you copies of a claimant's hearing recording or exhibited evidence on compact discs. We will grant you an extension of time and notify you in our letter that our records indicate you have access to the electronic folder.
- If a claimant has more than one claim pending at the same time (e.g., a claimant has a claim pending at the hearing level and at the AC), representatives will not have access to the electronic folder of either claim.
- A representative has access to a claimant's electronic folder for 90 days after the AC completes its action in a case. During the 90 days, only the representative recorded in our case control system at the time the case was closed has access to the electronic folder. If the claimant obtains a new representative to file a civil action, the new representative will not have access to the claimant's electronic folder.

Evidence Submissions

4.12 Submit any additional evidence or comments with the request for review.

For internal review and association purposes, it is very helpful if you submit the request for review and all evidence at the same time. Claimants must inform the agency about or submit to the agency all evidence, in its entirety, known to him or her that relates to whether he or she is blind or disabled. Representatives must help the claimant obtain the information or evidence that the claimant must submit. This duty applies at the AC level if the evidence relates to the period on or before the date of the administrative law judge (ALJ) decision.

4.13 If you have additional evidence, explain how it is material to the period at issue.

In regard to new evidence, the AC applies 20 CFR 404.970 and 416.1470. For disability claims filed in the Social Security Administration's Region I (Connecticut, Maine, Massachusetts, New Hampshire, Rhode Island, and Vermont), the AC applies 20 CFR 405.401 to new evidence submissions.

4.14 Avoid submitting duplicate evidence.

The AC has access to the entire record present at prior levels of adjudication, including the hearing level. Please do not resubmit information that is already available to the AC.

4.15 There are three ways to submit evidence to the AC.

You can submit evidence directly to the electronic folder by mail or fax, via the Electronic Records Express website, or by paper fax directly to the AC. Please see this Appointed Representative Guide to Requesting Appeals Council Review chart for a detailed explanation of each method. Please note, as discussed in section 4.2 above, you should never submit a request for review by the Electronic Records Express website.

4.16 When submitting evidence, organizing it chronologically and by source greatly aids case processing.

The AC reviews all evidence presented at prior levels of adjudication as well as evidence submitted while a claim is pending with the AC. Submitting evidence separately by source is the most effective way to assist the AC in completing a timely and accurate review of the record. Instead of submitting all new evidence into the record as one large exhibit, divide the evidence into separate exhibits containing the records from a single medical source. This allows the AC to associate new evidence with any previous medical or opinion evidence from the same source and helps the AC to review the claimant's case faster. Organizing records by date of medical service, oldest to newest, assists the AC in quickly and accurately reviewing the claimant's course of treatment with a particular source.

Clearly label newly submitted evidence with the source's name, the dates covered, and number of pages. For example: Attachment A – records from Mercy General Hospital, Topeka, KS, for the period 1/2012 through 6/2013, 16 pages; Attachment B – records from treating physician John Smith, M.D., Topeka, KS, for the period 12/2011 through 1/2013, 5 pages.

Contentions

4.17 Contentions should be specific.

The AC appreciates receiving concise, focused arguments. We recommend using 2,000 words or less if possible.

4.18 Contentions need not include a recitation of the jurisdictional history or evidence generally, unless related to a specific point of contention.

As the record is already before the AC and the AC reviews the entire record in each claim, a summary of the evidence is not necessary. There is also no need to send us a copy of the administrative law judge's decision or a copy of the hearing recording.

4.19 Cite to the record.

Citing specific exhibits and the pertinent page numbers of cited exhibits in support of a specific point of contention helps us review the record more efficiently.

Status Inquiries

4.20 Do not make automatic, multiple requests for the status of a request for review.

You can verify that the AC has received the request for review through the online status report available in the Social Security Administration's (SSA) Appointed Representative Services (ARS), by contacting your local Social Security office or local hearing office, or by calling our Congressional and Public Affairs Branch at 703-605-8000 and toll free at 1-877-670-2722.

4.21 Requirements to view the online AC status reports.

On August 26, 2013, SSA expanded ARS to include an online status report for cases pending at the AC. To have access to the AC status report, representatives must register with SSA for ARS. Additionally, the case must be pending before the AC with a record in our case control system, and the representative attempting to access the report must be shown as the claimant's representative in our case control system.

If you attempt to access ARS, are denied access, and the error message says, "Our system cannot accept the Social Security Number you entered" (see screenshot below):

- You may have entered the wrong Social Security Number (SSN); or
- You may not be shown as the appointed representative for this case in the Case Processing and Management System (CPMS) or the Appeals Review Processing System (ARPS).

If you are denied access and the error message says, "Your ability to use the Access Claimant's Electronic Folder service has been suspended" (see screenshot below), please call the telephone number provided in the message to reinstate your access. If you have already called to reinstate access and the problem persists, send your REP ID and contact information to **^ODAR HQ ARS** and request that they contact you to restore access to the electronic folder.

If you receive an error message saying "Unable to Process Your Request" (see screenshot below), it could be the result of one of the following problems:

- The case is not electronic;
- The case was closed more than 90 days ago;
- The case is not at the hearing office (HO) or AC level;
- The case has been remanded; or
- There are multiple pending cases at the HO or AC levels.

4.22 Representatives have three options for viewing their cases in real-time:

- Search for individual cases by SSN. (Cases must be active or closed within the last 90 days.)
- View a list of up to 100 of the oldest cases for all AC offices. (Cases must be active or closed within the last 90 days.)
- Download all cases for all AC offices in a spreadsheet file. (Cases must be active or closed within the last 90 days.)

4.23 The view only status report will display the following information:

- Claimant Name (Last, First)
- Last 4 of SSN
- Case Status/Status Date
- Appeals Office with Jurisdiction
- Transfer Information
- Electronic Case (Yes or No)
- Request Date
- Expedited (Yes or No)

4.24 The downloaded status report will display the following information:

- Claimant Name (Last, First)
- Last 4 of SSN
- Case Status/Status Date
- Claim Type
- Appeals Office with Jurisdiction
- Transfer Information
- Electronic Case (Yes or No)
- Request Date

- Expedited (Yes or No)
- Fee Agreement (Yes or No)
- Fee Petition (Yes or No)
- Title II and Title XVI (T2 & T16, respectively) Decision

NOTE: The Fee Agreement field displayed in the downloaded AC Status Report will always contain a **NO** unless the AC issues a favorable decision.

4.25 What it means if the T2 or T16 Decision field shows "Other".

The AC status report only provides detailed status information for the request for review workload. Therefore, the T2 & T16 Decision field will include denials, dismissals, favorables, unfavorables, and remands.

The workload types below will display the T2 & T16 disposition code "Other" when one of the following types of cases is closed.

BP	FORR	FORMAL RETURN
BP	INFR	INFORMAL RETURN
EOT	GRNT	GRANT EOT TO FILE CIVIL ACTION
EOT	OTHR	EXHIBITS / RECORDING SENT - NO EOT TO FILE CA
REO	FORR	FORMAL RETURN
URA	CONC	CONCUR WITH UNFAV ALJ DEC (ONE ADJUDICATOR)
URA	CON2	CONCUR WITH UNFAV ALJ DEC (TWO ADJUDICATORS)
URA	XCNC	CONCUR WITH UNFAV ALJ DEC (TWO ADJUDICATORS)
URR	EFC2	EFFECTUATE QA SENT TO EFFECTUATING COMPONENT
URR	EFEC	EFFECTUATE - SENT TO EFFECTUATING COMPONENT
URR	INFR	INFORMAL RETURN

4.26 Further descriptions of the "Case Status" field:

- New case – New request entered in control system pending further screening
- Case workup – Screening or case preparation actions (e.g., responses to claimant or rep initiated requests for extensions, file material, timeliness of filing)
- Pending analyst assignment – Preparation actions completed; in assignment queue
- Assigned to analyst – Assigned to analyst for workup and referral to adjudicator
- Assigned to adjudicator – With AC for disposition
- Document preparation – AC notice prepared for release

4.27 Other issues to note about the AC online status report:

- Only the representative recorded in the AC's case control system will have access to the status report. If a claimant's main representative changes, it is very important that you notify the AC right away so we can update our records. (The AC recognizes as the representative of record the person designated as the main representative on the Form SSA-1696 with the most recent date.)
- The AC online status report only provides information for active cases or cases closed within the last 90 days. Only the representative recorded in our case control system at the time the case was closed has access to the online status report.
- Federal court cases are excluded from the AC status report.

§280 Preparation as the Hearing Date Approaches

Order necessary medical and vocational records and reports early enough so that you will have them no later than three weeks before the hearing (because records are due 5 business days before the hearing). 20 C.F.R. § 404.935. As the time for the hearing approaches, turn your attention to final hearing preparation. Schedule an appointment with your client, arrange for witnesses, and consider the need for subpoenas. Also consider whether you have one of those novel cases in which a prehearing conference with the ALJ would be helpful in facilitating the hearing; and consider whether a hearing is necessary at all.

§281 Ask for a Prehearing Conference

An underutilized regulation provides for prehearing conferences between the parties to the hearing and the ALJ. Such a conference may be held on the ALJ's initiative or at the request of a party:

> to facilitate the hearing or the hearing decision. The administrative law judge shall tell the parties of the time, place and purpose of the conference at least seven days before the conference date, unless the parties have indicated in writing that they do not wish to receive a written notice of the conference. At the conference, the administrative law judge may consider matters in addition to those stated in the notice, if the parties consent in writing. A record of the conference will be made. The administrative law judge shall issue an order stating all agreements and actions resulting from the conference. If the parties do not object, the agreements and actions become part of the hearing record and are binding on all parties.

20 C.F.R. § 404.961

If your client's case is an appropriate one for requesting a prehearing conference, do so in writing and explain in detail why a conference is necessary, why such a conference may expedite the hearing, or why a conference may obviate the need for a hearing. Do not request a prehearing conference merely to open an opportunity to argue your client's case with the ALJ. This may be viewed by the ALJ as an abuse of the prehearing conference procedure which is designed for unusual situations involving difficult hearing issues or the potential for an on-the-record favorable decision.

Prehearing conferences may be held by telephone. Sometimes the ALJ is not involved in the prehearing conference. Instead, the conference may be scheduled to be conducted by a staff attorney, known as an attorney advisor. *See* HALLEX I-2-1-75. If this happens, do not be disappointed. The attorney will probably be the person who actually writes the decision in your client's case. Any efforts at persuading the attorney about the merits of your client's case will not be wasted.

§282 Request an On-the-Record Favorable Decision

20 C.F.R. § 404.948(a) provides that an ALJ may issue a wholly favorable decision without holding a hearing. Although this is totally within the ALJ's discretion and the regulation does not mention the possibility of a claimant requesting such a favorable decision, there is no harm in asking. Indeed, such a request is analogous to a summary judgment motion. If it is denied, you may proceed with the hearing with the ALJ already sensitized to the strength of your case and, if the ALJ tells you why he denied your request, you will know what he is looking for.

Be very sure, however, that your request for an on-the-record favorable decision pursuant to 20 C.F.R. § 404.948(a) is not construed as a waiver of your client's right to a hearing under 20 C.F.R. § 404.948(b).

§283 Never Waive a Hearing

A hearing is the best opportunity to impress upon the ALJ the degree to which your client is disabled. Never waive a hearing.

Some claimants are scared to death of hearings. Use all your persuasive powers to reassure them. You may represent claimants whose mental impairments are such that no amount of reassurance will convince them to go to the hearing. When this occurs, it is an issue for testimony by the claimant's friends and family when, after notifying the ALJ in advance, you attend the hearing without the claimant.

Make sure, though, that you understand the claimant's reasons for refusal to attend the hearing and explore the possibility that they can be accommodated. For example, some phobic claimants fear downtown buildings or elevators. If this is the reason, ask the ALJ to move the location of the hearing. Many ALJs will do so, especially if there is corroboration of this phobia in the medical records.

§284 Request Subpoenas

ALJs have subpoena power in disability cases. Subpoenas may be requested by a party and will be issued for witnesses or documents when "it is reasonably necessary for the full presentation of a case." 20 C.F.R. § 404.950(d)(1). A written request for a subpoena must be filed with the ALJ at least ten business days before the hearing.

> The written request must give the names of the witnesses or documents to be produced; describe the address or location of the witnesses or documents with sufficient detail to find them; state the important facts that the witness or document is expected to prove; and indicate why these facts could not be proven without issuing a subpoena.

20 C.F.R. § 404.950(d)(2). Costs of issuing the subpoena, witness fees and mileage will be borne by the Social Security Administration. 20 C.F.R. § 404.950(d)(3) & (4).

It is SSA's position that the claimant's right to subpoena is qualified. The request to issue a subpoena may be refused by an ALJ on the grounds that the testimony of the witness is not "reasonably necessary for the full presentation of the case." 20 C.F.R. § 404.950(d)(1). In order to comply with SSA's position, it is necessary to explain fully 1) what you expect the witness's testimony to prove and 2) why interrogatories are not an adequate substitute for live testimony.

Usually, the urge to subpoena a witness arises after an adverse report from that witness has been made a hearing exhibit by the ALJ. *See* §§222 and 223 of this book concerning state agency physicians and consulting physicians. In *Solis v. Schweiker*, 719 F.2d 301, 302 (9th Cir. 1983), the Ninth Circuit Court of Appeals held that "[a]lthough interrogatories can adequately replace in-court testimony where factual questions such as foundation or expertise are at issue, we agree with appellant that bias is better elicited through rigorous in-court scrutiny."

If your request for a subpoena is denied, make your record at the hearing, including a request that the report be stricken because the claimant has been denied his right to cross-examine an adverse witness. The United States Supreme Court held in *Richardson v. Perales*, 402 U.S. 389, 402 (1971), that failure of a claimant to request a subpoena precludes him from complaining later that he was denied the rights of confrontation and cross-examination of the author of an adverse medical report. *Richardson v. Perales* has been interpreted by some courts, contrary to SSA policy, to confer "an absolute right to subpoena a reporting physician." *See Lidy v. Sullivan*, 911 F.2d 1075, 1077 (5th Cir. 1990), adopted as an acquiescence ruling. AR 91-1(5).

§285 Submit Additional Evidence – The Five-Day Rule

You are required to inform the ALJ about or submit all evidence no later than five business days before the hearing. 20 C.F.R. § 404.935 provides:

> § 404.935 Submitting written evidence to an administrative law judge.
>
> (a) When you submit your request for hearing, you should also submit information or evidence as required by § 404.1512 or any summary of the evidence to the administrative law judge. Each party must make every effort to ensure that the administrative law judge receives all of the evidence and must inform us about or submit any written evidence, as required in § 404.1512, no later than 5 business days before the date of the scheduled hearing. If you do not comply with this requirement, the administrative law judge may decline to consider or obtain the evidence, unless the circumstances described in paragraph (b) of this section apply.
>
> (b) If you have evidence required under § 404.1512 but you have missed the deadline described in paragraph (a) of this section, the administrative law judge will accept the evidence if he or she has not yet issued a decision and you did not inform us about or submit the evidence before the deadline because:
>
> (1) Our action misled you;
>
> (2) You had a physical, mental, educational, or linguistic limitation(s) that prevented you from informing us about or submitting the evidence earlier; or
>
> (3) Some other unusual, unexpected, or unavoidable circumstance beyond your control prevented you from informing us about or submitting the evidence earlier. Examples include, but are not limited to:
>
> (i) You were seriously ill, and your illness prevented you from contacting us in person, in writing, or through a friend, relative, or other person;

(ii) There was a death or serious illness in your immediate family;

(iii) Important records were destroyed or damaged by fire or other accidental cause; or

(iv) You actively and diligently sought evidence from a source and the evidence was not received or was received less than 5 business days prior to the hearing.

It is best, if possible, to submit additional evidence well in advance of five business days before the hearing. (Note that ODAR's "best practices" memorandum, reprinted at § 279 of this book, recommends submitting evidence more than 15 business days before the hearing.) If you do this, the ALJ will have sufficient time to evaluate the new evidence before the hearing. This new evidence, which will fill gaps and correct misconceptions of the file, will be fresh in the ALJ's mind at the time when your client's testimony adds to the favorable impression. Also, the ALJ's staff will appreciate not getting the additional evidence at the last minute.

Practice Tip

About six business days before the hearing, check the file to make sure everything has been submitted. Write to the ALJ to inform the ALJ about any outstanding records requests or requests for medical source statements. Although the claimant's representative is supposed to assist the claimant in obtaining evidence, 20 C.F.R. § 404.1740(b)(2), your letter to the ALJ is not to shirk that responsibility. The purpose of your letter is to comply with the five-day rule and avoid giving the ALJ a reason to exclude evidence. You will be in compliance with 20 C.F.R. § 404.935(a) if you inform the ALJ about any evidence you have not yet received. You are required to "inform" SSA about "or submit any written evidence." 20 C.F.R. § 404.935(a). If you have timely informed the ALJ about the evidence, you ought to be be able to submit it later. The ALJ cannot use failure to meet the five-day rule as grounds to "decline to consider or obtain the evidence." 20 C.F.R. § 404.935(a). You have not missed the deadline.

If you have informed the ALJ about the evidence, you do not have to meet the requirements of 20 C.F.R. § 404.935(b), which require, in essence, that you show that being late is not your fault and not the fault of the claimant. In some cases, no matter how early you order the records and no matter how diligently you follow up, there will be ALJs who reject your plea based on 20 C.F.R. § 404.935(b)(3)(iv), saying "you should have ordered the records earlier" and decline to consider the evidence. In the introductory comments to the five-day rule regulation, 81 Fed. Reg. 90990 (2016), SSA stated: "If a claimant informs an ALJ about evidence 5 or more days before the hearing, there would be no need for the ALJ to find that an exception applies, because the claimant notified us prior to the deadline." Thus, informing the ALJ about the records avoids arguments about exceptions..

Practice Tip

Delegate to your office staff the job of putting together exhibits for your review before submitting them to the hearing office. The following memorandum, which is designed to help your staff prepare exhibits, may be edited to deal with preferences of local ALJs for how exhibits are submitted.

§285.1 Office Instructions for Submitting Hearing Exhibits

1. At least five business days before the hearing, we are required to inform the ALJ about or submit all evidence that "relates to" a claimant's disability. Revised 20 C.F.R. § 404.935, effective January 17, 2017, established the five-day rule. 20 C.F.R. § 404.1512, effective April 20, 2015, requires us submit all evidence that "relates to" a claimant's disability. The goal of the "all evidence" regulation was to require us to submit everything we get from medical and other sources without having to exercise legal judgment, though we may still have to determine if the evidence "relates to" the claimant's disability -- a broad standard. The primary impact of the regulation on our practice is that we'll be submitting more marginally relevant records, the sort of records that ALJs have told us in the past they do not want or need.
2. The all evidence rule does not require us to change how we request records from medical sources. We still do not need to request all records pertaining to a hospitalization after the alleged onset date. We still limit our requests to clinics and doctors by date range requesting only records after the last date of records received by the state agency. However, if we receive more than what we requested, we are supposed to submit everything. But see below. The "five-day rule" requires us to request evidence early enough that we can be reasonably assured we will have it five business days before the hearing

at the latest. Our goal is to submit evidence about three weeks before the date of the hearing.

3. Remove duplicates. The new 20 C.F.R. § 404.1512(c) says we're supposed to submit evidence we receive from a medical source "in its entirety, unless you previously submitted the same evidence to us or we instruct you otherwise." What if the state agency got the records and we receive duplicates? Letters from the hearing office still tell us not to submit duplicates. So if we receive duplicates of what the state agency gathered, we're not supposed to submit them because we have been instructed otherwise by the hearing office. A comment in the Federal Register said we should remove only "an exact duplicate of a document in the record, and not simply the substance of what is in the record." 80 Fed. Reg. 14834.
4. Documentation of what we received. Save the pdf file of records as we receive them. Create a working file that you "save as" another pdf file. It will be necessary to do this so that we can answer any future questions about what we received in the unlikely event SSA attempts to impose sanctions on us.
5. Worker's compensation records. Request medical and vocational opinion evidence and worker's compensation decisions. If we receive duplicate medical records, remove them.
6. Long term disability insurance carrier records. Request disability examiner analyses, opinions from doctors written at the request of the LTD carrier, i.e. treating doctor opinions and independent medical exams, and analysis by insurance company doctors. If we receive duplicate medical records, remove them.
7. Review hearing exhibits to get a feel for the case. Review the Table of Contents in the pdf hearing exhibit file. With a well-set up file, you'll be able to use the Table of Contents to help identify duplicates. But watch for mistakes on the date-range. That is, just because the Table of Contents says SSA got records from the Jones Clinic up to June 30, 2015, it doesn't necessarily mean that SSA got everything for this period. If we receive records from before June 30, 2015, you're going to have to flip through the records to make sure that they really are duplicates. If you find a mistake in the Table of Contents, identify it in the pdf hearing exhibit file with two pdf sticky notes, one on the Table of Contents page and one on the first page of the actual exhibit.
8. Review the attorney's "theory of the case." Figure out what the issues are. Watch for:
   a. Date last insured (DLI). As a rule, we will focus our attention on the time before the date last insured and several months after the DLI. We usually, but not always, also need to show continuing disability; therefore, we will need to submit some current records. Sometimes current records help explain what was going on before the date last insured; however, in a case where a client is clearly disabled after the DLI (and the exhibit file already has hundreds of pages of medical records showing this), try to figure out a way not to order irrelevant records. For example, judges don't want to have to read hundreds of pages having to do with the client's liver transplant that occurred two years after the DLI. If we receive many pages of marginally relevant records dated after the DLI, put them in a separate exhibit, which we will submit and identify as post-DLI.
   b. Remote onset date. When a claimant alleges an onset date of disability that is years ago, you're going to have to consult with the attorney about whether to order early records. We usually amend the alleged onset date to a more recent date. But sometimes all the good medical records are from years ago. Thus, we may want to stick with the early onset date alleged by the claimant. The state agency never orders medical records from more than one year prior to the date of application.
   c. Onset date appeal. In these cases, SSA has found our client disabled later than our client alleged. We will concentrate on gathering records relevant to the time our client alleges onset of disability. Consult with the attorney before you order current records. In many cases there is no issue over current disability. If so, an option to be exercised by the attorney, not the person ordering medical records, is to provide no records after the date the client has already been found disabled by SSA. Instead, the attorney will meet the requirements of the all evidence rule by providing a complete list of medical contacts and notify the ALJ that we will not be ordering records. In some cases, we will provide all current records, too. In some cases, we take a middle ground and gather just enough current information to show that our client has not improved. Find out the answers to these questions from the attorney before you order records.

d. Appeals Council remand with affirmation of finding of disability on subsequent application. Sometimes when our client has been found disabled on a later application, the Appeals Council's remand order will "affirm" the finding of disability on the later application. Consult with the attorney before you order medical records from the period after the disability finding.

e. Disabled Adult Child. We need to prove that our client was disabled before the age of 22 and remains disabled to the present.

f. What kind of case is this? Mental? Physical? Combination? This affects how we order records. For example, unless the disability has something to do with a gynecological disorder, we seldom order such records and if we get them, we submit them only if they are part of clinic records where our client was treated for other things, too or when they "relate to" our client's disability, i.e., when the gynecologist discusses the disabling impairment. Our clients generally regard gynecological records as private and irrelevant to their disabilities. There are exceptions for everything, though. Everything depends on what we are trying to prove. Every once in a while gynecological records show something useful for the case. We also may not need to order dermatologist records, ophthalmologist records, urologist records and routine mammogram records when the disability case has nothing to do with these things. Consult with the attorney before you order such records.

9. Organize new exhibits by medical care provider—clinic or doctor as appropriate. (This is not necessarily the same place we got the records.)

 a. This is a general rule, one that may be broken at your discretion. Here's a situation where this rule should be broken: For example, we obtain records from the claimant's primary doctor who has sent the claimant to several consultants for one-time evaluations. If those consultants do not find much of significance, rather than submitting several exhibits consisting of a page or two each, it is better to have one larger exhibit from the primary doctor. As a rule, though, we usually submit separate exhibits for each provider even if we got all the records from the primary doctor.

 b. As a rule, records from one clinic should not be broken up (unless the clinic itself treats the records as separate). For example, some clinics with multiple locations require us to order from one location so we submit those records as a group; other clinics require us to order from separate locations—in which case we should list each as if it were a separate clinic.

 c. We generally submit VA records as a unit from each VAMC, e.g., Milwaukee, North Chicago, even though there may be separate clinics involved. (VA records are now page-numbered when they are printed. If we move the records around, we are likely to invite questions. However, VA records now include hundreds of pages, many of which are duplicates. For example, "Consult Requests" are generally useless duplicates of other clinical information. Our records request should exclude "Consult Requests.")

 d. VA Regional Office records usually contain hundreds of pages of duplicate records from the VA Medical Center, which need to be removed from the records we submit. The most valuable items are the rating exam reports and the disability determinations by the VA. If the rating exam report is a thorough evaluation with conclusions that help our client's Social Security disability case, make it a separate exhibit. If the VA disability determination helps prove our client's case before SSA, make it a separate exhibit. If the records from the VA Regional Office do not go right to the heart of our client's case before SSA, lump the VA Regional Office records together.

10. If medical records are sequentially numbered by the provider, leave them in the order we receive them.

11. Unless the records are sequentially numbered by the provider, put them in order by date with the most recent on the bottom and the oldest on top. This is NOT the order we usually receive records from medical providers, so it is usually necessary to reverse the order. Lab reports are almost always together at the bottom of the stack. X-rays and other imaging reports are sometimes received from providers at the bottom of the stack and other times interspersed with treatment records. It is okay to leave the imaging reports in the order set by the medical provider.

12. Add reports we get from our client to records we receive from providers—or set up as separate exhibit. When we order medical records, despite the fact that we always ask for copies of all reports written by treating doctors, we often get

only progress notes. Our client, though, may have given us copies of forms or reports completed by the doctor. These forms or reports may be added to the records we receive from the provider or, if we want to emphasize the report, submitted as a separate exhibit.

13. Be sure to sort any records we may have received directly from our client looking for anything that isn't a duplicate of what we have already obtained from the provider or what already appears in the hearing exhibit file. Prepare these for submission. Be sure to notify the attorney if you think our client sanitized the records.
14. Duplicate removal procedure. Compare new exhibits to what is already in the hearing exhibit file and take out duplicates. Watch for duplicates within the new records we have gathered. Remove them unless the records are sequentially numbered and removing them leaves a page number gap that could invite questions. If you're working with paper, make a stack of duplicates from each provider clipped together with a post-it note on top saying, "Dupes from [name of provider]." Here is an exception: Sometimes a doctor will attach duplicates to one of our medical source statement forms on which the doctor answers one or more questions with "see attached." In this situation, even if the attached records are duplicates, for the judge to know what the doctor meant by "see attached," we need to leave those records attached.
15. Remove junk. Do not submit copies of our request, our consent forms, insurance forms, hospital face sheets, client's consent to treatment forms. If you're working with paper, clip the junk together by the provider and attach a post-it note that says "Junk from [name of provider]." If you're working with Acrobat, extract the junk to a separate file. Do not take anything out if taking it out is somehow misleading. Never take out things that look bad for the case.
16. Sometimes, however, we may need to submit some junk. Sometimes you will see a three-page report that is really a two-page report because the third page is blank except for the page number; but the pagination on the first and second pages indicates that there is a third page. If so, you need to include the blank page so that the judge won't think there is a page missing.
17. A notation from a medical provider that the provider has no records is usually junk that we do not submit. Sometimes, though, such notations are part of a mystery that the ALJ needs to know about. Consult with the attorney whenever our client insists that he or she was treated by the medical provider but the provider has no records.
18. Old records from long before our client's alleged onset date. Make a separate exhibit for the attorney to review. Whether to submit old records depends on whether they "relate to" our client's disability.
19. Sometimes, a doctor will send us redacted medical records. We see this most often in couples therapy where the doctor redacts information concerning our client's spouse. When this happens, we may need to notify the ALJ that it was the doctor who redacted the records.
20. Break up large exhibits. After you've removed the junk and duplicates, see to it that no one exhibit is larger than about 100 pages (at the most). When we get records from one provider that are larger than about 100 pages, try to find a logical way to break them up. For example, when we are submitting multiple years of records, see if you can make each individual year into separate exhibits to meet the page limit goal. If that doesn't work, consider using half years.
21. Pay attention to how we describe each exhibit in our transmittal letter:
    a. Are we providing enough information in the description of the exhibit? For example, when a client is treated primarily by one doctor at a clinic, the transmittal should show the name of the clinic followed by the doctor's name in parentheses. When there are more than two or three doctors who treated our client, list only the clinic name unless the majority of records are from one doctor.
    b. Are the dates correct? Are the page counts correct? Make corrections as necessary.
    c. Where a decision needs to be made NOT to submit something (because it does not "relate to" the client's disability), leave it up to the attorney to remove it. If you think it should not be submitted, write the attorney a note.
22. At least three weeks before the hearing, print a DRAFT of the submission letter and put it on the attorney's desk along with any notes about problem exhibits, missing records, etc.
23. If this case has a rare paper file at ODAR:
    a. After the attorney has reviewed the new exhibits, print the final version of the transmittal letter.

b. Use a pencil to sequentially number the pages in the lower right-hand corner of each page of each exhibit. Also on each page, include the total number of pages in the exhibit, so the page numbers for a 29-page exhibit will look like this: 1/29, 2/29, 3/29, etc.
c. Copy the new exhibits and transmit the originals to the hearing office. Make sure that the exhibits are stacked in the same order that they are listed on the transmittal letter. Hearing office staff ask that exhibits not be stapled—use paper clips or binder clips instead of staples.
d. Scan the individual exhibits (if they have not been scanned already).
e. Staple together our copies of the individual exhibits. Stack the exhibits in the same order that they are listed on the transmittal letter and, using a big binder clip, clip everything together with the transmittal letter on top. File immediately in the exhibits folder in the client's office file.

24. If this case has an electronic file at ODAR:
    a. After the attorney has reviewed the exhibits, print the final version of the transmittal letter.
    b. File exhibits and transmittal letter on the ERE website. Open the scanned copy of each exhibit to double-check it before you enter it on the ERE website. Make sure it is the correct exhibit and that the page counts correspond to the transmittal letter. Scroll through the entire exhibit to make sure there are no upside down pages; if there are, use Acrobat to fix the problem.
    c. Use the Acrobat printer to print the confirmation from the ERE website. If you print a paper copy of the confirmation, scan it. In our database, associate the pdf copy of each exhibit with the pdf confirmation.
25. Be sure to send our client a copy of the transmittal letter.

§286 Prepare a Hearing Brief or Proposed Decision

HALLEX I-2-8-13 provides:

A. Office of Disability Adjudication and Review (ODAR) Policy

All claimants and claimant representatives may submit a brief or written statement explaining why the evi-dence in the record supports a fully favorable decision. Such submissions are entirely voluntary and may be made at any time in the hearing process, from the filing of the request for hearing through any post-hearing time limit set by the administrative law judge (ALJ). Unrepresented claimants may submit a brief or written statement on their own or with the assistance of an advocate.

ODAR encourages representatives to submit briefs or written statements electronically. More information is available on the Social Security Administration website (http://www.socialsecurity.gov/appeals/otr.html).

B. Guidelines for Applying ODAR Policy
The following guidelines apply:
1. Hearing Offices should encourage claimants and representatives who wish to do so to provide a brief or written statement.
2. The submission of a brief or written statement is voluntary. An ALJ may not order any claimant or repre-sentative to submit a brief or written statement.
3. An ALJ is not required to use language or rationale from any submitted brief or written statement. An ALJ also is not required to provide reasons for not using the provided language or rationale in the decision.

On its website at http://www.socialsecurity.gov/appeals/otr.html, SSA says: "If you believe the evidence supports a fully favorable decision for your claimant, you may submit a brief to us, preferably before we hold a hearing. You may also submit a proposed check sheet in lieu of a brief, following the guidelines in HALLEX I-5-1-17." The check sheet to which SSA refers is the one used by ALJs for bench decisions, a copy of which is reproduced at §286.3.

When your case raises an unusual issue, it is especially useful to submit a brief on this issue before the hearing. Even in more routine cases, many ALJs appreciate concise pre-hearing briefs that analyze the significant medical evidence and step through the sequential evaluation process. At a minimum, submit a paragraph that states your theory of the case identifying the medical records or reports that support it and the regulatory basis under which a favorable decision may be issued.

Some attorneys submit proposed findings and a draft of the "decisional paragraph" that always appears at the end of a decision. A sample form appears at §286.1.

Some attorneys like to submit a more detailed memorandum. Milwaukee Attorney Bob Angermeier devised a prehearing memorandum worksheet from which his secretary prepares a memorandum based on his handwritten notes. A sample form based on his worksheet appears at §286.2.

§286.1 Form: Proposed Findings and Decision

RE: ______________________________

SSN: ______________________________

Findings

1. The claimant met the insured status requirements of the Act on [*insert onset date*], the date s/he states s/he became unable to work, and continues to meet these requirements through the date of this decision.

2. S/he has not performed any substantial gainful activity since the alleged onset date, [*insert onset date*].

3. The claimant has the following severe impairments: ______________________
____
____

4. The claimant's impairments do not meet or equal in severity the appropriate medical findings contained in 20 CFR Part 404, Appendix 1 to Subpart P (Listing of Impairments).

5. The claimant's allegations are found to be credible.

6. The claimant has the following residual functional capacity: ________________
____
____

7. The claimant is unable to perform his/her past relevant work as ______________

8. The claimant has no transferable work skills.

9. The claimant was _____ years old on the date the disability began and has a _____ grade education.

10. Based upon the claimant's residual functional capacity and vocational factors, there are no jobs existing in significant numbers which s/he can perform. This finding is based on [the framework of the] Medical-Vocational Guidelines, Rule ________, 20 CFR Part 404, Appendix 2 to Subpart P.

11. The claimant has been under a disability as defined by the Social Security Act and Regulations since the alleged onset date, [*insert onset date*].

Decision

Based on the Title II application filed on [*insert T2 application date*], the claimant is entitled to a period of disability beginning [*insert onset date*], and to disability insurance benefits under §§ 216(i) and 223, respectively, of the Social Security Act; and the claimant's disability has continued through at least the date of this decision.

[Add the following in a concurrent case]

It is the decision of the Administrative Law Judge that based on the Title XVI application filed on [*insert SSI application date*], the claimant has been disabled since [*insert onset date; note, however, in an SSI-only case you may use the date of the SSI application preceded by the words "at least"*], under section 1614(a)(3)(A) of the Social Security Act, and the claimant's disability has continued through the date of this decision.

The Social Security Administration must also determine whether the claimant meets the income and resources and other eligibility requirements for supplemental security income payments, and if the claimant is eligible, the amount and the month(s) for which the claimant will receive payment. The claimant will receive a notice from another office of the Social Security Administration when that office makes those determinations.

§286.2 Form: Prehearing Memorandum Worksheet

SOCIAL SECURITY ADMINISTRATION
OFFICE OF DISABILITY ADJUDICATION AND REVIEW

RE: Application for:

☐ Social Security Disability Benefits

☐ SSI

☐ Disabled Widow(er)'s Benefits

☐ Disabled Adult Child Benefits

___________________________, SSN: ____________________
Claimant

___________________________, SSN: ____________________
Wage Earner

PRE-HEARING MEMORANDUM

A. PROCEDURAL HISTORY

The procedural history is as follows:

1. An initial application was [☐ protectively] filed on ___________________.

2. The initial application was denied on ___________________.

3. A Request for Reconsideration was filed on ___________________.

4. The Request for Reconsideration was denied on ___________________.

5. A Request for Hearing was filed on ___________________.

B. ADMINISTRATIVE ACTION

The State Agency determined that the claimant has a medically determinable condition(s) consisting of:

1.

2.

3.

4.

☐ The State Agency determined that the claimant has the physical residual functional capacity for ☐ modified, ☐ sedentary, ☐ light, ☐ medium work.

☐ The State Agency found that the claimant's mental residual functional capacity was for ☐ routine, ☐ repetitive, ☐ low stress, ☐ unskilled work.

☐ The State Agency determined that the claimant could perform past relevant work as a ____________________________.

☐ The State Agency determined that the claimant cannot perform past relevant work.

☐ The State Agency determined that the claimant has not performed substantial gainful employment since ________________.

☐ SSA determined that work activity from ____________ to ____________ represented an unsuccessful work attempt.

C. STATEMENT OF FACTS

1. Preliminary Matters:

The claimant's date last insured is __________________.

The claimant's [☐ amended] alleged onset date is __________________.

☐ By this memorandum, the claimant hereby requests to amend the alleged onset date to __________________.

2. Reopening:

A prior application dated _____________ was initially denied on _____________.

☐ A request to reopen the prior application was filed on _______________.

☐ The current application, which alleges an onset date within the previously adjudicated period, constitutes an implied request to reopen within the meaning of HALLEX I-2-9-1.

☐ Reopening is hereby requested by this memorandum.

Basis for Reopening:

☐ Reopening is requested ☐ within one year for any reason. That reason is:

☐ Reopening is requested for good cause within the:

☐ 2-year good cause SSI time limit, 20 C.F.R. §§ 416.1488(b) and 416.1489

☐ 4-year Social Security disability good cause time limit, 20 C.F.R. §§ 404.988(b) and 404.989, measured from the date of the initial denial on the earlier claim.

☐ Good cause is demonstrated by the following new and material evidence: ____.

☐ Good cause is demonstrated by the fact that the evidence clearly shows on its face that an error was made, that is: ____________.

☐ Reopening of a Social Security disability application is appropriate at any time pursuant to 20 C.F.R. 404.988(c) because: ______________________.

HALLEX I-2-9-1 provides: "If an ALJ has jurisdiction to reopen and revise a determination or decision . . . and the conditions for reopening are met, the ALJ *must* reopen the determination or decision." (Emphasis added.)

3. Age and Education:

☐ The claimant is _____ years old (dob: _________).

☐ The claimant is ______ tall and weighs ______ pounds.

☐ Education—highest grade completed: ______.

☐ The claimant has had the following vocational training: ________________________.

D. PRIOR WORK HISTORY

1. Employment:

a. Employer: ____________________________

Dates of Employment: ____________________

Description of Work: _______________________________________

Exertional Demands: ______________________________________

Skill Level: ____

b. Employer: ____________________________

Dates of Employment: ____________________

Description of Work: _______________________________________

Exertional Demands: ______________________________________

Skill Level: ____

c. Employer: ____________________________

Dates of Employment: ____________________

Description of Work: _______________________________________

Exertional Demands: ______________________________________

Skill Level: ____

d. Employer: ____________________________

Dates of Employment: ____________________

Description of Work: ______________________________________

Exertional Demands: ______________________________________

Skill Level: ____

2. Unsuccessful Work Attempts:

a. Dates of Employment: __________________

Name of Employer: __________________________

Description of Work: ______________________________________

Reason Work Ended: ______________________________________

b. Dates of Employment: __________________

Name of Employer: __________________________

Description of Work: ______________________________________

Reason Work Ended: ______________________________________

3. Less Than SGA Work After Alleged Onset Date:

a. Dates of Employment: _______________

Name of Employer: _________________

Description of Work: ____________________________________

Monthly Earnings: __________________

IRWE: ____

b. Dates of Employment: _______________

Name of Employer: _________________

Description of Work: ____________________________________

Monthly Earnings: __________________

IRWE: ____

E. SIGNIFICANT MEDICAL HISTORY

1. Chronology of Medical Treatment:

____

____

2. Disabling Conditions:

a.

b.

c.

d.

e.

f.

3. Restrictions and Symptoms:

a.

b.

c.

d.

e.

f.

4. Medications:

Medication	Dosage	Condition
a.		
b.		
c.		
d.		
e.		
f.		

5. Treating Physicians:

a. Name: ______________________________

Specialty: ____________________________

Dates of Treatment: ____________________

b. Name: ______________________________

Specialty: ___________________________

Dates of Treatment: ___________________

c. Name: ______________________________

Specialty: ___________________________

Dates of Treatment: ___________________

F. THEORY OF THE CASE

☐ 1. Because of symptom-related limitations of function, the claimant is incapable of performing a full-time job of any sort, not even a sedentary one. As such, Rule 201.00(h) of the Medical-Vocational Guidelines provides the basis for finding the claimant disabled.

☐ 2. Because of symptom-related limitations of function, the claimant is incapable of performing past relevant work and is limited to performing work at the ☐ sedentary ☐ light/exertional level. As such, Rule _____ of the Medical-Vocational Guidelines requires that the claimant be found disabled.

☐ 3. ____

____

____

G. ISSUES OF LAW

1. Does the claimant's impairment meet or equal a "Listed" impairment? 20 C.F.R. § 404.1520(d).

2. Can the claimant perform past relevant work? 20 C.F.R. §§ 404.1520(f) and 404.1560(b).

3. Are there jobs in the national economy that the claimant can be expected to perform given the claimant's age, education and prior work experience? 20 C.F.R. §§ 404.1520(g) and 404.1560(c)(1).

☐ 4. What is the appropriate onset date? SSR 83-20.

☐ 5. Should the prior application be reopened? 20 C.F.R. § 404.988.

☐ 6. Is alcoholism or drug addiction a material factor? 20 C.F.R. § 404.1535.

H. RATIONALE

☐ The treating physician, Dr. ___________, is a board-certified specialist in ________________. This specialization entitles his medical opinion to greater weight. 20 C.F.R. § 404.1527(c)(5).

☐ Dr. _______________ is also a treating physician with significant longitudinal experience with the claimant. His opinions are well supported by diagnostic and clinical evidence.

☐ The State Agency physicians who evaluated this case are specialists in the fields of _________________ and ____________________. The professional qualifications of these physicians are a relevant consideration. 20 C.F.R. § 404.1527(c)(5). These State Agency physicians have not been involved in direct patient care for over ____ and ____ years respectively. They did not examine the claimant. Their medical opinions are entitled to less weight than examining sources. 20 C.F.R. § 404.1527(c)(1).

☐ Social Security Ruling 96-6p directs that State Agency physicians include in their evaluation consideration of "the existence and severity of the claimant's symptoms." Form SSA 4738-U8 is designed to elicit this assessment. The State Agency physicians failed to perform this assessment. (Exhibit _____, _____.) The claimant has previously put the agency on notice of a variety of symptoms that produced physical limitations. (Exhibits ___, ___, ___, ___, and ___.) Thus, the only medical opinions on the issue of the limitations arising from the claimant's symptoms are those supplied by the treating or examining physicians. (Exhibits ___, ____, ____, and ____.)

☐ "[B]ecause nonexamining sources have no examining or treating relationship . . . the weight [the Social Security Administration] will give their opinions will depend on the degree to which they provide supporting explanations for their opinions." 20 C.F.R. § 404.1527(c)(3). Form SSA 4734-U8 is designed to elicit this information. Exhibit ___ contains the purported explanation. It is deficient in the following respects:

☐ There are limited circumstances where the medical opinions of a state agency medical consultant can be given greater weight than those of treating or examining sources. SSR 96-6p. For example, SSR 96-6p explains that a state agency doctor's opinion may be entitled to greater weight than a treating source if it is based "on a *complete case record* that includes a medical report from a specialist in the individual's particular impairment which provides more detailed and comprehensive information than what was available to the individual's treating source." (Emphasis added.)

In the present case, the State Agency's medical opinion was not based upon a complete case record. (*See* Ex. ____, ____, ____, ____, _____, all of which were not part of the case record at the time the State Agency's medical opinion was generated.) There are no reports from a specialist on the claimant's particular impairment (______________, _________________, _______________) which provide more information than what was available to the individual's treating source. Thus, in the present case, the State Agency's medical opinions cannot be afforded greater weight than those of the treating/examining sources.

☐ The medical opinions offered by the State Agency consultant, Dr. _________, are inadmissible because that physician, a ______________, is not qualified by knowledge, training or experience to offer medical opinions pertaining to the claimant's condition.

I. PROPOSED FINDINGS

1. Insured Status/Widows:

   a. The claimant met the insured status requirements of the Act on ____________, (his/her) alleged onset date, and continues to meet them through _____________________.

   b. The claimant is the widow of the wage earner who died fully insured on ____________, and the claimant is not married. The period during which the claimant must establish that (he/she) was under a disability extends through ___________________.

2. Age/Date of Birth:

   a. The claimant was born on ______________.

   b. The claimant is ___ years old, which is defined as

      ☐ A "younger" individual.

      ☐ "Closely approaching advanced age" (50-54).

      ☐ "Advanced age" (55 to 59).

      ☐ "Closely approaching retirement age" (60 to 65).

   c. The claimant died on ________________.

d. The claimant was ___ years old at the time of the alleged onset of disability, and is ____ years old as of the date of the decision.

3. Education/Language Development:

a. ☐ The claimant is illiterate. That is, the claimant is unable to read or write simple messages. 20 C.F.R. § 404.1564(b)(1).

b. ☐ The claimant has a:

☐ "Marginal" education (6th grade or less).

☐ Limited education (7th through 11th grades).

☐ High school education (or more).

c ☐ Recent testing indicates that current functioning is at the grade level which corresponds to a "__________" education. 20 C.F.R. § 404.1564(b).

4. Severe Medical Impairments: Does Not Meet Listings:

a. The medical evidence establishes that the claimant has: ____, but that (he/she) does not have an impairment or combination of impairments listed in, or medically equal to, one listed in Appendix 1, Subpart P, Regulations No. 4. These impairments are "severe" under the Social Security Act and the Regulations.

5. Meets/Equals Listings:

☐ MENTAL

a. The severity of the claimant's mental dysfunction meets the requirements of Section 12.____, Appendix 1, Subpart P, Regulations No. 4 and has precluded him/her from working for at least 12 continuous months (20 C.F.R. § 404.1525). The claimant's restriction of activities of daily living is ☐ moderate/ ☐ marked/ ☐ extreme; the claimant's difficulties in maintaining social functioning is ☐ moderate/ ☐ marked/ ☐ extreme; the claimant's difficulties in maintaining concentration, persistence or pace are ☐ moderate/ ☐ marked/ ☐ extreme; the claimant has suffered ☐ no/ ☐ one or two/ ☐ three/ ☐ four or more episodes of decompensation.

☐ PHYSICAL

a. ☐ The claimant is suffering from a severe impairment, namely_____________, which meets the requirements of Listing Section _______, Appendix 1, Subpart P, Regulations No. 4.

b. ☐ The claimant's impairment is equal in severity to an impairment cited at Section ______ of the Listing of Impairments, 20 C.F.R. Part 404, Appendix 1 to Subpart P.

6. Date Last Worked/Unsuccessful Work Attempt:

a. ☐ The claimant did not engage in substantial gainful activity from ____________ through ______________.

b. ☐ The claimant has not performed any substantial gainful activity since the alleged onset date _________.

c. ☐ The claimant has not performed any substantial gainful activity since the [o protective] filing date for SSI, __________.

7. Function-by-Function Residual Functional Capacity:

The claimant can walk about _____ blocks before stopping. S/he can sit for about _____ minutes at one time and stand for about _____ minutes at one time. Out of an 8-hour working day, s/he can sit for a total of _____ hours and stand/walk for a total of _____ hours. S/he can occasionally lift and carry _____ lbs. and frequently lift and carry _____ lbs.

☐ S/he needs to walk around approximately every _____ minutes for about _____ minutes.

☐ S/he needs a job that permits shifting positions at will.

☐ The claimant needs to take unscheduled breaks [☐ to lie down] during an 8-hour working day. This is expected to happen ________________________; and s/he may need to rest ___________ minutes (on average) before returning to work.

☐ When sitting, the claimant needs to elevate his/her legs about _____% of the time during an 8-hour working day. S/he needs to elevate his/her legs about _____ high.

☐ The claimant needs a cane to walk.

☐ The claimant is limited to ☐ occasional fingering, ☐ occasional handling and ☐ occasional reaching during the working day.

☐ The claimant's mental residual functional capacity is as follows: ____.

8. Symptoms:

a. The claimant's medically determinable impairments could reasonably be expected to produce the claimant's symptoms.

b. The claimant's alleged limitations are consistent with the objective medical evidence and other evidence in the case record.

c. The claimant's testimony relative to the severity of (his/her) limitations is found to be credible.

9. Cannot Perform Past Relevant Work:

a. The claimant is unable to perform any of (his/her) past relevant jobs.

10. Transferability of Skills:

a. The claimant has no transferable work skills.

11. Occupational Base:

a. ☐ The claimant is limited to less than a full range of sedentary work. Based upon the claimant's residual functional capacity, and vocational factors, there are no jobs existing in significant numbers that the claimant can perform. This finding is based upon Rule 201.00(h) of the Medical-Vocational Guidelines, 20 C.F.R. Part 404, Appendix 2 to Subpart P, Regulations No. 4.

b. ☐ The claimant is limited to sedentary work. Based upon the claimant's residual functional capacity, and vocational factors, there are no jobs existing in significant numbers that the claimant can perform. This finding is based upon ☐ the framework of Medical-Vocational Rule 201.__, 20 C.F.R. Part 404, Appendix 2, Subpart P, Regulations No. 4.

c. ☐ The claimant is limited to light work. Based upon the claimant's residual functional capacity, and vocational factors, there are no jobs existing in significant numbers that the claimant can perform. This finding is based upon
☐ the framework of Medical-Vocational Rule 202.___, 20 C.F.R. Part 404, Appendix 2 to Subpart P, Regulations No. 4.

d. ☐ The claimant is limited to medium work. Based upon the claimant's residual functional capacity, and vocational factors, there are no jobs existing in significant numbers that the claimant can perform. This finding is based upon
☐ the framework of Medical-Vocational Rule 203.___, 20 C.F.R. Part 404, Appendix 2 to Subpart P, Regulations No. 4.

12. Occupational Base: Mental:

a. ☐ Due to the claimant's psychiatric impairments, the claimant does not have the residual functional capacity to perform unskilled/low-stress work on a sustained basis.

13. Occupational Base: Irregular Attendance:

a. ☐ Considering the claimant's education and skill levels, the claimant's medical impairments would produce frequent work absences to the extent that sustained work activity could not be achieved on an eight-hour-per-day, five-day-per-week basis.

14. Ability to Return to Work (Closed Period):

a. ☐ As of ______________, the claimant possessed the residual functional capacity for sedentary work and Medical-Vocational Rule 201.__ of Table No. 1, Appendix 2; Subpart P of Regulations No. 4 directs a finding that the claimant was no longer disabled.

b. ☐ Considering the claimant's condition within the framework of Vocational Rule ______, Appendix 2, Subpart P, Regulations No. 4, there are a substantial number of jobs in the economy that the claimant would be capable of performing after ______________.

15. Participation in Trial Work:

a. ☐ Since _____________, the claimant has been engaged in substantial gainful activity. Because the claimant has not medically improved, this work activity constitutes a period of "trial work." 20 C.F.R. §§ 404.1592 and 404.1594(f)(1).

16. Work Not SGA:

a. ☐ The claimant's part-time work activity since __________ as a ________________ for an average of ____ hours a week does not constitute substantial gainful activity within the meaning of the Regulations. 20 C.F.R. § 404.1574(b).

b. ☐ The claimant's work activity as a _________________ from _______________ to ________________ constitutes an unsuccessful work attempt within the meaning of the Regulations. 20 C.F.R. § 404.1574(c).

J. PROPOSED CONCLUSIONS

The claimant has been under a disability as defined by the Social Security Act and Regulations since ___________________.

K. PROPOSED DECISION

(Title II Only)

Based on the Title II application filed on _____________, the claimant is entitled to a period of disability beginning on ___________ and to disability insurance benefits under §§ 216(i) and 223, respectively, of the Social Security Act, and the claimant's disability has continued through at least the date of this decision.

(Concurrent)

It is the further finding of the Administrative Law Judge that as of ________, ____the protective filing date for supplemental security income benefits, the claimant was disabled within the meaning of § 1614(a)(3)(A) of the Social Security Act, and remained so through the date of this decision.

(SSI Only)

Since the date of the application filed on _____________, the claimant has been disabled under § 1614(a)(3)(A) of the Social Security Act.

(SSI and Concurrent)

The Social Security Administration must also determine whether the claimant meets the income and resources and other eligibility requirements for supplemental security income payments, and if the claimant is eligible, the amount and the month(s) for which the claimant will receive payment. The claimant will receive a notice from another office of the Social Security Administration when that office makes those determinations.

Dated this ____ day of ___________, 20___.

____

Attorney for Claimant

P.O. ADDRESS:

§286.3 ALJ Bench Decision Checksheet

ALJ Bench Decision Checksheet

Claimant Name: ____________________ **SSN:** ____________

DIB Application Date: ____________ **Hearing Date:** ____________

SSI Application Date: ____________ **DWB Application Date:** ____________

Date Last Insured: ____________ **Established Onset Date:** ____________

EOD is ☐ **AOD** ☐ **Amended AOD** ☐ **Current Appl. Date (SSI Only)** ☐ **Prior Appl. Date (SSI Only)**

☐ **EOD w/in Widow/Widower prescribed period**

☐ **Prior Application** ☐ **Reopened** ☐ **Not Reopened**

Prior Application Date(s): T2 ____________ **T16** ____________

Reason for Reopening ☐ **Within one year** ☐ **Good cause** ☐ **Grounds for reopening at any time**

☐ **Work After Onset** ☐ **UWA** ☐ **Not SGA** ☐ **TWP**

Severe Impairment(s) (singly or in combination):

☐ **Impairment(s) MEETS Listing #** ____________ ☐ **based on ME testimony**

☐ **Impairment(s) EQUALS Listing #** ____________ ☐ **based on ME testimony**

☐ **Child is Functionally Equal to Listings** ☐ **based on ME testimony**

Mrk	Extr		Mrk	Extr	
☐	☐	**1. Acquiring and Using Information**	☐	☐	**4. Moving about and Manipulating objects**
☐	☐	**2. Attending and Completing Tasks**	☐	☐	**5. Caring for Self**
☐	☐	**3. Interacting with Others**	☐	☐	**6. Health and Physical Well-being**

Mental Impairment Analysis (Part B)

Restriction of Activities of Daily Living ☐ **None** ☐ **Mild** ☐ **Moderate** ☐ **Marked** ☐ **Extreme**

Difficulties Maintaining Social Functioning ☐ **None** ☐ **Mild** ☐ **Moderate** ☐ **Marked** ☐ **Extreme**

Difficulties Maintaining Concentration-Pace ☐ **None** ☐ **Mild** ☐ **Moderate** ☐ **Marked** ☐ **Extreme**

Episodes of Decompensation ☐ **None** ☐ **One or Two** ☐ **Three** ☐ **Four or More**

Mental Impairment Analysis (Part C)

☐ **12.02, 12.03, or 12.04 w/ 2 yrs med. history & more than minimal limitation &**

☐ **Residual disease process w/ marginal adjustment so that minimal changes cause decomp.**

☐ **Current Hx. 1+years in highly supportive living arrangement w/ continuing need for same**

☐ **Repeated episodes of decompensation, each of extended duration**

☐ **12.06 (inability to function independently outside area of home)**

Residual Functional Capacity:

☐ **Full range of** ☐ **Sedentary** ☐ **Light** ☐ **Medium**

☐ **Less than full range of** ☐ **Sedentary** ☐ **Light** ☐ **Medium (describe below)**

☐ **Nonexertional only (describe below)**

Function by Function:

Rationale for Decision (Include Assessment of Credibility and Medical Opinions):

☐ **Claimant has PRW w/ Job Title(s):**

Claimant is unable to perform PRW as actually or normally performed ☐ **based on VE testimony**

PRW was ☐ **unskilled** ☐ **skilled/semiskilled**

Claimant "disabled" based on:

☐ **Direct application of Medical-Vocational Rule #** _________

☐ **Framework of Medical-Vocational Rule #** _________

☐ **based on VE testimony** ☐ **based on SSR#** _________

☐ **Section 204.00 Framework** ☐ **based on VE testimony** ☐ **based on SSR#** _________

☐ **Recommend Representative Payee**

☐ **Medical reexamination in** _________ **Months**

☐ **Evidence of Workers Compensation Claim/Payment**

☐ **Fee Agreement Approved-Representative Name:**

☐ **Fee Agreement Denied-Reason:**

ALJ: __________________________ DATE: ___________________

§287 Prepare Notes for the Hearing

Before you meet with your client for hearing preparation, make some brief notes which describe your theory of why your client is disabled, and list other issues in your client's case. It works best to consolidate your notes onto one page for use at the hearing. A one page form on which to summarize important information is provided at §288. You may complete the rest of the form during the meeting with your client.

Make sure you have identified all of the issues. Potential issues include:

- Objections to exhibits
- Correcting errors
- Explaining ambiguities in submissions by the claimant
- A date last insured problem
- Requesting a closed period of disability
- Reopening a prior application
- Amending the alleged onset date
- Unsuccessful work attempts
- Meeting the duration requirement
- Crucial elements of a Listing
- Capacity for a particular past job
- Whether a past job was SGA
- Whether a past job lasted long enough for the claimant to learn to do it
- Why work skills are not transferable
- Residual functional capacity
- The most important aspects of the claimant's limitation, e.g., inability to sit for six hours out of an eight-hour working day, inability to stand and walk for six hours out of eight, inability to lift more than a certain amount of weight, inability to relate to other people, inability to deal with work stress, and so on.

§288 Form: Social Security Hearing Sheet

ALJ: ____________________

NAME: ____________________ DATE/HEARING: ____________________

AGE: ____ DOB: ________ AGE/ONSET: ________ DATE/APPLICATION ____________________

SSD/SSI: ☐ SSD ONLY: ☐ SSI ONLY: ☐ DWB: ☐

LAST WORKED:______ ONSET DATE: ____LAST DATE INSURED: ____________________

THEORY: ____________________

ISSUES: ____________________

____

____

____

____

RECORD OPEN FOR RECEIPT OF: ____________________

SPOUSE'S NAME: ____________________ WITNESSES: ____________________

HIGHEST GRADE: ____________________ ____________________

CUSTOMARY WORK: ____________________ ____________________

EASIEST JOB/15 YRS: ____________________

MEDICAL CONDITIONS: ____________________

____

RESIDUAL FUNCTIONAL CAPACITY: ____________________

____

MED-VOC. RULE: ____________________ LISTINGS: ____________________

TYPICAL DAY/MISC.: ____________________

____

____

____

§289 Objections to Hearing Issues

The notice of hearing will "contain a statement of the specific issues to be decided." 20 C.F.R. § 404.938(b). The notice will state that if you object to the issues, "you must notify the administrative law judge in writing at the earliest possible opportunity but no later than 5 business days before the date set for the hearing." 20 C.F.R. § 404.939. If you make an objection, you must state the reasons. Your objection will be ruled on by the ALJ "either in writing or at the hearing." 20 C.F.R. § 404.939.

According to 20 C.F.R. § 404.946(a), the issues before an ALJ "include all the issues brought out in the initial, reconsideration or revised determination that were not decided entirely in your favor. However, if evidence presented before or during the hearing causes the administrative law judge to question a fully favorable determination, he or she will notify you and will consider it an issue at the hearing." 20 C.F. R. § 404.946(b)(1) states that the ALJ may consider a new issue if the ALJ "notifies you and all the parties about the new issue any time after receiving the hearing request and before mailing notice of the hearing decision." "Notice of the time and place of the hearing on any new issues will be given in the manner described in § 404.938," which pertains to the notice of hearing. 20 C.F.R. § 404.946(b)(2).

It is exceedingly rare in the usual case that there would be any objectionable issue. But in any case that is even a little out of the ordinary, it may be worthwhile to review the statement of issues and consider objecting if the statement of issues is, as so often happens, a boiler plate statement used in ordinary cases. The most common circumstance where this issue may arise is where your client has been found disabled but has appealed the onset date; but it could also arise in some termination cases, in some Appeals Council remands, or in other cases where your goal is to limit the issues before the ALJ.

See also §302.

§290 Preparing Witnesses to Testify

Preparing witnesses to testify is one of the most important—and difficult—things that a lawyer does in a Social Security disability case. You must begin preparing the claimant to testify with your first meeting. *See* §177. Your goal, of course, is for the claimant and lay witnesses to give relevant, credible testimony.

Since many common sense arguments offered by unprepared claimants are not relevant to SSA's hypothetical approach to disability analysis, you must explain SSA's view of disability determination. For example, when asked why he's unable to do a sit-down job, an unprepared claimant may reply that he's not qualified for sedentary work, there aren't any unskilled sedentary jobs available or that he'd never get a job like that. Considering the small size of the unskilled sedentary occupational base, these aren't bad answers. But the ALJ, who may have come to believe that the Medical-Vocational Guidelines accurately reflect the real world, may view any answer not immediately addressing physical or mental capacity for sedentary work as an implied admission that the claimant has the RFC for unskilled sedentary work.

Your worst enemy in establishing your client's credibility, the other main goal, is the claimant's own nervousness. Sufficient time spent explaining what will happen at the hearing can work wonders. But over preparing the claimant may have an equally adverse effect on credibility. You don't want the claimant to sound rehearsed. Because claimants are often unsophisticated and very literal in interpreting what they are told, it is important to exercise great care in giving any instructions about hearing testimony and behavior. Consider the following exchange at a hearing where one of the issues was whether the claimant could sit for six hours out of an eight-hour working day:

LJ: Why are you standing up?

Claimant: My lawyer told me to.

Different claimants respond to different approaches.

Less preparation is often appropriate for those with mental impairments—you want the ALJ to see such a claimant in his or her unvarnished state.

Claimants who have difficulty describing things may need more preparation. It is useful to have such claimants think about how their impairments have changed their lives. An activities questionnaire, sent a few days before the hearing, can be helpful. A sample questionnaire follows in §291.

§291 Form: Activities Questionnaire

To: ______________________________

____

____

Your disability hearing will be held soon. Please complete this Activities Questionnaire and bring it to the meeting we have scheduled to prepare you to testify.

Read through this form before you fill it out. Spend a few days thinking about the activities listed on the form and the many ways your life has changed because of your health problems. Talk with family members and friends about their observations. Then, in the days before you meet with us, complete the form in as much detail as possible.

For each of the activities listed, describe the way these things are done differently now (or not performed at all) compared to the way they were performed before you became disabled. For each activity, some possibilities are suggested in parentheses; but these are only suggestions to start you thinking. List changes in the way the activities are performed, however small the difference may seem. If you now perform these activities only on "good days," be sure to say so. State the reasons the activities are now performed differently. Explain. The details help.

Thank you.

1. DRIVING (no longer drive, drive less often, drive only short distances, difficulty getting into or out of the car, got handicapped parking permit, get lost while driving, use bigger car, accidents, make frequent stops):

____

____

____

____

____

2. COOKING and EATING (no longer cook, cook less often, cook simpler meals, cook only for myself, eat out more, skip meals, burn food, no appetite, drop cooking utensils, sit while cooking):

____

____

____

____

____

3. WASH DISHES (no longer wash dishes, wash less often, drop dishes, sit while washing dishes, only wash a few dishes at a time, let dirty dishes pile up, bought a dishwasher):

____

____

____

____

____

4. STRAIGHTEN UP HOUSE (house more of a mess, others help with cleaning, hired house-cleaner, rest after short periods of cleaning):

____

____

____

____

5. DUST:

____

____

6. VACUUM:

____

____

7. MOP FLOOR (use stick mop instead of scrubbing floor while kneeling):

____

____

8. LAUNDRY including washing, drying, ironing, folding (wash clothes less often, get assistance doing or carrying laundry, throw rather than carry laundry down the steps, stay in basement while doing laundry, carry only a few items at a time, take more clothes to cleaner, buy more permanent press clothes):

____

____

____

____

9. CLEAN BATHROOM:

____

____

10. MAKE BED:

____

____

11. YARD WORK including cutting grass, bagging clippings, gardening, raking, etc. (others cut grass, use self-propelled mower, stopped gardening, moved into condo):

____

____

____

12. SHOVEL SNOW:

____

____

13. FIX THINGS:

____

____

____

14. GROCERY SHOP (do not shop alone, shop when crowds are smaller and lines shorter, rest while shopping, lean on cart, smaller bags, use express checkout, delivery by store, buy smaller containers, get dropped off and picked up at store entrance, buy more convenience foods such as TV dinners, sandwiches, microwave foods):

____

____

____

____

15. PAY BILLS/HANDLE FINANCES:

____

____

____

16. WATCH/PLAY WITH CHILDREN:

____

____

____

17. WATCH TV/LISTEN TO RADIO (watch more, TV no longer keeps my interest, trouble concentrating on what is going on, shorter attention span, watch more while in bed or on recliner, more frequent breaks, noise makes me nervous):

____

____

____

____

____

18. READ (need to reread sections to understand, do not remember what was read, read for shorter periods of time, read shorter pieces such as magazines instead of novels, stopped reading the newspaper):

____

____

____

19. TALK WITH OTHERS, INCLUDING TELEPHONE (want to be left alone, initiate conversations less often, talk for shorter periods of time):

____

____

____

20. SLEEP AT NIGHT (different times to go to bed and get up, trouble falling asleep, restlessness, get out of bed during night, inability to sustain sleep, feel tired when getting up, use sleeping pills, extra pillows under head or legs):

____

____

____

____

____

21. SLEEP/REST DURING THE DAY (naps, rest periods, time spent in bed, couch or recliner):

___

___

___

22. DRESS AND GROOM SELF such as brush teeth, shave, wash, use toilet, comb hair, makeup application, shower, bath, (groom self less often, need reminders, guardrails in tub, others comb and wash hair, lean against sink while brushing teeth and shaving, shorter showers):

___

___

___

___

___

23. GO TO CHURCH:

___

___

24. PARTICIPATE IN CLUBS, ORGANIZATIONS OR CHURCH ACTIVITIES:

___

___

___

25. USE PUBLIC TRANSPORTATION (use bus schedules to reduce waiting time, sit on benches, hold onto rails while climbing steps, sit in front of bus, get ride to bus stop, ride bus when less crowded):

___

___

___

26. EXERCISING:

___

___

27. VISIT AND ACTIVITIES WITH FRIENDS, NEIGHBORS, FAMILY, RELATIVES (visit less often or for shorter periods, others come to my house, they visit in my bedroom or while I am lying down):

____

____

____

____

28. PLAY CARD/GAMES:

____

____

29. ATTEND SPORTING EVENTS/MOVIES/OUT TO DINNER:

____

____

30. IDENTIFY ALL INTERESTS AND HOBBIES you used to enjoy. Why and how you do them differently now or not at all? (for example, fishing, crossword puzzles, hunting, sports, knitting, collecting, rummage sales, musical instruments, woodworking, golfing):

____

____

____

____

____

____

____

31. WRITING:

____

____

____

32. SITTING (different chair/sofa, shorter periods, squirm, sit forward or lean to a side, elevate legs, difficulty arising from a chair, difficulties bending head down, using hands in front of myself, or reaching overhead while sitting, difficulty twisting while sitting):

____

33. <u>STANDING, WALKING AND CLIMBING STEPS</u> (use cane, lean against walls or furniture, stumble into things, fall or almost fall):

34. <u>LIFT AND CARRY</u> (smaller items, hold against body):

35. <u>USE ARMS/HANDS/FINGERS</u> (drop things, can't make fist, trembling or shaking, trouble picking up small items off the table, using hand tools, and opening containers, jars and doors, cannot reach into cupboards, write for short periods only, use slip-on instead of tie shoes, difficulty buttoning clothes):

36. "I CAN'T SEEM TO GET ANYTHING DONE ON TIME." (If this is true for you, explain why and give examples):

____

____

37. LEAVING THE HOME (less frequent walks, not leave home alone):

____

____

____

38. CARE FOR PETS:

____

____

____

OTHER COMMENTS:

____

____

____

§292 *Preparing Your Client to Testify*

§292.1 *Allay Your Client's Fears*

Meet with the claimant a day or so before the hearing to discuss your theory of disability, go through the issues in the case and prepare your client to testify. You will find that you will get much better testimony from a claimant if you are able to allay your client's fears about the hearing. You will not be successful in calming your client if you try to prepare your client to testify during a short meeting at the hearing office prior to the hearing.

Your goal is to prepare the claimant to give relevant, honest testimony which neither exaggerates nor minimizes impairments. It should be testimony that is filled with anecdotes, details, and examples of limitations. It should provide facts about strengths as well as weaknesses in a straight-forward manner.

A claimant is best prepared by giving information about the hearing. Tell your client about the hearing room, the judge, the judge's assistant who will record the hearing. Describe the recording device and the microphones and explain the necessity for audible answers to questions. Outline the areas of inquiry: education and training, work experience and work skills, medical condition, treatment history, physical abilities, mental abilities, and daily activities.

§292.2 *Explain the Theory of the Case*

Describe your theory of the case. Explain that you will be attempting to prove two things by your client's testimony:

First, that your client cannot do any of the jobs he or she has had in the past 15 years; and second that your client is not able to do any other jobs which exist in significant numbers. For the first element of proof, ask your client to describe the *easiest* job done in the past 15 years and explain why your client cannot do it now. Help your client refine the explanation by weeding out any reasons SSA has determined are irrelevant. For example, "The company went out of business." "They'd never rehire me with all my medical problems," etc. *See* 20 C.F.R. § 404.1566(c).

For the second element of proof, explain that you don't have to be bedridden to be incapable of performing jobs existing in significant numbers. Explain how Social Security regulations help with this proof by rather explicitly setting forth what needs to be shown, especially in an exertional im-pairment case. For example, for a 50-year-old poorly educated claimant with an unskilled heavy work background, explain that in addition to proving that your client cannot do his or her former heavy job, your client must also prove that he or she cannot do a light job, e.g., standing at a machine in a factory for six hours out of an eight-hour working day, frequently lifting ten pounds, occasionally lifting up to 20 pounds. Explain that even if the judge finds that your client is capable of a sit-down job, the judge will find him or her disabled.

§292.3 *Explain the Hypothetical Nature of Disability Evaluation*

Tell your client not to argue his or her own case. Explain that common sense arguments won't work, that disabil-ity determination is hypothetical. This is crucial for those difficult cases of claimants under age 50. Sort through the claimant's reasons that he or she cannot do a sit-down job and tell the claimant not to bring up the common sense reasons that SSA has deemed irrelevant: "I'm not qualified for a sit-down job." "I'd never be hired for a job like that." "There aren't any jobs like that around here." *See* 20 C.F.R. § 404.1566(c).

§292.4 *Minimize Medical Testimony From the Claimant*

If there are inconsistencies in the medical rec-ords, see if the claimant can help explain them. But, remember, there are always inconsistencies and, indeed, factual errors in medical records. Ignore most of them unless they are of a magnitude that cannot be disregarded. Unless the claimant has a very convincing explanation, you are best off deal-ing with these problems by asking a doctor to address them in a report. Try to keep the claimant's "medical" testimony (about things his doctor has said but which do not appear in the medical records, about his or her own medical theories, etc.) to a minimum. Such testimony is not usually helpful to the ALJ in understanding medical issues. Tell your client not to quote his or her doctor unless you or the judge specifically asks, "What did your doctor say about this?"

Point out to the claimant that if the ALJ asks, "What keeps you from working?" a good answer is *not* to state a diagnosis, such as arthritis. Lots of people work despite the fact that they have arthritis. The ALJ may have arthritis. The reason this claimant cannot work is the severity of symptoms, something which your client knows better than anyone. Thus, tell your client if he or she is asked that question, the door is open to launch into a full description of symptoms and limitations.

§292.5 Neither Exaggerate Nor Minimize Testimony About Pain or Limitations

When one hears "disabling pain" discussed, it sometimes conjures up the image of a claimant rolled into the fetal position, in so much pain that he or she is unable to get out of bed. Most claimants whose cases go to a hearing do not suffer such an extreme degree of pain. Indeed, if a claimant were suffering pain to this degree it would be legitimate for an ALJ to inquire how he or she was capable of attending the hearing. Explain to the claimant that it is not necessary for one to be in extreme incapacitating pain to be found disabled.

Try to guard against any tendencies of claimants to exaggerate pain testimony. At the same time, however, don't let them minimize it. Emphasize that the claimant will be testifying under oath and must tell the truth. When you are discussing testimony, if the claimant's description of pain deviates from that recorded in medical records, ask for an explanation.

Try to make sure the claimant understands how testimony about pain fits into the disability case. Go through with the claimant your theory of how pain prevents performing sub-stantial gainful activity, e.g., inability to sit, stand or walk for prolonged periods, inability to get through an eight-hour day without lying down, good days/bad days/missed work, inability to concentrate or pay attention on a consistent basis, irritability, etc.

§292.6 Avoid Rehearsing Testimony

Try to go through the claimant's testimony generally without rehearsing. Listen very carefully to what the claimant tells you. Look for those things in the claimant's explanation which need to be addressed in more detail and challenge the claimant to provide the additional details so that his or her testimony is not misconstrued. Use a nonconfrontational approach. For example, "I understand what you're telling me; but if you say it that way, this is how the judge is going to interpret it .... Is this what you mean?"

If, after sitting in your office for a half hour, the claimant estimates that sitting tolerance is only for 10-15 minutes, point out the inconsistency and ask for an explanation. You may find that the claimant has exaggerated sitting limitation. If so, encourage your client to come up with a more accurate estimate. More likely, however, you will find that the discrepancy is explained by the inherent ambiguity in the question: How long can you sit? A claimant can force himself or herself to sit for a period of time in a lawyer's office knowing that he or she will soon be able to go home and lie down. In estimating a sitting tolerance of 10-15 minutes, the claimant correctly perceived the question to ask for sitting tolerance in a work-type situation. To avoid any misunderstanding at the hearing, encourage the claimant to volunteer that he or she is estimating sitting, lifting, etc. tolerance in a work-type situation; or have your client answer the question by giving an example of overdoing it as well as an estimate of how long he or she can carry out an activity in a work-like environment.

§292.7 Encourage Testimony Filled With Examples and Anecdotes

The best way to obtain vivid description and detailed examples in the claimant's testimony is to make your client feel comfortable using his or her own words. One way to encourage natural testimony is to tell the claimant to prepare for talking to the ALJ, not the same way one would talk to a regular judge in a courtroom, but rather as if the ALJ were an old friend who wants to be brought up to date about all of the problems the claimant has been having lately.

Explain that when your client is asked about daily activities, your client is presented with a golden opportunity to describe limitations in the context of daily life. Tell the claimant to be sure to give enough details. Suggest that your client run through a usual day hour by hour for the judge, providing as much detail as possible, emphasizing those things that must be done differently now because of his or her impairments. Tell your client to describe how long he or she is active doing things and how long he or she rests afterwards. Tell your client to give details about resting—where he or she rests, whether it's sitting or lying down, whether it's on the couch or the bed or a recliner chair. Have the claimant tell how long it takes to do a project now compared to how long it used to take. Have your client describe all those things that he or she needs help from other people doing—and tell who those others are. Have your client give details and examples right down to the names of the television shows regularly watched, if that is what he or she does.

The more specifics your client can provide to the ALJ about daily activities, the more readily the ALJ will understand your client's testimony about symptoms and limitations.

§292.8 Explain the Mechanics of Issuing a Written Decision

At the conclusion of the prehearing preparation meeting with your client, explain that unless the ALJ issues a bench decision, the ALJ probably won't say at the hearing whether your client won or lost. Estimate how long it will take to get the decision. Remind your client about your agreement concerning fees and expenses; although SSA will pay the fee, your client will have to pay you directly for any expenses.

§292.9 Rules for Testifying

Before he or she leaves your office, give your client a summary to read the night before the hearing which outlines what you said during your meeting and which reiterates the general rules for testifying:

1. Tell the truth.
2. Neither exaggerate nor minimize your medi-cal symptoms.
3. Know your present abilities and limitations.
4. Provide relevant details and concrete exam-ples—but don't ramble on.
5. *Don't worry.* Your representative will be there to help you if you forget something or don't bring out the necessary details.

A sample memorandum which you may copy and give to your client to read follows at §293. Although this memorandum is long, it has been well received by many claimants.

§293 Memorandum: Testifying at Your Disability Hearing

Arrive Early

Unless your attorney asks you to be at the hearing office at a specific time, arrive for your hearing about a half an hour early. Any earlier is not necessary no matter what the hearing office may say in an automated phone call and no matter what your Notice of Hearing may say about coming early to review your file. Your lawyer has already reviewed your hearing exhibit file. It isn't necessary for you to review it (although you may if you want to). Disability hearings usually start on time—so whatever you do, don't be late.

Don't Talk About Your Case

When you come for your hearing, remember, Social Security hearings are serious business. Don't make jokes. Indeed, don't even talk about your case before or after your hearing in the waiting room, in the hallway, in the elevator or anywhere else where a stranger can overhear. A Social Security employee may misinterpret what you say and get the wrong impression about you. There may be a lot of Social Security employees in the building.

The Hearing Room

A Social Security hearing room is nothing more than a small conference room. It may have a few official trappings such as the seal of the Social Security Administration or an American flag. Hearing rooms are always equipped with a conference table. There also may be a small table for the judge's assistant. Usually there is a desk for the judge that sits on a small riser or she slightly above the level of the conference table where you and your attorney will sit.

The Recording Equipment

Each hearing room has its own audio recording equipment used to record your hearing. Because your hearing will be recorded, it is important for you to speak clearly when you answer questions. The microphones are very sensitive so that they will pick up your testimony from anywhere in the room if you speak loud enough for the judge to hear you. However, because these are only audio recordings, shaking your head won't do; neither will pointing at a part of your body without stating out loud what part of your body you are pointing at. Also, "uh huh" and "huh uh" answers do not transcribe as well as "yes" and "no" answers. So try to say "yes" and "no" if you can.

Persons Present in the Hearing Room

You will be seated at the conference table along with your attorney. Under some circumstances the judge may call a vocational witness or a doctor to testify. If so, they will be seated at the conference table, too.

Also seated at the conference table (or perhaps at a small table next to the conference table) will be the judge's assistant who operates a computer, which is used to make a CD-ROM that will contain the recording of the hearing.

You are allowed to bring observers into the hearing room. Some judges allow witnesses to be present for the entire hearing. Others make witnesses wait in the waiting room until it is time for their testimony. But the hearing is private. Anyone present other than the judge, the judge's staff and witnesses called by the judge must have your permission.

Social Security Hearings Are Informal

Social Security hearings are much less formal than court hearings. They were designed so that they would not be a threatening experience. The Social Security Administration (SSA) recognizes that if you can relax as much as possible, you will be the best witness for yourself. It's okay to let yourself be yourself.

Although this is an informal hearing, there are a few procedures that must be followed. Before you go into the hearing room, you must turn off your telephone and take off your hat. Once you are in the hearing room, you and all witnesses will testify under oath. It is important when you are testifying that you not ask anyone else in the room to help you answer questions and that your witnesses or friends do not chime in to help you testify. Only one person is allowed to testify at a time.

The Administrative Law Judge

The person who presides in a Social Security hearing is an administrative law judge (ALJ). Although many judges do not wear judicial robes and you will not be expected to stand up when the judge comes into the room, the Social Security judge is entitled to the same respect that you would pay to a court judge.

The judge's job is to issue an independent decision, which is not influenced by the fact that your case was denied at the time of your initial application and on reconsideration. The informal Social Security hearing is not supposed to be an "adversarial" hearing. That is, there is no lawyer on the other side who is going to cross-examine you.

Most judges do not try to trick a claimant into saying something he or she does not mean. Most judges do not act like your opponent. Most judges view their jobs as requiring them to find out the facts. While most judges do not "cross-examine" a claimant, if you say something different than what you said before, the best judges will ask you about it in order to give you a chance to explain.

Many people, by the time they get to a hearing before an administrative law judge, are angry at the Social Security system. Their applications for benefits have been denied twice, often without any logical reason given for the denial. This system is cumbersome. It is time-consuming with all of its appeals and delays, and it is frustrating.

But, it is important not to take your anger out on the judge. The judge did not create this system. The judge is not responsible for the problems that you have had with the system. Since the judge probably already knows all of the problems with the Social Security appeals system, you do not need to explain these problems. It also isn't helpful to ask the judge questions about your case, such as: "Why have I been denied?" "Why has it taken so long for me to have a hearing?" and so forth.

The only time you should ask the judge a question is when you do not understand what is being asked of you. Judges and lawyers sometimes ask simple questions in complicated ways. This is a shortcoming of the legal profession. Don't be intimidated by it. If you're not sure you understand a question, don't be embarrassed to ask politely for an explanation.

The best way to treat the judge is with the courtesy and candor that you would show an old friend whom you haven't seen for several years—someone that you want to bring up-to-date about all of your problems. In other words, it's okay for you to talk to the judge "regular." You do not have to use highfalutin words, lawyer words or doctor words. In fact, it's much better if you don't try to use such terminology. Just talk to the judge the same way you would talk to an old friend.

The Order in Which Things Happen at the Hearing

Many judges begin disability hearings by reciting the "case history" of your disability claim and stating the issues to be decided. Judges often state what you have to prove in your case but they seldom give a clear and simple explanation. They usually say that in order to be found disabled you must be "unable to perform substantial gainful activity which exists in significant numbers in the economy, considering your age, education and work experience." When they say this, it almost sounds like you've got to be bedridden to get disability benefits—but, as will be explained in more detail later, this isn't true.

The judge may question you first. Then the judge will give your lawyer a chance to ask you some questions. Occasionally, if a claimant is well prepared to testify, the lawyer doesn't have to ask any questions at all.

Some judges, however, expect lawyers to handle most of the questioning. If so, answer questions asked by your lawyer as if a stranger were the one asking them. Sometimes a claimant may give less than complete answers when his or her lawyer asks questions because the lawyer knows a lot about the case already. So, it is important to keep in mind that the judge, who will decide your case, doesn't know the answers until you say them. Although the judge probably will read your file before the hearing, when you're testifying, it is best to assume that the judge knows nothing about your case. Plan on explaining everything.

When you're done testifying, your lawyer will be allowed to question any witnesses you've brought to the hearing. It is really important for your case to bring at least one witness to testify in support of what you say, to give the judge details about your impairments and how they affect you, or to offer a different perspective on your medical problems.

Expert Witnesses

After your witness's testimony, any expert witnesses called by the judge will testify. If an expert witness—a medical or vocational expert—is going to testify, you will be given notice of this in the Notice of Hearing. Medical experts—a medical doctor or psychologist—testify in about 15 percent of cases nation-wide. The medical expert's job is to help the judge understand medical issues, particularly medical issues involving Social Security regulations. Medical experts are expected to be neutral witnesses.

Vocational experts, who are also supposed to be neutral witnesses, are called to testify much more often than medical experts. Some administrative law judges ask a vocational expert to testify in virtually all of their cases involving adult disability.

The vocational expert helps the judge understand the significant jobs you have done in the past 15 years, which is called your "past relevant work." The vocational expert will describe each of these jobs as you did it and also as the job is usually performed in the economy.

The vocational expert will describe the skill and exertional level of your past relevant work. Exertional level pertains to how much you had to lift and how much standing and walking was involved in these jobs. Skill level depends on how long it would take a new employee to learn to do your job with average proficiency. If it would take more than 30 days, it may mean that you have acquired work skills that could be transferable to other, easier jobs. If so, the vocational expert will describe your transferable skills, state what jobs these skills are transferable to and how many of these jobs there are in the economy.

Vocational experts are not supposed to provide their own evaluation of the medical evidence in your case, state whether job vacancies exist or whether you would be hired for a job, or state that you are or are not disabled. Instead, judges ask vocational experts a series of hypothetical questions based on different possible limitations in order to figure out whether you can do any past relevant work and whether other jobs exist in significant numbers in the economy for various different capacities for working. Then, often after the hearing is over, the judge will figure out which one of the hypothetical questions most closely describes you. The decision may be based on the vocational expert's answer to that question.

It is your lawyer's job to cross-examine any expert witnesses to make sure there is a legitimate basis for the expert's testimony.

At the Conclusion of the Hearing

At the end of the hearing, some judges will ask you if you have anything more to say. It's best if you don't try to argue your case at this point—let your lawyer do that. Most judges will give a lawyer the opportunity to make a closing argument either at the end of the hearing or to be submitted in writing.

Most judges won't tell you if you've won, although a few will. A few judges issue what is called a "bench decision," that is, a decision stated right at the hearing. Even if the judge issues a bench decision, the judge still must issue a short written decision, which will be mailed to you with a copy to your lawyer. The wonderful thing about the written part of the bench decision is that it comes only a few days after the hearing. When the judge issues a regular decision, sometimes it takes quite a while for the decision to come out.

What to Wear

A lot of people ask what to wear and whether they should dress up. You do not need to dress up. You do not need to wear the same clothes that you would wear to a wedding. This is an informal hearing. You may wear whatever makes you comfortable (within reason).

Testify Truthfully

The most important thing about a Social Security hearing is not what you wear. It is what you say. It is whether or not you are telling the truth.

Tell the truth. When the judge asks a question, don't try to figure out why the judge is asking that particular question or whether your answer will help or hurt your case. Be candid about your strengths as well as about your limitations. The best way to lose a good case is for the judge to think that you're not telling the truth. So, testify truthfully. While you can be caught in a lie, you can never be caught in the truth.

And, don't do any play-acting for the judge. That is, don't pretend to cry or be in more pain than you are. On the other hand, you need not suffer silently or minimize your problems when you tell the judge how you feel. If you need to take a break from the hearing, ask the judge for permission. If you are uncomfortable sitting and it would help to stand up for a while, you may do so, and you should not be embarrassed about it.

Medications on Hearing Day

Some people ask when they should take their medications on the day of the hearing. If medication side effects cause fuzzy thinking for a while, you need to figure out a time to take your medications—perhaps long before the hearing—so that you are the sharpest you can be at the time of the hearing. On the other hand, if without taking your medications the symptoms of your impairment are likely to interfere with you giving your best testimony, you need to take your medications closer to the time of the hearing so that you are at your best during the hearing. The goal is for you to give the best possible testimony.

Tell Your Story

This will be your chance to tell the judge everything we want the judge to know about why your condition prevents you from holding a job.

Many people think that since they are dealing with the government, they should keep their mouths shut, give the shortest possible answers and not volunteer anything. Although this is usually a good approach when the government is trying to do something to you, the opposite is true when you are asking the government to do something for you. You need to provide enough facts, details, and explanation in your testimony to make it clear to the judge that you are disabled. Details win cases.

Approximating Dates

If you are asked when something happened, the judge is likely to appreciate having the precise date. But if you don't remember the exact date, don't worry. Few people can remember precise dates for events in their lives. If you don't remember the exact date, say so. Then, do your best to give an approximate date, or a month and year, or a season and year, or, if you cannot remember more accurately, just the year. Getting dates wrong is something all of us, including the judge, do from time to time. Some people are worse than others with dates. The judge won't think you're being untruthful if it turns out that a date is wrong.

How the Judge Determines Disability

It is important that you understand some basic points about how the administrative law judge goes about determining whether someone is disabled. This process is complicated and technical, and it doesn't necessarily involve common sense. For example, most people think that if they cannot get a job because of their medical problems, this must prove that they are disabled. But, as we shall see, inability to get a job proves nothing.

Disability determination is what we call a "hypothetical" determination. It has very little to do with the real world. It has nothing to do with the fact that employers won't hire you because of your medical problems. The Social Security Administration looks only at whether you are capable of doing jobs, not whether you'd be hired. Thus, you may have to prove that you are unable to do jobs that you would never be hired for in a million years.

In some cases, the medical findings about your condition alone will cause the judge to find you disabled. In other cases, the majority of cases, we usually have to prove two things: First, we have to prove that your medical impairments prevent you from performing any significant job you've done in the past 15 years; and second, we have to prove that there aren't many other jobs you are capable of doing considering your age, education and work experience.

Think about all the jobs you've had in the past 15 years, and pick out the easiest one. If you did that easiest job long enough to learn how to do it and earned a minimum amount of money from that job, we have to prove that you cannot do that easiest job. We have to prove this even if we're dead certain you'd never be hired for that job again; and we have to prove it even if the company where you worked no longer exists and even if the job is no longer available elsewhere. Although this is rare, sometimes if you earned enough money at a job, we even have to prove you cannot do a part time job.

Proving the second thing—that considering your age, education and work experience you're unable to do very many other jobs—is even more complicated and opposed to common sense. In many cases we have to prove that you're incapable of doing jobs that we know you'd never actually be hired for.

A lot of people have heard the language "totally and permanently disabled." This phrase, which comes from workers' compensation cases, does not apply in Social Security disability and Supplemental Security Income (SSI) disability cases. For Social Security, you don't have to be "permanently" disabled; you only have to be disabled for 12 months. Although you have to be totally disabled in the sense that you are unable to perform jobs existing in significant numbers in the economy, this doesn't mean that you have to be unable to do anything. In fact, very few people who go in front of an administrative law judge are unable to do anything at all.

Everyone Can Do Something

Think about the job of bridge tender on a not-very-busy waterway. The bridge tender has a recliner chair in his room at the bridge. He sits in his recliner and when a boat comes along, a few times per hour, he flips a switch to raise the bridge. He is allowed to stand or sit or lie down as he chooses. Most claimants who go to hearings in front of Administrative Law Judges are able to do the bridge tender job. But thank goodness we don't have to prove you can't do that job in order to win your disability case. There are other similar jobs we don't have to prove you cannot perform in order to win your case. We usually do not have to prove you cannot do a part time job. We usually do not have to prove you cannot work from home over the Internet when you feel up to it.

Thinking about such jobs is important because one way to determine disability is to start by trying to figure out what you can do. Once we figure out what you can do, we can determine whether or not jobs within your capacity exist in significant numbers in the economy, considering your age, education and work experience. We do that either by looking at a fairly complicated set of rules or by asking some questions of a vocational expert.

Rules for Determining Disability

The rules that we use for determining disability apply most directly to impairments that limit your physical ability to stand, sit, walk, lift, bend or work with your hands. Mental impairments are a bit more complicated.

If you are unable to do certain kinds of manual labor, once we have shown that you cannot do any significant job you've done in the past 15 years, your lawyer will be able to look at the rules and figure out what you've got to prove to win your case. Here are some examples:

If you are under age 50, the general rule is that you've got to prove you can't do an easy sit-down job or even a job where you're allowed to alternate sitting and standing during the workday. You've got to prove this even though you might not be hired for such a job.

If you are age 50 through 54, the general rule is that you have to prove that you cannot do light work, that is, work involving being on your feet most of the day and lifting up to about 20 pounds. Thus, even though you might still be able to do a sit-down job, a desk job, you can still be found disabled.

If you are age 55 or older, it gets even easier. The general rule is that you have to prove that you cannot do "medium" work, that is, work involving being on your feet for most of the day, frequently lifting 25 pounds, occasionally up to 50 pounds. Thus, not only can you be capable of doing sedentary work, you can even be capable of doing light work and still be found disabled.

As you can see, we're not only going to prove what you can't do, we're also going to prove what you can do. As we noted above, in most cases, the judges just won't accept any sort of "I can't do anything" explanation for why you're disabled.

These are general rules. The issues can get more complicated when you've had jobs in the past where you've learned a lot of skills. The judge is going to want to know about your work skills. You are going to have to be able to explain them to the judge.

How do we go about proving all of this at the hearing? We do it through your testimony in response to questions from the judge and your lawyer at the hearing. Although your lawyer will remind you if you forget something, it's best if you can answer all questions thoroughly yourself. Otherwise, it could look like your lawyer is prodding you or putting words in your mouth.

Areas of Testimony

Questions are going to be asked of you at the hearing about your:

1. Work history;
2. Education;
3. Medical history;
4. Symptoms;
5. Your estimate of your work limitations; and
6. Your daily activities.

Work and Educational History

For work history, you will be asked to describe job duties on your last job and on all significant jobs you've had during the past fifteen years. For each job, the judge will want to know how much weight you had to lift and approximately how much time during the workday you spent sitting, standing and walking. The judge will also be interested in difficulties you had performing past jobs because of your health and why you left each former job, especially your last job.

The judge will also ask about job skills. If you have had semi-skilled or skilled work, it is important that you describe your skills accurately. Remember, though, this hearing is not like a job interview in which people often have a tendency to try to "puff up" their job skills. Just state the straight facts.

One test for determining the degree of skill involved in a job is how long it takes to learn to do that job. Be prepared to estimate how long it would take for an average person to learn to do your past jobs.

For education, you'll be asked the highest grade you completed in school, whether you had any training in the military, whether you have had any formal vocational training or on-the-job training.

If you have difficulty explaining why you can't now perform one of the jobs that you have done in the past 15 years, you'll want to go over this with your lawyer before your hearing. If you have recently completed some schooling that might qualify you for a skilled job, be sure your lawyer knows all about this schooling.

Medical History

Sometimes there are no questions whatsoever about your medical history. The judge will have your medical records from doctors, hospitals and others who have treated you and may let the medical records speak for themselves. It is your lawyer's job to see to it that all of the medical records the judge needs to see are in the hearing exhibit file and, when necessary, that there are letters from your doctors explaining your medical condition and their opinions about your limitations.

The judge may ask a few general questions about your medical history. The judge may want to know how often you see your doctor, what sort of treatment your doctor provides, what medications you are taking, how often you take them, how well the medications work and whether there are any side effects. You may be asked to describe the symptoms and treatment of your medical condition since it began, what doctors you have seen, where and when you were hospitalized, and so forth.

You will not be expected to explain technical medical things to the judge. Unless you are asked, it's better not even to try to explain what your doctor has told you or what your friends have told you or what you have read about your medical problem on the Internet unless you have first cleared it with your lawyer. However, if the judge asks you what your doctor has told you about your condition or your limitations, do your very best to quote your doctor as accurately as possible.

Symptoms

Symptoms are how you feel. No one knows how you feel better than you. You know where you hurt and when you hurt. You know when you get short of breath or dizzy or fatigued. So it's up to you to describe those symptoms to the judge in as much detail and as vividly as possible. After all, it's these symptoms that keep you from working. It's not because you have some particular label of disease like arthritis or a heart condition or a lung condition that you are unable to work. You cannot work because of how you feel.

So if the judge says to you, "Why can't you work?" Don't assume that telling the judge only the name of your impairment answers the question. If you say only, "It's because I have arthritis," you're really telling the judge very little. Lots of people with arthritis can and do work. The judge needs to know about the severity of your pain and other symptoms and how the symptoms limit you.

Be specific when you describe your symptoms. Don't just say, "It hurts." Describe what your symptoms feel like, the same way you have probably described your symptoms to members of your family. Describe the nature, intensity, and location of pain, whether it travels to different parts of your body, how often you have pain, and how long it lasts. Explain if you feel different from day to day. Explain what starts up your pain or other symptoms, what makes your symptoms worse and what helps relieve them.

Describe your symptoms to the judge the very best you can. Be precise and truthful. Don't exaggerate, but don't minimize your symptoms either.

If you exaggerate your symptoms in your testimony, if you testify about constant excruciating pain but the medical records don't back up what you say, the judge will not believe you. The judge is also going to wonder how you made it to the hearing if your pain is so bad. So be careful when you use words such as "extreme" or "excruciating" to describe pain; and don't say that you "always" or "constantly" hurt or that you "never" get any relief from pain if what you mean is something less.

On the other hand, if you minimize your symptoms by saying they're not so bad, and a lot of people do, the judge is not going to find you disabled because you will convince the judge that you have few limitations. This is not the time to be brave.

So try not to be a minimizer or an exaggerator. Try to describe your symptoms exactly as they are.

Estimate How Often You Have Pain or Other Symptoms

If your symptoms come and go, be prepared to explain how often this happens. Some people don't give enough information, especially when the frequency of symptoms varies a lot. It is never a good answer to say that something happens "sometimes" or "occasionally" or "once in a while." The judge won't know if you have the problem once a day, once a week or once a year. The judge could conclude that this means that your symptoms occur only a few times per year—which is not enough to be disabling. When the frequency of symptoms varies greatly, a lot of explanation and examples are necessary. For example, tell how often symptoms occur in a usual week. If you have weeks with no symptoms, estimate how many weeks out of a month or year are like that. The more information you give about how often you have symptoms, the better understanding the judge will have about why your symptoms keep you from working.

Estimate How Long Your Pain or Other Symptoms Last

For symptoms that come and go, be prepared to explain how long they last. Try to explain this without using the word "sometimes." Instead, try to estimate how long your symptoms usually last, then estimate how often the symptoms last longer and how often the symptoms are shorter.

Estimate the Intensity of Your Symptoms

You may be asked if your pain and other symptoms vary in intensity. If so, do your best to describe how your pain and other symptoms vary in intensity during a usual day or over a usual week. Often it is best to use the 1 to 10 scale sometimes used by therapists and doctors. On this scale, 1 is essentially no pain and 10 is the worst pain you've ever had. Be sure you understand this scale and use it correctly without exaggerating. Think about the worst pain you ever had. Did it cause you to go to the emergency room? Did you lie in your bed writhing in pain, finding it difficult to get up even to go to the bathroom? Did it cause you to roll up into a fetal position? These are the images that the judge will have about what it means to have pain at a 10 level. Some people with disability claims have pain that gets to this level once in a while. Most do not. People who testify that their pain is frequently at the 10 level do not understand the scale. Most judges will conclude that someone who testifies that his or her pain is at a 10 level during a hearing is not to be believed—because judges think there is no way a person could be at a hearing with pain that bad.

Estimate Your Limitations

The judge will ask how far you can walk, how much you can lift, how long you can stand, how long you can sit, etc. You must give the judge a genuine estimate of what you can do. So it is important to think about these things before your hearing.

If a friend asks you how far you can walk, you probably start thinking of places you have walked to recently, how you felt when you got there, whether you had to stop and rest along the way, and so forth. You are likely to answer your friend's question by giving one or more examples of walking someplace recently. If the judge asks this question, answer it the same way. Talk to the judge the same way that you would talk to an old friend.

A Social Security hearing is not a court hearing. If you are familiar with court hearings or have watched lawyer shows on television, wipe such things from your mind. In court hearings, lawyers are always advising people, "don't volunteer." What this means, of course, is don't give any examples or details, wait for the lawyer to ask. In Social Security hearings, this rule does not apply and, indeed, if you don't "volunteer" information, you will not be giving the judge the necessary information to decide your case.

Let's look at some examples. You decide which testimony is best. The person who has been advised by a lawyer not to volunteer in answering a question may answer this way:

Judge: How far can you walk?
Claimant: Two blocks.

A person who talks to a judge the same way he talks to a friend, as we're advising you to do, will answer the question this way:

Judge: How far can you walk?
Claimant: Judge, I can't walk more than about 2 blocks without stopping to rest. Just yesterday, I went to the store, which is only about a block and a half from my house. By the time I got there, my back felt like it had a hot spike driven into it. I started limping. All I bought at the store was a loaf of bread. I could barely carry it home. On the way home, I had to stop three times because my back hurt so much. When I got home I sat down in my recliner chair and put my legs up before I even put the bread away.

As you can see, the person who talks to the judge as an old friend provides a lot of important information, some good examples and some relevant details. This makes this example a much more effective answer than the one directly above it.

Also, be aware that there is a built-in problem with the way questions are asked about how long you can stand, how much you can lift, how far you can walk, and so forth. Judges always ask the question just this way: "How long can you stand?" The question should not be interpreted to mean, "How long can you stand before you are in so much pain that you must go home and go to bed?" If you interpret the question this way and say "one hour," without any explanation of your answer, you're likely to lead the judge to think you can stand much longer than you really can on a job. What the judge needs to know, of course, is how long you can stand in a work situation where you must stand for a while, are allowed to sit down, and then must stand again, repeating this several times during an 8-hour workday.

Many times it is best to answer the question more than one way. You could give the judge an example of overdoing it and having to go lie down. But if you give the judge that example, be sure to fully explain it. For example, explain that when you washed Thanksgiving dinner dishes for an hour, you had to go lie down for a half an hour. Otherwise, it will show up in the judge's decision that you have the capacity to stand for one hour at a time, when your true capacity in a work situation is much less. But also give other examples that demonstrate the work situation: for example, if you are going to stand for a period of time, then sit, then stand again, this second standing time may be much shorter.

The problem that we have with the way these questions are asked is even worse when the question comes to sitting. This sort of exchange happens all the time:

Judge: How long can you sit?
Claimant: Twenty minutes.

When the judge hears this answer, the judge may look at a clock and write down that the claimant had been sitting for 40 minutes when that question was answered. Thus, the judge could conclude that this claimant is a liar.

What this claimant meant, of course, is that he could sit for 20 minutes in a work situation, then stand or walk for a while and return to sitting. In all likelihood, a claimant with a sitting problem, after forcing himself to sit through an hour-long Social Security hearing, will go home and lie down in order to relieve the pain in his back. He answered the question truthfully. He can sit for only about 20 minutes in a work situation. If he forces himself, he can sit longer but then it takes some time to recuperate. It is important to explain all of this to the judge so that the judge can understand what you are able to do day in and day out in a work situation.

Some people testify that after sitting for a period of time they need to shift in the chair. But this is a point not worth making since all of us shift in our chairs. There is no impact on your ability to work caused by needing to shift in a chair. A person can shift and go right on working.

Here is an example of a good answer to a question about sitting:

Judge: How long can you sit?
Claimant: If I force myself, I can sit here for perhaps a whole hour; but after this, I'll have to go home and lie down, and I won't be much good for the rest of the day. When I am trying to do things around the house, like pay bills, I only sit for about 20 minutes at a time and then I get up and walk around for 15 or 20 minutes before I go back to sitting. If I were on a job where I could change positions between sitting and standing or walking, the length of time that I could sit would get shorter as the day wore on. Sitting is really hard on my back. It's better, though, if I can sit in my recliner chair with my legs up. I can sit in that chair for a long time but I find it really hard, for example, to pay bills sitting in that chair. I usually sit at the dining room table when I pay bills.

It is useful to provide information about what you need to do after sitting for a while. Can you sit for a while and then stand up, stretch, and sit back down and continue working? Do you need to alternate sitting and standing? Can you alternate sitting and standing at a work station all day long? Do you need to walk around after sitting or standing in one place? If so, how often do you need to walk around? How long do you need to walk around each time?

Most jobs give breaks from work every couple of hours. Do you need extra breaks from work? What do you need to do on such a break? Sit? Walk around? Lie down? Sit in a recliner? How often during the workday do you need such breaks? How long should each break be?

The judge or your lawyer may ask you how long out of an 8-hour working day you can sit. What the judge needs to know is the total length of time during an entire 8-hour working day that you are capable of sitting, even though sitting is in short stretches. You're going to have to add together all the short periods of sitting in order to come up with a total sitting estimate for an 8-hour working day. Think about this before the hearing so that you can give a realistic estimate. The judge may also want to know the same about standing.

Sometimes a problem for testimony comes up if you have good days and bad days. For example, on good days, you might be able to sit or stand or walk for much longer than you can on a bad day. If you have good days and bad days, describe what it's like on a good day and what it's like on a bad day. Be prepared, though, for the judge to ask you for your estimate of how many days out of a month are good days and how many days are bad days. A lot of people answer such questions as, "well, I never counted them." Count them. The judge will need this information.

Details. Details. Details. The more specifics that you can provide, the easier it is for the judge to understand your testimony about your symptoms and your limitations.

To give good testimony about your limitations, it is really important for you to know yourself, know your limitations, and neither exaggerate nor minimize them. This is hard to do. You will need to think about it, perhaps discuss your limitations with family members and definitely discuss these limitations with your attorney before the hearing.

Mental Limitations

This memorandum is not intended to help prepare people to testify who have only mental limitations, since the issues in such cases are different in many ways from those we have been discussing; and it is difficult to make general statements about how to prepare for such cases. If your case involves only mental limitations, you and your lawyer will need to go through these matters before the hearing. For those with mental limitations in combination with physical impairments, it is also necessary to discuss the mental limitations with your lawyer prior to your hearing; but there are a few things that we can say here about mental limitations in combination with physical impairments.

Many people who have serious physical problems, especially if they have been having pain for a long time, develop emotional aspects to their physical impairments. This is so common that it is surprising to find someone with a long-term physical problem who doesn't also have some emotional problem. But many people who suffer physical impairments are afraid to talk about this emotional component of pain for fear they will be viewed as crazy. Having such problems doesn't mean you're crazy. It probably means you're normal.

It is important for you to be willing and able to describe any emotional problems because it is often the emotional aspect of pain that interferes the greatest with the ability to work. Common problems include:

- Difficulty concentrating,
- Forgetfulness,
- Nervousness,
- A quick temper,
- Difficulty getting along with others,
- Avoiding other people,
- Crying spells, and
- Depression.

If you have some of these problems, you may also be asked about your ability to: understand, carry out and remember instructions, make judgments, respond to supervisors, co-workers and usual work situations, and how well you deal with changes in a routine work setting. You may be asked how well you deal with stress, which, you must remember, is a very individual thing. Different people find different things stressful. If the judge asks you about how well you deal with stress, be sure to tell the judge what sorts of things you find stressful, especially things at work.

Sometimes claimants have trouble putting their fingers on exactly what it is about work that they find stressful. Here's a list of examples of things some people find stressful in work:

- Meeting deadlines,
- Completing job tasks,
- Working with others,

- Dealing with the public,
- Working quickly,
- Trying to work with precision,
- Doing complex tasks,
- Making decisions,
- Working within a schedule,
- Dealing with supervisors,
- Being criticized by supervisors,
- Simply knowing that work is supervised,
- The monotony of routine,
- Getting to work regularly,
- Remaining at work for a full day,
- Fear of failure at work.

Sometimes people find routine, repetitive work stressful because of the monotony of routine, lack of opportunity for learning new things, little opportunity for decision-making, lack of collaboration on the job, underutilization of skills, or the lack of meaningfulness of work. Think about whether you find any of these things particularly stressful. If so, discuss them with your lawyer.

Daily Activities

Judges always ask about daily activities. They ask how you spend a usual day. They use your description to figure out whether or not your daily activities are consistent with the symptoms and limitations you describe. For example, if you claim to have trouble standing and walking because of severe pain in your legs, but you testify that you go out dancing every night, the judge is going to have some reason to doubt your testimony about your symptoms and limitations.

The judge's questioning about your daily activities provides you with a golden opportunity to help your case by giving a lot of details. Let me give you some examples of what happens if you don't give details:

Judge: What do you do on a usual day?
Claimant: Nothing.

This is not a good answer. Sitting and staring at a television set is doing something; sitting and staring out the window is doing something; sitting and staring at a blank wall or at the ceiling is doing something. So describe to the judge what you do; but don't do it this way. Here's another bad example:

Judge: What do you do on a usual day?
Claimant: Oh, I do some cleaning, cooking, straightening up the house, sometimes some laundry and going to the store.

This is a truthful answer since this person does all of these things; but it doesn't help his case at all. He has left out all of the important details. He failed to mention the fact that he cleans for only a few minutes at a time; he cooks only simple meals because he can't stand in the kitchen long enough to do anything more elaborate; he has help doing the laundry; and he never goes to the store alone; he always takes along his 15-year-old son to carry the groceries. He also failed to mention that he sits in his recliner several times during the day to relieve the pain in his back. In other words, the brief description of the things that he did during the day does not support his testimony about disability. But, the details about how he goes about doing these things do help his case.

To help the judge "live" your day with you, run through your usual day hour by hour. Emphasize those things that you do differently now because of your health problems. If you stop and think about it, you'll probably be able to come up with a long list of things you do differently now than you did before you became disabled. These things are important because they show how your disability has affected your life.

Describe how long you do an activity and how long you rest afterwards. Tell where you rest, whether it's sitting or lying down, whether it's on the couch or the bed or a recliner chair. Tell how long it takes you to do a project now compared to how long it used to take you. Describe all those things that you can't accomplish without help from other people—and tell who those other people are and what help they provide.

Some Things Not To Do

1. *Don't argue your case.* Your job is to testify to facts, describe your symptoms, give estimates of your limitations, outline your daily activities, and provide lots of examples of your problems. Leave arguing your case to your lawyer. For example, don't use the line that starts: "I worked all my life..." or don't say, "I know I can't work."

2. *Don't try to draw conclusions for the judge.* Let the judge draw his or her own conclusions. Don't say things such as, "If I could work, I would be working," or "I want to work." If you say either of these, it may cause the judge to think about Stephen Hawking who is wheelchair bound and unable to speak but is the world's leading expert on theoretical physics. There are many exceptional people with extreme disabilities who work; but that is not the issue in a Social Security disability case. It is also not relevant that there may be people less disabled than you who receive disability benefits.

3. *Don't compare yourself to others.* Popular lines are:

"I know a guy who has nothing wrong with him but he gets disability benefits."
"I know people less disabled than me who get disability benefits."
"If I were an alcoholic you'd give me disability benefits."

None of these comparisons helps your case.

4. *Don't try to play on the judge's sympathy.* It won't help. It might backfire. Judges have heard it all.

5. *Don't try to demonstrate what a "good" person you are.* Benefits are not awarded to the virtuous; they are awarded to the disabled. Sometimes claimants bring up things on their own only to demonstrate their virtue, thinking that this will influence the judge. Don't do it. This is just like trying to play on the judge's sympathy. It doesn't work. It may backfire.

6. *Don't tell the judge what an honest person you are.* Many genuinely honest claimants think that they need to tell the judge just how honest they are. "I am an honest person," such a claimant may say. Don't say it. Your honesty will be demonstrated by your totally truthful testimony on relevant matters. Telling the judge that you are honest may backfire.

7. *Don't engage in dramatics.* You are supposed to tell the truth at your hearing. If you are putting on a show for the judge, that is the same thing as not telling the truth. (At the same time, however, if you are having a genuine problem at the hearing and you need to stop the hearing for any reason, tell the judge and your lawyer.)

8. *Don't give irrelevant testimony.* Social Security regulations contain a list of irrelevant areas of testimony—areas that the judge can't and won't consider in deciding your case. This list is in the regulations:

(a) The fact that you are unable to get work is not relevant.
(b) The lack of work in your local area is not relevant.
(c) Hiring practices of employers are not relevant.
(d) Technological changes in the industry in which you have worked are not relevant.
(e) Cyclical economic conditions are not relevant.
(f) The fact that there are no job openings is not relevant.
(g) The fact that you would not actually be hired for a job is not relevant.
(h) The fact that you do not wish to work at a particular job is not relevant.

Also, it doesn't matter that a particular job doesn't pay well enough to support your family.

Problem Areas

There are three areas where there could be potential problems. So if any of these three things apply to your case, be sure to bring them to the attention of your lawyer before the hearing.

1. Think back over the 15 years before you became disabled. Pick out your easiest job. If you have trouble explaining why you can't now do that easiest job, even if that job no longer exists, be sure to discuss this with your lawyer.

2. If you received unemployment compensation at any time during the period that you are claiming to be disabled, make sure your lawyer knows about it before the hearing.

3. If you have been looking for work during any period that you claim to be disabled, tell your lawyer about it before the hearing.

Things To Do

Here's a list of things to do at your hearing:

1. Tell the truth.
2. Neither exaggerate nor minimize your symptoms.
3. Know your present abilities and limitations.
4. Provide relevant details and concrete examples, but don't ramble on.

Reminder

If you have a cell phone with you, don't forget to turn it off before the hearing starts. Don't just turn it to vibrate.

What Your Lawyer Does

Your hearing will be over in about an hour, maybe less. Hearings seldom take longer than an hour and a half. If you're well prepared because of this memorandum and your meeting with your lawyer before your hearing, your lawyer may not have to ask many questions at the hearing. In hearings with judges who like to ask most of the questions, the only time your lawyer needs to ask you anything is if your lawyer thinks that your testimony wasn't clear enough or there are issues that were not developed. In fact, it's better that way. The more information you give in answer to the judge's questions, the better it is for your case. Your case will be presented naturally and your testimony will flow freely. The judge will get to know you and your situation as you and the judge talk. And the judge won't think that it's your lawyer testifying rather than you. Your lawyer will, however, ask questions of any witnesses you bring along to the hearing; and it is the lawyer's job to question any expert witnesses called by the judge.

The most important part of what your lawyer does usually takes place outside of the hearing. That is, your lawyer gathers medical evidence, gets reports from doctors, does legal and medical research, and prepares witnesses to testify.

Your lawyer may make a closing argument either in writing or at the hearing. The best-developed cases, though, don't need a closing argument. If a case is well developed with medical evidence and with the claimant's testimony, a closing argument is often not necessary.

There is one thing that we lawyers cannot do, however: We are powerless to speed up the system. There may be a delay in getting the written decision. The written decision will be mailed to you with a copy to your lawyer. If you're lucky enough to have the judge issue a bench decision at the hearing, the short written bench decision summary usually comes within a week. Otherwise, don't expect a decision from the judge for at least a month—two months is common. Sometimes it takes even longer for a hearing decision to be mailed to you. Some judges are very slow.

There is seldom any way to speed up getting a decision out. So, as hard as it is, you must grit your teeth and wait. If more than three months pass, it's a good idea to make sure that your file hasn't been lost; and your lawyer can do that. But your lawyer can't do much more to speed things up.

Attorney Fees

If your fee agreement with your lawyer calls for the attorney fee to be 25 percent of back benefits up to a maximum amount set by the Commissioner of Social Security (currently $6,000), the Social Security Administration will withhold the attorney fee and, assuming neither you nor the judge objects to the fee, SSA will send that money to your lawyer. Although it's your money, you're not involved in paying it. But you will have to pay expenses directly to your lawyer if your fee agreement calls for you to reimburse your lawyer for expenses.

When You Get Your Decision

Although your lawyer may be able to find an electronic copy of your decision on SSA's website a few days before the paper copy arrives in the mail, when you receive your decision make sure that your lawyer knows about the decision. Your copy and your lawyer's paper copy of the decision are supposed to be mailed to each of you on the same day. But it happens every once in awhile that, because of a hearing office mistake, your lawyer may not be sent a copy of the decision. When this happens, your lawyer may not know what is going on in your case. Your lawyer may not know, for example, that the favorable decision contains an error which needs to be corrected right away; your lawyer may not know to monitor payment of your benefits; and your lawyer may not know if you received a denial decision that needs to be appealed. So, win or lose, call your lawyer's office when you get a decision to find out if your lawyer received a copy.

If You Lose

Sometimes good, well presented cases are lost. It is hard to figure out why, but it happens. There are usually some possibilities for appeal. If you lose, be sure to consult with your lawyer right away about appealing your case. Do this as soon as possible. It is absolutely essential that you appeal to the Appeals Council within 60 days of the judge's decision or you will lose your right to appeal.

§294 *The Importance of Lay Witness Testimony Is Recognized by SSA and the Courts*

Evidence in a disability claim "is anything you or anyone else submits to us or that we obtain that relates to your claim." 20 C.F.R. § 404.1512(b). This includes statements by "others" about the claimant's impairments, restrictions, daily activities, and efforts to work. 20 C.F.R. § 404.1512(b)(3). According to 20 C.F.R. § 404.1512(b)(4), evidence also includes "[i]nformation from other sources, as described in 404.1513(d)."

A regulation that deals with medical and other evidence about impairments, 20 C.F.R. § 404.1513, includes a subsection titled "other sources," which states that SSA may use evidence "from other sources to show the severity of your impairment(s) and how it affects your ability to work." 20 C.F.R. § 404.1513(d). Such other sources include "other non-medical sources (for example, spouses, parents and other caregivers, siblings, other relatives, friends, neighbors, and clergy)." 20 C.F.R. § 404.1513(d)(4).

SSR 83-20, which deals with determining the onset of disability, states that information may be obtained from family members, friends and former employers in those situations where medical evidence is not available. See also *Jones v. Chater*, 65 F.3d 102 (8th Cir. 1995).

SSA says that in evaluating lay witness testimony, "it would be appropriate to consider such factors as the nature and extent of the relationship, whether the evidence is consistent with other evidence, and any other factors that tend to support or refute the evidence." SSR 06-3p.

Step 2 Severity

Do not assume that lay testimony cannot be used to rebut a conclusion that a claimant's impairment is not severe. As long as there is a medically determinable impairment that *could cause* the claimant's symptoms, it is SSA's policy to evaluate symptoms at step 2 to determine if the claimant's impairment "significantly limits an individual's physical or mental abilities to do basic work activities." SSR 96-3p provides: "once the requisite relationship between the medically determinable impairment(s) and the alleged symptom(s) is established, the intensity, persistence, and limiting effects of the symptom(s) must be considered along with the objective medical and other evidence in determining whether the impairment or combination of impairments is severe." In determining the extent to which symptoms such as pain affect a claimant's capacity to perform basic work activities, 20 C.F.R. § 404.1529(c)(4), emphasis added, provides:

> We will consider your statements about the intensity, persistence, and limiting effects of your symptoms, and we will evaluate your statements in relation to the objective medical evidence *and other evidence*, in reaching a conclusion as to whether you are disabled. We will consider whether there are any inconsistencies in the evidence and the extent to which there are any conflicts between your statements and the rest of the evidence, including your history, the signs and laboratory findings, and statements by your treating or nontreating source *or other persons* about how your symptoms affect you. Your symptoms, including pain, will be determined to diminish your capacity for basic work activities to the extent that your alleged functional limitations and restrictions due to symptoms, such as pain, can reasonably be accepted as consistent with the objective medical evidence *and other evidence*.

Step 3 Listings

Although we tend to think of the Listing of Impairments as involving only medical evidence, there are impairments that may be documented by lay observations. For example, epilepsy must be documented by a detailed description of a typical seizure pattern, Listings 11.02 and 11.03, which can come from a lay witness. "Testimony of persons other than the claimant is essential for description of type and frequency of seizures if professional observation is not available." Listings 11.00A.

In mental impairment cases, when evaluating whether a claimant's impairment meets the "B criteria" of the mental Listings, lay witnesses are important in describing the claimant's daily activities, social functioning, concentration, persistence or pace and ability to tolerate stress. See § 12.00 D.1.c. of the Listing of Impairments.

In cases involving intellectual disability, Listing 12.05, description of "deficits in adaptive functioning initially manifested" before age 22 may come from lay witnesses.

Step 4 Past Relevant Work

According to 20 C.F.R. § 404.1565(b), when SSA cannot get all the information it needs about a claimant's past relevant work, SSA "will try, with your permission, to get it from your employer or other person who knows about your work, such as a member of your family or a co-worker."

Step 4 RFC

In assessing residual functional capacity, SSA will "also consider descriptions and observations of your limitations from your impairment(s), including limitations that result from your symptoms, such as pain, provided by you, your family, neighbors, friends, or other persons." 20 C.F.R. § 404.1545(a)(3). "Descriptions and observations of the claimant's restrictions by medical and nonmedical sources in addition to those made during formal medical examinations must also be considered in the determination of RFC." SSR 82-53. "The [RFC] assessment is based upon consideration of all relevant evidence in the case record, including medical evidence and relevant nonmedical evidence, such as observations of lay witnesses of an individual's apparent symptomatology . . . ." SSR 96-5p. "The RFC assessment must be based on *all* of the relevant evidence in the case record, such as . . . Lay evidence . . . ." SSR 96-8p, emphasis in original. "The [RFC] assessment is based upon consideration of all relevant evidence in the case record, including medical evidence and relevant nonmedical evidence, such as observations of lay witnesses of an individual's apparent symptomatology, or an individual's own statement of what he or she is able or unable to do." SSR 03-3p.

> In assessing mental residual functional capacity, SSR 85-16 provides:
>
> Other evidence also may play a vital role in the determination of the effects of impairment. To arrive at an overall assessment of the effects of mental impairment, relevant, reliable information, obtained from third party sources such as social workers, previous employers, family members, and staff members of halfway houses, mental health centers, and community centers, may be valuable in assessing an individual's level of activities of daily living. Information concerning an individual's performance in any work setting (including sheltered work and volunteer or competitive work), as well as the circumstances surrounding the termination of the work effort, may be pertinent in assessing the individual's ability to function in a competitive work environment.

Symptoms

The pain regulation, 20 C.F.R. § 404.1529, repeatedly states that "other evidence" or evidence from "other persons" in addition to objective medical evidence from doctors will be considered in evaluating a claimant's symptoms. "Other evidence" includes observations of lay witnesses. 20 C.F.R. § 404.1529(a). See also 20 C.F.R. § 404.1529(c)(3). Family and friends are identified in SSR 16-3p as a source of information that is "helpful to us in assessing the intensity, persistence, and limiting effects of symptoms."

SSR 03-2p, which deals with reflex sympathetic dystrophy, identifies lay witnesses as a source of information about day-to-day functioning:

> Information other than an individual's allegations and reports from the individual's treating sources helps to assess an individual's ability to function on a day-to-day basis and helps to depict the individual's capacities over a period of time, thus serving to establish a longitudinal picture of the individual's status. Such evidence includes, but is not limited to:
>
> • Information from neighbors, friends, relatives, or clergy;
>
> • Statements from such individuals as past employers, rehabilitation counselors, or teachers about the individual's impairment(s) and the effects of the impairment(s) on the individual's functioning in the work place, rehabilitation facility, or educational institution;
>
> • Statements from other practitioners with knowledge of the individual, e.g., nurse-practitioners, physicians' assistants, naturopaths, therapists, social workers, and chiropractors; or
>
> • Statements from other sources with knowledge of the individual's ability to function in daily activities.

SSR 03-1p, which deals with postpolio sequelae, says, "Evidence from employers and other third party sources may be valuable in documenting a loss of a previous level of functioning and should be sought when there is a discrepancy or a question of credibility in the evidence of record and a fully favorable determination or decision cannot be made based on the available evidence."

> In discussing documentation, SSR 12-2p which deals with fibromyalgia, states:
>
> Under our regulations and SSR 06-3p, information from nonmedical sources can also help us evaluate the severity and functional effects of a person's [fibromyalgia]. This information may help us to assess the person's ability to function day-to-day and over time. It may also help us when we make findings about the credibility of the person's allegations about symptoms and their effects. Examples of nonmedical sources include:
>
> a. Neighbors, friends, relatives, and clergy;
>
> b. Past employers, rehabilitation counselors, and teachers; and
>
> c. Statements from SSA personnel who interviewed the person.

SSR 12-2p also notes SSA will consider "statements by other people about the person's symptoms."

SSR 14-1p, dealing with evaluation of chronic fatigue syndrome, notes that third-party information may be very useful in assessing an individual's ability to function on a day-to-day basis. The ruling notes at III.A.3. that such evidence includes information from "[s]pouses, parents, siblings, other relatives, neighbors, friends, and clergy" as well as past employers, rehabilitation counselors and teachers.

ALJ Decisions

Although it is clearly SSA policy to treat lay witness evidence as important for understanding a claimant's case, many ALJs have a tendency to give such evidence short shrift. ALJs often resist taking evidence from lay witnesses at hearings, and many ALJ decisions do not even mention significant lay witness testimony or important letters from lay witnesses. SSR 06-3p states, "Although there is a distinction between what an adjudicator must consider and what the adjudicator must explain in the disability determination or decision, the adjudicator generally should explain the weight given to opinions from these 'other sources,' or otherwise ensure that the discussion the evidence in the determination or decision allows a claimant or subsequent reviewer to follow the adjudicator's reasoning, when such opinions may have an effect on the outcome of the case."

SSR 86-8 provides that the rationale of the disability decision "must reflect the sequential evaluation process; describe the weight attributed to the pertinent medical, nonmedical and vocational factors in the case; and reconcile any significant inconsistencies." Thus, significant inconsistencies between what a lay witness says and findings that purport to be based on medical evidence need to be reconciled in the decision.

Signed Statement with Knowledge of Penalty

In 20 C.F.R. § 404.702, the definition of "evidence" includes a "signed statement that helps to show whether you are eligible for benefits." SSA says that in "deciding that evidence is convincing," it will consider whether "information was given under oath or with witnesses present or with the knowledge that there was a penalty for giving false information." 20 C.F.R. § 404.708(c). This is the reason that our memorandums that describe for friends and family how to write a letter about someone's disability claim (§§297.5 and 297.6) ask the writer to close the letter with this language: "I understand that there is a penalty for giving false information in a claim for disability benefits from the Social Security Administration. I affirm that everything in this letter is true."

Federal Court Decisions

The federal courts have remanded cases in which the ALJ failed to give proper consideration to lay testimony. The leading circuit on this issue is the 9th. See, for example:

2nd Circuit

Williams on Behalf of Williams v. Bowen, 859 F.2d 255, 260-261 (2d Cir. 1988);

3rd Circuit

Burnett v. Commissioner of SSA, 220 F.3d 112, 122 (3d Cir. 2000);

Van Horn v. Schweiker, 717 F.2d 871, 873 (3d Cir. 1983);

6th Circuit

Lashley v. Secretary of Health & Human Services, 708 F.2d 1048, 1054 (6th Cir. 1983);

7th Circuit

Garcia v. Colvin, 741 F.3d 758, 761 (7th Cir. 2013);

Allord v. Barnhart, 455 F.3d 818, 821-822 (7th Cir. 2006);

Briscoe ex rel. Taylor v. Barnhart, 425 F.3d 345, 354 (7th Cir. 2005);

Behymer v. Apfel, 45 F. Supp. 2d 654, 663 (N.D. Ind. 1999); and

Munks v. Heckler, 580 F. Supp. 871, 874 (N.D. Ill. 1984).

8th Circuit

Willcockson v. Astrue, 540 F.3d 878, 880 (8th Cir. 2008)

Smith v. Heckler, 735 F.2d 312, 317 (8th Cir. 1984);

9th Circuit

Bruce v. Astrue, 557 F. 3d 1113, 1115 (9th Cir. 2009);

Stout v. Commissioner, 454 F.3d 1050, 1053 (9th Cir. 2006)

Nguyen v. Chater, 100 F. 3d 1462, 1467 (9th Cir. 1996);

Smolen v. Chater, 80 F.3d 1273, 1289 (9th Cir. 1996);

Dodrill v. Shalala, 12 F.3d 915, 918-919 (9th Cir. 1993);

Smith v. Bowen, 849 F.2d 1222, 1226 (9th Cir. 1988);

10th Circuit

Blea v. Barnhart, 466 F.3d 903, 914-916 (10th Cir. 2006);

DC Circuit

Narrol v. Heckler, 727 F.2d 1303, 1306-7 (D.C.Cir. 1984);

In *Schneider v. Commissioner of the SSA*, 223 F.3d 968, 976 (9th Cir. 2000), the court reversed the decision of the Commissioner and awarded benefits based on the strength of lay evidence that was ignored by the ALJ.

In *Stout v. Commissioner*, 454 F.3d 1050, 1053 (9th Cir. 2006) the court required an explicit credibility determination for each witness:

> In determining whether a claimant is disabled, an ALJ must consider lay witness testimony concerning a claimant's ability to work. See *Dodrill v. Shalala*, 12 F.3d 915, 919 (9th Cir.1993); 20 C.F.R. §§ 404.1513(d)(4) & (e), 416.913(d)(4) & (e). Indeed, "lay testimony as to a claimant's symptoms or how an impairment affects ability to work is competent evidence . . . and therefore cannot be disregarded without comment." *Nguyen v. Chater*, 100 F.3d 1462, 1467 (9th Cir.1996) (citations omitted). Consequently, "[i]f the ALJ wishes to discount the testimony of lay witnesses, he must give reasons that are germane to each witness." *Dodrill*, 12 F.3d at 919; see also *Lewis v. Apfel*, 236 F.3d 503, 511 ("Lay testimony as to a claimant's symptoms is

> competent evidence that an ALJ must take into account, unless he or she expressly determines to disregard such testimony and gives reasons germane to each witness for doing so." (citations omitted)).

In *Molina v. Astrue*, 674 F.3d 1104, 1114-1115 (9th Cir. 2012) the court held that failure to make a credibility determination for lay witness testimony can be harmless error, depending on the facts of the case:

> Lay testimony as to a claimant's symptoms or how an impairment affects the claimant's ability to work is competent evidence that the ALJ must take into account. *Nguyen v. Chater*, 100 F.3d 1462, 1467 (9th Cir.1996); *Dodrill v. Shalala*, 12 F.3d 915, 919 (9th Cir.1993). We have held that competent lay witness testimony "cannot be disregarded without comment," *Nguyen*, 100 F.3d at 1467, and that in order to discount competent lay witness testimony, the ALJ "must give reasons that are germane to each witness," *Dodrill*, 12 F.3d at 919. We have not, however, required the ALJ to discuss every witness's testimony on a individualized, witness-by-witness basis. Rather, if the ALJ gives germane reasons for rejecting testimony by one witness, the ALJ need only point to those reasons when rejecting similar testimony by a different witness. See *Valentine*, 574 F.3d at 694 (holding that because "the ALJ provided clear and convincing reasons for rejecting [the claimant's] own subjective complaints, and because [the lay witness's] testimony was similar to such complaints, it follows that the ALJ also gave germane reasons for rejecting [the lay witness's] testimony"). The applicable regulations are in accord; they require the ALJ to consider testimony from family and friends submitted on behalf of the claimant, see 20 C.F.R. §§ 404.1529(c)(3), 404.1545(a)(3), but do not require the ALJ to provide express reasons for rejecting testimony from each lay witness, see id.; see also SSR 06-03p (recognizing that "there is a distinction between what an adjudicator must consider and what the adjudicator must explain in the disability determination or decision").
>
> Here, the ALJ stated that the rationale for her credibility determination "include[d] reference to ... the third party statements submitted in support of the claimant." This statement establishes that the ALJ reviewed the lay witness testimony in the record, but it does not provide a reason for discounting the testimony. The ALJ gave reasons for rejecting Molina's testimony regarding her symptoms that were equally relevant to the similar testimony of the lay witnesses, and that would support a finding that the lay testimony was similarly not credible. But under our rule that lay witness testimony "cannot be disregarded without comment," *Nguyen*, 100 F.3d at 1467, the ALJ erred in failing to explain her reasons for disregarding the lay witness testimony, either individually or in the aggregate. Nevertheless, as discussed below, that error was harmless.

In *Garcia v. Colvin*, 741 F.3d 758, 761 (7th Cir. 2013), the court addressed the issue of whether lay witnesses could be treated as biased because of their relationship with the claimant:

> Besides the medical evidence, there was testimony by Garcia's fiancée that Garcia sometimes wakes up at night "moaning and crying from the pain." The administrative law judge gave her testimony only "some weight, recognizing the potential for bias" attributable to their relationship. The implication is that if a plaintiff or a defendant (or a relative of either — or a fiancée) testifies in a case, the testimony must automatically be discounted for bias. British and American courts used not to permit parties to a lawsuit (or their spouses) to testify at all, because of bias. The rule "preempted the jury's lie-detecting function by declaring certain witnesses to be likely liars as a matter of law." George Fisher, "The Jury's Rise as Lie Detector," 107 Yale L.J. 575, 624-25 (1997). When the rule was discarded, it wasn't replaced by a rule that the testimony of the parties or of other presumptively biased witness be given only half or a quarter or two-thirds the weight given the testimony of disinterested witnesses. The administrative law judge should have made clear whether he believed the fiancée's testimony or not, or which part he believed, or whether he had no idea how much of what she said was worthy of belief.

§295 Arrange for Lay Witness Testimony

Ask the claimant who would be the best witnesses and telephone them to discuss their observations of the claimant. Pick the best one or two witnesses (or in unusual cases more). Provide lay witnesses with information about the hearing and the sort of testimony expected. A letter to lay witnesses follows.

§296 *Sample: Letter to Lay Witness*

Name
Address

Re: Disability Hearing of [Claimant's Name]

Date of Hearing: ____________________

Time of Hearing: ____________________

Place of Hearing: ____________________
____
____

Dear ______________________:

This letter is to follow up our recent telephone conversation in which we discussed your testimony as a witness in a disability hearing. It is intended to give you general information.

A disability hearing is very different from a court hearing. There will be no audience or observers at the hearing like there often is at court hearings. A disability hearing is private. The hearing is quite informal, especially when compared to a court hearing. Just about the only formality is that you will be expected to testify under oath.

The hearing is held in a small conference room and is presided over by an administrative law judge. The judge is a neutral person whose job it is to find out all the facts about the claimant's disability. No lawyer represents the government in disability cases. Thus, no lawyer representing the government will cross-examine you.

An audio recording is made of hearing testimony. Therefore, it will be necessary for you to speak up and give audible answers to questions. Also, questions which can be answered yes or no ought to be answered that way since "uh huh" and "huh uh" answers don't transcribe well.

If someone else is testifying and you know the answer to a question but the person who is testifying doesn't know the answer, don't chime in. Don't offer to answer the question even if the person testifying asks you (unless the judge says it's okay). It is necessary for you to wait your turn.

At the hearing I will ask you questions. I always ask about who you are, your relationship with the claimant, how long you have known the claimant, and how often you get to see the claimant. These questions are to establish the basis for testimony about your observations. Then, I'll ask about those observations.

Essentially, we'll just have a conversation about the claimant. There aren't any peculiar rules for testifying at disability hearings like there are for court testimony such as the "don't volunteer" rule or even the "hearsay" rule. It is okay to talk to me just like we talked on the telephone. But don't assume that because we've spoken on the telephone that I already know the answer. The person you are really talking to at the hearing, of course, is the judge, not me. Therefore, if it helps, you may assume that I've forgotten everything you told me on the telephone and that you've got to tell it to me again.

You are expected to testify truthfully about things that you have observed. The best testimony is filled with examples of things you have seen with your own two eyes. Your job is to describe what you have seen.

Often, judges don't ask any questions of a witness such as you. However, if a judge does ask you any questions, I always regard it as a good sign. It means the judge is very interested in what you have to say. Judges, in my experience, don't "cross-examine" witnesses like you might have seen witnesses cross-examined on television. The judge is simply looking for all the facts in order to decide the case fairly. The judge certainly won't ask any trick questions or questions designed to embarrass.

There are only a few mistakes that occasionally people make in testifying. The worst is when a witness deliberately exaggerates the claimant's disability, thinking that this will help the claimant win the case. But this usually backfires because the judge simply doesn't believe it.

Other mistakes occur when a witness tries to give "medical" testimony, that is, offers medical conclusions that really ought to come from a doctor; or when a witness tries to take over the role of the lawyer and argues the claimant's case, such as when the witness tells the judge that the claimant can't work, or should be found disabled because he needs help, etc.

There really are only a few rules for testifying:

1. Tell the truth.
2. Don't exaggerate to try to "help" the claimant.
3. But don't minimize either.
4. Testify only about things that you've observed.
5. It is okay to give examples and explain your answers by describing those things you have observed.
6. But leave arguing the case to me.

I will meet with you just before the hearing. If you have any last minute questions, you can ask me then. Otherwise, if you have any questions about your testimony after reading this letter, please feel free to telephone me.

Sincerely,

(Name of Attorney)

§297 Written Statements From Lay Observers

For cases where you cannot get testimony from live witnesses, you should, by all means, use written statements. However, even more care should be used with written statements than with oral testimony.

§297.1 Form

In "deciding that evidence is convincing," SSA says it will consider whether "information was given under oath or with witnesses present or with the knowledge that there was a penalty for giving false information." 20 C.F.R. § 404.708(c). Having witnesses say that they realize there is a penalty for giving false information avoids having an ALJ reject such statements solely on the gounds that such statements are not given under oath. The statements do not necessarily need to be typewritten; a handwritten statement, well-phrased and to the point, can bear additional weight through its undeniable authenticity and sincerity. Even misspellings and bad grammar can sometimes help. However, a barely legible, semiliterate written statement might not get the attention it deserves.

§297.2 Content

The stereotyped letter is to be strongly avoided. A typed letter stating, in effect, "I have known Mr. Jones for 20 years; he is a hard worker and needs help because he is disabled," signed by 20 or 30 people is not worth much. Nor are carbon copies or photocopies of the same letter with different signatures. To be helpful, the statement should be individual. It should set out the relationship of the writer to the claimant, and the length of time they have known each other. It should indicate how the writer has special knowledge of the claimant, and should relate knowledge and observations in as much detail as possible.

§297.3 Illustration

A statement such as the following can be very effective:

> I am Mary Jones. I live across the street from Mrs. Smith who, I understand, has filed a claim for Social Security disability benefits. I have known Mrs. Smith for seven years; we worked together at the electronics company for five years. I saw her when she fell at the plant and hurt her back.
>
> I go to see her every day. I cook dinner for her and her family at times and twice a week go over and help her into the bathtub, since she can't get in or out of it by herself. I also take her to the doctor's office each week, since she takes medicine that makes her too dizzy to drive, according to what she tells me.
>
> She is an honest person, in my opinion, and has been a good worker and appears to have financial difficulties since she had to stop work. I don't believe she would be away from work if it weren't necessary.
>
> She spends most of her time in bed, has quit going to church and it's been over a month since I've seen her walking in her yard. Her main problem is with her back; she wears a back brace all the time.

§297.4 Other Tips

A written statement from a former employer or coworker should set out details of the work done by the claimant, the type of worker he or she was, and work absences, attitudes, and reason for leaving, especially if it was for health purposes. Benefit payments or sick leave should be detailed. Letters from ministers may not be too helpful, since they are almost always commendatory. However, letters setting out particular difficulties the claimant has in participating in religious activities can be helpful, especially if the claimant formerly was a mainstay of the activities of the church and now no longer participates, or participates to a much lesser extent.

Do not use any statements which are not based on personal knowledge, which contain any sort of implied (or actual) threat, or which broach the subject of race, religious conviction, or anything unrelated to your client's impairments and ultimately to your client's disability and possible entitlement to benefits.

A memorandum to send to friends, family, etc., about preparing a letter supporting a disability claim appears at §297.5, *infra*.

§297.5 Sample: Memorandum on Preparing a Letter for Use In a Disability Claim

Re: Preparing A Letter For Use In a Disability Claim
To: Friends, Family & Associates

You have been asked on behalf of someone you know, a claimant for disability benefits from the Social Security Administration, to write a letter providing your observations about the claimant's condition that we can submit as evidence in the claim. This memorandum is designed to answer questions people often have about how best to prepare such a letter.

To whom should I address the letter?

Address it and send it to me:

____
____
____
____

Write the letter as if you were simply writing an informative letter to a friend telling about the claimant's life. Write in your own words using language you would normally use.

Please include your address and telephone number in case someone has questions; and don't forget to sign and date the letter.

How do I start?

A good place to start is by explaining your relationship to the person on whose behalf you are writing, how long you've known him or her, and how often you get to see one another.

How should I refer to the claimant?

Refer to the claimant the same way you would normally refer to him or her. If you normally use the claimant's first name (or even a nickname), use that. At the beginning of your letter, though, make it clear who you are writing about.

Should I state that everything I say is true?

Yes. Please add the following language just above your signature:

I understand that there is a penalty for giving false information in a claim for disability benefits from the Social Security Administration. I affirm that everything in this letter is true.

Are there any general guidelines?

- Tell the truth.
- Don't exaggerate, but don't minimize the claimant's difficulties.
- Write from personal knowledge—your own observations, not what someone else has told you.
- Provide relevant details and examples but don't ramble.

[Add this heading and paragraph when dealing with a date last insured problem:]

Are there any special issues I should look out for?

Because of a peculiarity of this case, you need to discuss the claimant's capacity for doing things as it existed on or before **<u>date last insured</u>**. *Everything you describe should pertain to the period of time on or before **<u>date last insured</u>**.* Also, please note that the claimant alleges that disability began as of **<u>alleged onset date</u>**. Thus, the most important period of time is between these two dates: **<u>alleged onset date</u>** and **<u>date last insured</u>**.

What is the best approach?

Your letter may be most helpful if you describe the side of the claimant's life you know best. Rather than try to do too much, you might pick one or more of the following to write about:

- Explain how the claimant has changed since becoming disabled, describing his or her life both before and after the disability began.

- If you've observed the claimant having difficulty performing certain activities, tell about these.
- Outline the claimant's limited daily activities.
- Relate instances where even the most modest activities have necessitated a lengthy recuperation—if this is part of the claimant's problem.
- If the claimant has a history of being unable to participate in scheduled activities because the claimant's impairment is acting up, describe missed family dinners, weddings, reunions or other family occasions.
- If the claimant has a physical disability, describe difficulties you've observed with sitting, standing, walking, lifting, bending, etc.
- If the claimant has mental limitations, describe difficulties understanding, remembering and carrying out instructions, and in responding appropriately to supervisors, co-workers or work pressures, *etc.* It helps to include specific examples that you've noticed.
- Write about things you help the claimant with.
- Tell about other things you know the claimant needs help with.
- If pain is involved, you may have noticed difficulty concentrating, inability to pay attention to simple things, forgetfulness, a quick temper, avoiding other people, crying spells, or poor stress tolerance. These things often are good measures of how much pain a person has, and it is very helpful if people close to the claimant describe these observations in their letters.
- If the claimant has good days and bad days, describe what the claimant does on a good day and what he or she does on a bad day. Estimate how many times per month the claimant has a bad day.
- Sometimes a person's disability is what we call "episodic." That is, between episodes s/he is fairly normal; but the episodes are frequent enough that s/he would never be able to hold a job. If this is the claimant's problem, you can help by describing in detail an episode that you have observed and, if you know, estimating how often such episodes occur.
- If you know that the claimant had a hard time trying to work, tell about these problems and how the claimant tried to cope.

Is there anything that I shouldn't say?

As long as you tell the truth, write from personal knowledge and don't exaggerate the claimant's difficulty, there really is nothing you shouldn't say. But here are a few tips:

- Unless you have a medical background or have some other reason to know about the claimant's medical condition, don't write about medical issues. Leave that for the doctors.
- Don't focus on the time when someone was hospitalized. People often think it is helpful to describe how bad things were when someone was hospitalized. But we have hospital records for that; and everyone would agree that a patient cannot work while hospitalized. Instead, we need your help describing the claimant's life during more ordinary times.
- Don't try to play on the sympathy of the judge. The judge will find the claimant disabled based on inability to work, not because the claimant is a nice person or needs money, etc.
- Don't write about the claimant's inability *to get* a job. The Social Security Act says that the only thing that matters is the claimant's ability *to do* a job.
- Don't compare the claimant to others who seem less disabled but get disability benefits. Such comparisons don't help and may even give the wrong impression.
- Don't draw conclusions such as that the claimant can't work or is disabled. We'll let the judge draw his or her own conclusions based on the facts and descriptions you provide.
- Don't argue the case. Leave that to me.

§297.6 *Sample: Memorandum on Preparing a Letter for Use In a Disability Claim Involving a Mental Impairment*

Re: Preparing A Letter For Use In a Disability Claim Involving a Mental Impairment
To: Friends, Family & Associates

You have been asked on behalf of someone you know, a claimant for disability benefits from the Social Security Administration, to write a letter providing your observations about the claimant's condition that we can submit as evidence in the claim. This memorandum is designed to answer questions people often have about how best to prepare such a letter.

To whom should I address the letter?

Address it and send it to me:

____
____
____
____

Write the letter as if you were simply writing an informative letter to a friend telling about the claimant's life. Write in your own words using language you would normally use.

Please include your address and telephone number in case someone has questions; and don't forget to sign and date the letter.

How do I start?

A good place to start is by explaining your relationship to the person on whose behalf you are writing, how long you've known him or her, and how often you get to see one another.

How should I refer to the claimant?

Refer to the claimant the same way you would normally refer to him or her. If you normally use the claimant's first name (or even a nickname), use that. At the beginning of your letter, though, make it clear who you are writing about.

Should I state that everything I say is true?

Yes. Please add the following language just above your signature:

I understand that there is a penalty for giving false information in a claim for disability benefits from the Social Security Administration. I affirm that everything in this letter is true.

Are there any general guidelines?

- Tell the truth.
- Don't exaggerate, but don't minimize the claimant's difficulties.
- Write from personal knowledge—your own observations, not what someone else has told you.
- Provide relevant details and examples but don't ramble.

What is the best approach?

Your letter may be most helpful if you describe the side of the claimant's life you know best. Rather than try to do too much, you might pick one or more of the following to write about:

- Explain how the claimant has changed since becoming disabled, describing his or her life both before and after the disability began.
- If you've observed the claimant having difficulty performing certain activities, tell about these.
- Briefly describe how the claimant's disability has affected his/her ability to maintain social contacts, if applicable.
- If the claimant has a history of being unable to participate in scheduled activities because of his/her disability, describe missed family dinners, weddings, reunions or other family occasions.
- If the claimant has difficulty maintaining regular attendance or being punctual at scheduled activities, describe this problem and estimate how often it occurs.
- If the claimant needs special supervision in order to sustain an ordinary routine, describe this in detail.

- If the claimant has trouble performing at a consistent pace, describe this.
- If the claimant is unable to complete a normal workday or workweek, describe this problem.
- Describe difficulties understanding, remembering and carrying out instructions, and in responding appropriately to supervisors, co-workers or work pressures, *etc.* It helps to include specific examples that you've noticed.
- If there is difficulty maintaining socially appropriate behavior or adhering to basic standards of neatness and cleanliness, describe this problem.
- If the claimant has difficulty traveling in unfamiliar places, describe incidents that demonstrate this.
- Write about things you help the claimant with.
- Tell about other things you know the claimant needs help with.
- If you have noticed difficulty concentrating, inability to pay attention to simple things, forgetfulness, a quick temper, avoiding other people, crying spells, or poor stress tolerance, these things often are good measures of disability; and it is very helpful if people close to the claimant describe these observations in their letters.
- If the claimant has good days and bad days, describe what s/he does on a good day and what s/he does on a bad day. Estimate how many times per month s/he has a bad day.
- Sometimes a person's disability is what we call "episodic." That is, between episodes s/he is fairly normal; but the episodes are frequent enough that s/he would never be able to hold a job. If this is the claimant's problem, you can help by describing in detail an episode that you have observed and, if you know, how often such episodes occur.
- If you know that the claimant had a hard time trying to work, tell about these problems.

Is there anything that I shouldn't say?

As long as you tell the truth, write from personal knowledge and don't exaggerate the claimant's difficulty, there really is nothing you shouldn't say. But here are a few tips:

- Unless you have a medical background or have some other reason to know about the claimant's medical condition, don't write about medical issues. Leave that for the doctors.
- Don't focus on the ancient history of the claimant's problems, such as when the claimant was a child or, really, any time before the claimant became unable to work. We need your help describing the claimant's condition since around the time the claimant applied for disability benefits.
- Don't focus on the time when someone was hospitalized. People often think it is helpful to describe how bad things were when someone was hospitalized. But we have hospital records for that; and everyone would agree that a patient cannot work while hospitalized. Instead, we need your help describing the claimant's life during more ordinary times.
- Don't discuss your opinions about the *cause* of the claimant's problems. As long as we demonstrate that the claimant has problems, the ultimate cause does not matter and could become a distracting issue in the case.
- Don't try to play on the sympathy of the judge. The judge will find the claimant disabled based on inability to work, not because s/he is a nice person or needs money, *etc.*
- Don't write about the claimant's inability *to get* a job. The Social Security Act says that the only thing that matters is a claimant's ability *to do* a job.
- Don't compare the claimant to others who seem less disabled but get disability benefits. Such comparisons don't help and may even give the wrong impression.
- Don't draw conclusions such as that the claimant can't work or is disabled. We'll let the judge draw his or her own conclusions based on the facts and descriptions you provide.
- Don't argue the case. Leave that to me.

§298 Prehearing Checklist

1. Obtain a copy and review the hearing exhibit file.
2. Request additional medical records.
3. If necessary, obtain vocational records.
4. Develop a theory of disability based upon your client's condition and Social Security regulations.
5. Request medical reports from treating doctors that address the issues in your client's case.
6. Arrange for additional medical or vocational evaluations, if necessary.
7. Request letters from friends and family that provide observations of your client's limitations.
8. Submit additional evidence about three weeks before the date of the hearing.
9. Request a prehearing conference in a case that presents complicated issues.
10. Request an on-the-record fully favorable decision in a case that presents few or no issues.
11. Request subpoenas for witnesses or documents, if necessary, at least ten business days prior to the hearing date.
12. At least five business days before the hearing, review the file and notify the ALJ about any evidence not yet received.
13. Prepare a hearing brief, Submit the brief at least five business days before the hearing..
14. Submit written objections to hearing issues, if appropriate, at least five business days before the hearing.
15. Contact prospective witnesses and make arrangements for them to testify.
16. Prepare the claimant to testify.
17. If you want the "fee agreement process" to apply to your fee, check to make sure that the appropriate fee agreement signed by both you and the claimant has been submitted to the hearing office.
18. If you want direct payment of your fee, be sure you have submitted an SSA-1695 to the local office and received an acknowledgement.